Educational Assessment
of Students

Fifth Edition

Educational Assessment of Students

ANTHONY J. NITKO
University of Arizona

SUSAN M. BROOKHART
Duquesne University

Upper Saddle River, New Jersey

Columbus, Ohio

Library of Congress Cataloging in Publication Data

Nitko, Anthony J.
    Educational assessment of students / Anthony J. Nitko, Susan Brookhart.– 5th ed.
      p. cm.
    Includes bibliographical references and index.
    ISBN 0-13-171925-4
  1. Educational tests and measurements. I. Brookhart, Susan M. II. Title.
    LB3051.N57 2007
    371.26–dc22
                                                           2005034089

Vice President and Executive Publisher: Jeffery W. Johnston
Publisher: Kevin M. Davis
Development Editor: Autumn Crisp Benson
Editorial Assistant: Sarah N. Kenoyer
Production Editor: Mary Harlan
Production Coordinator: Carol Singer, GGS Book Services
Design Coordinator: Diane C. Lorenzo
Text Design and Illustrations: Brian Molloy, GGS Book Services
Cover Design: Jason Moore
Cover Image: Corbis
Production Manager: Laura Messerly
Director of Marketing: David Gesell
Marketing Manager: Autumn Purdy
Marketing Coordinator: Brian Mounts

This book was set in Garamond by GGS Book Services. It was printed and bound by Banta Book Group. The cover was printed by Phoenix Color Corp.

Pearson Prentice Hall™ is a trademark of Pearson Education, Inc.
Pearson® is a registered trademark of Pearson plc
Prentice Hall® is a registered trademark of Pearson Education, Inc.
Merrill® is a registered trademark of Pearson Education, Inc.

Pearson Education Ltd.
Pearson Education Singapore Pte. Ltd.
Pearson Education Canada, Ltd.
Pearson Education–Japan

Pearson Education Australia Pty. Limited
Pearson Education North Asia Ltd.
Pearson Educación de Mexico, S.A. de C.V.
Pearson Education Malaysia Pte. Ltd.

10 9 8 7

ISBN: 0-13-171925-4

To our loving spouses
Veronica Vail Nitko
and
Frank Brookhart

As for the previous editions, the goal of *Educational Assessment of Students*, Fifth Edition, is to help teachers and those in training to teach to improve their skills through better assessment of students. It focuses directly on the professional practices of elementary and secondary schoolteachers. This edition features:

- A continued strong emphasis on classroom assessment.
- Complete coverage of the basics as well as advanced topics.
- Practical advice and examples of how good and poor classroom assessments affect students' learning.

It is a core text written for a first course in educational testing and constructing classroom assessments, and it serves equally as the textbook for an undergraduate course or a first graduate course in educational assessment. No formal coursework in statistics or college mathematics is necessary to understand the text.

The book provides complete coverage of educational assessment, including developing plans that integrate teaching and assessment; crafting objective, performance, and portfolio assessments; evaluating students and discussing evaluations with parents; and interpreting state-mandated tests and standardized achievement tests.

It is important in a first course that students receive a balanced treatment of the topics. Because the book is a comprehensive treatment of traditional and alternative assessments, we give examples, discuss the pros and cons, and give guidance for crafting every assessment technique that we introduce. Research is cited that supports or refutes assessment and teaching practices.

The text prepares teachers and those in training to teach as professionals. We recognize that teachers' experiences and judgments are necessary for proper and valid use of educational assessment. We do not hesitate to point out teachers' and school administrators' erroneous judgments and assessment abuses, however, where good lessons can be learned from them. To ensure that the text material is in keeping with the competencies and standards held to be important by the profession, each chapter is keyed to the American Federation of Teachers, the National Council on Measurement in Education, and the National Education Association *Standards for Teacher Competence in Educational Assessment of Students* (reproduced in Appendix A).

New and Revised Content

In preparing this edition, we made a special effort to make it easy for the reader to apply the material to classroom practice through improved explanations, improved practical examples and illustrations, checklists, and step-by-step, how-to instructions. As with previous editions, we have written the text from the viewpoint that assessment is part of good teaching practice that helps the teacher improve students' learning. Material new to the fifth edition includes:

1. Redesign of the chapters for ease of learning.
2. Discussion of state and federal accountability and the No Child Left Behind Act in Chapter 1, along with suggestions in other chapters on how to apply the NCLB Act to assessment.
3. Updated information on federal laws applicable to assessment, accommodations, and testing students with disabilities.
4. Practical suggestions for aligning classroom assessments with state standards.
5. Discussion of the revised Bloom *Taxonomy*.
6. Improved discussion of ways to craft distractors in multiple-choice items so they have some diagnostic value to teachers.
7. Consolidation of practical suggestions for developing scoring rubrics from several chapters into Chapter 12.
8. Update of Websites related to assessment in most chapters.
9. Up-to-date discussion of published achievement tests, scholastic ability tests, and vocational interest inventories in Chapter 19.

Special Features

The following special features highlight the practicality of this text:

1. Examples of how to craft classroom assessments and what they typically look like.
2. Checklists with succinct tips for evaluating the quality of each type of assessment taught in the book.
3. Strategies for assessing higher-order thinking that serve as models and descriptions for developing problem-solving and critical-thinking assessments.
4. Chapter overviews that describe how the chapter is organized.
5. Chapter learning targets (objectives) that help students understand what they should be able to do after studying the chapter.
6. Important terms and concepts at the end of the chapter so students can focus their study on the new ideas a chapter introduces.
7. Chapter summaries in list form that highlight the major points and help students review the material.
8. End-of-chapter exercises and applications that let students apply their learning to practical situations.

9. Appendixes of statistical concepts with spreadsheet applications and tutorials for calculating reliability coefficients for instructors and students interested in a more quantitative approach than the text provides.
10. A glossary that defines the important terms and concepts introduced in the book so students can easily check meanings as they read.

Instructor's Manual/Test Bank

The on-line Instructor's Manual/Test Bank gives examples of performance activities for the instructor to use as class assignments, an example of a testing project, sample blueprints for a course examination, and sample syllabi. The majority of the manual is devoted to test items. The Instructor's Manual/Test Bank is available on-line so that the instructor can assemble and print objective-item tests.

To access the on-line instructor's manual, go to www.prenhall.com, click on the Instructor Support button, and then go to the Download Supplements section. Here you will be able to login or complete a one-time registration for a user name and password.

Companion Website

You can find the Companion Website for this text at www.prenhall.com/nitko. For each chapter of the book, the Companion Website presents *Chapter Objectives, Assess Yourself* (a Web-based quiz that is scored on-line; the results are given to the student and can be emailed automatically to the instructor), *Essays* (essay questions students can submit for grading on-line), *Key Terms* (an on-line Glossary), *Additional Readings* (bibliographical listings), and *Web Destinations* (hot links to a wide range of Websites related to the course).

Acknowledgments

A project of this magnitude requires the help of many persons. We are very much indebted to the reviewers whose critical reading contributed greatly to the technical accuracy, readability, and pedagogy of the fifth edition: Pamela Broadston, University of Arkansas at Little Rock; Anthony E. Kelly, George Mason University; Robert W. Lissitz, University of Maryland; and Leonard S. Feldt, University of Iowa.

We would also like to thank the reviewers for the second, third, and fourth editions: Peter W. Airasian, Boston College; Lawrence M. Aleamoni, University of Arizona; Carol E. Baker, University of Pittsburgh; W. L. Bashaw, University of

Georgia; Deborah Brown, West Chester University; Alice Corkill, University of Nevada at Las Vegas; Lee Doebler, University of Montevallo; Terry Fogg, Minnesota State University; Betty E. Gridley, Ball State University; Gretchen Guiton, University of Southern California; Thomas M. Haladyna, Arizona State University; Charles Hughes, Pennsylvania State University; Louise F. Jernigan, Eastern Michigan University; Suzanne Lane, University of Pittsburgh; Robert Lange, University of Central Florida; Craig Mertler, Bowling Green State University; William P. Moore, University of Kansas; Pamela A. Moss, University of Michigan; Robert Paugh, University of Central Florida; Susan E. Phillips, Michigan State University; Bruce Rogers, University of Northern Iowa; William M. Stallings, Georgia State University; Hoi K. Suen, Pennsylvania State University; James S. Terwilliger, University of Minnesota; Michael S. Trevisan, Washington State University; Anthony Truog, University of Wisconsin–Whitewater; Kinnard White, University of North Carolina; Richard Wolf, Teachers College, Columbia University; David R. Young, State University of New York–Cortland; and Michael J. Young, University of Pittsburgh.

We thank our students at the School of Education, University of Pittsburgh; the School of Education, Duquesne University; the College of Education, University of Arizona; the Curriculum Development and Evaluation Centre, Botswana Ministry of Education; teachers working with Jamaica Ministry of Education; teachers and assessors at the Examination Development Center, Indonesia Ministry of Education and Culture; and trainers with the Integrated Language Project in Egypt, who used the second, third, and fourth editions. They provided insightful feedback and corrections of errors that have greatly improved the usefulness of the text. Francis Amedahe helped classify chapter learning targets and write test items for the third edition. Sarah Bonner contributed test items, practical examples for classroom activities, and many elements of the Instructor's Manual for the fourth edition. Kevin Davis, Autumn Benson, and Mary Harlan of Merrill/Prentice Hall, as well as Carol Singer of GGS Book Services, applied their considerable knowledge and skill to producing the book. To all of these persons, and others we have failed to mention, we offer our most sincere thanks and appreciation.

Special thanks to Veronica Nitko, who made suggestions for improvement providing a teacher's perspective. She completed the entire permissions file, proving her ability to handle the most difficult cases of the grueling permissions process with grace and style. Special thanks also go to Frank Brookhart, whose support and encouragement were invaluable.

ABOUT THE AUTHORS

Anthony J. Nitko is an adjunct professor, Department of Educational Psychology, University of Arizona, and professor emeritus and former chairperson of the Department of Psychology in Education at the University of Pittsburgh. His research interests include curriculum-based criterion-referenced testing, integration of testing and instruction, classroom assessment, and the assessment of knowledge and higher-order thinking skills. His publications include the chapter "Designing Tests That Are Integrated with Instruction" in the third edition of *Educational Measurement* (1989). He co-authored (with C. M. Lindvall) *Measuring Pupil Achievement and Aptitude*; (with T. C. Hsu) *Pitt Educational Testing Aids* (PETA, a package of computer programs for classroom teachers); and (with R. Glaser) the chapter "Measurement in Learning and Instruction" in the second edition of *Educational Measurement* (1971).

Professor Nitko has been the editor of the journal *Educational Measurement: Issues and Practice* and also *d'News*, the AERA Division D newsletter. Some of the journals in which his research has appeared are *American Educational Research Journal, Applied Measurement in Education, Educational Evaluation and Policy Analysis, Educational Measurement: Issues and Practice, Educational Technology, Journal of Educational Measurement*, and *Research in Developmental Disabilities*.

Professor Nitko has been a member of several committees of the American Educational Research Association, was elected secretary of AERA Division D, served on committees of the National Council on Measurement in Education, and was elected to the board of directors and as president of the latter. He received Fulbright awards to Malawi and Barbados and has served as a consultant to various government and private agencies in Bangladesh, Barbados, Botswana, Egypt, Ethiopia, Indonesia, Jamaica, Malawi, Namibia, Oman, Singapore, the United States, and Vietnam.

Susan Brookhart is coordinator of assessment and evaluation for the School of Education at Duquesne University. Prior to this assignment, she was professor and chair of the Department of Educational Foundations and Leadership at Duquesne. Previous to her higher education experience, she taught both elementary and middle school. Her research interests include the role of classroom assessment in student motivation and achievement, the connection between classroom assessment and large-scale assessment, and grading.

Professor Brookhart is a past president of the American Educational Research Association's Special Interest Group on Classroom Assessment. She has been the education columnist for *National Forum*, the journal of Phi Kappa Phi. From 2003–2005 she served as newsletter editor for the National Council on Measurement in Education, and was program co-chair for the 2004 NCME annual meeting. She is the author of two books: *The Art and Science of Classroom Assessment* is a combination literature review and how-to book about classroom assessment in higher education; *Grading* is a textbook about grading in K–12 schools. She has written or co-authored over 40 articles on classroom assessment, educational measurement, program evaluation, and professional development, and serves on the editorial boards of *Teachers College Record* and *Applied Measurement in Education*.

**MERRILL
PRENTICE HALL**

Teacher Preparation Classroom

Your Class. Their Careers. Our Future. Will your students be prepared?

We invite you to explore our new, innovative and engaging website and all that it has to offer you, your course, and tomorrow's educators! Organized around the major courses pre-service teachers take, the Teacher Preparation site provides media, student/teacher artifacts, strategies, research articles, and other resources to equip your students with the quality tools needed to excel in their courses and prepare them for their first classroom.

This ultimate on-line education resource is available at no cost, when packaged with a Merrill text, and will provide you and your students access to:

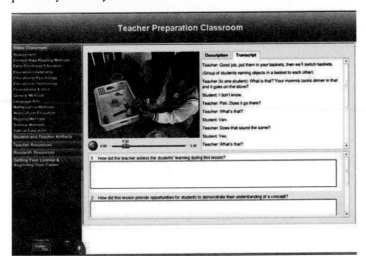

Online Video Library. More than 150 video clips—each tied to a course topic and framed by learning goals and Praxis-type questions—capture real teachers and students working in real classrooms, as well as in-depth interviews with both students and educators.

Student and Teacher Artifacts. More than 200 student and teacher classroom artifacts—each tied to a course topic and framed by learning goals and application questions—provide a wealth of materials and experiences to help make your study to become a professional teacher more concrete and hands-on.

Research Articles. Over 500 articles from ASCD's renowned journal *Educational Leadership*. The site also includes Research Navigator, a searchable database of additional educational journals.

Teaching Strategies. Over 500 strategies and lesson plans for you to use when you become a practicing professional.

Licensure and Career Tools. Resources devoted to helping you pass your licensure exam; learn standards, law, and public policies; plan a teaching portfolio; and succeed in your first year of teaching.

How to ORDER *Teacher Prep* for you and your students:
For students to receive a *Teacher Prep* Access Code with this text, instructors **must** provide a special value pack ISBN number on their textbook order form. To receive this special ISBN, please email **Merrill.marketing@pearsoned.com** and provide the following information:
- Name and Affiliation
- Author/Title/Edition of Merrill text

Upon ordering *Teacher Prep* for their students, instructors will be given a lifetime *Teacher Prep* Access Code.

BRIEF CONTENTS

CONTENTS

APPENDIXES

NOTE: Every effort has been made to provide accurate and current Internet information in this book. However, the Internet and information posted on it are constantly changing, so it is inevitable that some of the Internet addresses listed in this textbook will change.

1 | Classroom Decision Making and Using Assessment

LEARNING TARGETS

After studying this chapter, you should have learned the following:[1]

Teachers' Classroom Decisions

1. Give examples of teaching management decisions you need to make before, during, and after instruction. [4, 1, 2]

2. Give examples of assessment procedures that provide you with useful information for making the decisions you stated in Target 1. [1, 2, 3, 4]

Distinctions Among Assessments, Tests, Measurements, and Evaluations

3. Define and explain the relationships among teaching, assessment, testing, measurement, and evaluation. [6, 1]

4. Explain the principles that guide you in the process of selecting, developing, and using educationally meaningful assessments. [1, 3]

High-Stakes Assessment and Accountability

5. Explain the meaning of high-stakes testing and give examples. [6, 7]

6. Explain the purpose of accountability testing at the state and federal levels. [6, 7]

7. Describe the assessment requirements of the No Child Left Behind (NCLB) Act of 2001 and the consequences to schools that do not make adequate yearly progress toward achieving 100% proficiency of its student body attaining the state's standards. [7, 6]

8. State the positive and negative aspects of accountability testing in the NCLB framework. [7, 6, 4]

Assessment and Educational Decisions About Students

9. Describe and explain the range of educational decisions for which educators need quality assessments. [1, 6]

10. Distinguish between formative and summative evaluations. [1, 4]

11. Describe the type(s) of information assessments provide for making decisions about taking diagnostic/remedial actions, giving feedback to students/parents, giving feedback to teachers, motivating students, and assigning grades to students. [1, 3, 4]

12. Distinguish among selection decisions, placement decisions, classification decisions, counseling and guidance decisions, and credentialing/certification decisions. [1, 3, 6]

Acquiring the Competence to Assess Students

13. Explain how each of the *Standards for Teacher Competence in Educational Assessment of Students* is related to your teaching activities before, during, and after instruction. [6, 1, 7]

Important Terms and Concepts

14. Explain how the terms and concepts listed at the end of this chapter apply to educational assessments. [6]

[1]The Learning Targets that begin each chapter are cross-referenced to the American Federation of Teachers, National Council on Measurement in Education, and National Education Association (1990) *Standards for Teacher Competence in Educational Assessment of Students* (see Appendix A). The numbers that follow each learning target statement refer to one or more standards. The order of the standards represents the closeness on the match to the standards. The closest match is listed first. Francis Amedahe helped classify the learning targets.

Making good decisions in the classroom requires more than good intentions or previous experience. Good decisions, such as what to teach, how to teach it, and how to evaluate students' achievement, are based on high-quality information. Successful teachers obtain information about their students from high-quality assessments.

As you teach, don't fall into the trap of thinking that assessment involves simply testing and grading students or that assessment is separate from teaching. Rather, assessment involves gathering and using information to improve your teaching and your students' learning. When you use the assessment procedures you crafted, or when your district asks you to use specific assessment procedures, you need to be able to explain the results correctly to students, parents, other teachers, and school administrators. Further, as you develop professionally, you may have the opportunity to participate in local and state committees concerned with assessment issues. The mainstream media as well as educational publications emphasize assessment as a major concern and a newsworthy issue: It is likely to remain so for much of your professional career.

Studying the lessons taught by your instructor, studying the material in this book, and learning from your experience in the classroom will help you acquire the professional attitudes and competencies needed to assess your students validly.

ABOUT THIS CHAPTER

The first part of Chapter 1 looks at an example of how one student's assessments were interpreted and used by her parents and teachers. Next, the chapter discusses some of the many classroom decisions that teachers make and gives examples of the types of assessments that support these decisions. The third section looks more carefully at the meaning of assessment. We discuss how this concept is related to tests, measurements, and evaluations. Fourth, we explore the bigger picture of educational decision making. We look at the full range of educational decision making that assessments support. The final section covers the assessment competencies necessary to be an effective teacher.

EXAMPLE OF ASSESSMENTS USED FOR AN EDUCATIONAL DECISION

It is almost impossible for you to have attended school without having been exposed to a wide variety of educational and psychological assessment procedures. The fact that you are reading this book for a testing and measurement course places you not only among test takers, but also among successful test takers. Think for a few minutes: How many ways have you been assessed in your life? When did your assessment experiences begin? Consider this example:

Example

Meghan's educational assessment began in kindergarten with an interview and an observation. The state in which she lived had no mandatory kindergarten requirement. On registration day, Meghan and her mother came to school and were briefly interviewed. A teacher rated Meghan's cognitive and social-emotional skills. Her development was judged normal, and she attended kindergarten.

During the year, she experienced difficulty in paying attention to the teacher and participating in group activities, although she was neither aggressive nor hostile. She was given a "readiness test" at the end of kindergarten and performed as an average child. Her teacher recommended that she continue on to first grade, but her parents balked: They didn't think she was ready.

They took her to a child guidance clinic and requested further psychological assessment. The clinical psychologist administered an individual intelligence test and a "projective test" in which Meghan was asked to tell a story about what was happening in each of a set of pictures. The psychologist interviewed her, her parents, and her teacher. The psychologist described her as normal, both in cognitive ability and in social-emotional development.

Her parents withdrew her from the school she was attending and placed her in another school to repeat kindergarten. Later, they reported that whereas her first experience was difficult for her, her second kindergarten year was a great success. In their view, a teacher who was particularly sensitive to Meghan's needs helped accelerate her cognitive development. By the end of the year she had also become more confident in herself and regularly participated in group activities.

This brief anecdote shows assessments being used early in the person's life. Most of us recall more easily the assessments applied to us later in our lives, as older children, and as adults. You may not even associate the term *assessment* with Meghan's interviews. Yet, as shall be explained later, interviews are included in the broad definition of assessments.

Meghan's situation also illustrates that assessment results can contribute to a decision, but everyone concerned may not interpret the results in the same way. Although Meghan's parents may have been right to have her repeat kindergarten, there is no way of knowing what would have happened had she gone straight to first grade, because she didn't.

Decisions involve using different kinds of information. Sometimes test scores play a major role; at other times, less formal assessments play a more dominant role. In Meghan's case, both informal (teachers' observations, interviews) and formal (readiness test, intelligence test, projective test) assessments were administered.

This book discusses a variety of educational decisions that depend on assessments, especially in the classroom. Each time, it identifies the basic principles that relate to the evaluation and use of assessment information. It emphasizes basic principles rather than prescriptions to follow blindly (although you will find some of those, too). Once you understand the basic principles, however, you should be able to determine when those and other prescriptions are inappropriate.

TEACHERS' CLASSROOM DECISIONS

Teaching and learning require you to constantly gather information and make decisions. You might not realize it, but teachers make decisions about students at the rate of one every 2 to 3 minutes (Shavelson & Stern, 1981). That's about 20 decisions every class period! Sound teaching decisions require sound information. Sound assessment procedures gather sound information. Researchers estimate that teachers may spend from one third to one half of their time in assessment-related activities (Stiggins, Conklin, & Associates, 1992).

To help you think about the many decisions a teacher must make, we have organized a set of questions teachers must answer before, during, and after teaching. Examples of assessment methods that may give you useful information for making the decisions are listed in parentheses after each question.

Decisions Before Beginning Teaching

1.   What content do I need to cover during the next day, week, month, marking period, and so on? (Possible assessment methods: *Review the curriculum, the syllabus, and the textbook; examine copies of the standardized tests my students will need to pass.*)

2.   What abilities (cultural background factors, interests, skills, etc.) of my students do I need to take into account as I plan my teaching activities? (Possible assessment methods: *Informal observation of the students during class discussions; conversations with students' previous teachers; studying the students' permanent records to see their scholastic aptitude test results, past grades, and standardized test results; my knowledge of the student's personal family circumstances.*)

3.   What materials are appropriate for me to use with this group of students? (Possible assessment methods: *Class discussions in which I observe students' motivations, interests, beliefs, and experience with the topics I will teach, and their attitudes toward learning the topics; results from short pretests I administered; my study of the students' permanent records to learn the previous teacher's evaluations and the students' standardized achievement test results.*)

4.   With what learning activities will my students and I need to be engaged as I teach the lesson (unit, course)?

(Possible assessment methods: *My review of the types of activities I used previously that stimulated the interests of students; my analysis of the sequence of the learning activities students will follow; my review of how well the students achieved when those activities were used previously.*)

5.   What learning targets do I want my students to achieve as a result of my teaching? (Possible assessment methods: *My review of statements of goals and learning objectives; my review of test questions students should be able to answer; my review of the things students should be able to do and of the thinking skills students should be able to demonstrate after learning.*)

6.   How should I organize and arrange the students in the class for the upcoming lessons and activities? (Possible assessment methods: *My informal observation of students with special learning and social needs; my recollection of students' behavior during previous learning activities; information about what classroom arrangements worked best in the past when my students were learning similar targets.*)

Decisions During Teaching

1.   Is my lesson going well? Are students catching on (i.e., learning)? (Possible assessment methods: *My observations of students during learning activities; student responses to questions I have asked them; my observations of students' interactions.*)

2.   What should I do to make this lesson (activity) work better? (Possible assessment methods: *My diagnosis of the types of errors students made or misconceptions students are using; searching my memory for alternative ways to teach the material; my identifying which students are not participating or are acting inappropriately.*)

3.   What feedback should I give each student about how well he or she is learning? (Possible assessment methods: *My informal observation and experience on the amount and type of praise different students require; information about how close each student has come to achieving the learning target; students' homework and quiz results; my interviews of students.*)

4.   Are my students ready to move to the next activity in the learning sequence? (Possible assessment methods: *My informal observation and checking of students' completed work and questioning students about their understanding; my analysis of students' homework, quizzes, and test results.*)

Decisions After a Teaching Segment

1.   How well are my students achieving the short- and long-term instructional targets? (Possible assessment methods: *My classroom tests, projects, observations, interviews with students; my analysis of standardized test results.*)

2.   What strengths and weaknesses will I report to each student and to his or her guardian or parent? (Possible assessment methods: *My observations of each student's classroom participation; my review of each student's homework results; my review of each student's standardized achievement and*

scholastic aptitude test results when they become available; my review of information about a student's personal family circumstances.)

3. What grade should I give each student for the lesson or unit, marking period, or course? (Possible assessment methods: *My combining results from classroom learning activities, quizzes, tests, class projects, papers, labs, etc.; my observation about how well the student has attained the intended learning targets; my knowledge of the possible short- and long-term consequences to the student of reporting a particular grade.*)

4. How effectively did I teach this material to the students? (Possible assessment methods: *My review of summaries of the class's performance on the important instructional targets, on selected questions on standardized tests, and of how well the students liked the activities and lesson materials.*)

5. How effective are the curriculum and materials I used? (Possible assessment methods: *My review of summaries of informal observations of students' interests and reactions to the learning activities and materials; of the class's achievement on classroom tests that match the curriculum; and of several past classes' performance on selected areas of standardized tests.*)

These lists of questions and assessments are not exhaustive; you may wish to list several others. Later in this chapter we discuss several other educational decisions that need to be made by or for students. However, the preceding examples do illustrate that your teaching decisions require you to use many different types of information. Further, they illustrate that the exact type of information you need varies greatly from one teaching situation to the next. Remember that you cannot expect to make good decisions as you teach unless you can base these decisions on good-quality information.

DISTINCTIONS AMONG ASSESSMENTS, TESTS, MEASUREMENTS, AND EVALUATIONS

The general public often uses the terms *assessment, test, measurement,* and *evaluation* interchangeably, but it is important for you to distinguish among them. The meanings of the terms, as applied to situations in schools, are explained in the following paragraphs. This section explains the relationship among these terms (shown in Figure 1.1).

Assessments

Assessment is a broad term defined as a process for obtaining information that is used for making decisions about students; curricula, programs, and schools; and educational policy (see American Federation of Teachers, National Council on Measurement in Education, and National Education Association, 1990). Decisions about students include managing classroom instruction, placing them into different types of educational programs, assigning grades to

them, guiding and counseling them, selecting them for educational opportunities, and credentialing and certifying their competence. Decisions about curricula, programs, and schools include decisions about their effectiveness (summative evaluations) and about ways to improve them (formative evaluations). Decisions about educational policy are made at the local school district level, the state level, and the national level. Figure 1.2 illustrates some of the decisions and subdecisions for which educational assessments provide information.

When we say we are "assessing a student's competence," for example, we mean we are collecting information to help us decide the degree to which the student has achieved the learning targets. A large number of assessment techniques may be used to collect this information. These include formal and informal observations of a student; paper-and-pencil tests; a student's performance on homework, lab work, research papers, projects, and during oral questioning; and analyses of a student's records. This book will help you decide which of these techniques are best for your particular teaching situations.

Guidelines for Selecting and Using Classroom Assessments

Assessment is a process for obtaining information for making a particular educational decision. You should focus your assessment activities on the information you need to make particular educational decisions. This means that you need to become competent in selecting and using assessments. Here is a set of guiding principles that you should follow to select and use educational assessments meaningfully.

1. Be clear about the learning targets you want to assess.
2. Be sure that the assessment techniques you select match each learning target.
3. Be sure that the selected assessment techniques serve the needs of the learners.
4. Whenever possible, be sure to use multiple indicators of achievement for each learning target.
5. Be sure that when you interpret the results of assessments you take their limitations into account.

1. *Be clear about the learning targets you want to assess.* Before you can assess a student, you must know the kind(s) of student knowledge, skill(s), and performance(s) about which you need information. The knowledge, skills, and performances you want students to learn are sometimes called learning targets or standards. The more clearly you are able to specify the learning targets, the better you will be able to select the appropriate assessment techniques.

FIGURE 1.1
Relationship among the terms *assessments, tests, measurement,* and *evaluation.*

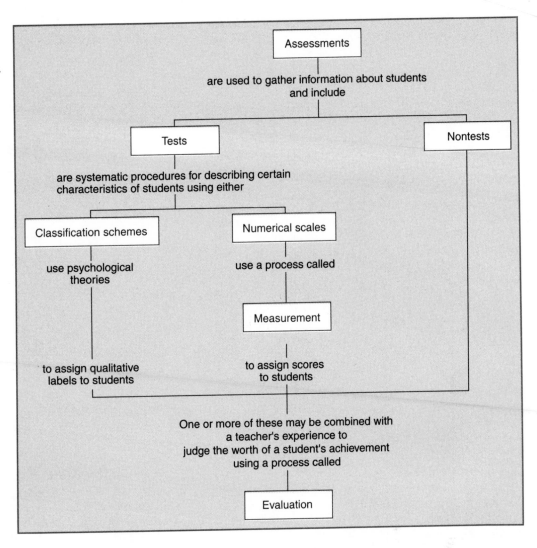

2. *Be sure that the assessment techniques you select match the learning target.* "Do we want to evaluate students' problem posing and problem solving in mathematics? Experimental research in science? Speaking, listening, and facilitating a discussion? Doing document-based historical inquiry? Thoroughly revising a piece of imaginative writing until it 'works' for the reader? Then let our assessment(s) be built out of such exemplary intellectual challenges" (Wiggins, 1990, p. 1). The assessment techniques selected should be as practical and efficient to use as possible, but practicality and efficiency should not be the overriding considerations.

3. *Be sure that the selected assessment techniques serve the needs of the learners.* Proper assessment tools are concrete examples for students of what they are expected to do with their learning. Assessment techniques should provide learners with opportunities for determining specifically what they have achieved and specifically what they must do to improve their performance. Therefore, you should select assessment methods that allow you to provide

meaningful feedback to the learners. You should be able to tell students how closely they have approximated the learning targets. Good assessment is good instruction.

4. *Whenever possible, be sure to use multiple indicators of performance for each learning target.* One format of assessment (such as short-answer questions or matching exercises) provides an incomplete picture of what a student has learned. Because one assessment format tends to emphasize only one aspect of a complex learning target, it typically underrepresents that learning target. Getting information about a student's achievement from several assessment modalities usually enhances the validity of your assessments. Matching exercises, for example, emphasize recall and recognition of factual information; essay questions emphasize organizing ideas and writing skill under the pressure of time limits; and a month-long project emphasizes freely using resources, research, and more thorough analyses of the topic. All three of these assessment techniques may be needed to ascertain the extent to which a student has achieved a given learning target.

6

FIGURE 1.2 **Examples of types of educational decisions for which assessments may be used.**

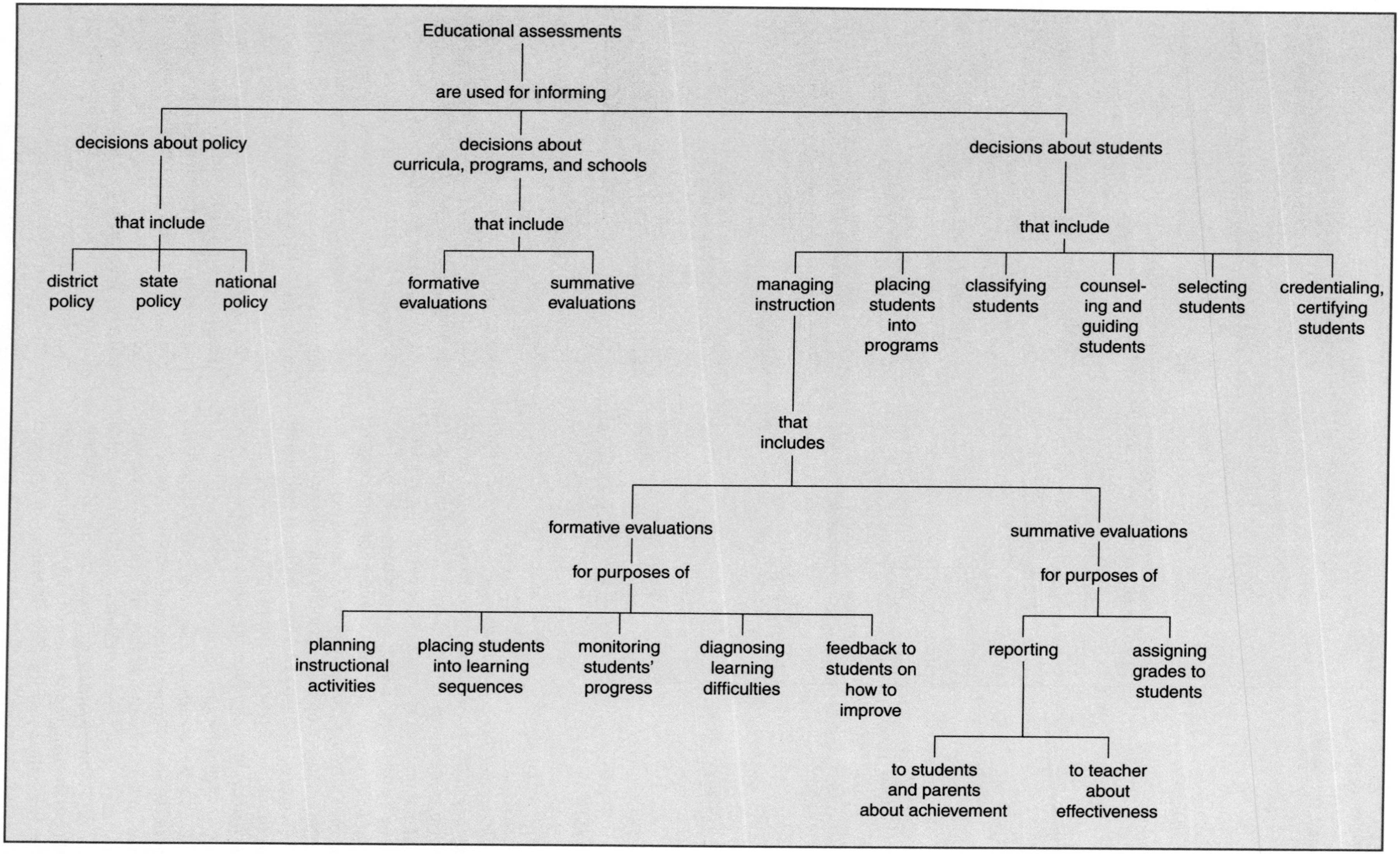

Educational assessments

are used for informing

decisions about policy
   that include
     district policy
     state policy
     national policy

decisions about curricula, programs, and schools
   that include
     formative evaluations
     summative evaluations

decisions about students
   that include
     managing instruction
     placing students into programs
     classifying students
     counseling and guiding students
     selecting students
     credentialing, certifying students

managing instruction
   that includes
     formative evaluations
       for purposes of
         planning instructional activities
         placing students into learning sequences
         monitoring students' progress
         diagnosing learning difficulties
         feedback to students on how to improve
     summative evaluations
       for purposes of
         assigning grades to students
         reporting
           to students and parents about achievement
           to teacher about effectiveness

5. *Be sure that when you interpret the results of assessments you take their limitations into account.* Although Guiding Principle 2 calls for increasing the authenticity or meaningfulness of the assessment techniques, assessments in schools cannot completely reproduce those things we want students to learn in "real life." The information we obtain, even when we use several different types of assessments, is only a sample of a student's attainment of a learning target. Because of this, information from assessment contains sampling error. Also, factors such as a student's physical and emotional conditions further limit the extent to which we can obtain truly accurate information. Teachers, and others, must make decisions nevertheless. The decisions, however, must keep these limitations in mind.

Tests

Testing Individuals A **test** is defined as an instrument or systematic procedure for observing and describing one or more characteristics of a student using either a numerical scale or a classification scheme. *Test* is a concept narrower than *assessment*. In schools, we usually think of a test as a paper-and-pencil instrument with a series of questions that students must answer. Teachers usually score these tests by adding together the "points" a student earned on each question. By using tests this way, teachers describe the student using a numerical scale. Similarly, a preschool child's cognitive development could be observed by using the *Wechsler Preschool and Primary Scale of Intelligence* (see Chapter 19) and described as having a percentile rank of 50 (see Chapter 17).

Not all tests use numerical scales. Other systematic observation procedures such as the play interview (Murphy, 1956) that child development specialists sometimes use with preschoolers describe the child using a classification scheme. For example, a child may be described as "ego centered" or "drive centered." These categories represent constructs based in Freudian psychological theories.

Survey Testing Programs Although it is natural to assume that tests are designed to provide information about an individual, this is not always true. States have testing programs designed to determine whether their *schools* have attained certain goals or standards. A federal law–the No Child Left Behind (NCLB) Act of 2001–mandates that each state use tests to evaluate whether schools are making adequate progress in improving students' achievement of the state's educational standards. Although these tests are administered to individual students, a state uses the results to measure the effectiveness of a school. In such cases, individual names are not associated with scores when reporting to the government. The "score" for the school system (or for a specific school at a specific grade level) is usually the percentage of the school's students who meet or exceed a state's standards.

Another example of an assessment program designed to survey the educational system rather than individual students is the National Assessment of Educational Progress (NAEP) (Merwin & Womer, 1969; Mullis, 1991; Tyler, 1966). The NAEP assesses the impact of the nation's educational efforts by describing what students are able to do.[2] Assessment tasks are assigned to students on a random sampling basis, so that not every student has the same or even comparable tasks. Thus, it is not meaningful to use the scores with individual students. The assessment is intended to pool the results from all students in the sample to show the progress of education in the entire country.

The NAEP surveys are efficient ways to gather information about the average performance of a group of students because they assess each student using very few tasks, but pool the results to estimate the average. This gain in efficiency of assessing the group is at the expense of being able to describe validly the achievement of individual students.

Measurement

Measurement is defined as a procedure for assigning numbers (usually called scores) to a specified attribute or characteristic of a person in such a way that the numbers describe the degree to which the person possesses the attribute. An important feature of the number-assigning procedure in measurement is that the resulting scores maintain the order that exists in the real world among the people being measured. At the minimum this would mean, for example, that if you are a better speller than us, a test that measures our spelling abilities should result in your score (your measurement) being higher than ours.

For many of the characteristics measured in education and psychology, the number-assigning procedure is to count the correct answers or to sum points earned on a test. Alternately, we may use a scale to rate quality of a student's product (for example, an essay or a response to an open-ended mathematics task) or performance (how well the student carries out chemistry lab procedures). (See Chapter 12 for examples.) There has been considerable debate in the field of psychometrics as to whether such procedures are sufficient to call measurement in psychology and education anything but crude (Campbell, 1928; Johnson, 1928, 1936; McGregor, 1935; Pfanzagl, 1968; Rozeboom, 1966; Stevens, 1951; Suppes & Zinnes, 1963). The debate about crudeness of educational measurement surfaces from time to time. Most measurement specialists would probably agree that although a counting or rating procedure is crude, as a practical matter, scores from assessments are useful when they are validated by using

[2]Details are found at http://nces.ed.gov/nationsreportcard.

data from research (Jones, 1971; Lord & Novick, 1968; Messick, 1989a; Rozeboom, 1966).

You can see from the preceding definitions that an assessment may or may not provide measurements. If a procedure describes a student by qualitative labels or categories, the student is assessed, but not measured in the sense used here. *Assessment* is a broader term than *test* or *measurement* because not all types of assessments yield measurements.

Evaluation

Evaluation is defined as the process of making a value judgment about the worth of a student's product or performance. For example, you may judge a student's writing as exceptionally good for his grade placement. This evaluation may lead you to encourage the student to enter a national essay competition. To make this evaluation, you would first have to assess his writing ability. You may gather information by reviewing the student's journal, comparing his writing to other students and to known quality standards of writing, and so on. Such assessments provide information you may use to judge the quality or worth of the student's writing. Your judgment that the student's writing is of high quality would lead you to decide to encourage him to enter the competition. Evaluations are the bases for decisions about what course of action to follow.

Evaluation may or may not be based on measurements or test results. Among others, evaluations may be based on counting things, using checklists, or using rating scales. Clearly, evaluation does occur in the absence of tests, measurements, and other objective information. You can—and probably often do—evaluate students on the basis of assessments such as systematic observation and qualitative description, without measuring them. Even if objective information is available and used, evaluators must integrate it into their own experiences to come to decisions. So degrees of subjectivity, inconsistency, and bias influence all evaluations. Testing and measurement, because they are more formal, standardized, and objective than other assessment techniques, reduce some of the inconsistency and subjectivity that influence evaluation. To say, however, that using tests and measurements (or, in general, quantitative information) "greatly improves" evaluation is itself a bias toward the technological.

Evaluation of Students You may evaluate students for formative or summative purposes. **Formative evaluation of students' achievement** means we are judging the quality of a student's achievement while the student is still in the process of learning. We make formative evaluations of students so we can guide their next learning steps. When you ask questions in class to see whether students understand the lesson, for example, you are obtaining information to formatively evaluate their learning. You can then adjust your lesson if students do not understand.

Summative evaluation of students' achievement means judging the quality or worth of a student's achievement after the instructional process is completed. Giving letter grades on report cards is one example of reporting your summative evaluation of a student's achievement.

Evaluation of Schools, Programs, or Materials Not all evaluations are of individual students. You also can evaluate a textbook, a set of instructional materials, an instructional procedure, a curriculum, an educational program, or a school. Each of these things may be evaluated during development as well as after they are completely developed. The terms *formative* and *summative* evaluation are also used to distinguish the roles of evaluation during these two periods (Cronbach, 1963; Lindvall & Cox, 1970; Scriven, 1967).

Formative evaluation of schools, programs or materials is judgment about quality or worth made during the design or development of instructional materials, instructional procedures, curricula, or educational programs. The evaluator uses these judgments to modify, form, or otherwise improve the school, program, or educational material. A teacher also engages in formative evaluation when revising lessons or learning materials based on information obtained from their previous use.

Summative evaluation of schools, programs, or materials is judgment about the quality or worth of schools, or already-completed instructional materials, instructional procedures, curricula, or educational programs. Such evaluations tend to summarize strengths and weaknesses; they describe the extent to which a properly implemented program or procedure has attained its stated goals and objectives. The results of summative evaluations, more than formative evaluations, suggest whether a particular educational product "works" and under which conditions or under what degree of implementation. Summative evaluations usually are directed less toward providing suggestions for improvement than are formative evaluations.

HIGH-STAKES ASSESSMENT AND ACCOUNTABILITY

It may not come as a surprise to you that what you teach and how you teach it are not entirely under your control. However, it may come as a shock to beginning teachers that assessments created externally to their classrooms will shape and influence what they teach and how they assess their students. Legally mandated assessment programs place constraints on your teaching. You need to be aware of these as you plan your instruction.

High-Stakes Testing

High-stakes assessments (tests) are used for decisions that result in serious consequences for school administrators, teachers, or students. Here are some examples:

Examples of High-Stakes Testing

Example 1. In a certain country, at the end of their secondary schooling, students must pass an examination for each subject they studied. The examinations cover the concepts and skills that are in the curriculum. Students are marked as A, B, C, D, and F for each examination. Students must get no Fs in order to be awarded the secondary school certificate. Persons without a secondary school certificate find it difficult to get a job in the country because employers see the certificate as indicating that candidates for a job have minimum competencies needed. Students who fail may study on their own time and take the examination again, but they cannot repeat the schooling because there are only a limited number of places in secondary schools. Students must have As and Bs but no Ds or Fs to be considered for a place in one of the few universities.

Example 2. In a certain state, students must pass tests in English, writing, and mathematics before Grade 12; otherwise they cannot receive a high school diploma. They begin taking the test in Grade 10, and once each year up to Grade 12 they may repeat the tests they failed. Students who do not pass all of the tests by the end of Grade 12 receive only an attendance certificate.

Example 3. In another state, students take the state-mandated tests annually in reading and mathematics from Grades 3 through 11. Students do not have to pass the tests, but each school is evaluated by how well its students do. If a school's students do not show a pattern of continued improvement on the tests, the state places a sanction on the school by dismissing the administrative staff and perhaps some of the teachers. It turns over the running of the school to a state-appointed team until the test scores show regular improvement.

In Example 1, the consequences of assessment are quite serious for individual students: If they fail to pass all subjects they may not get a job because the employers require a secondary school certificate; if they fail to do well on the examinations, they have no opportunity for attending a university. The stakes are high in Example 2, but not quite as high as in Example 1. Students can stay in school for several years, prepare for the tests, and retake the tests each year. In Example 3, there are high stakes for school administrators and teachers, but not for individual students. In fact, the tests may be low stakes for the students because there appear to be no consequences to them for doing poorly on the tests.

Accountability Testing

Although the use of high-stakes testing in the United States can be traced back to Horace Mann in the 1850s, modern high-stakes testing in the United States grew out of school reform movements that developed during the 1980s. Educational reformers and state legislators wanted to ensure that virtually all students could meet educational standards set by the state and demanded by employers. Employers needed to increase productivity and to be competitive in world markets. They needed a better-educated workforce to handle the demands of the rapidly increasing technology and greater intellectual skills needed in the workplace. State legislators considered testing to be one way of holding schools accountable for students learning the educational standards set by a state.

Assessment that is used to hold individual students or school officials responsible for ensuring that students meet state standards is called **accountability testing**. Usually accountability testing is accompanied by high-stakes consequences. A state's accountability testing may take several forms, as is shown by the examples above. A state may require both individual and school accountability, too. You should check your state's education department Website for its current regulations regarding individual and school accountability.

No Child Left Behind Act

The No Child Left Behind Act is important to our discussion of high-stakes assessment because it requires states to establish challenging content standards and performance standards (referred to as *achievement standards* in the NCLB Act literature), and to demonstrate by way of tests and other assessments how well students have attained high levels of achievement on these standards. A state's failure to provide this demonstration will result in loss of federal education funds that are authorized under the NCLB Act. Assessment under the NCLB Act is a school-level accountability tool.

Standards-Based Proficiency Requirements   **Content standards** describe the subject-matter facts, concepts, principles, and so on that students are expected to learn. **Performance standards** describe the things students can perform or do once the content standards are learned. (We discuss state standards and how to align your learning targets to them in Chapter 2.) When students are assessed on a state's standards, they are classified into one of three categories for purposes of reporting to the federal government: basic, proficient, and advanced. (A state may have more than three categories, but all must be aligned to these three.) Under the NCLB Act, the goal is for 100% of the students in each school to reach the proficient level or higher on the state's content and performance standards by 2014. In addition, schools must show *adequate yearly progress (AYP)* toward this goal, otherwise sanctions will be imposed.

Disaggregation   An important provision of the NCLB Act is that a state must report test summaries at the school level and must disaggregate the data. Disaggregate the test **results** means to separate the test results for the total population of students in order to report separately for subgroups of students—such as students who are poor, who are members of minority groups, who have limited English proficiency, and who have disabilities—in addition to reporting on the total student population. The reason for this requirement is that the federal government wants to ensure that states are accountable for all students learning the challenging state standards, including those in these subgroups. In some instances in the past, states reported only on the whole population of their students, thus masking the fact that some subgroups of students were not receiving quality education and were failing to meet the standards.

Assessment of Students With Disabilities   Under the NCLB Act all students must be assessed, including students with disabilities and students with limited English proficiency. Ninety-five percent of students with disabilities must participate in the assessment. Students' disabilities may be used as a basis for accommodations to the assessment process when they are unable to participate under the standardized conditions set for the general student population. Further, alternative assessment methods must be found to assess those students who cannot participate even with accommodations. States are now granted some limited flexibility in adjusting content and performance standards for students with severe cognitive impairments (U.S. Department of Education, 2005).

High-Stakes Sanctions   The sanctions and corrective actions that follow failure to make adequate yearly progress after 2 years include the following: (a) parents may choose to have their children attend another school in the district that is making AYP, (b) the school staff may be replaced, (c) a new curriculum may be implemented, (d) the authority of the administrative staff of the school may be changed, (e) the school year may be extended, (f) the school may be reorganized, (g) the school may be reopened as a charter school, (h) the state may contract with a private company to run the school, and (i) the school may be taken over by the state. We have already mentioned withholding federal education funding for noncompliance with NCLB. From these sanctions, you can see the high-stakes aspects of testing under NCLB.

Effectiveness of NCLB   Whether NCLB assessment and accountability requirements have improved or hindered education is controversial. Advocates of strong accountability testing support the federal government's position that "No Child Left Behind is designed to change the culture of America's schools by closing the achievement gap, offering more flexibility, giving parents more options, and teaching students based on what works" (U.S. Department of Education, n.d.). Assessment is seen as an objective way to ensure that all students demonstrate that learning has occurred. Some have prepared "instructionally

supportive accountability" assessments that "(1) measure students' mastery of only a modest number of extraordinarily significant curricular aims, (2) describe the nature of those aims for teachers with great clarity, and (3) provide aggregatable reports of each student's attainment of every curricular aim assessed" (Popham, 2005).

Critics point to the inevitable corruption of test scores when stakes are high, including the narrowing of the curriculum to easily tested objectives whenever the focus of the school is on improving scores on tests (e.g., Nichols & Berliner, 2005). (We discuss appropriate and ethical test preparation strategies that teachers and school administrators should use in both Chapters 5 and 14 of this book.) Others point out that "for special education students and the schools that serve them, the requirements of two federal education laws and their implementing regulations, the Individuals with Disabilities Education Act (IDEA) and the No Child Left Behind Act (NCLB), are in conflict" (Phillips, 2005). A number of states criticize NCLB because adequate funds for paying for the assessments and for educational improvements were promised but never delivered in sufficient amounts (Committee on Education and the Workforce, 2005, see also http://www.nclbgrassroots.org for a summary of the states' concerns).

Teachers Coping With NCLB and Other High-Stakes Testing

As you study this book, we will suggest many ways to improve your assessment competencies. We focus on using assessment results to improve your teaching and students' learning. High-stakes testing will require you to carefully determine how the content and learning targets of your teaching and your student assessments are aligned with your state's standards. Some school districts have already prepared curricular materials and sample assessments that show this alignment. Be thankful to the colleagues that preceded you! You should obtain these guidelines from your school office if they are available and use them as you develop your teaching and assessment plan.

We will help, too. In Chapter 2, we discuss how you can develop specific learning targets from statements of content and performance standards. In Chapter 5 we discuss some of your professional responsibilities and ethical behaviors that relate to preparing students for tests, including high-stakes accountability testing. In Chapter 6, we illustrate how to plan for assessments that are aligned with state standards and your own teaching. In Chapters 7–13 we provide the knowledge you need to develop the appropriate assessments. We expand on preparing students for taking tests in Chapter 14, where we offer some practical suggestions.

You must recognize that high-stakes assessment will have an impact on what and how you teach. The assessment skills you learn through your course instructor and in this book will help you with teaching and assessing in your professional practice.

ASSESSMENT AND EDUCATIONAL DECISIONS ABOUT STUDENTS

You now know that assessment provides information for decisions about students; schools, curricula, and programs; and educational policy. This section discusses several types of educational decisions made about students. It puts assessment into a broader context to give you a better idea of the purposes for which assessments are used (see Figure 1.2).

Understanding the features of different types of decisions will help you evaluate various assessment techniques that you may be thinking about using. There is no simple answer to the question, "Is this a good assessment procedure?" As you will learn in this course, an assessment procedure may serve some types of decisions very well, others not so well. Understanding the different types of decisions discussed in this section will also help you explain to parents why you used various assessments with their children. Finally, although you may not be required to make all of these types of student decisions yourself, by the time your students have completed their education they will have experienced virtually all of them.

Instructional Management Decisions

Your classroom is a decision-rich environment. You must make many decisions, including planning instructional activities, placing students into learning sequences, monitoring students' progress, diagnosing students' learning difficulties, providing students and parents with feedback about achievements, evaluating your teaching effectiveness, and assigning grades to students. We described previously some of the questions that need to be answered to make these decisions.

Instructional Diagnosis and Remediation Sometimes the instruction an individual student receives is not effective: The student may need special remedial help or special instruction that relies on alternative methods or materials. Assessments that provide some of the information needed to make this type of decision are called **diagnostic assessments**. Diagnostic decisions center on the question, "What learning activities should I use to best adapt to this student's individual requirements and thereby maximize the student's opportunities to attain the chosen learning target?" Diagnosis implies identifying both the appropriate content and the types of learning activities that will help a student attain the learning target (Glaser & Nitko, 1971; Nitko, 1989; Nitko & Hsu, 1974).

The art of diagnostic assessment is not well developed. There are at least five approaches to diagnosing a student's

learning difficulties. Chapter 13 describes them and offers suggestions for how to craft appropriate assessment techniques.

Feedback to Students Assessments also provide feedback to students about their learning. Feedback, however, is likely to improve learning only under certain conditions. Simply assessing students and reporting the results to them is not likely to affect their performance. Learners must review both correct and incorrect performance and, in addition, be able to correct their incorrect performance. In other words, feedback must give specific guidance to students about what they must do to improve their learning. Therefore, teachers who give students only their grade on a paper or test are not providing enough feedback to help students improve.

Assessments can be used to provide feedback that helps learning, provided you integrate them into your instructional process. Feedback from classroom assessment procedures will not help your students learn if the students lack a command of the prerequisite learning and/or have comprehended little or nothing of the lesson prior to the assessment. It is especially important that you correct students' errors—or that the students correct their own errors—before going on to new instruction. Similarly, frequent feedback during the lesson is essential. Additional discussion of feedback appears in Chapter 13.

Feedback to the Teacher Remember that assessments provide feedback to the teacher about how well students have learned and how well the teacher has taught. Of course, if students have failed to grasp important points, the teacher should reteach the material before proceeding to new material.

Modeling Learning Targets Assessments serve as examples for students by showing them what you want them to learn. Students can compare their current performance on the learning target with the desired performance. You may teach them to identify the way(s) in which their current performance matches the expected performance and how it is deficient. Your teaching can focus on how to remedy the deficiencies. In these ways, good assessment is good instruction. Also, as students evaluate their own performance, you may teach them the appropriate criteria for judging how well they are learning as well as teaching them what is important to learn.

Motivating Students Assessments may also motivate students to study. Unfortunately, some teachers use this form of accountability as a weapon rather than as a constructive force. Teachers may hope that using an assessment as a possible threat will encourage their students to take studying seriously. Sometimes teachers use the "surprise quiz" or "pop quiz" in this manner to encourage more frequent studying and less cramming.

Studies have not justified use of assessments this way. Rather, assessments ought to be viewed in a more positive light: as tools for instruction and feedback to students (Glaser & Nitko, 1971). Also, teachers or parents who stress test performance as the sole or major criterion for school success may create undue test anxiety for students. As a result, students may perform less well in the long run. This point is discussed again in Chapter 14.

Assigning Grades to Students   One of the most obvious reasons for giving classroom assessments is to help you assign grades to students. Although teachers continually assess their students' progress in informal ways, they also must officially record their evaluations of students' progress through grades. The grades or symbols (A, B, C, etc.) that you report represent your summative evaluations or judgments about how well your students have achieved important learning targets. Use a mixture of assessment formats to provide the information you need to make these evaluations. Good teaching practice and common sense indicate that grades should be based on more than test scores. Many teachers, however, fall back on test scores alone to justify the grades they assign. Assigning grades involves evaluative decisions, but subjective judgments are often difficult to justify and explain. Tests, especially those of the objective variety, seem to reduce judgment and subjectivity, even though this is not necessarily true. A more complete discussion of grading, including suggestions for assigning grades, appears in Chapter 15.

Selection Decisions

Most people are familiar with **selection decisions**: An institution or organization decides that some persons are acceptable, whereas others are not; those who are unacceptable are rejected and no longer are the concern of the institution or organization. This feature—rejection and the elimination of those rejected from immediate institutional concern—is central to a selection decision (Cronbach & Gleser, 1965).

An educational institution often uses test scores as one component for selection decisions. For example, college admissions are often selection decisions: Some candidates are admitted and others are not; those who are rejected are no longer the college's concern. Some critics may argue, however, that those rejected should still be of concern to society generally.

When an institution uses an assessment procedure for selection, it is important to show that candidates' results on these assessments bear a significant relationship to success in the program or job for which the institution is selecting persons. If data do not show that these assessment results can distinguish effectively between those candidates likely to succeed and those unlikely to succeed, then these assessment procedures should be improved or eliminated. In fact, it may be illegal to continue to use assessment results that bear no relationship to success on

the job (Equal Employment Opportunity Commission, Civil Service Commission, Department of Justice, Department of Labor, & Department of the Treasury, 1979; United States Supreme Court, 1971.).

Selection decisions need not be perfect to be useful, however. Assessment results cannot be expected to have perfect validity for selection, or any other, decisions (see Chapter 3). Figure 1.3 illustrates the use of imperfect assessments in selection. Some applicants would have been successful had they been selected instead of rejected; and some, even though they were accepted, turned out to be unsuccessful. Assessments can be evaluated, then, in terms of the consequences of the decisions made when using them. This subject is taken up in Chapter 3.

Placement Decisions

Placement decisions are characterized as follows: Persons are assigned to different levels of the same general type of instruction, education, or work; no one is rejected, but all remain within the institution to be assigned to some level (Cronbach, 1990; Cronbach & Gleser, 1965). Students not enrolled in honors sections, for example, must be placed at other educational levels. First-grade students with low scores on a reading readiness test, for example, cannot be sent home. They must be placed into appropriate educational levels and taught to read. You may recognize a decision as a placement decision by noting whether the institution must account for all candidates. The rejection of candidates and their elimination from the institution's concern that occurs with selection decisions is not possible in placement decisions.

Many, if not most, decisions in schools are placement decisions. Educators who use the language of selection often are using the language incorrectly. Upon closer examination, they are speaking about placement decisions. For example, when an educator speaks of "screening" students for a gifted and talented program, the decisions are actually placement decisions because their ultimate purpose is to place all students into appropriate educational programs. The schools are not free to teach some students and to reject the rest. If one instructional method is inappropriate for a particular student, then an appropriate alternative method needs to be found. In the end, all students are taught, and must learn.

Classification Decisions

Sometimes we must make a decision that results in a person being assigned to one of several different but unordered categories, jobs, or programs. These types of decisions are called **classification decisions** (Cronbach & Gleser, 1965). For example, educational legislation concerning persons with disabilities has given a legal status to many labels for classifying children with disabilities and

FIGURE 1.3 **A simplified illustration of how a selection situation uses assessments and the consequences of those decisions. The assessments and the decision rules are evaluated in terms of their consequences.**

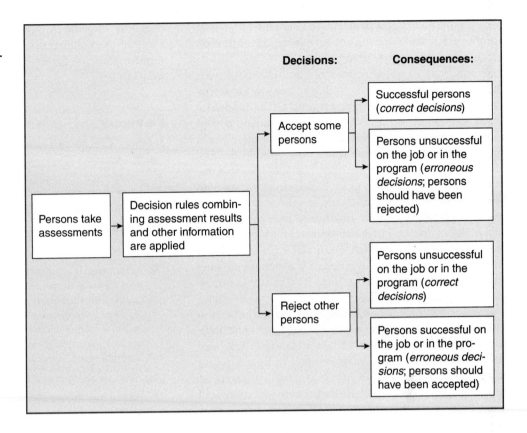

strongly encourages classifying them into one (or more) of a few designated categories. These categories are unordered (blindness is not higher or lower than deafness), so these are classification decisions rather than placement decisions.

You may consider *classification* as a more general term that subsumes *selection* and *placement* as special cases (Cronbach & Gleser, 1965). *Classification* refers to cases in which the categories are essentially unordered, *placement* refers to cases in which the categories represent ordered levels of education without rejection, and *selection* refers to cases in which students are accepted or rejected. This book considers the three types of decisions separately.

Counseling and Guidance Decisions

Assessment results frequently assist students in exploring, choosing, and preparing for careers. A single assessment result is not used for making guidance and counseling decisions. Rather, a *series of assessments* is administered, including an interview, an interest inventory, various aptitude tests, a personality questionnaire, and an achievement battery. Information from these assessments, along with additional background information, is discussed with the student during a series of counseling sessions. This facilitates a student's decision-making process and provides a beginning for exploring different careers. Exploring career options is likely to be an ongoing

and changing series of decisions that occur throughout a person's life.

Credentialing and Certification Decisions

Credentialing and certification decisions reflect whether a student has attained certain standards of learning. Student certification decisions may focus on whether a student has attained minimum competence or obtained a high standard, depending on the legal mandate. Certification and credentialing may be mandated by a state's legislation or may be voluntary. If a state law mandates that students achieve certain standards of performance, most often students are administered an assessment procedure created at the state level. Those who meet the standards are awarded a credential (such as a high school diploma).

These certification assessment procedures present special problems for validation. Individual students cannot reasonably be held accountable for instruction that the teacher failed to deliver or which was delivered poorly, even though, on the average, teaching was adequate. A critical point, therefore, is whether the quality of instruction corresponds to what the assessment procedure covers. The closer the correspondence, the fairer the certification is to the student. If students did not have the opportunity to learn how to perform the tasks that appear on the certification assessment procedure, either because a specific school lacked the necessary resources or a particular teacher failed to deliver appropriate instruction, the assessment-based certification process seems inherently unjust.

Often, it is not easy to resolve conflicts about what has been taught and what should appear on an assessment procedure. For example, suppose a state holds students accountable for a reading list of "important works." Suppose one group's teacher did not explain these works directly, but another group's teacher did. Should the first group be held accountable? Further, high standards in some states may require students to apply knowledge to new situations, to solve new problems, and to exhibit creativity. To assess application to new situations, assessments must include tasks that are unfamiliar or novel for students. This is accomplished by deliberately making the assessment materials different from the materials used during teaching (otherwise they would not be "novel"). The validity question is, "Is this fair to students?"

Another example is using assessments for teacher certification. Some states assess preservice teachers' knowledge using paper-and-pencil tests. Often a battery of tests will include basic skills, general knowledge, and professional knowledge. Some tests also include separate assessment of specialty areas such as biology, elementary education, and teaching students with hearing impairments. Some states also evaluate a teacher's classroom performance through observation or by assigning a master teacher to mentor a beginning teacher. The National Board for Professional Teaching Standards (NBPTS) has developed assessment procedures to certify experienced teachers who are outstanding in their teaching skills (see http://www.nbpts.org). Teachers are assessed in many areas and educational levels. Unlike the state-mandated assessments, NBPTS certification is voluntary. Also, the assessment procedures are heavily performance based. That is, teachers may submit portfolios of documents, student work samples, and perhaps videotapes to demonstrate their teaching competence. Their teaching may also be observed, and they may come to an assessment center to participate in simulated teaching activities such as instructional design, group interaction, parent-teacher conferences, peer collaboration, and staff development (Performance Assessment Laboratory, 1992).

ACQUIRING THE COMPETENCE TO ASSESS STUDENTS

To help you evaluate your present level of competence and focus on important areas of assessment skills, the American Federation of Teachers et al. (1990) published *Standards for Teacher Competence in Educational Assessment of Students*. These standards are reproduced in Appendix A. Each of these seven competencies is addressed throughout this book. We have keyed the learning targets at the beginning of each chapter to the specific competencies to which they refer. Because your assessment competence will

continue to grow throughout your professional career, some of the competencies listed in Appendix A may be more appropriate for experienced teachers than for beginning teachers.

Summary

Teachers' Classroom Decisions

- Teaching and learning require the continuous gathering of information for making decisions. Sound assessments are prerequisite to sound educational decisions.

Distinctions among Assessments, Tests, Measurements, and Evaluations

Assessments

- Assessment is a process for obtaining information that is used to make decisions about students, curricula and programs, and educational policy.
- Assessment techniques include paper-and-pencil tests; formal and informal observation; homework, exercises, and research papers; projects and exhibits; performances; portfolios; oral questioning; and analyses of students' records.

Guidelines for Selecting and Using Classroom Assessments

- Several important principles guide the selection and use of particular assessment techniques, including (a) being clear about the learning targets, (b) matching the assessment technique to the learning targets, (c) serving the needs of learners, (d) using multiple indicators of achievement, and (e) recognizing the limitations of each technique.

Tests

- A test is an instrument or systematic procedure for observing and describing one or more characteristics of a student, using either a numerical scale or a classification scheme. Tests can be for individual students or for surveying schools or nations.

Measurement

- Measurement is a procedure for assigning numbers (usually called scores) to a specified attribute or characteristic in such a way that the numbers describe the degree to which a person possesses the attribute.

Evaluation

- Evaluation is the process of making a value judgment about the worth of someone or something. Evaluations may or may not be based on information obtained from tests and other assessments.
- Formative evaluation of students are judgments about the quality of students' achievement while they are still in the process of learning and are made so we can guide their learning.
- Summative evaluation of students are judgments about the quality of students' achievement after instruction is complete and are made so we can report their achievement to parents and school authorities.
- Formative evaluations of educational actions are judgments about the worth of schools, curricula, materials, and programs while they are under development that result in suggestions for ways to redesign, refine, or improve them.

- Summative evaluations of educational actions are judgments about the value of schools, curricula, materials, and programs after they are completed; these evaluations suggest whether they should be continued, adopted, or used.

High-Stakes Assessment and Accountability

- High-stake assessments have very serious consequences to persons for whom the results are used.
- Accountability testing holds individual students or school officials responsible for ensuring that students achieve good test results.
- The No Child Left Behind (NCLB) Act of 2001 is a federal funding law that uses accountability testing to hold states responsible for students' achievement of the state's content and performance standards.
- According to NCLB, schools must make adequate yearly progress toward the goal of having 100% of students achieving at or above proficient levels on the state's standards by 2014.
- The NCLB requires that at least 95% of students with disabilities or limited English proficiency be administered assessments and be included in the state's results that are reported to the federal government.
- NCLB required high-stakes sanctions for schools that do not comply with the legislation or fail to make adequate yearly progress toward 100% proficiency.
- Advocates of the NCLB approach to accountability point to the legal need to ensure that all students achieve high standards and that tests help monitor this progress in an objective way.
- Critics of the NCLB approach to accountability point to the negative effects of testing that result in narrowing the curriculum that leads to corruption of test scores by teachers and school administrators, to inequities and contradictions for special education students, and to the lack of adequate federal funding to achieve the NCLB goals.
- Teachers will need to align their teaching and assessments with their state's content and performance standards in order that their students have an opportunity to achieve the standards.

Decisions About Educational Policy

- Educational policy decisions are made at the district, state, and national levels.
- Decisions about schools, curricula, materials, and programs may be made during their development or after they have been completed.

Assessment and Educational Decisions About Students

Instructional Management Decisions

- Managing instruction: planning instructional activities, placing students into learning sequences, monitoring students' progress, diagnosing students' learning difficulties, modeling learning targets, giving feedback to students and parents, deciding on one's own teaching effectiveness, and assigning grades to students.

Selection Decisions

- Selecting students: accepting some students and rejecting others for a job, program, or higher level of education.

Placement Decisions

- Placing students into programs: assigning students to different levels of learning programs.

Classification Decisions

- Classifying students: assigning students to different categories, such as by type of disability.

Counseling and Guidance Decisions

- Counseling and guidance: assisting students in exploring, choosing, and preparing for different careers; helping them adjust to home, school, and peer stress, which is part of normal growth and development.

Credentialing and Certification Decisions

- Credentialing and certifying students: deciding whether students meet standards of competence for a diploma or for a certificate that entitles them to apply for employment.

Acquiring the Competence to Assess Students

- The *Standards for Teacher Competence in Educational Assessment of Students* (American Federation of Teachers et al., 1990) identifies seven standards toward which teachers should strive to assess students properly. These are reproduced and explained in Appendix A. The learning targets of this book are keyed to these professional standards.

Important Terms and Concepts

accountability testing
assessment
classification decisions
content standards
credentialing
diagnostic assessments
disaggregate the test results
evaluation
formative evaluation of schools, programs, or materials
formative evaluation of students' achievement
high-stakes assessments (tests)
measurement
performance standards
placement decisions
selection decisions
summative evaluation of schools, programs, or materials
summative evaluation of students' achievement
test

Exercises and Applications

1. Self-reflect on a specific lesson you have taught or would like to teach. Make a list of the decisions you made (or need to make) before, during, and after this lesson. Next to each decision, identify how you will obtain the information needed to make the decision. What criterion might you use to judge the quality of each piece of information?
2. Check education magazines and newspapers during the past 4 months for articles on NCLB. (You may want to use their Websites to identify articles, for example go to http://www.edweek.org.) Also check the Websites of teachers' unions, state governors organizations, organizations of state boards of education, and parent advocacy

groups. Who are the persons or agencies concerned about NCLB? What are the major issues with which they are concerned? Summarize your results, present them to your class, and compare your results with those of the other students. What are the issues that teachers need to address in their classrooms that are related to NCLB?

3. Decide whether each of the following statements is true or false. Defend your answers.
   a. To make evaluations, one must use measurements.
   b. To measure an important educational attribute of a student, one must use a test.
   c. To evaluate a student, one must measure that student.
   d. To test a student, one must measure that student.
   e. Any piece of information a teacher obtains about a student is an assessment.
   f. To evaluate a student, one must assess that student.

4. Classify each of these statements as reflecting a selection, classification, placement, career guidance, diagnostic/remediation, or certification decision. Defend your answers.
   a. After students begin kindergarten, they are given a battery of perceptual skills tests to decide which children should receive special perceptual skills training and which should remain in the "regular" program.
   b. A school operates two different third-grade reading programs. At the end of third grade, the standardized reading test results are summarized separately for each program and compared.
   c. A child study team decides whether each child who has been administered a series of screening tests should be included in a particular category of disability (students with hearing impairments, learning disabilities, etc.).
   d. After a school psychologist assesses a student, local education authorities assign the student to the resource room, where the teacher for students with learning disabilities gives the student special instruction each day.
   e. Each graduate of this department of education is required to take and pass the state's test before being allowed to teach in the schools.

5. Self-reflect on each of the seven standards for teacher competence found in Appendix A. Under each standard, describe the kinds of competence you now have and those that you hope to have at the end of this course.

2 | Describing the Goals and Learning Targets of Instruction

LEARNING TARGETS

After studying this chapter, you should have learned the following:

Importance of Specifying Objectives

1. Describe how learning targets help direct the instructional process. [1, 4, 7]

2. List four ways in which learning targets contribute to improved classroom assessment. [1, 4]

Educational Goals, State Standards, and Learning Targets

3. Distinguish among content and performance standards, general and specific learning targets, and developmental and mastery learning targets. [2, 1]

Taxonomies of Learning Targets

4. Explain why taxonomies of thinking skills are useful for reviewing learning targets and assessment tasks. [2, 3, 1]

5. Classify learning targets using the Bloom et al. and Marzano et al. classifications of thinking skills. [2, 3, 1]

6. Explain the differences and similarities between the original and revised Bloom taxonomies. [2, 3, 1]

7. Name and define the major categories of at least one thinking skills taxonomy. [2, 1]

8. State the five criteria you may use to decide which taxonomy to use. [1, 4]

Selecting, Writing, and Evaluating Learning Targets

9. Name at least two sources for obtaining lists of learning targets for the lessons you plan to teach. [2, 1]

10. State the seven criteria that you may use to review and judge the quality of a list of learning targets for a unit or a course. [2, 1, 4]

11. Write specific learning targets for your subject area that meet the student-centered, performance-centered, and content-centered criteria for such statements. [2, 1, 4]

12. Develop learning targets that are aligned with your state standards. [2, 1, 4]

Making Sure Assessment Tasks Are Aligned to Learning Targets

13. Describe how you would decide whether your assessment matches the mastery learning targets you have set for your lessons. [3, 1, 6]

14. Explain why you need to use several assessment methods to evaluate students' achievement of developmental learning targets. [3, 1, 6]

15. Explain how you go about aligning your assessments and learning targets with your state's educational standards. [3, 1, 6]

Important Terms and Concepts

16. Explain how each of the terms and concepts listed at the end of this chapter may be applied to educational assessment. [6]

ABOUT THIS CHAPTER

Chapter 1 emphasized the need to be sure your assessment techniques actually match the learning targets of your teaching. In this chapter, you will learn what good learning targets are and how to prepare them for use in your teaching. First we discuss the importance of using learning targets in your teaching. Second, we focus on the differences among educational goals, general objectives, and learning targets. Third, we discuss different taxonomies of learning targets that help ensure that your teaching aligns with the important goals of the curriculum. Next we cover the skills you need to select, write, and evaluate the learning targets for teaching. Fifth, we discuss how to align the learning targets you specify for your teaching with the assessments you will use to evaluate the students.

IMPORTANCE OF SPECIFYING OBJECTIVES

A **learning objective** specifies what you would like students to achieve when they have completed an instructional segment. We use the term *objective* to emphasize that the goal of teaching involves more than "covering the material" and "keeping students actively engaged." The focus of your teaching should be on student achievements as well as on the learning process. A learning objective states what students should be able to do, value, or feel after you have taught them.

Although the formal term is *learning objective*, we will use the informal term **learning target** to mean the same thing as learning objective. Some authors use other synonyms such as *achievement targets*.

Learning Targets Help Direct the Instructional Process

Instruction is the process you use to provide students with the conditions that help them achieve the learning targets. Some learning targets are **cognitive**, meaning that they deal primarily with intellectual knowledge and thinking skills. For example, you may want students to read a claim made by a political figure and determine whether there is evidence available to support that claim. Other learning outcomes are **affective**, meaning that they deal with how students should feel or what they should value. For example, you may want students to value the right to vote in elections over other activities competing for their time. As another example, you may want students to feel comfortable when talking in front of their classmates about how to solve mathematics problems. Yet other learning targets are **psychomotor**, meaning that they deal primarily with motor skills and physical perceptions. For example, you may want students to set up, focus, and use a microscope properly during a science investigation of pond water.

Deciding the specific targets you expect students to learn is one important step in the teaching process. Instruction may be thought of as involving three fundamental but interrelated activities (Lindvall & Nitko, 1975):

1. Deciding what the student is to learn.
2. Carrying out the actual instruction.
3. Evaluating the learning.

Activity 1 requires you to articulate in some way what you expect students to be able to do after you have taught them. Usually, you do this by specifying learning targets or by providing several concrete examples of the tasks students should be able to do to demonstrate that the learning targets have been reached. Activity 1 informs you and the students about what is expected as a result of teaching and studying. Your understanding of the learning targets guides your teaching and provides a criterion for deciding whether students have attained the desired change.

Activity 2 is the heart of the teaching process itself. Here you provide the conditions and activities for students to learn. These include monitoring students' progress and giving them feedback on what they need to improve their achievement of the learning targets.

Activity 3, evaluating whether learning has occurred, is essential for good teaching. Through it you and your students come to know how well the learning targets have been reached. The more clearly you specify the learning targets, the more directed your teaching efforts and your students' learning efforts will be.

Interaction of the Three Teaching Activities

The three fundamental activities are interactive rather than a straight one-two-three process. Setting clear learning targets helps you plan your teaching efficiently, conduct your instruction effectively, and assess student outcomes validly. Assessing and evaluating students using clearly specified learning targets provides you with information about how to guide students' learning and how effective your instruction has been. This information, in turn, may be used to adjust your teaching, to plan the next instructional activities, or to specify the instructional targets better.

Additional Reasons for Using Specific Learning Targets

The three activities just presented are a simplified description of the teaching process. They do, however, illustrate that teaching can be easier when a teacher has clear learning targets in mind. Additional reasons why learning targets should be used in the classroom include (Gow, 1976):

1. They help teachers and/or curriculum designers make their own educational goals explicit.

2. They communicate the intent of instruction to students, parents, other teachers, school administrators, and the public.

3. They provide the basis for teachers to analyze what they teach and to construct learning activities.

4. They describe the specific performances against which teachers can evaluate the success of instruction.

5. They can help educators focus and clarify discussions of educational goals with parents (and others).

6. They communicate to students the performance they are expected to learn. This may empower them to direct their own learning.

7. They make it easier to individualize instruction.

8. They help teachers evaluate and improve both instructional procedures and learning targets.

Importance of Learning Targets for Classroom Assessment

Obviously, before you can craft procedures to evaluate students' learning, you should have clearly in mind the students' performances you want to evaluate. If you are not clear on which important learning outcomes you want to evaluate, you may easily fail to assess those outcomes validly. In this chapter, statements of specific learning targets are viewed as having value for at least the following aspects of classroom assessment:

1. *The general planning for an assessment procedure* is made easier by knowing the specific outcomes you wish students to achieve.

2. *Selecting and crafting assessment procedures* depend on your knowing which specific achievements you should assess.

3. *Evaluating an existing assessment procedure* you already crafted is easier when you know the specific learning targets.

4. *Properly judging the content relevance of an assessment procedure* requires you to know the specific achievements you should assess (see Chapter 3).

EDUCATIONAL GOALS, STATE STANDARDS, AND LEARNING TARGETS

This section discusses several closely related concepts. You might find it helpful to refer to Figure 2.1 when studying them.

Educational Goals Versus Specific Learning Targets

Schooling and other organized instruction help students attain educational goals. One of the many ways to define educational goals is that they "are those human activities which contribute to the functioning of a society (including the functioning of an individual in society), and which can be acquired through learning" (Gagné, Briggs, & Wagner, 1988, p. 39).

Educational goals are stated in broad terms. They give direction and purpose to planning overall educational activities. Examples of statements of broad educational goals appear in reports prepared by state departments of education, local school systems, and associations such as the National Council of Teachers of Mathematics, the American Association for the Advancement of Science, and the Association of American Geographers. Here is one example of an educational goal:

> **Example**
> Every student should acquire skills in using scientific measurement.

These types of broad goals are organized into subject-matter areas such as mathematics and history. The broad goals, and statements of subject-matter area and content-specific thinking processes, serve as a curriculum framework within which you and other educators can define specific learning targets. State education agencies take the process further by publishing expected learning outcomes or *standards*. In such cases, your school is held accountable for students' achieving these particular standards. You can obtain a copy of your state's standards from your school principal or central administration office. Also, check your state's education department Website to see what your state requires and download the standards if your school does not have a copy. Finally, check the Companion Website for this book to see what other states require.

General Learning Targets Versus Specific Learning Targets

There is an appropriate level of specificity for stating learning targets. If the description of a target is stated too broadly, teachers cannot use it for developing lesson plans and assessment procedures. The previously stated educational goal, for example, may help communicate a general educational aim, but is too broadly stated to be immediately useful to plan lessons and assessments.

A **general learning target** is a statement of an expected learning outcome that is derived from an educational goal. General learning targets are more specific than educational goals and usually clear enough for general planning of a course. However, they need to be made more specific before they can become learning targets that you use when planning your lessons. The following example of a general

FIGURE 2.1 **Relationships among the concepts of standards, goals, and learning targets.**

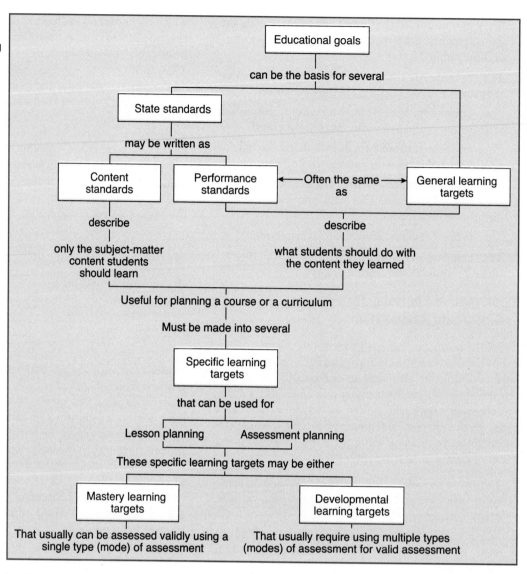

learning target might be stated for a primary school science unit on measurement in the metric system:

Example

Acquire the skills needed to use common instruments to measure length, volume, and mass in metric units.

When teaching students and assessing their attainment of this general learning target you may need to break it down into two or more specific learning targets. A **specific learning target** is a clear statement about what students are to achieve at the end of a unit of instruction. Here are three examples of specific learning targets that are derived from the preceding general learning target:

Example

1. Measure the length of objects to the nearest tenth of a meter using a meter stick.
2. Measure the mass of objects to the nearest tenth of a kilogram using a simple beam balance and one set of weights.
3. Measure the volume of liquids to the nearest tenth of a liter using a graduated cylinder.

Danger of Overly Specific Learning Targets

When learning targets are made more specific, the achievement you are to teach and to assess becomes clear. But beware of overspecificity. Long lists of very narrow "bits" of behavior can fragment the subject to be taught. The following examples show learning targets that are too specific, along with a suggested revision.

<hr>

Example

The student is able to:

Too specific: Estimate the number of beans in a jar.

Better: Solve practical problems using calculations and estimation.

Rationale: "Beans-in-a-jar" is not the real target of learning. Rather, it is but one of the many possible tasks that a student should complete to demonstrate achievement of estimation and calculation. The learning target statement should describe this less specific achievement.

<hr>

Example

The student is able to:

Too specific: Explain the meaning of the term *cold front*.

Better: Explain the meaning of key weather terms.

Rationale: "Cold front" is only one of several key weather terms that are included in a unit. Listing a separate learning target for each term taught in the unit fragments the unit's focus on general weather terminology.

<hr>

Example

The student is able to:

Too specific: Use question marks (?) correctly in paragraphs given to the student.

Better: Use end-of-sentence punctuation correctly.

Rationale: "Question marks" are but one type of end-of-sentence punctuation that students must learn. Punctuation applies both to editing paragraphs and to one's own writing: that is, to all situations involving written work. Listing a separate learning target for each type of terminal sentence punctuation taught in the unit fragments the unit's focus on using all terminal punctuation properly.

A second danger is that lists of specific objectives may become too long and are ignored. Identify a few of the most important learning targets for each instructional unit and focus on these.

Crafting Assessments That Require Students to Use Combinations of Learning Targets

It is important, too, to create learning and assessment situations that require students to use combinations of specific skills and knowledge to perform complex tasks and solve real-life problems. Figure 2.2 shows a beans-in-a-jar problem. In solving this problem students are expected to use several specific skills and knowledge (listed at the upper right of the figure) to accurately estimate the number of beans in the jar. "Beans-in-a-jar" is not the learning target itself, of course. Rather, it is only one example of many possible tasks in which the learning target is to apply a combination of proportional reasoning, estimation, measurement, and other skills to solve complex problems.

Notice that in this example, the most important outcomes teachers should assess are the processes and strategies students use to solve these problems. The criteria for these are listed under "Criterion-referenced interpretations" in Figure 2.1. An assessment procedure that focuses exclusively on the degree of correctness of students' answers to tasks like this would be invalid because it misses assessing the processes that students use.

State Standards Versus Learning Targets

Standards Your state may have mandated that students meet a set of educational standards. **Standards** are statements about what students are expected to learn. Some states call these statements *essential skills, learning expectations, learning outcomes, achievement expectations,* or other names. The NCLB Act requires all states to specify achievement standards and to assess students' attainment of them.

Often there are two sets of achievement standards. **Content standards** are statements about the subject-matter facts, concepts, principles, and so on that students are expected to learn. For example, a standard for life science might be, "Students should know that the cell nucleus is where genetic information is located in plants and animals." **Performance standards** are statements about the things students can perform or do once the content standards are learned.[1] For example, "students can

<hr>

[1]To make matters more confusing, some states define performance standards (or simply "standards") as certain ranges of test scores and then give these labels. For example, a student whose score is between 20 and 40 may be said to have reached the "basic level" of the standards; between 41 and 60 may be at the "proficient level"; and above 60 at the "advanced level." We shall not use the term *standards* in this way in this chapter.

FIGURE 2.2 **An assessment task used as a benchmark by the Toronto Board of Education.**

BEANS IN A JAR
Applying rate and ratio

In the task for this benchmark, students were first shown a jar filled with beans and asked to estimate the number of beans. They were then asked to work out the number of beans more accurately using any of the following materials: a calculator, a balance scale and masses, a ruler, a graduated cylinder, and a transparent centimeter-squared grid. They were told they could count some but not all of the beans. If the students did not know how to proceed, the evaluators suggested they weigh a small handful of beans. The students were asked to keep an ongoing record of their solutions. After they had solved the problem they were asked to describe the problem and their solutions.

Key objectives from the Ontario Ministry of Education and Toronto Board guidelines

- Apply ratio and rate in problem solving
- Consolidate conversions among commonly used metric units
- Collect and organize data
- Consolidate and apply operations with whole numbers and decimals with and without a calculator
- Apply estimation, rounding and reasonableness of results in calculations, in problem solving and in applications
- Develop facility in communication skills involving the use of the language and notation of mathematics
- Develop problem-solving abilities

Norm-referenced interpretations	Task score	Criterion-referenced interpretations
20% of the students scored 5 (80% scored lower than 5)	5	The student understands the problem and immediately begins to search for a strategy, perhaps experimenting with different methods and materials before proceeding. The student monitors the solution as it develops and may check and remeasure. The student uses the materials efficiently and accurately and keeps a good record of the data. All the calculations are performed accurately and a reasonable answer is produced. The student gives a clear explanation of the solution demonstrating sound reasoning with proportions. The student takes ownership of the task and enjoys its challenge.
19% of the students scored 4 (61% scored lower than 4)	4	The student may make some false starts and may be helped by the evaluator to get focused. The student may use some materials to no purpose or inaccurately, perhaps confusing volume and mass. The student reasons with proportions correctly. Although stuck at various points in the solution, the student perseveres and usually produces a reasonable answer. The student usually gives a clear explanation and enjoys the activity.
20% of the students attained 3 (41% scored lower than 3; the average score is 3.0)	3	There is some confusion in one or more aspects of the solution to the problem. The student may confuse units, make arithmetic errors or perform incorrect operations. The student may have some idea of proportionality but is unable to use it correctly. The student does not use the materials to the best advantage. The student seeks assistance from the evaluator. Although not totally confident, the student may persevere in an attempt to arrive at an answer to the problem.
24% of the students attained 2 (17% scored lower than 2)	2	The student may make a start at solving the problem but is unable to complete a solution. The student may repeatedly switch methods and materials, and be unable to find an effective strategy. There is considerable confusion with units and the interpretation of various measurements. The student usually guesses at the operations that should be performed with the data. The student lacks confidence and seeks a great deal of assistance from the evaluator.
17% of the students attained 1	1	The student may estimate the number of beans but gives no response or very limited response to working out the number more accurately..

Source: Adapted from John L. Clark (1992). The Toronto Board of Education's Benchmarks in Mathematics. *The Arithmetic Teacher: Mathematics Through the Middle Grades,* *39*(6), pp. 51–55. Adapted by permission.

identify the cell nucleus in microscopic slides of various plant and animal cells."

State education departments prepare standards used in schools. Local school districts are required to teach students to achieve these standards and are held accountable for students achieving them through the state's assessment system. Professional organizations can prepare standards, too. These organizations try to influence what is taught by publicly promoting their own standards. Examples of professional organizations with published standards are the National Academy of Sciences, National Council of Teachers of English, and National Council of Teachers of Mathematics. Most standards from professional organizations can be found on the organizations' Websites.

States' standards vary greatly in their quality and degree of specificity. Not all states have done a good job of writing standards. There seems to be no standard way (no pun intended) to write standards.

In the past, some states have established standards for only some grade levels (e.g., 4th, 8th, 10th, and 12th grades). Under the NCLB Act states must have standards for Grades 3 through 12 in reading/language arts and science by 2007. In response to this requirement, most states have prepared many standards for each grade level. Others, however, are experimenting with writing a select few standards for each grade and focusing assessment and teaching on these (Popham, 2005).

Learning Targets As you may have gathered from the preceding paragraphs, a state's standards are really learning targets. After officially adopting a state's standards, a school must make sure all students are taught and achieve those standards. Most state standards are written at a fairly general level. The better-written state performance standards are essentially the same as the general learning targets that we discussed earlier. Some states, however, have written only content standards, but in response to the NCLB Act requirements are in the process of preparing performance standards. In either case, you will need to break down each standard into two or more specific learning targets to teach and assess them. Thus, all of the material in this chapter applies to teaching and assessment whether your school and state use "objectives," "learning targets," or "standards." The example below shows how specific learning targets are developed from a state standard and compares statements of standards, general learning targets, and specific learning targets for third-grade reading in one school district. From this you can see that you need to derive specific learning targets from state standards.

Example

State standard

- Communicate well in writing for a variety of purposes.

General learning target

- Write for narrative, persuasive, imaginative, and expository purposes.

Specific learning targets

- Explains the difference between narrative, persuasive, imaginative, and expository writing purposes.
- Applies prewriting skills and strategies to generate ideas, clarify purpose, and define audience before beginning to write.
- After receiving feedback on the first draft in the areas of ideas, organization, voice, word choice, and sentence fluency, uses the feedback to revise the draft.
- Reviews and revises the second draft for grammatical correctness and proper use of standard writing conventions.

Specific Learning Targets as Mastery Statements

Assessment focuses on what you can see students doing. From this observation you will infer whether they have attained the learning targets. For example, a high school biology unit on living cells may have as a general learning target that students should "learn the organizations and functions of cells." But what can the student do to demonstrate learning of this general target? There may be several answers to this question, each phrased as a specific instructional objective and each describing what a student "can do," as shown in the following example:

Example

1. The student can draw models of various types of cells and label their parts.
2. The student can list the parts of a cell and describe the structures included in each.
3. The student can explain the functions that different cells perform and how these functions are related to each other.

Statements of what students can do at the end of instruction may be called **mastery learning targets**. Robert Forsyth (1976) referred to them as "can do" statements. They have also been called *specific learning outcomes* and *behavioral objectives*.

Mastery Learning Targets Versus Developmental Learning Targets

Some skills and abilities are more aptly stated at a somewhat higher level of abstraction than mastery learning targets to communicate that they are continuously developed throughout life. Consider the following examples.

Examples

1. Combine information and ideas from several sources to reach conclusions and solve problems.
2. Analyze and make critical judgments about the viewpoints expressed in passages.
3. Write several paragraphs that explain the author's point of view.
4. Use numerical concepts and measurements to describe real-world objects.
5. Interpret statistical data found in material from a variety of disciplines.
6. Write imaginative and creative stories.
7. Use examples from materials read to support your point of view.
8. Communicate your ideas using visual media such as drawings and figures.

Because of the lifelong nature of these targets they may be called *developmental objectives* (Gronlund, 1973) or **developmental learning targets**.

At first glance, it might seem that all one needs to do is to insert a "can do" phrase in front of each of the preceding statements to transform them to mastery learning targets. As Forsyth (1976) points out, however, it is not that simple. First, each statement represents a broad domain of loosely related (not highly correlated) performances. Second, each statement represents skills or abilities typically thought of as developing continuously to higher levels rather than the all-or-none dichotomy implied by the mastery learning targets.

The Problem of a Broad, Heterogeneous Domain Consider Developmental Learning Target 2 in the previous list. Now, think about questions you could ask students to assess how well they have achieved this learning target. Your questions need to require students to analyze a reading passage and make inferences based on information in it. The example below shows three possible questions. These questions are taken from the *Iowa Tests of Educational Development*, social studies reading subtest. The numbers in the brackets are the percentage of 10th-grade students answering each question correctly.

Example

1. From his manner and formal training, what opinion might people have formed of John Marshall? [28%]
2. What do the last two sentences suggest about Patasonian's acceptance of U.S. aid? [44%]
3. Suppose an uninsured and unemployed motorist damaged someone's car. Which speaker offers a plan that would allow the injured party to collect benefits? [64%] (Forsyth, 1976, p. 12)

You can see that each question refers to a different passage with different viewpoints expressed. Further, the percentage of students answering one question is quite different from the percentage answering another. Studies of these questions show that those who answer one question right are not necessarily the same students who get another question right (Forsyth, 1976).

We can conclude from this that Developmental Learning Target 2 represents a broad domain of reading passages and that mastering one part of the domain does not mean mastering another. This is the case with developmental learning targets like those listed previously.

The Issue of Continuous Development of Skill The second concern, the continuous or developmental nature of these learning targets, stems from the fact that "students cannot be expected to fully achieve such objectives. Even the simplest of these . . . is a matter of degree and can be continuously developed throughout life. All we can reasonably expect to do for a particular course or unit of instruction is to identify a sample of specific learning outcomes that represent degrees of progress toward the objectives" (Gronlund, 1973, p. 17). The essential concern here is that the skills represented by these learning targets are complex, the number of tasks that can be used to demonstrate learning is vast, and each represents goals to work toward continuously rather than to master completely (Gronlund, 1973).

Teaching and Assessing Developmental Learning Targets One way to begin designing instruction and assessing progress toward developmental objectives is to list several specific learning targets for each one. They should represent the *key* performances expected of a student at a particular *grade* or *age level*. This is illustrated in the following, which clarifies a broad instructional objective in science by listing several specific learning targets that support it:

Example[2]

Developmental learning target: Interprets and uses Boyle's Law to explain phenomena and solve problems.

Specific learning targets clarifying this developmental target.

1. States a definition of Boyle's Law.
2. States the domain to which Boyle's Law applies.
3. Describes the relationship between Boyle's Law and Charles' Law.
4. Uses Boyle's Law to explain an observation in a lab experiment.

[2]Based on Klopfer (1969).

5. Appropriately analyzes a new (to the student) situation in terms of Boyle's Law.

6. Solves a new problem or makes an appropriate choice for a course of action, taking into account the implications of Boyle's Law.

Although this list of six specific objectives might be made longer, the six objectives would likely be considered adequate for describing what is meant by "interpreting and using Boyle's Law" at the end of a first course in high school physics. Specific tasks could then be prepared for assessing achievement of the six specific objectives. Some tasks could assess only one of these learning targets; others could require a student to use several of these learning targets in combination. A student's overall score could be interpreted as indicating the degree to which a student has acquired the ability to interpret and use Boyle's Law, rather than as a "mastery/nonmastery" description.

TAXONOMIES OF LEARNING TARGETS

Simply writing learning targets "off the top of your head" can be frustrating because a seemingly endless number of possible targets exist. Further, if you are unaccustomed to writing learning targets, you are likely to write first those targets that have a very narrow focus, specify content topics, and represent lower level cognitive skills. A taxonomy can help you bring to mind the wide range of important learning targets and thinking skills.

Taxonomies of instructional learning targets are highly organized schemes for classifying learning targets into various levels of complexity. Generally, educational learning targets fall into one of three domains:[3]

1. *Cognitive domain:* Targets focus on knowledge and abilities requiring memory, thinking, and reasoning processes.

2. *Affective domain:* Targets focus on feelings, interests, attitudes, dispositions, and emotional states.

3. *Psychomotor domain:* Targets focus on motor skills and perceptual processes.

Learning targets within each domain may be classified by using a taxonomy for that domain. Because there is more than one way to define a classification scheme, several different taxonomies have been developed for sorting learning targets in a given domain. Only two of these taxonomies for the cognitive domain are described here. Other cognitive domain taxonomies are summarized in Appendixes D, E, and F. Chapter 6 will discuss using taxonomies to develop an assessment plan. You may want to review that chapter

[3]A single, real-life, complex performance will likely involve components of more than one domain.

briefly now. The other chapters in Part II discuss crafting tasks to assess learning targets at different taxonomy levels.

COGNITIVE DOMAIN TAXONOMIES
Bloom's *Taxonomy*

When developing a list of learning targets, you may find the *Taxonomy of Educational Objectives: The Classification of Educational Goals, Handbook I: Cognitive Domain* (Bloom, Englehart, Furst, Hill, & Krathwohl, 1956) to be of considerable value. This taxonomy is a comprehensive outline of a range of cognitive abilities that you might teach. The taxonomy classifies cognitive performances into six major headings arranged from simple to complex (Bloom et al., 1956).

The six main headings of the taxonomy are described here. To illustrate how this taxonomy can help you direct or focus your teaching and assessment strategies, we give an example of a learning target and a corresponding assessment item for each main heading as they may apply to teaching a language arts unit on short stories.

Suppose you are teaching students to understand the elements that authors use when writing short stories. Suppose the short stories you select all concern people's personal problems, and that the characters in these stories handle their personal problems inappropriately. The learning targets and questions that follow may be used to help you direct your assessment plans. Later chapters will detail how to craft assessment tasks. At this point we are studying only the range of thinking skills that should be taught and assessed.

1. **Knowledge** ... involves the recall of specifics and universals, the recall of methods and processes, or the recall of a pattern, structure, or setting. For measurement purposes, the recall situation involves little more than bringing to mind the appropriate material. (p. 201)

Example

Sample learning target: Recall the main characters in each of the short stories read and what they did.

Sample assessment items: (1) List the names of all of the characters in the *Witch's Forest*.

(2) In the *Witch's Forest*, what did Sally do when her mother refused to let her go into the forest?

2. **Comprehension** . . . represents the lowest level of understanding. It refers to a type of understanding or apprehension such that the individual knows what is being communicated and can make use of the material or idea being communicated without necessarily relating it to other material or seeing its fullest implications. (p. 204)

Example

Sample learning target:	Explain the main ideas and themes of the short stories that we read.
Sample assessment item:	Write using your own words what the *Witch's Forest* was all about.

3. **Application** . . . The use of abstractions in particular and concrete situations [to solve new or novel problems]. The abstractions may be in the form of general ideas, rules of procedures, or generalized methods. The abstractions may also be technical principles, ideas, and theories, which must be remembered and applied. (p. 205)

Example

Sample learning target:	Relate the personal problems of the characters in the short stories that were read to problems that real people face.
Sample assessment item:	Are the problems Sally had with her mother in the story similar to the problems you or someone you know have with their mother? Explain why or why not.

4. **Analysis** . . . The breakdown of a communication into its constituent elements or parts such that the relative hierarchy of ideas is made clear and/or the relations between the ideas expressed are made explicit. Such analyses are intended to clarify the communication, to indicate how the communication is organized, and the way in which it manages to convey its effects, as well as its basis and arrangements. (p. 205)

Example

Sample learning target:	Identify the literary devices that authors use to convey their characters' feelings to the reader.

Sample assessment item:	In *Witch's Forest*, Sally was upset with her mother. In *Dog Long Gone*, Billy was upset with his brother. What words and phrases did the authors of these two stories use to show how upset these characters were? Explain and give examples.

5. **Synthesis** . . . The putting together of elements and parts so as to form a whole. This involves the process of working with pieces, parts, elements, etc., and arranging and combining them in such a way as to constitute a pattern or structure not clearly there before. (p. 206)

Example

Sample learning target:	Describe, across all of the stories read, the general approach that the characters used to resolve their problems unsuccessfully.
Sample assessment item:	So far we have read *Witch's Forest, Dog Long Gone, Simon's Top,* and *Woman With No Manners.* In every story one character was not able to solve the personal problem he or she faced. What were the ways these characters tried to solve their problems? What do these unsuccessful ways to solve problems have in common?

6. **Evaluation** . . . Judgments about the value of material and methods for given purposes. Quantitative and qualitative judgments about the extent to which materials and methods satisfy criteria. Use of a standard of appraisal. The criteria may be those determined by the student or given to him. (p. 207)

Example

Sample learning targets:	(1) Develop one's own set of three or four criteria for judging the quality of a short story.
	(2) Use the three or four criteria to evaluate several new stories that were not read in class.

Sample assessment items: (1) So far we have read four short stories. What are three or four different traits that make a story high quality? Use these traits to develop three or four criteria that you could use to evaluate the quality of any short story.

(2) Read the two new short stories assigned to you. Use the criteria you developed to evaluate these two stories. Evaluate each story on every criterion. Summarize your findings.

Figure 2.3 shows how learning targets in science and social studies may be classified in the *Taxonomy*. Examples of other learning targets and test items from each level of this taxonomy are described in detail in Bloom et al. (1956). (See Appendix D for additional examples.) The value of such a taxonomy is that it calls your attention to the variety of abilities and skills toward which you can direct instruction and assessment.

Revised Bloom's *Taxonomy*

Relationship of the Revision to the Original The original *Taxonomy of Educational Objectives* is still in wide use in schools. However, this taxonomy has now been revised as *A Taxonomy for Learning, Teaching, and Assessing: A Revision of Bloom's Taxonomy of Educational Objectives* (Anderson et al., 2001). The revised *Taxonomy* improves on the original by giving a two-dimensional framework into which you may classify learning targets and assessment items. The two dimensions, which were derived from the original taxonomy, are Knowledge Dimension and Cognitive Process Dimension. They are related to the original as follows (Anderson et al., 2001):

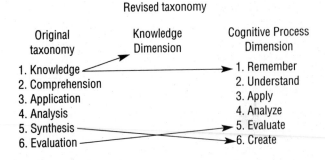

FIGURE 2.3 **How different outcomes for science and social studies may be classified using the Bloom et al.** *Taxonomy.*

Bloom et al. Category	Science	Social Studies
Knowledge	• Recall the names of parts of a flower • Identify and label the parts of insects • List the steps in a process	• List known causes of the Civil War • Recall general principles of migration of peoples of Africa
Comprehension	• Find real examples of types of coleoptera • Find real examples of igneous rock and mineral formations • Explain the digestive processes in one's own words	• Explain the meaning of technical concepts in one's own words • Give examples of propaganda usage from current events
Application	• Use scientific principles to make a simple machine • Use a learned process to conduct a new experiment	• Use specified critical thinking skills to explain current events • Carry out a survey and collect data from the field
Analysis	• Show how scientific principles or concepts are applied when designing a refrigerator	• Identify the credible and noncredible claims of an advertisement for clothing • Show the different component parts of a political speech
Synthesis	• Determine what the rule is that underlies the results obtained from several experiments or investigations	• Show the similarities among several schools of social thought • Develop plans for peace among two countries
Evaluation	• Use criteria or standards to evaluate the conclusions drawn from the research findings • Use criteria to evaluate the soundness of a research study	• Use a specific set of criteria to evaluate several political speeches

You can see that the Knowledge category has been divided into two parts: Knowledge Dimension and Remember. The Knowledge Dimension has four subcategories (shown later in Figure 2.4): Factual Knowledge, Conceptual Knowledge, Procedural Knowledge, and Metacognitive Knowledge. The details of these are given in Appendix D. The Knowledge Dimension contains the type of content a learning target refers to: a fact, a concept, a procedure, or a metacognitive content. The meaning of metacognition is explained in Appendix F.

The Taxonomy Table A two-dimensional table, the *Taxonomy Table* is constructed to describe the location of a learning target and its corresponding assessment on both dimensions simultaneously. (see Figure 2.4). The figure shows 24 cells, each defined by one knowledge and one cognitive process subcategory. Note that the subcategories of the Knowledge Dimension are lettered, whereas the subcategories of the Cognitive Process Dimension are numbered. As a shortcut, we can refer to a particular cell by its letter and number. Thus, a learning target that requires students to remember some factual knowledge is placed in cell 1A.

Classifying Learning Targets and Assessment Items In the previous section, we gave examples of learning targets and assessment items for each of the six categories of the original *Taxonomy*. How would these same items be classified in the revised Taxonomy? The examples under the original taxonomy's Knowledge category, for instance, would be classified in cell 1A because it requires students to remember specific facts about the characters in the short stories. The examples under the original taxonomy's Comprehension category would be classified in cell 2B because the main ideas and themes of the short stories are conceptual knowledge and paraphrasing these in one's own words show understanding. We would classify the other examples from the original *Taxonomy* into the revised *Taxonomy* as follows: Application examples as 3B, Analysis examples as 4C, Synthesis examples as 6C, and Evaluation examples as 5C. Do you agree? Why or why not?

Advantage of the Revised Taxonomy The advantage of the revised Taxonomy is that it allows you to consider a broader range of learning targets than the one-dimensional original taxonomy. If you classify your learning targets, your assessment items, and your teaching activities into the Taxonomy Table shown in Figure 2.4, you can immediately see the types of knowledge and thinking on which your instructional unit focuses. Not every unit should have learning targets and assessments in every one of the 24 cells, of course. But over the semester, your teaching should be addressing and evaluating students' learning in all (or nearly all) of them.

Taxonomies Are Not Teaching Hierarchies

Do not assume that this taxonomy is a teaching hierarchy. For example, you should not teach "knowledge" first and "comprehension" second. Its only purpose is to classify various learning targets and assessment tasks.

Different Modes of Assessments for Different Taxonomy Levels

Note that learning targets classified in the first three cognitive categories are more easily assessed with short-answer, true-false, multiple-choice, or matching test items. Learning targets classified in the last three cognitive categories might be partially tested by such item formats, but their assessment

FIGURE 2.4 **Taxonomy Table from the revised *Taxonomy*.**

Knowledge Dimension	Cognitive Process Dimension					
	1. Remember	2. Understand	3. Apply	4. Analyze	5. Evaluate	6. Create
A. Factual Knowledge						
B. Conceptual Knowledge						
C. Procedural Knowledge						
D. Metacognitive Knowledge						

Source: From Lorin W. Anderson & David R. Krathwohl, *A Taxonomy for Learning, Teaching, and Assessing* © 2001. Published by Allyn and Bacon, Boston, MA. Copyright © 2001 by Pearson Education. Reprinted by permission of the publisher.

usually requires a variety of other procedures such as essay questions, homework, class projects, observing performance in labs, and portfolios. Learning targets at more complex thinking levels require students to actually produce or create something, rather than simply to answer questions. Carefully reading the various subcategories of the taxonomy in Appendix D should make this more apparent.

Condensing the Taxonomy Because it is sometimes difficult for teachers to classify their learning targets into all six cognitive categories, some schools have used a shorter version of the Bloom et al. *Taxonomy*. For example, some have reduced it to three categories: Knowledge, Comprehension, and Higher Order Thinking. The "Higher Order Thinking" category collapses Application, Analysis, Synthesis, and Evaluation learning targets into one group. Other schools formed three categories somewhat differently: Knowledge (including Comprehension), Application, and Higher Order Thinking (including Analysis, Synthesis, and Evaluation). The advantage of these condensations is that they eliminate the need for struggling with how to classify learning targets into one of the top three categories of the *Taxonomy*.

A serious disadvantage of using a condensed version of the *Taxonomy* is that teachers may stop trying to teach learning targets in the Synthesis and Evaluation categories. Because, after condensing, Application and Analysis will be in the same category as Synthesis and Evaluation, it is easy to avoid making the necessary distinctions among these four. As a result, a teacher may settle for not including the highest two categories of learning targets in lesson and assessment plans.

Dimensions of Learning Model

Marzano, Pickering, and McTighe (1993) developed another way of classifying types of thinking using the Dimensions of Learning Model developed at the McREL Institute in Colorado. This taxonomy uses seven broad categories. The seven categories and corresponding examples of learning targets are shown here. Appendix E provides a more detailed summary, which includes 13 subtypes of complex thinking skills.

To illustrate how you could use this taxonomy to guide your teaching and assessment, we give examples of a learning target and an assessment item for each category. These examples apply the taxonomy to a social studies research project.

Suppose students are asked to work together in groups to complete a research project. In this project, they interview other students in the school, asking their opinions on ways to resolve certain local community issues. Although students work together to design the study and collect data, students write their research reports individually. Your learning targets and assessments for this complex project should focus on several dimensions of learning as the examples that follow illustrate.

1. **Declarative knowledge**—This category of learning targets asks students to learn the facts, ideas, generalizations, and/or theories of a subject.

Example

Sample learning target:	The student states issues that are currently of major concern to the local community.
Sample assessment item:	List the major community issues that you will include in your project survey.

2. **Procedural knowledge**—This category of learning targets asks students to demonstrate procedures or ways of doing things.

Example

Sample learning target:	The student uses proper interview techniques when conducting research.
Sample assessment item:	Observe each student as the student conducts an interview of other students. Use a checklist of proper interview techniques to assess whether the interview is conducted properly.

3. **Complex thinking**—This category of learning targets asks students to apply their knowledge and/or to use different types of reasoning strategies. (See Appendix E for details about 13 subtypes of complex reasoning skills included in this category.)

Example

Sample learning target:	The student supports research conclusions using the data collected during the research study.
Sample assessment item:	The teacher reads the conclusion section of the students' research reports. The teacher uses a rating scale to assess the degree to which each student used the data collected during the study to support the conclusions made.

4. **Information processing**—This category of learning targets asks students to demonstrate different ways of gathering, synthesizing, and/or evaluating information needed for a particular purpose. The category includes learning targets that ask students to identify what information is needed for a particular purpose.

Example

Sample learning target:	From among all the information given to the student during an interview, the student uses the relevant information for the research study.
Sample assessment item:	The teacher reads the students' research reports, paying careful attention to the information the students collected and how it was used to describe opinions about resolving community issues. The teacher uses a rating scale to assess the degree to which each student used relevant information from the interviews for the study.

5. **Effective communication**—These learning targets ask students to demonstrate their communication skills such as communicating to the right audience, using the most appropriate communication method for the purpose at hand, and developing appropriate communication products.

Example

Sample learning target:	The student makes an effective and clear oral presentation of the results of his/her research study to an audience of peers.
Sample assessment item:	The teacher observes each student making an oral presentation to the class. The teacher uses a rating scale to rate how effective and clear the presentation was.

6. **Collaboration and cooperation**—These learning targets ask students to demonstrate their group skills such as working toward the group's goals, using interpersonal skills, performing functions that keep the group working on relevant activities, and/or serving multiple roles during group activities.

Example

Sample learning target:	The student works cooperatively with other group members to design the research study and collect the interview data effectively.
Sample assessment item:	The teacher observes the group during the study's design and data collection phase. The teacher uses a rating scale to assess each student's group participation including working toward group goals, interpersonal skills, group maintenance activities, and roles performed in the group.

7. **Habits of mind**—These learning targets ask students to demonstrate their ability for self-regulation, critical thinking, and/or creative thinking.

Example

Sample learning target:	The student plans and organizes the interview data collection methods and activities.
Sample assessment item:	The teacher meets with each student before the student begins the interview process, asking the student to describe the plan for selecting interviewees, conducting interviews, and collecting and recording information from the interview. The teacher previews the student's interview question sheet and recording sheet. Using a rating scale, the teacher evaluates how well the student has planned for and organized the data collection phase of the study.

We recognize that you may not be familiar with some of the techniques (e.g., rating scales and checklists) used in the preceding assessment samples. You will learn these later in the course, so it is not necessary that you understand them completely at this point. Suggestions for crafting complex performance assessments and their corresponding scoring rubrics are found in Chapter 12.

The categories of the Dimensions of Learning Model were derived from research and writings on cognitive psychology, higher-order thinking, and critical thinking. Unlike the Bloom et al. *Taxonomy*, the categories are not meant to be hierarchical. They are, however, meant to be a framework for organizing curricula and focusing teaching.

Problems When Classifying Learning Targets Using a Taxonomy

It is important to recognize that (a) thinking skill categories may not be hierarchical, and (b) student performance on complex tasks involves using several thinking skills at the same time. It is possible, therefore, to classify a given learning target or assessment task into more than one taxonomy category. The authors of the revised *Taxonomy*, in fact, encourage you to do so (Krathwohl, 2002).

The main purpose for suggesting that you use a taxonomy for assessment is to give you a tool to judge whether you have taught and assessed a wide enough range of higher- and lower-order thinking skills. A taxonomy may help you find the gaps. Including a wide range of thinking skills in an assessment usually improves its validity.

If this is your first introduction to taxonomies, however, you should begin by classifying your learning targets or assessment tasks into only one category of the taxonomy. Doing so would simplify your understanding of learning targets and assessment tasks, even though this may be somewhat artificial. As you do this, keep in mind that you should use the one category that represents the thinking skill that is (a) most prominently used by or (b) the main intent of the learning target or assessment task. Once completed, you should use the classification to decide if some important skills have received too little or too much attention in your teaching and assessment.

CHOOSING A TAXONOMY

We have discussed two different schemes for classifying cognitive learning targets. There are many more taxonomies or schemes that we have not discussed, some of which are in Appendixes D and E of this book (see DeLandsheere, 1988, for a review). Which one should you use? That depends on whether this is a personal decision for use in your classroom only or a more general decision

in which the taxonomy will be used throughout your school system.

An example of criteria you can apply to help you choose among the various taxonomies follows. Apply these practical criteria to judge each taxonomy or classification scheme you are considering. If the decision is a personal one for a single classroom, then not all criteria may apply.

Example

Practical Criteria for Selecting a Taxonomy of Cognitive Learning Targets

1. *Completeness:* To what degree can your major learning targets be classified within each taxonomy?
2. *Point of view:* To what extent can each taxonomy be used as a platform for explaining your teaching methods or your curriculum characteristics to others?
3. *Reform:* To what extent can each taxonomy help you evaluate your curriculum or your learning targets and lead you to revise the learning targets?
4. *Simplicity:* How easy is it for parents, teachers, and education officials to understand each taxonomy?
5. *Reporting:* How useful is each taxonomy in organizing reports of assessment results for individual students, educational officials, government officials, or the public?

SOURCES FOR LOCATING LEARNING TARGETS

You may find lists of learning targets in instructional materials and teachers' manuals, local and state curriculum frameworks, state Websites containing performance standards, reports of the National Assessment of Educational Progress, books on teaching methods, manuals accompanying tests (especially criterion-referenced tests), and reports from educational associations. More than likely you will have to adapt the learning targets you find in these sources to your own situation. Nevertheless, these sources and the taxonomies do provide a starting place: It is much easier to adapt and revise learning target statements than to write them without any assistance.

Also, a learning target often will cut across several lessons or subject areas. The ability to use library and print resources to obtain information for a report, for example, is likely to be a learning target common to social studies, mathematics, and language arts curricula. In this regard, the categories provided by the taxonomies shown in this chapter were created so that each would apply across several curricular areas.

EVALUATING THE LEARNING TARGETS OF A COURSE OR UNIT

Never teach a unit until you list the learning targets for that unit. It is important to develop a complete or comprehensive list of learning targets. A complete list is not necessarily long, however. Apply the following practical criteria to evaluate your list of learning targets:

Practical Criteria for Evaluating a List of Learning Targets for a Course or Unit

1. Be sure all the learning targets are appropriate for students' educational level.
2. Be sure the list of learning targets is limited to only the important outcomes for the course.
3. Be sure all the learning targets are consistent with your state's published learning standards.
4. Be sure all the learning targets are consistent with your local school's philosophy and general goals.
5. Be sure all the learning targets can be defended by currently accepted learning principles.
6. Be sure all the learning targets can be taught in the time limits of the course.
7. Be sure all the learning targets can be taught with available teaching resources.

HOW TO WRITE SPECIFIC LEARNING TARGETS

The following minimum criteria for learning targets ensures their usefulness as a basis for classroom instruction and crafting assessment instruments (Lindvall, 1964, 1967):

1. *Student centered:* Learning targets should focus on the student.

2. *Performance centered:* Learning targets should be worded in terms of what a student can perform after the required learning experiences.

3. *Content centered:* Learning targets should state the specific content to which the student should apply the performance.

Student Centered

Because instruction focuses on changes in student performance, learning targets should describe student performances. It is not unusual, however, for some teacher guides, curriculum frameworks, and other materials to contain statements that do not focus on the student. Consider this statement:

Example

Poor: Provide the opportunity for students to express their opinions in classroom discussions about why peace is so difficult to attain.

The problem with the preceding statement is that it is an activity statement *for teachers* rather than a learning target for students. You may "provide the opportunity for students to express their opinions," yet each student may not express his or her opinion. Learning targets need to be student centered if they are to be the basis for crafting assessment procedures. Thus, you should say:

Example

Better: A student will express his or her opinion in classroom discussions about why peace is so difficult to attain.

Student-centered learning targets allow you to decide whether the students actually have achieved what you intended from the lesson.

Performance Centered

Not only should a learning target refer to a student, it should state a performance—that is, an observable activity. This can be accomplished by being sure that the statement includes an **action verb** that specifies a student performance.

To help beginners write learning targets that describe students' performances, Figure 2.5 lists further examples of various action verbs. These verbs are organized according to the Bloom and Krathwohl et al. cognitive and affective taxonomies discussed in Appendix D. When verbs such as these are used in statements of learning targets, the learning targets will usually satisfy the second criterion of expressing observable student performance. A balance is necessary between verbs that are too broad (and thus imply too many nonequivalent performances) and those that are too specific (and which are often just ways of marking answers). Consider this learning target, which is stated too specifically:

Example

Poor: The student is able to put an *X* on the picture of the correct geometric shape (circle, triangle, rectangle, square, or ellipse) when the name of the shape is given.

The main intent of such an objective is to select or identify the correct shape, not just to make *X*s. Any response that indicates the student has correctly identified the

FIGURE 2.5 Action verbs to use when writing learning targets. (See Appendix D for additional examples.)

I. **Cognitive domain (Bloom et al., 1956)**
   a. **Knowledge:** define, describe, identify, label, list, match, name, outline, select, state
   b. **Comprehension:** convert, distinguish, estimate, explain, extend, generalize, give examples, infer, paraphrase, predict, rewrite, summarize
   c. **Application:** change, compute, demonstrate, discover, manipulate, modify, operate, predict, prepare, produce, relate, show, solve, use
   d. **Analysis:** break down, diagram, differentiate, discriminate, distinguish, identify, illustrate, infer, outline, point out, relate, select, separate, subdivide
   e. **Synthesis:** categorize, combine, compile, compose, create, design, devise, rewrite, summarize, tell, write
   f. **Evaluation:** appraise, compare, conclude, contrast, criticize, describe, discriminate, explain, justify, interpret, relate, summarize, support

II. **Affective domain (Krathwohl et al., 1964)**
   a. **Receiving:** ask, choose, describe, follow, give, hold, identify, locate, name, point to, reply, select, sit erect, use
   b. **Responding:** answer, assist, comply, conform, discuss, greet, help, label, perform, practice, present, read, report, respond, select, tell, write
   c. **Valuing:** complete, demonstrate, describe, differentiate, explain, follow, form, initiate, invite, join, justify, propose, read, recognize, report, select, share, study, work, write
   d. **Organizing:** adhere, alter, arrange, combine, compare, complete, defend, explain, generalize, identify, integrate, modify, organize, order, prepare, relate, synthesize
   e. **Characterizing by a value or value complex:** act, discriminate, display, influence, listen, modify, perform, practice, propose, qualify, question, revise, serve, solve, use, verify

Source: From *Testing for Teachers* 2nd edition by Tuckman. © 1988. Reprinted with permission of Wadsworth, a division of Thomson Learning: www.thomsonrights.com. Fax 800 730-2215.

required shape is acceptable. Thus, the learning target should be written as:

Example

Better: The student is able to identify a picture of a geometric shape (circle, triangle, rectangle, square, or ellipse) when the name of the shape is given.

Figure 2.6 suggests some verbs that maintain this balance and illustrates other verbs that are too specific or too broad to make useful learning target statements.

Content Oriented

When stating a learning target, you should indicate the content to which a student's performance is to apply. The following learning target is poor because it lacks a reference to content:

Example

Poor: The student is able to write definitions of the important terms used in the text.

To modify this learning target you need to include a reference to a specific list of "important words" or in some other way describe them:

Example

Better: The student is able to write definitions of the terms listed in the "Important Terms and Concepts" section of Chapters 1–5 of the textbook.

If you do not refer to content in your learning target statement, you will be uncertain whether an assessment task is valid for evaluating the student. For example, the assessment may require students to define words that, although in the text, may be unimportant. Without knowing the content, it is difficult for anyone to determine what, if anything, was learned.

MAKING SURE ASSESSMENT TASKS ARE ALIGNED WITH LEARNING TARGETS

Chapters 6 through 15 discuss the details of crafting high-quality assessments. Here we wish to point out that the basic purpose of any assessment is to determine the extent to which each student has achieved the stated learning targets. Although this purpose sounds straightforward, it is not always an easy criterion to meet. The validity of your assessment results determines the quality of your evaluation. Validity is the subject of the next chapter; here we discuss validity only in relation to matching or aligning assessment tasks to learning targets.

FIGURE 2.6 Action verbs sometimes used in learning targets.

Specific but acceptable verbs			
add, total	describe	match	rename
alphabetize	divide	measure	rephrase
choose	draw	multiply	select
complete, supply	explain	name	sort, classify
construct, make	identify	order, arrange	state
convert	label	pick out	subtract, take away
count	list	regroup	weigh
delete			

Too broad, unacceptable verbs			
apply	examine	interpret	respond
deduce	generate	observe	test
do	infer	perform	use

Too specific, essentially indicator verbs			
check	draw a line between	put a mark on	underline
circle	draw a ring around	put an X on	write the letter of
color the same as	put a box around	shade	write the number of

Toss-up verbs, requiring further clarification			
answer	contrast	differentiate	give
collect, synthesize	demonstrate	discriminate	locate
compare	determine	distinguish	predict

Source: From "Criteria for Stating IPI Objectives" by C. M. Lindvall, 1976, pp. 214–215. In D. T. Gow (Ed.). *Design and Development of Curricular Materials: Instructional Design Articles* (Volume 2). Pittsburgh, PA: University of Pittsburgh, University Center for International Studies.

Aligning Assessments to Mastery Learning Targets

The specific tasks or procedures you use in an assessment should require the student to display the skill or knowledge stated in the learning target. For instance, if the main intent of your learning target is for a student to build an apparatus, write a poem, or perform a physical skill, your assessment procedure must give the student the opportunity to *perform*. Assessment procedures that require a student only to name the parts of an apparatus, to analyze an existing poem, or to describe the sequence of steps needed for performing a physical skill do not require the performance stated in these learning targets. Therefore, they would be invalid for assessing them: They are not aligned to the learning targets' main intents. A very basic requirement for the validity of classroom assessment procedures is that the assessment procedures should be aligned with the intentions of the specific learning targets that you include in your assessment plan. The methods of developing assessment plans are treated in Chapter 6.

Aligning Assessments to Developmental Learning Targets

As is often the case, developmental learning targets imply a broad domain of performance application. To ensure the validity of your classroom assessment, you may need to assess the same learning target in several different ways. For example, you might assess spelling achievement both by scoring several samples of students' written assignments and by using a dictated spelling test. The test provides the opportunity to assess a student's spelling of word patterns that might not appear in the natural course of the student's writing, but that may well be part of the learning target. Observing a student's natural writing habits permits you to infer how well the student is likely to spell in typical writing situations. Using both procedures increases how comprehensively you assess the student's spelling ability and the validity of your evaluation.

Another reason for using more than one assessment procedure is to obtain more reliable results. Your subjective evaluation of a student's written essay on a topic might be supplemented by a test made up of more objectively scored items. Combining the less reliable information about the student's written work (that is, your subjective evaluation) with the more reliable information (the objectively scored test) yields a more reliable overall evaluation result. Reliability is discussed in more detail in Chapter 4.

Aligning Assessments to State Standards

Earlier in this chapter we showed how you can derive your learning targets from your state's standards. It is important that you maintain consistency by aligning your classroom assessments as well as the learning targets with the state's standards. Aligning your assessments with the learning targets that you derive from the state's standards (in the manner we showed earlier) is one way to ensure this. You will want to ensure that your assessments match the span of content covered by the standards, the depth of thinking implied by the standards, and the topical emphasis in the standards, and to require students to make the same types of performances as are specified in the standards.

Summary

Importance of Specifying Objectives

- Learning targets are important because specifying them helps you direct your teaching toward the important student achievements that you, the school, and parents have in mind.
- Among the benefits of using specific learning target statements are (a) making educational goals explicit, (b) communicating instructional intent to others, (c) analyzing and sequencing what is to be taught, (d) evaluating instructional procedures, (e) providing focus in discussions with parents, (f) clarifying to students what is expected of them, (g) facilitating individualized instruction, and (h) facilitating the revision of instructional procedures.
- Specifying learning targets has a practical value for your classroom assessments by (a) facilitating your general planning for assessment, (b) clarifying the specific performances for which you should craft or select assessment tasks, (c) facilitating your evaluation of an existing assessment procedure, and (d) facilitating your judgment of the validity of an assessment.

Educational Goals, State Standards, and Learning Targets

- Statements of general educational goals help guide the overall educational enterprise, but you must make them more specific before you can implement them in the classroom.
- You achieve specificity by organizing goals into subject-matter areas and then developing several general learning targets for each goal. You subsequently define each general learning target by more specific performances that you can teach and assess. You use assessment results from these specific learning targets to infer the degree to which students have attained general learning targets and goals.
- Content standards describe what subject-matter content students are expected to learn. Performance standards describe what students are expected to do with their content knowledge. Standards are often statements of general learning targets.

Therefore, teachers need to break standards into more specific learning targets for purposes of teaching and assessment.

- At least two kinds or levels of learning targets useful for classroom instruction can be identified: specific, mastery learning targets; and broader, developmental learning targets.
- Students never fully achieve developmental learning targets. However, you can teach and assess the degree of students' achievement at a particular educational level by writing several important, specific learning targets that define appropriate educational development at that level. You use students' performances on this sample of learning targets to estimate the progress students have made in achieving the developmental learning target.
- Developmental learning targets cannot be considered mastery learning targets because (a) they imply several performances that are not highly related to each other; and (b) it is reasonable to expect degrees of development or growth in certain achievement areas, rather than complete mastery.

Taxonomies of Learning Targets and Sources for Locating Learning Targets

- When writing the learning targets for a lesson or unit and for crafting a classroom assessment, it is important to identify the full range of student performance to be achieved. This is done by (a) referring to taxonomies of cognitive, affective, and/or psychomotor objectives; (b) reviewing instructional materials and teachers' manuals; (c) consulting curriculum frameworks from various sources; (d) reviewing books on methods of teaching the subject; (e) reviewing the criterion-referenced tests of a subject; (f) consulting your state's mandated standards; and (g) reviewing reports from professional organizations.

Cognitive Domain Taxonomies

- The Bloom et al. (1956) *Taxonomy* orders levels of cognitive learning targets from simplest to most complex. These are knowledge, comprehension, application, analysis, synthesis, and evaluation. (See Figure D.1 of Appendix D for details.)
- The revised *Taxonomy* (Anderson et al., 2001) transforms the original Bloom taxonomy from a one-dimensional classification to a two-dimensional classification system. The Knowledge Dimension includes Factual Knowledge, Conceptual Knowledge, Procedural Knowledge, and Metacognitive Knowledge. The Cognitive Dimension includes Remember, Understand, Apply, Analyze, Evaluate, and Create.
- The Dimensions of Learning Model approach defines seven broad categories of learning targets: declarative knowledge, procedural knowledge, complex thinking, information processing, effective communication, collaboration and cooperation, and habits of mind.
- The Dimensions of Learning Model approach is not hierarchical, but the Bloom et al. Taxonomy is.
- Taxonomies for the affective and psychomotor domains are presented in Appendix D (Figures D.4 and D.5).

Choosing a Taxonomy

- Criteria for choosing which cognitive taxonomy to use were listed.

Evaluating the Learning Targets of a Course or Unit

● Criteria for evaluating the quality and importance of the learning targets you select for a unit or a course were listed.

How to Write Specific Learning Targets

● A written statement of a specific learning target should be worded (a) in terms of the student, rather than in terms of a teacher or a school; (b) in terms of observable student performance; and (c) so the specific content to which a student's performance is applied is clear.

● Specific examples for action verbs that describe student performance appear in Figures 2.5 and 2.6.

Making Sure Assessment Tasks Are Aligned With Learning Targets

● The validity of assessment results increases if the assessment closely matches the intent of the learning targets.

● Sometimes you need to use several different methods of assessing a student's performance before you can validly conclude that the student has met the intent of the learning target.

● Align your assessments with the state's standards by making sure to include the content covered by the standards, the depth of thinking implied by the standards, the topical emphasis implied by the standards, and the same types of performance as are implied by the standards.

Important Terms and Concepts

action verb
affective domain
analysis, application, comprehension, evaluation, knowledge, synthesis
cognitive domain
collaboration and cooperation, complex thinking, declarative knowledge, effective communication, habits of mind, information processing, procedural knowledge
content centered
content standards
developmental learning targets
educational goals
general learning target
instruction
learning objective
learning target
mastery learning targets
matching assessment tasks to learning targets
performance centered
performance standards
psychomotor domain
specific learning target
standards
student centered
taxonomies of instructional learning targets

Exercises and Applications

1. Write three specific learning targets for a lesson you plan to teach. Explain how each learning target meets the three criteria: student centered, performance centered, and content centered.

2. Here are three learning targets. Decide whether each implies a homogeneous or a heterogeneous domain. Write a brief statement justifying your choice.
   a. When given a Roman numeral, the student is able to write the corresponding Arabic numeral.
   b. Students are able to recognize examples of deductive and inductive reasoning.
   c. Students are able to write a definition of deductive and inductive reasoning.

3. Following are three learning targets. Decide whether each is a mastery learning target or a developmental learning target. Explain your choices.
   a. The student is able to take the square root of any number using a handheld calculator.
   b. The student is able to determine whether the thesis of the argument is supported adequately.
   c. When given data, the student is able to construct a graph to describe the trend in the data.

4. Decide whether each learning target listed here belongs to the cognitive, affective, or psychomotor domain. Does the performance of each learning target require some use of elements from domains other than the one into which you classified it? Which one(s)? Explain why. Does this mean you should reclassify that learning target? Explain.
   a. The student is able to tune a color television set to get the best color resolution.
   b. The student demonstrates knowledge of parliamentary law by conducting a meeting without violating parliamentary procedures.
   c. The student contributes to group maintenance when working with classmates on a science project.
   d. The student makes five baskets out of 10 tries on the basketball court while standing at the foul line.

5. a. Obtain a copy of your state's (or neighboring state's) standards. Analyze the suitability of these statements (i) for planning units and lessons and (ii) for developing assessment exercises. Prepare a criticism of these standards from your point of view as a teacher of a specific grade and subject. In your criticism, be sure to emphasize assessment-related issues. Hint: Log on to your state education department's Website and search for links to the education standards. See also the Companion Website for this textbook.
   b. Select one unit you are teaching or plan to teach in the future that includes one or more of your state's standards. Explain what you would need to do to align your classroom learning targets and your student assessments with the state's standards. Summarize the results and report them to your class.

3 Validity of Assessment Results

LEARNING TARGETS

After studying this chapter, you should have learned the following:

General Nature of and Principles for Validation

1. Explain the concept of validity and how it applies to all educational assessment results. [3, 4, 6]
2. Explain the four principles for validation. [3, 6, 7]

Validity of Teacher-Crafted Classroom Assessment Results

3. Apply the validity criteria in Figure 3.1 to your own classroom assessment results. [5, 4, 2, 7]

Categories of Validity Evidence

4. Describe each of the eight types of evidence needed to validate interpretations and uses of extraclassroom assessment results. [6, 3, 7]
5. Explain the concept of correlation and how it is used in validating assessment results. [6, 3]
6. Explain how scatter diagrams and expectancy tables may be used to interpret relationships between two sets of assessment results. [3, 6]
7. Explain how various factors affect the magnitude of correlation coefficients. [6, 3]

8. Explain how to evaluate the criterion measures used in validation studies. [6, 4, 3]
9. Describe the difference between concurrent and predictive validity evidence. [6, 4, 3]
10. Explain the special validity problems that arise when using extraclassroom assessment instruments to evaluate curricula, schools, and educational innovations. [6, 4, 1]

Combining Evidence for Validity Judgments

11. Explain the three steps needed to develop a validation argument. [6, 4, 3]

Validity Issues When Accommodating Students With Disabilities

12. Describe how the purpose of assessment is linked to the validity of accommodations made when assessing students with disabilities.
13. Describe the validity concerns of testing with accommodations.

Important Terms and Concepts

14. Explain how each of the terms and concepts listed at the end of this chapter apply to the validation of educational assessment results. [6]

ABOUT THIS CHAPTER

The chapter begins by discussing the meaning of validity: What does it mean when we ask if our assessment results are valid? Second, it discusses how to validate the assessments you craft for classroom use: What are the criteria for validating the results of your own assessments? Next, we discuss the validation of other assessments used in schools such as standardized achievement tests: What evidence should we look for to support the valid use of tests in schools? Fourth, it covers ways to combine evidence to build an argument for the valid use of assessments: What do schools and test publishers need to do to present their case for valid uses of their tests? Last, it discusses validity issues when you modify a test to accommodate students with disabilities: Are modified tests still valid assessments?

GENERAL NATURE OF VALIDITY

Do you remember the guiding principles for selecting and using assessment that we discussed in Chapter 1? Applying those principles leads to meaningful assessment results. Meaningful assessment is one way to talk about validity. **Validity** is the soundness of your interpretations and uses of students' assessment results. To validate your interpretations and uses of students' assessment results, you must combine evidence from a variety of sources that demonstrates these interpretations and uses are appropriate. You must also demonstrate that students experience no serious negative consequences when results are used as you intend.

The question "Are these assessment results valid?" has many different answers *depending on how the results are interpreted and used.* For example, suppose your school administers the *ABC Reading Test* and wishes to use the scores for one or more of the following purposes: to describe students' growth in reading comprehension; to place students into high, middle, and low reading groups; or to evaluate the school's reading program. The scores from this hypothetical test may have a high degree of validity for one of these purposes but may not for the others.

When discussing the validity of assessment results, keep in mind the following points:

1. *The concept of validity applies to the ways we interpret and use the assessment results and not to the assessment procedure itself.* Thus, we may not say, "Is the *ABC Reading Test* valid?" except as an informal, shorthand way of speaking. Rather, we must ask more specific questions such as, "Is it valid to interpret the scores from the *ABC Reading Test* as measuring reading comprehension?" or "Is it valid to use *ABC Reading Test* scores to place students into reading groups?" and so on.

2. *The assessment results have different degrees of validity for different purposes and for different situations.* The scores from our hypothetical *ABC Reading Test*, for example, may

be highly valid when used to evaluate the reading program in your school district because the items on it match the district's reading program objectives quite well. On the other hand, scores from the same test may have poor validity for evaluating your neighboring district's reading program because the items match that district's reading program objectives poorly.

3. *You should make judgments about the validity of your interpretations or uses of assessment results only after studying and combining several types of validity evidence.* As an example, before coming to a conclusion about the validity of a proposed interpretation or the use of the *ABC Reading Test*'s scores, you need to collect evidence concerning how well it samples the reading domain. You also need to decide whether the skills assessed represent "authentic" or appropriate reading, whether the scores are unduly influenced by irrelevant factors such as the students' moods or their motivation to be tested, how closely the tested skills match your school district's reading objectives, whether the scores are reliable, and so on.

Validity is not established by presenting the evidence about only one of these areas. Rather, it is a judgment you make *after considering evidence from all relevant areas.* Until you have collected, reviewed, weighed, and combined all relevant evidence, your evaluation of the validity of the results is incomplete. In effect, validating specific interpretations and uses of assessment results requires making a convincing argument that the evidence supports them (Kane, 1992).

FOUR PRINCIPLES FOR VALIDATION

Four principles for validation will help you decide how valid your assessment results are (Messick, 1989b, 1994a) (remember to base your validity judgment on all four principles, not just on one of them):

1. The *interpretations* (or meanings) you give to your students' assessment results are valid only to the degree that you can point to evidence that supports their appropriateness and correctness.

2. The *uses* you may make of your assessment results are valid only to the degree to which you can point to evidence that supports their correctness and appropriateness.

3. The interpretations and uses of your assessment results are valid only when the *values* implied by them are appropriate.

4. The interpretations and uses you make of your assessment results are valid only when the *consequences* of these interpretations and uses are consistent with appropriate values.

These principles are explained in the following paragraphs.

Appropriate Interpretations

Consider, for example, a Lincoln School student, Hiram. Hiram has taken the *ABC Reading Test* each year, but his scores suddenly rose this year. How would you interpret Hiram's sudden score rise? Here are several possible interpretations: (a) his reading comprehension has improved, (b) his motivation to do well on reading comprehension tests has improved, and (c) his skill in answering multiple-choice reading comprehension test items has improved. These interpretations are not mutually exclusive. Hiram may have improved in one or more of these areas.

The Lincoln School staff may like to interpret Hiram's assessments to mean an improvement in his reading comprehension. Before they can claim that such an interpretation has some degree of validity, however, they need to offer evidence. First, they need to show that the *ABC Reading Test* measures reading comprehension in the way reading specialists define comprehension. Second, they need evidence to show that Hiram's increased test performance is due primarily to his improved reading, rather than simply a result of his increased motivation to do well on the test and his improved test-taking skills. Third, they need to use other evidence that exists in the school: Hiram's reading teacher and/or classroom teacher should compare his test performance with his classroom reading performance. If, for example, the staff finds contradictory evidence in the assessment research literature that test scores are easily increased by a student's motivation and test-taking skills, then continuing to interpret Hiram's scores as measuring purely reading comprehension would be unsound or invalid. Figure 3.10 (later in this chapter) shows an example of a research study that explores the impact of motivation on a reading test.

Appropriate Uses

We distinguish between *interpretations*—the meaning you give to the scores—and *uses*—what actions you take based on the scores. What are some of the test uses that the Lincoln School staff might have in mind? They may want, for example, to (a) certify that Hiram is reading at an appropriate level for his grade; (b) diagnose or identify the types of reading comprehension problems Hiram may be experiencing; (c) place Hiram into a remedial, regular, or advanced reading group; and (d) continually monitor Hiram's growth in reading comprehension. The Lincoln School staff may wish to use Hiram's scores for more than one of these purposes. However, the validity of any of Lincoln School's uses of the *ABC Reading Test* scores depends on the evidence teachers and school officials can find to support each use. For example, what evidence can Lincoln School provide to demonstrate that students assigned to remedial reading groups on the basis of their *ABC Reading Test* scores will learn to read better than if they were assigned to the regular reading classes? Evidence should be provided separately for each intended use of assessment results. For published standardized tests, much of this evidence may be available already in the test's technical manual so a school may not need to do its own research. This is not always the case, however.

Notice that the Lincoln School examples used wording that implied a reading comprehension *interpretation* of the test results. This illustrates an important point about the assessment validation process: *To validate a particular usage of assessment results, you must also employ a validated interpretation or meaning of those results.* Thus, Lincoln School must first establish the degree to which the *ABC Reading Test* measures reading comprehension. If it cannot do this, the school would not be able to validate any further use of the test scores that *are based on the assumption that the test measures reading comprehension.*

Appropriate Values

The interpretations you give to and the uses you make of your students' assessment results arise from your educational and social values. What values were implied when Lincoln School's staff interpreted Hiram's *ABC Reading Test* scores as measuring reading comprehension and used them to describe and to plan his reading development?

First, the very choice of the *ABC Reading Test* implied that the staff valued the format and content of the test items. Suppose that the *ABC Reading Test* consists of several short passages (less than 500 words each), each followed by several multiple-choice questions. Further, suppose the themes of the reading passages ignore (or are irrelevant to) African American, Hispanic, Native American, or other minority cultural experiences. Using and interpreting this test as a measure of reading comprehension implies the staff accepted that such cultural and ethnic experiences are unimportant in assessing a student's reading comprehension.

Second, using a multiple-choice format for assessing reading comprehension is also a value judgment: Should longer, more "authentic" reading passages and open-ended questions be used instead? Does the less expensive multiple-choice test have more value than the more costly authentic assessment?

Third, the staff's use of the test scores to assign students to different reading groups implies that they value homogeneous grouping for reading instruction. This also implies that the benefits received from being taught with others of similar reading ability outweigh the benefits received from being taught in a more mixed reading ability group.

Again notice that the discussion of value judgments in the preceding paragraphs uses a reading comprehension interpretation of the test results *AND* describes specific ways of using the scores. This illustrates that *you must consider proper interpretations, relevant uses, and appropriate values when asking how valid your assessment results are.*

Appropriate Consequences

Whenever you interpret and use your students' assessment results, intended and unintended consequences result: Every action you take has a consequence. You must consider these consequences when judging whether you are using the assessment results validly. What are the intended and unintended consequences for Lincoln School? Lincoln School's intended consequence for placing children with low *ABC Reading Test* scores into remedial reading groups was to improve these children's reading ability as rapidly as possible. As the students' reading comprehension improves, the staff believes, so will their other schoolwork and their self-esteem.

But suppose something unintended and unvalued happens instead. Suppose the remedial reading students quickly come to see themselves as incompetent, and their self-esteem declines. Suppose, too, that out of frustration their teachers begin drilling them on material the students do not understand (instead of building on what they already know). Suppose that eventually the students never leave the remedial reading track. In the face of these unintended and negative consequences, would Lincoln School's use of the *ABC Reading Test* scores to form remedial groups still be highly valid? Even if the test measured reading comprehension, when such negative consequences occur its continued use would be devastating to these children. Interpretations and uses of assessment results must have positively valued consequences (and avoid negatively valued consequences) to have a high degree of validity.

This example uses a reading comprehension interpretation of the test results, describes a specific use of the results (placement into remedial reading groups), and incorporates a positively valued intention (improved student reading and self-esteem). The example also shows, however, that positively valued consequences may not result for all students. *You must consider appropriate interpretations, appropriate uses, appropriate values, AND appropriate consequences when asking how valid your assessment results are.*

VALIDITY OF TEACHER-CRAFTED CLASSROOM ASSESSMENT RESULTS

What does the preceding discussion mean for classroom assessment? This section considers criteria for validating the results of classroom assessment methods. Although validity criteria apply to all types of classroom assessments, including brief assignments, long-term assignments, and quizzes, we illustrate the application of these criteria with only one example. The reason for doing this is that judgment of validity depends on knowing the specific interpretation, uses, values, and consequences of the assessment. The one example provides that specific focus we use to illustrate the ideas.

An Example of Assessment Interpretation and Use

The example in this section assumes three things. First, it assumes that a teacher will interpret the classroom assessment results as one of the summative evaluations of the students' mastery of the material. The assessment purpose includes using the results to assign letter grades to students. Second, it assumes also that the teacher will use the results of this assessment as only one of several important pieces of information in assigning letter grades to students. Finally, it assumes that the assessment covers a sizable "chunk" of learning, such as a unit, a marking period, or a semester. The criteria we discuss apply to any assessment technique used for this purpose; the technique may or may not be a paper-and-pencil test.

Validity Criteria for Improving Classroom Assessments

Several criteria may be used to improve the validity of using your assessment results for grading students. These criteria are summarized in Figure 3.1, which organizes them into several categories discussed in this section.

Content Representativeness and Relevance

The validity of your classroom assessment results depends very much on how well your assessment samples the learning targets. To create valid assessments, you must (a) clearly identify the important learning targets and (b) be sure they are well sampled by the assessment procedure. This is why Chapter 2 was devoted to the topic of learning targets.

You must place the learning targets you teach and assess into the appropriate context of your school district, your state standards, and the discipline you are teaching. This means that the tasks included on your assessment should reflect the important content and learning outcomes specified in your school's and state's standards. A thinking skills taxonomy, one of the topics in Chapter 2, is a useful tool in this regard. You should also review each assessment task to ensure that from the content perspective it is relevant, important, stated accurately, has an accurate key or scoring rubric, and represents something that is meaningful to learn.

When evaluating your classroom assessment method in relation to representativeness and relevance, you should focus on the following questions:

1. *Does my assessment procedure emphasize what I have taught?* Students have a right to expect to be evaluated on what you have emphasized in class. If you have spent lots of time in one area of the material, the assessment should feature that area prominently. This is a common error: Teachers uncritically use the tests that come with the

FIGURE 3.1 Criteria for improving the validity of scores from classroom assessments used for assigning grades to students.

Category	Criteria to be attained. Your assessment should:
Content representativeness and relevance	1. Emphasize what you taught 2. Represent school's stated curricular content 3. Represent current thinking about the subject 4. Contain content worth learning
Thinking processes and skills represented	5. Require students to integrate and use several thinking skills 6. Represent thinking processes and skills stated in school's curriculum 7. Contain tasks that cannot be completed without using intended thinking skills 8. Allow enough time for students to use complex skills and processes
Consistency with other classroom assessments	9. Yield pattern of results consistent with your other assessments of the class 10. Contain individual tasks (items) not too easy or too difficult
Reliability and objectivity	11. Use a systematic procedure for every student to assign quality ratings or marks 12. Provide each student with several opportunities to demonstrate competence for each learning target assessed
Fairness to different types of students	13. Contain tasks that are interpreted appropriately by students with different backgrounds 14. Accommodate students with disabilities or learning difficulties, if necessary 15. Be free of ethnic, racial, and gender bias
Economy, efficiency, practicality, instructional features	16. Require a reasonable amount of time for you to construct and administer 17. Represent appropriate use of students' class time 18. Represent appropriate use of your class time
Multiple assessment usage	19. Be used in conjunction with other assessment results for important decisions

curriculum materials or the textbook. Often, the items on these tests are of poor quality, emphasize low-level thinking skills (Center for the Study of Testing, Evaluation, and Educational Policy, 1992), or emphasize different content than was emphasized during teaching.[1] We recall a tragic anecdote in this regard. A teacher used one of these tests without carefully reviewing it. The day of the test, the teacher discovered that 10 of the 40 items covered material that she had not taught. In desperation, the teacher used the first 15 minutes of testing time to try to teach these concepts and then gave the test. Of course, this assessment not only lacked validity but also produced student frustration and disastrous results. This case is an example, too, of unethical test use on the part of the teacher.

2.   *Do my assessment tasks accurately represent the outcomes specified in my school's and state's curriculum framework?* Assessments that you use in grading should reflect the learning targets that the school district and state identify as important. Students' grades will be recorded and eventually be interpreted by persons who have seen the curriculum but who are not familiar with what you taught in the classroom. They will expect the grades to reflect the district's learning targets and the state's standards. Because grades are based on your assessments, your assessments should reflect these learning outcomes.

3.   *Are my assessment tasks in line with the current thinking about what should be taught and how it should be assessed?* Educators, philosophers, curriculum theorists, researchers, and others are constantly redefining what is worth learning. Professional teachers keep abreast of these developments and implement them in their teaching and assessment practices.

4.   *Is the content in my assessment important and worth learning?* Content included in your assessment should be of great value or significance to a student's further learning or life skills. The curriculum and content you teach contain many specifics. You must be certain that the assessed content relates directly, rather than tangentially, to important student learning targets.

[1]You can increase the validity of your classroom assessments if you craft your own instruments. The second part of this book is devoted to teaching you how to craft valid classroom assessments.

Most worthwhile learning involves students' applying combinations of skills and content rather than using isolated skills or memorizing bits of content. Teaching and assessment, therefore, should also require students to apply several aspects of such knowledge, skills, and processes in combination.

Thinking Processes and Skills Represented

Closely related to content representativeness and relevance is whether your assessment method permits you to evaluate students on a sufficiently wide range of thinking skills and processes. Assessment instruments that cover broad areas of learning—a unit, marking period, or semester—should comprehensively assess different types of thinking skills. We stressed using taxonomies in Chapter 2 because of the importance of this comprehensiveness. A taxonomy is used along with a content outline to write an assessment blueprint. This blueprint helps you ensure that your assessment covers the important thinking skills and content. Such comprehensiveness can be accomplished only by consciously planning for it. Chapter 6 discusses how to develop assessment plans, and Figure 6.5 shows an example of a test blueprint.

The following questions will help you judge the validity of your classroom assessment in relation to thinking skills and processes:

5. *Do the tasks on my assessment instrument require students to use important thinking skills and processes?* Every classroom assessment procedure should require students to use a mixture of thinking skills and processes. The issue here, however, is the degree to which your assessment mirrors the important thinking skills used in the discipline and the state standards you are teaching. The answer is a matter of emphasis and of knowing what curriculum experts have recommended as learning targets for the students at a particular grade level.

Your assessment should gather information about a student's ability to use strategies and processes that are commonly used in the discipline. For example, a mathematics assessment should help you assess whether a student uses good mathematics thinking when solving problems, not only whether the student can obtain the right answer. Assessment in social studies should help you assess how students think critically and apply the material to their daily lives, rather than simply assessing whether they can "compare and contrast" or "list the factors that caused. . . ." Important and worthwhile learning can be applied to real-life situations. Assessment tasks should at least simulate real-life applications at levels appropriate for the students you teach. They should require students to use combinations of several skills and knowledge whenever possible.

6. *Does my assessment instrument represent the kinds of thinking skills that my school's curriculum framework and state's standards view as important?* Local curricula and state standards often include certain types of higher-order, critical thinking, and performances as goals of instruction (Chapter 10 discusses these thinking skills in detail). Your teaching should foster this kind of thinking, and you should assess your students' abilities to use it appropriately.

7. *Do students actually use during the assessment the types of thinking I expect them to use?* If you are going to interpret students' assessment as reflecting complex thinking skills, then you should be sure that students are actually using them when completing the assessment. Check this by observing the strategies your students appear to use during the assessment. You may interview a few students, asking them to "think aloud" as they solve assessment tasks. You may also review the tasks on your assessment. Poorly constructed test items will give clues to the correct answers and lower the chances that students will need to use the important thinking skills you want them to use. Similarly, ambiguously worded questions confuse students, interfering with their use of important strategies, and lower the validity of their scores.

8. *Do I allow enough time for students to demonstrate the type of thinking I am trying to assess?* Complex thinking, meaningful problem solving, and creative applications require considerable time for most students to demonstrate. A 40- to 50-minute classroom period is usually too short to permit valid assessment of such thinking. You may need to assess students over a longer period for the results to be validly interpreted as reflecting these types of learning outcomes. This means that you may need to give a test over a longer time or assess some learning targets using projects or portfolios.

Consistency With Other Classroom Assessments

Over the course of the unit, marking period, or semester, you will have observed the individuals in your class many times. You will have collected much information that is relevant to evaluating each student's attainments. The results of a student's assessment for grading should be consistent with the student's pattern of performance throughout the period. Some students may perform better or worse than you expect, of course, and you should try to determine why. However, the pattern of assessment results for the entire class should not surprise you. If it is a surprise, there may be a validity problem with your assessment procedure. Evaluate this possibility by focusing on these questions:

9. *Is the pattern of results in the class consistent with what I expected based on my other assessments of them?* If the pattern for the class is quite different from what you were expecting, review your assessment procedure in relation to Questions 1–8. Perhaps the emphasis of your test, for

example, did not match the emphasis of your teaching. Perhaps it did not match the content emphasis of the other assessments on which you based your expectations. If these reasons explain the discrepancy, you may not be able to interpret the assessment results as mastery or use them for validly grading the students.

10.   *Do I make the assessment tasks too difficult or too easy for my students?* When the tasks are too difficult or too easy, the assessment results will not be consistent with your other student observations. When the assessment is too easy or too difficult, all students will attain nearly the same result, and you will be unable to distinguish reliable individual differences among them. This may lower the validity of the results for grading. Also, too difficult an assessment frustrates the students, making them feel as if their study time was wasted. Such a situation is a negative consequence and does not reveal students' best performances. Assessment tasks should be challenging, of course, but not so difficult that only one or two students in the class can perform well on them.

The order of tasks in your assessment instrument is important. The easiest tasks should appear first. If the more difficult tasks are first, students may spend too much time on them. As a result, they may run out of time before attempting the easier tasks that they probably are able to perform. Also, students who are test-anxious may experience debilitating anxiety when faced with difficult tasks early in the assessment. Your assessment results are less valid in these situations because they do not offer students a fair chance to demonstrate their achievement.

Reliability and Objectivity

Reliability refers to the consistency of assessment results. Reliability is the subject of a separate chapter (Chapter 4) but is highly related to valid assessment results. If your students' scores on your assessments are so inconsistent as to be essentially random numbers, your assessment cannot be valid. Inconsistencies that lower the validity of your classroom assessment scores are caused by such factors as using too short a test, failing to use proper scoring rubrics, and your own day-to-day fluctuations in judgment. Chapter 4 will address these factors in more detail.

Objectivity is the degree to which two or more qualified evaluators will agree on what quality rating or score to assign a student's performance. Objectivity is not an all-or-nothing characteristic, of course. It is a matter of degree: All assessment results are more or less objective.

This does not mean that the more subjective assessment procedures should be eliminated. As a professional and expert teacher, your judgments are extremely valuable and important to students. It would be unethical for you to refuse to evaluate student performance and achievement simply because such evaluations are subjective.

What students seek is consistency and fairness in your professional judgment. Personal flaws that result in unprofessional, idiosyncratic, or erratic behavior should be held in check. Chapter 4 and other chapters will suggest ways of improving the reliability of classroom assessment results.

When evaluating your classroom assessment procedures, keep focused on these questions:

11.   *Do I use a scoring guide for obtaining quality ratings or scores from students' performance on the assessment?* Such a guide may be a scoring key, a scoring rubric, or a rating scale with each rating level clearly defined. Apply your scoring guide to every student you are assessing (do not stop using your scoring rubric after the first few students). Your scoring guide should be crafted well enough that a qualified teaching colleague could use it and obtain the same results as you do.

12.   *Is my assessment instrument long enough to be a representative sample of the types of learning outcomes I am assessing?* Be sure that your assessment instrument contains several opportunities for students to demonstrate their knowledge and skill for each learning target. If practical constraints do not allow for a more complete assessment in one class period, consider using another class period, a take-home assessment, or a combination of results from several assessments administered over the marking period.

Fairness to Different Types of Students

Your assessment procedures should be fair to students from all ethnic and socioeconomic backgrounds, as well as students with disabilities who are mainstreamed in your class. For example, a deaf student may understand the concepts you have taught but not be able to express that understanding on your written or oral assessment. Deaf students' general vocabulary and verbal skills usually lag behind their hearing peers', even though their content knowledge may be on par. In such cases, a more valid assessment of a student's understanding may be obtained through a special assessment with a lower verbal load (e.g., simplifying or explaining the nontechnical or nonsubject-specific vocabulary) or through an alternative communication mode (e.g., using a signed language). Chapter 5 discusses assessment accommodation strategies; the last section of this chapter discusses important validity issues concerning accommodation strategies.

Similarly, your assessment should not contain material that is subtly or blatantly offensive to any subgroup of students or that perpetuates **ethnic and gender stereotypes**. For example, you would be perpetuating stereotypes if your assessment materials depict (in words or pictures) only majority race members or males as leaders, technically trained, professional, and so on, or minority race(s) or females only as followers, unskilled, or technically backward (see Zoref & Williams, 1980).

As you evaluate your classroom assessment procedure for fairness, focus on the following questions:

13. *Do I word the problems or tasks on my assessment so students with different ethnic and socioeconomic backgrounds will interpret them in appropriate ways?* "Appropriate interpretations" of assessment tasks does not mean that everyone has identical interpretations: There may be several appropriate ways to interpret the same task. Good classroom assessments will permit you to evaluate the richness in diversity of your students' thinking. You may wish to interview a few students to understand how they interpreted the tasks you set. You should also check whether all students understood the assessment directions and the scoring rules. If students do not understand your directions, they may respond inappropriately through no fault of their own. If this happens, the assessment results will not be valid for purposes of grading.

14. *Do I modify the wording or the administrative conditions of the assessment tasks to accommodate students with disabilities or special learning problems?* The basic interpretation you wish to make is whether the students have achieved the learning targets you are assessing. If the way that you organize your assessment materials inhibits students' ability to communicate their understanding, your assessment results are less valid. Some teachers may balk at the types of assessment adaptations implied here. They may claim that such adaptations for a few students make the assessment unstandardized and unfair to the majority of students. But fairness is not a matter of voting for how to obtain information in which the majority wins. Valid assessment results give us a clear picture of what each student is capable of doing in relation to the learning targets. This may require using somewhat modified assessment procedures for some students in the class. (See Chapter 5 for details.)

15. *Do the pictures, stories, verbal statements, or other aspects of my assessment procedure perpetuate racial, ethnic, or gender stereotypes?* Assessments need not be free of any reference to race, ethnicity, or gender. Rather, you should eliminate stereotypes and balance the references among various groups. Balanced references represent the diversity of peoples and views in the country.

Economy, Efficiency, Practicality, Instructional Features

Your assessments should be efficient. Although assessing students is a very important part of teaching, you must still teach the students. Assessment activities should not consume all of your time. Assessing students is not the same as teaching them: You can't fatten a calf by weighing it!

The validity of classroom assessment results also depends on whether they can inform and guide your teaching toward important learning goals. When evaluating your assessment, focus on these questions:

16. *Is the assessment relatively easy for me to construct and not too cumbersome to use to evaluate students?* Two practical concerns to keep in mind are how easy it is to create the assessment tasks and how easy it is to obtain quality ratings or scores. It is simpler to develop essay questions, for example, than to develop complex problem-solving performance tasks or good multiple-choice items. Once developed, however, multiple-choice items are easier to score and may be reused for next year's class. Problem-solving performance tasks set in real-life settings are difficult to construct properly. However, they let you assess more completely whether students can use what they learned than do either the typical teacher-crafted multiple-choice items or short-answer questions. Thus, teacher convenience or ease of crafting should not be the overriding criteria for evaluating validity.

17. *Would the time needed to use this assessment be better spent directly teaching my students instead?* Your assessments must be balanced against the best way to use students' time in class. Some procedures, such as interviews and individual observations of students' performance, require a long time to complete. Also, while interviewing or observing one student, you need to keep the remainder of the class meaningfully engaged in learning. Group tests, on the other hand, are more efficient because you administer them to all the students at the same time. You must judge according to the circumstances of your own classroom the appropriate balance between occupying a student's time with assessment activities versus occupying it with other activities.

18. *Does my assessment represent the best use of my time?* Essay tests, term papers, projects, and lengthy written works generally require much student time to complete and much teacher time to grade and evaluate. When using these procedures, you must decide whether they are a wise investment of your time. But remember, the grading time and student-learning time need not be entirely separate. For example, you may be able to evaluate a term paper or a project with the student present. If you can do this in a nonthreatening way, "talking through" the reasons for your evaluation with the student, it gives the student a chance to understand the quality of work you are expecting. This opportunity may also let the student ask questions, clarify the criteria you are using, contribute to the evaluation itself, and otherwise improve her grasp of the learning targets. Such rich interaction is often not possible with multiple-choice testing, which usually yields only one score.

When such student-teacher interactions do occur, the time you spend assessing is identical with the student's instructional time. Assessment and instruction blend together. Learners can look forward to assessment as feedback about their accomplishments and as opportunities for coaching and guidance toward their chosen goals.

Multiple Assessment Usage

19.   *Do I use one assessment result in conjunction with other assessment results?* Even though you ask the preceding questions of your assessment technique, you will discover that it does not produce perfectly valid results. The technique will stand up well under the scrutiny of some questions but do poorly under others. Even if you modify your technique to improve its validity, it will not be perfect because a single assessment procedure cannot yield results that are perfectly valid for a given purpose. A **multiple-assessment strategy** combines the results from several different types of assessments (such as homework, class performance, quizzes, projects, and tests) to improve the validity of your decisions about a student's attainments. Weighing one assessment result too heavily in relation to others (like making the student's semester grade depend almost exclusively on his end-of-semester test performance) results in lowered validity.

VALIDITY OF EXTRACLASSROOM ASSESSMENTS

Besides the assessments you craft for use in the classroom, many other educational assessments are used in schools. You will be required to administer and interpret some of them. These *extraclassroom assessments* include district- and state-mandated assessments, standardized achievement and aptitude tests, attitude inventories, and individually administered intelligence tests, to name only a few. These and other assessment methods are described in Part III of this book. In this section we discuss the types of evidence required to support the valid interpretation and use of their results. Understanding these kinds of validity evidence will help you to locate the proper information to evaluate and select an assessment instrument.

Evidence Used to Judge Validity

At least eight types of validity evidence must be considered before you reach a decision about the validity of assessment results for a particular interpretation and use. Each type of evidence does not carry the same weight, however, because assessment results are interpreted and used differently in different settings. Each setting requires a somewhat different emphasis on various types of evidence.

Figure 3.2 summarizes eight types of evidence that validity theorists (Cronbach, 1988, 1989; Linn, Baker, & Dunbar, 1991; Messick, 1989a, 1989b) have identified as important. In addition, the figure lists the typical questions each type of evidence addresses and the typical procedures used to gather the evidence.

You will notice the similarity between some of the types of evidence and questions in Figure 3.2 and the material presented in the previous section on validating teacher-crafted assessments. This is no coincidence. All educational assessment methods share the validity concerns of teacher-crafted assessment procedures. The purposes for using these extraclassroom assessments are usually different from those of teacher-crafted assessments, however. For example, extraclassroom assessments are not used for assigning grades. Therefore, the emphases and mixes of evidence used to judge validity differ also. This section focuses primarily on evidence concerning the validity of extraclassroom assessments.

Before we discuss the details of these types of evidence, you should note the following:

1.   *The importance of each type of evidence changes as interpretations and uses of assessment results change.* All of the evidence types in Figure 3.2 apply to nearly every kind of assessment procedure. However, different interpretations and uses of assessment procedure results will require some types of evidence to be stronger than others. For example, the *SAT Reasoning Test* is intended to predict first-year college grade point averages. Thus, a university or college should weigh more heavily the test's predictive powers and its potential for negative consequences, such as reducing the number of men it selects, than evidence that the test matches curriculum objectives and content. However, evidence about how the *SAT Reasoning Test* scores reflect students' high school performance in academic core curriculum areas should not be entirely ignored.

2.   *Providing evidence is the responsibility of both the publisher and the user.* Both the user of assessment results and the publisher of the assessment instrument should provide evidence about validity. Publishers and other agencies that produce assessments are responsible for providing data that support the reliability, validity, and other technical aspects of assessment results. These responsibilities are described in the *Standards for Educational and Psychological Testing* (American Educational Research Association, American Psychological Association, & National Council on Measurement in Education, 1999). The responsibilities of persons who *use* assessment procedures produced by others are described in a number of resources such as the *Code of Fair Testing Practices in Education* (2004), reproduced in Appendix B, and *Responsibilities of Users of Standardized Tests (RUST)* (3rd ed.) (Association for Assessment in Counseling and Education, 2003).

3.   *You must always be concerned about the validity of your assessment results even if you cannot afford to conduct validity studies.* Educators at different levels have differing amounts of resources and opportunities for gathering evidence about the validity of results. Teachers have the fewest opportunities and resources; school district administrators have more; and state-level educators even more. This fact does not relieve those with fewer resources (e.g., teachers) from the requirement of validating their interpretations and uses of assessment results. Rather, it demands that they be honest and admit that they do not have the resources to validate satisfactorily the way they use the

FIGURE 3.2 Summary of the different types of validity evidence for educational assessments.

Type of evidence	Examples of questions needing to be answered	Techniques often used to obtain answers
1. Content representativeness and relevance (called *content evidence*)	a. How well do the assessment tasks represent the domain of important content? b. How well do the assessment tasks represent the curriculum as you define it? c. How well do the assessment tasks reflect current thinking about what should be taught and assessed? d. Are the assessment tasks worthy of being learned? e. How well do tasks align with state standards?	A description of the curriculum and content to be learned is obtained. Each assessment task is checked to see if it matches important content and learning outcomes. Each assessment task is rated for its relevance, importance, accuracy, and meaningfulness. The assessment procedure is viewed as a whole, and judgments are made about representativeness and relevance of the entire collection of tasks.
2. Types of thinking skills and processes required (called *substantive evidence*)	a. How much do the assessment tasks require students to use important thinking skills and processes? b. How well do the assessment tasks represent the types of thinking skills espoused as important curriculum outcomes? c. Are the thinking skills and processes that students actually use to complete the assessment procedure the same ones claimed to be assessed? d. Do thinking skills required by the test align with thinking skills required by state standards?	The assessment procedure is analyzed to reveal the types of cognitions required to perform the tasks successfully. The relationship between the strategies students are taught to use and those they are required to use during the assessment are determined. Students may be asked to "think aloud" while performing the assessment tasks and the resultant protocols analyzed to identify cognitions the students used. Judgments are made about the assessment procedure as a whole to decide whether desirable, representative, and relevant thinking skills and processes are being assessed.
3. Relationships among the assessment tasks or parts of the assessment (called *internal structure evidence*)	a. Do all the assessment tasks "work together" so that each task contributes positively toward assessing the quality of interest? b. If the different parts of the assessment procedure are supposed to provide unique information, do the results support this uniqueness? c. If the different parts of the assessment procedure are supposed to provide the same or similar information, do the results support this? d. Are the students' responses scored in a way that is consistent with the constructs and theory on which the assessment is based?	a. If students' performance on each task is quantified, correlations of task scores with total scores from the assessment are studied to decide whether all tasks contribute positively. b. Each part of the assessment may be scored separately and these part scores intercorrelated to see whether the desired pattern of relationships emerges. c. Logic, substantive knowledge, and experience are used to generate explanations for high and low performance on the assessment. Not all hypotheses should be consistent with the intended interpretations of how the parts function. d. Empirical studies, both experimental and correlational, are conducted to support or refute the hypotheses generated in (c) above.
4. Relationships of assessment results to the results of other variables (called *external structure evidence*)	a. Are the results of this assessment consistent with the results of other similar assessments for these students? b. How well does performance on this assessment procedure reflect the quality or trait that is measured by other tests? c. How well does performance on this assessment procedure predict current or future performance on other valued tasks or measures (criteria)? d. How well can the assessment results be used to select persons for jobs, schools, etc.? What is the magnitude of error? e. How well can the assessment results be used to assign pupils to different types of instruction? Is learning better when pupils are assigned this way?	a. The criterion tasks are identified and analyzed. Assessment of their important characteristics is created. b. Scores from the assessment are compared to scores on the criterion to be predicted. c. Studies of various classification and prediction errors are made. d. Studies show whether the results from this assessment converge with or diverge from results from other assessments in the way expected when the proposed interpretation of the students' performance is used (called *convergent and discriminant evidence*).

5. Reliability over time, assessors, and content domain (called *reliability evidence*)	a. Will the same students obtain nearly the same results if the assessment procedure was applied on another occasion? What is the margin of error expected? b. If different persons administered, graded, or scored the assessment results, would the students' outcomes be the same? What is the margin of error? c. If a second, alternate form of the assessment procedure were to be developed, with similar content, would the students' results be very similar? What is the margin of error?	Studies are conducted focusing on the consistency (reliability) of the assessment results. These studies are described in more detail in Chapter 4
6. Generalization of interpretations over different types of people, under different conditions, or with special instruction/intervention (called *generalization evidence*)	a. Does the assessment procedure give significantly different results when it is used with students from different socioeconomic and ethnic backgrounds, but of the same ability? If so, is this fair or unbiased? b. Will students' results from the assessment procedure be altered drastically if they are given special incentives or motives? If so, should this change how the assessment results are interpreted? c. Will special intervention, changes in instructions, or special coaching significantly alter the results students obtain on the assessment? If so, should this change how the assessment results are interpreted?	a. Logic, substantive knowledge, and experience are used to generate explanations (hypotheses) about how the interpretation of the assessment results might change when the procedure is applied to different types of people, under different conditions, or with special instruction (intervention). b. Empirical studies, both experimental and correlational, are conducted to support or refute the hypotheses generated in (a) above.
7. Value of the intended and/or unintended consequences (called *consequential evidence*)	a. What do we expect to happen to the students if we interpret and use the assessment results in this particular way? To what degree do these expected consequences happen, and is that good? b. What side effects do we anticipate happening to the students if we interpret and use the assessment results in this particular way? To what degree are these anticipated side effects occurring, and are they positive or negative? c. What unanticipated negative side effects happened to the students for whom we interpreted and used the assessment results in this particular way? Can these negative side effects be avoided by using other assessment procedures/techniques or by altering our interpretations?	a. Studies are conducted to describe the intended outcomes of using the given assessment procedure and to determine the degree to which these outcomes are realized for all students. b. Studies are conducted to determine whether anticipated or unanticipated side effects have resulted from interpreting and using the given assessment procedure in a certain way.
8. Cost, efficiency, practicality, instructional features (called *practicality evidence*)	a. Can the assessment procedure accommodate typical numbers of students? b. Is the assessment procedure easy for teachers to use? c. Can the assessment procedure give quick results to guide instruction? d. Do teachers agree that the theoretical concepts behind the assessment procedure reflect the key understandings they are teaching? e. Do the assessment results meaningfully explain individual differences? f. Do the assessment results identify misunderstandings that need to be corrected? g. Would an alternative assessment procedure be more efficient?	Logical analyses, cost analyses, reviews by teachers, and field trial data are used to come to decisions about the factors of cost, efficiency, practicality, and usefulness of instructional features.

Note: These types of validity evidence have been suggested by Messick (1989b, 1994b) and Linn, Baker, and Dunbar (1991).

assessment. They also must admit that because they do not have the evidence, their interpretations and uses may have low validity.

There is a professional obligation to raise issues about the validity of the assessments being used and to seek help in establishing their validity. If you are the only person in your school who has taken a recent course on validity, you have a special obligation to raise validity issues with your colleagues or your school. Your additional knowledge brings with it increased professional responsibility.

CATEGORIES OF VALIDITY EVIDENCE

Measurement specialists now recommend that validity be used as a unitary concept (American Educational Research Association et al., 1999; Messick, 1989b). This book follows this recommendation.[2] Thus, you should think of the following as types of evidence that support an assessment's validity, not as different kinds of validity.

Content Representativeness and Relevance: Content Evidence

The idea of content representativeness and relevance applies to all sorts of assessments: achievement tests, aptitude tests, personality tests, student-teacher observation procedures, performance rating scales, and so on. This section focuses mostly on extraclassroom achievement tests.

Domain Definition   As shown in Figure 3.2, this type of evidence comes from judging the content of the tasks or items on an instrument. Evidence of an assessment's **content representativeness** comes from judgments of informed persons that focus on whether the assessment tasks are a representative sample from a larger domain of performance. Any assessment is but a sample of the items that could be presented to students. Because we cannot present every possible task to a student, we must sample from the domain in such a way that our sample represents the domain fairly. (Think of *re*-presenting the domain in a smaller version.) Evidence of an assessment's **content relevance** comes from judgments of informed persons that focus on how much of the test user's domain definition includes the assessment tasks.

One question that arises is whose definition of the domain is appropriate: the assessment developer's or the assessment user's? The *ABC Reading Test*, for example, may

emphasize paragraph and sentence reading but may not separately measure word attack skills or vocabulary. School personnel selecting a reading test may view these latter areas as relevant to the definition of the reading domain. Here, the test developer and the test user disagree on the definition of the domain and, therefore, on what is or is not to be included in the assessment. Making separate judgments about how well the tasks on the assessment represent (a) the developer's domain and (b) the user's domain will clarify whether the evidence supports a school's intended use of the assessment procedure. See Nitko, Al-Sarimi, Amedahe, Wang, and Wingert (1998) for an example of how this can be done.

Table of Specifications   A test developer often defines the domain assessed in an accompanying manual or technical publication. Within the manual a typical tool for defining the domain for standardized survey achievement tests is a **table of specifications**. This table contains the major content categories and skills that are assessed. It describes the percentage of tasks (items) for each content-skills combination. The percentage of tasks per combination is a rough measure of the weight that a combination contributes to the student's total score. Chapter 6 and Appendix G show examples of tables of specifications.

Curricular Relevance and Content Domains   An assessment method is relevant to a school's definition of the achievement domain to the extent that it matches the school's curriculum learning targets. Evidence of an assessment's **curricular relevance** comes from judgments by informed persons of the degree of overlap between a curriculum and the items contained in the assessment instrument. Studying Figure 3.3 may help clarify the distinction between matching the assessment to the developer's achievement domain and the curricular relevance of the assessment. The developer's definition of achievement and the sample of tasks comprising a particular assessment are shown in the center of the figure. The assessment matches the developer's domain if the tasks on it adequately represent the developer's definition. (Both the solid and broken straight lines show these tasks.) The assessment's curricular relevance is based on how well the tasks on the instrument represent your school's curriculum framework. (In Figure 3.3, the solid straight lines show this.) As the figure shows, the assessment illustrated has more curriculum relevance for School A than for School B: A considerable proportion of School A's curriculum is not assessed, however.

This is typical: A school's curriculum framework is usually much broader and richer than any single extraclassroom assessment instrument. Thus, even though the assessment instrument illustrated has more curricular relevance for School A than for School B, that degree of relevance still may not be sufficient for the school to use the instrument.

---

[2] Some textbooks and many standardized test manuals still recognize three kinds of validity: content validity, criterion-related validity, and construct validity. Many other terms have been used, including curricular validity, instructional validity, synthetic validity, predictive validity, concurrent validity, convergent validity, factorial validity, nomological validity, and "face" validity. "In general, such terms refer to specific procedures for evaluating validity rather than to new kinds of interpretive inferences from test scores" (American Psychological Association, 1974, p. 26).

FIGURE 3.3 **A schematic illustration of the relationship between an assessment instrument, a developer's content domain, and the curriculum-specific domains of two schools. An assessment may match the developer's domain yet may lack curricular relevance for some schools.**

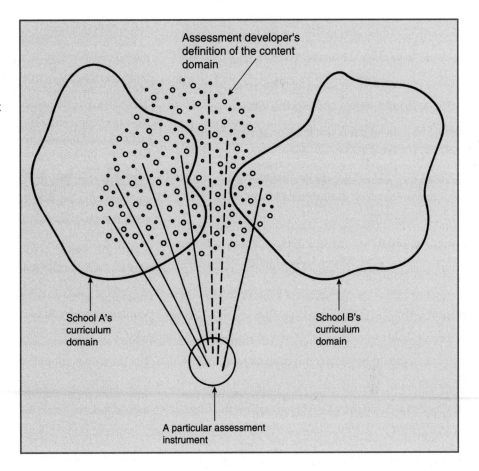

You should keep in mind the questions in Figure 3.2 for this area. Curricular relevance is more than a simple proportion of the content that matches the curriculum. The instrument must be reviewed as a whole to judge whether different content areas receive emphasis in keeping with the local curriculum's learning targets. The individual tasks on the assessment must also (a) reflect current thinking of subject-matter experts about what is important to teach and to assess, (b) accurately portray the subject matter, (c) be keyed correctly, and (d) contain meaningful and important content. In addition, the individual assessment tasks must be crafted well. Poorly crafted tasks may "clue" answers to less knowledgeable students or introduce bias and ambiguity, which prevent some students from performing to their best levels.

Alignment of State Standards and Accountability Tests One important issue for states and schools is the alignment of the assessments used for accountability and the educational standards states specify. The NCLB Act requires states to provide evidence that the educational assessments used to report to the federal government are aligned with the state's standards. As a result, a state often contracts with organizations to conduct alignment studies. **Alignment studies** are empirical studies involving the

collection of ratings from trained judges and summaries of students' responses to test items that have the aim of describing, in the most objective ways possible, the degree to which the actual test items on a state's assessment instrument(s) are aligned to the educational content and performance standards set by that state. These studies provide evidence that falls into the content and substantive categories of Figure 3.2.

It is beyond the scope of this textbook to describe the details of how to conduct alignment studies. However, you will hear or read of such studies in connection with your state's assessment program. You should be aware that, at the minimum, such studies should provide information about how well their state's assessment(s) match the:

1. *Content* span, ideas, and detail that are specified by their state's standards.

2. *Depth* of understanding, cognitive complexity, and ability to apply the knowledge described in the state's standards.

3. *Emphasis* of different topics and cognitive processes that are reflected in the state's standards.

4. *Performances* expected of the students as these are described by the state's standards.

5. *Implied applicability* of the state's standards to all students. (For example, does the assessment allow all students, regardless of disability or limited English proficiency, to display completely and fairly their achievement of the state's standards?) (La Marca, Redfield, Winter, Bailey, & Despriet, 2000)

It should be pointed out that alignment studies often take into account several years of state assessments rather than only one year's testing. This is because, as we have stated earlier, one test is but a sample of the possible domain of items that could be presented to students. Alignment over several years is sometimes a more appropriate criterion. Additional information about alignment of assessments with state standards may be found in Achieve (2004); Blank (2002); Council of Chief State School Officers (2005); Porter and Smithson (2001); and Webb (1999).

Thinking Skills and Processes: Substantive Evidence

An assessment should be judged not only in terms of the content it covers but also in terms of the thinking processes and skills students must use to complete the tasks successfully. As discussed in the section on the validity of classroom assessment results, achievement assessments should require students to use important thinking processes and skills as defined by the curriculum framework, the state's standards, and by experts in the subject matter being assessed. Assessment instruments sometimes ask students to use combinations of skills and knowledge together to work on "real-life" applications.

To validate a claim that the tasks require students to use higher-order thinking processes and skills, assessment developers should provide you with student-based data to support their claims. This should include (a) a detailed description of the processes and abilities that they claim to be assessing, (b) a clear demonstration of how each type of task or assessment exercise assesses each of these processes and skills, and (c) evidence from research studies showing that, when responding successfully, students use the thinking processes and skills that are claimed. The latter may take the form of small studies conducted in *cognitive labs*. Students are asked to "think aloud" as they work through the tasks on the instrument. Their thinking is organized into "protocols" and analyzed to reveal the types of thinking strategies students say they have used (Ericsson & Simon, 1999). Zucker, Sassman, and Case (2004) give an example of how one test publisher uses the cognitive lab approach to develop and validate a standardized test.

More rigorous experiments may be reported concerning the strategies students use, but these are rare. These studies should also demonstrate that students do not use inappropriate processes to solve the tasks. For example, suppose a multiple-choice mathematics test developer claims to be assessing students' higher-order problem-solving ability.

The developer should provide evidence that students do, in fact, use the intended higher-order abilities.

Relationships Among Parts of Assessment: Internal Structure Evidence

An assessment instrument should not be only a hodge-podge collection of assessment tasks or test questions. Each task in the procedure should contribute positively to the total result. The **internal structure** of an assessment instrument is described by the interrelationships among the tasks and the relationship between the tasks and the total results. The internal and external structures of an assessment procedure are important in interpreting the assessment results as indicators of a person's standing on an educational or psychological construct. For example, a test may claim to have a unidimensional internal structure that assesses only one student ability, such as arithmetic problem solving. To be certain that you are truly interpreting the assessment results as measuring only this student's ability, you must locate evidence that supports this claim. The developer should provide evidence that each task on this assessment differentiates students along this single dimension (here, arithmetic problem solving). Often, however, assessment tasks measure more than one dimension. For example, solving an arithmetic problem may depend heavily on reading skill, vocabulary knowledge, computational speed, and general speed of working, as well as arithmetic problem solving. In this case, you may not validly interpret the results as reflecting only the students' arithmetic problem-solving ability.

On the other hand, some assessment instruments are deliberately crafted to assess two or more dimensions. For example, some scholastic aptitude tests provide measures of verbal ability, quantitative ability, and nonverbal ability. (See Chapter 19 for examples.) If so, then the technical manual should contain evidence that verbal, quantitative, and nonverbal test scores are meaningfully different. Evidence from research studies should demonstrate that, although students' scores on the three parts of the test might be moderately related (because they are aspects of a global or general scholastic aptitude), they are different enough to be interpreted as three different aspects of scholastic aptitude.

Test developers often use *correlation coefficients* as evidence to support the validity of these types of interpretations. These coefficients measure the degree of relationship between two or more sets of assessment scores. Correlation coefficients are explained later in this chapter.

Relationships of Results to Other Variables: External Structure Evidence

Evidence about the validity of assessment results must go beyond demonstrating how well the tasks sample content and thinking processes or how scores on different tasks correlate with one another. Evidence also comes from how well the assessment results correlate with other variables or criteria. For example, the *SAT Reasoning Test* measures both verbal and mathematics abilities. Its validity depends in part on its internal structure–whether the verbal items in fact measure verbal ability, mathematics items measure mathematics ability, and the scores on the two parts of the test are meaningfully different. However, the primary use of the *SAT Reasoning Test* is to provide information that helps admissions officers select applicants who are likely to succeed in college. The most important validity evidence must come, therefore, from studies that establish the correlation of the *SAT Reasoning Test* scores with an external variable, namely, grades in college. The **external structure** of an assessment is the pattern of relationships between assessment results (scores) and scores from variables external to the assessment.

The specific evidence you need depends on how you want to interpret and use the assessment results. If you want to use the assessment results to help select candidates for college, for example, then you need to establish that the assessment results are positively correlated with a college success criterion such as grade point average. Sometimes we want to validate that a new assessment measures the same ability as one that already exists. For example, we may want to validate that a multiple-choice and an oral assessment both measure reading comprehension. If they both measure the same ability, you would expect their scores to be positively correlated: Students with high scores on one should also have high scores on the other. If the scores on the two assessments differ significantly, it is likely that they measure different attributes. Additional research would be needed to establish which score, if any, measures reading comprehension. A researcher generates hypotheses and counterhypotheses about the relationships of assessment results to external criteria result from logical analysis, experience, previous research, and a theory about the nature of the traits or characteristics being assessed.

Notice from these two examples that some evidence helps predict future performance (such as success in college), and some evidence estimates the individual's current status on a variable. **Predictive validity evidence** refers to the extent to which individuals' *future performance* on a criterion can be predicted from their prior performance on an assessment instrument. For example, we could collect high school students' grade point averages, wait until they finish one year of college, collect their college grade point averages, and correlate high school grades with them. Prediction over time is the aim. **Concurrent validity evidence** refers to the extent to which individuals' *current status* on a criterion can be estimated from their current performance on an assessment instrument. For example, we can study students already in college, give them a special aptitude test, and collect their current grade point averages. The relationship between the grades and the test

is concurrent validity evidence because the two measures were collected at the same time. The distinction is important because the time interval between administering the assessment instrument and obtaining criterion results affects the strength of the relationship between the two results: Usually the longer the time interval between the two results, the lower the correlation between them.

To understand the external structure information that test developers usually offer, it is necessary to know a little bit about *correlation coefficients*. We turn to this necessary digression in the following paragraphs.

Correlation Coefficient

The **correlation coefficient** is a statistical index that quantifies the degree of relationship between the scores from one assessment and the scores from another. The index is reported on a scale of -1 to $+1$. (This section focuses on concepts. Computations are illustrated in Appendix I.)

Students' Scores on Different Tests An example showing the relationship between the scores from several tests will help explain correlation. The example Figure 3.4 shows the scores of 11 students on each of three tests. The students have been arranged in descending order according to their verbal aptitude scores (V). Look at the first two columns of scores and notice that the verbal scores and the reading scores (R) order the students in about the same way. This is not a perfect ordering, however. Notice, too, that the relationship between the verbal and arithmetic scores (A) is less strong: The order of the students is not as similar on these tests as it is on the verbal and reading tests.

Comparing Students' Rank Orders This correspondence is clearer when we transform each score to a rank, as in the last three columns of the example in Figure 3.4. The ranks of the students on verbal aptitude and reading, though not identical in every case, are quite close. The ranks of the students on verbal aptitude and arithmetic correspond less closely, but the ranks are still similar. There is more shifting in the students' ranks from verbal aptitude to arithmetic than there was from verbal aptitude to reading. Comparing students' rank orders on two assessments is one way of studying how correlated the results are.

Scatter Diagrams Another way to study the correlation between the scores from assessments is graphically with a **scatter diagram** (sometimes called a **scattergram**). A scatter diagram is a graph on which the paired scores are plotted. The example in Figure 3.5 shows these plots for V vs. R and V vs. A. When completed, the graph shows the relationship between the paired scores for the entire group of 11 students.

FIGURE 3.4 Hypothetical scores for 11 pupils on a verbal aptitude test, a reading test, and an arithmetic test.

Pupil	Verbal score (V)	Reading score (R)	Arithmetic score (A)	Verbal rank order	Reading rank order	Arithmetic rank order
A	82	59	48	1	1	4
B	77	54	65	2	4	1
C	70	55	43	3	3	7
D	65	58	58	4	2	2
E	59	51	40	5	5	8.5
F	53	44	47	6	6	5
G	45	38	55	7	7	3
H	41	34	44	8	9	6
I	34	35	25	9	8	11
J	30	30	40	10	10	8.5
K	23	26	33	11	11	10

Source: Adapted from *Measuring Pupil Achievement and Aptitude,* 2nd Ed., by C. M. Lindvall and A. J. Nitko, New York: Harcourt, Brace Jovanovich, © 1975 by C. M. Lindvall and A. J. Nitko.

FIGURE 3.5 Scatter diagram of the verbal aptitude versus reading test scores and the verbal aptitude versus arithmetic test scores for the 11 pupils shown in Figure 3.4.

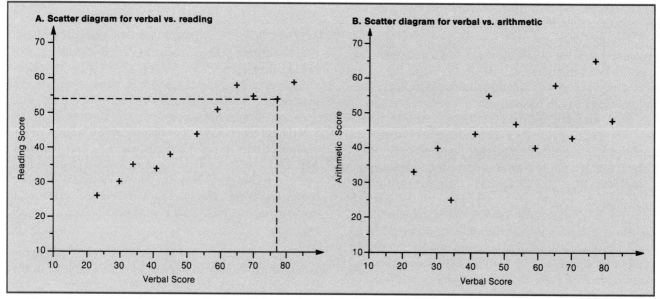

You can obtain considerable insight into how the scores on two assessments are related by making a scatter diagram. In Figure 3.5(A), the plots lie along an almost straight line from the lower left of the graph to the upper right. In Figure 3.5(B), however, the plots do not come as close to a straight line. However, there is a trend in the graph from the lower left of the graph to the upper right.

The tendency for points of a scatter diagram to lie along a straight line is central to the concept of correlation. The higher the degree of correlation between two sets of scores, the closer the points come to lying along a straight line. As the degree of correlation lessens, the points tend to scatter away from this straight line. These points scatter in an elliptical shape: the narrower the elliptical pattern in the

scattergram, the higher the degree of correlation; the less the degree of correlation, the wider these elliptical patterns of the scatter diagrams. When the two sets of scores have no relationship, the pattern will widen until it is circular, rather than elliptical.

Pearson Product-Moment Correlation Coefficients Visually comparing rank orders of scores and plotting scatter diagrams are two qualitative ways of studying the correlation between the scores. Most published assessment material uses a quantitative measure of correlation called the **Pearson product-moment correlation coefficient**, which is denoted by r. Of the many different types of correlation coefficients, r is most commonly used in validity studies. For sake of simplicity, we shall refer to r as the *correlation coefficient* in this text.

A correlation coefficient has a possible range of values from −1.00 through 0.00 to +1.00. A correlation of 0.00 means that the two sets of scores are unrelated: Students' scores on one assessment cannot be predicted from their scores on the other assessment. A perfect positive relationship would have a correlation coefficient of +1.00: A student's score on one assessment can perfectly predict his score on the other assessment. In **positive correlations,** high scores on one assessment are associated with high scores on another. A perfect negative relationship would have a correlation coefficient of −1.00. In **negative correlations,** high scores on one assessment are associated with low scores on another. For perfect negative relationships, a student's score from one assessment is perfectly predicted from her score on the other, too; but here we predict that high scores on one will associate with low scores on the other, and low scores on one will associate with high scores on the other.

Numerical Values of the Correlation Coefficients for Scores in Figure 3.4 What are the numerical values of the correlation coefficients for the scores in the example in Figure 3.4? We do not consider calculations in this chapter. Rather, we

focus on conceptual understanding. You may wish to calculate the correlation coefficients on your own, however. If so, use the procedure shown in Appendix I. If you applied the procedure described in Appendix I, you would find that the correlation between the verbal and reading test scores is 0.97 and between the verbal and arithmetic scores is 0.71. You can see that these correlation coefficients are consistent with the impression you had when you compared the rank orders of the scores in the table and studied the scatter diagrams. The number 0.97 reflects a high positive relationship (it is close to 1.00), whereas 0.71 indicates a weaker relationship.

Degrees of Relationship It is helpful in understanding correlation coefficients to relate them to scatter diagrams. Figure 3.6 shows the scatter diagrams and corresponding correlation coefficients for paired scores that have different degrees of relationships. Each dot represents a pair of scores for a person. The scatter diagrams are arranged to illustrate that positive and negative correlation coefficients having the same absolute numerical value (i.e., the number without the algebraic sign) represent the same strength or degree of relationship.

FIGURE 3.6 Scatter diagrams for different degrees of correlation.

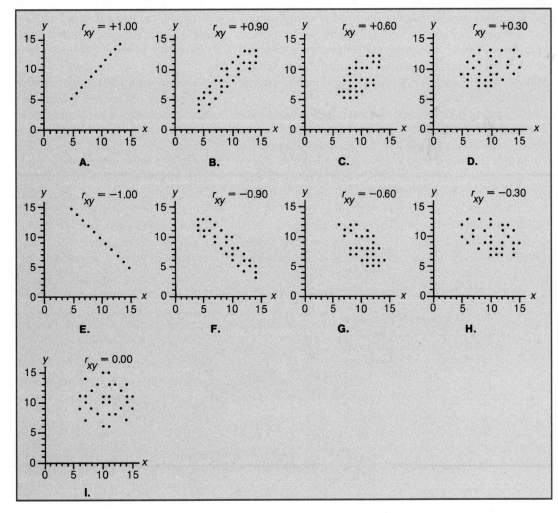

Compare Scatter Diagrams A and E, for example. Both show perfect correlation, but Diagram A shows a perfect positive correlation, whereas Diagram E shows a perfect negative correlation. The *strength* of the relationship is identical in both cases, but the *direction* of the relationship differs. The negative sign on the correlation coefficient shows that the direction of the relationship is negative. Because the correlation is perfect in both cases, knowing a person's score on one assessment would allow us to predict exactly the score the person obtained on the second assessment: Perfect correlation means perfect prediction.

Perfect correlations are seldom found in practical work with educational and psychological assessment scores. There are many reasons for this, such as the assessments containing random error of measurement, the units of measurement being unequal, the distributions of the scores not having identical shapes, and the two assessment results not being related in a simple, linear manner (Carroll, 1961).

Other degrees of relationship are shown in Figure 3.6. In B and F, the correlations are −0.90 and +0.90, respectively. Correlations of this magnitude indicate that the assessment results are highly related. Again, the degree of relationship is the same in B and F, but the directions of the relationships are opposite. In both cases, the plotted points in the scatter diagram tend to fall along straight lines, even though they do not fall exactly on the lines as they do in A and E. Although perfect prediction of scores on one assessment from scores on another is not possible when the correlation is −.90 or +.90, reasonably accurate predictions are possible.

Comparing B with F, and C with G, we see that as the correlation between the scores declines, a greater scatter occurs away from a straight line. It is still possible to predict a person's score on *Y* from knowledge of the person's score on *X*, but such predictions would have to be made with broader margins of error than in the case when $r = -0.90$ or $r = +0.90$. In D and H the correlations are +0.40 and −0.40, respectively. The elliptical patterns are broader still.

Finally, scatter Diagram I illustrates a complete lack of correlation between two sets of scores. A person with a high score on Assessment *X* could have either a high, middle, or low score on Assessment *Y*. Thus, the scores are said to be unrelated or uncorrelated, and $r = 0.00$. Note the circular pattern of the points in the scatter diagram.

In practical work with assessments, correlations of exactly 0.00, −1.00, and −1.00 are rare. These particular numerical values, however, serve as benchmarks: Actual correlation coefficients take on meaning in the context of these limiting values.

Correlation and Causation If the scores from two assessments correlate, this does not necessarily mean that the underlying traits are causally related. For example, there is a positive correlation between shoe sizes and reading comprehension grade-equivalent scores for a population of elementary school children (compare Blommers & Forsyth, 1977). Children with larger feet read better: They are older and have had more reading instruction. The larger feet are in eighth grade and, relative to first and second graders, so are the better readers. A third variable, amount of reading instruction, not size of foot, is the most likely "cause" of the correlation between shoe size and reading scores. Of course, we wouldn't recommend a reading readiness program in which we stretched each child's feet. Yet some educators have erroneously recommended instructional procedures primarily on the basis of correlations rather than on demonstrations of their effectiveness (Cronbach & Snow, 1977).

Correlation Coefficients and Sample Sizes The correlation coefficients reported in studies of assessments and in test manuals are based on scores obtained from *samples of persons*, not on the scores of all persons in the population. A correlation computed from a sample only estimates the numerical value of the correlation in the complete population. You should have less confidence in the exact values of correlations computed from smaller samples than you would from correlations computed from larger samples. In small samples, even one pair of scores can affect the numerical value of the correlation coefficient substantially. The example in Figure 3.7 demonstrates this. The correlation of

FIGURE 3.7 **An example of how a change in only one pair of scores can alter the correlation coefficient. In this example, N = 25 pairs of scores.**

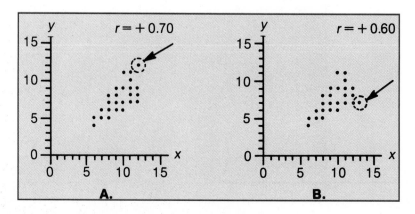

FIGURE 3.8 **Factors affecting the magnitude of correlation coefficients.**

Factor	Effect on correlation coefficient	Example
Similarity of traits assessed	The more similar the traits, the higher the correlation.	Verbal aptitude and reading comprehension test scores will be more highly correlated than verbal aptitude and mathematics aptitude test scores.
Reliability of the scores	Less reliable scores correlate lower than more reliable scores.	Subjective rating of students' correct English usage from essay examinations correlate lower with reading comprehension test scores than do correct English usage scores from multiple-choice tests.
Range or spread of scores	The large the range (spread) of scores, the higher the correlation is likely to be.	Algebra aptitude test scores will correlate higher with end-of-semester mathematics grades when all first-year high school students are included in the sample than when only those first-year students in honors mathematics are included.
Similarity of distribution shapes	The more different the shapes of the distribution of scores on the two assessments, the lower the correlation.	Scores from an achievement test that is very difficult and scores from one that is very easy for a particular group of students will correlate less than if the two tests were moderately difficult for this group.
Time interval between assessment administrations	The shorter the time interval between assessment administrations, the higher the correlation is likely to be.	An algebra aptitude test is administered at the beginning of the school year. The correlation between its scores and mathematics grades at the end of the first semester will be higher than with mathematics grades of the same students after 2 years.

0.70 in Diagram A drops to 0.60 in Diagram B when the person with $X = 12$, $Y = 12$ is replaced by another person with $X = 13$, $Y = 7$, even though all the other scores remain the same.

Factors That Raise or Lower Correlation Coefficients Correlation coefficients appear in test manuals and research reports. When we encounter them, our first tendency is to interpret them as reporting the true relationship between the characteristics our instruments assess. In fact, the similarity of the characteristics being assessed is only one factor that affects the magnitude of the correlation coefficient reported. In general, higher correlations result when (a) the traits being assessed are alike, (b) the reliability of the scores on both assessments is high, (c) the range of scores on both assessments is large, (d) the shapes of the scores distributions on the two assessments are alike, and (e) the time interval between administering the two assessments is short. Figure 3.8 summarizes these factors and gives an example of each. Often, more than one of these factors operates at the same time. Read reports of correlational validity evidence cautiously, keeping these factors in mind as possible explanations of the numerical correlation values you are interpreting.

Validity Coefficients

The usual procedure when collecting predictive or concurrent validation evidence is to compute correlations between scores from the assessment instrument and criterion scores.

Such a correlation is sometimes referred to as a **validity coefficient,** although, as you can easily see from Figure 3.6, no single number is appropriate to judge the validity of assessment results. In selection situations, however, high validity coefficients typically are strong evidence that the selection test is useful for selecting people who will be successful.[3] This is because high correlations are evidence that predictions of success will be reasonably accurate (recall our discussion of Figure 3.6). Note that realistically you would expect neither a perfect (error-free) prediction nor a correlation of 1.00.

Expectancy Tables

Another way to display predictive validity data is to make an expectancy table. An **expectancy table** is a grid or two-way table that permits predictions about how likely it is for a person with a specific assessment result to attain each

[3]Note that you cannot judge from the correlation coefficient the likely size of the errors that may be made when the assessment results are used to predict criterion scores. For example, if you were predicting college grade point averages, the correlation would not tell you how many GPA units your prediction is likely to be in error. An index that can estimate the likely size of errors of prediction is called the *standard error of estimate.* Its equation is

$$SD_{est} = SD_y \sqrt{1 - r^2}.$$

The symbol SD_y denotes a standard deviation, which is explained in Appendix I.

FIGURE 3.9 The develop-
ment of an expectancy table
for a hypothetical set of 100
pupils. The expectancy table
shows the percentage of
pupils at each predictor test
level earning each grade level
in the course. These percentages are interpreted as probabilities.

A. Frequency of grades for each predictor score level

| Predictor test score | Number of pupils receiving each grade | | | | | |
	F	D	C	B	A	Totals
80–89			1	3	1	5
70–79		1	4	5	2	12
60–69		3	5	6	1	15
50–59		4	8	5	1	18
40–49	1	5	8	4		18
30–39	1	6	5	3		15
20–29	2	5	4	1		12
10–19	1	2	1			4
0–9	1					1
Totals	6	26	36	27	5	100

B. Expectancy table made by converting frequencies into percentages

| Predictor test score | Percentage of pupils receiving each grade | | | | | |
	F	D	C	B	A	Totals
80–89			20	60	20	100
70–79		8	33	42	17	100
60–69		20	33	40	7	100
50–59		22	44	28	6	100
40–49	6	28	44	22		100
30–39	7	40	33	20		100
20–29	17	42	33	8		100
10–19	25	50	25			100
0–9	100					100

criterion score level. Figure 3.9 illustrates how an expectancy table is developed to indicate the probability that students at particular aptitude score levels will attain each letter grade in a course. (Of course, expectancy tables can be developed to predict other criteria such as supervisors' ratings, amount of sales, success in clinical treatment, and other relevant criteria.)

First a table is constructed, such as in Figure 3.9 (A), in which each cell contains the number of persons with a particular score who attained each course grade (criterion score level). For example, 15 students had aptitude test scores between 60 and 69. This number is shown in the right margin of the 60–69 row. Three of these 15 attained a course grade of D, five a grade of C, six a grade of B, and one a grade of A.

Second, each cell frequency in Figure 3.9 (A) is divided by its corresponding row total, converted to a percentage, and put into an expectancy table such as Figure 3.9 (B). These percentages may be interpreted as probabilities or chances out of 100 to answer such questions as, "At this school, what is the probability that a person with an aptitude test score of 65 will succeed in this course?" First, note that a person with a score of 65 is a member of the

group whose scores are between 60 and 69. Second, if we define *succeed* to mean *a grade of C or better*, then 33% + 40% + 7% = 80% of the students with aptitude scores between 60 and 69 were successful. Since a person with an aptitude score of 65 is a member of this group, the answer to the question is, "A person with an aptitude score of 65 has an 80% chance of being successful in this course."

Expectancy tables can help parents and students interpret assessment results, too. For example, suppose an expectancy table is made for a particular college showing how admissions test scores are related to first-year-student grade point averages. Persons reading the table can then interpret the admission test results in terms of a student's chances of obtaining various grade point averages. Such interpretations of admissions test scores give more information than a scaled score or percentile rank (the typical report of results students receive).[4]

If you interpret assessment results using expectancy tables, you should observe commonsense cautions. For

[4]Scaled scores and percentile ranks are described in Chapter 17 and Appendix I.

example, assessment instruments used to predict success seldom, if ever, measure students' initiative, persistence, or motivation. Thus, they cannot predict with certainty what a *particular student* will do. Rather, the table represents the experience of other students in the past and can offer some guidance only. Therefore, never tell a student that the data in the table "prove" the student can (or cannot) be successful. You must explain that the data show the experience of other students similar to him or her.

The Criterion

Your judgment about whether the assessment developer has provided appropriate validity evidence depends in part on whether the assessment results have been correlated with relevant criteria. Obtaining suitable criterion measures to use in validating assessment results is so difficult that this has been dubbed the *criterion problem* (Thorndike, 1949).

Kinds of Criteria A variety of criteria are used to provide validity evidence. Personnel classification and selection research in government and industry use four general types: production (quantity and quality of goods, sales), personal data (accidents on the job, length of service, group membership, training course grades), samples of actual or simulated job performance, and judgments by others (checklists, supervisors' ratings) (Lawshe & Balma, 1966). In education, criteria fall into three types: (a) achievement test scores; (b) ratings, grades, and other quantified judgments of teachers; and (c) career data. A common example is a reading readiness test given at the beginning of first grade. Scores are often validated by correlating them with scores from a reading achievement test (the criterion) administered at the end of first grade. Using grade point averages to validate scores from aptitude and admissions tests was mentioned already. Sometimes teachers' ratings of students' self-concept, sociability, and so on are used as criterion measures. Scores from vocational interest inventories are validated in part by relating them to career data. (See Chapter 19.)

You should note that any single criterion measure is incomplete. Each represents partial attainment of the ultimate performance that an assessment procedure would like to predict. For this reason, the validation process for a test claiming to be useful in predicting performance should include several studies of how the test's scores relate to various criteria. You will need to review all of these studies before deciding the predictive validity of a test.

Judging the Worth of Criteria The criterion measures used in a validity study are themselves evaluated in four broad areas (Thorndike, 1949): (a) relevance to the long-term or ultimate real-life performance, (b) degree of reliability, (c) extent of bias against individuals or groups, and (d) practical problems of availability and convenience. Most

often of interest in a predictive validity study are one or more ultimate real-life performances (Cronbach, 1971; Lindquist, 1951; Messick, 1989b; Thorndike, 1949). But such ultimate criteria frequently do not occur until many years after the developer initially obtains the assessment results. In such cases, intermediate criteria are used. A developer must present a suitable rationale for using an intermediate criterion before you can accept the data as part of the predictive validity evidence (Cronbach, 1971; Thorndike, 1949).

Low Criterion Reliability Limits Validity Reliability is the topic of Chapter 4. But you should be aware that if assessment results have low reliability, they will correlate lower with other measures than if they had high reliability. Frequently, predictor instruments will have good reliability, but the criterion scores with which they are correlated are unreliable. No assessment instrument will be able to predict unreliable criterion scores.

Systematic Errors Systematic errors in criterion measurement may lead you to the wrong conclusion about the validity of an instrument's scores. For example, a validity study may correlate the test's scores with teachers' ratings of students. If these ratings favor boys over girls, or students with high verbal skills over those with lower verbal skills, the criterion measures themselves may be inappropriate. Systematic biases such as these introduce irrelevant factors into the validation process; they "contaminate" the criterion scores. Thus, before accepting correlation results as evidence for predictive validity, think carefully about the possibility that the scores on the criteria themselves may be biased or invalid.

Practical Considerations Ideally, scores from an instrument should be validated using data from ultimate real-life criteria. However, practical considerations limit the degree to which a developer can do this. Practicality should not be the sole driving force in a developer's decision to select criterion measures, however. Sometimes a developer could, with very little extra expense and effort, obtain criterion measures that are more appropriate than the surrogates the developer uses in a validation study.

Reliability Over Time, Assessors, and Content Domains: Reliability Evidence

Reliability refers to the consistency of the assessment results if and when they are repeated. For example, suppose the scores from the *ABC Reading Test* administered today correlated 0.00 with the scores from this test administered next week. This correlation is evidence that the scores have no consistency over this period. You would question the validity of this test if students' scores had little or no consistency from one week to the next because you believe that reading ability should be stable over a short period. If an assessment instrument produces inconsistent or unstable results, you can have little confidence in those results. Inconsistency means unreliability. Therefore, the reliability of an assessment's results limits its validity. This point is discussed in greater detail in Chapter 4, which is devoted entirely to estimating the reliability of assessment results.

Generalization of Interpretation Over People, Conditions, or Special Instructions and Interventions: Generalization Evidence

This category of validation evidence addresses how broadly you may interpret and use assessment results. For example, does the *ABC Reading Test* measure the type of reading comprehension required of students in higher levels of schooling and in real life? Does it measure reading comprehension for nonwhite students in the same way that it measures white students? Is it appropriate to use the scores from this test for remedial reading groups of Spanish-speaking students? Do scores on the *ABC Reading Test* greatly depend on students' moods or motivations at the time the test is administered? If students receive special instruction on what strategies to use to answer the questions on this test (e.g., read the question first, then look for the answer in the text), will this greatly affect their scores?

Answers to questions such as these help us see the assessment results in a broader perspective. Usually the answers show that our interpretations of assessment results cannot be simplistic. The validity of our interpretations and uses of the results are limited to certain conditions.

Consider the following illustration:[5]: Suppose the *ABC Reading Test* had the typical format—a passage of one or two paragraphs followed by several multiple-choice questions. The test directions call for the student to read each passage and to answer the questions that follow it by marking a separate answer sheet. At first glance, it appears that the student needs to read and understand the questions.

Vernon (1962) did a thorough, logical analysis of this type of reading comprehension task. That analysis led to hypothesizing several factors, in addition to reading comprehension, which might account for a student's test performance. If these factors alter the student's score, then you cannot interpret the test as a pure measure of reading comprehension. Further, you cannot make decisions about students using scores that depend on such a pure reading comprehension interpretation. Among the factors that may alter a student's reading score are the following:

1. *Content Bias.* A passage may refer to a specific topic, theme, or experience about which some students may have a lot of prior knowledge. For these students, the

test is a different kind of task than for students who lack this specific knowledge.

2. *Passage Independence.* Students may answer questions without reading the passage because of prior knowledge or poor-quality test items. **Passage dependency** describes the degree to which answers to questions depend on reading and comprehending the passage. In other words, if a student can answer the questions without reading the passage, the questions are not passage-dependent. Thus, they cannot be said to assess reading comprehension.

3. *Speededness.* Many tests are timed. If the time limits are not generous enough, the score may depend on reading speed rather than reading comprehension only.

4. *Attitudes and Motivation.* If the way the test is presented or administered affects performance, the test will not be a pure measure of reading comprehension. Highly motivated students are likely to score much better than poorly motivated ones when the test is presented poorly.

5. *Students' Sophistication.* Students who are "testwise" or who have good test-taking strategies are likely to score higher than their peers of equal ability who do not have such skills.

6. *Test Directions.* If a student misunderstands test directions, performance probably will be affected adversely.

7. *Ability to Mark Answers.* Most published multiple-choice tests use separate answer sheets that can be machine scored. Students will differ in the speed and accuracy with which they mark the correct answers. Frequently the type of answer sheet affects the test score.

The preceding list is by no means exhaustive. These questions stand as counterhypotheses to the intended interpretation of the scores as measures of reading comprehension. As you raise these questions, you should look in the publisher's manual and technical reports for research evidence concerning them. Not all evidence will be included in the publisher's materials, however, especially if it is unfavorable evidence. You may have to review research literature to obtain additional information. The *Mental Measurement Yearbooks* (see Chapter 18) contain reviews of tests and bibliographies of research in which the particular test appeared. You may search online using the Educational Research Information Center (ERIC) as well.

Figure 3.10 offers an example of a research study that sought to determine the effects of motivation on a reading test's scores. One study cannot provide all the evidence needed to support the validity of assessment interpretations, of course. A series of studies is necessary. Further, you should not assume from Figure 3.10 that simple incentives, such as pep talks, prizes, or money, would influence

[5]This illustration is based in part on an example in Cronbach (1971).

FIGURE 3.10 **Can test scores go up if prizes are offered?**

Tuinman, Farr, and Blanton (1972) sought to determine the extent to which reading test scores could be increased by offering prizes immediately before giving a posttest that followed an instructional period. Nonproblem readers in the seventh and eighth grades were randomly selected and randomly assigned to either an experimental (E) or control (C) group. All students took the *Nelson Reading Test*, Form A (1962) twice; there was a 4-week interval between testings. Between the two testing sessions, students took their regular school program.

Directions for retesting the E and C groups were different. The C group was told that the reason they were to be retested was to find out how much they had learned. The E group was shown prizes (6 transistor radios, 9 Indiana University sweatshirts, and large candy bars) and given the following directions (p. 217):

"A few weeks ago you took a test and we have now scored your test. We would like to have you try to beat your first test score. We have some prizes for you if you can do better on this than you did on the last test. We don't care who makes the highest score. We want to see who can make *more points* on this test than on the first test. All you need to do is *raise your own score* by as many points as you can. The students who raise their scores the most will win prizes. *Remember,* it's not the student who scores highest that wins; it's the student who *raises his score the most.*

"If you are one of the top six students who gains the most points you will win a transistor radio—NOT the six highest scores but the six who improve the most.

"If you are one of the next nine students who raises your score the most points, you will win one of these IU shirts.

"And if you raise your score even as little as one point, you get one of these candy bars. So everyone who gets even just one point higher will get a prize.

If you do not score any higher on this test than the first test there are no prizes.

"It's not hard, just try to beat your own score. Compete with no one but yourself. All you have to do is work harder and try to do more items and more of them correctly than you did last time. Raise your score and take home one of the prizes."

Some of the results of the study appear here.

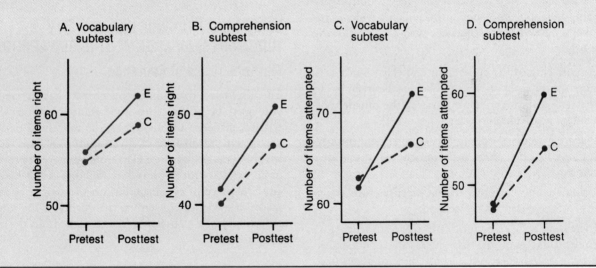

the results of all assessments for all types of students. Nor should you assume that motivation is the only factor that affects students' performance.

Intended and Unintended Consequences: Consequential Evidence

As mentioned at the beginning of this chapter in connection with the four principles for validation, the meanings and uses you give to assessment results arise from your educational and social values. We also discussed the consequences and pressures on school curricula when there is a mismatch between the a priori domain sampled by an assessment instrument and the curricular and instructional domains in a local school system. We have also discussed accountability assessment and the sanctions imposed by failure to meet the requirements of the NCLB Act. As Moss (1992) notes, "many of the arguments raging today about externally imposed versus classroom-generated assessments or about multiple-choice versus performance assessments are warranted, not in terms of technical validity considerations, but in terms of the consequences for instruction and learning and equity" (p. 236).

Most state assessment and accountability programs, for example, are intended to have the following positive consequences (Lane & Stone, 2002):

- Increase the educational efforts of students, teachers, and school administrators.

- Improve curriculum content and instructional strategies.

- Improve all students' learning.

- Improve teachers' professional development and a school's support for that development.

- Improve the focus and nature of how students are prepared for assessments.

- Increase the students', teachers', administrators', and public's awareness of the value of standards, criteria, and assessments to evaluate schools.

Evidence about how well these intended consequences are achieved becomes part of the case for the validating state assessment programs.

It is not enough, however, to collect evidence only about whether a program's intended consequences have been achieved. A state's assessment and accountability program validation effort should also look for evidence for negative, unintended consequences such as the following (Lane & Stone, 2002):

- A narrowing of the curriculum and classroom teaching to focus only on what is likely to be included in the state assessment, while ignoring the broader curriculum goals and purposes.

- Preparing students only to take tests without improving the quality their achievement of the state's standards.

- Using unethical test preparation practices such as giving out the questions beforehand.

- Increasing achievement of only some students (e.g., students in schools that have high socioeconomic levels of parents) whereas the achievement of others (e.g., students in schools from lower socioeconomic levels of parents) remains low or decreases.

- An increase in inappropriate uses of assessment results such as transferring or punishing teachers and principals whose students have low scores.

- A decrease in some students' motivation to learn and achieve because of past poor performance on the assessments.

A validation program should look for evidence of negative, unintended consequences as well as evidence of achieving the positive, intended consequences of an assessment program.

Cost, Efficiency, Practicality, and Instructional Features: Practicality Evidence

Assessment results may be technically sound, but practical barriers may impede their proper (and therefore valid) use. For example, if an assessment procedure is too complex for teachers to use, they will not use it properly. If the proper administration of an assessment requires more training than teachers have, the assessment is likely to be administered improperly and yield results of low validity. Further, the validity of an assessment instrument will improve if it is administered and interpreted properly. Some assessment instruments may be accompanied by computerized score reports that help a teacher identify students needing special help. The availability of these and other auxiliary materials increases the likelihood that results will be used as intended.

Although assessment cost is not a major consideration for validity, it is a consideration nevertheless. Of concern here is that from among various choices of similar assessment instruments, which one will be most cost effective? Which one will deliver the most valid results under the practical circumstances in a particular school setting? Will the cheapest alternative be the most valid alternative?

COMBINING EVIDENCE FOR VALIDITY JUDGMENTS: AN ARGUMENT-BASED APPROACH
Multiple Types of Evidence

The discussion throughout this chapter has stressed that you must be prepared to review and combine several types of evidence before judging the validity of particular assessment results for a given purpose. This is true whether you are judging a classroom assessment procedure or an extraclassroom procedure. Validity is not based on any one piece of evidence, but on the weight of several pieces of evidence concerning the quality of the interpretations and uses you would like to make from the assessment results.

Prioritizing Your Validity Evidence

Each type of evidence in Figure 3.2 has some usefulness for validating the ways you intend to interpret and use assessment results. Unless you identify which types of evidence are more important for your particular case, however, confusion can result. Shepard (1993) suggests that you organize and focus validity evidence to answer questions such as these:

1. What does my assessment practice claim to do?
2. What evidence supports or refutes my claim that my assessment practice achieves what I intend?

3. When I use my assessment practice in an educational setting, what does it do, for good or bad, other than what I claim for it?

The idea is that you prioritize the types of evidence described in Figure 3.2 and present the evidence in such a way that you can answer these three questions. The term **assessment practice** means the way you intend to interpret and use the assessment results in your particular situation. Therefore, different persons may answer these questions in different ways for the same assessment procedure. This reinforces the point we made at the beginning of this chapter: The question, "Are these assessment results valid?" has many different answers depending on how the results will be interpreted and used.

Argument-Based Approach to Validation

Kane (1992, 2001, 2002) suggests organizing answers to questions such as these in the form of a persuasive argument. In other words, use a combination of logic and data that convinces others that your interpretations and uses of the assessment results are valid. This approach to validity requires you to (a) state clearly what interpretations and uses you intend to make of the assessment results, (b) present a logically coherent argument to support your claim that the assessment results can be interpreted and used as you intend, and (c) support your logical argument by citing evidence for and against your intended interpretation(s) and use(s). This approach is called the **argument-based approach to validation** (Kane, 1992).

The evidence to support your validity argument and refute potential counterarguments comes from the various categories described in Figure 3.2. The types of evidence you emphasize in your argument will depend on the assessment practice you want to validate. Kane (1992) gives the following example. Suppose that you wanted to validate using an algebra placement test to assign students either to a remedial algebra course or to a calculus course. To validate this assessment practice, Kane points out that you need arguments supported by evidence (such as those described in Figure 3.2) that the following are reasonable:

1. You can appropriately assess students' success in the calculus course (i.e., a suitable criterion assessment procedure is available).
2. You can identify the algebra concepts and thinking skills that students will use frequently in the calculus course.
3. The algebra content and thinking skills assessed by the placement test match those frequently used in the calculus course.
4. The remedial course to which low-scoring students will be assigned will succeed in teaching students the algebra concepts and skills needed in the calculus course.
5. Scores on the placement test are reliable (i.e., students' scores are consistent across different samples of test items, different testing occasions, and different persons scoring the test).
6. It is not helpful for students with high ability in algebra to take the remedial algebra course (i.e., students who score high on the placement tests will not significantly improve their chances of success in calculus by first taking this particular remedial algebra course).
7. The placement test scores are not affected by systematic errors that would lower the validity of your interpretation that the placement test measures algebra knowledge and thinking skills.

VALIDITY ISSUES WHEN ACCOMMODATING STUDENTS WITH DISABILITIES

In Chapter 1 we discussed accountability assessments and the fact that under the NCLB Act, all students must be assessed, including students with disabilities. Ninety-five percent of students with disabilities must participate in the assessment. The students' disabilities may be used as a basis for accommodations to the assessment process for those students unable to participate in the assessment under the standardized conditions set for the general school population. Further, alternative assessment methods must be found to assess those students who cannot participate even with accommodations. **Assessment accommodations** or **assessment modifications** are changes in either the conditions or materials of assessment that allow the achievement of students with disabilities to be evaluated in the same areas as students who are evaluated with unmodified assessments.

Issues and Controversies

Standardized test accommodations for students with physical disabilities are less controversial than accommodations for students with cognitive disabilities such as learning disabilities (Phillips, 1994). One concern is the validity of the test result interpretations: If a test was administered under accommodating conditions, do the scores mean the same thing as the scores for students who took the test under standard conditions? Another concern is violation of students' privacy rights. Should the results for students administered the test under accommodating conditions be identified or flagged in the record or score report? There are no simple answers to either concern. In this section we discuss the validity concern. In Chapter 5 we discuss the concern about flagging scores of students with disabilities.

Validity of Scores From Test Accommodations

The validity of interpretations depends on the type of test administered, the purpose of the testing, the type of accommodation, the type of disability the student has, and the nature of the interpretation itself. If the purpose of testing, for example, is to assess a student's knowledge and ability in a subject such as social studies or mathematics, then it may be appropriate for a student with a severe reading disability to have a reader (someone to read the test questions). In this case, the concepts, principles, and procedures of the subject are independent of the printed medium in which they are presented on the test. Thus it is logical for you to assess a student's understanding of them through an appropriate accommodation.

If you can reasonably argue that reading is not part of the knowledge and ability being assessed, you could also argue that poor readers without learning disabilities should also have their mathematics and social studies tests read to them. Under this scenario, it would be considered fair, for example, to provide a reader for both students with learning disabilities and for poor readers, if they so desired.

On the other hand, a student with a severe reading disability (such as dyslexia) may be unable to complete the reading comprehension section of a standardized achievement test. If the purpose of testing were to assess a student's ability to read standard printed English, it would be invalid to provide a reader for the student on such a test.

However, suppose the student can read some material if given more time to answer. This accommodation violates the standardization conditions, thus invalidating the usual norm-referenced interpretations such as grade equivalents, percentile ranks, and standard scores. Nevertheless, by giving the student more time, you discovered what test material he or she could read when the time element is removed. Your interpretation of the results cannot ignore the accommodations, however; you would need to preface your norm-referenced interpretation with something like the following example.

Example

"Here is how Sally compares to other students. The other students took the test under standard conditions and with limited time. However, Sally took the test under nonstandard conditions and with no time limits because [give your rationale]."

This emphasizes a point we made earlier in this chapter: *Validity refers to your interpretations of the scores.*

How Should Accommodated Norm-Referenced Scores Be Reported? The issue of whether to report any norm-referenced information about a student's performance when the test administration violated the standardized

testing conditions (e.g., failing to keep to the time limits) remains controversial. If a test's standardized administration conditions are violated, some would view the following as inappropriate: (a) reporting any type of norm-referencing information for the accommodated students and (b) including in school averages the results from the students that had accommodated administrations of the test (Phillips, personal communication, 2001). Legal requirements, such as the NCLB Act reporting requirements, state that the percentage of students achieving the proficient level or better on a state's standards needs to be reported, regardless of accommodations.

How Should Accommodated Criterion-Referenced Scores Be Reported? A criterion-referenced interpretation (e.g., an interpretation of the type of material read and types of questions answered) is often made for test results. However, speed of reading is also part of this interpretation for standardized achievement tests because of the limits imposed by the standardization conditions. Therefore, your criterion-referenced interpretation would need to be stated in a manner that reflects the nonstandard administration, such as in the following example.

Example

"These are the types of materials and questions Sally was able to read when she took the test under nonstandard conditions and with no time limits."

It is sometimes possible to report two results: the student's performance under standard conditions and the student's performance under accommodated conditions.

Problems Will Remain

Problems still arise, however, when trying to interpret the results of the accommodation in the preceding paragraphs. Nonaccommodated students took the test under standard conditions in which they had to read the test materials and the questions themselves. Even your criterion-referenced interpretation of the student's results (e.g., how well the student understands the concepts, principles, and procedures) needs to be qualified. You will need to state that these accommodated students cannot express or have difficulty expressing their understanding in standard printed English tests.

If you provide accommodations, such as reading the test items to students, there may be controversy. The controversy may intensify if you read the test items to students with disabilities other than the learning disability illustrated in the preceding example. The intensity of the controversy may increase, too, if the purpose for testing changed from strictly describing a student's achievement to other purposes such as assessing general scholastic aptitude, testing for admission to higher education, or granting a high school diploma.

Measurement Perspective on Accommodations

From a strict measurement perspective, in which the validity of a testing program is a primary concern, the following questions might be considered:

1. Will changes in format or testing conditions change the skill being measured?

2. Will the scores of examinees tested under standard conditions have a different meaning than scores for examinees tested with the requested accommodation?

3. Would examinees who do not need accommodations benefit if they were nevertheless allowed the same accommodations?

4. Do examinees requesting or granted accommodations have any capacity for adjusting to standard test administration conditions?

5. Is the disability evidence or testing accommodation policy based on procedures with doubtful validity and reliability? (Adapted from Phillips, 1994, p. 104)

Phillips argues that if you answer yes to any of these questions, a test accommodation is not appropriate because it would compromise the validity of the test results. She points out the potential conflict between providing maximum participation in society for persons with disabilities and maintaining test validity. You should be cautious when interpreting yes answers to these five questions. A mean-spirited or a misinformed person could respond yes and be wrong. Further, answering some of these questions would demand valid research results that do not exist. Nevertheless, the point that validity of assessment is a prime issue is an important consideration.

Measurement Experts Can Disagree

Not all would agree, however, with Phillips's conclusions. For example, even though accommodations may change the skill assessed or the meaning of the scores (see Questions 1 and 2), such changes may be more, rather than less, valid. Phillips's argument assumes that administering the test under standard conditions is the criterion against which accommodations should be judged. It also assumes that the skill or ability assessed by the test under standard conditions is the relevant skill and ability to be assessed. These assumptions may not be correct. For example, reading short passages and answering questions under timed standard conditions (the typical reading comprehension test) is not the ultimate learning target for education, nor is it a direct assessment of "real-world" reading. Accommodations to the standard test conditions may change both the skill required and the meaning of the

results in a more positive direction. This, in turn, may make the accommodated test results more like the ultimate learning targets in the real world—especially for students with certain disabilities. This is more likely to be the case as the Americans with Disabilities Act of 1990 begins to alter the conditions, accommodation patterns, and attitudes in the workplace. The basis for judging the validity of assessment results changes over time as we learn more about the capabilities and contributions of persons with disabilities. For example, for many jobs and real-world situations, reading with accommodations (such as using more time) is permitted and acceptable.

Summary

General Nature of Validity

- Validity refers to the soundness of your interpretations and uses of assessment results, rather than to the assessment instrument itself.
- Assessment results have different degrees of validity, depending on how the results are interpreted and used.

Four Principles for Validation

- Validity of assessment results may be determined only after combining several types of evidence and judging that combination in relation to the particular interpretation and use you wish to make of the results.
- The validity of assessment results depends also on the appropriateness of the values implied by the way you use the assessment results and on the social consequences of that use.

Validity of Teacher-Crafted Classroom Assessment Results

- Classroom-based assessments used for assigning grades to students should meet the validity criteria in the following categories. (Figure 3.1 lists the specific criteria for each category.)
  - Content representativeness and relevance
  - Thinking processes and skills
  - Consistency with other classroom assessments
  - Reliability and objectivity
  - Fairness to different students
  - Economy, efficiency, practicality, instructional features
  - Multiple assessment usage

Categories of Validity Evidence

- The validity of results from standardized tests and other extraclassroom assessments should be based on evidence from the following eight categories. Figure 3.2 summarizes examples of specific questions and validation procedures for each category.
  - Content representativeness and relevance (*content evidence*)
  - Types of thinking skills and processes required (*substantive evidence*)
  - Relationships among the tasks or parts of the assessment (*internal structure evidence*)
  - Relationships of the assessment results to other variables (*external structure evidence*)
  - Reliability over time, assessors, and content domains (*reliability evidence*)
  - Generalization of interpretation over different types of people, different conditions, or special instructions and interventions (*generalization evidence*)

- Value of the intended and unintended consequences (*consequential evidence*)
- Cost, efficiency, practicality, and instructional features (*practicality evidence*)
- You will need to weigh the evidence from different categories differently depending on the types of interpretations and uses that you wish to make from the results.

Alignment of State Standards and Accountability Tests

- The NCLB Act requires that states provide evidence that their accountability assessments are aligned with their content and performance standards.
- Alignment studies are used to describe the extent to which a state's assessments are aligned with the state's standards. These studies describe alignment in terms of content match, depth of cognitive process match, assessments versus standards emphasis, performance expectation match, and accessibility match. These alignment areas are types of content and substantive evidence as described in Figure 3.2.

Further Validity Concerns

- Providing validity evidence is the joint responsibility of the publisher of the assessment and the person using the results. Appendix B summarizes many of these joint responsibilities.
- It is improper to ignore the need to validate your interpretations and uses of assessment results just because you cannot afford to carry out the necessary validity studies.
- Several types of validity evidence depend on the correlation between two or more sets of assessment scores. Predictive validity evidence indicates how well scores on the assessment instrument predict future scores on a criterion. Concurrent validity evidence reflects the extent to which individuals' current status on a criterion can be estimated from the scores on the assessment instrument. In some cases, correlation coefficients or expectancy tables may provide the validity evidence needed.
- The criterion problem arises because it is difficult to obtain measures of criteria suitable for validating assessment results. Criteria are judged by their (a) relevance to ultimate real-life performance, (b) degree of reliability, (c) extent of bias against individuals or groups, and (d) availability and convenience.

Combining Evidence for Validity Judgments

- Because most persons interpret a student's assessment performance in a broad way that infers the student's status on an educational or psychological construct like reading comprehension or intelligence, it is necessary to integrate a rather large and diverse amount of information concerning the factors that influence a student's assessment performance. This information comes from all eight categories of Figure 3.2.
- You need to establish priorities among the eight categories of evidence in Figure 3.2 by considering how you intend to interpret and use the assessment results. You prepare a validation argument by addressing these questions: (a) What does my assessment practice claim to do? (b) What evidence supports or refutes assertions that my assessment practice achieves what I claim? (c) When I use my assessment practice in the educational system, what does it do, for good or for bad, other than what I claim for it?

- Your validation argument must: (a) state clearly what interpretations and uses you intend to make of the assessment results, (b) present a logically coherent argument to support your claim that the results can be interpreted and used as you intend, and (c) support your logical argument by citing evidence for and against your intended interpretation(s) and use(s).

Validity Issues When Accommodating Students With Disabilities

- Students with disabilities may have the testing conditions or materials changed to accommodate their disabilities and to better assess their achievement.
- Changes and modifications to assessment materials or conditions often violate the standardization requirements of a test and therefore invalidate the norm-referenced score reporting.
- It may be necessary to report that a student's score has resulted from an assessment modification or accommodation in order to properly interpret and use it.
- Although some assessment specialists argue that accommodations or modifications to the testing procedure lower the validity of the results, others argue that validity of the results may be increased if the scores are properly interpreted.

Important Terms and Concepts

alignment studies
argument-based approach to validation
assessment accommodations or assessment modifications
assessment practice
concurrent validity evidence
content relevance
content representativeness
correlation coefficient
curricular relevance
ethnic and gender stereotypes
expectancy table
external structure
four principles for validation
internal structure
multiple-assessment strategy
negative correlation
objectivity
passage dependency
Pearson product-moment correlation coefficient
positive correlation
predictive validity evidence
scatter diagram (scattergram)
table of specifications
validity
validity coefficient

Exercises and Applications

1. Obtain a teacher-crafted assessment instrument that has been used for assigning students' marks or letter grades. Using the criteria listed in Figure 3.1, and, if possible, an interview with the teacher, evaluate the validity of using the assessment results for grading students. Then briefly describe how valid this assessment is for this purpose and why. Finally, using the criteria in Figure 3.1, describe how you could improve the validity of this assessment instrument.

2. Obtain a teacher-crafted assessment instrument (either of your own construction or from someone else). Identify the main or intended interpretations of student results from that assessment instrument. Analyze the assessment logically. Playing "devil's advocate," identify three counterinterpretations (i.e., possible alternative interpretations that raise questions about the validity of the intended interpretation). Then specify the kind(s) of evidence that could be collected to verify the intended interpretation and invalidate each of the three counterinterpretations. Attach this test to this exercise.

3. Assume that a new high school science aptitude test is being developed, and in the course of that development several procedures and techniques have been used to provide evidence for its validity. These procedures are listed in the following statements. For each statement, decide which type of evidence in Figure 3.2 is directly addressed. Explain why you made the choice you did.

   a. For a sample of 150 10th graders, scores on the odd-numbered items were correlated with scores on the even-numbered items.

   b. Scores from 300 first-year students obtained from a September administration of the test were correlated with scores of the same group obtained from a February administration.

   c. Scores of 200 first-year students obtained from a September administration of the test were correlated with the general science course grades of these same students obtained from school records in January.

   d. Scores of students who had taken one, two, three, and four science courses were compared to see if they differed on the average.

   e. A section of the test manual describes seven aspects of science aptitude and the number of items measuring each aspect.

4. Each of the following statements is a question that an educator can ask about an assessment procedure. Using Figure 3.2, identify for each statement the type(s) of validity evidence that is (are) most important to answering the question directly. Then briefly explain your choice.

   a. "Is this spelling test from a book publisher representative of the type of spelling patterns we teach our sixth graders?"

   b. "Can scores on this reading test help me assign students to different instructional groups?"

   c. "I'm using this performance assessment to select persons for a special training program. Are the results significantly influenced by the personality of the person administering the assessment?"

   d. "Does this mathematics performance assessment really assess the mathematics ability of these students?"

   e. "We now use a procedure to rate student teachers. Does this procedure permit a student teacher to be observed in the broad range of classroom situations likely to be encountered when teaching in this state?"

5. Read each statement and decide whether it is true or false. Then explain why you marked it the way you did.

   a. A verbal reasoning test is given at the start of 9th grade. Scores on this test are correlated with English grades assigned in 9th, 10th, 11th, and 12th grades. The correlations between the test scores and the 12th-grade marks will likely be the lowest of the four correlations.

   b. A certain predictor test has perfect reliability (reliability coefficient = 1.00). This means that the predictor test is likely to have very high correlation with just about any criterion measure an investigator wants to use.

   c. Another predictor test has zero reliability (reliability coefficient = 0.00). This means that the predictor test will likely correlate zero with just about any criterion measure the investigator wants to use.

4 | Reliability of Assessment Results

LEARNING TARGETS

After studying this chapter, you should have learned the following:

General Nature of Reliability

1. Explain the concept of reliability and how it relates to inconsistency in students' assessment results. [3, 6]

2. Explain the relationship between reliability, validity, and the quality of educational decisions. [3, 6]

Causes of Measurement Error or Inconsistency

3. Describe several causes of measurement error and how such error may lead to improper interpretations of students' assessment results. [3, 6, 7]

Types of Reliability Coefficients

4. Explain why assessment results might be reliable for some purposes but not for others. [6, 3]

5. Name the different types of reliability coefficients and describe how data are collected for their calculation. [6, 3]

6. Identify the specific reliability coefficient(s) that provides information for answering questions about an instrument's various measurement errors. [3, 1, 6, 7]

Obtained Scores, True Scores, and Error Scores

7. Explain the meaning of observed, true, and error scores. [6]

8. Explain the meaning of standard error of measurement, its relationship to reliability, and how it is used to interpret scores. [3, 6, 4]

9. Give examples of the factors affecting reliability coefficients and standard errors of measurement. [3, 6, 7]

Reliability of Mastery and Pass-Fail Decisions

10. Explain the meaning of decision consistency in relation to using a procedure for assessing mastery and pass-fail decisions. [6, 3, 1]

How to Improve Reliability

11. Describe nine ways to improve the reliability of your assessments. [3, 6, 4]

12. Describe the types of education decisions that require very high levels of assessment reliability and the types for which more moderate levels may be tolerated. [3, 6, 4]

Important Terms and Concepts

13. Explain how each term and concept listed at the end of this chapter applies to educational measurement. [6]

ABOUT THIS CHAPTER

You know, of course, that your assessments are not perfect. In the last chapter, you learned how to improve their validity. This chapter will teach you how to improve their reliability.

This chapter begins with a discussion of the overall concept of reliability and how it relates to validity. Second, we explain some of the basic causes of measurement error that creeps into your assessment results. Third, we study some of the common reliability indexes that help us describe how reliable our test scores are. Fourth, we study how a student's score can be thought of as comprising two components: a true component and an error component. Fifth, we see how we can estimate the size of this error component. Sixth, we describe several additional factors that will increase the reliability of your assessments. Seventh, we consider how errors in our assessments affect our decisions about whether a student has mastered learning targets. Finally, we consider what a desirable level of reliability is.

GENERAL NATURE OF RELIABILITY

Reliability Defined

Suppose you asked students today to write an essay explaining the pros and cons of democratic elections. Suppose, further, that you repeated this same essay with the same students a month from now. If your marks of each student's essay responses are essentially the same on both occasions, we say that the results are consistent over this period. We say the results are reliable over a month's time.

Now suppose that you marked each student's essay tonight. Then tomorrow, without revealing the marks you assigned, you give the essays to a teaching colleague to mark. If the marks you assigned each student essentially agree with the marks independently assigned by your colleague, we would say that results are consistent or reliable with respect to different graders.

To use another example, suppose you rephrased the essay question in a different but equivalent way and asked the students to write essays for both versions. If the qualities of each student's essays were essentially the same on the two versions of the task, we would say that the students' responses are consistent or reliable with respect to equivalent versions of the same task.

Reliability, then, is the degree to which students' results remain consistent over replications of an assessment procedure. That is, reliability is the degree to which students' assessment results are the same when (a) they complete the same task(s) on two or more different occasions; (b) two or more teachers mark their performance on the same task(s); or (c) they complete two or more different but equivalent tasks on the same or different occasions. Consistent scores over repeated assessment is the key to understanding reliability. As with validity, reliability refers to the students' assessment results or scores, not to the assessment instrument itself.

You can see that consistency is an important concept to consider in deciding how much confidence to place in your students' assessment results. Later in this chapter we describe this qualitative concept in more specific ways. This will lead to various indices of the degree of reliability. First, however, we briefly discuss the relationship between reliability and validity.

Reliability Limits Validity

Validity, as we discussed in the last chapter, relates to the confidence we may have in interpreting students' assessment results and in using them to make decisions. Your interpretations and decisions are less valid when your students' assessment results are inconsistent, however. *An assessment result's degree of reliability limits its degree of validity.*

High Reliability Does Not Guarantee Validity Although high degrees of validity require high degrees of reliability, the reverse is not true. A highly reliable assessment does not guarantee that you can make highly valid interpretations or decisions. This is because reliability is only one of many validity criteria (see Figures 3.1 and 3.2).

As an illustration, consider this example. Ms. Cortez teaches seventh-grade arithmetic. She reflects on the kinds of computations that her students will be expected to perform as they go through their daily lives in the local community and lists these skills. She then creates a computation and problem-solving test to assess her students' ability to perform these skills. Because this paper-and-pencil test has a moderately large number of items, Ms. Cortez can be confident that the resulting scores will be very reliable.

Knowing that these scores are reliable, however, is not enough to conclude they are valid. These are among the questions Ms. Cortez should answer before deciding how valid the assessment results are: Is this test a representative sample of the domain of computations to which she wishes to generalize the results? Are the test items' formats appropriate for assessing the students at this point in their educational development? Are the time limits for the test appropriate? Does reading ability affect performance on the test seriously? Will scores on the test help her plan instruction for these students? Will using these types of test items inadvertently convey to students that computations and problem solving in school are isolated from "real-world" or "authentic" mathematics problems? A negative answer to any of these questions would undermine the validity of the test for the types of interpretations she apparently has in mind, even though the scores may be highly reliable.

Reliability Is Necessary for Validity An assessment's reliability affects the quality (validity) of decisions. Here is an example.

Example

Ms. Cortez decided that mastering 80% of the targeted domain of computations is passing. The test is only a sample from the domain, however. If the test scores were of low reliability, it is very likely that among all those students who actually mastered 80% or more of the targeted *domain*, some would have *test scores* below 80%. These students would be erroneously classified as failures. On the other hand, among the students who truly know slightly less than 80% of the targeted *domain*, some are very likely to *pass the test*. These students would be erroneously classified as having sufficient competence.

Here is another example:

Example

A counselor wants to know whether a student's mathematical ability or verbal ability is higher. A student's score on a test of mathematical ability is not likely to be identical to her score on a test of verbal ability. The validity question is, "Do scores that are different mean that the student is truly different in these two abilities?" For the counselor to say that the student's ability in one area exceeds that in the other, the counselor needs to know how much scores are likely to differ from the true ability scores due only to measurement error. If scores fluctuate widely, they are unreliable. If the scores are unreliable, the counselor can have little confidence that differences in the scores indicate a difference in verbal and mathematical ability.

Inconsistencies like those that are of concern in these two examples are called *measurement errors*. Errors of measurement are always of concern to persons needing to make decisions about a student or interpret a student's profile of scores validly, as in diagnostic assessment or vocational counseling assessment.

CAUSES OF MEASUREMENT ERROR OR INCONSISTENCY

Reliability and *measurement error* are complementary ways of speaking about the same assessment phenomenon. The concept of reliability focuses on the consistency of assessment results; the concept of measurement error focuses on their inconsistencies. Inconsistencies have different causes. Not every cause, however, is equally important to your particular interpretation and use of assessment results.

Consider the following situation. Suppose all of the tasks that might be appropriate for assessing achievement for a particular set of learning targets could be described. This description of possible tasks is called a **domain of achievement**. For example, the domain could be all the open-ended tasks that might be used to assess fifth-grade students' ability to solve mathematical problems involving proportions. The large circle on the left of Figure 4.1 represents this domain.

Now suppose you wish to determine the percentage of the domain a student knows. Rather than administering

FIGURE 4.1   **A schematic diagram illustrating how changes in performance on an assessment relate to content samples and occasions of assessment.**

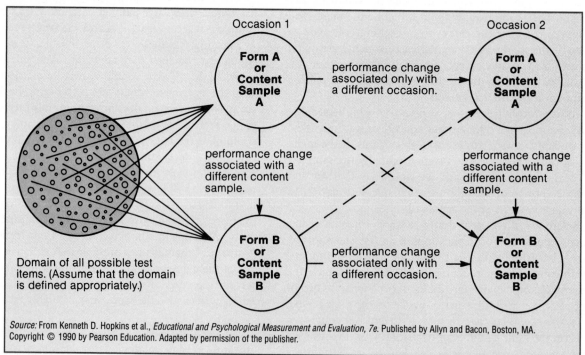

Source: From Kenneth D. Hopkins et al., *Educational and Psychological Measurement and Evaluation, 7e.* Published by Allyn and Bacon, Boston, MA. Copyright © 1990 by Pearson Education. Adapted by permission of the publisher.

the entire domain, an impossible feat, you select from the domain a random sample of 10 tasks and administer them to the student. Clearly, the student's score on this assessment depends on which tasks happen to be included in the sample. A different sample of 10 tasks would be easier or harder than the first sample, resulting in a higher or lower score for the student. Suppose the student's results are 80% right on the first sample and 50% right on the second. What causes this inconsistency? As shown by Figure 4.1, it is a result of using a different content sample (or "form" of the assessment procedure).

Next consider this second situation: Suppose you administer the first sample of 10 tasks on Tuesday, which is a "bad day" for a student, and the student attains 40% right. Perhaps the student had an upsetting encounter on the playground before class, had eaten no breakfast, or had allergies acting up making concentration difficult. For whatever reason, on Tuesday the student's performance is off. Suppose, now, that the same 10 tasks were administered on Friday. Perhaps Friday was a very good day, and the student performed much better than normal, attaining 70%. As shown in Figure 4.1, this type of inconsistency is a result of sampling on a different occasion. The identical content sample (i.e., the same 10 tasks) was administered on both Tuesday and Friday, so any source of the scoring inconsistency cannot be content sampling.

This description considers two of the **factors influencing consistency of assessment performance**: (a) the content or particular sample of tasks appearing on any form of the assessment and (b) the occasion on which the assessment is administered. Solid arrows in the schematic diagram of Figure 4.1 indicate these factors. The figure also shows (via diagonal dashed arrows) the additional possibility that both content and occasion may work together to influence assessment performance.

We can draw several important conclusions from this discussion and Figure 4.1. Interpreting assessment results a student obtained on a particular occasion with a particular sample of tasks has definite limitations. Assessment results must be reasonably consistent (perfect consistency is not possible) over different samples of content, tasks, and occasions; otherwise, we can have little confidence in them.

Figure 4.1 also shows that there are different kinds of consistencies. Assessment results may be consistent in some ways but not in others. For example, students' assessment results may not be consistent over repeated assessment on different samples of tasks administered on the same occasion, but may be very consistent over repeated assessment on the same sample of tasks over a month. You must keep in mind what type of repeated assessment is most appropriate to the way you want to use the results; otherwise, you will be misled. If your assessment concern is to generalize today's performance by a student to how well that student is likely to perform next month on the

same sample of tasks, then consistency over a month is more relevant to you than information about score consistency over different samples of tasks. On the other hand, if you know the students are learning rapidly and changing constantly, then consistency of scores over time is less relevant. If you keep in mind the potential interpretations and uses for your assessment, you will be able to better gauge the most important type of consistency for the assessment results.

TYPES OF RELIABILITY COEFFICIENTS

Quantifying the Consistency of Assessment Results

We have just described reliability and measurement errors. It also is possible to quantify these concepts. Statistical methods can indicate the degree of reliability and the approximate size of the measurement errors in the assessment results. Such indices are possible only when an assessment yields quantitative scores or measurements of the students.

The advantage of using these indices is that they can provide guidance on the quality of your assessment results. A low reliability index means that the assessment results are not very consistent. As a result, the quality of your assessment information is poor. The decisions you make using poor quality information will not be optimal.

The general strategy to obtain reliability coefficients is to administer the assessment to a group of students one or more times and obtain the scores. Then, one of two approaches is used to examine consistency. One approach is to correlate the scores from the two administrations. As discussed in Chapter 3, a correlation coefficient is an index of whether the relative standing of students in the group (as determined by their scores) differs from one assessment to the next. In the context of score consistency, this correlation is called a **reliability coefficient**. A second approach is to estimate the amount by which we can expect a student's score to change from one administration to the next. The index expressing this variation in score consistency is called the *standard error of measurement* (to be discussed later). Reliability coefficients are most useful when you are comparing assessment procedures that report students' scores on different scales. Standard errors of measurement are more useful than reliability coefficients when you are using a particular instrument and are concerned with interpreting students' scores.

Because both indices are so widely used in describing the quality of assessment methods, you should understand the basic ideas behind them to interpret your assessments properly. Understanding these indices is an important part of your professional development and essential for using assessment results responsibly, even if you do not actually calculate them. We first discuss various types of reliability coefficients, and then address the standard error of measurement. Our approach is conceptual and does not emphasize calculations. Appendix J shows how to calculate these indices.

Overview of Reliability Coefficients

This section discusses ways of estimating reliability coefficients. The different reliability coefficients build on the ideas introduced in Figure 4.1. We discuss three categories of reliability coefficients: (a) those that focus on the consistency of student scores over time (as shown by the horizontal arrows in Figure 4.1); (b) those that focus on consistency of scores from one sample of content to another (the vertical arrows in Figure 4.1); and (c) those that focus on the consistency of marks or ratings of student responses (this category is not represented in Figure 4.1).

Figure 4.2 shows these three categories, lists each of the coefficients we discuss in each category, the major questions for which the coefficients provide answers, and the type of measurement error each addresses. As you examine this figure and study this section, you will realize that the

question "Are these scores reliable?" has many different answers depending on the types of measurement errors that concern you. Refer to this figure frequently when you read this chapter so you don't lose your bearing on why different reliability coefficients are used.

Estimating Reliability Over Time

Suppose we ask questions such as: To what extent are scores on identical tasks likely to be different because they were administered on different occasions? Or, if a student teacher were observed on a Monday, would the ratings agree with the ratings from observations made on Wednesday? Or if Dr. Adams rates the teacher on Monday and Dr. Meyers rates on Thursday, would the two ratings be likely to agree? (Recall Figure 4.1.) Procedures for estimating reliability in situations like these are the subject of this section.

Test-Retest Reliability The first reliability question in the preceding paragraph centers on the *stability of scores* on a fixed sample of assessment tasks over a specified time period. Studying data obtained from administering the

FIGURE 4.2 Summary of reliability coefficients.

Type of coefficient	Major question(s) answered	What is counted as measurement error or inconsistency
I. Influence of occasions or time		
Test-retest	a. How are scores on the identical content sample affected by testing on another occasion? b. How stable are scores on this particular test form over time?	Time or occasion sampling
Alternate forms (with time interval)	a. How consistent are the test scores regardless of form used or occasion on which it is administered? b. How stable are scores on this trial over time (and content samples)?	Time or occasion sampling and content sampling
II. Influence of different content samples		
Alternate forms (no time interval)	a. Are scores affected by sampling different content on the same occasion?	Content sampling
	b. Are two carefully matched test forms interchangeable (equivalent, parallel)?	Content sampling
Split-halves	a. Same as above. b. What is an estimate of the alternate-forms reliability coefficient?	
Kuder-Richardson formulas 20 and 21, coefficient alpha	a. Same as above, except equivalence or parallelism of forms may not concern the investigator. b. What is a crude estimate of test homogeneity? c. How consistent are responses from item to item? d. Are scores affected by content sampling on the same occasion?	Content sampling and homogeneity
III. Influence of different scores		
Scorer reliability	a. To what extent will the scores be different if different scorers (raters, judges) are used? b. To what extent is the test objective? c. Are the results from different scorers (observers, raters, judges) interchangeable?	Scorer sampling

identical tasks to a group of students on two separate occasions will answer this question. Because the same tasks (rather than equivalent tasks) are administered at two different times, the correlation between the scores on the two occasions is known as the **test-retest reliability coefficient**. Sometimes it is also called a **stability coefficient**.

This paradigm is as follows:

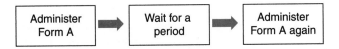

You may recall that a correlation of 0.00 represents no relationship between two sets of scores, and a correlation of 1.00 is a perfect positive relationship. Reliability coefficients have a range of 0.00 to 1.00. A completely unreliable (inconsistent) set of scores has a reliability coefficient of 0.00. A perfectly reliable set, containing no measurement errors, has a reliability coefficient of 1.00. If students were tested on two occasions, and if their scores were identical, they would be ranked identically on the two tests, thus the test-retest coefficient would be 1.00. Test-retest coefficients of 1.00 rarely occur, however. Typically, test-retest coefficients for standardized achievement and aptitude tests are between 0.80 and 0.90 when the interval between testing is 3 to 6 months.

It is important when you interpret these test-retest coefficients to know (a) the length of time between the two administrations of the assessment and (b) the expected stability of the performance being measured. In general, the longer the interval between the repeated administrations, the lower the reliability. Further, the less stable the performance of students, the lower the reliability. For example, some performances of infants and young children are not consistent from one day to the next. You would expect the test-retest reliability of assessments of these performances to be low, too. On the other hand, traits such as older students' general scholastic aptitude tend to remain stable over a semester or a year. Test-retest reliability of assessments of this trait usually will be relatively high over a longer period, and assessments of general scholastic aptitude tend to be useful in predicting future performance over these periods. The validity of assessment results as predictors of future performance lessens when the results lack stability.

The teacher's concern with whether a student is having an "off day" concentrates on whether the student's performance is consistent over a relatively short time interval. The teacher may not expect the student's performance to stay the same over a longer period, such as a month, because the teacher is teaching the student and the student is learning more each day. Changes in level of performance over a longer time interval would likely reflect actual changes in student ability rather than random fluctuations due to the circumstances of a particular occasion or off day. However, such actual changes in ability do reduce the correlation of scores obtained on the two occasions because different students have different rates of changes or growth.

Alternate-Forms Reliability (With Time Interval) Another procedure for estimating reliability is to administer one form of an assessment on one occasion and an alternate form on another occasion. This permits both content and occasion to vary. (See the diagonal line in Figure 4.1.) The correlation between the scores on the two occasions is influenced by differences in both content and in occasion. This paradigm is depicted as follows:

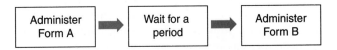

This correlation is known as the **delayed alternate-forms reliability coefficient** or the *delayed equivalent-forms reliability coefficient*. The two forms are built to the same content specifications (i.e., same blueprint) and level of difficulty, but they contain different questions or tasks. When this paradigm is applied, the reliability coefficient reflects both the equivalence of the assessment techniques and the stability of students' performance.

The comments about the time interval for the test-retest reliability coefficient also apply to the delayed alternate-forms coefficient. However, because a new sample of tasks is administered (Form B), this eliminates the effects of students' remembering specific assessment questions (but it does not eliminate general practice effects).

Delayed alternate-forms reliability is important when you want to generalize your interpretation of assessment results over both occasions and content samples. You may ask, for example, "How well does this test assess the ability to solve mathematics problems, regardless of test form used or occasion on which I administer the test?" Many interpretations of assessment results can use this framework. For example, in estimating a student teacher's "teaching ability," a supervisor may want to focus on the consistency of ratings obtained on different occasions and from different raters. Rarely is teaching ability defined in terms of only a single occasion (e.g., many supervisors' ratings on Tuesday, October 5) or a specific supervisor's ratings over several occasions (e.g., Mr. Washington's ratings of teachers throughout the year).

The *meaning of occasions* needs to be carefully specified when interpreting delayed alternate-forms reliability coefficients. For instance, if children are observed while learning a subject they happen to enjoy very much or with an exceptionally enthralling teacher, their attentiveness may fluctuate little from day to day. But relatively large fluctuations in attentiveness might occur within the same day as students move from mathematics instruction to language arts to gym. These moment-to-moment or subject-to-subject fluctuations in attentiveness might surpass day-to-day fluctuations (Goodwin, 1966). What this means is that to interpret whether students' performances are consistent from subject to subject, you should examine data representing subject-to-subject performance.

Deciding the appropriateness of a particular time interval and a particular stability coefficient is based on an informed professional judgment. You need to use your knowledge of the population of students for whom you are using the assessment results. In addition, you need to be knowledgeable about (a) the domain of performance being assessed, (b) the theory and facts concerning which factors influence students' performance in that domain, and (c) the intended use of the assessment results. You have a wealth of knowledge about assessment interpretation. Combining knowledge of reliability and professional experience permits you to evaluate the usefulness of a particular assessment and its accompanying reliability information.

Estimating Reliability on a Single Occasion

Alternate-Forms Reliability (No Time Interval) When attempting to interpret students' assessment results, you may wonder whether the results would have been different with a different sample of assessment tasks. If so, your primary concern is the consistency of two sets of results (one set from each of two comparable forms) obtained on the same occasion.

One way to provide the type of reliability information this question implies is to administer two forms of an assessment to the same group of students on the same (or nearly the same) occasion and to correlate the scores. This correlation is known as the **alternate-forms reliability coefficient** or the *equivalent-forms reliability coefficient*. This coefficient is most often used with standardized tests that have two interchangeable forms. Look for alternate-forms reliability coefficients in the publisher's test manual whenever you intend to use two or more forms of a test. Because teachers usually do not build two forms of a test, this coefficient is seldom available for teacher-crafted tests. Nevertheless, the ideas that form the basis for this reliability coefficient are important for proper interpretation of teacher-made tests.

When interpreting this coefficient, remember that only inconsistencies due to fluctuations in content samples are counted as measurement error. Other factors such as practice effects, fatigue, and boredom—all of which may occur on this one occasion—are considered part of the students' true scores.

Two forms of an assessment that are made up of tasks carefully matched to the same blueprint are called *parallel forms* (American Psychological Association [APA], American Educational Research Association, and National Council on Measurement in Education, 1974). In this case, the correlation of the scores from the two forms is referred to as a **parallel-forms reliability coefficient.**

Ideally, scores from **parallel forms** of a test should (a) have equal observed score means and standard deviations, (b) measure students with equal accuracy (i.e., have equal standard errors of measurement), (c) correlate equally with other measurements, and (d) measure the same attribute in precisely the same way. If the two forms of the assessment meet these criteria, it wouldn't matter to the student which form he or she takes: They are interchangeable. Alternate forms that are "built" simply by drawing random samples of tasks from the same domain are not strictly parallel because chance will determine the composition of each form.

Any systematic score differences from one form to another are especially important when an individual's scores are to be interpreted on their own merits rather than on the basis of the individual's relative standing in a group. Here is an example:

Example

A test is used to certify teachers. It has a passing score. Candidates with test scores above the passing score are certified; those below the passing score are not. It doesn't matter how one candidate's scores on the test compare to others: It only matters whether the candidate's score is above the passing mark. If different candidates take different forms of the certification test, they expect the forms to be equivalent.

Note that in this example, candidates are not served well when the different forms of such a certification test lack equivalence. If one form is more difficult than an alternate form, more candidates than necessary are failed. A less difficult alternate form has the opposite consequence: Many students are certified who may not be qualified. A correlation coefficient of the scores from the two forms won't reveal such consequences because the coefficient reflects only rank order rather than the exact values of the scores.

Parallel Forms Do Not Always Exist Although in principle several parallel forms of an assessment might exist, in practice many assessments have no parallel form. Further, assessments that do have parallel forms seldom have more than two or three forms. When any of the following occurs, a developer usually does not create a parallel form of the assessment:

1. *The assessment procedure will be used only once with each student.* Repeated testing for practical decisions is not anticipated.

2. *The very act of taking the assessment may change the student* (Thorndike, 1951). For example, if tasks are crafted to assess the strategies students use to solve unfamiliar problems, completing the assessment tasks themselves may result in the student becoming more familiar

with the different types of problems and better at the strategies for solving them.

3. *Only one way exists to assess the ability of interest* (Thorndike, 1951).

4. *It is too costly to build a parallel form of the assessment.*

In situations such as the preceding, methods other than alternate-forms reliability are used to evaluate the extent to which content sampling affects observed scores. We discuss two such methods in this section: split-halves and Kuder-Richardson.

Split-Halves Reliability Coefficients The first way that alternate-forms reliability may be estimated from a single form of an assessment is by a method known as the split-halves procedure. In applying the **split-halves procedure**, the entire test is administered once to the students. Then the test's items are organized into two equivalent halves. Each half (called a *split*) is considered to be a separate (albeit smaller) sample of tasks. For purposes of analysis, every student receives a score for each half of the test. These half-test scores form the basis for estimating the extent of error due to content sampling for the full-length assessment. There are many possible split-halves procedures (Feldt & Brennan, 1989; Stanley, 1971; Thorndike, 1951). We discuss only one here: the *Spearman-Brown double length formula* (Brown, 1910; Spearman, 1910).[1]

Spearman-Brown Double Length Formula The **Spearman-Brown double length formula** (sometimes called the *Spearman-Brown prophecy formula*) is an estimate of the parallel-forms correlation. Students receive scores on each half of the test. Their scores on the halves are correlated. Because this correlation reflects the correspondence of two sets of scores from only half test rather than the full-length assessment, this correlation is adjusted or "stepped up" to estimate the reliability of the whole test. The Spearman-Brown formula is simple to use:

$$\text{Whole test reliability} = \frac{2 \times \text{correlation between half test scores}}{1 + \text{correlation between half test scores}} \quad [\text{Eq. 4.1}]$$

For example, assume that the correlation between the half-test scores is 0.60. The Spearman-Brown double length reliability estimate for the full-length test is:

$$\text{Whole test reliability} = \frac{2 \times 0.60}{1 + 0.60} = \frac{1.20}{1.60} = 0.75$$

The double length formula is often used to estimate a parallel form's reliability coefficient. To do so properly requires organizing the assessment's items into parallel halves, making the halves equivalent in terms of content coverage, difficulty level, and variability in essentially the same manner as when two parallel forms are constructed.

An assessment's items may be organized into halves in many ways,[2] but not all prove satisfactory when applying split-halves procedures. The most commonly used procedure to organize the items is to let the odd-numbered items (1, 3, 5, 7, . . .) comprise one of the halves and the even-numbered (2, 4, 6, 8, . . .) comprise the other half. This is known as the **odd-even split-halves procedure**. Splitting the assessment and instrument into halves this way works fine as long as (a) the odd half and the even half can be considered parallel content samples, and (b) the assessment is not speeded. A **speeded assessment** is one for which there is not enough time for everyone to consider and attempt to answer each item. If an assessment is speeded, agreement among students' scores on the two halves is spuriously high. In general, split-halves procedures should not be used with speeded or partially speeded assessments unless precautions are taken to administer and time each half separately. The odd-even split-halves procedure is inappropriate when groups of items are linked together, such as when a cluster of items requires answers based on the same reading selection (or on the same data table, figure, graph, etc.), or when items are grouped in homogeneous clusters in a matching exercise (Thorndike, 1951).

Kuder-Richardson Reliability Coefficients A second way to obtain a reliability estimate from a single form of the test is by using one of the Kuder and Richardson (1937) procedures. The two discussed here, **Kuder-Richardson formula 20 (KR20)** and **Kuder-Richardson formula 21 (KR21)**, are used when test items are scored dichotomously (0 or 1). The names of these procedures derive from the numbering scheme Kuder and Richardson used to identify the formulas in their 1937 paper.

The Kuder-Richardson formula 20, like the split-half formula, estimates reliability from a single administration of a test. Unlike the split-half procedure, however, KR20 does not require splitting the test in half. Instead it uses data on the proportion of persons answering each item correctly and the standard deviation of the total scores. The Kuder-Richardson formula 21 procedure is a simpler version of KR20: It uses only the mean and standard deviation of the total scores. Appendix J illustrates the computation of these reliability estimates. The KR20 formula is most often used in published reports of standardized tests and is often provided as output in computer programs that analyze classroom test data.

Kuder-Richardson formulas 20 and 21 are used when the test contains only dichotomously scored items. Not all

---

[1]Appendix J provides a computing guide for the Spearman-Brown formula as well as for another split-half method, the Rulon (1939) method.

[2]For a 4-item test there are 3 possible ways to split the test into halves. A 6-item test may be split into halves 10 ways; an 8-item test, 35 ways; and a 10-item test, 126 ways. For a general formula see Thorndike (1951, p. 579), Stanley (1971, p. 408), or Feldt and Brennan (1989, p. 120).

assessments contain only items scored that way. Some assessments contain a mixture of item types; essay tests are scored more continuously; attitude scales require the student to express agreement with each item on a scale of, say, 1 to 4; and performance assessments may rate a student on a scale from 1 to 5, for example. In these cases, a more general version of KR20 is used. This reliability estimate is known as **coefficient alpha** (Cronbach, 1951). Appendix J shows an example of how to calculate this coefficient also. Because coefficient alpha is a more general version of KR20, it can be used with items scored either 0 or 1; or on a more continuous scale (e.g., 0, 1, 2, 3, and 5). Rating scales, essays, and rubrics, for example, use a more continuous scale.

The split-half and Kuder-Richardson procedures assume that the consistency with which students respond from one assessment task to the next is a good foundation to estimate the reliability coefficient for the total scores. This focus on task-to-task consistency within an assessment has led to these coefficients being called *internal consistency reliability estimates*.

These three procedures are sensitive to the homogeneity of the tasks as well as to their specific content. **Homogeneous tasks** all measure the same trait or attribute. An assessment procedure in which different tasks measure different traits is said to contain *heterogeneous tasks*. If assessment tasks are homogeneous, the KR20 and coefficient alpha procedures will give nearly the same results as the split-halves procedure. When the assessment tasks are heterogeneous, results from the KR20 and coefficient alpha procedures are lower than the split-halves procedure. For this reason, KR20 and coefficient alpha are often called *lower bound estimates of reliability*.

It should be noted that KR20 and coefficient alpha are equal to the average of all possible split-half reliability coefficients that could be computed for the assessment procedure in question (see Cronbach, 1951). "All possible split-halves" means not just the odd-even split, but also all different splits that could divide a test into halves.[3]

Also, the length of the test as well as its homogeneity influences the numerical values of KR20 and coefficient alpha. Longer tests will tend to have higher values of KR20 or coefficient alpha, even though they may be heterogeneous. The KR20, KR21, and alpha coefficients are influenced by speed in the same manner as split-halves coefficients. They should not be used with speeded or partially speeded tests.

The KR20 and coefficient alpha procedures are usually not appropriate to use when a test is composed of items organized in clusters (e.g., several different types of reading passage, each with several items that are based on the respective reading passage) or containing a mixture of assessment formats (e.g., a combination of multiple-choice, short-answer, and performance assessments). For tests comprised of such heterogeneous exercise formats,

another index, called a *congeneric reliability coefficient*, should be used because if KR20 and coefficient alpha were to be used, they would underestimate the test's internal consistency reliability (Feldt, 2002). For an explanation of the congeneric coefficient refer to more advanced resources (e.g., Feldt & Brennan, 1989).

Finally, as you may notice in Figure 4.1, KR20, KR21, coefficient alpha, and the split-half methods do not consider sampling of occasions or sampling of raters as sources of measurement error. To estimate the degree of inconsistency attributed to students' day-to-day fluctuations in performance, you must use test-retest or delayed alternate-forms coefficients. To estimate the degree of inconsistency attributed to persons who rate or mark an assessment, you must use inter-rater reliability coefficients (see the next section). If KR20 or coefficient alpha are used inappropriately to describe assessment reliability for these other types of inconsistency questions, they will overestimate the assessment reliability (Brennan, 2001). In other words, using KR20 or coefficient alpha inappropriately will lead you to believe the assessment results are more consistent than they really are.

Estimating Inter-Rater Reliability

Yet another source of measurement error arises from the persons (or machines) that score students' work. Here concern focuses on questions such as: (a) To what extent would a student obtain the same score if a different teacher had scored the paper or rated the performance? (b) To what extent might the assessment procedure be said to be objective? and (c) Are the results obtained from different scorers (observers, raters, judges) interchangeable?

Inter-rater reliability is especially important if you use essay questions, open-ended questions, performance assessments, and portfolio assessment. To improve the reliability of scoring these types of assessments, you should develop and use *scoring rubrics*. You will learn how to craft scoring rubrics in Chapter 12. Here we show how to evaluate the reliability of scores.

Correlating Raters' Scores The most straightforward way to estimate this type of reliability is to have two persons score each student's paper or rate each student's performance. The two scores for each student—one score from each scorer—are then correlated. (Correlation is explained in Chapter 3.) This correlation coefficient is called **scorer reliability** or **inter-rater reliability**. It is an index of the scorers' consistency in marking the same students. In this case, *consistency* is defined as similarity of students' rank ordering by the two teachers or judges. The group of four students' ratings in Figure 4.3 illustrates this point in an admittedly exaggerated situation.

The ratings in this illustration don't "agree" in the absolute sense. Agreement in the absolute sense happens when two scorers assign identical scores or ratings to each

---

[3]See footnote 2.

FIGURE 4.3 Ratings and rank order of four students.

Students	Ratings from:		Ratings converted to ranks	
	Rater A	Rater B	Rank from A	Rank from B
Tony	4	8	1	1
Marya	3	7	2	2
Bobby	2	6	3	3
Meghan	1	5	4	4
Mean	2.5	6.5	$r_{AB} = 1.00$	
SD	1.12	1.12		

student. But they do agree perfectly in the relative sense because the rankings are in perfect agreement: The correlation coefficient of 1.00 reflects this.

Percentage Agreement The extent to which this identical assignment of scorers occurs is sometimes expressed as a **percentage of agreement**, which is defined as an index of the consistency of decisions made by two independent judges. (Percentage of agreement is discussed further and calculated later in this chapter.) If scorers always agree in their assignment of scores, there is 100% agreement; if they never agree, the percentage of agreement is zero; partial agreement is expressed as a percentage falling between these two values.

Percentage of agreement is quite a different concept than a reliability coefficient based on a correlation coefficient: In general, the numerical values of the two will differ. The choice between a percentage of agreement index and a correlation index of inter-rater reliability depends on whether a student's absolute (actual) or relative (rank order) score level is important for a particular interpretation and use. Suppose that in Figure 4.3 a rating of 5 or better was needed to "pass." If the scores of Rater A were used, then everyone "failed," but if the scores of Rater B were used, everyone passed. For interpretations of pass and fail, the actual score level is important. A serious source of error (in this example) is the particular scorer or rater employed: The raters do not seem to agree on the scores that rate the students. Only the percentage of agreement will show this. Suppose, on the other hand, that only the rank order of the scores is important, such as when you want to know who in the class is the best, next best, and so on. In this case, the two observers agree perfectly on who the "best" and the "next best" are. In other words, they agree perfectly on their ranking or relative level of accomplishment. The correlation inter-rater reliability coefficient shows this.

OBTAINED SCORES, TRUE SCORES, AND ERROR SCORES

In the preceding sections we often referred to students' scores. In this section, we dig more deeply into the idea that students' assessment results are reported as scores. The scores students receive when you assess them are called **obtained scores**. Obtained scores include ratings from open-ended tasks such as essays, number-right scores from multiple-choice or short-answer tests, and standard scores or grade-equivalent scores from norm-referenced standardized tests. You may think of each student's obtained score as containing some measurement error. This means that the obtained score is really composed of two parts: a true score and an error score. The sum of these two scores equals the obtained score. Whenever we assess a student, we really want to know the student's true score. However, we are always "stuck" with the obtained score because the true score is not available to us. The obtained scores from our assessments are only *estimates* of the students' true status. Because obtained scores contain errors, we must learn to live with measurement errors—and to be cautious in our interpretation of obtained scores.

If you could quantify the amount of error in a student's obtained score, you would have the **error score**. (Often the error score is referred to as **measurement error**.) The **true score** is the remaining portion of the observed score and contains no measurement error. In other words, if we subtract the error score from the student's obtained score, the result is the student's true score.

As an illustration, suppose you had two students, Suzanne and Georgia. Assume that you gave them the same problem-solving test and that both students scored 52. The score, 52, is their obtained score, the only score you see. You might be tempted to use these results to conclude that Suzanne and Georgia have the same problem-solving ability. Don't yield to this temptation! You cannot conclude these two students have identical problem-solving ability based solely on the fact they have the identical test score, 52. The score, 52, contains measurement error that needs to be acknowledged.

Let us further assume that Suzanne's true score is 50 and that Georgia's true score is 53. If you could create a problem-solving test that resulted in scores without measurement error, you would see that Georgia has somewhat more ability than Suzanne. Unfortunately, creating such a perfect test is impossible. Consequently, both students ended up getting identical obtained scores of 52.

How much measurement error is in their obtained scores? In our example, Georgia's true score is 53. Thus, her error score is $52 - 53 = -1$. Suzanne's true score, on the other hand, is 50, so her error score is $52 - 50 = +2$. This illustrates that errors of measurement may be either positive (e.g., $+2$) or negative (e.g., -1).

Although we illustrated two students having different true scores but the same obtained score, other possibilities exist. Two students may have the *same true score*, but as a result of measurement errors, they may receive *different obtained scores*. The point is, you need to treat an observed test score as an imperfect piece of information. How can you improve assessment to get a better estimate of a person's true score? To estimate a student's true score better, you need to include more than one test in your overall evaluation.

A student's true score is not some hidden property that your assessment procedure seeks to discover or some set of quantities assigned to the student at birth. It is not an "ultimate fact in the book of the recording angel" (Stanley, 1971, p. 361). Rather, a student's true score for a particular assessment procedure is defined as the hypothetical average (mean) of the observed scores the student would obtain if repeatedly assessed under the same conditions (Lord & Novick, 1968).

Because a true score is an average, it is constant from one administration of an assessment procedure to the next. (Different students will have different true scores, however.) For each separate administration of the assessment procedure, a student's error score is different. On any one occasion the student's error score may be either positive, negative, or zero. These measurement errors result in the student's obtained scores being higher or lower than the student's true score. One consequence of these measurement errors is that scores obtained from any two administrations of an assessment procedure do not rank students in identical order.

STANDARD ERROR OF MEASUREMENT

Meaning of the Standard Error of Measurement

Because no procedure assesses with perfect consistency, your score interpretations are improved if you take into account the likely size of measurement errors. One way to describe the inconsistency of assessment scores is to assess a student repeatedly and note how much scores vary. This can only be done hypothetically, however. If you could assess a student many times (without changing the student's ability with respect to the trait you are assessing), you would obtain a collection of the student's obtained scores. Some scores would be higher than others, but most would cluster around an average (mean) value. This average is the true score to which we referred earlier. The standard deviation or spread of this distribution is the **standard error of measurement (SEM)**. The *SEM*

estimates the likely difference of students' obtained scores from their true scores.

In practice you cannot repeatedly reassess students without changing them, so the standard error of measurement is not calculated by actually reassessing students. Instead it is estimated using the following equation.

$$SEM = SD_x\sqrt{1 - \text{reliability coefficient}} \qquad \text{[Eq. 4.2]}$$

where SD_x is the standard deviation of the obtained scores of the assessment. (See Appendix I for a description of standard deviation.)

The *SEM* is an estimate of the standard deviation of the errors of measurement. For example, if SD_x was equal to 10 and the reliability coefficient equaled 0.84, then

$$SEM = 10\sqrt{1 - .84} = 10\sqrt{.16} = 10(.4) = 4$$

The standard error of measurement helps us understand the size of measurement error for a particular assessment procedure. One interpretation is that the numerical value of *SEM* estimates the amount by which a student's observed scores are likely to deviate from her true score. Thus, in the preceding example, $SEM = 4.0$ means that a student's obtained scores are likely to be about 4 points above or below her true score. Because of this likely deviation from true score, you must interpret the obtained score as only an estimate of the student's true score.

Another interpretation of *SEM* uses a normal distribution. It is assumed that the hypothetical distribution of obtained scores, resulting from repeatedly assessing a student, is normal in form. (See Chapter 17 for a discussion of normal distributions.) The mean of this distribution is the student's true score, whereas the standard deviation is the standard error of measurement. Using the relationship between standard deviation and percent of cases under a normal curve from Chapter 17, it can be said that 68% of the time the student's obtained scores will be within a distance of one *SEM* from the true score.

This meaning of the *SEM* is illustrated in Figure 4.4 for a hypothetical student with a true score of 52 and *SEM* of 4.0. Following the normal curve interpretation, one-third (32%) of the time that a student is retested, her obtained scores will be outside the bounds shown at the bottom of the shaded area in Figure 4.4: They will be greater than 56 ($52 + 4$) about one sixth (16%) of the time and less than 48 ($52 - 4$) about one sixth of the time.

Reliability Coefficients and *SEMs*

As you study Figure 4.4, you may notice that if the standard error of measurement became smaller, observed scores would cluster more closely around the true score because two-thirds of the time they are within ± 1 *SEM* of the true score. This illustrates graphically what we mean by

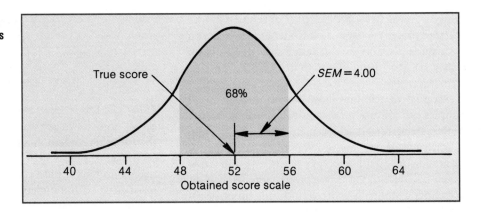

FIGURE 4.4 **A hypothetical normal distribution of scores resulting from repeated assessment of one student whose "true" score is 52.**

consistency: If the observed assessment scores tend to be very near a student's true score, the scores are consistent. More consistency means smaller measurement errors.

The size of the standard error of measurement, however, depends on both the reliability coefficient and the standard deviation of the obtained scores. In the preceding example, if $SD_x = 5$ instead of 10, then $SEM = 2.0$. Thus, while the reliability remained at 0.84, SEM becomes smaller when SD_x is smaller. This smaller SEM illustrates that the standard deviation of the scores should be taken into account when interpreting the consistency of assessment results.

Because different assessment procedures have different units of measurement as well as different standard deviations, it is usually true that the only way to compare the consistency of the scores from two different assessment methods is by looking at their reliability coefficients. An SEM calculated for students' raw scores would have radically different numerical value than the SEM calculated for the same students after these same raw scores are converted into grade-equivalent scores on the same test.

The relationship between the SD_x, the reliability coefficient, and the SEM is shown in Figure 4.5. When the reliability coefficient is fixed, SEM becomes larger as SD_x

increases. When the SD_x is fixed, SEM becomes smaller as the reliability coefficient becomes larger. If a test manual does not report SEM, Figure 4.5 can provide a rough estimate once the SD_x and the reliability coefficient are known.

Finally, remember that the type of reliability coefficient you use in the SEM formula is important. Each reliability coefficient estimates the reliability for different types of measurement error (see column 3 of Figure 4.2). This means that the SEM will estimate the likely size of the same type of measurement error as the reliability coefficient used in the formula.

Using the *SEM* to Set Confidence Bands

You should not interpret assessment results as if they had great precision. An obtained score is likely to be near, but not exactly equal to, the student's true score. You can use the SEM to help express how students' true scores can differ from their obtained scores. To accomplish this, you add to and subtract the value of the SEM from each student's obtained score, thus forming the boundaries of a **score band** or **uncertainty interval** for scores. This kind of

FIGURE 4.5 **Standard error of measurement for various standard deviations and reliability coefficients.**

Reliability coefficient	Standard deviation					
	5	10	15	20	25	30
.98	0.7	1.4	2.1	2.8	3.5	4.2
.95	1.1	2.2	3.4	4.5	5.6	6.7
.90	1.6	3.2	4.7	6.2	7.9	9.5
.85	1.9	3.9	5.8	7.7	9.7	11.6
.80	2.2	4.5	6.7	8.9	11.1	13.4
.75	2.5	5.0	7.5	10.0	12.5	15.0
.70	2.7	5.5	8.2	11.0	13.7	16.4
.65	3.0	5.9	8.9	11.8	14.8	17.7
.60	3.2	6.3	9.5	12.6	15.8	19.0
.50	3.5	7.1	10.6	14.1	17.7	21.2
.20	4.5	8.9	13.4	17.9	22.4	26.8
.10	4.7	9.5	14.2	19.0	23.7	28.5

uncertainty interval has a 68% chance of containing the student's true score. You can use this method to help you interpret a student's score on one test, a student's score on two tests, or two different students' scores on the same test.

The examples that follow show how to do this. In all the examples we will use grade-equivalent scores from a hypothetical standardized achievement test that has a reliability coefficient of 0.84 and a standard deviation of 1.0 (on the grade-equivalent scale). For this test, the *SEM* would then be equal to 0.4. It would be quite likely that, upon retesting, a student's score would shift up or down the scale 4 grade-equivalent months (0.4).

Uncertainty Interval for One Student's Score To show the uncertainty interval for a student, you would add +0.4 to the student's obtained score to compute the upper limit of the uncertainty interval and subtract 0.4 from the student's obtained score to find the lower limit of the band. Any number between the upper and the lower limits of the interval could be the student's true score.

Example

Suppose Harry's obtained grade-equivalent score in science is 7.8. After making the uncertainty interval, our interpretation is that Harry's true grade-equivalent score is probably between 7.4 and 8.2.

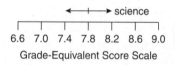

Using SEM *to Interpret the Difference Between Two Scores* When a student takes a battery of achievement tests, the student usually has two or more scores, one for each subject. These scores may not be identical. We can set an uncertainty interval around each of these scores. If the intervals for two scores overlap, it is likely that the student's true scores are not meaningfully different. If the intervals overlap, the observed-score differences for the student could have come about 68% of the time simply by measurement error.

Example

Harry's obtained grade-equivalent score in science is 7.8, whereas in mathematics it is 7.4. Does this mean he is stronger in science than in math? No. The uncertainty interval for science is 7.4 to 8.2; for math it is 7.0 to 7.8. Because the uncertainty intervals overlap, it is likely that his true scores on the two tests are not meaningfully different.

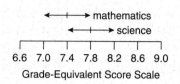

Using SEM *to Interpret the Difference Between Two Students' Scores* Sometimes you want to see if one student is stronger than another student in a subject by comparing their scores on the same achievement test. The students' obtained scores may be different, but because the scores contain measurement error, are the students' true scores different? To answer this question, form an uncertainty interval around each student's score. Then, see if the intervals overlap. No overlap means that the students' true scores are probably meaningfully different. If the intervals do overlap, there may be no meaningful differences in the two students' true scores because differences of the size observed could arise simply by errors of measurement 68% of the time.

Example

In reading, Sally's obtained grade-equivalent score was 8.2 whereas Jane's was 7.0. The uncertainty interval for Sally is 7.8 to 8.6; for Jane it is 6.6 to 7.4. Does this mean Sally is a stronger reader than Jane? Yes, because the intervals do not overlap.

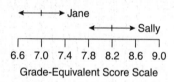

You should be cautious about **overinterpreting** small differences in scores by acting as if small differences in scores have an important meaning. You should not be so conservative, however, as to err by **underinterpreting** by ignoring meaningful score differences. Perhaps a more widespread problem than overinterpreting scores is a "do-nothing pattern": failing to interpret score changes or ups and downs of profiles because of overdemanding criteria of 68%, 90%, or 95% uncertainty intervals (Feldt, 1967). To avoid wasting valuable information, corroborate the information obtained from one assessment with information from other sources that you already have (such as classroom performance), thereby reducing the probability of overinterpretation errors (Feldt, 1967).

ADDITIONAL FACTORS AFFECTING RELIABILITY AND *SEM*

You should keep a number of factors in mind when interpreting reliability and *SEM* information, especially when comparing such information from two or more assessment procedures.

1. *Longer assessment procedures are more reliable than shorter procedures.* The greater the number of items, judges, occasions of observation, and so on that enter into formulation of a score, the more reliable that score will be. This means, for example, that you should put little confidence in a student's score based on only one task, or even on clusters of two or three tasks. The general Spearman-Brown formula shows the relation between lengthening an assessment by adding similar tasks and the reliability of the resultant assessment procedure. Appendix J shows a computational example.

2. *The numerical value computed for a reliability coefficient will fluctuate from one sample to another.* The reliability coefficients reported in a test manual are based on samples of students. These numerical values will fluctuate from one sample to the next, so that any one published number is only an estimate of what the reliability coefficient would be if the entire population of students was tested. Sampling fluctuations are greater for small samples drawn from the population than from large samples.

3. *The narrower the range of a group's ability, the lower the reliability coefficient tends to be.* Many educators use assessment results to make decisions about students with similar abilities, grade levels, and ages. It is much easier, however, to distinguish individual differences in ability when students vary widely from one another. Therefore, look in test manuals for reliability coefficients calculated on data from students whose abilities are as close together as those with whom you must deal. Put less stock in a published high-reliability coefficient that was derived by pooling samples from groups with wide ranges of ability or from groups spanning many age levels. This is especially true when you will be using the assessment to evaluate students whose abilities are close.

4. *Students at different achievement levels may be assessed with different degrees of accuracy.* The *SEM*, being a single number for an entire test, represents only an average amount of score inconsistency. The consistency of results, however, varies with the achievement level. The *SEM* may be larger in the middle of the score range than at the extremes. If so, very high and very low scoring students are assessed with somewhat more consistency than are middle-range students. The technical manual of a published test should tell you which achievement levels are more consistently assessed.

5. *The longer the interval between testing, the lower test-retest and alternate-forms reliability coefficients will tend to be.* If the same assessment is administered twice, the students' scores will be more similar when the time between the administrations is short than when it is long.

6. *More objectively scored assessment results are more reliable.* Objectivity is the degree to which two qualified observers assign the same scores to the same student performances. We called this inter-rater reliability. Remember, however, that reliability and objectivity apply even to qualitative assessments, such as observing and classifying students. This is why we stress developing formal rating scales and scoring schemes for open-ended and performance assessments. (See Chapters 11 and 12 for details.) As with multiple-choice and true-false questions, alternative assessment methods should be marked as objectively as possible. Increasing objectivity increases reliability, and this will have a positive effect on the validity.

7. *Different methods of estimating reliability will not give the same result.* The reliability coefficients differ because they include different sources of error, as described in Figure 4.2. Be careful to use the proper coefficient in your interpretation of assessments. Using the improper reliability coefficient will mean incorrectly describing an assessment's quality.

RELIABILITY OF MASTERY AND PASS-FAIL DECISIONS

We have been discussing consistency of students' scores. This consistency is of concern no matter what type of assessment method you are using. There are certain classroom situations, however, when the consistency of the exact score a student receives is less important than the consistency of the decision made about the student. For example, you may set the passing score on a mastery test as 80% correct. A student who gets 85% receives the same decision (i.e., pass), as does the student who gets 92%. Similarly, two students with 50% and 65%, respectively, both fail.

In this type of assessment interpretation, it makes more sense to speak of *decision consistency* than of score consistency. A **decision consistency index** describes how consistent the classification decisions are rather than how consistent the scores are. For example, suppose you crafted two equivalent forms of a mastery test. Such indexes answer the question, "Would both tests classify the same students as masters and nonmasters?"

Error of Classification

Figure 4.6 illustrates how measurement error may cause an assessment to mask a student's true mastery status. Whenever a student's true status is not revealed by the assessment results, a decision error or error of misclassification occurs.

Several factors influence how often decision errors occur when assessing mastery.

1. *The assessment tool may contain tasks that have weak validity for assessing the type of mastery you have in mind.* This may happen, for example, when you use the test questions that come with the published curriculum materials you use in class. Very often these questions are poorly worded or assess content that you omitted or deemphasized in your teaching. Weak validity increases decision errors.

FIGURE 4.6 Relationship between a student's true mastery status and possible errors of classification when drawing conclusions from assessment results.

		True status of a student with respect to the degree of domain proficiency	
		Master	Nonmaster
Conclusion the teacher drew about the student from the assessment results	The assessment results are interpreted as mastery	*There is no misclassification:* Both the student's true status and the conclusion the teacher drew from the assessment results agree.	*An error of classification:* The student is a nonmaster, but the teacher concluded that the assessment results showed mastery.
	The assessment results are interpreted as nonmastery	*An error of classification:* Student is a master, but the teacher concluded that the assessment results showed nonmastery.	*There is no misclassification:* Both the student's true status and the conclusion the teacher drew from the assessment results agree.

2.   *Longer assessment methods usually lead to more accurate mastery decisions.* Judging mastery from a short test (e.g., fewer than 10 response-choice items) or from one project or one performance activity usually raises decision errors to unacceptably high levels. You should use several different pieces of assessment information before finalizing a mastery decision about a student.

3.   *Low inter-rater reliability is associated with high rates of mastery decision errors.* More reliable assessments generally lead to more accurate mastery decisions.

4.   *The passing score you set for deciding mastery affects the rate of decision errors.* In general, setting the passing score very high (90% or 95%) or very low (20% or 30%) will increase errors of classification.

5.   *Students whose true mastery status is very close to the passing score you set are the ones who are most likely to be misclassified.* For example, if you set the passing score at 80%, students whose true mastery status is in the range of 70% to 90% will have higher rates of erroneous classification than students outside this range. When students' assessment results are close to the passing score, you should use information from other sources (such as performance in class, homework, project performance) in addition to the main assessment before making a final mastery decision.

Percentage Agreement

A quantitative index of decision consistency can be calculated by administering two parallel forms of a mastery test to the same group of students and studying whether students are consistently classified as masters or nonmasters. Two indices may be calculated: percentage of agreement (P_A) and kappa coefficient (κ) (Cohen, 1960). Here we show the calculation of P_A. Appendix J shows an example of calculating kappa coefficient.

As stated earlier, the percentage of agreement is an index of the consistency of decisions made by two independent judges: It is the percentage of students for whom

the two judges reached the same decision. The percentage of agreement is calculated by the following formula when the assessments classify students into two categories (e.g., "mastery" and "nonmastery"):

$$P_A = \begin{bmatrix} \text{Percentage consistent} \\ \text{mastery decisions} \end{bmatrix} + \begin{bmatrix} \text{Percentage consistent} \\ \text{nonmastery decisions} \end{bmatrix}$$
[Eq. 4.3]

Example

Two forms of an assessment, A and B, were administered to a group of 25 students, and the mastery criterion on each form was 80%. Figure 4.7 summarizes how consistently the two assessment results classified these students. Eleven students were classified as masters by both forms, 9 as nonmasters by both forms, and the others as masters by one and nonmasters by the other. For this example, the percent of agreement is calculated as follows:

$$P_A = \frac{11}{25} + \frac{9}{25} = \frac{20}{25} = 0.80$$

The percentage agreement, $P_A = 0.80$ in this example, is the "total proportion of consistent classification that occurs for whatever reason on the two tests" (Subkoviak, 1980, p. 152).

As described by Equation 4.3 and as illustrated here, percentage agreement requires administering two forms of the assessment to the same group of students. Instead of using two forms, you may also use a test-retest paradigm or two independent judges of mastery. The latter may be especially important whenever you are using assessments that are not paper-and-pencil tests, such as judging whether a student's product or project meets minimum standards.

FIGURE 4.7 Hypothetical example of how 25 students were classified using the scores from two forms of a mastery test.

		Results from Form A		
		Mastery	Nonmastery	Marginal totals
Results from Form B	Mastery	11	4	15
	Nonmastery	1	9	10
	Marginal totals	12	13	25

The percentage agreement need not be limited to the simple, two-category case illustrated here: More than two categories could be used for classifying students. One example is the situation in which you assign letter grades of A, B, C, D, and F to students' projects or performances. Formulas for computing percentage agreement (and kappa coefficient) for such situations can be found in Cohen (1960) and Swaminathan, Hambleton, & Algina (1974). You may also estimate percentage agreement from only one administration of the assessment (see Huynh, 1976; Subkoviak, 1976).

HOW TO IMPROVE RELIABILITY

Students of educational assessment often ask, "Is thus-and-such reliability coefficient good enough?" You realize by now that perfect reliability is indicated by a coefficient of 1.00. This value is virtually unattainable in practice, however, because most assessment results have some degree of inconsistency in every population of students. What can you do to improve the reliability of your assessment results? Figure 4.8 gives nine suggestions. (Also see Chapter 12, page 285.)

Different types of assessment instruments have different levels of reliability. Standardized multiple-choice achievement tests typically have reliability coefficients in the .85 to .95 range. Open-ended paper-and-pencil assessments are typically in the .65 to .80 range. Portfolio scoring may have reliability in the .40 to .60 range.

A general rule for estimating "how close to 1.00" a reliability coefficient for a single assessment instrument should be is as follows: *The more important and the less reversible is the decision about an individual based on the assessment instrument, the higher the reliability should be.* Decisions such as whether a person is awarded a diploma, admitted to a higher educational program, put into a special education classroom, and given a job are examples of high-stakes decisions which, if erroneous, would have serious consequences for an individual. *The results of a single assessment instrument should not be used alone to make high-stakes decisions. High-reliability coefficients, equal to .90 or higher, should be demanded for each instrument used for such decisions.* (Another reason for using more than one instrument in these situations is that they require high validity, as well as high reliability. A single assessment instrument seldom has sufficient validity to be used alone.)

FIGURE 4.8 How to improve the reliability of assessment results.

1. *Lengthen the assessment procedure.* Whenever practical, give more time, use more questions, more observations, and so on.

2. *Broaden the scope of the procedure.* Use procedures that assess all of the essential and important aspects of the largest learning performance.

3. *Improve objectivity.* Use a systematic, more formal procedure for scoring student performance (e.g., a scoring schema or rubric.)

4. *Use multiple markers.* Whenever possible, have more than one qualified person score each student's essay, term paper, performance, portfolio, or open-ended assessment task. Average the results or confer to reconcile differences.

5. *Combine results from several assessments.* When making important educational decisions, use a combination of the results from several different assessment methods rather than a single assessment result.

6. *Provide sufficient time to students.* Within practical limits, be sure that every student has enough time to complete the assessment procedure.

7. *Teach students how to perform their best.* Provide practice and training to students on how to "put their best foot forward," strategies to use, and so on before using an assessment method.

8. *Match the assessment difficulty to students' ability levels.* Be sure the assessment procedure contains tasks that are not too easy or too difficult for the students. Tailor the assessment to each student's ability level, if possible.

9. *Differentiate among students.* Select assessment tasks that do a good job of differentiating the best students from the least able students.

A classroom is an information-rich environment, and you have many opportunities to assess students. Further, classroom decisions should not be high-stakes decisions. That is, students should have many different opportunities to recover from their learning failures and to be retaught. Classroom assessment results typically have moderate reliability levels, but you can (and should) combine assessment results from several procedures before making important classroom decisions (e.g., before assigning marking period grades). Thus, you may tolerate moderate levels of reliability of .70 or higher for any one assessment result *as long as several pieces of information are combined for classroom decisions.*

Summary

General Nature of Reliability

- Reliability refers to the consistency of assessment results, rather than to the assessment instrument itself.
- Reliability is a limiting factor for validity. Unreliable assessment results cannot be highly valid.
- Reliability is one criterion for validity of assessment results, but not the only criterion. Thus, highly reliable assessment results may not be valid if they fail to meet other validity criteria.

Causes of Measurement Error or Inconsistency

- There are several causes of unreliable assessment results. Four were discussed:
  - *Content factors*—Inconsistent results caused by the different content or tasks included in two equivalent assessments.
  - *Time factors*—Inconsistent results caused by the temporary and permanent changes that a student experiences when assessed on different occasions.
  - *Scorer factors*—Inconsistent results caused by the idiosyncrasies of the persons who mark a student's performance.
  - *Combined factors*—Inconsistent results caused by a combination of these (and other) factors.

Types of Reliability Coefficients

- Two types of quantitative indicators of inconsistency were discussed: reliability coefficients and the standard errors of measurement.
- A reliability coefficient is more useful when comparing the consistency of results from different assessment procedures. A standard error of measurement is more useful when estimating the size of typical measurement errors when you are using a particular assessment procedure.
- Several types of reliability coefficients were discussed:
  - *Test-retest reliability* measures the stability of scores.
  - *Alternate-forms reliability (different occasions)* measures stability and equivalence of the forms.
  - *Alternate-forms reliability (same occasion)* measures the equivalence of two versions of an assessment instrument.
  - *Spearman-Brown (split-halves)* reliability estimates the equivalence of an assessment instrument using information about the internal consistency of students' responses. This coefficient is not appropriate for speeded assessment instruments.

- *Kuder-Richardson and coefficient alpha reliability* also estimate the equivalence of an assessment instrument using the internal consistency of students' responses. These formulas also are not to be used when the assessment is speeded.
- *Inter-rater reliability* measures the consistency with which two judges or evaluators assign ratings to student performance on an assessment instrument.
- *Percentage agreement* is not a reliability coefficient but it measures the consistency of the decisions reached independently, using the results from two equivalent assessment instruments.

Standard Error of Measurement

- The standard error of measurement is a measure of the amount of inconsistency expected for individuals' assessment results.
- The numerical value of the standard error of measurement may be added to and subtracted from a person's score. The result is a "band" or range of scores that probably includes the person's true score.

Additional Factors Affecting Reliability and *SEM*

- Various factors affecting the reliability and the standard error of measurement are described:
  - Longer assessments are more reliable than shorter assessments.
  - Reliability coefficients reported in test manuals are only estimates from samples.
  - Reliability is low when the spread of scores is small.
  - The standard error of measurement may be different at various ability levels.
  - The meaning of the standard error of measurement depends on the types of reliability coefficients used in its calculation.
  - As the time interval between administering assessments increases, test-retest and alternate-forms reliability coefficients become smaller.
  - The more objective the scoring of assessment performance, the higher the reliability.

Reliability of Mastery and Pass-Fail Decisions

- Several factors influence the frequency with which mastery or pass-fail decision errors are made including:
  - The degree of validity of your assessment product.
  - The length of the assessment procedure.
  - The degree of inter-rater reliability of the scores.
  - The numerical value of the passing score.
  - How close the students' true scores are to the passing score.

Desired Levels of Reliability

- Higher levels of reliability are needed when assessment results factor into important and irreversible decisions about individuals. Moderate levels may be tolerated when decisions are reversible, less important, and based on information from several assessment results.
- Several suggestions are given in Figure 4.8 for improving the reliability of your assessments.

Important Terms and Concepts

decision consistency index
domain of achievement
error score, obtained score, true score

factors influencing consistency of assessment performance
homogeneous tasks
inter-rater reliability
measurement error
parallel forms
percentage of agreement
reliability
reliability coefficient
scorer reliability
speeded assessment
stability coefficient
standard error of measurement (*SEM*)
types of reliability coefficients (alternate forms/same occasion, coefficient alpha, delayed alternate forms, Kuder-Richardson formulas 20 and 21, odd-even split-halves procedure, parallel forms, Spearman-Brown double length formula, split-halves procedure, test-retest)
uncertainty interval (score band)
underinterpreting versus overinterpreting score differences

Exercises and Applications

1. Which type(s) of reliability coefficient(s), if any, would be a major source of information needed to answer each of the following questions?
   a. A teacher wonders whether her student Meghan's test score could be a result of her having an off day.
   b. An 8th-grade teacher wonders whether the students' aptitude test scores will predict their success in ninth grade.
   c. A 10th-grade English teacher wonders whether the grades he assigns to his students' essays are equivalent to the grades his colleague would assign them.
   d. A 12th-grade physics teacher wonders whether her final exam this year is equivalent to her final exam last year.
   e. An 8th-grade English teacher has students create portfolios of their work over the semester. Using the portfolios, she classifies the students into three groups: excellent, satisfactory, and unsatisfactory. The teacher wonders whether her classification of students can be made with fewer errors.

2. The correlation between students' scores on the odd and even items of a test is .40. The teacher claims that the students would attain the same scores if he used an equivalent test. Is the teacher's claim justifiable? Support your conclusion using an appropriate reliability coefficient.

3. A test-retest reliability coefficient is .75 and the test standard deviation is 15. By how many points can we expect individual students' test scores to differ when we test them on two different occasions? (Use Figure 4.5 to help you.)

4. The examples on pages 77–78 illustrate the use of the *SEM* to form confidence bands for students to help us interpret their scores. Suppose that for the students in the figure, the *SEM* equals 0.2 instead of 0.4. How, if at all, would the interpretations of each of the three illustrations in the examples change?

5. For each of the following types of assessment procedures, explain which cause(s) of measurement error is (are) of most concern and why:
   a. Student essays in social studies exams
   b. Science projects
   c. Grades on art projects
   d. True-false tests in science
   e. Portfolios in English courses
   f. Mathematics homework problems
   g. A teacher's marks for students' daily participation in class
   h. A paper-and-pencil test for a unit in social studies consisting of multiple-choice, matching, and short-answer questions

5 Professional Responsibilities, Ethical Behavior, and Legal Requirements in Educational Assessments

LEARNING TARGETS

After studying this chapter, you should have learned the following:

A Teacher's Professional Responsibilities in Assessment

1. Explain why you have a professional responsibility to use quality assessment information to make classroom decisions. [7]

2. Describe the six areas of professional assessment responsibility for teachers. [7, 6]

3. Identify examples of professionally responsible and irresponsible classroom assessment practices in each of the six areas. [7, 2]

4. Explain specific professional responsibilities when crafting your own classroom assessment procedures and when using published assessment procedures for classroom assessment. [7, 2, 4]

5. Explain several responsibilities you have when scoring your own classroom assessments. [3, 7]

Students' Rights and Responsibilities as Test Takers

6. Describe students' rights and ethical responsibilities and teachers' responsibilities in relation to assessment. [7, 6]

7. Explain the assessment rights and access to information that students have under the U.S. Constitution and federal legislation. [7, 6]

Secrecy, Access, Privacy, Confidentiality, and the Teacher

8. Explain and give examples of ethical and professional responsibility issues surrounding (a) access to student data for research purposes, (b) purging and correcting students' records, (c) confidentiality of students' achievement records, and (d) informed consent. [7, 6]

Accommodations for Students With Disabilities and Legal Defensibility of Accommodations

9. Describe ways classroom assessments may be modified to accommodate students with disabilities. [2, 3]

10. Explain how the validity and score-reporting concerns differ for classroom assessments and standardized tests when they are modified to accommodate students with disabilities. [3, 4, 5]

11. Describe steps that can be taken to process students' requests for accommodations and make testing accommodation programs legally defensible. [5, 6, 7]

Testing Challenged in Court and Bias in Educational Assessment

12. Explain and give examples of some of the major psychometric assessment issues presented in court. [7, 6]

13. Explain and give examples of some of the nonpsychometric assessment issues presented in court. [7, 6]

14. Identify and give examples of the types of test or assessment bias found in the news media and professional literature. [7, 5, 6]

15. Explain assessment as test fairness applies to both classroom and extraclassroom assessments. [7, 5, 6]

Important Terms and Concepts

16. Explain the meaning and educational significance of each of the important terms and concepts listed at the end of this chapter. [6, 7]

ABOUT THIS CHAPTER

Classroom assessment involves much more than knowing how to develop tools for gathering information. Assessments factor into decisions about students; along with those decision-making powers come professional responsibilities. These professional responsibilities, ethical principles, and legal requirements are the subjects of this chapter.

The first part of this chapter discusses a teacher's responsibilities in assessing students, organizing these responsibilities around six main assessment activities, from crafting the assessments through communicating the results to students and parents. Second, because students also have rights and responsibilities, we discuss these next. Third, we discuss legal requirements for confidentiality of student information. We then turn to the requirements for accommodating students with disabilities who are mainstreamed in your classes. Schools and state agencies have been taken to court for using assessments in certain ways. We examine the psychometric and nonpsychometric issues that have been brought to the courts. Sixth, we discuss the concept of educational assessment bias, how to guard against it, and what is the future of test fairness.

A TEACHER'S PROFESSIONAL RESPONSIBILITIES IN ASSESSMENT
Responsibility to Use Quality Information to Make Decisions

Independence Makes You Responsible You have nearly complete control in your classroom to gather and use information to improve your students' learning. Along with this independence comes **professional responsibility** for gathering and using information appropriately. You must follow professional standards of practice and ethical principles of behavior to fulfill your responsibilities.

Decisions Have Consequences You must make hundreds of decisions as you teach. Formal and informal assessment tools help you gather useful information for making decisions about your students. If you are as human as the rest of us, not all of your decisions will be correct. Correct or not, each decision you make will have **positive or negative consequences** for your students.

The consequences differ in their degree of seriousness for the students. **Serious consequences of decisions** occur when students benefit or lose something very valuable and cannot easily recover from an incorrect initial decision. Sometimes, these are called *high-stakes decisions*. For example, your decision to give a student a low final grade in chemistry may lower the student's chances of being admitted as a chemistry major at a particular college. **Less serious consequences of decisions** occur when students

benefit or lose something less valuable and can easily recover from an incorrect initial decision. Sometimes, these are called *low-stakes decisions*. For example, you may decide to reteach a particular chemistry concept to a student, but as you are reteaching you discover that the student already does understand the concept. It is easy for you to readjust your teaching, and the student can easily recover from your incorrect initial decision. The point here is that when the consequences of a decision are serious, you have an added responsibility to use the best available information in your decision-making process.

High-Quality Information Leads to Correct Decisions Assessment is the process of gathering appropriate information for making educational decisions. One way to improve your decisions is to use **high-quality information**: information that is highly valid and highly reliable for the decisions at hand. Of course, using high-quality information does not guarantee that your decisions will be correct. However, if you base your decisions on poor-quality or erroneous information, you are very likely to make an incorrect decision. This may be harmful to a student. If you cause harm to your students, either deliberately or through negligence, your actions are unprofessional, unethical, and/or illegal.

Code of Professional Responsibility in Educational Measurement

Professional Associations' Ethical Codes Professional associations often develop and enforce codes of ethical behavior for their members. These codes provide guidance on how to act responsibly. Codes of ethics commonly cover such areas as the professional's role in society, conflicts of interest, and communication with clients and the public (Schmeiser, 1992). Figure 5.1 lists some of the codes that contain statements of professional responsibility when using assessments.

Much of the information in this chapter is adapted from the principles described in the National Council on Measurement in Education's (NCME) *Code of Professional Responsibilities in Educational Measurement (CPR)*. A copy of the *CPR* is reproduced in Appendix C. The focus in this chapter is on ethical, professional, and legal responsibilities of classroom teacher assessment. The *CPR*, however, offers guidance to a wide range of educational professionals who are involved in assessment activities. These educational professionals include teachers; school and district administrators; professional support staff (supervisors, counselors, school psychologists, etc.); technical, legislative, and policy staff members of research, evaluation, and assessment organizations; test preparation service providers; faculty members and administrators at colleges and universities; and professionals in business who implement educational programs (National Council on Measurement in Education [NCME], 1995).

FIGURE 5.1 Professional association codes of professional responsibilities related to using educational assessments.

American Counseling Association. (1995). *The ACA code of ethics.* Alexandria, VA: Author. Available from http://www.counseling.org/resources/ethics.htm

American Educational Research Association, American Psychological Association, & National Council on Measurement in Education. (1999). *Standards for educational and psychological testing.* Washington, DC: American Educational Research Association.

American Educational Research Association. (2000). *Ethical standards of the American Educational Research Association.* Washington, DC: Author. Available from http://www.aera.net

American Federation of Teachers, National Council on Measurement in Education, & National Education Association. (1990). *Standards for teacher competence in educational assessment of students.* Washington, DC: National Council on Measurement in Education. Available from http://www.unl.edu/buros/bimm/html/subarts.html

American Psychological Association. (2002). *Ethical principles of psychologists and code of conduct.* Washington, DC: Author. Available from http://www.apa.org/ethics/homepage.html

American School Counselor Association. (2004). *Ethical standards for school counselors.* Alexandria, VA: Author. Available from http://www.schoolcounselor.org

Association for Assessment in Counseling and Education. (2003). *Rights and responsibilities of test takers: Guidelines and expectations.* Alexandria, VA: American Counseling Association. Available from http://aac.ncat.edu/documents/ttrr.html

Joint Advisory Committee. (1993). *Principles for fair student assessment practices for education in Canada.* Edmonton, Alberta: Author, Centre for Research in Applied Measurement and Evaluation, University of Alberta.

Joint Committee on Standards for Educational Evaluation. (1988). *The personnel evaluation standards: How to assess systems for evaluating educators.* Thousand Oaks, CA: Corwin Press. Available from http://www.wmich.edu/evalctr/jc

Joint Committee on Standards for Educational Evaluation. (1994). *The program evaluation standards: How to assess evaluations of educational programs.* Thousand Oaks, CA: Sage. Available from http://www.wmich.edu/evalctr/jc

Joint Committee on Standards for Educational Evaluation. (2002). *The student evaluation standards: How to improve evaluations of students.* Thousand Oaks, CA: Corwin Press.

Joint Committee on Testing Practices. (2004). *Code of fair testing practices in education (revised).* Washington, DC: Science Directorate, American Psychological Association. Available from http://www.apa.org/science/fairtestcode.html

National Association of College Admission Counselors. (2003). *Statement of principles of good practices.* Alexandria, VA: Author. Available from http://www.nacac.com/downloads/policy_spgp.pdf

National Board of Certified Counselors. (2005). *NBCC code of ethics.* Greensboro, NC: Author. Available from http://www.nbcc.org/ethics2

National Council on Measurement in Education (NCME). (1995). *Code of professional responsibilities in educational measurement (CPR).* Washington, DC: Author. Available from http://www.unl.edu/buros/bimm/html/article2.html

Related Standards of Conduct The *CPR* assumes that an informed user of educational assessments will behave in accordance with other assessment-related professional standards. These include the **Code of Fair Testing Practices in Education (Revised)** (Joint Committee on Testing Practices, 2004) and the *Standards for Educational and Psychological Testing* (AERA et al., 1999). The *Code of Fair Testing Practices in Education (Revised)* is reproduced in this book as Appendix B. The *Standards* are discussed in Chapter 18 but are not reproduced in this book.

General Principles of Professional Behavior As we discuss your professional responsibilities when using educational assessments, keep in mind that you are expected to uphold the principles of professional conduct. You are expected to:

1. protect the safety, health, and welfare of all examinees;
2. be knowledgeable about, and behave in compliance with, state and federal laws relevant to the conduct of professional activities;
3. maintain and improve [your]. . . professional competence in educational assessment;
4. provide assessment services only in areas of [your]. . . competence and experience, affording full disclosure of [your] professional qualifications;

5. promote the understanding of sound assessment practices in education;
6. adhere to the highest standards of conduct and promote professionally responsible conduct with educational institutions and agencies that provide educational services; and
7. perform all professional responsibilities with honesty, integrity, due care, and fairness. (NCME, 1995, p. 2)

Six Categories of Responsibility for Teachers

Your teaching involves six categories of assessment-related activities. Each has its own specific professional and ethical concerns:

1. *Crafting assessment procedures*—When you develop your own assessment procedures, you have a responsibility to ensure they are of high quality.

2. *Choosing assessment procedures*—When you choose or select assessment procedures that others have crafted, you have a responsibility to make sure they are appropriate for your intended use

3. *Administering assessment procedures*—When you administer assessment procedures, you have a responsibility to ensure that your administration process is fair to all students and will not result in uninterpretable results.

4. *Scoring assessment results*—When you score students' responses to an assessment, you have a responsibility to evaluate the responses accurately and to report the results to students in a timely manner.

5. *Interpreting and using assessment results*—When you interpret and use assessment results, you have a responsibility to ensure that your interpretations are as valid as possible, are used to promote positive student outcomes, and are used to minimize negative student outcomes.

6. *Communicating assessment results*—When you communicate assessment results, you have a responsibility to provide complete, useful, and correct information about students' performance that will promote positive student outcomes and minimize negative student outcomes.

The next sections discuss teachers' professional responsibilities in each of these six areas. Although the *CPR* influences this discussion, you should not construe this discussion as being endorsed by the sponsors of the *CPR*.

Responsibilities When Crafting Assessment Procedures

General Responsibilities If no appropriate assessment procedure is available, you must craft one. In this case, your professional responsibilities focus on producing an assessment procedure that provides results that (a) are as valid as possible for the interpretations and use you intend to make of them, and (b) are as reliable as needed for the seriousness of the consequences of the decisions you will make. *Validity* refers to how you interpret and use the results (see Chapter 3).

Example

Suppose a state's standards require schools to teach how well a student is able to solve real-life problems using mathematics principles and generalizations. A teacher's responsibility is not only to teach, but also to craft assessment tasks that require students to engage in real-life problem-solving thinking and activities.

In the preceding example, the teacher would not be acting responsibly if the teacher's assessment procedure required students only to recall facts and generalizations, to solve problems that are unlike real life, and to demonstrate general comprehension of mathematics concepts. As important as these learning outcomes may be, they are not real-life problem-solving tasks.

Reliability refers to how consistent the assessment results are (see Chapter 4). Consider the following example.

Example

A teacher is deciding what grade to give a student for the term. The teacher should not expect a student's performance on one question (or on a short test) to be a highly consistent indicator of term-long learning. Therefore, the teacher would be acting irresponsibly if the teacher based the term-grade decision on only a few questions or a short performance assessment.

You may increase the reliability of the information you use by combining the results from several assessments of the same learning targets such as quizzes, daily class performance, projects, and tests. This "triangulation" of results gives you a more reliable, hence, more valid picture of the student's achievement. Thus, it demonstrates a more responsible assessment strategy on your part.

Specific Responsibilities In addition to this general responsibility to craft valid and reliable assessment procedures, teachers have more specific responsibilities. As a teacher, you have a professional responsibility to:

1. *Apply sound principles* of assessment planning, assessment design, task development, item writing, rubric development, and assessment marking to each formal assessment you use.

2. *Craft assessment procedures* that are free from characteristics irrelevant to assessing the learning target. Assessment procedures should be free of gender, ethnic, race, social class, and religious bias and stereotypes.

3. *Accommodate in appropriate ways* students in your class with disabilities or special needs.

4. *Obtain permission* necessary to use copyrighted material in assessments you craft.

5. *Present the assessment results in a way that encourages* students and others to interpret them properly.

6. *Ensure that assessment materials do not contain errors* and inaccuracies in the content, instructions, and scoring key (or rubrics). If errors and inaccuracies are discovered after administering the assessment, you should correct them as soon as possible and rescore responses. Test questions containing errors should not be counted in the total score. You may need to readminister the assessment if rescoring cannot correct the error and if the decision it depends on is a serious one.

You can find the knowledge you need to fulfill these responsibilities in several chapters in this textbook as well as in many other texts. Your instructor may provide you with additional knowledge and perhaps some supervised practice. Practice and experience will hone your skills.

Responsibilities When Choosing Assessment Procedures

Choosing Assessments for Classroom Use Although you will often have to craft your own assessment techniques, you will no doubt also use assessment procedures developed by others. Many times these will be assessments that accompany published learning materials: quizzes and tests in the teacher's edition of the book, separate tests and performance tasks sold to accompany instructional units, specimen items and tasks on the Internet and in teachers' magazines and journals, and so on. Your main professional obligations in using these assessments are the same as those you apply when crafting your own: The results from them must (a) be valid for your intended interpretation and use and (b) have a degree of reliability appropriate to the importance of the decision(s) you will make using the results. In addition, many of the six specific responsibilities listed in the last section also apply to assessments you obtain from other sources.

Responsibility to Use Quality Assessment Materials In some ways, fulfilling your professional responsibilities when using others' assessment tools is more difficult than when you design your own. Others' assessment tasks often do not match the content, emphasis, vocabulary, or methods you used in teaching. If these differences are serious, using them will be unfair to your students and yield invalid results. In short, you violate your professional responsibility by using such assessments without carefully checking and improving their quality. Often you may need to rewrite or recraft others' assessment tools to suit your own classroom circumstances. You should improve a classroom assessment instead of using it "straight out of the box" if it does not match your teaching.

Publication Does Not Guarantee Quality You should be aware, too, that the publication of an assessment task or tool is no guarantee of the accuracy of its content or its quality as an assessment tool. Most of the assessment tasks available through the previously mentioned sources are not prepared or reviewed by professional assessment task developers. Many were not prepared personally by the author(s) of the curriculum materials or textbooks, but by others such as students of these authors. Consequently, many poor-quality assessment tasks are available to you. It would be irresponsible for you to use these assessment materials without carefully evaluating them, because you are putting your students' assessment results in jeopardy. Chapters 6 through 12 of this text help you evaluate these materials.

Serving on Assessment Selection Committees More experienced teachers sometimes serve on committees at the district or state level to review and select published assessments. Local education authorities should include teachers on assessment selection panels. The *CPR* states that persons providing such service have a special responsibility "to make sure that the assessments are appropriate for their intended use" (NCME, 1995, p. 5).

If you review the 10 specific professional responsibilities in Section 3 of the *CPR* (Appendix C), you will see that those engaged in assessment selection activities must have considerable knowledge of both the subject matter to be assessed and the technical principles of educational assessment. By studying the material in this and other textbooks on educational assessment you may learn much of this knowledge. (Chapters 16 and 18 of this book are devoted to procedures for evaluating published achievement tests.) The *Code of Fair Testing Practices in Education (Revised)* (Appendix B) contains additional principles and responsibilities for those who select and use published tests.

In addition, the *CPR* specifies that selectors of assessment procedures have a professional responsibility to consider the potential misuses and misinterpretations of an assessment procedure, as well as its potential for fulfilling the intended purposes. As discussed in Chapter 3, this relates to the question of validity. You cannot fulfill this professional responsibility if your school experience is narrow, if you have failed to pay attention to how other districts and states have used similar assessments, and if you are unaware of unintended consequences that may result. Thus, you should read widely to keep current about assessment and its educational use. Such reading is necessary for professional development if you intend to be involved in evaluating and selecting assessment tools as you fulfill your professional role outside the confines of your classroom. One source for learning about how other districts and states are using and misusing assessments is the news publication *Education Week*.

Responsibilities When Administering Assessments

Give Students Sufficient Information Usually, classroom assessments are meant to be opportunities for students to demonstrate their maximum performance. (See Chapter 14 for how to prepare students to do their best.) For students to perform at their maximum, they need basic information about the assessment, including (a) when it will be given, (b) the conditions under which they are expected to perform, (c) the content and abilities that will be assessed, (d) what the assessment will emphasize, (e) the standard or level of performance expected, (f) how the assessment performance will be scored, and (g) the effect the results of this assessment will have on any decisions (e.g., grades) you will make from the results. (The details of these information elements are described in Chapters 6 and 15.) It is your professional obligation to provide this information to students. If you do not give students the complete information as described in these seven points, you are not acting as a responsible professional.

Conduct the Administration Professionally A special concern in administering classroom assessments is the assessment environment you establish. Rushing students unnecessarily or making the assessment tasks too long for the available time creates unfair conditions if the goal is to have the student demonstrate maximum performance. Similarly, if you make students nervous by standing near them or chatting to them as they try to perform the assessment, you create unfair conditions. Sometimes a teacher will be rude, short, or gruff to a student who asks an honest question about the assessment tasks (especially when the teacher did not craft the task or its directions carefully and as a result created some ambiguity). Your professional responsibility is to provide "reasonable opportunities for individuals to ask questions about the assessment procedures or directions prior to and at appropriate times during administration" (NCME, 1995, p. 6).

Accommodate Students With Disabilities It is not unusual to have students with disabilities in your class. You have a professional and possibly legal responsibility to make reasonable accommodations to assess them properly. **Assessment accommodations** or **modifications** are changes in either the conditions or materials of assessment that allow the achievement of students with disabilities to be evaluated in the same areas as students who are evaluated with unmodified assessments. They are intended to make the assessment for students with disabilities more fair and more valid by "leveling the field" for all students. Learning and assessment should not be impeded by the student's disability.

Accommodations may be grouped into four types (National Center on Educational Outcomes, 2005):

- *Presentation of the test* (e.g., repeat directions, read aloud, use of larger bubbles, etc.)
- *Response of students* (e.g., mark answers in book, use reference aids, point, etc.)
- *Setting where test is administered* (e.g., study carrel, special lighting, separate room, etc.)
- *Timing/Scheduling* of the test administration (e.g., extended time, frequent breaks, etc.)

As a general rule, the accommodations necessary for a classroom learning environment would be appropriate accommodations for administering a classroom assessment. The classroom learning environment accommodations are described in a student's **individual education plan** (IEP), and teachers have a legal responsibility to implement those accommodations. Each student's IEP is developed by a child study team from the school and is approved by a student's parents. It specifies learning targets, appropriate teaching methods, and classroom accommodations for the student. Often assessment conditions and accommodations are specified, too. It is important to recognize that you should not introduce accommodations for the first time during the assessment (National Center on Educational Outcomes, 2005). They should be incorporated into the teaching and learning process.

You must treat each student as an individual rather than as a stereotype of a disability category. For example, not all blind students can read Braille, and not all deaf students can understand a signed language. The severity of students' disabilities varies widely, students' cognitive abilities vary widely, and many students have multiple disabilities. In addition, students may need accommodation for some domains of learning but not for others. The needs for accommodation found in their IEPs may not adequately describe the learning targets (domains) for which students need assessment accommodations (Reschly, 1993). Thus you should not rely on IEPs alone to determine the type of assessment accommodation a student needs. However, if an accommodation is stated in the IEP, there is a legal mandate to provide it.

Figure 5.2 describes some of the assessment accommodations or assessment modifications that may be appropriate for students with different disabilities. If your school does not have facilities or services for accommodating students, they may be available through your state or county itinerant service provider, a community agency that specializes in assisting persons with disabilities, or the office of services for students with disabilities at a local college or university.

Your school's administrators, and the school's special-service professionals share professional responsibility in this area. Nevertheless, as the person most in touch with the students on a daily basis, you have a special obligation to identify reasonable accommodations for classroom assessment activities and to seek the help of the appropriate school personnel.

Students with disabilities are often very aware of what accommodations they may or may not need to be assessed in your class. Whenever possible, you should consult with the students themselves before you impose an inappropriate assessment accommodation on them. Remember, however, that sometimes a student or a parent may believe that an accommodation will lead to a higher score. Getting higher scores is not the point. Rather, valid scores are the primary consideration. An accommodation should increase the validity of the scores so they reflect students' true achievements. As such, the scores after accommodation may not be higher, yet may be more valid. We discuss this point in more detail later in this chapter.

Standardized and Mandated Tests **Mandated tests** are tests required by school district policy or state law. **Standardized tests** are developed by professional agencies and use the same test materials and same administration procedures for all students. (See Chapter 16.) Your professional

FIGURE 5.2 Examples of types of modifications that may be appropriate for classroom assessment of students with disabilities.

Type of disability	Examples of possible assessment modifications
Blindness	Extended time, voice-recorded questions, Braille translation of assessment tasks, raised line drawing, a notetaker/scribe, computer, voice-recorded answers, reader to explain diagrams and read questions, scribe to write answers.
Low vision	Extended time, large print, magnifier for standard print, voice-recorded questions, special lighting, modified format for recording written answers, voice-recorded answers, reader to read questions and explain diagrams, scribe to write answers.
Hearing impairment	Extended time, notetaker, sign language interpreter, language-simplified questions, modified answer format (e.g., allowing answers to be made in American Sign Language, then having the answer interpreted into standard English).
Physical impairment	Extended time, scribe/notetaker, modified answer format (e.g., allowing oral responses), modified question format, computer, large surface desk.
Learning disabilities	Extended time, environment controls (e.g., freedom from extraneous noise, distractions), calculator, computer (instead of handwriting the answers), voice-recorded questions or a reader, scribe to write answers, modified answer format.
Health- and stress-related disabilities	Extended time, environment controls.

Note: No universal guidelines exist for when to use these modifications. Much depends on the purpose of the assessment and the way the scores are to be used. Within a disability category, not every student should be granted every modification. Types of modifications may differ, also, depending on whether the test is a classroom test or a standardized test. There are many students with multiple disabilities, and severity varies widely. Therefore you have hove a professional responsibility not to stereotype students but to treat them as individuals.

Source: Based on information in Algozzine (1993); King & Janow (1990); and Roberts (1994).

responsibilities in this area are similar to those you have in administering your own assessments, with additional responsibilities related to (a) fully informing students and parents about the testing and how the results will be used, (b) carefully following the administration instructions in the test manual, (c) maintaining security, and (d) maintaining testing conditions appropriate for maximum performance. These and other responsibilities are described in Section 4 of the *CPR* in Appendix C. Chapter 16 describes how to administer standardized tests in more detail.

You should be aware that the same modifications you make in your classroom assessments might not be appropriate for standardized and state-mandated tests. This is especially true if a student's score is to be interpreted using national norms. You should follow the test administration instructions from your school's test director and the state's guidelines. Since the passage of the NCLB Act, a state's accountability assessment program specifies what accommodations are permitted and the criteria students must meet in order for those accommodations to be permitted. Visit the National Center on Educational Outcomes Website (http://www.education.umn.edu/nceo/TopicAreas/Accommodations/StatesAccomm.htm) to see the latest requirements of each state.

Preparing Students to Take Standardized Tests A special concern for teachers is their professional responsibility in preparing students for standardized tests. Teachers feel pressure when they perceive potential personal consequences if students do not perform well. Nichols and Berliner (2005) document many unethical assessment practices in high-stakes testing programs. It is clearly

unethical for you to tell students the answers to questions they are unable to answer, give clues to students about which answer is correct, or to change student answers to improve their scores. If you see a colleague engaging in these or other unethical behaviors, you should report him or her to school authorities. A more complete discussion of your responsibilities in preparing students and administering standardized tests is given in Chapter 16 (see Figure 16.5). In Chapter 16, ethical test preparation practices are discussed also, drawing on analyses by Mehrens and Kaminski (1989) and Popham (1991). You should review the appropriate section of Chapter 16 at this time.

Responsibilities When Scoring Assessments

Your Own Classroom Assessments Your professional obligations are:

1. *To score student responses accurately* by using the appropriate tools such as scoring keys, scoring rubrics, checklists, or rating scales. Chapter 12 explains how to craft and use these accuracy-improving aids.

2. *To score students fairly* by removing from the scoring process anything that would cause unfair results. Examples of acting responsibly include using objective items and a scoring key when appropriate, having students place their names on the back of their essay examinations so you are not influenced by the name, scoring all student responses to one question before moving on to another, scoring performance tasks with a scoring rubric, periodically rescoring a sample of student responses as a check against your initial scoring, and having a colleague rescore a sample or all of your papers.

Suggestions for improving the fairness of scoring essay and performance assessments are given in Chapter 12.

3. *To provide students with feedback that helps them improve their learning.* Your professional responsibility goes beyond simply giving students the score or the letter grade earned on the assessment. You have a professional responsibility to show students what they did incorrectly and what their expected performance level is. A teacher who simply gives the score without even permitting students to see the questions they missed and explaining the correct answers is acting irresponsibly. Students must have the opportunity to learn from the assessment how they need to improve. Chapter 13 discusses how to craft assessments that detect why a student has failed to perform correctly. Final examinations may be problematic in this regard, because students and teachers may leave at the end of the term or the academic year. Nevertheless, if a student requests clarification and information, serious efforts should be made to provide it. Convenience is not the primary criterion here.

4. *To explain to students the rationale for the correct answers and for the scoring rubrics you use.* By explaining how you arrived at the score and what standards and criteria you used, you teach students what is important to learn about the learning target. This clarifies the learning target and teaches students the standards they are expected to meet.

5. *To give students the opportunity to review their evaluations individually.* Students have a right to know how their responses were marked and evaluated. They have a right to be assured that scoring was done accurately and fairly. You have the professional responsibility to go over your evaluation of a student's response with a student who requests it.

6. *To correct errors in scoring and make necessary adjustments as quickly as possible.* Because you are human, you will make scoring errors, even if you use multiple-choice tests and a scoring stencil. You should not be threatened by a request from a student or a parent to rescore an assessment. Should you discover scoring errors (even if no one else discovers them), honesty dictates that you correct all errors and readjust the scores accordingly. This should be done in a timely manner.

7. *To score and return results in a timely manner.* For feedback to be effective, it must be timely. Further, failure to return results as quickly as possible does not allow a student to effectively monitor her progress or permit the student to adjust her study strategy. Slowness in returning assessment results does not give you or parents enough time to provide remediation to a student who is having difficulty. As a general rule, you should return students' results within a week or two after the assessment occurs—sooner, if possible. You do not act in a professionally responsible manner when you delay returning results for longer periods without good reason.

Standardized and Mandated Tests Occasionally you may be asked to score standardized tests or other tests mandated by your school district or state. In such cases, *you*

have a responsibility to follow the scoring procedures given in the test manual or in other materials. Read these materials beforehand and be sure that you understand how to apply the scoring guidelines. Teachers frequently make mistakes in applying scoring keys to multiple-choice items and when looking up norm-referenced scores (e.g., percentile ranks or grade equivalents) in the tables accompanying the test materials. A common error is to use the norm tables for the wrong time of year (e.g., referring to the fall norms table when the test was administered in the spring). *It is your professional responsibility to ensure that your scoring is accurate and to check the quality of your work.*

Many times teachers will be required to score open-ended tasks, performance tasks, and portfolios for mandated state assessment programs. Districts or states requiring teachers to do this have the obligation to provide high-quality scoring rubrics and to train teachers to use them with high degrees of consistency. As a teacher, your responsibility is to learn how to use the rubrics and to apply them fairly and consistently. Using scoring rubrics is discussed in Chapter 12.

In some states, schools may receive financial rewards or negative sanctions depending on their performance on state assessments. For example, a school may be declared "at risk," its principal replaced, and an outside team brought in to run it. In some communities real estate agencies publish neighborhood school assessment results. Pressures are thus put on teachers to raise scores by inappropriate test preparation practices. (See Chapter 16 for details.) It should go without saying that you have a professional responsibility to score and report scores honestly. Unfortunately, some teachers feel pressured to report the scores as more favorable than they are. It is irresponsible for educational authorities to create a situation that pressures teachers (or makes them feel pressured) into reporting high scores. However, it is still your responsibility to resist this pressure, score students' responses honestly, and report the actual results. Some communities may turn over the operation of a school to a private profit-making organization. Sometimes the organization's profits depend on the students' performance on standardized tests. This "payment by results" situation may increase pressures for teachers and administrators to prepare students inappropriately for the tests or to be less than honest in scoring them.

Responsibilities When Interpreting and Using Assessment Results

Results From Your Own Assessments Your professional obligations in this area are:

1. *To interpret students' performance on one assessment by first considering the learning targets you taught and emphasized in your teaching.* Students should be held accountable for

the learning targets you taught. When you emphasize particular content or a particular learning target, you communicate its importance to students. It would be irresponsible and perhaps deceptive to base a large part of students' evaluations on their performance in areas that you did not emphasize.

2. *To interpret students' performance on one assessment by considering the results from other assessments.* No single assessment procedure is comprehensive enough to cover every important learning target. You should allow students multiple opportunities and modes to express their abilities with respect to the curriculum learning targets. You act irresponsibly if you base your evaluation of a student only on his performance on one assessment.

3. *To interpret a student's performance by realizing the limitations of the assessment procedure you used.* Not only does a single assessment procedure lack comprehensiveness, it is also not perfectly reliable. A student's score would likely change if you gave an assessment again tomorrow or next week, or if you used slightly different questions or content. If someone else marked the responses, the grader may come up with different marks. You act irresponsibly, therefore, if you do not consider these limitations when using your own assessment procedure. For example, you act irresponsibly if you tell a student that her grade depends completely on her test performance, or if you do not seriously consider rescoring after an honest query about how you marked a paper.

4. *To help students and parents properly interpret the assessment results.* Parents and students may not understand the limitations of tests and other assessments. They may not understand, for example, the limitations of your classroom assessments resulting from their low reliability. You must communicate these limitations and place results of all the assessments into their proper interpretive context.

5. *To help students and parents understand the consequences of improperly interpreting your classroom assessment results.* Some parents make too much of a test score or the result of a single assessment. Others do not see the pattern of success or failure that develops over time. You act responsibly when you help them understand the negative consequences of their wrong interpretations (e.g., discouraging a student's further learning) and the positive consequences of a correct interpretation (a steady improvement over the course of the marking period).

6. *To interpret a student's performance as a way of evaluating his attainment of learning targets rather than as a weapon for punishing or controlling students' behavior.* Although upcoming assessments may motivate students, they are poor weapons for controlling student behavior. You act irresponsibly if you threaten students with tests or try to manipulate them through some assessment procedure.

7. *To keep classroom assessment results confidential and to protect students' rights of privacy.* You act irresponsibly when you post students' names and assessment results on the classroom wall, or when you reveal your students' results to other teachers who have no right to know them. Sometimes a parent will ask how a neighbor's child performed in relation to the parent's own child. You should not honor this request even if it is for the relative comparison instead of the exact score.

Standardized and Mandated Test Results   Because external tests do not exactly match the curriculum learning targets and your teaching emphasis, they often are misinterpreted by students, parents, and the public, who are unaware of the impact of school factors on the test results. Further, the test results are often reported as norm-referenced scores (e.g., percentile ranks, grade equivalents), many of which are not easy to interpret properly. Your school administrators and/or state education authorities have serious obligations and responsibilities to properly interpret the results and to see to it that improper interpretations are avoided or at least minimized. Section 6 of the *CPR* (Appendix C) lists these responsibilities. Many of them apply to the classroom teacher as well. You should review these responsibilities at this time.

Because standardized test results are often sent home through the teacher, teachers are often the first people contacted when parents have questions. For you to fulfill the professional responsibilities listed in Section 6 of the *CPR*, you need to understand reliability, validity, norm-referencing, criterion-referencing, and standardized tests. Chapters 3, 4, 16, 17, 18, and 19 are devoted to these topics. Studying them will help you fulfill your responsibilities in this area.

Responsibilities When Communicating Assessment Results

Communicating assessment results means communicating the proper interpretations of the results to students, parents, and school authorities. Your responsibility here is to develop proper means of communicating correct interpretations. You must determine the level of understanding of the students, parents, or school officials and tailor your communication to that level. It may involve teaching a parent the meaning of certain types of scores or assessment concepts. It would not be professionally responsible, for example, to use educational measurement jargon (e.g., *percentiles, T-scores, reliability, validity*) with parents unless they understood its meaning.

In addition to the level of communication, you have an obligation to communicate frequently. You have a professional responsibility to establish and follow a regular communication schedule to report student progress to parents. Your school may have a policy to communicate progress to parents when grades are sent home. These policies usually specify minimum communication patterns. You may need more frequent communication depending on the community and the students you teach. However, you should not overdo it: Daily progress reports may be inappropriate for students beyond preschool.

STUDENTS' RIGHTS AS TEST TAKERS

Your school district and state department of education will have assessment and school-record policies and procedures covering students' and parents' rights. There are two main issues: participation and accommodation (Salvia & Ysseldyke, 2004). **Participation** means that students with disabilities have the right, and sometimes the obligation, to be assessed, including taking part in accountability assessment programs. In the past, students with disabilities were often excluded from taking accountability tests because officials believed including them would lower the test averages. This lowering, it was believed, would have impact on funding and the public image of a district or a school. Thus, when students with disabilities were not served well by existing school programs, their exclusion resulted in schools not being accountable for their failure to learn the state standards. Accommodations or assessment modifications are changes in either the conditions or materials of assessment that allow the achievement of students with disabilities to be evaluated in the same areas as students who are evaluated with unmodified assessments.

Federal laws now cover matters of participation and accommodation that apply to school districts and states receiving federal funds. These include the Fifth and Fourteenth Amendments to the U.S. Constitution, Section 504 of the Rehabilitation Act of 1973 (Public Law 93–112), the Family Educational Rights and Privacy Act of 1974 (FERPA; Public Law 93–380), the Education of All Handicapped Children Act of 1975 (Public Law 94–142), the Education of the Handicapped Act Amendment of 1986 (Public Law 99–457), the Individuals with Disabilities Education Act Amendments of 1990 (IDEA; Public Law 101–476), the Rehabilitation Act of 1973 (Public Law 93–112), and the Americans with Disabilities Act of 1992 (ADA; Public Law 101–336), 1997 Amendments to the Individuals with Disabilities Education Act (Public Law 105–17), and the No Child Left Behind Act of 2001 (NCLB; Public Law 107–110). Figure 5.3 summarizes some of the student and parental rights under the laws.

Whether or not there is a legal requirement to do so, professional ethics may suggest that some principles underlying the rights summarized in Figure 5.3 can apply to classroom assessment practices. You should check with the superintendent of your school district for information on your state's requirements regarding student and family rights. Your school should also have its own written policy on (a) maintenance and release of assessment results, (b) release of nonconfidential information, (c) nondiscrimination, and (d) representational consent information.

In addition to legal requirements, professional organizations are working on statements of test-takers' rights. The *CPR*, for example, suggests several areas for which test takers (e.g., students) have rights. The Test-Takers' Rights Working Group (1999) of the Joint Committee on Testing Practices has prepared **test-takers' rights** statements. A test taker has the right of: (a) being informed of the rights and responsibilities of a test taker; (b) being treated with respect and courtesy regardless of personal characteristics and orientations; (c) being tested with tests that are appropriate for the purpose for which they are to be used and that have been developed to meet professional standards; (d) receiving an explanation prior to being tested about the purpose for testing, who will receive the test results, and what the plans are for using the results; (e) being told what accommodations are available and then being tested with appropriate accommodations; (f) being informed in advance about when the test will be administered, when the examinee will receive the results, and the cost of testing; (g) having the test administered and interpreted by appropriately trained persons who follow professional codes of responsibility; (h) being told the consequences of not taking a test, not completing a test, or canceling the scores on a test already taken; (i) being given an explanation of the results of testing in easily understood language and in a timely manner; (j) having test results kept confidential within the limits of law; and (k) being able to present his or her concerns about the testing process or results and having those concerns reviewed seriously. The Joint Committee on Testing Practices, whose subcommittee prepared this "bill of rights for test takers" consists of representatives from several professional associations: American Educational Research Association, the American Psychological Association, the National Council on Measurement in Education, the American Counseling Association, the American Speech-Language-Hearing Association, the National Association of School Psychologists, and the National Association of Test Directors. Teachers should be aware of these associations' test-takers' rights efforts and consider their own assessment practices in relation to them. Among the major issues for a classroom teacher are fairness to each student, respecting students, opening up student evaluation processes, and correcting errors in student evaluations as soon as possible.

STUDENTS' RESPONSIBILITIES

The theme of this chapter is your professional responsibilities regarding assessment. Students also have responsibilities in an assessment situation. Students have the responsibility of studying and preparing for tests and examinations in their classes. The same Test-Takers' Rights Working Group (1999) that prepared test-takers' rights has prepared a list of test-takers' responsibilities. These include the responsibility to: (a) attend to explanations of one's rights and

FIGURE 5.3   Some student and parent testing and school records rights mandated by federal legislation. (Not all of these are absolute rights under the cited legislation. Some exceptions may be granted by the courts. See the footnotes.)

I. **The Family Educational Rights and Privacy Act of 1974**
   A. **Right to inspect records**
      1. Right to see all of a child's test records that are part of the child's official school record.
      2. Right to have test results explained.
      3. Written requests to see test results must be honored in 45 days.
      4. If a child is over 18, only the child has the right to the record.
   B. **Right to privacy:** Rights here limit access to the official school records (including test scores) to those who have legitimate educational needs.
      Additional Information: Family Educational Rights and Privacy Act (FERPA) Office, U.S. Department of Education, 400 Maryland Avenue, S.W., Washington, DC 20201.

II. **The individuals with Disabilities Education Act Amendments of 1991 (IDEA) and the Rehabilitation Act of 1973**
   A. **Right to parent involvement**
      1. The first time a child is considered for special education placement, the parents must be given written notice in their native language, and their permission must be obtained to test the child.
      2. Right to challenge the accuracy of test scores used to plan the child's program.
      3. Right to file a written request to have the child tested by other than the school staff.
      4. Right to request a hearing if not satisfied with the school's decision as to what are the best services for the child.
   B. **Right to fairness in testing[a,b]**
      1. Right of the child to be tested in the language spoken at home
      2. Tests given for placement cannot discriminate on the basis of race, sex, or socioeconomic status. The tests cannot be culturally biased.
      3. Right to be tested with a test that meets special needs (e.g., in Braille, orally, etc.).
      4. No single test score can be used to make special education decisions. Right to be tested in several different ways.
      Additional Information: National Institute on Disabilities and Rehabilitation, U.S. Department of Education, Switzer Building, Room 3132, 330 C Street, S.W., Washington, DC 20202-2524.

III. **The Americans with Disabilities Act of 1990 (ADA)[b]**
   A. **Right to accommodated testing**
      1. Right of a qualified person with disabilities to be tested in a way that he or she can understand what is being asked and in a way that he or she can respond.
      2. The test administrator is expected to provide all the necessary test locations, services, aids, or accommodations at no extra charge to the examinee.
      Additional Information: National Institute on Disabilities and Rehabilitation, U.S. Department of Education, Switzer Building, Room 3132, 330 C Street, S.W., Washington, DC 20202-2524. (Also contact your regional ADA Technical Assistance Center.)

Notes: (a) It may be argued in court that limited English proficiency is not a student disability. Rather, it is a temporary condition that can be overcome by instruction and study. It may be reasonable to treat English language limitations separately from disability issues (Phillips, personal communication, 2002).

(b) As interpreted by the courts, IDEA and ADA require "reasonable accommodations" to adjust extraneous factors affecting test outcomes, and not modifications that alter the skills and abilities tested.

Sources: Adapted from "The Americans with Disabilities Act: Implications for Measurement," by R. J. Fischer, 1994. *Educational Measurement: Issues and Practice, 13*(4), pp. 17–26, 37, *Your Child and Testing,* by E. B. Herndon, 1980. Washington, DC: National Institute of Education and Phillips (1994; personal communication, 1999, 2001).

---

responsibilities as a test taker; (b) be respectful and courteous toward others during testing; (c) ask questions and clarify before the testing when uncertain about the purpose of testing, the manner in which it will be administered, what one will be expected to do, and how the results will be reported and used; (d) attend to instructions that are presented in writing or orally; (e) inform the examiner in advance of what accommodations or modifications are needed; (f) inform the examiner in advance of any current illness that may affect one's performance; (g) inform the examiner if one had difficulty understanding the language of the test; (h) learn the date, time, and place of the test; (i) pay for the test if necessary; (j) arrive for the testing on time, with the requisite materials, and prepared to begin the test; (k) follow the examiner's instructions; (l) respond and behave honestly during the examination; (m) understand the consequences of not taking the test and be prepared to accept those consequences if one chooses not to take it; (n) tell the appropriate persons if one believes that the testing conditions adversely affected one's performance; (o) find out about the confidentiality of the results; and (p) present any concerns one has about the testing process or the results to the appropriate persons in a timely manner.

Students who cheat are dishonest and behave unethically. Plagiarism in the form of copying homework or purchasing papers for projects and other take-home assignments should not be tolerated. Parents, teachers, school administrators, and students should work collaboratively to understand the seriousness of cheating and other forms of intellectual dishonesty. School policies and due-process procedures for handling dishonesty should be written and taught to students before enforcing them. "While teachers must do their part, they also have the right to expect ethical behavior from their students and to not be pressured to lower standards, water down courses, or give high grades for minimal work" (Phillips, personal communication, May 1999).

SECRECY, ACCESS, PRIVACY, CONFIDENTIALITY, AND THE TEACHER

Secrecy and Access

Secrecy and test security have been the hallmarks of the testing industry since the late 1920s and early 1930s, when large-scale abuse of testing abounded. Withholding test information—either about the items on the test or the exact score(s) a student attained—often was justified on the grounds that **access to assessment results** would do more harm than good. For example:

- A student might attempt to memorize only specific answers ("a" or "b") rather than focusing on mastery of the general skills the test was designed to measure; this behavior would distort the measurement of knowledge and ability.

- Tests that measure highly sensitive and personal characteristics may require a high degree of professional training to interpret the scores; examinees lacking this training might cause themselves harm by misinterpreting the results.

- Releasing test items might result in their being used by unqualified examiners who would misinterpret scores, causing examinees harm.

- Releasing copies of old forms of a test might require the test developer to spend unreasonable sums of money to develop new forms, assuming that new forms of the test could, in fact, be developed.

In recent years, however, the public has become aware that *some test abuses have resulted from such secrecy*. For example:

- Professionals themselves vary in qualifications and have, in fact, misinterpreted tests or abused results.

- Decisions made about educational placement, ostensibly on the basis of valid and objective test results, have later been discovered to be biased, misinterpreted, or otherwise invalid.

- Errors in scoring that could not be detected occurred because those having the greatest stake in their accuracy—the students and parents—could not scrutinize the tests.

- Although some tests publicly were declared to assess learned skills and abilities, examinees were unable to check their content to decide whether their preparation had been adequate or whether they should seek special remediation or training.

- Although professionals may have interpreted assessment results properly, records were often open to other persons, who used the results either unprofessionally or in a manner unauthorized by and detrimental to the examinee.

Problems such as these spawned a renewed public interest in the ethics of secrecy and the right of students and parents to know. A number of state and federal laws and court decisions have arisen, mandating greater access for students and parents to assessment results and toward greater participation in the assessment-based decision-making process. Figure 5.3 lists some of these access and participation rights under federal legislation. Your own school district should have written policies regarding students' and families' rights regarding access to records and assessment results.

Access to Student Data for Research Purposes

Another point concerns the use of records for research. Usually, obtaining assessment results for research purposes is not considered a violation of privacy provided the identity of the student remains anonymous. The Department of Health and Human Services issues regulations protecting the welfare of human subjects in research projects. Although you are not a researcher, you should be sensitive to **ethical principles** of privacy and confidentiality because you may need to collect data to use on your research projects for graduate courses and degrees, and you may have to protect the rights of students under your care when others (within and outside the school) request student information.

Purging and Correcting School Records

Another issue is the **purging** of outdated files and other student records and correcting erroneous information. Certainly, if you give an incorrect grade you should correct the affected student's record. Sometimes the teacher (or others) will score a standardized test incorrectly, discovering this fact after the information has been entered on the record. This will necessitate changing the record also. Computerized databases are relatively easy to update, despite the often-used excuse by some school officials that it is "too late because the data are in the computer." You have a professional responsibility to correct mistakes in the records. Information such as your anecdotal records should be purged when it is no longer necessary (usually within a year or two). Some schools have policies for systematic purging of student records. Others may depend on a student's parents to come in and periodically review the records for unnecessary, damaging, or erroneous information.

Privacy, Confidentiality, and the Teacher

An important question is whether a student has the right to expect certain information to be held in confidence. **Privacy** and **confidentiality** affect you in several ways. In the classroom itself, for example, teachers sometimes keep charts or post students' progress. Other teachers have students mark each other's papers and call out the marks for reporting. Such public displays may or may not be in the form of grades. These practices raise the question of whether the evaluations should be confidential. The ethical nature of confidentiality may or may not be covered by existing laws. For example, the Supreme Court ruled that peer marking and calling out peers' marks to the teacher was not forbidden by the Family Educational Rights and Privacy Act (FERPA), even though the parents objected to the teacher's practice, because that act referred only to official school records (*Owasso Independent School District No. I0011 vs. Falvo*, 2002).

Another example is the practice of keeping scores, grades, and anecdotal comments in a student's official school records. Ethical questions arise about who has authorized access to these files. Teachers and certain other persons have legitimate rights to obtain necessary information from them to help teach a given student. Many schools have forms or other means to keep records of who has used a student's records and for what purposes. Usually a student's test scores and other records cannot be transferred to another institution without that student's (or parents') written authorization. Unlike the informal peer-grading situation cited in the preceding paragraph, the FERPA covers official school records.

Wagging tongues in teachers' lounges are still another way confidentiality can be violated. It is your professional responsibility not to use the teachers' lounge as a place to gossip and spread confidential information about students.

Informed Consent

Privacy is not violated if persons give consent to others to obtain and use personal information. Without going into a detailed ethical analysis of the matter, we shall state that there are at least four levels of consent (McCormick, 1974; O'Donnell, 1974): informed consent, presumed consent, implied consent, and proxy consent. **Informed consent** is obtained directly from the student and presumes that the student, in giving that consent, has received and understands the following information (Boruch, 1971): (a) the exact nature and extent to which personal information will remain anonymous, (b) to what extent participation is voluntary rather than required, (c) who (or what agency) is requesting the information and for what purpose, and (d) what will happen to the information after it is collected (including whether and/or when it will be destroyed).

Obviously, few young students will be able to understand the implications of all of this information, so their consent may not be truly informed. Often consent must come from a *proxy*, such as a parent or a school official. The extent to which school officials can grant permission for collecting and using pupil information will depend, among other things, on the degree to which such consent is *presumed* or *implied* by the fact that students are entrusted to their care. This is sometimes referred to as *representational consent*.

Flagged Scores May Violate Confidentiality

Another serious issue that arises when making accommodations and interpretations is *identification*. Should we identify (*flag*) in the school record and score reports those students for whom accommodations were made? In effect, this flagging of scores means that you would identify the person as disabled and perhaps even identify the nature of the disability. This information is generally considered to be confidential and private (Phillips, 1994). Persons with disabilities may fear that such disclosure makes them vulnerable to prejudice or misinformed test interpretations by persons who might use the assessment results. Oftentimes, assessment results used for one purpose are later used in different circumstances. Unfortunately, once the scores and flags are on the record, there is little control over how they might be misused in the future. Others might argue that an employer or a postsecondary institution has a right to know whether an applicant needs an accommodation, and therefore flagging the assessment results is necessary and appropriate (Phillips, 1994). Others argue that a test with accommodations provides an unfair advantage to students with disabilities or that accommodations make a test score less valid. Those holding these latter positions say that scores should be flagged. A number of admissions tests such as the Graduate Management Admissions Test, the SAT, and the ACT have stopped flagging tests taken with accommodations (Sireci, 2005). The main issues about whether to flag scores of students with disabilities who take tests with accommodations is the validity of the scores. We discussed the validity of accommodated scores in Chapter 3.

LEGALLY DEFENSIBLE ASSESSMENT ACCOMMODATION POLICIES
Only Reasonable Accommodations May Be Required

As you may have inferred from the preceding discussion, issues of accommodation and inclusion are controversial. They may also result in legal action against a school district or a state. Because the Americans with Disabilities Act requires reasonable accommodations when they are necessary in the workplace, educational authorities must develop accommodation policies and procedures that preserve assessment validity in the broad sense, are fair and respectful of rights of persons with disabilities, and comply with the law. Recently, the NCLB Act requires necessary accommodations or alternative assessment for students with disabilities so they can participate in a state's accountability assessment program.

A related issue concerns the NCLB Act requirement that 95% of the students with disabilities be tested on grade-level standards in a state's accountability assessment program. This requirement is in conflict with the IDEA legislation that permits the development of an individual education plan. That IEP may result in students with disabilities being taught a curriculum that is below their grade level. Thus, one law, the NCLB Act, requires students to be tested at levels for which they have not been taught, but their curriculum has been authorized by another law, IDEA (Phillips, 2005). States are now granted some limited flexibility in adjusting content and performance standards for students with severe cognitive impairments (U.S. Department of Education, 2005).

Don't Cater to Only One Advocacy Group

Educational authorities are urged to seek the advice of their legal counselors and of advocates of persons with disabilities as they draw up accommodation policies. Authorities should keep in mind, however, that because of the large differences in students' abilities among (and within) disability categories, consulting only one advocacy group is likely to yield inappropriate policies and practices. For example, the reasonable accommodations required for students with mental retardation are likely to be quite inappropriate for students with hearing losses who have no cognitive disabilities. You should be aware, too, that although the law may require "reasonable accommodations," exactly what that means is unclear. The teacher, the school officials, and the student (or parents) will need to base accommodations on reasonableness and validity, not on a parent's negotiating skill (Phillips, personal communications, 1999).

Suggestions to Improve Legal Defensibility of Accommodations

The following suggestions are adapted from Phillips (1994), who is both an assessment specialist and a lawyer. Phillips's suggestions are for a state or school district program. Her suggestions help make the process more legally defensible. You are urged to consult the reference before attempting to implement these suggestions.

1. Prepare a written set of instructions for how a student (parent) should request an assessment accommodation. Protect students' due-process rights by making sure students and parents are aware of these instructions.

2. Prepare a standard form for requesting accommodations, and describe clearly how to return the form and what the deadline is.

3. Require students (parents) requesting accommodations to document their disability. Require:
    a. Verification of the qualifications and disability-related experience of the professional who is describing the disability.
    b. A letter signed by the qualified professional specifying the type(s) of accommodations required.
    c. The professional to provide you with test results and the procedures used to make the diagnosis.
    d. A verification that the professional conducted an in-person evaluation within the past 12 months.
    e. Additional documentation for questionable cases, including documentation of the professional's qualifications and the requesting of student's medical records.

4. Determine if the student's IEP requires a particular accommodation.

5. If you will flag the scores resulting from the accommodated assessment, notify the students and/or the parents of this in writing. Require them to sign statements that they have been notified.

6. Designate a single professional staff member to review and act on all requests. Call in a qualified consultant to handle borderline cases.

7. Develop general guidelines for how to accommodate persons with similar disability patterns, but act only on an individual, case-by-case basis. (You will want to treat similarly situated persons consistently, but because there are so many individual differences within a category, you need to work with students directly.)

8. Designate a professional staff member to collect data that can be used to assess the validity of various accommodations for different types of students. Use this validity data to refine policies and procedures.

9. If you deny an accommodation request, provide for a speedy review of the case. Be sure all information and documentation are available to the reviewer(s) and that the reviewer(s) is (are) qualified to evaluate the decision.

10. Develop a formal appeal procedure and a process for the student whose accommodation is denied. Require the student, parent, or guardian to make a written request to appeal. Allow for new evidence and for representation by legal counsel.

11. Students who are protected by the Individuals with Disabilities Education Act of 1991, Section 504 of

the Rehabilitation Act of 1973, and the Americans with Disabilities Act of 1990 probably cannot be asked to pay for additional services and accommodations.

12. Institutionalize or legalize your accommodation policies so they can be sustained as personnel changes occur over the years. Do not depend on the goodwill of one person to implement the policies.

Caveat The preceding suggestions are designed to protect educational authorities and assessment organizations from legal action while ensuring due process for students with disabilities. They appear to place a heavy responsibility on the student and his or her legal guardian for documenting disabilities and justifying needed accommodations. They also appear to be set in an adversarial context, rather than a conciliatory or cooperative context.

Classroom Versus External Assessments In your classroom, you need not be so formal. However, be sure to use assessment modifications in a legally appropriate way, as outlined in this chapter. If parents challenge your assessment and student evaluation practices, you will then be able to defend your practices within the legal guidelines summarized in this chapter.

TESTING CHALLENGED IN COURT

Plaintiffs seeking legal redress for real and/or perceived violations of rights may bring testing programs to the courts. Notable among legal issues are race or gender discrimination, a test's contribution toward segregation in schools and other disparate impact issues, unfairness of particular tests, and the violation of due process—such as failure to give sufficient notice for a test or failure to give opportunities for hearings and appeals. Educational testing practices resulting in court cases include minimum-competency testing programs designed to control graduation, teacher certification tests designed to control who can teach in a state, and college admissions testing.

Court cases sometimes involve class-action suits in which the plaintiffs represent an entire group of persons, and the judgments handed down by the court apply to all members. This was true, for example, in the *Debra P. vs. Turlington* (1979, 1981) case, which challenged Florida's minimum-competency test. The court recognized the following classes: "(a) . . . all present and future twelfth grade public school students in the State of Florida who have failed or who hereafter fail the SSAT-II [i.e., the State Student Assessment, Part II]. (b) . . . all present and future twelfth grade African-American public school students in the State of Florida who have failed or who hereafter fail the SSAT-II. (c) . . . all present and future twelfth grade African-American public school students in Hillsborough County, Florida who have failed or who hereafter fail the SSAT-II" (Fisher, 1980, p. 7).

Psychometric Issues Presented in Court

Some issues raised in court focus on the technical aspects of testing. We refer to these as **psychometric issues**. The following aspects of testing have been questioned in courts in connection with high-stakes testing such as graduation tests (Fisher, 1980; Langenfeld & Crocker, 1994; Mehrens & Popham, 1992; Phillips, 1994, personal communication, 2001). They appear, however, to apply to many court cases involving other tests.

1. *Test security.* Plaintiffs and special interest groups may want to know the content of the test, sometimes before the test is used. Related to this issue are matters of test security, applicable state and federal "sunshine" laws, and "truth-in-testing" legislation.

2. *AERA, APA, and NCME Standards.* The AERA, APA, and NCME (1999) *Standards* were mentioned earlier in this chapter. The *Uniform Guidelines on Employee Selection and Procedures* (Equal Employment Opportunity Commission [EEOC], Civil Service Commission, Department of Labor, & Department of Justice, 1978) are used also when adverse impact is an issue. These guidelines may not strictly apply to student testing and to teacher certification (Phillips, personal communication, 1999). The EEOC guidelines apply only to employment testing. Student testing is covered under the Fourteenth Amendment of the U.S. Constitution. Some legal opinion holds that a state that requires licensing is not doing so as an employer. Although not a legal document, the *Standards* do represent a consensus of professional opinion and values as to what constitutes good test development practices. Plaintiffs sometimes use these *Standards* as a basis for arguing against the quality or use of a particular test or testing program.

3. *Reliability.* (See Chapter 4.) Plaintiffs may challenge either the magnitude of a test's reliability data or the appropriateness of using particular techniques for ascertaining reliability.

4. *Validity and opportunity to learn.* (See Chapter 3.) With educational tests designed to certify minimum competence, the relationship of content on the test to content taught in the classroom is likely to be challenged. (This is sometimes called *curriculum relevance* or *curricular validity*.)

5. *Test development procedures.* Every stage of test development may be challenged in a particular case: the test plan; the qualifications of the item writers; the correspondence between items and objectives; the readability level; the correct and alternative options to multiple-choice items; the tryout and field procedures; the correctness of the scanning and reporting; and steps taken to reduce or minimize culture, race, gender, and/or regional bias.

6. *Passing scores.* Several methods for setting passing scores exist, all of which plaintiffs may attack. Such attacks may not succeed if a large group, legally empowered to do

so, sets the passing score by following acceptable standard-setting practices (see Jaeger, 1989, 1990; Mehrens & Popham, 1992).

7. *Mechanical issues.* Plaintiffs can criticize mechanical aspects of the test, such as the quality of instructions and directions for administering, the ink color, the print size (some states have laws on this for certain grade levels), and other physical features of the test.

8. *Accommodations for persons with disabilities.* Plaintiffs with mental or physical disabilities can challenge a test if appropriate accommodations are denied. Accommodations include access to the testing room as well as accommodations such as those listed in Figure 5.2.

9. *Testing using English.* Plaintiffs may challenge a test if it is not in the first language of the student, especially if the student has had only a limited opportunity to learn English.

Nonpsychometric Issues Presented in Court

Nonpsychometric issues that are the basis for legal redress in the use of tests include:

1. *Legal authority.* Plaintiffs may challenge a test or testing program, not so much on the basis of whether the test is of high quality, but whether the program has been legally authorized or whether individuals making the decisions about testing have the legal authority to do so.

2. *Segregation in the schools.* Here the challenge can be that the tests are biased against the lower scoring group and/or that they reflect and perpetuate past segregation in the schools, which lowered the quality of education. Thus, the plaintiffs should not be denied access or certification based on test results. (Test bias is discussed later in this chapter.)

3. *Equal protection.* If tests are used for sanctions and rewards, the distribution should allow schools with high percentages of minorities or poor students the same opportunity to achieve these rewards as schools with low numbers of minorities or poor students (Parkes & Stevens, 2002).

4. *Property interests in a diploma.* The theory is that "the student has the right to expect that a diploma will be forthcoming assuming that all courses were passed, and any substantive change in the graduation requirements cannot take place without due notice to the student" (Fisher, 1980, p. 4). In a landmark case (*Debra P. vs. Turlington,* 1984) concerning the Florida minimum-competency graduation test, the court held that "a diploma is a property right subject to the Fourteenth Amendment protections" (Phillips, 1994, p. 108).

5. *Due process.* This could be either substantive or procedural **due process**. *Substantive due process* concerns the appropriateness of the requirement (e.g., passing the

teacher-certification test) and the purpose (e.g., maintaining high-quality teaching). *Procedural due process* focuses on how fairly the examinee was treated. Fairness includes notifying the examinee in advance of the requirement, test date, and so forth; giving opportunity for hearings and appeals; and making sure that the hearing is conducted fairly. One recent due-process case, *GI Forum vs. Texas Education Agency* (2000), was decided in the U.S District Court. It centered on whether the use of the *Texas Assessment of Academic Skills* as a graduation requirement adversely affected Texas minority students and violated their due-process rights of the law under the U.S. Constitution. The court upheld the use of the test for such purposes.

The No Child Left Behind Act of 2001 (Public Law 107–110) requires states to impose sanctions and rewards on schools based on their test performance over time. A few of the due-process legal challenges that could arise are (Parkes & Stevens, 2002):

a. *Lack of adequate notice*–1 to 4 years may not be enough time to implement the sanctions.
b. *Holding schools accountable for their demographics* rather than the performance of teachers–punishing schools with high percentages of poor children, for example.
c. *Lack of justification for what constitutes the achievement index* and the weights that the components are given in the reward or sanction decision.

6. *Stigmatization.* The results of the test may be used to deny a diploma or certificate or to label a person. A plaintiff's challenge may be that such occurrences that result from testing are illegal because they stigmatize a person, especially if the case can be linked to ethnic or gender bias.

Notice that in matters of test use and abuse, the application of particular laws is seldom clear. A court decision depends on the particular circumstances surrounding a given case, the evidence brought to bear in the case, and the opinion of the judge and jury involved.

BIAS IN EDUCATIONAL ASSESSMENT
Definitions of Bias

One of the concerns surrounding the suitability of assessments for various decisions is whether a particular assessment is biased against particular groups. It is not always clear exactly what "biased assessment" means, because many definitions of **assessment** or **test bias** exist in the media and the professional literature. Sometimes persons who discuss bias have more than one type of bias in mind, although they may not distinguish between types. The following catalog of assessment bias definitions is adapted from Flaugher (1978).

Assessment Bias As Mean Differences

Many use the **bias as mean differences** approach. According to this approach, an assessment is biased against a particular group when the average (mean) score of that group falls short of the average score of another group. (The mean is explained in Appendix I.) Most assessment specialists would not subscribe to this definition of bias because average differences in groups' performances could represent real differences in the level of their attainment, rather than an artificial difference. Bias implies "unfair" or "unjust." Thus, *differences as differences* may not represent bias. If one group receives an inferior education or has been socialized away from learning or developing certain skills, a test measuring these things will likely result in lower average scores for this group versus another group that has had the opportunity or encouragement to learn.

Although differences in groups' means do not necessarily indicate a biased assessment procedure, one should still try to explain why the groups differ. Such differences may indicate that the groups have been treated unfairly (not given equal opportunity to acquire the abilities assessed), and thus they have developed different ability levels. However, such mean differences in groups may mean that the assessment procedure is biased, too. In other words, several factors can cause a mean difference between groups, including a biased assessment. Unfortunately, knowing only that such differences exist does not explain why they exist.

Assessment Bias As Differential Item Functioning (DIF)

Instead of studying average total score differences among groups, some assessment developers study differences at the individual test item or assessment task level. An individual test question may favor one group over another; but the assessment, as a whole, may not show any difference. The approach here is not to look simply at overall average differences in an item's performance. Rather, it involves looking at whether persons of the same ability performed differently on the item. For example, you would study how boys of low ability compared to girls of low ability, boys of average ability compared to girls of average ability, and boys of high ability compared to girls of high ability. If these comparisons show that students in the two groups who are of the same ability perform differently on a task, this may indicate that the task is biased. However, just as average total test scores do not necessarily confirm a test is biased, so, too, do such item differences not necessarily confirm item bias. In other words, test items may function differently in two groups, but there may be no discernible bias. Because these differences do not prove bias, assessment specialists refer to the differences as **differential item functioning (DIF)** rather than as item bias.

Assessment Bias As Misinterpretation of Scores

Bias as misinterpretation of scores can creep into the interpretations of assessment results when someone tries to make inappropriate inferences about students' performances that go beyond the content domain of the assessment (Cole, 1978; Cole & Moss, 1989). It is one thing to say, for example, that a female has difficulty solving two-step arithmetic word problems that involve knowledge of male suburban experiences; it's another to interpret performance on the assessment as an indication that females have lower arithmetic reasoning skills than males. The latter interpretation goes beyond the content domain and demands more than cursory evidence to support a claim that the interpretation is unbiased.

Assessment Bias As Sexist and Racist Content: Facial Bias

Facial bias is the use of offensive stereotypes in the language and pictures that make up assessment tasks and materials. Ours has been a white, male-dominated, Anglocentric culture. A goal is not to perpetuate this image through the use of language and pictures in assessment (and other) materials. You can judge the content of assessment tasks (and other material) according to whether they represent male or female, white or nonwhite, as well as whether the content depicts certain **role stereotypes**. Figure 5.4 shows one set of criteria for such judging. Under the definition of bias described here, an assessment would be biased if its tasks perpetuated undesirable role stereotypes, **race stereotypes**, or **gender stereotypes**. This judgment about the offensive nature of assessment content can be called facial bias (Cole & Nitko, 1981). Criteria such as those in Figure 5.4 have been applied to achievement tests and intelligence tests. Special concerns for race and gender facial bias exist in vocational interest inventories. The goal is not to produce faceless, gender-free, ethnic-free assessment materials. Rather, it is to represent gender and ethnic groups in a balanced, inoffensive, and fair way in those materials.

Assessment Bias As Differential Validity

Predictive validity refers to evidence that describes the extent to which a test is able to estimate a person's probable standing on a second measure called a criterion (see Chapter 3). The criterion of interest in assessment bias is usually some measure of job or school success. Under the definition of **bias as differential validity**, an assessment would be biased if it predicted criterion scores better for one group of persons (e.g., whites) than for another (e.g., African Americans) (Cole & Moss, 1989). A "fair" or

FIGURE 5.4   Criteria for judging assessment tasks for racial and sexist content.

Gender representation: the extent to which an item can be characterized as representing a male or female.

1. *Pictorial items.* Which gender does the item picture? Features checked include attire, length of hair, facial characteristics and make-up (e.g., barrettes in a baby's hair mean the illustration presents a female).

2. *Verbal items.* Nouns and pronouns indicate gender: *he/she, him/her, John/Jane* (e.g., "Marion bought a bell for his bike," describes a male).

Gender role-stereotype: the extent to which an item can be characterized as depicting a male or female stereotyped role. Male role-stereotyped items depict males as intelligent, strong, vigorous, rugged, contributing to history, mechanically apt, professional, famous, etc. Female role-stereotyped items depict females as domestic, passive, generally inactive, crying, physically attractive, and nonintellectual.

1. *Pictorial items.* Does the picture illustrate a gender role-stereotype (e.g., woman fixing a meal, little girl playing with dolls, man carrying a picnic basket while escorting woman to park, man watching contact sports, or boy being mischievous)?

2. *Verbal items.* Does the item contain statements that are gender role-stereotyped (e.g., question; "Who invented the electric light bulb?" [male role-stereotype] or story theme: brother and sister get a horse, boy rides horse while sister watches and laughs when brother falls in mud [female role-stereotype])? (Bias is implied when nearly all questions represent single-gender, negative stereotypes, rather than a balance of gender accomplishments.)

Race representation: the extent to which an item can be characterized as representing a white or nonwhite person.

1. *Pictorial items.* Are physical features such as skin color, eye shape and color, hair color and texture varied?

2. *Verbal items.* Do famous persons to be identified come from various races (e.g., George Washington, Martin Luther King, Jr.)?

Race role-stereotype: the extent to which an item can be characterized as depicting a white or nonwhite role-stereotype. White role-stereotyped items depict whites as wealthy, technically or academically trained, professional, intelligent, and inclined toward academic or intellectual pursuits. Pictures or verbal themes show whites operating instrument such as stethoscopes or surveying transoms. Nonwhite role-stereotyped items depict nonwhites as poor, unskilled, athletic (e.g., boxer, football lineman), culturally primitive, and religiously pagan.

1. *Pictorial items.* Are role-stereotypes depicted (e.g., white male executive, Oriental coolies, Native American warriors, and black bellboys)?

2. *Verbal items.* Does the verbal content or story theme represent a role-stereotype (e.g., "Who wrote *Hamlet?*")?

Source: From "A Look at Content Bias in IQ Tests," by L. Zoref and P. Williams, 1980, *Journal of Educational Measurement, 17,* pp. 313–322. Copyright 1980. National Council on Measurement in Education, Washington, DC. Adapted by permission of Blackwell Publishing.

---

unbiased assessment would, according to this definition, predict criterion scores with equal accuracy for all groups assessed. There have been a number of empirical studies of differential bias, but the overall conclusion is that few tests exhibit this pattern of differential correlation with educational success criteria. That is, educational selection tests seem to predict educational success equally well (or equally poorly) for most groups.

Assessment Bias As Content and Experience Differential

The definition of bias as **content/experience differential** is that an assessment is biased if the content of the assessment tasks differs radically from a particular subgroup of students' life experiences *and* the assessment results are interpreted without taking such differences into proper consideration. For example, consider two high school vocabulary tests, one consisting of word meanings likely to be learned in a white, middle-class suburban high school and the other comprised of slang word meanings likely to be learned only by urban, streetwise, African American youths. Would either or both tests be biased? The answer

depends on the use and interpretation of results. Clearly, one would expect African American youths to perform better than white youths on the latter test (Williams, 1975). However, if the purpose of the latter test were to gauge knowledge of this culture-specific vocabulary domain, then it would not be biased against white youths who lack the experience needed to acquire this learning. Content evidence (see Chapter 3) could be brought forward to support the use of this test for this limited purpose.

On the other hand, if the culture-specific vocabulary test were interpreted as a broad measure of general verbal ability, it might well be biased against white youths. Similarly, the middle-class suburban vocabulary test might be biased against urban African American youths, if it were interpreted as a broad measure of verbal ability. But the suburban vocabulary test might validly measure the white, culture-specific verbal ability of white suburban youths as developed by their experience, where as the culture-specific African American urban vocabulary test might do the same for African American youths.

When students' experiences and an assessment's content differ radically, it is probably not possible to offer the same construct interpretation (e.g., general verbal ability) for one subgroup's performance as that offered for another subgroup whose experience and assessment content more nearly match. If you restrict your assessment interpretations to the limited domain from which the tasks are sampled (e.g., white middle-class vocabulary knowledge or knowledge of urban African American slang), the issue of content bias is less likely to be raised. Seldom, however, does a teacher, counselor, or other assessment interpreter limit interpretation to the narrow content domain: Most often, even for achievement tests, we use broad-construct interpretations such as math concepts, listening comprehension, and spelling ability (Cole, 1978).

Assessment Bias As the Statistical Model Used for Selection Decisions

When many applicants vie for a limited number of openings, some procedure will be used to narrow the field. Most persons in this culture would reject the lottery (random drawing) as a means of selection, because a random process is uncorrelated with the ability to succeed on the job or in school. Most people believe that selection decisions should be based on "merits." Combinations of various assessments provide information that ranks applicants in order of merit. Among the information-gathering tools are interviews and the application form itself, as well as a variety of performance assessments and paper-and-pencil tests. All assessments used for selection must show some positive relationship to job or school success. The problem arises when certain subgroups score consistently lower on one or more of the assessments used in the selection process, and when the assessments have slightly different relationships with the measures of the success criterion. The **bias as the statistical model** definition focuses on whether the statistical procedure used for selection is fair to all persons, regardless of group membership.

At least 10 actuarial or statistical models for reducing selection bias have appeared in the literature (Cleary, 1968; Cole, 1973; Cole & Moss, 1989; Darlington, 1971, 1976; Einhorn & Bass, 1971; Gross & Su, 1975; Linn, 1973; Novick & Peterson, 1976; Ravelo & Nitko, 1988; Thorndike, 1971).

Assessment Bias As the Wrong Criterion Measure

Selection tests are used to predict success on a second measure called a criterion. But the criterion measure itself may be biased, making the selection process biased, even if the test is unbiased. That is **bias as the wrong criterion**. For example, suppose a job did not require reading skills and that on-the-job performance is the relevant criterion. Suppose further that an employer used a paper-and-pencil test of job knowledge as a substitute or proxy criterion measure instead of using a measure of actual job performance. Because in this case the paper-and-pencil test

would be interpreted erroneously as the "ability to do the job," it would be a biased assessment against those who could not read or who were poor paper-and-pencil test takers but might well be able to perform the job. Some criteria represent traditional cultural values (e.g., supervisors' ratings, grade point average) and may be used as proxies to an ultimate criterion measure such as job performance. Persons able to perform well on the ultimate criterion may not necessarily perform well on these proxy measures.

Bias Stemming From the Atmosphere and Conditions of Assessment

Basic test-taking stresses, such as test anxiety, feeling unwelcome, or being tested by a member of the opposite gender or another race, can adversely affect the performance of some groups. Others have argued that it is unfair to students and teachers in schools in impoverished areas to use an officially mandated test that serves "to inflict on them periodic, detailed documentation of just how very far away from anything approaching the norm they are" (Flaugher, 1978, p. 677). These situations describe **bias stemming from testing conditions**.

POSSIBLE FUTURE DIRECTIONS OF TEST FAIRNESS

As the preceding discussion suggests, there is not just one definition of test bias or assessment fairness. One thread of commonality you can see from all of these approaches is that test bias and **assessment or test fairness** reflect test validity. A fair assessment or test is one that provides scores that (a) are interpreted and used appropriately for specific purposes, (b) do not have negative or adverse consequences as a result of the way they are interpreted or used, and (c) promote appropriate values. In the future, assessment developers will need to focus on four issues to make assessment instruments fairer (Cole & Zieky, 2001):

1. Reduce group difference by controlling early in the development process what constructs to assess, what formats to assess them with, and the specific questions to include.

2. Recognize that because any one assessment contains only a limited representation of the ultimate learning targets, a student's achievement may not be assessed well by a particular procedure.

3. Develop methods for identifying misuses of an assessment and how to deal with these misuses.

4. Develop procedures for accommodating individual students recognizing that different methods of assessment may be required to assess the same achievement with different students.

Summary

A Teacher's Professional Responsibilities in Assessment

- You have professional, ethical, and legal responsibilities concerning the way you craft, use, and report the results of your classroom assessments.
- Professional associations have developed codes of ethical and professional responsibilities. The *Code of Professional Responsibilities in Educational Measurement* (Appendix C) is one of them.
- You have ethical and professional responsibility in six main areas of assessment activities: (a) crafting assessments, (b) choosing assessments, (c) administering assessments, (d) scoring assessments, (e) interpreting and using assessment results, and (f) communicating assessment results.
- When crafting assessment procedures, your professional responsibility is to develop a procedure that closely fits your intended purpose and has a degree of reliability appropriate to the seriousness of the decision for which you will use the results.
- Your professional responsibilities include ensuring that (a) your assessment-crafting process uses the sound and well-known principles of assessment development, (b) your assessments are free from characteristics that are irrelevant to assessing the learning target, (c) your assessments accommodate students with disabilities who are in your class, (d) you obtain necessary permission to use copyrighted material in your assessment, (e) you present the assessments in a way that encourages their proper use, and (f) your assessment materials do not contain errors or inaccuracies.
- When choosing assessment procedures that come with curricular materials or that are separately purchased, you have a professional responsibility to (a) not use them if they fail to match your classroom teaching, vocabulary, reading level, or content emphasis; (b) recraft them, if necessary, before using them; and (c) ensure that you meet the same six professional responsibilities as you do when you craft your own assessment procedures.
- When serving on a committee to select a standardized test for your school district or for a state assessment program, you have a professional responsibility to be knowledgeable about (a) educational assessment quality characteristics, (b) the AERA, APA, and NCME *Standards* and the *Code of Fair Testing Practices in Education (Revised)*, (c) the procedures and criteria used to evaluate an educational assessment, and (d) the ways similar assessments have been used in other places and the consequences of such usage.
- When administering assessments to students, you have a professional responsibility to (a) give students sufficient advance notice of the assessment, (b) give students complete information about the coverage of the assessment and the conditions under which it will be given, and (c) conduct the assessment in a professional manner that encourages each student to do his or her best.
- You have a professional responsibility to ensure that students with disabilities in your class receive the assessment accommodations necessary for them to demonstrate their learning. Figure 5.2 shows examples of various types of assessment accommodations.
- In accommodating students with disabilities, you should treat each as an individual rather than stereotyping his or her assessment accommodation needs.
- When administrating standardized or state-mandated tests, you have a professional responsibility to (a) fully inform students about the testing and its purpose; (b) carefully follow the directions for administering the test; (c) maintain the necessary test security; (d) maintain testing conditions appropriate for maximum performance; (e) provide for necessary accommodations for students with disabilities; and (f) avoid cheating, teaching specific answers to test items, and unethical test-preparation practices.
- When scoring your own classroom assessments, you have a professional responsibility to (a) score students' responses accurately, (b) score students fairly, (c) provide students with appropriate feedback, (d) explain to students the rationale for the correct answers and for the scoring rubrics you used, (e) give students the opportunity to review their evaluations individually, (f) correct scoring errors as quickly as possible, and (g) score and return assessment results in a timely manner.
- When scoring standardized and state-mandated assessments, you have a professional responsibility to (a) follow the manual's directions exactly, (b) ensure that your scoring is accurate, (c) monitor the quality of your scoring, and (d) learn how to use and to fairly apply the scoring rubrics.
- When using and interpreting assessment results, you have the professional responsibility to interpret students' performance (a) in the context of the learning targets you emphasized in class; (b) in relation to the results from several assessments, not just one; (c) in relation to the limitations of the assessment procedure; (d) properly to parents; (e) as assessments of learning targets rather than as tools for controlling students; and (f) in ways that protect students' rights of privacy.
- You have a professional responsibility to learn the meaning of standardized test score-reporting schemes that affect your students (e.g., grade equivalents and standard scores) and to interpret these properly.
- You have a professional responsibility to (a) communicate correctly and accurately the results of assessments to students, parents, colleagues, and school officials; (b) tailor your communication to each of these groups so they make proper interpretations themselves; (c) communicate in a way that minimizes the likelihood of misinterpretations on the part of the information recipient; and (d) establish an appropriate and frequent pattern of communication of assessment results with parents and students.

Students' Rights and Responsibilities as Test Takers

- Students have rights as test takers. The U.S. Constitution and federal legislation protect some of these rights (see Figure 5.3). Others follow from your ethical and professional responsibilities. The chapter identifies 13 areas of rights that should be considered.
- Students also have responsibilities as test takers. The chapter lists 15 such responsibilities. They have the responsibility to study and prepare for assessments. They have the responsibility not to pressure teachers to lower standards.

Secrecy, Access, Privacy, Confidentiality, and the Teacher

- Students' assessment results and classroom performance are generally considered confidential, and you have a professional responsibility to help protect the students' rights to privacy. Responsibilities include requiring researchers to seek permission and informed consent from students or their parents before releasing data.

- You have a professional responsibility to correct, on students' records (including computerized records), any errors you make in reporting assessment results or grading students. Your obligation is not lessened if only you know the error. Nor is your obligation lessened if the information has already been entered into the computer "system."
- You have a professional responsibility to limit your posting or display of students' assessment results to protect their rights to privacy. You also have a professional responsibility not to gossip about students with other teachers or to spread confidential information about them.
- Informed consent means that the student understands (a) the nature and extent to which personal information will remain anonymous, (b) the extent to which participation is voluntary, (c) who is requesting information and the purpose of the request, and (d) what will happen to information collected.

Legally Defensible Assessment Accommodation Policies

- The persons for whom accommodations are needed are usually specified in state and federal laws.
- Conflicts arise if two laws provide different recommendations as to what content standards are appropriate for teaching and accountability regarding students with disabilities.
- The chapter presents several suggestions that will make accommodations and modification of assessments for students with disabilities legally defensible.

Testing Challenged in Court and Bias in Educational Assessment

- Testing programs have been challenged in courts. Plaintiffs may be individuals or classes of persons. They may challenge the psychometric properties of tests or nonpsychometric properties. Examples are given in the chapter.
- Test bias takes many forms. Eight are described in the chapter.

Possible Future Directions of Test Fairness

- A fair test (assessment) is one that provides scores that (a) are interpreted and used appropriately for specific purposes, (b) do not have negative or adverse consequences as a result of the way they are interpreted or used, and (c) promote appropriate values.
- Suggestions for improving test fairness include developing assessment methods that (a) reduce differences among groups that are caused by factors unrelated to the achievement being assessed, (b) recognize that any one assessment contains only a limited representation of the ultimate learning targets so that one procedure may not assess a student's achievement well, (c) identify misuses of an assessment and how to deal with these misuses, and (d) recognize that different methods of assessment may be required to assess the same achievement with different students.

Important Terms and Concepts

access to assessment results
assessment or test bias
assessment or test fairness
bias as content/experience differential
bias as differential validity
bias as mean differences
bias as misinterpretation of scores
bias as the statistical model
bias as the wrong criterion
bias stemming from testing conditions
Code of Fair Testing Practices in Education (Revised)
Code of Professional Responsibility in Educational Measurement (CPR)
confidentiality
differential item functioning (DIF)
due process
ethical principles
facial bias
fair assessment or test
gender representation
gender stereotype
high-quality information
individual education plan (IEP)
informed consent
mandated tests
participation in assessment
positive or negative consequences of decisions
privacy
professional responsibility
psychometric issues
purging records
race representation
race stereotype
role stereotypes
serious versus less serious consequences of decisions
standardized tests
test-takers' rights

Exercises and Applications

1. Each of these statements describes a situation in which a teacher crafts an assessment procedure. Read each statement and decide whether a violation of professional responsibility has occurred. After deciding, write an explanation justifying your decision. Discuss your findings with other members of your class.
   a. Mrs. Jones schedules a short quiz in social studies every Friday. She announces this at the beginning of the semester, and every student is aware that this will occur. She jots down the questions on Friday mornings before class and photocopies them to give out during class. She has never taken a course in assessment, nor has she ever read a book on how to improve assessments.
   b. Mr. Roberts teaches science. There is a deaf student in his class. When a test is scheduled, he gives a copy of the test a few days ahead of schedule to the student's sign language interpreter, who simplifies the language of the questions but keeps the technical or scientific terminology. When other students are sitting for the test, the deaf student is in another room being administered the test by the student's sign language interpreter, who signs the questions to the student.
2. Each of these statements describes a situation in which a teacher chooses or helps choose an assessment procedure the teacher did not develop. Read each statement and decide whether a violation of professional responsibility has

occurred. After deciding, write an explanation justifying your decision. Discuss your findings with other members of your class.

   a. Mr. Smith teaches biology. His teacher's guide comes with a printed multiple-choice test covering the materials in the chapter he just taught. He gives the test to the office secretary for duplication a few days ahead of schedule. On the day he is to give the test, he goes over it to make an answer key. He discovers that out of 40 items, 10 cover material he either did not cover or did not thoroughly teach. He spends the first 15 minutes of class teaching these concepts, and then gives the test. All 40 items count toward students' grades.

   b. Mr. Williams teaches history. The authors of the textbook used in his class provide multiple-choice unit tests. One of the students brings the test home after the results are returned. The student's father goes over it and notices that for 5 of the 40 items, his son's answers are correct according to the information in the textbook but were marked wrong by Mr. Williams. He writes a note to Mr. Williams describing the situation and citing the textbook pages to support his claim. Mr. Williams writes back saying the test was written by the textbook authors and is published, so it would be absurd to question the items' correctness. He refuses to reconsider the items or rescore the papers.

3. Each of the following statements describes a situation in which a teacher administers an assessment. Read each statement and decide whether a violation of professional responsibility has occurred. After deciding, write an explanation justifying your decision. Discuss your findings with other members of your class.

   a. Mr. Gordon likes to give "pop" quizzes or surprise quizzes to keep his students "on their toes." These quizzes count 50% of the students' grades.

   b. Mrs. Stravinski believed that the standardized test she was requested to give in reading was too speeded. Consequently she gave the students an extra 10 minutes. She did not report this to anyone.

4. Each of these statements describes a situation in which a teacher scores an assessment. Read each statement and decide whether a violation of professional responsibility has occurred. Write an explanation justifying your decision. Discuss your findings with other members of your class.

   a. Mrs. Appleton is an itinerant teacher for students with hearing impairments who assists with the education of mainstreamed students at Mountain View High School. Billy David is a senior deaf student to whom she administers a standardized achievement test battery using an appropriate signed language. She knows that Billy's results will be sent to postsecondary schools for deaf students, and that they will use the results as part of the admission decision. When scoring the test by hand, she noticed that Billy's scores were unexpectedly low. She reviewed the questions he missed and said to herself, "I know he really knows the answers to these." So she changed his answers to about 25% of the questions to give him a higher score. She rationalized her actions by thinking, "He really is a good student, and if I simply sent in the scores he got he would not be given the chance I know he deserves."

   b. Mr. Pennel gives essay questions and performance tasks as a major part of his assessment. He seldom bothers with developing scoring rubrics because he doesn't know how to do so and they take time to develop. He'd rather spend the time teaching.

   c. Mrs. Dingle marks the assessments of John and Robert. They both receive the same score, which is on the borderline between an A and a B. She gives John an A and Robert a B. The boys are friends and they compare papers, discovering the different grades for the same score. John goes to Mrs. Dingle and tells her that Robert deserves the A. Mrs. Dingle says, "John, everyone knows that you are an A student, whereas Robert is a B student. My grades just reflect this fact so I won't change his grade."

5. What definition(s) of assessment bias is (are) implied by each of the following statements? Justify your classification and share your findings with other members of your class.

   a. "This performance assessment is biased because it requires doing work outside school, and the students from wealthier families have more resources to help them do it well."

   b. "This performance task is biased because it requires females to be familiar with automobiles and airplanes, something they are unlikely to be in this community."

   c. "This performance assessment is biased because, overall, students from African American families do better on it than students from white families."

   d. "This assessment is biased because on Tasks 3 and 7 boys score higher than girls at every ability level."

   e. "This assessment is biased because all the pictorial material shows white males in professional roles but females and minorities in passive and subservient roles."

   f. "This portfolio assessment is biased because the male teacher favors boys' responses that agree with his positions on controversial matters."

6 Planning for Integrating Assessment and Instruction

LEARNING TARGETS

After studying this chapter, you should have learned the following:

Making Your Own Assessments Improves Your Teaching

1. Describe several ways in which learning to craft assessment tools can improve your teaching. [1, 2]

Are You Assessing for Formative or Summative Purposes?

2. Describe and give examples of common formative and summative uses of assessment results. [4, 1, 3]

Assessment Planning for a Marking Period

3. Craft a formative and summative assessment plan for a marking period. [1, 2, 4]

Assessment Planning for One Unit of Instruction

4. Design a formative and summative assessment plan for one unit of instruction. [1, 2, 3]

5. Explain how to integrate assessment and instruction through an assessment plan. [1, 2, 4]

Pretesting to Plan Your Teaching

6. Use a preinstruction framework to craft an instrument for assessing students prior to teaching a unit in your area. [2, 1]

Crafting a Plan for One Summative Assessment

7. Craft a blueprint for a summative assessment instrument for a unit in your area. [2, 1]

8. Explain the major decisions you make when crafting your summative assessment blueprint. [2, 1]

9. Apply the validity criteria from Chapter 3 to the classroom assessment instrument described by your blueprint, and to any accommodations made to it. [2, 1, 3, 7]

Blueprints for Student-Centered Assessment

10. Describe how sharing your summative assessment blueprint improves the student-centeredness of the assessment.

Criteria for Improving Assessment Plans

11. Apply the criteria in Figure 6.7 to improve your assessment plans.

What Assessment Options Are Available to You?

12. State the advantages and disadvantages of commonly used formative and summative assessment techniques. [4, 1, 3]

Validity of Different Assessment Options

13. Describe the potential validity of using the results from each of the common assessment techniques. [4, 1, 3, 6]

14. Explain why no single assessment technique should be used for all classroom decisions. [1, 3, 6, 7]

Important Terms and Concepts

15. Explain how each of the terms and concepts found at the end of this chapter may be applied to the creation of plans for assessment and instruction in your classroom. [6]

ABOUT THIS CHAPTER

Plans for teaching are incomplete unless they contain plans for assessment. This chapter focuses on how to improve your **assessment planning**, first by discussing how crafting your own assessments improves your teaching. Second, we describe two major purposes for classroom assessment: formative and summative. Knowing the purpose for the assessment is critical to effective planning. Not having the purpose clearly in mind can easily make for poor assessment and, in turn, ineffective teaching. Next, we show how to make assessment plans. This third section discusses planning for longer periods: a year, a term, or a marking period. The fourth section examines more detailed planning that you need for teaching one instructional unit. After that, we turn to more specialized topics. Our fifth section discusses assessing students' attitudes, knowledge, beliefs, and experiences to plan your teaching. Sixth, we turn to crafting blueprints for one summative assessment, such as a unit test or an end-of-semester test. A blueprint ensures that you include both higher-order and lower-order thinking skills in your assessment instrument. Seventh, we discuss how you can share your assessment blueprint with students to make your assessments more student-centered. Eighth, we show how to evaluate your assessment plans, especially when the purpose of the plan is to help you assign grades to students. Ninth, we give an overview of the many options you have for crafting formative and summative assessments. Knowing your options and the advantages and disadvantages of each will help you become a better assessment planner. The chapter concludes by evaluating the validity of each of the assessment options for each of several assessment purposes. You will see that for some teaching decisions, certain assessment methods have very low validity and should not be used. Knowing the validity of assessment options will help you choose the assessment procedure that provides the most valid information about your students' achievements.

HOW MAKING YOUR OWN ASSESSMENTS IMPROVES YOUR TEACHING

You can expect the following benefits to your teaching as your assessment-crafting skills improve.

1. *Knowing how to choose or to craft quality assessments increases the quality of your teaching decisions.* By assessing how your students use their knowledge and skills, you are able to monitor and evaluate their progress. This allows you to plan better teaching.

2. *What and how you assess communicates in a powerful way what you really value in your students' learning.* For example, you may tell your students how important it is for them to be independent and critical thinkers, but your words are empty if your assessments consist of only a few matching exercises based on facts from the textbook or handouts. On the other hand, if your assessments require students to integrate their knowledge and skills to solve "real-life" problems, they learn that you expect them to develop integrating and problem-solving abilities.

3. *When you carefully define assessment tasks, you are clarifying what you want students to learn.* When you craft assessment tasks, you learn how to create situations in which students can demonstrate their achievement. These skills apply directly to your teaching, because to teach effectively you must have clearly in mind how students should demonstrate their achievement.

4. *You use your knowledge of how to craft quality assessment tasks when you evaluate assessment materials available from other sources.* Your knowledge of the craft will also help you evaluate and become a critical consumer of assessment procedures, whether they are part of your curriculum materials or are imposed by or on your school district, such as standardized achievement tests and state-mandated assessments.

5. *Learning to craft assessment tasks increases your freedom to design lessons* (Stiggins et al., 1986). Knowing how to assess students validly, especially in relation to higher-order thinking skills, means that you are no longer chained to the assessment procedures already prepared by textbook publishers and others. You can use a wider variety of teaching strategies because you are able to assess students using your own assessment procedures.

6. *You will improve the validity of your interpretations and uses of assessment results.* Research shows that teachers who have studied assessment, either through coursework or in-service training, are able to recognize and produce better assessments (Boothroyd, McMorris, & Pruzek, 1992; Plake, Impara, & Fager, 1993).

7. *You will improve your appreciation of the strengths and limitations of each type of assessment procedure.* As a professional, you must have the knowledge and skill to independently evaluate proposed assessment approaches. You must evaluate their general educational value and their technical quality. Without both evaluations, you cannot determine whether these approaches can make good on the promises implied by their promoters. To fulfill your professional responsibility, you need a solid foundation in the basic principles of assessment development and in the criteria for valid use of the assessment results.

ARE YOU ASSESSING FOR FORMATIVE OR SUMMATIVE PURPOSES?

A major point to keep in mind is that you must assess for both *formative* and *summative* purposes, but usually with different assessment methods. We introduced these concepts in Chapter 1. In this chapter we discuss how to apply them to assessment planning. Figure 6.1 shows

FIGURE 6.1   Examples of basic purposes for which classroom assessment results are used.

I.   *Formative uses* help teachers monitor or guide student learning while it is still in progress.
   A.   *Sizing-up uses* help a teacher form initial impressions of students' strengths, weaknesses, learning characteristics, and personalities at the beginning of the year or course.
   B.   *Diagnosing individual students' learning needs* helps a teacher and the student identify what the student has learned and what still needs to be learned, decide how instruction needs to be adapted, and decide what feedback the student needs about how to improve.
   C.   *Diagnosing the group's learning needs* helps a teacher identify how the class as a whole has progressed in its learning, what might need to be reinforced or retaught, and when the group is ready to move on to new learning.
   D.   *Providing specific feedback* gives students information about how to improve.
   E.   *Planning instructional uses* help a teacher design and implement appropriate learning and instruction activities, decide what content to include or emphasize, and organize and manage the classroom as a learning environment.
II. *Summative uses* help a teacher evaluate student learning after teaching one or more units of a course of study.
   A.   *Assigning grades for report cards* is a way in which a teacher records evaluations of each student's learning progress to communicate evaluations to students, their parents, and responsible educational authorities.
   B.   *Placing students into remedial and advanced courses* is a way in which a teacher attempts to adapt instruction to individuals' needs when teaching is group based. Students who do poorly in the teacher's class may be placed into remedial classes that provide either alternate or supplemental instruction that is more suitable for the students' current level of educational development. Similarly, students whose educational

development in the subject is above that of the rest of the class may be placed into a higher level or more enriched class.
   C.   *Evaluating one's own teaching* requires a teacher to review the learning that students have been able to demonstrate after the lessons are complete, identify which lessons were successful with which students, and formulate modifications in teaching strategies that will lead to improved student performance the next time the lessons are taught.
III. *Other uses* help in teaching generally but may not be directly linked to evaluating individuals.
   A.   *Using assessment procedures as teaching tools* is a way in which a teacher uses the assessment process as a teaching strategy. For example, a teacher may give practice tests or "mock exams" to help students understand the types of tasks used on the assessment, practice answering and recording answers in the desired way, or improve the speed at which they respond. In some cases, the performance assessed is identical or nearly identical to the desired learning target so that "practicing the assessment" is akin to teaching the desired learning target.
   B.   *Communicating achievement expectations* to students is a use in which a teacher helps clarify for students exactly what they are expected to be able to perform when their learning is complete. This may be done by showing the actual assessment tasks or by reviewing the various levels or degrees of performance of previous students on specific assessment tasks so that current students may be clear about the level of learning expected of them.
   C.   *Controlling students' behavior* is a use in which a teacher hopes to motivate students to study and learn by using performance on an assessment instrument as a vehicle for student accountability. The higher the stakes for the student in doing well on the assessment, the greater the incentive to "get a good grade" or "pass" the assessment. Some teachers believe that without such external rewards students will not study and learn the material.

common uses for classroom assessment results. The uses are organized into three groups: formative, summative, and other uses.

Formative Purposes of Assessment

Formative Uses of Assessment **Formative uses of assessment** help you guide or monitor student learning while it is still in progress. High-quality formative assessment and **feedback** increases student learning (Black & Wiliam, 1998). You use a variety of formal and informal assessment results to make formative decisions and to provide formative feedback to students. In general, formative assessments are less formal. We recommend that you record the results of these assessments to help your memory; however, you do not use them to report official letter grades or achievement progress. (As you can see from Figure 6.1, each of the formative uses helps you plan what and how to teach.)

Sizing-Up Uses Typically, you use the most informal assessments for sizing-up purposes. **Sizing up** means to form a general impression of a student's strengths, weaknesses, learning characteristics, and personality at the

beginning of a course or at the start of the year. The following example illustrates how a teacher pulled together various informally obtained pieces of information to size up Joslyn, a fifth-grade student:

> Joslyn walks into class each day with a worried and tired look on her face. Praising her work, or even the smallest positive action, will crack a smile on her cheeks, though the impact is brief. She is inattentive, even during the exercises we do step by step as a class together. She is shy, but sometimes will ask for help, but before she gives herself a chance, she will put her head down on her desk and close her eyes. I don't know why she lacks motivation so severely. Possibly it's a chemical imbalance or maybe problems at home. She will probably be this way all year. (Airasian, 1991a, p. 37)

You can see that this teacher was using information about Joslyn's cognitive, affective, and psychomotor traits. The teacher's impression of Joslyn helps form a general strategy for how to teach her and deal with her in class.

Other Formative Uses Typically, you make other formative decisions that require quality information. These include diagnosing individual students' learning needs, diagnosing the group's learning needs, providing feedback, and planning instruction. Chapter 13 discusses diagnosis in detail. These decisions were also described in the first two chapters of this book. We mention them here to underscore the need to use valid information when making these decisions correctly. The validity of your assessment rises, of course, when you have carefully planned the assessment.

Student Self-Assessment Every important learning target should offer students ways to think about evaluating their own learning. This is known as **student self-assessment**. Ways to do this include applying criteria to their own work in progress, discussions with peers about their work, and reflections on their work after its completion. Students need to be taught effective self-assessment techniques.

Summative Purposes of Assessment

Summative uses of assessment help you evaluate your students and your own teaching after you finish teaching one or more units. Often we use summative information about a student's achievement to count toward her grade for a marking period. Parents and school authorities interpret those grades as the progress students have made toward achieving the curriculum's learning targets. Often this reporting is done through a home report or a report card. Because of the importance of summative assessment, you should prepare to keep records of students' results on those assessments that will be used in the grades. Figure 6.1 lists three examples of summative uses for assessment results. Because assigning grades is an important assessment use for all teachers, we devote Chapter 15 to that topic. However, in Figure 3.1 (Chapter 3), we discussed how to improve the validity of results from an assessment you use for assigning grades. You may wish to review that now. The validity criteria will be helpful in this chapter as you study ways to select and plan assessments.

Other Uses

Figure 6.1 lists three other uses for classroom assessment: as a teaching tool, to communicate what you expect students to know and perform, and to control students' behaviors. We will discuss these uses in Chapters 7 through 15. At this point, however, you should recognize that using assessments to control students' behaviors is a common and sometimes unethical practice. Controlling students through assessments turns a process of information gathering into a process of threatening and punishing. Using assessment results to intimidate or to punish students has negative consequences for their learning and self-esteem.

ASSESSMENT PLANNING FOR A MARKING PERIOD

Keeping in mind that you need to plan for both formative and summative assessment, the next thing to consider is the period for the plan. You may plan for a year, a semester, a marking period, a unit, or a lesson. Your plans for larger segments of your teaching will be less detailed than your plans for smaller segments.

Plans for a year or a semester set out the general approaches and strategies you shall use to teach and to assess. Such a plan contains an outline of the topics you will teach, the general learning targets your students will achieve, and the main strategies you will use to assess them.

Plans for a marking period usually apply to two or three units of instruction. A **marking period** is the number of weeks you must teach before you need to prepare a grade for each student's report card. In a typical academic year a marking period consists of 9 weeks. A **unit of instruction** is a teaching sequence covering from 1 to 7 weeks of lessons, depending on the students and topics you are teaching. You use plans for instructional units to break down and organize the larger curriculum into manageable teaching, learning, and assessment sequences. Planning for several units at one time allows for sequencing the units and for keeping your teaching and assessment approaches consistent. It also allows you to describe your plans for formative and summative assessment.

Plans for only one unit will necessarily be more detailed. You will describe the specific content, concepts, procedures, terminology, and thinking skills your students will learn and use. You also describe your teaching activities and your students' learning activities. You identify the learning targets of the lessons, the specific formative and summative assessments you will use, and when you will use them.

The shortest term for planning is for one day or one lesson. As you teach, you will begin to reflect on what you have previously taught these students and how well your students have achieved the unit's learning targets to date. This reflection is an opportunity for you to adjust your unit plan. Your teaching and assessment strategies become more fine-tuned, adapting to your students' abilities. Each day, you adjust your teaching as you gather new information about your students and your teaching.

This latter point illustrates that your teaching and assessment plans are not set in stone. They are guidelines for teaching and assessing. They are flexible and subject to change as new information about your students' achievements accumulates.

Example of How to Develop an Assessment Plan for a Marking Period

To stimulate your thinking about assessment planning, let's look at a simple example. Because this is an assessment book we shall emphasize the assessment aspects of planning, but your planning will include instructional ties also. Suppose you are teaching middle school science. Suppose, further, that you are planning for a 9-week marking period. Perhaps you plan to teach two units: one on the water cycle and one on weather and weather systems. For each unit you would outline the major points of content you will cover, the general sequence and timing of the units, and, most important, the learning targets your students will achieve from each unit. Your plan is beginning to take shape.

You need to plan more on the teaching side. You need to answer questions such as the following: What overall approach and teaching strategy will you adopt? The water cycle and weather units are related; how will you make that clear to students? What kinds of learning activities will you need to create and use (e.g., creating a demonstration of condensation, cloud simulation, building a diorama of the water cycle, drawing weather maps, measuring variables related to weather such as wind speed and precipitation, collecting and reading weather maps, or conducting a weather prediction activity)?

Part of your teaching plan must include student evaluation. How will you evaluate students' achievement of the learning targets? What are your general strategies for formative evaluation? Perhaps you plan for some in-class activities and exercises that will allow you to evaluate how well students are progressing. These also allow you to give students appropriate feedback. Perhaps you plan homework exercises. These allow you to evaluate whether students have mastered the basic concepts. Your thinking should include planning for how often you assess. At what points in the lessons will homework or quizzes be appropriate, for example?

To provide formative feedback to students, you will have to mark and evaluate their work. Will you do all the marking? Will students' peers evaluate performance? If so, students will need evaluation criteria and scoring rubrics. When you use oral questioning, what levels of the taxonomy will you emphasize most? How will you respond to intermediate steps toward larger projects (plans, outlines, drafts, etc.)?

A very important point is this: *Plan to use the formative feedback to help students improve their learning.* In order for formative feedback to be effective, you will probably have to teach your students how to use this feedback in their learning. For example, you may need to teach them how to review and evaluate their own work as they proceed through the lessons.

Your summative evaluation strategy needs to be planned also. You have many options, but not all options are equally valid. (We will discuss this point further later in this chapter.) The point is that you need to think ahead, so that you can evaluate students on what you taught them and on the learning targets they should achieve. You might use a paper-and-pencil test at the end of each unit. You might use a project for one unit and a performance activity

for another. For example, students may collect weather data and use them to predict the weather. For some other subjects, term papers, independent investigations, or portfolios might prove useful for summative evaluation. You will want to build in formative assessment opportunities along the way for the larger projects.

Your plan must include the weighting of each component as part of a final grade: How much will the tests, homework, projects, and so forth count toward the grade? Will each count equally, or will some weigh more heavily than others? To be fair, you will need to explain the weighting to students in advance. (Grading students is an important topic; we devote Chapter 15 entirely to grading.)

Example of an Assessment Plan for a Marking Period

Figure 6.2 shows an assessment plan that a hypothetical teacher created when teaching the two science units referred to in the preceding paragraphs. Although this plan is well organized and neatly typed, your own plan need not be so neat. It may be handwritten, put into your teaching folder, and used as a working document as you teach. The main points are that by planning you have (a) decided ahead about when and how you will assess, (b) recorded this thinking so that you do not forget, and (c) followed a systematic plan to achieve your assessment goals.

ASSESSMENT PLANNING FOR ONE UNIT OF INSTRUCTION

Developing an Assessment Plan for One Instructional Unit

Designing an assessment plan for one unit is a bit more detailed. You need to lay out the lesson sequences and the learning targets. Then you need to choose what methods of assessment you will use. Finally, you should identify why you need to use each type, how the assessments are related to the lessons, and what actions you will take once you have information about the students' achievement.

Example of an Assessment Plan for One Unit

Figure 6.3 shows an example of an assessment plan for one of the science units in Figure 6.3. When you are studying Figure 6.3, keep in mind that it includes all the thinking a teacher might use when deciding what assessments to conduct. Your own plan might not be so detailed because the thinking remains in your head. The important points are that you can explain when and why you are using different assessment methods, that you match the assessment methods with the learning target(s) for which they are

FIGURE 6.2 **A long-term plan for a marking period in which two elementary science units will be taught.**

Unit 1. The Water Cycle	
General learning target:	Understanding what the water cycle is, how it works, and how it helps living things. Ability to explain the water cycle and apply it to real life.
Time frame:	It will take 2 weeks to complete.
Formative assessment:	(a) Three homework assignments (taken from Chapter 8)
	(b) Condensation demonstrations (Group activity; I will ask students to explain what they are doing, how it relates to the water cycle, and how it relates to real life.)
	(c) Short quiz on the basic concepts at the end of Week 1
Summative assessment:	A written test at the end of the unit (short-answer and an essay)
Weights:	(a) Homework 10%
	(b) Quiz 10%
	(c) End-of-unit test 80%
Unit 2. Weather Systems and Predicting Weather	
General learning target:	Understanding basic weather patterns, their movements, and their influence on local climate. Ability to understand weather maps, weather forecasts; ability to collect weather data and use them to make simple predictions.
Time frame:	It will take 7 weeks to complete.
Formative assessment:	(a) Seven homework assignments (taken from Chapter 8 and my own)
	(b) Seatwork on drawing a simple weather map with symbols (I will circulate among students and ask questions to check their understanding.)
	(c) Correct use of simple instruments to gather weather-related data (I will have each student demonstrate each instrument's use and give them feedback when necessary.)
	(d) Collection of weather maps and forecasts (I will discuss with students what the maps and forecasts mean and be sure they understand them.)
	(e) Four quizzes on the major concepts and a performance activity (Week 1, Week 3, Week 4, and Week 5)
Summative assessment:	(a) Map drawing (I will provide weather information; students will draw corresponding maps independently. This will be Quiz 4.)
	(b) End-of-unit test (short-answer, matching, map identification, essay question)
	(c) Independent investigation (Collect weather data for 2 weeks and make daily 2-day weather predictions. I will structure this activity. It will be done toward the end of the unit.)
Weights:	(a) Homework 10%
	(b) Quizzes 10%
	(c) Independent investigation 30%
	(d) Map drawing 20%
	(e) End-of-unit test 30%
Marking Period Grade	
	Unit 1 marks count 30%
	Unit 2 marks count 70%

appropriate, and that you can state what teaching action you will take once the information is gathered. *Assessments are useless if you do not take action when you see the results.*

Observe carefully how Figure 6.3 is organized. Notice that in this example seven lessons are planned. Directly below each lesson is a brief statement of the lesson's main learning target. The various types or methods of assessment (pretest, observation, homework, quizzes, independent investigations, end-of-unit test) are listed in the leftmost column. Notice that as you go down the column, the purposes of assessment become more summative and the assessment procedure becomes more formal. The most summative purposes require the most formal and most carefully crafted assessments.

FIGURE 6.3 An assessment activity plan for one unit of instruction.

More Formative in Nature / More Summative in Nature	Assessment techniques	Description of assessment purpose, activity, and follow-up action (use)						
	Pretest	About a week before beginning this unit, I will give a very brief pretest to get a sense of students' attitudes, experiences, knowledge, and belief about weather. (See Figure 6.4.) *Action:* I will use this information to help me develop discussions in class, to develop lessons that overcome students' misconceptions and fears about the weather, and to build on what students already know.						
		Lesson 1 Comprehending basic weather concepts	**Lesson 2** Distinguishing weather patterns and systems	**Lesson 3** Identifying local weather conditions and patterns	**Lesson 4** Using basic tools for measuring weather	**Lesson 5** Understanding and making weather maps	**Lesson 6** Collecting and recording local weather data	**Lesson 7** Using data to predict local weather
	Observation and oral questioning	In every lesson, I will observe students and ask questions during the lesson to assess how well they are responding to the material, how well they seem to understand the daily activities and assignments, and whether they have any misconceptions about the weather concepts we are studying. *Action:* I'll adjust my teaching if most of the class is having difficulty. If only a few are experiencing difficulty, I'll work with them individually, in small groups, or ask another student to teach the concept.						
	Homework	I will assign homework after every lesson. Homework activities will focus on observing and discovering real-world examples of the weather concepts we learn in class. Students will record their observations and write explanations of them using proper scientific language learned in the unit. *Action:* As I read students' homework responses, I will note for each student how accurately and fluently the student uses scientific language to discuss the weather. I will also evaluate their observational and recording skills. I will reteach those materials for which many students experience difficulty. If only a few are having difficulty, I will work with them individually.						
	Quizzes	**Quiz 1** (covers Lesson 1): Short-answer questions testing basic vocabulary *Action:* Students not mastering the basic concepts will be retaught.	**Quiz 2** (covers Lessons 2 and 3): Short-answer questions with some diagrams. Focuses on weather patterns: local, national, and international. *Action:* I will use this quiz to monitor students' understanding of weather patterns and systems. I'll reteach or move on, depending on the outcomes.		**Quiz 3** (covers Lesson 4): This will be a performance activity. I want to be sure each student can use with accuracy the weather-measuring tools and can record data properly. *Action:* I will correct errors on the spot.	**Quiz 4** (covers Lesson 5): I want students to read, interpret, and draw simple weather maps. I will give weather data to the students and ask them to draw an appropriate map using the weather data. I will also give maps already drawn and ask students to interpret them. *Action:* I will reteach if there are problems.		
	Independent investigation (performance assessment)				**Predicting the Weather** (begins after Lesson 4, and includes Lessons 5 and 6): This performance assessment will help me evaluate whether students can apply the concepts from the lessons to the real world. It will help me evaluate whether they can synthesize and use criteria to evaluate the data they collect. Students will collect and measure weather data, record it, and use it to predict the local weather for two days in advance. They will repeat the exercise every day for at least 2 weeks. They will work independently. They will prepare a report describing what they did and evaluating their investigation and its accuracy. *Action:* This is a type of summative evaluation. I will use the exercise to help me decide how well the students have learned the concepts and principles in this unit. I should have a pretty good idea whether students can apply what they learned in class.			
	End-of-unit test							**Unit Test** (covers all lessons): This will come at the end of all the lessons. It will be a paper-and-pencil test given in class. (I may give it over 2 days.) It will be comprehensive, covering most of the important learning targets in the unit.) *Action:* I will use the results of this test along with the results from homework, quizzes, drawing, and the independent investigation to assign a grade to the students for the unit. (Weights are given in Figure 6.2.)

The statements written in the body of this figure describe the purpose, procedure, and action to be taken for each assessment. The **teaching actions after assessing** are steps the teacher will take to improve students' achievement based on the assessment results.

When the statements in Figure 6.3 are spread across the page, that means the assessment's purpose, procedure, and actions apply to all of the lessons. In the figure, observation, oral questioning, and homework are of this character. Statements that appear directly below one or two lessons mean that the assessment applies to only those one or two lessons. The quizzes, independent investigation, and end-of-unit test are of this character. Because the seven lessons are spread out in sequence over time, the plan shows that some assessments occur at different times throughout the unit. Study Figure 6.3 before reading further.

PRETESTING TO PLAN YOUR TEACHING

Notice in Figure 6.3 that the teacher gave a pretest about a week before teaching this unit. The pretest results were not used to grade students. Rather, they were used primarily to help the teacher understand the students' attitudes, knowledge, beliefs, and experiences about the weather so that the teacher could better teach the unit.

Importance of Preinstructional Unit Assessment

As you plan instruction for a unit, you must consider more than covering the material. In most subjects, students bring to the unit a complex combination of knowledge, experiences, skills, beliefs, and attitudes that are especially related to the topics to be taught. If you understand your students' thinking before teaching them, you can build your instruction on it. The "pretest" does not need to be a formal test. You may, for example, have a class discussion about some of the topics that you will be teaching in an upcoming unit. From this discussion you can gauge how much the class already knows about the topics and what kinds of

misconceptions they may have. Use this information to plan your teaching of the unit.

Often students' beliefs about a topic are contrary to what you will teach. Even after you present the information, students' beliefs may not change. If students do not believe what you are teaching, then they do not integrate new concepts into their existing ways of thinking, and they will be unable to apply that information in the future. For example, youngsters know that wearing sweaters keeps them warm. When teaching a science unit on insulating properties, you may teach that air has insulating properties. If you ask youngsters what happens to the temperature of a cold bottle of soft drink when you wrap it in a sweater, many may say it gets very warm. If you tell them it will stay cold, many will not believe you because they know sweaters keep them warm. Knowing this, your teaching will have to include activities that change students' beliefs by building on their prior experiences and knowledge. Your instruction will have to offer a real demonstration and comprehensive explanation—for example, why a sweater keeps the student warm *and* the soft drink cool—before that instruction can alter their beliefs.

A Framework for Constructing Instruments

A **preinstruction unit assessment framework** is a plan you use to help you assess cognitive and affective learning targets of an upcoming unit. Preinstruction assessments should be relatively short, however, so focus your assessment on only a few core elements. Do a written assessment so you can easily summarize the information and use it to make your planning decisions. You could also organize a class discussion around the results.

It is especially helpful if you adopt a set framework and use it to generate assessment questions for every unit you teach. This establishes a comprehensive and consistent approach to gathering and using information. The framework in Figure 6.4 is useful to follow for several subject matters. It uses six categories of information. It was originally developed for middle school science.

FIGURE 6.4 Framework for crafting a written assessment of students' attitudes, knowledge, beliefs, and experiences about a topic.

Area assessed	Example question
1. Student's attitudes about the topic.	"I think meteorology is *boring, interesting*, etc."
2. Student's school experiences with the topics.	"Have you ever studied meteorology or the weather? When?"
3. Students' knowledge of an explanatory model centrally important in the unit.	"Explain what makes it rain. Include a diagram if you wish."
4. Students' awareness of common knowledge associated with the topic.	"Imagine you are a TV or radio weather announcer. Write a forecast for what the weather will be tomorrow."
5. Students' knowledge of technical terms associated with the topic.	"Describe what each of these instruments does or is used for: barometer, thermometer, and weather vane."
6. Students' personal experiences with some aspect of the topic.	"Describe your most unusual or scary experience involving weather."

Source: Adapted from "Instructional Assessments: Lever for Systematic Change in Science Education Classrooms," by B. Gong, R. Venezky, and D. Mioduser, 1992. *Journal of Science Education and Technology, 1*(3), pp. 164–165. With kind permission of Springer Science and Business Media and the author.

Pretesting for Metacognition Skills

Some teachers have found it useful to pretest students' abilities to monitor and control their own thinking as they perform learning activities (Tittle, 1989; Tittle, Hecht, & Moore, 1993). If students are aware that learning one thing is more difficult than another, if they are able habitually to check statements before accepting them as facts, or if they habitually plan their work before beginning it, they are using *metacognitive skills*. You may wish to assess these skills before teaching so you will have a better idea of how well your students can monitor and control their thinking about the assignments you will make during the unit. You may wish to integrate teaching some of the metacognitive skills into the unit. The details for doing this are presented in Appendix F.

CRAFTING A PLAN FOR ONE SUMMATIVE ASSESSMENT

This section focuses on one assessment purpose: using the results to help assign grades to students. This is an important responsibility, and you should not base this action on only one test. Chapter 15 will discuss in great detail strategies and techniques for assigning grades. In this section,

however, our focus is narrower—*how to develop a plan* for one formal assessment instrument you will use for this summative purpose.

Organizing a Blueprint

Before crafting an instrument, you need to make a blueprint. The **blueprint** describes both the content the assessment should cover and the performance expected of the student in relation to that content. Some authors call the blueprint a **table of specifications**. The blueprint serves as a basis for setting the number of assessment tasks and for ensuring that the assessment will have the desired emphasis and balance. Thus, the **elements of a complete test plan** include (a) content topics to assess, (b) types of thinking skills to assess, (c) specific learning targets to assess, and (d) emphasis (number of item or points) for each learning target to be assessed. Figure 6.5 illustrates such a blueprint for a science unit on forces. See Appendix G for examples of alternate procedures for test blueprints.

The row headings along the left margin list the major topics the assessment will cover. You can use a more detailed outline if you wish. The column headings across the top list the major classifications of Bloom et al. taxonomy of cognitive education objectives. You may use one

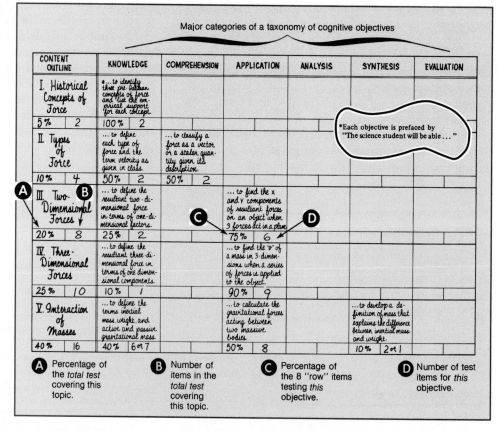

FIGURE 6.5 Example of a blueprint for summative assessment of a science unit.

Source: Adapted from *Developing Classroom Tests* (p. 42), by W. J. Kryspin and J. F. Feldhusen, 1974, Edina, MN: Burgess. Adapted by permission of Pearson Custom Publishing, Boston.

of the other taxonomies, described in more detail in Appendixes D and E, if you prefer. Notice that from left to right the types of performances implied by the column headings are increasingly complex. Performances that demonstrate knowledge or comprehension, for example, are lower level cognitive performances. Those reflecting the ability to synthesize or evaluate are higher level cognitive performances.

The body of the blueprint lists the specific learning targets. Both a content topic and a level of complexity of the taxonomic category thus doubly classify the learning targets. In this example, most of the learning targets are at the lower and middle levels of the taxonomy. For a different emphasis, you would use the blueprint to identify the cells in which to write other objectives to assess.

Rigorous Classification Is Unnecessary

It is difficult to classify learning objectives and items into the categories of some of the taxonomies. This approach to assessment planning is still useful, however. The purpose of formally laying out this two-way grid is not to promote exact or rigorous classification. Rather, it is a tool to help you recall the higher-order cognitive skills that need to be systematically taught and evaluated in the classroom.

Blueprint Specifies Assessment Emphasis

The numbers in the blueprint in Figure 6.5 describe the emphasis of the assessment, both in terms of percentage of the total number of tasks and in terms of the percentage of tasks within each row or content category. You decide how many tasks to include on an assessment after you consider (a) the importance of each learning target, (b) type of tasks, (c) content to be assessed, (d) what you emphasized in your teaching, and (e) amount of time available for assessment. The example in Figure 6.6 illustrates how the blueprint in Figure 6.5 is made. The example assumes an objective test, where each item is worth 1 point. The same procedure should be followed for tests with multipoint items (for example, essay questions or problems to solve). Five points from the blueprint could be five 1-point items, or one 5-point item, or any combination of items worth 5 points.

Students will expect the various numbers of points on the assessment to correspond to the amount of time devoted to the material in class and to the emphasis they perceive you have placed on that material. If the assessment you are planning does not meet this expectation, it seems fair to notify the students of this fact well in advance of administering it.

FIGURE 6.6 Example of teacher thinking for constructing a test blueprint.

The major topics of the unit are listed in the leftmost column. The teacher decided that Topic I will have 5% of the marks for the test, Topic II will have 10%, Topic III will have 20%, Topic IV will have 25%, and Topic V will have 40% of the marks. The teacher decided these percentages based on how important the topics were and how much emphasis they were given during instruction.

Suppose the teacher plans to use 40 test items for this unit. The blueprint shows that of these 40, the teacher decided that 2 items, or 5% of 40, should be devoted to Topic I. Thus, a 2 is entered in the space next to 5% in Column 1. Similarly, 20% of 40, or 8 items, will be used to test instructional learning targets that deal with Topic III. This process is continued until the number of items for each topic is calculated and recorded in Column 1.

Next the teacher selected the learning targets to assess. The teacher selected the most important learning targets for each of the topics, and then slotted them under the taxonomy category to which each belonged. Topic I, for example, has only one learning target and it is slotted under the knowledge category.

After slotting the learning targets, the teacher decided what percentage of the items previously decided for each topic should be allotted to each learning target. For example, Topic I has only one learning target, so 100% of the items allotted to Topic I are to be used to assess this learning target. Notice there are two learning targets for Topic III—one at the Knowledge level and one at the Application level. Of the 8 items allotted to Topic III, the teacher decided that 25% should deal with the Knowledge-level learning target and 75% with the Application-level learning target. These percentages were selected based on the teacher's professional judgment of the importance of these two learning targets. That is, the Application-level learning target was judged to be three times more important than the Knowledge-level learning target. The percentages are recorded below each learning target. Notice that for each *row*, the sum of the percentages under the learning targets *for that row* equals 100%.

The percentages recorded below each learning target need to be translated into the number of items that will assess each learning target. This is done by multiplying the percentage assigned to a learning target by the number of items listed in the leftmost column for that respective topic. The teacher wants Topic III, for example, to be assessed by 8 items (see leftmost column). The Knowledge-level learning target should have 25% of these 8 items. Thus, that learning target should be assessed by 25% of 8, or 2 items. The number of items is recorded in the space just below the Knowledge-level learning target for Topic III. In the same way, the Application-level learning target for Topic III is assigned 75% or 6 of the 8 items for this topic. Notice that for each row, the sum of the items under the learning targets for that row equals the number of items allotted to the topic for that row.

The teacher reviewed the blueprint after slotting in all the learning targets and after calculating all of the items needed for assessing them. The teacher noticed that 25 (= 6 + 9 + 8 + 2) of the items were to assess the higher-order thinking levels of Application and Synthesis. That means that 63% (25 of the 40) of the *assessment questions* will deal with the higher taxonomic levels, even though there are many *learning targets* at the lower levels of the taxonomy. This example illustrates that the weighting or emphasis of an assessment instrument is related to the number of tasks or points included in a particular category, not the number of learning targets. It reflects that some learning targets are more important for summative student evaluation than others.

The teacher was satisfied with the distribution of items across topics, thinking skills levels, and learning targets. Had the teacher not been satisfied, the plan could have been changed to better reflect the emphasis the teacher wanted.

This advanced planning for developing a summative classroom assessment allows you to view the assessment as a whole. In this way, you can maintain whatever balance or emphasis of content coverage and whatever complexity of performance you believe is necessary to match your teaching, and the assessment will neither be too easy nor too hard for your students. Plus, it simplifies the task of writing the test. It is easier to do that when a blueprint tells you exactly what kind of tasks and items you need.

Using the Blueprint to Improve Validity

A blueprint is an important tool to improve the validity of your instrument's results. The criteria for improving the validity of your assessment results are listed in Figure 3.1 in Chapter 3. Review that figure at this time, and note that the blueprint is an excellent way to ensure that many of the criteria for improving validity are met.

In addition to Figure 3.1, you should also consult Figure G.1 in Appendix G. This figure is a checklist for judging the quality of the your blueprint.

Craft Blueprints Over Time

The assessment-planning procedures described here are a lot of work. Given the many other responsibilities and activities competing for your time, you cannot always follow them completely. Because the validity of your grading decisions is important, however, you need to use some type of systematic plan to develop unit assessments. But, you need not attempt to devise a formal plan for all units in one semester or year. If you develop a blueprint for a few units each year, after a few years most units will have blueprints. As the learning targets change, you can update these blueprints with less work than originally required. Also, several teachers could draft blueprints for different units in a subject and exchange them. Even if a colleague's blueprint has to be modified to suit your particular teaching approach, you will likely save considerable time. When changes in the blueprints do occur, you should revise and redistribute the blueprints.

Simplified Specifications

The blueprint shown in Figure 6.5 is rather complete. It is possible to create other useful but less complete specifications. Appendix G offers examples of other types of blueprints.

Accommodations to the Summative Assessment

Any modifications you have made to the items on the test, conditions of administration, or student response modes in order to accommodate students with disabilities must give you assessment information that is valid. Review the discussion of accommodations in Chapter 5 and the list in Figure 5.2. Make sure that your accommodations for students who have IEPs are consistent with these educational plans. For example, if you are using a modified set of learning objectives for a student, consistent with the IEP, then a modified blueprint should be used to ensure the test reflects those learning objectives. If a student's IEP specifies that test items should be read to her, then (unless the test is a reading test) you should plan the logistics (the reader, a quiet location, etc.) to allow this to happen.

BLUEPRINTS FOR STUDENT-CENTERED ASSESSMENT

As you can see, the assessment blueprint is a concise way to explain what is important for students to learn and to decide how much to emphasize each learning target in students' summative evaluations. Blueprints are useful instructional tools, too, especially with students in middle and senior high school. Therefore, share your assessment blueprints with your students.

Ideally, you should do this sharing when you begin the unit. You should review and discuss the blueprint thoroughly with the students to ensure they (a) have no misunderstandings, (b) understand the unit's emphasis, (c) understand what they will be held accountable for performing, and (d) see how the summative assessment factors into their overall grades. In Chapter 5 we discussed your professional responsibility to give students sufficient information when administering assessments. A blueprint is a very good way of providing this information for middle and senior high school students. Older students may offer suggestions for changing the emphasis or manner of assessment, thus more fully engaging in their own learning and evaluation. Students can write test questions for each blueprint cell. Use them for a practice test.

CRITERIA FOR IMPROVING THE VALIDITY OF ASSESSMENT PLANS

By now you have an idea of the general process of developing an assessment plan. The general steps required to move from initial assessment ideas to a draft of the assessment instrument are:

1. Define the purpose for assessment at this time.
2. Use the blueprint to specify the content and thinking processes you wish to observe and assess.
3. Use the blueprint to specify the learning targets and their weight in the assessment.
4. Identify the tasks and other techniques you need to use.
5. Develop the initial drafts of these tasks and techniques.

So far, we have discussed the first three steps. Step four is the subject of the rest of this chapter. The last step, developing the tasks and assessment exercises, is the subject of Chapters 7 through 14.

In this section, we emphasize some of the general **criteria for evaluating a planned assessment.** These include (a) matching tasks to learning targets, (b) covering important skills, (c) selecting appropriate assessment task formats, (d) making assessments understandable, (e) satisfying validity criteria, (f) satisfying reliability criteria, (g) ensuring equivalence, and (h) identifying appropriate complexity and difficulty of tasks.

The discussion in this section necessarily will be general because we assume that you are not yet familiar with the technical aspects of crafting an assessment. This section, however, will show how you can integrate the knowledge you have already acquired through studying this book into the initial planning stages of a classroom assessment. Figure 6.7 summarizes the main points.

Matching Assessment Tasks to Learning Targets

Your teaching is most effective when your lesson plans, teaching activities, and learning targets are all aligned. All three should also be aligned with your state's curriculum framework and standards (see Chapter 2). Your assessment plans specify the important learning targets to be taught and assessed. It is most important, therefore, that the actual tasks students perform on the assessment match those learning targets. To be valid, assessment procedures must match the learning targets.

FIGURE 6.7 Criteria and ways to improve the validity of your summative assessments.

Criteria to use	Ways to evaluate your assessment plan
Align assessment tasks with curriculum, standards, and instruction	• Be sure you clearly understand the main intent of the learning target to be taught and assessed. • *Think:* What is the main intent of the learning target? Does the assessment task require a student to do exactly as the main intent requires? • Analyze the assessment task to identify which part(s) may not match the learning target. Eliminate or rewrite the nonmatching parts.
Assess only important learning targets	• Review the learning targets taught and assessed; prioritize them from most to least important. Eliminate assessments matching low-priority learning targets. • Be sure your state's standards or learning expectations are assessed by one or more of your assessments. • Craft assessments that require students to demonstrate more than one high-priority learning target through the same task.
Use appropriate multiple assessment formats	• Become skilled in crafting many types of assessment formats. • Learn the strengths and limitations of each type of assessment format. • Analyze each learning target. *Think:* What are several different ways I can assess this achievement? How can I use two or more ways? • Analyze the assessment tasks to identify which parts may not match the learning target. Eliminate or rewrite the nonmatching parts. • Plan for assessing each important learning target in two or more ways
Make assessments understandable	• Be sure each assessment procedure has clear directions to the student, and that you have prepared students concerning each assessment. (See "Preparing Students for the Assessment" in Chapter 14.) • Learn to craft assessments well so they will satisfy the criteria and checklists contained in Chapters 7, 8, 9, 10, 11, 12, and 14. • Learn to craft scoring rubrics well so they will satisfy the criteria and checklists in Chapters 9 and 12.
Follow appropriate validity criteria	• Use the criteria described in Chapter 3, Figure 3.1.
Use appropriate length of assessments	• Be sure all students who know the material can finish within the time limits. • Follow the suggestions for improving reliability given in Chapter 4. • Follow the guidelines in Figure 6.8 until you have considerable experience with your students.
Ensure equivalence across years	• Use blueprints from previous years to guide you in crafting this year's assessment blueprints. • Be sure to make the difficulty and complexity of this year's assessment tasks equivalent to last year's tasks.
Ensure appropriate difficulty and complexity of assessment tasks	• Be sure the conditions and tools for students to use during the assessment are appropriate for the learning targets and the students' educational development. • Add appropriate accommodations for students with disabilities (see Figure 5.2). • Follow the guidelines in Figure 6.9.

Assessment tasks must match the targets. For example, if a learning target calls for a student to build a model, write a poem, collect data, or perform a physical skill, the students should be administered a performance assessment. If your assessment task requires students only to list the parts of a model, to analyze an existing poem, to summarize data already collected, or to describe the sequence of steps needed for performing the physical skill, it does not match these learning targets. The validity of your classroom assessment results plummets when even *some* of the tasks do not match the stated learning targets.

As an example, consider the ninth-grade social studies learning target stated here and the three assessment tasks that follow it:

Example

Learning target: Students will explain in their own words the meaning of the concept of *culture*.

Task 1. Name three things that are important to the *culture* of indigenous Americans.

Task 2. Give a short talk to the class comparing three different *cultures*. In your talk, make sure you describe the similarities and differences among the cultures you have chosen.

Task 3. Write a paragraph telling in your own words what is meant by the term *culture*.

Only Task 3 matches the stated learning target. Consider Task 1: The performance required applies to a specific cultural situation rather than to the general concept of culture as intended by the learning target. Task 1 should not be used for the assessment of this learning target. The performances required in Task 2 are to "compare" and to "describe" ("giving a talk" is only the way the student has to indicate she is describing similarities and differences among the cultures). Although these are worthwhile activities, they seem to go beyond the more limited scope and main intent of the learning target. Because this task fails to match the learning target, it should not appear on the assessment either.

What should you do if you create or identify a "great" task that does not match the stated learning target? You have only three choices: disregard the task, modify the task so it matches the learning target, or modify the learning target so it matches the task. Often, crafting an excellent assessment task helps further clarify a learning target: we see the full meaning of the learning target, which was not previously clear from its verbal statement. If this is the case, then you should modify the stated learning target so it more clearly expresses what you intend.

Be careful, however. If you have already communicated the assessment plan to students, you need to be sure that you do not "surprise" them with a more complex or difficult task than the type for which they are preparing themselves. Changing the rules in midstream is often unethical. Usually, it guarantees that you lose the respect of at least some students. Rather than completely discarding the task, you could either modify it to suit the stated learning target or save it until the next time you teach the unit. At that time you can more clearly specify the learning target.

Covering Only Important Learning Targets

We want to reinforce here that your summative assessment should cover only the important content and learning targets of the unit. Carefully planning the assessment ensures this. Blueprints are the major vehicles for summarizing and evaluating your assessment plans.

Using Appropriate Multiple Assessment Task Formats

Many varieties of assessments are available. In the next section we describe the advantages and disadvantages of each. The most important consideration is the validity of your assessment results. In this section we are focusing on summative evaluation for purposes of grading. (Chapter 13 discusses formative evaluation.)

One of the criteria we discussed in Chapter 3 (Figure 3.1) is to present students with multiple ways to demonstrate their competence. The validity of your assessment results usually improves, therefore, if you use several task formats to assess students. The many specific **task formats** from which you can choose include:

I. Paper-and-pencil formats
   A. Choice formats ("objective" items)
      1. True-false (Chapter 7)
      2. Multiple-choice (Chapters 8 and 10)
      3. Matching exercises (Chapter 8)
      4. Other formats (Chapter 8)
   B. Short-answer and completion format (Chapter 7)
   C. Essay format (Chapter 9)
      1. Restricted response
      2. Extended response
II. Performance formats (Chapters 11 and 12)
   A. Checklists
   B. Rating scales
   C. Sign and category systems
III. Long-term activity formats (Chapters 11 and 12)
   A. Projects
   B. Extended written assignments
   C. Laboratory exercises
   D. Portfolios
IV. Personal communication formats (Chapters 10 and 13)
   A. In-depth interviews, observation
   B. Oral questioning

activities, to diagnose the causes of students' learning difficulties, and to give students information about how to improve. In fact, it is questionable whether we should call assessment "formative" unless students actually can use the information for improvement.

You must gather this information while you are still teaching the material and while students are still learning it. As a result, these are **informal assessment techniques**. That is, they occur spontaneously as you need information, and you rarely stop teaching to do the assessment. Figure 6.10 summarizes eight categories of formative assessment options. The eight categories fall into three groups as described in the following paragraphs.

Oral Assessment Techniques   You may gather information to improve students' learning without creating tests or other paper-and-pencil tasks. Conversations with teachers who have taught a student may give you insight into the student's background and which approaches have worked in the past. These conversations may also help as you size up the class at the beginning of the term. Conversations with students give you additional insight into their feelings, attitudes, interests, and motivations.

As you teach a lesson, you question students about the material. These questions should encourage students to think about the material and to reveal their understandings, including misconceptions. This will help you guide your teaching. Avoid the "recitation" type of questioning in which you seek short answers to your questions. This style of questioning provides little insight into students' thinking and, therefore, provides little formative information. Avoid the tendency to ignore or ask only simple questions of the shy and less verbal students (Brophy & Good, 1999).

A good way to plan your oral questioning is to use a thinking skills taxonomy. In every lesson, be sure you ask several questions from the higher-order thinking categories of the taxonomy. Below are examples of some questions a teacher might ask students who have been studying the short story as a literary form:

Example	
Knowledge	"Who was the main character in the last story we read?"
Comprehension	"What were some of the personal problems that the characters in this story had to solve?"
Application	"Are the characters' problems in any way similar to the problems you or someone you know have had? Tell us about that. Don't use real names if you will embarrass the person."
Analysis	"What literary devices, style of writing, or 'writing trick' did the author use to help the reader really understand how the characters were feeling? Explain how this was done."
Synthesis	"So far this semester, we have read eight short stories. In each one, a character (sometimes two characters) wasn't able to solve his or her problem satisfactorily—even though each character tried to do so. Why is that? What do they all have in common that resulted in failure to solve their problems? What general problem-solving approach did all of these characters use that resulted in their failure?"
Evaluation	"What are three or four criteria that we can apply to all of the stories so we can compare and evaluate their literary quality?"

Paper-and-Pencil Assessment Techniques   Each day you give students seatwork and homework. These **paper-and-pencil assessments** let students practice the learning targets and perhaps extend their learning beyond the specific material you taught. You should review the results of seatwork and homework not just for correctness, but for whether the work reveals students' errors or faulty thinking that needs correction. If a student is exhibiting a pattern of errors, the student may have a misconception or may be using a rule consistently but inappropriately. (See Chapter 13, especially Figure 13.1, for an example.) Providing that specific information as feedback to students who need it is a powerful way of personalizing learning and helps students change.

You also periodically craft and administer short quizzes and tests. These monitor the progress students are making toward achieving learning targets. Tests and exams tend to be somewhat formal and are more useful for summative evaluation of students than for formative evaluation. However, if you use open-ended response items and carefully review students' responses for insights into their thinking, you will be able to derive some diagnostic information from these techniques.

Portfolios   Other formative evaluation techniques are somewhat more labor intensive than the ones we have discussed so far. A **growth and learning-progress portfolio** is a selected sequence of a student's work that demonstrates progress or development toward achieving the learning target(s). By containing "not-so-good works," "improved works," and "best works," it shows progress and learning during the course.

Typically, both the teacher and the student decide what a portfolio should include. Further, students are usually

FIGURE 6.10 Advantages, limitations, and pitfalls of alternative types of classroom assessment techniques.

Assessment alternatives	Advantages for teachers	Disadvantages for teachers	Suggestions for improved use
		Formative assessment techniques	
1. Conversations and comments from other teachers	(a) Fast way to obtain certain types of background information about a student. (b) Permit colleagues to share experiences with specific students in other learning contexts, thereby broadening the perspective about the learners. (c) Permit attainment of information about a student's family, siblings, or peer problems that may be affecting the student's learning.	(a) Tend to reinforce stereotypes and biases toward a family or social class. (b) Students' learning under another teacher or in another context may be quite unlike their learning in the current context. (c) Others' opinions are not objective, often based on incomplete information, personal life view, or personal theory of personality.	(a) Do not believe hearsay, rumors, biases of others. (b) Do not gossip or reveal private and confidential information about students. (c) Keep the conversation on a professional level focused on facts rather than speculation and confidential so it is not overheard by others.
2. Casual conversations with students	(a) Provide relaxed, informal setting for obtaining information. (b) Students may reveal their attitudes and motivations toward learning that are not exhibited in class.	(a) A student's mind may not be focused on the learning target being assessed. (b) Inadequate sampling of students' knowledge; too few students assessed. (c) Inefficient students' conversation may be irrelevant to assessing their achievement.	(a) Do not appear as an inquisitor, always probing students. (b) Be careful not to misperceive a student's attitude or a student's degree of understanding.
3. Questioning students during instruction	(a) Permits judgments about students' thinking and learning progress during the course of teaching; gives teachers immediate feedback. (b) Permits teachers to ask questions requiring higher-order thinking and elaborated responses. (c) Permits student-to-student interaction to be assessed. (d) Permits assessment of students' ability to discuss issues with others orally and in some depth.	(a) Some students cannot express themselves well in front of other students. (b) Requires education in how to ask proper questions and to plan for asking specific types of questions during the lesson. (c) Information obtained tends to be only a small sample of the learning outcomes and of the students in the class. (d) Some learning targets cannot be assessed by spontaneous and short oral responses; they require longer time frames in which students are free to think, create, and respond. (e) Records of students' responses are kept only in the teacher's mind, which may be unreliable.	(a) Be sure to ask questions of students who are reticent or slow to respond. Avoid focusing on verbally aggressive and pleasant "stars." (b) Wait 5–10 seconds for a student to respond before moving on to another. (c) Avoid limiting questions to those requiring facts or a definite correct answer, thereby narrowing the focus of the assessment inappropriately. (d) Do not punish students for failing to participate in class question sessions or inappropriately reward those verbally aggressive students who participate fully. (e) Remember that students' verbal and nonverbal behavior in class may not indicate their true attitudes/values.
4. Daily homework and seatwork	(a) Provide formative information about how learning is progressing. (b) Allow errors to be diagnosed and corrected. (c) Combine practice, reinforcement, and assessment.	(a) Tend to focus on narrow segments of learning rather than integrating large complexes of skills and knowledge. (b) Sample only a small variety of content and skills on any one assignment. (c) Assignment may not be complete or may be copied from others.	(a) Remember that this method assesses learning that is only in the formative stages. It may be inappropriate to assign summative letter grades from the results. (b) Failure to complete homework or completing it late is no reason to punish students by embarrassing them in front of others or by lowering their overall grade. Learning may be subsequently demonstrated through other assessments. (c) Do not inappropriately attribute poor test performance to the student not doing the homework.

	Strengths	Weaknesses	Cautions / Suggestions
(continued from previous item)			(d) Do not overemphasize the homework grade and overuse homework as a teaching strategy (e.g., using it as a primary teaching method.)
5. Teacher-made quizzes and tests	(a) Although primarily useful for summative evaluation, they may permit diagnosis of errors and faulty thinking. (b) Provide for students' written expression of knowledge.	(a) Require time to craft good tasks useful for diagnosis. (b) Focus exclusively on cognitive learning targets.	(a) Do not overemphasize lower level thinking skills. (b) Use open-ended or constructed-response tasks to gain insight into a student's thinking processes and errors. (c) For better diagnosis of a student's thinking, use tasks that require students to apply and use their knowledge to "real-life" situations.
6. In-depth interviews of individual students	(a) Permit in-depth probing of students' understandings, thinking patterns, and problem-solving strategies. (b) Permit follow-up questions tailored to a student's responses and allow a student to elaborate answers. (c) Permit diagnosis of faulty thinking and errors in performances.	(a) Require a lot of time to complete. (b) Require keeping the rest of the class occupied while one student is being interviewed. (c) Require learning skills in effective educational achievement interviewing and diagnosis.	(a) If assessing students' thinking patterns, problem-solving strategies, etc., avoid prompting student toward a prescribed way of problem solving. (b) Some students need their self-confidence bolstered before they feel comfortable revealing their mistakes.
7. Growth and learning-progress portfolios	(a) Allow large segments of a student's learning experiences to be reviewed. (b) Allow monitoring a student's growth and progress. (c) Communicate to students that growth and progress are more important than test results. (d) Allow student to participate in selecting and evaluating material to include in the portfolio. (e) Can become a focus of teaching and learning.	(a) Require a long time to accumulate evidence of growth and progress. (b) Require special effort to teach students how to use appropriate and realistic self-assessment techniques. (c) Require high-level knowledge of the subject matter to diagnose and guide students. (d) Require the ability to recognize complex and subtle pattern of growth and progress in the subjects. (e) Results tend to be inconsistent from teacher to teacher.	(a) Be very clear about the learning targets toward which you are monitoring progress. (b) Use a conceptual framework or learning progress model to guide your diagnosis and monitoring. (c) Coordinate portfolio development and assessment with other teachers. (d) Develop scoring rubrics to define standards and maintain consistency.
8. Attitude and values questionnaires	(a) Assess affective characteristics of students. (b) Knowing student's attitudes and values in relation to a specific topic or subject matter may be useful in planning teaching. (c) May provide insights into students' motivations.	(a) The results are sensitive to the way questions are worded. Students may misinterpret, not understand, or react differently than the assessor intended. (b) Can be easily "faked" by older and testwise students.	(a) Remember that the way questions are worded significantly affects how students respond. (b) Remember that attitude questionnaire responses may change drastically from one occasion or context to another. (c) Remember that your personal theory of personality or personal value system may lead to incorrect interpretations of students' responses.

Summative assessment techniques

	Strengths	Weaknesses	Cautions / Suggestions
1. Teacher-made tests and quizzes.	(a) Can assess a wide range of content and cognitive skills. (b) Can be aligned with what was actually taught. (c) Use a variety of task formats. (d) Allow for assessment of written expression.	(a) Difficult to assess complex skills or ability to use combinations of skills. (b) Require time to create, edit, and produce good items. (c) Class period is often too short for a complete assessment. (d) Focus exclusively on cognitive outcomes.	(a) Do not overemphasize lower level thinking skills. (b) Do not overuse short-answer and response-choice items. (c) Craft task requiring students to apply knowledge to "real life."

(continued)

FIGURE 6.10 (*Continued*)

Assessment alternatives	Advantages for teachers	Disadvantages for teachers	Suggestions for improved use
2. Task focusing on procedures and processes	(a) Allow assessments of nonverbal as well as verbal responses. (b) Allow students to integrate several simple skills and knowledge to perform a complex, realistic task. (c) Allow for group and cooperative performance and assessment. (d) Allow assessment of steps used to complete an assignment.	(a) Focus on a narrow range of content knowledge and cognitive skills. (b) Require a great deal of time to properly formulate, administer, and rate. (c) May have low interrater reliability unless scoring rubrics are used. (d) Results are often specific to the combination of student and task. Students' performance quality is not easily generalized across different content and tasks. (e) Tasks that students perceive as uninteresting, boring, or irrelevant do not elicit the students' best efforts.	(a) Investigate carefully the reason for student's failure to complete the task successfully. (b) Use a scoring rubric to increase the reliability and validity of results. (c) Do not confuse the evaluation of the process a student uses with the need to evaluate the correctness of the answers. (d) Allow sufficient time for students to adequately demonstrate the performance.
3. Projects and tasks focusing on products	(a) Same as 2(a), (b), and (c). (b) Permit several equally valid processes to be used to produce the product or complete the project. (c) Allow assessment of the quality of the product. (d) Allow longer time than class period to complete the tasks.	(a) Same as 2(a), (b), (c), (d), and (e). (b) Students may have unauthorized help outside class to complete the product or project. (c) All students in the class must have the same opportunity to use all appropriate materials and tools in order for the assessment to be fair.	(a) Same as 2(a), (b), (c), and (d). (b) Give adequate instruction to students on the criteria that will be used to evaluate their work, the standards that will be applied, and how students can use these criteria and standards to monitor their own progress in completing the work. (c) Do not mistake the aesthetic appearance of the product for substance and thoughtfulness. (d) Do not punish tardiness in completing the project or product by lowering the student's grade.
4. Best works portfolios	(a) Allow large segments of a student's learning experience to be assessed. (b) May allow students to participate in the selection of the material to be included in the portfolio. (c) Allow either quantitative or qualitative assessment of the works in the portfolio.	(a) Require waiting a long time before reporting assessment results. (b) Students must be taught how to select work to include as well as how to present it effectively. (c) Teachers must learn to use a scoring rubric that assesses a wide variety of pieces of work.	(a) Be very clear about the learning targets to be assessed to avoid confusion and invalid portfolio assessment results. (b) Teach a student to use appropriate criteria to choose the work to include. (c) Do not collect too much material to evaluate.

	Strengths	Weaknesses	Recommendations
	(d) Permit a much broader assessment of learning targets than tests.	(d) Interrater reliability is low from teacher to teacher. (e) Require high levels of subject-matter knowledge to evaluate students' work properly.	(d) Coordinate portfolio development with other teachers. (e) Develop and use scoring rubrics to define standards and maintain consistency.
5. Textbook-supplied tests and quizzes	(a) Allow for assessment of written expression. (b) Already prepared, save teachers' time. (c) Match the content and sequence of the textbook or curricular materials.	(a) Often do not assess complex skills or ability to use combinations of skills. (b) Often do not match the emphases and presentations in class. (c) Focus on cognitive sills. (d) Class period is often too short for a complete assessment.	(a) Be skeptical that the items were made by professionals and are of high quality. (b) Carefully edit or rewrite the item to match what you have taught. (c) Remember that you are personally responsible for using a poor-quality test. You must not appeal to the authority of the textbook.
6. Standardized achievement tests	(a) Assess a wide range of cognitive abilities and skills that cover a year's learning. (b) Assess content and skills common to many schools across the country. (c) Items developed and screened by professionals, resulting in only the best items being included. (d) Corroborate what teachers know about pupils; sometimes indicate unexpected results for specific students. (e) Provide norm-referenced information that permits evaluation of students' progress in relation to students nationwide. (f) Provide legitimate comparisons of a student's achievement in two or more curricular areas. (g) Provide growth scales so students' long-term educational development can be monitored. (h) Useful for curriculum evaluation.	(a) Focus exclusively on cognitive outcomes. (b) Often the emphasis on a particular test is different from the emphasis of a particular teacher. (c) Do not provide diagnostic information. (d) Results usually take too long to get back to teachers, so are not directly useful for instructional planning.	(a) Avoid narrowing your instruction to prepare students for these tests when administrators put pressure on teachers. (b) Do not use these tests to evaluate teachers. (c) Do not confuse the quality of the learning that did occur in the classroom with the results on standardized tests when interpreting them. (d) Educate parents about the tests, limited validity for assessing a student's learning potentials.

...

...

asked to describe the work they included, why they selected it, what it demonstrates about their learning, and their affective reactions to the material and to their learning experiences. Because a portfolio is built up over time, it permits closer integration of assessments with instruction than with some of the other techniques. These attributes are considered advantages of portfolios over "one-shot" assessment techniques because of the richness of information they provide the teacher.

Growth and learning-progress portfolios are usually evaluated qualitatively, although rating scales are sometimes used. Evaluating the evidence qualitatively requires a significant amount of skill and knowledge about student learning and the subject matter. The following excerpt from an evaluation of the language arts portfolio of an eighth-grade student illustrates both the richness of the information in the portfolio and the deep level of teacher knowledge required to evaluate it:

Example

Our experience is that growth is often manifested in qualitative changes in the writing—changes in the complexity of the problems that students undertake, which may involve losing control over other features of the writing like organization or mechanics. Take Gretchen . . . who included two pieces of expository response to literature in her portfolio. In one sense, the second piece is not as strong as the first—it is not well organized or coherent— but it is a richer interpretation. Unlike the first piece, which simply compares two groups of characters from *Lord of the Flies* . . . the second piece, on *Animal Farm*, has a thematic framework about the role of scapegoats that is played out with evidence from Gretchen's own personal experience, from the novel, and from a definition of the term acquired from another resource. A comparison of Gretchen's revisions in the two pieces shows a newly developed awareness of the need for elaboration and for evidence on particular points. (Moss et al., 1992, p. 13)

You need to learn how to craft portfolios before you can use them effectively. Novice portfolio users too often include nearly every scrap of a student's work in the portfolio and omit an organizational framework for the material. This makes the portfolio cumbersome and reduces its usefulness for assessing major trends in educational growth. You will learn to craft portfolios by studying Chapters 11 and 12.

Interviews In addition to portfolios, you may conduct *interviews with individual students*. Interviews can give you additional insights into students' thinking and learning difficulties. These interviews are more effective if you organize them around key concepts or specific problem-solving tasks. For example, you could work with the

student to create a mental map of the relevant concepts in a unit and discuss with the student how he believes the concepts to be related to one another. Concept map interviews are discussed in detail in Chapter 13. You may also administer a simple questionnaire to your class to gain insight into students' attitudes and values associated with the concepts you are about to teach. We saw this strategy being used in Figure 6.3.

Summative Assessment Options

You use summative assessments to help you formally evaluate students' learning-target achievement so you can report to students, parents, and school officials. This evaluation results in a home report or a report card grade. Summative assessment techniques are usually more formal than formative assessment techniques. Keep in mind, however, that formative and summative are not always distinct. For example, after you teach a unit, you may give a summative unit test. However, you may find students who have not achieved the learning targets. This will usually require you to reteach the students or provide remedial instruction. Because you have used the summative assessment to guide your teaching, it has provided formative assessment information.

Figure 6.10 shows six categories of summative assessment options. We may separate these into two groups: teacher-crafted techniques and external (extraclassroom) techniques.

Teacher-Crafted Techniques We have already mentioned tests and quizzes. These paper-and-pencil techniques may include open-ended questions (such as essays and other constructed-response formats), multiple-choice, true-false, and matching exercises. Chapters 7 through 10 discuss how to craft these formats.

But paper-and-pencil techniques are limited primarily to verbal expressions of knowledge. Students must read and respond to the assessment materials using some type of written response, ranging from simple marks and single words to complex and elaborated essays. Students' abilities to carry out actual experiments, to carry out library research, or to build a model, for example, are not assessed directly with paper-and-pencil techniques. Further, it is usually difficult for teachers to craft paper-and-pencil tasks that require students to apply knowledge and skills from several areas to solve real-life or "authentic" problems. Chapter 10 suggests crafting techniques that assess higher-order thinking skills.

Performance assessment techniques require students to physically carry out a complex, extended **process** (e.g., present an argument orally, play a musical piece, or climb a knotted rope) or produce an important **product** (e.g., write a poem, report on an experiment, or create a painting). The performances you assess should (a) be very close to the ultimate learning targets, (b) require students to use combinations of many different abilities and skills, and (c) require students to perform under "realistic conditions" (especially requiring student self-pacing, self-motivation, and self-evaluation). Some performance assessments require paper-and-pencil as a medium for expression (e.g., writing a research paper or a short story), but the emphasis in these performances is on the complexity of the product, and students are allowed appropriate time limits. This distinguishes such performance assessments from the short answers, decontextualized math problems, or brief (one class period) essay tasks found on typical paper-and-pencil assessments.

Because some performance assessments very closely measure the ultimate learning targets of schooling, they may be used as instructional tools. For example, you may instruct a student on presenting arguments orally and require the student to perform the task several times over the course of the term. You might repeat the teaching-performance combination several times until the student has learned the technique to the degree of expertise appropriate to the student's level of educational development.

Principal disadvantages are that a great deal of time is required to craft appropriate tasks, to prepare marking schemes or rating scales, to carry out the assessment itself, and to administer several tasks. The last point relates to the validity of interpreting students' results. Seldom can you generalize a student's performance on one task to performance on another. That is, how well a student performs depends on the specific content and task to which the performance is linked (Baker, 1992; Linn, 1994). A student may write a good poem about the people in her neighborhood but an awful poem about the traffic in Los Angeles. How good is the student as a poet in such cases? Quality performance assessment requires a very clear vision of an important learning target and a high level of skill to translate that vision into appropriate tasks and grading criteria (Arter & Stiggins, 1992).

Previously, we discussed the growth and learning-progress portfolio as a formative assessment tool. Portfolios may also be used for summative evaluation. The **best works portfolio** is a representative selection of a student's best products (productions) that provides evidence of the degree to which the student has achieved specified learning targets. In an art course it might be the student's best works in drawing, painting, sculpture, craftwork, and, perhaps, a medium chosen by the student. In mathematics it might include reports on mathematical investigations, examples of how the student applied mathematics to a real problem, writings about mathematics or mathematicians, and examples of how to use mathematics in social studies, English, and science. Best works portfolios focus on summative evaluation. To improve reliability of portfolio evaluations, you need to craft a scoring rubric. You need also to share the rubric with students and teach them how to select their best work in light of those rubrics. You will learn more

details on portfolio assessments, including how to craft them, by studying Chapters 11 and 12.

External (Extraclassroom) Techniques Teachers often use two other techniques. One is the *quizzes and tests supplied by textbook publishers*. These are convenient because you don't have to craft them yourself, and they match the book you are using. The problem is that these assessment materials are often of *poor quality*: they may not match local learning targets very well, they tend to focus on low-level thinking skills, and they can be poorly crafted. As we mentioned in Chapter 5, you have a professional responsibility to improve these assessment materials before using them.

Standardized Achievement Test Standardized tests also provide summative assessment information. Unlike textbook tests, these materials are usually very well crafted and supported by research on the validity of the scores. The tests consist of a battery of subtests, each covering a different curriculum area. Because the same group of students (norm group) took all subtests, the publisher's percentile norms allow you to compare a student's development in two or more curricular areas; and the publisher's score scales allow you to monitor a student's growth over time. Your own or your school district's tests cannot provide these types of information. A standardized test battery does not match your curriculum or your teaching goals exactly. Therefore, use it to assess broad goals (e.g., reading comprehension) rather than the specific learning targets in your classroom. You will learn more details about this assessment option by studying Chapters 16 through 18.

VALIDITY OF DIFFERENT CLASSROOM ASSESSMENT OPTIONS

Validity Principles to Guide Planning

Your classroom assessment plans must focus on obtaining the most valid assessment results for your specific interpretations and uses. We summarized the most common classroom purposes in Figure 6.1. This section discusses the relationship between these purposes and the validity of the results from assessment options in Figure 6.10. This should help you understand that *different assessment options are not equally valid for all purposes.*

Two important validity principles from Chapter 3 should guide your assessment plans. You should keep these principles at the forefront of your thinking, whether planning for a single assessment or multiple assessments:

1. Assessment results are valid only for specific interpretations and uses, not for all interpretations or uses.

2. Because no single assessment method gives perfectly valid results, more than one method should be used to assess the same achievement.

Assessment alternatives		Formative uses					Summative uses			Other uses		
		Sizing up	Diagnosing individuals' needs	Diagnosing a group's needs	Planning instruction	Providing feedback	Assigning grades for report cards	Placing students into remedial or advanced classes	Evaluating your own teaching	Assessment as a teaching tool	Controlling students' behavior	Communicating achievement expectations to students
Formative assessment techniques	Comments from other teachers	L/M	L	L	L	L	L	L	L	L	L	L
	Casual conversations with students	L	L	L	L	L	L	L	L	L	L	L
	Questioning students during instruction	L	M	L	M	M	L	L	M	L	L	M/H
	Daily homework and seatwork	L	H	H	H	H	L/M	L	L/M	M	L	H/M
	Teacher-made quizzes and tests	M	H	H	H	H	H	M	H	M	L	H
	Interviewing students individually	H	H	M	H	H	M	M	L/M	L	L	L/M
	Growth and learning-progress portfolios	L	M/H	L	L/M	H	L/M	L/M	M	H	L	H
	Attitude and values questionnaires	M/H	M/L	L	M	L/M	L	L/M	L	L	L	L
Summative assessment techniques	Teacher-made tests and quizzes	M	H	H	H	H	H	M	H	M	L	H
	Tasks focusing on procedures and processes	L	L/M	L/M	H	H	H	L/M	M/H	H	L	H
	Tasks focusing on products and projects	L	L/M	L/M	H	H	H	L/M	M/H	H	L	H
	Best works portfolios	L	L	L	L/M	M/H	M/H	L/M	M	H	L	H
	Textbook tests and quizzes	M	M	M	L	L/M	L/M	M/H	L/M	L	L	L/M
	Standardized tests	M	L/M	M	L/M	L	L	H	L/M	L	L	L/M

Note: H = results tend to have *high validity* for the indicated purpose
M = results tend to have *moderate validity* for the indicated purpose
L = results tend to have *low validity* for the indicated purpose

Various uses for the assessment results

Potential Validity of Assessment Options

Because the validity of assessment results depends on the specific details of how you use them in your classroom, we cannot predict the validity you will actually attain if you use a specific option. However, we can offer some guidance. Figure 6.11 shows the assessment uses and alternatives discussed previously. The figure shows, for each combination of use and assessment option, the *potential* validity of using that option for that particular type of decision. For example, Figure 6.11 shows that the results from teacher-made tests and quizzes have the potential of being highly valid for such purposes as planning instruction and assigning grades. The results are moderately valid for sizing up students and placing them into remedial or advanced classes. Finally, the results have low validity for controlling student behavior.

Interpreting Validity Guides

As you develop your assessment plans, you should refer to Figures 6.10 and 6.11 for guidance about what assessment options are appropriate. When interpreting Figure 6.11, you should keep the following points in mind:

1. *Under certain conditions, your assessment results have validity quite different from those shown in the figure.* You can think of the results as estimates of potential validity. A teacher could, for example, craft an exceptionally poor paper-and-pencil test that has very low validity for grading students, even though we show high validity in the figure. In this example, the teacher's paper-and-pencil test would not reach its potential.

2. *You must still apply the validity criteria described in Chapter 3 to the specific classroom assessment procedures you use.* Figure 6.11 gives *general* guidance, but you still have a professional obligation to develop your own argument for the validity of your assessment results. (See Chapters 3 and 5 for further discussion of this point.)

3. *The estimates of potential validity displayed in Figure 6.11 are the authors' judgments and not the results of scientific experiments.* In making these judgments, we used personal knowledge of the assessment option and our experience of how very good, experienced teachers typically craft and use them. We also used personal experience of the ways in which the purposes are *typically* carried out in classrooms. Finally, we applied to each combination of purpose and assessment method the criteria listed in Figure 3.2 to *typical* instruments or procedures of that assessment type. We focused on classroom use rather than on external or accountability uses. Perhaps in the future someone will conduct more scientific studies of the validity of classroom assessment results for each decision, but as it stands now, such scientific evidence is weak or lacking. Therefore, we believe the validities in Figure 6.11 are what you can reasonably expect to attain if you acquire and apply the knowledge and skills outlined in this textbook.

4. *In Figure 6.11, "high validity" does not mean perfect validity.* No single assessment instrument or assessment option has perfect validity.

5. *Combining the results from several types of assessments, each with low or moderate validity, will often result in a higher validity than for the individual components considered alone.* Although this is generally true, it may not be true in your case. For example, when combining grades from several assessments you may, for some strange reason, weight most heavily the assessment with the poorest validity. This practice will lower the validity of the combination. Or perhaps each of the components is so terrible that even the combination does not result in improved validity.

Summary

Making Your Own Assessments Improves Your Teaching

- High-quality assessment and high-quality instruction are part of the seamless fabric of high-quality teaching.
- The ability to craft and to interpret high-quality assessments improves your teaching because it
  - Increases the validity of the information you use.
  - Communicates to students your standards for performance.
  - Helps you more clearly define the learning targets.
  - Helps you evaluate assessment materials acquired from other sources.
  - Increases your freedom to design the instruction plans you want.
  - Improves the fairness of student assessment.
  - Helps you recognize the limitations of various types of assessment procedures.

Are You Assessing for Formative or Summative Purposes?

- Common classroom uses of assessment results are (see also Figure 6.1):
  - *Formative uses*—Sizing up, diagnosing individual students' learning needs, diagnosing the group's learning needs, planning instruction, and providing feedback to students.
  - *Summative uses*—Assigning grades for report cards, placing students into remedial or advanced courses, and evaluating one's own teaching.
  - *Other uses*—Using assessment procedures as teaching tools, controlling students' behavior, and communicating achievement expectations to students.

Assessment Planning for a Marking Period
and for One Unit of Instruction

- Planning for different time frames was discussed. Examples of planning assessment for a marking period (Figure 6.2) and for an instructional unit (Figure 6.3) were given. These examples illustrated planning for both formative and summative assessment, including a wide range of assessment techniques, matching techniques with appropriate lessons and learning targets, and using assessment results to take action for improving students' learning.

Pretesting to Plan Your Teaching

- The importance of obtaining preinstruction assessment information for planning an instructional unit was discussed. A framework for planning and crafting such instruments was discussed. The framework suggests assessing students'
  - Attitudes about the topic.
  - School experiences with the topic.
  - Knowledge of an explanatory model centrally important in the unit.
  - Awareness of common knowledge associated with the topic.
  - Knowledge of technical terms associated with the topic.
  - Personal experiences with some aspect of the topic.

Crafting a Plan for One Summative Assessment

- The chapter described an assessment blueprint (or table of specifications) for a summative assessment, including
  - How to organize the blueprint.
  - How to use the blueprint to determine the content and skill emphasis of the assessment.
  - How to use the blueprint as a teaching tool.
- Several types of blueprints were described: two-way grids with learning targets, two-way grids without learning targets, lists of learning targets, and content outlines.
- When crafting your own classroom assessment procedure, you should follow these steps:
  - Define the purpose for which you will use the assessment results.
  - Craft a blueprint to specify the learning targets and content you will assess.
  - Specify the weight each learning target will carry in the assessment.
  - Identify the tasks and assessment options that match the blueprint.
  - Craft initial drafts of the tasks and options.

Criteria for Improving Assessment Plans

- General criteria for evaluating your planned assessment are
  - Matching assessment tasks to learning targets.
  - Covering only important learning targets.
  - Using appropriate multiple-task formats.
  - Making assessments understandable to students.
  - Satisfying appropriate validity criteria.
  - Satisfying appropriate reliability criteria.
  - Ensuring equivalence.
  - Identifying appropriate complexity and difficulty of tasks.

What Assessment Options Are Available to You?

- These assessment options were described and the advantages, limitations, and suggestions for using them were discussed (see Figure 6.10):
  - *Formative assessment options*—Conversations and comments from other teachers, casual conversations with students, questioning students during instruction, daily home-work and seatwork, teacher-made quizzes and tests, in-depth interviews of individual students, growth and learning-progress portfolios, and attitude and values questionnaires.
  - *Summative assessment options*—Teacher-made tests and quizzes, tasks focusing on procedures and processes, tasks focusing on products and projects, best works portfolios, textbook-supplied tests and quizzes, and standardized achievement tests.
- All teachers are urged to learn the advantages and disadvantages of these assessment procedures before planning their assessment strategies.

Validity of Different Assessment Options

- The validity results from each of these assessment options, for each of the common classroom purposes, were estimated (see Figure 6.11), illustrating that:
  - No technique yields perfectly valid results for any one purpose.
  - Some options yield results with uniformly low validity for virtually all purposes.
  - Some options yield results with low validity for certain purposes and high validity for others.
  - A combination of different types of assessments usually yields results with more validity.

Important Terms and Concepts

assessment planning
best works portfolio
blueprint (table of specifications, assessment plan)
criteria for evaluating a planned assessment
elements of a complete test plan
equivalence
feedback to students
formative uses of assessment
growth and learning-progress portfolio
informal assessment techniques
item difficulty level
marking period
paper-and-pencil assessments
performance assessment techniques
preinstruction unit assessment framework
product versus process assessment
relative achievement
sizing-up uses
student self-assessment
summative uses of assessment
task formats
teaching actions after assessing
unit of instruction

Exercises and Applications

1. Visit a classroom (if you are not an in-service teacher) or use your own teaching experience to complete the following:
   a. Identify one or more specific examples of each classroom assessment purpose described in Figure 6.1.
   b. For each example, describe what assessment tools and information the teacher used to make that decision.
   c. Classify each tool or technique into one of the assessment-option categories shown in Figure 6.10.
   d. Create a table with row and column headings similar to Figure 6.11 to show which assessment tools were used for what purposes.
   e. Evaluate the validity of using the results of assessments for those decisions. Use the criteria listed in Figure 3.1 to help your evaluation.

2. Visit a classroom, or look around your own classroom, and list all the instructional resources that provide assessment or assessment-like tools.
   a. Classify each as true-false, multiple-choice, matching, essay, short-answer, completion, performance assessments, projects, portfolios, oral questioning strategies, observation strategies, or in-depth interviewing strategies.
   b. Which type(s) is (are) dominant?
   c. Tally the thinking skill levels each appears to assess. Which levels of thinking do the majority seem to assess?
   d. Judge the quality of each of these materials using the criteria in Figure 3.1.
3. Select a unit in your area for which you might craft a summative assessment instrument. Develop a complete blueprint for this assessment, using Figure 6.5 as a model.

Describe the kinds of tasks you would include, and explain how you would decide whether the tasks matched the learning targets. Estimate the amount of time it would take students to complete your assessment.

4. Develop an assessment plan for a unit of instruction in your area. Using Figure 6.3 as a model, list lessons and learning targets, types of assessment, purpose(s) of assessment, and actions to take using assessment results. Share your results with your classmates.
5. Develop an assessment plan for a marking period or a semester in an area you teach. Using Figure 6.2 as a model, include the time frame for the units, the formative and summative assessment strategies, and the weighting of the assessments within units and across units (i.e., for the entire time periods). Share your results with your classmates.

7 Completion, Short-Answer, and True-False Items

LEARNING TARGETS

After studying this chapter, you should have learned the following:

Three Fundamental Principles for Crafting Assessments

1. State the three fundamental principles for crafting assessments and explain how they apply to your own classroom situation. [2, 4]

Short-Answer Items

2. Name and give examples of the major variations of short-answer assessment tasks. [2, 1]

3. State the lower- and higher-order abilities that short-answer items can assess. [2, 1, 3]

4. Explain the strengths and shortcomings of short-answer items as they apply to assessing students in the area(s) you teach. [2, 4, 3]

5. Construct short-answer items in the area(s) you teach that are free from commonly encountered item-writing flaws. [2]

6. Use the checklist for judging the quality of short-answer and completion items to identify and correct flawed items of your own creation and those that are provided with instructional materials. [2, 1]

True-False Items

7. Name and give examples of the six major variations of true-false assessment tasks. [2, 1]

8. State the lower- and higher-order abilities that can be assessed by the varieties of true-false items. [2, 1, 1]

9. Explain the strengths and shortcomings of true-false items as they apply to assessing students in your teaching area(s). [2, 4, 3]

10. Explain the roles of blind and informed guessing on true-false tests. [6]

11. List five suggestions for how to begin writing true-false items that are free from the most common criticisms. [2, 1]

12. Construct various types of true-false items that are free from commonly encountered item-writing flaws. [2]

13. Use the checklist for judging the quality of true-false items to identify and correct flawed items of your own creation and those that are provided with instructional materials in your teaching area(s). [2, 1]

14. Explain the strengths and shortcomings of multiple true-false items as they apply to your teaching area(s). [2, 4, 3]

Important Terms and Concepts

15. Explain how each term and concept listed at the end of this chapter applies to educational assessments. [6]

ABOUT THIS CHAPTER

In this chapter we discuss how to craft simple forms of items suitable for paper-and-pencil quizzes and tests: short-answer and true-false items. If you follow the simple guidelines in this chapter, you will produce items that are valid for assessing a wide range of lower-order—as well as some higher-order—thinking skills.

The chapter begins with a discussion of three fundamental assessment design principles. These principles are the key points of sound student evaluation no matter what type of assessment—paper-and-pencil or not—you are using. Second, we discuss how to craft short-answer items. We give practical guidelines for crafting these formats well. Third, we discuss how to craft true-false items. We provide practical guidelines for constructing these items, also.

Chapters 7, 8, and 9 focus on paper-and-pencil tests and quizzes. In Chapter 10 we consider more advanced forms of assessment: items assessing complex skills, problem solving, and higher-order thinking. Chapters 11 and 12 discuss crafting performance assessments and student portfolios. Informal observation and diagnostic assessment are discussed in Chapter 13.

THREE FUNDAMENTAL PRINCIPLES FOR CRAFTING ASSESSMENTS

You will want your assessment to conform to the **three fundamental principles for crafting assessments**:

1. Focus each assessment task entirely on important learning targets (content and performance).
2. Craft each assessment task to elicit from students only the knowledge and performance that are relevant to the learning targets you are assessing.
3. Craft each assessment task to neither prevent nor inhibit a student's ability to demonstrate attainment of the learning targets you are assessing.

The first principle is a strong one. It implies that assessing whether students have learned trivial performances or minor points of content is a waste of time. You should limit the assessment tasks to those that focus on only educationally important learning targets.

To apply the second fundamental principle, you need a very clear idea of what the learning target is. If a student has achieved the desired degree of learning, the student should complete the relevant assessment task correctly. If, on the other hand, a student has not achieved the desired degree of learning, the deficiency should also be apparent in the assessment results.

The second principle recognizes, however, that sometimes teachers construct such poor assessments that the tasks elicit unwanted behaviors from students such as bluffing, fear, wild guessing, craftiness, or testwise skills. Testwiseness is the ability to use assessment-taking strategies,

clues from poorly written items, and experience in taking assessments to improve one's score beyond what one would otherwise attain from mastery of the subject matter itself. (Testwiseness is described in more detail in Chapter 14.) These extra, unwanted behaviors may lead you to an inaccurate evaluation. As a result, you may erroneously conclude that a truly knowledgeable student did not achieve the learning target; or, conversely, that a poorly prepared student did achieve the target. Many of the suggestions in the next several chapters are specific ways to help you apply the second principle.

The third fundamental principle recognizes that imprecise wording in a question, for example, may make an item so ambiguous that a student who has the knowledge may answer it wrong. Similarly, simple matters such as inappropriate vocabulary, poorly worded directions, or poorly drawn diagrams may lead an otherwise knowledgeable student to respond incorrectly. Even the format or arrangement of an item on the page can inhibit some students from responding correctly. The third principle is amplified and applied to each item format discussed in this and the subsequent chapters.

Not all assessment experts would agree that there are only three basic principles, but most are likely to agree that these three are the important and fundamental principles for constructing classroom assessment tasks. These three encompass most of the specific suggestions that assessment experts have made over the years except, perhaps, those practical suggestions for efficient scoring.

SHORT-ANSWER ITEMS[1]

Varieties of Short-Answer Formats

Short-answer items require a word, short phrase, number, or symbol response. There are three types of short-answer items: question, completion, and association (Odell, 1928; Wesman, 1971). The **question variety** asks a direct question and the students give short answers. (A question that requires the student to write paragraphs or longer responses is called an *essay item*. We will discuss essay items in Chapter 9.) Here are a few examples:

> **Example**
>
> 1. What is the capital city of Pennsylvania? _(Harrisburg)_
> 2. What is the Greek letter commonly used as a symbol for the standard deviation? _(σ)_
> 3. How many microns make up one millimeter? _(1,000)_

[1]When referring specifically to paper-and-pencil assessment tasks, we shall use the terms *item* and *test item*.

The **completion variety** presents a student with an incomplete sentence and requires the student to add one or more words to complete it. Here are two examples:

Example

1. The capital city of Pennsylvania is ___(Harrisburg)___
2. $4 + (6 \div 2) =$ ___(7)___

The **association variety** consists of a list of terms or a picture for which students have to recall numbers, labels, symbols, or other terms. This type of question is also called the *identification* variety. Some examples:

Example

On the blank next to the name of each chemical element, write the symbol used for it.

Element	Symbol
Barium	(Ba)
Calcium	(Ca)
Chlorine	(Cl)
Potassium	(K)
Zinc	(Zn)

Usefulness of Short-Answer Items

Abilities Assessed It seems obvious that short-answer items can assess students' performance of lower-order thinking skills such as recall and comprehension of information. The short-answer format also can be used to assess higher-level abilities such as the following (Gronlund, 1976):

1. Ability to make simple interpretations of data and applications of rules (e.g., counting the number of syllables in a word, demonstrating knowledge of place value in a number system, identifying the parts of an organism or apparatus in a picture, applying the definition of an isosceles triangle).

2. Ability to solve numerical problems in science and mathematics.

3. Ability to manipulate mathematical symbols and balance mathematical and chemical equations.

Figure 7.1 lists a large number of examples of short-answer items. As you will see in other chapters, multiple-choice and other objective items can also assess these abilities. The generic items from Figure 7.1 are not matched to specific learning targets. An item used directly from this table is unlikely to assess the learning target you have taught.

Thus, you must review each item and match it to your learning targets to be sure it will function validly.

Strengths and Shortcomings The short-answer format is popular because it is relatively easy to construct and can be scored objectively. But short-answer items are not free of subjectivity in scoring. You cannot anticipate all possible responses students will make. Therefore, you often have to make subjective judgments as to the correctness of what the students wrote. Spelling errors, grammatical errors, and legibility tend to complicate the scoring process further. For example, to the question "What is the name of the author of *Alice in Wonderland*?" students may respond Carroll Lewis, Louis Carroll, Charles Dodgson, Lutwidge Dodgson, or Lewis Carroll Dodgson. Which, if any, should be considered correct? Although subjective judgment is proper, it does slow down the scoring process. It also tends to lower the reliability of the obtained scores.

An advantage of the short-answer format is that it lowers the probability of getting the answer correct by random guessing. A student who guesses randomly on a true-false item has a 50–50 chance of guessing correctly; on a four-option multiple-choice item, the student has one chance in four of randomly guessing the correct answer. For most short-answer items, however, the probability of randomly guessing the correct answer is zero. Short-answer items do not prevent students from attempting to guess the answer—they only lower the probability of the students guessing correctly.

In principle, guessing can be distinguished from using one's partial knowledge to help formulate an answer. Partial knowledge is not likely to result in the (exact) correct answer in short-answer items. Teachers, however, often give **partial credit** for responses judged to be partially correct. This is an appropriate practice and can result in more reliable scores *if* you use a **scoring key** that shows the kinds of answers eligible for partial credit. Using such a scoring key makes your assignment of partial credit more consistent from student to student, improving reliability.

Crafting Short-Answer Items

Short-answer items are easy to construct, but you must follow a few simple guidelines. The checklist summarizes these guidelines in the form of yes–no questions. Use this checklist to review items before you put them on your test. A no answer to any one question is sufficient reason for you to omit an item from tests until you correct the flaw. The guidelines are really applications of the three fundamental principles for crafting assessments. In the following paragraphs, we examine the checklist's guidelines in more detail.

FIGURE 7.1 Examples of short-answer items assessing different types of lower-order thinking skills.

	Examples of generic questions*	Examples of actual questions
Knowledge of terminology	What is a ____? What does ____ mean? Define the meaning of ____?	What is a *geode*?
Knowledge of specific facts	Who did ____? When did ____? Why did ____ happen? Name the causes of ____.	What is the title of the person who heads the executive branch of government?
Knowledge of conventions	What are ____ usually called? Where are ____ usually found? What is the proper way to ____? Who usually ____?	What are magnetic poles usually named?
Knowledge of trends and sequences	In what order does ____ happen? Name the stages in ____. After ____, what happens next? Over the last ____ years, what has happened to ____? List the causes of the ____.	Write the life cycle stages of the moth in their correct order. 1st ____ 2nd ____ 3rd ____ 4th ____
Knowledge of classifications and categories	To what group do ____ belong? In what category would you classify ____? Which ____ does not belong with the others? List the advantages and disadvantages of ____.	Mars, Earth, Jupiter, and Venus are all ____
Knowledge of criteria*	By what criteria would you judge ____? What standards should ____ meet? How do you know if ____ is of high quality?	What is the main criterion against which an organization such as Greenpeace would judge the voting record of a congressional representative?
Knowledge of methods, principles, techniques	How do you test for ____ When ____ increases, what happens to ____ What should you do to ____ to get the ____ effect?	Today the sun's rays are more oblique to Centerville than they were 4 months ago. How does Centerville's temperature today compare with its temperature 4 months ago?
Comprehension	Write ____ in your own words. Explain ____ in your own words. Draw a simple diagram to show ____	What do these two lines from Shakespeare's Sonnet XV mean? "When I consider everything that grows, Holds in perfection but a little moment . . . "
Simple interpretations	Identify the ____ in the ____. How many ____ are shown below? Label ____ What is the ____ in ____	In the blank, write the adjective in each phrase below. *Phrase* 1. A beautiful girl ____ 2. A mouse is a small rodent ____ 3. John found the muddy river ____
Solving numerical problems	(Problem statements or figures to calculate would be placed here.) Use the data above to find the ____	Draw a graph to show John's activities between 2:00 p.m. and 2:45 p.m. • John left home at 2:00 p.m. • John ran from 2:00 p.m. to 2:15 p.m. • John walked from 2:15 p.m. to 2:30 p.m. • John sat from 2:30 p.m. to 2:45 p.m.
Manipulating symbols, equations	Balance these equations. Derive the formula for ____ Show that ____ equals ____ Factor the expressions below.	Balance this equation ____ Cu + ____ H_2SO_4 = ____ $CuSO_4$ + ____ H_2O + SO_2

*The "blanks" in the generic items are for you to fill in. The generic items are simply suggestions to get you started. You generate your own items suitable for testing your students. Your items must match your learning targets to be valid.

✓ *Checklist*

A Checklist for Reviewing the Quality of Short-Answer Items

Ask these questions of every item you write. If you answer "no" to one or more questions, revise the item accordingly.

1. Does the item assess an important aspect of the unit's instructional targets?

2. Does the item match your assessment plan in terms of performance, emphasis, and number of points?

3. If possible, is the item written in question format?

4. Is the item worded clearly so that the correct answer is a brief phrase, single word, or single number?

5. Is the blank or answer space toward the end of the sentence?

6. Is the item paraphrased rather than a sentence copied from learning materials?

7. If the item is in the completion format, is the omitted word an important word rather than a trivial word?

8. Are there only one or two blanks?

9. Is the blank or answer space in this item (a) the same length as the blank in other items, or (b) arranged in an appropriate column?

10. If appropriate, does the item (or the directions) tell the student the appropriate the degree of detail, specificity, precision, or units you want the answer to have?

11. Does the item avoid grammatical (and other irrelevant) clues to the correct answer?

Sources: Based on ideas from: Ebel, 1951, 1979; Greene, Jorgensen, & Gerberich, 1942; Gronlund, 1976; Hopkins, Stanley, & Hopkins, 1990; Lindvall & Nitko, 1975; Mehrens & Lehman, 1991; Nitko & Hsu, 1987; Odell, 1928; Sax, 1974; Stalnaker, 1951; Thorndike & Hagen, 1977.

1–2. The first two guidelines concern the importance of what is assessed and how the item matches the test blueprint. We have already discussed why you should assess only important performance and content and match tasks to your learning targets and the assessment plan. Even if you perform no other evaluation of your assessment, you should make it a habit to evaluate every test item using these two criteria.

3. *The question format is the preferred format for a short-answer item.* The question format of a short-answer item is preferred over the completion format. Here's why: The completion format always implies a question. The student must read the incomplete sentence and mentally convert it to a question before answering. Therefore, the most straightforward thing to do is ask a direct question in the first place. If you scrutinize most completion items, you will see that they could be phrased as questions.

Further, the meaning of the items is often clearer if you phrase them as questions instead of incomplete sentences. Consider how a completion item can be improved by converting it into a direct question:

Example

Poor: The author of *Alice in Wonderland* was _____.

Better: What is the pen name of the author of *Alice in Wonderland*?

(Lewis Carroll)

Because the first version is not written in a question format, many correct answers are possible, including "a story writer," "a mathematician," "an Englishman," and "buried in 1898." The second version phrases the statement as a question, **focusing the item** on the specific knowledge sought.

As with all such rules, this one does have exceptions. Occasionally the question form of the item incorrectly suggests the need for a longer or more complex answer. In this case, the incomplete sentence serves better. Here is an example of how the question form of an item may imply a longer than necessary answer:

Example

Poor: Why are scoring guides recommended for use with essay tests?

Better: The main reason for using a scoring guide with an essay test is to increase the (objectivity) of the scoring.

Although the first version in the example implies that the teacher wants a paragraph or more, the teacher really had a very simple response in mind. This miscommunication is corrected by the second, revised version of the item.

Most of the time, the question format produces better items. Your first impulse, therefore, should be to write questions, not incomplete sentences.

4. *Word the items specifically and clearly.* Usually, short-answer items require a single correct answer. You should word the question or incomplete sentence so this is clear to the student. Illustrations of how using the correct wording communicates that the teacher wants a single, specific answer include the following:

Example

Poor: Where is Pittsburgh, Pennsylvania, located?

_____

Better: Pittsburgh, Pennsylvania, is located at the confluence of what two rivers? (Allegheny and Monongahela)

Better: What city is located at the confluence of the Allegheny and Monongahela rivers? (Pittsburgh, Pennsylvania)

Several answers to the first version are possible, depending on how specific you want the answer to be: "western Pennsylvania," "southwestern corner of Pennsylvania," "Ohio River," "Monongahela and Allegheny rivers," and so on are all correct. If you want a specific answer, you must phrase the question in a focused and structured way. If you want to focus on the rivers, for example, the first rephrased version may be used. To focus on the city, use the second rephrased version.

Focusing the item is important because you want a certain answer. Some students who know the desired answer will not give it because they misinterpreted the question. This is especially likely for students at the elementary levels who interpret questions literally. For example, in one classroom, fourth graders were given a bar graph to interpret. The teacher then asked the poorly phrased question below.

> **Example**
>
> *Poor*:   Was the population of Mexico greater in 1941 or 1951?   _____

One hapless student examined the graph and responded, "yes." We'll leave the revision of this item to you.

5. *Put the blank toward the end of the sentence.* This fifth guideline applies to completion items. If blanks are placed at the beginning or in the middle of the sentence, the student has to mentally rearrange the item as a question before responding to it. Even a knowledgeable student will have to read the item twice to answer it. The examples below show how to improve an item by putting the blank at the end.

> **Example**
>
> *Poor*:   _____ is the name of the capital city of Illinois.
> *Better*:   The name of the capital city of Illinois is (Springfield).

Teachers of elementary-level arithmetic recognize that the ability to solve missing addend problems (e.g., "5 + ____ = 12" or "____+ 5 = 12") is quite difficult to learn. When blanks are not placed at the end of a sentence, the verbal item functions like these arithmetic problems. Unlike missing addend problems, however, putting blanks at the beginning of a sentence places an unintended barrier in the path of a youngster who has command of the relevant knowledge. Such barriers lower the validity of your assessments. Elementary students are sometimes observed stopping and puzzling at a blank without reading the entire item: They realize that they should write an answer there, but they lack the experience to read ahead and mentally rearrange the item as a question. If you rephrase the item as a direct question or place the blank at the end, these youngsters are able to display the knowledge they have acquired.

6. *Do not copy statements verbatim.* When you copy material, you encourage students' rote memorization rather than their comprehension and understanding. Further, textbook statements used as test items are usually quoted out of context. This may lead to item ambiguity or to more than one correct answer. One suggestion is to think first of the answer and then make up a question to which that answer is the only correct response (Ebel, 1979).

7. *A completion item should omit important words and not trivial words.* Use the item to assess a student's knowledge of an important fact or concept. This means, for example, that you should not make the blanks the verbs in the statement. An exception, of course, is a language usage item that focuses on the correct verb form (Thorndike, Cunningham, Thorndike, & Hagen, 1991).

8. *Limit blanks to one or two.* With more than one or two blanks, a completion item usually becomes unintelligible or ambiguous so that several unintended answers could be considered correct. Consider the following example:

> **Example**
>
> *Poor*:   _____ and _____ are two methods of scoring _____.
> *Better*:   Two different methods of scoring essay tests are the (analytic) and (holistic) methods.

9. *Testwise students sometimes use the length of the blank as a clue to the answer, so you should attend to length and arrangement of blanks in completion items.* To avoid such unintended clues, keep all blanks the same length. When testing older students, you can save yourself considerable scoring time by using short blanks in the item and by placing spaces for students to record answers at the right or left margin of the paper or on a separate answer sheet. You can then lay a **strip key** with the correct answers along the edge of each student's paper and score papers quickly. Typing the items so that all blanks occur in a column accomplishes the same purpose. For example, instead of spreading the items across the page, you can arrange them as follows:

> **Example**
>
> *Poor*:   Decisions for which rejection of some students is permitted are called _____ decisions.
>
> Decisions for which every student must be assigned to one of several educational programs are called _____.
>
> *Better*:   Which type of decision permits rejection of some students?   _____
>
> Which type of decision requires that every student be assigned to one of several educational programs?   _____

10. *Specify the precision you expect in the answer.* In a short-answer test involving dates or numerical answers, be sure to specify the numerical units you expect the students to use, or how precise or accurate you want the answers to be. This clarifies the task. It also saves time for students who strive for a degree of precision beyond your intentions. These examples illustrate how to state the degree of precision expected in the answers.

Example

Poor: If each letter to be mailed weighs 1 1/8 oz., how much will 10 letters weigh? _____

Better: If each letter to be mailed weighs 1 1/8 oz., how much (to the nearest whole oz.) will 10 letters weigh? (11 oz.)

Better: A kilogram is equal to (2.2) pounds. (Express your answer to one decimal place.)

If there are more than one or two numerical items, you can describe the level of precision you expect in the general directions at the beginning of the set of questions, rather than adding words to each item.

11. *Avoid irrelevant clues.* A test item is crafted to assess a specific learning target, but sometimes the wording provides an irrelevant clue. When this happens, a student may answer correctly without having achieved the learning target. The verb in a sentence, for example, may unintentionally clue the student that the answer you want is plural or singular. An indefinite article may be a clue that the answer you want begins with a vowel. The next example shows the same item with and without clues:

Example

Poor: A specialist in urban planning is called an   (urbanist)

Better: A specialist in city planning is called a(n)   (urbanist)

The poor version has two clues to the right answer: It uses *urban planning*, which clues *urbanist*, and it uses the indefinite article, *an*, which clues the student that the expected answer begins with a vowel sound. The better version corrects these flaws by substituting a synonym (*city planning*) and using *a(n)* for the indefinite article form.

TRUE-FALSE ITEMS

Varieties of True-False Items

A **true-false item** consists of a statement or a **proposition** that a student must judge and mark as either true or false. There are at least six varieties: true-false, yes-no, right-wrong,

correction, multiple true-false, and yes-no with explanation. The **true-false** variety presents a proposition that a student judges true or false. Here is an example:

Example

The sum of all the angles in any four-sided closed figure equals 360 degrees.   T   F

The **yes-no** variety asks a direct question, to which a student answers yes or no. This is an example:

Example

Is it possible for a presidential candidate to become president of the United States without obtaining a majority of the votes cast on election day?   Yes   No

The **right-wrong** variety presents a computation, equation, or language sentence that the student judges as correct or incorrect (right or wrong). Here are two examples:

Example

Example assessing an arithmetic principle

$5 + 3 \times 2 = 16$ R   W

Example assessing grammatical correctness

Did she know whom it was?   C   I

The **correction** variety requires a student to judge a proposition, as does the true-false variety, but the student is also required to correct any false statement to make it true. Here is an example along with the directions to the students:

Example

Read each statement below and decide if it is correct or incorrect. If it is incorrect, change the underlined word or phrase to make the statement correct.

The new student, who we met today, came from Greece.   C   I

The **multiple true-false** variety looks similar to a multiple-choice item. However, instead of selecting one option as correct, the student treats every option as a separate true-false statement. (More than one choice may be true.) Each choice is scored as a separate item. For example:

Example

Under the Bill of Rights, freedom of the press means that newspapers:

1. have the right to print anything they wish without restrictions.   T   F
2. can be stopped from printing criticisms of the government.   T   F
3. have the right to attend any meeting of the executive branch of the federal government.   T   F

The **yes-no with explanation** variety asks a direct question and requires the student to respond yes or no. In addition, the student must explain why his or her choice is correct. Here are some examples:

Example

*Situation.**

A poll was taken of 500 city Democrats and 500 city Republicans. Each person was asked whether he or she agreed with the statement: "That government is best which governs least." These are the results:

Democratic male	Agree 12%	Disagree 35%
Democratic female	Agree 3%	Disagree 14%
Republican male	Agree 48%	Disagree 12%
Republican female	Agree 28%	Disagree 7%

1. I assert that this poll proves that most people want the government to do very little. Am I correct?   Yes   No
2. If you say "No," explain why I am wrong: _____

*The situation portion of this item is adapted from Sanders, 1966, p. 117.

USEFULNESS OF TRUE-FALSE ITEMS

Advantages and Criticisms

Teachers often use true-false items because (a) certain aspects of the subject matter readily lend themselves to verbal propositions that can be judged true or false, (b) they are relatively easy to write, (c) they can be scored easily and objectively, and (d) they can cover a wide range of content within a relatively short period. But some educators have severely criticized true-false items—*especially poorly constructed true-false items.* Among the more frequent criticisms are that poorly constructed true-false items assess only specific, frequently trivial facts; are ambiguously worded; are answered correctly by random guessing; and encourage students to study and accept only oversimplified statements of truth and factual details. If you follow the suggestions in this

chapter for improving true-false items, you can avoid these criticisms.

Assess More Than Simple Recall

Well-written true-false items can assess a student's ability to identify the correctness or appropriateness of a variety of meaningful propositions, including the following (Ebel, 1972):

1. *Generalizations* in a subject area.
2. *Comparisons* among concepts.
3. *Causal or conditional propositions.*
4. *Relationships* between two events, concepts, facts, or principles.
5. *Explanations* for why events or phenomena occurred.
6. *Instances or examples* of a concept or principle.
7. *Evidential statements.*
8. *Predictions* about phenomena or events.
9. *Steps* in a procedure or process.
10. *Computations* (or other kinds of results obtained from applying a procedure).
11. *Evaluations* of events or phenomena.

Examples of items of each of these types are shown in Figure 7.2. Some of the key phrases used to construct items in each category appear, too. You may want to refer to Figure 7.2 from time to time to glean suggestions for writing true-false items. However, be sure that you don't follow Figure 7.2 blindly. When you use a key phrase the final item should assess your intended thinking skill and learning target. However, using a key phrase from the figure does not guarantee that the item you craft will assess the thinking skill shown.

Validity of the True-False Item Format

Ebel, perhaps more than any other measurement specialist, defended the use of well-written true-false items for classroom assessment. He offered the following argument for the validity of this format:

1. The essence of educational achievement is the command of useful verbal knowledge.
2. All verbal knowledge can be expressed in propositions.
3. A proposition is any sentence that can be said to be true or false.
4. The extent of a student's command of a particular area of knowledge is indicated by his success in judging the truth or falsity of propositions related to it. (Ebel, 1979, pp. 111–112)

FIGURE 7.2 Types of statements that could form the basis for your true-false items.

Type of statement	Examples of introductory words or phrases	Examples of true-false items
Generalization	All . . . Most . . . Many . . .	All adverbs modify verbs. (F)
Comparative	The difference between . . . is . . . Both . . . and . . . require . . .	Both dependent and independent clauses contain subjects and verbs. (T)
Conditional	If . . . (then) . . . When . . .	When there is no coordinating conjunction between two independent clauses, they should be separated by a colon. (F)
Relational	The larger . . . The higher . . . The lower . . . Making . . . us likely to . . . Increasing . . . tends to . . . How much . . . depends on . . .	The amount of technical vocabulary you should include in an essay depends on your intended audience. (T)
Explanatory	The main reason for . . . The purpose of . . . One of the actors that adversely affect . . . Since . . . Although . . .	One of the factors affecting changes in rules governing English grammar and style is changes in how people use the language. (T)
Exemplary	An example of . . . One instance of . . .	The movie title *The Man Who Came to Dinner* contains a nonrestrictive clause. (F)
Evidential	Studies of . . . reveal . . .	Studies of contemporary literature show that some authors deliberately violate style and usage rules to create literary effects. (T)
Predictive	One could expect . . . Increasing . . . would result in . . .	Increasing the number of clauses in sentences usually increases the reading difficulty of a passage. (T)
Procedural	To find . . . one must . . . In order to . . . one must . . . One method of . . . is to . . . One essential step . . . is to . . . Use . . . of . . . The first step toward . . .	The first step toward composing a good essay is to write a rough draft. (F)
Computational	(Item includes numerical data and requires computation or estimation.)	There are two adjectives in the sentence "The quick brown fox jumped over the lazy dog." (F)
Evaluative	A good . . . It is better to . . . than . . . The best . . . is . . . The maximum . . . is . . . The easiest method of . . . is to . . . It is easy to demonstrate that . . . It is difficult to . . . It is possible to . . . It is reasonable to . . . It is necessary to . . . in order to . . . The major drawback to . . . is . . .	It is generally better to express complex ideas as two or more shorter sentences rather than one longer sentence. (T)

Note: To be valid, the items must match specific learning targets.

Source: Adapted from *Essentials of Educational Measurement* (pp. 183–185), by R. L. Ebel, 1972, Upper Saddle River, NJ: Prentice Hall. Adapted by permission of the copyright holder.

Note that requiring students to identify the truth or falsity of propositions is not the only means of ascertaining their command of knowledge. Other ways of assessing command of knowledge are discussed further in the remaining chapters of this book.

Verbal knowledge is an important element of several learning targets, however. Nevertheless, as we saw in Chapter 2 and 6 and will see more of in Chapters 10, 11, and 12, wide ranges of thinking skills and performance outcomes form the learning targets of education. Thus,

FIGURE 7.3 Chances of a student obtaining various "good scores" by using only random guessing for all items on true-false tests of various lengths.

Number of T-F items on the test	Chances of getting the following percentage of T-F questions right:		
	60% or better	80% or better	100%
5	50 in 100	19 in 100	3 in 100
10	38 in 100	6 in 100	1 in 1,000
15	30 in 100	2 in 100	3 in 100,000
20	25 in 100	6 in 1,000	1 in 1,000,000
25	21 in 100	2 in 1,000	3 in 100,000,000

Note: Computations are based on binomial probability theory.

true-false items can assess some thinking skills and performances beyond simple recall, but you cannot use them exclusively to create valid assessment results. They must be used in combination with other assessment formats to achieve results that can be judged valid by the criteria in Chapter 3.

Guessing on True-False Items: An Ill Wind?

Charles Schulz's "Peanuts" character Linus once observed, "Taking a true-false test is like having the wind at your back." This reflects a common criticism of true-false tests: They are subject to error because students can answer them with random guesses. It is well known that for a single true-false item, there is a 50–50 chance of answering the item correctly if true or false is selected at random. This means that persons guessing randomly can expect to get *on the average* one half of the true-false items correct.[2] Several points, however, blunt this criticism (Ebel, 1972):

1. Blind (completely random) guessing is quite unlike informed guessing (guessing based on partial knowledge).

2. Well-motivated students (at least at the college level) tend to guess blindly on only a small percentage of the questions on a test.

3. It is very difficult to obtain a good score on a test by blind guessing alone.

4. The fact that a given true-false test has a high reliability coefficient[3] would be evidence that scores on that test are not seriously affected by blind guessing.

Random guessing, of the type that is assumed by the "50–50 chance" statement, is by definition random responding. Random guessing is sometimes called *blind guessing*. But most everyone's experience is that students

rarely respond this way to test questions. Rather, students tend to use whatever **partial knowledge** they have about the subject of the questions and/or about the context in which the questions are embedded to make an informed guess. Such informed guessers have a higher than 50–50 chance of success on true-false items (but how much higher, we are unable to say). This means that scores from true-false items (as with other item types) are measures of partial knowledge when informed guessing occurs. (Of course, persons who actually know the answer have a 100% chance of answering correctly!)

Although a student who is responding randomly on a single true-false item will have a 50–50 chance of being correct, the laws of chance indicate that the probability of getting a good score by random guessing on a test made up of many true-false items is quite small, especially for longer tests. This is illustrated in Figure 7.3. Chances are only 2 in 100, for example, that a student who has guessed randomly on all the items on a 15-item test will get 80% or more of the items correct. If the test has 20 true-false questions and a student guesses randomly on all items, that student has only 2 chances in 1,000 of getting 80% or more items correct. Chances of a perfect (100% correct) paper are even smaller.

Suggestions for Getting Started Properly

To write good true-false items, you must be able to identify propositions that (a) represent important ideas, (b) can be defended by competent critics as true or false, and (c) are not obviously correct to persons with general knowledge or good common sense who have not studied the subject (Ebel, 1972). These propositions are then used as starting points to derive true-false items.

In this regard, Ebel (1972) suggested that you should think of a segment of knowledge as being represented by a paragraph; the propositions are the main ideas of that paragraph. You can then use these main ideas as starting points for writing true-false items. Figure 7.2 offers suggestions on how to get started in phrasing true-false items from these propositions.

[2]For example, the average guessing score (called the *expected chance score*) for a true-false test of 50 items is 25; for 10 T-F items is 5; etc.
[3]See Chapter 4 for an explanation of reliability coefficients.

Frisbie and Becker (1990) offer these additional suggestions for getting started:

1. *Create pairs of items, one true and one false, related to the same idea, even though you will use only one.* Creating pairs of items helps you check on a statement's ambiguity and whether you need to include qualifications in the wording. Frisbie and Becker suggest that your false item is not worth using if you can only write a true version of it by inserting the word *not*.

2. *If your statement asks students to make evaluative judgments ("The best . . . is . . . ," "The most important . . . is . . . ," etc.), try to rephrase it as a comparative statement ("Compared to . . . , A is better than . . . ").* The comparative statement allows you to put into the item itself the comparisons you want students to make. Usually, when you write "What is the best way of . . . ," for example, you raise in the mind of the student the question, "compared to what?" Thus, if you include your intended comparison in the statement itself, this clears up the ambiguity.

3. *Write false statements that reflect the actual misconceptions held by students who have not achieved the learning targets.* To do this, you have to know your students well and try to think about a proposition the way a misinformed or poorly prepared student thinks about it. As you teach, you may notice these misconceptions. Take notes so you can recall them as you write items.

4. *You may wish to convert a multiple-choice item into two or more true-false items.* Because the foils (or incorrect options) of a multiple-choice item are not correct, they may be used as a basis for writing false statements.

Suggestions for Improving True-False Items

You should review and revise the first drafts of all your assessment tasks. We will say this many times in the book: *Your first drafts of assessment tasks are not fit for human consumption.* Editing assessment tasks is an important step in the assessment development process. The checklist summarizes principles for improving the quality of true-false items. These are written as questions you can ask when you review your item drafts. You should always use the checklist to review true-false items that come with your textbook and curriculum materials, because these true-false items are notorious for their poor quality. The principles implied by the checklist are explained and illustrated in the following section.

✓ Checklist

A Checklist for Judging the Quality of True-False Items

Revise every item for which you answered "no" to one or more questions.

1. Does the item assess an important aspect of the unit's instructional targets?

2. Does the item match your assessment plan in terms of performance, emphasis, and number of points?

3. Does the item assess important ideas, knowledge, or understanding (rather than trivia, general knowledge, or common sense)?

4. Is the statement either definitely true or definitely false without adding further qualifications or conditions?

5. Is the statement paraphrased rather than copied verbatim from learning materials?

6. Are the word-lengths of true statements about the same as those of false statements?

7. Did you avoid presenting items in a repetitive or easily learned pattern (e.g., TTFFTT . . . , TFTFTF . . .)?

8. Is the item free of verbal clues that give away the answer?

9. If the statement represents an opinion, have you stated the source of the opinion?

10. If the statement does not assess knowledge of the relationship between two ideas, does it focus on only one important idea?

Sources: Based on ideas from: Ebel, 1951, 1979; Greene, Jorgensen, & Gerberich, 1942; Gronlund, 1976; Hopkins, Stanley, & Hopkins, 1990; Lindquist, 1936; Lindvall, 1967; Nitko & Hsu, 1987; Thorndike & Hagen, 1977; Weidemann, 1926; Wesman, 1971.

1–2. *The first items on the checklist cover the importance of what is assessed and its match to the test blueprint.* As always, the first two criteria that your assessment tasks should meet are importance and match to your assessment plan. Eliminate every item failing to meet these two criteria.

3. *Assess important ideas, rather than trivia, general knowledge, or common sense.* Although this guideline applies to all assessment tasks, you need to be especially sensitive to this point when writing true-false items. It is easy to write items that assess trivial knowledge. Here are some examples of how to improve items so they focus on more important ideas:

Example

Poor:	George Washington had wooden teeth.	T	F
Better:	George Washington actively participated in the Constitutional Convention.	T	F
Poor:	The author of the textbook provides six suggestions for writing true-false items.	T	F
Better:	A good procedure for developing true-false items is to insert the word *not* into a true proposition taken from a textbook.	T	F

The first item focuses on trivia rather than important information about Washington's role in the early days of the nation. The revised version at least asks a more significant fact about him. The second poor item does not assess anything important. The revised version of this item assesses a student's understanding of an item-writing principle rather than a questionable idiosyncratic fact.

Incidentally, the answer to the second revised item is "false." The practice of taking a textbook sentence and making it false by inserting negative function words (e.g., *not, neither . . . nor*) makes the item you write tricky for students. Tricky items do not belong on your assessment instruments. Even well-prepared students can overlook the negative word (Ebel, 1979). If you follow the suggestions in this chapter for getting started, you are unlikely to create such a flawed item.

4. *Make sure the item is either definitely true or definitely false.* A proposition should not be so general that a knowledgeable student can find exceptions that change the intended truth or falsity of the statement. Make sure the item is phrased in a way that makes it unambiguous to the *knowledgeable* student. (Items should, of course, appear ambiguous to the unprepared or unknowledgeable student.) A few suggestions for reducing item ambiguity include the following (Lindvall & Nitko, 1975):

a. *Use short statements where possible.* This makes it easier to identify the idea you want the student to judge true or false. Complex, cumbersome statements make identifying the essential element in the item difficult for even knowledgeable students (Ebel, 1951). If the information you want to describe in the statement is complex, use different sentences to separate the description from the statement students must judge true or false. Frequently, you can shorten a long, complex statement that contains extraneous material by simply editing it.[4] An example of improving an item by editing it to make it more concise and to the point follows:

Example

Poor:	Although a single item is generally an unreliable measure, and although it is frequently difficult to write additional items, a test's reliability usually can be improved by making the test longer and thereby increasing the number of times the students' behaviors are observed.	T F
Better:	Tests containing more items are usually less reliable than shorter tests.	T F

b. *Use exact language.* Frequently, quantitative terms can clarify an otherwise ambiguous statement. For example, instead of saying "equal to approximately $5.00" or "approximately one half of . . . ," say "between $4.00 and $6.00" or "between 45% and 55%."

c. *Use positive statements and avoid* **double negatives**, which many students find especially confusing. Here are some examples of improving items by avoiding negatives and double negatives:

Example

1. *Poor*:	It is not undesirable to use double negatives inadvertently in a true-false item.[*]	T F
2. *Poor*:	The Monongahela River does not flow northward.	T F
3. *Better*:	The Monongahela River flows southward.	T F

[*]*Principles of Educational and Psychological Measurement and Evaluation*, 3rd edition, by G Sax © 1989. Reprinted with permission of Wadsworth Publishing, a division of Thomson Learning: www.thomsonrights.com. Fax 800 730-2215.

If you must use a negative function word, be sure to underline it or use all capital letters so it is NOT overlooked.

5. *Avoid copying sentences verbatim.* Students often find sentences copied from a text uninterpretable because they have been taken out of context. In addition, such statements are likely to communicate to students that the text's exact (and often idiosyncratic) phrasing is important, rather than their own comprehension. This encourages students to engage in rote learning of textbook sentences. Recall from Figure 3.2 that one factor in the validity of your assessment is that it does not have such negative consequences.

Copying items from a text is more likely when a teacher is testing for knowledge of verbal concepts (including definitions) and statements of principles (rules). But testing for comprehension demands paraphrasing at the minimum, and enhancing a student's comprehension of concepts and principles seems to be a more important educational goal than encouraging a student to memorize textbook statements word for word. Again, if you follow the earlier-stated suggestions for initially deriving items, you are not likely to copy statements from a textbook.

6. *True and false statements should have approximately the same number of words.* Teachers tend to make true statements more qualified and wordy than false statements. Testwise students can pick up on this irrelevant clue and get the item right without achieving the learning target. The easiest way to correct this type of flaw is to keep a watchful editorial eye and to rewrite inappropriate statements.

7. *Don't present items in a repetitive or easily learned pattern* (e.g., TFTF . . . , TTFFTT . . . , TFFTFF . . .). Some

---

[4]This suggestion applies to all item types, of course.

teachers develop such patterns because they are easy to remember and thus make scoring easier. But if it's easy for a teacher to remember, it will be easy for testwise students to learn also. Assessment results will then be invalid. You should also avoid a consistent practice of having many more true answers than false, or many more false answers than true. If students notice, for example, that you seldom use a false statement, they will (rightly) avoid choosing false when they are uncertain of the answer. Upper-grade students discover these patterns quickly when a teacher uses lots of true-false items.

Not all educational assessment specialists agree on the proportion of true-to-false answers to include (Frisbie & Becker, 1990). Some specialists (Ebel & Frisbie, 1991; Popham, 1991) recommend having more false items than true ones, because false items have been shown to discriminate[5] better than true items (Barker & Ebel, 1981; Oosterhof & Glasnap, 1974). *Discriminate* in this context means that false items tend to differentiate the most knowledgeable students from the least knowledgeable better than true items. Increased item discrimination improves the reliability of the total test scores.

8. *Do not use **verbal clues (specific determiners) that give away the answer**.* A **specific determiner**[6] is a word or phrase in a true-false or multiple-choice item that "overqualifies" a given statement and gives the student an unintended clue to the correct answer (Sarnacki, 1979). Words such as *always*, *never*, and *every* tend to make propositions false. Words such as *often*, *usually*, and *frequently* tend to make propositions true. Testwise students will use these clues to respond correctly even though they do not have command of the requisite knowledge. Some examples of poor items using specific determiners follow:

Example

Poor:	It is always better to use a longer test than a shorter one.	T	F
Poor:	Frequently, it is better to use a longer test than a shorter test.	T	F

You should note that *some* propositions are "always" or "never" true, or "often" or "usually" false. For this reason some assessment specialists suggest that using specific determiners in reverse helps distinguish the knowledgeable student from the merely testwise one (Ebel, 1979; Ebel & Frisbie, 1991). We wouldn't recommend using such tactics with elementary school students. Some evidence (Slakter, Koehler, & Hampton, 1970) indicates that youngsters do not attend to specific determiner

clues in multiple-choice items until the ninth grade, even though they do use other types of test-wiseness skills as early as fifth grade. The same seems likely to be valid for true-false items.

9. *Attribute the opinion in a statement to an appropriate source.* If your true-false item expresses an opinion, value, or attitude, you should attribute the statement to an appropriate source. You can use an introductory clause, such as "According to the text . . . " or "In the opinion of most specialists in this area . . . " or "In Jones's view. . . . " This referencing reduces ambiguity in two ways: (a) it makes clear that the statement is not to be judged in general, but rather in terms of the specific source; and (b) it makes clear that you are not asking for the student's personal opinion.

10. *Focus on one idea.* Have only one idea per item, unless the item is crafted to assess knowledge of the relationship between two ideas. The following example shows how an item can be improved by focusing it on only one idea:

Example

Poor:	The Monongahela River flows north to join the Allegheny River at Columbus, where they form the Ohio River.	T	F
Better:	The Monongahela River and the Allegheny River join to form the Ohio River.	T	F

In the poor item, a student may respond with the correct answer, F, for an appropriate reason: The student may think (erroneously) that the Monongahela River does not flow north, may be unaware that the confluence of the rivers is at Pittsburgh, or may lack any knowledge about the three rivers. Thus, the student would get the item right without having the knowledge that getting the right answers implies. A separate statement for each idea may be necessary to identify precisely what the student knows.

Crafting Multiple True-False Items

A multiple true-false item looks like a multiple-choice item in that it has a stem followed by several alternatives. Unlike when responding to a multiple-choice item, however, the student does not select the single correct or best answer; she responds true or false to every alternative. In turn, each alternative is scored correct or incorrect. Because of this, the item may be crafted to have several correct (true) alternatives instead of only one. The examples that follow illustrate this.

---

[5]*Discrimination* is a technical term used in analysis of item response data. See Chapter 14 for an explanation.
[6]C. C. Weidemann (1926) was probably the first person to use this term in connection with true-false items.

Examples

**Under current collective bargaining laws, workers have the right to bargain for

1. how much workers of each skill level
   should be paid   T   F
2. how much managers should be paid.   T   F
3. what new products the company should
   produce.   T   F
4. which workers should be laid off first.   T   F

**The following statements are arguments used by some people before the Civil War to justify slavery. Read each statement and decide if it is an argument based on democratic ideas.

5. Slavery is right because it existed through
   most of history.   T   F
6. Slavery is right because the men who wrote
   the United States Constitution accepted it.   T   F
7. Slavery is right because the great Greek,
   Aristotle, supported it.   T   F

Source: Adapted from Sanders, 1966, pp. 53 & 132.

Format Notice three things about the format of the preceding examples. First, unlike multiple-choice items, the *options are numbered* consecutively, and asterisks set off the different clusters' stems. Second, you do not need to have a balance of true or false correct answers within one cluster. Some clusters, like the second one, may not have any true or any yes answers. Third, all of the statements within a cluster must relate to the same stem or question. Each statement within a cluster is treated as a separate true-false item. Thus, the example contains seven items, not two items.

Advantages This item format has the following advantages (Ebel & Frisbie, 1991; Frisbie, 1992): (a) Students can make two or three multiple true-false responses in the same time it takes them to answer one multiple-choice item; (b) a multiple true-false test created from multiple-choice items has a higher reliability than the original multiple-choice test; (c) multiple true-false items can assess the same abilities as straight multiple-choice items that are crafted to assess parallel content; (d) students believe that multiple true-false items do a better job of assessing their knowledge than straight multiple-choice items; (e) students perceive multiple true-false items to be slightly harder than straight multiple-choice items; and (f) multiple true-false items may be easier to write than multiple-choice items because you are not limited to creating only one correct answer.

Limitations The multiple true-false item format shares many of the same limitations as multiple-choice items. These limitations are discussed in Chapter 8. Some research shows that standard multiple-choice items may be more appropriate than multiple true-false items for assessing

higher-order thinking skills and when criterion-related validity evidence is important (Downing, Baranowski, Grosso, & Norcini, 1995).

Summary

Three Fundamental Principles for Crafting Assessments

- Three fundamental principles guide most recommendations for crafting assessment tasks:
  - Focus only on educationally important learning targets.
  - Elicit only the performances that are relevant to the learning target being assessed.
  - Neither prevent nor inhibit a student's ability to demonstrate that he has attained the learning target.

Short-Answer Items

- Short-answer items require the student to respond with a word, short phrase, number, or symbol.
- Three types of short-answer items were identified: the question variety, the completion variety, and the association variety.
- Short-answer items assess various abilities, including
  - Simply recalling terminology, facts, symbols, and classifications.
  - Applying rules and making simple interpretations of data and other information.
  - Solving simple science and mathematics problems.
  - Manipulating symbols and balancing mathematical and chemical equations.
- Short-answer items are more objective than essay items but are not free of subjectivity in scoring.
- The chance of a student randomly guessing the correct answer on a short-answer item is much less than on a true-false or a multiple-choice item.
- A checklist for judging the quality of short-answer items is presented.

True-False Items

- A true-false item consists of a statement or proposition that the student must judge as true or false. Varieties include true-false, yes-no, right-wrong, correction, multiple true-false, and yes-no with explanation.
- True-false items are frequently criticized because they can:
  - Be used to assess specific, trivial facts.
  - Be ambiguously worded.
  - Be answered correctly by blind guessing.
  - Encourage students to study factual details and to accept oversimplified statements of truth.
- Carefully constructed true-false questions frequently reach beyond factual details. They are not ambiguously worded, nor do they assess trivial facts. Examples are given in Figure 7.2.
- Advantages of true-false items include
  - Ease of construction.
  - Objectivity and ease of scoring.
  - Increased coverage of content per unit of testing time.
- One logical argument for the validity of true-false items concludes that a student's judgments of the truth of propositions in an area of knowledge reflect the student's command or mastery of that area.

- It is possible to guess randomly on true-false items, but it is difficult to get good scores by this process when the test has many items (see Figure 7.3).
- A random guess is a completely random response, much like flipping a coin; an informed guess is a response based on partial knowledge and testwiseness.
- Most well-prepared and well-motivated students are unlikely to use random guessing, but they may use informed guessing.
- Your ability to write good quality true-false items begins with your ability to identify propositions in a subject area that:
  - Reflect important concepts.
  - Competent authorities can defend as true.
  - Are not obvious or common knowledge.
- The chapter describes how to get started in writing quality true-false items.
- As with all assessment tasks, you should carefully review and edit true-false items.
- A checklist for judging the quality of true-false items is provided.

Important Terms and Concepts

double negatives
focusing the item
partial credit
partial knowledge
proposition
random guessing
scoring key
short-answer varieties (association, completion, question)
strip key
three fundamental principles for crafting assessments
true-false varieties (correction, multiple true-false, right-wrong, true-false, yes-no, yes-no with explanation)
verbal clues (specific determiners)

Exercises and Applications

1. Write short-answer or completion items in your teaching area(s) that assess each of the lower-order thinking skills listed in Figure 7.1.
2. Each of the following completion items contains one or more flaws. For each item, use the checklist for short-answer items to identify the flaw(s), and rewrite the item so it remedies the flaw(s) you identified but creates no new flaws.
   a. _____ is the substance that helps plants turn light energy to food.
   b. The Johnstown Flood occurred during _____.
   c. The _____ is the major reason why _____ and _____ exhibit _____.
   d. San Francisco was named after _____.
   e. A kilogram is equivalent to _____.
   f. Was the population greater in 1941 or 1951?
3. Obtain a teacher's edition of a textbook (or other curricular materials) that covers the material for the teaching unit you selected for Exercise 3 of Chapter 6. Locate the completion and true-false items presented in the teacher's edition or textbook for this unit. Match those items to the learning targets included in the assessment blueprint you crafted for Exercise 3. To what extent do these items match the learning targets and the blueprint? What do your findings suggest about the way you should use the items the textbook gives you? About your need to craft items yourself? Prepare a short report and share your findings with others in this course.
4. Write one true-false item in your teaching area(s) that assesses a student's use of each of the categories of propositions listed in Figure 7.2.
5. Each of the following true-false items contains one or more flaws. For each item, use the checklist on p. 142 to identify the flaw(s), and rewrite it, correcting the flaw(s) identified. Be sure your rewritten items do not exhibit new flaws.
   a. The two categories, plants and animals, are all that biologists need to classify every living thing.   T   F
   b. In the United States, it is warm in the winter.   T   F
   c. Editing assessment tasks is an important step in the assessment development process.   T   F
   d. The major problem in the world today is that too many people want more than their "fair share" of the Earth's resources.   T   F
   e. There were more teachers on strike in 1982 than in 1942, even though the employment rate was lower in 1942 than in 1982.   T   F

8 Multiple-Choice and Matching Exercises

LEARNING TARGETS

After studying this chapter, you should have learned the following:

Multiple-Choice Item Format

1. State the basic purpose that any assessment task must serve. [4, 6]
2. Name and describe the function of each part of a multiple-choice item. [2, 6]

Considerations Before Crafting Items

3. Describe each of the major varieties of multiple-choice items. [1, 2]
4. State the abilities that can and cannot be directly assessed by multiple-choice items. [1, 2]

Advantages and Criticisms of Multiple-Choice Items

5. Explain the advantages and criticisms of multiple-choice items. [1, 2, 6]
6. Describe the situations when you should not use multiple-choice items, even though it appears that they would be applicable. [1, 6]

Crafting Basic Multiple-Choice Items and Using a Checklist

7. Construct multiple-choice items in the area(s) you teach that are free from commonly encountered item-writing flaws. [2]
8. Use the checklist provided in the textbook for basic multiple-choice items to evaluate the quality and correct the flaws in items of your own crafting and items provided with instructional materials in your own teaching area(s). [2]

Crafting Alternative Varieties of Multiple-Choice Items

9. Craft usable items of the following types in your teaching area(s): greater-less-same, best-answer, experiment-interpretation, and statement-and-comment. [2]
10. Describe the advantages and disadvantages of each of the alternative types of multiple-choice items listed in Learning Target 9. [1, 2, 6]
11. Explain the value of using the item types listed in Learning Target 9 over traditional true-false, multiple-choice, matching, and short-answer items. [1, 2, 3]
12. For the types of items in Learning Target 9, use the checklists provided in the textbook to evaluate the quality and correct the flaws in items you have designed and items provided with instructional materials in your own teaching area(s). [2, 6]

Matching Exercise Format and Its Advantages and Criticisms

13. Name and describe the function of each part of a matching exercise. [2, 6]
14. State the abilities that can and cannot be directly assessed by matching exercises. [1, 2]
15. Explain the advantages and criticisms of matching exercises. [1, 2, 6]

Crafting Basic Matching Exercises

16. Construct matching exercises that are free from commonly encountered item-writing flaws. [2]
17. Use the checklist for judging the quality of matching exercises to identify and correct flawed items of your

own creation and those provided with instructional materials in your teaching area(s). [2, 1]

Crafting Alternative Varieties of Matching Exercises

18. Craft usable items in your teaching area of each of the following alternative types of matching exercises: masterlist (keylist) and tabular (matrix). [2, 1]

19. Explain the advantages and criticisms of the masterlist and tabular matching exercise formats. [1, 2, 6]

20. Describe the types of knowledge and skills assessed by the masterlist and tabular item formats. [1, 2, 6]

21. Explain the advantages of the masterlist and tabular item formats over the traditional

true-false, multiple choice, and matching item formats. [1, 2, 6]

22. For the masterlist and tabular matching exercise formats, use the checklists provided in the textbook to evaluate the quality and correct the flaws in items of your own crafting and items provided with instructional materials in your own teaching area(s). [2, 6]

23. Score tabular (matrix) item sets using the procedures described in this chapter. [3]

Important Terms and Concepts

24. Explain how terms and concepts listed at the end of this chapter apply to the construction of assessment tasks. [6]

ABOUT THIS CHAPTER

We begin the chapter by discussing the usefulness of multiple-choice items: their characteristics, varieties, advantages and criticisms, and when not to use them. Next, we offer suggestions for crafting multiple-choice items in three areas: improving the item stem, improving the alternatives, and wording the correct answer. Illustrating alternative varieties of multiple-choice items that assess different types and levels of thinking skills concludes the section.

After discussing multiple-choice item writing, we discuss crafting matching exercises. Suggestions for improving both the exercises you craft and the exercises you adapt from commercial instructional and curricular materials are given. The chapter concludes with a discussion of alternative varieties of matching items. These alternatives assess different levels of thinking skills. They may provide useful ways to assess some otherwise difficult-to-assess learning targets.

MULTIPLE-CHOICE ITEM FORMAT

A **multiple-choice item** consists of one or more introductory sentences followed by a list of two or more suggested responses. The student must choose the **correct answer** from among the responses you list. The following example illustrates this format.

Example

Which of the following, combined with the revolution of the sun, causes the seasons?   **Stem**

  A The frequency of sunspot occurrences

  B The gravitational pull of the moon   **Distractors**

  C The intensity of light emitted by the sun

  *D The tilt of the Earth's axis   **Keyed alternative**

Note: Correct answers to multiple-choice items will appear with an asterisk (*) throughout this book.

Source: From *The Geography Learning of High-School Seniors* (p. 44), by R. Allen, N. Bettis, D. Kurfman, W. MacDonald, I. V. S. Mullis, and C. Salter (1990), Princeton, NJ: National Assessment of Educational Progress, Educational Testing Service. Reprinted by permission.

Stem

The **stem** is the part of the item that asks the question, sets the task a student must perform, or states the problem a student must solve. You write the stem so that a student understands what task to perform or what question to answer.

FIGURE 8.1 Item with interpretive material.

Interpretive Material →		Jan	Feb	Mar	Apr	May	June	July	Aug	Sept	Oct	Nov	Dec	Annual
	Mean Temperature (in degrees)	79	79	80	81	81	80	81	81	82	82	82	80	80.7
	Total Precipitation (in inches)	7	6	6	7	11	12	10	7	3	2	6	11	88

Which of the following regions would have the range of monthly temperature and precipitation in the chart above?

 A Savanna

 B Semiarid desert

 *C Tropical rain forest

 D Tundra

Source: From *The Geography Learning of High-School Seniors* (p. 45), by R. Allen, N. Bettis, D. Kurfman, W. MacDonald, I. V. S. Mullis, and C. Salter (1990), Princeton, NJ: National Assessment of Educational Progress. Educational Testing Service. Reprinted by permission.

Alternatives

Teachers call the list of suggested responses by various names: **alternatives, responses, choices,** and **options.** The alternatives should always be arranged in a meaningful way (logically, numerically, alphabetically, etc.). The chronological sequence in which events occur and the size of objects (large, medium, small) are examples of logical orders. If no logical or numerical order exists among them, the alternatives should be arranged in alphabetical order. In the preceding example, alternatives are in alphabetical order. The reason for this is that you do not want to establish a pattern that can clue the answer for students who do not know it. Second, following this rule saves the students time.

Keyed Alternative and Distractors

The alternative that is the correct or best answer to the question or problem you pose is called the **keyed answer, keyed alternative,** or simply the **key.** The remaining incorrect alternatives are called **distractors** or **foils.** The purpose of the latter is to present plausible (but incorrect) answers to the question or solutions to the problem in the stem. These foils should be plausible only to students who do not have the level of knowledge or understanding required by your learning target—those who haven't learned the material well enough. Conversely, the foils should not be plausible to students who have the degree of knowledge you desire.

Interpretive Material

In some cases, you may need to add information to make a question clearer or more authentic. You may wish to assess a learning target, for example, that requires students

to apply their knowledge to data in a table or a graph, to a situation described in a paragraph, to an object, or to an event simulated by a picture. If adding this kind of information makes the stem more than one or two sentences long, then the information is placed in a section that comes before the stem. This information is called **interpretive material,** and the items that refer to it are called **context-dependent items, interpretive exercises,** or **linked items** (the items are "linked" to the interpretive material). Figure 8.1 illustrates this assessment technique. The table of weather data is the interpretive material. We give more elaborate suggestions for crafting context-dependent items in Chapter 10.

CONSIDERATIONS BEFORE CRAFTING ITEMS

Similarity of Distractors

Think of a student as being located at some point along a **continuum of learning** for a given learning target.[1] You can construct a test item for students at a specific level of this learning continuum. The students who are at this level (or above it) should be able to answer the item correctly; others, lower on the continuum of learning, will not.

---

[1]This is not an entirely satisfactory conceptualization from a strictly scientific viewpoint, but it does have pedagogical value.

Consider the following items:

> **Example**
>
> 1. In what year did the United States enter World War I?
>   A 1776
>   B 1812
>   *C 1917
>   D 1981
>
> 2. In what year did the United States enter World War I?
>   A 1901
>   *B 1917
>   C 1941
>   D 1950
>
> 3. In what year did the United States enter World War I?
>   A 1913
>   B 1915
>   C 1916
>   *D 1917

All three items ask the same question, but the specificity of knowledge that is required to answer that question increases from Item 1 to Item 3. In this example, you can easily see how the *alternatives operate to make the item easy or difficult*: The alternatives require the students to make finer distinctions among the dates. Some research supports the idea that similarity among the alternatives increases the difficulty of an item (Green, 1984). Although the example uses dates, similarities can also be the result of using certain words or concepts. Of course, manipulating the alternatives is not the only way to create more difficult items.

For which level of knowledge should an item be written? There is no general rule, but keep in mind these main points: the type of students, the level of instruction, the purpose for which you will use the assessment results, and the level of knowledge your students need to attain at this point in their educational development. Be sure, too, that you consider the taxonomy thinking levels your test will assess. (Review these thinking levels in Chapter 6.) In effect, you need to decide, at least roughly, which level of proficiency is sufficient for each important learning target. Then you construct test items that will allow you to distinguish students who lack sufficient proficiency from those who have acquired it. Or if you are trying to map students along a range of proficiencies (A, B, C, D, F, for example; or Basic, Proficient, Advanced; etc.), you should include items along the range of the continuum, so that each category of students will have some items that indicate the proficiency level.

Basic Purpose of Assessment Tasks

The preceding description represents an idealized situation. Seldom will your real assessment tasks separate students this neatly. Some less knowledgeable students probably will answer some tasks correctly, and other, more knowledgeable students will not. In general, though, keep in mind this principle:

> The **basic purpose of an assessment task**, whether or not it is a multiple-choice item, is to identify students who have attained a sufficient (or necessary) level of knowledge (skill, ability, or performance) of the learning target being assessed.

Varieties of Multiple-Choice Items

Teachers and professional test developers use several **varieties of multiple-choice items**. Some of these are shown in Figure 8.2.

Teachers usually find that the correct-answer, best-answer, incomplete-statement, and negative varieties in Figure 8.2 are the most useful. As you grow more skilled at evaluating students, you will find that you need to use several of these variations to obtain valid results. Space does not permit us, however, to describe each one in this textbook. If you would like more detail about a particular variety, you should read Ebel (1951) or Wesman (1971), as well as the material listed at the end of this chapter. After we present material about the basics of crafting multiple-choice items, we will discuss the more advanced multiple-choice varieties.

Direct Versus Indirect Assessment

Lindvall (1967) distinguished between direct and indirect assessment of educational outcomes. A multiple-choice test can be a **direct assessment** of certain abilities. Well-written multiple-choice items, especially those requiring the use of interpretive materials, can help directly assess a student's ability to discriminate and make correct choices; to comprehend concepts, principles, and generalizations; to make judgments about and choices among various courses of action; to infer and reason; to compute; to interpret new data or new information; and to apply information and knowledge in structured situations.

Multiple-choice items are only **indirect assessments** of other important educational outcomes, such as the ability to recall (as opposed to recognize) information under minimal prompting conditions, to articulate explanations and give examples, to produce and express unique or original ideas, to solve problems that are not well structured, to organize personal thoughts, to display thought processes or patterns of reasoning, to work in groups, and to construct or build things. These are important abilities. Many of them can be assessed directly with other paper-and-pencil formats such as extended written assignments. Others require alternative assessment techniques such as observing a student over an extended period working alone or in a group; interviewing a student; or assessing a student's performance, product, or creation. These latter techniques are discussed in Chapters 11, 12, and 13.

FIGURE 8.2 Varieties of multiple-choice items.

A. *The correct-answer variety*

Who invented the sewing machine?
- A. Fulton
- *B. Howe
- C. Singer
- D. White
- E. Whitney

B. *The best-answer variety*

What was the basic purpose of the Marshall Plan?
- A. military defended western Europe
- *B. reestablish business and industry in western Europe
- C. settle United States' differences with Russia
- D. directly help the hungry and homeless in Europe

C. *The multiple-response variety*

What factors are principally responsible for the clotting of blood?
- A. contact of blood with a foreign substance
- *B. contact of blood with injured tissue
- C. oxidation of hemoglobin
- D. presence of unchanged prothrombin

D. *The incomplete-statement variety*

Millions of dollars of corn, oats, wheat, and rye are destroyed annually in the United States by
- A. mildews.
- B. molds.
- C. rusts.
- *D. smuts.

E. *The negative variety*

Which of these is NOT true of viruses?
- A. Viruses live only in plants and animals.
- B. Viruses reproduce themselves.
- *C. Viruses are composed of very large living cells.
- D. Viruses can cause diseases.

F. *The substitution variety*

Passage to be read

Surely the forces of education should be fully utilized to acquaint youth with the real nature of the dangers to democracy, <u>*for*</u> no other place
1

offers <u>*as good or better opportunities than*</u> the school
2

for a <u>*rational*</u> consideration of the problems involved.
3

Items to be answered
1. *A. , for
    B. . For
    C. - for
    D. no punctuation needed
2. A. As good or better opportunities than
    B. as good opportunities or better than
    C. as good opportunities as or better than
    *D. better opportunities than
3. *A. rational
    B. radical
    C. reasonable
    D. realistic

G. *The incomplete-alternative variety*[a]

An apple that has a sharp, pungent, but not disagreeably sour or bitter, taste is said to be (4)
- A. p
- B. q
- *C. t
- D. v
- E. w

H. *The combined response variety*

In what order should these sentences be written in order to make a coherent paragraph?
- a. A sharp distinction must be drawn between table manners and sporting manners.
- b. This kind of handling of a spoon at the table, however, is likely to produce nothing more than an angry protest against squirting grapefruit juice about.
- c. Thus, for example, a fly ball caught by an outfielder in baseball or a completed pass in football is a subject for applause.
- d. Similarly, the dexterous handling of a spoon in golf to release a ball from a sand trap may win a championship match.
- e. But a biscuit or a muffin tossed and caught at table produces scorn and reproach.

- A. a, b, c, d, e
- *B. a, c, e, d, b
- C. a, e, c, d, b
- D. b, e, d, c, a

[a]The numeral in parentheses indicates the number of letters in the correct answer (which in this case is "tart"). Using this number rules out borderline correct answers.

Sources: Adapted from "Writing the Test Item," by R. L. Ebel, in *Educational Measurement* (pp. 194–195), by E. F. Lindquist (Ed.), 1951, Washington, DC: American Council on Education. Also adapted from "Writing the Test Item," by A. G. Wesman, in *Educational Measurement* (2nd ed.), (pp. 94–97), by R. L. Thorndike (Ed.). 1971, Washington, DC: American Council on Education. Adapted by permission.

ADVANTAGES AND CRITICISMS OF MULTIPLE-CHOICE ITEMS

Advantages

The following are advantages of multiple-choice items:

1. *The multiple-choice format can be used to assess a greater variety of learning targets than other formats of response-choice items.* The various abilities were discussed in the preceding paragraphs.

2. *Multiple-choice items*[2] do not require students to write out and elaborate their answers and thus minimize the opportunity for less knowledgeable students to "bluff" or "dress up" their answers (Wood, 1977). This lack of

[2]These advantages apply to other types of response-choice tasks as well.

opportunity to write answers is considered a disadvantage to some.[3]

3. *Multiple-choice tests focus on reading and thinking.* They do not require students to use writing processes under examination conditions.

4. *Students have less chance to guess the correct answer to a multiple-choice item than to a true-false item or to a poorly constructed matching exercise.* The probability of a student blindly guessing the correct answer to a three-alternative item is 1/3; to a four-alternative item it is 1/4; and so on.

5. *The distractor a student chooses may give you diagnostic insight into difficulties the student is experiencing.* However, for distractors to work this way you must carefully craft them so they are attractive to students who make common errors or who hold common misconceptions. Note, too, that a single item is not a very reliable basis for a diagnosis. You will have to follow up to confirm your diagnosis.

Criticisms

Wood (1977) has summarized several criticisms of multiple-choice tests. Of course, most of the criticisms expressed in this section can also be true of any type of assessment procedure. However, in other assessment formats these flaws may show up in the way a teacher sets the task or in the rubrics a teacher uses for scoring students' responses.

1. *Students must choose from among a fixed list of options, rather than creating or expressing their own ideas or solutions.* If you rely exclusively on multiple-choice testing, you will risk giving your students little or no opportunity to write about the topics in the subject they are learning.

2. *Poorly written multiple-choice items can be superficial, trivial, and limited to factual knowledge.* Of course, so can any poorly constructed assessment format. Gaining the knowledge and skill to overcome this criticism is the reason you are taking this course!

3. *Because usually only one option of an item is keyed as correct, brighter students may be penalized for not choosing it.* Brighter students may detect flaws in multiple-choice items due to ambiguities of wording, divergent viewpoints, or additional knowledge of the subject, whereas other students may not.

4. *Multiple-choice items tend to be based on "standardized," "vulgarized," or "approved" knowledge.* The problems students solve on multiple-choice items tend to be very structured and closed (having one correct answer). This gives the impression that all problems in a subject area have a single correct answer, which may encourage students to place too much faith in an authority figure's correctness or may misrepresent a subject area as having a fixed and limited knowledge base. Further, if you use multiple-choice tests that

fail to use items linked to realistic interpretive materials, this results in tests not having a real-world context. This is referred to as **decontextualized knowledge**. As a result, your tests may not assess whether students can use what they have learned in a meaningful and authentic context.

5. *Exclusive use of multiple-choice testing for important or high-stakes assessments may shape education in undesirable ways.* Those objecting to multiple-choice tests point out that the type of examination you use can shape the content and nature of instruction you deliver to students. If a high-stakes assessment's multiple-choice items focus on factual knowledge, teachers tend to use drill-and-practice techniques to prepare students for it. If the test contains multiple-choice items that assess using knowledge and applying higher-order thinking skills, drill-and-practice teaching strategies are less effective.

WHEN NOT TO USE MULTIPLE-CHOICE ITEMS

Definite "Don'ts"

As indicated in previous chapters (especially Chapter 6), test items must be aligned with the student achievements you want them to assess. You would not, for example, substitute multiple-choice questions on English mechanics and grammar for actual samples of writing when your learning target calls for students to write. Nor would you use multiple-choice items when your main learning target requires students to organize their own ideas, develop their own logical arguments, express their own thoughts and feelings, or otherwise demonstrate their self-expression abilities.

When You Have a Choice

At times, you have a choice between using short-answer items for the entire test and using multiple-choice items for the entire test. Perhaps on the surface, either format seems appropriate. One of these instances is when you are assessing students' simple recall of information. However, multiple-choice items should not be used in certain classroom tests (Lindquist & Mann, 1936). If most or all of the items in your test will assess students' simple recall, a short-answer test is preferred when:

1. each of the items has only one correct answer and the correct answers are almost always a single word or number.

2. all of the items are computational problems calling for numerical answers.

3. almost all of the items have only two possible plausible responses (e.g., yes vs. no, male vs. female, positive vs. negative).

4. the answer to each test item is short enough so that writing the answers doesn't take the student any longer than marking the answer to multiple-choice questions on an answer sheet.

[3]You may be surprised to learn that what some persons praise as advantages, others damn with a vengeance!

When any one of these situations exist, it will be difficult for you to write good multiple-choice items requiring students to demonstrate the required degree of recollection and computation. Further, as in Situations 2 and 4, sometimes there is no advantage to the multiple-choice format over the more direct short-answer format.

Exceptions

There are exceptions to these suggestions, of course. When you need to assess a large number of students over large areas of content, and when you have readily available machine scoring, multiple-choice items may be the only practical assessment. Or when you already have a test that includes lots of good multiple-choice items but only one or two of those items fit one of the four situations previously listed, it is more efficient to use the multiple-choice format for these items.

If your students will be administered a standardized achievement test (either by your school district or by the state), it will be to their advantage to have experience answering multiple-choice items. In fact, some educational measurement specialists argue that in such instances you would be remiss if you did not give your students practice in taking multiple-choice tests. Therefore, you may wish to use multiple-choice items for at least some parts of your assessments to give students appropriate practice, even though one of the four situations exists.

Classroom assessment generally benefits from a mixture of assessment formats. You should specifically craft each task to assess learning targets giving the most valid results. The validity of your results, rather than your own convenience, should be your first priority.

Other "Don'ts" and Exceptions

Some writers advise against including multiple-choice items when the test will be used only once, or when there are few students. It is easier to formulate short-answer questions than to write good multiple-choice items, and scoring will not be time consuming when there are few students. However, even when the number of students is small, if you plan to teach the same subject at the same level in subsequent years, it is usually worthwhile to develop a "pool" of multiple-choice items over time. You can then select items from this pool for future tests.

CRAFTING BASIC MULTIPLE-CHOICE ITEMS

Five Basic Skills of the Craft

You will craft useful multiple-choice items if you learn how to do five things: (a) focus items to assess specific learning targets; (b) prepare the stem as a question or problem to be solved; (c) write a concise, correct alternative; (d) write distractors that are plausible; and (e) edit the item to remove irrelevant clues to the correct answer. You must remember that when a multiple-choice item first comes out of your thoughts, it is only a crude item. *The first draft of any assessment task is unfit for human consumption.* It should not be put on a test until it is edited and polished. Dashing off multiple-choice items to put on a test at the last minute is a dead giveaway that you are not living up to your professional responsibilities (see Chapter 5). Editing items is a necessary step, even for the most experienced item writers. This section presents several item-writing guidelines for improving items in this editorial stage.

If you are a beginner, do not be discouraged by the difficulty you experience in writing good multiple-choice items. As with other forms of functional writing, crafting high-quality assessment tasks requires practice, frequent rewriting, and editing. This type of writing is unlike freewheeling, expressive writing in which few extrinsic standards apply.

It will be most helpful if you have your items critiqued by your instructor or classmates. Critics should keep in mind, however, that a lot of ego is invested in the creation of an item and that, to the uninitiated, critiquing a person's item is frequently perceived as a personal affront. Nevertheless, criticism is a valuable aid to learning skills in item writing.

Suggestions for crafting multiple-choice items are organized into three groups: suggestions for the stem, suggestions for the foils, and suggestions for the correct alternative. Suggestions for improving the quality of the stem portion of multiple-choice items are summarized in Figure 8.3 and discussed in more detail in the following section.

Crafting the Stem of the Item

Direct Question Asked or Implied After reading the stem, a student should understand the main intent of the item—what type of response you expect. The stem should ask a direct question or should clearly formulate a problem for the student to solve.

Incomplete sentences sometimes make good stems, but experience and research (Haladyna & Downing, 1989a) indicate that item writers usually produce better items when they phrase the stem as a direct question. The reason is probably that when a teacher does not ask a direct question, the student must mentally rephrase the stem as a question appropriate to the alternatives presented. This increases the cognitive complexity of the student's task, perhaps beyond what you may intend. When this happens you are violating the second and third fundamental principles of crafting assessments. When an incomplete sentence is used, a question is implied, of course. Older and brighter students are sometimes able to do this rephrasing without difficulty. However, younger, more average students, and perhaps those experiencing some learning difficulties may find that this extra process increases their difficulty in expressing what they know.

A simple way to check for this flaw is to cover the alternatives with your hand. Then, read the stem. *On the basis of that stem alone, can you determine what is expected of the student?*

FIGURE 8.3 Suggestions for improving the quality of the stems of multiple-choice items.

To do	To avoid
1. If possible, write as a direct question.	1. Avoid extraneous, superfluous, and non-functioning words and phrases that are mere "window dressing."

2. If an incomplete sentence is used, be sure
  a. it implies a direct question.
  b. the alternatives come at the end (rather than in the middle) of the sentence.
	2. Avoid (or use sparingly) negatively worded items.

3. Control the wording so that vocabulary and sentence structure are at a relatively low and non-technical level.	3. Avoid phrasing the item so that the personal opinion of the examinee is an option.
	4. Avoid textbook wording and "textbookish" or stereo-typed phraseology.
4. In items testing definitions, place the word or term in the stem and use definitions or descriptions as alternatives.	5. Avoid "cluing" and "linking" items (i.e., having the correct answer to one item be clued or linked to the correctness of the answer to a previous item).

Sources: Ebel, 1951, 1979, Greene, Jorgensen, & Gerberich 1942, 1943; Gronlund, 1976; Hopkins, Stanley, & Hopkins 1990; Lindquist & Mann, 1936; Lindvall, 1967; Millman, 1972; Sax, 1974; Thorndike, Cunningham, Thorndike, & Hagen 1991; Wesman, 1971.

If not, the stem is incomplete and you should rewrite it. The example that follows shows how an item is improved by rephrasing the incomplete stem as a question.

Example

Poor: Incomplete stem

1. W. E. B. DuBois

  *A actively pressed for complete political participation and full rights for African Americans.

  B taught that the immediate need was for African Americans to raise their economic status by learning trades and crafts.

  C emphasized helping African Americans through the National Urban League.

  D founded the Association for the Study of Negro Life and History.

Better: Asks a question

2. Which of the following comes closest to expressing W. E. B. DuBois's ideas about priorities of activities of African Americans during the early 20th century?

  A African Americans should first improve their economic condition before becoming fully involved in politics.

  B African Americans should postpone the fight for equal access to higher education until their majority acquire salable trade skills.

  C African Americans should withdraw from white society to form a separate state in which they have complete political and economic control.

  *D African Americans should become active, seeking out complete citizenship and full political participation immediately.

Example 1 is poor because the stem does not set a task or ask a question. (Cover the alternative. What task or problem does the stem set?) The student must read the entire item and infer that the teacher must be trying to find out something about W. E. B. DuBois's ideas. The student may very well know DuBois's ideas, but if the student makes the wrong inference about the teacher's intent, the student may answer the item incorrectly. Example 2 is better because the intent of the item is clear after the student reads the stem.

Put Alternatives at the End If you fail to follow this rule, you will encounter problems similar to those encountered with completion items when the blank is not placed at the end of the incomplete sentence (Chapter 7). The following example shows how an item is improved by listing alternatives at the end of the stem.

Example

Poor: Options in the middle of the stem

1. Before the Civil War, the South's

  *A emphasis on staple-crop production

  B lack of suitable supply of raw materials

  C short supply of personnel capable of operating the necessary machinery

was one of the major reasons manufacturing developed more slowly than it did in the North.

Better: Options put at the end

2. Before the Civil War, why did manufacturing develop more slowly in the South than in the North?

  *A The South emphasized staple-crop production.

  B The South lacked a suitable supply of raw materials.

  C The South had a short supply of people capable of operating the necessary machinery.

Control Vocabulary and Sentence Structure When testing for subject-matter learning, make sure you phrase the item at a level suitable for the students. You don't want long sentences, difficult vocabulary, and unnecessarily complex sentence structures to interfere with students' ability to answer the item. This may be especially true when you have students with disabilities mainstreamed in your class. For example, deaf and hard-of-hearing students frequently have relatively large language and vocabulary deficits. These students may very well have acquired the specific knowledge, concept, or principle you are assessing, but the way you phrase an item may interfere with their ability to demonstrate this knowledge (see Suppes, 1974). Check Chapter 5 for appropriate accommodations for students.

The example illustrates how a simple information item can be complicated by uncontrolled language. The item is improved by making it more concise.

Example

Poor: Unnecessary wordiness and complexity

1. Given the present-day utilization of the automobile in urban settings, which of the following represents an important contribution of Garrett A. Morgan's genius?
   A automobile safety belts
   B crosswalk markers
   *C traffic lights
   D vulcanized rubber tires

Better: More concise

2. Which of the following did Garrett A. Morgan invent?
   A automobile safety belts
   B crosswalk markers
   *C traffic lights
   D vulcanized rubber tires

Avoid "Window Dressing" Item 1 in the preceding example demonstrates how extraneous wording can complicate an item unnecessarily. Less obvious is the use of words that tend to "dress up" a stem to make it sound as though it is testing something of practical importance (Ebel, 1965). Often such **window dressing** creeps into an item when you are struggling to measure higher-level cognitive abilities, such as applications. Window dressing makes an item appear to measure applications, when it does not. The next example shows how window dressing makes an item more difficult, less discriminating, less reliable, and less valid (Haladyna & Downing, 1989a). The item is improved by eliminating the window dressing.

Example

Poor: Window dressing

1. There are 10 preservice teachers in the Department of Education who recently registered for the college-sponsored weight loss program. At the beginning of the program each was weighed, and the 10 had a mean weight of 139.4 pounds. Suppose there were but three men in this group, and that their mean weight was 180 pounds. What was the mean weight of the women at the beginning of the program?
   A 115.0 pounds
   *B 122.0 pounds
   C 140.0 pounds
   D 159.7 pounds

Better: More concise

2 Ten persons have a mean weight of 139.4 pounds. The mean weight of three of them is 180 pounds. What is the mean weight of the remaining seven persons?
   A 115.0 pounds
   *B 122.0 pounds
   C 140.0 pounds
   D 159.7 pounds

Every word used in an item should have a purpose. Sometimes names, places, and other "facts" about a situation are necessary pieces of information: They can give the student the basis for determining the correct answer. The following example shows an acceptable inclusion of facts in an item stem.

Example

A company owns a fleet of cars for which it pays all fuel expenses. Three readily available types of gasoline were tested to see which type was giving better mileage. The results are shown below in miles per gallon.

	Mean	Median
Type A	19.1	18.5
Type B	18.5	19.1
Type C	18.8	18.9

1. Assuming they all cost the same, which type of gasoline should the company use?
   *A Type A
   B Type B
   C Type C

Avoid Negatively Worded Stems Phrase items positively if possible. **Negatively worded stems,** such as "which of the following is not. . . ," tend to confuse students, especially the younger or less careful ones. Even well-prepared students often overlook the *not* in an examination question. Positively worded items are easier for students than the corresponding negatively worded items (Haladyna & Downing, 1989a; Haladyna, Downing, & Rodriguez, 2002). The following example shows how to improve an item by using positive wording.

Example

Poor: Negatively phrased stem

1. Sometimes a teacher finds it necessary to use a mild form of punishment. When this occurs, which of the following should not happen?
   A Children should not believe all of their behavior is bad.
   B Children should understand the reason(s) why they are being punished.
   *C Children should understand that the teacher, not them, controls when the punishment will end.

Better: Positively phrased stem

2. Sometimes a teacher finds it necessary to use a mild form of punishment. When this occurs, it is important that the children understand
   A that it may be a long time before happy times return to the classroom.
   *B the reason(s) why they are being punished.
   C that the teacher, not the children, controls when their punishment will end.

If negatively phrased items must be used, use the negative word only in the stem or only in an option (not both), and either underline the negative word or place it in CAPITAL LETTERS.

Avoid Grading Personal Opinions Do not ask for students' personal opinions in the context of a multiple-choice test in which the students need to select one option as best or correct. Everyone is entitled to an opinion. If you ask for students' opinions in a multiple-choice item, every option could be correct. The following example illustrates this point.

Example

Poor: Makes the correct answer a matter of personal opinion

1. Which of the following men contributed most toward the improvement of the self-confidence of African Americans?
   A W. E. B. DuBois
   B Eugene K. Jones
   C Booker T. Washington
   D Carter G. Woodson

There is no single correct answer to the preceding question, because each man's contributions can be judged and evaluated in different ways. The question could form the basis for an extended-response essay or a term paper in which the students support their opinions with evidence and logical argument. However, do not grade the opinions or the positions taken. Rather, evaluate the way the students use the evidence to support their opinions.

Avoid Textbookish Wording As with true-false items, when you copy sentences verbatim from the text you end up with a poor item because (a) frequently, a sentence loses its meaning when you take it out of context, (b) you encourage rote memory of textbook material instead of comprehension, (c) you are likely to produce awkwardly worded items with implausible distractors, and (d) learners who have only a superficial understanding of the underlying concept or principle may obtain clues to the correct answer by simply recalling the textbook phrasing. You must use a new, perhaps less familiar, wording of the stem and correct option to test a deeper comprehension of a concept or principle (Lindquist & Mann, 1936). You should avoid **textbookish phrasing**. Even though you paraphrase, you may word the item so it reads very much like the textbook. The procedure we discussed earlier in Chapter 7—stating main ideas of textbook passages in your own words and rephrasing these as questions—is a practical one for avoiding textbookish phrasing. Study the following example.

Example

Poor: Uses texbookish phrasing

1. The annual incomes of five employees are $8,000, $8,000, $10,000, $11,000, and $25,000, respectively. Which index should be used to summarize the typical employee's income?
   A mean
   *B median
   C mode

Better: Novel situation for students

A teacher keeps a record of how long it takes students to complete the 50-question final exam. The mean time was 46 minutes and the median time was 20 minutes. The teacher used this information to set the next exam's time at 20 minutes. The teacher reasoned that these data demonstrate that the typical student could complete the test in that time.

2. In all likelihood, this time limit is
   A just about right.
   *B too short.
   C too long.

The first item is weak because most introductory statistics books associate the term typical with median and often use income examples to illustrate the application of the median. By knowing these superficial facts, the student can mark "B" without demonstrating an in-depth understanding of this statistical index. The better item, Question 2, assesses a different learning target. It is better because it presents a novel situation and requires an application of the concept.

When testing older students, you may find it helpful to use stereotyped phraseology, certain "pat phrases," and verbal associations to make distractors plausible to students lacking the required degree of knowledge. These phrases may be put into the stem or into the distractors. Item 2, although it is a bit wordy and places a premium on reading, does just this. A student who interprets the correctness of using a particular statistical index only on the basis of the verbal association of typical with median will not answer the item correctly. Such a student will fail to notice that if the teacher set the time limit for the test at 20 minutes, only half of the class will have enough time to complete it. Surely this is inappropriate for a classroom test.

Create Independent Items With the possible exception of context-dependent items,[4] each item should assess a distinct performance, and the correct answer to an item should not be clued by another item. Two flaws to avoid are linking and clueing. **Linking** means that the answer to one or more items depends on obtaining the correct answer to a previous item. Linked items frequently result in a double penalty for a student for an incorrect answer, as when a computational result from one item is required to answer a subsequent item. **Clueing** means that a hint to the correct answer to one item is found in the contents of another item in the test. In the next example, Questions 1 and 2 illustrate linked items.

Example

Preceding item

1. The perimeter of a rectangle is 350 centimeters. The length of the rectangle is 3 centimeters longer than the width. What is the width?
   A 18.7 cm.
   *B 86.0 cm.
   C 89.0 cm.
   D 116.7 cm.

Poor subsequent item: Linked to Item 1

2. What is the area of the rectangle described in Question 1?
   A 1,050 sq. cm.
   B 7,396 sq. cm.
   *C 7,654 sq. cm.
   D 8,188 sq. cm.

Better subsequent item: Independent of Item 1

3. The width of a rectangle is 4 centimeters and the length is 3 centimeters. What is the area?
   A 9 sq. cm.
   *B 12 sq. cm.
   C 16 sq. cm.
   D 17 sq. cm.

The "preceding item" is primarily computational. The poor subsequent item (Item 2) is linked to it. A student could make an incorrect computation in Item 1, obtaining 89.0, for example. Having already made a mistake in Item 1, the student would get Item 2 wrong also, because $89 \times (89 + 3) = 8,188$ is keyed as the wrong answer. One solution to the problem is shown in the better subsequent item: You present a new numerical value for the student to use, which is independent of the preceding item. Thus, Item 3 is not linked to Item 1.

Of course, items may provide clues to other items even though they are not linked. You should review all the items in your test to see if any item suggests an answer to other items.

Definitions Go in the Alternatives Teachers frequently assess whether students know the meaning of special terms or vocabulary words. Multiple-choice items are often used for this purpose. A common flaw, however, is to put the definition of the term in the stem and to use a list of words as alternatives. The flaw with this approach is that it increases the likelihood that students will get the answer correct by using only superficial knowledge of the definition being assessed. Students can obtain the correct answer by knowing only that the words in the definition "look like" (seem similar to) a word in the alternatives (Lindquist & Mann, 1936). To assess whether students have in-depth knowledge of a term, put the term in the stem and write various definitions in the alternatives. The item can be made easier or harder depending on how similar the alternatives are. The following example shows how to improve a definition item by putting the term in the stem and using different definitions as alternatives.

[4]Context-dependent items are discussed in Chapter 10.

Example

Poor: Definition in the stem

1. The increase in length per unit of length of a metal rod for each degree rise in temperature (Centigrade) is known as the
   *A coefficient of linear expansion of the metal.
   B elasticity of the metal.
   C specific heat of the metal.
   D surface tension of the metal.

Better: Definitions in the alternatives

2. What is the *coefficient of linear expansion* of a metal rod?
   A the increase in length of the rod when its temperature is raised 1°C
   *B the increase in length when the temperature is raised 1°C divided by the total length of the rod at its original temperature
   C the ratio of its length at 100 to its length at 0°C
   D the rise in temperature (degrees Centigrade) that is necessary to cause the length of the rod to expand 1 percent

Source: Adapted from "The Construction of Tests," by E. F. Lindquist and C. R. Mann, in *The Construction and Use of Achievement Examinations: A Manual for Secondary School Teachers* (pp. 145–146), by. H. E. Hawkes, E. F. Lindquist, and C. R. Mann (Eds.), 1936, Boston: Houghton Mifflin.

Crafting Alternatives or Foils

The alternatives of a multiple-choice item present choices to the students. All of the choices must be appropriate to the stem. If they are not, they may be confusing to knowledgeable students or may be easily eliminated by less knowledgeable ones. When all alternatives are appropriate to the stem, the item functions better as a complete unit. Suggestions for improving the quality of the alternatives are summarized in Figure 8.4 and discussed in more detail in the following text.

Plausible and Functional Alternatives Many of the suggestions that follow will help you craft plausible distractors. **Plausible distractors** are incorrect alternatives that appear to be correct to students who have not mastered the assessed learning target. To make distractors plausible, base them on errors students commonly make, such as computational errors, conceptual errors, or errors resulting from faulty common knowledge. In this way, your analysis of students' responses could help you identify their specific difficulties.

Figure 8.4 calls for using from three to five functional alternatives. A **functional alternative** serves the purpose for which it is written. This means that an alternative that is a distractor attracts at least one of the students who do not have the degree of knowledge that you expect of all students. Also, an alternative that is the keyed answer is functional if all students who do have the degree of knowledge you expect select it.

For example, an item may have five alternatives. If even the most superficial learner easily eliminates two of the distractors, however, only the remaining three are seriously considered plausible answers. In reality, then, the item has only three *functional* alternatives. For practical purposes you may as well delete the two nonfunctional alternatives. Nonfunctional distractors are called **"deadwood"** or **filler alternatives**.

Teachers sometimes ask if each multiple-choice item should have the same number of alternatives and, if so, how many there should be. Assessment specialists have long recognized that there is no virtue in having the same number of alternatives for each item (Ebel, 1965; Lindquist & Mann, 1936). This is especially true for classroom assessment. Research supports the rule that you should write as many functional distractors as is feasible; as Haladyna and Downing (1989b) point out, "The key to

FIGURE 8.4 Suggestions for improving the alternatives of multiple-choice items.

To do	To avoid
1. In general strive for creating three to five functional alternatives.	1. Avoid overlapping alternatives.
2. All alternatives should be homogeneous and appropriate to the stem.	2. Avoid making the alternatives a collection of true-false items.
3. Put repeated words and phrases in the stem.	3. Avoid using "not given," "none of the above," etc. as an alternative in *best-answer* type of items (use only with *correct-answer* variety).
4. Use consistent and correct punctuation in relation to the stem.	
5. Arrange alternatives in a list format rather than in tandem.	4. Avoid using "all of the above": limit its use to the *correct-answer* variety.
6. Arrange alternatives in a logical or meaningful order.	5. Avoid using verbal clues in the alternatives.
7. All distractors should be grammatically correct with respect to the stem.	6. Avoid using technical terms, unknown words or names and "silly" terms or names as distractors.
	7. Avoid making it harder to eliminate a distractor than to choose the keyed alternative.

Sources: Ebel, 1951, 1979, Greene, Jorgensen, & Gerberich 1942, 1943; Gronlund, 1976; Hopkins, Stanley, & Hopkins 1990; Lindquist & Mann, 1936; Lindvall, 1957; Millman, 1972; Sax, 1974; Thorndike, Cunningham, Thorndike, & Hagen 1991; Wesman, 1971.

distractor development is not the *number* of distractors but the *quality* of distractors" (p. 59).

If you can write three to five functional alternatives, then the item is more likely to distinguish those who have the desired degree of knowledge from those who do not. Research suggests that having three functional alternatives is best, on balance (Rodriguez, 2005). The more alternatives you try to write, the harder it will be to make them functional. As a rule of thumb, strive to write three functional alternatives for most purposes, and use up to five functional alternatives if there is a justification for each (for example, if each distractor exemplifies a common kind of error). Don't waste your time trying to create the same number of alternatives for each item if by so doing you are creating nonfunctional fillers or deadwood. If a separate answer sheet is used for machine scoring, check the maximum spaces allowed per item and adjust the maximum number of alternatives accordingly.

Homogeneous Alternatives Lack of homogeneity is a primary reason why distractors do not function. An item is said to have **homogeneous alternatives** when each alternative belongs to the same set of "things" *and* each alternative is appropriate to the question asked or problem posed by the stem. For example, if the stem asks students to identify the name of someone who invented a particular machine, then each alternative should be a name and each name should be an inventor to be appropriate to the stem.

An item has **heterogeneous alternatives** when one or more of its alternatives do not belong to the same set of things. An example that shows how to improve an item by making its alternatives homogeneous follows.

Example

Poor: Heterogeneous alternatives that do not belong to the same category

1. What is the official state bird of Pennsylvania?
   A mountain laurel
   B Philadelphia
   *C ruffed grouse
   D Susquehanna River

Better: Homogeneous alternatives that belong to the same category

2. What is the official state bird of Pennsylvania?
   A goldfinch
   B robin
   *C ruffed grouse
   D wild turkey

You may also adjust the degree of homogeneity to control the difficulty of an item. As students' perception that the distractors are similar increases, the difficulty of the item increases (Green, 1984). The World War I items in the

"Considerations Before Crafting Items" section illustrated this point previously. Whether alternatives are perceived to be homogeneous by the students you are assessing depends on their level of educational development. Item 2 in the preceding example could be made more homogeneous (and more difficult) by using as alternatives the scientific names of several different species of grouse, for example. The World War I items in the "Considerations Before Crafting Items" section illustrate this point, too: The alternatives in Item 1 in that section may appear homogeneous to less knowledgeable, younger students, but they will likely appear to be quite heterogeneous alternatives to knowledgeable, older students.

Put Repeated Words in the Stem In general, it is better to put into the stem words or phrases that are repeated in each alternative. A more complete stem reduces the amount of reading required of the students and makes the task clearer to the student. To accomplish this, you may find it necessary to rephrase the stem to focus it on the critical point of the learning target. The next example shows how to improve an item by eliminating words that are repeated in each alternative.

Example

Poor: Words repeated in each alternative

1. Which of the following is the best definition of *seismograph*?
   A an apparatus for measuring sound waves
   B an apparatus for measuring heat waves
   *C an apparatus for measuring earthquake waves
   D an apparatus for measuring ocean waves

Better: Stem is more focused and repeated words are incorporated into the stem

2. What type of waves does a *seismograph* measure?
   *A earthquake waves
   B heat waves
   C ocean waves
   D sound waves

Consistent, Correct Punctuation If the stem asks a question directly (i.e., it ends in a question mark), the options can be either (a) complete sentences; (b) single words, terms, names, or phrases; or (c) other incomplete sentences. Complete sentences begin with a capital letter and end with an appropriate punctuation mark; do not use a semicolon or other inappropriate terminal punctuation. If the options are single words or incomplete sentences, do not use terminal punctuation. However, use a consistent rule for capitalizing the initial word in each option: Throughout the test, either capitalize *all* initial words or capitalize *no* initial word (except a proper noun, of course).

An **incomplete stem** contains an incomplete sentence that the student must complete by choosing the correct alternative. In this case, you must choose plausible alternatives to complete the sentence for students who have not mastered the learning target. When writing this type of item, begin each alternative with a lowercase letter (unless an alternative's initial word is a proper noun) and end it with the appropriate terminal punctuation.

There are exceptions to these rules, of course, as when the purpose of an item is to assess knowledge of grammar rules. The next item illustrates this exception to the rule of using consistent punctuation.

Example

Choose the phrases that correctly complete the sentence.

1. Julia became very frightened and shouted,
   A "Please save me."
   B "Please save me?"
   *C "Please save me!"

Arrangement of the Alternatives Alternatives are less confusing and easier to read when they are arranged one below the other in list form rather than in **tandem** or beside one another. The following item shows a poor (tandem) arrangement of the alternatives.

Example

Poor: Tandem arrangement of alternatives

1. A test-retest reliability coefficient is calculated from test scores separated by a one-week time interval. Which of the following would likely lower the numerical value of the coefficient? (A) Differences in the extent to which students have learned the information required to answer the particular items on the test. (B) The fact that some students have a better command of general test-taking skills than do others. (C) The fact that a few students do better on the particular types of items used. *(D) Some students became upset during the second administration. (E) All of the above would likely lower the test-retest reliability coefficient for a particular test.

Alternatives should be arranged in **meaningful order**, such as order of magnitude or size, degree to which they reflect a given quality, chronologically, or alphabetically. Such arrangements make locating the correct answer easier for the knowledgeable student, reduce reading and search time, and lessen the chance of careless errors. The next examples show acceptable arrangements of alternatives.

Example

Alphabetical arrangement of alternatives

1. Which of the following is made from the shells of tiny animals?
   *A chalk
   B clay
   C shale

Numerical arrangement of alternatives

2. A student's percentile rank is 4. What is the stanine corresponding to this percentile rank?
   A 4
   B 3
   C 2
   *D 1

Grammatically Correct Relationship to the Stem Items that contain grammatical clues to the correct answer are easier and less reliable than items without such clues (Haladyna & Downing, 1989a). Don't clue the correct answer or permit distractors to be eliminated on superficial bases. Examples of inappropriate grammatical clues include lack of subject-verb agreement, inappropriate indefinite article, and singular/plural confusion. Below are examples of improving items by eliminating grammatical clues to the correct answers.

Example

Poor: The definite article "a" at the end of the stem and plural usage of "angles" in the alternatives clue the correct answer.

1. A 90° angle is called a
   A acute angles.
   B obtuse angles.
   *C right angle.

Better: Writing the stem as a direct question eliminates the grammatical clue.

2. What are 90° angles called?
   A acute angles
   B obtuse angles
   *C right angles

Poor: Only one alternative uses the conjunction in a grammatically correct relationship to the stem.

3. Green plants may lose their color when
   A are forming flowers.
   *B grown in the dark.
   C are placed in strong light.
   D temperature drops.

Better: Ask a direct question to focus the item.

4. When may green plants lose their color?
   A when they form flowers.
   *B when they are grown in the dark.
   C when they are placed in strong light.
   D when the surrounding temperatures drop.

Poor: Use of "are" in the stem gives a cue that the answer must contain more than one thing.

5. Which of the following are called *scarves*?
   A band of cloth worn around the neck
   B type of wood joint
   *C both (a) and (b) are scarves

Better: Ask a direct question to focus the item.

6. What is a *scarf*?
   A band of cloth worn around the neck
   B type of wood joint
   C a tool for trimming shrubs
   *D both (A) and (B) are scarves

The indefinite article *a* in Item 1 gives the student the clue that Alternative C is correct. The other two alternatives begin with vowels and thus require the indefinite article *an*. In Item 3, the conjunction *when* is appropriate only to the phrasing of Alternative B. Item 5, a plural verb form in the stem, clues students to choose more than one definition.

Overlapping Alternatives Each alternative should be distinct and not a logical subset of another alternative. Alternatives that include some or all of one another are called **overlapping alternatives**. If you write an item containing overlapping alternatives, you give the less knowledgeable, but testwise, student clues to the correct answer. Several examples of improving items written with overlapping alternatives follow.

Example

Poor: Use of "over" makes Alternatives A and B overlap with C.

1. What is the population of Modesto, CA?
   A over 200,000
   B over 180,000
   *C over 160,000

Better: Numerical values of the alternatives do not overlap.

2. The population of Modesto, CA, is approximately
   *A 200,000.
   B 180,000.
   C 160,000.

Poor: All alternatives have essentially the same meaning.

3 Why is there a shortage of water in the lower basin of the Colorado River?
   A The hot sun almost always shines.
   B There is a wide, hot desert.
   C The temperatures are very hot.
   *D All of the above are reasons why.

Better: Each alternative has a distinct meaning.

4. Why is there a shortage of water in the lower basin of the Colorado River?
   *A There is low rainfall and few tributaries at that region.
   B The desert soaks up water quickly.
   C A dam in the upper part made the lower part dry up.

Poor: Alternatives B, C, and D are essentially the same and, thus, can be eliminated.

5. How long does a perennial plant live?
   *A It continues to live year after year.
   B It lives only for one growing season.
   C It needs to be replanted every year.
   D It dies after the first year.

Better: The alternatives are refocused to ask about the number of years directly.

6. How long does a perennial plant live?
   *A It continues to live for several years.
   B It lives for only two years.
   C It lives for only one year.

In Item 1, Option C overlaps with Options A and B. Even if a student didn't know the correct answer, the student is likely to choose Option C. In Item 3, Options A, B, and C essentially say the same thing: A testwise student, recognizing this overlap, would likely choose Option D even if the student knew nothing about the need for water in the lower Colorado River basin. Similarly, for Item 5, Options B, C, and D all say essentially the same thing, but here "all of the above" is not one of the choices. Therefore, the testwise student will know that Option A must be correct.

Avoid a Collection of True-False Alternatives A frequent cause of this type of flaw is that the teacher did not have in mind a clear problem or question when creating the item. Here is an example of improving an item by refocusing the collection of true-false alternatives.

Example

Poor: Alternatives are an unfocused collection of true-false statements.

1. A *linear function* is
   *A completely determined if we know two points.
   B completely determined if we know one point.
   C unrelated to the point-slope formula.
   D the same as the *y* intercept.

Better: The stem focuses on a problem.

2. In which of the following situations would it be possible to write the *equation for a linear function*?
   *A We know the line passes through the points (3,5) and (4,6).
   B We know the slope is 1.
   C We know the *y* intercept is (0,2).

In Item 1, it is difficult to identify any single question to which a student must respond. All options are related only by the fact that they could begin with the phrase, "A linear function is." Options B, C, and D, when used with that phrase, become false statements. This item is unfocused because it really embeds three ideas: how two points determine a line, the definition of the point-slope formula, and the definition of *y* intercept. Only one of these ideas should be selected and used as a basis for a revised item, as is done with Item 2. (However, to craft *multiple true-false items*, review Chapter 7.)

Avoid "None of the Above" Research on the phrase **"none of the above"** as an option in multiple-choice items indicates that it results in less reliable, more difficult items (Haladyna et al., 2002). Therefore, be very cautious when using this phrase as an option. This option should never be used with the best-answer variety (see the example given earlier in the chapter) of multiple-choice items. The very nature of a best-answer question requires that all of the options are to some degree incorrect, but one of them is "best." It seems illogical to require students to choose "none of the above" under these conditions.

It does make sense, however, to use "none of the above" with some correct-answer questions, when students look for one option that is completely correct. In areas such as arithmetic, certain English mechanics, spelling, and the like, a single, completely correct answer can be definitely established and defended. Some assessment experts recommend using "none of the above" only when students are more likely to solve a problem first before looking at the options, as opposed to searching through the distractors before proceeding with the solution to the problem (Wood, 1977).

Two special problems associated with using "none of the above" are (a) students may not believe that this choice can be correct and, therefore, they do not think it is plausible; and (b) students who choose it may be given credit when their thinking is incorrect (Ebel, 1951). To avoid the first problem, use "none of these" as the correct answer to a few easy items near the beginning of the test. This conditions students to seriously consider "none of the above" as a possible correct answer for the remainder of the test. It may then be used as either a correct or incorrect answer later in the test. The second problem is handled by using "none of the above" as a *correct answer* in an item when the distractors encompass most of the wrong answers that can be expected (see Item 1 below), or using it as a *distractor* for items in which most of the probable wrong answers cannot be incorporated into the distractors (Ebel, 1951) (see Item 2).

Example

Acceptable use of "none of the above": As a correct answer

1. What is the difference?

   $$106$$
   $$-21$$
   $$?$$

   A 81
   B 89
   C 101
   *D None of the above

Acceptable use of "none of the above": As a plausible distractor

2. What is the sum?

   $$46$$
   $$47$$
   $$48$$
   $$?$$

   A 161
   B 171
   *C 141
   D None of the above

More than likely, however, items such as 1 and 2 would be better as completion (short-answer) items than as multiple-choice items. If you used completion items, you would be able to check the students' wrong answers to determine why they responded incorrectly; then you could remediate the students.

Two final comments on this point. Avoid using "none of the above" as a filler to increase the number of distractors. Remember that distractors must be plausible. Second, as an option, "none of the above" is probably more confusing to younger students than to older ones.

Avoid "All of the Above" Research on the use of **"all of the above"** is inconclusive (Haladyna et al., 2002). This option, if used at all, should be limited to correct-answer varieties of multiple-choice items. It cannot be used with best-answer varieties because "all of the options" cannot be simultaneously best. Two further difficulties arise: (a) Students who know that one option is correct may simply choose it and inadvertently go on to the next item without reviewing the remaining options, and (b) students who know that two out of four options are correct can choose "all of the above" without knowing the correctness of the third option. The first difficulty can be reduced to some extent by making the first choice in the list read "all of the following are correct." However, this wording can also confuse elementary and junior high students. Generally, the recommendation is to avoid using "all of the above." Rewrite items with multiple answers as two or more items and avoid these problems. Alternately, rewrite the item as a multiple true-false item (see Chapter 7).

Avoid Verbal Clues Failure to follow this rule makes items easier and lowers the test reliability (Haladyna & Downing, 1989b). **Verbal clues** include using overlapping alternatives, silly or absurd distractors, **clang** (i.e., sound-alike words) or other associations between words in the stem and in the correct alternatives, repetition or resemblance between the correct alternative and the stem, and specific determiners. Verbal clues in the alternative frequently lead the less knowledgeable but verbally able student to the correct answer. Examples of poorly worded items with verbal clues are shown next.

Example

Poor: Answered by association of words in stem and in correct answer

1. Which government agency is most concerned with our nation's agricultural policies?
   *A Department of Agriculture
   B Department of Education
   C Department of the Interior
   D Department of Labor

2. In which journal can you find articles about recent research in educational testing?
   A *American Psychologist*
   *B *Journal of Educational Measurement*
   C *Journal of Abnormal Child Psychology*
   D *Memory and Cognition*

Poor: Specific determiners can be used to eliminate distractors.

3. Which of the following was one of E. L. Thorndike's contributions to educational measurement?
   A He invented all of the types of multiple-choice items now in use.
   B He constructed every educational test published between 1900 and 1920.
   *C He helped educational testing gain scientific respectability.

Item 1, for example, uses *agriculture* in both stems and alternative. This creates a "Who is buried in Grant's tomb?" type of question. Similarly, in Item 2, one can easily associate the terms *educational testing* and *educational measurement* to come up with the correct answer without knowing the contents of any of the journals listed.

Specific determiners are words that overqualify a statement so that it is always true or always false. We saw how these operated with true-false items in Chapter 7; they can occur in multiple-choice items. Item 3 in the previous example shows this. Alternatives A and B can be easily eliminated: No one "invented all" of anything, nor would anyone "construct every . . . test published." After these are eliminated, only Alternative C remains.

Avoid Technical and Unfamiliar Wording Teachers writing multiple-choice items sometimes use highly technical or unfamiliar words as distractors. Words beyond students' knowledge base may require more ability to reject the wrong answer than to choose the correct answer (Ebel, 1951). Some studies indicate, however, that students view options containing unfamiliar technical words as less plausible, thereby making such alternatives nonfunctional. In one study, when college students were instructed to mark answers to items for which, unknown to them, no real answer existed, students chose options containing familiar, nontechnical words more frequently than options containing either familiar technical words, vaguely familiar technical words, or unfamiliar technical words (Strang, 1977).

Do Not Make a Distractor Too Plausible Incorrect alternatives sometimes may be made so plausible that generally good students get the item wrong, whereas less able students respond correctly. (Such items are said to be *negatively discriminating*; see Chapter 14.) The good students' knowledge, though perhaps normally sufficient for selection of the correct answer when embedded in another context, may be insufficient for rejection of all the distractors in a particular item (Lindquist, 1936). The U.S. history items in Figure 8.5 illustrate how students' insufficient knowledge and wrong learning can result in poorly functioning items.

FIGURE 8.5 Effects of insufficient or incorrect learning.

THE EFFECT OF INSUFFICIENT LEARNING OR UNDERSTANDING

The failure of an item to function because of insufficient or wrong learning is something beyond the control of the test constructor. . . .

What was one of the most important immediate results of the War of 1812?

1. The introduction of a period of intense sectionalism (39%)
2. The destruction of the United States Bank (7%)
3. The defeat of the Jeffersonian Party (7%)
4. The final collapse of the Federalist Party (4% omitted the item) (43%)

The correct response is Option 4. Nevertheless, the pupils who selected the first and incorrect response were, on the average, superior in general achievement to those who selected the correct response (4). Again, the pupils selecting the first and incorrect response apparently did so because of positive but insufficient learning. They did know that a period of intense sectionalism set in before the middle of the century, and therefore chose the first response. Apparently they did not know, or failed to recall, that a short period of intense nationalism was an immediate result of the Second War with Great Britain, and that this war, therefore, could not be considered as "introducing" an era of sectional strife. Other pupils, with less knowledge in general, were able to select the correct response because they were not attracted to the first response by a certain knowledge that intense sectionalism did develop in the 19th century. (It should be noted, however, that for an abler group of pupils, capable of making the judgment called for, this same item might have shown a high positive index of discrimination.)

THE EFFECT OF WRONG LEARNING

Wrong learning, as well as insufficient learning, on the part of pupils for whom the test is intended may cause an item in that test to show a negative index of discrimination.

In the second half of the 15th century the Portuguese were searching for an alternate water route to India because

1. they wished to rediscover the route traveled by Marco Polo (4%).
2. the Turks had closed the old routes (59%).
3. the Spanish had proved that it was possible to reach the east by sailing westward (10%).
4. an all-water route would make possible greater profits (1% omitted the item) (26%).

It will be noted that more than half of the pupils selected Response 2. The negative index of discrimination indicates furthermore that the average achievement of the pupils who selected this response was superior to that of the 25% of the pupils who selected the correct response (4). Authoritative historians no longer would accept the second response as a sufficient explanation of Portuguese attempts to round Africa, nor would they deny that Response 4 is the best of those given. An analysis of current textbooks in American history, however, will reveal that these lag behind research and that many of them still present the now-disproved explanation: "The Turks closed the old routes." It is not surprising, therefore, that the superior pupils are more likely to select this response than those who have made little or no effective attempt to learn the facts contained in the textbooks. This being the case, the inclusion of this item in the test not only contributed nothing to its effectiveness but also even detracted from it. There can be little question, however, that the item is free from technical imperfections or ambiguities, and that it does hold the pupil responsible for an established fact of considerable significance in history.

Source: Adapted from *The Construction and Use of Achievement Examinations: A Manual for Secondary School Teachers* (pp. 56–63), by H. E. Hawkes, E. F. Lindquist, and C. R. Mann (Eds.), 1936, Boston: Houghton Mifflin, ©1936 by Houghton Mifflin Company. Adapted by permission of the publisher.

Crafting the Correct Alternative

You should word the correct alternative so that students *without* the requisite knowledge are *not clued* as to the correct answer and those students *with* the requisite knowledge *are able* to select the correct answer.

1. *In general, there should be only one correct or best answer to a multiple-choice item.* It is possible to write items that have more than one correct alternative. However, such items may not be as valid as you intend, especially with elementary and junior high school students. Students may, for example, mark the first correct alternative they encounter and skip to the next item without considering all of the alternatives. Some beginning item writers attempt to compensate for this behavior by using the combined response variety of multiple-choice items (see the example of this type given earlier in this chapter) or by using "all of the above." This usually results in poorer quality items.

2. *Be sure that competent authorities can agree that the answer keyed as correct (or best) is in fact correct (or best).* If you violate this rule, you may come into conflict with the more able student (or the student's parent). Further, if you insist there is only one correct answer when students also see another choice as equally logical and correct, students will likely see you as arbitrary and capricious. To avoid such embarrassment and negative consequences, have a knowledgeable colleague review the correctness of your keyed answers and the incorrectness of your distractors before you use them. The best way to do this is to have your colleague take your test without the correct answers marked. If the colleague chooses an answer that you did not key as correct, then there may be a problem with the correctness of your key.

3. *The correct alternative should be a grammatically correct response to the stem.* The knowledgeable student faces a conflict if the content of the keyed response is correct, but the grammar is incorrect.

4. *Check over the entire test to ensure that the correct alternatives do not follow an easily learned pattern.* Use the answer key you develop to tabulate the number of As, Bs, Cs, and so on that are keyed as correct. Sometimes teachers

favor one or two positions (e.g., B and C) for the correct answers. Students will quickly catch on to this pattern, which lowers the validity of your assessment. Also, avoid repetitive, easily learned patterns, such as AABBCCDD or ABCDABCD. If you arrange your alternatives in a logical, numerical, or alphabetical order, you should not have any problems. By using a scoring stencil, you can score exams just as quickly without resorting to set patterns of correct answers.

5.   *Avoid phrasing the correct alternative in a textbookish or stereotyped manner.*   To assess comprehension and understanding, you must at least paraphrase textbook statements. Students quickly learn the idiosyncratic or stereotyped way in which you and the textbook phrase certain ideas. If your test items also reflect such idiosyncrasies, you will be encouraging students to select answers that "sound right" to them but that they do not understand. For more mature students, however, stereotyped phrases that have a "ring of truth" in the distractors may serve to distinguish those who have fully grasped the concept from those with only superficial knowledge (Ebel, 1979). Use this tactic with senior high school and college students, but not with elementary and junior high school students.

6.   *The correct alternative should be of approximately the same overall length as the distractors.*   Teachers sometimes make the correct option longer than the incorrect options by phrasing it in a more completely explained or more qualified manner. The testwise student can pick up on this and mark the longest or most complete answer without having the requisite knowledge. Research supports the generalization that if you violate this rule you will make the item easier (Haladyna & Downing, 1989b). Don't be too scrupulous in counting words, however. If your correct answer is one or two words longer, don't worry about it.

7.   *An advantage of a multiple-choice test is that it reduces the amount of time required for writing answers, thus allowing the assessment to cover more content.*   Don't defeat this purpose by requiring students to write out their answers. Have the students either mark (circle, check, etc.) the letter of the alternative they choose, write the letter on a blank next to the stem created for that purpose, or use a separate answer sheet. Separate answer sheets are not recommended for children below fourth or fifth grade (see Aleyideino, 1968; Beck, 1974; Cashen & Ramseyer, 1969; Davis & Trimble, 1978; Gaffney & Maguire, 1971; Moss, Cole, & Trent, 1979; Muller, Calhoun, & Orling, 1972; Ramseyer & Cashen, 1971). If your state has a testing program that uses separate answer sheets in the primary grades, however, use answer sheets with some of your classroom tests to give the children practice. This is good teaching practice.

Encoding Meaning Into Distractor Choices

Thus far we have discussed distractors that all serve the same purpose, namely, to appear plausible to those who do not know the correct answer. In scoring, all are equally "wrong." On a right-wrong, 1-0 item scoring scale, choosing a distractor gets a student 0 points. Several different programs of research have investigated encoding more meaning into distractors than simply "wrong."

It is possible to write distractors that help teachers identify what next steps a student should take. These can be based on cognitive developmental models of how children learn (Pellegrino, Chudowsky, & Glaser, 2001). So, for example, one of the distractors could represent what a student who is in the beginning stages of concept development would select, another distractor would represent what a student who has progressed to a second stage of concept development would select, and so on. In problem solving, distractors can be crafted to represent different kinds of mistakes. For example, for the problem $115-97=$, one of the distractors might be 22, which is what a student who always subtracted the smaller number from the larger might select. Another distractor might be 28, which is what a student who knew how to borrow in the one's place, but not how to change the value in the ten's place, would select.

Harcourt Assessment, Inc. has developed a **distractor rationale taxonomy** (King, Gardner, Zucker, & Jorgensen, 2004) for multiple-choice items in reading and mathematics. These taxonomies describe types of errors in reading and mathematics, respectively, that correspond with different levels of understanding. The advantage is that one distractor can be written for each level. A student whose incorrect answers are typically at a specific level can be given instruction targeted to that level of understanding. Figure 8.6 presents the distractor taxonomy for reading items and examples to illustrate its use. Readers who would like to see the mathematics distractor rationale taxonomy and additional examples should refer to the reference.

A CHECKLIST FOR EVALUATING MULTIPLE-CHOICE ITEMS

Practicing the preceding rules will help you write better multiple-choice items. It is difficult to keep all of the rules in mind, however. Some of the most useful rules are presented in the checklist. You can use this checklist to review the items you have written or those you have found in the quizzes and tests that come with your textbook or teaching materials. As we pointed out earlier, professional item writers seldom write the tests that come with textbooks and curricular materials, so the items may be poorly written. Before using them, use the checklist to review each item. Revise every item that does not pass your checklist evaluation before you use it.

FIGURE 8.6 A distractor rationale taxonomy for reading items related to the main idea and vocabulary in context.

Level of understanding	Student error
LEVEL 1	Makes errors that reflect focus on decoding and retrieving facts or details that are not necessarily related to the text or item. Student invokes prior knowledge related to the general topic of the passage, but response is not text-based. These errors indicate that the student is grabbing bits and pieces of the text as he or she understands them, but the pieces are unrelated to the information required by the question being asked.
LEVEL 2	Makes errors that reflect initial understanding of facts or details in the text, but inability to relate them to each other or apply them to come to even a weak conclusion of inference. The student may be focusing on literal aspects of a text or on superficial connections to arrive at a response.
LEVEL 3	Makes errors that reflect analysis and interpretation, but conclusions or inferences arrived at are secondary or weaker than ones required for correct response. A distractor may be related to the correct response in meaning, but be too narrow or broad given the circumstances.
LEVEL 4	Correct response.

The examples are associated with a Grade 3 reading passage titled "Frogs and Toads."
The first example uses this taxonomy:

WHAT IS THE MAIN IDEA OF THE PASSAGE "FROGS AND TOADS"?
A.　Frogs and toads are cute. [Level 1: prior knowledge, not text-based]
B.　Toads have shorter legs than frogs have. [Level 2: text-based detail unrelated to main idea]
C.　Frogs are different than toads. [Level 3: only part of main idea]
*D.　Frogs and toads share many differences and similarities. [Level 4: correct response]

The second example presents a traditional version of an item with the same stem, for contrast.

WHAT IS THE MAIN IDEA OF THE PASSAGE "FROGS AND TOADS"?
A.　Frogs live closer to water than toads.　　　　All distractors are essentially Level 3: Each is related to the
B.　Frogs and toads are like cousins.　　　　　　main idea but is not the *best* answer.
C.　Frogs are different than toads.
*D.　Frogs and toads share many differences and similarities.

✓ *Checklist*

A checklist for Reviewing the Quality of Multiple-Choice Items

Ask these questions of every item you write. If you answer "no" to one or more questions, revise the item accordingly.

1. Does the item assess an important aspect of the unit's instructional targets?

2. Does the item match your assessment plan in terms of performance, emphasis, and number of points?

3. Does the stem ask a direct question or set a specific problem?

4. Is the item based on a paraphrase rather than words lifted directly from a textbook?

5. Are the vocabulary and sentence structure at a relatively low and nontechnical level?

6. Is each alternative (foil) plausible so that a student who lacks knowledge of the correct answer cannot view it as absurd or silly?

7. If possible, is every incorrect alternative based on a common student error or misconception?

8. Is the correct answer to this item independent of the correct answers of other items?

9. Are all of the alternatives homogeneous and appropriate to the content of the stem?

10. Did you avoid using "all of the above" or "none of the above" as much as possible?

11. Is there only one correct or best answer to the item?

Source: Adapted from *Teacher's Guide to Better Classroom Testing: A Judgmental Approach* (p. 35), by A. J. Nitko and T-C Hsu, 1987, Pittsburgh, PA: Institute for Practice and Research in Education, School of Education, University of Pittsburgh. Adapted by permission of copyright holders.

CRAFTING ALTERNATIVE VARIETIES OF MULTIPLE-CHOICE ITEMS

A number of multiple-choice item formats are usually not taught in traditional assessment courses, but they have considerable usefulness. The value of these item formats is fourfold. First, some of them will fit your learning targets much more closely than do typical true-false, matching, and multiple-choice formats, thus increasing the validity of your classroom assessments. It is most important that you craft assessment tasks that closely match the targets you intended students to learn. Second, the formats are objectively scored. As you know, the more objective your scoring, the more likely you are to have reliable scores for evaluating your students. Third, because these tasks take students a relatively short time to complete, your assessment coverage of the content and learning targets you taught is more thorough. That is, because you have only a limited amount of time to assess students, you can assess a wider range of content and learning targets by using one or more of these formats in addition to your traditional assessment formats. Fourth, these formats are relatively easy to craft. In most cases they are easier to write than traditional multiple-choice and matching items.

The section discusses four item formats: greater-less-same, best-answer, experiment-interpretation, and statement-and-comment. Many of the ideas for this discussion are adapted from Carlson (1985) and Gulliksen (1986). After each format is illustrated, we discuss advantages and criticisms, then offer suggestions for improving the way you craft the items.

GREATER-LESS-SAME ITEMS

Format

The **greater-less-same item** format consists of a pair of concepts, phrases, quantities, and so on that have a greater-than, same-as, or less-than relationship. The greater-less-same item

format is used to assess qualitative, quantitative, or temporal relationships between two concepts. Several examples are shown in Figure 8.7.

The student's task is to identify the relationship between the concepts and record an answer. You may use before-during-after, more-same-less, heavier-same-lighter, or other ordered triads, depending on the context of the items. Also, instead of spelling out the words *greater*, *less*, *same*, you can use the letters *G*, *L*, and *S*, respectively. Using letters instead of words may be more appropriate for older students.

Advantages and Criticisms

Advantages The greater-less-same format is especially suited for assessing whether students understand the order or relationships between two concepts, events, or outcomes. These include greater than versus less than, more of versus less of, before versus after, more correct versus less correct, more preferred versus less preferred, heavier versus lighter, and higher quality versus lesser quality. When you teach the relationships in class or when students learn the relationships from the textbook, this item assesses recall and recognition. However, this item format need not be limited to recall or remembering. You may teach a principle or a set of criteria and give several examples of its application in class. Then, when assessing the students, *present new examples*. A student can

FIGURE 8.7 **Examples of greater-less-same items.**

Directions: The numbered items below contain pairs of statements. Compare the two members of each pair. If the thing described on the *left* is greater than the thing described on the right, circle the word "greater"; if the *left* is less than the right, circle "less"; and if the *left* and the right are essentially the same, circle "same."

1.	Total area of Lake Erie	Greater / Same / (Less)	Total area of Lake Huron
2.	Meaning of the prefix mono-	Greater / (Same) / Less	Meaning of the prefix uni-
3.	Radius of Mars	Greater / Same / (Less)	Radius of Venus
4.	Number of Christians in Africa	(Greater) / Same / Less	Number of Muslims in Africa
5.	Atomic weight of Ca	(Greater) / Same / Less	Atomic weight of C
6.	$\sqrt{3^2 + 7^2}$	Greater / Same / (Less)	$\sqrt{3^2} + \sqrt{7^2}$
7.	First U.S. passenger railroad opened	Before / Same / (After)	Erie Canal opened

then apply the principle(s) or criteria you taught to *deduce the relationship* between the concept pairs. This elevates the item so it requires a higher level of thinking than remembering.

Criticisms The criticisms of greater-less-same items are similar to those for matching and true-false items. That is, teachers often use them to assess rote association and disconnected bits of knowledge. Also, this format limits assessment to relationships among pairs of concepts. If you wish to assess a student's ability to order larger members of a set of events or facts, then use an item format that requires students to rank the members.

Crafting Suggestions

Begin to craft items by first identifying the learning targets you want to assess. This item format assesses learning targets that include the ability to identify the relationships between two ideas, concepts, or situations. You should make a list of concept pairs that are related; add to this list other paired relationships that your students can deduce from principles or criteria they have learned. Rephrase the members of each pair so they are clearly stated and fit the item format. When arranging the pairs, be sure that you do not have all the "greaters" on one side of the pair.

Write a set of directions for students that explains the basis on which they are to choose greater-same-less (before-during-after, etc.). Normally, *the set of items should refer to the same general topic.* In the preceding examples this is not the case, because we wanted to illustrate items from different subject areas. Therefore, the directions in our preceding examples are too general. Your directions should be more focused on the set of items you are using and very clear. Notice, too, that Item 7 does not "fit" the directions.

The first time you use this format, you may need to give your students some sample items to help them understand what they are to do. Be sure the directions tell the students *which member* (i.e., *left* or *right member*) of the pairs in the set they are to use as a referent.

Organize all the items of this format into one section of your assessment. Put the directions and the sample item at the beginning of the set. The numbered items should follow. Be sure that the correct answers do not follow a set pattern (such as GSLGSL or GGLLSS). Review the set to be sure the items are concisely worded, the task is clear, and the relationships are not ambiguous.

The checklist summarizes the suggestions in this section for judging the quality of greater-less-same items. Use the checklist to guide you in crafting this type of item format. Use it, too, to evaluate the item sets you have already crafted.

✓ *Checklist*

A Checklist for Reviewing the Quality of Greater-Less-Same Items

Ask these questions of every item you write. If you answer "no" to one or more questions, revise the item accordingly.

1. Does each item in the greater-less-same set assess an important aspect of the unit's instructional targets?
2. Does each item in the greater-less-same set match your assessment plan in terms of performance, emphasis, and number of points?
3. Do some of the items in the greater-less-same set require students to apply their knowledge and skill to new situations, examples, or events?
4. Do your directions clearly and completely explain the basis you intend students to use when judging "greater than," "less than," or "same as" for each pair of statements?
5. Do your directions state which pair member (left or right) is the referent?
6. Did you avoid using a pattern (GGSSLLGGSSLL, etc.) for the correct answers?

BEST-ANSWER ITEMS
Format

Best-answer items are multiple-choice items for which every option is at least partly correct. The student's task is to select the best or most correct option. Here are two examples of best-answer items.

Example

1. Which statement best describes why William attacked England?
   A William felt that his ties to the kings of England qualified him to take the throne when Edward the Confessor died.
   B The king of Norway, Harold Hardrada, asked William to help him conquer England. William agreed, hoping to dispose of Harold later.
   C William felt that Edward the Confessor had promised him the throne and Harold, Earl of Wessex, had sworn personal loyalty to him. When the Witan chose to be king, William felt betrayed.
   D William's cousin, Harold of Wessex, was being held for ransom by Edward the Confessor and William wanted to help release him and then to ask him to swear loyalty to William as king of England.

Directions: In the paragraph below is a set of facts about the way two gases, P and Q, react with each other. Following the facts is a hypothesis and a brief description of possible experiments to test the hypothesis. In light of the facts, select the experiment that will best test the hypothesis.

Facts:

Two gases, P and Q, react quickly when mixed in a glass flask. However, if you heat the flask until very hot and then let it cool just before you introduce the gases into it, they do not react. Also, if you use a copper container, the gases do not react at all.

2. Hypothesis: Water is necessary for the gases to react.
   A. *Experiment*: Before introducing the gases into the flask, you should dry the flask but do not heat it.
   B. *Experiment*: After you introduce the gases into the flask, you should leave the flask open.
   C. *Experiment*: Before you introduce the gases into the flask, you should moisten the walls of the flask with water.
   D. *Experiment*: Before you introduce the gases into the flask, you should heat the flask until very hot, let it cool, and then leave it open for several days.
   E. This hypothesis is untenable or cannot be tested experimentally.

Sources: Item 1 is adapted from *Creative Classroom Testing: Ten Designs for Assessment and Instruction* (p. 182), by S. B. Carlson, 1985, Princeton, NJ: Educational Testing Service. Materials selected from Creative Classroom Testing, 1985. Reprinted by permission of Educational Testing Service, the copyright owner. Item 2 is adapted from *Handbook on Formative and Summative Evaluation of Student Learning* (p. 199), by B. S. Bloom, J. T. Hastings, and G. F. Madaus, 1971, New York: McGraw-Hill. Adapted by permission.

In this item format, each distractor contains partial misinterpretations or omissions. The keyed or best answer contains neither misinterpretations nor omissions. A distractor that contains omissions is an incomplete answer to the stem and, therefore, is not as good a choice as the best answer. Only one option can be the "best." Therefore, you should never use "all of the above" or "none of the above" with this format. Neither can some combination of choices (such as "both A and C") be the keyed answer.

Advantages and Criticisms

Advantages   Best-answer items assess students' ability to make relatively fine distinctions among the choices. They must comprehend the question and the criteria used to judge the "best" option. Thus, best-answer items assess relatively high-order verbal reasoning skills.

Criticisms   The best-answer item format is difficult to craft. You must know your subject and your students' faulty thinking patterns quite well. You need to create distractors that are partially correct, yet less defensible than the keyed answers. This is unlike typical multiple-choice items for which one option is the only correct one and the others

are incorrect. Another criticism is that this format may be unsuitable for some students because their level of educational development is not high enough to make the fine distinctions necessary to select the best answer.

A third criticism is that different teachers may not teach consistently across sections of the same course. Thus, what is legitimately a best answer in one teacher's class (given what students have been taught) is not the best answer in another teacher's class. A fourth criticism is that best implies a set of criteria that students may not have been taught or may fail to understand. No answer is unequivocally best unless it is evaluated by applying these criteria. Your students must internalize criteria to apply them. Also, your own knowledge of the subject may be limited. As a result, what you consider the best answer may in fact not be best, because you do not understand other criteria by which the options may be evaluated. A fifth criticism is that a teacher may easily write a **tricky** item—that is, an item in which an option's correctness depends on a trivial fact, an idiosyncratic standard, or an easily overlooked word or phrase.

Design Suggestions   As always, first identify the learning targets you want to assess. Learning targets that require students to choose among several partially correct alternatives may be assessed using this format. Before using this type of item, be sure you have taught your students to use criteria for selecting the best among several partially correct explanations, descriptions, and ideas. These are higher-order thinking skills (often called critical-thinking skills) in that students must use criteria (such as "completeness of response" and "no misinformation") to evaluate alternatives.

Begin writing by first drafting the question for the stem. Second, write several ways in which students' responses to that question are typically partially correct. These become the basis for crafting distractors. You could also give your students several open-ended short-answer questions as homework. Then, select from among the students' responses those that represent excellent, good, and poor answers. Edited versions of these could be used as a basis for creating the options. (You should not use students' responses verbatim as alternatives. They may be poorly phrased or contain too many other errors to function well as partially correct nonkeyed response options.)

Because the best-answer format is a multiple-choice format, you should follow the basic rules of writing multiple-choice items discussed earlier. You should review the checklist for evaluating the quality of multiple-choice items at this point to be certain you understand what these basic rules are. A typical flaw with best-answer items is that the best or keyed answer is the one with the longest wording because it contains the most complete information. Avoid this flaw by being sure the options have approximately equal numbers of words.

Use the checklist for judging the quality of best-answer items. Use it, too, as an evaluation guide as you review and edit the items you have already crafted.

✓ *Checklist*

A Checklist for Reviewing the Quality of Best-Answer Items

Ask these questions of every item you write. If you answer "no" to one or more questions, revise the item accordingly.

1. Does each best-answer item assess an important aspect of the unit's instructional targets?

2. Does each best-answer item match your assessment plan in terms of performance, emphasis, and number of points?

3. Does each best-answer item require students to apply their knowledge and skill in some manner to new situations, examples, or events?

4. Do your directions clearly and completely explain the basis you intend students to use when judging "best"? (Have your students been given practice in using the appropriate criteria for judging "best"?)

5. Are all the options correct to some degree?

6. Is the keyed answer the only one that can be defended as "the best" by applying the criteria you specify in the directions?

7. Is each distractor based on an important misconception, misunderstanding, or way of being an incomplete answer? (Did you avoid tricky or trivial ways of making a distractor partially correct or contain misinformation?)

8. Are all of the options of equal length (within five words of each other)?

9. Did you avoid (a) having more than one "best" answer and (b) using "all of the above" or "none of the above"?

10. Did you apply all of the multiple-choice item-writing guidelines described in the multiple-choice checklist?

EXPERIMENT-INTERPRETATION ITEMS

Format

The **experiment-interpretation item** consists of a description of an experiment followed by a multiple-choice item requiring students to recognize the best interpretation of the results from the experiment. Figure 8.8 presents three examples.

Items 1 and 2 are for a unit in general or physical science; Item 3 is for a social studies unit or a mathematics unit on statistical methods. We use the term *experiment* loosely in this section: It means any data-based research study. Scientific or controlled studies are included in the term, but we do not limit its use to only those types of studies. The experiment-interpretation item is similar to the best-answer format because very often the multiple-choice options will all have some degree of correctness, but only one is the best answer.

A variation is to use a short-answer item along with or instead of the multiple-choice items. For example, you may ask a student to justify her choice on the multiple-choice item. Alternatively, you could use a short-answer question instead of the multiple-choice one. Example items 4–7 on p. 171 show alternate ways to craft the experiment-interpretation item format. These examples are based on Item 3 in the preceding examples.

FIGURE 8.8 Examples of experiment-interpretation items.

Use the following information to answer Question 1.

Billy and Jesse were walking through an empty lot near their home. Billy picked up a whitish rock. "Look," he said, "I found a limestone rock. I know it is a limestone rock because I found a rock last year that has the same color and it was limestone."

Jesse said, "Just because it looks the same it doesn't have to be the same."

1. Which of the following explanations best supports *Jesse's* point of view?
   A. During the year the chemical properties of limestone probably changed.
   B. Different minerals have very similar physical properties.
   C. One year is not long enough for the minerals in a rock to change their physical properties.

Use the following information to answer Question 2.

Billy took the rock home and did an experiment with it. He put a piece of the rock in a clear glass and poured vinegar over it. The piece of rock bubbled and foamed. "There!" he said to Jesse, "That proves the rock is limestone."

Jesse said, "No! You are wrong. You haven't proved it!"

2. Why was Jesse correct?
   A. Billy did the experiment only once. He needs to repeat the same type of experiment many times with different bits of the rock. If the mixture bubbles every time, that will prove it.

Source: Items 1 and 2 are based on ideas found in Klopfer (1971).

B. The experiment is correct but Billy misinterpreted the results. Limestone does not bubble and foam in vinegar.
C. Billy should do many different kinds of experiments, not just vinegar tests, because many different kinds of substances bubble and foam in vinegar.
D. Billy should not have used vinegar. He should have used distilled water. If the rock made the water warm, that would prove it is limestone.

Use the following information when answering Question 3.

For a social studies project, a class interviewed all the 10th-grade students. They asked how many hours per week students worked at after-school jobs. They also asked what their average grades were last term. They found that students with Fs and Ds worked 8 to 10 hours per week, students with Cs and Bs worked 10 to 20 hours per week, and students with As worked 8 to 10 hours per week.

3. Which of the following is the most valid interpretation of these findings?
   A. If you work 10 to 20 hours per week you will only get Cs and Bs.
   B. A student who works 10 to 20 hours per week is probably not an A-student or a B-student.
   C. Working after school is not related to your grades.
   D. The more hours a student works after school, the higher will be that student's grades.

Example

Use the following information when answering the questions below.

For a social studies project, a class interviewed all the 10th-grade students. They asked how many hours per week students worked at after-school jobs. They also asked what their average grades were last term. They found that students with Fs and Ds worked 8 to 10 hours per week, students with Cs and Bs worked 10 to 20 hours per week, and students with As worked 8 to 10 hours per week.

Alternative Format A

Students choose from among teacher-provided interpretations but are required to write a justification of their choice.

4. Which of the following is the most valid interpretation of these findings?
   A If you work 10 to 20 hours per week you will only get Cs and Bs.
   B Working after school is not related to your grades.
   C A student who works 10 to 20 hours per week is probably not an A-student or a B-student.
   D The more hours a student works after school, the higher will be that student's grades.

5. Write a brief explanation of why your answer to Question 4 is the most valid interpretation of these findings.

   _____

   _____

   _____

   _____

Alternative Format B

Students supply their own interpretation and write a justification of it.

6. What is the most valid interpretation of the relationship the class found between the number of hours students worked and their grades?

   _____

   _____

   _____

   _____

7. Write a brief explanation of why your interpretation of these findings is the most valid one.

   _____

   _____

   _____

   _____

   _____

You should note that the three variations (multiple-choice only, multiple-choice with short-answer, and short-answer only) assess somewhat different abilities. Using multiple-choice only (Item 3) assesses a student's ability to evaluate each of *the interpretations you provide* and select the best one. Thus you do not know a student's reasoning behind his selection. The multiple-choice with short-answer combination (Items 4 and 5) assesses a student's ability to explain or justify her choice from among the interpretations you provide as options. This helps you assess the reasoning behind students' choices. The short-answer *without the multiple-choice items* (Items 6 and 7) assess both a student's ability to interpret the experiment's results and his ability to explain his reasoning. In this latter format, there may be multiple correct responses to the constructed-response questions. As with other constructed-response items, you may want to give students partial credit if their response is not completely correct.

Advantages and Criticisms

Advantages You may use the experiment-interpretation format to assess a student's ability to evaluate explanations, interpretations, and inferences from data. The multiple-choice-only version allows you to score the items more quickly and more objectively than the other versions. Because students are required only to select the correct answer, their response times are shorter. Therefore, you can use more items and cover more content within a shorter assessment period than with short-answer items.

If the experiments and findings you present in the items are new to the students, your items will assess your students' ability to apply principles and criteria from your subject area. Using experiments and data new to your students in assessment tasks requires you to teach students how to apply criteria and principles to a variety of situations. You will need to give students sufficient practice in applying criteria and principles before assessing them for summative evaluation purposes. This will move your teaching away from teaching facts and results, and toward teaching students to actively apply their knowledge and skill.

If you require students to justify their multiple-choice answers, you will have some information about their reasoning processes. Students often make the correct choice from among the possible interpretations you give them, but they cannot explain why they made the choice, or they give faulty explanations. If you require a student both to supply his interpretation and to justify it, you can assess whether the student can generate and explain his own interpretations of experimental findings.

Criticisms Like the best-answer item format, the experiment-interpretation format is not easy to craft. You must know your subject matter and your students' thinking patterns well enough to craft items that allow you to identify faulty thinking as well as correct answers. Faulty thinking must be reflected in your multiple-choice distractors. This means you must be able to create partially correct interpretations and incorrect interpretations that people typically make.

Criticism is leveled at teachers who use this format to assess whether a student can remember the "correct" interpretations of specific experimental results that the teacher taught. These teachers are not assessing the higher-order thinking ability that this format is capable of gauging. Using this item format to assess remembering encourages students to look to the teacher or the text as the source of fixed knowledge. It discourages students from learning skills required to interpret the empirical results of experiments.

Crafting Suggestions

First, identify the learning targets you want to assess. The experiment-interpretation assessment format is appropriate when a learning target requires students to understand and interpret the results of empirical research. Before using this format for summative student evaluation, be sure you have taught and have given practice in interpreting the findings from empirical research studies.

Write the item to assess the student's ability to apply specific principles. This means that you first identify the principles or rules you want students to apply, then craft the item so it requires students to use the principle in a new situation. For example, items in the preceding examples are crafted around the following principles:

- Different substances may share the same or similar physical properties such as color, texture, and solubility. [Item 1]
- Different substances may share the same or similar chemical properties, such as their reactivity with acids. [Item 2]
- Some patterns of relationships among variables are not strictly increasing or decreasing but are curvilinear. [Item 3 and Items 4 through 7]

After identifying the principle(s), you create the item in such a way that it requires students to use or apply the principle(s). Usually, this means writing a description of the experiment or research study that results in findings that a student can then interpret using the principle(s). (See the interpretive text that immediately precedes Items 1, 2, 3, 4/5, and 6/7 in the previous examples.)

Next, draft a stem that asks the student to interpret or explain the experimental findings you describe. You may then list several correct or partially correct interpretations. You may also list incorrect interpretations that result from incomplete or faulty reasoning. Avoid using as distractors interpretations that are completely unrelated to the experiment you describe in the interpretive material or distractors that are "silly" or "tricky." For example, it would be inappropriate for you to use in Item 1 a distractor such as "Jesse knows that Billy is a liar."

As with the best-answer item format, distractors for this format should contain interpretations or explanations that contain your students' typical misconceptions. To determine these misinterpretations, you could assign several open-ended questions as homework and select from among the students' responses those that are excellent, good, and poor. Use these selections as a basis for crafting multiple-choice options.

If you use the multiple-choice versions of this format, you should follow the basic rules of writing multiple-choice items that we discussed earlier and that are summarized in the multiple-choice checklist. You may wish to review these rules at this time. If you use one of the short-answer versions of this format, you should follow the basic rules of short-answer item writing. We discussed and summarized these in the short-answer checklist in Chapter 7. You may wish to review these at this time also. The checklist offers specific guidance for the experiment-interpretation item format. Use it to review the items you craft.

✓ Checklist

A Checklist for Reviewing the Quality of Experiment-Interpretation Items

Ask these questions of every item you write. If you answer "no" to one or more questions, revise the item accordingly.

1. Does each item assess an important aspect of the unit's instructional targets?

2. Does each experiment-interpretation item match your assessment plan in terms of performance, emphasis, and number of points?

3. Does each item focus on requiring students to apply one or more important principles or criteria to new situations, examples, or events?

4. Have you given students opportunity to practice applying the appropriate criteria or principles for judging the "best" or "most valid" interpretation?

5. Did you describe an experiment or research study in concise but sufficient detail that a student can use the appropriate criteria or principles to interpret the results?

6. Is the keyed answer the only one that can be defended as the "best" or "most valid" interpretation?

7. Is each distractor based on an important misconception, misinterpretation, or misapplication of a criterion or principle? (Did you avoid tricky or trivial ways of making a distractor partially correct or contain misinformation?)

8. Did you avoid (a) having more than one "best" or "most valid" answer and (b) using "all of the above" or "none of the above"?

9. Did you apply all of the appropriate item-writing guidelines described in the multiple-choice checklist?

10. If you used short-answer items, did you apply all of the appropriate item-writing guidelines described in the short-answer checklist?

STATEMENT-AND-COMMENT ITEMS

Format

A **statement-and-comment item** presents a statement about some relevant subject matter and requires the student either to write a comment about the statement or to select the most appropriate comment from among a list you provide. Figure 8.9 shows examples of statement-and-comment items.

The subject-matter area of the items is Shakespeare's play *Julius Caesar*. The statements are three of the play's themes, which the class discussed. These themes are shown in quotation marks. In the multiple-choice version, a student selects from among several alternate choices the best meaning of the quoted theme. The multiple-choice version is a special case of the best-answer item format. The alternatives should be phrased in language different from the "pat phrases" learned in class. In the short-answer version, a student must comment directly, writing her own interpretation of the quoted statement.

Advantages and Criticisms

Advantages The statement-and-comment item format assesses a student's ability to evaluate interpretations of a given statement. The multiple-choice version assesses whether students can identify the best interpretation or explanation from among several. Explanations should not use the same wording used in class. Rather, they should be comments typically made by students when interpreting the quoted statement. In this way, a student must rely on her comprehension of the quoted phrase instead of her memory of a "set" comment.

The open-ended version assesses a student's ability to recall and write about the meaning of the quoted statement. Although it may be an advantage to have students construct their own comments about the quoted statement, there is a downside. Students may just write an explanation or commentary they memorized from the class discussion or from a textbook. You have some control over what kinds of comments they must evaluate if you present the multiple-choice version.

The short-answer version could assess some higher-order thinking if the quoted statement was from outside the course but can be commented on or evaluated using the knowledge and skills taught in the course. For example, the quote can be from a public official's statement in the newspaper. The task could be to evaluate or criticize the statement using specified principles.

Criticisms The statement-and-comment item format has limited applications. You must identify appropriate statements that students should interpret. Although there are

FIGURE 8.9 Examples of statement-and-comment items

A. Multiple-choice version of statement-and-comment items
Directions: The quote in each numbered statement expresses a theme about the play *Julius Caesar*. Below the quote are several comments about the meaning of the statements in quotes. Choose the one comment that best expresses how the quoted theme applies to the play.

1. "Power corrupts."
    A. Caesar wanted to be crowned king.
    B. Brutus feared that one man would control Rome. Therefore, he plotted against Caesar.
    C. Cassius wanted power so much he led a conspiracy against Caesar.

2. "Cowards die many times before their deaths."
    A. Caesar ignored the warning he was given because he was not a coward.
    B. Brutus and Cassius ran away because they were afraid of being killed.
    C. Brutus and Cassius led lives of shame and defeat after running away from Rome.

3. "The evil that men do lives after them."
    A. Romans would remember Brutus and Cassius for the murderers they committed instead of the "noble" motive they had for committing the murders.
    B. Caesar's murderers considered only his bad qualities, not his good qualities.
    C. Anthony remembered only the evil side of Cassius.

Directions: The quote in each numbered statement below expresses a theme about the play *Julius Caesar*. Below the quote, write an explanation of the meaning of the statement in quotes. Your comments should explain how the theme applies to the play.

4. "Power corrupts."

    _____

    _____

    _____

5. "Cowards die many times before their deaths."

    _____

    _____

    _____

6. "The evil that men do lives after them."

    _____

    _____

    _____

Source: Items A and B are adapted from *Creative Classroom Testing: Ten Designs for Assessment and Instruction* (pp. 124–125), by S. B. Carlson, 1985, Princeton, NJ: Educational Testing Service. Reprinted by permission of Educational Testing Service, the copyright owner.

many subjects for which such statements exist, the task itself represents a small range of learning targets. The short-answer version of the task does provide an opportunity for students to display their comprehension of the quoted statement. However, students may simply repeat the phrases they learned in class.

Crafting Suggestions

First, as always, identify the learning targets you want to assess. This assessment format is appropriate when a learning target requires a student to comprehend statements and themes. For example, a learning target that focuses on understanding of the themes that underlie the play *Julius Caesar* could use this format.

If you give students the short-answer version as a homework exercise, you may use excellent, good, and poor student responses as a basis for creating the alternatives for the multiple-choice version. As with the best-answer variety, of which this may be considered a special case, you usually cannot use students' responses verbatim as multiple-choice options; paraphrase them. Because the multiple-choice version of the statement-and-comment is a type of best-answer item, follow the guidelines suggested in the best-answer item checklist.

MATCHING EXERCISE FORMAT

A **matching exercise** presents a student with three things: (1) **directions for matching**, (2) a list of **premises**, and (3) a list of **responses**. The student's task is to match each premise with one of the responses, using as a basis for matching the criteria described in the directions. Figure 8.10 shows a matching exercise with its various parts labeled.

This sample exercise requires simple matching based on associations that a student must remember. You may create matching exercises, however, to assess students' comprehension of concepts and principles. Examples of these latter types appear later in the chapter.

Study the example. Premises are listed in the left column and responses in the right column.[5] Each premise is numbered because each is a separately scorable item. You can craft matching exercises with more responses than premises, more premises than responses, or an equal number of each. When there is an equal number of premise statements and response statements, this is called **perfect matching**. Most assessment *specialists consider perfect matching to be undesirable* because, if a student knows four of the five answers, the student automatically gets the fifth (last) choice correct, whether or not he knows the answer. This reduces the validity of the assessment results.

Matching exercises are very much like multiple-choice items. Each premise functions as a separate item. The elements in the list of responses function as alternatives. You could rewrite a matching exercise as a series of multiple-choice items: Each premise would then be a multiple-choice stem, but the same alternatives would be repeated for each of these stems. This leads to an important principle for crafting matching exercises: *Use matching exercises only when you have several multiple-choice items that require repeating the identical set of alternatives (foils).*

[5]The responses may also be put vertically above the premises. See the masterlist variety of matching exercise.

FIGURE 8.10 Example of a matching exercise.

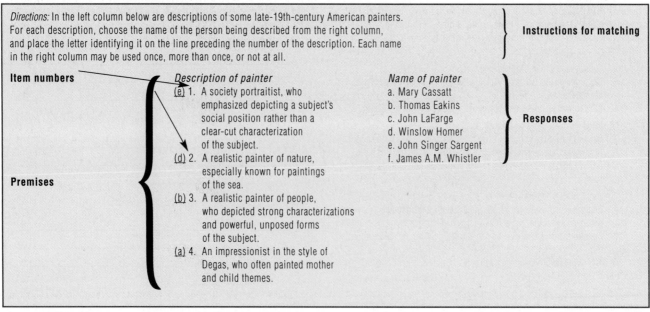

Directions: In the left column below are descriptions of some late-19th-century American painters. For each description, choose the name of the person being described from the right column, and place the letter identifying it on the line preceding the number of the description. Each name in the right column may be used once, more than once, or not at all.   } **Instructions for matching**

Item numbers

Description of painter
(e) 1. A society portraitist, who emphasized depicting a subject's social position rather than a clear-cut characterization of the subject.
(d) 2. A realistic painter of nature, especially known for paintings of the sea.
(b) 3. A realistic painter of people, who depicted strong characterizations and powerful, unposed forms of the subject.
(a) 4. An impressionist in the style of Degas, who often painted mother and child themes.

Premises

Name of painter
a. Mary Cassatt
b. Thomas Eakins
c. John LaFarge
d. Winslow Homer
e. John Singer Sargent
f. James A.M. Whistler   } **Responses**

FIGURE 8.11 Examples of different foundations for developing matching exercises.

Possible premise sets	Associated response sets
Accomplished	Persons
Noted events	Dates
Definitions	Terms and phrases
Examples, applications	Rules, principles, and classifications
Concepts (ideas, operations, quantities, and qualities)	Symbols and signs
Titles of works	Authors and artists
Foreign words and phrases	English correspondence
Uses and functions	Parts and machines
Names of objects	Pictures of objects

ADVANTAGES AND CRITICISMS OF MATCHING EXERCISES

Advantages

A matching exercise can be a space-saving and objective way to assess a number of important learning targets, such as a student's ability to identify associations or relationships between two sets of things. You can also develop matching exercises using pictorial materials to assess the students' abilities to match words and phrases with pictures of objects or with locations on maps and diagrams. Figure 8.11 gives examples of relationships that you may use as a basis for developing matching exercises (Gronlund, 1976).

Criticisms

Detractors criticize the matching exercise because students can use rote memorization to learn the elements in two lists, and because teachers often use matching exercises only to assess such rote associations as names and dates. As a result, critics often see this assessment format as limited to the assessment of memorized factual information.

Thoughtful teachers, however, also use matching exercises to assess aspects of a student's comprehension of concepts, principles, or schemes for classifying objects, ideas, or events (we will see examples later). *If you want to assess students on these higher-level abilities, craft exercises that present new examples or instances of the concept or principle to the students.* Then require the students to match these examples with the names of appropriate concepts or principles. In this context, *new examples* are instances of concepts that students have not been previously taught or encountered. Similarly, a matching task can describe a situation novel to the student, and the student can decide which of several rules, principles, or classifications is likely to apply. An example of this type of matching exercise follows.

Example

Directions: Each numbered statement below describes a testing situation in which ONE decision is represented. On the blank next to each statement, write the letter:

A   if the decision is primarily concerned with *placement*

B   if the decision is primarily concerned with *selection*

C   if the decision is primarily concerned with *program improvement*

D   if the decision is primarily concerned with *theory development*

E   if the decision is primarily concerned with *motivating students*

(A) 1.   After children are admitted to kindergarten, they are given a screening test to determine which children should be given special training in perceptual skills.

(A) 2.   At the end of the third grade, all students are given an extensive battery of reading tests, and reading profiles are developed for each child. On the basis of these profiles, some children are given a special reading program, whereas others continue on with the regular program.

(B) 3.   High school seniors take a national scholastic aptitude test and send their scores to colleges they wish to attend. On the basis of these scores, colleges admit some students and do not admit others.

(E) 4.   Students are informed about the learning targets their examination will cover and about how many points each examination question will be worth.

This exercise assesses a student's understanding of five concepts related to using tests for decision making. The placement of the response list above the premise list creates a type of matching exercise called the **masterlist variety**. It is also called the **classification** or **keylist variety**. Later in this chapter we present suggestions for creating this type of matching exercise as well as the double matching exercise or tabular exercise.

Homogeneous premises and responses means that the elements in the premises list and the elements in the responses list together refer to the same category of things. In the preceding example, for instance, all premises and responses refer to some type of educational decision. In the example about painters, all premises and responses refer to late-19th-century painters.

Why should you create matching exercises with homogeneous premises and responses? Because the *entire* list of response choices has to be plausible for *every* premise. If it is not, the students' matching task may be trivial. As an example, consider the nonhomogeneous, poor-quality matching exercise shown here.

Example

Poor: Premises and response set are not homogeneous

(d) 1. Pennsylvania's official state flower
(a) 2. Pennsylvania's official state bird
(b) 3. Major steel-producing city in the 1940s
(c) 4. 1970 population of Philadelphia

a. Ruffed grouse
b. Pittsburgh
c. 1,950,098
d. Mountain laurel
e. Allegheny River

Not all of the responses in this example are plausible distractors for *each* premise. As a result, students can answer the items on the basis of general knowledge of a few of the associations and common sense, rather than on any special knowledge learned from the curriculum.

This matching exercise is poor for another, perhaps more important, reason: *The main focus of the exercise seems lost.* Even if you tried to improve it, your efforts would probably be self-defeating. You may attempt to make the exercise's responses more homogeneous, but this may result in an exercise that does not assess the intended learning target. For example, you could make all the premises refer to different states and all the premises to different official state birds: The task would be to match the birds with the states. Your local curriculum, however, may only require students to identify their own state bird (or other facts and symbols about their own state). Creating a homogeneous exercise, as in this example, may result in a test that does not match the curriculum and, therefore, cannot be used. Remember that the learning targets determine the type of assessment.

Could anything be done to salvage this exercise? Remember the rule mentioned earlier in this chapter: You should reserve the matching exercise for situations when several multiple-choice items require the same set of responses. Returning to the example, note that each premise could be turned into a separate multiple-choice item, each with a different set of plausible options. Plausible options for a multiple-choice item on Pennsylvania's official state flower, for example, would include only flowers native to the Pennsylvania region (e.g., daisies, roses, violets, etc.). Similarly, separate multiple-choice items could assess knowledge of the official state bird, names of cities, and size of cities.

CRAFTING BASIC MATCHING EXERCISES

Many of the suggestions for crafting multiple-choice items apply to matching exercises as well. A few maxims, however, apply particularly to matching exercises. If you follow these, your assessment quality will improve. These suggestions are summarized in a checklist and discussed here. You should use the checklist to evaluate your own matching exercises or those that you adapt from teachers' texts or other curricular materials.

✓ Checklist

A Checklist for Reviewing the Quality of Matching Exercises

Ask these questions of every item you write. If you answer "no" to one or more questions, revise the item accordingly.

1. Does the exercise assess an important aspect of the unit's instructional targets?
2. Does the exercise match your assessment plan in terms of performance, emphasis, and number of points?
3. Within this exercise, does every premise and response belong to the same category of things?
4. Do your directions clearly state the basis you intend students to use to complete the matching correctly?
5. Does every element in the response list function as a plausible alternative to every element in the premise list?
6. Are there fewer than 10 responses in this matching exercise?
7. Did you avoid "perfect matching"?
8. Are the longer statements in the premise list and the shorter statements (names, words, symbols, etc.) in the response list?
9. If possible, are the elements in the response list ordered in a meaningful way (logically, numerically, alphabetically, etc.)?
10. Are the premises numbered and the responses lettered?

Source: Adapted from *Teacher's Guide to Better Classroom Testing: A Judgmental Approach* (p. 34), by A. J. Nitko and T-C Hsu, 1987, Pittsburgh, PA: Institute for Practice and Research in Education, School of Education, University of Pittsburgh. Adapted by permission of copyright holders.

Crafting Suggestions

1 and 2. *Importance of what is assessed and its match to assessment plan.* As always, your assessment tasks should meet the dual criteria of importance and fit with your assessment plan. Eliminate every item that fails to meet these two criteria.

3. *Make a matching exercise homogeneous.* Although we have discussed this point previously, here we add that often the degree to which students perceive the exercise as homogeneous varies with their maturity and educational development (Gronlund, 1976; Lindquist & Mann, 1936). What may be a homogeneous exercise for primary school-children may be less so for middle school youngsters and even less so for high schoolers. Consider, for example, the following matching exercise.

Example

Directions: Column A below lists important events in U.S. history. For each event, find in Column B the date it happened. Write the letter of the date on the blank to the left of each event. Each date in Column B may be used once, more than once, or not at all.

Column A (events)	Column B (dates)
(f) 1. United States entered World War I	a. 1492
	b. 1607
(d) 2. Lincoln became president	c. 1776
(g) 3. Truman became president	d. 1861
(b) 4. Pilgrims landed at Cape Cod	e. 1880
	f. 1917
	g. 1945

The students' task is to match U.S. historical events with their dates. For younger, less experienced students, such a matching task would likely be difficult. It would appear homogeneous, however, because for these children all responses would be plausible options for each premise. High school students would find the task easier—even though they didn't know the exact dates—because they could use partial knowledge to organize the dates into early, middle, and recent history. For them, only Options f and g would be plausible for Item 1.

4. *Explain completely the intended basis for matching.* You must make clear what basis you want students to use to match the premises and the responses. The example below shows how to improve the directions by explaining the basis for the matching.

Example

Poor: Directions are incomplete

Match Column A with Column B. Write your answer on the blank to the left.

Better: Directions explain basis for matching

Column A lists parts of a plant cell. For each cell part, choose from Column B the main purpose of that cell part. Write the letter of that purpose on the blank to the left of the cell part.

Elementary students may need oral explanations and, perhaps, some practice with this format before you assess them. The masterlist variety of matching exercise usually requires more elaborate directions and may require special oral explanations even for high school students. Avoid long, involved written directions, however. These place an unnecessary premium on reading skill.

5. *All responses should function as plausible options for each premise.* Homogeneous premises and responses will minimize plausibility problems. Also, avoid using specific determiners and grammatical clues. For example, avoid beginning some premises or responses with *an* and others with *a,* having some plural whereas others are singular, stating some in the past tense whereas others are stated in the present or future tense. These clue the answer unnecessarily.

Avoid using incomplete sentences as premises. If you use incomplete sentences for premises, it becomes difficult to make all responses homogeneous and easier for students to respond correctly on the basis of superficial features such as grammatical clues or sentence structure (Lindquist & Mann, 1936). Here is an example of a poor matching exercise that comes about when incomplete sentences are used.

Example

Poor: Uses incomplete sentences

(c) 1. Most normally green plants lose their color when	a. through their stomata.
(e) 2. The common characteristic of a flowering plant is	b. contracts into a rounded mass.
	c. grown in the dark.
(d) 3. Almost all plants that form coal	d. are now extinct.
(b) 4. When an expanded amoebae is strongly stimulated it	e. the formation of a reproductive body.

Source: From *The Construction and Use of Achievement Examinations* (p. 69), by H. E. Hawkes, E. F. Lindquist, and C. R. Mann (Eds.), 1936, by American Council of Education. Used by permission. Adapted from an illustration in *Traditional Examinations and New Type Tests* (p. 380), by C. W. Odell, 1928, New York: Century Co.

6. *Use short lists of responses and premises.* For a single matching exercise, put no more than 5 to 10 elements in a response list. The reasons are that (a) longer lists make it difficult for you to develop homogeneous exercises, (b) longer matching exercises overload a test with one kind of performance, and (c) longer lists require too much student searching time (Ebel, 1951). Finally, (d) some evidence suggests that students attain a lower percentage of correct answers with longer matching exercises than with shorter exercises (Shannon, 1973).

Shorter matching exercises make it easier to keep everything belonging to a single exercise on the same page. For some students, having to turn the page back and forth to answer the exercise may interfere with their ability to show you what they know. For these students, splitting an exercise between two pages increases the likelihood of carelessness, confusion, and short-term memory lapses. In short, a student's ability to answer a test item while flipping pages is not relevant to the learning target you want to assess.

To fix an exercise that is too long, separate it into two or more shorter exercises. Or you can use each response as a correct answer more than once. When you do this, alert students through either oral or written directions. One standard phrase you may use to do this is "You may use each of the [names, dates, etc.] once, more than once, or not at all" (see the painters' example we presented at the beginning of this section).

7.   *Avoid "perfect matching."*   As we discussed previously, perfect matching is undesirable. It gives away at least one answer to the student who knows all but one of them. This student's final choice will be automatically correct because it is the only one left, thus lowering the validity of your assessment. You can avoid perfect matching by including one or more responses that do not match any of the premises and by using a response as the correct answer for more than one premise.

8.   *Longer phrases appear in the premise list; shorter phrases in the response list.*   Consider how a student approaches the matching exercise: (a) first reading a premise, (b) then searching through the response list for the correct answer, and (c) rereading the response list for each premise. It is, therefore, more efficient and less time consuming if students read the longer phrases only once. They can reread or scan the shorter phrases (words, symbols) as often as necessary.

9.   *Arrange the response list in a logical order.*   A student saves time if the response list is arranged in some meaningful order: Dates arranged chronologically, numbers in order of magnitude, words and names alphabetically, and qualitative phrases in a logical sequence. Such arrangements also may contribute to the clarity of the task, reduce student confusion, and lower incidence of student carelessness and oversight.

10.   *Identify premises with numbers and responses with letters.*   Remember, each premise is a separately scored item. Therefore, premises should carry numbers, which indicate their position in the sequence of items. For example, if the first 10 items are multiple-choice, and these are followed by a five-premise matching exercise, the five premises should be consecutively numbered 11 through 15.

CRAFTING ALTERNATIVE VARIETIES OF MATCHING EXERCISES

Two types of matching exercises—masterlist and tabular—may fit some of your learning targets better than the more basic matching exercise. As with the alternative varieties of multiple-choice items we discussed previously, these matching formats are objectively scored, do not take students a long time to complete, and are often easier for you to craft than the basic matching format.

MASTERLIST (KEYLIST) ITEMS

Format

A masterlist (or keylist or classification) matching exercise has three parts: (a) directions to students, (b) the masterlist of options, and (c) a list or set of stems. To respond to a masterlist item set, a student reads each numbered stem and applies one of the options from the masterlist. Each stem is scored separately. Figure 8.12 shows a masterlist matching exercise for a 10th-grade civics course.

The content learning target for this masterlist exercise is the students' ability to relate constitutional *values and principles* to specific modern-day, concrete examples of actions or events. Therefore, in crafting this item you would ensure that each masterlist response choice (A, B, C, D) is a value or principle expressed by the U.S. Constitution, rather than a Preamble goal or some other aspect of the Constitution.

Notice that each numbered stem is a brief, realistic, and concrete example of an action or event that illustrates one of the four values in the masterlist. Because the learning target calls for students to relate constitutional principles to concrete examples, each stem must be a concrete example. You would not use textbook abstractions or general descriptions. (For example, you would not word a stem in general language such as, "A law takes effect when the majority of Congress votes to approve it," because this statement describes a general principle rather than a concrete example.) Although the preceding exercise shows only four stems, you need not limit the stems to four. Use as many stems as are appropriate, as long as each stem is an example of one of the masterlist options. Further, although not the case in this example, each stem in a masterlist set may have more than one correct answer from the masterlist.

Advantages and Criticisms

Advantages   A masterlist item set is a variation of the matching exercise format, and it has many of the same advantages as that format. It is a space-saving, compact, and objective way to assess learning targets for which you want students to identify associations between two sets of things. However, it is best used to assess a student's *understanding of concepts*. The preceding masterlist exercise, for instance, requires a student to analyze the specific example in each stem and to classify it as an illustration of one of the constitutional principles in the masterlist. Each constitutional principle is a different concept.

FIGURE 8.12 Example of a masterlist matching exercise.

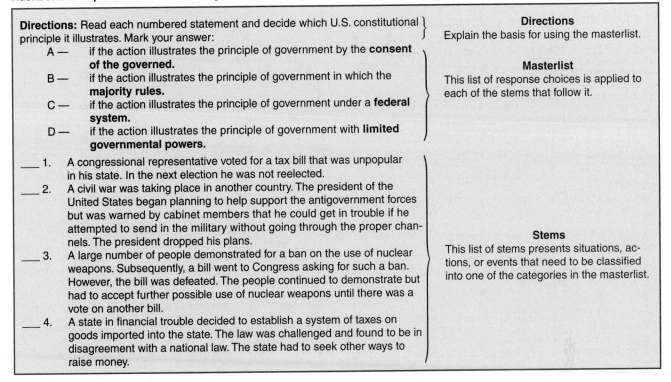

When using this format to assess concept understanding, the examples you give students to classify cannot be the same examples you illustrated in class or that appeared in the textbook or assignments. If your examples are not "new to the students," then the masterlist item set becomes simply an alternate way to assess students' recall and recognition of verbal information. As with other matching exercises, you can use pictures, maps, symbols, or diagrams as stems.

The masterlist item also is an efficient way to assess a student's ability to (a) analyze a passage, table, or graph and (b) recognize an appropriate interpretation or conclusion drawn from this interpretative material. Figure 8.13 shows this type of masterlist exercise.

Criticisms Because masterlist item sets are "cousins" to matching exercises, they share the same criticisms. Critics point out that teachers often limit using the format to assess rote associations such as names and dates, memorized lists of causes and effects, lists of symbols and definitions, and so on. Although some learning targets do focus on memorization and recall of information, many do not and should not. Therefore, you should craft masterlist item sets to assess students' (a) comprehension of concepts, principles, or schemes for classifying objects, events, and ideas and (b) ability to analyze appropriate interpretations and conclusions. Do this by presenting new examples or new interpretations in the stems and requiring students to apply the masterlist.

Crafting Suggestions

To craft your masterlist item set, first identify the learning target you want to assess. For example, this might be "the students' ability to recognize whether data support interpretations about what events occurred." Next write the masterlist of options on which you want to focus. For example, for the constitutional principles exercise given previously, you would list the four constitutional principles; for the masterlist exercise in Figure 8.13, you would list *supportive, contradictory,* and *neither.* If you will use a table, graph, or other interpretive material, prepare it next.

Select one of the options from the masterlist and write as many stems for it as you can. For example, you might select "consent of the governed" as a principle and write four or five concrete examples that illustrate that principle in a real-world application. Continue selecting options and writing stems until you have several items for each option. Review the stems to be sure that they require students to apply their knowledge and skills to new real-world situations, examples, or events.

Create the directions last. Be sure the directions clearly describe the basis on which the student is to solve the masterlist item set. For example, in the civics course exercise, the directions tell students they must read the examples in the statements and decide which constitutional principle each represents. In the graph interpretation example, the directions tell the student that the statements are interpretations of the graph and that the student must decide whether the

FIGURE 8.13 A masterlist item set that requires students to recognize proper interpretations of a graph.

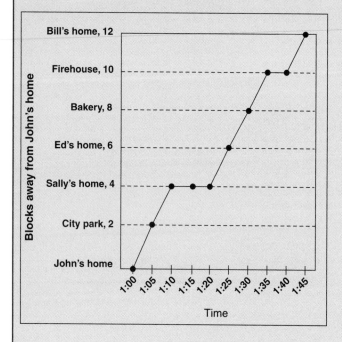

Use the graph below to help you answer Questions 1 through 5.

The graph shows that John left his home at 1:00 and arrived at his friend Bill's home at 1:45. The graph shows where John was in the community at different times.

Directions: The numbered statements below tell what different students said about this graph. Read each statement and decide whether the information in the graph is consistent with a student's statement. Mark answer:

A — if the information in the graph **is consistent** with the statement.

B — if the information in the graph **contradicts** the statement.

C — if the information in the graph **neither contradicts nor is consistent** with the statement.

_____ 1. John ran or walked very fast between his house and the city park.

_____ 2. John stopped at Sally's home on his way to Bill's home.

_____ 3. John stopped at Ed's home on his way to Bill's home.

_____ 4. John stopped to buy something at the bakery before he got to Bill's home.

_____ 5. John traveled faster after he passed by Sally's home than before he reached her home.

graph supports or contradicts the interpretation. If your masterlist item set refers to interpretive material such as this, your directions should clearly describe the material and how students should use it.

After completing the preceding steps, polish your masterlist item set. Organize the interpretive material, if any, at the beginning of the set. Next, place the masterlist before the stems. *Assign letters to the masterlist response choices* that the students may use. If you will not use a machine-scorable answer sheet, your letters do not have to be *A, B, C, D,* or *E.* For example, in the civics course exercise, you could use *C* for "consent of the governed," *M* for "majority rules," and so on.

The stems are always numbered and follow the masterlist. If you are not using a separate answer sheet, put a blank *before* the stem number rather than at the end of the stem. You will score the papers much more quickly and accurately if the blank is before the number of the stem. Scramble the stems so that all the stems matching one masterlist option are not together, and make sure there is no discernible pattern to the answers (avoid ABCDABCD, etc.). If you have written too many

stems, select the best ones and save the others for revision and use at a later date. Edit the stems to make them grammatically correct, clear, and concise. Limit each stem to 40 or fewer words. However, the stems and the other parts of the item set must provide enough information for the student to apply the rule or principle. For example, in the civics course exercise, Stem 2 would not have had sufficient information if it contained only these words:

2. A civil war was taking place in another country. The president of the United States began planning to help support the civil war.

More details are needed to know to what principle the stem refers.

The checklist summarizes the suggestions in this section as a masterlist checklist. Use this checklist to guide you in crafting your masterlist item set. Use it also to evaluate the draft of your masterlist item set. Remember, if you answer no to one or more questions, you need to revise the item set.

A Checklist for Reviewing the Quality of Masterlist Exercises

Ask these questions of every item you write. If you answer "no" to one or more questions, revise the item accordingly.

1. Does the masterlist exercise assess an important aspect of the unit's instructional targets?
2. Does the masterlist exercise match your assessment plan in terms of performance, emphasis, and number of points?
3. Does the masterlist exercise require the students to apply their knowledge and skill to new situations, examples, or events?
4. Did you provide enough information so that knowledgeable students are able to apply the knowledge and skill called for by the item?
5. Do your directions to the students clearly and completely explain the basis you intend them to use when applying masterlist response choices to the stems?
6. Within this masterlist exercise, does every stem and every response choice in the masterlist belong to the same category of things?
7. Does every response choice in the masterlist function as a plausible alternative for every stem?
8. Did you avoid "perfect matching"?
9. If possible, are the options in the masterlist ordered in a meaningful way (logically, numerically, alphabetically, etc.)?
10. Are the stems numbered and the masterlist response choices lettered?

TABULAR (MATRIX) ITEMS

Format

A **tabular (or matrix) item** format is a type of matching exercise in which elements from several lists of *responses* (e.g., presidents, political parties, famous firsts, and important events) are matched with elements from a common list of premises. The students' task is to select one or more elements from each response list and match the elements with one of the numbered premises. An example of a tabular item format is shown in Figure 8.14.

You can see that the example is a quadruple matching exercise: (a) match year and president, (b) match year and president's political party, (c) match year and famous first, and (d) match year and important event. One premise list and several response lists that correspond to it can be efficiently organized into a tabular or matrix item format. Notice that each premise is *numbered*. Thus, each premise is scored as a separate item.

Another example is shown in Figure 8.15. In this example there is one premise list (planet descriptions) and one response list (planet names). Notice that each premise in the list is numbered. Unlike an ordinary match exercise, however, in the tabular item set each premise may apply to more than one response element. For example, many of the planets are named after Greek or Roman gods, so the students would mark an *X* in every cell for Item 8 that is under a planet named for a god.

Advantages and Criticisms

Advantages The tabular or matrix item is a useful way to assess whether students can pull together facts and ideas into an organized format such as a table. It is easy to craft when assessing recall of verbal information, such as facts, dates, generalizations, terminology, and characteristics of theories. It is also very efficient when you have one list of premises and many different lists of responses. You may recall that when crafting a *basic* matching item, the responses within a list should be homogeneous: that is, all should belong to the same category. When you are crafting a basic matching exercise and find the response list becoming heterogeneous, you may wish to reorganize the exercise into a tabular item set.

Criticisms Although it may be possible to create tabular item sets that assess complex or higher-order thinking skills, it is difficult to do so. Most teachers find this format most useful for assessing recall and recognition of verbal information. Because the format is easy to construct, some teachers overuse it (or its cousin, basic matching) and are therefore subject to criticism of focusing on facts rather than problem-solving, critical-thinking, or other higher-order cognitive skills. Also, scoring the set is problematic. We discuss this problem and possible solutions to it later in this section.

Crafting Suggestions

First, as always, identify the learning targets you wish to assess. Targets for which students must cross-classify facts or examples, or for which they must identify several characteristics or properties of dates, events, or objects, are most suitable.

You should first construct a list of premises. For instance, in the earlier example, the premises were the four-year time spans defining a U.S. president's term of office. In the planets example, the premises were planets' descriptions. Next, create lists of responses organized into homogeneous groups. You need two or more homogeneous response lists. You should add to each list at least one *plausible* response that does not match any of the premises. This will eliminate the perfect-matching flaw we discussed previously. For instance, in the earlier example,

FIGURE 8.14 **A tabular or matrix item set.**

Directions: Match the names, political parties, famous firsts, and important events in the columns with the dates in the table below. Write the letter in the proper column in the table. You may use a letter once, more than once, or not at all in any cell in the table.

Presidents	Presidents' political parties	Famous firsts	Important event
A. Coolidge	K. Democrat	N. First airplane fight	U. Atomic bomb on Hiroshima
B. Eisenhower	L. Independent	O. First airplane flight across U.S.	V. Great Depression begins
C. Harding	M. Republican	P. First automobile trip across U.S.	W. NAACP founded
D. Hoover		Q. First telephone talk across U.S.	X. New Deal legislation passed
E. McKinley		R. First transatlantic solo flight	Y. North Pole reached
F. Roosevelt, F.D.		S. First U.S. satellite in space	Z. Panama Canal opened
G. Roosevelt, T.		T. First woman in cabinet	AA. Panama Canal Treaty signed
H. Taft			BB. Social Security Act passed
I. Truman			CC. United Nations founded
J. Wilson			DD. World War I ends
			EE. Korean Conflict begins

	Year	President	President's political party	Famous first	Important event		Score
1.	1901–1904						1. _____
2.	1905–1908						2. _____
3.	1909–1912						3. _____
4.	1913–1916						4. _____
5.	1917–1920						5. _____
6.	1921–1924						6. _____
7.	1925–1928						7. _____
8.	1929–1932						8. _____
9.	1933–1936						9. _____
10.	1937–1940						10. _____
11.	1941–1944						11. _____
12.	1945–1948						12. _____

"Eisenhower," "Independent," "First U.S. satellite in space," and "Korean Conflict begins" do not match any of the premises (dates).

Create the table or matrix to correspond to your premise and response lists. Be sure to *number the premises.* Label the columns with the same headings you used for the response lists. For convenience, make a place to record scores at the right of the table, as is shown in the presidential term example.

Directions to students are created next. The directions should clearly tell the students what they are to match, the basis for matching, how they should record their answers, and that a response may be used once, more than once, or not at all.

Craft the exercise in a layout modeled after the two preceding examples (depending on the type of response required). Put the directions at the top and the lists of responses below the directions and above the table. The exercise is easier to understand with this arrangement than when the response lists follow the table. It is also easier for students to read and keep track of the responses if they appear first. Use letters to identify each response. There are fewer student clerical errors if the lettering continues consecutively across the lists as in the presidential term example. Finally, place the table and make places to record scores. A grid is easier for students to use and for you to score.

Edit and polish all your work. Check spelling. Alphabetize the elements within each list separately. Keep the response lists side by side (as in the example) if at all possible. This makes it easier for students to read the lists. Organize the list of premises into logical,

FIGURE 8.15 Example of an alternate tabular or matrix item set.

Directions: For each planet description, place an *X* in the box below the name of the planet that fits the description.

Planets

Planet descriptions	EARTH	JUPITER	MARS	MERCURY	NEPTUNE	PLUTO	SATURN	URANUS	VENUS
1. has only one moon									
2. has no moons									
3. larger than Earth									
4. has no atmosphere									
5. composed mostly of gas									
6. can support life									
7. has moon with atmosphere									
8. named after Roman or Greek god									

Source: Adapted from *Creative Classroom Testing: Ten Designs for Assessment and Instruction* (p. 138), by S. B. Carlson, 1985, Princeton, NJ: Educational Testing Service. Reprinted by permission of Educational Testing Service, the copyright owner.

numerical, or chronological order. Check that the premises are numbered. If possible, keep the entire exercise on the same page. This reduces the clerical errors and frustrations students experience when they have to flip pages back and forth when answering the items. A word processor or spreadsheet program is helpful in crafting the final version. Use the features of your word processor or spreadsheet program that create tables for both the table itself and for creating the lists of responses.

The checklist for tabular items summarizes the suggestions in this section. Use it as a guideline when crafting the tabular item set and to evaluate your item set when it is complete. Because the tabular item set is closely related to the basic matching exercise, you should review the suggestions for creating basic matching exercises. The matching exercise checklist for basic matching exercises and is a convenient way for you to review the fundamentals of crafting matching exercises.

✓ *Checklist*

A Checklist for Reviewing the Quality of Tabular (Matrix) Exercises

Ask these questions of every item you write. If you answer "no" to one or more questions, revise the item accordingly.

1. Does the tabular exercise assess an important aspect of the unit's instructional targets?

2. Does the tabular exercise match your assessment plan in terms of performance, emphasis, and number of points?

3. Do your directions to students clearly explain (a) the basis you intend students to use when matching the responses to the premises, (b) how to mark their answers, and (c) that a response choice may be used once, more than once, or not at all?

4. Do the response choices within each response list all belong to the same category of things?

5. Does every response choice function as a plausible alternative to every premise?

6. Did you avoid "perfect matching"?

7. If possible, are the response choices ordered in a meaningful way (logically, numerically, alphabetically, etc.)?

8. Are the premises numbered and the response choices lettered?

9. On the test page are the directions placed first, the response choices second, and the table third?

10. If possible, is the entire exercise printed on one page rather than split between two pages?

Scoring   Scoring is a special concern with the tabular or matrix item format. Two options for scoring are available:

1. *You may score each numbered row as completely correct or incorrect* (for example, score each row as a 1

[completely correct] or a 0 [one or more elements are incorrect]).

2. *You may score each row according to how many elements should be placed in its cells.* For instance, in the planets example, each row has 9 elements (planets), so scores for a row could range from 0 to 9. Each cell within a row is scored 0 to 1 according to whether an *X* or a blank is properly placed in it. For example, a student who places an *X* in Row 8 under Earth is marked wrong (given a 0 for this cell), because Earth is not named after a Greek or Roman god. Similarly, a student who leaves this cell blank is marked correct (given a 1 for this cell).

Of these two options, we prefer the second: It gives partial credit and yields more reliable scores.

Special problems may arise when (a) the correct answer requires placing more than one response in a cell but a student enters *fewer or more responses* than should be entered and (b) the correct answer is a blank but a student enters *some response(s)* in that cell. In the presidential term example, for instance, both Roosevelt and Truman were president in the span 1945–1948: Roosevelt died in office while Truman was the vice president. A student may place an *E*, an *H*, or both into the corresponding cell in the "President" column. How should this cell be scored? The correct answer is "E and H," so clearly this should be given full credit or 2 points (1 point for each). Students who mark only *E* or only *H* could be given partial credit (1 point), or they could be given no credit (0 points). Giving partial credit would seem to be the fairest thing to do.

Suppose, however, a student responded with both C and H. Option C is clearly incorrect, but Option H is correct yet incomplete. Some teachers are tempted to punish students by deducting marks for the C response. This way of marking seems arbitrary and unfair. We recommend giving partial credit (1 point) for the correct portion and not subtracting points for the incorrect Option C. You could make a note to the student that Option C is incorrectly placed, however. Arbitrarily subtracting marks makes the exercise difficult for you to score, increasing the likelihood that you will make clerical errors in marking. Also, arbitrarily subtracting points is likely to lead to scores that do not accurately reflect a student's partial knowledge.

One way a clever student may attempt to "beat the system" is to put the letter of every response option in every cell of the table. Because the correct option(s) would always be included in a cell (along with all the other incorrect options), the student would get 100% if our suggestions for scoring were followed. What should you do if this happens? We suggest that you return the test paper to the student (without penalty) and ask the student to enter in the table cells only those few choices the student believes are correct. You could also alter the directions in

future tests to make it clear that you want only a few choices per cell.

Summary

Multiple-Choice Item Format and Considerations Before Crafting

- The suggestions for writing multiple-choice items represent the clinical lore of experienced item writers, and nearly all of them can be subsumed under the three fundamental principles in Chapter 7.
- A multiple-choice item consists of one or more introductory sentences followed by two or more suggested responses, from which the student chooses the correct answers. Varieties are illustrated.
- Each part of a multiple-choice item must work properly before the item as a whole will work:
  - The purpose of the stem is to ask a question, set the task to be performed, or state the problem to be solved.
  - The purpose of the alternatives (responses or options) is to suggest answers to the question or problem specified by the stem. One alternative is usually the correct or best response.
  - The purpose of the distractors (foils) is to appear plausible to students who do not possess sufficient knowledge to select the correct alternative.

Advantages and Criticisms of Multiple-Choice Items

- The basic purpose of any assessment task is to distinguish students who have attained the learning target from those who have not.
- Among the objective types of items, the multiple-choice item is considered the most highly valued, applicable, and versatile.
- Multiple-choice items are only indirect procedures for observing such important learning outcomes as the ability to:
  - Recall with minimal prompts.
  - Produce and express unique ideas.
  - Articulate explanations and give examples.
  - Organize personal thoughts.
  - Display thought processes or patterns of reasoning.
- Multiple-choice items can provide opportunities to observe directly such important learning outcomes as the ability to:
  - Discriminate and make correct choices.
  - Comprehend concepts, principles, and generalizations.
  - Make judgments about and choices among various courses of action.
  - Infer and reason.
  - Compute.
  - Interpret new information.
  - Apply information and knowledge.
- The advantages of multiple-choice items include their:
  - Versatility in assessing a variety of learning targets.
  - Reduction of opportunities for the student to bluff or dress up an answer.
  - Focus on reading and thinking and thereby not on writing under examination conditions.
  - Reduced chances for a student to obtain the correct answer by blind guessing.

- Usefulness in obtaining diagnostic insight when distractors are based on common student errors or misconceptions.
- Criticisms of multiple-choice items include the following:
  - Such items require students to choose from among fixed options and do not let them express their own ideas.
  - Poorly written items can focus on trivial facts.
  - Brighter students who are forced to choose a single option may be penalized if they have detected ambiguities, recognize a divergent viewpoint, or have additional knowledge of the topic.
  - The possibility of getting the item right through blind guessing cannot be eliminated entirely.
  - Multiple-choice items tend to be based on "standardized" conceptions of knowledge, which may lead students to believe that a single, correct answer will be found for every problem in life.
  - Multiple-choice items may shape the content and nature of instruction in undesirable ways, limiting instruction to only those skills measured by the test.

When Not to Use Multiple-Choice Items

- Among instances in the classroom for which multiple-choice items are not recommended (even though they would be appropriate) are
  - Problems or questions requiring a single-word or single-number answer.
  - Computational problems in general.
  - Questions with only two plausible answers (e.g., yes-no).
  - Items for which writing the answer doesn't take any longer than marking an answer to the multiple-choice item.

Crafting Basic Multiple-Choice Items and Using a Checklist

- As with all types of assessment tasks, multiple-choice items should be carefully edited before being administered.
- Suggestions for crafting the stems of multiple-choice items are summarized in Figure 8.3. Illustrative examples follow.
- Suggestions for crafting the alternatives in multiple-choice items are summarized by the maxims in Figure 8.4. Illustrative examples follow.
- Special care should be taken to phrase the correct alternative in a way that:
  - Permits those who have the minimum desired degree of knowledge to select the correct alternative.
  - Does not permit students who lack the requisite knowledge to select the correct alternative on the basis of testwiseness or superficial clues.
- Suggestions for crafting the correct alternative are discussed.
- A checklist is included for you to use for judging the quality of multiple-choice items that you craft or obtain from curricular materials.

Crafting Alternative Varieties of Multiple-Choice Items

- The alternative varieties of multiple-choice and matching items in this chapter have the following general advantages: (a) They better match many learning targets; (b) they can be scored objectively; (c) they are efficient, covering more content in a given time span; and (d) they are relatively easy to craft.
- Greater-less-same items may be used to assess students' ability to compare the quantitative, qualitative, or order relationships between pairs of concepts.
- Greater-less-same items may be criticized because teachers use them to assess recall of verbal information rather than to assess application of criteria and principles to new situations. They are also criticized because they assess relationships between only two concepts at a time.
- Suggestions for crafting and evaluating greater-less-same items are presented in a checklist format.
- Best-answer items may be used to assess students' ability to distinguish between degrees of correctness of various answers or solutions. They assess students' ability to apply criteria to judge qualitatively different answers.
- Best-answer items may be criticized because (a) they are difficult to craft well; (b) they are unsuitable for students with lower levels of educational development; (c) for the same item, different teachers may disagree as to what is the best answer; (d) the criteria for selecting the best-answer choice may not be taught to the students; and (e) some teachers produce options that are tricky for students.
- Suggestions for crafting and evaluating best-answer items are summarized in a checklist format.
- Experiment-interpretation items may be used to assess students' ability to recognize appropriate interpretations of empirical research study results, appropriate explanations of results, and appropriate inferences from data.
- Open-ended variations of the experiment-interpretation items may be used to assess students' ability to explain and justify their answers.
- Experiment-interpretation items may be criticized because (a) they are difficult to craft well, and (b) some teachers use them to assess memorized or "fixed" interpretations.
- Suggestions for crafting and evaluating experiment-interpretation items are summarized in a checklist format.
- Statement-and-comment items may be used to assess students' ability to evaluate a given set of interpretations of quoted comments using learned criteria.
- Open-ended versions assess students' ability to recall and write about the meaning of a quoted comment.
- Statement-and-comment items may be criticized because they (a) focus on a relatively narrow set of learning targets and (b) are used by some teachers to assess students' recall of interpretations the teacher presented in class.
- Because the statement-and-comment item format is a special type of best-answer format, you can use the best-answer checklist as a guide for crafting and evaluating these items.

Matching Exercise Format

- A matching exercise consists of a list of premises, a list of responses, and a set of directions for matching the elements of the two lists.
- Matching exercises are like multiple-choice items in that each premise functions as a separate item. Unlike most multiple-choice items, however, each premise has the same list of options (or response choices).
- You should use matching exercises whenever several multiple-choice items would require repetition of the same set of alternatives.

Advantages and Criticisms of Matching Exercises

- The advantages of the matching exercise include
  - It is compact, space-saving, and objectively scorable.
  - It assesses the ability to identify relationships.

- It assesses the ability to classify things.
- A criticism of matching exercises is that teachers frequently use them exclusively for assessing rote associations rather than the abilities to comprehend or classify.

Crafting Basic Matching Exercises

- You can avoid "giving away" answers to matching exercises by crafting homogeneous premises and responses so that each response is a plausible option to each premise. The homogeneity of premises and responses is usually a function of students' educational development as well as the content of the exercise.
- Suggestions for constructing matching exercises are presented along with illustrative exercises.
- A checklist is provided that you can use to judge the quality of the matching exercises you create or adapt from curricular materials.

Crafting Alternative Varieties of Matching Exercises

- Masterlist items may be used to assess students' ability to classify new examples into learned classification frameworks and the ability to apply principles to new situations.
- Masterlist items may be criticized because teachers often use them to assess recall of verbal information rather than to assess application of learning to new situations.
- Suggestions for crafting and evaluating masterlist items are presented in a checklist format.
- Tabular (matrix) items may be used to assess students' ability to match facts and concepts across several categories of classification and pull together information in a table format.
- The tabular item format may be criticized for the same reasons matching exercises are criticized: Teachers tend to use the format to assess students' ability to recall facts and other bits of verbal information.
- Suggestions for crafting and evaluating tabular items are summarized in a checklist format.
- Tabular items may present scoring problems. The chapter recommends that each row of the matrix (table) be scored according to how many of the student's entries are correct.

Important Terms and Concepts

"all of the above"
alternatives, choices, options, responses
basic purpose of an assessment task
best-answer item
clueing, linking
context-dependent items, interpretive exercises, interpretive materials, linked items
continuum of learning
correct-answer variety of multiple choice item
decontextualized knowledge
direct assessment, indirect assessment
directions for matching
distractor rationale taxonomy
distractors, foils
experiment-interpretation items
filler alternatives, deadwood alternatives
greater-less-same items

homogeneous alternatives, heterogeneous alternatives
homogeneous premises and responses
incomplete stem
keyed alternative, key, keyed answer
masterlist items, classification items, keylist items
matching exercise (basic)
meaningfully arranged alternatives
multiple-choice items (interpretative material)
multiple-choice item
negatively worded stem
"none of the above"
overlapping alternatives
perfect matching
plausible distractors, functional alternatives
premises, premise list
responses, response list
specific determiner
statement-and-comment items
stem
tabular (matrix) items
tandem arrangement of options
textbookish phrasing
tricky item
varieties of multiple-choice items
verbal clues, clang associations, grammatical clues
window dressing

Exercises and Applications

1. For the subject you teach, or one with which you are most familiar, construct one flawless multiple-choice item to assess each of the following abilities. Before writing each item, write a specific learning target that the item will assess. After writing the items, use the checklist for multiple-choice items to evaluate and revise your items. Share your items with the other members of your class.
   a. Ability to discriminate two verbal concepts
   b. Ability to comprehend a principle or rule
   c. Ability to select an appropriate course of action
   d. Ability to interpret new data or new information
2. For the subject you teach, obtain curricular material that has multiple-choice items for teachers and students to use. Select from this material 10 items that would be appropriate for a unit you might teach. Evaluate each item using the multiple-choice checklist. Identify the flaw(s) in each item, and then revise the item to correct the flaw(s). (Be sure to evaluate your revised items so they are flawless.) Discuss your findings with the class.
3. For the subject you teach, obtain curricular material that has matching exercises for teachers and students to use. Select two exercises that would be appropriate for a unit you might teach. Evaluate each exercise using the matching exercise checklist. Identify the flaw(s) in each exercise, and then revise the exercises to correct the flaw(s). (Be sure to evaluate your revised exercises so they are flawless.) Discuss your findings with the class.
4. Choose two different kinds of relationships from the following list and craft matching exercises for the subject you teach: accomplishments of persons; dates of noted events; definitions of terms; examples of applications of principles or rules; symbols for concepts; authors or artists and their

specific works; English equivalents of foreign phrases; functions of specific parts of a mechanism; or names of pictured objects. Develop matching exercises for each of the two you chose. Evaluate and revise your exercises using the matching exercise checklist to eliminate all flaws. Present your matching exercises to your class.

5. Evaluate the matching exercise below using the matching exercise checklist. Prepare a list of the flaws found. For each flaw listed, explain why it is a flaw in this exercise. After completing your analysis, revise the exercise so it has no flaws. Share your findings with your class.

Instructions: Match the two columns

A	B
1. chlorophyll	A. Green plants contain this substance
2. igneous	B. Type of rock formed when melted rock hardens
3. photosynthesis	C. A substance made up of both hydrogen and oxygen
4. water	D. Process by which green plants produce their food

9 Essay Assessment Tasks

LEARNING TARGETS

After studying this chapter, you should have learned the following:

Formats for Essay Items

1. Explain the strengths and weaknesses of restricted and extended response items. [1, 2]

2. Describe the types of learning targets that you should assess. [1, 2]

3. Explain why you should not use essay items to assess learning targets that are limited to recall and comprehension of verbal information. [1]

Usefulness of Essay Assessments

4. State the likely influence of using essay items on the study habits of your students. [1, 2, 3, 4]

5. State the types of learning targets that are better assessed using objective items rather than essay items. [1, 2, 3, 4]

Constructing Essays Assessing Subject-Matter Learning and Using Optional Questions

6. Write good essay questions, free from flaws, that assess a variety of students' thinking skills. [2]

7. Use a checklist of essay-writing criteria to evaluate and improve the quality of your essay questions. [2, 1]

8. Explain why allowing your students a choice of questions to answer on a summative evaluation is generally not a sound assessment practice. [2]

Constructing Prompts for Assessing Writing Achievement

9. Explain how writing instruction and writing assessment should be integrated. [1, 2, 3, 4]

10. Explain the multiple steps in a writing process, how each of the traits of good writing is assessed, and how each is used as a student develops a piece of writing. [2, 4, 3]

11. Explain the qualities or dimensions of good writing (including the Six + 1 Traits®) that should be taught and assessed so that students' writing can be improved. [4, 5, 3]

12. Explain how using a traits framework (e.g., Six + 1 Traits®) for teaching and assessing writing can improve students' writing across subjects and grade levels. [4, 5, 3]

13. Explain how writing standards and scoring guides (rubrics) are used to assess students' achievement in writing ability. [4, 5, 3]

14. Craft high-quality writing prompts for narrative, imaginative, expository, and persuasive writing. [4, 5, 3]

Scoring Essay Assessments

15. List the factors that lower the reliability of your students' essay scores and explain how you can improve this reliability. [2, 3]

16. List several ways you can improve your essay assessment scoring procedures. [2, 3]

17. List several techniques that will give your students feedback on their responses to your essay questions. [3, 4]

Important Terms and Concepts

18. Explain how the important terms and concepts listed at the end of this chapter apply to educational assessment. [6]

ABOUT THIS CHAPTER

The chapter begins by discussing two common formats of essay items—restricted response and extended response. We discuss the advantages and disadvantages of these formats and illustrate them with examples. Second, the chapter discusses several general concerns about using essays. We discuss, for example, which skills and abilities are best assessed with essays, how using essays affects students' study habits, and whether essays sacrifice breadth of content coverage for depth of coverage. Third, the chapter provides suggestions for how to craft essay items that assess subject-matter learning. We give lots of suggestions for improving your essay items and illustrate these with examples. Fourth, the chapter provides suggestions for essay prompts used for assessing students' writing ability. We illustrate how your assessment of writing ability can be highly integrated into your teaching of writing. We discuss the writing process, the traits or qualities of writing that should be assessed (including the Six + 1 Traits®) and different genres of writing. We illustrate different genre writing prompts with examples. Finally, the chapter discusses how to improve the weakest part of essay assessment—the scoring. We identify the most common errors teachers make when scoring classroom assessment and offer suggestions for how to correct these errors.

On the whole, this chapter focuses on helping you learn the fundamentals of crafting quality essay items. Chapter 10, and especially Chapters 11 and 12, describe the more complex uses of written responses. This chapter is more basic, explaining the fundamentals of creating quality essay tasks.

FORMATS FOR ESSAY ITEMS

Essay formats are usually classified into two groups: restricted response items and extended response items. Both types are useful tools, but for different purposes.

Restricted Response Varieties

Definition **Restricted response essay items** restrict or limit both the content of students' answers and the form of their written responses. This is done by the way you phrase a restricted response task. Two examples follow.

Example

1. Write a brief essay comparing and contrasting the terms *measurement* and *assessment* as they relate to (a) the degree of quantification of the quality of students' responses, (b) the process of obtaining information, and (c) the way in which students' responses are recorded.

2. List five of the suggestions for writing essay questions that your text presented. For each suggestion you list, write a short statement explaining why that suggestion is useful for improving the validity of your essay assessments.

Assessing More Than Recall and Comprehension Restricted response items should require students to apply their skills to solve new problems or to analyze novel situations. One way to do this is to include interpretive material with the assessment. Interpretive material could be, for example, a paragraph or two describing a particular problem or social situation, an extract from a literary work, or a description of a scientific experiment or finding. Essay (and response-choice) items based on this kind of material are called **interpretive exercises** or **context-dependent tasks** (introduced in Chapter 8). Interpretive exercises ask students to read, listen to, analyze, or otherwise interpret the accompanying material and then to complete one or more items based on it. The following examples illustrate restricted response items and, by way of contrast, an extended response item that requires students to analyze a particular poem in various ways. The items are intended for a high school literature course.

Example

Interpretive material

On First Looking Into Chapman's Homer

Much have I travell'd in the realms of gold,
And many goodly states and kingdoms seen;
Round many western islands have I been
Which bards in fealty to Apollo hold.
Oft of one wide expanse have I been told
That deep-brow'd Homer ruled as his demesne;
Yet did I never breathe its pure serene
Till I heard Chapman speak out loud and bold:
Then felt I like some watcher of the skies
When a new planet swims into his ken;
Or like stout Cortez when with eagle eyes
He star'd at the Pacific—and all his men
Look'd at each other with a wild surmise—
Silent, upon a peak in Darien.

John Keats

Restricted response questions

1. What is the poet's attitude toward literature as is apparent in lines 1 to 8? What words in these lines make that attitude apparent?
2. Summarize the mood described in lines 9 to 14.
3. What is the relationship between the attitude described in lines 1 to 8 and the mood established in lines 9 to 14?

Extended response questions

4. Describe the way in which the structure of the poem reinforces the speaker's mood as it is presented in lines 9 to 14. In your essay show how the attitude in the first part of the poem is related to the mood at the end of the poem.

Source: From "Evaluation of Learning in Literature," by A. C. Purves, in *Handbook on Formative and Summative Evaluation of Student Learning* (pp. 736, 755–756), by B. S. Bloom, J. T. Hastings, and G. F. Madaus (Eds.), 1971, New York: McGraw-Hill. Reprinted by permission.

Often restricted response items are limited to only certain aspects or components of very complex learning. The restricted response items above, written at the "analysis" level of the Bloom et al. *Taxonomy,* ask a few of the many (perhaps 15 or 20) questions that a teacher might write to assess students' ability to analyze the mood of a poem. The extended response item, by contrast, attempts to elicit from the student a rather complete and integrated analysis of the poem.

Advantages of Restricted Response This format narrows the focus of your assessment to a specific and well-defined performance. The nature of these items makes it more likely that your students will interpret each question the way you intended. You are in a better position to assess the correctness of student answers when a question is focused and all students interpret it in the same way. When you are clear about what makes up correct answers, it improves your scoring reliability, hence the scores' validity.

Other Assessment Options Multiple-choice interpretive exercises assess many abilities more reliably than restricted response essays. This is illustrated in Figure 9.1. You are not using restricted response essays properly if you use them only to assess students' recall of factual information. You can assess a student's ability to recall factual information better through completion, true-false, multiple-choice, and matching items.

Extended Response Varieties

Definition **Extended response essay items** require students to write essays in which they are free to express their own ideas and interrelationships among their ideas and to use their own organization of their answers. Usually no single answer is considered correct. A student is free to choose the way to respond, and degrees of correctness or merit of a student's response can be judged only by a skilled teacher who is informed on the subject (Stalnaker, 1951).

Two Purposes The two broad uses for the extended response essay format are to assess students' (a) **general writing ability** and (b) **subject-matter knowledge**. This chapter discusses both of these essay purposes.

Writing Assessment If your intention is to assess only writing ability, your essay must present the students with a prompt. A **prompt** is a brief statement that suggests a topic to write about, provides general guidance to the student, motivates the student to write, and elicits the students' best performance. You evaluate students' performance by using a scoring rubric that defines various characteristics or qualities of writing.

FIGURE 9.1 Examples of varieties of learning outcomes that can be assessed using objective interpretive exercises and essay items.

Type of test item	Examples of complex learning outcomes that can be measured
Objective interpretive exercises	Ability to— identify cause-effect relationships identify the application of principles identify the relevance of arguments identify tenable hypotheses identify valid conclusions identify unstated assumptions identify the limitations of data identify the adequacy of procedures (and similar outcomes based on the pupil's ability to *select* the answer)
Restricted response essay questions	Ability to— explain cause-effect relationships describe applications of principles present relevant arguments formulate tenable hypotheses formulate valid conclusions state necessary assumptions describe the limitations of data explain methods and procedures (and similar outcomes based on the pupil's ability to *supply* the answer)
Extended response essay questions	Ability to— produce, organize, and express ideas integrate learnings in different areas create original forms (e.g., designing an experiment) evaluate the worth of ideas

Source: Adapted from *Measurement and Evaluation in Teaching* (7th ed), p. 224, by R.L. Linn and N.E. Gronlund, 1995. Upper Saddle River, NJ: Prentice Hall. © 1995. Adapted by permission.

Example

Extended response writing prompt

Sometimes people write just for the fun of it. This is a chance for you to have some fun writing. Pretend you are a pair of tennis shoes. You've done all kinds of things with your owner in all kinds of weather. Now you are being picked up again by your owner. Tell what you, as the tennis shoes, think about what's going to happen to you. Tell how you feel about your owner. Space is provided below and on the next two pages.

Source: From *Composing Childhood Experience: An Approach to Writing and Learning in the Elementary Grades* (Experimental Version, p. 14), by C. H. Klaus, R. Lloyd-Jones, R. Brown, W. Littlefair, I. Mullis, D. Miller, and D. Verity, 1979, St. Louis: CEMREL. Reprinted by permission of the author.

In this example, the prompt stimulates the student to write in an imaginative way. The student is asked to use expressive writing ability to play an imaginative role, tennis shoes, and to elaborate this role by explaining the "feelings" and "thoughts" of tennis shoes. Later in this chapter we will discuss criteria for evaluating students' writing.

Subject-Matter Knowledge Assessment If the primary purpose of your assessment is to evaluate students' knowledge, understanding, and reasoning in a subject, then a different kind of prompt and essay structure is needed. Here is an example in the subject of social studies.

Example

Extended response subject-matter essay prompt

Devise a plan to determine whether the Democrats and Republicans are evenly distributed throughout the city, or whether the supporters of each party are concentrated in certain wards.

Source: From *Classroom Questions: What Kinds?* (p. 136), by N. M. Sanders, 1966, New York: Harper & Row. Reprinted by permission.

In this example the prompt set the task for the student by describing the general purpose of the plan the student is expected to develop. Students' responses are evaluated primarily using subject-matter criteria—how well a student understands the structure of wards in the city, how well the plan addresses data collection issues, and so forth. The essay is designed to assess students' competence in reasoning and applying knowledge in the subject of social studies. In the Bloom et al. *Taxonomy*, one aspect of synthesis is the ability to formulate a plan of action for a particular purpose. This essay requires just that.

Advantages Some of your learning targets center around a student's ability to organize ideas, develop a logical argument, discuss evaluations of certain positions or data, communicate thoughts and feelings, or demonstrate original

thinking. The restricted response essay format does not lend itself to assessing these types of learning targets. Students need opportunities for more extended responses to demonstrate such skills and abilities. The extended response essay is suited to assessing learning targets that require students to use a combination of skills such as interpreting material, solving a problem, and explaining the problem and its solution coherently.

Disadvantages One disadvantage of an extended response essay is poor **scoring reliability**. It is difficult to score an extended response objectively. A common problem is that, without special training, different teachers will award different marks to the same essays. When the grades or marks for the same responses are inconsistent from one teacher to the next, the validity of the assessment results is lowered. Another common problem with teachers' marks of essays is that they evaluate different students' essays using different criteria. For example, you may attend mainly to the quality of ideas in Johnny's paper, to the neatness and grammatical elegance of Sally's, and to the poor spelling in Harry's. When you mark in this way, you evaluate each student on a different basis. As a result of your student-to-student inconsistency, the assessment results are less valid.

A second disadvantage is that scoring essays is often time consuming, especially if you want to give feedback to students so they can improve their learning. When you have many essays to mark, that leaves little time for giving detailed comments to students on how to improve their work.

A scoring rubric may improve the reliability (consistency), hence the validity, of scoring essays. Using a scoring rubric also reduces scoring time. Suggestions for crafting scoring rubrics are explained in more detail in Chapter 12.

USEFULNESS OF ESSAY ASSESSMENTS

Abilities and Skills Assessed by Essay Items

The preceding paragraphs described some of the abilities and skills that essays let the student demonstrate. Figure 9.1 provides a concise summary of these skills and abilities. Note that the outcomes listed are suggestive, rather than exhaustive (Linn & Gronlund, 1995). Notice also that multiple-choice items can measure some of these same abilities. Suggestions for developing multiple-choice and essay items to measure higher-level abilities are given in Chapters 10, 11, and 12.

What is perhaps unique about the essay format is that it offers students the opportunity to display their abilities to write about, to organize, to express, and to explain interrelationships among ideas. You may assess memory, recall, and comprehension more easily with short-answer and response-choice items. An important point: *Select an assessment format that will assess exactly the learning target you want students to achieve.*

Ideas for Phrasing Essay Questions to Assess Different Abilities

You may find it helpful to study different ways of phrasing questions, which will allow you to craft items that encourage a student to use higher-level cognitive processes and skills. Figure 9.2 shows some examples of ways to phrase essay questions so they assess different learning targets.

If you craft questions in a manner similar to those given above, you will encourage essays assessing higher-order thinking skills. Notice that many of the questions use interpretive materials that are new or novel for the students. Also notice that most of the questions ask the students to give reasons or explain their choices. Without asking for such explanations or reasons, you will not be assessing the higher-order thinking processes the students use. Several authors have attempted to catalog or classify such "thought" questions as the preceding examples. Monroe and Carter (1923); Odell (1928); Curtis (1943); Wesley and Wronski (1958); and Bloom, Hastings, and Madaus (1971) have provided similar classifications. You may check these additional resources for more examples.

Influence on Studying Strategies

You may use assessment to motivate students to study. It seems reasonable that the type of performances you expect from students on tests will influence their methods of study. Some research indicates that when students know that essay questions will be asked, they tend to focus on learning broad concepts and on articulating interrelationships, contrasting, comparing, and so on; those preparing for response-choice questions focus on recalling facts, details, and specific ideas (Douglas & Tallmadge, 1934; Terry, 1933). But despite reporting that they prepare differently for different types of assessments, students do not necessarily perform differently on the different forms. Some studies have found little, if any, difference in *performance* on essay or response-choice assessments even though students reported using different study strategies (Hakstain, 1969; Vallance, 1947).

When a state department of education uses essay questions on its accountability tests, that motivates teachers to require students to write more, and they report that students' writing skills improve (Evaluation Center, 1995). Outside observers report, however, that although students write more, they do not necessarily write better (Viadero, 1995).

Because both essay and response-choice formats can call for knowledge of specific facts, and both can call for application of complex reasoning skills, the questions' format may not be the key issue in how students plan their study strategies (Ebel, 1979). The kinds of study strategies your students use in preparing for your assessments are more likely to reflect the type of the thinking skills your assessment tasks require rather than the format (essay or not essay) of the tasks. If two different assessment formats

FIGURE 9.2 How to phrase essay questions to assess learning targets.

1. *Concept understanding:* Identifying examples, producing examples
   - Read the newspaper articles attached. Which events illustrate the concept of *political compromise?*
   - Explain in your own words the meaning of *prejudice.* Give an example of prejudice from your own experience.
2. *Concept understanding:* Classifying examples
   - Read the five mathematics word problems attached. Sort these problems into two groups. Explain why the problems in each group are similar and belong together. Explain how the two groups differ.
   - Study the pictures of the 10 paintings that are attached. Organize these paintings into two or more groups according to their style. Explain the reasons behind your grouping.
3. *Analysis*
   - Look at the family photo attached. Describe the mood or feeling in the photo as well as the body language of the people. Use metaphors or similes to make these descriptions.
   - Read the attached newspaper article. Which statements are opinions? Explain why.
4. *Comparison*
   - Compare Artist A's use of color in her paintings with Artist B's use of color in his mask. How are they similar and different? What moods do the colors convey in each piece?
   - Read the attached statements of Senator A and Senator B. In what ways are their points of view similar? Explain the reasons for your conclusions.
5. *Using principles and rules:* Inference, prediction
   - Read the situation above about the Basarwa, a cultural group we did not study. Based on what we did study about cultural groups, what would you predict would happen to the Basarwa in the next 20 years? Explain the principles you used to make your predictions.
   - Suppose the government of South Africa ordered all of the white citrus farmers to leave the country. Where would you expect them to go? Explain the principles you used to make these predictions.
6. *Inferences:* Deductions, predictions, generalizations
   - Compare the information in Table A with the information in Figure A. What conclusions do you draw about how successful rice farming will be in the region to which the data apply? Explain the reasons for your conclusions.
   - Read the attached statements from a scientist, senator, and newspaper editor about the consequences of continuing to use gasoline-powered automobile engines. What generalization can you make about the continued use of these engines in developed countries?
   - Study the data in the table above. What would you expect to happen to our exports of wheat over the next 5 years? Explain the assumptions you made for your predictions to be valid.
7. *Evaluation*
   - Above are the criteria we use to judge how well an author has used "voice" in writing. Attached is a short piece of writing by a student in a nearby school. Use the criteria to evaluate the writer's use of voice. Explain why good voice is or is not used by this writer. Use examples from the piece to illustrate your evaluation.
   - Use your daily log and records of your plant's growth to explain the present state of your plant. Explain why your plant is better or worse than your classmates' plants. What could you have done differently? What effect would that have had on your plant's present state?

require students to use the same kind of thinking skills, the formats ought to require the same types of study strategies. If your "essays" are really a regurgitation of facts, students' study strategies will focus on remembering and recalling facts. Thus, the advantages of essays and other open-ended response formats will not be realized in your classroom.

If you believe students must learn to write about ideas in a particular subject area, perhaps the best advice is to be sure you explain and teach writing about the subject to students in your class. You need to assign students a significant number of writing tasks so they can learn to write in this subject area. Do not limit writing tasks to examinations. Various written assignments such as short compositions and longer term papers can help your students achieve these writing-oriented goals. This often means relying less on the questions and homework assignments that are in the back of the students' textbook chapters and more on your own assignments. Keep in mind, however, that assessment results are more valid if you use multiple assessment formats. Your summative assessments should include, therefore, both essay and response-choice items so they cover a proper range of learning targets.

Depth and Breadth of Content Sampling

Answering essay questions takes a long time and limits the breadth of content about which the student can write. If your students can answer one or two response-choice items in 1 minute, then they can answer 30 to 60 response-choice items in a half hour. Sixty items can cover a very broad area of content and at least parts of many instructional objectives. In the same 30 minutes, these same students can probably answer only one or two essay questions. Thus, you can assess in-depth learning of a narrower topic using one essay or broad, less in-depth, general coverage using many objective items. To improve the content coverage of their assessment, many teachers use both essay and objective test items.

To overcome the shortcoming of an essay's limited content sampling, use a series of compositions that students can write over a longer period (Coffman, 1971). You can accumulate these in portfolios. Several out-of-class essays written over a marking period may better assess a particular learning target than a single essay written during a brief examination period. You must remember, too, that asking students to write under the time pressure of an examination may not be the best method to assess their maximum ability.

Efficient Use of Teacher Time

Essays and compositions take a long time to mark properly. This time is well spent if these are the best ways to assess important learning targets, if performing them is a meaningful student activity, and if the students benefit from your feedback on the quality of their responses. Sometimes, however, because teachers must score large numbers of essays or because they are under the pressures of the day, they score essays carelessly: This is a breach of

professional ethics and an abuse of responsibility. Assessing and evaluating students is serious business. Careful planning, including deciding whether the essay format is the most valid method of assessment, can greatly alleviate inappropriate scoring of essay assessments.

Influence of Scoring Criteria and Exemplars

It is very important to use well-defined criteria to evaluate students' essay responses. The criteria should be taught and explained to students. Local school districts and state educational authorities have recognized the importance of developing these criteria. As a result, teachers may be engaged in professional development activities to help define these criteria and to improve their application to students' responses. Much of this effort is focused on defining criteria or rubrics that are used with performance assessment, of which essay assessment can be considered a part. (See Chapters 11 and 12 for details.)

The professional development approach gives teachers insight from students into what constitutes quality responses. Through collaboration with other teachers, they have crafted criteria that clarify the meaning of statements of state standards and of learning targets in the curriculum.

Similarly, sharing quality criteria and examples of work at different quality levels with students will better integrate your assessment and instruction. Students learn what the characteristics of quality performance are and, through examples, learn what quality performance looks like. Chapters 11 and 12 describe this point in greater detail.

CONSTRUCTING ESSAYS ASSESSING SUBJECT-MATTER LEARNING

The checklist summarizes suggestions for improving essay items. As with previous checklists, an answer of no to any one of the checklist questions is sufficient reason not to use that essay item until you correct the flaw. The suggestions are discussed later in the chapter. First, we will look at a poorly crafted essay item and apply the checklist to it. This will give you an idea of how the item should be improved.

✓ Checklist

A Checklist for Evaluating the Quality of Essays Assessing Subject-Matter Learning

Ask these questions of every item you write. If you answer "no" to one or more questions, revise the item accordingly.

---

1. Does the essay assess an important aspect of the unit's instructional targets?

2. Does the essay match your assessment plan in terms of performance, emphasis, and number of points?

3. Does the essay require students to apply their knowledge to a new or novel situation?

4. When viewed in relation to other items on the test, does this item contribute to covering the range of content and thinking skills specified in your assessment plan?

5. Is the prompt focused? Does it define a task with specific directions, rather than leave the assignment so broad that virtually any response can satisfy the question?

6. Is the task defined by the prompt within the level of complexity that is appropriate for the educational maturity of the students?

7. To get a good mark on the item is the student required to demonstrate more than recall of facts, definitions, lists, ideas, generalizations, etc.?

8. Is the prompt worded in a way that leads all students to interpret the assignment in the way you intended?

9. Does the wording of the prompt make clear to students all of the following:
    a. Magnitude or length of the required wirting?
    b. Purpose for which they are writing?
    c. Amount of time to be devoted to answering this item?
    d. Basis on which their answers will be evaluated?

10. If the essay prompt asks students to state and support their opinions on controversial matters, does the wording make it clear that the students' assessment will be based on the logic and evidence supporting their arguments, rather than on the actual position taken or opinion stated?

Source: Adapted from *Teacher's Guide to Better Classroom Testing: A Judgmental Approach* (p. 31), by A.J. Nitko and T-C Hsu, 1987, Pittsburgh, PA: Institute for Practice and Research in Education, School of Education, University of Pittsburgh. Adapted by permission of copyright holders.

Case Study of a Poorly Crafted Essay Item

Before we discuss the suggestions in the checklist in detail, let's study a poorly worded essay question and use the checklist to evaluate it. This exercise should help you understand how to evaluate your own essay questions and will make the checklist explanations more meaningful to you.

The Poor Item Suppose a teacher wanted to assess the following 10th-grade U.S. history learning target:

Example

Tenth-grade learning target to be assessed

Analyze reasons for success of the Colonials during the American War of Independence and explain what alternative actions the British or the Colonials could have taken to alter the outcomes.

The teacher wrote the following essay question to assess this learning target. Overall, the teacher's essay item does not assess the learning target very well. Read this item, then we shall evaluate it using the checklist.

Example

A poorly crafted essay item

Analyze the defeat of the British by the Colonials by listing the four factors discussed in class that led to the defeat.

Evaluation Using the Checklist Here is a point-by-point analysis using the checklist. The numbers refer to the point in the checklist.

Example

1. Yes, the factors contributing to the success of the Colonials are important to the learning outcome of this unit.

2. No, the learning target calls for students to analyze reasons for success and explain alternative possibilities. The item requires neither analysis nor explanation.

3. No, the item requires only listing (recalling) information presented during the class.

4. Yes, this item, in relation to other items (not shown), contributes to the breadth of coverage the teacher had in mind for the unit.

5. Yes, what the student is to do (i.e., list) is clearly stated.

6. No, the learning target implies that the students should be capable of more than the item requires. (The task set by the item, "listing from memory," is within the capability of the students, but it is below the appropriate level of complexity as specified by the learning target.)

7. No, the item requires only recalling verbal information.

8. Questionable; some students may be confused by the word *analyze* but most will probably make a *list*.

9. a. Yes, the item says students should list four reasons.
    b. Perhaps the purpose is simply to repeat what was taught in class, but the purpose isn't stated.
    c. No, a time limit is not stated.
    d. No, but simply being right or wrong seems to be the implied basis for evaluation.

10. Not applicable; no opinion asked.

The Revised Item After using the checklist, the teacher rethought the item in relation to the learning target and what he had taught. The teacher recrafted the item to make it more in line with the learning target. Here is the revised item.

Example

An improved essay task

A. List four of the factors that led to the Colonial victory over the British in the War of Independence   (4 points)

B. For every factor you list, write a short explanation of how that factor helped the Colonists defeat the British.   (4 points)

C. Choose one of these factors that in your opinion the British could have changed or overcome. Explain what actions the British could have taken to change or overcome this factor.   (4 points)

D. What probably would have happened in the war if the British had taken the actions you stated? Why do you think this would have happened?   (8 points)

Grading: Parts A and B will be marked on how correct your answers are. Parts C and D will be marked on how well you support your opinion, but not on what position you take.

Time limit: 40 minutes.

The revised item is more complex and more difficult than the original, but it comes closer to assessing the learning target. Notice that the revised item is expanded to include recalling information, explaining the recalled information, and using higher-level skills. These higher-level skills require students to explain why they hold logically deduced opinions and to describe probable consequences of actions. The teacher's basis for grading is specified, as is a time limit. Because the class period at this school is 50 minutes long, this essay will probably be the only assessment that the teacher could do that day. To cover other aspects of the unit the teacher would need additional assessments, including quizzes, homework, class discussions, and an objective test over the unit's content.

Discussion of the Checklist

1 and 2. *Importance of what is assessed and correspondence to the assessment plan.* We have stressed that each of your assessment tasks, no matter what their format, must focus on important learning targets and must match your assessment plan. Learning targets that require essays may be difficult for you to state because the target may be complex and abstract. Further, when assessing these complex learning targets, you may need to use more than one type of

assessment tasks. For example, you may want a student to demonstrate the ability to analyze critically and evaluate passages expressing different points of view about the equality of men and women. This complex learning target will require assessing the student using several different tasks before you conclude the student has attained this objective.

You should focus on the type of response you wish the student to make, rather than worrying about how well the learning target is stated. You could, for example, write a specimen answer—an outline of the major points you want the students to make. Or you could state the way(s) you expect the student to approach the problem in an essay question. Then you can refine the essay question to clarify what you wish the student to do.

3. *Essential knowledge applied to new situations.* The essay question format has the potential of assessing a student's command of higher cognitive processes and skills. The best way to do this is to require a student to apply thinking skills to new or novel problems and situations. If a student is asked to write only information recalled from the textbook or class discussion, you are assessing only lower cognitive processes. A student's ability to recall verbal information is an important educational goal and reflects general competence, but you can better assess recall of information by using other assessment formats such as completion or short-answer items.

4. *Covering the range of content and thinking skills.* As you read in Chapter 6, your assessment plan should cover your learning targets' full range of content and thinking skills. Your plan plays a key role in guiding your assessment activities. It helps you to take into account all appropriate learning targets. Review your essay questions in relation to the full range of your learning targets to be sure that they contribute properly to the goal of full coverage and, hence, to the improved validity of your assessments. You should remember that sometimes one essay question may assess several specific learning targets and may be related to more than one thinking-skill category.

Essay items, unlike short objective items, require significant student assessment time. Thus, you have to balance the available assessment time against the range of coverage you have planned. You may need to revise your essay (either by narrowing it or by broadening it) in conjunction with the other assessment formats you could also use. For example, you could make your essay focus more on higher-order thinking than on recall. Given the fixed amount of time in one class period, you may have to reduce the number of nonessay items, or, alternately, carry out essay assessments one day and objective format assessment on another day.

5. *Focus questions; clarify limits and purposes.* You should phrase a question to focus attention on the issues or points on which you want the students to write. If you do not craft the questions carefully, your students are apt

to interpret your question in so many different ways it will be impossible to evaluate their responses. Consider the extended response example about analyzing a Keats poem. An unfocused version of this item might read: "Write an essay analyzing the poem." It is unlikely that such an unfocused item would result in an analysis of the poem's "mood," which is what the teacher had in mind. If an item is not focused, you will find it impossible to distinguish those students who can perform the learning target—but misinterpreted your question—from those who simply cannot apply the skills you taught.

Sometimes, if you find it difficult to state the nature of the task itself clearly, specifying the manner and criteria by which you will evaluate students' responses may increase clarity. For example, sometimes a teacher will give students an extract from a newspaper expressing a point of view and want students to evaluate the extracted statement by applying the strategies and criteria taught in class. However, the teacher's poorly stated question may simply say, "Do you agree or disagree with this article's position?" There's no telling what kind of responses students would make: Their responses would likely range from a simple yes or no through long-winded polemic entanglements. The teacher should focus the item more by specifying which aspects of the extract the students should address. Also, the teacher should tell the students that their essays will not be evaluated on whether they agree or disagree with the extract, but on how well they frame the argument and the quality of the outside information they bring to the essay to support their positions.

Focusing the question and specifying limits of the intended response do not mean providing information that gives away the answer. If you want the essay to assess the ability to organize a written argument or identify the central issue in a "fuzzy problem," for example, you should not provide students with a particular organization in the question. However, you should tell students that the way they choose to organize the answer is important, and that you will evaluate the paper on how well it is organized.

An important practical suggestion here is to have a colleague or friend review the questions and, if possible, to try the item with a few students. You can then revise the questions if necessary. Following such steps greatly improves the quality of essay questions.

6. *Complexity should be appropriate to educational level.* Because answering an essay requires students to read, think, and write, you must be sure that the item is appropriate to your students' level of educational development. Avoid the use of complicated sentence structures and phrasings for elementary students. Avoid phrases that are indirect or that add unnecessary reading to the question. Do not, however, oversimplify essays for more advanced students. Essays should challenge students to do their best thinking and use their best writing skills. Because essays

require writing, your students must have the level of writing proficiency needed to answer the question. If students do not have sufficient writing skill to express their knowledge on your essay question, you should consider using another means of assessment.

7. *Require more than recall of verbal information.* Although students must learn various facts, ideas, lists, definitions, and generalizations, you should not use the essay format to assess this type of learning. Instead, use short-answer, completion, true-false, matching, and multiple-choice formats to **assess simple recall** of verbal information. These latter formats are better for assessing such recall because they sample more of a student's verbal information store in a fixed time with nonessay items than with essays. Using short-answer and response-choice items increases the content coverage and the validity of the results for assessing recall.

Do use essays to **assess higher-order thinking**, including the ability to express one's own ideas, to compare, and explain reasons. One assessment strategy is to organize a small group or class discussion about the upcoming essays. The students discuss the problem posed in the essay. The discussions familiarize students with the content covered and various ways to solve the problem stated in the essay. In the following class period, students respond to the essay individually. Another assessment strategy gives students some essay tasks to complete over several days or as take-home assignments. This gives students the opportunity to think, to use prewriting skills, to organize, and to revise their answers. This process is more like the ultimate situations in which your students will be writing.

8. *Make the intention of the essay clear.* You should carefully craft your essay question to be sure it communicates clearly to the students the framework in which they are to respond: the issues their essays are to address; the amount of justification or evidence, the information they are expected to bring to bear in their responses; and the level of detail you expect in their responses.

9. *Clarify response length, purpose, time limits, and evaluation criteria.* You should tell students (a) the approximate length you expect their response to be, (b) the purpose for which they are writing, (c) the goal toward which their essay should aim, and (d) the audience for whom they should target their responses. If you impose time limits, you should clearly announce these to your students. If more than one answer can be correct, your students should know this. If you will deduct points for incorrect spelling, poor language usage, or poor penmanship, tell students before they respond. Failing to provide this information for an important summative evaluation of students is professionally irresponsible. (See Chapter 5 for more professional responsibilities.)

10. *Clarify how students' opinions will be evaluated.* Often an essay will require students to state and support their

opinions on controversial or nonroutine matters. These essays provide excellent opportunities to assess students' abilities to analyze, synthesize, and evaluate. In such items, you should make clear that students' answers will be evaluated on the logic shown in their answers and how well they use evidence to support their positions. You should reassure them that the opinions or positions they state will not be marked right or wrong per se.

OPTIONAL QUESTIONS

When the purpose for assessment is summative evaluation, you should require all students to answer the same questions. This is especially important if you grade students based on ranking or comparing them to each other. The validity of your ranking is increased if you compare your students on the same questions.

Some teachers believe that offering students **optional essay questions** (a choice of questions) is fairer because it permits students to "put their best foot forward." Research doesn't bear out this belief, however (Coffman, 1971; Stalnaker, 1951; Wilson, 1976). Some students will choose to answer questions on which they do less well (Cowan, 1972; Meyer, 1939; Stalnaker, 1936; Taylor & Nuttall, 1974). Further, the topics on which questions are based vary in familiarity and difficulty for the students. We have already mentioned how difficult it is to generalize from one essay to the next. In addition, teachers marking essays frequently change their ratings based on their own perceptions of the nature and difficulty of topics. It is extremely difficult, often impossible, to compare tests equitably when students have taken different items (Wang, Wainer, & Thissen, 1995). If all the questions asked on an assessment represent important learning targets, then it seems logical and fair to hold all students accountable for answering all of them (Ebel, 1979).

Perhaps the story would be different if general writing ability were being assessed, rather than subject-matter competence (Coffman, 1971). You could argue that students may demonstrate general writing ability by writing on any one of a number of topics. If you follow this practice, you should score papers on each topic separately, rather than mixing topics together. This will reduce the topic-to-topic differences that tend to raise or lower your rating of an essay quite apart from its merits. As we pointed out earlier in this chapter, however, the topic and the prompt of the essay questions are important determinants of how well a student performs. A student can write well about some topics and poorly about others. You might, for example, write a better essay on the frustrations of a teacher than on the frustrations of a professional golfer, simply because you know more about one area than the other. Similarly, the topics students choose or are assigned do affect their ability to answer appropriately. Even if you are assessing general writing ability, interpret cautiously students' responses to different topics and prompts. The most important thing for you to do is to use multiple topics and assess students over longer periods, rather than base your evaluation on a single essay.

CONSTRUCTING PROMPTS FOR ASSESSING WRITING ACHIEVEMENT

Assessing students' writing achievement requires special attention to both writing prompts and scoring rubrics. In this section we discuss writing prompts. Scoring rubrics for writing assessment are discussed in the next section.

Before we begin, you should note that some school district or state assessment programs have adopted very specific writing instruction and assessment frameworks. We cannot discuss all of these in this book. We will discuss a few so you have an idea about writing assessment. However, you should follow your school's or state's mandated program to be fair to your students. It is possible for you to adapt some of the guidelines in this book to your local situation.

Writing instruction and formative student assessment need to be tightly integrated. Thus, although this is an assessment book, our discussion includes a brief review of the pedagogy of writing instruction at the elementary, junior, and high school levels. We did this to illustrate how assessment and instruction may be integrated. The discussion is not meant to replace a course in methods of teaching writing. Our point is that assessment provides a teacher with information about what feedback students need to improve their writing. This makes this section a bit different than what you have been used to reading so far in this book.

General Suggestions for Integrating Writing Assessment and Instruction

Focus on the Characteristics of Good Writing For classroom purposes, teaching and evaluating students' writing should concentrate on characteristics or qualities of good writing, especially those that students can be taught to improve. Sometimes these writing qualities are called **writing traits** or **writing dimensions**. Teaching and assessing writing need to be highly integrated because to improve, students need to know in some detail (a) what dimensions of their writing need improving and (b) how to make these improvements. Information from assessment should allow you to give students specific feedback that guides their writing improvement.

What Are the Characteristics of Good Writing? You need to know which writing traits to teach and to assess. Educators differ as to what constitutes good student writing. State standards and school district guidelines will differ in the number and type of traits that define good writing. Many schools and states have adopted or adapted some or all of the

Six + 1 Traits® of Writing developed by the Northwest Regional Educational Laboratory (http://www.nwrel.org/assessment/toolkit98.php). These are:

Example

1. Ideas
2. Organization
3. Voice
4. Word choice
5. Sentence fluency
6. Conventions
7. Presentation

For example, Arizona (http://www.ade.az.gov/sbtl/6traits/) uses the first six traits (all but *presentation*). Oregon (http://www.ode.state.or.us/teachlearn/testing/scoring/guides/student/mswrtg.pdf) uses six traits, plus an additional one, "Citing Sources," for classroom work that requires research.

The Pennsylvania Department of Education evaluates five traits (http://www.pde.state.pa.us/a_and_t/lib/a_and_t/WritingHighlights2005.pdf).

Example

Writing traits used by Pennsylvania

1. Focus
2. Content
3. Organization
4. Style
5. Conventions

You use the writing traits you adopt as a framework around which you organize your assessment *and* teaching to help students understand what constitutes good writing. Using the traits as a framework for feedback avoids giving feedback that is too general to be helpful (Examples of overly general feedback are: "This is a B paper." "You need to improve your writing." etc.)

Teach Students What Good Writing Is Students in your class need to understand that good writing has certain qualities that can be stated, learned, and put into practice. These traits or qualities are the criteria by which most writing can be evaluated. How well students put them into practice can be evaluated. Students learn that your feedback on how well they have put these traits to work in their writing helps them improve. When the trait framework is made clear to students, you and they will have a shared vision of what good writing is. If this vision is shared across teachers and grades, then students will come to internalize the traits and use them to improve their daily writing.

Integrate Writing Traits With a Clearly Defined Writing Process Part of writing instruction is to teach students that there is an orderly process for developing a piece of writing. All too often, students have the mistaken idea that they should write a final piece at one sitting. Often their view of the process is: Teacher makes a writing assignment, student completes the assignment and turns it in, and teacher gives a grade—end of story! That's it—no development of ideas, no revisions, no editing, and no polishing the piece.

This is a far cry from how good writers work. Students need to understand that most writing results from an orderly process that includes drafting, feedback, revisions, and polishing. There is more than one step in this process.

The **writing process** presented in Figure 9.3 is adapted from suggestions developed by the Northwest Regional Educational Laboratory. Note (a) how the assessment is built into this process and (b) that some of the steps in the writing process depend on the feedback that the assessment provided.

Define Standards or Levels of Achievement for Each Writing Trait For assessment-based feedback to be meaningful, you must use standards that clearly identify the student's achievement level on each trait. You can think of achievement as developing along a continuum from very poor achievement at one end to very high-level attainment at the other. The points along this continuum need to be defined so you can pinpoint the students' current level of achievement. Once a student's current level is known, the continuum's definitions of more advanced levels help you guide the student to achieving that next level. Figure 9.4 shows how Oregon's State Department of Education defined the different levels of attainment for the ideas and content trait at the middle school level (http://www.ode.state.or.us/teachlearn/testing/scoring/guides/student/mswrtg.pdf). These definitions take the form of a scoring guide.

If your state or school has also adopted a particular framework for writing traits, it probably has also adopted the definitions of different levels of achievement for each of these traits. You will need to use these, rather than craft your own, because students will be expected to write according to them. These descriptions are usually in the form of scoring rubrics or scoring guides. We will discuss rubrics later in this chapter and in Chapter 12.

Rubrics and Trait Definitions Should Apply Across Different Types of Writing Students will be working with different genres or types of writing, as well as writing for different audiences. Because students are novice writers, it is likely to be confusing if each genre and purpose had very different criteria or traits. Pedagogically it would seem better if the same few traits could be applied to many different types of writing. In this way students can learn all the traits and apply them to all their writing. It is possible, for example, that each type of writing can be evaluated for common

FIGURE 9.3 How the writing traits may be integrated into a writing process.

1. *Prewriting activities*—Before writing, a writer clarifies the purpose for writing, begins to organize thoughts, brainstorms, and tries out new ideas. The writer discusses the ideas with others, decides the format and approach to writing, and determines the primary audience. A plan for the piece develops. The teacher may wish to schedule a content conference (Darden, 2000) to help students focus the ideas and content for the piece.

2. *Draft the piece*—The writer works up a preliminary draft of the piece to reflect the prewriting ideas. Ideas and plans change as the draft develops. The purpose for the writing is further clarified (even changed). The draft begins to take shape and ideas and content start to develop. The preliminary organization of the piece is developed so that a beginning, middle, and end begin to emerge. The draft is considered a work in progress, not the final piece.

3. *Obtain feedback for improving the draft*—Based on assessment, the writer gets feedback from the teacher, peers, or others. The assessment is used to make the feedback specific to the traits that have been adopted to define good writing (e.g., ideas, organization, choice of words, use of sentence variety). The teacher may wish to schedule a *drafting* conference (Darden, 2000) with the student to give some of the feedback.

4. *Revise the piece*—The writer uses specific feedback from the assessment to improve the piece in each of the trait areas. For example, as a result of specific feedback, the writer may incorporate more colorful or more exciting words into a story.

5. *Repeat Steps 3 and 4 if necessary*—The writer may not have implemented the suggestions from the feedback properly. Or, the writer may not understand the feedback and may need more instruction. Writing is not strictly a linear process; it may require many iterations. Student writers must learn that completing the assignment and turning it in is not a final step. The teacher may wish to schedule a process conference (Darden, 2000) with the student to discuss the choices the student made and suggest how to proceed with the revision.

6. *Edit*—The writer edits the revised piece by checking for correct English mechanics: specific points of spelling, grammar, punctuation, etc. English mechanics is one of the traits of good writing. The teacher may evaluate the written piece for how well the student has implemented mechanics, but note that in this particular writing process, English mechanics are assessed late in the writing process because the pedagogy is to have the student concentrate first on ideas, organization, word choice, etc. as the piece is being developed. This helps the writer be more creative and concentrate on the substance of the piece while it is in the formative stages.

7. *Finalize and make the piece presentable*—The writer puts the piece into final form for presentation to the teacher or class or for mailing. Depending on the grade level, purpose, and resources, this may mean writing neatly with even margins, or fancy word processing. Note that attention to appearance is left to the very end, after the piece is revised and polished.

Source: Based on the authors' interpretations of the ideas and suggestions developed at the Northwest Regional Educational Laboratory. Endorsement by the Northwest Regional Educational Laboratory should not be inferred.

traits such as for ideas and content, for organization, for word choice, and so on. If you and the students evaluate all writing using these same traits, students will learn them more quickly and internalize the traits' meanings. As a result, students will automatically apply the traits to all their writing.

Crafting Writing Prompts

Rhetorical Specifications You ask students to write for different purposes and audiences and in different genres. To stimulate students to do this, you will need to build into your writing prompts rhetorical clues that elicit the kind of writing that you have in mind. The prompts you write should include statements containing the following elements (Albertson, 1998):

1. *Subject*–inform the student whom or what the piece is supposed to be about.

2. *Occasion*–inform the student about the occasion or situation that requires the piece to be written.

3. *Audience*–inform the student whom the intended audience is.

4. *Purpose*–inform the student what the writing purpose is supposed to be: Is it to inform or narrate? to be imaginative? to be persuasive? (Sometimes the acronym **SOAP** is used for the four preceding elements.)

5. *Writer's role*–inform the student what role he or she is to play while writing (e.g., a friend, a student, a parent, etc.).

6. *Form*–inform the student if you expect the piece to take a certain form such as a poem, letter, paragraph, essay, and so on.

The following example shows how to improve a writing prompt by adding these rhetorical clues.

Example

Poor: No SOAP—Writing prompt does not provide suggestions for the subject, occasion, audience, or purpose of the piece.

Write a letter telling about an event.

Better: SOAP is built into the prompt

Recall something important that you saw or that happened to you recently. It could be that you saw an accident, a crime, a good deed someone did. Maybe something funny happened to you recently.

Write a letter to a friend to describe what you saw or what happened to you, just the way it happened. Describe the event clearly so your friend who was not there can tell exactly what it was like and how you felt about it.

Crafting Writing Prompts for Different Genres You teach students to write for different audiences and different purposes. The writing prompts you provide guide them in writing the specific type of piece you have in mind. Typically, classroom writing takes one of four forms: narrative, imaginative, expository, and persuasive.

FIGURE 9.4 How different levels of achievement on the Ideas and Content writing trait are defined by the Oregon Department of Education.

Ideas/Content		
6 The writing is exceptionally clear, focused, and interesting. It holds the reader's attention throughout. Main ideas stand out and are developed by strong support and rich details suitable to audience and purpose. The writing is characterized by • clarity, focus, and control. • main idea(s) that stand out. • supporting, relevant, carefully selected details; when appropriate, use of resources provides strong, accurate, credible support. • a thorough, balanced, in-depth explanation / exploration of the topic; the writing makes connections and shares insights. • content and selected details that are well-suited to audience and purpose.	**5** The writing is clear, focused and interesting. It holds the reader's attention. Main ideas stand out and are developed by supporting details suitable to audience and purpose. The writing is characterized by • clarity, focus, and control. • main idea(s) that stand out. • supporting, relevant, carefully selected details; when appropriate, use of resources provides strong, accurate, credible support. • a thorough, balanced explanation / exploration of the topic; the writing makes connections and shares insights. • content and selected details that are well-suited to audience and purpose.	**4** The writing is clear and focused. The reader can easily understand the main ideas. Support is present, although it may be limited or rather general. The writing is characterized by • an easily identifiable purpose. • clear main idea(s). • supporting details that are relevant, but may be overly general or limited in places; when appropriate, resources are used to provide accurate support. • a topic that is explored / explained, although developmental details may occasionally be out of balance with the main idea(s); some connections and insights may be present. • content and selected details that are relevant, but perhaps not consistently well-chosen for audience and purpose.
3 The reader can understand the main ideas, although they may be overly broad or simplistic, and the results may not be effective. Supporting detail is often limited, insubstantial, overly general, or occasionally slightly off-topic. The writing is characterized by • an easily identifiable purpose and main idea(s). • predictable or overly-obvious main ideas or plot; conclusions or main points seem to echo observations heard elsewhere. • support that is attempted, but developmental details that are often limited in scope, uneven, somewhat off-topic, predictable, or overly general. • details that may not be well-grounded in credible resources; they may be based on clichés, stereotypes or questionable sources of information. • difficulties when moving from general observations to specifics.	**2** Main ideas and purpose are somewhat unclear or development is attempted but minimal. The writing is characterized by • a purpose and main idea(s) that may require extensive inferences by the reader. • minimal development; insufficient details. • irrelevant details that clutter the text. • extensive repetition of detail.	**1** The writing lacks a central idea or purpose. The writing is characterized by • ideas that are extremely limited or simply unclear. • attempts at development that are minimal or non-existent; the paper is too short to demonstrate the development of an idea.

Source: From *Writing Scoring Guide* (p. 1), by Oregon Department of Education, 1996, Salem, OR: Office of Assessment and Evaluation, author. Reprinted by permission.

Narrative writing describes something that really happened, usually a personal experience of a student. Following is an example of a prompt that elicits narrative writing from a student.

Example

Narrative prompt

Think of one HAPPY thing that happened to you in the past. Maybe it was something that happened at home or at school or someplace else.

Write an essay that tells what happened. Be sure to give specific details that explain why this was a happy thing.

Imaginative writing describes something that did not, often could not, happen. A student uses imagination and creativity to tell a story. Here is an example:

Example

Imaginative prompt

Suppose that one day you woke up and found that you were a FISH. What would your life be like? What would happen to you?

Write a story that we can put into our class magazine that tells what happens to you when you are a fish. Be sure to give specific details about what your life as a fish is like.

Expository writing gives an explanation and information. The student is asked to give details, clarify things, and explain things. Here is an example:

Example

Expository prompt

Animals change a lot when they grow. Think about ONE ANIMAL that you know a lot about.

Write an essay that explains how this animal changes as it grows. Be sure to explain very carefully and clearly so that your classmates reading your explanation can understand.

Students often use expository writing when answering subject-matter essay questions.

Persuasive writing convinces the reader of the writer's point of view. The writer may want the reader to accept his or her idea or to take some actions that the writer supports. Here is an example:

Example

Persuasive prompt

Suppose students in this school had 30 minutes of free time each week. The school principal wants your suggestions about ONE THING students should do with this free time. What is the one thing you would suggest?

Write an essay to the school principal that would CONVINCE the principal that your idea is the best. Explain why your idea about using the free time is the best and should be followed. Give reasons to support your position.

Additional Suggestions for Writing Prompts

There are some special considerations when preparing classroom assessments that evaluate students' ability to write. Albertson (1998) offers the following suggestions.

Do not prepare prompts that:

- demand specialized knowledge on the part of students.
- ask students to write narratives about experiences that they may not have because of cultural or social background.
- ask for students' opinions about personal values, religious beliefs, or sensitive or controversial matters that parents would object to.
- encourage complaints and criticisms about the school, students' parents, or persons in the community.

Do prepare prompts that:

- refer to specific situations rather than abstract situations.
- will be interesting to students.

- will be interesting to you when you evaluate students' writing.
- are in the realm of the students' experiences.

SCORING ESSAY ASSESSMENTS

Essay questions should be scored with scoring scales that fit the point values planned in the test blueprint (see Chapter 6). Rubrics or rating scales should be used for this purpose. Chapter 12 gives specific details about how to write and apply scoring rubrics. Briefly, rubrics can be categorized in two ways: according to how many scales are used (*analytic* rubrics use several scales; *holistic* rubrics use one) and according to whether the rubrics are *task-specific* or *generic* (or *general*) rubrics.

You may want to go to Chapter 12 now and read the section on rubrics. As an example to have in mind as you read the practical suggestions for scoring essays (below), Figure 9.5 shows two sets of task-specific scoring rubrics for the Keats poem on page 189.

Rubrics have many positive features. Probably the most important is that the descriptions of the qualities of work in general rubrics define what "good work" is and help students conceptualize the kind of performance they are aiming for. The writing trait rubrics shown earlier are an excellent example of this. Thus rubrics are a powerful instructional tool as well as an assessment tool.

Suggestions for Scoring Essays

Principles for scoring essays are summarized in Figure 9.6. We discuss them in the following paragraphs.

Scoring Rubrics Scoring rubrics and model answers were illustrated in the previous example. The point of using these tools is to improve the consistency of your scoring so that you apply the same standards from paper to paper. Some states have adopted general rubrics that you should use. Check your state's requirements on its Website.

Score One Question at a Time If there is more than one essay question, score all students on the first question before moving on. Then grade all answers to the next question. This method improves the uniformity with which you apply scoring standards to each student. It also makes you more familiar with the scoring guide for a given question, and you are less likely to be distracted by responses to other questions (Mehrens & Lehmann, 1991). Finally, using this method helps reduce the carryover error discussed earlier. You can reduce carryover errors further by reshuffling the papers after scoring each question.

Score Subject-Matter Correctness Separately From Other Factors When marking subject-matter essays, factors other than an answer's content often affect your evaluation. Among such factors are spelling, penmanship, neatness, and language usage. To avoid blending your judgment of

FIGURE 9.5 Example of task-specific scoring rubrics.

The second essay question about our Keats poem read, "Summarize the mood described in lines 9 to 14." First, you must know what a good answer would say. That means you have to understand the poem very well yourself. Chapman did the first good English translations of Homer's *Iliad* and *Odyssey* (which, of course, were written in Greek). At that time (early 1600s), therefore, a whole body of classic literature became available to English-speaking people. This poem is about a reader who reads these works for the first time. He likens literature to a wonderful land ("realms of gold"; lines 1 to 8) and explains that coming across these works of Homer was like discovering a new land. He uses two images: the image of an astronomer discovering a new planet (lines 9–10) and the image of the explorer Cortez discovering the Pacific Ocean (lines 11–14).

Suppose you decided, then, that good student essays would identify these images and conclude that the mood was one of discovery, with its attendant feelings of surprise and delight. You also wanted good essays to be well organized for readers and written according to standard English grammar and usage conventions. These three dimensions (content, organization, and grammar/usage) are your criteria. You might use the following set of rubrics. Note that the content rubric ("description of mood") is task-specific. You could not share this rubric with the students before they wrote their essays because that would analyze the poem for them. Also note that the weights for the content rubric are doubled, making the ideas worth half (6 points) and the writing worth half (6 points).

EXAMPLE OF ANALYTIC SCORING RUBRICS FOR ESSAY QUESTION #2 (PAGE 189)

3 criteria, 12 points possible

Description of Mood (Discovery)

6   Identifies both astronomer and explorer images as discovery images and gives clear explanation
4   Identifies mood but explanation absent or unclear
2   Mood not identified or incorrectly identified

Organization

3   Thesis is clearly stated in topic sentence; how details support thesis is explicitly stated
2   Topic sentence includes thesis; supporting details are present
1   No topic/thesis sentence and/or no supporting details

Grammar/Usage

3   No errors or minor ones that do not impede reading
2   Some errors in grammar or usage, but meaning is clear
1   So many errors that meaning is unclear

Use analytic scoring (above) if feedback on different aspects of performance is required (for example, so a student knows what to work on to improve). Use holistic scoring (below) if one overall judgment is required (for example, on a final exam whose results a student might not see). Notice, however, that the holistic rubrics use the same criteria: content, organization, and grammar/usage. Assign the grade or score whose description most closely matches the student's essay.

EXAMPLE OF HOLISTIC SCORING RUBRICS FOR ESSAY QUESTION #2 (PAGE 189)

A   Mood of discovery is clearly identified; support for this is derived from images of astronomer and explorer; writing is clear and well organized.
B   Mood of discovery is identified; support is implied but not made explicit in discussion of images of astronomer and explorer; writing is clear and organized.
C   Mood of discovery is identified; one of the images is described; organization is minimal; writing needs editing.
D   Mood is not clearly identified or is incorrectly identified; writing is not clear or well organized.
E   Essay is not about mood and/or so many errors in grammar and usage make meaning impossible to interpret.

Notice that your standards of achievement are embodied in these scoring levels. It would be possible to have "harder" or "easier" rubrics, for example, where the D in this scale might be an F in another.

FIGURE 9.6 Summary of principles for scoring responses to subject-matter essay items.

1. Prepare some type of scoring guide (e.g., an outline, a rubric, an "ideal" answer, or "specimen" responses from past administrations).
2. Grade all responses to one question before moving on to the next question.
3. Periodically rescore previously scored papers.
4. Score penmanship, general neatness, spelling, use of prescribed format, and English mechanics separately from subject-matter correctness.
5. Score papers without knowing the name of the pupil writing the response.
6. Provide pupils with feedback on the strengths and weaknesses of their responses.
7. When the grading decision is crucial, have two or more readers score the essays independently.

Sources: Coffman, 1971; Ebel, 1979; Greene, Jorgensen, & Gerberich, 1942; Gronlund, 1976; Hopkins, Stanley, & Hopkins, 1990; Lindvall & Nitko, 1975; Mehrens & Lehmann, 1991; Sax, 1989; Stalnaker, 1951; Thorndike, Cunningham, Thorndike, & Hagen, 1991.

the quality of the ideas or substantive content of a student's answer with these other factors, score the other factors separately—perhaps by using a rating scale (see Chapter 12).

Scoring separately for quality of ideas, correctness of content, and other factors also gives you the freedom to weight each factor appropriately in calculating the grade. For example, you can weight spelling zero or more heavily, depending on the state policy, school policy, or your classroom practice. You still report the results on the zero-weighted factor (e.g., spelling) to the student; you just do not make it part of the grade. But if a factor is to receive a

weight of zero, why bother marking and reporting it separately? The answer is that you are influenced unknowingly by factors such as penmanship, spelling, and neatness even when you are consciously trying to grade on the basis of ideas or content alone (Marshall, 1967; Marshall & Powers, 1969; Scannell & Marshall, 1966). Separately scoring such factors lessens their influence on essay grades, letting you better assess the content learning target.

Score Essays Anonymously Scoring is more valid when you do not know the name of the student who wrote the response. Anonymous scoring of essays prevents the halo error described below. Further, if students know that you score papers anonymously, they are likely to perceive the grading process as fair (Mehrens & Lehmann, 1991). One suggestion for maintaining anonymity is to have students write their names on the back of the answer sheet or exam booklet. Other, more elaborate methods, such as using student numbers or other codes, are also effective.

Give Students Feedback An important reason for using essays is the opportunity they give you to assess students' expressive abilities and thought processes. You should note strengths and weaknesses in these areas for each student and explain how you arrived at the grade you assigned. In this way the essay assessment provides an opportunity for further student learning. The following list offers suggestions for commenting on students' compositions when your focus is on teaching general writing skills. The suggestions, however, also apply to subject-matter essay questions.

1. Comment on just two or three points in any paper. . . .
2. Select those matters for comment which are most important for an individual student at a particular time. . . .
3. Summarize the commentary in usable form.
4. Begin writing comments only after a rapid analysis of the paper as a whole. . . .
5. Choose those comments which will be likely to induce the greatest assessment improvement in the intrinsic effectiveness of the student's next paper. . . .
6. State the comments in an encouraging manner.
7. Do not hesitate to repeat a comment over several papers. . . .
8. Keep track of the comments, so that nothing of great importance for a particular student is omitted during the course. . . .
9. Make clear from the tone of the comments that they deal with a craft to be learned and not with the teacher's personal taste. (Hirsch, 1977, pp. 160–161)

Another suggestion for giving feedback is to hold student conferences–that is, meet with each student individually to review answers and comments. A brief conference of 10 to 20 minutes with each student is more personal and can provide clearer guidance to the student than written comments in the paper's margin. A short, direct conference with each student may also save you hours of writing copious notes and commentary to clarify a point for the student.

Independent Scoring The quirks of individual teachers do affect essay scores. The suggestions in Figure 9.6 help reduce the impact of your quirks, but they do not entirely eliminate them. The ancient Chinese realized that when important decisions rest on the scores from essays, more than one reader is necessary (Kracke, 1953). Realistically, however, even though everyday grading decisions are important, it is unlikely that you will find the time or consistent cooperation of colleagues to carry out **independent scoring of essays**. Nevertheless, such a practice would improve the consistency of your scoring.

Scoring Reliability

The essay format often has very low inter-rater reliability. You can make a deliberate effort to overcome some of the negative factors that lower the reliability of essay scoring. We discuss these factors in the following paragraphs. Attending to these factors will reduce the measurement errors in your evaluations of students' work. You can also improve the inter-rater reliability of essay scores by using scoring rubrics. Reviews of research studies on these aspects of essay scoring can be found in Coffman (1971); Hopkins, Stanley, and Hopkins (1990); and Stalnaker (1951).

Inconsistent Standards Grades assigned to a student's response may vary widely from one reader to the next, both because of the readers' inconsistencies and because of their differences in grading standards. Further, the same reader may mark the same essay differently from one day to the next. The lack of inconsistent standards in evaluating essays was a major justification for turning to true-false and multiple-choice assessments in education in the early 1900s. A way to overcome this consistency is to have all teachers use the same scoring rubrics.

Rater Drift Even if scoring criteria are well-defined, raters tend either to not pay attention to criteria over time or to interpret them differently as time passes. This tendency to change the way scoring criteria are applied over time occurs slowly and is called **rater drift**. The practical application is that you have to periodically stop and determine whether you are applying the scoring standards the same way to later-scored papers as you did to earlier-scored papers.

Changes in the Topic and Prompt Another factor that causes your assessment results to be inconsistent is the topic (subject) of the essay. A student's scores may vary widely, even when marked by the same reader, because of the topic, prompt, or questions (Breland, Camp, Jones, Morris, & Rock, 1987; Dunbar, Koretz, & Hoover, 1991). This is a serious problem: If you base your evaluation of a student on one essay question, you will not be able to make general statements about this student's performance on different topics. If your statements about a student are limited to only the one essay a student wrote, the validity of your overall evaluation (e.g., grades) is lowered. This is a strong reason for basing a student's marking period grade on multiple assessments collected over the entire marking period. This means, of course, that you must have an assessment plan for the marking period that identifies what different kinds of assessment formats you will use. (See Chapter 6 for devising assessment plans.)

Halo Effect The **halo effect** error occurs when your judgments of one characteristic of a person reflect your judgments of other characteristics or your general impression of that person. Thus, you may tend to grade a particular essay more leniently for a student you admire because you know in your heart that the student has command of the objective or topic. The halo effect works the other way, too: You may give a lower grade to a particular essay by a student because you know in your heart that he or she is not a "good student." One way to correct this flaw is to mark essays only after concealing the students' names.

Carryover Effect A **carryover effect** error occurs when your judgment of a student's response to Question 1 affects your judgment of the student's response to Question 2. For example, a student may have a brilliant answer to Question 1 but a mediocre answer to Question 2. The carryover effect occurs when you mark Question 2 right after marking Question 1: You mark Question 2 more favorably because you "carried over" your favorable impression from Question 1. Unless you use the scoring suggestion that follows, the scores you assign to adjacent questions will likely be more similar regardless of the quality of the students' answers than scores on nonadjacent questions. The suggestion is this: Score Question 1 for all students first, then go back and score Question 2 for all, and so on.

Summary

Formats for Essay Items

- Essay items require the student to write a somewhat lengthy response to a question or problem.
- Restricted response essays restrict or limit both the substantive content and the form of the written response.
- Extended response essays permit the student to make fuller use of written verbal reasoning and writing skills, including a full elaboration of the answer to a substantive question.
- A summary of the different learning outcomes that can be assessed by objective items, restricted response essays, and extended response essays is given in Figure 9.1.
- The restricted response format:
  - Should be used to measure a variety of complex learning outcomes.
  - Narrows the focus of the item to more specific content and to well-defined problem situations.
  - Can be used as context-dependent or interpretive exercises.
  - Is likely to result in nearly all pupils interpreting the intent of the item in basically the same way.
  - Is likely to be more reliably scored than the extended response format.
- The extended response format:
  - Should be used to measure a more complex variety of learning targets.
  - Should be used to assess either the ability to write about the subject matter or the student's general writing ability.
  - Has the unique feature of permitting the student to display the abilities needed for written production, organization, and expression of ideas and the interrelationships among these abilities.
  - Should not be used to elicit lower-level thinking processes, such as simple recall of information.

Usefulness of Essay Assessments

- Students may study differently when preparing for essay assessments than when preparing for more objective assessments. Study habits are more likely influenced by the substantive nature of the questions and the abilities required to answer them than whether they are essay or objective tasks.
- Essay questions sample a narrower range of content than briefer, objective questions, but they generally require students to show a more in-depth understanding of the content. This is a disadvantage if the learning targets require broad content assessment.

Constructing Essays Assessing Subject-Matter Learning

- To grade fairly and for students to benefit from an essay assessment, you should carefully plan for essay testing.
- The checklist for improving essay questions summarizes 10 suggestions for crafting essay assessments.
- Ideas and examples for phrasing essay questions are given.

Optional Questions

- For summative assessment of subject-matter achievement, all students should answer the same questions. This is especially true if students are to be ranked on the basis of their achievement.
- When students choose the question to answer, there is no guarantee that they will choose the question on which they will respond best. It is also problematic to try to equate students' responses to different prompts and content.
- For assessing writing achievement, especially for formative purposes, having students choose topics for writing within the same genre is often desirable. Usually, this means crafting one prompt in a single genre that all students respond to but with their personal choice of how to respond.

Constructing Prompts for Assessing Writing Achievement

- Effective writing instruction requires assessment to be formative and highly integrated into instruction.
- Assessment and instruction require that you concentrate on the characteristics or traits of good writing such as ideas and content, organization, voice, word choice, sentence fluency, and English mechanics. The chapter gave several examples of these traits. Appendix H shows how to define them in detail.
- Writing assessment is seen as primarily formative with different type of feedback provided at each stage of writing. An example of a writing process integrated with assessment is given in the chapter.
- When you craft writing prompts you should be sure that each prompt contains sufficient rhetorical clues so that students will understand what it is you want them to write. Among the rhetorical clues you should include are SOAP (subject, occasion, audience, purpose), writer's role, and form.
- The chapter provides a number of dos and don'ts for preparing writing prompts.
- Prompts should be crafted for different genres and purposes of writing in order to meet all of the learning targets in a writing curriculum. Among the common genres are narrative, imaginative, expository, and persuasive writing.

Scoring Essay Assessments

- The subjectivity involved in grading essays presents a serious threat to the reliability and validity of the scores:
  - A given reader may be inconsistent.

- There are often large reader-to-reader differences in the scores of the same students.
- The type and topic of the question influence a reader's scoring.
- Halo effects, carryover effects, bluffing, penmanship, spelling, and grammar all influence scoring.

Important Terms and Concepts

assessing general writing ability
assessing subject-matter knowledge
assessment of higher-order thinking
assessment of simple recall
carryover effect
expository writing
extended response essay items
halo effect
imaginative writing
independent scoring of essays
interpretive exercises (context-dependent tasks)
narrative writing
optional essay questions
persuasive writing
prewriting activities
prompt
rater drift
restricted response essay items
scoring reliability
Six + 1 Traits® of Writing
SOAP
writing process
writing traits (writing dimensions)

Exercises and Applications

1. For each subject you teach (or plan to teach), identify different types of material that can accompany context-dependent items.
   a. For each type, state the educational level of the students for which it is intended.
   b. For each thinking-skill category in the examples given in the section titled "Ideas for Phrasing Essay Questions to Assess Different Abilities," craft at least one essay item based on the material you identified. Use the examples in the section as models for phrasing your essay prompts.
2. For each essay item you wrote in Exercise 1(b), apply the checklist for improving the quality of essay items. Revise any item for which you answered no to a checklist question. Exchange your items with one or more of the students in this course. Review each other's essay items using the checklist. Discuss with your classmates the reasons for assigning a no to an item. Discuss how to improve each item.
3. Each of these two essay items has one or more flaws. Using the checklist for improving the quality of essay items, identify the flaw(s), then rewrite each item to eliminate the flaw(s). Check your rewritten essay item to be sure you have not added another flaw.
   a. Item A: State the two examples of prejudices we discussed in class.

   b. Item B: Evaluate the effect of air pollution on the quality of life in the western part of this state.
4. Following are four restricted response essay questions that together constitute a science unit test. After each question is the keyed answer provided by the teacher and Jane Smith's answer. You are to do two things: First, decide the maximum marks (points) of each question. (The entire test has a maximum score of 50 points, so you need to distribute these among the four questions according to what you believe is appropriate.) Second, evaluate Jane Smith's answers against the answer key and award her points according to her answers' degree of correctness.

   Question 1   *What is the shape of a quartz crystal?*
   Answer key: Hexagonal
   Maximum marks: _____
   Jane's answer: "Six-sided hectogon."
   Jane's score: _____

   Question 2   *What is a saturated solution?*
   Answer key: A solution that contains as much dissolved substance as it can for a particular temperature.
   Maximum marks: _____
   Jane's answer: "Large crystals contain a great deal of substance that has been formed. This process of forming crystals is called crystallization. It occurs both in the laboratory and in nature."
   Jane's score: _____

   Question 3   *Write a paragraph describing how you can grow very large crystals.*
   Answer key: Any answer that says size of crystal is directly related to the rate of crystallization.
   Maximum marks: _____
   Jane's answer: "Large crystals contain a great deal of substance that has been formed. This process of forming crystals is called crystallization. It occurs both in the laboratory and in nature."
   Jane's score: _____

   Question 4   *Name three major categories of rocks.*
   Answer key: Igneous, sedimentary, and metamorphic
   Maximum marks: _____
   Jane's answer: "The three kinds are fire-formed, settled, and those that have changed their form."
   Jane's score: _____

5. This exercise should be done during your class.
   a. Compare the maximum marks you assigned to each question in Exercise 4 with those assigned by other persons in this course. (Put the distributions of maximum marks on the board.) For which questions is there more agreement? For which is there less agreement?
   b. Discuss during class the reasons for agreement and disagreement. Make a list of the factors that seem to affect the maximum value that your classmates assign to each question.

c. Suggest ways of reducing the variability among persons assigning maximum values to questions. Make sure the suggestions are specific to these four questions.

d. Compare the scores you gave Jane on each question with the scores given by others in this course. On which items is there more agreement? On which is there less agreement?

e. Discuss during class the reasons for an agreement and disagreement in marking. Make a list of the factors that seem to affect the scores assigned to Jane for each question.

f. Are the questions on which there is more agreement in scoring Jane's responses the same questions on which there is more agreement for maximum marks? Explain.

10

Higher-Order Thinking, Problem Solving, and Critical Thinking

LEARNING TARGETS

After studying this chapter, you should have learned the following:

Assessing Higher-Order Thinking with Context-Dependent Item Sets

1. Explain why you must use novel material to assess higher-order thinking. [1, 2]

2. Explain the advantages, disadvantages, and layout characteristics of context-dependent item sets. [2, 1]

Assessing Learning of Concepts

3. Explain concept learning and how concepts are linked to students' schemata. [4, 6, 1]

4. Craft tasks to assess whether a student has learned concrete and defined concepts. [2]

5. Craft performance tasks to assess a student's deeper understanding of concepts. [2]

Assessing Comprehension of Rules and Principles

6. Explain the meaning of rule-governed (principle-governed) thinking and the basic strategies for assessing a student's comprehension of principles and rules. [4, 6, 1]

7. Craft tasks to assess a student's comprehension of principles and rules. [2]

Assessing Problem-Solving Ability

8. Explain the nature of problem solving and the ways students may use general and subject-matter problem-solving abilities, and give examples of problem-solving heuristics. [4]

9. Craft tasks to assess students' ability to perform the following problem-solving abilities: identifying and recognizing problems, defining and representing problems, exploring possible solutions strategies, and acting on and looking back on problem-solution strategies. [2]

Assessing Critical-Thinking Ability

10. Explain the meaning of critical thinking and its relation to problem solving. [4, 3]

11. Craft checklists and simple rating scales for assessing students' dispositions toward critical thinking. [2]

12. Craft tasks for assessing the following categories of critical-thinking abilities: elementary clarification abilities, basic support abilities, inference abilities, advanced clarification abilities, and strategic and tactical abilities. [2]

13. Explain why it is necessary to assess both students' ability to use problem-solving and critical-thinking activities in combination as well as assess components of these skills separately. [4, 5, 3]

Assessing Other Higher-Order Skills and Abilities

14. Craft tasks to assess students' ability to use reference materials, to read graphs and tables, to read maps, and to read print materials. [2]

15. Craft enhanced multiple-choice items. [2]

Important Terms and Concepts

16. Explain how the terms and concepts listed at the end of this chapter apply to educational assessments. [6]

ABOUT THIS CHAPTER

The chapter begins with a brief discussion of context-dependent item sets. This item format is especially suited for assessing higher-order thinking, problem solving, and critical thinking. Next, we discuss the meaning and assessment of concept learning. Because ensuring that students' understand the major concepts of a subject is a large part of your teaching, this is an important place to begin discussing higher-order thinking. We discuss eight strategies for conducting these assessments. Third, we discuss how to assess students' understanding of rules and principles that are the learning targets of most school subjects. A key to this discussion is how to craft your assessments so students can demonstrate that they can apply the rules and principles of the subject to real-world situations. We discuss seven strategies for assessing in this area. Fourth, we focus on problem-solving assessment. We discuss the meaning of problem solving and present 17 strategies you can use to assess students in this area. Fifth, we turn to critical thinking. We discuss the meaning of critical thinking and nine strategies for assessing students in this area. The last part of the chapter discusses strategies for assessing higher-order thinking in such specialized areas as (a) use of reference materials, graphs, tables, and maps; and (b) reading comprehension and language arts skills.

ASSESSING HIGHER-ORDER THINKING

A basic rule for assessment of higher-order thinking skills is to craft tasks requiring use of knowledge and skill in new or novel situations. If you only assess students' ability to recall what is in the textbook or what you say, you will not know whether they understand or can apply the reasons, explanations, and interpretations. In short, you must use **novel materials** to assess higher-order thinking.

CONTEXT-DEPENDENT ITEM SETS

Characteristics

Context-dependent item sets consist of introductory material followed by several items. You craft the items so that a student must think about and use the information in the introductory material to answer the questions, solve the problems, or otherwise complete the assessment tasks. Context-dependent item sets are sometimes called **interpretive exercises**. The introductory material may be extracts from reading materials, pictures, graphs, drawings, paragraphs, poems, formulas, tables of numbers, lists of words or symbols, specimens, maps, films, and sound recordings. If you want to assess higher-order thinking skills of the type described in this chapter, you need to use context-dependent item sets. Here is one example.

Example

Below is part of a dictionary. Use it to answer Questions 1, 2, and 3.

---

ru·bi·ous (roo´bē-əs) *adj.* Of the color of a ruby : red.
ru·ble (roo´bəl) *n.* var. of ROUBLE.
ru·bric (roo´brĭk) *n.* [ME *rubrike* < OFr. *rubriche* < Lat. *rubrica*, rubric, red chalk < *ruber*, red.] **1.** A part of a manuscript or book, as a heading, title, or initial letter, that appears in decorative red lettering or is otherwise distinguished from the rest of the text. **2.** A title or heading of a statute or chapter in a code of law. **3. a.** A class or category. **b.** A title : name. **4.** A direction in a liturgical book, as a missal or hymnal. **5.** An authoritative direction or rule. **6.** A short commentary or explanation covering a broad subject. **7.** Red ocher. —*adj.*, **1.** Red or reddish. **2.** Written in red. —**ru´bri·cal** *adj.*
ru·bri·cate (roo´brĭ-kāt´) *vt.* **-cat, ed, -cat- ing, -cates.** [Lat. *rubricate, rubricat-*, to color red < *rubrica*, rubric.] **1.** To write, arrange, or print as a rubric. **2.** To provide with rubrics. **3.** To establish rules for. —**ru´bri·ca´tion** *n.* —**ru´bri·ca´tor** *n.*
ru·bri·cian (roo-brĭsh´ən) *n.* One learned in the rubrics of ecclesiastical ritual.
ru·by (roo´bē) *n., pl.* **-bies.** [ME < OFr. *rubi, rubis* < Med. Lat. *rubinus (lapis)*, red (stone) < Lat. *rubeus*, red.] **1.** A deep-red translucent corundum highly valued as a precious stone. **2.** Something, as a watch bearing, made from a ruby. **3.** A dark or deep red to deep purplish red. —*adj.* Of the color ruby.

Source: Copyright © 2005 by Houghton Mifflin Company. Adapted and reproduced by permission from Webster's II New College Dictionary.

---

1. The *u* in *rubric* is pronounced like
   A *u* in *but*
   *B *oo* in *boot*
   C *u* in *lunch*
   D *oo* in *cook*

2. Which meaning of *rubric* is used in the following sentence: "Our teacher told us to use the rubric when we mark our papers."
   A 1
   B 4
   *C 5
   D 6

3. What part of speech is the word *rubrication*?
   A adjective
   B adverb
   *C noun
   D transitive verb

In this example, the interpretive material is an extract from a dictionary. This extract "simulates" a dictionary page and thus presents a concrete, realistic example. A student must analyze or process the material in this example to answer the questions. The example shows multiple-choice items. Context-dependent item sets may be used, however, with any type of item format.

Advantages and Disadvantages

Advantages A context-dependent item set has these advantages: (a) It provides an opportunity to assess students on materials that are relatively close to the real-world contexts, (b) it provides, through the introductory material, the same context for all students, (c) its introductory material lessens the burden of memorizing and may moderate the effects of prior experience with the specific content, and (d) frequently it is the only means to test certain intellectual abilities.

Disadvantages Some disadvantages of a context-dependent item set are (a) the set may be difficult to construct, (b) you must carefully create the introductory material to assess higher-order thinking skills, (c) a student's performance on one context-dependent item set may not generalize well to performance on another similar set, (d) the set often requires students to use additional abilities (such as reading comprehension and writing skills) that may go beyond the major focus of the assessment tasks, and (e) you may need special facilities (such as a photocopy machine and/or drawing skill and equipment) to produce them that may not be available.

Layout

The way context-dependent material is arranged on the pages of a test booklet is important because a poor arrangement may lead a student to misread or misinterpret the item set. Thus, a poor arrangement can jeopardize the validity of your assessment results. The next example shows one acceptable arrangement.

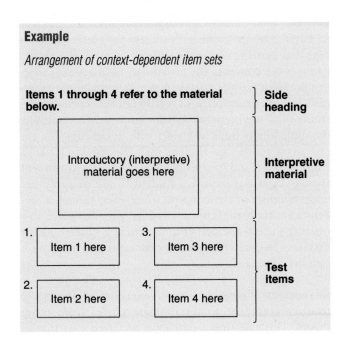

Example

Arrangement of context-dependent item sets

Items 1 through 4 refer to the material below. — Side heading

Introductory (interpretive) material goes here — Interpretive material

1. Item 1 here
2. Item 2 here
3. Item 3 here
4. Item 4 here
— Test items

Note that a side heading (underlined, in bold, or in capital letters) directs the students to the introductory material and to the particular tasks based on it. Some students may skip over introductory material or become confused about the items to which it refers. A side heading helps avoid this. The introductory material is placed in the center of the page. The items may be stacked or placed as shown in the last example.

A drawing should be neat, clear, and, if necessary, labeled. Photographs and magazine pictures may not be legible when photocopied, so check the reproduction equipment you will use beforehand. If the introductory material is a passage or poem, centering and single spacing are usually acceptable, but young children and those with certain disabilities may have difficulty with this arrangement. You may need to use enlarged print for some students. Remember to seek permission when using copyrighted material.

Page Arrangement

Keep the introductory material and all items that refer to it on the same page, if possible. Otherwise, students will be distracted as they flip pages back and forth while completing the assessment. Students with poor short-term attention and memory may lose their place or make careless errors.

CONCEPTS AND CONCEPT LEARNING

What Are Concepts?

A **concept** is a class or category of similar things (objects, people, events, or relations). Many of the things you teach are concepts. Students' understanding of concepts forms the basis for their higher-order learning. When we speak of the concept *red*, for example, we refer to a category of objects with a similar color. A student is said to have learned the concept *red* if the student (a) can identify examples or instances of red things (red tricycle, red book, red lipstick, etc.) *and* (b) does not refer to nonred things (green tricycle, purple book, pink lipstick, etc.) as red. Concepts are ideas or abstractions: Only specific examples of a concept exist in the world. The individual members of the concept category are called *instances*, *examples*, or **exemplars**.

Concrete Versus Defined Concepts

A distinction can be made between concrete concepts and defined concepts (Gagné, 1970). A **concrete concept** refers to a class, the members of which have in common one or more physical, tangible qualities that can be heard, seen, tasted, felt, or smelled. Examples of concrete concepts include *large*, *triangle*, *green*, *house*, and *dog*. A **defined concept** refers to a class, the members of which can be defined in the same way by attributes that are not tangible and that frequently involve relationships among other concepts. Defined concepts are sometimes called abstract or **relational concepts** (Gagné, 1970). Defined concepts are usually learned by definitions. Gagné gives an example of the defined concept *diagonal*, which is defined as a line connecting the opposite corners of a quadrilateral figure. The relationship is "connecting." The related concepts are "opposite corners," "quadrilateral figure," and "line." Other examples of defined concepts include *beside*, *friendliness*, *uncle*, and *mother*. Some concepts are learned initially as concrete concepts and later as defined concepts.

Understanding a Concept

Understanding a concept goes beyond simply identifying examples of it. Concepts are related to each other and linked together in complex ways through schemata or networks. A **schema** is the way knowledge is represented in our minds through networks of connected concepts, information, rules, problem-solving strategies, and conditions for actions (Marshall, 1990). For example, Woolfolk (2005) points out that we know counterfeit money is not real, even though it fits the *money* concept prototype and examples. We know it is counterfeit money because we link our concept of money to other concepts, such as the concepts of authority to print, crime, forgery, and so on. You need to help students connect concepts to their existing networks and schemata of knowledge before they can fully understand these concepts. Woolfolk (2005) summarizes recommended lesson structures for teaching a concept.

ASSESSING CONCRETE CONCEPT LEARNING

Three Assessment Strategies

Three commonly used strategies can assess whether a student has learned a concrete concept. Strategy 1 is *give the name*: You ask for the name of the concept after you present the student with different exemplars of it. Here is an example of assessing whether a student has learned the shape circle.

Example

Strategy 1. Give the name: Students give the concept name after seeing exemplars

1. What are the shapes in this group called? [Ans.: Circles]

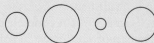

Strategy 2 is *distinguish exemplars from nonexemplars*: You present the student with several exemplars of the target concept and several nonexemplars, all arranged in a scrambled order, provide the name of the target concept, and ask the student to identify which are the exemplars of the concept. Here is an example assessing whether a student has learned the concept *circle*.

Example

Strategy 2. Discriminate exemplars from nonexemplars: Students must discriminate the concept exemplars from the nonexemplars

2. Which of these shapes are circles? [Ans.: A, D, G]

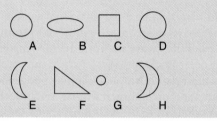

Strategy 3 is *produce new exemplars*: You ask a student to produce new exemplars after you tell the student the concept name. Here is an example of the third strategy for the concept *circle*.

Example

Strategy 3. Produce new example: Students produce their own exemplars when given the concept name.

3. Draw three circles. Be sure each is different from the others.

Criticisms of the Three Strategies

Give the Name Strategy 1 is usually an unsatisfactory way to assess concept learning. A student may learn the concept and perhaps can use it without learning the proper name of the concept. The give-the-name assessment strategy does not require a student to discriminate the exemplars from nonexemplars, so you do not know whether the student has **overgeneralized the concept**. For example, the student may think all shapes with round edges are circles. As a result, the student may confuse circles with ellipses (ovals) and spheres (balls). Finally, this assessment strategy does not require a student to use or apply her understanding of the concept. Thus, even though a student can state the concept name, you do not know whether she has the deeper understanding of the concept necessary to connect it to other concepts and integrate it into her schemata.

Discriminate Exemplars From Nonexemplars Strategy 2 requires a student to discriminate circles from other shapes. This assessment strategy is preferred over that of

Strategy 1 because it (1) does not require a student to produce the concept name to complete the task[1] and (2) allows you to control the assessment situation. You need to control (a) the degree to which the exemplars and nonexemplars are familiar to the students, (b) how typical the exemplars are of the concept, (c) the number and type of discriminations between exemplars and nonexemplars, and (d) the total number of exemplars you present. To use this strategy you must present at least two exemplars for the student to identify; otherwise you do not know whether the student has **undergeneralized the concept**. Undergeneralizing means that the student thinks only one example is the same as the whole concept (e.g., thinking that the circle you showed in class on the board is the only circle). As with Strategy 1, this strategy does not require students to use or apply their understanding of a concept. Thus, it does not permit you to assess students' deeper understanding of it.

Produce New Exemplars Strategy 3 requires (a) the student to think up examples, (b) you to judge the correctness of the examples, and (c) you to judge whether the student's examples were explicitly taught (i.e., whether they are "new"; see Jenkins & Deno, 1971). Keep in mind, however, that a student's ability to generate new examples may not be a requirement for learning a concept. Thus, although this strategy may be useful for assessing simple concepts (such as circle), it is not preferred for more complex concept assessment because it does not permit you to assess students' deeper understanding.

ASSESSING CONCEPT UNDERSTANDING AT A DEEPER LEVEL

We saw in the previous section that all three commonly used strategies had some weaknesses. None of them assessed a student's deeper understanding of a concept. However, a student needs a deeper understanding before using a concept for further learning and for higher-order thinking. In this section we discuss a better strategy for assessing deeper understandings of a concept.

Performance Assessment for Deeper Understanding

Students show their deeper understanding when they are able to (a) use the concepts to solve problems, (b) relate the concepts to other concepts, principles (rules), and generalizations they have learned, and (c) use concepts to learn new material. To assess students' deeper understanding, you

must craft assessments that are more complex and require more application of the concepts than was illustrated by the previous items. The example that follows shows this deeper assessment is possible, even with simple concrete concepts.

Example

Strategy 4. Deeper level understanding: A performance assessment assessing concept understanding at a deeper level

The teacher explains the task orally

We have been studying two shapes: circles and squares. Yesterday we walked through the school neighborhood to look at the shapes of the buildings, people, and cars. Today, you will draw a picture of the school neighborhood, your neighborhood, or a city. Your drawing must include buildings, people, and cars. However, you cannot use any circles or squares in your drawing.

As you work, ask a friend to keep checking your picture to see if you have used either of these shapes. If you have, change your drawing so it has no circles or squares.

When you are finished I will look to see if you have used either of the shapes. While you are working, I will ask you to explain to me, using the words for the shapes we have studied, what you have learned in this assignment about the importance of shapes in our world. I will ask you to explain to me what makes drawing a picture like this without circles and squares so difficult.

Before you begin I will show you some examples of pictures, explain what I will be looking for, and the kinds of answers I will be expecting of you.

Source: Adapted from *Assessing Student Outcomes: Performance Assessment Using the Dimensions of Learning Model* (pp. 61–62), by R. J. Marzano, D. Pickering, and J. McTighe, 1993, Alexandria, VA: Association for Supervision and Curriculum Development. Reproduced with permission of McREL Institute, 2550 S. Parker Rd., Suite 500, Aurora, CO 80014. Telephone (303) 337-0990. © 1993 by McREL Institute. All rights reserved.

The example shows a *performance task*, meaning that students have to do something with their knowledge (see Chapters 11 and 12 for a complete discussion of performance assessment). This assessment can be used to evaluate the following learning:

I. Content targets (in combination)
   A. Identifies circles and squares
   B. Discriminates circles and squares from other shapes
   C. Understands the importance of shapes in the world
II. Complex thinking target (problem solving)
   A. Identifies things that keep you from solving a problem

The assessment in this example takes a relatively long time to administer, probably two or three 40-minute mathematics periods. The main performance is this: Make a

---

[1]You can separately assess a student's ability to name a concept if you wish.

drawing of the neighborhood that includes buildings, cars, and people but that does not use circles and squares. This drawing presents a problem to be solved: How can you make buildings, cars, and people, yet not use circles and squares? This is a difficult problem for a first grader because circles and squares are basic shapes comprising much of the student's experience. The student must distinguish among circles, squares, and other shapes to solve the problem. Notice, too, that the assessment requires you to do more than collect the drawings. You must interview or have a conference with each student using the drawing to prompt or draw out from the student information about how well the learning targets have been attained.

To evaluate students you will need to use scoring rubrics. Figure 10.1 illustrates some examples.

All learning targets are represented in the scoring rubrics. However, you do not treat each rubric as a separate test item. You assess this task overall, rather than piece-by-piece. You use a combination of reviewing a student's drawing, conferencing with a student, and prompting a student to discuss the mathematical content to obtain lots of information about the student's achievement of the learning targets. Only then do you evaluate how well the student has learned each target.

Advantage of This Strategy

An advantage of using Strategy 4 for assessing concepts through complex performance tasks, such as the one in the example, is that students use the concepts in realistic situations. These situations activate students' cognitive frameworks and schemata. They require students to link the concepts to many others as they complete the task. If you focus on a student's way(s) of using the target concepts while he engages in problem solving, you assess whether the student understands the concepts beyond simply naming and identifying them.

ASSESSING DEFINED CONCEPT LEARNING

Four Assessment Strategies

Four strategies can help assess students' learning of abstract or defined concepts. Strategy 1 *requires students to produce a correct definition* of a concept (Jenkins & Deno, 1971). Here is an example:

> **Example**
>
> *Strategy 1: Requiring students to produce a definition*
>
> 1. Define a *prejudiced act* in your own words.
> 2. Tell what is meant by *lonesome*.

Strategy 2 *requires students to produce a new or novel example* of a concept (Jenkins & Deno, 1971). This is an example:

> **Example**
>
> *Strategy 2: Requiring students to produce examples*
>
> 3. Describe two examples of *acts of prejudice* that were not discussed in class or in the text but which you witnessed or experienced during the past few weeks.

Strategy 3 requires students to *identify exemplars and nonexemplars* of a concept (Jenkins & Deno, 1971). Matching and multiple-choice items lend themselves to this strategy.

FIGURE 10.1 Scoring rubrics for the circle and squares drawing problem.

Identifies and discriminates circles and squares

4 Always identifies circles and squares with little or no prompting.
3 Identifies circles and squares but needs some prompting.
2 Sometimes confuses circles and squares with ellipses or other curves; sometimes confuses squares with rectangles or other shapes.
1 Demonstrates severe misunderstanding of circles and/or squares.

Understands importance of circles and squares as the basic shapes comprising objects in the world

4 Demonstrates a thorough understanding of how circles and squares are the basic shapes that make up most objects in the world and provides new insights into some aspect of their use.
3 Displays a complete and accurate understanding of how circles and squares are used in the world but doesn't provide new insights into an aspect of their use.

2 Displays an incomplete understanding of how circles and squares are used in the world and has some notable misconceptions about their use.
1 Has a severe misconception about how circles and squares are used in the world.

Understands that not being able to use circles and squares is an obstacle to depicting real-world objects accurately

4 Accurately and thoroughly describes that not using circles and squares in drawings results in distortions or inability to represent objects in drawings. Addresses obstacles or constraints that are not immediately apparent.
3 Accurately identifies the most important obstacles or constraints imposed by not being able to use circles and squares in drawings of objects.
2 Identifies some constraints or obstacles about not using circles and squares that are accurate but also includes some that are inaccurate or irrelevant to the drawing problem.
1 Omits the most significant constraints or obstacles imposed by not being able to use circles and squares to solve the drawing problem.

Example

Strategy 3: Requiring students to discriminate exemplars from nonexemplars

Matching exercise

Directions: Read each numbered statement. In front of the statement mark:

P–If it is most likely an example of an act of prejudice.
NP–If it is most likely *not* an example of an act of prejudice.

(NP) 4. Sam, a white man, was overcharged by an African American cashier at the company cafeteria. He became upset and refused to speak with the cashier for two weeks afterward.

(P) 5. Ron, a white man, makes it a personal rule never to socialize with his fellow workers who are African American, unless he is forced to do so.

(P) 6. John, an African American manager of a local drug store, is convinced that women are incompetent pharmacists.

(NP) 7. Bill, a professional golfer, stated that in his professional career no woman against whom he competed ever beat him.

Multiple-choice exercise

8. Which statement *most nearly* describes the concept of *lonesome?*
   A Ten-year-old Meghan decides to play alone today with her dollhouse, even though her friends asked her to play with them.
   B Each morning Professor Cory closes her office door to be by herself to write up her research reports.
   *C Each lunch period 15-year-old Marya stands by herself, not speaking to anyone in the crowded school cafeteria.
   D Clarisse, a cloistered nun, speaks to no one and spends many hours alone while praying.

Strategy 4 requires students to analyze the defined concept to identify its component concepts and state the relationships among them (Gagné & Briggs, 1979). This is an example:

Example

Strategy 4: Requiring students to identify components and demonstrate relationships

   (Picture of earth with person on it omitted to save space)

9. In the picture above, draw lines and an angle (or angles) to show the location of the zenith in relation to the person. Label the angle(s) and the zenith.

Source: Item 9 is based on ideas in Gagné & Briggs, 1979, p. 227.

Of the four strategies, Strategy 1, requiring students to produce a definition, and Strategy 2, requiring students to produce new exemplars of the concept, are the weaker strategies and may not be suitable for younger students (Nitko, 1983). Strategy 3, requiring students to discriminate exemplars from nonexemplars, and Strategy 4, requiring students to identify components and demonstrate relationships, are the stronger strategies. Their main advantage is that they require students to recognize new exemplars, ensuring that they do not respond with only a memorized definition. The performance (drawing and labeling) aspect of Item 9 (Strategy 4) has the additional advantage of not depending solely on highly developed verbal skills. (See Nitko, 1983, for further details.)

Limitations of Verbal Items Assessing Certain Defined Concepts

You cannot assess a student's comprehension of some concepts using the types of items shown in the preceding examples. Two of these are (a) relational concepts (e.g., uncle, aunt) and (b) concepts whose exemplars can be described verbally only by repeating the concept name for each exemplar (Anderson, 1972). An *aunt* is a sister of a mother or father. If you tried to write an "instance" of *aunt*, you would need to mention this relationship in the options.

The concept *wings* is an example of the second type of concept (Anderson, 1972). Each exemplar you write would have to include the word *wings* (airplane wings, bird wings, angel wings, etc.), and so a test item would be answerable on the basis of matching a word in the stem with a word in the options. However, you can assess a concept such as *tools* by the types of items shown in the examples because instances of tools (screwdriver, wrench, saw) can be written without repeating the term *tool*.

ASSESSING WHETHER STUDENTS' THINKING USES RULES

Another important area of learning is rule-governed or principle-governed thinking. A **principle** is a rule that relates two or more concepts. Students learn abstract principles in later elementary and high school. Following are some examples.

Example

Abstract principles learned in high school

- When performance is followed by a reinforcing event the probability of that performance reoccurring increases.
- Experimental studies allow conclusions regarding functional relations while correlational studies allow only statements of co-occurrence.

- People tend to immigrate to, and find success in, physical environments closely resembling those from which they came.
- The status of a group in a society is positively related to the priorities of that society.
- The rate of increase in law enforcement officials is negatively related to the stability of the society.
- The record of the past is irremediably fragmentary, selective and biased. (Jenkins & Deno, 1971, p. 96)

We say a student uses **principle-governed thinking** when she can apply a principle or rule appropriately in a variety of "new" situations. You must assess students' understanding of a principle by asking them to apply it to a new situation rather than by simply mimicking your classroom.

ASSESSING COMPREHENSION OF RULES AND PRINCIPLES

Basic Strategies for Creating Tasks

Most principles operate under certain conditions and not under others. Further, when the conditions exist and when a principle does operate, it leads to certain consequences and not to others. This suggests three basic strategies for crafting tasks to assess students' comprehension of principles.

Identify Consequences Strategy 1 presents students with a situation in which the principle can operate and *requires students to produce or identify the consequences* (see Anderson, 1972). For instance, suppose the principle students must understand is: A behavior that is reinforced intermittently (as contrasted with not being reinforced or being reinforced all the time) is highly resistant to extinction. Here is an example of assessing comprehension of that principle by applying it to a classroom situation.

Example

Strategy 1: Require students to produce or identify consequences

Use the information below when answering Item 1.

A student eager for attention blurts out jokes several times during social studies class. For the first 3 days, the teacher and class laugh at some but not all of the jokes. On the fourth day everyone simply ignores the jokes as if they did not occur. They show no animosity toward the jokester.

1. Assuming that the situation described above remains the same, what is the jokester student most likely to do with regard to his joking behavior?
   A Become angry with the teacher and/or class.
   B Stop telling jokes immediately.
   *C Continue telling jokes for a long time even though no one laughs.
   D Tell even more jokes on the fourth and fifth days, but then stop altogether.

The question in the example asks what will happen when the reinforcing laughter stops. To answer this question, you need to know the reinforcement conditions that preceded the laughter stopping. If the teacher and the classmates laughed at every joke attempt, the jokester would stop very soon after the laughter stopped. However, because the preceding laughter was intermittent, it is likely that the jokester will continue in the same manner for a rather long time, according to the principle. Although the item in the example is in a multiple-choice format, it also could be presented as a short-answer, open-ended task.

Produce Consequences and Explanations Strategy 2 *requires students to produce or recall from experience their own consequences*, rather than select from among choices you provide, and to explain them. The explanation should be based on a student's comprehension of the principle you are assessing. In the next example, the principle students are expected to use is: People tend to immigrate to and find success in physical environments most closely resembling those from which they came.

Example

Strategy 2: Require students to produce the consequences and explain why

2. Suppose President Smith forced all the farmers from the flatlands of the Midwest to leave the country. Name two or more geographical locations in the world you would expect them to move. Explain your choices.

Source: Adapted from "Assessing Knowledge of Concepts and Principles," by J. R. Jenkins and S. J. Deno, 1971, *Journal of Educational Measurement*, 8(1), p. 100. Adapted by permission of Blackwell Publishing. © 1971 by the National Council on Measurement in Education.

The stem of this constructed response item provides the context in which students are required to (a) recognize or deduce which principle is applicable, (b) apply that principle to deduce possible consequences, and (c) write an appropriate explanation using the principle to justify the stated consequences. Notice that the item requires students to have knowledge beyond recalling the principle and recognizing. To answer the item correctly, students have to know not only the principle, but also geography well enough to state two or more "geographical locations" that resemble the "flatlands of the Midwest." Further, the usual criterion requires that the students use new examples.

Limitations These requirements make this type of task difficult, especially for younger, inexperienced learners who are not well-read. Further, a student's performance on such tasks may be difficult to interpret. Here are some of the questions you have to answer about a student's response to evaluate it properly:

- Are the student's examples new, or were they presented in the class or in the assigned materials?

- Why can't a student give a good example?
- If the student cannot write an explanation, does he understand the principle?
- Is there weak knowledge of the specific content to which you have asked the principle to be applied?

Produce the Principle That Explains the Consequences
Strategy 3 presents students with the conditions and consequences and *requires students to produce a possible explanation of those consequences* in terms of the principle. The difference between this strategy and Strategy 2 is that with Strategy 3 the student is not required to come up with the consequences, only to explain them. Here is an example:

Example

Strategy 3: Produce an explanation only

Use the information below when answering Item 3.

During a recent visit to a classroom, Principal Larson noticed that Mrs. Hewmenist was having difficulty working with one of the children, Dizzy Ordur. Dizzy would work as long as Mrs. Hewmenist remained with him, but as soon as she would leave Dizzy he would "talk out" or leave his seat and she would have to return to get him back to work. Mr. Larson observed this once in the first 10 minutes, three times in the second 10 minutes, and four times in the third 10 minutes.

3. Why do you think Mrs. Hewmenist was having so much trouble with Dizzy Ordur?

Source: Adapted from "Assessing Knowledge of Concepts and Principles," by J. R. Jenkins and S. J. Deno, 1971, *Journal of Educational Measurement,* 8(1), p. 101. Adapted by permission of Blackwell Publishing. © 1971 by the National Council on Measurement in Education.

This type of item requires students to recall the principle without prompting and articulate it. Students unable to do these two things will not answer correctly. Further, there may be more than one correct explanation for the phenomena stated in your example. This occurs often where the "truth" of the principle or its applicability to all situations is open to question. As discussed earlier, principles usually apply only under certain conditions. These conditions may not be stated properly in your item or its introductory material. This problem, incidentally, may exist in any of the assessment strategies presented in this chapter.

Identify the Proper Conclusion Using a Principle Strategy 4 presents students with a situation from which they can draw several conclusions and *requires them to select the appropriate conclusion* after applying the principle. In the following item, the principle students are expected to remember and apply is: Correlational studies do not allow conclusions that one variable causes another but only that the measures of one are related to the measures of the other.

Example

Strategy 4: Identify a conclusion based on application of a principle

Use the information below when answering Item 4.

A researcher drew random samples of children from three socioeconomic levels (SES): upper, middle, and lower. He determined through interviews and observations how frequently children from each level engaged in aggressive behavior (fighting). He found that low SES children were significantly more aggressive than middle and upper SES children, and that middle SES children exhibited significantly more aggressive behavior than upper SES children.

4. On the basis of the results of this study, which of the following conclusions is most valid?
   A SES influences aggressiveness.
   B Placing children from a low SES environment into a high SES environment will decrease their aggressiveness.
   *C SES is related to aggressiveness.

Source: Adapted from "Assessing Knowledge of Concepts and Principles," by J. R. Jenkins and S. J. Deno, 1971, *Journal of Educational Measurement,* 8(1), p. 99. Adapted by permission of Blackwell Publishing. © 1971 by the National Council on Measurement in Education.

The interpretive material accompanying this item describes a correlational study. The students are expected to recognize this, to recall the principle, use it to evaluate the list of conclusions presented in the alternatives, and finally, to select the most appropriate conclusion.

Limitations Because the items implementing Strategies 1 through 4 are highly verbal, they are likely to require a good level of reading comprehension. Students with poor reading skills who actually understand the principle may miss the item. You may try reading the item situations to poor readers to see if they will respond better. You may be able to simplify the reading level, too.

PROBLEM SOLVING

The Nature of Problem Solving

What Is a Problem? A student incurs a **problem** when the student wants to reach a specific outcome or goal but does not automatically recognize the proper path or solution to use to reach it. The problem to solve is how to reach the desired goal. Because a student cannot automatically recognize the proper way to reach the desired goal, she must use one or more higher-order thinking processes. These thinking processes are called *problem-solving thinking.* For instance, in our earlier example of drawing without using circles or squares, students are asked to draw a picture of a car without using the circle shape. Attaining this goal is a problem for most kindergarten and first-grade students because some of the common things in their environment are circular. A car, for example, has wheels, a steering wheel, and headlights that are circular. Will a car with non-circular wheels still be a car? Will it move? Most young students do not immediately know the path or solution to this problem: They will need to engage in problem-solving thinking to complete their drawings.

"No-Brainers" Are Not Problems If the procedure for attaining a goal is so well known to a student that he can complete the task without having to reason, he does not have to use problem-solving skills. Older students have a name for these kinds of tasks: They call them "no-brainers." They recognize that there is no problem to solve if you do not have to think about the proper solution.

This intuitive concept, no-brainer, should be a useful clue when you craft tasks to assess problem-solving ability. If the tasks require students simply to repeat a procedure you taught them in a situation that is more or less identical to the one you used in class, you created a no-brainer task, and not a problem-solving task. To apply problem-solving skills, a student needs a task that is somehow different or new to her. (The task need not be new to the world, just new to the student.)

Well-Structured and Ill-Structured Problems Most of the problem tasks in teachers' editions of textbooks and in the end-of-chapter exercises are a few notches above no-brainers. They present tasks that are clearly laid out: All the information students need is given, the situations are very much the same as you have taught in class, and there is usually one correct answer that students can reach by applying a procedure you taught. These are known as **well-structured problems** (Frederiksen, 1984). Well-structured problems serve a useful purpose in giving students opportunities to rehearse the procedures or algorithms you taught.

However, well-structured problems are unlike the real-life or authentic problems students will eventually have to face. Most authentic problems are **ill-structured** (Simon, 1973). For ill-structured problems, students must (a) organize the information to understand it; (b) clarify the problem itself; (c) obtain all the information needed, which may not be immediately available; and (d) recognize that there may be several equally correct answers. A problem with a single correct answer is called a **closed-response task**; a problem with multiple correct answers is called an **open-response task** (see Collis, 1991). We discuss this point further in Chapter 11.

Components of Problem Solving A task presents a problem to a student if it contains one or more obstacles that the student must overcome to reach the desired outcome. A

good problem solver exhibits the following performances in relation to a problem:

- Accurately identifies constraints or obstacles.
- Identifies [creative, plausible] . . . and important alternatives for overcoming the constraints or obstacles.
- Selects and [carries out valid and extensive trials of the] . . . alternatives.
- If [several] . . . alternatives were tried, accurately articulates and supports the reasoning behind the order of their selection, and the extent to which each overcame the obstacles or constraints. (Marzano et al., 1993, p. 79)

Schema-Driven Problem Solving To solve a problem, a student must engage in a sequence of thinking that leads either to an immediately successful solution strategy or to an appropriate search for a solution strategy. Figure 10.2 offers one way to characterize this problem-solving thinking process.

The figure diagrams a **schema-driven problem-solving process** (Gick, 1986). A schema helps us recognize familiar things about a situation, what we can expect to happen, and how we typically act in a situation. If we recognize a particular problem as part of or very similar to one of our existing schemata, we can apply the solution strategy stored in that schema. For example, if we recognize that a mathematics problem is a time problem rather than a cost problem, this activates the "time problem schema" that contains our

FIGURE 10.2 Steps in the problem-solving process.

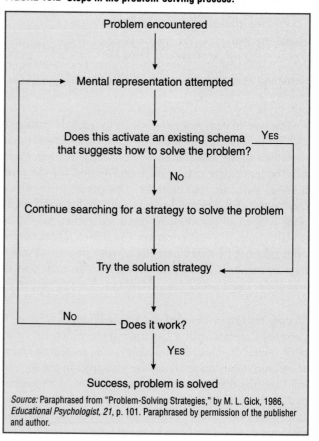

Source: Paraphrased from "Problem-Solving Strategies," by M. L. Gick, 1986, *Educational Psychologist, 21,* p. 101. Paraphrased by permission of the publisher and author.

stored memories of this type of problem and the strategies we typically use to solve these kinds of problems.

How is a schema for a particular problem activated or triggered? One way this is done is by characterizing or representing the problem properly. This is called a **mental model** of the problem. If for some reason you misrepresent a time problem as a cost problem, you will trigger cost-problem solution strategies that, of course, will not work. If a solution strategy you apply does not work, you have to continue looking for other strategies. You might try reconceptualizing the problem—that is, try a different mental model that will trigger an appropriate schema.

Keeping the basic components and processes of problem solving in mind can focus your teaching on what students need to know to become good problem solvers. When you are crafting assessment tasks, be sure they require students to demonstrate command of these problem-solving components and processes.

General Versus Subject-Specific Problem Solving

Power Versus Generalizability Controversies still exist among cognitive scientists, psychologists, and educators concerning whether we should teach students problem-solving strategies that are general or specific to each curriculum area—strategies specific, for example, to mathematics, history, or art. Strategies for solving curriculum-specific problems are less applicable across different subjects but more powerful within the specific curriculum; the general approach applies somewhat to every curriculum area but has limited power within any specific curriculum (Marzano et al., 1988).

It appears that people actually use both general and specific strategies (Alexander, 1992; Perkins & Salomon, 1989; Shuell, 1990). Persons working in an area who have a great deal of knowledge and expertise apply well-known problem-solving strategies to solve problems specific to their area. However, if they work outside their area of expertise, the specific strategies no longer apply: They resort, then, to more general problem-solving strategies. However, as they develop expertise in an initially unfamiliar area, the general strategies are dropped in favor of more area-specific strategies.

The IDEAL Problem Solver General problem-solving skills may be organized into a five-stage process that Bransford and Stein (1984) call the **IDEAL problem solver**:

I   Identify the problem

D   Define and represent the problem

E   Explore possible strategies

A   Act on the strategies

L   Look back and evaluate the effects of your activities

These skill areas are very similar to those shown in Figure 10.2.

Heuristics for Solving Problems

Knowledge-based problem-solving methods within a particular domain provide much better solution strategies than the general methods suggested in this section (Anderson, 1987; Royer, Cisero, & Carlo, 1993). Nevertheless, when a student does not have a knowledge-based strategy, a heuristic should be tried. A **heuristic** is a general problem-solving strategy that may help solve a given problem. The following is a list of 10 problem-solving heuristics (Cyert, 1980; Frederiksen, 1984):

1. Try to see the whole picture; do not focus only on details.

2. Withhold your judgment; do not rush to a solution too quickly.

3. Create a model for a problem using pictures, sketches, diagrams, graphs, equations, or symbols.

4. If one way of modeling or representing the problem does not work, try another way.

5. State the problem as a question; change the question if the original does not suggest a solution.

6. Be flexible: Look for unconventional or new ways to use the available tools; see the conventional in new ways; try responding to the situation from a different angle or point of view; think divergently.

7. Try working backward by starting with the goal and going backward to find the solution strategy.

8. Keep track of your partial solutions so you can come back to them and resume where you left off.

9. Use analogical thinking: Ask, "What is this problem like?" "Where have I seen something similar to this?"

10. Talk about and through a problem; keep talking about it until a solution suggests itself.

ASSESSING PROBLEM-SOLVING SKILLS

Seventeen Assessment Strategies

Because the more powerful problem-solving strategies are specific to a domain or subject matter, it is difficult within space permitted in this book to present detailed examples. Further, the variety of problems within a curriculum area is very large, so even a sample of problems may not do justice to the subject. For example, in junior high school mathematics, you could craft many problems in content areas such as number and operations, patterns, pre-algebra, geometry and measurement, and data analysis (Lane, Parke, & Moskal, 1992).

If you evaluate only whether an answer is correct or incorrect, you are likely to miss the opportunity to evaluate a student's thinking skills in general and problem-solving skills in particular. *Assessing students' problem-solving skills requires set tasks that allow you to systematically evaluate students' thinking about problem solving.* You need to craft different types of tasks to assess the different aspects of problem solving.

In this section we illustrate assessment strategies to show the direction your assessment crafting might take. The assessment strategies are grouped according to the IDEAL problem solver categories. The strategies are descriptions of how to approach the assessment; they suggest the general layout or structure of the tasks: You need to apply them specifically to your own teaching area.

Identifying and Recognizing Problems

Assessment Strategy 1. Identifying the Problem This strategy presents a description of a situation in which a person or persons are inconvenienced or put into unpleasant circumstances. Students are required to identify the problem to be solved. This approach is shown in Item 1 in the following example.

Example

Read the description below, and then answer the question.

A young deaf couple has their first child. The infant needs to be fed and changed whenever it cries in the night, but neither the mother nor the father is able to hear the baby. The couple does not wish to bring the baby into their bed for fear of rolling on it and suffocating it. They also do not wish to put the baby on a strict schedule of changing and feeding at fixed times.

1. Explain the problem that needs to be solved in the above situation.

Defining and Representing Problems

Assessment Strategy 2. Posing Questions [2] Strategy 2 presents a statement that contains the problem and requires students to pose the question (or questions), using the language and concepts of the subject you are teaching, that needs to be answered to solve the problem. (For example, in mathematics, what mathematical question needs to be answered? In social studies, what political question needs to be addressed?)

Assessment Strategy 3. Linguistic Understanding Strategy 3 presents several problems students should be able to solve and underlines the key phrases and common vocabulary they need to know to comprehend the context of the problem. Students are required to explain in their own words the meaning of these linguistic features of the problem.

---

[2] Strategies 2, 7, 10, 11, and 12 were adapted from junior high school mathematics performance assessments described by Lane, Parke, and Moskal (1992). We stripped their definitions of mathematical content to suggest the general structure of the strategy. Using this structure, you should be able to craft tasks specific to your own subject area.

The students understood the phrase in Figure 10.3, "makes buckets the fastest," differently than was intended by the task crafter. Thus, students could not solve this problem correctly.

Assessment Strategy 4. Identifying Irrelevancies Strategy 4 presents interpretive materials and a problem statement and requires students to identify all the *irrelevant* information. Be sure the interpretive material contains information that is both relevant and irrelevant to the problem solution.

Assessment Strategy 5. Sorting Problem Cards Strategy 5 presents a collection of two or more examples of each of several *different types* of problem statements and requires students to (a) sort the problems into categories or groups of their own choosing and (b) explain why the problems they grouped belong together. Write each problem statement on a separate card, but do not specify the type of problem it is. Focus your assessment on whether students are attending to only the wording or other surface features of the problem or, more appropriately, to the deeper features of the problem. (For example, students should group all problems that can be solved using the same mathematical principle, the same scientific law, etc., even though the problems are worded differently or are applied to different content.)

Assessment Strategy 6. Identifying Assumptions Strategy 6 presents students a problem statement and requires students to state (a) a tentative solution and (b) what assumptions about the current and future problem situation they have made in reaching their solution. Here is an example:

Example

Strategy 6: Identifying assumptions behind the proposed solution

Read the description below, and then answer the question.

A young deaf couple has their first child. The infant needs to be fed and changed whenever it cries in the night, but neither the mother nor the father is able to hear the baby. The couple does not wish to bring the baby into their bed for fear of rolling on it and suffocating it. They also do not wish to put the baby on a strict schedule of changing and feeding at fixed times.

2. What assumptions about the couple, their baby, their home life, and so on did you make to come up with the solution to this problem?

Assessment Strategy 7. Describing Multiple Strategies Strategy 7 presents a statement of a problem and requires students to

FIGURE 10.3 Example of a flawed problem-solving task.

The following task was given to sixth-grade students.

The Robinson family owns a company that makes cleaning supplies. They need to buy a new machine that makes buckets.

They see the three advertisements below.

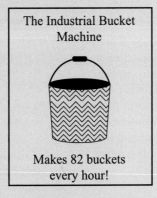

The Galaxy Bucket Machine — Makes 21 buckets in just 15 minutes!

The Industrial Bucket Machine — Makes 82 buckets every hour!

The Heavy Duty Bucket Machine — Makes 44 buckets in only 30 minutes!

The family wants to buy the machine that makes buckets the fastest.

A. Which machine do you think they should buy?

Answer: _____

B. Why do you think they should buy this machine?

Many students misinterpreted the phrase, "the machine that makes buckets the fastest." The assessors wanted the "task to assess students' ability to choose the machine that made buckets at the fastest rate (or the largest number for a fixed time period)" (p. 24). However, the students perceived "fastest" in terms of *waiting time*. For example, they thought you had to wait only 15 minutes for the Galaxy Buckets, 60 minutes for the Industrial Buckets, and 30 minutes for the Heavy Duty Buckets. Thus, they chose Galaxy Buckets because the "wait time" was perceived to be the shortest. The students' interpretation is not wrong, but it makes the task a less interesting mathematical problem to solve. As a result, the assessors had to eliminate the task because it did not result in the type of mathematics problem-solving thinking desired.

Source: From *Principles for Developing Performance Assessments*, by S. Lane, C. Parke, and B. Moskal, 1992, a paper presented at the annual meeting of the American Educational Research Association. Reprinted by permission of the authors.

(a) solve the problem in two or more ways and (b) show their solutions using pictures, diagrams, or graphs. Here is an example:

Example

Strategy 7: Solve the problem in two or more ways

Mickey has an album of baseball cards. He has six empty pages. Each page holds nine cards. How many baseball cards does Mickey need to fill his six empty album pages?

3. Show two or more ways to answer the question in the above problem. Use numbers, pictures, drawings, or graphs to show how you arrived at your answer.

Some of the students' responses:

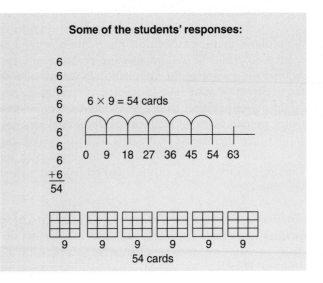

Assessment Strategy 8. Modeling Problem Strategy 8 presents a statement of a problem and requires students to draw a diagram or picture showing the problem situation. Focus your assessment on how the students represent the problem rather than on whether the problem is correctly solved. Drawings of time problems in mathematics, for example, should depict time lines, not scales for weighing.

Assessment Strategy 9. Identifying Obstacles Strategy 9 presents a difficult problem to solve, perhaps one missing a key piece of information, and requires students to explain (a) why it is difficult to complete the task, (b) what the obstacles are, and/or (c) what additional information they need to overcome the obstacles. Focus your assessment on whether students can identify the obstacle to solving the problem. (See the circles and squares drawing problem and scoring rubric we discussed earlier for an example.)

Exploring Possible Solution Strategies

Assessment Strategy 10. Justifying Solutions Strategy 10 presents a problem statement along with two or more possible solutions to the problem and requires students to (a) select one solution they believe is correct and (b) justify why it is correct.

Assessment Strategy 11. Justifying Strategies Used Strategy 11 presents a problem statement and two or more strategies for solving the problem and requires students to explain why both strategies are correct. When you craft an item using this assessment strategy, be certain both strategies yield the correct solution. In writing an item you might, for example, state that these were different ways that two fictional students solved the problem.

Assessment Strategy 12. Integrating Data Strategy 12 presents several types of interpretive material (story, cartoon, graph, data table) and a statement of a problem that requires using information from two or more of the interpretive material types, then requires students to (a) solve the problem and (b) explain the procedure they used to reach a solution. Be certain that the problem solution requires using some of the information in two or more of the interpretive materials. In science, for example, you might present rainfall tables, soil analyses, temperature tables, tomato nutrition requirements for several varieties, and fertilizer ingredients and require students to select the best variety to plant locally and to develop a plan for watering and feeding the plants based on the information you gave them.

Assessment Strategy 13. Producing Alternate Strategies Strategy 13 presents a problem statement and requires students to state two or more alternative solutions to the problem. Here is an example:

Example

Strategy 13: Producing alternative strategies to solve a problem

Read the description below, and then answer the question.

A young deaf couple has their first child. The infant needs to be fed and changed whenever it cries in the night, but neither the mother nor the father is able to hear the baby. The couple does not wish to bring the baby into their bed for fear of rolling on it and suffocating it. They also do not wish to put the baby on a strict schedule of changing and feeding at fixed times.

3. Suggest at least three solutions to the problem. Be very specific in describing your proposed solutions.

An alternative approach is to present, along with the problem statement, one strategy that solves the problem, and require students to show you another way the problem could be solved.

Assessment Strategy 14. Using Analogies Strategy 14 presents a problem statement and a solution strategy for correctly solving the problem and requires students to (a) describe other problems that could (by analogy) be solved by using this same solution strategy and (b) explain why the solution to the problem they generated is like the solution to the problem you gave them. Focus your assessment on the analogical relationship of the students' solution strategy to the solution strategy you gave them. You want to find out if students can use analogies as a heuristic method to solve different problems. Here is an example:

Example

Strategy 14: Using analogies to help solve another problem

Questions 1 and 2 refer to the situation below.

Members of a certain congressional committee talked a lot during committee hearings. Some members talked to explain their own views, some treated a witness as hostile and tried to discredit that witness's testimony, some wanted to prevent their opponents on the committee from speaking, and some wanted to prolong the debate and the hearing to postpone or prolong a committee vote. To solve this problem rules were established to give each committee member a fixed amount of time to speak and to ask questions of a witness. Under these rules, a committee member is allowed to give another member all or part of his allotted time.

1. Describe several other problems in different situations that could be solved by using a set of rules similar to those that the congressional committee used.

2. For each of the problems you listed, explain how the rules might be modified and why this would solve the problem you listed.

Assessment Strategy 15. Solving Backward Strategy 15 presents a complex problem situation or a complex (multi-step) task to complete, and requires students to work backward from the desired outcome to develop a plan or a strategy for completing the task or solving the problem. (For example, develop the steps and time frame needed to complete a library research paper; develop a plan to gather information to answer the question, "Do students in this school favor curfews for persons under 18 years old?") Focus your assessment on how well students use backward solution strategies.

Example

Strategy 15: Solving a problem using a backward heuristic

A student survey has been completed to determine whether students in a school favor curfews for persons under 18 years old. The results showed that among the girls, 56% favored the curfew (10% did not respond) and among the boys, 48% favored the curfew (9% did not respond). The results were based only on a sample of the students.

3. Working backward from the information above, develop a plan to show how this survey and the results were obtained. Be sure your plan covers all parts of the research.

Acting on and Looking Back on Problem-Solution Strategies

Assessment Strategy 16. Evaluating the Quality of the Solution Strategy 14 presents a problem statement and requires students to evaluate several different strategies for solving the problem. You can ask students to produce several different solutions or you can provide several solutions and ask them to evaluate those provided. If you provide solutions to evaluate, be certain to vary their correctness and quality, so that students can display their ability to evaluate. (For example, some may be more efficient, some may have negative consequences, and some may not work at all.) Ask students to try to implement each strategy and to thoroughly evaluate it. Ask them to determine the best strategy, explain why some strategies worked better than others, and why some did not work at all. Focus your assessment on the students' ability to justify the hierarchical ordering of the strategies' quality. Here is an example:

Example

Strategy 16: Evaluating the quality of problem solutions

Read the description below, then answer the question.

A young deaf couple has their first child. The infant needs to be fed and changed whenever it cries in the night, but neither the mother nor the father is able to hear the baby. The couple does not wish to bring the baby into their bed for fear of rolling on it and suffocating it. They also do not wish to put the baby on a strict schedule of changing and feeding at fixed times.

4. Which of the solutions that you proposed in Question 3 is best? Justify your choice by explaining its advantages and disadvantages.
5. Explain why each of the other solutions is not as good as the one you decided was best.

Assessment Strategy 17. Systematically Evaluating Strategies Strategy 17 uses the same types of tasks as in Assessment Strategy 16, but you focus your evaluation on the extent to which a student follows systematic *procedures* to evaluate each of the solution strategies you proposed.

OTHER PROMISING APPROACHES FOR ASSESSING PROBLEM SOLVING

In the preceding section we suggest that you could assess whether students have the skills associated with each step in the problem-solving process. Other approaches to assessing problem solving show promise, but are still in the experimental and validation states (Royer, Cisero, & Carlo, 1993). Space does not permit our discussion of these methods, however. You may wish to follow up on this topic by checking some of the references listed at the back of the textbook (e.g., Glaser, Lesgold, and Lajoie, 1985; Nitko, 1996; Parke, Lane, Silver, & Magone, 2003). You may wish to review also the assessment of students' knowledge structures in Chapter 13 (Approach 5).

CRITICAL THINKING

Curriculum frameworks frequently state that developing students' abilities for critical thinking is an important educational goal. Critical-thinking educational goals focus on developing students who are fair-minded, are objective, reach sound conclusions, and are disposed toward seeking clarity and accuracy (Marzano et al., 1988). What is critical thinking? Psychologists do not agree on all the skills that constitute it (Kuhn, 1999; Woolfolk, 1995). Discussions of critical thinking often use many of the same terms used in discussions of problem solving: The two areas are closely related.

In this chapter, we shall adopt the following definition: **"Critical thinking** is reasonable, reflective thinking that is focused on deciding what to believe or do" (Ennis, 1985, p. 54). This definition implies the following (Norris & Ennis, 1989):

1. *Reasonable thinking*—using good reasons
2. *Reflective thinking*—being conscious of looking for and using good reasons

3. *Focused thinking*—thinking for a particular purpose or goal

4. *Deciding what to believe or do*—evaluating both statements (what to believe) and actions (what to do)

5. *Abilities and dispositions*—both cognitive skills (abilities) and tendency to use the abilities (dispositions)

ASSESSING DISPOSITIONS TOWARD CRITICAL THINKING

What Are Dispositions?

Dispositions are **habits of mind** or tendencies to use appropriate critical-thinking behaviors often. Students who are disposed toward critical thinking:

1. seek a statement of the thesis or question;
2. seek reasons;
3. try to be well informed;
4. use credible sources and mention them;
5. take into account the total situation;
6. keep their thinking relevant to the main point;
7. keep in mind the original or most basic concern;
8. look for alternatives;
9. are open-minded and
   a. seriously consider points of view other than their own;
   b. reason from starting points with which they disagree without letting the disagreement interfere with their reasoning;
   c. withhold judgment when the evidence and reasons are insufficient;
10. take a position and change a position when the evidence and reasons are sufficient to do so;
11. seek as much precision as the subject permits;
12. deal in an orderly manner with the parts of a complex whole;
13. employ their critical thinking abilities;
14. are sensitive to the feelings, level of knowledge, and degree of sophistication of others.

Source: From *Evaluating Critical Thinking* (p. 12), by S. P. Norris and R. H. Ennis, 1989, Pacific Grove, CA: Critical Thinking Books and Software. Reprinted by permission.

Assessing Dispositions

Although you can assess a student's use of a critical-thinking ability or skill on one occasion, *assessment of a student's disposition requires you to focus on her long-term habits.* Your assessment should report how frequently over a marking period, term, or year a student uses critical thinking in the curriculum subject matter. You assess dispositions using either a checklist or a rating scale.

Checklists A **checklist** is a tool that contains a list of behaviors. You observe a student over a period of time and make a checkmark (√) next to the behavior you have observed. You then have a record of which disposition

behaviors a student exhibited. The more behaviors you checked, the greater the student's disposition toward critical thinking. Chapter 12 gives specific suggestions for crafting these types of assessment devices. An example checklist that could be used to assess a student's dispositions toward critical thinking is shown in Figure 10.4.

This checklist could help you keep track of a student's critical-thinking actions over the course of a unit. You can see from the checklist that the student exhibited a number of dispositions frequently (e.g., "2. Looks for explanations and reasons," "6. Open-minded") and others not very frequently (e.g., "5. Looks for alternatives"). You can use this information to help the student develop his critical thinking by teaching him to develop the habit of always looking for alternatives.

Rating Scales A simple **rating scale** is a device to record your judgments of the quality level of a student's dispositions toward each critical-thinking behavior. A rating scale usually has a line with points on it that range from poor quality to excellent quality. Usually, four or five quality points are further defined by describing what the behavior looks like at each point. These descriptions are called anchors. Figure 10.5 is an example of some of the dispositions toward critical thinking that a teacher might observe as a student completes an assignment. The anchor points on the items' rating scales were adapted from the Marzano et al. (1993) analysis of habits of mind.

In this example, each item's scale shows the degree to which a student is disposed toward using a particular critical-thinking habit. The numerical ratings on the scale are anchored by descriptions of specific and observable behaviors. Over time you can observe the student with respect to these habits. Then, at the end of the period, you use the rating scale to assess the student's disposition on each habit.

ASSESSING CRITICAL-THINKING ABILITIES

Abilities to Assess

Critical-thinking abilities are specific cognitive skills that are used when a student exhibits critical-thinking behavior. Here are some of the abilities typically considered in discussions of critical thinking that could be assessed. They are grouped into five areas.

Elementary clarification
1. Focus on a question
2. Analyze arguments
3. Asking and answering questions that clarify and challenge

Basic support
4. Judging the credibility of a source
5. Making and judging observations

Inference
6. Making and judging deductions
7. Making and judging inductions
8. Making and judging value judgments

FIGURE 10.4 Example of a checklist to keep track of a student's use of critical-thinking dispositions throughout a teaching unit.

Individual Student's Critical-Thinking Disposition Record					
Student's name:			**Class period:**		**Dates:**
Subject/unit: U.S. History/Unit III. Beginning a Government, 1780–1800					
	Assignment/activity				
Critical-thinking dispositions	Class discussion of the Articles of the Confederation	Essay discussing arguments for and against ratification of the Constitution	Scrapbook collecting and analyzing events reported in the newspaper using concepts from the Constitution	Teams debate the issue, "Have political parties made the United States goverment better?"	Essay evaluating Washington as president
1. Seeks statements of the main point or question	√	—	√	√	NA
2. Looks for explanations and reasons	√	√	√	√	√
3. Uses and cites credible sources	—	√	—	√	—
4. Keeps to the main and relevant point(s)	—	—	NA	√	√
5. Looks for alternatives	—	—	NA	—	NA
6. Open-minded	√	√	√	NA	—
7. Takes a position on an issue		√	—	√	—
8. Changes position on an issue with good reason(s)	NA	—	NA	NA	NA
9. Seeks to be accurate and precise in statements and work	NA	—	√	√	—
10. Sensitive to the feelings, levels of knowledge of others	√	NA	NA	—	NA

FIGURE 10.5 Sample rating scale assessing the quality of some of a student's dispositions toward critical thinking that a teacher might observe as the student completes an assignment.

Rating Scale for Critical Thinking Dispositions			
Student's name:		Date:	
Assignment:			

1. Did the student consider different points of view?

0	1	2	3
Acts as if own point of view is accepted by everyone	Aware that own point of view is not accepted by everyone	Shows awareness that others have legitimate points of view that differ from own	Actively looks for and encourages others to express points of view different from or opposing own

2. How did the student treat others' points of view?

0	1	2	3
Acts in a way that avoids or discourages others' points of view	Shows some attention to others' points of view	Makes a serious effort to consider others' points of view, but is not consistently objective or rational	Attends seriously to others' points of view and consistently reviews them objectively and rationally

3. Did the student communicate well with others who had less knowledge or ability?

0	1	2	3
Cannot work or communicate with others who have less knowledge or ability	Attempts to work or communicate with others who have less knowledge or ability, but is less than adequate in doing so	Works and communicates adequately with others who have less knowledge or ability	Works and communicates excellently with others who have less knowledge or ability

4. Was the student sensitive to the feelings of others with less knowledge or ability?

0	1	2	3
Acts apathetically or cruelly toward others who have less knowledge and ability	Does the minimum to help or encourage respect for the feelings of others who have less knowledge and ability	Offers good encouragement and respect for the feelings of others who have less knowledge and ability	Actively seeks to bolster and increase respect for the feelings of others who have less knowledge and ability

Advanced clarification
9. Defining terms and judging definitions
10. Identifying assumptions

Strategies and tactics
11. Deciding on an action
12. Interacting with others

Source: From *Evaluating Critical Thinking* (p. 14), by S. P. Norris and R. H. Ennis, 1989, Pacific Grove, CA: Critical Thinking Books and Software. Reprinted by permission.

The ultimate goal of education in critical thinking is to have students use these abilities spontaneously in school and in their lives after school. For example, students would be expected to spontaneously clarify the main point of an argument that someone was stating unclearly by asking the person, "What is your main point?" or "Can I say that your main point is _____?" As stated in Point 13 of our list of critical-thinking dispositions, students should be regularly using the abilities in this list.

Critical Thinking in Context

For the most part, critical-thinking abilities are best taught and assessed in the context of individual subjects. Ultimately students will apply critical thinking to specific events in their lives, so they must learn to apply these abilities in different

contexts. You should keep in mind that what constitutes "reasonable reflective thinking" about a subject such as visual arts may be quite different from what constitutes "reasonable reflective thinking" about a subject such as science: Different subject matters have different types of arguments and criteria for verifying truth or credibility. The example on page 274 (Chapter 12) shows how middle school students can use science criteria to evaluate their projects critically.

For these reasons, and for the practical reason of limited space, we cannot illustrate meaningful items for assessing critical-thinking abilities in many different subjects. However, we do show the *strategies* you could use when crafting assessment tasks for these abilities. Some of these are illustrated with sample items. You need to practice applying these strategies to the subject(s) you teach.

The material that follows is organized around the headings used to organize the preceding list of critical-thinking abilities. We first explain a critical-thinking ability, then describe and illustrate how to assess it, before moving on to the next.

Elementary Clarification Abilities

Focusing on a Question Students possessing the ability to **focus on a question** can critically review an action, a verbal statement, a piece of discourse, a scientific or political argument, or even a cartoon to determine its main point(s) or the essence of the argument. Subskills include (a) formulating or identifying the question or issue being posed, (b) formulating or selecting the proper criteria to use in evaluating the material presented, and (c) keeping the issue and its proper context in mind (Ennis, 1985). Here is a strategy for crafting items to assess this ability.

Strategy

Strategy 1: How to assess the ability to focus on a question

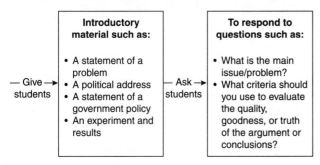

Note: For this and subsequent assessment strategies, you will need to rephrase the questions so they are written at the educational level of your students.

Item 1 in the next example below shows a multiple-choice item assessing a student's ability to focus on the main issue in a political cartoon.

Example

Strategies applied: Focusing on the main question and drawing conclusions after analyzing

Questions 1 and 2 refer to the cartoon above.

1. The cartoon illustrates which of the following characteristics of the party system in the United States?
   *A Strong party discipline is often lacking.
   B The parties are responsive to the will of the voters.

C The parties are often more concerned with the politics than with the national welfare
D Bipartisanship often exists in name only.

2. The situation shown in the cartoon is least likely to occur at which of the following times?
   A During the first sessions of a new Congress
   B During a political convention
   C During a primary election campaign
   *D During a presidential election campaign

Source: From *Making the Classroom Test: A Guide for Teachers* (No. 4. Evaluation and Advisory Services, pp. 18–19), by Q. Stodola, 1961, Princeton, NJ: Educational Testing Service. Cartoon courtesy of Army Times Publishing Company. Reprinted by permission of Educational Testing Service, the copyright owner.

Analyzing Arguments Students possessing the ability to **analyze arguments** are able to analyze the *details* of the arguments presented in verbal statements, discussions, scientific or political reports, cartoons, and so on. The subskills include (a) identifying the conclusions in a statement, (b) identifying the stated and unstated reasons behind an argument, (c) seeing similarities and differences among two or more arguments, (d) finding, pointing out, and ignoring (when appropriate) irrelevancies appearing in an argument, (e) representing the logic or structure of an argument, and (f) summarizing an argument (Ennis, 1985). When crafting tasks to assess this ability, use Strategy 2. An example follows.

Strategy

Strategy 2: How to assess the ability to analyze arguments

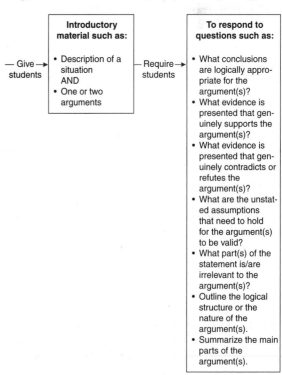

FIGURE 10.6 Examples of assessing subskills of the ability to analyze arguments.

Identifying assumptions (Item 1), identifying the structure of an argument (Item 2), identifying similarities among several sources (Item 3), identifying differences in two arguments (Item 4)

Items 1 and 2 are based on the reading from Clayton's book.

> A reading from Clayton's book accompanies each copy of the test

1. What assumption does Clayton's argument make?
    A   Cattle-raising will remain Botswana's most basic economic activity.
    B   The Botswana government should follow a laissez-faire policy for foreign trade.
    C   The economic conditions for ordinary people can be improved by the government helping certain industries.
    D   The Botswana income is not distributed equitably among all people.
2. The fundamental structure of Clayton's argument is that Botswana's people are strongly motivated by their
    A   desire to maximize their individual gains.
    B   desire to place nationalism before their individual gains.
    C   faith that competition in the marketplace will overcome present difficulties.
    D   sincere concern for the welfare of all people in the country.

Item 3 is based on the five readings listed below.

> Reading A accompanies the test   Reading B accompanies the test   Reading C accompanies the test
> Reading D accompanies the test   Reading E accompanies the test

3. Based on your reading of the five articles, list two or three principles on which the government might base its domestic policy.

Item 4 is based on the readings from Clayton's book and Mmualefe's book.

> Readings from Clayton's book accompany the test   Readings from Mmualefe's book accompany the test

4. What is the most fundamental difference between Clayton and Mmualefe regarding Botswana's economic situation?
    A   They differ on whether a competitive economy is desirable.
    B   They differ on the role that morality plays in economic life.
    C   They differ in their prediction of whether the government will become corrupt.
    D   They differ in the degree to which they believe that government should encourage foreign investment in Botswana.

Note: Theses items are for illustration only. The readings and persons referred to are fictitious.

One of the subskills for this area is identifying conclusions. Item 2 in the political cartoon item presented previously is an example of assessing those subskills. Figure 10.6 shows four social studies items that assess various subskills of the ability to analyze arguments. Note that in practice the items would be accompanied by introductory material for students to read before answering the questions.

Questioning to Clarify and Challenge Students possessing the ability to **ask clarifying questions** can do two things: (a) ask appropriate questions of someone who is presenting an argument, and (b) answer critical questions appropriately when making an argument themselves. Among the questions that students should ask and be able to answer are: Why? What would not be an example? How does that apply in this situation? What are the facts that support your position? (Ennis, 1985).

You may find it difficult to assess this ability directly, because you must either observe a student while he is attending to someone who is presenting an argument or

have the student present an argument and ask questions yourself. The first approach is problematic for several reasons: It may be impolite to interrupt a speaker; a student may be shy about asking questions afterward; a speaker's argument may be well presented so that few critical questions are appropriate; or a speaker's presentation may be so poor that students lose interest in it.

Having the student present an argument is less problematic, but it, too, contains elements that threaten the validity of the results. For instance, all students do not have the same degree of knowledge of a topic. Differences in topical knowledge will affect the quality of students' presentations and the questions that are appropriate for you to ask. Also, it would be tedious to have 25 or more students present the same or similar arguments to you or to the class. Probably the best way to assess this ability is to collect information about it over a long period, use a variety of assignments and tasks, and use a systematic procedure for recording your assessments such as a checklist (see Figure 10.4) or a rating scale (Figure 10.5).

Basic Support of an Argument

Judging the Credibility of a Source Students with this ability can evaluate the quality of the evidence someone uses in supporting a position. Standards or criteria a student should be able to use when **judging credibility** include (a) the expertise of the person giving the evidence, (b) whether the person giving the evidence has a conflict of interest, (c) whether different sources of evidence agree, (d) whether the source of evidence has a reputation for being accurate and correct, (e) whether the evidence was obtained by established procedures that give it validity, and (f) whether there are good reasons for using the evidence under the given circumstances (Ennis, 1985). Each discipline will have specific rules of evidence, too.

When crafting tasks to assess this ability, you can use the strategy that follows.

Strategy

Strategy 3: How to assess the ability to judge credibility

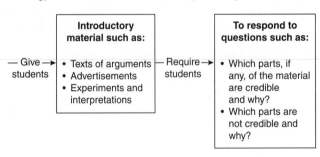

The objective item formats that help assess this critical-thinking ability include (a) masterlist, (b) best-answer, (c) experiment-interpretation, (d) statement-and-comment, and (e) rank-order.[3] Examples of the first four formats are given in Chapter 8. Short-answer formats may also be used. An example is shown here:

Example

Using Strategy 3 to assess students' ability to judge the credibility of an argument or statement

Question 1 refers to the information below.

The board of directors announced that last year's sales of the XYZ automobile increased 25% over the previous year. Mr. Hereto, the president of the XYZ Automobile Company, stated that the reason for this increase is that the automobile buyers in this country recognize that the XYZ cars are the best cars available today.

---

[3]*Rank-order items* present students with a randomly arranged list and ask students to order the list on the basis of a given criterion. For example, ordering statements according to their degree of credibility.

1. Analyze this statement indicating which part(s) of it is/are credible and which part(s), if any, is/are not credible. Give reasons for each of your choices. You may organize your answers in the format below.

Credible part(s):	Reason(s) why:
_____	_____
_____	_____
_____	_____
_____	_____
_____	_____

Part(s) not credible:	Reason(s) why:
_____	_____
_____	_____
_____	_____
_____	_____

To validly assess this ability, you must be careful to include introductory material that was not part of examples in class or the assigned reading, and pose questions that require students to explain the reasoning behind their evaluations of the credibility of each part of the material. *Assessing students on material you have already analyzed and judged for them produces an invalid assessment of the students' ability to judge the credibility of a source for themselves.* Also, if you fail to ask students to explain the reasoning they used to evaluate the credibility of a source, you will not know whether students have used appropriate criteria and critical thinking to arrive at their answer.

Observing and Judging Observation Reports This is the ability of students to evaluate the quality of information obtained from eyewitness or direct observation of an event, phenomenon, or person. Among the standards or criteria students should be able to use when making these judgments are whether (a) an observer reports with minimal referral to others' observations; (b) the time between the event and the report by the observer is short; (c) an observer is not reporting hearsay; (d) an observer keeps records of the observation; (e) the observations reported are corroborated by others; (f) an observer had good access to the event or person so direct observation can be accurate; (g) an observer records the observations properly; and (h) an observer is a credible source (Ennis, 1985). Each discipline may have more specific criteria as well. Here is the strategy for assessing this ability.

Strategy

Strategy 4: How to assess the ability to judge observation reports

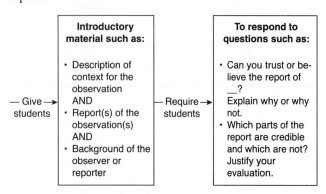

Strategy

Strategy 5(A): How to assess the ability to make and judge conclusions by comparing different conclusions

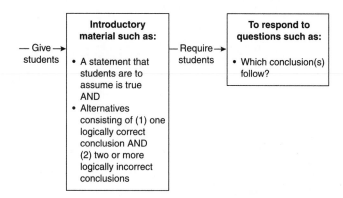

Strategy 5(B): How to assess the ability to make and judge conclusions by judging the truth of a conclusion

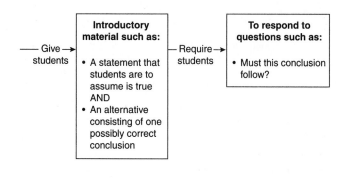

Assessing this ability requires you to present students with (a) observation reports, (b) information about the context within which the observations were made, and (c) information about the person making or recording the observations. In other words, students must have sufficient information to evaluate, using the criteria just listed. This may be difficult to do without making the task unwieldy and without giving away the answer. Further, to obtain valid assessment results, you must use introductory materials that were not used as examples in class or in assigned reading and require students to explain the reason(s) for their evaluations of the reported observations. *The validity of the assessment results suffers if you do not include these two elements in your task.*

Newspaper articles related to your subject area may be useful sources for introductory material, provided competent reporters write them. A competent reporter usually includes information about the nature of the observation, the background of the observer or reporter (e.g., political affiliation, source of funding for a study), and whether there was corroboration of observations.

Inferences

Deducing and Judging Deductions Students able to **judge deductions** apply logical thinking when they analyze statements and conclusions. Subskills include (a) using the logic of class inclusion (what elements or members should be logically included in a class or category), (b) using conditional logic (identifying the conditions under which something is true or false), and (c) properly interpreting statements using logical strategies (negatives; double negatives; necessary vs. sufficient conditions; and words such as *if, or, some, not, both*) (Ennis, 1985). To design an objective task to assess this ability, you can use one of the strategies that follows (Norris & Ennis, 1989).

An example of Strategy 5(A) is shown in Item 1 below. Strategy 5(B) has been applied to Item 2.

Example

Examples of items assessing students' ability to judge logical conclusions

Questions 1 and 2 are based on the information below.

If this substance is calcium carbonate, then it will bubble when acid is added. But there were no bubbles when I added the acid.

An item applying Strategy 5(A): Comparing different conclusions

1. Based on the above information, which of the following is correct?
   A This substance cannot produce bubbles.
   B This substance is calcium carbonate.
   C This substance is not calcium carbonate.
   D This substance is calcium chloride.

An item applying Strategy 5(B): Judging the truth of one conclusion

2. Based on the above information, is it true that this substance is calcium carbonate?
   A Yes, it must be true.
   B No, it cannot be true.
   C We cannot be certain it is true from the information given.

Inducing and Judging Inductions Students who have the ability to induce can draw valid conclusions by generalizing from given information. Students who have the ability to **judge inductions** identify the conclusions that best explain the given evidence (Norris & Ennis, 1989). Subskills for generalizing from the data include (a) identifying and using typical features or patterns in the data to make inferences, (b) using appropriate techniques to make inferences from sample data, and (c) using patterns and trends shown in tables and graphs to make inferences (Ennis, 1985). Subskills for identifying the conclusion that best explains the given evidence include (a) understanding and using different types of hypotheses and explanations (recognizing causal claims, recognizing historical claims, etc.); (b) understanding and using valid ways of collecting relevant information (designing empirical research studies, methods of seeking evidence and counterevidence, etc.); and (c) being able to use criteria to evaluate the extent to which the information (data) supports the conclusion (Ennis, 1985).

Both response-choice and constructed-response tasks can assess students' ability to reach a conclusion. Two assessment strategies follow.

Strategy

Strategy 6(A): How to assess the ability to judge inductions using response-choice items

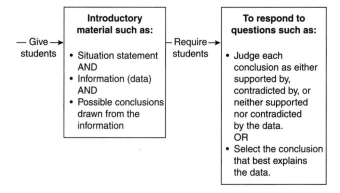

Strategy 6(B): How to assess the ability to judge inductions using constructed response items

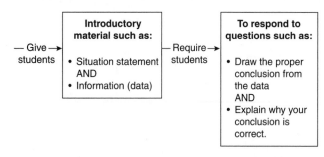

The item formats that are especially suited for assessing students in this area of critical thinking are the formats we discussed in Chapters 7 and 8, especially the *best-answer* (see p. 169, Item 2), *experiment-interpretation* (see p. 170, Items 1–3), *experiment-interpretation with written justification* supplied by students (see p. 171, Items 4–7), *masterlist* (see page 179, Items 1–4), and *short-answer* (see p. 135, Figure 7.1). Suggestions for constructing these task formats are presented in Chapter 8.

You should note that having students justify their answers is a very important way to assess whether they can make or judge inductions appropriately. Students may choose the correct conclusion for the wrong reasons, or choose an incorrect conclusion because they do not have enough information to interpret the context of the situation you gave them correctly. For example, in the graph interpretation item on page 180 of Chapter 8, Items 1–5, students may not comprehend how long a city block is and, therefore, may draw incorrect inferences about the graph. Their critical thinking may be well developed, yet their knowledge base may be lacking in specific areas.

Again, you must present students with situations and information for which you did not already teach the proper conclusion. This is absolutely necessary to assess their abilities to make conclusions. You don't want to assess the students' ability to recall the induction you made.

Making Value Judgments Not all critical-thinking inferences are made using data and syllogisms. Some are based on **judging value definitions**. Students with this critical-thinking ability are able to identify when inferences have been made on the basis of values, what these values are, and when to use their own values to make inferences. Subskills of this ability include (a) gathering and using appropriate background information before judging, (b) identifying the consequences of the inferences that could be drawn and weighing the consequences before drawing conclusions, (c) identifying alternative actions and their value, and (d) balancing alternatives, weighing consequences, and deciding rationally (Ennis, 1985).

To assess this ability, you must require students to explain the value, worth, or importance behind their inferences. Also, you must assess whether they recognize that different inferences or conclusions imply actions that have different consequences. You want, therefore, to craft an assessment task that requires students to create or judge different courses of action using different values as criteria. For the most part, you would need to ask students to supply their reasons either in writing or orally. You can use the assessment strategy shown here:

Strategy

Strategy 7: How to assess the ability to make judgments about values

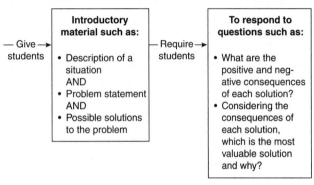

Students' use of consequences and values may appear in assessment tasks that are not originally intended to assess critical thinking. For instance, study the arithmetic problem below that might be used with junior high school students (Silver, Smith, & Nelson, 1995).

Example

Arithmetic item in which students are given the opportunity to explain the value-basis of their answers

Juanita must decide whether to buy a weekly bus pass or to pay the fare each day. She must ride the bus to work and back home again on Monday, Tuesday, and Wednesday. She must ride the bus to work on Thursday and Friday, but she receives car rides home from her friends on these 2 days. Here are the costs of the bus:

one-way fare $1.00
weekly pass $9.00

1. Which option, weekly pass or pay every day, should Juanita choose? Explain your answer.

Teachers reasoned that the correct answer to the problem is the daily payment because it is the more economical option (3 days × $2 per day + 2 days × $1 per day = $8; this is less than the $9 weekly pass). However, many students reasoned that the $9 weekly pass was more economical

because the weekly pass could be used not only by Juanita, but also in the evenings and on weekends by various family members. Thus, students applied their knowledge of urban life and their values of sharing limited resources with family members to choose an alternative the teachers originally did not consider correct. This example points out the importance of using a wide variety of classroom situations and constructed response tasks to identify how well students can use critical-thinking skills.

Advanced Clarification

Defining Terms and Judging Definitions Students possessing this ability are able to analyze the meanings and definitions of the terms used in the course of arguments, statements, and events to evaluate them critically. Among the subskills of this ability are (a) knowing the various forms that key terms may take and how these forms function in the context of an argument, (b) knowing how different strategies are used to define key terms in arguments, and (c) knowing the validity of the content of the definition itself (Ennis, 1985).

Assessment of this critical-thinking ability must go beyond simply asking for definitions or meanings of words in context (although this is related to the ability). The idea is to assess whether a student can recognize that words may be defined in certain ways to make a point, distort an argument, or deceive a listener or reader. For example, there may be two or more meanings for a key term. In an argumentative presentation, a writer may shift from one meaning to another (Ennis, 1985). Students skilled in this aspect of critical thinking should be able to detect the shift of meaning and describe the impact of the shift on the quality of the argument. A strategy for assessing this skill is shown next.

Strategy

Strategy 8: How to assess the ability to judge definitions

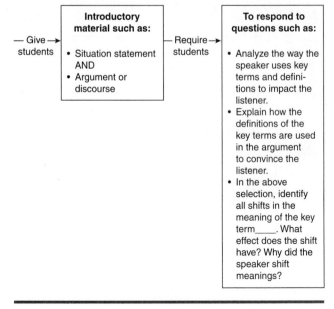

Identifying Assumptions Students possessing this ability are able to **identify assumptions** that are part of someone's reasoning about what to believe or to do. Norris and Ennis (1989) point out that there are three meanings of *assumption*, but only one is appropriate in the context of this critical-thinking ability:

1. *A tentatively held conclusion* ("I assume you are going to eat because you got out the plate and dish.")

2. *Pejorative sense of assumption* ("I wouldn't put much faith in her story. Her tale is just an assumption.")

3. *An unstated basis for someone's reasoning* (John said, "Because half the students have baseball cards, at least half the students are males." Sally said, "You are assuming that only male students have baseball cards.")

For purposes of our discussion of critical thinking in this chapter, we use only the third meaning, which is usually intended when educational goals state that identifying implicit assumptions is a critical-thinking skill (Norris & Ennis, 1989).

Confusion over the meaning of *assumption* can lead you to set poor-quality assessment tasks. Norris and Ennis point out that short-answer tasks usually result in poor assessment results because students interpret the word *assumption* in its first meaning, when you want them to use the third meaning. As a result, students' responses are likely to consist of tentative conclusions for which they believe there is little support in the introductory material that you gave them. If all students do not interpret the task the way you intended, the quality of your assessment results would be poor.

A second way you may create poor-quality assessment of this ability is when you use the term *assumption* improperly in an assessment task. A common flaw, as pointed out earlier, is to confuse assumption with conclusion. The examples below show how to improve items that contain this flaw.

Example

Poor: Confuses assumptions with conclusions

According to the Federal Election Commission, the percentages of the voting population who voted in the presidential election years 1932–1988 were:

Year	%	Year	%	Year	%	Year	%
1932	52.4	1948	51.1	1964	61.9	1980	54.0
1936	56.0	1952	61.6	1968	60.9	1984	53.1
1940	58.9	1956	59.3	1972	55.2	1988	50.1
1944	56.0	1960	62.8	1976	53.5		

1. From the above data you can assume that
   A in 1988 most voters were unhappy with the candidates.
   B in 1988 voter turnout was at an all-time low.
   C voter turnout declined from 1980 to 1988.
   D the majority of the voters did not vote.

Better: Gives conclusion and asks for the assumption needed to reach conclusion

FACTS: According to the Federal Election Commission, the percentage of the voting population who voted in the presidential election years 1932–1988 were:

Year	%	Year	%	Year	%	Year	%
1932	52.4	1948	51.1	1964	61.9	1980	54.0
1936	56.0	1952	61.6	1968	60.9	1984	53.1
1940	58.9	1956	59.3	1972	55.2	1988	50.1
1944	56.0	1960	62.8	1976	53.5		

CONCLUSION: The number of persons voting in national elections in presidential election years 1932–1988 was at its lowest in 1988.

2. For this conclusion to be true, it must be assumed that
   A the number of voting-age persons in 1988 was the same as or less than each of the other presidential election years in 1932–1988.
   B the number of voting-age persons increased from 1932 to 1988.
   C the percentage of voting-age persons who voted in each of the other presidential election years was less than 50.1%.

The problem with Item 1 is that, even though it uses the word *assume*, it actually requires students to draw conclusions from the given data: A student is not required to identify an implicit or unstated assumption that might be the basis for a conclusion. Item 2 is an improvement because it is rewritten to focus on implicit assumptions.

To craft quality tasks that assess students' ability to identify implicit assumptions, you must attend carefully to the concerns described in the preceding paragraphs. The overall assessment strategy below seems most appropriate for this area of critical-thinking skills (Norris & Ennis, 1989).

Strategy

Strategy 9: How to assess the ability to identify implicit assumptions with response-choice items

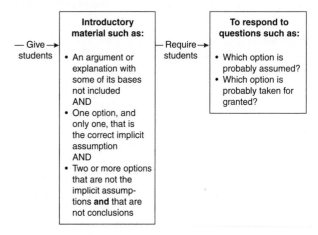

FIGURE 10.7 Example of a simple rating scale to use as a scoring rubric for assessing the quality of a student's oral or written presentation of an argument.

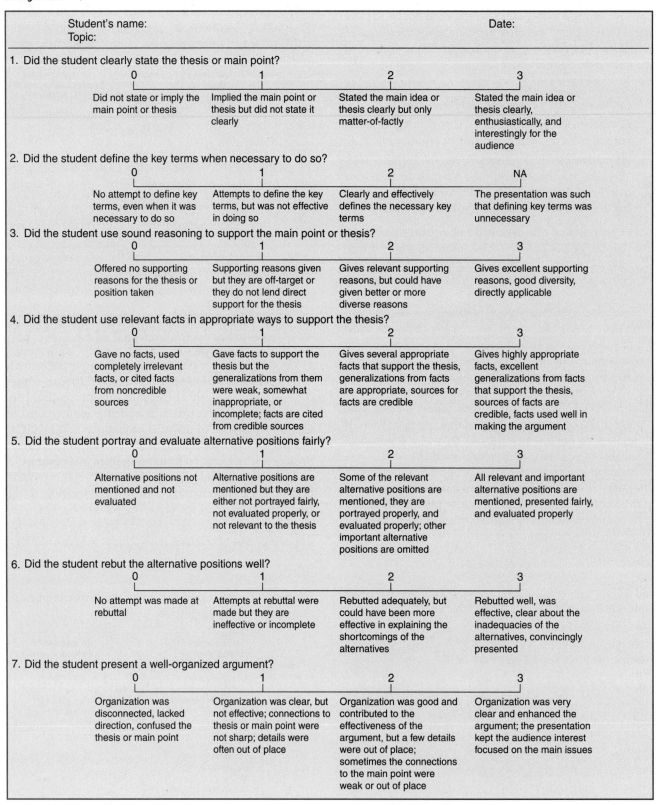

Do not ask students to identify the same assumption for the same material that you illustrated during the lesson. Also, be sure that the interpretive material you use in fact has an implicit assumption. This means you cannot include passages for which the author makes his or her assumptions explicit. It also means you cannot use material for which no assumptions have been made to reach the conclusion. To craft appropriate items, you may have to rewrite some of the passages you select from documents and other sources.

Strategies and Tactics As Critical-Thinking Skills

Deciding on an Action Students who can **decide on an action** are essentially good problem solvers. The subskills are those we discussed earlier in this chapter on problem solving: defining problems, formulating and evaluating solutions, viewing the total problem and taking action, and evaluating the action taken. The assessment strategies for this ability are the same as those you would use in assessing problem-solving skills.

Interacting With Others Students who are good at **interacting with others** are able to identify and use rhetorical devices to persuade, explain, or argue. Among the rhetorical devices the student should be able to identify and use are (a) argumentative verbal tactics (appeal to authority, strawman, etc.), (b) logical strategies, and (c) skillful organization and presentation (Ennis, 1985).

Assessment of this ability may take several forms. One form is to ask students to present argumentative or persuasive work of their own creation. The media and purposes of the presentation may vary widely, depending on the subject matter you are teaching. For example, product or service advertisements are designed to persuade people and may use different media such as printing, still photography, or motion pictures (videos). Debates, on the other hand, are usually more structured.

Assessing students' performances requires use of a scoring scheme, most likely in the form of a rating scale. Without a rating scale, you are not likely to be fair or helpful to the student. Using a rating scale serves several purposes: (a) It makes clear the criteria you use to evaluate students; (b) you can give the scale to students, so they can internalize standards for performance; and (c) it greatly improves the consistency (reliability) of your marking. Figure 10.7 shows an example of a rating scale for evaluating an argumentative presentation.

You may also wish to assess whether students can identify the rhetorical mechanisms and tactics that are used in a particular piece of writing, speech, advertisement, or other persuasive material. Two assessment strategies for doing this follow.

Strategy

Strategy 10(A): How to assess the ability to identify rhetorical mechanisms and tactics by analyzing one piece to identify what is misleading

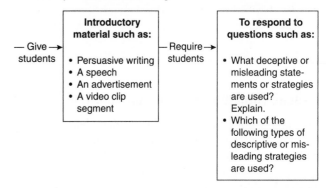

Strategy 10(B): How to assess the ability to identify rhetorical mechanisms and tactics by identifying the misleading piece from among several pieces that are not misleading

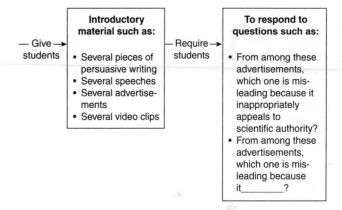

Here are two examples that implement this strategy with the multiple-choice format.

Example

Items using Strategy 10(B) to assess the ability to identify misleading approaches in persuasive material (e.g., advertisements)

Questions 1 and 2 refer to the advertisements below.

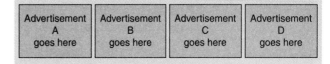

1. Which of the advertisements above should be considered misleading because it inappropriately appeals to scientific authority?
   A
   B
   C
   D

2. Which of the advertisements above should be considered misleading because it focuses on the consumer keeping up with the crowd or joining the bandwagon?

A

B

C

D

Critical-Thinking Skills in Combination

You should not lose sight of this ultimate learning goal: When faced with real-world applications, the student must spontaneously decide to use critical-thinking abilities and use them in selective combinations that fit the circumstances. You need to give students instruction and practice in deciding on the appropriate analyses and when to use combinations of critical-thinking skills in different circumstances. Your assessment tasks themselves must provide realistic situations that require students to use combinations of several critical-thinking abilities. Performance tasks, discussed in Chapter 11, offer assessment opportunities for doing this.

Finally, if students are to learn to be disposed toward using critical thinking in their daily activities, you should assess their dispositions continuously throughout the term or year. If some students are not exhibiting a critical-thinking disposition, you should alter your teaching of those students so they do. If you do not assess critical-thinking dispositions, both you and your students will come to believe they are unimportant learning goals.

OTHER SPECIFIC HIGHER-ORDER SKILLS AND ABILITIES

Ability to Use Reference Materials

Undoubtedly it is important to develop the ability to use both general reference materials and special subject-matter-specific materials. Among the reference-using skills you may teach and assess are: alphabetizing, using tables of contents and indexes, using encyclopedias, using dictionaries, using general reference materials (calendars, maps and globes, textbooks, periodical indexes, atlases, *Who's Who in America*, and magazines), and using a library and its catalog (Hoover, Hieronymus, Frisbie, & Dunbar, 1993b). The Internet and computer-based CDs are also reference materials. Skills in using these media should also be taught and assessed. The dictionary items on page 208 illustrate how to assess these dictionary-entry skills: using the phonetic spelling, locating the meaning in particular usage, and identifying a word's part of speech.

Earlier we spoke of using interpretive materials. In this assessment area interpretive materials include: a section of

an index, a section of a table of contents, a part of an atlas, a list of words to alphabetize, a reproduction of a library, and a catalog entry card, a section of the Dewey or Library of Congress classification system, a picture of a computer screen, and a section of a periodical guide (index). Many times, however, you will have to rewrite or modify these materials before they are suitable for use in assessment, because (a) they contain material irrelevant or extraneous to assessing the objective at hand; (b) they are too long; or (c) the extract is out of context and is therefore not clear to students. You may need to obtain written permission to reproduce copyrighted materials. You may, of course, use entire volumes or take students to the library for the assessment. To do so, you will need sufficient materials (or computers) for all students, as well as sufficient uninterrupted time to administer this type of performance assessment.

Graphs and Tables

Much information is condensed in tables and graphs. **Graph and table reading abilities** are important to further learning in many areas, both in and out of school. Following are examples of some of the graph- and table-reading abilities that you can teach and assess.

Example

1. To comprehend from the title the topic on which a table or graph gives information

2. To recognize from subtitles and row or column headings what is shown by each part of a graph or table

3. To read amounts
   A by using the scale (or scales) on bar, line, and picture graphs
   B by interpreting the sectors of a circle on circle graphs
   C by locating a cell in a table
   D by using special symbols and a key

4. To compare two or more values read from a graph or a table
   A by determining rank
   B by determining differences between amounts
   C by determining how many times greater one amount is than another

5. To determine relative rates or trends

6. To determine underlying relationships through correct interpretation of a graph

7. To grasp the outstanding facts portrayed by a graph or a table

FIGURE 10.8 Examples of items written to assess graph and table reading skills.

Use the table below to answer Questions 1 and 2.

	2000		*2001*		*2002*		*2003*	
Average Temperature and Rainfall at Windy Hill Town								
	Temp	**Rain**	**Temp**	**Rain**	**Temp**	**Rain**	**Temp**	**Rain**
September	64°	0.1 in	63°	0.2 in	66°	0.0 in	64°	0.3 in
October	72°	0.4 in	71°	0.5 in	74°	0.4 in	71°	0.6 in
November	77°	0.9 in	75°	1.0 in	78°	0.8 in	76°	0.7 in
December	81°	2.0 in	80°	2.7 in	85°	1.5 in	80°	2.1 in

Example of assessing the ability to locate and compare information from a table

1. When did the highest average rainfall occur?
    A   November of 2000
    B   November of 2001
    *C   December of 2001
    D   December of 2003

Example of assessing the ability to draw inferences based on trends and other information in a table

2. Which of the following even most likely to have occurred between September and December of 2002?
    A   The roads were covered with ice and snow.
    *B   The town's water reserves were very low.
    C   The river flowing through the town overflowed its banks.

Item 1 of Figure 10.8 requires a student to read the table and locate the information in a cell [Capability 3(c) in the preceding list] and to compare several values read from the table to determine which is largest [Capability 4(a) in the list]. Item 2 requires a student to make an inference concerning the likelihood of an event based on understanding the trends and facts presented (Capabilities 6 and 7).

Next is an illustration of how you could use a graph and multiple-choice items to assess capabilities to draw inference based on the displayed rates or trends (Capability 5), underlying relationships (Capability 6), and facts.

Example

Use the information below to answer Questions 1 and 2

Before the exercise period began, the teacher divided the class into two groups. Group 1 was to walk around the track two times. Group 2 was to run around the track one time. All students took their pulses both before and after going around the track. The average pulse for each group is shown in the graph below.

Example of an item to assess the ability to draw an inference from a graph

1. According to the graph, which type of exercise made students' hearts beat faster?
    *A   Running
    B   Walking
    C   Neither—they had the same result with either walking or running

Example of an item assessing the ability to interpret trends underlying a graph

2. What would be the heart beats about one hour after the exercise period when all the students are reading in the library?
    *A   About 70 for both groups
    B   About 70 for the group that walked twice around and about 130 for the group that ran once around
    C   About 90 for the group that walked twice around and about 130 for the group that ran once around
    D   Lower than 60 for both groups

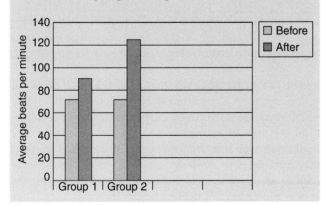

Maps

It is important to teach and assess general **map-reading ability**. Here are some examples of specific abilities that comprise map-reading ability:

Example

1. Ability to orient maps and determine direction
   a. to determine direction from orientation
   b. to determine direction from parallels or meridians
   c. to determine direction of river flows or slope of land
2. Ability to locate and/or describe places on maps and globes
   a. through the use of standard map symbols
   b. through the use of a key
   c. through the use of distance and/or direction
   d. through the use of latitude or longitude
3. Ability to determine distances
   a. determining distances on a road map
   b. determining distances by using a scale of units
   c. determining distances on a globe
   d. comparing distances
4. Ability to determine or trace routes of travel
5. Ability to determine seasonal variations, sun patterns, and time differences
6. Ability to read and compare facts from one or more pattern maps
7. Ability to visualize landscape features
8. Ability to infer man's activities or way of living
   a. from outline maps
   b. from pattern maps

Source: Copyright © 1971 by The University of Iowa. All rights reserved. Reproduced from the *Iowa Tests of Basic Skills, Teachers Guide to Administration, Interpretation, and Use, Levels Edition,* Form 6, p. 44, with permission of the Riverside Publishing Company.

Suggestions for teaching these skills and a bibliography of teaching materials are given in Hoover et al. (1993b). Figure 10.9 lists some examples of items that assess these abilities.

Reading Skills

Traditional Procedure Having students read material in a subject area and answer questions based on that material is a desirable way to assess reading skills. Although developing passages followed by questions is not easy, you may need to do so, especially when teaching subjects for which you lack adequate assessment procedures or study booklets covering these skills. To develop such assessments, the reading materials need to be carefully selected to represent the kind of material students should be able to read. Also, the reading material may need to be rewritten so that the interpretive questions can be answered primarily on the basis of the material presented. Finally, questions need to be phrased in a way that does not require a student to have more background or special information than you deem appropriate for the level of students and subject matter at hand (Ebel, 1951; Wesman, 1971).

The steps for building a set of assessment questions requiring reading and interpreting of a printed passage follow (Ebel, 1951; Wesman, 1971):

1. *Locate a promising passage.* Examine sources (texts, periodicals, reference works, specialized books, and collections and anthologies) until you find a passage for which you can write several interpretive items.
2. *Write initial test items.* Write as many items for the passage as you can. Try to exploit all of the possibilities for interpretation of the passage that fit your original assessment plan.
3. *Rewrite the passage.* After you have a tentative set of items, rewrite the passage to eliminate unessential material that does not contribute to the items you have written.
4. *Consider rewriting some of the items.* Changes in the passage may require revising or eliminating some of the items you already wrote. The goal of steps 3 and 4 is to produce a condensed and efficient passage and item set.
5. *Repeat steps 3 and 4 as often as necessary,* until you are satisfied that you have an efficient set of items.

Most commercial survey achievement tests contain reading comprehension subtests. You should consult these for examples of using passages to assess reading comprehension.

Authentic Reading Assessment If you are most interested in reading comprehension, rather than the students' ability to interpret subject-matter materials, the preceding type of condensation may be undesirable, especially if part of what you want to assess is the ability to read naturally occurring materials and the capacity to distinguish between relevant and extraneous material (Wesman, 1971). Critics of standardized reading comprehension tests argue that the passages and questions created by the traditional five-step procedure are too artificial. The critics would rather use materials that students need to read in the real world or in further schooling. They claim that students exposed to traditional reading comprehension tests come to believe that reading (a) consists of short passages, (b) requires answering questions whose answers are known by the authorities that set them, and (c) has little to do with interpreting the written word (Resnick, 1989).

Passages are considered authentic if they are drawn from the primary sources of a discipline, age-appropriate books and magazines, newspapers, and textbooks students may encounter. In addition, authentic reading tasks may require students to read longer passages than typically appear on traditional reading comprehension tests. They

FIGURE 10.9 Items assessing the ability to read maps.

The map below shows five states. The cities are in alphabetical order beginning at the top. The key below the map tells what the signs on the map mean.

Item 1 assesses the ability to determine the direction of places on maps from a given orientation [Capability 1(a)].

1. Which of these cities is farthest south?
   A Eton
   B Follet
   C Gull
   *D Hart

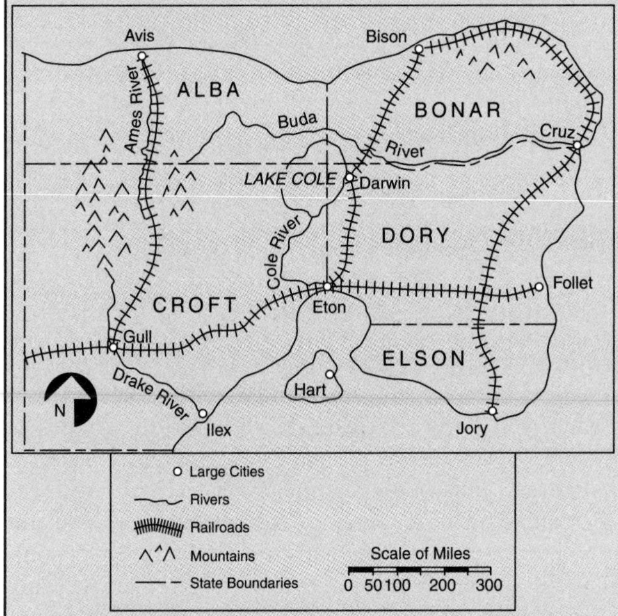

O Large Cities
Rivers
Railroads
∧∧∧ Mountains
State Boundaries
Scale of Miles
0 50 100 200 300

Item 2 assesses the ability to visualize landscape features (Capability 7).

2. On which train trip could one see the mountains on one side and the ocean on the other?
   A Avis to Gull
   *B Bison to Cruz
   C Bison to Darwin
   D Darwin to Eton

Item 3 assesses the student's ability to determine distance using a scale of miles [Capability 3(b)].

3. About how far is it from Hart to the mainland at the closest point?
   A 5 miles
   B 15 miles
   *C 50 miles
   D 85 miles

Item 4 assesses the ability to determine the direction a river flows [Capability 1(c)].

4. Which way does the Ames River flow?
   *A North
   B South
   C East
   D West

may also require students to read from several sources to compare points of view or obtain reliable and complete information. For example, a student may read four different accounts of an event or of a procedure and then answer questions about the event or procedure, or about comparisons among the different accounts read.

Alternately, you may want to combine reading, writing, and subject-matter exercises, such as conducting science experiments. For instance, students can individually read several pieces and answer questions about them. Then you can organize students into groups to discuss the pieces they read and to share their insights into interpreting them. Next, students can individually write essays or set up experiments to extend or synthesize the material they have read and discussed. The purpose of the intermediate discussion is to offer all students the opportunity, through group discussion, to clarify points, obtain information they may have missed through their reading, and "level the playing field" somewhat before the writing phase of the assessment begins.

Longer and more authentic reading tasks use more of your class time for assessment than does the traditional method. An assessment that requires reading several original texts and writing essays after a class discussion may take several class periods to complete. You need to balance your assessment time against your teaching time before deciding which assessment strategy to use. You could try some combination of both. You could use more authentic assessment methods on some occasions and more efficient assessment methods on others. Compare students' performance and the type of information you obtain under the different approaches. This may give you some insight into the validity of the assessment results from each method. (Assessment validity is discussed in Chapter 3.)

The MAZE Item Type Reading comprehension can be assessed through a multiple-choice variety of the **cloze reading exercise** known as **MAZE**. The basic idea is to find an appropriate passage and embed a multiple-choice question in the passage that students can answer only if they comprehend the meaning of the surrounding passage. To better understand this procedure, consider the following multiple-choice item, which requires students to select the word that best completes the sentence, "The baby _____."

Example

MAZE multiple-choice item <u>before</u> it is embedded in text

The baby ___1___.
   1. A cried
      B laughed
      C slept
      D walked

Notice that all options correctly complete this sentence when it is read outside the context of a reading passage. Now, consider the same item when it is embedded in a brief passage as shown in Item 2 below.

Example

MAZE multiple-choice item <u>after</u> it is embedded in text

Mother and her six-month-old baby played for a long time. The baby ___1___. He enjoyed being tickled under the arms.
   2. A cried
     *B laughed
      C slept
      D walked

Option B is correct because of the context in which the item is embedded. Item 2 shows a simple paragraph of a few short sentences; this technique also can, and should, be applied to longer and more complex prose passages.

MAZE items appear to have a considerable advantage over the usual cloze exercises, in which only the blank appears and students must fill in the missing word. They (a) assess whether students can construct meaning from the passages, (b) are objectively scored, (c) do not result in a student filling in blanks with words that leave you wondering whether a student understands the passage, and (d) do not require students to have a great deal of outside knowledge for you to assess their ability to read.

The following suggestions for formulating MAZE test items are based on those used for the *Degrees of Reading Power* (Touchstone Applied Science Associates, 1995a, 1995b) test.

1. *Design the items so that a student needs to read and understand the passage to answer correctly.* As in the preceding example, when an item is considered in isolation, each option should make the sentence grammatically

and semantically correct. However, once the item is embedded in the text, only one option should be correct.

2. *The passage should contain all the content information a student needs to answer the item correctly.* For the item to assess reading ability, a student should not have to depend on recall of special experiences to find the correct answer. This usually means the passages must be written specifically for the test.

3. *All of the items' options should be common words.* All students should recognize and understand the meaning of each option. This ensures that when a student misses an item, the fault lies with the student's inability to comprehend the reading passage rather than the student's lack of knowledge about the meaning of the words in the item.

ENHANCED MULTIPLE-CHOICE ITEMS

Tasks Requiring Combinations of Abilities

A criticism of teacher-made tests is that they often assess skills and knowledge in fragmented "bits." That is, often teachers will assess knowledge taken out of the context or application in which it ultimately will be used. A teacher may assess skills one at a time. Or a teacher may focus assessment on outcomes or "correct answers" and not attend to the processes students use to reach their answers. One way to correct these deficiencies is to increase usage of complex performance tasks in assessments. We discuss these in the next two chapters. Another way is to be sure that each of your response-choice items requires students to use knowledge and skills in meaningful situations. This usually entails creating items that require students to apply more than one skill at a time.

Multiple-Choice Items

Response-choice scored items, such as multiple-choice, can address many of the preceding criticisms by using enhanced items. **Enhanced multiple-choice items** require students to use knowledge and skills in combinations, often through a carefully crafted context-dependent item set. Enhanced multiple-choice items differ from simple forms of multiple-choice items in the following ways (Psychological Corporation, 1992a):

1. They require students to use knowledge and skill in a context that is similar to real life or to know how the knowledge and skill will be used in new classroom learning.
2. They assess how well students use the thinking and "doing" processes required by the discipline underlying the subject matter.
3. Insofar as possible with paper-and-pencil tasks, they require students to perform actual skills that are the ultimate purpose

of a learning target. Some performances are mental activities (decision making, identifying problem solutions, computations, reading, etc.). These cognitive performances can be assessed efficiently with paper-and-pencil tasks.

4. They require students to use processes and knowledge in combination, sometimes from different subjects or from different teaching units of the same subject matter. This allows you to assess "constellations" of skills and abilities rather than only discrete pieces of learning.

The examples in Figure 10.10 show enhanced multiple-choice items from different curriculum areas. Chapter 8 described how to write more advanced formats for multiple-choice items.

FIGURE 10.10 Examples of enhanced multiple-choice items.

A. Items in language usage

For a class assignment, Tanya is going to write a report about her work at the recycling center.

> **Here is the first part of Tanya's report. Use it to answer Questions 6 and 7.**
>
> Our town has a new recycling center. I work there every
> (1)   (2)
> Saturday. My friend Bob works at the car wash. I have
> (3)   (4)
> learned that our city's dump is getting too full. It is too
> (5)
> full to take any more garbage.

1. Which sentence contains information that does not belong?
   A 2
   B 3
   C 4
   D 5

> **Read the next part of Tanya's report and answer Question 8. This section has groups of underlined words. The questions ask about them.**
>
> Recycling means reusing things instead of throwing
> (6)
> them away. People bring things to the center. Then
> (7)   (8)
> the center sells these things to companies that reuse
> them. This way, natural resources are saved.
> (9)

2. In Sentence 8, how should *Then the center sells* be written?
   A   Then the Center sells
   B   Then the center sells
   C   Then The Center sells

B. Items in science

1. If all of the wasps are killed, which of these will increase first?

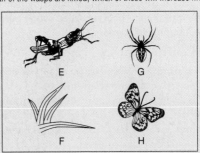

C. Items in social studies

HOW COLE EARNED HIS MONEY

How Cole Earned His Money

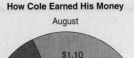

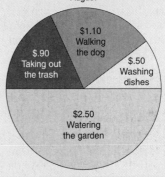

1. Which statement is true based on these graphs?
   A   Cole earned less money watering the garden in September than in August.
   B   Cole earned more money walking the dog in September than August.
   C   Cole washed dishes less often in September than in August.
   D   Cole does not take out the trash on school days.

Source: Adapted from *Focus on: Enhanced Multiple-Choice Questions* (pp. 4, 6–7), by the Psychological Corporation, 1992, by Harcourt, Inc. Reprinted by permission. All rights reserved.

Summary

Assessing Higher-Order Thinking with Context-Dependent Item Sets

- A basic rule for developing tasks to assess higher-order thinking abilities is that the assessment materials should be new or novel to the student: They should not repeat the specific examples you used during instruction and should be phrased in language different from what you used in teaching.
- To assess higher-order thinking abilities, it is often necessary to develop tasks for which the solutions or answers depend on a particular piece (or pieces) of introductory material presented along with them. These are called context-dependent item sets or interpretive exercises.

Concepts and Concept Learning

- A concept is a name that represents a category of things such as persons, objects, events, or relationships.
- A student has learned a concept if the student can identify various new exemplars or instances of it and does not refer to noninstances as exemplars. Tasks assessing concept acquisition need to preserve this criterion.
- You may distinguish between concrete concepts and defined concepts:
  - A concrete concept refers to a category, the members of which have in common one or more physical, tangible qualities that can be heard, seen, tasted, felt, and/or smelled.
  - A defined concept or relational concept refers to a class, the members of which have in common some abstract quality or some relational quality.

Assessing Concrete Concept Learning

- Concrete concepts have been assessed by three procedures:
  - Presenting examples to the student and requiring the student to give the concept a name or label.
  - Presenting a mixture of examples and nonexamples of the concept along with the concept name and requiring the student to identify the examples of the concept.
  - Giving the name of the concept and requiring the student to produce new examples of the concept.
- Assessing concept understanding often requires calling for an indicator performance on the part of the student. You should take care to ensure that the indicator behavior is within the repertoire of the student and to avoid confusing the inability to make an indicator response (e.g., stating the concept name) with lack of understanding the concept.
- Considering the appropriateness of an indicator response is very important when testing young children, bilingual learners, students with special learning difficulties, and students with disabilities.

Assessing Defined Concept Learning

- Defined concepts have been assessed by:
  - Requiring a student to produce a correct definition of a concept.
  - Presenting instances and noninstances of the concept and requiring students to identify the instances of the concept.
  - Giving the name of the concept and requiring a student to produce new instances of the concept.
  - Requiring students to identify the components of a defined concept and give an example of the relationship among the components.

Assessing Concept Understanding at a Deeper Level

- Using complex performance assessments in which students apply the concept to a new situation and connect it to other concepts and relations best assesses a student's deep understanding of a concept. The chapter presents examples of strategies for assessing this understanding.

Assessing Comprehension of Rules and Principles

- A person's behavior is rule-governed or principle-governed if the person regularly responds to a class of concepts with a class of appropriate relational responses.
- To assess whether a student comprehends a rule, you must be certain that the tasks assess more than the student's ability to verbalize or state the rule. You must require the student to apply the rule to a new or novel situation.
- As with assessments of concept understanding, tasks for assessing whether a student comprehends a principle need to present the student with situations that are different from those you used as examples during instruction and phrased in language that is not identical with what you used during instruction.
- Tasks must not become so dependent on reading comprehension that they interfere with identifying students who, although they comprehend the rule, cannot read well.
- Two basic strategies for crafting verbal items that assess comprehension of rules or principles are
  - Presenting the student with the antecedent conditions that are specified in the principle and requiring the student to state or select an example of the consequences that would follow if the rule were to be applied.
  - Presenting the student with the consequences and requiring the student to state or select the antecedent conditions that would have to exist according to the rule to produce the consequences.
- Varieties of tasks similar to the preceding two basic types include
  - Requiring the student to identify inferences or predictions consistent with the application of a principle in a given situation.
  - Requiring the student to produce a new example of an inference or the consequence of applying a principle in a given situation.
  - Requiring the student to produce a statement of the principle that explains a particular situation or set of events.

Assessing Problem-Solving Ability

- Problem solving involves identifying obstacles to attaining a desired outcome and using appropriate ways to overcome these obstacles so the goal is attained. Problem solving can be considered from several perspectives, including whether the problems are well structured or ill structured, whether the solutions are schema driven, and whether solution strategies are subject-matter specific or general. Understanding these perspectives is essential to identifying the appropriate assessment strategy.
- Using the IDEAL problem solver as a framework, the chapter describes and gives examples of tasks you can use to assess specific problem-solving abilities. Strategies are presented for

assessing students' ability to identify and recognize problems, define and represent problems, explore and use heuristics and other solution strategies, and look back and evaluate problem solutions.

Assessing Critical-Thinking Ability

- Critical thinking is the ability to use reasonable, reflective, and effective thinking processes to decide what to do or believe. To assess critical thinking, you must assess both the disposition toward using critical thinking and the ability to apply critical-thinking skills in appropriate ways.
- Dispositions toward critical thinking are the tendencies or habitual uses of critical-thinking abilities. These are listed on page 222. Simple checklists and rating scales for assessing these dispositions were provided.
- Critical-thinking abilities consist of skills and abilities that enable students to analyze actions and statements to determine their credibility, logical consistency, and value implications so the student knows what to do or to believe. The specific abilities comprising critical thinking are listed on page 222–224. The chapter provides strategies and examples of tasks for assessing each of these abilities.

Assessing Other Higher-Order Skills and Abilities

- Using a variety of introductory material such as pictures, maps, graphs, drawings, and paragraphs helps in assessing many learning targets. The examples illustrate the use of context-dependent item sets to assess:
  - Ability to use reference materials.
  - Ability to use graphs and tables.
  - Ability to use maps.
- To develop assessment exercises requiring a student to read and interpret a passage of one or more paragraphs, you should follow the five-step process described in the chapter.
- Critics of those who use short passages for assessing reading comprehension suggest that you should give students one or more longer passages to read that have not been edited for purposes of assessment. Such passages are said to be more realistic and similar to those students are likely to encounter in the real world.
- MAZE items seem more effective than the usual cloze items for assessing reading comprehension.
- Enhanced multiple-choice items assess combinations of skills and knowledge in ways that require students to apply what they know. Examples of the types of items are given in the chapter.
- The ultimate learning targets are those that require students to use their abilities in applications they encounter after schooling is completed. Students will be expected to use combinations of abilities in relatively ill-defined problem situations. Therefore, you should both teach and assess students in ways that foster their growth toward these ultimate learning targets.

Important Terms and Concepts

analyze arguments
ask clarifying questions
checklist
closed-response task
cloze reading exercise
concept

concrete concept
context-dependent item sets
critical thinking
deciding on an action
defined concept
dispositions
enhanced multiple-choice items
exemplar
focus on a question
graph and table reading abilities
habits of mind
heuristic
IDEAL problem solver
identifying assumptions
ill-structured problems
interacting with others
interpretive exercises
judging credibility
judging deductions
judging inductions
judging value definitions
map-reading abilities
MAZE item type
mental model
novel material
open-response task
overgeneralizing a concept
principle
principle-governed thinking
problem
rating scale
relational concepts
schema (schemata)
schema-driven problem solving
undergeneralizing a concept
well-structured problems

Exercises and Applications

1. Identify a principle or rule in a subject you teach or plan to teach. Then complete these tasks:
   a. State the subject and the grade level.
   b. State the principle and give its name.
   c. Describe in general terms the conditions under which it is appropriate to use the principle to solve a problem or explain a phenomenon.
   d. Using general terms, describe the most likely kinds of faulty inferences made or conclusions drawn by students who misinterpret or misapply the principle.
   e. Using the example for Strategy 4: Identifying the consequences of applying a principle on page 215 as a model for format, prepare one multiple-choice item to assess a student's ability to identify an appropriate conclusion to be made when applying this rule. Use the information in your answer to the previous question as a basis for formulating distractors. Use the checklist for judging the quality of multiple-choice items to improve your item.
   f. Using the example for Strategy 2: Producing an example for utilizing a principle on page 214 as a format model, prepare a constructed-response item to assess a student's ability to produce examples of conclusions after applying

the principle. This item should assess the same principle that you used for constructing the multiple-choice item just written.

g. Administer both of these items, one at a time, to a student at the appropriate grade level. Administer the constructed-response item first, then remove it from the student before administering the multiple-choice item.

h. Compare the results you obtained. What were the similarities and differences in the quality of information you received? Which task is more valid? Why?

i. Share your results with others in this class. How do your results compare with theirs? Were there differences with respect to subject matter and grade level assessed? What conclusions can the class draw from its collective experience?

2. For the subject you teach or plan to teach, develop a notebook with well-crafted tasks that assess different problem-solving abilities. Organize your tasks according to the categories of the IDEAL problem solver. Structure your notebook as follows:

a. Craft one assessment task using each of the 17 assessment strategies for problem-solving assessment presented in this chapter.

b. Type one assessment task per page. Label the task with the subject, teaching unit, student grade level, assessment strategy, and category of the IDEAL problem solver the task assesses.

c. On a separate page, craft a scoring rubric for the task and write a sample ideal response.

d. Review your work carefully. Be sure that the content of each task and the scoring rubric are accurate and that the tasks are well crafted.

e. Share your notebook with the other participants in this course.

3. Select a subject and grade level you teach or plan to teach, for which critical thinking is an important learning outcome. Then, complete the following tasks:

a. Identify and briefly describe (in general terms) one or more teaching units in which critical-thinking abilities can be taught and practiced.

b. On a large sheet of paper, create a table in which each row heading is one of the 12 critical-thinking abilities listed on pages 222–224.

c. Label the columns with the teaching and learning activities in the unit(s) that lend themselves to teaching and practicing critical-thinking abilities.

d. For each cell in the body of the table, briefly describe how a student would demonstrate that he or she was engaging in the corresponding critical-thinking ability. Not every cell will be filled, because not every ability can be demonstrated with every activity you list. However, in the table as a whole, all abilities should be demonstrated at least once. If they are not, then add a unit or an activity to your table.

e. Present your table to the others in this course. Discuss your activities and demonstrations. Revise your table on the basis of the discussion. Then share it with the other class members.

4. For the same subject and grade level you identified in Exercise 3, develop a notebook containing samples of tasks assessing each of the 12 critical-thinking abilities listed on pages 222–224. Structure your notebook around the 12 abilities as follows:

a. Craft one assessment task using each of the critical-thinking assessment strategies described in this chapter.

b. Type one assessment task per page. Label the task with the subject, teaching unit, student grade level, assessment strategy, and critical-thinking ability the task assesses.

c. On a separate page, craft a scoring rubric or scoring guide for the task and write a sample ideal response.

d. Review your work carefully. Be sure the content of each task and scoring rubric is accurate. Be sure the tasks are well crafted.

e. Share your notebook with the other members of this course.

5. For a subject and grade level you teach or plan to teach, identify a graph and a table (chart) the students should be able to use:

a. Craft a context-dependent item set for the graph assessing the students' ability to use it beyond simply reading values from it. Craft at least two tasks for the set. Review the items using the appropriate checklists from Chapters 7 and 8. Attach a completed checklist for each item.

b. Share your context-dependent item sets with the other members of this course.

11 | Performance, Portfolio, and Authentic Assessments: An Overview

LEARNING TARGETS

After studying this chapter, you should have learned the following:

What Is Performance Assessment?

1. Distinguish performance tasks from other assessment formats. [1, 3, 6]
2. Distinguish classroom performance activities from performance assessment tasks. [1, 4]

Types of Performance Assessments

3. List, explain, and give examples of the major types of performance assessment. [1, 4, 6]

Authentic Assessments

4. Explain the meaning of authentic assessment and its essential characteristics. [1, 6]

Advantages and Criticisms of Performance Assessments

5. Explain the major advantages and disadvantages of using performance assessment. [1, 6]

How Using Performance Assessment Can Improve Your Teaching

6. Describe how using performance assessments can improve teaching, learning, and assessment validity. [4, 1, 3, 6]

Multiple-Intelligences Perspective on Performance Assessments

7. Explain the strengths and weaknesses of using performance assessments when teaching from a multiple-intelligences perspective. [1, 6]

Important Terms and Concepts

8. Explain how the terms and concepts listed at the end of this chapter apply to educational assessment. [6, 1, 4]

ABOUT THIS CHAPTER

This chapter gives an introduction to performance assessment. First we discuss the meanings and roles of performance assessments in your teaching and helping students to achieve learning targets. Second, we describe the many types of performance assessments and their uses. A map of the performance assessment landscape is included. Third, we discuss authentic assessment, which mirrors the real-world activities for which schools are preparing students. Next, we discuss the advantages and disadvantages of performance assessment for you as a teacher. Fifth, we discuss how you can use performance assessments to your advantage to improve your teaching and students' learning. Last, we discuss the theory of multiple intelligences and its relation to performance assessment. We discuss the special validity concerns that arise when adopting this approach to teaching. In the next chapter, we discuss the details of how to craft performance assessments for your own assessment needs, including projects and portfolios.

WHAT IS PERFORMANCE ASSESSMENT?

Definition

A **performance assessment** (a) presents a task requiring students to do an activity that requires applying their knowledge and skills from several learning targets and (b) uses clearly defined criteria to evaluate how well the student has achieved this application. A performance assessment requires students to do something with their knowledge, such as make something (build a bookshelf), produce a report (report on a group project that surveyed parents' attitudes), or demonstrate a process (show how to measure mass on a laboratory scale). Figure 11.1 shows a decision-making task that a history teacher constructed. The teacher used this one task to assess several types of learning targets derived from the Dimensions of Learning Model (Marzano et al., 1992). (See Appendix E for a summary of these types.)

Balancing Assessment Formats

You should not assess every learning target with performance assessments. Every curriculum is very diverse, and not every learning target requires students to apply their knowledge and skills. Therefore, before choosing an assessment method, you must first be clear what learning target you want to assess, then match the method to it. Some learning targets, for example, require students to learn facts (such as the structure of the nation's government, the main provisions of the Constitution and the Bill of Rights), comprehend an event or a theory, or compare two or more concepts. You should use traditional item formats to obtain valid results when assessing these types of learning targets. You should use performance tasks, on the other hand, to assess learning targets that require students to apply their knowledge and skills as they perform something. A good rule of thumb to remember is that simple learning targets require simple assessment formats; complex learning targets require complex assessment (Arter, 1998).

Essential Characteristics of Performance Assessments

A performance assessment must have two components: the performance task itself and a clear rubric for scoring. A common misconception is that any performance learning activity used in teaching is also an assessment. Nothing can be further from the truth. Classroom assessment requires that you deliberately gather information about how well each student has achieved stated learning targets. This means going beyond simply doing an activity. It means focusing an activity on specific learning targets and evaluating achievement of these learning targets against established criteria. Usually, classroom performance activities lack this scoring rubric component, and thus cannot qualify as assessments.

The Performance Task A **performance task** is an assessment activity that requires a student to demonstrate her achievement by producing an extended written or spoken answer, by engaging in group or individual activities, or by creating a specific product. The high school history example we presented earlier is one such activity. When you use a performance task, you require students to demonstrate directly their achievement of a learning target. You require only indirect demonstration if you ask students simply for a brief answer (e.g., completion items or short-answer) or to select an answer from among options you present to them (matching exercises, true-false items, or multiple-choice items).

The performance task you administered may be used to assess the **product** the student produces and/or the **process** a student uses to complete the product. Depending on the learning target, you may want to evaluate either or both of these aspects. In Chapter 12, you will read more about this distinction and learn how to craft tasks and rubrics that assess product and process.

The Rubrics for Scoring A **scoring rubric** is a coherent set of rules you use to assess the quality of a student's performance: The rules guide your judgments and ensure that you apply your judgments consistently. The rules may be in the form of a rating scale or a checklist. Complex performances require that you assess several learning targets or several parts of the performance. To do this, you use several scoring rubrics: one for each learning target or part. See Chapter 12 for details on how to construct scoring rubrics.

A *rating scale* consists of numerals, such as 0 to 3, or 1 to 4, that reflect the quality levels of performance. Each

FIGURE 11.1 A performance assessment task for a high school history course.

DECISION-MAKING TASK

Suppose you lived in the 1940s and President Harry S. Truman requested that you serve on a White House task force. The goal is to decide on how to force the unconditional surrender of Japan, yet provide for a secure post-war world.

You are a member of the committee of four and have reached the point at which you are trying to decide whether to drop the bomb. Identify the alternatives you are considering and the criteria you are using to make the decision. Explain the values that influenced the selection of the criteria you are using to make the decision. Also explain how your decision has helped you better understand this statement: "War forces people to confront inherent conflicts of values."

Before you begin your task, establish a clear goal and write it down. Then write down a plan for accomplishing your goal. When you are finished with the task, be prepared to describe the changes you had to make in your plan along the way.

As you work on your task, try a variety of sources of information: books, magazine articles, newspapers, and people who lived through the war. Keep a list of those sources and be prepared to describe how you determined which information was most relevant and which information was not very useful. Present your conclusions and findings in at least two of the following ways:

- A written report
- A letter to the president following the completion of the committee meeting
- An article written for *Time* magazine, complete with suggested photos and charts
- A videotape of a dramatization of the committee meeting
- An audio tape
- A newscast
- A mock interview

You will be provided rubrics for and be assessed on each of the following learning targets:

Content Learning Target
1. Your understanding of the principle that war forces sensitive issues to surface and causes people to confront inherent conflicts of values and beliefs.

Information Processing Learning Targets
2. Your ability to review and evaluate how valuable each source of information is to the parts of your project.

Complex Thinking Learning Targets: Decision Making
3. Your ability to identify important and appropriate alternatives to dropping the bomb.
4. Your ability to identify important and appropriate criteria to evaluate each alternative to be considered.
5. Your ability to accurately evaluate the extent to which each of your alternatives meets each criterion.
6. Your ability to select the alternative(s) that adequately meets (meet) the criteria and answer the initial decision question.

Habits of Mind Learning Target
7. Your ability to effectively define your goal in this assignment and to explain your plan for attaining this goal.

Effective Communication Learning Target
8. Your ability to communicate your conclusions and findings in two or more ways.

Source: Adapted from *Assessing Student Outcomes: Performance Assessment Using the Dimensions of Learning Model* (pp. 27–29), by R. J. Marzano, D. Pickering, and J. McTighe, 1993, Alexandria, VA: Association for Supervision and Curriculum Development. Adapted by permission of McREL Institute, 2550 S. Parker Rd., Suite 500, Aurora, CO 80014. Telephone (303) 337-0990. © by McREL Institute. All rights reserved.

numeral corresponds to a verbal description of the quality level it represents. (We present an example in the following paragraphs.) Instead of verbal descriptions, examples of students' work may serve as concrete illustrations of each quality level.

What Makes Your Classroom Performance Assessments Valid?

You must attend to three major points to improve the validity of your student evaluations when you use performance assessment:

1. *Be sure that what you require students to do in your performance activity matches the learning targets and that your scoring rubrics evaluate those same learning targets.* For example, if the learning target says the student must weigh chemicals on the laboratory scale, the performance task must require actual weighing, not an essay on how to use the scale. In addition, you must have a scoring rubric to help you decide how well the student weighs chemicals and not simply specify that chemicals were weighed.

2. *Be sure the performance tasks you craft require students to use curriculum-specified thinking processes.* Once students begin performing these tasks, you can then evaluate those processes.

3. *Be sure to use many different types of assessment procedures (short-answer items, objective items, and a variety of long-term and short-term performance tasks) to sample the breadth of your state's standards and your local curriculum's learning targets.* If your evaluations are based only on one type of assessment format (e.g., if you rely only on performance tasks), you are likely to have an incomplete picture of each student's learning.

TYPES OF PERFORMANCE ASSESSMENTS

Many types of tasks fit the broad definition we adopted here. Figure 11.2 lists most of these. In the paragraphs that follow, we describe them and give examples.

Structured, On-Demand Tasks

You use **structured, on-demand tasks** or exercises when you are the one who decides what and when materials should be used, specifies the instructions for performance, describes the kinds of outcomes toward which students should work, tells the students they are being assessed, and gives students opportunities to prepare themselves for the assessment. Such tasks are also called on-demand (or controlled) tasks.

FIGURE 11.2 Types of performance assessment techniques.

A. Structured, on-demand tasks for individual students, groups, or both
   1. Paper-and-pencil tasks
   2. Tasks requiring equipment and resources beyond paper and pencil
B. Naturally occurring or typical performance tasks
C. Longer-term projects for individual students, groups, or both
D. Portfolios
   1. Best works portfolios
   2. Growth and learning-progress portfolios
	E. Demonstrations
	F. Experiments
	G. Oral presentations and dramatizations
	H. Simulations and contrived situations
	   1. Actors and "standard patients"
	   2. Computerized adaptive audio-visual scenarios
	   3. Computerized adaptive text scenarios
	   4. Computerized audio-visual simulations

Paper-and-Pencil Tasks We have already studied many types of **paper-and-pencil tasks**. In Chapters 7, 9, and 10 we discussed constructed-response and essay items. These formats permit students not only to record their answers but also to give explanations, articulate their reasoning, and express their own approaches toward solving a problem. Sometimes your main focus is on the written product itself, such as the story, report, or drawing a student creates. At other times, you may be more interested in the process the student uses (for example, when a student records the steps he used to complete an experiment or explains how he solved a problem). Here are some additional examples:

Example

Examples of on-demand paper-and-pencil performance tasks

1. Solve this arithmetic story problem and explain how you solved it.
2. Study the following graph that shows how Sally uses her time. Then, write a story about a typical day in Sally's life using the information from the graph.
3. Draw a diagram to illustrate the mathematical ideas in the following word problem.

Tasks Requiring Other Equipment and Resources In subjects such as mathematics, science, mechanical drawing, art, first aid and life-saving, home economics, and driver's education, important outcomes require students to do something with equipment and resources rather than write about how to do it. In some academic subjects, performing a **non-paper-and-pencil task** might be a better option than using a written response, even though either could be done.

For example, in elementary school general science, you would *directly assess* students' understanding and use of the metric system if you required them to measure objects, volume, mass, and so on. You use *indirect assessment* if you require students only to perform numerical conversions from one system or unit of measurement to another, or to answer questions based on pictures of measuring equipment. You could assess students' estimation skills, measuring skills, and systematic thinking skills, for example, all in one task by giving students a jar of beans and some simple

tools. After giving students suitable directions, you can observe how the students solve the problem of estimating the number of beans in the jar. (See Figure 2.2 for an example.) Here are some other examples.

Example

Examples of structured, on-demand, non-paper-and-pencil performance tasks

1. Build as many geometric shapes as possible from this set of four triangles.
2. Talk on this telephone to ask about a job and to request a job application.
3. Show me how to mix acid and water.

You may use non-paper-and-pencil tasks to present problems to be solved by a group, an individual, or some combination of group and individual work. In the latter case, the group may work cooperatively on the task; after the group solves the problem, individuals describe or write up what the group did and the solution to the problem. Non-paper-and-pencil tasks may also be **open response**, allowing for alternative correct performances, or **closed response**, allowing only one best or correct answer. An example of an open-response, non-paper-and-pencil performance task is given next. Notice that in this example the focus is on the *process* students use rather than on the end product.

Example

An open-response science task requiring resources beyond paper and pencil

Task description:

Students must find one or more methods that remove the most debris from dirty water.

Equipment resources for each student:

3 clear plastic graduated cups; 2 clear plastic cups; 30 cc of aquarium charcoal; 30 cc of clean aquarium sand; 4 cotton balls; pencils; transparent tape; paper sacks; a student book containing an outline and a space for answers.

Directions in booklet:

The owner of Finny Fishes Pet Store wants to use some water from a pond in the store's aquariums. The water is not very clean. The owner needs your help to find a method that will take the most dirt out of the water. You will need to keep a record to show the owner of Finny Fishes. [The booklet provides spaces for students to record (a) questions they need to ask to solve the problem, (b) the procedures they use, (c) diagrams and explanatory drawings, (d) the measures they made and the data they collected, and (e) a report of the experiment.]

Directions from teacher:

The teacher reviews the material and booklet; demonstrates how to make one type of filter; encourages asking many different questions, making different filters, recording observations and data, and experimenting with different ways of solving the problem; and assures students that they will be assessed on how they go about solving the problem rather than on finding a single right answer.

Scoring:

Scoring is both holistic and analytic. The analytic scoring includes separate scores for experimenting, collecting data, drawing conclusions, and communicating.

Source: Adapted from *Task 981, Clean Water, Integrated Assessment System: Directions for Administering.* From the Integrated Assessment System: Science Performance Assessment. Copyright © 1992 by Harcourt Assessment Inc. Reproduced by permission. All rights reserved.

Naturally Occurring or Typical Performance Tasks

In opposition to structured, on-demand performances are naturally occurring performances. **Naturally occurring tasks** require you to observe and assess students in natural settings: in typical classroom settings, while on the playground, or while at home. In these settings you are likely to see the way a student typically performs on a learning target, such as cooperating with members of a group to achieve a goal. In natural settings you do not tell students they are being assessed, nor do you control the situation in any way. Here are some examples.

Example

Examples of naturally occurring or typical performance tasks

1. Observe a student's way of dealing with conflicts on the playground.
2. Collect all pieces that each student wrote in every subject and analyze them for grammatical, spelling, and syntactic errors to determine a student's typical language usage (at least in school assignments).
3. Observe whether a student makes change correctly when running a refreshment stand at the school fair.

Although a naturally occurring setting may let you assess a student's typical performance, this is not always

the case. In natural settings you have to wait for the opportunity to arise for a particular student to perform the particular activity you would like to assess. The acivity may not occur while you are observing. This waiting lowers the efficiency of this assessment mode. For example, Task 2, above, is unlikely to provide you with all the information you need to determine a student's command of even the mechanics of writing. Not all spelling patterns and forms of sentence structure a student needs to learn, for example, are likely to appear in every student's writings. Thus, you would have no way of thoroughly assessing students' use of sentence structures.

This simple example illustrates the difficulty of using naturally occurring events as a major source of assessment tasks. Here are the major shortcomings:

- A lot of your time is consumed by waiting.
- You have little control over what performances will occur and when they will occur.
- You cannot ensure that all students will perform the same task.
- You cannot ensure that all students will perform a task under desirable or even similar conditions.
- Teacher time is used inefficiently.

Longer-Term Projects

Individual Student Projects An **individual project** is a long-term activity that results in a student product: a model, a functional object, a substantial report, or a collection. Here are some examples:

Example

Examples of individual student projects

1. Collect and classify newspaper and magazine advertisements in the months before each holiday during the semester.
2. Build a small piece of furniture using the hand tools you learned to use during the semester.
3. Build a working model of a camera using the optical principles taught in this unit.
4. Using resources in the school library, write a research paper on why voter turnout is so low during primary elections.

Figure 11.3 shows that properly crafted projects require students to apply and integrate a wide range of abilities and knowledge; and use creativity, originality, and some sense of aesthetics. When a student writes a library research paper, for example, the student must apply the skills of locating and using reference materials and sources: outlining, organizing, and planning a report; communicating using written language, word processing, and presentation style; and demonstrating his understanding of the

FIGURE 11.3 **Features of projects.**

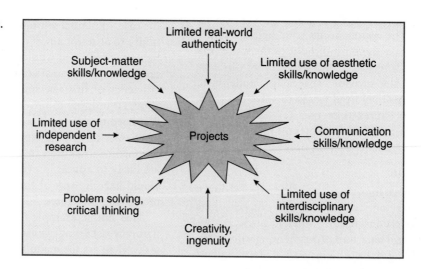

topic. A good project will engage her in critical thinking, creative thinking, and problem solving (see Chapter 10).

Although projects are usually worthwhile educational activities, their usefulness as *assessment tools* for individual students depends on how well you craft them. We discuss how to craft projects in Chapter 12.

Group Projects   A **group project** requires two or more students to work together on a longer project. The major purpose of a group project *as an assessment technique* is to evaluate whether students can work together cooperatively and appropriately to create a high-quality product. The learning targets for a group project depend on the subject matter and the level of the students you are assessing. For example, group projects may focus on:

- *Action-oriented learning targets* (creating a newsletter).
- *Student-interest-oriented learning targets* (writing a paper on a topic they're interested in).
- *Subject-matter-oriented learning targets* (understanding how rivers are formed).
- *Interdisciplinary learning targets* (designing an ideal city) (Harmin, 1994).

We provide suggestions for improving group projects in Chapter 12. An example of a subject-oriented group project is shown in Figure 11.4.

FIGURE 11.4 **A group project in a U.S. history course for students in middle school or high school.**

HISTORICAL INVESTIGATION TASK

In recent years controversy has arisen over the status of Christopher Columbus. Was he a hero or villain? As we study Columbus we will read from a number of resources penned by different historians that will present their views of Columbus.

In cooperative groups, choose at least two resources that describe conflicting reports of events that took place upon Columbus's "discovery" of the New World and during its settlement. Discuss the contradictions you find and try to determine why the historians reported the events differently. Using the resources available, develop a clear explanation of the reasons for the contradictions or present a scenario that clears up the contradictions.

Your group will explain to the class why historians seem to report the same event differently. In addition, your group will offer to the class its ideas for resolving the contradictions. Your group's presentation to the class may be either a dramatization, a panel discussion, or a debate.

Your project will be due 3 weeks from today. Every Friday one member of your group will tell the class the progress you made on the project during the past week, any problems the group had in completing the assignment, and what the group plans to complete during the next week.

Each member of the group will be assessed on the learning targets that follow. You will be provided rubrics for each of the learning targets so you may see more clearly what the assessment will be.

Social Studies Content Learning Target
1. Your understanding that recorded history is influenced by the perspective of the historian.
2. Your understanding of the events surrounding Columbus's discovery and settlement of the New World.

Complex Thinking Learning Targets: Historical Investigation
1. Your ability to identify and explain the confusion, uncertainty, or contradiction surrounding a past event.
2. Your ability to develop and defend a logical and plausible resolution to the confusion, uncertainty, or contradiction surrounding a past event.

Effective Communication Learning Targets
1. Your ability to communicate for a variety of purposes.
2. Your ability to communicate in a variety of ways.

Collaboration Learning Targets
1. Your ability to work with all of the students in your group to complete the project successfully.
2. Your ability to contribute good ideas and resources for presenting the findings to the class.
3. Your ability to do several different kinds of activities to help the group complete the project successfully.

Source: Adapted from *Assessing Student Outcomes: Performance Assessment Using the Dimensions of Learning Model* (p. 60), by R. J. Marzano, D. Pickering, and J. McTighe, 1993, Alexandria, VA: Association for Supervision and Curriculum Development. Adapted by permission of McREL Institute, 2550 S. Parker Rd., Suite 500, Aurora, CO 80014. Telephone (303) 337-0990. © by McREL Institute. All rights reserved.

FIGURE 11.5 General rubrics for assessing collaboration and cooperation as students work in groups.

Learning Target A: Works toward the achievement of group goals.
4   Actively helps to identify group goals and works hard to meet them.
3   Communicates commitment to the group goals and effectively carries out assigned roles.
2   Communicates commitment to the group's goals but does not carry out assigned roles.
1   Does not work toward group goals or actively works against them.

Learning Target B: Demonstrates effective interpersonal skills.
4   Actively promotes effective group interaction and the expression of ideas and opinions in a way that is sensitive to the feelings and knowledge base of others.
3   Participates in group interaction with prompting. Expresses ideas and opinions in a way that is sensitive to the feelings and knowledge base of others.
2   Participates in group interaction without prompting or expresses ideas and opinions without considering the feelings and knowledge base of others.
1   Does not participate in group interaction, even with prompting, or expresses ideas and opinions in a way that is insensitive to the feelings and knowledge base of others.

Learning Target C: Contributes to group maintenance.
4   Actively helps the group to identify changes or modifications necessary in the group process and works toward carrying out those changes.
3   Helps identify changes or modifications necessary in the group process and works toward carrying out those changes.
2   When prompted, helps identify changes or modifications necessary in the group process, or is only minimally involved in carrying out those changes.
1   Does not attempt to identify changes or modifications necessary in the group process, even when prompted, or refuses to work toward carrying out those changes.

Learning Target D: Effectively performs a variety of roles within a group.
4   Effectively performs multiple roles within the group.
3   Effectively performs two roles within the group.
2   Makes an attempt to perform more than one role within the group but has little success with secondary roles.
1   Rejects opportunities or requests to perform more than one role in the group.

Source: Adapted from *Assessing Student Outcomes: Performance Assessment Using the Dimensions of Learning Model* (pp. 87–88), by R. J. Marzano, D. Pickering, and J. McTighe, 1993, Alexandria, VA: Association for Supervision and Curriculum Development. Adapted by permission of McREL Institute, 2550 S. Parker Rd., Suite 500, Aurora, CO 80014. Telephone (303) 337-0990. © by McREL Institute. All rights reserved.

Rubrics for Scoring Project Work Students' performance in this project is assessed along several dimensions or categories of learning targets as described in the section titled "Dimensions of Learning Model" in Chapter 2 and in Appendix E. To assess students, you must develop scoring rubrics that are specific to the project (or adapt the rubrics from other sources). Figure 11.5 displays a set of general scoring rubrics for assessing collaboration and cooperation while working with group tasks. All of these rubrics and anchor points could be rewritten so they apply to the specific project at hand.

Combining Group and Individual Projects In a **combined group and individual project**, groups of students work on a long-term project together, and after the group activities are completed, individuals prepare their own reports without assistance from the other group members. The combination approach is useful when a project is complex and requires the collaborative talents of several students to complete in a reasonable time frame, yet the learning target requires that individual students have the ability to prepare final reports, interpret results on their own, and so on. To assess students in this performance setting you must prepare both group and individual learning targets and scoring rubrics.

Cooperative Learning Strategies Research on cooperative learning indicates that students achieve most when the learning setting requires both group goals and individual accountability:

> Two conditions are essential if the achievement effects of cooperative learning are to be realized. First, the cooperating groups must have a group goal that is important to them. For example, groups may be working to earn certificates or other recognition, to receive a few minutes extra of recess, or to earn bonus points on their grades (although I am philosophically opposed to having grades largely determined by team performance). . . . Second, the success of the group must depend on the individual learning of all group members. That is, there must be individual accountability as well as group accountability. For example, groups might be rewarded based on the average of their members' individual quiz scores. (Slavin, 1988, p. 31)

Assessment in this type of combined group and individual learning project requires assessing a group's joint success on the project as well as the degree to which individuals attained the learning targets.

Portfolios

For purposes of assessment, a **portfolio** is a limited collection of a student's work used either to present the student's best work(s) or to demonstrate the student's educational growth over a given time. A portfolio is not simply a collection of all of a student's work: The works put into a portfolio are limited to those that best serve the portfolio's purpose. A portfolio is neither a scrapbook nor a "dumping ground" for all the student's accomplishments. Items included in a portfolio are carefully and deliberately selected so the collection as a whole accomplishes its purpose. Although there are other purposes for creating a portfolio, this chapter discusses only two assessment purposes:[1] presenting one's best work and demonstrating educational growth.

---

[1]Three other purposes for portfolios include (1) showcasing, in which the student selects his or her favorite works (Paulson, Paulson, & Meyer, 1991); (2) process documenting, in which the student places commentary and documentation for a long-term project (Wolf, 1989); and (3) demonstrating the composite achievement of a group of students (Arter & Spandel, 1992).

Best Works Portfolios A **best works portfolio** contains a student's best final products. You use best works portfolios primarily for summative purposes. Here are examples of some of the purposes that best works portfolios serve.

Example

Examples of best works portfolios

General purpose: Evaluation of individual students

Possible specific purposes

- Evidence of subject-matter mastery and learning.
- Evidence of high-level accomplishment in an area such as art or writing.
- Evidence of minimal competence in a subject for purposes of graduation.
- Evidence of a school district's accomplishments.

Contents of the portfolio

- A student's best works are selected to provide convincing evidence that the student has achieved specific learning targets.

General purpose: Communications

Possible specific purposes

- A student's showcase for his or her parents.
- Pass on information about a student to the next teacher.
- A school's showcase.

Contents of the portfolio

- Examples of accomplishments that may be typical or may impress others.

Very often the contents of the best works portfolio are prescribed. For example, to certify a student's accomplishment in art, educational authorities may require a drawing, a painting, a sculpture, a craft product, and one work in a medium of the student's choosing. In mathematics, an educational authority may require that a student's portfolio contain a table of contents, a letter telling the portfolio evaluator about the entries included, and five to seven best works involving a variety of types of activities, tools, and topics (Kentucky Department of Education, 1993a).

Students need to learn how to create a best works portfolio to present themselves in the best possible way. Among the portfolio-making skills students need to learn are deciding exactly what they want to communicate or accomplish through the portfolio; how to choose the pieces to include in the portfolio; how best to present the pieces chosen; and evaluating the qualities of the pieces selected using the scoring rubrics that will be applied to their portfolios.

As with other forms of performance assessment, you assess best works portfolios only after you have developed a scoring rubric. Scoring rubrics for portfolios usually apply to the entire portfolio rather than to each piece separately, but there are exceptions. We will discuss rubrics for portfolios in Chapter 12.

Growth and Learning-Progress Portfolios A **growth and learning-progress portfolio** contains examples of a student's work, along with comments, that demonstrate how well the student's learning has progressed over a given period. It does not focus on the final products a student produces. Instead, you and the student use the portfolio for formative purposes to monitor the student's learning and thinking progress, to diagnose learning and thinking difficulties, and to guide new learning and thinking. The student plays a significant role in deciding what should be included in this portfolio and learns to use the portfolio to understand and evaluate her own progress. Here are some examples:

Example

Examples of growth and learning-progress portfolios

General purpose: Monitoring progress of individual students

Possible specific purposes

- Teachers and/or students want to review progress and change in achievement.
- Student needs to look over his or her work to see the "long view" or "whole picture" of what has been accomplished.

Contents of the portfolio

- A student's products or works that appear at intermediate stages in the course of the student's learning. These may include early drafts, records of thinking, and rewrites. The final product is placed into the portfolio, too.

General purpose: Daily instruction

Possible specific purposes

- A basis for discussing with the student his ideas and work.
- Keep a record of changes in a student's thinking and conceptual explanations.
- A basis for diagnosing a student's learning difficulties in a subject.

Contents of the portfolio

- Examples of a student's recently completed work, data the student collected, recent findings from an ongoing investigation in the subject matter, a student's own explanations of the work that is underway, etc.

General purpose: Self-reflection and self-guidance

Possible specific purposes

- Reflect on one's own progress in subject knowledge and skill (e.g., in reading).

- Reflect on own changes in how one thinks about events (e.g., how one explains a scientific phenomenon).

- Reflect on one's own progress after reviewing other students' portfolios.

Contents of the portfolio

- Examples of work completed at several points separated in time, records of a student's past and present conceptual thinking about a particular issue in the subject, records of a student's past and present evaluations of his or her own work, etc.

For a growth and learning-progress portfolio to be effective, it must be carefully crafted. We discuss crafting them in Chapter 12.

Using these portfolios requires significant knowledge, skill, and ability. Also, you need to be very well versed in the discipline for which you are assessing progress. You should notice, too, that this type of portfolio assessment activity is considerably more spontaneous and less formal than assessing with best works portfolios. These characteristics are not necessarily weaknesses because the portfolio is used with interactive instruction and as a formative evaluation tool.

Demonstrations

A **demonstration** is an on-demand performance in which a student shows he can use knowledge and skills to complete a well-defined, complex task. Demonstrations are not as long or as complex as projects. Demonstrations are usually closed-response tasks. Tasks comprising a demonstration are often well defined and the "right" or "best way" is often known to both the student and the evaluator. However, individual variations are permitted; style and manner of presentation often count when a student presents a demonstration. The 4-H Clubs often use demonstrations: Boys and girls demonstrate their skills in a variety of agricultural and homemaking areas.

In schools, students may demonstrate their skills in proper techniques such as in the following examples.

Example

Examples of demonstrations for assessment

1. Demonstrate the proper way to knead dough for bread.

2. Demonstrate how to set up the microscope for viewing stained slides.

3. Demonstrate how to climb a rope.

4. Demonstrate how to look up information on the Internet.

For the most part, demonstrations focus on how well a student uses her skills, rather than on how well the student can explain her thinking or articulate the principles underlying a phenomenon. If you use a demonstration for assessment purposes, you should carefully identify the appropriate learning target and use an appropriate scoring rubric.

Experiments

An **experiment** or *investigation* is an on-demand performance in which a student plans, conducts, and interprets the results of an empirical research study. The study focuses on answering specific research questions (e.g., "Do most students in this school support the death-penalty laws of this state?") or on investigating specific research hypotheses ("A brightly colored advertisement will be remembered longer"). As defined here, experiments or investigations include a wide range of research activities that occur in both natural and social science disciplines. They include field and survey research investigations as well as laboratory and control-group experiments and may be conducted as individual or as group activities.

Experiments let you assess whether students use proper inquiry skills and methods. You can also assess whether students have developed proper conceptual frameworks and theoretical, discipline-based explanations of the phenomena they have investigated. To assess these latter aspects, focus on the quality of students' frames of reference, their mental representations of the problem they are studying, how well they plan or design the research, the quality of the questions or hypotheses they can specify, and the quality of explanations they offer for why the data relationships exist.

To assess these abilities, craft your experiment or investigation task so that students must:

1. Make estimates and predictions before they begin collecting data.

2. Gather their own data, analyze them, and display the results of the analyses.

3. Draw conclusions and support them by citing the appropriate evidence they collected.

4. State their assumptions and identify possible sources of error in their methods or data.

5. Effectively communicate the findings of the experiment or investigation. (Barone, 1991)

Oral Presentations and Dramatizations

Oral presentations permit students to verbalize their knowledge and use their oral skills in the form of interviews, speeches, or oral presentations. Decide which learning targets should be the focus of the oral presentations. In language and language-arts curricula, for example, many learning targets focus on style and communication skills rather than on the correctness of the content. Fluency of speaking a foreign language is an important learning target in some curricula. Here is an example of the major anchor points in a proficiency-level scale suggested for use in an oral proficiency interview in a foreign language:

Example

Example of a description of competency levels for assessing oral proficiency in a foreign language

Proficiency level	Description
Superior	The Superior level is characterized by the speaker's ability to: • participate effectively in most formal and informal conversations on practical, social, professional, and abstract topics; and • support opinions and hypotheses using natural and idiomatic discourse strategies.
Advanced	The Advanced level is characterized by the speaker's ability to: • converse in a clear, participatory fashion; • initiate, sustain, and bring to closure a wide variety of communicative tasks, including those that require an increased ability to convey meaning with diverse language strategies due to a complication or an unforeseen turn of events; • satisfy the requirements of school and work situations; and narrate and describe with paragraph-length connected discourse.
Intermediate	The Intermediate level is characterized by the speaker's ability to: • create with the language by combining and recombining learned elements, though primarily in a reactive mode; • initiate, minimally sustain, and close in a simple way basic communicative tasks; and • ask and answer questions.
Novice	The Novice level is characterized by the ability to communicate minimally with learned material.

Source: Adapted from *Oral Proficiency Interview: Tester Training Manual*, by American Council on the Teaching of Foreign Languages, 1989, Yonkers, NY: Author. Adapted with permission.

Another area in which oral presentations are especially useful is in speaking to a group. Figure 11.6 shows a simple scale for assessing the delivery of a classroom speech.

Debates are a special type of oral performance. A **debate** pits one student against another to argue issues logically in a formal exchange of views. Assessment focuses on the logical and persuasive quality of the argument and the rebuttals. Other *forensic activities* include poetry reading and oratories.

Dramatizations combine verbalizations, oral and elocution skills, and movement performances. Students may express their understanding of fictional characters or historical persons, for example, by acting a role showing ideological positions and personal characteristics of these persons. Although dramatizations usually involve oral skills, occasionally they may not. For example, after reading about Huck Finn, a teacher could ask the student to pantomime the way Huck Finn might act in a classroom (Armstrong, 1994).

Simulations and Contrived Situations

Actors and "Standardized Patients" **Simulations** are on-demand events that happen under controlled conditions and attempt to mimic naturally occurring events. When the performance to be evaluated is the ability to interact with another person, an actor may be trained to play the role of the other person. Originally the **standardized patient format** was used to assess the clinical skills of medical candidates and practicing doctors. The actor is trained to display the symptoms of a particular disorder. Each medical candidate meets and interviews this standardized patient to diagnose the illness and to prescribe treatment. A panel of evaluators observes this interaction and assesses the candidate.

Computerized Adaptive Audiovisual Scenarios The combined technologies of video, CD-ROM, audio, and computers may be used to present realistic situations to students. A computer then evaluates students' responses to these presentations. If the situation presented is reasonably structured and the number of possible actions is limited, an **adaptive assessment task** can be built whereby a student's response to one situation will determine what the next presentation will be. For example, the media present a **scenario** to the student and ask a question or call for a decision. The student responds, and the presentation continues in a way that depends on the response. In this way each student receives a somewhat different scenario, depending on his choices of action.

Computerized Adaptive Text Scenarios This assessment format is similar to the adaptive audiovisual scenario format, except that text displays replace multimedia presentation.

Computerized Audiovisual Simulations With rapid advances in technology and software, multimedia simulations have become more realistic and complex. In middle school science, for example, computers can simulate hands-on investigations (Shavelson & Baxter, 1991). In a sow bug investigation, students investigate what the "computer sow

FIGURE 11.6 Example of a simple rating scale for assessing the quality of a student's oral presentation.

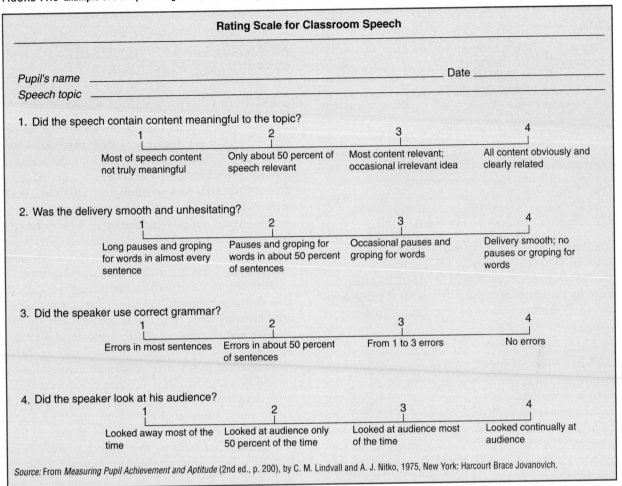

Source: From *Measuring Pupil Achievement and Aptitude* (2nd ed., p. 200), by C. M. Lindvall and A. J. Nitko, 1975, New York: Harcourt Brace Jovanovich.

bugs" do when simulated light and moisture are varied. Virtual reality technology offers more promise in this area. Flight simulators are examples of how technology combines with a sophisticated knowledge base of the conditions of the live performance and the consequences of different actions.

The advantages of this and the preceding formats are greater economy and consistency compared to real life, and the potential for computerized scoring (Jones, 1994). The further away from actual situations and real people the simulation gets, the less realistic and meaningful it is. Often, classroom teachers cannot use simulations because they are unavailable. These are the principal disadvantages of these formats.

AUTHENTIC ASSESSMENTS

Performance assessment is sometimes called **alternative assessment** or **authentic assessment**. These terms are not interchangeable, however. The "alternative" in *alternative assessment* usually means in opposition to standardized

achievement tests and to multiple-choice (true-false, matching, completion) item formats. From an educational philosophy perspective, the "authentic" in *authentic assessment* usually means presenting students with tasks that are directly meaningful to their education instead of indirectly meaningful. For example, reading several long works and using them to compare and contrast different social viewpoints is directly meaningful because it is the kind of thoughtful reading educated citizens do. Reading short paragraphs and answering questions about the "main idea" or about what the characters in the passage did, on the other hand, is indirectly meaningful because it is only one fragment or component of the ultimate learning target of realistic reading. "Realistic" and "meaningful" are terms educators writing about authentic assessment often use. As we shall discuss later, these terms also beg further questions, such as, "Realistic in which context?" and "Meaningful for whom?"

Authentic Characteristics Performance assessment material you read outside this textbook makes reference to authentic assessment. This usually means that students are assessed on tasks that are directly educationally meaningful. **Authentic tasks** have the following characteristics (Wiggins, 1990):

1. They require students to use their knowledge to do a meaningful task.
2. They are complex and require students to use combinations of different knowledge, skills, and abilities.
3. They require high-quality polished, complete, and justifiable responses, performances, or products.
4. They clearly specify standards and criteria for assessing the possibly multiple correct answers, performances, or products.
5. They simulate the ways in which students should use combinations of knowledge, skills, and abilities in the real world.
6. They present to students ill-structured "challenges and roles" that are similar to those roles and tasks they are likely to encounter as adults at work and at home.

Your review of the types of performance tasks shows that not all of them exhibit all of Wiggins's authenticity characteristics. Further, you should recognize that there are **degrees of authenticity**: tasks will vary in the degree to which they meet any one of the characteristics just described.

Valuable in Their Own Right   Rhetoric surrounding authentic assessment tasks often justifies them by criticizing formats such as multiple-choice, matching, true-false, and short-answer tasks (Hambleton & Murphy, 1992). Such discussions also criticize the use of standardized tests (see Chapter 16 for a summary of these criticisms). Those educators who do not distinguish their criticisms about how standardized tests' results are used from their criticisms about the merits of using objective assessment tasks mislead and confuse you. Further, such "test bashing" often is unnecessary: Compelling arguments can be made for using performance assessment without putting down either objective tasks or standardized tests.

Practical Considerations   Reviews of the authentic assessment literature (Barone, 1991; Horvath, 1991; Jones, 1994) suggest that you should incorporate the following four features into authentic assessments:

1. *Emphasize applications*—Assess whether a student can use his knowledge in addition to assessing what the student knows.
2. *Focus on direct assessment*—Assess the stated learning target directly as contrasted with indirect assessment.
3. *Use realistic problems*—Frame the tasks in a highly realistic way so that students can recognize them as a part of everyday life.
4. *Encourage open-ended thinking*—Frame the tasks to encourage more than one correct answer, more than one way of expressing the answer, groups of students working together, and taking a relatively long time to complete (e.g., several days, weeks, months).

We shall discuss the details of constructing performance assessment in Chapter 12.

ADVANTAGES AND CRITICISMS OF PERFORMANCE ASSESSMENTS

Classroom Activities Versus Assessment

You now have a good idea of the wide range of performance assessment techniques and that choosing the proper technique depends very much on the learning targets you wish to assess. You should recognize, however, that not all **classroom performance activities** are assessment tasks. When you teach, you use many learning activities to engage students' interest, to give them experience, and to give practice with the learning targets. Many of these activities are useful teaching tools and resemble the performance tasks described in the preceding section.

Performance tasks become assessment tools when you craft the tasks primarily for their value as assessment procedures rather than primarily as opportunities for student practice and enrichment. Assessments must also include criteria and a scoring rubric.

This is not to say that performance assessment tasks should be radically different from practices and enrichment activities. However, you use the tasks primarily to gather information about students' progress on specific learning targets rather than primarily as student learning activities for those targets. This distinction is similar to the formative and summative student evaluation distinction discussed in Chapter 6. That is, you can use all student activities as occasions for informally gathering formative information about students' progress, but summative evaluation requires a more careful focus on gathering high-quality information from tasks you create specifically for this purpose.

Advantages of Performance Assessment   Performance assessments have several advantages over other assessments. These advantages (Hambleton & Murphy, 1992; Linn & Gronlund, 1995; Oosterhof, 1994; Rudner & Boston, 1994; Shepard, 1991; Stiggins, 1994; Wiggins, 1990) are summarized here:

1. *Performance tasks clarify the meaning of complex learning targets.* Authentic performance tasks match complex learning targets to a close degree. When you present them to students and share them with parents, you make the learning goals clear through actual example.

2. *Performance tasks assess the ability "to do."* An important school outcome is the ability to use knowledge and skill to solve problems and lead a useful life, rather than simply to answer questions about doing.

3. *Performance assessment is consistent with modern learning theory.* Modern learning theory emphasizes that students should use their previous knowledge to build new

knowledge structures, be actively involved in exploration and inquiry through task like activities, and construct meaning for themselves from educational experience. This is called the constructivist approach to learning. Most performance assessments engage students and actively involve them with complex tasks. Many performance tasks require exploration and inquiry.

4. *Performance tasks require integration of knowledge, skills, and abilities.* Complex performance tasks, especially those that span longer periods, usually require students to use many different skills and abilities. Portfolio assessment, projects, and research reports, for example, require a student to use knowledge from several different subject areas and many different abilities.

5. *Performance assessments may be linked more closely with teaching activities.* When your teaching requires students to be actively involved in inquiry and performance activities, performance assessments are a meaningful component. This is not an advantage of performance assessment if your teaching is primarily teacher directed or uses lecture style.

6. *Performance tasks broaden the approach to student assessment.* Introducing performance assessment along with traditional objective formats broadens the types of learning targets you assess and offers students a variety of ways of expressing their learning. This increases the validity of your student evaluations.

7. *Performance tasks let teachers assess the processes students use as well as the products they produce.* Many performance tasks offer you the opportunity to watch the way a student goes about solving a problem or completing a task. Appropriate scoring rubrics help you collect information about the quality of the processes and strategies students use, as well as assess the quality of the finished product.

Disadvantages of Performance Assessments

Although performance assessments offer several advantages over traditional objective assessment procedures, they have some distinct disadvantages (Hambleton & Murphy, 1992; Linn & Gronlund, 1995; Miller & Seraphine, 1993; Oosterhof, 1994; Rudner & Boston, 1994):

1. *High-quality performance tasks are difficult to craft.* Good performance assessments match complex learning targets. You will need to learn a significant number of skills to create high-quality tasks. We discuss how to craft performance tasks in Chapter 12.

2. *High-quality scoring rubrics are difficult to craft.* This is especially true when you want to assess complex reasoning ability or permit multiple correct answers and products. Scoring rubric creation is also covered in Chapter 12.

3. *Completing performance tasks takes students a lot of time.* Even short on-demand paper-and-pencil tasks take 10 to 20 minutes per task to complete. Most authentic tasks take days or weeks to complete. If your assessments are not part of

your instructional procedures themselves, this means either administering fewer tasks (thereby reducing the reliability of the results) or reducing the amount of instructional time.

4. *Scoring performance task responses takes a lot of time.* The more complex the performance and the product, the more time you can expect to spend on scoring. You can reduce the scoring time by crafting high-quality scoring rubrics. Holistic scoring is quicker than analytic scoring.

5. *Scores from performance tasks may have lower scorer reliability.* With complex tasks, multiple correct answers, and fast-paced performances, scoring depends on your own scoring competence. If two teachers use different frameworks, have different levels of competence, use a different scoring rubric, or use no scoring rubrics at all, they will mark the same student's performance or product quite differently. Inconsistent scoring is not only frustrating to a student, it also lowers the reliability and validity of the assessment results. High levels of scorer reliability can be obtained, however, if scorers use the same well-defined rubrics, are well trained, and are monitored so they don't drift away from the standards set in the rubrics (Linn, 1993). Scorer reliability is especially problematic for portfolio assessment (Koretz, Stecher, Klein, & McCaffrey, 1994). However, portfolio scorer reliability can be improved.

6. *Students' performance on one task provides little information about their performance on other tasks.* A serious problem with performance assessments is that a student's performance on a task very much depends on her prior knowledge, the particular wording and phrasing of the task, the context in which it is administered, and the specific subject-matter content embedded in the task (Lane et al., 1992; Linn, 1993; Shavelson & Baxter, 1991). This results in low reliability from the content-sampling point of view. (See Chapter 4.) In other words, you may have to use six or seven performance tasks to evaluate reliably a student in a unit of instruction.

The educational importance of these findings is this: Whenever a learning target implies that a student should be able to perform several quite different tasks under varied conditions and in several contexts (which is almost always!), your assessment must include many different types of tasks, not just one. The validity of your assessment results is low whenever you use too few tasks.

7. *Performance tasks do not assess all learning targets well.* If a learning target focuses on memorizing and recalling, then objective format items such as short-answer, multiple-choice, matching, and true-false are better assessment choices. If your learning targets emphasize logical thinking, understanding concepts, or verbal reasoning, objective formats may still be a better choice than performance formats. They allow a much broader content to be assessed and can assess that broad coverage in less time. Further, objective formats are easier to score and the results from them are more reliable. A balanced assessment approach is recommended.

8. *Completing performance tasks may be discouraging to less able students.* Complex tasks that require students to sustain their interest and intensity over a long period may discourage less able students. They may see the high standards implied by such tasks as beyond their reach. They may have partial knowledge of the learning target but may fail to complete the task because it does not allow them to use or express this partial knowledge effectively. Group projects may help by permitting peers to share the work, use each other's partial knowledge and differential skills, and motivate one another.

9. *Performance assessments may underrepresent the learning of some cultural groups.* Although performance assessments allow the opportunity for students to use their backgrounds in diverse ways and allow multiple correct solutions, you may find it difficult to craft tasks—especially scoring rubrics—to take advantage of this diversity. If you are not knowledgeable about how different cultural groups express their higher thinking skills, you may systematically bias your assessments of them. Further, some groups perform better on some types of tasks than others (e.g., word problems vs. computational mathematics).

Performance tasks will not wash away differences among cultural groups; in fact, they are likely to make such differences more apparent. Multiple assessment formats may improve this situation somewhat because they allow knowledge, skills, and ability to be expressed in different formats and media, thus allowing students with different backgrounds to express their achievement of the learning targets in different ways. After reviewing the research literature regarding performance assessments and equity, Baker and O'Neil (1994) drew this conclusion:

> If it is believed that performance-based assessment, if not the only solution, is at least a critical component of integrative educational reform, then attempts must be made to remedy its obvious potential for injury. These remedies include improving the design measures and scoring procedures so that differences in students' world knowledge, specific prior knowledge, perception of meaningfulness, and language facility are considered explicitly. Administration conditions, including climate, setting, and logistical support, must also be comparable. Furthermore, qualifications of raters including their training to avoid ethnic interactions, the models of student performance, and comparable standards of judgment must be made public and subject to independent review. Of course, the real key is that students receive truly comparable and equitable teaching offered in safe environments from qualified teachers with high expectations. Research into all these aspects needs to continue. (p. 24)

10. *Performance assessments may be corruptible.* As you use performance assessments, you will teach your students how to do well on them. This amounts to coaching them how to perform (often called "teaching to the test"). If your coaching amounts to teaching all aspects of your state's standards

and your school's curriculum framework's learning targets, you are doing the right thing. However, if you focus primarily on only one aspect of the learning targets (e.g., how to write answers to constructed-response social studies items), you will lower the validity of your results.

In Chapters 2 and 10, we said that a student's use of higher-order thinking is best assessed when the student faces new or novel tasks. Coaching tends to reduce the novelty of the task or change it from an "application" task to a "following-the-solution-strategy-the-teacher-taught-me" task. These types of coaching reduce the validity of your results because they do not assess the main intent of learning targets that want students to learn to solve new and ill-structured problems. The quality of a student's education is thereby reduced.

HOW USING PERFORMANCE ASSESSMENT CAN IMPROVE YOUR TEACHING

You may improve your teaching by using performance assessments and performance learning activities as follows:

1. *Require students to complete a well-crafted performance task, giving them the opportunity to apply their learning to a new situation.* This shows them that learning must not be limited to repeating what teacher said.

2. *Craft performance tasks to help students make connections between the skills and abilities they learned in separate subjects.* For example, students must integrate skills and abilities in language arts, mathematics, science, and social studies when they conduct, analyze, and write up a survey of students' opinions in their school.

3. *Craft performance tasks to help students realize the connections between "schoolhouse" learning and real-world activities.* This realization is likely when performance tasks are the same as those people use in real life (planning a trip using a map, using a bus timetable, and making a travel budget) or tasks that involve current events (comparing local politicians' points of view as expressed in speeches, advertisements, and daily newspapers).

4. *Share your scoring rubrics with students to clarify the learning targets for them.* The more students understand the skills and abilities they should use, the better they are able to identify where they should focus their practice and study efforts.

MULTIPLE INTELLIGENCES PERSPECTIVE ON PERFORMANCE ASSESSMENTS

Theory of Multiple Intelligences

In some schools teachers organize their teaching around Howard Gardner's (1983, 1991, 1993) **theory of multiple intelligences**. This theory says that all persons have not

FIGURE 11.7 Summary of the eight intelligences described in Gardner's work.

Intelligence Type	Description
Linguistic intelligence	Capacity to use your own and other languages to express yourself and to understand others.
Logical-mathematical intelligence	Capacity to understand underlying causal principles in ways similar to scientists or logicians, or to use quantitative and mathematical reasoning in ways similar to mathematics.
Spatial intelligence	Capacity to represent the spatial aspects of the world in your mind in ways similar to airplane pilot navigators, chess players, painters, sculptors, or architects.
Bodily kinesthetic intelligence	Capacity to use part or all of your body to solve a problem, make a product, or perform in ways similar to athletes, actors, or dancers.
Musical intelligence	Capacity to mentally process music in a way that recognizes patterns, remembers patterns, and manipulates music to solve problems or to express understanding.
Interpersonal intelligence	Capacity to understand and meaningfully relate to other people. This is accomplished through understanding other persons: what they are able to do, how they approach the world and others, what their reactions are likely to be, what they like, what they avoid, and what they might be feeling.
Intrapersonal intelligence	Capacity to understand yourself, knowing who you are, your strengths and limitations, your goals and aspirations, how you feel, what you should avoid, and how you will react in various situations.
Naturalist intelligence	Capacity to understand nature and the modern world by discriminating among and classifying living and nonliving natural things, as well as among human-made things.

Source: Adapted and paraphrased from Howard Gardner's statements in "The First Seven. . . and the Eighth: A Conversation with Howard Gardner," by K. Checkley, 1997, *Educational Leadership, 55*(1), 12.

one, but eight intelligences, although some persons are stronger in some of these areas than others. These intelligences are briefly described in Figure 11.7.

These particular capacities were selected as intelligences because they fit certain criteria. They are (a) necessary for our survival, (b) evolutionary capacities (i.e., existing to some extent in nonhuman animals), and (c) detected by specific brain activities. This theory has inspired an educational philosophy and numerous classroom practices that teach students to (a) be aware that they can be smart in several different ways; (b) appreciate the value of different intelligences in themselves and others; (c) use, practice, and improve all of their intelligences to the best of their ability; and (d) demonstrate their achievement of learning targets by using two or more intelligences (Campbell, 1997).

Performance Assessment Is Part of the Multiple Intelligences Approach

It is not our purpose to endorse or even expand on the multiple intelligences educational approach. You should be aware that advocates of this approach value using performance assessments. They believe performance assessments allow students' achievements to be demonstrated and evaluated in several different ways. As Gardner writes, "The current emphasis on performance assessment is well supported by the theory of multiple intelligences. . . . One, let's not look at things through the filter of a short-answer test. Let's look instead at the performance that we

value, whether it is linguistic, logical, aesthetic, or social performance; and, two, let's never pin our assessments of understanding on just one particular measure, but let's always allow students to show their understanding in a variety of ways" (interview in Checkley, 1997).

Using Assessment Menus

If you wish to assess in a way that is consistent with this educational approach, you would need to hold high standards for students' achievement of learning targets, and at the same time allow students to demonstrate that achievement in multiple ways. Figure 11.8 shows one example of a **multiple intelligences assessment menu**. Within each type of intelligence the menu contains several suggestions for different performances a student might select to demonstrate her achievement of the learning target. Advocates of the approach would ask students to demonstrate their achievement by using one method from each of two or more intelligences (e.g., Campbell, 1997; Silver, Strong, & Perini, 1997).

Concerns About the Validity of Multiple Intelligences Assessment Menus

Menus Not Tied to Learning Targets and Scoring Criteria Are Missing You should be aware that although much has been written about this approach to teaching, there is very little sound research to demonstrate the validity of the corresponding assessments. If you read the testimonies of

FIGURE 11.8 Example of a multiple intelligences assessment menu. Students are allowed to demonstrate their achievement of learning targets by choosing an assessment model from one or more of the intelligences categories.

Multiple Intelligences Menus

Linguistic Menu
Use storytelling to explain _____
Conduct a debate on _____
Write a poem, myth, legend, short play, or news article
  about _____
Create a talk show radio program about _____
Conduct an interview of _____ on _____

Logical-Mathematical Menu
Translate a _____ into a mathematical formula
Design and conduct an experiment on _____
Make up syllogisms to demonstrate _____
Make up analogies to explain _____
Describe the patterns or symmetry in _____
Others of your choice _____

Bodily-Kinesthetic Menu
Create a movement or sequence of movements to
  explain _____
Make task or puzzle cards for _____
Build or construct a _____
Plan and attend a field trip that will _____
Bring hands-on materials to demonstrate _____

Visual Menu
Chart, map, cluster, or graph _____
Create a slide show, videotape, or photo album of _____
Create a piece of art that demonstrates _____
Invent a board or card game to demonstrate _____
Illustrate, draw, paint, sketch, or sculpt _____

Musical Menu
Give a presentation with appropriate musical accompaniment
  on _____
Sing a rap or song that explains _____
Indicate the rhythmical patterns in _____
Explain how the music of a song is similar to _____
Make an instrument and use it to demonstrate _____

Interpersonal Menu
Conduct a meeting to address _____
Intentionally use _____ social skills to learn about _____
Participate in a service project to _____
Teach someone about _____
Practice giving and receiving feedback on _____
Use technology to _____

Intrapersonal Menu
Describe qualities you possess that will help you successfully
  complete _____
Set and pursue a goal to _____
Describe one of your personal values about _____
Write a journal entry on _____
Assess your own work in _____

Naturalist Menu
Create observation notebooks of _____
Describe changes in the local or global environment _____
Care for pets, wildlife, gardens, or parks _____
Use binoculars, telescopes, microscopes, or
  magnifiers to _____
Draw or photograph natural objects _____

Source: From "Variations on a Theme: How Teachers Interpret MI Theory," by L. Campbell, 1997, *Educational Leadership, 55*(1) 14–18 (figure on page 18). Permission granted by Educational Leadership Association for Supervision and Curriculum Development, Alexandria, VA.

the enthusiasts, you will see very useful and interesting performance activities. Students will no doubt enjoy these activities. Often, however, *well-crafted criteria are either not provided or only vaguely described.* Often, too, the enthusiast has not described the specific curriculum learning targets for which the activity is specifically designed. Gardner himself advocates that teachers use combinations of intelligences to help students be successful in school-based learning targets, rather than teaching only the intelligences themselves (interview in Checkley, 1997). This point is sometimes lost in discussions of the assessment part of multiple intelligences teaching.

Activities in the Menu Are Not Equivalent Other validity issues that have not been addressed are the generalization and meaning of students' assessment results from different menu formats in Figure 11.8. It should be clear to you that each of the entries in the menu is qualitatively different—the activities are nonequivalent; they cannot be simply interchanged. Here are some questions you must answer if you use a multiple intelligences assessment menu in your classroom assessment:

- Although students can use different demonstrations, do the different demonstrations address the same learning target in the same way?

- Are the modalities of the different formats such that some of them do not assess the main intent of the particular learning target?

- Is it unclear whether the same standards and criteria can (or should) apply across modalities?

- Would the same criteria or same scoring rubric apply, for example, to a student's movement sequence that explains when an airplane should begin its landing descent from 30,000 feet as would singing a rap song for the same explanation? (For further discussion of this point, see the "Response Mode" section on page 267 in Chapter 12.)

Will Students Craft Valid Tasks? Finally, there is the issue of who will craft the scoring rubrics and the tasks themselves. It is one matter to have students select from among several well-crafted tasks that have been carefully prepared to be equivalent demonstrations of a learning target. It is another to expect students to develop their own assessment tasks and scoring rubrics.

Performance Activities Versus Performance Assessment

The area of multiple intelligences is a good one to emphasize the differences between performance learning experiences on one hand and performance assessment on the other. Assessment is not just the activity. Good assessment requires that criteria and scoring rubrics be well defined and validly applied. An assessment must describe how well a student has achieved. Classroom activities do not have such requirements: If students and teachers enjoy them, and through engaging in several activities, students learn something, then the activities are successful. Appropriate assessment is needed, however, before you can describe specifically how well each student has achieved the learning targets.

Suggestion for Improving Validity of Multiple Intelligences Assessment

Align Activities to Learning Targets and Use Well-Defined Scoring Criteria If you wish to use performance assessments in a multiple intelligences program, you will need to worry about the validity of your assessment results. We suggest that you state clearly the particular academic learning targets to be taught by this approach. Do use multiple methods of assessment that are consistent with the intentions of the approach. However, be very clear about the achievement criteria and scoring rubrics. Perhaps it will be appropriate to use the same scoring rubrics to evaluate the academic learning target for all ways of assessment a student chooses from the menu.

Craft Tasks for Students and Have Common Tasks You may need to craft the performance tasks for students to obtain the information you need to evaluate the student, rather than relying on student-crafted tasks. It may be useful, too, to have one performance task that all students must do and then allow for alternatives after that. Keeping one task in common will help you decide the weakness and/or the value-added information for assessing a student that comes from the student-selected alternatives.

Summary

What Is Performance Assessment?

- Performance assessments require students to demonstrate their ability to complete a task using their knowledge and skills from several areas rather than simply recalling information or saying how to do a task.
- Because curricular areas are very diverse, not all learning targets focus on performance, and thus not all assessments should be performance assessments.

- Performance assessments must have two components: (a) a task to perform and (b) a rubric for evaluating the quality of students' performance on the task.
- Scoring rubrics should fit together into a coherent assessment framework that matches the emphasis of the curriculum framework. This usually means creating a general rubric describing the main content and process areas to be assessed and a specific rubric that applies all these areas to the particular task at hand.
- Performance assessments can improve the validity of classroom assessment results if they are appropriately matched to the curriculum framework's learning targets, match your teaching emphasis, and are included with more objective assessment formats so that all important learning targets are assessed.

Types of Performance Assessments

- You can choose from a wide variety of performance task formats, but all are not equally valid. Format choice is guided primarily by its match to the main intent of your curriculum framework's learning targets. A mismatch between task format and learning targets or teaching emphasis will lower the validity of the results, even if authentic performance tasks are used.
- These are the major performance task formats: structured, on-demand tasks (paper-and-pencil and non-paper-and-pencil); naturally occurring or typical performance; longer-term projects (individual, group, and combined); portfolios (best works, and growth and learning-progress); demonstrations; experiments or investigations; oral presentations and dramatizations (includes debates); and simulations (standardized patients, computerized adaptive audiovisual scenarios, computerized text scenarios, simulations).
- A portfolio culture model uses growth and learning progress as the focus of instructional activity. The portfolio used with this model includes authentic work, examples of a student's growth in conceptual understanding and examples of a student's use of reflective thinking.
- Although performance types of classroom activities may be worthwhile teaching techniques, not all such activities lend themselves to high-quality formative and summative assessments. An assessment task—performance or not—needs to be crafted carefully to achieve its purpose.

Authentic Assessments

- Authentic performance assessment tasks emphasize applications, focus on direct assessment, use realistic problems, and encourage open-ended thinking. Not all performance assessment tasks are authentic.
- Performance assessments can and should be justified in their own right rather than by bashing other assessment tools and formats. Teachers should not be fooled by spurious arguments. They should demand that advocates of any assessment technique justify the technique in its own right.
- A performance assessment task need not be authentic to be interesting, challenging, and engaging.

Advantages and Criticisms of Performance Assessments

- Advantages of performance assessments include their potential to clarify learning targets; assess "doing"; be consistent with modern learning theory; assess integration of knowledge, skills, and abilities; link with teaching activities; broaden the basis for assessment when combined with other assessment formats; and assess students' use of processes as well as products.

- Disadvantages of performance assessment techniques include their difficulty to craft and score; requirement for large amounts of assessment and scoring time; unreliable scoring; low generalization across different task content; tendency to focus on a narrow set of learning targets; tendency to discourage less able students; tendency to underrepresent the learning of some cultural groups; and possibile corruptibility.

How Using Performance Assessment Can Improve Your Teaching

- Performance assessments may improve teaching and learning if they are well integrated with instruction, if criteria for performance is clearly stated and understood by all students, if these performance criteria are used appropriately and consistently by the teacher and students, and if students received detailed feedback.

Multiple Intelligences Perspective on Performance Assessments

- Advocates of Gardner's multiple intelligences approach encourage using performance activities in the classroom, but often do not provide teachers with performance assessment tools. Multiple intelligences discussions of performance activities often ignore the issues of matching performance activities to specific learning targets and providing well-crafted scoring rubrics.
- Assessment menus for multiple intelligences lack validity because they fail to match classroom learning targets, do not provide adequate scoring rubrics, imply an equivalence of different activities that is unjustified, and imply that students will craft their own tasks well.

Important Terms and Concepts

adaptive assessment task
alternative assessment
authentic assessment
authentic task
best works portfolio
classroom activity versus assessment task
closed-response task
combined group and individual project
debate
degree of authenticity
demonstration
dramatization

experiment
group project
growth and learning-progress portfolio
individual student project
multiple intelligences assessment menu
multiple intelligences theory
naturally occurring performance
non-paper-and-pencil task
on-demand task
open-response task
oral presentation
paper-and-pencil task
performance assessment
performance task
portfolio
product versus process
scenario
scoring rubric
simulation
standardized patient format
structured task (exercise)

Exercises and Applications

1. Apply the ideas in Figure 11.2 to a subject you teach or plan to teach. For each category and subcategory, describe one performance assessment applicable to your subject. (Do not use the examples given in the text, but you can adapt them.) You do not have to actually create a workable task. Rather, in one or two sentences describe a task that could be created. Which types of tasks are not applicable to your teaching situation? Explain.

2. Do you have any experience with classroom performance activities? Performance assessment? Teaching in a multiple intelligences framework? Share these experiences with others in your course. Do you agree with the author that performance assessments have potential for improving your teaching? Defend your answer.

3. Make three columns on a sheet of paper. In the first column list the four characteristics of authentic performance tasks. Select two performance tasks from either your own experience or from this chapter. Identify the second column with one of these two tasks; the third column with the other. Then, in each cell of the table, evaluate each task against each of the four characteristics: Describe how well each characteristic is exhibited by each task. Share your findings with others in this course.

12 How to Craft Performance Tasks, Projects, Portfolios, Rating Scales, and Scoring Rubrics

LEARNING TARGETS

After studying this chapter, you should have learned the following:

Crafting Performance Tasks and Rubrics

1. Describe the stages and steps necessary to craft high-quality performance tasks. [2, 1]

2. Apply criteria to evaluate achievement dimensions your tasks will assess. [2,1]

3. Craft performance assessment tasks and their corresponding scoring rubrics. [2]

4. Apply criteria for evaluating the quality of your performance assessment tasks. [2, 1]

5. Describe the major types of scoring rubrics, their advantages, and the process used to develop them. [2, 3, 5]

6. Apply criteria to evaluate the quality of your scoring rubrics. [2, 3, 5]

Crafting Checklists and Rating Scales

7. Craft a checklist tool for assessing a student's product or the procedures (process) a student uses to complete a performance. [2, 3]

8. Describe the advantages and disadvantages of the major types of rating scales. [1, 6]

9. Craft rating scales for assessing student performance. [2, 3, 5]

10. Apply criteria to evaluate your checklists and rating scales. [2, 3, 5]

Crafting Projects

11. Describe the conditions under which projects can be useful for assessing students. [1, 6]

12. Craft a classroom project that is useful for assessing students. [2, 3]

13. Explain a teacher's classroom management goals and strategies for ensuring a successful project. [1, 2, 6]

Crafting Portfolios, Including Electronic Portfolios

14. Describe and give examples of the different purposes for portfolios. [1, 6]

15. Explain why different uses of portfolios require different organizations, evaluations, and types or entries. [1, 6, 3]

16. Describe what must be decided in each of the six steps for crafting a portfolio system. [2, 1, 4]

17. Craft a plan for a portfolio system to use with your students. [2, 4, 6]

18. Describe how electronic portfolios are organized and used. [1, 2, 3]

Important Terms and Concepts

19. Explain how the important terms and concepts listed at the end of this chapter apply to educational assessment. [6, 1, 4]

ABOUT THIS CHAPTER

The chapter begins by describing a three-stage process for developing performance assessments. We discuss how to get started, how to identify the proper achievement dimensions to assess, and how to frame levels of achievement. Second, we discuss the actual crafting of the performance task: how to begin, how to revise, and how to extend the task to include assessment of several achievement dimensions such as problem-solving and critical-thinking skills. Third, we discuss how to craft scoring rubrics that will validly assess your students' achievement. Part of this discussion includes how to craft, use, and improve rating scales and checklists. Fourth, we turn to the crafting of long-term student projects. We discuss how to manage the projects so that worthwhile educational achievements are assessed. Last, we turn to the design and crafting of portfolios. We discuss how to craft growth and learning-progress portfolios as well as best works portfolios.

STAGES IN CRAFTING PERFORMANCE TASKS AND RUBRICS

It is best to use a systematic approach for crafting performance tasks. The process has three stages (Stiggins, 1994): (a) being very clear about the performance you want to assess, (b) crafting the task, and (c) crafting a way to score and record the results. The following sections suggest ways to improve your performance task crafting in each stage.

STAGE ONE: BEING CLEAR ABOUT THE PERFORMANCE TO ASSESS

Because performance tasks assess complex learning targets, you must be quite clear about what you will assess. You must know whether the curriculum learning targets you wish to assess are mainly about the process a student uses, the product produced, or both. You must answer these questions:

- Which important learning targets will I assess?
- On what content achievement dimension will the task focus?
- On what complex thinking skills should I focus this task?
- What other achievement dimensions shall I assess along with the content dimension and the thinking-skills dimension?
- Does the learning target imply assessing a process, a product, or both?

Select the Learning Target(s) to Assess

When crafting performance assessment, your state's and school's curriculum framework, state and school standards, and specific learning targets in the subject(s) taught should

guide you. Any performance assessment must be consistent with those guides. You may decide that two or three learning targets can be assessed by the same complex performance assessment. Some learning targets may cut across curricula (e.g., effective communication).

Recall from Chapter 11 that not every learning target can or should be assessed by performance tasks: Select only those that can and should. Recall from Chapter 6 that you should have an assessment plan and that the performance assessment you craft should fit into this assessment plan. Finally, recall from Chapter 7 that a fundamental principle of assessment is to focus only on important learning targets; thus, your assessment should assess worthwhile learning targets.

Assess Achievement Dimensions

Perhaps the most important part of the first stage in performance assessment crafting is specifying the achievement dimensions against which you will assess students' performance (see Marzano et al., 1993; Stiggins, 1987). **Achievement dimensions** are the knowledge, skills, and abilities that you want students to learn as a result of your teaching. Dimensions include content or subject-matter-specific learning targets and lifelong learning targets. **Content achievement dimensions** include the specific declarative and procedural learning targets you want students to achieve. Declarative learning targets are the facts, ideas, generalizations, and theories you want a student to learn. Procedural learning targets are the skills, methods, and procedures you want a student to learn. **Lifelong achievement dimensions** include outcomes that cut across curricula or may be useful outside school, such as complex thinking, information processing, effective communication, cooperation and collaboration, and habits of mind (Marzano et al., 1993). Appendix E shows these categories of learning targets. You should frame your performance task around them or some other framework that your school district requires you to use.

Limit Number of Dimensions Assessed You should not try to assess all of the achievement dimensions in Appendix E in one performance task, otherwise the task will become unwieldy and confusing. Marzano and colleagues (1993) suggest that every performance task should assess one achievement dimension from each of these four categories: content, complex thinking, information processing, and effective communication. Assessing one achievement dimension from each of the other two categories (collaboration/cooperation and habits of mind) is optional. The high school history decision-making task and the history group investigation task, both presented in Chapter 11, are examples of two performance tasks developed around the achievement dimensions outlined in Appendix E.

Define Quality Levels

Each achievement dimension you assess actually represents a continuum of educational growth. Different students will attain different levels of achievement on each dimension. Further, one student may perform with high competence on some dimensions but with less competence on others. Thus, part of crafting your performance task is to define an achievement scale for each dimension. You define this scale by spelling out the different degrees of achievement–from low to high–on each dimension. This continuum forms the basis for crafting scoring rubrics, which we discuss later in this chapter. In Chapter 11, we showed examples of rubrics that assessed students on the collaboration/cooperation dimensions of knowledge (p. 249).

Assessing Student Outcomes: Performance Assessment Using the Dimensions of Learning Model (Marzano et al., 1993) gives general scoring rubrics and quality levels for each of the dimensions shown in Appendix E. You must adapt these general achievement dimensions to your own tasks before you can use them. Nevertheless, the achievement levels listed in the book are useful ways to start.

Evaluate the Achievement Dimensions You Select

You may wonder whether the achievement dimensions you selected are appropriately stated. The checklist provides criteria for evaluating these achievement dimensions.

✓ Checklist

A Checklist for Judging the Quality of the Achievement Dimensions You Intend to Use to Evaluate Students on a Performance Task

Ask these questions of every item you write. If you answer "no" to one or more questions, revise the item accordingly.

1. *Do the achievements you are assessing have significance within the broader context of the curriculum and real-world applications?*
   Explanation.   Your achievement dimensions for your task should specify only the most important components; they should include high-level content learning targets and reflect several lifelong or real-world learning targets, including complex reasoning, information processing, effective communication, and, where appropriate, habits of mind and cooperative learning targets.

2. *Do the achievements you are assessing have authenticity and fidelity to the way the task should be performed outside the assessment context?*
   Explanation.   Your achievement dimensions should be stated in a way that they would apply equally if the student were to perform a similar task in the real world. They should reflect factors such as the resources typically available when the task is performed in the real

world, as well as specifying the types of structure and assistance (i.e., scaffolding) a student would have available to complete the task in the real world.

3. *Have you applied a general achievement framework to your scoring rubrics for this task?*
   Explanation.   Your rubrics, although specific to the performance task you are using, should fit into a general scheme or general rubric framework so it is easy to see how a student has performed over several similar tasks belonging to the same category, but under different conditions or at different times. This type of general framework will make it easier for you and other teachers to apply the rubric consistently across different tasks within the same curriculum.

4. *Do your achievement dimensions fit within a broader framework of educational competence?*
   Explanation.   Your achievement dimensions should be (a) stated in a sound educational development way so it is easy to see as extending from novice to expert performance, (b) located within a broader framework but in a way that is appropriate for the grade and age levels of the students you are assessing, and (c) worded to describe the performance expected at each level (as contrasted with being stated as values such as "poor").

5. *Are your achievement dimensions easy to understand by students, parents, and teachers?*
   Explanation.   Your achievement dimensions should be stated in clear language so students, parents, teachers, and the community easily understand them. You may want to have a plain language version and a technical language version, the former for students and parents and the latter for other teachers in your field.

6. *Are your achievement dimensions useful for pointing to the ways students can improve?*
   Explanation.   Your achievement dimensions and their continua should be focused on those features of performance that students can improve. Your dimensions should be able to communicate to students (and others) what they need to concentrate on to improve.

Source: Based on criteria and ideas in Quellmalz (1991).

Should You Assess Process, Products, or Both?

Sometimes a learning target asks the student to demonstrate a process or a procedure. Here are some examples.

Example

Examples of learning targets that require students to demonstrate a certain process

1. Use the long-division algorithm.
2. Use the posted safety procedures when handling laboratory chemicals.

In some cases, the learning target permits several correct processes. In a mathematics curriculum, for example, a learning target may ask students to learn several different procedures for division rather than a single correct algorithm.

At other times, even though you teach a specific process, the curriculum framework clearly implies that the major focus is the product a student produces. The specific process you teach is only one of several that a student may use. Here are two examples.

Example

Examples of learning targets that require students to produce a product

1. Write haiku poems based on everyday experience.
2. Prepare a research term paper on the causes of volcanic eruptions.

There may be several equally good methods for completing such tasks, but the focus is on the result or products.

Sometimes *both product and process* are of equal importance. For example:

Example

Examples of learning targets that require students to produce a product by performing a certain process

1. Write a research term paper by following the steps provided in the textbook.
2. Using the long-division algorithm, solve 90% of the problems presented in the chapter quiz.

When to Assess the Process Focus your assessment on the *process a student uses* if you are able to answer yes to these questions (Highland, 1955):

1. Did you teach students to use a particular procedure? Can you specify those steps?
2. Can you accurately assess the extent to which a student has deviated from the accepted procedure(s)?
3. Is most or all the evidence about a student's achievement of the learning target found in the way the performance is carried out? Is little or none of the evidence you need to evaluate the student present in the product itself?
4. Do you have enough time or assistance to observe, record, and score the procedures a student uses?

When to Assess the Product Focus your assessment on the *product a student produces* if you can answer yes to the following (Highland, 1955):

1. Can you assess the product accurately and objectively?
2. Is most or all of the evidence about a student's achievement of the learning targets found in the product itself? Is little or none of the evidence you need to evaluate the student

found in the procedure a student uses or the way the student performs?
3. Are you unable to determine the proper sequence(s) of steps to follow to perform the learning target? Was a specific set of procedures not taught? Although everyone knows the steps, are they difficult to perform?
4. Do you have enough time or assistance to evaluate the product a student produces?

Craft Your Tasks to Accommodate Students

As you craft an assessment task, you need to be sure that performing the tasks is within the students' ability range. Performance assessments differ depending on the students' educational level and the mix of general scholastic ability in your class. Further, some students with disabilities may need to have the tasks modified before they can participate in the performance assessment. In Chapter 5 we discussed the general principles for modifying assessments to accommodate students with disabilities.

Tasks Should Suit Class Size

The more students you have in your class, the less elaborate the performance assessment tasks you can set. The fewer the number in your class, the more time you have per student for scoring. Your assessment planning should reflect the realities of your classroom.

STAGE TWO: CRAFTING PERFORMANCE TASKS

When you have a clear understanding of the achievement you want to assess, the next step is to craft the task(s) that will assess this achievement. Further, the types of tasks you craft will depend on the learning targets you are assessing. Some targets imply that the tasks should be structured; others require unstructured tasks; tasks can be structured in various ways. The questions you must answer as you craft your tasks include

- What ranges of tasks do the learning targets imply?
- Should the tasks be structured or unstructured?
- Which parts of the tasks should be structured, and to what degree?
- Does each task require students to perform all the important elements implied by the learning targets?
- Are the tasks crafted to allow me to assess the achievement dimensions I need to assess?
- What must I tell students about the task and its scoring to communicate to them what they need to perform?
- Will students with different ethnic and social backgrounds interpret my task appropriately?

Create Meaningful Tasks

The tasks you craft should be meaningful to the students. This lets students become personally involved in solving a problem or doing well on the task. The following suggestions (Barone, 1991) will help you identify appropriate ideas around which you can craft your tasks:

1. Choose a situation or task that is likely to have personal meaning for most of your students.
2. Carefully blend the familiar and the novel so students will be challenged by the task. Do not make the task so demanding or strange that it becomes frustrating for your students.
3. Choose some situations or tasks that are grounded in the real-world experience of the students you are teaching.
4. Choose some situations or tasks that require your students to apply the knowledge and skills they have acquired outside of your class.
5. Choose situations or tasks that assess whether students have the ability to transfer their knowledge and skills from classroom activities and examples to similar but new (for them) formats.

Develop Tasks in Stages

You should not expect to "knock out" a high-quality performance task quickly. Remember that your first drafts are not fit for human consumption. You need to craft tasks through stages. You first identify the learning targets and dimensions you want to assess and then develop a task around these targets. This ensures that your task lets you evaluate students on these targets. The following steps (Marzano et al., 1993) may be used:

Step 1. Select a content achievement dimension to build your task around. This may be either a declarative or procedural knowledge dimension.

Step 2. Using this content dimension as a guide, select one of the complex-thinking achievement dimensions (see Appendix E) that is closely related to the content dimension. These two achievement dimensions will be the main focus of your task.

Step 3. Using the content and thinking dimensions, draft your performance task. Craft the task so that your students know they are required to apply the appropriate thinking skills learning targets to the content.

Step 4. Select one appropriate information-processing achievement dimension that is consistent with your content- and thinking-skills dimensions and with the task you are crafting. Rewrite the task to include instructions concerning your expectations about applying the information-processing dimension.

Step 5. (Optional) If your task is a group task, select a collaboration/cooperation achievement dimension to assess in conjunction with the dimensions you already have selected. You may also wish to assess a "habit of mind" achievement dimension. (You may wish to do so even if the task is not a group task.)

Step 6. Rewrite your performance task if you decided to use one or more of the achievement dimensions described in Step 5.

Step 7. Select an effective communication achievement dimension you believe is important to assess with this task.

Step 8. Rewrite your performance task to incorporate the effective communication dimension.

Step 9. Review and edit the task. For each dimension, specify several quality levels of performance competence. (This will be the basis for your scoring rubric.)

Figure 12.1 diagrams this process. It implies that you need to develop three or four drafts before the task is well crafted. At this point, refer to the historical decision-making (p. 245) and historical investigation (p. 248) tasks from Chapter 11. These performance tasks were developed using the preceding steps.

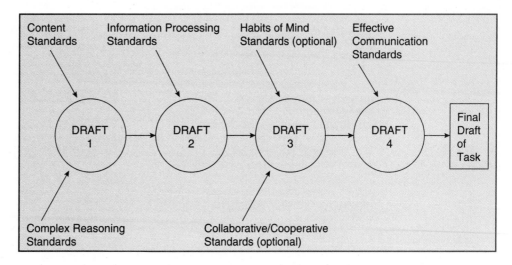

FIGURE 12.1 Process for performance task development.

Importance of Task Tryout

Experience with performance assessments has shown that many of the tasks that seem great on the drawing board are flops as assessment tools. Although a systematic and careful development process can minimize flawed tasks, it does not eliminate them. Flaws become especially noticeable when you try to apply scoring rubrics to many students' responses—by then, it is usually too late to "fix" the task.

Trying out assessment tasks (whether performance or traditional paper-and-pencil) before using them is next to impossible for classroom teachers. You can, however, have your colleagues review and criticize your tasks before you use them. The next best thing to live student tryouts can and should be done: After you use an assessment task, use the information you obtain about flaws in the task or in the rubrics to revise the task or rubric; then reuse the task and rubric next year with a new class of students.

Things to Control to Craft Valid Tasks

You should be aware of the ways in which tasks assessing the same content learning target can differ from one another. These differences make some tasks useful for assessing different types of lifelong learning targets. Figure 12.2 shows five properties of a task that you must control to produce a well-crafted task (some of which we discussed in earlier chapters). Study your task's learning target to decide how to control these properties to make your task more valid.

Time Needed to Complete the Work Some learning targets can be assessed in a relatively short period of 15 to 40 minutes. For example, the ability to work in groups, write an essay or an explanation, plot a graph, or carry out simple experiments can be assessed with **short tasks**. Many learning targets and dimensions, however, imply that students complete **long tasks**. For example, doing an opinion survey and writing it up, building a model town, and developing complex plans for community action require a month or more, and much of the work may need to be done outside class. Task time limits must match the intent of the learning target and dimensions rather than your own convenience—if your goal is to use the results to make valid interpretations about how well a student has achieved that learning target.

Task Structure It may be misleading to talk about structured versus unstructured performance because you can **structure a task** in various ways (Davey & Rindone, 1990), including the way you define the problem, scaffold the instructions, require alternate strategies, and require alternate solutions. At one extreme your task may *define a problem* for a student to solve (structured); at the other extreme you may require the student himself to identify what the problem is (unstructured or ill-defined).

Scaffolding is the degree of support, guidance, and direction you provide the students when they set out to complete the task. You may suggest how to attack the problem, what books or material to use, and the general

FIGURE 12.2 Properties of tasks that you can vary to better align students' performance with the requirements of the achievement dimensions and learning targets.

Task property	Variations in the task requirements	Task property	Variations in the task requirements
Time to complete the task	*Short tasks* can be done in one class period or less. *Long tasks* require a month or more, and work may need to be done outside class.	Participation of groups	The task may require: *Individual work* only throughout all phases of performance. *Mixed individual and group work* in which some of the performance occurs in groups and some is strictly individual effort. *Group work* only throughout all phases of performance.
Task structure provided	Structure may vary in: *Problem definition:* High structure means you carefully define the problem the student must solve. Low structure means the student is free to select and define the problem. *Scaffolding:* High structure means the student is given lots of guidance or directions in how to begin a solution and what materials to use. Low structure means a student has little or no guidance and must decide for him or herself. *Alternate strategies:* High structure means there are very few correct or appropriate pathways to get to the correct answer. Low structure means there are many correct or appropriate approaches to get an acceptable answer. *Alternate solutions:* High structure means there is a correct answer to the task. Low structure means there is no single correct answer to this task.	Product and process focus	The task may require: *Process assessment* only in which the student's performance of the steps and procedures and not the outcome are observed and evaluated. *Both process and product assessment* in which both the steps and the concrete outcome (product) are evaluated. *Product assessment* only in which only the concrete product or outcome is evaluated.
		Performance modality	The task may require: *A single modality* in which the performance is limited to one mode (e.g., oral, written, wood model, etc.). *Multiple modality* in which the performance must be done in several modes (e.g., do both a written and an oral report).

Source: Based on ideas in Davey & Rindone (1990).

nature of the end product you require. These directions and guidance statements add structure to the task. Less scaffolding means less structure.

If your task can be performed or solved using only one or two procedures or strategies, it has fewer **alternate solution strategies** and is more structured in this respect. Unstructured alternatives mean that there are a great many equally correct pathways to the correct answer or to producing the correct product. A similar analysis applies to the solution or the product itself: A task is unstructured in this respect when it has many correct or *acceptable solutions or products*. Just how a task may vary in these elements is shown in the following example:

Example

Example showing how controlling properties can change a performance task

Assume that students have been asked simply to build a scale model of the solar system. As far as problem definition goes, this task has fairly high structure—you have a specified goal to meet. However, there is very little scaffolding—students are not told what materials to use, or what proportions to use, or where to get information on the planetary distances and orbits. There are a lot of alternative pathways to the solution—consider the fact that no two models will look exactly alike, and will vary in terms of materials used, scale employed, special features included (such as neurons, orbital speeds, etc.), and in a way there's one best solution, a perfectly scaled model of the solar system. (Davey & Rindone, 1990, p. 5)

Participation of Groups Learning targets and the dimensions guide your task construction. If your learning targets call for cooperative or collaborative learning (or using other group-based skills), you should set a task using, at least in part, group activities. Appendix E shows some of the possible group collaboration dimensions you may choose to assess.

Product and Process If you want to assess process, you need to do the assessing while a student is performing. You may take away a product, on the other hand, and evaluate it at your convenience. Further, you cannot assess cognitive processes (mental activities) directly, only indirectly through some intermediate or "partial" products. For example, you can ask students to tell you or to write what they were thinking about while they were doing the task. Or you may ask them to record the early drafts they made and ideas they used.

Your indirect assessments of a student's mental activities and thinking processes depend on the student having abilities other than those required to complete the task. They depend, for example, on the accuracy of the students' memories, their skills in understanding the thinking processes they used, and their abilities to describe these thinking processes orally or in writing. Because you assess cognitive processes only indirectly, your inferences and judgments about how well a student uses them—that is, the validity of your evaluation of a student's use of cognitive processes—might be weak. Other processes, such as group processes and behavior that occurs in a sequence of steps, are more directly assessed because you can observe them directly.

Response Mode Some learning targets specify that students should be able to communicate their knowledge in several ways, solve a problem using several methods, or express themselves in a variety of modalities. For example, the history decision-making task in Chapter 11 (p. 245) asks students to report their results in two or more modalities. You should not use multiple response modes on a whim, however. You need to align the modalities with the learning targets, state standards, and curriculum framework. Also, you should use alternate modes to accommodate students with disabilities or cultural differences if the mainstream, single mode is not appropriate for them.

Accommodating a student's response mode also has meaning in the context of educational programs following a multiple intelligences framework (see Chapter 11). However, you need to focus assessment tasks for these alternatives on the main intents of learning targets and achievement dimensions. For example, if the main intent of a learning target is communicating through the written word, then singing a song, pantomiming an answer, or drawing a picture will not be appropriate (valid), even though these are alternative modalities. But if the learning targets focus on content understanding, thinking skills, and problem solving, a written response is not the only way to express competent performance. Even though you may expect most students to express their problem solutions in writing, you may assess some students by permitting alternative performances.

Make the Task Clear to Students

When crafting performance tasks, you write the learning target(s), the criteria by which you will evaluate performance, and the instructions for completing the task. Task wording and directions should depend on the educational maturity of your students. Make sure to state clearly the time limits and the conditions under which you want the task done. Be sure students understand how long a response you are expecting. Share with students the rubrics you will use to assess their performance.

When students misinterpret the task, you cannot validly interpret their assessment results in the same way as you do those students who interpreted the task correctly. Students from certain ethnic, linguistic, or gender groups may not interpret your wording as you expect them to (Duran, 1989; Lane et al., 1992). (See also the discussion of projects later in this chapter.)

The validity of assessment is problematic for teachers using multiple intelligences menus (Figure 11.8). Letting students choose different response modes may be popular, but not all response modes are valid for assessing a learning target. The first priority, especially for summative assessment, is to match the assessment format to the main intent of the learning targets.

Number of Tasks

As a general rule, the fewer the number of tasks, the fewer learning targets you can assess, the lower the score reliability, and the lower the validity of your interpretations. The number of performance tasks to include in your assessment depends on several factors; however, some of these factors you cannot control. You need to resolve the following issues to decide on the appropriate number of tasks:

1. *Crucial decisions.* Certification, promotion, and graduation are examples of very crucial decisions. Assessments for crucial decisions such as these, in which the consequences of failing are severe, are called **high-stakes assessments**. These assessments require more tasks and longer assessment times to gather sufficiently reliable information. High-stakes decisions should not depend on information from only one assessment session. Letter-grade assignments are also crucial decisions, especially if you are unwilling or unable to change the grade if a mistake is made. Grading may be less crucial a decision than certification, but grades for a term or a marking period should not be based on a single assessment, either. Daily instructional decisions for formative evaluation of learning can be easily changed if wrong decisions are made. These less crucial decisions can be based on lower-quality information if need be.

2. *Scope of your assessment.* How much instruction are you covering with this assessment—a unit or only one lesson? How much content is covered in a unit? The broader the scope of your assessment, the more tasks you will need.

3. *Mixture of assessment formats.* If you mix objective formats with performance tasks, you will be able to cover more aspects of the learning targets, balance your assessment, and broaden your assessment scope. In this case, you may need fewer performance tasks because your assessment scope will be broader than if you used performance tasks alone.

4. *Complexity of the learning target.* A complex learning target requires integration of many skills and abilities and may need to be performed over a long time. In this case, practicality limits the number of tasks of this type you may give. However, because more time is devoted to one (or at most a few) such tasks, the information may be of high quality (i.e., reliable). Nevertheless, the scope or span of your assessment may not be very broad. This could present a validity problem.

5. *Time needed to complete each task.* As a practical matter, you can administer only a few tasks during a typical class period. Decide how much time one task will take a student to complete, and divide this into the length of the class period to determine the maximum number of tasks possible. Students usually take longer to complete a task than you think, so allow for that.

6. *Time available for the total assessment.* You may be willing to devote more or less than one period to assessment. The number of tasks may shrink or expand depending on the available time.

7. *Diagnostic detail needed.* If you need a lot of detail to diagnose a student's learning or conceptual problems, you need to craft tasks that provide this rich detail. This usually means fewer tasks, more detailed performance, and more detailed scoring of the responses. If you assess many students for diagnostic purposes, practicalities of time for performance and scoring will usually limit you to only a few tasks per student.

8. *Available human resources.* If you have an aide or a parent to help you administer or score the assessments, this may free up some time so that you can give a few more tasks. You can also teach students to score the assessments; although this is educationally useful, it is unlikely to lead to increasing the number of tasks.

Evaluate Your Performance Tasks

The more important suggestions for improving performance tasks are shown in the checklist. You can use this checklist to evaluate individual performance tasks. In a way that is similar to how you used the checklists for objective items in earlier chapters: A "no" answer to one question in the checklist is sufficient cause for you to revise the task before administering it to students.

✓ *Checklist*

A Checklist for Judging the Quality of Performance Tasks

Ask these questions of every item you write. If you answer "no" to one or more questions, revise the item accordingly.

---

1. Does the task focus on an important aspect of the unit's learning targets?
2. Does the task match your assessment plan in terms of performance, emphasis, and number of points (marks)?
3. Does the task actually require a student to *do* something (i.e., a performance) rather than requiring only writing about how to do it, or simply to recall or copy information?
4. Do you allow enough time so all of your students can complete the task under your specified conditions?

5. *If this is an open-response task*, do your wording and directions make it clear to students that they may use a variety of approaches and strategies, that you will accept more than one answer as correct, and that they need to fully elaborate their response?

6. *If the task is intended to be authentic or realistic*, do you present a situation that your level of students will recognize as coming from the real world?

7. *If this task requires using resources and locating information outside the classroom*, will all of your students have fair and equal access to the expected resources?

8. Do your directions and other wording:

   a. define a task that is appropriate to the educational maturity of your students?

   b. lead all students, including those from diverse cultural and ethnic backgrounds, to interpret the task requirements in the way you intend?

   c. make clear the purpose or goal of the task?

   d. make clear the length or the degree of elaboration of the response that you expect?

   e. make clear the bases on which you will evaluate the responses to the task?

9. Are the drawings, graphs, diagrams, charts, manipulatives, and other task materials clearly drawn, properly constructed, appropriate to the intended performance, and in good working order?

10. *If you have students with disabilities in your class*, have you modified or adapted the task to accommodate their needs?

STAGE THREE: CRAFTING RUBRICS, CHECKLISTS, AND RATING SCALES

Rubrics not only improve scoring consistency, they also improve validity by clarifying the standards of achievement you will use to evaluate your students. As you craft scoring rubrics and ways of recording results, you will need to address questions such as:

- What important criteria and learning targets do I need to assess?

- What are the levels of development (achievement) for each of these criteria and learning targets?

- Should I use a holistic or an analytic scoring rubric?

- Do I need to use a rating scale or a checklist as my scoring scheme?

- Should my students be involved in rating their own performance?

- How can I make my scoring efficient and less time consuming?

- What do I need to record as the result of my assessments?

TYPES OF SCORING RUBRICS

Rubrics can be categorized according to whether they use one scale or several and according to whether the descriptions of work quality are general (i.e., can be applied to many different tasks) or specific to the task, essay, or assignment. An **analytic scoring rubric** (also called *scoring key*, *point scale*, or *trait scale*) requires you to evaluate specific dimensions, traits, or elements of a student's response. A **holistic scoring rubric** (also called global, sorting, or rating) requires you to make a judgment about the overall quality or of each student's response. **Generic rubrics** (also called *general rubrics*) describe performance quality in general terms so the scoring can be applied to many different tasks. **Task-specific rubrics** describe performance quality in terms that include reference to the specific assignment. Note that whether a rubric is analytic or holistic is independent of whether it is generic or task-specific. Rubrics can be described on both factors. For example, the writing rubrics in Appendix H are generic (general) and analytic.

Analytic Scoring Rubrics

List Major Criteria An analytic scoring rubric requires that you list the major criteria of good work (sometimes called *dimensions* or *traits*) and prepare a rubric for each of these criteria. The analytic scoring rubric for the Ideas/Content dimension shown in the Oregon example in Appendix H is a rubric for only one trait. As such, it is only a part of the analytic scoring rubric for scoring writing. Rubrics for all six traits would constitute an analytic scoring rubric for writing. The complete analytic scoring rubric for writing assessment of the state of Oregon is given in Appendix H.

Determine Number of Points You decide the number of points to award to students for each criterion. An example of an analytic, task-specific scoring rubric for a restricted response essay was presented in Chapter 9. Examples of generic analytic rubrics for evaluating collaboration and cooperation were presented in Chapter 11. The scales may all be of equal weight, or you may decide one or more of the aspects of performance is worth more points.

Usually students' responses will match the scoring rubric to various degrees. Assigning a rubric level to particular student work is like a "choose the best answer" type of multiple-choice question. The score is the one whose description most closely matches a student's work. The top and bottom of a rubric scale are usually easier categories to decide than the middle. When you match student work to rubric levels in an inconsistent way you lower the reliability of the scoring process.

Holistic Scoring Rubrics

Holistic scoring is appropriate for extended response subject-matter essays or papers involving a student's abilities to synthesize and create when no single description of good work can be prespecified. It is also appropriate for final exams or projects where giving feedback to students is not a consideration. States that do large-scale assessment of either writing or subject-matter essay responses often prefer holistic scoring. The large numbers of papers to be marked often precludes the detailed scoring required by analytic rubrics. An example of a holistic, task-specific scoring rubric for a restricted response essay was presented on page 202.

Develop and Use Holistic Scoring Rubrics To craft holistic rubrics, you still need to identify the criteria for good work on which your scoring will be based. The difference is that for analytic rubrics, descriptions of levels of performance on each criterion are considered separately. For holistic rubrics, levels of performance on all criteria are considered simultaneously. The description that best fits the student work identifies the score to be given.

Number of Categories of Overall Quality One way to implement the holistic method is to decide beforehand on the number of categories of the overall quality of the work into which you will sort the students' responses to each question. Usually, you can use between three and five categories, such as A, B, C, D, and F; distinguished, proficient, apprentice, and novice; or 4, 3, 2, and 1. A very important point in deciding the number of categories is to be sure they correspond to your school's grading system. If your school uses grades A through F, for example, then you need five categories. Using only three quality levels in a scoring rubric will make your student evaluations unnecessarily complicated.

Define the Meaning of Each Category After deciding on the number of categories, define the *quality* of the papers that belong in each category. This means, for example, describing what an A performance is, a B performance, and so on. It is best to revise your scoring rubric after you have tried out the draft version on several performances (papers, assignments, projects). Trying out the rubric will allow you to identify parts of it that are problematic, then add qualities of student responses that you may have failed to include in the original draft. After categorizing all of the students' work, you should reexamine the performances within categories to be sure they are enough alike in quality to receive the same grade or quality rating.

Use Exemplars A refinement that will help you use the rubrics more reliably, and make them even easier to use the next time, is to select *specimens* or **exemplars** that are good examples of each scoring category. You can then compare the current students' answers to the exemplars that define each quality level. Finally, you decide into which category to place them.

Ranking An alternative way of implementing holistic scoring is to consider all the papers, projects, or assignments and compare one with another to decide which are the best, the

next best, and so on. This will result in a rough ranking of all the papers. The best-ranked papers are placed in the highest category, the next best in the second category, and so on. This approach, however, does not work very well with a large number of students, and it is inconsistent with a criterion-referenced approach to teaching, which bases instruction on learning objectives and assessment on the degree to which each student met the objectives.

Annotated Holistic Scoring Rubrics

Some educators have successfully used a third type of scoring rubric that is a hybrid of the analytic and holistic rubrics. The **annotated holistic rubric** is an approach that uses holistic scoring but adds feedback to students on a few of the traits in a way similar to the analytic scoring. With this approach, quality levels are defined and the papers are scored holistically. After reaching a holistic judgment, you write on the student's paper very brief comments, based on the prespecified traits, that point out one or two strengths of the response and one or two weaknesses. You write only about what led you to reach your holistic judgment of the paper.

Generic (General) Rubrics

Generic (general) rubrics use descriptions of work that apply to a whole family or set of assignments. Generic rubrics for writing, math problem solving, science laboratory work, analyzing literature, and so on are important instructional as well as assessment tools. As students practice and perform many different learning targets in a subject throughout the school year, their learning improves if they apply the same general evaluation framework to all of the same type of work in that subject. Some research evidence supports the idea that when students routinely use generic, but analytic, rubrics in the classroom, their achievement improves (Khattri, Reeve, & Adamson, 1997). The Oregon writing assessment rubric in Appendix H is an example of this type of generic, analytic rubric. The Chicago Public Schools Website (http://intranet.cps.k12.il.us/Assessments/index.html) has a library of generic rubrics in various topic areas.

A generic (general) scoring rubric contains guidelines for scoring that apply across many different tasks of a similar type (for example, writing, or math problem solving), not just to one specific instance of that kind of task. The generic rubric can serve as a general framework for developing more specific rubrics, or it can be used as is. Following is an example of a generic scoring guide for assessing the content learning target of any high school history task similar to the one we presented previously. A task centered on the Gulf War and President Bush, for example, would be an alternative task that could assess this content learning target.

Example

General rubric that could be applied to a high school history task

Content learning target being assessed:

Understands that war forces sensitive issues to the surface and causes people to confront inherent conflicts of values and beliefs.

4 Demonstrates a thorough understanding of the generalized concepts and facts specific to the task or situation. Provides new insights into some aspect of that information.

3 Displays a complete and accurate understanding of the generalizations, concepts, and facts specific to the task or situation.

2 Displays an incomplete understanding of the generalizations, concepts, and facts specific to the task or situation.

1 Demonstrates severe misconceptions about the generalizations, concepts, and facts specific to the task or situation.

Source: Adapted from *Assessing Student Outcomes: Performance Assessment Using the Dimensions of Learning Model* (pp. 29–30), by R. J. Marzano, D. Pickering, and J. McTighe, 1993, Alexandria, VA: Association for Supervision and Curriculum Development. Adapted by permission of McREL Institute, 2550 S. Parker Rd., Suite 500, Aurora, CO 80014. Telephone (303) 337–0990. © by McREL Institute. All rights reserved.

Example

Specific rubric that could be applied to the high school history task

Content learning target being assessed:

Understands that war forces sensitive issues to the surface and causes people to confront inherent conflicts of values and beliefs.

4 Demonstrates a thorough understanding of the generalization that war forces sensitive issues to the surface and causes people to confront inherent conflicts of values and beliefs. Provides new insights into people's behavior during wartime.

3 Displays a complete and accurate understanding of the generalization that war forces sensitive issues to the surface and causes people to confront inherent conflicts of values and beliefs.

2 Displays an incomplete understanding of the generalization that war forces sensitive issues to the surface and causes people to confront inherent conflicts of values and beliefs. Has some notable misconceptions about this generalization.

1 Demonstrates severe misconceptions about the generalization that war forces sensitive issues to the surface and causes people to confront inherent conflicts of values and beliefs.

Source: Adapted from *Assessing Student Outcomes: Performance Assessment Using the Dimensions of Learning Model* (pp. 29–30), by R. J. Marzano, D. Pickering, and J. McTighe, 1993, Alexandria, VA: Association for Supervision and Curriculum Development. Adapted by permission of McREL Institute, 2550 S. Parker Rd., Suite 500, Aurora, CO 80014. Telephone (303) 337–0990. © by McREL Institute. All rights reserved.

Task-Specific Rubrics

A **task-specific scoring rubric** is a scoring scale that applies the general scoring framework to a particular task. Carefully applying the generic scoring framework to craft a specific scoring rubric ensures that your specific rubric assesses students in a way that is aligned with the general scoring framework. This process would be very helpful when you use the state's generic rubric to develop a specific rubric for your classroom because it helps you align your class assessments with the state standards. Here is the specific scoring rubric that a history teacher used to assess students' performance on the high school history decision-making task presented earlier. It uses the preceding general scoring rubric as a framework.

You can use a general framework to develop scoring rubrics specific to a particular task. In this way you are applying the same general framework in a consistent manner to each new performance task. The reliability and validity of your scores improve when you use a general scoring framework as a guideline to craft specific scoring rubrics.

Advantages and Disadvantages of the Methods

Different scoring approaches are not interchangeable. They serve different purposes for scoring your students' performance. Figure 12.3 gives advantages and disadvantages for each type of rubrics.

A clear advantage of the analytic scoring rubric is that it provides you and your students with much more detail about their strengths and weaknesses. If you use an analytic scoring rubric, take advantage of this added information to enhance your teaching and to give students guidance concerning what they need to do to improve. For example, you could identify which elements or parts of the entire class's answers are weakest and direct your reteaching to that aspect. You will also be able to give your students specific praise for those parts of the answer on which they did well.

An advantage of using a holistic scoring rubric is the time it saves. It is faster to score a student's essay holistically than analytically. Often the time saved is considerable, on the order of two or three to one.

FIGURE 12.3 **Advantages and disadvantages of different types of rubrics.**

Type of rubric	Definition	Advantages	Disadvantages
Holistic or Analytic: One or Several Judgments?			
Analytic	• Each criterion (dimension, trait) is evaluated separately.	• Gives diagnostic information to teacher • Gives formative feedback to students • Easier to link to instruction than holistic rubrics • Good for formative assessment; adaptable for summative assessment; if you need an overall score for grading, you can combine the scores	• Takes more time to score than holistic rubrics • Takes more time to achieve inter-rater reliability than with holistic rubrics
Holistic	• All criteria (dimensions, traits) are evaluated simultaneously.	• Scoring is faster than with analytic rubrics • Requires less time to achieve inter-rater reliability • Good for summative assessment	• Single overall score does not communicate information about what to do to improve • Not good for formative assessment
Description of Performance: Generic or Task-Specific?			
Generic	• Description of work gives characteristics that apply to a whole family of tasks (e.g., writing, problem solving).	• Can share with students, explicitly linking assessment and instruction • Reuse same rubrics with several tasks or assignments • Supports learning by helping students see "good work" as bigger than one task • Support student self-evaluation • Students can help construct generic rubrics	• Lower reliability at first than with task-specific rubrics • Requires practice to apply well
Task-specific	• Description of work refers to the specific content of a particular task (e.g., gives an answer, specifies a conclusion).	• Teachers sometimes say using these makes scoring "easier" • Requires less time to achieve inter-rater reliability	• Cannot share with students (would give away answers) • Need to write new rubrics for each task • For open-ended tasks, good answers not listed in rubrics may be evaluated poorly

Holistic scoring rubrics are easier to use and take less time per student. They permit an overall evaluation, which allows the rater to report a general impression over all aspects of the performance. An analytic scoring rubric is more time consuming to use because the rater must look for and separately rate each component of a performance. This level of detail is useful when your focus is diagnosis or helping students understand your expectations for each part of the performance. This may be especially useful for helping students learn, even if it is more time consuming. Using a general, analytic trait rubric (e.g., the type illustrated in Appendix H) in a consistent way through the entire year may improve learning if students understand it and if they receive feedback linked to it.

The annotated holistic scoring rubric is a restricted combination of the holistic and analytic rubrics. The additional analytic feedback is restricted to only a few characteristics, which do not change the initial holistic rating. The advantage is that it allows you to rate the papers quickly and to support your rating with a few salient points. These points give feedback to students but may not be useful for diagnosis. In order to provide a complete diagnosis and feedback, you still need analytic rubrics that rate each component of the performance separately.

Note that holistic and analytic scoring rubrics probably assess a student's performance differently (Taylor, 1998). Analytic trait scoring may be more valid if it allows you to evaluate several dimensions of performance as well as how the student integrates those dimensions when performing the task.

Task-specific scoring rubrics cannot be shared with students ahead of time. They contain specific information about the responses the students are expected to make, for example, "answers" to problems students are to solve, or lists of facts or concepts students should provide. And you obviously have to come up with a new rubric for each task. However, task-specific rubrics are very useful for some purposes. They make for reliable and efficient scoring of essay questions or show-the-work problems on exams. This is probably their best use. Because of the instructional and formative assessment advantages, generic (general), analytic rubrics are the kind you aim to use whenever students are involved in the assessment process—which should be most of the time.

Crafting Scoring Rubrics: Before You Begin

Scoring rubrics are necessary for all of the performance assessment methods described in this and the previous chapter, including projects and portfolios, and for scoring essays and show-the-work problems. In Stage One of the crafting process, you identified achievement dimensions and a scale of progress for each dimension, from very low progress to very high progress. To craft a scoring rubric you need to refine these descriptions of performance levels to be sure they are clear. You may associate each level with a numerical value (illustrated in Chapter 11 on pages 249 and 253). Alternately, you may associate each level with a qualitative description such as novice, apprentice, proficient, and distinguished. These qualitative descriptions are illustrated in the foreign language proficiency-rating example on page 252.

It is necessary to describe the characteristics of a student's performance that distinguish one achievement level from another, because these descriptions anchor the scale at each level. It is important to have as many achievement levels as your school has letter grades. In that way rubrics can support your grades.

CRAFTING SCORING RUBRICS: HOW TO DO IT

Top-Down Approach

The **top-down approach** begins with a conceptual framework that you can use to evaluate students' performance to develop scoring rubrics; follow these steps:

Step 1. Adapt or create a conceptual framework of achievement dimensions that describes the content and performance that you should assess.
Step 2. Develop a detailed outline that arranges the content and performance from Step 1 in a way that identifies what you should include in the general rubric.
Step 3. Craft a general scoring rubric that conforms to this detailed outline and focuses on the important aspects of content and process to be assessed across different tasks. The general rubric can be shared with students. It can be

used as is to score student work, or it can be used to craft specific rubrics.
Step 4. Craft a specific scoring rubric for the specific performance task you are going to use.
Step 5. Use the specific scoring rubric to assess the performances of several students; use this experience to revise the rubric as necessary.

In the top-down approach you need a framework-based organization to develop a rubric. Thus, Steps 1, 2, and 3 may be difficult to achieve on your own and may require you to work with groups of teachers. Figure 12.4 illustrates a simple assessment framework for middle school science. No rubrics are provided for it, however.

Figure 12.5 shows an example of a holistic scoring rubric for middle school mathematics that has been organized around a three-part conceptual framework: mathematical knowledge, strategic knowledge, and communication (Lane, 1992). This three-part organization helps define the specific standards within each level of the rubric. Similarly, Appendix E shows a framework for organizing general rubrics that are consistent with the Dimensions of Learning Model.

When we discussed writing assessment in Chapter 9, we discussed scoring organized in a six-part framework: ideas and content, organization, voice, word choice, sentence fluency, and conventions. An analytic rubric for implementing this framework is reproduced in Appendix H.

Bottom-Up Approach

With the **bottom-up approach** you begin with samples of students' work, using actual responses to create your own framework. Use examples of different quality levels to help you identify the dimensions along which students can be assessed. The following steps may be helpful:

Step 1. Obtain copies of about 10 to 12 students' actual responses to a performance item. Be sure the responses you select illustrate various levels of quality of the general achievement you are assessing (e.g., science understanding, letter writing, critical reasoning, etc.).
Step 2. Read the responses and sort all of them into three groups: high-quality responses, medium-quality responses, and low-quality responses. Alternatively, you can ask students to do this. For tasks with which they have some experience (for example, writing), and for which they therefore have some basis to begin to judge quality, this is a particularly powerful learning experience. The resulting bottom-up rubrics that students have helped create can be used for student self-evaluation and teacher-provided formative feedback.
Step 3. After sorting, carefully study each student's responses within the groups, and write (or have students write) very specific reasons why you put that response into that particular group. How are the students' responses in one group (e.g., high-quality group) different from the responses in each of the other groups? Be as specific as you can. For example, don't

- What is it about the students' responses that distinguish the poor, acceptable, and excellent student?
- Are there samples of student work (excellent and poor) that I can contrast to identify the characteristics that differentiate them?
- Does my school district, state assessment program, a national curriculum panel, or a professional society have examples of rubrics or curriculum frameworks that show standards and criteria?
- Are there any suggestions in teachers' magazines, state teacher's newsletters, professional journals, or textbooks?

Compare the generic (general) rubric you draft with those developed by other districts, state assessment programs, national curriculum panels, or professional societies. Refine yours to make it clearer and more complete.

If you do not create a general rubric or a conceptual framework, your scoring rubrics across all your performance tasks will lack coherence and consistency. Coherence applies not only to your assessment but also to your teaching, and it helps your students understand the standards that their learning should meet.

Administer the performance task to your students, then apply the general or specific rubric that you developed. If you have difficulty rating a student's performance, you should reexamine your rubric to see where it is unclear. Often you will need to expand the descriptions of each quality level in the rubric to include an example or to describe an aspect of a student's performance you initially forgot to include.

CRAFTING CHECKLISTS

Several useful ways to record your assessments of students' performance are briefly described in Figure 12.6. Although each of the ways listed in the figure has a special use, checklists and rating scales are the most frequently used with performance tasks. Suggestions for developing checklists are in this section. Suggestions for rating scales are in the next section.

Types of Checklists

A **checklist** consists of a list of specific behaviors, characteristics, or activities and a place for marking whether each is present or absent. You may use a checklist for assessing a

FIGURE 12.6 **Some useful methods of recording students' responses to performance tasks.**

Recording method	Description	Recommended use	Example of uses
Anecdotal records	You observe the performance and write a description of what the student did.	These are primarily useful for keeping records of unanticipated or naturally occurring performances. Usually you can record only one student at a time.	A student shows unusual insights into current events and you want to keep a record of these to put into his portfolio or to recommend the student for a summer program for leadership.
Behavior tallies	You create a list of specific behaviors of which you want to keep a record for a student. As you observe the performance you tally how many times each behavior occurs. The list is usually limited to only a few behaviors.	These are primarily useful for well-defined lists of behaviors that you can expect to occur frequently. They may be useful to keep track of undesirable behaviors, too.	As a communications teacher, you keep track of how often a student uses "uh-h-h" when speaking in front of the class.
Checklists	You create a list of specific steps in a procedure or specific behaviors. You check each behavior that occurs. The list may be long.	These are primarily useful if the behaviors are in a sequence or if all the sub-tasks that make up the complete performance can be listed.	You are a science teacher and want to be sure that each student performs the steps in setting up a microscope properly. You are an automotive shop teacher and want to be sure that each student properly completes all the tasks necessary to change the oil in a car.
Rating scales	You create standards or criteria for evaluating a performance. Each standard has levels of competence, and you rate students according to how well they performed each standard as they complete the task.	These are especially useful if each standard can be judged according to the level or the degree of quality rather than as simply being present or absent.	You are an art teacher and rate each student's painting on its composition, texture, theme, and technique. You are a mathematics teacher and rate a student's problem solution according to how well the student demonstrates mathematical knowledge, uses a good strategy to solve the problem, and communicates her explanation of the solution in writing.

procedure a student uses, a product a student produces, or behaviors a student exhibits. Students may use checklists to evaluate their own performance.

Procedure Checklist A **procedure checklist** assesses whether a student follows the appropriate steps in a process or procedure. For example, a checklist may assess whether a student is able to use a microscope properly. The form represents both the presence or absence of each step and the sequence that a particular student used to perform the task. Sometimes the major flaw in a student's performance is the order in which he performs the steps. Recording the correct sequence and the student's sequence on the form will help you attend to this aspect of performance.

Product Checklist A **product checklist** focuses on the quality of the thing a student makes. Products include drawings, constructed models, essays, and term papers. These checklists identify the parts or other properties a product is supposed to have. You then inspect each product, checking whether those properties are present.

Behavior Checklist A **behavior checklist** consists of a list of discrete behaviors related to a specific area of a student's performance. For example, you may wish to identify the particular difficulties a student is having in the phonological, semantic, and syntactic aspects of spoken language. The behavior checklist might have items such as "uses only simple sentence structure" or "responds without delay to questions." Figure 12.7 illustrates such a checklist.

Self-Evaluation Checklist Students use a **self-evaluation checklist** to review and evaluate their own work. You could use the checklist students complete as a basis for a student-teacher conference in which you discuss a student's progress. As an example, consider the situation in which a student produces a best works mathematics portfolio. To create this portfolio, a student has to complete mathematics tasks and decide which of these completed tasks she should include in the portfolio. A student must select six or seven completed tasks to put into the best works portfolio. A checklist can help a student evaluate each entry and decide what to put into the portfolio. It can also serve as a basis for discussing the entries with peers, parents, or teachers. Because the checklist focuses on portfolio entries, it focuses students' attention on the portfolio scoring rubric. However, the checklist is phrased in simpler and less formal language than the scoring rubric used by teachers. An adaptation of this checklist is shown in Figure 12.8.

How to Craft Checklists

To craft a checklist, you need a thorough understanding of the subject matter as well as the procedure or the product you want to assess. Without this knowledge you will find it difficult to identify critical performance and steps, critical flaws in the product, and potential student errors. Thus, for you to craft checklists you must complete a detailed analysis of the procedure you are evaluating or a careful specification of the precise characteristics of the desired student product.

Before crafting a *product checklist*, you should examine several students' products–especially those products that differ greatly in quality. Careful study of these products will help you identify the characteristics and flaws you want to include in your checklist.

When crafting a *procedure checklist*, first observe and study students performing so you can identify all the appropriate steps. You may find the following steps (Linn & Gronlund, 1995) helpful when crafting procedure checklists:

Step 1. List and describe clearly each specific subperformance or step in the procedure you want the student to follow.
Step 2. Add to the list specific errors that students commonly make (avoid unwieldy lists, however).
Step 3. Order the correct steps and the errors in the approximate sequence in which they should occur.
Step 4. Make sure you include a way either to check the steps as the student performs them or to number the sequence in which the student performs them.

If several equally correct procedures for accomplishing the learning target are available, developing a checklist this way will not be useful.

CRAFTING RATING SCALES

Why Rating Scales Are Useful

Need to Evaluate the Degree of Achievement Checklists help you evaluate whether a given step, a specific property, or particular action is present. Many times you are concerned with more than the presence or absence of these elements. A **rating scale** assesses the *degree to which* students have attained the achievement dimensions in the performance task. As an example, consider assessing the quality of a student's oral presentation to the class. You would probably identify several dimensions of a "good oral presentation" and then judge the degree to which a student demonstrates each of them. A good oral presentation might include such characteristics as the degree to which a student presents material relevant to the topic; speaks in a smooth, unhesitating manner; uses correct grammar and language patterns; and makes visual contact with the audience (Lindvall, 1967). You need to assess and record the degree to which a student demonstrates each dimension, rather than assessing on an all-or-none, present-or-absent basis. A simple rating scale for doing this was shown in Chapter 11 (Figure 11.6). You have seen other examples of rating scales in Chapter 10: a scale for rating critical thinking dispositions (Figure 10.5) and one for evaluating an oral presentation of an argument (Figure 10.7).

FIGURE 12.7 Example of a portion of a checklist used to report a high school student's speaking behavior.

Speaking Behavior DATES ▶				
Speaks clearly and audibly				
Speaks fluently in home language				
Expresses thoughts in complete sentences				
Uses appropriate phrasing and sentence patterns				
Chooses appropriate topic for presentation				
Organizes material				
▲ Presents both introductory and concluding statements				
▲ Uses notes or note cards				
▲ Uses appropriate visual aids or other support material				
▲				
▲				
Establishes and maintains eye contact to ensure listener attention				
Varies tone, stress, and volume to convey meaning				
Displays good posture while speaking				
Demonstrates poise and confidence				
Uses appropriate gestures and body language to convey meaning				
Uses appropriate language for the form of communication				
Emphasizes main idea(s)				
Uses persuasive devices (e.g., glad names, bad names, bandwagon, testimonial)				
Conveys intended purpose when speaking				

Source: From *Listening and Speaking Checklist*, grades 9–12 (p.4), *California Achievement Tests*, 5th Edition, by permission of the publisher, CTB/McGraw-Hill LLC, a subsidiary of The McGraw-Hill Companies, Inc. Copyright © 1992 by CTB/McGraw-Hill LLC. All rights reserved.

Using Rating Scales in Teaching Rating scales can be used for teaching purposes as well as assessment:

1. *The rating scale helps students understand the learning target and focus their attention on the important aspects of the performance.* You can give it to students as they prepare for the performance task.

2. *The completed rating scale gives specific feedback to a student concerning the strengths and weaknesses of the performance.* You can give the rating scale to students after you have used it to evaluate their performance.

3. *Students not only achieve the learning targets but also may internalize the criteria used to evaluate their achievement.* This means that they will automatically apply the

FIGURE 12.8 Example of a checklist that students use to evaluate their own entries for a best works portfolio.

Mathematics Self-Assessment and Conference Form

Name: _____

Entry title: _____

Conference with:
_____ Classmate   Date: _____
_____ Teacher   Date: _____
_____ My parent   Date: _____

Mathematics Area	Did I . . .	Comments about strengths and needs
Problem solving	1. understand the problem? 2. use more than one strategy to solve the problem? 3. solve the problem? 4. review, revise, or expand the problem? 5. show and explain all my work or my thinking?	
Reasoning	6. make predictions by observing data or recognizing patterns? 7. test my predictions by using logical arguments, using my past knowledge, or collecting additional data? 8. explain and justify my solution?	
Mathematics communication	9. use mathematical words, symbols, graphs, manipulatives, etc. to communicate ideas and thinking? 10. communicate my ideas and thinking through written, oral, or other means?	
Understanding and connecting core concepts	11. show that I understood mathematical topics and ideas? 12. recognize and use mathematics in other subjects or in everyday life? 13. recognize connections and relationships with mathematics?	

Do the following with your teacher

Type of entry	14. Circle the kind(s) of entry this is: writing investigation/discovery application interdisciplinary nonroutine problem project	
Core concepts & principles I used	15. Circle the mathematical concepts that you used in this entry: change measurement data number mathematical procedures space & dimensionality mathematical structure	
Tools I used	16. Circle the mathematical tools you used in this entry: algebra tiles fraction bars base 10 blocks geoboards beans pattern blocks calculator protractor compass rulers computer scales decimal squares other	
Type of entry	17. Circle the kind of entry this is: individual group	

Do you want to revise, edit, or polish this entry?	Yes No	Is this entry one that you want to publish in your assessment portfolio? Yes No

Possible changes:

Source: Adapted from *Teacher's Guide: Kentucky Mathematics Portfolio,* by Kentucky Department of Education, 1993, Frankfort, KY: Office of Assessment and Accountability, Author. Reprinted by permission.

Name _____ Date __5-11-92__

Self-Evaluation

Have you changed as a reader? What are your strengths and weaknesses? As I reader I haven't gone through many changes. My only weakness is getting into a book, but once I'm started my strengths take over me. I love to read!!!!

How have you changed as a writer? What are your strengths and weaknesses? As a writer I have relized that it takes many reworkings to come up with a final copy. Spelling is my main weakness and my strengths include sentence structure + punctuation.

Having looked at your work what goals would you set for yourself as a reader and writer? As a reader I plan to widen my spread of books and as a writer I'm going to look more deeply into my work.

Self-Reflection

When you look at your portfolio, how do you feel about yourself as a writer? Tell why you feel that way. I feel great about myself as a writer. I started off rather slow, but have improved 95%, since the start of this year + I plan to keep improving untill the end.

When you look at your portfolio, how do you feel about yourself as a reader? Tell why you feel that way. I feel extra great as a reader. I love reading + I love the feeling that I get when I finish a really good book.

Source: Adapted from "Literacy Portfolios for Teaching, Learning, and Accountability: The Bellevue Literacy Project," by S. W. Valencia and N. A. Place, in *Authentic Reading Assessment: Practice and Possibilities* (p. 146), by Sheila W. Valencia, E. H. Hiebert, and Peter P. Afferbach (Eds.). Copyright © 1994 by the International Reading Association. Adapted by permission.

Without such organization, it would be easy for the portfolio to become too disorganized for the teachers to use efficiently in class. Figure 12.13 is an example of one of these entry forms completed by a student.

Using Growth and Learning-Progress Portfolios in Your Teaching

Creating a Portfolio Classroom Culture Growth and learning-progress portfolios, like other assessments, work best when integrated fully into your teaching. Some writers advocate making the portfolio the center of your instructional planning and teaching activities so you and your students will interact intensively with the portfolio contents. This is called the **portfolio culture model** of conceptual change (Duschl & Gitomer, 1991; Niyogi, 1995). In a portfolio culture, instructional activities and projects are opportunities for students to record their intermediate progress, their progressive understanding of concepts and phenomena, and their interactions with peers and teachers. Duschl and Gitomer suggest the work included must have certain characteristics to be useful in a portfolio culture educational setting that focuses on restructuring students' conceptual development. The following suggestions are consistent with their views:

1. *Include authentic work.* The work that a student includes in the portfolio must provide a direct opportunity for him to engage in the types of thinking and abilities typically used by those working in the field or discipline. For example, in a science portfolio a student should work on evaluating evidence, using scientific explanations to account for data, or collecting data to support or refute explanations.

2. *Record conceptual development.* Portfolio entries must record a student's own explanations, understandings, and conceptual frameworks. This record must be frequently updated as the student progresses through a project or a problem solution to show changes in the student's conceptual framework and thinking as the project develops. It is not enough to include only the finished work. For example, a student should periodically record in a science portfolio her current scientific explanation of the events encountered, results observed, and concepts being studied.

3. *Engage in reflective activity.* The student uses the portfolio contents as a basis for discussions with the teacher about his understanding of concepts, principles, and theories that underlie the work. The teacher guides the discussion so that the student uses the same thinking strategies and abilities used by workers in the fields or discipline. For example, if the student is working on a scientific problem, she should use the portfolio contents to engage in scientific thinking and activities. The student should record changes in her explanations as new evidence accumulates.

You Must Be Knowledgeable and Spontaneous Using these portfolios requires that you have significant knowledge, skill, and ability. Also, you need to be very well versed in the discipline for which you are assessing progress. You should notice, too, that this type of portfolio assessment activity is considerably more spontaneous and less formal than assessing with best works portfolios. These characteristics are not necessarily weaknesses because the portfolio is used with interactive instruction and as a formative evaluation tool.

Best Works Portfolio Organization and Contents

Organizing a Best Works Portfolio A **best works portfolio** is organized around learning targets, too. For example, a portfolio may be designed to assess learning targets in the areas of problem solving, mathematical reasoning, mathematical communication, and understanding the core curriculum concepts. Thus each portfolio must contain examples of mathematics investigations, applications, solutions to nonroutine problems, projects, interdisciplinary problem solutions, and writing about mathematics.

Students prepare entries throughout the year. There is no mandated time schedule except the date on which the portfolio is due. However, to help the students prepare, teachers give students explanations and suggestions for deciding which examples the student should include. Figure 12.14 shows some of the explanations and self-reflection questions a teacher gave to students preparing their best works mathematics portfolios.

Best Works Portfolios Should Fit the Curriculum To be effective, portfolios must be consistent with the goals, standards, and learning targets of the state or school district curriculum framework and your daily teaching activities. Keep in mind the following points as you plan your portfolio organization and contents (Arter & Spandel, 1992):

- Portfolios should emphasize the same standards, curriculum goals, and learning targets emphasized in your daily instruction.

- The criteria used to evaluate students' portfolio entries should be the same as those used in daily instruction.

- The way you organize and use a portfolio should be consistent with the values you convey through your teaching activities (e.g., if your teaching emphasizes students taking responsibility for their own learning, the portfolio procedure you use should be consistent with this approach).

What Counts as Evidence in Best Works Portfolios? The issue here is what should be included in or excluded from the portfolio. The purpose of a best works portfolio is to provide evidence that the major learning targets have been accomplished. Therefore, these learning targets determine what to include. You will need to decide whether a portfolio is the best method of assessing accomplishments on these learning targets, too. The portfolio, like other performance assessments, should not be used to assess every learning target in curriculum. As students mature and take more responsibility for their own learning, they can decide for themselves what constitutes appropriate evidence of accomplishment. In that case, you will need to give students clear statements of learning targets and of the criteria by which you will judge their entries.

FIGURE 12.14 Example of suggestions given to fourth-grade students on how to prepare their mathematics portfolios.

WHAT WORKS?	CHECK IT OUT!
Here are the types of pieces you should include in your portfolio: • investigations—studying a mathematical topic or doing a mathematical experiment • applications—using mathematics to solve real world problems • non-routine—combining or inventing problem-solving strategies to arrive at solutions or results • projects—completing problems that take several days or longer • interdisciplinary—using mathematics with other subjects • writing—writing about mathematics to explain your thinking or solution These pieces should also show that you can do these things: • understand ways to solve problems and do more with the problem (problem solving) • think by using mathematical ideas and prove your solution is correct by using logical explanations (reasoning) • explain mathematics to others using mathematical language, symbols, and drawings (mathematical communication) • understand mathematical topics and use mathematics in other subjects and everyday life (understanding/connecting core concepts)	Ask yourself these questions when choosing pieces for your portfolio: • Did I solve the problem in different ways? • Have I done other things with the problem? • Is my answer correct and does it make sense? • Did I use correct mathematical language, symbols, and/or drawings? • Is my mathematics connected to other subjects and everyday life? • Have I listed the mathematical tools (calculators, blocks, beans, etc.) I used? • Did I explain my thinking and show all my work? • Does my explanation show that I understand mathematics? • Have I edited and corrected my work so this is my best effort? • Have I chosen different types of pieces for my portfolio? • Did I show all the mathematical topics (core concepts)? • If I chose a group entry, did I include my own ideas and explanations? • Have I talked with my teacher about the pieces in my portfolio?

Source: From *Portfolios and You* (p. 3), by the Kentucky Department of Education, 1993, Frankfort, KY: Office of Assessment and Accountability. Reprinted by permission.

Entry Captions for Best Works Portfolios A portfolio can quickly become a mess of materials and papers that is difficult to assess. To improve the situation, each entry should have an appropriate **portfolio entry sheet** (or **caption**) containing the following information:

- Name of the student
- Date of entry
- Title or description of the entry. For example, "Comparison of the Population Growth of Canada and the United States."
- Some indication of the learning target or purpose for including the entry. A student may write, "This entry shows that I can use numbers in real-world situations to draw conclusions about how populations grow. I can use growth rates and draw conclusions about when the two populations will be the same."
- Why this particular entry is important or valuable. For example, "I think this was a good piece to include because it shows an actual situation in which I had to use mathematics. Population growth is a social studies topic that I applied mathematics to solve. Also, I had to use a computer spreadsheet program to make the calculations many times in order to discover that the two countries will have the same population in about 59 years."

Limits to a Best Works Portfolio The size of a portfolio is no small matter! A portfolio that contains too many entries is difficult to understand and may be confusing to students who can get lost in the mass of materials. Also, evaluating long portfolios is difficult and time consuming.

Portfolio size is related to validity and reliability. Does the portfolio represent the student's attainment? How many entries and what varieties of entries are needed to ensure a representative sample of the student's work? Will a long portfolio be scored less consistently than a short portfolio?

Self-Reflection on Portfolio Entries

How to Encourage Students' Self-Reflection For some teaching purposes, a student's review of and self-reflection on the portfolio's contents are the major concerns. However, doing self-reflection well can enhance the learning process if the reflection is substantive (not simply comments like "I worked hard") because it requires students to reason with the subject matter. Reflection also develops metacognitive skills. Arter and Spandel (1992) suggest asking students the following types of questions to prompt self-reflective activities:

- What is the process you went through to complete this assignment? Include where you got ideas, how you explored the subject, what problems you encountered, and what revision strategies you used.

- What were the points made by the group as it reviewed your work? Describe your response to each point—did you agree or disagree? Why? What did you do as the result of their feedback?

- What makes your most effective piece different from your least effective piece?

- How does this activity relate to what you have learned before?

- What are the strengths of your work? What still makes you uneasy? (p. 40)

Metacognition Although such questions prompt students to review and evaluate their work, the list does not comprise an assessment method per se. Keep in mind that self-reflection is a mental activity. Your assessment of this activity must, therefore, be indirect. Further, although self-reflection appears to be a worthwhile instructional activity, it is not clear educationally that it is either desirable or appropriate to assess formally students' ability to do these self-reflective activities. They may best be handled as informal formative evaluation. In Appendix F we discuss a related area, *metacognition*. Figure F.1 illustrates a student self-assessment questionnaire regarding different aspects of metacognition. You may want to adapt this questionnaire to assess portfolio self-reflection.

Special Concerns About Portfolio Contents

If one or two teachers work out a portfolio system for use in one or two classes, the system will likely meet their immediate needs as an informal assessment of students' progress. On the other hand, if central educational authorities at the state or local levels mandate a portfolio system, it becomes an "add-on" to already existing classroom activities. As a result, special steps are needed to convince and educate teachers about the usefulness of the mandated portfolio. A portfolio is not well integrated with instruction, for example, if students see one day a week as "portfolio day." They perceive portfolios as a separate subject!

At one time, Kentucky's department of education mandated portfolios as part of the school accountability system. Patterns of portfolio crafting and usage illustrated this lack of integration in the early stages of the mandate. Buren and Lewis (1994) observed the following patterns of portfolio usage for writing.

- *High-investment portfolios.* These portfolios showed the students were highly invested in the portfolio contents. Each portfolio was highly individual, and the contents were clearly the students' choices. The portfolios generally showed higher writing proficiency than the types described later. This was highly desirable.

- *Cookie-cutter portfolios.* Not very desirable. All portfolios from the same class look nearly identical. All students write about the same topics and use the same prompts. Students don't choose the contents and there is low student investment. These portfolios typically showed low writing proficiency.

- *Portfolio-week portfolios.* Not very desirable. All portfolios from the same classroom bore the same dates on all pieces. The pieces were not polished or rewritten. Rather, they were completed just before the deadline for submission to the state. The contents do not show high individual student choices or investment. These portfolios typically showed low writing proficiency.

- *Teacher-generated portfolio prompts.* Not very desirable. All portfolios from the same class were based on the same set of prompts. There was little student choice of topics and low student investment. The teacher-generated prompts were inappropriate or limited students' ability to write for different purposes or to different audiences.

- *Content-limited portfolios.* Not very desirable. These portfolios may exhibit any of the foregoing patterns. However, some of the pieces are writings from curriculum areas outside of the language arts area. The content areas are limited, and the portfolios generally show that students' writing outside language arts classes needs further improvement. The portfolios demonstrate that writing skill is not being applied or integrated across different curriculum areas.

Obviously, you do not want to create a system that produces any of the inappropriate portfolio types. As you follow the steps described in the next section, keep the purpose of your portfolio clearly in mind.

Six Steps for Crafting a Portfolio System

Because portfolios are used for such a wide range of formative and summative purposes, a single set of design guidelines is difficult to devise. The six steps that follow are general enough, however, to give you overall guidance in the portfolio-crafting process. You should adapt the steps to suit your particular purposes. The steps express an assessment point of view, namely that assessment should be highly aligned to curriculum and teaching.

Following each step is a set of portfolio-crafting questions to sharpen the focus of your development efforts. Notice that after answering the questions in Step 1, you may decide *not* to develop a portfolio system. Steps 2 through 5 assume that you have completed Step 1 and have decided to use a portfolio system. If you decide to develop a portfolio system, the answers to the questions in Step 1 will set the boundaries and context as you apply the last five steps.

Step 1. Identify Portfolio's Purpose and Focus

- Why do I want a portfolio?
- What learning targets and curriculum goals will it serve?
- Will other methods of assessment serve these learning targets better?

- Should the portfolio focus on best work, growth and learning progress, or both?
- Will the portfolio be used for students' summative evaluation, formative evaluation, or both?
- Who should be involved in defining the purpose, focus, and organization of the portfolio (e.g., students, teachers, parents)?

Step 2. Identify the General Achievement Dimensions to Be Assessed

- Do I need to use the same content and thinking processes framework as I do for individual performance tasks?
- Should I focus primarily on how well the student uses the portfolio to reflect on his or her progress or growth?
- What kinds of knowledge, skills, and abilities will be the major focus of the portfolio?
- If I require a growth and learning-progress portfolio, what do I want to learn about students' self-reflections?

Step 3. Identify Appropriate Organization

- What types of entries (student products and activity records) will provide assessment information about the content and process dimensions identified in Step 2?
- What should the outline or table of contents for each portfolio contain?
- Define each category or type of entry:
  - Which content and process dimension does it assess?
  - What will the teacher or the student "get out of" each entry?
  - What is the time frame for each entry being put into the portfolio?
  - When will the entries be evaluated?
  - What are the minimum and maximum numbers of entries per category?
  - How will the entries within a student's portfolio be organized?
  - Will this set of entries fully represent the student's attainment or growth and learning progress?
  - What type of container will I need to hold all of the students' entries, and where will I keep them?

Step 4. Portfolio's Use in Practice

- When will the students work on or use their portfolios (e.g., 15 minutes of every class period)?
- How will the portfolio fit into the classroom routine?
- Will the teacher, student, or both decide what to include in the portfolio?
- Do I need to create a special climate in the classroom to promote the good use of portfolios?

- When will the student and/or the teacher review and evaluate the portfolio?
- How will the portfolio be weighted, if at all, when the time comes to assign letter grades for the marking period?
- Will I schedule a conference to go over the portfolio with the student?
- Will the portfolio be shared with parents? Other teachers? Other students?

Step 5.　Evaluation of Portfolios and Entries

- Are scoring rubrics already available for each type of entry?
- Does an evaluation framework or general scoring rubric exist for each type of entry?
- Are the general and specific rubrics aligned with the state standards and school district's curriculum framework?
- Will students, teachers, or both evaluate entries? Which ones?
- Will evaluations of every entry count toward a marking-period grade?
- Given its purpose, is it necessary to have an overall score for the portfolio?
- Should the rubric be holistic, analytic, or annotated holistic?
- Who will score the portfolio (e.g., student, teacher, outsider)?
- How often will the whole portfolio need to be scored (e.g., each week or each marking period)?
- Does an evaluation framework or general scoring rubric exist for evaluating the portfolio as a whole?

Step 6.　Evaluation of Rubrics

- Are scoring rubrics available that are consistent with the purpose of the portfolio? With the way each individual entry was evaluated? With the overall curriculum framework?
- Has the scoring rubric been tried on portfolios from different students? From students with different teachers? With what results?
- Does the scoring rubric give the same results for the same students when applied by different teachers?

ELECTRONIC PORTFOLIOS

Textbook publishers and software developers have created products that allow a best works portfolio to be presented digitally. These are called **electronic portfolios**. One use of such a portfolio is for teacher education students to present their teaching credentials when applying for positions. The digitized portfolio can reside on a local computer, a compact disk (CD), or a Website. The software provides an organization for the portfolio contents. Persons then add electronic documents and images in various categories. For example, a portfolio for a teacher candidate may have categories such as (a) candidate's overview statement, (b) resume, (c) state teaching standards met, (d) lesson plans developed, (e) teaching units developed, and (f) student assessment tools crafted. The software provides a template for the organization and sometimes for the entries.

The person creating the portfolio uploads various digital files containing documents and artifacts into the electronic portfolio in the appropriate categories such as lesson plans, resumes, essays on teaching philosophy, and so on. Some more sophisticated software allows uploading of video clips, so a person can show the portfolio evaluator a video of himself or herself teaching a lesson. Photos of artifacts (e.g., performance tasks crafted) can be scanned (or made with a digital camera) and uploaded. If the electronic portfolio resides on a Website, then a prospective employer anywhere can be given access to view it. Alternately, the completed electronic portfolio can be copied onto a CD and sent to employers.

Barrett (2000) described six levels of electronic portfolio development, closely tied to the technology skills of the person developing the portfolio:

- Level 0—All documents are in paper format. Some portfolio data may be stored on videotape.
- Level 1—All documents are in digital file formats, using word processing or other commonly used software, and stored in electronic folders on a hard drive, floppy disk, or LAN server.
- Level 2—Portfolio data are entered into a structured format, such as a database or HyperStudio template or slide show (such as PowerPoint or AppleWorks) and stored on a hard drive, Zip, floppy disk, or LAN.
- Level 3—Documents are translated into Portable Document Format with hyperlinks between standards, artifacts, and reflections using Adobe Acrobat Exchange and stored on a hard drive, Zip, Jaz, CD-R/W, or LAN server.
- Level 4—Documents are translated into HTML, complete with hyperlinks between standards, artifacts, and reflections, using a Web authoring program and posted to a Web server.
- Level 5—Portfolio is organized with a multimedia authoring program, incorporating digital sound and video. Then it is converted to digital format and pressed to CD-R/W or posted to the Web in streaming format.

Summary

Crafting Performance Tasks and Rubrics

- Performance assessments are developed in three stages: defining and clarifying the performance to be assessed, constructing the performance task, and creating scoring rubrics. In practice, the stages are iterative, not linear.

- The chapter provides numerous suggestions for defining and clarifying the performance to assess. Included are suggestions for using a framework in guiding the definitions of the achievement dimensions on which the assessment will focus. A checklist for evaluating achievement dimensions is given.
- The chapter provides numerous suggestions for constructing performance tasks: how to identify meaningful tasks, how to develop a task around important content and thinking-process achievement dimensions, and how to incorporate a variety of task features into the design. A checklist for evaluating performance tasks is given.
- The number of performance tasks to include on an assessment is critical because such tasks take a long time to complete, and thus there are fewer of them on any one assessment. The chapter reviews how several factors affect the decision of how many tasks to use, including criticalness of the decisions, scope of the assessment, mixture of assessment formats, complexity of learning targets, time needed to complete the tasks, time available for assessment, diagnostic detail needed, and available human resources.
- The chapter provides numerous suggestions for crafting scoring rubrics and recording assessment results. Suggestions include developing and using a conceptual framework to organize the rubrics. A checklist for evaluating scoring rubrics is given.
- Rubrics differ according to whether they require one or several judgments (holistic or analytic) and according to whether the performance descriptions are generic or task-specific. Advantages and disadvantages of each type were presented in Figure 12.3.

Crafting Checklists and Rating Scales

- The chapter provides guidelines for crafting checklists and examples of using them for assessing processes and procedures as well as products.
- Guidelines for crafting rating scales and examples of their use in implementing scoring rubrics are provided.
- Errors teachers could make when using rating scales as scoring rubrics are described.
- Suggestions are made for improving the reliability of rating scales. A checklist for evaluating scoring rubrics is given.

Crafting Projects

- Guidelines and suggestions for crafting projects that can be used as assessment tools are given.
- The chapter provides guidance for managing classroom projects, including management goals and strategies for attaining these goals.

Crafting Portfolios Including Electronic Portfolios

- Guidelines and suggestions for constructing portfolio systems describe issues surrounding content and purposes of portfolios. The chapter presents a six-step procedure for crafting portfolios.
- The chapter discusses how electronic portfolios are organized and used.

Important Terms and Concepts

achievement dimensions
alternate solution strategies
behavior checklist
best works portfolio
bottom-up approach to rubric crafting
central tendency error
checklist
content achievement dimensions
descriptive graphic rating scale
electronic portfolio
exemplars
graphic rating scale
growth and learning-progress portfolio
halo effect
high-stakes assessment
leniency error
lifelong achievement dimensions
logical error
numerical rating scale
personal bias
portfolio culture model
portfolio entry sheet (caption)
procedure checklist
product checklist
product versus process
rater drift
rating scale
reliability decay
reliability of ratings
rubrics (analytic, annotated holistic, holistic, generic (general), task-specific)
scaffolding
self-evaluation checklist
severity error
short task versus long task
stages in crafting performance tasks
standard or quality dimension
structure a task
top-down approach to rubric crafting

Exercises and Applications

1. For a subject you teach (or plan to teach), identify learning targets that would be appropriately assessed with on-demand performance tasks using a paper-and-pencil format, and with on-demand performance tasks not using paper and pencil.
   a. Using these results, create one on-demand performance task using paper and pencil and one on-demand performance task not using paper and pencil. For both tasks, follow the Marzano et al. (1993) procedure described in the text.
   b. Exchange your tasks with another student in the course. Evaluate each other's task by applying the checklist for judging the quality of performance tasks. If a task resulted in a "no" answer to one of the checklist items, explain why. Revise the tasks where necessary.
   c. Share your results with others in the course.
2. Select one performance task that you created in Exercise 1, or that you obtained from other sources. Following the procedures in this chapter, prepare general and specific scoring rubrics. (You may use the framework in Appendix E or another one that your instructor approves.)
   a. Write a description of each step you used to craft the rubrics.

b. Exchange your rubrics with another student in the course. Evaluate each other's specific rubrics using the checklist for judging the quality of scoring rubrics. Whenever your rubrics received a "no" answer to one of the checklist items, explain why. Revise the rubrics where necessary.

c. Share your results with others in your course.

3. Select two or more learning targets that can be assessed by one performance task and a corresponding specific scoring rubric (of your own or others' creation). Justify your selection by explaining how this task best assesses these learning targets.

a. Administer the performance task to at least five students. Score the task using the scoring rubric.

b. Write a short essay describing your scoring experience. Was the scoring rubric adequate? Were there any reliability problems in using it? Why or why not? Make suggestions for improving the scoring rubric based on your experience.

c. Prepare a summary of your students' results.

4. Apply the checklist for judging the quality of performance tasks to the following examples from the text in Chapter 11. Write a report of your findings. Be sure to make suggestions on how to improve the tasks. Send a copy of your report to the textbook author.

a. "Decision Making" (p. 245)

b. "Clean Water" (p. 246–247)

c. "Historical Investigation" (p. 248)

5. Design a best works portfolio system for assessing students in the subject you teach (or plan to teach). Follow the six-step procedure suggested in the chapter.

a. Prepare a report describing the portfolio system you designed. Be sure your report addresses all of the questions listed under each step.

b. Discuss your portfolio system in class with other students.

13 Formative Evaluation Using Informal Diagnostic Assessments

LEARNING TARGETS

After studying this chapter, you should have learned the following:

Diagnostic Assessment

1. Explain the dual purpose of diagnostic assessment of learning difficulties. [1, 4]

Integrating Teaching With the Six Approaches to Diagnosis

2. Describe six approaches to diagnostic assessment and give examples of each. [1, 4]

3. Craft diagnostic assessment procedures using each of the six approaches described in this chapter. [2, 3, 4]

4. Explain the strengths and weaknesses of each diagnostic assessment approach. [1, 4]

5. Show through words and/or diagrams how the teaching, diagnosis, and assessment processes may be integrated. [4, 3, 1]

Interviewing Students

6. Explain how to improve diagnostic assessment interviews of students. [2, 4]

Important Terms and Concepts

7. Explain the importance to educational assessment of the terms and concepts listed at the end of this chapter. [6, 4]

ABOUT THIS CHAPTER

We begin the chapter by discussing the purposes of diagnostic assessment and formative evaluation using six different approaches. We discuss how these approaches complement one another and fit into a teaching sequence. Each approach is discussed and we describe how you may implement it. We close the chapter by discussing suggestions for interviewing students expressly to discover why they do not understand some concepts and principles.

DIAGNOSTIC ASSESSMENT

Two Purposes of Classroom Diagnostic Assessment

Diagnostic assessment of learning difficulties serves two related purposes: (a) to identify which learning targets a student has not mastered and (b) to suggest possible causes or reasons why the student has not mastered the learning targets. If you know what specific learning targets a student has not mastered, you can focus your remedial teaching on those specific targets. However, unless you also know or can hypothesize why the student cannot perform a learning target, you will be unsure how to focus your remedial teaching.

Six Approaches to Diagnosis of Learning Problems

Different approaches to diagnosis provide different levels of detail about students' **deficits in learning**. They also differ in the degree to which they emphasize the first or second of the purposes of diagnosis described previously. These are the six approaches we shall discuss:

1. The **profiling content areas strengths and weaknesses** approach, in which a deficit is defined as a student's low standing, relative to peers, in a broad learning outcome area in a subject. For example, a student may have less ability in subtraction and division than in addition and multiplication compared to peers.

2. The **prerequisite knowledge and skills deficits approach**, in which a deficit is defined as a student's failure to have learned concepts and skills necessary to profit from instruction in a course or a unit.

FIGURE 13.1 Examples of how different approaches to diagnostic assessment interpret the same student's performance.

Examples of items along with responses of a hypothetical student								
(a)	(b)	(c)	(d)	(e)	(f)	(g)	(h)	(i)
17	15	43	337	654	43	63	562	667
−12	−13	−32	−226	−423	−25	−57	−453	−374
5	2	11	111	231	√ 22	√ 14	√ 111	√ 313

Total score for subtraction = 5/9 or 56%. Percentile rank = 18

Approach 1. Profile of strengths and weaknesses

The score on the subtraction subtest shown above is compared to the scores on other subtests such as addition, multiplication, division, etc. A profile of strengths and weaknesses in arithmetic is created for each student.

Example: The score of 5 correct has a percentile rank of 18 and is lower than other subtest scores.

Interpretation of the results: The student is weak in subtraction.

Approaches 2 and 3. Prerequisite hierarchy combined with mastery of specific objectives

The items above may be derived from a hierarchy of prerequisite arithmetic skills and the mastery of each skill in the hierarchy is assessed. (Skill statements are based on Ferguson [1970].)

Example:	*Hierarchy of Skills*	*Score*
	(4) Subtract 3-digit numbers requiring borrowing from either tens' or hundreds' place. [Items (h) and (i)]	0/2 or 0 %
	(3) Subtract 2-digit numbers with borrowing from tens' place. [Items (f) and (g)]	1/2 or 50 %
	(2) Subtract two 2-digit and two 3-digit numbers when borrowing is not needed. [Items (c), (d), and (e)]	3/3 or 100 %
	(1) Subtract 2-digit numbers when numbers are less than 20. [Items (a) and (b)]	2/2 or 100 %

Interpretation of the results: The student has mastered the prerequisite Objectives 1 and 2, but has not mastered Objectives 3 and 4. Instruction should begin with Objective 3.

Approach 4. Identifying Errors

The subtraction item(s) that the student answered incorrectly are studied and the student's errors are identified.

Example: The student's responses to Items (f), (g), (h), and (i) are wrong. These are studied to identify the type(s) of errors the student made.

Interpretation of the results: The student is not renaming (regrouping) from tens' to units' place and from hundreds' to tens' place.

3. The **mastery of specific objectives approach**, in which a deficit is defined as a student's failure to master one or more end-of-instruction learning targets.

4. The **identifying students' errors in performance approach**, in which a deficit is defined as the type(s) of errors a student makes.

5. The **knowledge structure approach**, in which a deficit is defined as a student's inappropriate or incorrect mental organization of concepts and their interrelationships.

6. The **component competencies of problem solving approach**, in which a deficit is defined as a student's inability to perform one or more of the components necessary to solve a word problem.

Each approach will be described and evaluated in terms of how well it meets the second purpose of diagnostic testing: identifying probable causes of a student's learning difficulty. Figure 13.1 illustrates each of the first four approaches with a specific example and serves as a device for comparing the approaches. The last two approaches,

illustrated later, are more in line with cognitively oriented instructional psychology.

INTEGRATING TEACHING, DIAGNOSIS, AND ASSESSMENT

Feedback from assessment of students' learning guides your next steps as you proceed in teaching. The teaching process is complex and cannot be completely captured in simple diagrams. Nevertheless, we use a simplified diagram in Figure 13.2 to show you how the various diagnostic approaches fit into the teaching process. The example assumes that you are planning to teach a new unit to the students.

The steps in Figure 13.2 are described here.

1. *Have the students learned the prerequisites for the new unit?* If not, you will need to identify the deficit prerequisites, then teach them before beginning the new material. Otherwise students will not profit from the new unit.

2. *Teach the new unit.* If students have learned the necessary prerequisites, you can begin to teach the new material.

FIGURE 13.2 Example of how the six approaches to diagnosing learning difficulties may be integrated into the teaching process.

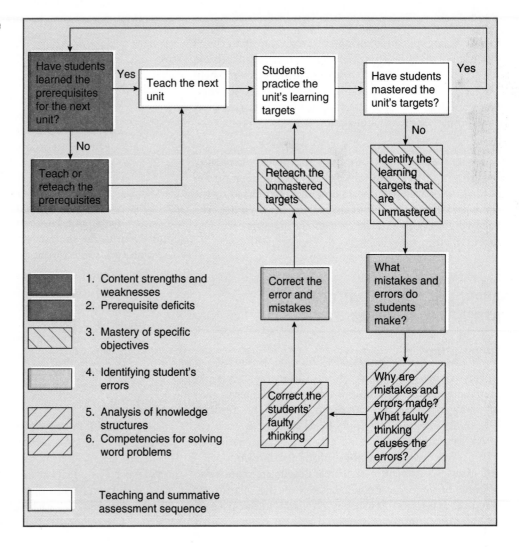

3. *Students are given practice on the units' learning targets.* Students must practice to master the learning targets.

4. *Have students mastered the units' learning targets?* At this step you can conduct a more formal summative assessment of the students by implementing the assessment plans described in Chapter 6. If students have mastered the material, you can proceed to the next unit. If they have not, you may need to reteach at least some part of the unit.

5. *What learning targets have students not mastered?* Your reteaching should focus on these learning targets. Depending on the content and educational level of your students, simply knowing which targets were not learned sufficiently may be enough information for you to carry out your remedial lesson(s).

6. *What mistakes or errors do students make?* Often you will need to look beyond the learning target deficits to identify the errors or mistakes a student makes. Your reteaching can focus on correcting the mistakes or errors you identify.

7. *Why are the mistakes/errors made? What is the faulty thinking that students use when they make mistakes?* Students' errors are very often the result of not understanding concepts, not relating concepts to existing knowledge, applying the wrong rule, or knowing how to do some part of the task but not all of it. If you can identify these deeper thinking errors, you can organize your remedial teaching to help students correct their thinking. This should reduce their errors and lead to their mastery of the learning targets. (See, for example, Approach 4 in Figure 13.1.)

Figure 13.2 describes these steps in a more dynamic way by using a process flow chart. Parts of the diagram are shaded differently to indicate how they are related to the six approaches to diagnostic assessment listed earlier. The following sections discuss each of the six approaches in more detail.

APPROACH 1: PROFILING CONTENT STRENGTHS AND WEAKNESSES

Description

In this approach, a school subject—say, elementary arithmetic or elementary reading—is subdivided into areas, each of which is treated as a separate trait or ability. *KeyMath Diagnostic Arithmetic Test* (Connolly, Nachtman, & Pritchett, 1976), for example, divides primary school arithmetic into 14 areas (numeration, fractions, addition, subtraction, etc.) and assesses a student in each area. Results are reported as a profile of strengths and weaknesses over the 14 areas. As is typical of tests in this category, strengths and weaknesses are interpreted in norm-referenced ways: A student with a

"weakness" is significantly below the norm. Percentile ranks (discussed in Chapter 17) are the primary type of norm-referenced score used in this context.

Classroom Application

The following steps describe how to craft this type of diagnostic assessment for classroom use.

1. *Identify two or more content areas over which you want to profile students.* Each content area should be related to the learning targets you will be teaching during the term. For example, you may wish to obtain a diagnostic profile in mathematics for addition, subtraction, multiplication, division, place value, fractions, and word problems. Try to limit the number of areas to eight to keep the assessment of reasonable length.

2. *Craft items to span the basic concepts in each content area.* The items should match the learning targets in each area.

   a. For classroom purposes, it is best to use constructed-response or short-answer items for diagnostic tests of this type. This reduces chances of students answering correctly by blind guessing or because you crafted the response-choice items poorly.

   b. If possible, use 12 to 25 items per content area. This will result in more reliable profiles.

   c. The items should cover the most basic concepts and procedures in each content area. You are trying to identify those few students who are most in need of remediation in an area. The items for each content area should be easy for students who have achieved an acceptable level of learning in each area.

3. *Assemble the items into separate **subtests**, with one subtest for each content area.* For example, put all the addition items together, all the subtraction, and so on. Arrange the items within each subtest from easiest to most difficult.

4. *Administer each subtest separately, using separate directions and timing.* All students should work on the same subtest, stopping and starting a subtest together. Students should not go back to a subtest once the class has moved onto the next subtest. When the students have completed all of the subtests, score each subtest separately. The subtest scores are the ones you interpret diagnostically. The total score (summed over all subtests) has no diagnostic value.

Figure 13.3 shows the hypothetical results of administering this type of diagnostic test to a group of students. The test covers French I and would likely be administered to French II students at the beginning of the term to give the teacher an idea of the strengths and weaknesses of the incoming class. For each subtest, a student receives two scores: (a) the number right, expressed as a fraction of the

FIGURE 13.3 Example of students' strengths and weaknesses profiles resulting from a teacher-made diagnostic test of French I.

	Areas of French I									
	Idioms		Vocab.		Grammar		Para. Reading		Listen. Compre.	
	Correct	Rank	Correct	Rank	Correct	Rank	Correct	Rank	Correct	Rank
Ali	10/12	3.5	11/15	3	11/13	3	9/12	4	3/15	(5)
Isaac	11/12	2	10/15	4.5	3/13	(6)	11/12	2	10/15	3
Leslie	12/12	1	15/15	1	12/13	2	11/12	2	14/15	1
Miriam	3/12	(6)	10/15	4.5	10/13	4.5	2/12	(6)	1/15	(6)
Rebecca	5/12	(5)	3/15	(6)	10/13	4.5	6/12	(5)	4/15	4
Sharonda	10/12	3.5	14/15	2	13/13	1	11/12	2	12/15	2

maximum possible score, and (b) the student's rank. (Figure I.2 in Appendix I explains ranks.) Including the ranks helps you identify the poorest students quickly. Note that the *smaller* the rank, the *better* the student (i.e., the top-scoring student receives a rank of 1). In the example, the worst scores are circled.

You interpret the students' strengths and weaknesses using their ranks. Ali, for example, has a weakness in listening comprehension compared to other students in the group. Isaac, who generally did well, is weak in grammar. Leslie is strong in all areas, as is Sharonda. Miriam and Rebecca are weak in several areas but are average in grammar. This norm-referenced approach is useful for forming classroom groups for review and practice. Heterogeneous groups that contain some stronger and some weaker students should function well.

Strengths and Weaknesses

Strengths This approach to diagnostic assessment is most useful when you want to obtain a general idea about students' performance in subareas of a subject matter. If you know little about an incoming class of students, administering this type of assessment as a pretest at the beginning of the term can help you plan your teaching around the students' profiles. It is easy to craft. It can be scored quickly, which is a benefit if you have a large class or several sections.

Weaknesses For these profiles to be valid, the items you construct must assess the appropriate knowledge and skills, all students must take the same subtests, and the subtests must be reliable. If the subtests each contain only a handful of assessment tasks, the subtest scores probably will be unreliable. Unreliable subtest scores result in an **unreliable profile** over the different subareas. As a result, the students' strengths and weaknesses may be exaggerated or masked by chance errors of measurement. Note that this approach does not tell you about attainment of particular learning goals in the absolute sense; rather, it gives relative strengths and weaknesses within the group.

Diagnosis with such tests provides you with only general information about where their problems lie. It is much like saying, "The treasure lies to the north." The information is helpful, but it leaves you with a lot of work to do before the Grail can be found.

A good educational diagnostician will use the initial test results to formulate hypotheses concerning students' difficulties. You confirm or reject these hypotheses by following up and gathering additional information. Thus, although the initial profile of strengths and weaknesses is likely to be unreliable, the final diagnosis will be much more reliable if a skilled diagnostician who incorporates into that diagnosis appropriate additional information makes it. This is not to say, however, that the reliability of the profile-generating test should be ignored: High initial reliability helps focus the initial set of hypotheses, and prevents a large number of false leads. A test with very low profile reliability wastes the diagnostician's resources because many false leads are pursued.

APPROACH 2: IDENTIFYING PREREQUISITE DEFICITS

Description

This approach explores whether students have fallen behind because they have not learned the specific knowledge and skills necessary to profit from upcoming instruction. Among the approaches relying upon identification of learning prerequisites are Gagné's **learning hierarchies** (Gagné, 1962, 1968; Gagné, Major, Garstens, & Paradise, 1962; Gagné & Paradise, 1961).

The first step in creating a hierarchy is to select one learning target the student must be able to perform. The next steps involve analyzing it to identify the prerequisites a student must learn in order to achieve the target. For each prerequisite identified, you repeat the same analysis, generating a hierarchy of prerequisite performances. This backward analytic procedure identifies critical prior learning, the lack of which could cause students problems in subsequent learning.

The difference between this approach and the previous one is that here you focus on whether each prerequisite was learned rather than on the pattern of profile strengths and weaknesses. Your interpretation of results is criterion-referenced rather than norm-referenced.

Metropolitan Performance Assessment (Nurss, 1994), for example, contains several assessment components to survey prekindergarten and kindergarten students' learning of the basic skills and processes needed for beginning the first grade. One of the assessment components is the *Metropolitan Integrated Performance Tasks*, which assesses readiness skills such as following oral directions, understanding rhyming words, matching uppercase and lowercase letters, copying printed letters, drawing pictures, basic concepts (e.g., top, bottom, middle, under), rote counting, correspondence of number to numerals, counting forward and backward, and reading simple graphs. Preschool and kindergarten teachers use information on mastering prerequisites from the *Metropolitan Performance Assessment* to prepare students for first-grade work.

Classroom Application

You can identify prerequisites for a single unit of instruction or for a term. Use the hierarchical approach, or simply identify necessary prerequisites that are not in a teaching order. To develop a learning hierarchy, you should follow the procedure described earlier in relation to the Gagné learning hierarchies. For each learning target, ask yourself, "What must a student be able to do before he is ready to learn this learning target?" Focus on what needs to be learned immediately before. Once you identify that immediately prior (prerequisite) performance, you ask the same question about it. You may identify one or more performances that are immediately prerequisite. Continue this backward analysis until you have reached the point at which you can safely assume that nearly all the incoming students have learned the prerequisites.

Figure 13.4 shows an example of a learning hierarchy for computational subtraction based on an analysis by Ferguson (1970). The final learning target, "subtracting two 3-digit numbers with borrowing from both the tens' and hundreds' place," is at the top. All the other performances are prerequisite to it. Notice that Performance 5 is prerequisite to 4, but that both 2 and 3 are prerequisite to 4. The 2 and 3 performances are not prerequisite to each other, however, so they are shown in parallel branches.

Once you have created the hierarchy, you assess each student with several items for each of the prerequisites identified. At a minimum, you should use four or five items per prerequisite in the hierarchy.

If the hierarchy is small, you can start at the bottom and proceed upward, assessing one node at a time. Stop assessing

FIGURE 13.4 Prerequisite hierarchy of a subtraction unit.

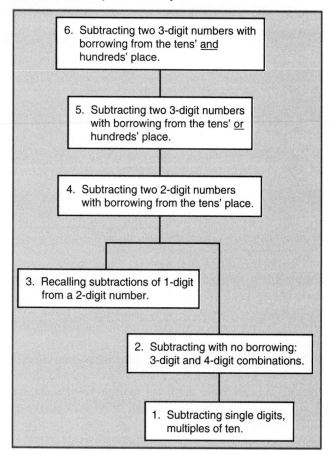

6. Subtracting two 3-digit numbers with borrowing from the tens' <u>and</u> hundreds' place.

5. Subtracting two 3-digit numbers with borrowing from the tens' <u>or</u> hundreds' place.

4. Subtracting two 2-digit numbers with borrowing from the tens' place.

3. Recalling subtractions of 1-digit from a 2-digit number.

2. Subtracting with no borrowing: 3-digit and 4-digit combinations.

1. Subtracting single digits, multiples of ten.

a student when the student reaches a point where she can do none or only one or two of the items at a node. If the hierarchy is very large, you can use an **adaptive testing strategy**. Begin with the node at the middle of the hierarchy. If a student does well on those items, branch upward to the next node and continue assessing until the student reaches a point where it is obvious that he cannot proceed further. Because the nodes are in a prerequisite order, the lower nodes in the hierarchy are not tested; you assume the student can perform them. If a student does poorly, you can branch downward to the next lower node, continuing to assess until it is obvious the student knows all the remaining lower nodes. In this case, you assume that the student has learned the prerequisites below that point.

Without a hierarchy, you can still identify the prerequisite learning for the term material or unit you are about to teach. You can identify these prerequisites in a manner similar to the procedure for developing a hierarchy. That is, ask yourself, "What does a student need to know how to do before I can teach the student this learning target?" The answers to such questions should result in a list of prerequisites that students should know before learning the new targets. Once these are identified, you develop four to five assessment tasks for each prerequisite.

Whether or not you use a hierarchy, your ultimate purpose for assessment is to identify for each student the prerequisites that are mastered and those that are not. You then remediate by teaching students the prerequisites they do not know before beginning new instruction.

Strengths and Weaknesses

Strengths This approach very specifically identifies skills that students need to learn before they are ready to be taught new learning targets. A hierarchy suggests the sequence for teaching the prerequisites. Assessments of prerequisite knowledge and skills are most helpful when you know very little about the students, especially when you expect large differences in their mastery of the prerequisites. Once you know each student's command of the prerequisites, you can tailor your teaching to meet his or her needs.

To be most effective, the prerequisites you identify should be specific to your curriculum and to your teaching approach. Different curricula and different teachers will approach the subject differently. This means that the prerequisites for students you teach may be somewhat different than the prerequisites for students a colleague teaches. (They should not be radically different, however, when both teachers are teaching comparable students the same material.)

Weaknesses This approach is limited by the care and accuracy with which you analyze the learning requirements of your curriculum. If you do not identify the proper prerequisites, your assessment will lack validity. Further, in a continuous-progress curriculum, the distinction between prerequisites and "regular learning" is arbitrary, based more or less on instructional convenience.

The learning theory underlying this approach assumes that learning proceeds best by first teaching the prerequisites. This is a building-block approach, in which prerequisite performances build one on another to facilitate the learning of new targets. It is not clear that this building-block approach to learning is an appropriate teaching strategy for all subjects and for all students.

Prerequisites derived from logical analyses of learning targets have at least two weaknesses that make it difficult to begin remedial instruction: (a) They identify certain, but not all, types of knowledge and skills students require to learn new material, and (b) they fail to provide information about the way students organize or structure their partial knowledge about the content to be learned (see Champagne, Klopfer, & Gunstone, 1982).

Champagne et al. (1982) reviewed the instructional implications of cognitive researcher's findings concerning teaching basic principles of mechanics. They found that logical analysis of learning targets failed to identify (a) the ways in which students entering a physics course mentally organized and understood mechanical principles in their everyday experience, (b) that students need to be taught how to qualitatively analyze problems before attempting to solve them quantitatively (i.e., before applying an equation), and (c) that one goal of instruction is to change students' entering knowledge schemata so that they approach the schemata of experts. (Chapter 10 discusses schemata.) It often is not simply the students' lack of content knowledge that is the primary cause of learning difficulty, but also the conflicts between the students' preconceptions of how the concepts in a subject are related to each other and how the textbook or teacher says the concepts are related. (See the discussion of pretesting in Chapter 6.)

APPROACH 3: IDENTIFYING OBJECTIVES NOT MASTERED

Description

This approach centers the assessment on the important, specific targets students are expected to learn. Short tests assess each objective. The difference between this approach and the identifying prerequisite deficits approach is that here you assess only the objectives that are the outcomes of the unit or the course, not the prerequisite objectives.

This approach has become the dominant one for diagnosis and is often recommended as the method of choice to classroom teachers, as well as to more specialized educational diagnosticians. Despite the many techniques and potential uses of criterion-referencing (Nitko, 1980), many educators consider the concepts of diagnosis, behavioral objectives, and criterion-referencing inseparable, as the following extract illustrates:

> Diagnosing and monitoring student learning progress has become an operating feature of programs aimed at adapting instruction to student differences. A key component of such programs is the use of criterion-referenced assessments, that is [assessments] designed to determine the presence or absence of certain specific competencies, providing teachers with the necessary information to determine skills and knowledge already possessed by students so that their appropriate entrance into the learning sequence can be insured. Furthermore, the use of such clear-cut descriptions of the students' capabilities insures that they neither repeat tasks they have already mastered nor work on objectives for which they lack critical prerequisites. (Wang, 1980, p. 5)

The idea of teaching to specific learning objectives dates back at least to the seminal work of Waples and Tyler (Tyler, 1934; Waples & Tyler, 1930). Teachers in the 1930s and 1940s, however, generally did not write statements of behavior or develop diagnostic assessments based on them.

The current widespread popularity of objectives-based assessment and instruction is principally a result of the commercial availability of integrated sets of objectives and tests. Publishers moved toward such integrated materials in the late 1970s and early 1980s, after educators enthusiastically greeted the concept of criterion-referencing tests (Glaser, 1963; Nitko, 1980). Instructional methods were developed that integrated objectives, learning material, and diagnostic tests. The major prototypes were the mastery learning model (Bloom, 1968; Carroll, 1963), Individually Prescribed Instruction (Glaser, 1968; Lindvall & Bolvin, 1967), Program for Learning in Accordance with Needs (Flanagan, 1967, 1969), Individually Guided Instruction (Klausmeier, 1975), and Personalized System of Instruction (Keller, 1968; Keller & Sherman, 1974).

Classroom Applications

The diagnostic information you want to obtain from this approach is a list of learning targets (objectives) that a student has mastered and not mastered. This means that for each teaching unit you must carefully identify and state the important learning targets. Follow these steps:

Step 1. Identify and write statements of the learning targets that are the main outcomes of the unit or the course.
Step 2. For each learning target, craft four to eight test items.
Step 3. If possible, have another teacher review each item and rate how closely it matches the learning targets. Revise the items as necessary to obtain a closer match.
Step 4. Assemble the items into a single instrument if the list of learning targets is relatively short (less than six); otherwise, depending on the students' educational development, you may need to divide the assessment into two or more instruments. For ease of scoring, keep all the items assessing the same objective together in the instrument.

Step 5. Set a "mastery" or passing score for each learning target. A frequently used **passing score** is 80% (or as near as you can come to this with the number of items you have for assessing a learning target). There is no educational justification for 80%, however. The important point is not the exact value of the passing score or passing percentage. Rather, it is the minimum level of knowledge a student needs to demonstrate with respect to each learning target to benefit from further instruction. This may vary from one learning target to the next. Use your own judgment, remembering that setting a standard too low or too high results in misclassifying students as masters or nonmasters.
Step 6. Administer the assessment to the students. After administering the assessment, separately score each learning target. Prepare a class list and chart in which you can record the students' scores on each learning target. This lets you identify students with similar deficits. Figure 13.5 shows an example of such a chart. The scores circled on the chart indicate a lack of mastery. Students should be given remedial instruction on these objectives.

Strengths and Weaknesses

Strengths Diagnostic assessments based on specific objectives are appealing because they (a) focus on specific and limited learning targets to teach, (b) communicate learning targets in an easy-to-understand form, and (c) focus your attention on students' observed performance. These features make assessment easier, instructional decision making simpler, and public accountability clearer.

Weaknesses Objectives-based diagnostic assessments are generally plagued with measurement error, primarily because the assessments tend to have too few items per

FIGURE 13.5 Hypothetical example of diagnosis of specific objectives mastered and not mastered on a teacher-made, objectives-based diagnostic test. Circles mean nonmastery.

Objectives	Ali	Isaac	Leslie	Miriam	Rebecca	Sharonda
1. Names and tells functions of each cell part. [8 items, mastery = 7/8]	7/8	8/8	7/8	(2/8)	(5/8)	(6/8)
2. Lists substances diffused and not diffused through cell membrane. [6 items, mastery = 5/6]	(4/6)	6/6	5/6	5/6	(3/6)	(1/6)
3. Labels parts of animal and plant cells. [6 items, mastery = 5/6]	5/6	5/6	5/6	(4/6)	(2/6)	(4/6)
4. Applies concepts of diffusion, oxidation, fusion, division, chromosomes, and DNA to explain reproduction. [8 items, mastery = 7/8]	(5/8)	7/8	7/8	7/8	(3/8)	(6/8)

objective. If you use a diagnostic assessment to decide whether a student has "mastered" an objective, you should evaluate its quality using an index such as percentage agreement, rather than a traditional reliability coefficient. Percentage agreement is discussed in Chapter 4. A **percentage agreement index** estimates how likely students are to be classified in the same category when either the same assessment is readministered or an alternate form of the assessment is administered. (See Appendix J for examples of how to calculate this index.) Consistency of classification (i.e., of mastery or nonmastery) is the main focus, rather than consistency of students' exact scores.

The behavioral objectives approach to diagnostic assessment has other serious limitations. The information obtained reflects only one aspect of diagnosis: the observable behavior or performance of what is to be learned. This gives you little information about how to remediate the deficits discovered. You know only that a student has not mastered an objective. Like the other approaches we have discussed, behavioral objectives-based assessments are not fully diagnostic.

The behavioral objectives approach can also be criticized for implying an inappropriate theory of how knowledge and skill are acquired. A student's knowledge base is seen as a simple sum of previously learned specific behaviors. Further, critics point out that behavior-based tests fail to assess students' knowledge schemata, problem-solving disabilities, and abilities to think in new real-world contexts (Haertel & Calfee, 1983). In recent years, instructional and cognitive psychology have stressed the importance of learning a student's internal representation (or schema) of knowledge, the relationships a student makes between knowledge elements, the way students construct meaning from their learning experiences, and the knowledge-processing skills a student commands (Glaser, 1982, 1984; Greeno, 1976).

Finally, focusing on isolated and specific learning targets can make the curriculum seem fragmented. That is, the general themes and the learning goals that express integration of many specific knowledge and skill components are often neglected in favor of the isolated specific objectives.

APPROACH 4: IDENTIFYING STUDENTS' ERRORS

Description

The goal of this approach is to identify a student's errors, rather than simply making a mastery-nonmastery decision about the student's overall performance on a particular behavioral objective. Examples of errors are failure to regroup when "borrowing" in subtraction, improper pronunciation of vowels when reading, reversing *i* and *e* when spelling, and producing a sentence fragment when writing. Once you identify and classify a student's errors, you can attempt to provide instruction to remediate (eliminate) them (see Figures 13.1 and 13.2).

Related to the error classification approach are methods that analyze complex performance into two or more component performances. If a student cannot perform the entire complex performance, diagnostic assessment identifies which component behaviors are lacking. Resnick and her associates (Resnick, 1975, 1976; Resnick, Wang, & Kaplan, 1973), for example, broke complex preschool mathematics skills into their component skills and identified the sequence in which these subskills should be performed. Burton (1982) identified all the subskills needed for a student to solve a problem correctly. The measurement of each of these less complex subskills in isolation is the basis of diagnosis. Gagné (1970, 1979) proposed a two-stage procedure to assess problem-solving ability. When a student fails to solve the problem presented, a second-stage assessment is used to determine which, if any, of the principles the student knows, whether all of the principles are known, and whether the student understands how to combine them.

Classroom Applications

It is not easy to apply this approach because it takes considerable experience and skill to identify students' errors, and there may be more than one cause for an error. Consider the subtraction problems in Figure 13.1, for example. An inexperienced or unskilled teacher may not recognize the possible cause of the student's mistakes. Oftentimes, such teachers will say the student was "not careful" or "made careless errors." However, students' errors are rarely careless or random. Rather, *students' errors are often systematic.* Students may apply a rule or a procedure consistently in both appropriate and inappropriate situations. For instance, in Figure 13.1, the student appears to have consistently applied this rule: "Subtract the smaller digit from the larger digit." This rule works for problems (a) through (e), but does not work for Problems (f) through (i). *It is important, therefore, that you consider every error a student makes as having some systematic cause.* Try to identify what caused the error, or what rule the student is using, before you dismiss it as careless or random.

Interviewing students best discovers many student errors. You can ask them to explain how they solved a problem, to explain why they responded the way they did, to tell you the rule for solving the problem, or to talk aloud as they go through the solutions to problems. These informal assessment procedures often reveal the types of errors a student is making.

Chapter 10 discussed higher-order thinking and problem-solving assessment. Those assessment strategies are useful for discovering what types of problem-solving errors a student tends to make.

Strengths and Weaknesses

Strengths The chief advantage of the error classification approach over the behavioral objectives approach is that you discover not only *that* a learning target cannot be performed but also which aspects of the student's performance are flawed. This narrows your search for possible causes of poor performance. A skilled teacher can use this information to identify quickly one or more instructional procedures that have previously worked (remediated the error) with similar students.

Weaknesses Error classification procedures have serious drawbacks, however. There are several practical problems. Students make many different kinds of errors, and these are difficult to classify and to keep in mind while analyzing a student's performance. Frequently students demonstrate the same error for different reasons, so remedial instruction could be misdirected. Also, the amount of individual assessment and interpretation required seems prohibitive, given the amount of instructional time available.

More serious than practical problems of implementation, however, is the problem that, if diagnosis only classifies errors, it still fails to identify the thinking processes a student has used to produce the errors. Just knowing the type of error (failing to borrow in subtraction) does not tell you the appropriate knowledge structures and cognitive processes a student needs to reach the desired outcome. Error enumeration and classification focus on the negative aspects of performance and are insufficient for understanding why students produce errors (Bejar, 1984). Of course, cognitive analyses could be incorporated into error diagnostic procedures. We turn next to this possibility.

APPROACH 5: IDENTIFYING STUDENT KNOWLEDGE STRUCTURES

Description

A shortcoming of the diagnostic assessment approaches already mentioned is their strong ties to the **surface features** of subject-matter information and problem solving. Diagnosis should focus more on how a student perceives the structure or organization of that content (i.e., the student's knowledge structures) and how she processes information and knowledge to solve problems using that content knowledge. As Sternberg has pointed out in other contexts (Sternberg, 1984; Wagner & Sternberg, 1984), behaviorist and psychometric approaches are not exactly wrong, but they are incomplete. A better approach would describe a student's mental processes that help change thinking.

We showed one assessment technique for gathering this information in Chapter 6 (Figure 6.1). Frequently, students' **everyday understandings of terms and phenomena** are at odds with subject-matter experts' and textbooks' understandings. Further, students' everyday understanding of technical and nontechnical concepts varies from culture to culture, so that instruction geared to certain technical forms of knowledge might need to be adapted to different

settings (Urevbu, 1984). These conflicts can interfere with your teaching of technical or specialized knowledge, unless you explicitly address students' knowledge schemata in the course of your teaching (Champagne et al., 1982).

One example of preinstructional assessment is our Chapter 6 discussion of a cold drink and a sweater. If you ask younger students what will happen to the temperature of a bottle of cold soft drink when it is wrapped up in a wool sweater, many will say that the sweater will warm the drink. In their schemata, "sweater" is something that Mother tells you to put on to keep warm. Thus, even though you may explain things clearly, they do not believe that a sweater has insulating properties that will keep a cold drink cold. You must relate the new concepts to their current thinking and schemata. You must help them reconstruct their knowledge structures. They need to understand how keeping their bodies warm and keeping the soft drink cold are linked by the concept of insulation. To believe it they need to understand the principles of insulation and how a sweater works as an insulator. You may need to conduct some experiments to support their new beliefs and understandings further.

There is considerable evidence that a person's knowledge structure is important to learning (Anderson, 1977, 1984; Glaser, 1984; Haertel & Calfee, 1983; Kintsch, 1974; Minstrell & Stimpson, 1990; Prichert & Anderson, 1977; Shank & Ableson, 1977; Shavelson, 1985). This research documents the role of knowledge structures in recalling information, reasoning, acquiring understanding, representing problems, and identifying clues, heuristics, and constraints in solving problems.

Several methods are used for assessing students' knowledge structures. These methods share the common perspective that as individuals become more proficient, their knowledge becomes more interconnected, more deeply organized, and more accessible. Knowledge organization assessment has a long history, with early studies using free recall and later studies using word association (Preece, 1976, is one example). Other methods include free sorting of cards (Hambleton & Sheehan, 1977); similarity rating (Johnson, 1967); tree or hierarchical graph building (Fillenbaum & Rapoport, 1971); ordered tree hierarchical recovery (Reitman & Rueter, 1980); modified ordered tree (MOT) hierarchy recovery (Naveh-Benjamin, McKeachie, Lin, & Tucker, 1986); analysis of protocols (Greeno, 1976, 1978; Hewson & Hamlyn, 1984); mapping tests (Surber, 1984; Surber & Smith, 1981); structure formation (SLT) (Ballstaedt & Mandl, 1986); MicoCAM concept mapping (Ju, 1989; Young, 1993); and concept structuring analysis (ConSAT) (Champagne & Klopfer, 1980). These techniques vary in theoretical perspective and the type of knowledge organization they represent. Techniques that make similar assumptions about the theoretical constructs and underlying knowledge structure and how this structure is reflected in what the student records have convergent validity sufficient for classroom assessment purposes

(Champagne, Hoz, & Klopfer, 1984; Shavelson & Stanton, 1975).

Classroom Applications

A **concept map** is a graphic way to represent how a student understands the relationships among the major concepts in the subject. An example of how a student might organize concepts related to a science unit on rocks is shown in Figure 13.6.

Notice that this concept map shows that the student has fairly well-organized knowledge of this unit's concepts. However, some important concept linkages are missing. For the most part, the student understands the concepts hierarchically (e.g., *granite* and *pumice* are included in the category called *igneous*, which is a type of *rock*). The student shows only one connection that is related to change or transformation of specific rocks or categories of rocks (*shale* changes to *slate*). The student can't fit into the map the concept *sediment* and so doesn't know that sediment can form *shale* or *limestone*. Other linkages are missing, too: Igneous rocks can weather and transform into sediment and sedimentary rocks; sedimentary rocks can form metamorphic rocks, which in turn can weather and return back to sedimentary rocks; and limestone can change into marble (Champagne & Klopfer, 1980).

Suggestions for how to capture a student's concept map are given in Figure 13.7. For this task, the teacher shows a student the list of concepts at the top of Figure 13.6 and works with the student individually, following the procedure described in Figure 13.7, to create the concept map. As each concept is used in the map, it is crossed off the list.

As you can see from the example, using this approach to diagnosing requires individually assessing students, knowing the subject very well so you can identify where a student has a missing link, and using considerable judgment when interpreting the resulting concept map. The validity of your judgments improves if you corroborate your assessment of a student's "missing links" with other evidence about how a student understands the concepts, such as problem-solving tasks and a student's essays and class responses. Also, keep in mind that there may be more than one correct way to relate the information; more than one schema may be correct.

Strengths and Weaknesses

Strengths This diagnostic approach focuses your attention on how a student thinks about the concepts and their interrelationships. It gives you some insight into how the student sees the concepts organized and, perhaps, how they might be related to other concepts and procedures a student has learned. These insights may help you explain why students are making errors, or why they are having difficulty solving problems.

Weaknesses Although assessment of knowledge structures and problem representation may offer you insight into a student's thinking, these clinical procedures are experimental. We do not know the degree to which the results are valid, or whether different teachers would reach the same diagnosis for the same student. The way a student reacts to the interviewer (teacher) and the interviewing situation may drastically affect the results. You will need to be cautious, therefore, when you interpret the results.

In large classrooms, these procedures present practical problems. Because you must assess one student at a time, you need to keep the rest of the class occupied. Although

FIGURE 13.6 Hypothetical example of a student's concept map of rocks.

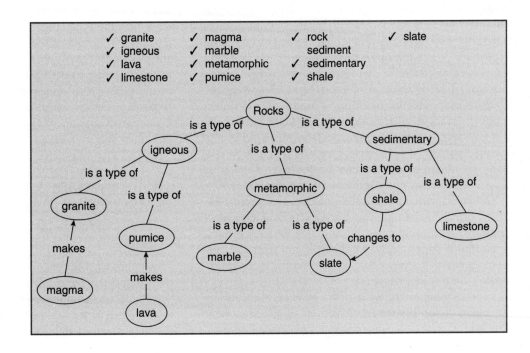

FIGURE 13.7 **Suggestions for conducting a student interview to create a concept map useful for assessment.**

Step	The focus of your interviewing and probing
1. Identify major concepts	Start with giving the student a few of the major concepts in the area you are probing. You could put these on cards. Ask students to tell you about these concepts, what they mean to the student, and some of the other things about which they make the student think. Write every concept the student mentions in a list.
2. Create an arrangement of the concepts to match the student's thinking	Use a large sheet of paper. Review the list created in Step 1 with the student. Ask the student which of the concepts (including the ones you initially showed on the cards) is the major or most important one. Even if the student does not identify one as the major one, ask the student to pick one with which to start. Write this concept in the middle of the page. Ask the student to select another that is most closely related to the one on the page. Write this near the one already on the page. Continue asking for the ones nearest to the central one. Write these around the central concept. Continue with the remaining concepts, asking where they belong. These may be further from the central one and may be near some of the secondary concepts.
3. Establish how the student relates the concepts to one another.	Begin with the central concept, work with the nearest ones to it, one at a time, and take each pair in turn. Ask the student whether the two are related and, if so, why or how they are related. Connect the related concepts with a line. Do not connect the concepts the student says are unrelated, even if you think they should be. Remember, you are trying to picture how the student is thinking. Assure the student frequently that there is no correct answer you are looking for but that you seek to help the student explain how he or she is thinking about these concepts. After connecting the related concepts with a line, write on the line the type of relationship the student tells you. (e.g., "is an example of," "is a," "causes," "is part of," "it makes it go," etc.) If a student just says, "They are related," probe further to understand what the relationship is.
4. Give feedback to the student and rearrange the map	Show the student the map so far. Talk about the arrangement. Give feedback to the student what the map tells you about the student's thinking and ask if this is correct. Rearrange the map so that it better represents the student's thinking and understanding of the concepts. Talk about each concept and its relationships. Add new concepts if the student mentions them and determine how they are linked to the mapped concepts. Redraw the map if necessary.
5. Elaborate the map to show new concepts, linkages, and examples	Discuss the rearranged map further with the student. Ask the student to tell you more: What else does the student know about these concepts, what are some examples, why are the concepts related, etc. Incorporate this new information into the map and add branches and expansions as necessary to depict the student's thinking.
6. Explore cross-linkages and complex relationships	Go over the map drawn to this point with the student. Ask the student about the pairs of concepts previously unconnected and about the connections of new concepts mentioned in Step 5. Ask the student if he or she thinks three or four concepts should be connected together and why. Record these complex relationships.
7. Give feedback to the student and rearrange to make the final map	Show the map to the student and discuss with the student what the map tells you about the student's thinking. Ask the student if this is accurate and rearrange the map to make it more accurately describe the student's organization of the concepts. You may stop here if you have sufficient detail to understand the student's organization of the concepts. Otherwise, repeat Steps 5 and 6.

some of the procedures listed earlier are group oriented, it is not clear that they lead to the same results as the individual interview methods recommended here. Some authors (Clarke, 1990) recommend teaching students to use concept maps. It is not clear, however, whether the skills students need to create the maps help or hinder their expression of their knowledge organizations. Drawing the concept map and diagramming a model of a problem require spatial skills that all students may not have. Further, it is not clear that all concepts and relationships can be represented spatially. For example, how would you show spatially the relationship between family love, respect for neighbors, and peaceful coexistence in the community?

Other diagrams can better represent some topics. For example, when the concepts have a strictly hierarchical relationship, a table or an outline may better represent them than a concept map. Similarly, if you want to represent a process or a procedure, a flow chart is more appropriate than a concept map.

Especially important to classroom practice, therefore, are the practical and **instructional features of an assessment procedure**. Can the procedure accommodate typical numbers of students? Is it easy for you to use? Can it give quick results to guide your teaching? Will other teachers agree that the theoretical concept of knowledge structure reflects the key understandings they are teaching? Can knowledge structure assessment help explain individual differences among students? Can these assessments identify the most important student misunderstandings that need to be corrected? Answers to these questions help you build an argument to support the validity of using this assessment technique. (See also Chapter 3.)

APPROACH 6: IDENTIFYING COMPETENCIES FOR SOLVING WORD PROBLEMS

Description

This approach focuses on diagnosing whether students understand the components of word problems. Solving word problems comprises a significant number of learning targets in social studies, mathematics, and science. A word problem is a short verbal account of a more or less realistic situation that requires students to use the given information to answer a question (Marshall, Pribe, & Smith, 1987). Consider the following word problem:

> **Example**
>
> A bus is carrying 38 passengers. It stops at a bus stop, where 23 passengers get off the bus and 11 other passengers get on. How many passengers are on the bus as it pulls away from this bus stop?

To solve this problem, a student must mentally process it using knowledge from long-term memory in several ways (Mayer, Larkin, & Kadane, 1984):

1. *Translation*—The student must understand each statement in the problem. This requires a student to use factual and **linguistic knowledge**.

> **Example**
>
> For example, in the preceding problem, a student must understand the concepts of *bus*, *carrying passengers*, *bus stop*, *get off the bus*, *get on the bus*, and *pulls away from this bus stop*. Linguistically, the student has to understand the meaning of the question, "How many passengers are on the bus as it pulls away from this bus stop?"

2. *Understanding*—The student must form a mental representation or model of the problem. In other words, the student must use **schematic knowledge** to recognize how the problem fits into a general framework to identify the type of problem it is. (See Chapter 10 for a discussion of schemata.)

> **Example**
>
> In the preceding problem, a student must recognize that this is an arithmetic problem involving only addition and subtraction.

3. *Planning*—The student must form a strategy or plan for solving the problem. The student must use **strategic knowledge**. (See Chapter 10 for a discussion of assessing solution strategies.)

> **Example**
>
> A student must recognize that to know how many passengers are on the bus as it leaves the bus stop, you must subtract from the 38 on the bus those 23 who got off at the stop and add to that remainder the 11 who got on at the stop. Arithmetically, the strategy is: $(38 - 23) + 11$.
>
> (*Note*: Many problems may have more than one correct strategy.)

4. *Execution*—The student must use an appropriate algorithm (procedure) and carry out the calculations or steps properly. The student must use **algorithmic knowledge**.

> **Example**
>
> The student must be able to correctly calculate: $(38 - 23) + 11 = 26$ passengers on the bus as it leaves the bus stop.

The diagnosis in this approach is to identify students who are unable to solve word problems and whether their deficits lie in linguistic and factual knowledge, schematic knowledge, strategic knowledge, or algorithmic knowledge. A student may be unable to solve a problem because the student lacks one or more of these four types of knowledge. Your remedial instruction focuses on teaching students to use the type of knowledge in which they are deficient.

Classroom Applications

You apply this approach by identifying the critical types of linguistic, schematic, strategic, and algorithmic knowledge in each word problem. This means you must analyze each word problem and use the results of your analysis as a basis for asking diagnostic questions. Here is an example, similar to that used by Ismail (1994), of how you could phrase diagnostic items.

> **Example**
>
> *Examples of diagnostic items for assessing students' knowledge of the component competencies of word problems*
>
> *Focal Word Problem*
>
> The weight of an empty cookie tin is 3 ounces. When it is filled with cookies it weighs 1 pound. How many ounces do the cookies inside the tin weigh?
>
> *Linguistic Knowledge Diagnostic Items*
>
> 1. What is a cookie tin?
> 2. What do you think the following question means: "How many ounces do the cookies inside the tin weigh?"
>
> *Schematic Knowledge Diagnostic Items*
>
> 3. What are the arithmetic operations you need to solve this problem?
>
> *Strategic Knowledge Diagnostic Items*
>
> 4. How many ounces are in one pound?
> 5. What steps should you take to solve this problem? (Or, how would you go about solving this problem?)
> 6. Which of these is a correct way to solve this problem?
>   A $(1 \times 16) - 3$
>   B $(3 - 1)\,16$
>   C (1×3)
>   D $3 + 1$
>   E $3 - 1$
>
> *Algorithmic Knowledge Diagnostic Item*
>
> 7. $(1 \times 16) - 3 =$

The following suggestions will help you craft items for using with this type of diagnostic procedure.

1. *To assess linguistic knowledge,* focus your questions on the key terms and key phrases a student must understand to translate the statement into a mental model of the problem. You may need to ask several questions and probe a student's answers to discover his level of understanding of the words and phrases in a problem.

2. *To assess schematic knowledge,* ask students questions to see if they know which rules or principles they must use to solve the problem. For arithmetic problems, this may mean asking what operations should be used.

3. *To assess strategic knowledge,* focus on the student's ability to identify the proper sequence of steps or the proper processes needed to reach the answer. For arithmetic word problems, this means determining whether the student knows which numbers to use, which operations to use with those numbers, and the proper order of applying the operations. It may be easier to show the student several sequences and ask which is the appropriate one for the given problem (Ismail, 1994). All the numbers in the alternative solution strategies should relate to the word problem at hand.

4. *To assess algorithmic knowledge,* craft an item that presents the proper sequence and the proper numbers. The focus is on whether the student can follow the algorithm without the context of the word problem. To avoid clueing the student as to the proper schema and strategy, present the algorithmic item after you have completed questioning for linguistic, schematic, and strategic knowledge (Ismail, 1994).

Although it is useful to identify in which of the four types of component knowledge a student is deficient, it is more useful to assess whether a student's deficits have a pattern that persists over several different problems. To identify this pattern, select two word problems in each of several different categories of problems. For each problem, craft diagnostic questions for each of the four types of knowledge previously described. Administer the items in this sequence:

1. Administer all the word problems first.
2. For each word problem, administer the linguistic, schematic, and strategic knowledge items.
3. Administer all the algorithmic knowledge items.

To identify a student's patterns, review the student's answers to the linguistic items across all types of problems. Does the student do consistently well or poorly, or is there difficulty with only one word problem or category of problem? Repeat this review for the schematic items, then the strategic, then the algorithmic. Base your diagnosis on the consistency of a student's responses.

It is possible to craft multiple-choice items that follow this approach (Ismail, 1994). However, it is more informative if you assess students individually with constructed-response items, for which you can probe or follow up to

clarify a student's answers. You can have a student respond orally, and you can record the answers for the student.

Strengths and Weaknesses

Strengths This approach is most appropriate when you have word problems that are solved by applying a formula or a set of arithmetic operations in an algorithm. These include arithmetic word problems (such as money, time, rate, and cost), word problems in algebra, statistics word problems, social studies word problems involving mathematics, and science word problems. The framework you use to interpret the diagnosis (linguistic, schematic, strategic, and algorithmic knowledge) can be applied consistently across many categories of problems. The framework also suggests how you could remediate a student's deficits.

Weaknesses This approach requires many items per knowledge category to ensure sufficient reliability. Patterns you observe for one type of problem (e.g., money) may not emerge in other problem types (e.g., time). This makes diagnosis less valid if you try to generalize a student's deficits across problem types. Because many items are required, and because individual administration of items is the most appropriate assessment approach, the procedure is time consuming. The validity of the approach also depends very much on how well you are able to identify key phrases, appropriate schemata, and appropriate strategies for solving the problems. If multiple strategies for problem solving are appropriate, you must be careful to allow students to express these and not confuse the diagnosis by discounting them. Nevertheless, you can use this approach in a very informal way, perhaps asking questions orally, to get some insight into why a student is having difficulty with word problems.

INTERVIEWING STUDENTS

Many of the diagnostic approaches discussed in this chapter require you to work individually with students. Many times you will need to ask students to explain their thinking or ask other questions to follow up on a student's response to gather informal diagnosis information. Here are some suggestions for using an interview for gathering diagnostic information:

1. *Remember that the main purpose of the interview is to gather information about a student's thinking, errors, faulty processes, or faulty approaches to the subject.* You are not looking for a "correct" answer to the questions you pose.

2. *Prepare for an interview as you would prepare for other assessments.* Have in mind the types of information you are seeking, know the general strategy you will use to probe for answers, have necessary materials at hand, prepare a quiet place for the interview that is free from distractions, make plans to keep the rest of the class occupied, and plan to limit the interview to a few minutes.

3. *Do not intimidate or frighten the student.* Use an informal, friendly conversational manner.

4. *Do not barrage the student with large numbers of rapid-fire questions.*

5. *Wait for the student to respond.* A 5- or 10-second waiting time may be a minimum when you are asking students to think or tell you how they process information.

6. *Begin with broader questions and gradually ask more specific and focused questions.* Keep the questions focused on the types of diagnostic information you seek.

7. *Keep notes so you do not have to rely on your memory and can follow up when planning remedial instruction.*

Summary

Diagnostic Assessment

- Diagnostic assessment of learning difficulties has two related purposes: (a) identifying which learning targets a student has not mastered and (b) suggesting possible causes or reasons why a student has not mastered the learning targets.

Integrating Teaching With the Six Approaches to Diagnosis

- The chapter presented six different approaches to diagnosing learning problems: (a) profiling content areas strengths and weaknesses, (b) identifying prerequisite knowledge and skills, (c) identifying nonmastered specific objectives, (d) identifying a student's errors, (e) identifying a student's knowledge structure, and (f) identifying deficits in knowledge components or problem solving.

- Figure 13.2 summarizes how the six diagnostic approaches fit into the teaching process.

- The profiling content areas strengths and weaknesses approach presents a student's norm-referenced profile on several topical areas. The approach is useful when you know little about an incoming group of students and want to get a rough idea of their needs. The rough profile of the students provides only general guidance for teaching and must be followed up with more detailed diagnosis. The profile is often unreliable, too. The chapter gives suggestions for crafting and using tests that follow this approach.

- The identifying deficits in prerequisite knowledge and skills approach focuses on what a student already needs to know before she can profit from new instruction. The approach uses task analysis to identify entry requirements and may also identify a learning hierarchy of prerequisites. The approach identifies the specific skills that students need to learn before they are ready for learning new material. The approach views learning as cumulative and does not give specific guidance on how to teach the prerequisites. The chapter suggests ways to identify prerequisites and to craft assessment procedures based on them.

- The identifying specific objectives that are not mastered approach focuses on end-of-instruction learning targets. The approach identifies which learning targets are mastered and which are not. The approach is useful because it (a) focuses on specific and limited learning targets to teach, (b) communicates learning targets in an easy-to-understand form, and (c) focuses your attention on student performance.

Assessments of the specific objectives are usually short and, therefore, are plagued with measurement error that results in misclassifying some masters as nonmasters and vice versa. The approach focuses only on observable performance and fosters a building-block, fragmented approach to learning. The chapter describes ways to craft assessments consistent with this approach.

- The identifying students' errors approach goes beyond identifying nonmastered objectives to identify and classify the types of errors students make when they have not mastered a learning target. The advantage of the approach is that you are able to discover what aspects of a student's performance are flawed. The approach does not identify the causes of the errors or flaws in students' thinking that may make errors consistent rather than random or careless. The chapter suggests ways to implement the approach in classrooms.

- The identifying students' knowledge structures approach focuses on how a student (a) perceives the structure or organization of the concepts and facts of the subject, and (b) processes concepts and facts to solve problems in the subject. The advantage is that this approach requires you to analyze how students think about the interrelated concepts. Attention to this facet of student learning helps you gather information about why students make errors or why they have difficulty solving problems. The procedures for obtaining this information are experimental, and their degree of validity is not known. The procedures require working intensively with individual students and thus are somewhat impractical in large classes with only one teacher. The chapter suggests ways to implement this approach with individual students.

- The identifying component competencies for solving word problems approach focuses on word problems in social studies, mathematics, and science. To solve a word problem, students must use linguistic, schematic, strategic, and algorithmic knowledge. Assessment focuses on identifying whether students have sufficient problem-specific knowledge in each of these areas. The approach is most useful for closed-response problems that can be solved by applying appropriate formulas. The framework of types of knowledge can be applied across a wide range of problems and is useful for focusing students' remedial instruction. The approach can be plagued by measurement error if only a few tasks assess each type of knowledge. It is also a time-consuming approach whose validity depends on the quality of your analysis of the word problems. Suggestions for crafting this type of diagnostic assessment are presented in the chapter.

Interviewing Students

- Many diagnostic assessment strategies require intensive work with individual students in an interview situation. The chapter provides suggestions for improving diagnostic interviews.

Important Terms and Concepts

adaptive testing strategy
algorithmic knowledge
component competencies of problem-solving
concept mapping
deficits in learning
diagnostic assessment
everyday understandings of terms and phenomena
identifying errors in performance

instructional features of an assessment procedure
knowledge structure
learning hierarchy
linguistic knowledge
mastery of specific objectives
passing score
percentage agreement index
prerequisite knowledge and skill deficits
profile of strengths and weaknesses
schematic knowledge
strategic knowledge
subtest
surface feature
unreliable profile

Exercises and Applications

1. For a subject you teach or plan to teach, craft a diagnostic assessment procedure for Approaches 1, 2, 3, and 4. If there is time, try each approach with students who are experiencing learning difficulties. Revise your assessment procedure based on these student trials. Share the final versions of your assessment procedures with others in your course.

2. Each of these statements describes an instructional decision-making situation. Read each statement and decide the approach(es) to diagnostic assessment that may provide needed information.
   a. A teacher wonders whether Larissa missed several arithmetic story problems because she doesn't know her number facts.
   b. Trinh missed several addition computational problems involving mixed decimal fractions. His teacher wonders whether Trinh is counting the number of decimal places in each addend and using this count as the basis for placing the decimal point in the final answer.
   c. Lou missed several whole-number arithmetic problems involving carrying (regrouping). His teacher wonders whether Lou has not remembered to add his "carries" to the sum of the digits in the next column.
   d. Janet is a slow reader who frequently misses comprehension questions following a passage. Her teacher wonders whether Janet has reading reversals that cause her to misread some words in the passage.

3. Sometimes students learn an incorrect rule or apply a correct rule at the wrong time. To diagnose a student's learning difficulty in this case, you must identify the rule the student actually used to solve the problem and then decide whether this is an appropriate rule. For example, consider this arithmetic story problem:

   Sally was given 6 pieces of candy. Then she went to the store and bought some candy. Now she has 8 pieces of candy altogether. How many pieces of candy did Sally buy?

One student gave 14 as the answer to this problem. When the teacher interviewed the student, the teacher discovered that the student was using this erroneous rule: "Whenever you see the word altogether in a story problem, you add the two numbers they give you." Thus, the student added, $6 + 8 = 14$, instead of subtracting, $8 - 6 = 2$.

   a. Consider the subject and the students you teach or plan to teach. Identify two wrong rules you have seen students use. (If you are inexperienced, you may need to work with a few students before proceeding with this exercise.) Below, state the wrong rule, the correct rule, and an example to illustrate each point (as was done in the preceding passage).
      Subject, grade level: _____
      i. Correct rule: _____
      ii. Student's incorrect rule: _____
      iii. Illustrative example: _____
   b. Subject, grade level: _____
      i. Correct rule:_____
      ii. Student's incorrect rule: _____
      iii. Illustrative example: _____
   c. Share and discuss your findings with others in this course.

4. Reconsider the arithmetic story problem given in Exercise 3. Analyze the story problem according to linguistic knowledge, schematic knowledge, strategic knowledge, and algorithmic knowledge.
   a. Describe the specifics of each type of knowledge required to solve this problem.
   b. Using the items in the example on page 307 as a model, craft similar items in each category to diagnose students' level of understanding of each type of knowledge.
   c. If there is time, administer your diagnostic assessment tasks to several students, some of whom did not answer the word problem correctly. Share your findings with others in this course.

5. Apply the teaching diagnosis process chart shown in Figure 13.2 to a unit of content you teach or plan to teach.
   a. Describe the unit and the learning targets (performances) toward which it is directed.
   b. Identify the prerequisites and explain whether you must diagnose students with respect to them.
   c. Identify the learning targets for which you can diagnose mastery or nonmastery at the end of the unit.
   d. Identify the kinds of errors students often make when completing the tasks assessing each learning target.
   e. For each error identified, explain the faulty thinking that is likely to cause each error.
   f. If there is time, teach the unit and collect information about the validity of your assertions for (a) through (e) above.

14 Preparing Your Students to Be Assessed and Using Students' Results to Improve Your Assessments

LEARNING TARGETS

After studying this chapter, you should have learned the following:

Section I: Getting Students Ready

1. Describe how to prepare students for an upcoming assessment, including the minimum information students need to perform their best. [3]

2. Describe necessary test-taking skills and how to teach them to students. [1, 4]

3. Describe testwiseness and when it might lower the validity of your assessment results. [3, 2]

4. Describe test anxiety, its components, and what you can do to help students who experience it. [4, 3]

Section II: Putting the Assessment Together

5. Explain why the way you assemble and administer an assessment affects the validity of the scores. [3, 4]

6. List the kinds of information that should be included in test directions. [2, 3]

7. List the preparations for scoring you need to make before giving a test. [3]

8. Explain the correction for guessing, and list the factors to consider when deciding whether to use a correction. [4]

Section III: Using Students' Responses to Improve Assessments

9. Describe the important reasons for using item analysis for classroom assessments. [2]

10. Carry out a simple item analysis, including item difficulty and discrimination. [2, 3]

11. Use item analysis results to improve the quality of true-false, matching, and multiple-choice items. [2]

12. Describe how item analysis data are used to select items for tests having different purposes. [2, 1]

Important Terms and Concepts

13. Explain how the terms and concepts listed at the end of this chapter may be applied to educational assessment. [6]

ITEM DIFFICULTY INDEX

Effect on Test Score Distribution

Shape of the Distribution The difficulty of test items affects the shape of the distribution of total test scores. Very difficult tests, containing items with *p*-values < 0.25, will tend to be positively skewed, whereas easy tests, containing items with *p*-values > 0.80, will tend to be negatively skewed. (See Figure I.7 in Appendix I for an explanation of distribution shapes.) The shapes of total score distributions for other kinds of assessments are not so easily deduced.

Average or Mean Test Score The difficulty of items affects the average or mean test score: The average test score (*M*) is equal to the sum of the difficulties of the items. The relationship is given here:

$$M = \sum p \qquad \text{[Eq. 14.7]}$$

The mean (*M*) test score is equal to the sum of the difficulty values (that is, the *p*-values) of the items comprising the test. When the assessment contains only performance or constructed-response items, the mean is simply the sum of the item means, *not* the sum of the *p** values from Equation 14.5.

Spread of Scores The spread of item difficulties and the spread of test scores are related. A test with all *p*-values clustered around 0.50 has the largest spread of test scores, whereas tests with difficulties distributed between 0.10 and 0.90 have smaller score spreads.

Item difficulties (*p*-values) are not the sole factor contributing to the spread of test scores. Another factor is the correlation (Appendix I) among the items: The higher these item intercorrelations, the larger the test's standard deviation. However, the correlations among items may be affected by the *p*-values: Items for which $p = 0.00$ or 1.00 have correlations of 0.00.

Uses of Item Difficulty Information

Figure 14.4 summarizes some of the ways in which teachers and school officials can use *p*-values and *p**-values in assessment and instruction. For the teacher, perhaps identifying concepts to be retaught and giving students feedback about their learning are the more important uses of item difficulty data. Using item information to determine curriculum strengths or to identify suspected item bias requires districtwide cooperation. Such analyses tend to be employed

FIGURE 14.4 Examples of ways in which item difficulty indices can be used in testing and instruction.

Purpose	Procedure	Comments
Identifying concepts that need to be retaught	Find items with small *p*-values. These items may point to objectives needing to be retaught.	a. Poor test performance may not reflect poor teaching: Poor performance may reflect poorly written items, incorrect prior learning, or poor motivation on tests. b. A score based on several similar items is more reliable than performance on a single item.
Providing clues to possible strengths and weaknesses in school curricula	Calculate *p*-values for clusters of similar items for a school building or district. Compare these to *p*-values of the same items from the publisher's national norm-group. Note areas of strength and weakness.	a. See a and b above. b. This procedure applies to standardized tests only. c. Items must correspond to local curriculum objectives and instruction. d. No published test will cover all the objectives of a school district.
Giving feedback to students	Report *p*-value of each item to student along with ID number of the items missed.	a. Such reporting is more useful for high school and college students.
Providing clues to possible item bias	Separate test papers into groups to be contrasted (e.g., males vs. females, blacks vs. whites). Compute *p*-values for each item separately for each group. Items for which *p*-value differences are unusually large are studied further to see if they may be biased.	a. This is only a crude method and not a scientifically satisfactory method (Lord, 1977). b. This procedure is not very useful in small samples of examinees because of sampling fluctuations.
Building tests that have certain statistical properties	See Figure 14.5.	

Ambiguous Alternatives

Student responses can provide leads to **ambiguous alternatives**. In this context, alternatives are ambiguous if *upper group students* are unable to distinguish between the keyed answer and one or more of the distractors (Sax, 1989). When this happens, the upper group tends to choose a distractor with about the same frequency as the keyed response, as illustrated in the following example.

Example

Example of an upper group distractor response pattern showing ambiguous alternatives

On which river is the city of Pittsburgh, Pennsylvania, located?	Upper group	Lower group
A Delaware River	0	3
B Ohio River	5	3
C Monongahela River	4	1
D Susquehanna River	1	3

The confluence of the Allegheny and Monongahela Rivers forms the Ohio River at Pittsburgh. The upper group in the example chose B and C with approximately equal frequency, thus reflecting the students' ambiguity in selecting only one of these two alternatives as a correct answer. This item should be rewritten so that only one answer is clearly correct or best.

You might notice that very often the lower group is equally divided among two or more alternatives. This is usually *not* an indication that you must revise the item. Rather, it means that students with less knowledge will find many alternatives equally plausible, and so the task becomes an ambiguous one for them. The cause of these students' ambiguity is likely to be insufficient knowledge.

Before concluding that you need to revise an item, however, you must study the item in relation to the students taking the test and judge whether the ambiguity stems from the students' lack of knowledge rather than from a poorly written item (Sax, 1974). Consider the next example, which shows how incomplete learning may produce a response pattern that gives the appearance of ambiguous alternatives.

Example

Example of how incomplete learning may result in a response pattern that gives the appearance of ambiguous alternatives

$$3 + 5 \times 2 = ?$$

	Upper group	Lower group
A 10	0	2
*B 13	5	3
C 16	5	3
D 30	0	2

This item requires applying arithmetic operations in a certain order: multiplication first, then addition. Option B reflects this order, whereas Option C is the answer obtained by adding first and then multiplying. Apparently half the upper group followed this erroneous procedure and chose C. The item is not technically flawed, but the responses indicate to the teacher that a number of students need to learn this principle. (The entire group's responses to this item should be checked, of course.)

Miskeyed Items

You may have **miskeyed** an item if a larger number of upper group students selects a particular wrong response. When this happens, check to be sure that the answer key is correct. Look at this example:

Example

Example of an upper group distractor response pattern showing a possible miskeyed item

Who was the fourth president of the United States?	Upper group	Lower group
A John Quincy Adams	0	3
B Thomas Jefferson	1	2
C James Madison	9	3
*D James Monroe	0	2

In the example, C is the correct answer, but the teacher inadvertently used Alternative D as the answer key. The response pattern in the figure is typical of such an item.

Again, be sure to check the item content. The numbers from the item analysis only warn of possible miskeying–perhaps there is no miskeying and the upper group simply lacks the required knowledge.

Random Guessing

Students may be **guessing randomly** if many of the alternatives are equally plausible to the upper-scoring group. If the upper group students guess randomly, each option tends to be chosen an approximately equal number of times, as illustrated in this example:

Example

Example of an upper group distractor response pattern showing possible random guess or confusion

In what year did the United States enter World War II?	Upper group	Lower group
A 1913	2	3
B 1915	2	2
C 1916	3	3
*D 1917	3	2

Remember to look at the pattern of responses of the upper group, *not* the lower group, to find items on which many students may be guessing. Guessing among the most knowledgeable students may signal widespread confusion in the class. Lower-scoring students may in fact be guessing on the more difficult items, too, but this indicates you need to reteach them rather than simply revise the test item. Random guessing adds errors of measurement to the scores, thereby reducing reliability and validity.

SELECTING TEST ITEMS

Another Purpose for Item Analysis

Most teachers using item analysis procedures will do so for one or more of the following reasons: (a) to check whether the items are functioning as intended, (b) to give students feedback on their assessment performance, (c) to acquire feedback for themselves about students' difficulties, (d) to identify areas of the curriculum that may need improvement, and (e) to obtain objective data that signal the need for revising their items. You can also use item analysis for selecting some items and culling others from a pool of items.

Purpose of Assessment Helps Select Items

No statistical item selection rule is helpful if it is inconsistent with your purpose for conducting assessments. Further, any procedure you use for selecting some items over others changes the definition of the domain of performance. Those performances represented by items you eliminate are never assessed.

Relative Versus Absolute Student Attainment Careful selection of items results in shorter, more efficient, and more reliable assessments. In the classroom, *statistically based item selection* seems to apply most when you are concerned primarily with students' relative achievement rather than their absolute achievement. You focus on assessing relative achievement when your priority is to rank students with respect to what they have learned. You focus on assessing absolute achievement when your priority is to determine the precise content (or performance) each student has learned.

As an example, suppose you wanted to assess students' learning of the 100 simple addition facts typically taught in first and second grades. If you want to know only the relative achievement of the students (which student knows the most, next most, and so on), you could use a relatively short test, made up of only addition facts that best discriminate among the students. This test would probably contain mostly the middle and upper parts of the addition table. Addition facts that almost everyone knows (such as $1 + 1 = 2$) would not be included on such a test because these items would not discriminate ($D = 0$) and thus would not provide information to rank the students.

However, excluding certain addition facts from the assessment because they do not discriminate well means that you will be unable to observe a student's performance on all 100 addition facts.

On the other hand, suppose your purpose for assessment is to identify the particular addition combinations with which a student has difficulty. In this case, finding out the absolute level of achievement would be your main assessment focus. You may find it necessary to use a longer, less efficient test (or several shorter ones), perhaps assessing all 100 facts.

Absolute, rather than relative, achievement is more important for diagnostic assessments intended to identify such things as whether a student has acquired particular reading skills, learned a certain percentage of facts in some specified domain, or has the ability to solve certain types of problems. Relative achievement is more important when you are assessing a student's general educational development in a subject area.

Complete Versus Partial Ordering For some educational decisions, you may need to accurately rank all students using their test performance, called a **complete ordering of students**. On the other hand, you may only want to separate students into five ordered categories so you can assign grades (A, B, C, D, and F). In so doing, you may not wish to make precise distinctions among the students within each category. Similarly, you may wish to divide the class into two groups, such as mastery/nonmastery or faster/slower readers. We say there is **partial ordering** when the categories themselves are ordered, but there is *no ordering of individuals within a category*. Categorizing students by their grades, or into fail-pass groups, are examples of partial ordering.

When you focus your assessment on either partial or complete ordering, it is inefficient to include items that do not contribute to ordering and distinguishing students. Such items therefore are culled from the pool. To cull, you try out items with students before creating the final version of the test (or you use items from past administrations of the test for which you have data). You calculate item statistics (p and D). You select and assemble into the final test those items with high, positive discrimination indices. Select items with p-values (difficulty) at each level of performance where you wish to have information (e.g., A through F). A "C" student, for example, should not just be a C student because he or she got right, partly by chance, a portion of the items an A student is expected to get. A "C" student should be in that category because he or she scored correctly on items at that level of difficulty.

Realities, Content Coverage, and Compromise

In practice, you must include test items with less than ideal statistical properties so a test can match its blueprint. Actual assessment construction tends to be a compromise between considerations of subject-matter coverage and psychometric properties (Henrysson, 1971). The general principle is: *Select the best available items that cover the important areas of content as defined by the blueprint, even though the discrimination and difficulty indices of these items have values that are less than ideal.*

Rules of Thumb for Selecting Test Items

Figure 14.5 summarizes guidelines for selecting items for classroom tests, keeping in mind our discussion of the differences between building a test to measure relative achievement and building one to measure absolute achievement. Note that coverage of content and learning targets has primacy over statistical indices when selecting test items by the procedures recommended here. The guidelines shown in Figure 14.5 require you to understand whether the prospective test should assess only one ability or a combination of several abilities. A **homogeneous test** will measure one ability, whereas a **heterogeneous test** will assess a combination of abilities. If your test contains some items for which students can get the right answer by random guessing (such as with multiple-choice items), then the items you select should be approximately 5% easier than shown in the figure.

When crafting a test of relative achievement, remember that in choosing between two items assessing the same learning target, good item discrimination takes precedence over obtaining the ideal item difficulty level. That is, if two items assess the same learning target and are of approximately the same difficulty level, use the one that discriminates better.

When you design a criterion-referenced classroom test, item statistics play a lesser role for selecting and culling items. You should still calculate item statistics to obtain data on how the items might be improved, however. Items exhibiting zero or negative discrimination frequently contain technical flaws that you may not notice unless you do an item analysis. You should also make sure that the item difficulties cover the range of expected performance.

USING COMPUTERS FOR TEST ASSEMBLY AND ITEM ANALYSES

The calculations and tabulations illustrated in this chapter can be done with a handheld calculator. They can also be done using a computer program. In some schools, students' responses on special answer sheets can be scanned directly into a program that does all the item analyses illustrated in this chapter. In other schools the scanner creates a computer file, but you must use your own program to analyze the data. You can duplicate much of the analysis done by specialized programs using a standard spreadsheet program that comes with office suite programs.

Vendors have also created software that allows banking or storing test items in a computer file (i.e., both the item's

FIGURE 14.5 Guidelines for selecting items.

	Relative achievement is the focus		Absolute achievement is the focus
	Complete ordering	**Partial ordering (two groups)**	
General concerns	Ranking all the pupils in terms of their relative attainment in a subject area.	Dividing pupils into two groups on the basis of their relative attainment. Pupils within each group will be treated alike.	Assess the absolute status (achievement) of the pupil with respect to a well-defined domain of instructionally relevant tasks.
Specific focus of test	Seek to accurately describe differences in relative achievement between individual pupils.	Seek to accurately classify persons into two categories.	Seek to accurately estimate the percentage of the domain each pupil can perform successfully.
Attention to the test's blueprint	Be sure that items cover all important topics and objectives within the blueprint.	Be sure that items cover all important topics and objectives within the blueprint.	Be sure items are a representative, random sample from the defined domain which the blueprint operationalizes.
How the difficulty index (p) is used	Within each topical area of the blueprint, select those items with: (1) p between 0.16 and 0.84 if performance on the test represents a single ability. (2) p between 0.40 and 0.60 if performance on the test represents several different abilities. *Note:* Items should be easier than described above if guessing is a factor.	Within each topical area of the blueprint, select those items with p-values slightly larger than the percentage of persons to be classified in the upper group (e.g., if the class is to be divided in half [0.50] then items with p-value of about 0.60 should be selected; if the division is lower 75% vs. upper 25%, items should have $p = 0.35$ [approximately]). *Note:* The above suggestion assumes the test measures a single ability.	Don't select items on the basis of their p-values, but study each p to see if it is signaling a poorly written item. Make sure there is a sufficient number of items with p values at each level of performance.
How the discrimination index (D) is used	Within each topical area of the blueprint, select items with D greater than or equal to $+0.30$.	Within each topical area of the blueprint, select items with D greater than or equal to $+0.30$.	All items should have D greater than or equal to 0.00. Unless there is a rational explanation to the contrary, revise those items not possessing this property.

text and graphics). The software then allows you to select items from the bank, assemble tests, and print them for duplication. Some software permits tests to be administered via intranet or Internet. Other software products offer even more organization: You can align your assignments with your state's standards and school's curriculum objectives, then compare each student's progress against these standards and objectives.

Software, hardware, and related products vary greatly, not only in their quality, cost, and user friendliness but also in how well they match your teaching and school's instructional goals. Some programs can be run right out of the box, whereas others require considerable training. We are not able to review the products here. You can visit the *T.H.E. Journal* Website (http://www.thejournal.com) or Websites of firms that produce assessment and item-analysis software (e.g., Assessment Systems Corporation at http://www.assess.com).

Summary

Section I: Getting Students Ready

- Students should demonstrate their maximum performance on classroom assessments.
- If you handle your classroom assessments properly, you can help students demonstrate their maximum capability.
- Before an upcoming assessment, you should tell students the number and kind of items, the assessment's time limits, how you expect them to answer questions, the penalty, if any, you will impose for guessing, and whether there is a general strategy they should follow when responding to the items.
- Give students at least 48 hours' notice before assessing them in a subject. Surprise quizzes do not seem to have the motivating effects frequently attributed to them, and students sometimes view them as unfair.
- Nine test-taking skills are presented. These are the minimum skills your students will need, beyond subject-matter knowledge, to display maximum capabilities on your assessment. Teach all of these skills.
- Testwiseness refers to a student's ability to use the characteristics of both the assessment materials and the assessment situation to attain a higher score.
- Testwiseness skills and knowledge can be classified into two broad areas: those that students can use regardless of the purpose for taking the assessment or who developed the assessment procedure, and those that students can use with assessments developed for certain purposes or by certain persons. These skills and knowledge are outlined in Figure 14.1.
- Students' testwiseness and general test-taking skills become more sophisticated as they progress through the grades, but students' abilities vary greatly. Those with few skills and little testwiseness are usually at a disadvantage when they take tests with more skilled and testwise peers.

Section II: Putting the Assessment Together

- You facilitate students' maximum assessment performance by attending carefully to the assessment materials, including their overall appearance, the arrangement of the assessment tasks, and the way you present the assessment to your students.

- When crafting the format and procedures for a formal assessment, you should be sensitive to the visual and auditory abilities of your students and how these abilities may affect their assessment performance.
- Arrange tasks in an assessment to help students do their best.
- You should prepare the procedures for marking and a scoring key (or marking guide) before you administer the assessment to your students.

Test Anxiety

- Anxiety associated with taking a test is thought to elicit in examinees task-relevant responses, which facilitate performance on the test, and task-irrelevant responses, which interfere with test performance.
- Task-irrelevant thoughts can debilitate highly test-anxious persons who are preoccupied with their own inadequacy, helplessness, and possible failure.
- Test anxiety consists of a cognitive, worry component and an emotionality component. Alternately, four components may be identified: (a) tension, (b) worry, (c) task-irrelevant thinking, and (d) bodily reactions.
- Three groups of highly test-anxious students are (a) students with poor study habits who have not learned the material assessed, (b) students with good study skills who have developed fears of being assessed, and (c) students who incorrectly believe they have good study skills but do poorly on assessments.
- Suggestions for helping test-anxious students are provided.

Correction for Guessing

- Correction for guessing formulas attempt to discourage students from guessing blindly on multiple-choice and true-false items, but only a few of the many explanations of why a student marked or didn't mark an answer appear to fit the rationales needed for using a correction formula. Further, correction for guessing neither corrects for students' good luck nor compensates for bad luck.
- Figure 14.2 lists things to consider before deciding whether to use a correction for guessing formula on a classroom test.
- Your assessment's directions to students should clearly indicate whether you will apply a correction and the students' best strategy when responding to the assessment tasks.
- You should teach the important skills and knowledge that will appear on an assessment, but it is unethical to teach students only the answers to specific items that will appear on the assessment.

Section III: Using Students' Responses to Improve Assessments

- Item analysis refers to the process of collecting, summarizing, and using information about students' responses to each assessment task.
- Important uses of item analyses of classroom assessments are (a) indicating whether the assessment tasks function as you intend, (b) giving students feedback on their performance and creating a basis for class discussion, (c) providing feedback about the students' learning deficits, (d) suggesting areas for teaching improvement, (e) suggesting how the assessment tasks may be revised, and (f) helping you improve your skills in setting assessment tasks.

- A measure of an item's difficulty is p, the fraction of the total group responding correctly to the item. The most difficult items have p close to 0.00, and the easiest items have p close to 1.00.
- A measure of an item's discrimination power is D, the difference between the fraction of the upper extreme group answering the item correctly and the fraction of the lower extreme group answering it correctly. This index ranges from -1.00 to $+1.00$. Items that do not discriminate have D-values near zero. Many test developers strive to have items with $D > +0.30$.
- The shape of your assessment score distribution, its mean, and its spread of scores are affected by the p-values of the items on the assessment.
- Factors affecting an assessment task's difficulty include the effectiveness of your teaching, the assessment task's technical quality, the students' background and previous learning, and the students' motivation when taking the assessment.
- The magnitude of the item discrimination indices in an assessment affects the spread of assessment scores, is limited by the difficulty of the items, and affects the reliability of the assessment scores.
- You can identify poorly functioning distractors on multiple-choice items by tabulating the number of students choosing each alternative. The tabulation is done separately for an upper-scoring and a lower-scoring group. As a general rule, every incorrect alternative should have at least one lower group student choosing it, and more lower group than upper group students should choose each incorrect alternative.
- Alternatives are ambiguous if higher-scoring students are unable to distinguish between the correct answer and one or more of the incorrect alternatives. A poorly written item or students' lack of knowledge may create ambiguity.
- You should check an item for inadvertent miskeying if a large number of higher-scoring students chooses a particular wrong response.
- You should suspect that students are engaging in considerable random guessing if an approximately equal number of higher-scoring students are choosing each alternative.
- The assessment of relative achievement focuses mainly on ranking students with respect to what they have learned (who has learned most, next most, and so on). Assessment of absolute achievement focuses mainly on describing the content or performance each student has learned. Absolute achievement is of more concern when attempting to diagnose student learning deficits; relative achievement is of more concern in ascertaining a student's general educational development in an area.
- The p and D indices can be used together with the assessment blueprint to select from a larger pool of items that will best measure relative achievement. Rules of thumb for item selections are summarized in Figure 14.5.
- The p and D indices generally play a lesser role in selecting items when the focus of the assessment is on absolute achievement.

Important Terms and Concepts

ambiguous alternatives
bodily reactions to anxiety
cognitive interference
complete versus partial ordering of students
content analysis of the responses
correction for guessing formulas
dichotomous item scoring
emotionality
homogeneous versus heterogeneous test
item analysis
item bank
item difficulty index (p and p^*)
item discrimination index (D and D^*)
item file
maximum performance assessment
minimum assessment-taking skills
miskeyed items
negatively discriminating item
nondiscriminating item
poorly functioning distractor
positively discriminating item
random guessing
relative versus absolute achievement
task-directed versus task-irrelevant thoughts
tension
test anxiety
testwiseness
types of test-anxious students
typical performance assessment
upper, middle, and lower scoring groups
worry

Exercises and Applications

1. The following statements are thoughts that students might have during an assessment situation. Read each statement and decide whether it is a task-relevant (TR) thought or a task-irrelevant (TI) thought.
   a. "I have to be very careful in answering this problem. My teacher takes points off for computational errors."
   b. "I am really dumb. I just can't do it!"
   c. "If I don't pass this test, Dad will kill me!"
   d. "I know I don't know the answer to this question. It's no use trying to fool Mr. Jones. He'll just think I'm dumber than I am."
   e. "Oops! I forgot to study the material this question is asking. Oh well, I'd better write something down. I usually am able to get a few points from Mr. Jones!"
2. What testwise strategies do the following statements represent?
   a. "When Mr. Jones gives a true-false test, I mark true when in doubt because he always has more true than false items on his tests."
   b. "When writing essays for a philosophy course I always use words such as *ergo, being,* and *thing.* This makes my answer sound more philosophical."
   c. "The first thing I do is mark B in all the answer spaces. Then I go back and read the questions. If B was wrong, I change it to the correct answer. At least I have a mark on every answer before time is called."
3. Explain the meaning of each of the following values of D.
   a. $+1.00$
   b. $+0.50$
   c. 0.00
   d. -0.50
   e. -1.00

FIGURE 14.6 Item analysis summary for use with Exercise 4.

Item number	Groups	Options A	B	C	D	Faulty distractors	Miskeying	Ambiguous	Guessing
1.	Upper	0	2	*9	0	—	—	—	—
	Middle			*5					
	Lower	1	2	*4	4		$p =$ ——	$D =$ ——	
2.	Upper	2	*7	0	2	—	—	—	—
	Middle		*4						
	Lower	0	*9	1	1		$p =$ ——	$D =$ ——	
3.	Upper	9	*1	1	0	—	—	—	—
	Middle		*1						
	Lower	6	*2	2	1		$p =$ ——	$D =$ ——	
4.	Upper	*5	5	0	1	—	—	—	—
	Middle	*8							
	Lower	*3	3	3	2		$p =$ ——	$D =$ ——	
5.	Upper	3	2	3	*3	—	—	—	—
	Middle				*4				
	Lower	3	2	3	*3		$p =$ ——	$D =$ ——	

Note: This idea for this exercise came from Sax, 1980, pp. 109–112.

4. Figure 14.6 shows a summary of item analysis data for five multiple-choice items for a class of 30 students. There are 11 students in the upper group and 11 students in the lower group. The keyed answer to each item is marked with an asterisk. For each item, calculate the difficulty index (p) and the discrimination index (D), then decide whether the item has poor distractors; is possibly miskeyed, the upper group is possibly guessing, or two options seem to be ambiguous.

5. The following questions refer to your analysis of the item data in Exercise 4.
   a. Which item is a negative discriminator?
   b. Which item is the easiest?
   c. Which item is the most difficult?
   d. For which items do more upper group students than lower group students choose a distractor?
   e. Which item has the highest discrimination index?
   f. Which item has the lowest discrimination index?
   g. What is the average (mean) score on this five-item test for the 30 students who took it?

15 Evaluating and Grading Student Progress

LEARNING TARGETS

After studying this chapter, you should have learned the following:

Section I: The Meanings and Purposes of Grades

1. Explain why grading students is an important teacher responsibility. [5, 6]

2. Explain the various decisions made from grades and how different stakeholders use grades differently. [5, 4, 6, 7]

3. Explain the arguments for and against using grades to motivate students. [5, 7, 4]

Section II: Report Cards and Other Official Reports of Student Progress

4. Describe the different methods for reporting student progress and their advantages and disadvantages. [4, 6, 5]

5. Plan a parent-teacher conference that is effective and educationally productive. [5, 3]

6. Describe the components of a multiple-marking-system report card. [5, 6, 4]

Section III: Choosing a Grading Model

7. Develop your own grading philosophy that is consistent with your teaching approach, is effective for formative and summative purposes, and is valid for reporting students' achievement of standards and learning targets. [5, 6]

8. Explain the advantages and disadvantages of using the three major grade-referencing frameworks: criterion-referencing (absolute standards), norm-referencing (relative standards), and self-referencing (growth standards). [5, 4, 6]

9. Defend your grading system against various criticisms. [5, 4, 6]

Section IV: Sensible Grading Practices

10. Differentiate among assessment variables, reporting variables, and grading variables. [5]

11. Explain how to make your assessment scales consistent across different assignments. [5, 3, 6]

12. Explain how the number of points on your grading scale affects the precision of your grades. [5, 3, 6]

13. Apply the following factors to the components of grading to decide how much weight to give each component: (a) representatives and relevance, (b) emphasis on what you taught, (c) thinking processes and skills required, (d) overlap among the components, (e) fairness to all students, and (f) reliability and objectivity of the assessment results. [5, 3, 6]

14. Explain how you set grade boundaries across different assignments. [5]

15. Explain how you handle the grading of students who are at the boundaries between two grades. [5]

16. Explain the meaning of failure grades and how you handle grading of students who fail to try. [4, 5, 6]

17. Explain how lowering grades for late assignments and giving zero marks for not turning in assignments result in lowering the validity of grades. [5, 4, 6]

Section V: Techniques for Setting Grade Boundaries and Combining Scores

18. Grade students using each of the following methods of grading: (a) grading on the curve, (b) the standard deviation method, (c) adjusting for the class's ability level,

(d) transforming scores to *SS*-scores, (e) the total points method, (f) the fixed-percentage method, (g) the content-based or quality-level method, and (h) weighting components for absolute standard systems. [5]

19. Explain why using grades to punish students, to control them, and so on violates your ethical obligations to them. [1, 4, 3]

Important Terms and Concepts

20. Explain how the terms and concepts listed at the end of this chapter apply to educational assessment. [6]

ABOUT THIS CHAPTER

This chapter is divided into five sections. In Section I, we discuss the meaning and purposes of grading. We evaluate the pros and cons of grading and examine who uses grades and for what purposes. In Section II, we discuss report cards and other methods for reporting educational progress to parents and students. Among the alternatives discussed are checklists, narrative progress reports, and parent-teacher conferences. We also discuss how to design a report card that reports cognitive and noncognitive student achievement. Section III teaches you how to choose a grading model that matches your teaching approach. Three grading frameworks are discussed: criterion-referenced, norm-referenced, and self-referenced. In Section IV, we discuss sensible grading practices. We distinguish among assessment, reporting, and grading variables. We discuss how to make your grading scale consistent across assignments, how to think about students who may be failing, and the devastation of giving a zero to a student for not turning in an assignment. Section V teaches eight methods for setting grade boundaries and assigning grades. It also teaches methods for combining grades from different components into a single score that will be used for grading.

Section I: The Meanings and Purposes of Grades

WHAT ARE YOUR ATTITUDES TOWARD MARKS AND GRADES?

Before starting this chapter, consider how you feel about assigning grades and marks. Read each of the statements in Figure 15.1. Next to each one, check A if you agree, D if you disagree, and U if you are undecided. Compare your answers with those of your classmates and your instructor. Keep these attitudes in mind as you study this chapter and think about how to apply the concepts to your own teaching. Revisit your answers after you study this chapter. How many answers did you change?

CONTINUOUS ASSESSMENT AND GRADING

Formative and Summative Assessment

Formative Assessment **Continuous assessment** is the daily process by which you gather information about students' progress in achieving the curriculum's learning targets (Nitko, 1995). Continuous assessment has both formative and summative aspects. You use formative continuous assessment to make decisions about daily lesson planning and how well your day's lesson is going. You do not formally record formative evaluations on a report card or a permanent record card. Many are reported directly to the student. (For example, "Meghan, I want you to pay special attention to the lesson today," or "Bob, Monday we are going to learn how to do word problems. Please review the number facts with your dad this weekend.") Other formative evaluations are discussed with parents in a personal conference, by telephone, or in a letter or note to the home.

Summative Assessment This chapter emphasizes how to use grades to report your summative continuous assessments of students' achievement of the curriculum's major learning targets. **Grading** (or marking) refers primarily to the process of using a system of symbols (usually letters) for reporting various types of students' progress. **Grading for summative purposes** lets you provide yourself, other teachers, school officials, students, parents, postsecondary educational institutions, and potential employers with a report about how well a student has achieved the curriculum learning targets. You usually are required to report students' grades several times a year to parents or guardians. The report covers several weeks of school, called a **marking period**; this is often each fourth of the academic year. The grades you give students are reported to the school administration on a permanent record card or folder. In the later years of schooling, they become part of the student's transcript. The school reports grades to students and parents through various means such as report cards, conferences, or letters.

FIGURE 15.1 What are your feelings about marks and grades (A = agree, U = undecided, D = disagree)?

	A U D
1. When academic marks are used, more than three marking categories are desirable.	___ ___ ___
2. There are justifiable reasons why the marks of some teachers, courses, and departments average consistently higher than others.	___ ___ ___
3. If a student fails a course but subsequently passes it, the initial failing mark should remain on his permanent record.	___ ___ ___
4. College students should have a substantial role in the evaluation and marking of their own individual achievements in academic areas.	___ ___ ___
5. Academic marks should be based more on achievement status than on growth or progress.	___ ___ ___
6. If academic marks are used, they should be numerals, not letters.	___ ___ ___
7. Students' academic marks should be determined solely by their academic achievements and not by attendance, citizenship, effort, and attitudes.	___ ___ ___
8. Schools that use marks should adopt and enforce a clearly defined institutional marking policy.	___ ___ ___
9. If academic marks are assigned to students, they should be viewed as measurements, not evaluations.	___ ___ ___
10. About the same proportion of high marks should be given to classes of slow learners as to classes of rapid learners.	___ ___ ___
11. Most teachers use too few appropriate statistical techniques in evaluating and marking their students.	___ ___ ___
12. In the absence of an institutional marking policy, marks should not be used in determining students' eligibility for academic courses and programs.	___ ___ ___

	A U D
13. Most current criticisms of marks refer to the act of marking per se and not the specific marking practices.	___ ___ ___
14. Absolute standards are more desirable than relative standards in evaluating and marking students in academic areas.	___ ___ ___
15. In the absence of an institutional marking policy, marks should not be used in determining eligibility for athletics and other extraclass activities.	___ ___ ___
16. "Pass/fail" or "credit/no credit" are more desirable than marking systems with three or more categories for academic classes.	___ ___ ___
17. Allowing students to contract for their own marks is preferable to marking on a relative basis.	___ ___ ___
18. The majority of teachers rely too much on their subjective judgments in evaluating their students.	___ ___ ___
19. Some type of numerical or letter marking system is essential to good educational practice.	___ ___ ___
20. Typical marking practices create too much undesirable competition among students.	___ ___ ___
21. Final course marks should be based on achievement status at the end and not on the average achievement throughout the course.	___ ___ ___
22. Factors like attitudes and interests should be used deliberately in determining students' marks.	___ ___ ___
23. "If something exists, it exists in some amount, and therefore can be measured."	___ ___ ___
24. Teachers should attempt to evaluate and mark students in such areas as interests, attitudes, and motivation.	___ ___ ___

Source: From "Agreement Among NCME Members on Selected Issues in Education Measurement," by W. S. Harris, 1973, *Journal of Educational Measurement, 10,* pp. 67–70. Washington, DC: NCME. Copyright 1973 by the National Council on Measurement in Education. Reprinted by permission of the publisher.

Validity Is Required Grades serving official summative evaluation purposes must be based on formal, continuous assessments that are aligned with your school's standards, official curriculum's learning targets, and educational psychology. As one fourth-grade teacher said (cited in Azwell & Schmar, 1995, pp. 7–9):

I don't know how other teachers feel, but anytime I send out an official report with my name on it, it is the equivalent of a legal document. The information in that report declares itself to be the best and latest educational information on a child. This may sound overly dramatic, but parents are expecting that report to tell them about an important chunk of their child's life. It is supposed to be true, and it is official.

Because many **stakeholders** will use your summative grades for many different purposes, the grades must be validly prepared and based on high-quality assessments. Assessments contributing to grades come from several sources: curriculum materials, quizzes and tests, performance tasks you create, projects and other long-term tasks, products students produce, portfolios you and your students assemble, and assessments set by groups of teachers working together.

It seems unfair to base a student's final grade on a single examination (assessment). This "big bang" approach to evaluation ignores several important factors about assessing students: (a) Only a limited amount of time is available during one teaching period for assessing; (b) in a limited time, only a small sample of tasks can be administered to students; (c) students may know much more than what appeared on the "one shot" assessment; (d) students' illness or family problems can interfere with their ability to demonstrate the required achievement; (e) students can demonstrate their achievement in several ways other than the one way you decided to assess it; and (f) some important learning targets are best assessed through longer-term projects, papers, or out-of-school assignments.

Why Teachers Dislike Grading

Grading for many teachers is one of the most difficult and troublesome aspects of teaching. This has been so for many generations. Why is this? Ebel (1979) cites the following reasons:

1. Educational achievements are difficult to evaluate properly.

2. Differing educational opinions and philosophies imply different methods for assessing, evaluating, and reporting students' progress.

3. Grading requires teachers to judge students, and many of these judgments are difficult and/or unpleasant to make.

In spite of teachers' dislike of grading, it is a required part of the job. This is one reason why you need to learn how to grade students as validly as possible.

HOW PEOPLE PERCEIVE AND USE GRADES

Validity, Decisions, and Stakeholders

Figure 15.2 gives examples of information frequently found on formal student progress reports and various kinds of decisions that may be based on such information. Study these decisions to become familiar with the ways in which others will use the grades you assign. This will help you better understand the rest of this chapter.

As you learn to grade, keep in mind that different persons will use grades in different ways. Figure 15.3 shows several different types of stakeholders and the ways they use grades. This figure illustrates that grades have serious meaning beyond your classroom. The grades you assign must be clear to judge whether any of these uses are valid.

Although assessment specialists generally recommend that you keep the meaning of grades clear by basing them only on a student's achievement of your course's learning targets, we know that many teachers do not follow this advice (Brookhart, 1991; Stiggins, Frisbie, & Griswold, 1989; Waltman & Frisbie, 1994). Brookhart states the issue clearly:

> The adjustments teachers make to compensate for grade use and misuse, however, are not uniform and are not necessarily valid either. A hodgepodge grade of attitude, effort, and achievement, created in an attempt to provide positive feedback to the student, is not the answer. Such a hodgepodge grade also falls down under a validity check; it does not possess the characteristic of interpretability. What teachers seem to intend when they add nonachievement factors to grades is to mitigate negative social consequences, but grades are not the appropriate tool for

FIGURE 15.2 **Examples of the types of information found on report cards and the types of decisions made from that information.**

Information in report	Decisions that can be made			
	Selection	Placement remediation	Guidance, counseling	Course improvement
1. Content or objectives learned	Promotion, probation, graduation, admissions	Selecting courses to take, remedial help needed	Selecting next courses to take, additional schooling needed, career-related choices	Deciding where instruction can be improved
2. Comparison of performance in different subjects	Admission	Selecting advanced and/or remedial courses	Determining pattern of a pupil's strengths and weaknesses	Identifying areas that are strong points of school
3. Performance relative to other people	Scholarships, prizes, admission	Estimating likely success, eligibility for special programs	Estimating likely success in certain areas	
4. Social behavior		Matching personal characteristics to course and teacher placement	Determining need for adjustment, likes, dislikes, ability to get along with others	Identifying problems with a course or with a teacher

FIGURE 15.3 Various uses to which grades are put by different stakeholders.

Usage for grades	Student	Parents	Teacher	Guidance counselor	School administrators	Postsecondary educational institutions	Employers
					Stakeholder likely to use the grades in the way indicated		
1. Reaffirm what is already known about classroom achievement	✓						
2. Document educational progress and course completion	✓	✓	✓	✓	✓	✓	✓
3. Obtain extrinsic rewards/punishments	✓	✓					
4. Obtain social attention or teacher attention	✓						
5. Request new educational placement		✓	✓	✓	✓		
6. Judge a teacher's competence or fairness		✓		✓	✓		
7. Indicate school problems for a student		✓	✓	✓	✓		
8. Support vocational or career guidance explorations	✓	✓					
9. Limit or exclude student's participation in extracurricular activities			✓		✓		
10. Promote or retain			✓		✓		
11. Grant graduation/diploma					✓		
12. Determine whether student has necessary prerequisite for a higher level course			✓	✓	✓		
13. Select for postsecondary education						✓	
14. Decide whether an individual has basic skills needed for a particular job							✓

social engineering. Teachers' intuition about social consequences, however, is useful because it points us to the other half of the validity issue: what happens when grades are used for decisions and actions. (p. 36)

Parents' Versus Teachers' Understanding

Communicating to parents is especially challenging. Some research shows that parents' and teachers' understanding of what report card grades mean are often far apart (Waltman & Frisbie, 1994). For example, parents may see grades as reflecting pure achievement. Or, they may see grades as predictive of future success on the job or in postsecondary school.

Grades Communicate Your Values

For the teacher, grades communicate more than achievement information about a student. The grades you assign communicate your (and your school's) values. If obedience to your classroom rules is rewarded by an A or "performing satisfactorily" in *reading*, but "fooling around" during class means the *reading grade* is lowered, in spite of successful reading performance, you have communicated that obedience is valued more than reading well. The teacher who gives an unsatisfactory grade to the student whose academic performance is satisfactory and then says, "I warned you about passing notes during class!" is perhaps communicating vindictiveness. You may value both social behavior (e.g., conformity) and achievement, but if the grade you report intertwines the two, you are communicating poorly and are encouraging confusion. To clarify matters, you must separate your evaluations of achievement from your evaluations of noncognitive student characteristics.

Grades as Motivators

Can and should grades be used to motivate students? Educational assessment experts are divided on whether it is appropriate to use the traditional marking system (A, B, C, . . .) to motivate students. Some (such as Ebel, 1979) have held that grades are important motivators for students. To serve this function, many assessment specialists believe that grades must validly and accurately reflect only achievement—students who attain the performance standards to the highest degree should receive the highest grades (Ebel & Frisbie, 1991; Hills, 1990; Linn & Gronlund, 1995; Oosterhof, 1994; Stiggins et al., 1989; Terwilliger, 1989).

Others offer another view of the motivating effects of grades. Cronbach (1977), for example, gave four principles of motivation: (a) There should be learning targets that students want to achieve, (b) students should believe they can achieve these learning targets, (c) students should understand how near they are to achieving these learning targets, and (d) achieving classroom learning targets should lead students to apply their learning in authentic settings.

Cronbach's analysis of traditional A, B, C grading in terms of these principles stated that (a) grades do serve as goals that at least some students seek to attain; (b) grades do not motivate students who feel high grades are out of reach—a condition likely when grades include only a student's final level of attainment, rather than progress in a course that takes initial readiness into account; (c) students can use grades to judge their progress if the teacher continually gives them the results of assessments that clearly explain what students' final performance is supposed look like; (d) grades tend to be holistic judgments rather than descriptions of strengths and weaknesses; and (e) grades alone do not tell students what they need to do better to improve their current achievement so it more closely resembles the desired achievement.

CRITICISMS OF GRADES AND MARKS

Types of Criticisms

Educators have voiced a number of criticisms of grades over the years. You need to be aware of these criticisms to explain the rationale for your own grading policy to parents and other educators. Many of these criticisms can be summarized under the four headings in Figure 15.4.

Responses to Criticism

The following comments are offered in response to these criticisms (Ebel, 1974):

1. *Grades are essentially meaningless.* There is some truth in each of the criticisms under this heading. However, Criticisms 1, 2, 4, and 5 in Figure 15.4 can be used as arguments supporting the need to improve and strengthen grading practices rather than eliminating them. Criticism 3 attributes to grades more than they were ever intended to convey. Summative grades were never intended to substitute for the complex details of achievement needed for daily instructional planning. Grades are summary reports of a student's general level of achievement.

2. *Grades are educationally unimportant.* Criticisms here are a mixture of value statements and unnecessary comparisons. Certainly grades are symbols, but it doesn't follow that symbols are unimportant. Some persons work for concrete, tangible rewards; others work with and for symbolic rewards. To value intangible outcomes exclusively would be to hold that nothing of any value in education can be observed or assessed. This seems untenable. To pit a teacher's grades against a student's self-evaluations implies that only one or the other can be used. There is reason to believe, however, that both should be used. Further, evaluations by teachers help individuals realistically evaluate themselves. Grades do predict subsequent academic achievement (i.e., subsequent grades), and they do predict some types of out-of-class accomplishments. Grades

FIGURE 15.4 **Commonly expressed criticisms of grades.**

A. Grades are essentially meaningless
  1. There is great diversity among institutions and teachers in grading practices.
  2. Many schools lack definite grading policies.
  3. A single symbol cannot possibly report adequately the complex details of an educational achievement.
  4. Teachers are often casual or even careless in grading.
  5. Grades are frequently used to punish or to enforce discipline rather than to report achievement accurately.

B. Grades are educationally unimportant.
  6. Grades are only symbols.
  7. The most important outcomes are intangible and hence cannot be assessed or graded.
  8. A teacher's grades are less important to a pupil than his own self-evaluations.
  9. Grades do not predict later achievement correctly.
  10. What should be evaluated is the educational program, not the pupils.

C. Grades are unnecessary.
  11. Grades are ineffective motivators of real achievement in education.

  12. When students learn mastery, as they should, no differential levels of achievement remain to be graded.
  13. Grades have persisted in schools mainly because teachers cling to traditional practices.

D. Grades are harmful
  14. Low grades may discourage the less able pupils from efforts to learn.
  15. Grading makes failure inevitable for some pupils.
  16. Parents sometimes punish pupils for low grades, and reward high grades inappropriately.
  17. Grades set universal standards for all pupils despite their great individual differences.
  18. Grading emphasizes common goals for all pupils and discourages individuality in learning.
  19. Grading rewards conformity and penalizes creativity.
  20. Grading fosters competition rather than cooperation.
  21. Pressure to get high grades leads some pupils to cheat.
  22. Grading is more compatible with subject-centered education than with humanistic, child-centered education.

Source: From "Shall We Get Rid of Grades?" by R. L. Ebel, 1974, *Measurement in Education, 5* (4), pp. 1–2. Washington, DC: NCME. Copyright 1974 by the National Council on Measurement in Education. Reprinted with permission of the publisher.

cannot be expected to be perfect or near-perfect predictors. Much goes into subsequent accomplishment including opportunity, effort, quality of instruction, and luck. Further, valid grades should reflect what students were taught. If the curriculum learning targets fail to match the skills, abilities, and attitudes necessary for job success, then you would not expect grades to predict job performance, even if grades perfectly described what students have learned.

3. *Grades are unnecessary.* The preceding points show that, although grades are not necessary for all evaluative functions, they cannot be entirely eliminated. Some type of summary report is needed for guidance and counseling and for accountability—both of the students to the school and the school to students and parents. You need to summarize large amounts of achievement data before they are understood. Thus, imperfect as grades are, they serve summary and record-keeping functions. Parents need to know, for example, how their children are doing in arithmetic, on the whole, as well as the specific kinds of arithmetic competence the student possesses. Overly detailed reports, however, will be incomprehensible. A high school student, for example, may want to know whether to register for advanced placement calculus or regular calculus. The counselor reaches for this semester's precalculus course grade, not a list of specific mathematics concepts learned in the last 9 weeks. As another example, a student may want to know whether she is progressing satisfactorily. The school is obliged to offer its judgment, possibly summarized in a grade, not simply a description of her placement in a curriculum.

4. *Grades are harmful.* Unfortunately, some teachers do use grades punitively and vindictively, as weapons rather

than as tools. Some parents do overstress the importance of grades, putting undesirable pressure on their children to achieve at all costs. But to what extent these harmful activities are occurring is not clear. For example, are 1 or 2 or 10 parents per classroom overly ambitious for their children? Are 1 in 20 teachers vindictive? No one knows for sure.

A real concern among elementary teachers is the discouraging effect of low grades. Cronbach's analysis of the motivating effects of grades suggests some ways in which teacher evaluations can be improved to avoid discouragement. Even though grades may only report learning failure, and cannot be entirely to blame for this failure, it is still important to consider the effects such reports can have on children. As Brookhart (1991) put it, "What do we say when we define an important indicator [of a student's school success] in a way that is guaranteed to defeat some children?" (p. 35).

Section II: Report Cards and Other Official Reports of Student Progress

STUDENT PROGRESS REPORTING METHODS

Advantages and Disadvantages

Student progress reporting methods are ways that schools communicate to students and parents, as well as ways of keeping records of students' achievement. Figure 15.5 summarizes the advantages and disadvantages of different methods. Your school district may use more than one method of reporting student progress because different methods may serve different purposes and

FIGURE 15.5 **Advantages and disadvantages of some commonly used methods of reporting student progress.**

Name	Type of code used	Advantages	Disadvantages
Letter grades	A, B, C, etc., also "+" and "−" may be added.	a. Administratively easy to use b. Believed to be easy to interpret c. Concisely summarize overall performance	a. Meaning of a grade varies widely with subject, teacher, school b. Do not describe strengths and weaknesses c. Kindergarten and primary school children may feel defeated by them
Number or percentage grade	Integers (5, 4, 3 . . .) or percentages (99, 98, . . .)	a. Same as points a, b, and c above b. More continuous than letter grades c. May be used along with letter grades	a. Same as points a, b, and c above b. Meaning not immediately apparent unless explanation accompanies them
Two-category grade	Pass-fail, satisfactory-unsatisfactory, credit-entry	a. Less devastating to younger students b. Can encourage older students to take courses normally neglected because of fear of lowered GPA	a. Less reliable than more continuous system b. Does not communicate enough information about pupil's performance for others to judge progress
Checklist and rating scales	Checks (✓) next to objectives mastered or numerical ratings of degree of mastery	a. Give the details of what the pupil achieved b. May be combined with letter grades or with group-referenced data	a. May become too detailed for parents to comprehend b. Administratively cumbersome for record keeping
Narrative report	None, but may refer to one or more of the above; however, usually does not refer to grades	a. Allows teacher the opportunity to describe a student's educational development b. Shows a student's progress in terms of standards, indicators of achievement, learning targets, or a continuum of educational growth c. Provides opportunity to open dialogue and other types of communication with parents and students	a. Very time consuming b. Requires excellent writing skill and effective communication skills on the teacher's part c. May require translation into language read by parents, with possible loss of meaning in the translation d. Parents who are not skilled readers may misunderstand it or may be put off e. Parents may be overwhelmed and not respond f. Often modified to include checklist-like list of indicators with short teacher comments
Pupil-teacher conference	Usually none, but any of the above may be discussed	a. Offers opportunity to discuss progress personally b. Can be an ongoing process that is integrated into instruction	a. Teacher needs skill in offering positive as well as negative comments b. Can be time consuming c. Can be threatening to some pupils d. Doesn't offer the institution the kind of summary record desired
Parent-teacher conference	None, but often one or more of the above may be discussed	a. Allows parents and teachers to discuss concerns and clarify misunderstandings b. Teachers can show samples of students' work and explain basis for judgments made c. May lead to improved home-school relations	a. Time consuming b. Requires teacher to prepare ahead of time c. May provoke too much anxiety for some teachers and parents d. Inadequate means of reporting large amounts of information e. May be inconvenient for parent to attend
Letter to parents	None, but may refer to one or more of the above	a. Useful supplement to other progress-reporting methods	a. Short letters inadequately communicate pupil progress b. Requires exceptional writing skill and much teacher time

different audiences. You can find useful summaries of the practical pros and cons of various student-reporting methods in the additional readings listed on the Companion Website. When evaluating your school district's reporting methods, keep the following points in mind:

1. *Teachers use some methods of reporting student progress more frequently at certain grade levels.* Letter grades, for example, are used with high frequency in the upper elementary, junior high, and senior high school levels. Parent-teacher conferences do not occur often in junior and senior high schools.

2. *Often schools use combinations of methods on the same report card.* For example, letter grades may report a student's subject-matter achievement; rating scales may report the student's attitudes and deportment. A parent-teacher conference may convey information on achievement, effort, attitudes, and behavior. Schools may use a combination of nearly all methods.

3. *Conflicts may arise between methods.* School administrators need a concise summary of each student's progress for accountability and record keeping. Parents and teachers may need slightly more detailed explanations of the content

taught, the standards mastered, and how a student's educational development compares with members of a peer group.[1] The most detailed methods of reporting identified in Figure 15.5 are the checklist and the narrative.

Checklists

A checklist contains a list of many specific behaviors; a teacher checks off or rates each behavior as a student performs it during the year. Figure 12.7 shows part of a checklist one test publisher offers for assessing high school students' progress in speaking.

Narrative Reports

Narrative reports are detailed, written accounts of what each student has learned in relation to the school's curriculum framework and the student's effort in class. The hope is that narrative reports will replace the shortcomings of letter grades because the latter tend to condense too much information into a single symbol. Narratives also allow teachers to include unique information about students' learning or something unique the teacher has done for that student—things that would not appear on a standardized form (Power & Chandler, 1998).

Advantages The concept of providing a rich description of a student's learning and educational development is laudable. When done well, these descriptions can mean much more to parents and students than the simple summaries that grades provide. This would be useful for describing elementary students' learning, especially if a state or school has defined a continuum of learning targets and performance standards over several grades, with benchmarks defined for each grade.

Limitations Narrative reports can be poorly or insensitively written, of course. Even teachers with good intentions find them difficult to write well. They may confuse or overwhelm parents, who may be asked to read 5 to 10 pages of narrative to understand what their children are learning. Using narrative reports should not be undertaken without considerable teacher development. A mean teacher can be just as mean in narrative writing as in letter grading. One mean teacher wrote, "Johnny thinks like a chicken!" Sensitivity and constructive comments are necessary. It would be important to base teacher development on the successful experience of teachers in schools outside of one's own district to gain perspective and practical advice. Lots of guided practice is needed in writing nonthreatening and nonblaming comments.

Modified Narrative Reports Because meaningful long narrative reports are very time consuming for teachers to prepare, some schools have modified the reporting process. One way to do this is by combining the checklist or rating-scale procedure with short written comments about each student. Figure 15.6 shows one section of a primary-school pupil narrative report. The full report is four pages and includes a few pages showing the school's educational developmental continuum (Egawa & Azwell, 1995).

You can see from the example that the indicators function in a way similar to checklists (even if you do not actually tick them) and provide a kind of framework for interpreting the teacher's brief comments. The presence of the indicators reduces the need for a teacher to explain what curricular activities were used and evaluated for each student.

Along the same lines is the *standards-based report card*, developed in the Tucson Unified School System (Clarridge & Whitaker, 1997). Figure 15.7 shows an example.

For each curriculum area, standards were written for Grades 1–2 and 3–6. Each standard was adopted from the state's standards and written to match the district's core curriculum. In that way, standards were linked to specific learning targets. (See Chapter 2 for an example.) If a student achieves a state's standard, the teacher gives the student a quality score of 4. Teachers also prepared verbal descriptions of levels 3, 2, and 1 for each standard to explain the meaning of lesser levels of achievement; much in the same way one would develop general scoring rubrics. (See Chapter 12 for information on scoring rubrics.) All of these verbal descriptions were computerized using a database program.

Each marking period, each student's progress along the levels of the "rubric" for each standard is the basis for marking. To use the system, the teacher enters a student's name and, for each state standard taught in each curriculum area, a numeral from 1 to 4 that describes the student's progress in achieving that standard. The computer prepares a report by automatically printing the words describing the level of achievement the numeral represents. Teachers' own brief comments can be added and printed, too. Thus, this is a criterion-referenced reporting system.

The use of technology relieves much of the burden for teachers (Clarridge & Whitaker, 1997). Student-learner qualities (self-direction, collaboration/cooperation, problem solving, citizenship, and quality of work produced) were also reported using the same standards and rubric-based procedure. Teachers must be trained so they avoid corrupting the system by using the 1, 2, 3, and 4 ratings as simple substitutes for A, B, C, and D.

---

[1]Note that parents may seek norm-referenced information because they have had little experience with students of a given age or grade. After 5 years of teaching, for example, a teacher may have experienced hundreds of students of a given grade. After 20 years of parenting, parents have experienced only their own children and a few children of friends, relatives, and neighbors.

FIGURE 15.6 Example of a section of a primary-level narrative student progress report using indicators and teacher comments.

Primary Progress Report

Name _____   Class _____

Parents _____   Teacher _____

Reporting Period _____   Phone _____

Days Present _____ Absent _____ Tardies _____

Note to parents: *Under each area of curriculum I have listed indicators which I look for when assessing and evaluating students. Student should be demonstrating or working toward these goals. These indicators are on the left hand side of the report. Specific comments about your child are to right of the indicators.* ** *These items will be emphasized in the spring.*

Learning & Social Skills
The members of our school community focus on the following:
- doing their personal best
- being trustworthy
- being truthful
- actively listening to others
- not "putting down" others

- contributes to the learning of other class members
- settles down quickly in appropriate area
- works cooperatively with others
- actively participates in discussions and projects
- takes responsibility for learning
- cleans up before starting the next activity
- respects classroom materials and the property of others
- pays attention when others are speaking

Personal comments are added here for each child:

Reading and the Language Arts
Activities of the curriculum included in this category include: classroom newspaper, dialogue journals, personal notebook and sketchpad, author's folders, literature study, literacy strategies and the arts (drama, music, art)

Classroom Newspaper
- volunteers stories to the weekly news
- contributes conventions (punctuation, spelling, calendar information, temperature, etc.) at teacher request
- joins in the re-reading or shared reading of the dictated news of classmates
- contributes his or her own writing to the second page*
- actively participates and pays attention while others share
- stays in place/seat
- illustrates his/her own news

Parent Comments:

The newspaper is created daily on a plastic overlay that is projected on a large screen. The students contribute information as the teacher writes. *Personal comments are added here for each child:*

Source: Telling the Story: Narrative Reports," reprinted by permission of Kathy Egawa and Tara Azwell. In *Report on Report Cards: Alternatives to Consider* edited by Tara Azwell and Elizabeth Schmar. (Heinemann, a division of Reed Elsevier Inc., Portsmouth, NH, 1995.) Figure 9-1, p. 103.

Parent-Teacher Conferences

Conducting Conferences **Parent-teacher conferences** are one of the best ways to build strong connections with parents, to provide them with an understanding of their children's learning strengths and needs, and to help them be involved in their children's learning. However, you need to conduct them carefully and skillfully if they are to be successful. Figure 15.8 lists some of the things to do before, during, and after the conference to keep it on target. Additional suggestions are given in Shalaway's (1998) *Learning to Teach . . . Not Just for Beginners.*

Limitations of Conferences Parent-teacher conferences have their drawbacks, however. They are time consuming for the teacher, both in preparation time and in actual contact time. Schools frequently schedule 1 or 2 days during which you are to hold conferences during school hours; some

FIGURE 15.7 **Example of a section of a computer-assisted narrative student progress report using standards-and rubric-based procedure along with teacher comments**

	Semester			
	1st	2nd	3rd	4th
Self-Directed Learner	3			
Student often sets achievable goals, considers risks, and makes some choices about what to do and in what order to do them, usually reviews progress, and often takes responsibility for own actions.	Comments:			
Collaborative Worker	2			
Student is developing the abililty to work in groups, has positive relationships with other students, and is learning to work toward group goals.	Comments:			
Problem Solver	4			
Student reasons, makes decisions, and solves complex problems in many situations, and uses these skills regularly, independently, and efficiently.	Comments:			

Note: The report is for the first marking period (4 = the highest rating).

Source: Reprinted by permission from *Rolling the Elephant Over: How to Effect Large-Scale Change in the Reporting Process* by P. B. Clarridge and E. M. Whittaker. Copyright © 1997 by P. B. Clarridge and E. M. Whittaker. Published by Heinemann, a division of Reed Elsevier, Inc., Portsmouth, NH. All rights reserved.

FIGURE 15.8 **Suggestions for organizing and conducting a parent conference.**

SET PURPOSE

- Set goals for the conference.
- Decide what information you need to communicate with parents.
- Decide how, if at all, students will be involved, and what their role and tasks will be at the conference.

PLAN LOGISTICS

- If possible, send home report cards or other information about a week before, so parents have time to prepare questions and talk with their child.
- Schedule times and locations for each appointment. Include breaks for yourself at regular intervals.
- Keep to the schedule to respect everyone's time.
- Arrange for a waiting area where waiting parents cannot overhear your conference with other parents.
- Arrange a comfortable setting (chairs, tables, etc.) where you can converse easily.

COLLECT EVIDENCE

- Have grades, portfolios, student work samples, checklists, anecdotal records, etc., as appropriate, organized to share with parents. Work samples should illustrate the general level of student work and help parents understand their student's grades, current achievement level, and next steps.
- Involve students in the collection of evidence whenever possible.

INTERPRET EVIDENCE

- Prepare your main points ahead of time. Don't rely on spur-of-the moment thinking to convey important information about students. Clear oral communication requires just as much preparation as written comments do.
- Prepare questions you may have for parents about their child's work, interests, activities, etc.
- If you are well prepared, you can communicate clearly and remain confident.

COMMUNICATE

- Aim for clarity of expression; make your points clearly and briefly and support them with evidence.
- Listen carefully to what parents say. Respond to their concerns. Be open to learning more about the student than you know from the school setting.
- Use interpersonal skills: communicate genuine care for the student, develop rapport, and reflect parents' feelings.
- If the child is present, include him or her in the communication; if the child is not present, plan with parents how to share what went on so the child does not experience the conference as "people talking behind my back."
- Plan the next steps for the student jointly with parents.
- Do not allow antagonistic parents to derail communication. Your job is to understand the child's work and behavior as best you can, not to become the family's counselor or to become afraid or anxious. Listen and try to understand.

Source: Based on ideas from Brookhart (2004); Newman (1997–1998); Perl (1995); Swiderek (1997).

schedule evening hours for the convenience of working parents. Sometimes schools neglect to give teachers time to plan and prepare for the conferences, assuming that teachers either need little or no planning time, or that they will do the necessary preparation after hours. In addition, parent-teacher conferences can be frustrating and produce anxiety for both teacher and parent, especially if the parties lack confidence in each other.

Attendance may also be a problem. Not all parents will come to conferences. Parents may be working, ill, embarrassed about their poor English or their poverty, unwilling to attend, or otherwise unable to come. Some parents are courteous and will notify you that they cannot attend, but you should not expect most parents to do this.

Finally, teachers and/or parents may have too much information, too many issues, or too many concerns to discuss in the brief time allotted to the conference. Often about 20 minutes is allotted for the conference. Also, some parents (and teachers) talk too much and use up more than their share of time. Scheduling another conference with the parents may be necessary.

Privacy Parent conferences should be private and between one teacher and the parent(s) of one student. The school principal should provide facilities to allow confidential discussions. Avoid holding a conference where other teachers, other students, or other parents can overhear what is being said. This protects the rights of all involved. It may be difficult to limit the conference to one teacher and the parent(s), especially in schools where students have different teachers for different subjects.

Multiple Marking Systems

A Report Card Example When a school uses more than one method to report students' progress, such as a report card with several kinds of marks or symbols, this is called a **multiple marking system**. A report card, especially for the elementary schools, usually uses a multiple marking system. Figure 15.9 shows an example of a **report card** employing a multiple marking system for Grades 4 through 6 in one school district.

Reporting Achievement for Each Subject Notice the card has four marking periods, called "report periods," each approximately 9 weeks long. Words (*experiencing difficulty, performing successfully,* and *commendable*) define levels of accomplishment and serve as a rating scale for other areas. These are repeated as column headings under each marking period. For each marking period, the teacher uses a checkmark for reporting the student's achievement in each curriculum area. A dash (–) and an "I" also are used to communicate. In this report card, each curriculum area is divided into two to four subareas that contain the major learning targets of the curriculum in this school district. Reporting progress on each of them provides both parents and the following year's teacher with more specific information about what a student has achieved in the curriculum.

Reporting Noncognitive Achievement Progress in nonacademic areas is reported on the right side of the report card in the last example. Most schools rate citizenship, behavior, and so on separately from achievement, but this provision varies with the grade level (Kunder & Porwoll, 1977). For kindergarten, primary, and upper elementary grades, most schools provide this separation; somewhat fewer schools do so at the junior high school and senior high levels. Notice that in the example report card, the nonacademic areas are defined by specific, observable student performances. Thus, instead of asking teachers to rate general traits such as "personality" or "deportment," the school district asks the teacher to focus on specific student performances that can be observed and assessed.

Permanent Record Cards A **permanent record card** is the official record of a student's school performance. Not all information needs to appear on a student's permanent record card. Putting elementary students' letter grades in a permanent record card is controversial. Many educators (and some professional associations) argue that reporting or recording grades at the elementary level is inappropriate. However, students and parents may become upset if, for the first time in junior high, a student receives a C (or lower) in a subject, when previously the student has received only "performing satisfactorily" checks on the elementary report card or a narrative report.

Some intermediate policy may help a student with this transition from the elementary school marking code to a new marking code at the junior high. A school may decide, for example, to have teachers prepare letter grades for fifth and sixth graders, but not to report them on report cards or on permanent record cards. Parents, however, are apprised of these grades. Thus, a "performing satisfactorily" can mean a C for some students and a B for others. At the end of the year, the letter-grades records are destroyed.

CRAFTING A MULTIPLE REPORTING SYSTEM

No matter which type of system you adopt, you first need to put progress reports into a grading framework so everyone can clearly interpret information about students. Basic grading frameworks include norm-referencing (relative standards), criterion-referencing (absolute standards), and self-referencing (growth standards).[2] Each way of referencing provides a different perspective on a student. These frameworks are explained in Section III of this chapter.

---

[2]Norm-referencing is sometimes called group-referencing, whereas criterion-referencing is sometimes called absolute marking, objectives-referencing, or task-referencing.

FIGURE 15.9 Example of a multiple marking system report card for Grades 4, 5, 6.

KEY

A dash (—) indicates that performance was not measured during the report period.
(I) indicates improved performance.

The evaluations in this section refer to personal interaction and task-related skill development as viewed by your child's regular subject teacher(s). Special subject teachers may use these numerals to explain improvement needed in their respective areas.

YOUR CHILD IN SCHOOL

Personal Interaction Skills

1 Is courteous in speech and actions
2 Shows respect for others
3 Responds positively to help and correction
4 Respects property of the school and others
5 Takes care of personal belongings
6 Demonstrates self-control
7 Observes rules and regulations

Task-related skills

8 Follows directions
9 Utilizes time effectively
10 Listens attentively
11 Works independently when necessary
12 Starts and finishes work on time
13 Completes assigned work
14 Contributes to class discussion
15 Observes standards of neatness
16 Works quietly
17 Brings necessary material to class

ESTHETIC DEVELOPMENT

Vocal Music

Develops basic performing skills
Comprehends and interprets musical elements
Participates appropriately in activities
Performs commendably

Art

Manipulates a variety of materials
Applies principles of design in projects
Participates appropriately in activities
Uses constructive imagination in art projects
Performs commendably

PHYSICAL DEVELOPMENT

Physical Education

Displays good sportsmanship
Participates in activities
Maintains minimal fitness level
Behaves appropriately

Health

Performs commendably
Demonstrates knowledge of health concepts
Behaves appropriately

Days Absent
Times Tardy
Times Excused Early
Absences affecting progress

EXPLANATION OF MARKING

Experiencing Difficulty — Basic skills have not been acquired, the student has not reached the performance level set for his or her group or set for the child individually.

Performing Successfully — The student has attained the performance level set for his or her group or set for the child individually. Knowledge and skills have developed satisfactorily.

Commendable — Knowledge and skills are well developed. The student has exceeded the expectations set for him or her individually or for the group. Performance is praiseworthy.

THE LANGUAGE ARTS

Reading

Reads with understanding
Recognizes and applies vocabulary
Uses study and reference skills
Understands elements of literature

Spelling

Spells assigned words accurately
Spells accurately in written communication

Language

Recognizes parts of speech
Applies correct sentence structure
Uses conventional punctuation
Expresses ideas clearly

Handwriting

Writes legibly

MATHEMATICS

Understands concepts
Recalls basic facts (+, −, ×, ÷)
Works accurately
Uses reasoning in solving word problems
Applies principles of measurement and geometry

SOCIAL STUDIES

Understands basic concepts
Uses research skills

SCIENCE

Understands basic concepts.
Uses process skills.

Lower Int.	Middle Int.	Upper Int.	Grade 7			
Book 4	Book 5	Book 6	Book 7			

Intermediate basal reading materials used to date

*A check mark indicates the performance level in the basal reading program which has been covered.

REPORT PERIOD — 1st, 2nd, 3rd, 4th — Performing Successfully / Experiencing Difficulty

REPORT PERIOD — 1st, 2nd, 3rd, 4th — Commendable / Performing Successfully / Experiencing Difficulty

Source: Courtesy of the Mt. Lebanon, Pennsylvania, Public Schools.

FIGURE 15.11 Examples of definitions of grades under three different referencing frameworks.

Absolute scale: task-referenced, criterion-referenced	Relative scale: group-referenced, norm-referenced	Growth scale: self-referenced, change scale
Grade *Relative to the learning targets specified in the curriculum, the student has:*	*Relative to the other students in the class, the student is:*	*Relative to the ability and knowledge this student brought to the learning situation, the student:*
A • Excellent command of concepts, principles, strategies implied by the learning targets • High level of performance of the learning targets and skills • Excellent preparation for more advanced learning	• Far above the class average	• Made significant gains • Performed significantly above what the teacher expected
B • Solid, beyond the minimum, but not an excellent, command of the concepts, principles, strategies implied by the learning targets • Advanced level of performance of the learning targets and of most skills • Prepared well for more advanced learning	• Above the class average	• Made very good gains • Performed somewhat higher than what the teacher expected
C • Minimum command of concepts, principles, strategies implied by the learning targets • Demonstrated minimum ability to perform the learning targets and to use basic skills • Deficiencies in a few prerequisites needed for later learning	• At or very near the class average	• Made good gains • Met the performance level the teacher expected
D • Not learned some of the *essential* concepts, principles, and strategies implied by the learning targets • Not demonstrated ability to perform some *very essential* learning targets and basic skills • Deficiencies in many, but not all, of the prerequisites needed for later learning	• Below the class average	• Made some good gains • Did not quite meet the level of performance the teacher expected
F • Not learned *most* of the basic concepts, principles, and strategies implied by the learning targets • Not learned most of the *very essential* learning targets and basic skills • Not acquired most of the prerequisites needed for later learning	• Far below the class average	• Made insignificant or no gains • Performed far below what the teacher expected

Note: This figure is an adaptation of some of the ideas in Frisbie & Waltman (1992).

describing achievement of learning targets or standards, (b) the performance of others in a specific group (such as classmates), or (c) the student's starting point or overall ability. At this point, however, you may wish to review Figure 2.2 and the related text in Chapter 2. Before discussing which of these frameworks you should use, we shall explain each one separately.

Criterion Referencing: Absolute Standards **Criterion-referenced grading** is also referred to as using **absolute standards grading** or **task-referenced grading**. You assign grades by comparing a student's performance to a defined set of standards to be achieved, targets to be learned, or knowledge to be acquired: Students who complete the tasks, achieve the standards completely, or learn the targets are given the better grades, regardless of how well other

students perform or whether they have worked up to their potential. Thus, it is possible that you may give all students As and Bs if they all meet the absolute standards specified by the learning targets. Similarly, when you use this framework you must be prepared to assign all students Fs and Ds if none of them meet the standards set by the learning targets.

Learning targets and standards need to be realistic. For example, suppose the students are typical for the grade you teach, and you teach well. Further, suppose the learning target specifies that the students should be able to create meaningful mathematics word problems that mirror real-life situations. If all or most of your students cannot perform this learning target, it may be misplaced in the curriculum. If you are using a criterion-referenced grading framework, you might be tempted to give all students low grades. However, common sense requires you to discuss the placement of the learning target with other teachers and the curriculum coordinator. Failing students when they are not ready to learn the tasks is inappropriate. (Of course, you must be sure that the standards are in fact inappropriate and that you have in fact taught well. If you taught poorly or used a poor-quality assessment procedure, then you should reteach or assess properly.) This also means that absolute standards must be set using norm-referenced information: What is appropriate or typical for the population of students you are teaching? Both norm-referencing and criterion-referencing are necessary to interpret assessment results properly.

Criterion-referenced grading is most meaningful when you have a well-defined domain of performance for students to learn. The recent educational movement to set standards at the state level has put pressure on school districts to use these standards to set specific learning targets at the classroom level. The teachers in a school district often are left to align the specific learning targets with the standards. The aligned learning targets serve as the well-defined domain of performance students are expected to learn. Achievement of these learning targets becomes the basis for assigning grades. (See Chapters 2 and 3 for discussions of alignment.)

Arguments both for and against criterion-referencing, in general, center on whether it is of value to know exactly what the student has learned independently of the student's own capability and the learning of others. Bellanca and Kirschenbaum (1976) summarize these arguments.

Norm-Referencing: Relative Standards Norm-referencing is also called **grading with relative standards** or **group-referenced grading**. In this approach, you assign grades based on how a student's performance compared with others in the class: Students performing better than most classmates receive the higher grades. Advocates of group-referencing base their arguments on the necessity of competition in life, the value of knowing one's standing in relation to peers, and the idea that relative achievement is more important than absolute achievement. Arguments against norm-referenced grading center on the ill effects of competition, that the knowledge of standing in a peer group does not describe what a student has learned, and that ascertaining the absolute level of achievement is more important than ascertaining relative achievement. Bellanca and Kirschenbaum (1976) offer a more detailed summary of these arguments.

With group-referenced grading, you must define the reference group against which you compare a student. Is the reference group the other students in this section of the course, in all sections taking the course this year, or all students taking the course during the past five years? Just as the criterion-referenced framework requires defining learning targets clearly for grades to be meaningful, so too does a group-referenced framework require defining the reference group clearly.

A grade based purely on a student's relative standing in a group does not convey to parents and school officials what the student is capable of doing relative to the curriculum's learning targets. Further, to act consistently within this framework, you should give good grades to the "top" students, even though they may not possess the level of competence specified by standards or the curriculum's learning targets. Similarly, you should give poor grades to the low-ranking students even though they may have met the minimum level of competence that the curriculum's learning targets specify.

Just as the criterion-referenced framework needs to be grounded in the standards appropriate for the grade level you are teaching, so too must the group-referenced framework be adjusted. Your responsibility as a teacher includes making sure the students learn the curriculum's specified learning targets. It would be irresponsible to give As, Bs, and Cs to students who have not met the standards even though they may be the top students. Those who use the grades you assign will count on you to make the grades reflect these learning targets. Thus, we return to the earlier principle that both norm-referenced and criterion-referenced information is needed to properly interpret the grades.

Don't waffle and retrofit. You may start out wanting to grade using criterion-referencing and standards, but then discover that your students have done poorly. Being afraid to give poor grades, you may then waffle and start to "grade on the curve" (i.e., use norm-referencing). This retrofitting of a norm-referenced framework simply does not fit either approach and is not good educational practice. If the standards you set are grade appropriate and if students performed poorly, then you must determine why. Perhaps your assessment instruments were poorly crafted (e.g., you may have used poor-quality testing materials that came with your curriculum). If so, then your assessments are invalid and no amount of norm-referencing can make them more valid. Perhaps your teaching was inadequate. Then reteaching is in order. Or perhaps the standards are simply not grade appropriate or are inappropriate for the educational development of the students you teach. This is a matter that needs to be addressed by your principal or by the curriculum coordinator. In this case you need to adjust the standards, and then reteach: Grading on the curve in this instance distorts the real educational problem and is, therefore, not acting in a professionally responsible way.

Self-Referencing: Growth Standards Self-referencing is also called **growth-based grading** or **change-based grading**. You assign grades by comparing a student's performance with your perceptions of his capability: Students performing at or above the level at which you believe them capable of performing receive the better grades, regardless of their absolute levels of attainment or their relative standing in the group. A student who came to the class with very little previous knowledge but who has made great strides may be given the same grade as a student who has learned more but who initially came to the class with a great deal more previous learning. A variation of this approach is grading on the basis of improvement, growth, or change.

Arguments in favor of self-referenced grading center on the possibility of reducing competition among students and the concept that grades can be adjusted to motivate, to encourage, and to meet the students' needs. Arguments against the system center on the unreliable nature of teachers' judgments of capability, the need for parents and students to know standing relative to peers, the idea that this procedure tends to be applied mostly to lower ability students, and the possibility that this system may eventually lead to grading based solely on effort (Dunbar, Float, & Lyman, 1980). Additionally, students may not achieve the state's standards set for the grade.

From a statistical viewpoint, grading purely on growth or change may result in a negative correlation between the students' initial level of achievement and their growth: Students coming into class with the highest levels of achievement tend to have the smallest amount of measurable improvement or change, even though their final absolute levels of achievement remain the highest. (Terwilliger, 1971, illustrates how this can happen.) This presents an irony: Students knowing most when they come into the course will tend to get the lowest grades because, even though in an absolute sense they may know more than most other students at the end of the course, they have shown a smaller amount of growth or change.

CHOOSING YOUR GRADING MODEL

Integrating Teaching Approach, Evaluation Purpose, and Grading Framework

Now that you are familiar with the frameworks for grading, and have thought about your teaching approach and the formative and summative purposes for grading, you must consider how to put these together in a logically consistent manner. Which framework should you use? Or should you use more than one framework?

Figure 15.12 offers some guidance. The figure shows how the different grading approaches complement teaching approaches and purposes for grading. *Self-referenced grading*, for example, is consistent with a teaching approach that focuses on standards or learning targets, but only when the purpose of grading is for formative evaluation that gives a student feedback on how well he has progressed from his starting point or within the limits of his ability. This combination of purpose and teaching approach is the only one consistent with using self-referenced grading.

Criterion-referenced grading, on the other hand, is not consistent with a teaching approach that emphasizes competition among classmates. As shown in Figure 15.12, criterion-referenced grading is consistent with teaching

that focuses on standards or learning targets, but is not consistent with all of the purposes for grading within that teaching approach. Criterion-referenced grading is appropriate for giving students feedback on how close they are to achieving learning targets or to meeting standards. This is a formative evaluation purpose. This grading framework is also appropriate for summative evaluation when the intent is to officially report students' levels of accomplishment in relation to learning targets or performance standards. The following quote from two experienced teachers in the Tucson Unified School District (Clarridge & Whitaker, 1997) reinforces this point:

> If you support the use of performance assessments and portfolios, or if there are state or district mandates in that direction, you will most likely find the rubric [i.e., criterion-referenced] system of grading easier to explain, use, and integrate with your approach to assessment. Be sure to consider the assessment requirements and initiatives of your district before developing a reporting system. (p. 20)

Norm-referenced grading is not appropriate for use in a standards-based or learning-target-based teaching approach. It is consistent with a teaching approach that emphasizes comparisons among peers or classmates. With this teaching approach, the only formative purpose served by norm-referenced grading is giving students feedback on how they compare or rank relative to each other. The only summative purpose norm-referenced grading serves is to report officially students' standing relative to their peers.

It should be clear from Figure 15.12 that one grading framework couldn't serve all teaching philosophies and all purposes for wanting to assign grades. You may find that your own teaching does not have a clear philosophy or approach: If so, it will be difficult for you to approach grading in a consistent way. The point of Figure 15.12 is that if you select one or more appropriate grading frameworks, you need to work within a clear teaching approach and understand that some grading frameworks are appropriate for certain formative and summative purposes but not for others.

School District Policy and Local Grading Culture

Your school district's grading policy and a grading culture are important factors in selecting a grading framework. Not every school district has a clearly written grading policy, but if your school district has a grading policy, you will be required to work within its guidelines. If it is a poor or inconsistent policy, you may wish to suggest ways to improve it. If you are a new teacher, your suggestions may not be taken seriously until the administration has confidence in your ability to teach. Press on with your reforms after you have taught for a year or two: Begin by working out your ideas with your most valued teaching colleagues. Don't ever give up on improving education for your students.

FIGURE 15.12 Recommendations for choosing a grading framework that is consistent with teaching approaches.

	Teaching approaches, philosophies	
	Approach Type A. Standards-based, performance-based, focused on learning targets, focused on learning objectives. High achievement means meeting the standards achieving the learning targets. Self-esteem comes from intrinsic or internal motivation that results from meeting goals and standards.	**Approach Type B.** High achievement means achieving more than one's peers. Education should make one competitive. Self-esteem is achieved by being better than one's peers.
Purposes of grading		
	Formative evaluation (Feedback to students and teachers; monitoring learners' progress)	
1. Feedback on how much a student has progressed from his/her own starting point or within the limits of his/her capacity.	• *Self-referenced (growth) grading* is consistent with this purpose and teaching approach. It is assumed that knowing one's progress in relation to one's ability will stimulate more effort to learn and be less discouraging to students.	
2. Feedback on how close a student is to achieving the learning targets or to meeting the standards.	• *Criterion-referenced (task-referenced) grading* is consistent with this purpose and teaching approach. It is assumed that understanding what quality learning looks like and what one's own status in relation to that level of learning is will motivate further learning and effort to meet the high standards.	
3. Feedback on how a student is achieving relative to peers at this point in instruction.		• *Norm-referenced (group-referenced) grading* is consistent with this purpose and teaching approach. It is assumed that knowing one's current rank in class will motivate one to work harder to achieve more.
	Summative evaluation (Official recording of achievement at end of marking period or end of term; official report of achievement)	
4. Reporting a student's level of performance in relation to learning targets and to standards.	• *Criterion-referenced (task referenced) grading* is consistent with this purpose and teaching approach.	
5. Reporting a student's standing relative to classmates and peers.		• *Norm-referenced (group-referenced) grading* is consistent with this purpose and teaching approach.

Grades for Report Cards

A school probably finds some merit in each of the systems of referencing because each addresses a different aspect of a student's performance: the curriculum, other students, and self. Thus, in the long run, a report card may need to contain all three types of information. A given school district will likely emphasize one of the referencing frameworks at some grade levels and other frameworks at other grade levels.

Section IV: Sensible Grading Practices

This section focuses in more detail on using your assessment plan for summative grading. As you implement summative grading you must address at least seven issues so that your grades are valid.

1. Consider what types of student performance you should grade. We will discuss three categories of student performances: those assessed, those reported, and those graded.

2. Consider how to make your marking scales consistent across all assignments throughout the marking period. We discuss both the practical and the validity aspects of this issue.

3. Decide the components making up the grade and their weighting in relation to the final grade. Our discussion of this issue shall emphasize the validity of the grades.

4. Consider the standards or boundaries for each letter grade: How are they set and are they meaningful?

5. What about borderline cases? What do you do with students who are just at the border between two letter grades?

6. Be concerned with the issue of failures (Fs). What does failure mean?

7. Be concerned with the practice of assigning zero for a mark on one or more components going into a grade: What is the impact of this practice? When should a zero not be given?

TYPES OF PERFORMANCE TO ASSESS

Link Your Grading to Your Assessment Plan

In Chapter 6 we discussed how to craft an assessment plan. Your assessment plan describes what component assessments will make up the summative assessment for each instructional unit and for the marking period. In addition, you specify the weights the components will carry in the grade for each unit as well as the units' weights in calculating the final grade for the marking period. Figure 6.3 shows an example of this type of assessment plan. The assessment plan becomes critical to assigning grades. Without a plan, you will be unable to integrate all the assessment components meaningfully into a valid grade. You will also be unable to explain your grading to students, parents, and school administrators.

What to Assess, Report, and Grade

Assessment Variables In Chapter 6 we discussed the types of student information you need when teaching, including sizing up the class, diagnoses of students' needs, prerequisite student achievements, students' attitudes, students' work habits, students' study skills, and students' motivation and effort in school. The complete set of these characteristics for which you gather information are called **assessment variables** (sometimes called **evaluation variables** [Frisbie & Waltman, 1992]). However, not all variables you assess need to be recorded and reported. Clearly, you will use some of the information to plan and guide your own teaching. This information is primarily formative. It should not make its way into a grade. A grade is a summative evaluation of a student's achievement.

Reporting Variables Your school district will expect you to report a subset of the assessment variables to parents and for official purposes. These are called **reporting variables** (Frisbie & Waltman, 1992). They often include the students' achievement in the subject, study skills, social behavior and interpersonal skills, motivation and study efforts in class, leadership skills, and aesthetic talents. This is illustrated by the multiple-marking system report card example shown earlier in this chapter.

Grading Variables Reporting variables represent important school outcomes and therefore should be appropriately reported to parents and others. They should not be confused, however, with grades for course achievement. That is, from among all the reporting variables, there is a more limited subset on which you may base your grades. The variables in this limited subset are called **grading variables** (Frisbie & Waltman, 1992). You use the grading variables to describe a student's accomplishments in the subject. You assess these achievements by crafting more formal procedures such as performance tasks, portfolios, projects, tests, and quizzes. They are the most valid and reasonable bases for assigning grades.

Relationships Among Variables It is important that you keep the meaning of these variables in mind as you assign grades. Figure 15.13 will help you understand the relationships among these variables and how they are used.

Eliminate Mixing If you mix grading variables with other variables, you create grades that have confusing and invalid meaning. For example, if you punish a student by lowering her grade for failing to turn in an assignment or for turning it in late, then you have confused the student's achievement with the student's deportment. Similarly, if you lower a science or social studies grade because of poor language usage or poor appearance, your grade is a less valid assessment of the student's achievement of the science or social studies curriculum learning targets. Consider the following:

> If the social studies essay scores of some students are reduced because of deficiencies in writing mechanics, how well do those scores describe achievement? If a teacher assigns an A to a group project, what does this mean for a member of the group who made little contribution to planning, conducting, or summarizing the project activities? If the grade on a paper is dropped a full letter grade each day it is late, what does the final grade on the paper indicate about achievement in language arts? If a student has an unexcused absence on the day of a test, what does an F grade for that test do to a quarter grade that is supposed to describe achievement? . . . Tainted component scores cause tainted composites. Tainted composites lead to misinterpretation. (Frisbie & Waltman, 1992, pp. 37–38)

The preceding paragraph does not mean that language usage or turning in work on time is irrelevant to a student's school experience. Rather, the intention is clarity of meaning for grades so they become more valid indicators of achievement. Some schools, for example, use a "writing across the curriculum" approach. This means that social studies, history, mathematics, and science work is evaluated for both the subject-matter correctness and language usage. Evaluations of the students' language usage are reported as part of the language grade, whereas evaluations of students' subject-matter achievement become part of the subject grade. Similarly, tardiness, failure to complete work, and other problems can be reported separately from achievement and may be used to explain a student's lack of school accomplishment.

Eliminate Formative Evaluation Components Not all achievement variables should be included as grading variables (Frisbie & Waltman, 1992). Many achievement variables are formative in nature. Homework, quizzes, and oral responses

FIGURE 15.13 **Relationships among different types of assessment variables and grading variables.**

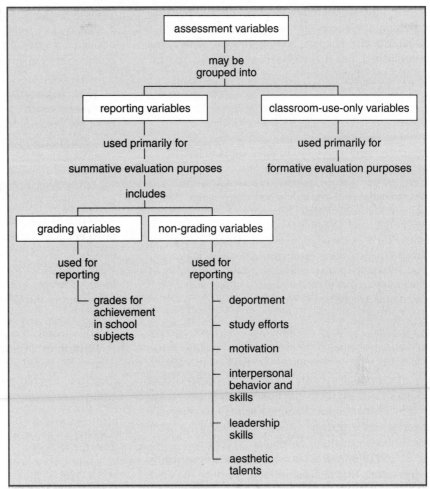

to classroom activities, for example, may serve mostly formative purposes—to help you decide whether individual students need more reinforcement, whether your lessons are going well, and to use as a basis for helping students to improve their performance. These formative assessments *should not* be included in the subject grade for the marking period. Not all out-of-class assignments are formative, of course. Some homework, most projects, and most research papers can be used for summative evaluation. The general rule, then, is to *include in the grade the assessments that you establish as useful for summative evaluation and exclude all assessments established primarily for formative evaluation.*

CONSISTENT GRADING THROUGHOUT THE MARKING PERIOD

Craft Marking Scales to Be Consistent Across Different Assessments

Incompatibility of Scales You need to think ahead to make your assessment scales compatible across all the components that go into the summative grade. The assessment

plan for the weather unit in Figure 6.2, for example, shows five components entering into the summative grade for the unit: homework, quizzes, independent investigation, map drawing, and the end-of-unit test. Suppose each of these is marked on a different scale as follows:

Component	*Scale*
Homework	0–10
Quizzes	0–5
Independent investigation	1–20
Map drawing	1–4
End-of-unit test	0–100

If you simply add students' marks from each of these components using these scales, you will have difficulty because they are incompatible. The map-drawing scale, for example, may be based on a rubric with four levels of quality whereas the end-of-unit test is based on a percentage scale from 0% to 100%. Such incompatibilities make a *simple sum of the marks* an invalid basis for a grade. You will need to mark each assessment in a way that makes scales compatible.

The planning stages are the time to prevent this situation. You may use one of several options, which we shall discuss later in this chapter. Solving this problem is not that complicated, but it is best solved up front. The following anecdote illustrates this point:

> In a school district I work with, eighth-grade teachers were faced with the task of combining percentage-correct scores from conventional language arts tests and writing performances scored on a 4-point rubric into five levels for report card grades (A, B, C, D, F). Several of the teachers did not have the quantitative reasoning background to understand why or how scale conversions could be made, and it had not occurred to any one of the several people who adopted the 4-point writing rubric that it would not be very helpful for assigning five levels of grades. This is a more complicated problem to solve after the fact than to solve at the design stage, when it would be appropriate to choose rubrics and construct decision rules. (Brookhart, 1999, p. 8)

Losing Precision The most reliable scores are those that are able to distinguish small differences in the quality of students' learning. A scale that allows you to demonstrate that Sally's command of a learning target is slightly better than Johnny's is more reliable than a scale that cannot tell the difference between their learning levels. To allow reliable detection of small differences between students, a score scale needs many gradations or "points." A scale that shows Sally at 89 and Johnny at 82 displays their learning quality better than a scale that shows them both receiving the same rating of B.

You lose precision when you transform scores from a fine-grained scale (e.g., percentage correct scale) to a coarse-grained one (e.g., letter grades). If a B were defined to be a score from 80 to 89, then both Sally and Johnny would receive the same grade, B. Because they both receive the same grade, their true difference cannot be distinguished with the letter-grade scale. By transforming the 89 and 82 both to a B, you have lost reliability.

You should not think that all percentage scales are fine-grained. For example, if you have five test questions, each worth 1 point, then the only possible percentages are 0, 20, 40, 60, 80, and 100. Thus, only six possible percentage values are used, not the 100 values you usually associate with a percentage scale. In this example, the percentage scale is just as coarse as the letter-grade scale. A test of 10 questions, each worth 1 point, is similarly not very fine-grained. Keep in mind that scales reporting fine differences among students must use many numerical values to be reliable assessments of the achievement differences among students. *If you use only a few of the many possible values of a scale, then you lose precision.*

Although you lose precision when you move from a fine-grained scale to a coarse-grained scale, you *do not gain precision by moving from a coarse-grained to a fine one.* If we have only the coarse scores initially, no transformation will make them more precise. Suppose, for example, you had

the following writing scale: 4 = advanced, 3 = proficient, 3 = basic, 1 = unacceptable. Suppose your scoring rubric evaluated a student's writing as a 3 on this 4-point scale. You could transform the 3 to a percentage–3 out of 4 points means 75%. You have not gained any precision, however, in distinguishing among students because all students who received 3s now receive 75%. Unfortunately, from the precision standpoint, the scale has only 4 points after the transformation (25%, 50%, 75%, and 100%), the same as before the transformation. Only the labels have changed. In addition, because the 100% scale implies there are other possible percentages between those reported (especially between 75% and 100%), you have changed the meaning of the scale from advanced, proficient, basic, unacceptable (if those were the rubric levels) to an implied (from the percents) scale of A = 100%, C = 75%, F = 50%, and F = 25%. You can see that these so-called grades have a corrupted meaning–they are not aligned the original meaning intended by the verbal labels of the writing scale.

The impact of scale precision, positive or negative, is something in addition to the positive impact made by using well-crafted assessment instruments. It will pay you, therefore, to craft your scoring scales as carefully as you craft your assessment instruments.

COMPONENTS OF A GRADE

Weighting the Components

You should not weight every assessment equally when grading. You decide how much weight to assign to the components—home assignments, tests, quizzes, term papers, and other elements—after you decide their importance to the description of a student's achievement of the learning targets. Begin by making a list of all the components you want to use for evaluating achievement of the grade. Next, decide how these components relate to the learning objectives and determine how important each is (and thus how heavily each will weigh) in relation to the overall summative grade.

Consider at least six factors when deciding how much to weight each component:

1. Components that assess more of the important learning targets and content should be weighted more heavily than those that focus only on one or a few targets.

2. Components that focus on what you spent the most time teaching the students should receive the most weight in determining the grade.

3. Components that require students to integrate and apply their learning should receive more weight than those that require students simply to parrot what was taught.

4. When two components assess some of the same learning targets, each should be given less weight

individually than other components that assess an equal number of unique learning targets (i.e., nonoverlapping components) (Frisbie & Waltman, 1992).

5.   If you know that one of the components you want to count toward the grade has some degree of unfairness to certain groups of students, you should be very cautious in using it for grading. If you decide that on the whole it is still appropriate to use it, you should weight it less, especially for students for whom it is less fair. For example, you may find that a timed, written test does not adequately assess students with certain disabilities. In such cases, it would be appropriate to weight this procedure less for these students and to give other, more appropriate procedures more weight in determining their grades.

6.   *Components that are less reliable and less objective should be weighted less heavily than those that are more reliable and objective.* However, this is not to say that you should avoid using less objectively scored assessments such as essays and portfolios for assigning grades. Rather, you should use scoring rubrics for marking them so the marks are more reliable. (See Chapter 12, page 285.)

GRADE BOUNDARIES

Standards or Boundaries Between Grades

An important practical consideration is how to establish boundaries between the grades. What constitutes an A, B, and so on? The answer will depend on (a) which framework you are using and (b) your school district's policy. The procedure for setting norm-referenced grading boundaries is very different from the procedure for setting criterion-referenced grading boundaries. You will need to follow the boundary-setting method consistent with your teaching approach. We discuss the details of these boundary-setting procedures later in this chapter.

It is important at this point, however, to recognize that your grade boundaries must have the same meaning across all assessments that will make up the grade. This doesn't mean that you need to use the same number of marks (points) for each assessment. It does mean, however, that an A on one assessment should be of approximately the same standard of quality across all assessments. For example, if each assessment is marked according to the percentage correct, then the same percentage range (e.g., 90%–100%) should be used for an A across all assessments.

Borderline Cases

You will always have **borderline cases**—students whose composite marks are very near or or right on the boundary between two grades. What do you do? How close to the grade boundary does a student have to be before you adjust a letter grade upward or downward? Many teachers

are comfortable reviewing students' work and raising grades for those who are just under the borderline, but do not consider lowering the grades of those just above the borderline (Brookhart, 1993). Nevertheless, lowering borderline grades is just as valid as raising them when additional achievement evidence justifies it.

As you learned in Chapter 4, assessment results contain errors of measurement, so students whose scores are on or near the border are likely to have true scores that are *different* from their observed scores. This argues against being hard-nosed and telling a student that she missed the next higher grade by 1 or 2 points. You should think of scores near the grade boundary as in an "uncertainty band" much like the one discussed in Chapter 4. You should use additional achievement information about the student to help you decide whether the student's true score is above or below the boundary. Using additional *achievement* information to help make boundary decisions is *more valid than using information about how much effort a student put forth in studying* (Brookhart, 1999). If you are still in doubt, it is better pedagogy to give the next higher grade than to give the lower grade.

FAILURE GRADES

The Meaning of Failure

As Frisbie and Waltman (1992) point out, the grade F carries a lot of emotion with it because there are usually negative consequences for students who receive it. What should an F mean? Your answer should be consistent with your grading framework. The least confusing way to assign a **failing grade** (F) is to set reasonable minimum standards regarding performance on the curriculum learning targets. Students who *consistently* perform below these minimum performance standards receive an F.

Let's get to the practical side of assigning a failing grade. Darnell does not turn in an important assignment, even though he knew the deadline and you made several announcements in class. You decide to give Darnell a zero. James, on the other hand, turns in the assignment on time, but the work is so poor you must give it a 55, which is in the F range. Both James and Darnell receive Fs. The question is, do these Fs mean the same thing? If not, how meaningful (i.e., valid) is using an F? We will address this issue momentarily, but first another example.

Many scoring rubrics for performance assessments and constructed-response items use a scoring scale from 1 to 4. Our concern is with the meaning of the lowest category, 1. Usually, the rubric describes 1 as very poor quality work, amounting to failure. However, the 1 is often assigned to students who did nothing, failed to turn in the work, or wrote gibberish. Does a score of 1 mean the same for every student? If not, how valid is it? This issue is not necessarily resolved by using a scoring rubric that goes from 0 to 4.

If the zero is given to students who failed to turn in an assignment, as well as to those who turned it in but wrote poorly, the zero has two different meanings. This type of confusion lowers the validity of the marks.

One way to frame this issue is to consider two categories of student performance (Brookhart, 1999): (a) doing work that is of very poor quality, that is, **failing work** and (b) not doing the work at all, that is, **failing to try**. The first category describes the student's achievement: the student's status compared to the standards or learning targets. The meaning of failure marks or grades for such students is reasonably clear.

The second category reflects a student's motivation (and perhaps attitudes and personality characteristics, such as lack of self-confidence, test anxiety, rebelliousness, etc.). Darnell's failure to turn in an assignment might be a signal to you that he has not understood what you taught. Darnell may have failed to do the assignment because he didn't know how. This calls for working with Darnell and his parent(s) to see that he receives the help he needs. Darnell may be insecure and afraid to admit his failure to learn: Not every failure to try is malicious. Sometimes children who have an emotional crisis at home actually do the work in school but do not turn it in because they have given up being successful students. In "failure-to-try" cases, giving a failing grade (or lowering a grade) is always invalid because the resulting grade does not accurately describe achievement. This does not mean that you should avoid reporting failure to try; it does mean that describing these two types of student responses with the same mark (0) or with the same grade (F) is not valid.

A closely related question is, "Should I lower a student's grade when the assignment is turned in *late*?" Some teachers, for example, mark assignments that are turned in late, but deduct points from the mark or otherwise limit the highest mark possible for this assignment. Again, such a practice lowers the validity of the marks and the resulting grades because it mixes up their meaning: Do not use the same grade to describe for some students only achievement, but for other students a mixture of achievement, attitudes, and personality evaluations.

Abhorrent grading practices like these are practiced because teachers face difficult teaching conditions. They seek to use grades (and student evaluations, in general) to control students' behavior. As we discussed in Chapter 5, you act irresponsibly when you threaten, punish, or otherwise try to manipulate students by lowering achievement grades for behavior that is unrelated to achievement. The issue of what to do with missing and late assignments is a real one with which you and your colleagues must struggle, but it is not a measurement problem per se. It is a result of the conditions of teaching, school policies, and assumptions people make about the way one should educate (Brookhart, 1999).

A school district's policy needs to address how to handle students who do not turn in assignments or who turn them in late. A culture for punctuality and completing assigned work on time needs to be developed. A policy needs to be legal, fair, and valid, and it needs to meet criteria for sound educational philosophy. Punishing, threatening, or manipulating students should be eliminated from any policy.

From strictly a measurement point of view, assigning an "incomplete" when assignments are not turned in seems reasonable. Students who complete the work beyond the deadline may be given full credit from a measurement perspective. The report card could contain a notation that some of the work on which the grade is based was completed after the due date. Repeated notations of this type describe tardiness but do not detract from describing achievement.

These measurement "solutions," however, do not address all the concerns of teachers. You can raise questions such as: Is it fair to students who habitually complete their work on time to allow other students not to complete theirs on time? Are there circumstances under which late work is allowed (without penalty or commentary) or appropriate (e.g., illness, personal tragedy)? Will a flexible policy on when to turn in work result in classroom chaos? Is the assignment of an invalid grade or a grade with low validity more ethical than addressing the issues of why students do not behave properly or do not turn in assignments? You may tackle these issues with your instructor and teaching colleagues.

The Deadly Zero

Do you recognize how much a zero can affect a composite score? Suppose Ashley is a good student, capable of B work. What happens to her average marks if she fails to turn in one assignment and you give her a zero for it? Are you surprised to learn that her average grade could drop from a B to a D?

The impact of a zero, of course, depends on the component marks a student receives, how many marks enter into the composite grade, the weights assigned to the component, and the mark the student would have received had she turned in the assignment. Figure 15.14 may help you understand the impact of zero on a student's grade.

In this example, there are five assignments. To keep things simple, let us assume they are equally weighted. As a point of reference, suppose Ashley's "true performance," what she would have received had she completed all her assignments, is shown in Panel A. Ashley is a B student.

Panel B shows what will happen to Ashley if she fails to turn in one assignment and if you were to give her zero for that assignment. The impact on her grades is dramatic: One missing assignment results in her dropping two whole grades, from a B to a D. This happens no matter which assignment she fails to turn in.

Using a zero means that you have given Ashley the lowest possible failing mark as a substitute for her missing

FIGURE 15.14 **Hypothetical example of the impact of substituting zero or 59 for one assignment a student did not turn in.**

		1	2	3	4	5	Avg	Grd
A. True Performance		80	70	85	75	90	80	B
B. Strategy 1—Substitute zero for the missing assessment								
	Case 1	(0)	70	85	75	90	64	D
	Case 2	80	(0)	85	75	90	66	D
	Case 3	80	70	(0)	75	90	63	D
	Case 4	80	70	85	(0)	90	65	D
	Case 5	80	70	85	75	(0)	62	D
C. Strategy 2—Substitute the highest possible failing mark (i.e., 59) for the missing assessment								
	Case 1	(59)	70	85	75	90	76	C
	Case 2	80	(59)	85	75	90	76	C
	Case 3	80	70	(59)	75	90	75	C
	Case 4	80	70	85	(59)	90	75	C
	Case 5	80	70	85	75	(59)	74	C
D. Strategy 3—Base the grade on only those assignments that were turned in								
	Case 1	—	70	85	75	90	80	B
	Case 2	80	—	85	75	90	83	B
	Case 3	80	70	—	75	90	79	C
	Case 4	80	70	85	—	90	81	B
	Case 5	80	70	85	75	—	76	C

Note: Substituted values are shown in parentheses. (Assume A = 90–100, B = 80–89, C = 70–79, D = 60–69, F = 0–59.)

assignment. Instead, you could give her the highest possible failing mark. In this example, the F range is from 0 to 59, so 59 is the highest possible failing mark. Panel C shows what happens to Ashley's grade if you follow this strategy. Ashley goes from a B average (Panel A) to a C average (Panel C). Still, one missing assignment has resulted in her average dropping one whole grade.

Other strategies could be used. One is shown in Panel D. Here you simply ignore the missing assignment, basing your grade on the remaining four. As shown in Panel D, the impact on her grade depends on which assignment she failed to turn in. If she failed to turn in one of the two on which she could have scored the highest (Case 3, where Assignment 3 was 85, or Case 5, where Assignment 5 was 90), her grade would drop a whole grade; in the other cases it would remain at B. Other strategies (not shown) could be used (Brookhart, 1999), such as using the median grade, using 50 instead of 59, or substituting the average of the four completed assignments for the missing assignment. In Ashley's case these other approaches give the same letter-grade results as shown in Panel D.

From the measurement perspective, Strategy 3 (basing the grade only on assignments turned in) would be the best of the three when (a) assignments are of approximately equal difficulty for the students, (b) assignments are weighted equally (or are worth the same number of points), and (c) there are several assignments and only one or two are missing. This recommendation does not consider other factors, such as whether (a) the "missing assignment" is the most important one to complete (e.g., a

project or a final examination), (b) a student fails to turn in an assignment because of illness or personal tragedy, (c) a student fails to complete the assignment because she didn't understand how to do the work, and (d) a student has made a habit of not turning in work on time. As we stated previously, these are not measurement issues per se but matters of educational practice, classroom management, and school policy.

Section V: Techniques for Setting Grade Boundaries and Combining Scores

ASSIGNING NORM-REFERENCED LETTER GRADES

Several methods of assigning grades use relative or norm-referenced standards.[3] One method, called **grading on the curve**, uses the rank order of students' marks: Students' marks are ordered from highest to lowest, and grades (A, B, C, etc.) are assigned on the basis of this ranking. A second, called the **standard deviation method**, uses the standard deviation (see Appendix I) as a unit: A teacher computes the standard deviation of the scores and uses this number to mark off segments on the number line that define the

---

[3]Your instructor may ask you to postpone studying this section until you have studied Chapter 17.

boundaries for grade assignment. The two methods do not necessarily give the same results. We explain how to use the methods next.

Grading a Single Test or Assessment

Grading on the Curve To use the grading on the curve method to assign letter grades, you decide on the percentage of As, Bs, Cs, and so on to award. For example, you may decide as follows:

Example

Example of one possible set of percentages to use for grading on the curve

top 20% of the students get A
next 30% get B
next 30% get C
next 15% get D
lowest 5% get F

There are no rules on how you would select the percentages to use. They are chosen arbitrarily based on your experience as to what is realistic in your school for a distribution of letter grades. This approach does not require using a normal or bell curve.

Another way to set the percentages is to divide the range of a normal or bell curve (see Chapter 17) into five equal-length intervals. The example below shows the resulting percentages of students receiving each grade.

Example

Example of one possible set of percentages to use for grading using the normal curve with five equal intervals

top 3.6% of the students get A
next 23.8% get B
next 45.2% get C
next 23.8% get D
lowest 3.6% get F

This set of percentages assumes that the true achievement in the group of students in your class is normally distributed, an assumption which, in the authors' view, is hard for you or any teacher to justify. Notice that (a) the width of the interval that determines the percentages is completely arbitrary, (b) the assessment scores must be valid measures of the desired achievement, and (c) there is no reference to the learning targets, skills, or competence the letter grades represent (except that higher-ranked students have more competence than lower-ranked students). If you do decide to grade on a curve, then you

must provide a convincing and educationally sound argument to justify the validity of the particular percentages that you use; otherwise, your grades are likely to be unsound.

Standard Deviation Method To use the standard deviation method, you first decide on the score that defines the lower limit for a *grade of A*. You do this by deciding how many multiples of a standard deviation the lower limit of A will lie above the median (50th percentile) of the group (Ebel, 1965; Ebel & Stuit, 1954). You then mark off the score scale into four more[4] segments: The width of each of these four segments equals the numerical value of the standard deviation; you begin at the lower limit of A and go downward. (Appendix I explains the standard deviation and how to calculate it.) Figure 15.15 shows the steps for doing this, along with an example.

Adjustment for the Average Ability of Your Class Rather than use the same percentage of As, Bs, Cs, and so on for every class, it seems reasonable for this norm-referenced grading method to change the percentages as the ability of the class changes. For example, if the class is very bright, then you would expect to give more As and fewer Ds than if the class was average. The method outlined in the preceding example adjusts the number of each letter grade assigned to suit the general scholastic ability of students in your class. Thus, the first step is to estimate the ability level of the group (poor to exceptional) using either students' previous grade point averages or scores on an ability test all students have taken. With this method, the choice of what interval width to use and the lower limit for A are arbitrary, just as the choice of percentages for grading on the curve were arbitrary. Further, as with the grading on the curve method, reference is made only to the person's relative achievement, rather than to an absolute description of the competence the students may possess.

The method assumes that for "average" ability students, the underlying achievement follows a normal distribution, even though the distribution on the test or other assessment being graded does not. The assumptions about the distribution of achievement for above- and below-average students are represented by the "percentage of marks" in the rows of tables in the example. A decided advantage is that this approach helps make grades more comparable among all teachers who use it.

Grading a Composite of Several Scores

This section discusses how to combine the scores from several grading components into a single (composite) mark. The procedure will be consistent with the

---

[4]This assumes an A, B, C, D, F scale. If there are six grades, the intervals will be narrower; if three letter grades, wider; and so on.

FIGURE 15.15 Example of applying the Ebel-Stuit standard deviation method for setting grade boundaries.

Letter Mark Distribution Statistics for Classes at Seven Levels of Ability

Class ability level	Lower limit of A's	Percent of marks					Ability measures	
		A	B	C	D	F	GPA	Percentile
Exceptional	0.7	24	38	29	8	1	2.80	79
Superior	0.9	18	36	32	12	2	2.60	73
Good	1.1	14	32	36	15	3	2.40	66
Fair	1.3	10	29	37	20	4	2.20	68
Average	1.5	7	24	38	24	7	2.00	50
Weak	1.7	4	20	37	29	10	1.80	42
Poor	1.9	3	15	36	32	14	1.60	34

Four steps are involved in this process of assigning marks.

1. Select from [the above table]…a distribution of marks appropriate to the level of ability of the class being graded.

2. Calculate the median and the standard deviation of the scores on which the marks are to be based.

3. Determine the lower score limits of the A, B, C, and D mark intervals, using the median, the standard deviation, and the appropriate lower limit factor from [the table].

4. Assign the designated marks to the students whose scores fall in intervals determined for each mark.

Sample Problem in Letter Mark Assignment

A. Data for the problem
  1. Measures of class ability level
     a. Mean GPA on previous years' courses: 2.17
     b. Mean percentile on aptitude test: 56.3
     c. Appropriate grade distribution [from above table]: *fair*
  2. Achievement scores (number of students = 38)

112	100	93	84	78	72	66	51
109	97	91	83	75	71	62	47
106	97	90	82	75	70	59	44
105	95	89	81	75	69	59	
104	95	84	80	74	68	58	

B. Calculations from the data

  1. Median = 80.5   2. Standard deviation = 17.6

Marks	Lower limits	Intervals	Number	Percent
A	80.5 + (1.3 × 17.6) = 103.4	103–112	5	13
B	103.4 − 17.6 = 85.8	86–102	9	24
C	85.8 − 17.6 = 68.2	68–85	16	42
D	68.2 − 17.6 = 50.6	51–67	6	16
F		44–50	2	5
			38	100

norm-referenced grading framework. Later we discuss combining marks from components in a way that is consistent with the criterion-referenced grading framework. Usually a report card grade reflects a student's performance on several assessments such as assignments, quizzes, reports, and perhaps an examination. We discussed previously the factors you need to consider when assigning weights to each component of the grade. There is no agreement as to exactly what weights are proper for each grading component.

Weighting Guidelines When norm-referenced grading is adopted, the component that contributes the most to the final rankings of the students in the group carries the most weight. This principle is likely to be violated if you simply multiply the component scores by some arbitrary weights and then add the weighted scores to form a composite. The reason is that the rank of a composite score is influenced by the standard deviations of the components making up the composite (and by the intercorrelations among components). To illustrate this, consider the next example.

Example

Hypothetical example showing how a grading component can work in the opposite way the teacher intends when norm-referenced grading is used

Suppose that the final grades are based on the sum of the marks from one exam and one project. Suppose further that the project is intended to weigh twice as much as the exam. In an attempt to accomplish this, the teacher decides to give twice as many points to the project as to the exam: 100 points for the project and 50 points for the exam. Remember that in a norm-referenced grading framework, those who rank highest should receive the highest grades. Here are the marks and ranks of five students.

	Exam (50 points)		Project (100 points)		Total	
Student	Marks	Ranks	Marks	Ranks	Marks	Ranks
Anthony	44	1	77	5	120	1
Ashley	33	2	78	4	111	2
Billy	26	3	79	3	105	3
Chad	22	4	80	2	102	4
Vanessa	15	5	81	1	96	5

Notice that the project ranks students exactly opposite from the exam. The final order is exactly the same as the exam, however, even though the teacher weighted the project more. This is because the ranking of the students on the total marks depends on the spread of scores rather than on the teacher's intended weighting. The spread of scores is measured by the standard deviation. (See Appendix I.) The project scores are close to each other, so their standard deviation is small, whereas the exam scores are quite different from each other, so their standard deviation is large. Because of the exam score's larger standard deviation, the students' *exam ranking* dominates their final total ranking in spite of the teacher's intention to make the project the dominant component. In general, when using norm-referenced grading, the larger the standard deviation of one component's scores, the more that component influences the final ranking of students when a composite is formed.

Using SS-Score Method The **SS-score method** preserves the influence (weights) you want the components to have, by first adjusting the values of the components' standard deviations. After adjusting, you may then apply the

weights you desire. There are three steps: First, change all of the scores on each component into SS-scores (SS means linear standard score; see Chapter 17). This makes all of the standard deviations equal. Second, multiply the components' SS-scores by the weights you want. Finally, add these products to form the composite mark for each student. The following formula summarizes these steps.

$$\text{weighted composite score} = \Sigma(\text{weight} \times SS) \quad [\text{Eq.15.1}]$$

where

$$\text{weight} = \text{weight you want the component to have}$$
$$SS = \text{the linear } SS\text{-score for the component}$$
$$= [10(X - M)/SD] + 50$$

The procedure is illustrated in Figure 15.16.

Note that these weighted composite scores are not themselves SS-scores. However, the weighted composite scores do provide a way to rank students so that the component weightings you specify will have the desired influence on the students' final standings.

To appreciate the influence of the SS-score method on the students' ranking in the final weighted composite, recall our earlier example in which the teacher's attempt to make the project dominate the ranking of the students failed. This time, let's apply the SS-score method to those same marks:

Example

Hypothetical example showing using the SS-score method can help the teacher weigh the assignments as intended when norm-referenced grading is used.

	Exam (Weight = 1)			Project (Weight = 2)			Total	
Student	Marks	SS	Ranks	Marks	SS	Ranks	Composite	Ranks
Anthony	44	66	1	77	36	5	138	5
Ashley	33	55	2	78	43	4	141	4
Billy	26	48	3	79	50	3	148	3
Chad	22	44	4	80	57	2	158	2
Vanessa	15	37	5	81	64	1	165	1

Compare the final rankings in this example with the final rankings in the earlier example. Now the project dominates the rankings based on the composite instead of the exam. This result is what the teacher initially intended. Transforming the marks to SS-scores first made the exam marks' and project marks' standard deviations equal.[5] Then when the weight of 2 was applied, the composite better matched the teacher's intent.

---

[5]As an exercise, verify this example using the standard deviation formula in Appendix I.

FIGURE 15.16 **Example of calculating composite marks using the *SS*-scores method.**

	Components entering into the grade			
	Quizzes	**Homework**	**Term paper**	**Exam**
Mean (*M*)	70	85	75	65
Standard deviation (*SD*)	5	8	15	20
Teacher's weight	20%	10%	20%	50%
Calculation for *SS*[a]	$SS = 10(\text{Mark} - 70)/5 + 50$	$SS = 10(\text{Mark} - 85)/8 + 50$	$SS = 10(\text{Mark} - 75)/15 + 50$	$SS = 10(\text{Mark} - 65)/20 + 50$

[a]*SS*-scores are calculated by subtracting the component mean from a student's raw score, dividing the difference by the standard deviation, multiplying by 10, and adding 50 to the product. The results for each student are shown below. For example:

The quizzes *SS*-score for Bob	$= 10(87 - 70)/5 + 50$	$= 84$
The quizzes *SS*-score for Chad	$= 10(85 - 70)/5 + 50$	$= 80$
The quizzes *SS*-score for Susan	$= 10(75 - 70)/5 + 50$	$= 60$
The quizzes *SS*-score for Theresa	$= 10(70 - 70)/5 + 50$	$= 50$

	Raw scores on components				*SS*-scores on components				
Students	**Quizzes**	**Home-work**	**Term paper**	**Exam**	**Quizzes**	**Home-work**	**Term paper**	**Exam**	**Weighted composite**
Bob	87	85	70	80	84	50	47	58	60
Chad	85	80	80	70	80	44	53	53	58
Susan	75	82	85	60	60	46	57	48	51
Theresa	70	78	75	65	50	41	50	50	49

Composite scores are calculated by multiplying the component *SS*-score by the corresponding teacher's component weights and summing the products. For example:

Composite score for Bob	$= .2(84) + .1(50) + .2(47) + .5(58) = 60$
Composite score for Chad	$= .2(80) + .1(44) + .2(53) + .5(53) = 58$
Composite score for Susan	$= .2(60) + .1(46) + .2(57) + .5(48) = 51$
Composite score for Theresa	$= .2(50) + .1(41) + .2(50) + .5(50) = 49$

Source: From *Essentials of Educational Measurement* (3rd ed., pp. 248–251), by R. L. Ebel, 1979, Englewood Cliffs, NJ: Prentice Hall. Copyright 1979. Adapted by permission of the copyright holder.

ASSIGNING CRITERION-REFERENCED LETTER GRADES

There are several methods for grading using the criterion-referencing grading framework. In this book we shall discuss only three. One method is known as the **fixed-percentage method**: The scores on each component entering into the composite are first converted to percentage correct (or percent of total points); then the percentages are translated to grades. For each component, you must use the same percentage to define the letter-grade boundaries.

A second method is called the **total points method**: Each component included in the final composite grade is assigned a maximum point value (e.g., quizzes may count 10 points, exams may count a maximum of 50 points each, and projects may count a maximum of 40 points each); the letter grades are assigned based on the number of total points a student accumulated over the marking period.

A third method is the **quality-level method** or the **rubric method**. It is sometimes called the **content-based method**

(Frisbie & Waltman, 1992). In this method, you describe the quality level of performance a student must demonstrate for each letter grade—what types of performance will constitute an A, B, C, and so on. (An example of these definitions of quality is shown in Figure 15.11 in column one.) Given these definitions, you evaluate the student's work on each component, decide the quality level of work, and then assign the corresponding grade. This method is very similar to using scoring rubrics for performance tasks (see Chapter 12 for details about scoring rubrics). When you develop rubrics for a component, you must be sure the number of quality levels corresponds to the number of letter-grade levels.

Grading a Single Test or Assessment

Fixed-Percentage Method Teachers frequently use percentages as bases for marking and grading papers. The relationship between percentage correct and letter grade is arbitrary. In some schools, 80% is an A; in others, 85% is an A. In still others, 90% is an A. Some school boards have a policy on this matter. The following is an example of one such set of percentages that defines letter grades:

Note that a percentage begs the question, "percentage of what?" Often, the only answer that you can defend is that the score represents the percentage of the maximum points on the test or the assignment. This answer ignores the broader concern: The test should be a representative sample from a well-defined domain of performance implied by the curriculum learning targets. If you have not defined this domain and have not built the assessment to sample the domain representatively, then you cannot use the percentage grade to estimate the student's status accurately on that broader domain. Such tests (or assessments), and consequently such percentages, cannot be considered criterion-referenced.

The percentage that defines each grade should take into account a teacher's experience with the kinds of students being taught and the difficulty of tests the teacher develops. Thus, norm-referenced information helps establish a criterion-referenced grading system. If the school district does not have a defined set of percentages for each letter grade, it may take you several years to work out a percentage grading scheme that is both fair to the students and represents reasonable standards of scholarship. If you are a new teacher, you should check with colleagues to be sure that your grading scheme is reasonable and not unnecessarily out of line with the rest of the teachers.

One limitation of this fixed-percentage method stems from the fact that every assessment you create has a different level of difficulty, which you may not know in advance. This method, however, uses the same fixed percentages for A, B, and so on for every component. Thus, if you create a test that is too difficult for your class, you may end up giving too many low grades based on the percentages you fixed in advance. This will be frustrating for students and may put you into a position where you have to change the grading system.

A second limitation is that this method encourages you to focus more strongly on the difficulty level of the assessment than on the learning targets it should assess. For example, if you fix the percentages, you will be looking for ways to make the assessment easy enough or difficult enough so that you get a reasonable distribution of letter grades for your class. This seems to go against the principles of absolute or criterion-referenced grading.

Total Points Method To use this method, you must decide in advance all the components that will enter into the end-of-a-marking-period grade. Then, also in advance, you decide the maximum number of points for each component. Your assessment plan should do this. The maximum number of points each component is worth mirrors the weight you assign to each component. If you want the unit test(s) to count more toward the grade, for example, you would assign the unit tests more of the total points. Finally, you sum all the maximum points for components and use that maximum possible total to set letter-grade boundaries. Notice that, unlike for the fixed percentage method, you do not assign letter grades for each component, but only for the total summed over all components.

As an example, suppose you used the same four components that were used in one of our earlier examples: quizzes, homework, a term paper, and an exam.

Having decided on the components and their maximum point values, you then set the boundaries for assigning letter grades to the total points that students accumulate in the marking period. For example,

Total point grade boundaries	Grade
180–200	A
160–179	B
140–159	C
120–139	D
0–119	F

Notice that these total point grade *boundaries* correspond to percentages of 90%, 80%, 70%, and 60% of the 200 total points for A, B, C, and D, respectively. (For example, for an A, $180 \div 200 = 0.90$ or 90%.) You may use other percentages to define the letter-grade boundaries. Adjust the total point boundaries accordingly.

One limitation of the total points method is that it makes it too easy for you to give "extra credit" assignments to boost the total points of low-scoring students. Extra credit assignments tend to distort the meaning of the grades, especially when these assignments do not properly assess the same learning targets as the original set of components. For example, if a student did poorly on the term paper, you may be tempted to have the student read and summarize a current events magazine article to boost the student's score instead of writing another term paper. The meaning of the total points for this student would be distorted relative to other students. As a result, your grades are less valid.

Another limitation of this method is that by defining the maximum number of points before creating the assessments, you may be faced with an unacceptable choice when you do create an assessment tool. Consider this situation:

> Suppose I need a 50-point test to fit my [total points] grading scheme, but find that I need 32 multiple-choice items to sample the content domain thoroughly. I find this unsatisfactory (or inconvenient) because 32 does not divide into 50 very nicely. (It's 1.56!) To make life simpler, I could drop 7 items and use a 25-item test with 2 points per item. If I did that, my points total would be in fine shape, but my test would be an incomplete measure of the important unit objectives. The fact that I had to commit to 50 points prematurely dealt a serious blow to obtaining meaningful assessment results. (Frisbie & Waltman, 1992, p. 41)

Quality-Level Method When you grade an individual assignment with a rubric or grading scale, you make a judgment based on the quality level of the work, overall or according to several criteria. In fact, as you saw in Chapter 12, performance levels for rubrics are specifically written to be descriptions of work at various quality levels. Whether the rubric scale is defined as 1, 2, 3, and 4 or as A, B, C, D, and F, or some other scale, assigning a level to a piece of work in this manner is an example of the quality-level method.

Grading a Composite of Several Scores

This section discusses how to combine scores from several components into a single composite mark. The discussion is consistent with the criterion-referenced grading framework. When using a criterion-referenced framework, as with norm-referenced grading, you must be careful when assigning weights to components. If weights are assigned improperly, the composite results will not maintain the importance you seek for each component.

Fixed-Percentage Method If you use a fixed-percentage grading method, you will have a percentage score for each student for each component. Then, you multiply each component percentage by its corresponding weight, add these products together, and divide the sum of products by the sum of the weights. This procedure may be summarized by the following formula:

$$\text{composite percentage score} = \frac{\Sigma(\text{weight} \times \text{percentage score})}{\Sigma(\text{weight})}$$

[Eq. 15.2]

where

Σ = sum of

weight = weight you give to a component

percentage score = the percentage you gave the student on the component

To illustrate, consider Figure 15.17.

If you did not use the weights, each component would count equally toward the composite. This procedure should not be used with norm-referenced grading because the weights assigned here fail to reflect the standard deviations of the components.

Total Points Method The way we described the total points method in the previous section automatically grades composites. The composite score for a student is the total of the points the student accumulates. However, make sure that the points you assign for each component reflect the weight you want each component to contribute to the total composite. For example, if the weights you want for the components are quizzes 20%, homework 10%, term paper 20%, and exam 50%, then points for each component should reflect these percentages of the total maximum points. Thus, if the maximum total points is 200, then all of the quizzes are worth a maximum of 40 points (= 20% of 200), all of the homework a maximum of 20 points, term paper 40 points, and exam 100 points.

Quality-Level Methods You can derive a grade from a set of rubric scores on various assignments in one of several ways: summing across components, using the median score, or using rules for minimum attainment. These methods may also be used when the components are a mixture of percentage scores on tests and quizzes, and rubrics-based scores. As we pointed out in our discussions of the other methods, be careful to place all of the component marks on comparable scales before combining them into a composite for grade assignment. So for instance, all components marks may be converted into an A, B, C, D, and F quality scale before combining them to arrive at a final grade. These letter grades (as well as rubrics-based marks) represent achievement scales on which students are *partially ordered*. (See Chapter 14 for a discussion of partial ordering.)

Summing Across Components Convert each score to a percentage, and then used the fixed-percentage method to combine them. We do not recommend this method, however, because it has a severe limitation that affects the validity of grade interpretation. As we discussed in the section "Consistent Grading Throughout the Marking Period," turning rubrics into percents usually distorts the intended meaning of the grade. For example, a 3 on a 4-point writing rubric may describe acceptable writing, of the sort you might consider B work. However, 3 out of

FIGURE 15.17 Example of how to calculate the composite score using the fixed-percentage method.

Suppose you had four components (quizzes, homework, term paper, and exam) that you want to combine into a composite score for the end of a marking period. Suppose, further, that each component was originally marked as a percentage correct. Suppose, too, you did not want to weigh each component the same. Finally, suppose that the students' marks and weights for each component were as follows:

Student	Quizzes (wt. = 20%)	Homework (wt. = 10%)	Term paper (wt. = 20%)	Exam (wt. = 50%)	Weighted composite percentage
Bob	87	85	70	80	80
Chad	85	80	80	70	75
Susan	75	82	85	60	65
Theresa	70	78	75	65	69

You calculate the weighted composite score (last column) and compare that score to the boundaries you set for the letter grades. You use Equation 15.2 to calculate the weighted composite score. The calculations are as follows:

$$\text{weighted composite score for Bob} = [20 \times 87 + 10 \times 85 + 20 \times 70 + 50 \times 80] \div [100] = 80$$

$$\text{weighted composite score for Chad} = [20 \times 85 + 10 \times 80 + 20 \times 80 + 50 \times 70] \div [100] = 75$$

$$\text{weighted composite score for Susan} = [20 \times 75 + 10 \times 82 + 20 \times 85 + 50 \times 60] \div [100] = 65$$

$$\text{weighted composite score for Theresa} = [20 \times 70 + 10 \times 78 + 20 \times 75 + 50 \times 65] \div [100] = 69$$

Suppose your grade boundaries were:

$$A = 90–100; B = 80–89; C = 70–79; D = 60–69; \text{and } F = 0–59$$

Then using the weighted composite percentages as calculated, the grades for these students are:

$$\text{Bob} = B; \text{Chad} = C; \text{Susan} = D; \text{and Theresa} = D$$

4 points is 75%, which in many grading policies would constitute a C or even a D.

Using the Median Score   This works well for components that include a mixture of rubrics and percent-correct scores. The **median score method** approach treats all component marks as ordinal data (i.e., essentially as ranks) and uses the student's median mark to calculate the grade instead of using the sum of marks or the average mark. Before taking the median, convert all scores (rubrics, percents, and so on) to the same scale (for example, A, B, C, D, F). The median is discussed in Appendix I. See Brookhart (2004) for a more complete explanation of this method.

Using Minimum Attainment   The **minimum attainment method** bases the composite grades on whether students meet minimum standards on the most important assessments that comprise the final grade, while at the same time allowing somewhat lower performance on a few of the less important components. Although this method could be used in a variety of circumstances, it is suitable when you have marked the components using quality-level scores such as letter grades (see Figure 15.11), rubric scores (see Figure 12.6), or quality-level labels (e.g., basic, proficient, advanced) but you do not want to convert these quality-level marks to percentages.

The minimum attainment rules method is a *noncompensatory approach to grading.*[6] A teacher sets the minimum marks on some important assessment components that the students must meet in order to receive a particular grade. If a student fails meet the minimum standards on these specified assessments, she cannot receive high grades, no matter how well she did on the other, less important, assessments. Students who *do* meet the minimum standards on the specified assessment also must meet some standards on the other, less important components. The minimum attainment rules method is only one such noncompensatory approach to grading.

To use this method, you first determine what components will be included in students' final grades, and which of those are more important to demonstrating the students' achievement of the learning targets. Second, you must specify, for each of these "more important" components, the minimum level of performance you will accept for each of the final grade levels of A, B, C, D, and so on. Third, you establish rules for what levels of performance you will accept, at each final grade level, on each of the "less important" components. These rules form a set of decision rules for how to assign grades. An example of how to use these rules follows.

[6]The methods whereby you add together scores from the components are called *compensatory* methods because a student's low score on one component can be compensated by a high grade on another.

Example

Example of the minimum attainment method for grading

Assume an English class with one test (graded in percentages that are then converted to letter grades), four small writing assignments (graded with rubrics as A, B, C, D, F), and one longer paper (also graded with rubrics as A, B, C, D, F). That is, six components go into the final grade. Assume, also, you wanted the combined test and paper marks to be worth twice as much as the four smaller assignments.

If a student scores	Then the grade is
As on at least three of the writing assignments, *and* As on the paper and test, or an A on one and a B on the other	A
As or Bs on at least three of the writing assignments, *and* at least Bs on the paper and test, or an A on one and a C on the other	B
C or better on at least three of the writing assignments, *and* at least Cs on the paper and test, or a B or better on one and a D or better on the other	C
D or better on at least three of the writing assignments, *and* at least Ds on the paper and test, or a C or better on one and an F on the other	D
A combination lower than the above	F

Here is an example of how these rules would be applied for eight students:

Example

Example of applying the minimum attainment method for grading in the preceding example to eight students

	Writing 1	Writing 2	Writing 3	Writing 4	Long paper	Test	Final grade
Aiden	A	A	C	A	A	A	A
Anthony	A	B	A	A	A	B	A
Ashley	A	B	B	C	B	B	B
Billy	A	B	B	C	B	B	B
Blake	C	C	C	A	C	C	C
Chad	D	D	D	A	D	D	D
Jesse	D	D	D	A	F	C	D
Sophia	D	D	F	F	D	D	F

You may notice from the example that the rules are similar to the rules in set theory arithmetic used in elementary schools because they use *if, not, and, or,* and *then.* In the preceding example, for instance, the rule for an A grade states: "IF (writing assignments = 3 As or more) AND [(both paper and test = A) OR (paper and test have A and B)] THEN overall grade = A. Sometimes this method of grading is referred to as the **logic rule method** (Arter & McTighe, 2001).

Of course, you may use other decision rules beside the ones we used in the example. Other decision rules might describe minimum attainment in the manner of an holistic rubric (as in Figure 15.11), for example.

GRADEBOOK COMPUTER PROGRAMS

A number of the procedures described for calculating composite grades are somewhat complex and involve some tedious multiplication and addition. All these calculations can be made with the help of a handheld calculator, of course. If you have a personal computer, you may also want to use a simple spreadsheet program to make the calculations. Several **gradebook programs** in the marketplace can also help you. The advantage is that a gradebook program provides you with a spreadsheet already set up for recording and reporting grades. The better programs combine spreadsheets and database functions. These will allow you to choose from a variety of grading frameworks, keep a class roster, keep attendance, record comments about students' assignments, obtain class summaries, and print reports for the total class or for one student to take home.

You may search for gradebook programs that work on the PC, the Macintosh, or handheld PDA (e.g., Palm). The more reputable vendors will permit you to download the program for a trial period. Take advantage of that offer and use the program to see if it suits your needs. Try to find a program that will allow you to use one or more of the grading methods you learned in this chapter. The program should allow you to keep grades and records for multiple classes or multiple subjects.

School districts sometimes provide—and require—teachers to use a particular gradebook program. These programs are sometimes linked to the district's administrative software so that report cards can be printed without the extra step of "turning in grades." Some of these programs are linked to a Website where parents, with password and identification, can log in and check their students' grades at any time, and sometimes even compare their student's grade with the rest of the class. This opens up new opportunities for home-school communication. It also requires even clearer grading plans and policies, so that students and parents who check incomplete records for a marking period correctly interpret the information in front of them. Smith and Walker (2002) recommend that before implementing a building-wide electronic gradebook system, principals should consider (a) teachers' technology comfort level, (b) computer availability, (c) network capability, (d) interface with student information management system, (e) staff development, (f) ongoing support, and (g) principal's commitment.

One disadvantage of some gradebook programs is that they may limit the type of grading you may employ, or they may not permit you to use your own grading method to override the method(s) build into the program. We have seen a gradebook program advertised that claims to "think like an elementary school teacher" and includes ways to encode "effort" into students' grades! Be careful to be a critical consumer of any program you choose. If your district chooses a gradebook program for you, you should still investigate what kind of framework it uses for its calculations and adjust default settings to what you intend for your grades whenever possible.

Software for delivering online courses also includes gradebook capability. If you are teaching online, use the same approach to these gradebooks as you would for a gradebook program you use for a face-to-face class. Find out what its capabilities are, what kinds of data it will accommodate, and how it will display summaries or print reports. Most important, find out what framework it uses for combining individual grades or scores into composite marks and check that the method is what you intend. If not, adjust the program's settings.

Summary

Section I: The Meanings and Purposes of Grades

- Although good teaching requires continuous assessment, not all assessment results should become part of a student's grade. Only summative assessments of achievement should be part of the grade.
- Grades are important summaries of a student's achievements and are used by students, parents, other teachers, guidance counselors, school officials, postsecondary educational institutions, and employers. Therefore, you must assign grades with utmost care and maintain their validity.
- Marks and grades are difficult for many teachers to assign because educational achievement is difficult to measure, marking systems are frequently controversial, and grading may require difficult or unpleasant decisions about students.
- The ways you and your school district assign grades communicate your own values and attitudes as well as student progress information.
- Measurement specialists are divided on the issue of whether traditional grades are effective motivators of academic performance. One analysis indicates that traditional grades (a) can serve as goals for some students, (b) reduce motivation when they are perceived by a student as being out of reach, (c) seldom provide continuous information the student can use to judge progress, and (d) provide little information the student can use to improve learning. If the last four conditions exist, then grades are less likely to be effective motivators of student learning.
- Grades have been criticized on many different grounds. These are summarized in Figure 15.4.

Section II: Report Cards and Other Official Reports of Student Progress

- Among the methods of reporting student progress in the United States, the most popular are letter grades, numbers or percentages, two-category systems, checklists and rating scales, narrative reports, student-teacher conferences, parent-teacher conferences, and letters to parents. Advantages and disadvantages of the various methods are shown in Figure 15.5.
- Schools often use more than one method of reporting student progress, and different methods are used at different educational levels.
- Figure 15.8 summarizes suggestions for conducting parent-teacher conferences.
- Multiple marking systems are needed when a school reports several kinds of symbols and marks students on several kinds of objectives. Figure 15.10 offers suggestions for developing multiple marking systems.
- It is unlikely that one best system for reporting student progress exists. Schools might consider the total informational needs of different students and parents and design multiple reporting systems tailored to community circumstances.

Section III: Choosing a Grading Model

- Letter grades are assigned within certain grade-referencing frameworks: norm-referencing (relative standards), criterion-referencing (absolute standards), and self-referencing (growth standards).
- Before you can assign valid grades, you need to choose a grading framework that matches your (a) teaching approach and (b) formative and summative information purposes. These factors determine which grade-referencing framework is appropriate.
- A norm-referenced approach assigns grades to students on the basis of how well their performances compare with one another.
- A self-referenced approach assigns grades on the basis of the teacher's perception of the student's capability and subsequent educational growth.
- A criterion-referenced approach assigns grades by comparing a student's performance with a defined set of standards, performances to learn, or knowledge to acquire. This approach can be considered criterion-referenced only if you use a well-defined domain of tasks and draw representative samples from the domain on which to observe and assess students. Most teachers do not do this.

Section IV: Sensible Grading Practices

- Your grading plan must be based on your assessment plan (see Chapter 6).
- To make your summative grades sensible, you need to:
  - Focus only on grading variables.
  - Eliminate mixing nongrading variables into a grade.
  - Make your marking scales consistent across all components.
  - Assign weights to the components rationally.

- Use additional achievement assessment information to evaluate students near the grade boundaries.
  - Set grade boundaries using techniques that match your grade-referencing framework.
  - Use F to represent low achievement rather than "failing to try" or "failing to turn in assignments."
  - Avoid giving zeros for failing to turn in assignments or as punishment.
- Grading variables are a subset of reporting variables, and reporting variables are a subset of assessment variables. Grading variables are limited to assessment variables that reflect summative student achievement of a curriculum's learning targets, which you must report on official school records.
- You should weight each of the categories of assessment components comprising grades differently. Among the factors you should consider in weighting the components are representatives and relevance, emphasis on what you taught, thinking processes and skills required, overlap among the components, fairness to all students, and reliability and objectivity of the assessment results.
- You need to consider the meaning of failure and its impact on students. The chapter discusses some of the issues and offers suggestions for how you should view failing grades in the light of your school district's policy.
- You should understand the serious impact of assigning a zero grade to a student when the student does not complete an assignment. Alternatives to assigning a zero are suggested.

Section V: Techniques for Setting Grade Boundaries and Combining Scores

- The chapter explained several techniques for assigning grades, including grading on a curve, the standard deviation method, adjusting for the class's ability level, transforming scores to SS-scores, the total points method, the fixed-percentage method, the quality-level method, and weight components for absolute standards systems.
- Computerized gradebook programs are available that allow you to use complex grading procedures rather easily. They also help you easily prepare a number of useful summaries of your grades and reports to submit to students, parents, and school officials.

Important Terms and Concepts

assessment variables (evaluation variables)
borderline cases
continuous assessment
criterion-referenced grading framework (absolute standards, task-referenced)
failing grade
failing work versus failing to try
fixed-percentage method for grading
gradebook program
grading
grading for summative purposes
grading framework
grading on a curve
grading variables
logic rule method for grading
marking period

median score method
minimum attainment method
multiple marking system
narrative report
norm-referenced grading framework (group-referenced, relative standards)
permanent record card
quality-level method for grading (content-based method, rubric method)
report card
reporting variables
self-referenced grading framework (change-based, growth standards)
SS-score method for making composites
stakeholders
standard deviation method of grading
student progress reporting method (checklist, letter grades, letter to parents, narrative reports, numbers, parent-teacher conferences, percentages, pupil-teacher conferences, rating scale, two-category)
total points method for grading

Exercises and Applications

1. Prepare a brief paper explaining the grading system you use (or plan to use). In a separate section explain the educational rationale for using this system, including an explanation of how your system has improved (or will improve) your students' educational development. In your paper, show how you used Figure 15.12 to frame your thinking. Discuss your grading point of view with others in your class. Prepare at least one paragraph explaining each of the following:
   a. The meaning of your grade symbols.
   b. The meaning of failure in your class.
   c. How you distinguish between "failure" and "failure to try."
   d. How you handle late work or work not handed in.
   e. How you avoid the "deadly zero."
   f. What student performances count toward grades you assign your student.
   g. The number of each letter (or other symbol) grade you typically assign (or will assign) in your class.
   h. What components go (or will go) into the end-of-term grade for your students.
   i. How much weight each component in Item h should receive.
   j. What boundaries you use (or would use) for each grade.
   k. How you handle students who are on the borderline between grades.
   l. Any other factors you take into account.
2. Talk with school administrators and teachers at several grade levels in the school district in which you live or work. Bring Figure 15.5 with you.
   a. What method(s) of student progress reporting is (are) used?
   b. Is the district satisfied with the method(s) it uses?
   c. Which of the advantages and disadvantages listed in Figure 15.5 has the school district experienced? Explain.
   d. Obtain copies of the district's report card(s). Share all your findings with the other members of your class.
   e. Summarize the similarities and differences among the district represented in your class and offer suggestions for improving student progress reporting.

FIGURE 15.18 List of students and the marks they received on each component during one marking period. Use this table for Exercise 5.

Pupil	Last year's grade average	Teacher's judgment of ability	Deportment	Homework 1	2	3	Project	Quizzes 1	2	Test score
A	B	Average	Very good	10	3	8	12	8	4	25
B	C	Average	Very good	9	2	7	15	7	4	20
C	A	Very high	Poor	10	0	9	15	10	5	29
D	A	Above average	Excellent	10	4	10	15	6	5	28
E	D	Average	Poor	0	2	5	0	5	3	10
F	B	Average	Good	10	1	2	10	5	3	18
G	C	Below average	Good	10	3	9	8	6	2	15
H	C	Above average	Poor	10	1	4	15	8	4	12
I	C	Above average	Excellent	10	1	3	13	8	3	21
J	C	Above average	Very good	10	1	5	10	8	2	23
Maximum possible score:				10	10	10	15	10	5	30
Mean				8.9	1.8	6.2	11.3	7.1	3.5	20.1
Standard deviation:				3.0	1.2	2.6	4.5	1.5	1.0	6.1
Teacher's weights:				5%	5%	5%	15%	10%	10%	50%

3. Identify a unit that you have taught or will teach.
   a. In the context of your teaching situation and this unit, identify the assessment variables, the reporting variables, and the grading variables.
   b. Prepare a three-column table listing these variables and describing how you have assessed (or will assess) each one.
   c. Share your findings with the others in your class.
4. Name several kinds of student performances (homework, class participation, performance tasks, tests, etc.) that you believe should be included in each of the following levels: primary, middle school, or high school.
   a. State what weight should be assigned to each type of performance. Explain the reasons for these weights by discussing each of the six factors stated in the chapter in relation to each kind of performance.
   b. Would the weights vary with different grade levels or with different subjects? Explain.

5. Figure 15.18 contains information about the performance of a class of 10 students. Use it to complete this exercise.
   a. Determine an overall report card grade for each student using the following methods: (i) self-referencing; (ii) criterion-referencing, fixed-percentage; (iii) criterion-referencing, total points; (iv) norm-referencing, grading on the curve; (v) norm-referencing, standard deviation method; and (vi) norm-referencing, Ebel-Stuit method. (*Hint*: Average the marks within categories—for example, within homework—before applying the teacher's weight.)
   b. Prepare a table with the students' names as the row headings and the four different methods as the column headings. Enter the students' grades under each method and compare the results.
   c. Share your results with the others in your class. Where do you see the most agreement and most disagreement?
   d. List the reasons for agreements and disagreements for each method.

16 | Standardized Achievement Tests

LEARNING TARGETS

After studying this chapter, you should have learned the following:

Types of Tests and Standardized Survey Batteries

1. Name and describe the major categories of educational achievement tests. [4, 6, 1]
2. Explain the advantages of each type of educational achievement test. [4, 3, 1]
3. Explain the benefits to a school of using standardized educational survey tests that have been developed using empirical research. [4, 3, 1]
4. Describe the features that standardized achievement batteries have in common. [1, 6, 7]
5. Describe the major dimensions along which the standardized achievement batteries differ. [1, 6, 7]
6. Interpret computer-prepared reports that come with a standardized testing program including item analysis (cluster) reports, school (building) reports, and student (home) reports. [1, 6, 7]

State-Mandated Customized Tests

7. Describe how state-mandated testing programs get their tests. [6, 5]
8. Describe how state-mandated testing programs typically operate. [6, 5]

Nonstandardized Achievement Tests

9. Explain what you gain and lose when you use the tests that come with your curriculum materials. [1, 4]
10. Describe the advantages and disadvantages of teacher-made assessments over published assessments. [1, 4]

Appropriate Uses of Standardized Test Results

11. Describe and illustrate the appropriate uses of standardized achievement tests for within-classroom decisions. [3, 1, 4]

12. Describe and illustrate the appropriate uses of standardized achievement tests for decisions external to the classroom. [3, 4, 6]

Inappropriate Uses of Standardized Test Results

13. Describe and illustrate the common criticisms and misuses of standardized achievement tests in schools. [7, 3]

Choosing Standardized Tests

14. Identify the factors that a school must keep in mind when selecting a standardized achievement test for elementary and secondary schools. [1, 7, 6]
15. Describe factors to keep in mind when you want to choose a standardized test to complement your state-mandated assessment. [5, 6, 7]

How to Administer Standardized Tests

16. Describe what you need to do before and during the administration of a standardized assessment procedure. [3]

Ethical and Unethical Student Practice for Standardized Assessments

17. Identify ethical and unethical teacher practices for preparing students for standardized assessments. [6, 3, 4]
18. Apply the two principles for judging the ethics of a teacher's standardized assessment–preparation practices. [6, 3, 4]

Important Terms and Concepts

19. Explain how the terms and concepts listed at the end of this chapter apply to educational assessment. [6]

ABOUT THIS CHAPTER

We begin the chapter by looking at the full range of published tests. We discuss how you know whether a test is standardized. Next, we look at the advantages of different types of tests, including teacher-made tests. Third, we discuss state-mandated tests and how they differ from ordinary standardized tests. Fourth, we discuss appropriate ways to use standardized test results for decisions in the classroom and for decisions external to the classroom. Fifth, we discuss criticisms and misuses of standardized test results. Sixth, we make suggestions for choosing a standardized test. We consider what you need to keep in mind when you want a standardized test to complement your state-mandated test. Seventh, we offer suggestions for how to administer a standardized test, including how to prepare your students for the test. Finally, we discuss ethical and unethical ways of giving students practice for standardized tests. In Chapter 18 we shall discuss how a published test is developed and evaluated.

TYPES OF TESTS

Overview

Published achievement tests vary in their purpose, usefulness, and quality. To appreciate their variety, you may find it helpful to classify them. Here is one classifying scheme:

I. Published achievement tests
    A. *Standardized, **empirically documented tests*** have a high degree of standardization. **Standardized tests** follow the development procedures outlined in Chapter 18, especially the steps that require using empirical data to document their effectiveness. The following types are in this group:
        1. *Multilevel survey batteries* are the familiar, annually administered tests that survey students' general educational growth or basic skill development in each of several curricular areas. *Multilevel* means that the test content spans several grade levels; *battery* means that several curricular areas are assessed by different subtests.
        2. *Multilevel criterion-referenced tests for a single curricular area* provide detailed information about students' status for a well-defined domain of performance in a single subject area (e.g., mathematics). The test spans several grade levels.
        3. *Other multilevel tests for a single curricular area* are noncriterion-referenced tests that assess students in a broader way than do subtests in a survey battery.
        4. *Single-level standardized tests for one course or subject* are developed for assessing achievement at only one educational level or for one course (e.g., Algebra I). Usually they are stand-alone tests, neither coordinated with tests from other courses nor normed on the same students as other tests.
    B. *State-mandated customized tests* are developed by publishers of standardized multilevel survey batteries for use only in a particular state. The tests are said to be *customized* because a publisher contracts with a state to prepare standardized tests that are aligned with the state's standards and are secure so they can be used for accountability purposes. Since the NCLB Act, the grades typically covered are 3 through 12 and the subjects tested are reading, language arts, mathematics, and, perhaps, science.
    C. *Nonstandardized tests, without adequate empirical data to document* their effectiveness make little or no attempt to standardize and do not follow all the development procedures outlined in Chapter 18. Publishers do not spend the time and money to document their effectiveness or their quality empirically.
        1. *Some criterion-referenced tests* estimate students' status with respect to a well-defined domain of performance (usually specified by specific behavioral objectives), but they lack standardization and empirical documentation of worth.
        2. *Textbook or curricular accompaniments* are tests or test items found in teacher's editions, at the end of textbook chapters, at the back of the book, supplements that come with textbook series, or built into instructional materials. They are called different names, such as pretests, posttests, placement tests, progress checks, unit tests, review tests, or curriculum-embedded tests. They lack standardization and empirical data to document their quality (although there are a few exceptions). As a teacher, you must keep in mind that these tests are seldom the products of professional item writers, usually measure low-level cognitive skills, and very often have several incorrectly keyed answers.
II. *Teacher-made tests* are crafted by you to measure the specific learning targets your curriculum framework emphasizes. These tests help you in making day-to-day instructional decisions.

The focus of this chapter is limited to standardized tests having empirical data to document their effectiveness. The full range of tests in the classification is not discussed.

Multilevel Survey Batteries

The workhorse of standardized achievement testing is the **multilevel survey battery**. Although each publisher's test battery emphasizes different details of content and skill, the batteries are organized similarly.

Organization of Batteries Each battery is group administered and each contains several subtests. A **subtest** assesses one area, such as reading, mathematics, listening skills, English usage (mechanics), writing, spelling (recognition), vocabulary (word meaning), or skills in using library and reference materials. Not all questions on these subtests are multiple-choice: In recent years, publishers have added constructed-response items or performance tasks to several subtests or have offered them as separate subtests. Separate scores are given for each subtest. Usually, a battery has subtests for six to eight curriculum areas. Different publishers may have different subtest names for the same curriculum area.

Each subtest is made up of a coordinated series of **test levels** that spans the grades. For example, a reading subtest may be organized into four levels: one level for Grades 1 and 2, another for Grades 3 and 4, another for 5 and 6, and a fourth for 7 and 8. It is not unusual for a publisher to have adjacent levels with overlapping grades (e.g., one level covering Grades 3–4–5 and the next level covering Grades 5–6–7).

Figure 16.1 shows the curriculum areas, subtests, and grade levels covered by some of the more popular standardized achievement tests.

Although different publishers' survey batteries are similar in their surface features, they are not interchangeable, even though subtest names may sound similar. The specific content emphasized, the cognitive skills students are required to use to complete the tasks, and the way the norms and scales are developed will be very different from publisher to publisher.

Tests vary in how well they match any school district's curriculum or state's standards. In some curricula, such as reading and perhaps mathematics, the curricula differ very little from one school district to another within a state. The tests and these curricula may match closely. In other curricula such as science and social studies, especially in

FIGURE 16.1 Examples of curriculum areas and grade levels assessed by survey batteries.

Curriculum area/subarea[a]	Stanford Achievement Test (10th edition)	Metropolitan Achievement Tests (8th edition)	Iowa Tests of Basic Skills (Form A)	Iowa Tests of Educational Development (Form A)	TerraNova CTBS Complete Battery Plus
Reading multiple-choice					
Alphabet knowledge	K.0–1.5	K.0–K.5	K.1–1.9		
Word/sentence reading	K.0–2.5	1.5–4.5	K.8–3.5		K–4.2
Phonetic/structural analysis	1.5–3.5	K.0–4.5	K.0–3.5		K–4.2
Decoding skills	K.0–1.5	K.0–1.5			K–4.2
Vocabulary	2.5–12.9	1.5–12.9	K.0–8.9	9.0–12.9	K–12.9
Comprehension	1.5–12.9	1.5–12.9	K.8–8.9	9.0–12.9	K.0–12.9
Reading performance assessment	1.5–12.9[b]	1.5–12.9[b]	3.0–8.9[b]	9.0–12.9[b]	1.6–12.9[c]
Language multiple-choice					
Punctuation	1.5–12.9	1.5–12.9	3.0–8.5	9.0–12.9	1.6–12.9
Capitalization	1.5–12.9	1.5–12.9	3.0–8.9	9.0–12.9	1.6–12.9
Usage	1.5–12.9	1.5–12.9	3.0–8.9	9.0–12.9	1.6–12.9
Listening	K.0–9.9	K.0–3.5	K.0–8.9		K.6–2.6
Sentence/paragraph organization	1.5–12.9	3.0–8.9		9.0–12.9	1.6–12.9
Language/writing performance assessment	3.5–12.9[b]	1.5–12.9[b]	1.0–8.9[b]	9.0–12.9[b]	1.6–12.9[c]
Spelling multiple-choice	1.5–12.9	1.5–12.9	1.7–8.9	9.0–12.9	2.0–12.9
Spelling performance assessment					
Mathematics multiple-choice					
Computation	K.0–12.9	K.5–9.5	1.7–8.9	9.0–12.9	1.6–12.9
Concepts	K.0–12.9	K.5–12.9	K.0–8.9	9.0–12.9	K.0–12.9
Problem solving	K.5–12.9	1.5–12.9	1.7–8.9	9.0–12.9	K.6–12.9
Mathematics performance assessment	1.5–12.9[b]	1.5–12.9[b]	1.0–8.9[b]	9.0–12.9[b]	1.6–12.9[c]
Study skills multiple-choice					
Maps, graphs, tables	4.5–12.9	3.5–12.9	1.7–8.9	9.0–12.9	1.6–12.9
Library/reference materials	4.5–12.9	3.5–12.9	1.7–8.9	9.0–12.9	1.6–12.9
Study skills performance assessment		K.0–8.9[b]		9.0–12.9[b]	1.6–12.9
Science multiple-choice	K.0–12.9	1.5–12.9	1.7–8.9	9.0–12.9	1.6–12.9
Science performance assessment	1.5–12.9[b]	1.5–12.9[b]	1.0–8.9[b]	9.0–12.9[b]	1.6–12.9[c]
Social studies multiple-choice	3.5–12.9	1.5–12.9	1.7–8.9	9.0–12.9	1.6–12.9
Social studies performance assessment	1.5–12.9[b]	1.5–12.9[b]	1.0–8.9[b]	9.0–12.9[b]	1.6–12.9[c]

Notes:[a]Publishers may have somewhat different names for these areas than those used here. Separate scores are not provided for every area.
[b]Assessments in these areas are available as supplements or additional purchase components that are not part of the battery itself.
[c]Part of the Multiple Assessments Edition.

the elementary schools, there are much larger variations between school districts. For a teacher this means that the different subtests in the battery have less value in assessing the specifics of what the teacher taught during the year. However, such subtests can assess general information and general ability to apply knowledge and skill.

These differences make it necessary for school officials to actually inspect the test items before they adopt a battery, matching their local curriculum to the battery's content and skills emphasis. If there is a wide gap between your local curriculum's learning targets and the battery's tasks, do not adopt the survey battery.

Publishers think of each subtest (e.g., reading comprehension) as assessing a continuous dimension that grows or develops over a range of grades. Because each subtest is a graded series of assessments, the publisher can use empirical data to link the levels together and to place the scores of students from every grade on one numerical scale that spans all the grades. The scale allows achievement to be expressed quantitatively (that is, to be measured). This allows you to use a multilevel subtest to measure a student's year-to-year educational development and growth in a curricular area. Different types of educational development scales are explained in Chapter 17.

Each publisher norms and standardizes its tests on different samples of students, so the samples and the resulting norm-referenced scores are not comparable. However, all the subtests in one publisher's survey battery are administered to the same national sample of students. The major advantage of administering all subtests to the same students is that the different subtest results can be referenced to the same norm group, allowing you to compare a student's relative strengths and weaknesses across the different curricular areas. You can assess these strengths and weaknesses, however, only by comparing a student's percentile rank in one curricular area to that student's percentile rank in another. An example of the kind of comparison you make follows:

Example

Shanna is better in mathematics than she is in social studies because her score in mathematics is higher than 98% of the students at her grade level, whereas her score in social studies is higher than only 60% of students at her grade level.

Survey batteries report grade-equivalent scores and standard scores, too, but you should not use them to compare a student's achievement in two curricular areas. Percentile ranks, standard scores, and grade-equivalent scores are explained in Chapter 17.

Common Learning Targets It is important to keep in mind that virtually all published standardized tests cover content and learning targets judged to be common to many schools rather than one specific school district. Therefore, standardized achievement tests are not focused on the teaching emphasis of one teacher, one school, one textbook, or one set of curricular materials. This is an advantage because it gives you an "external" or "objective" view of what your students have learned. It is also a disadvantage because the cognitive skills and knowledge assessed by the test may not have been taught to the students before they were tested. Therefore, it is imperative that a school district carefully compares a test's content and *when* that content is taught in their schools, item by item, to the state's standards and the school district's curriculum framework before deciding to adopt it. Sometimes as few as three or four misaligned items can have a serious impact on the results. Also, a teacher must develop and use his or her own assessment procedures for day-to-day instructional decisions (e.g., whether a student has mastered a specific concept). (See "Content Representativeness and Relevance: Content Evidence" in Chapter 3.)

Auxiliary Materials Most publishers of standardized, empirically documented tests provide auxiliary materials to help you interpret and use the assessment results. Teacher's manuals describe in considerable detail the intended purpose and uses of the results, often suggesting ways to improve students' skills by using assessment results for instructional planning. Some publishers provide separate manuals for curriculum coordinators and school administrators to help them use assessment results in curriculum evaluation and reports to the school board. Most publishers provide nicely printed score reports that the school district may use both within the school and with students and parents.

Multilevel Criterion-Referenced Tests

Multilevel criterion-referenced tests provide information about a student's status with respect to the specific learning targets in a domain. Although some survey batteries also provide this information, most surveys assess very broadly or globally defined educational development. Multilevel criterion-referenced tests tend to focus on a more narrowly defined set of learning targets. Some publishers make efforts to align their tests with states' standards.

Other Multilevel Tests

Other types of multilevel tests are stand-alone products that cover one curricular area, such as reading or mathematics, across several grades. These assessments provide a deeper and broader sampling of content than a corresponding subtest of a survey battery. Thus, more time is devoted to assessing students in a single curricular area than when you use a survey battery subtest. However, if the same sample of students was not used to norm a stand-alone multilevel test concurrently with tests from other curricular areas, you cannot use the stand-alone tests to compare a student's relative strengths and weaknesses across curricular areas. For example, you could not say a student is better in reading than in mathematics.

Single-Level Standardized Tests

If you do not want to measure growth or development, a **single-level test** may be useful. Rather than cover several grade or age levels, such tests are directed toward one level or a particular course. Usually these assessments are built for high school and college courses. There are, for example, tests for Algebra 1, first-year college chemistry, and first-year college French.

Each test is a stand-alone product and is not coordinated with other tests. Thus, these test results cannot be used to compare a student's relative standing in several subjects. Scores from this group of achievement tests are most often interpreted using norm-referencing schemes such as percentile ranks and standard scores.

STANDARDIZED SURVEY BATTERIES

Benefits of Standardized Tests

Standardizing is necessary if you want the results to be comparable from time to time, place to place, and person to person. If an assessment procedure is standardized, you are better able to properly interpret students' scores on it. The quality of any assessment procedure is demonstrated by using empirical data to document its validity and effectiveness. These data provide the test developers with a basis for (a) improving and selecting tasks, (b) establishing reliability and validity, (c) describing how well the assessment works in the target population of students, (d) creating scales to measure growth, (e) equating scores (making scores comparable from grade to grade and from one form of the assessment to another), and (f) developing a variety of norm-referenced scores.

Common Features

Most group-administered survey batteries have the following features in common (Iwanicki, 1980).

1. *Test development features.* Manuals and other materials describe for each subtest the (a) content and learning targets covered, (b) types of norms and how they were developed, (c) type of criterion-referencing provided, (d) reliability data, and (e) techniques used to screen items for offensiveness and possible gender, ethnic, and racial bias.

2. *Test administration features.* Tests generally (a) have two equivalent forms; (b) require a total administration time of 2 to 3 hours, spread among several testing sessions over several school days (although tests vary widely in length and administration time); (c) provide practice booklets for students to use before being tested; (d) have

separate, machine-scorable answer sheets for upper grades (students in lower grades mark answers directly on the machine-scorable test booklets); and (e) permit both **in-level** and **out-of-level testing**.[1]

3. *Test norming features.* Tests generally use broadly representative national sampling for norms development and provide both fall and spring individual student norms. Sometimes **special norms** such as the following are provided: (a) large-city norms, (b) norms for students in special government entitlement programs, (c) norms for high-income communities, (d) norms for nonpublic schools, (e) regional norms, and (f) norms for school-building averages.

4. *Test score features.* Tests provide raw scores for each subtest and the following norm-referenced scores: percentile ranks, normal curve equivalents, stanines, extended normalized standard scores, and grade-equivalents (or some similar grade-level indicator score). Attitudes toward using grade-equivalents vary. Some tests provide instructional reading-level scores that are keyed to commonly used basal readers. (We discuss these scores in the next chapter.)

5. *Test score reporting and interpretation features.* Tests generally have interpretive manuals for teachers, school administrators, and/or counselors. Most group tests provide **computer-prepared narrative reports** that contain summaries of district, school building, and classroom test results. Such reports are not free, of course. Figures 16.2 to 16.4 show reports that you would be expected to be able to read and interpret for your students.

Differences

Although survey batteries share common features, they are definitely not interchangeable. Scores obtained from different publishers' batteries, even on subtests with similar-sounding titles, will be different and cannot be compared directly. Among the features that are different and that seriously affect comparability of scores are the following:

1. *Emphasis within content areas.* Subtest scores on batteries from different test publishers have different meanings. For example, a study of the mathematics subtests of four standardized survey batteries for the fourth-grade level indicated that the percentage of items covering a topic such as fractions varied widely among tests—from 5.4% to 14.4% (Freeman, Kuhs, Knappen, & Porter, 1982). This difference in coverage affects pupils' scores significantly. Because each test publisher chooses to emphasize

[1]Test booklets are organized by level; each level is designed for use with a few grades. A student is said to be tested *in-level* if the test booklet level corresponds to the student's actual grade placement. If a student's level of academic functioning is either above or below the actual grade placement, the school may administer the test level that more nearly corresponds to the student's functioning level. This is called *out-of-level testing.* A student is measured best when a test is tailored to the student's functioning level.

FIGURE 16.2 Example of a report that analyzes your class's performance on clusters of items. This report is for mathematics subtests. It reports the percent correct (%C) for each item and for clusters of items. Comparisons are made for your class, the district at your grade level, and the nation at your grade level. This type of report helps you see where in the mathematics area your class is strong and weak.

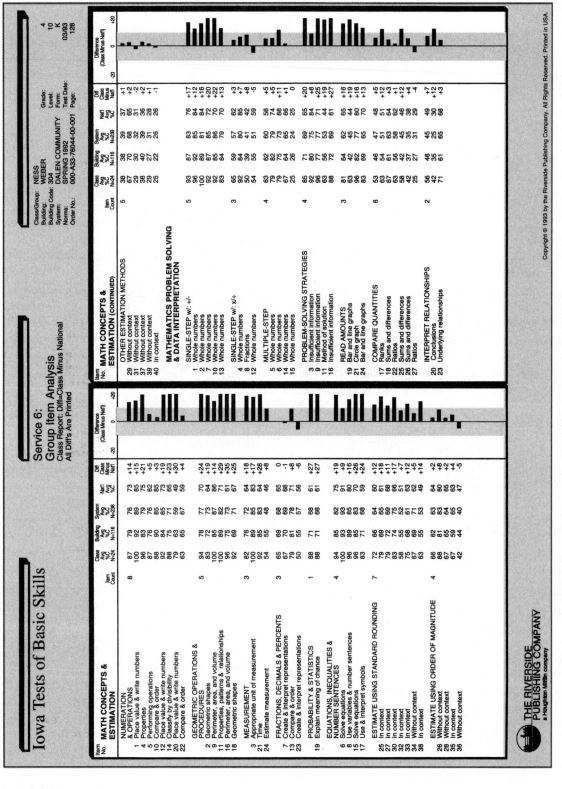

Source: H. D. Hoover, A. N. Hieronymus, D. A. Frisbie, and S. Dunbar, 1993b. Copyright © 1993 by The University of Iowa. All rights reserved. Reproduced from the *Iowa Tests of Basic Skills, Interpretive Guide for Teachers and Counselors, Levels 9–14,* p. 60, with permission of the Riverside Publishing Company.

FIGURE 16.3 Example of a building report showing the performance of a school's Grade 4 students on each subtest. This report shows (a) how the local 90th, 75th, 50th, 25th, and 10th percentile students performed relative to the national norm group; (b) how the local quarters performed relative to the national norm group; (c) how many local students were in each quarter of the national norm group; and (d) what percentage of the local students were in each quarter of the national norm group.

TerraNova

MULTIPLE ASSESSMENTS

Evaluation Summary Report

School: WINFIELD

Grade 4

Purpose

This page gives administrators numeric information to evaluate the overall effectiveness of the educational program. This page displays a comprehensive numeric description of your students' achievement. This page is for those who prefer to analyze the data in tabular form.

Simulated Data

No. of Students: 89

Form/Level: A-14
Test Date: 11/01/99   Scoring: PATTERN (IRT)
QM: 08   Norms Date: 1996

District: Winfield USD

City/State: Metropolis, CA

	Reading	Lang.	Math	Total Score*	Science	Social Studies
Number of Students	86	87	89	86	88	88
Mean Scores & Standard Deviations						
Grade Mean Equivalent	4.6	5.0	4.5	4.8	4.6	4.3
Standard Deviation	1.5	2.0	1.9	1.3	1.7	1.8
Mean Normal Curve Equiv.	48.0	52.0	49.5	51.4	49.9	47.0
Standard Deviation	13.9	14.9	19.3	15.7	18.2	18.1
NP of the Mean NCE	46	54	49	53	50	44
Mean Scale Scores	696.7	715.3	694.4	696.7	700.5	696.1
Standard Deviation	35.2	33.2	45.4	31.0	40.5	48.3
Local Percentiles/Quartiles						
90th Local Percentile						
National Percentile	84.3	91.2	89.0	88.3	88.9	86.1
Grade Equivalent	8.5	9.9	7.8	7.4	8.2	9.0
Normal Curve Equiv.	71.2	78.3	76.4	75.4	76.2	73.0
Scale Score	748.1	765.3	754.4	744.2	756.6	758.5
75th Local Percentile Q3						
National Percentile	62.8	75.4	72.3	70.2	74.3	65.6
Grade Equivalent	5.4	6.8	5.8	5.5	5.8	5.4
Normal Curve Equiv.	56.9	64.4	62.7	61.0	63.9	58.7
Scale Score	719.8	741.5	725.3	719.7	731.3	726.6
50th Percentile (median) Q2						
National Percentile	41.8	53.3	54.0	52.7	56.7	49.8
Grade Equivalent	4.3	4.8	4.8	4.6	4.6	4.6
Normal Curve Equiv.	45.9	52.0	52.0	50.2	53.3	50.6
Scale Score	695.3	719.3	704.0	699.7	711.3	707.8
25th Local Percentile Q1						
National Percentile	30.0	36.1	24.8	30.1	26.0	29.0
Grade Equivalent	3.6	3.5	3.3	3.7	3.4	3.5
Normal Curve Equiv.	39.0	42.4	35.5	38.9	36.5	38.5
Scale Score	678.0	698.2	665.5	678.0	647.0	679.0
10th Local Percentile						
National Percentile	12.1	15.5	10.9	13.2	11.0	12.3
Grade Equivalent	2.6	2.7	2.9	2.9	2.6	2.7
Normal Curve Equiv.	25.2	29.0	24.3	26.1	24.1	25.6
Scale Score	635.3	661.0	639.7	646.9	647.0	644.3
National Quarters						
Local/Number 76-99	10	22	19	16	20	13
Per Quarter 51-75	24	25	26	30	27	30
26-50	38	26	21	25	20	26
01-25	14	14	23	15	21	19
Local/Percent 76-99	11.6	25.3	21.3	18.6	22.7	14.8
Per Quarter 51-75	27.9	28.7	29.2	34.9	30.7	34.1
26-50	44.2	29.9	23.6	29.1	22.7	29.5
01-25	16.3	16.1	25.8	17.4	23.9	21.6

*Total Score consists of Reading, Language, and Mathematics.

Source: From Score Reports for TerraNova, 2nd Edition, by permission of the publisher, CTB/McGraw-Hill LLC, a subsidiary of The McGraw-Hill Companies, Inc. Copyright © 2000 by CTB/McGraw-Hill LLC. All rights reserved.

could account for all the factors that affect the learning of students in a particular community.

All of these purposes relate in some way to accountability. But accountability is poorly determined if the assessment instrument used does not correspond to what is happening in the classroom. Further, when school officials overemphasize standardized tests, pressures may intrude into your classroom practices. As a result, you may believe that having the students "pass the test" is more important than teaching them the important abilities defined in the broader curriculum framework. This unfortunate attitude ultimately leads to a narrowing of the curriculum in undesirable ways, such as teaching only what will appear on the test.

INAPPROPRIATE USES OF STANDARDIZED TEST RESULTS

Criticisms of Standardized Tests

Criticisms of norm-referenced standardized achievement tests are very common. Some critics find the very idea of a commercial, external, norm-referenced, summative, and/or quantitative device for measuring educational outcomes repugnant and ludicrous. Of course, any assessment procedure–standardized or not, norm-referenced or criterion-referenced, formative or summative, external or teacher-made, qualitative and quantitative–can be misused. Much of this misuse, moreover, comes not from something inherent in a particular standardized test, but from the invalid claims that persons make for some assessments or the unscrupulous way(s) in which an assessment might be used. Throughout this text, we discuss appropriate uses and emphasize the need to validate claims made for assessments. You must use

professional judgment in administering and interpreting all assessment procedures. The *Code of Professional Responsibilities in Educational Measurement* (Appendix C) and the *Code of Fair Testing Practices in Education (Revised)* (Appendix B) describe your responsibilities with regard to standardized achievement tests.

Figure 16.5 summarizes some of the many criticisms of standardized survey achievement batteries. As the figure shows, criticisms may focus on some intrinsic characteristic of a test, such as its content coverage; something that is not part of a test, such as its failure to test certain student characteristics; or the misuse of test results, such as inappropriately using a test to classify or label a student.

Airasian (1979) discussed several aspects of these three domains of criticisms:

1. *Critics often describe perceived misuses of tests using arguments from more than one of the three domains.* For example, they may say that tests (a) measure only a small portion of what is taught in the classroom (intrinsic characteristic), (b) do not measure the real goals of an educational program (characteristics not measured), and (c) foster undesirable changes in school curricula or teacher emphasis (misuse of test results).

2. *Some criticisms are contradictory.* The same test may be criticized by some persons because its focus is too narrow and by others because its scores are influenced by too broad a range of human characteristics.

3. *Many of the criticisms can be overcome.* You may overcome many problems by either using the test in the way the publisher intended it to be used or by choosing another, more appropriate test.

4. *A single test cannot be expected to measure the "whole person."* Human characteristics are too rich and too diverse

---

FIGURE 16.5 Examples of three categories of criticisms of standardized, norm-referenced, and survey achievement tests.

> **A. Criticisms directed toward an intrinsic test characteristic:**
>   1. Tests assume that everyone values the skills tested.
>   2. Tests assume a homogeneous culture and/or a common curriculum.
>   3. Tests are biased, favoring white, middle-class pupils.
>   4. Tests assume that approximately half the pupils are below average.
>   5. Tests are too impersonal, vague, undemocratic, and/or irrelevant.
>   6. Tests cover only a small fraction of what schools try to accomplish.
>   7. Tests are invalid measures of behaviors specifically learned in schools.
>
> **B. Criticisms directed toward a characteristic not measured by a test:**
>   1. Tests are not diagnostic.
>   2. Tests do not measure the objectives of innovative instructional programs.
>   3. Tests do not measure creativity, interest, initiative, and/or values.
>   4. Tests compare students rather than measure an individual's learning.
>
> **C. Criticisms directed toward the effects of using a test:**
>   1. Children are "labeled" (or "mislabeled").
>   2. Test use alters the school curriculum by encouraging teaching toward the test.
>   3. Tests result in competition among learners.
>   4. Tests cause fear.
>
> *Source:* Adapted from "A Perspective on the Uses and Misuses of Standardized Achievement Tests," by P. W. Airasian, 1979, *Measurement in Education, 10*(3). Copyright 1979, National Council on Measurement in Education. Reprinted by permission of NCME.

to be assessed by any one assessment. It is an open question, furthermore, whether some human characteristics (interests, attitudes, values, emotional states, etc.) ought to be assessed regularly by a school district.

5. *A criticism of a test may or may not be the same thing as a misuse of a test.* Educators can criticize a test for not measuring a certain student characteristic (e.g., feelings toward someone), but such a failure may not be a misuse. Sometimes, measuring that characteristic (feelings toward someone) may be the misuse (by violating a student's privacy). (See Chapter 5 and Appendix C for professional responsibilities concerning assessment.)

Misuses

You should always strive to use the results of achievement assessments—survey batteries, performance assessments, or authentic tasks—in valid, professional ways. One of the "fatal errors" you will be tempted to make in your career is to use a single assessment result to make an important decision about a student. For example, you may be tempted to base a student's grade exclusively on the student's examination score, ignoring daily classroom performance or the student's personal situation when the student took the test. Teachers and school administrators misuse standardized test results in similar ways. Inappropriate uses of a survey achievement battery are listed here. You should also note that using a state-mandated assessment in these ways is also inappropriate (Hoover et al., 1993b).

1. *Placing a student in a special instructional program solely on results from a standardized achievement test.* Special programs include remedial programs as well as programs for students who are gifted and talented. School officials can overcome this misuse by using many pieces of information when making these decisions. They should include students' daily classroom performance, teachers' assessments, and results from other assessments in addition to the survey achievement battery.

2. *Retaining a student in a grade solely on the results from a standardized test.* First, you should recognize that the wisdom of retaining students is very much an open educational question, and the common practice of retention in the early grades often does not help students (Karweit & Wasik, 1992). Second, your daily observation, teaching, and evaluation of a student are the most relevant types of information that a school official should use when making this decision. Third, parents have information about a child that school officials and teachers do not. Although standardized achievement test scores may have some bearing on this type of decision, their importance should have little weight in the final decision.

3. *Judging an entire school program's quality solely on the basis of the results from a standardized achievement test.* School programs are complex. They teach many things other than those assessed by standardized tests. You know, too, that even within a curriculum area assessed by a test, there is no perfect match between what is assessed and all the instructional targets in the curriculum framework. (Figure 18.5 lists many of the school and community factors that should be considered when using survey battery scores for curriculum evaluation.) School officials can overcome misuse by aggressively placing program evaluation decisions in a broader context of the full curriculum framework and the full context of school and community factors.

4. *Using a survey achievement battery to prescribe specific content teachers should teach at certain grade levels.* You know that a test only samples the many tasks that students could be asked to perform. Although test tasks are important, each task is not an end in itself. If the tasks are a representative sample from this larger domain, they allow you to generalize beyond them to estimate a student's performance on the domain. If school officials manipulate the sample or try to limit the curriculum domain primarily to the sample appearing on a test, they destroy the ability to generalize. School officials may overcome this misuse by developing curriculum frameworks using appropriate principles drawn from educational development, child development, learning, and the subject-matter disciplines. They should then select the test that best matches the important curriculum learning targets, rather than vice versa.

5. *Attributing a student's poor assessment results to only one cause.* Sometimes a teacher or school administrator interprets a student's assessment result as though it was entirely the result of the student's own shortcomings rather than the result of several interacting conditions. A student's poor assessment result may very well reflect the quality of previous teaching, the nature of the student's home environment, or other personal experiences.

6. *School officials or parents trying to blame the teacher if the class does poorly on a standardized test.* Before a person can attribute the rise (or fall) of a class's test scores solely to a particular teacher, that person would have to consider how each of several factors influences the scores: Did the content of the test match the breadth and emphasis of what was taught in the classroom? Did the students in this year's class have, on the whole, better or worse general school aptitude than classes in the past (or classes assigned to other teachers)? Were students in this (or another) class taught the answers to the items or otherwise given an unfair advantage? Did last year's teacher do an exceptionally good (or poor) job of teaching, and did this influence carry over to this year? What home factors influenced the students' successes (or lack thereof)? Did the school principal (or other instructional leader) facilitate or inhibit the teacher's teaching or the students' learning? You can probably name other factors to consider when trying to find the reasons for a class's test results. Unlike an automobile manufacturer or a pizzeria owner, schools and teachers have relatively little control over their raw materials and the conditions under which they must operate (Feldt, 1976).

MULTILEVEL SURVEY BATTERIES

Many achievement survey batteries are available in the marketplace. (Each edition of the *Mental Measurements Yearbook* lists dozens of different tests.) Here, in alphabetical order, are the most widely used batteries. The grade ranges they cover are noted in parentheses.

Iowa Tests of Basic Skills (K–8)
Iowa Tests of Educational Development (9–12)
Metropolitan Achievement Tests (K–12)
Peabody Individual Achievement Test (K–adult)
Stanford Achievement Test Series (K–12)
STS Educational Development Series (2–12)
TerraNova Comprehensive Tests of Basic Skills (CTBS) (K–12)
TerraNova, Second Edition (CAT/6), (K–12)
Tests of Achievement and Proficiency (9–12)
Wide Range Achievement Test (K–adult)

These are all group-administered tests, except for the *Peabody* and the *Wide Range,* which are individually administered. Publishers are listed in Appendixes K and L. Details about each battery can be obtained from the publishers' catalogs and Websites. Critical reviews are found in the *Mental Measurements Yearbooks, Test Critiques,* and other sources identified in Chapter 18.

Group-Administered Survey Batteries

Group-administered survey batteries have several subtests, each assessing a different curricular area. Although each multilevel survey battery emphasizes different content and skills, Figure 16.1 shows areas typically measured by each of several batteries. Separate scores are provided for several (usually six to eight) areas; different publishers may have different names for an area.

Individually Administered Surveys

Individually administered achievement batteries are commonly used for students with special needs, such as students with disabilities who otherwise would have difficulty taking assessments in group settings. Students who cannot be assessed in groups often can be validly assessed in individual sessions where the assessment administrator can provide the special accommodations they need and can establish greater rapport than is possible in a group. (See Chapter 5, Figure 5.2, for examples of ways to modify tests.)

Sometimes individual achievement batteries are used as "screening" tests to identify students with learning difficulties, or as part of a broader series of individual assessments when a school psychologist conducts a general psychological evaluation. A school district may use individual achievement survey batteries to assess the general educational development of a newly transferred student, or as a double-check on a previously administered group survey test when the results are being questioned for a particular student.

Because both the content and norms of an individual assessment are different from the group test, you should proceed very cautiously when double-checking. You can expect a student's results from the two types of tests to correspond only very roughly.

Two commonly administered individual survey achievement tests are the *Wide Range Achievement Test, Third Edition (WRAT-3)* and the *Peabody Individual Achievement Test–Revised-Normative Update (PIAT-R/NU).* These single instruments contain items that span many ages or grades (essentially ages 5 to adult). Thus, by their very nature they contain few items specifically associated with a given age or grade level. Such tests do not have as much in-depth coverage as group survey tests that have separate levels for each age or grade level. This comment is not necessarily a criticism of these tests. These wide-range tests make a quick assessment of a student's strengths in several basic curricular areas. This quickly obtained assessment helps the teacher determine relatively weak areas needing more in-depth diagnostic follow-up.

The *PIAT-R/NU*'s items are printed on a small easel. Students do not write responses to the multiple-choice items; they must only say or point to the option. Within each subtest the items are arranged in order of difficulty. A student does not take each item; a starting point (called a basal level) and an ending point (called a ceiling level) are established, based on the student's pattern of correct answers and errors.

Using Results to Plan Instruction

Figure 16.6 outlines suggestions for using survey battery information in planning classroom instruction. Other procedures for reviewing test scores appear in Chapter 17. You should review these at this time.

CHOOSING STANDARDIZED TESTS

Survey Achievement Battery Selection

As mentioned, you must examine and review each test individually to decide whether it is appropriate for your school. School officials should keep the following advice in mind before selecting an elementary school survey battery (Gronlund, 1976):

1. Survey batteries measure only part of the outcomes desired for elementary schools. Use additional assessment procedures to evaluate the other outcomes.

2. Specific content in subjects such as social studies and science may become dated quickly. Tests designed to measure broad cognitive skills or levels of educational development become dated less quickly.

3. Tests measuring broad cognitive skills or levels of educational development need to be supplemented by teacher-crafted or standardized tests of specific content.

FIGURE 16.6 A systematic procedure for using the results of a standardized achievement test to plan instruction for a class.

Step 1. Review the class report to determine weaknesses
Use a report that summarizes performance on clusters of items for all students in your class. Within each curriculum area, identify on which clusters your students need improvement most. Match the clusters to your state's standards and determine the class's weakness and strengths with respect to the standards. Use your knowledge of the subject and of your students to verify the areas of greatest need. Don't be afraid to contradict the picture given by the test if you have good evidence that supports the fact that the students know more than they have shown on the test.

Step 2. Establish instructional priorities
Review your list of instructional needs. Put them into an order for instruction. Be sure to teach prerequisite needs first. Concentrate on the most important areas—those that will help students in their further understanding of concepts and principles in the subject.

Step 3. Organize the class for instruction
The test information may help you form small groups of students who have similar instructional needs. Alternately, you could form small groups that have students at different levels of learning so that those who already know the material can help instruct those who have not yet mastered it. You will need to use your own resources to organize your class, as the test cannot do that directly.

Step 4. Plan your instruction before you begin
Be clear about your instructional targets. Look at the test items to get an idea of the types of tasks you want students to learn to do, but remember that you are trying to teach generalizable skills and abilities. The tasks on the test are only a small sample of the domain of tasks implied by the curriculum.

Look to the curriculum to see where the areas of need fit into the larger scheme. Teach within this larger framework, rather than narrowing your teaching to the test items. Create your own assessment instrument for each of the areas of need so you can clarify what you will expect students to do at the end of the lessons. Organize your teaching activities to accomplish these ends.

Step 5. Assess students' progress toward your instructional targets and state's standards
Monitor students' progress through both informal and formal assessments. Observe students as they complete the assignments you give them to see if they are making progress toward your learning targets and state standards. Use performance and paper-and-pencil assessments to monitor their progress in more formal ways. Adjust your teaching for those students who are not making appropriate progress. Give feedback to students by showing them what they are expected to do (i.e., the learning target or state standard), explaining to them what their performance is like now, how it is different from the target performance, and what they have yet to learn to accomplish the target performance.

Step 6. Carry out summative assessment
Use a variety of assessment techniques to assess each student so that you are certain that the student has learned the target and can apply the concepts and principles to appropriate realistic situations. Use performance assessments, extended responses, and objective items in appropriate combinations. Do not limit your assessment to only one format.

4. Each battery has a different mix and emphasis of content and behavior; each is accompanied by various kinds of interpretive aids. Examine a test battery carefully before deciding to purchase it.

Because high school curricula vary so much, choosing a survey battery for this educational level is difficult. Choosing a test at this level requires complete knowledge of a school's major curriculum emphasis and philosophy. School officials should keep the following points in mind before selecting a high school test battery (Gronlund, 1976):

1. Survey batteries that emphasize basic skills (reading, mathematics, language) may be more useful as measures of high school readiness than as measures of high school outcomes (unless a high school program is especially directed toward basic skills development).

2. Some tests are more oriented toward testing specific content than educational development broadly defined. If you want a content-oriented test, review each item on the test carefully to see if the test measures what the school intends.

3. Tests stressing the measurement of levels of educational development that cut across several subject areas rather than measure knowledge and specific content tend to measure more complex skills and global processes.

4. The variety of course offerings at the high school level makes it more necessary than at the elementary level to examine the content of each survey battery carefully.

5. You may find it necessary to supplement a high school survey battery with assessments measuring content knowledge of specific subjects.

6. A practical consideration is the continuity of measurement from elementary to secondary levels. This often means purchasing a high school battery from the same company that published the elementary school battery.

COMPLEMENTING YOUR STATE ASSESSMENT

If your state mandates its own assessment, you will need to take its coverage into account before choosing a published standardized test. Most state assessments have accountability as their main purpose. This is not the case for a published standardized test, which is used primarily to measure individual students' educational growth. Keep the following points in mind if you are trying to select a standardized multilevel achievement test when you are also faced with a state-mandated assessment.

1. *All things being equal, choose a standardized test that requires students to demonstrate learning that is very consistent with your state's standards or curriculum framework.*

2. *If your community does not like the focus of your state-mandated assessment, choose a multilevel achievement test that reflects the community's concerns.* For example, your community may not wish to limit assessment to the higher-order thinking and complex problem solving on which the state assessment focuses. The community may wish to know whether basic skills such as computation, reading comprehension, English writing mechanics, and spelling are being learned.

3. *Plan to use the chosen test over a period of at least 5 years, so that you can track changes in your school district.*

4. *Test at grade levels not tested by the state-mandated assessment to avoid overburdening students and teachers.*

Uses for Single-Subject Tests

If you are teaching in a single subject area, such as Algebra I or 19th-Century English Literature, you may be interested in assessing how well students are performing in just that subject. Multilevel tests are often inappropriate for such courses because they span several grades with relatively few items and thus lack content relevance for a particular course. *For most purposes, a teacher-made test for a subject is most appropriate: It is closest to the course content and contains the emphasis you desire.*

Single-subject or course tests have been found most useful for such purposes as: pretesting to determine the general background of students coming into a course; advanced placement in college courses; exemption from required or introductory courses; contests and scholarship programs that reward general knowledge of a particular subject; and granting college credit for knowledge acquired by independent study, work experience, or other types of nontraditional education. Many tests for specific subjects are listed in the *Mental Measurements Yearbooks*.

HOW TO ADMINISTER STANDARDIZED TESTS

You certainly will be required to administer a standardized assessment to your students, most likely one or more per year. These assessments may be standardized achievement tests, performance assessments, or assessments mandated by your state department of education. Part of the validity of your students' results will depend on how well you follow the standardization procedure specified in the teacher's administration manual.

The Right Way to Prepare Yourself and Students for a Standardized Test

There are two important areas of assessment administration that you directly control and that directly affect the validity of your students' results. One area is how you prepare yourself and the students for the assessment. Standardized assessments, regardless of whether they are performance or multiple-choice formats, require students to be aware of (a) the fact that they will be assessed, (b) what they will be assessed on, (c) the reasons for the assessment, and (d) how their results will be used. Students should be prepared to do their best. You must also be prepared to administer, and perhaps to mark, the assessments. That means you must be familiar with the assessment procedures and materials, prepare the assessment environment so that a valid assessment can be done, understand how to administer the assessment—including what you are permitted to say to the students—and know how to prepare the students for the assessment.

The Right Way to Administer a Standardized Test

A second area in which you need to perform well is in actually administering the assessment. Valid assessment results will depend on how well you carry out your responsibilities during the administration phase. You need to follow the procedures stated in the manual exactly: Otherwise, the assessment results will not be comparable across students and using the norms will be invalid. Also, you need to monitor students to be sure they are following directions, marking their answers in the proper manner, and otherwise attending to the tasks. Figure 16.7 is a checklist of what you

FIGURE 16.7 Checklist for administering a standardized assessment procedure to your students.

Before the assessment date
1. Prepare a schedule for assessment, including dates and times for each component you need to administer.
2. Discuss the upcoming assessments with the students.
   a. Explain the purpose of the assessment.
   b. Explain what they will be doing.
   c. Explain when and how they will receive the results.
   d. Explain how the results will be used.
3. Become familiar with the assessment procedure and the directions for administering it. (Practice taking the assessment yourself.)
4. If proctors are necessary, schedule and train them.
5. Be sure that all the assessment materials are available, that students have pencils and other necessary tools, and that scratch paper and other materials are available.
6. Make any necessary physical adjustments to the room.
7. Make a sign that reads, "Assessing. Please do not disturb us!" Use the sign during the assessment sessions.

During the assessment
1. Follow the directions exactly as given in the directions manual.
2. Monitor students to be sure they are working on the correct pages and activities and are recording their responses properly.
3. Supervise the work of any proctors that are present.
4. Make notes describing any irregularities, either for individual students or for the entire group.

Source: H. D. Hoover, A. N. Hieronymus, D. A. Frisbie, and S. B. Dunbar, 1993a. Copyright © 1993 by The University of Iowa. All rights reserved. Adapted from the *Iowa Tests of Basic Skills, Directions for Administration, Forms K and L., Levels 9–14*, p. 15, with permission of the Riverside Publishing Company.

must do to administer a standardized assessment without lowering its validity.

ETHICAL AND UNETHICAL STUDENT PRACTICE FOR STANDARDIZED TESTS

The question of what type of practice to give students before they take a standardized assessment is an important one for you to answer. Educators do not agree about what is appropriate (Cohen & Hyman, 1991; Mehrens, 1991; Mehrens & Kaminski, 1989; Popham, 1991). The controversy concerns **ethical test preparation practices**. If you prepare students in inappropriate ways, then the validity of their assessment results is questionable. Do certain pre-assessment activities give your students unwarranted advantages that are not available to other students? If your students receive certain types of practice, can you or others still validly interpret their scores? If you teach your students certain responses or answers, can you generalize their assessment results properly?

A Clearly Unethical Teaching Practice

One of the guiding principles for ensuring validity is the **generalizability of assessment results**. (See Figure 3.2.) That is, can you infer a student's performance on the entire curriculum domain from the specific items the student took? If not, the validity of the results is low. For example, suppose there are 100 key concepts in a particular area of social studies. Further, suppose that instead of teaching students strategies for organizing and understanding these concepts and principles, you picked only the four concepts that will appear on a standardized social studies test and taught answers only to the questions about those four concepts. Assuming you are a good teacher, your students would do very well on the test questions related to these concepts, and their test scores would be higher. However, your students would most likely not understand or integrate the broader social studies framework and the full set of concepts the course was supposed to teach. In other words, by narrowing your teaching to only those few tasks that appear on a specific test, you have failed to provide your students with empowering strategies to organize social studies concepts and principles. Further, you cannot interpret their test results as reflecting their general knowledge of the course concepts and principles. By teaching only those four concepts, you invalidated the students' test results and corrupted the students' education.

When you assess a student, you want to generalize from the student's performance to the larger and broader domain of abilities and knowledge that the curriculum framework is supposed to foster. Responses on a particular test or assessment are only signs or pointers to the student's possible performance in the larger domain implied by the learning targets of the curriculum framework.

However, if you give specific practice only on the questions or tasks on the assessment, you focus a student's learning only on these few tasks. It is very unlikely that such narrowly focused instruction and learning can generalize to the broader learning targets that are the real goals of education.

The Range of Ethical to Unethical Practices

You can provide a variety of practice activities to help students improve their performance on an assessment. Which of these is appropriate? The following is list of assessment preparation activities, arranged in order from the most to least legitimate (Mehrens & Kaminski, 1989):

1. Teaching the learning targets in the curriculum without narrowing your teaching to those targets that appear on a standardized assessment.

2. Teaching general test-taking strategies, such as those discussed in Chapter 14.

3. Teaching only those learning targets that specifically match the targets that will appear on the standardized assessment your students will take.

4. Teaching only those learning targets that specifically match the targets that will appear on the standardized assessment your students will take and giving practice using the same types of task formats that will appear on the assessment.

5. Giving your students practice on a published parallel form of the assessment they will take.

6. Giving your students practice on the same questions and tasks that they will take later.

Most educators would agree that the first activity is always ethical because it is the teacher's job to teach the official curriculum. Most educators would also agree that the second activity, teaching students how to take tests and do their best on them, is not unethical. The fifth and sixth activities would always be considered unethical because they narrow instruction to only the specific assessment tasks that your students will be administered and practically eliminate your ability to generalize from the assessment results to the performance domain specified by the curriculum.

Thus, Mehrens and Kaminski (1989) indicate that the boundary between ethical and unethical test preparation practices is somewhere between Activities 3 and 5. They indicate that the deciding factor lies in the degree to which a school wishes to generalize the test results. The closer the activity is to the fifth one, the less able are school officials to generalize students' assessment results to the official curriculum—unless, of course, the official curriculum is identical to the assessment instrument. School officials must realize that the goal of education is to improve students' competence, knowledge, cultural awareness, and thinking skills—not to improve test scores.

Two Guiding Principles

Popham (1991) provides two ethical standards that summarize the principles illustrated in the preceding discussion. You may use them to judge whether you or others in your school are preparing students appropriately for standardized assessments:

- *Professional ethics:* No test-preparation practice should violate the ethical standards of the education profession (p. 13).
- *Educational defensibility:* No test-preparation practice should increase students' test scores without simultaneously increasing student mastery of the content domain tested. (p. 13)

Summary

Types of Tests and Standardized Survey Batteries

- A variety of published achievement tests are available. The chapter distinguished two broad groups: standardized, empirically documented tests and nonstandardized, not empirically documented tests.
- Standardized, empirically documented tests include multilevel tests designed to span several grade levels or age levels and single-level tests designed for only one grade level or course.
- Multilevel tests include achievement survey batteries and criterion-referenced and/or norm-referenced tests in particular curricular areas such as mathematics or reading.
- Single-level tests measure achievement in a particular subject or course such as Algebra I or French II.
- The features of group-administered and individually administered multilevel achievement tests were described and illustrated along with suggestions for interpreting scores and using test results for instructional planning. Specific tests are listed in Appendix K.
- Nonstandardized, not empirically documented tests fail to employ empirical data from samples of subjects to improve and refine tests and to document their degree of reliability and validity.

Appropriate Uses of Standardized Test Results

- Standardized achievement tests can be used for a variety of within-classroom and extraclassroom purposes. The usefulness of a particular standardized achievement test for any of these purposes depends on its curricular relevance to a given school.

Inappropriate Uses of Standardized Test Results

- Criticisms of standardized achievement batteries have been directed toward their intrinsic properties, missing properties, and effects on students and school curricula. Proper test selection and use can overcome many criticisms.
- Among the misuses of achievement test scores are (a) failing to consider the possibility of measurement error, (b) using a single score as the only criterion for important decisions, (c) uncritically accepting a score as a pure measure of a characteristic, and (d) failing to recognize that students' test performances are caused by a complex set of antecedent conditions.

How to Administer Standardized Tests

- You must prepare yourself and your students for taking a standardized assessment, whether this assessment is a paper-and-pencil test or a performance test. The chapter offers suggestions for appropriate ways to undertake these preparations.

Ethical and Unethical Student Practice for Standardized Assessments

- There are also inappropriate or unethical ways to prepare students to take assessments. The chapter describes a continuum of assessment preparation activities from most to least illegitimate, so that you can judge your own behavior using this continuum.

Important Terms and Concepts

Code of Fair Testing Practices in Education (Revised)
Code of Professional Responsibilities in Educational Measurement
computer-prepared narrative reports (building report, item analysis report, profile report)
empirically documented tests
ethical test preparation practices
external uses of test results
generalizability of assessment results
in-level versus out-of-level testing
multilevel survey battery versus single-level test
Professional Ethics Principle and Educational Defensibility Principle
special norms
standardized tests
state-mandated assessments
subtest
test levels
within-classroom uses of test results

Exercises and Applications

1. Using test publishers' catalogs, the *Mental Measurements Yearbooks*, and other resources, identify one published test that fits into each category of the author's scheme for classifying published achievement tests. Share your findings with your classmates.

2. Describe the students, their community, and subject(s) that you teach (or plan to teach). Through self-reflection, give specific examples of how you may misuse achievement test results in this context in each of the following ways. Share your findings with the others in your course.
   a. Failing to consider measurement error when interpreting a student's scores.
   b. Using only the test results for making a decision about a student.
   c. Uncritically interpreting a student's score as measuring a pure trait.
   d. Failing to consider the complex nature of the causes for a particular student's test performance.

3. Evaluate the appropriateness of each of the following standardized test preparation practices using Popham's two ethical principles.
   a. The school uses the latest version of a certain test. A teacher uses a version of the test that is no longer being administered in the school to give students special practice.

FIGURE 16.8 Comparisons of the characteristics of various kinds of published tests with teacher-made tests.

Characteristic	Published tests in the marketplace							Teacher-made tests
	Standardized, empirically documented					Nonstandardized, not empirically documented		
	Multilevel		Single-level			Criterion-referenced tests	Textbook accompaniments	
	Survey batteries	Criterion-referenced tests	Other single-area tests	State-mandated accountability test	Single-course tests			
Content/ objectives covered 1. Common to many schools 2. Specific to one teacher/ school 3. Specific to one text or set of materials								
Intended to measure 1. Growth over time 2. Status on each specific objective in domain 3. Profile of strengths and weaknesses								
Norm-referencing provided 1. Several types of scores 2. Several types of norm groups 3. Spans several grades								
Criterion-referencing provided 1. Many items per objective 2. Diagnosis possible								
Provides materials for interpreting scores to 1. Students 2. Parents 3. Teachers 4. Administrators								
Technical quality 1. Professionally written items. 2. Empirical data on reliability and validity								

b. A teacher copies items from a test that is currently being used in the school and gives these to students for practice.

c. A teacher teaches students general rules and strategies for taking standardized tests, such as how to eliminate options and "guess" when they are not certain, and how to plan their testing time wisely.

d. The curriculum framework calls for learning the grammar rules covered by the test the school uses. The teacher teaches the students how to use these rules to answer the same format of questions that will appear on the test, but does not provide practice in more natural contexts of writing sentences and paragraphs.

e. The curriculum framework calls for learning the grammar rules covered by the test the school uses. The teacher teaches the students how to use these rules to answer the same format of question that will appear on the test, but also teaches them how to apply the rules in their own writing of sentences and paragraphs.

f. A deaf student who is mainstreamed in an inclusive program plans to go to a special postsecondary school for deaf students. For admission, the postsecondary school requires the student to submit results from standardized reading and mathematics tests. The teacher gives the upcoming tests to the student to take home to read a few days ahead of time, then answers any clarifying questions the student has about the vocabulary and the type of strategies that should be used when answering the questions. Later in the week the teacher administers the tests to the student under standardized conditions but with the help of a sign language interpreter.

4. Figure 16.8 lists various types of tests across the top and various characteristics as row headings. For each characteristic, describe the extent to which it is found in each type of test. In the cells in the body of the table, mark:

a. ++ if most tests in that category exhibit this characteristic.

b. + if a few tests in that category exhibit this characteristic.

c. 0 if it is very rare that tests in that category exhibit this characteristic.

5. Using the Internet, locate three states' education departments and descriptions of their state assessment program. (A list of all states' Websites is found on the U.S. Department of Education's Website: http://wdcrobcolp01.ed.gov/Programs/EROD/org_list.cfm?category_ID=SEA.) If your state has an assessment program, be sure to include it as one of the three. Compare the assessment programs in terms of student versus school accountability; objective versus constructed-response assessment; use of standards, teacher development and capacity building; and general objectives and purposes. Share your findings with others in this course.

17 | Interpreting Norm-Referenced Scores

LEARNING TARGETS

After studying this chapter, you should have learned the following:

Three Referencing Frameworks

1. Explain why it is necessary to use both norm-referencing and criterion-referencing frameworks to understand a student's assessment performance properly. [3, 6, 4]

2. Explain the advantages and disadvantages of various types of criterion-referenced scores. [3, 4, 6]

3. Explain the advantages and disadvantages of norm-referenced scores. [3, 4, 6]

4. Explain how a standards-referenced framework combines elements of criterion-referencing and norm-referencing [3, 6, 4]

Using Norms

5. Explain the purposes and usefulness of local, national, and special norm-group comparisons. [3, 4]

6. Apply criteria of relevance, representativeness, and recency to evaluate the quality of norm data. [3, 4]

Norm-Referenced Scores

7. Accurately look up students' norm-referenced scores in standardized test publishers' norm tables. [3]

8. Correctly explain to parents the meaning of the norm-referenced scores their children obtained on standardized tests. [6, 4]

Normal Distributions

9. State the most common misconceptions that some teachers and school administrators hold about normal distributions of student aptitudes, intelligences, and achievements. [6, 4, 7]

Grade-Equivalent Scores

10. State the seven most common misconceptions that some teachers and school administrators hold about grade-equivalent scores. [6, 4, 7]

Interpreting Scores to Parents

11. Use standardized test reports of the students in your class to confirm your own observations about them, identify their patterns of strengths, find possible weaknesses needing remediation, and understand how the group performed as a whole. [3, 4]

Important Terms and Concepts

12. Explain how the terms and concepts listed at the end of this chapter apply to interpreting educational assessment results. [6]

ABOUT THIS CHAPTER

The chapter is organized as follows. First, we explain the three frameworks for interpreting scores: norm-referencing, criterion-referencing, and standards-referencing. Second, we discuss the publishers' norms. We describe the different types of norms, how to use them, and how to evaluate their quality. Third, we show a concept map of the different types of criterion-referenced and norm-referenced scores and how they are related. Fourth, we explain the meaning, use, and interpretation of norm-referenced scores. We discuss percentile ranks, standard scores, normal curve-based scores, and grade-equivalent scores, among others. Fifth, we compare the meaning of the norm-referenced scores and provide guidelines for you to interpret them and explain them to parents.

THREE REFERENCING FRAMEWORKS

Suppose that you took a spelling test and your score was 45, found by giving one point for each correctly spelled word. How well have you performed? Knowing only that your task was "a spelling test" and that your score was 45 leaves you unable to interpret your performance.

Raw scores are the number of points (marks) you assign to a student's performance on an assessment. You may obtain these marks by adding the number of correct answers, the ratings for each task, or the number of points awarded to separate parts of the assessment. As in the preceding spelling score example, a raw score tells a student what he or she "got," but tells very little about the *meaning of the score*.

Practically all educational and psychological assessments require you to use some type of referencing framework to interpret students' performance. A *referencing framework* is a structure you use to compare a student's performance to something external to the assessment itself. An external framework enhances your interpretation of a student's assessment results.

Norm-Referencing Framework

Norm-Referencing You use a **norm-referencing framework** to interpret a student's assessment performance by comparing it to the performance of a well-defined group of other students who have taken the same assessment. The well-defined group of other students is called the **norm group**. To make valid norm-referenced interpretations, all persons in the norm group must have been given the same assessment as your students and under the same conditions (same time limits, directions, equipment and materials, etc.). This is why you must follow administration instructions exactly when administering a standardized achievement test whose results you later will want to interpret through a norm-referenced framework.

To understand a norm-referenced interpretation, let's return to your score on the spelling test. Suppose your raw score of 45 means that your percentile rank (*PR*) is 99—that is, 99% of the persons who took the spelling test have scored lower than 45. Before you congratulate yourself, however, you should determine who is in the norm group to which your raw score is being referenced. You would interpret your performance differently if you knew the norm group was comprised of third graders than if the norm group was comprised of adults.

Validity of Norm-Referenced Interpretations Your norm-referenced interpretations are less valid when the norm group is not well defined. The more you know about who is in the norm group, the better you can interpret a student's performance in a norm-referenced framework. Consider the difference in interpreting your performance on the spelling test, for example, when the norm group is adults in general versus a norm group comprised of adults who have won prizes in national spelling contests.

Norm-Referenced Scores Derived scores make norm-referenced interpretations easier. A more or less standard set of derived scores is now routinely reported for most published tests in education:

1. *Percentile ranks* tell the percentage of persons in a norm group scoring lower than a particular raw score.
2. *Linear standard scores* tell the location of a particular raw score in relation to the mean and standard deviation of a norm group.
3. *Normalized standard scores* tell the location of a particular raw score in relation to a normal distribution fitted to a norm group.
4. *Grade-equivalent scores* tell the grade placement for which a particular raw score is the average for a norm group.

Criterion-Referencing Framework

Beyond Norm-Referencing Norm-referencing is not enough to interpret your score fully: You may be a better speller than other people—whoever they happen to be—but what can you spell? At a minimum, you would need to know the kinds of words in the pool from which those on the spelling test were selected, the number of words selected, and the process used to select the words. Were they really words, or were they nonsense syllables? Were they English words? Were they selected from a list of the most difficult (or easiest) English words? Did the test have 45 words or 500 words? Did the words on the test represent some larger class or domain? Did spelling the words require you to use certain mental processes or to apply certain spelling rules?

These questions are especially important when you need to make absolute interpretations of students' assessment performance—for example, when you need to know which specific learning target your students are having trouble mastering. Norm-referencing provides information to help in your relative interpretations of scores, but frequently these are not enough. Scores that reflect relative achievement such as rank order, for example, may be helpful in picking the best readers, or in sectioning a class into better, good, and poor readers. However, to plan appropriate instruction, eventually you need to know each student's specific reading skills and the particular types of difficulties each student is experiencing. When your diagnosis and prescription are based on students' error patterns or on your analysis of their faulty reasoning or thinking processes, as described in Chapter 13, you must put aside the norm-referencing framework and use a criterion-referencing framework.

Criterion-Referencing You use a **criterion-referencing framework** to infer the kinds of performances a student can do in a domain, rather than the student's relative standing in a norm group. This domain of performance to which you reference a student's assessment results is called the *criterion*. When you teach, the criterion that is of most interest is the domain of performance implied by your state's standards, your curriculum framework, and your lessons' learning targets.

Validity of Criterion-Referenced Interpretations Your criterion-referenced assessment interpretations lose validity when the domain of performances to which you wish to infer your students' status is poorly defined, or when your assessment is a poor sample from that domain. The more you know about the domain from which the tasks on your assessment were sampled, the more validly you can interpret their results. For example, if you did not construct your assessment using clearly defined statements of learning targets, or if your assessment inadequately represents the wide range of performance implied by a clearly defined set of learning targets, then you have only a weak basis for making criterion-referenced interpretations.

You can easily see why by reviewing the spelling example again. Suppose you knew that the spelling domain was the 10,000 most frequently misspelled English words, and that the assessment had been constructed as a sample of 100 words representative of the spelling patterns in this domain. In this case you may interpret your score of 45 on a 100-word assessment as an estimate of the proportion of those 10,000 words you know how to spell. You can see that if there were only 50 words on the assessment, your estimate would be less accurate than when there are 100. A sample of 10 words is even less accurate. Further, if the 100 words did not sample the domain representatively, your estimate would be less accurate also, even though there were 100 words. For example, the 100 words may contain only regular spelling patterns and ignore others. Thus, both the number of items on the assessment and how well they represent the domain contribute to how valid your criterion-referenced interpretation is.

Criterion-Referenced Scores Criterion-referenced assessments do not have well-developed, derived score systems like norm-referenced assessments. Nevertheless, certain types of scores are often used with these assessments:

1. *Percentage*—a number telling the proportion of the maximum points earned by the student (percentage correct, percentage of objectives mastered, etc.).
2. *Speed of performance*—the time a student takes to complete a task, or the number of tasks completed in a fixed amount of time (typing 40 words per minute, running a mile in 5 minutes, completing 25 number facts correctly in 1 minute, etc.).
3. *Quality ratings*—the quality level at which a student performs ("Excellent," rating of "5," "mastery," etc.).
4. *Precision of performance*—the degree of accuracy with which a student completes a task (measuring accurately to the nearest 10th of a meter, weighing accurately to the nearest gram, fewer than 10 typing errors, etc.).

Standards-Referencing Framework

Meeting Standards The NCLB Act of 2001 required states to report the percentage of students who have achieved at three levels—basic, proficient, and advanced—in meeting a state's reading, language arts, mathematics, and science standards. The three levels of achievement in each subject area are specific to a state's particular standards. States use tests that are aligned with their standards to classify a student as attaining basic, proficient, and advanced achievement in each subject area. Because the goal of the NCLB Act is to have all students achieve at the proficient or higher levels (as these levels are defined in each state), there is an additional federal mandate that a state show that it is making adequate yearly progress toward achieving this goal.

Standards-Referencing All of this accountability assessment requires that students' scores on a test be referenced to the standards-defined achievement levels. The immediate testing question that faces a state is what range of test scores is to be called "basic," what range is called "proficient," and what range is called "advanced." Once these ranges of scores are defined, students' scores are referenced to those ranges and interpreted to mean basic, proficient, or advanced achievement in a subject. This is called a **standards-referencing framework** (Young & Zucker, 2004).

Combining Frameworks The standards-referencing framework is accomplished by combining aspects of the criterion-referencing and the norm-referencing frameworks. On the criterion-referencing side, test items are selected to match or align with the state's standards. On the norm-referencing side, the state administers the test to the students and gathers information about the performance of students on each test item. A common procedure is then to order the items from easiest to most difficult. Panels of experts (including teachers) use this ordered list of test items, along with their knowledge of the subject area and students, to set the score that forms the boundary between each achievement level. If a student's score falls between the lower and upper boundaries of a category, the proficiency category, for example, then the student is classified into that category (e.g., proficient.)

Adequate Yearly Progress The boundaries for basic, proficient, and advanced are set using the population of students who took the test the first year. This group serves as the baseline group, so that in subsequent years, the state can measure whether its yearly progress is adequate. It does this by determining each year the percentage of students that have scores within each achievement level. Statistical and practical rules are established to determine whether the percentage of students in the proficient and above categories increase enough to represent adequate yearly progress. The goal, as we said, is for all students in a state to have scores within or above the proficient level.

USING NORMS

Importance of Norms

Norm-referencing indicates how one student's performance compares to the performances of others. You should realize, however, that simply comparing students with one another is not a very good reason for assessing them (Hoover et al., 1993b). Here are the major reasons for assessing students:

1. To describe, within each subject area, the performances a student has achieved.
2. To describe, within each subject area, student deficiencies that need further improvement.
3. To describe, across the curriculum, which subjects are the student's strengths and weaknesses.
4. To describe, within each subject area, the amount of educational development (progress) a student has made over the course of one or more years.

The first two purposes are best served within a criterion-referencing framework. In essence, this requires you to look carefully at a student's performance, item by item, and compare it to your learning targets.

The second two purposes are best served within a norm-referencing framework. A student's relative strength in reading and mathematics, for example, cannot be described on purely a criterion-referenced basis. You can describe what a student can do in each area, but you need a norm basis to conclude whether these are relative strengths or weaknesses. A teacher may say, for example, that a student is able to solve routine linear and quadratic equations in mathematics and is able to read with comprehension age-appropriate stories. However, which is the stronger area? Normative information can determine this.

Standardized tests describe students' relative strengths and weaknesses in different curricular areas because of the normative information they provide. The same group of students at the same grade level (the norm group) is administered tests covering several curricular areas. Thus, if fourth-grader Blake ranks at the top of the norm group in mathematics but in the middle of the norm group in reading, we know that of the two subjects, Blake is stronger in mathematics.

The fourth purpose mentioned earlier—measuring educational growth and development—also requires norm-referencing. Norm groups provide the basis for defining an educational development scale (such as the grade-equivalent scale) across different grade levels. We assess a student once every year or two, each time referencing the results to this developmental scale. We measure growth by the student's progress along this scale.

The remainder of this chapter discusses the various norm-referenced scores and scales used in educational assessment. As a teacher, you will not be required to create growth scales or calculate scale scores. However, you will be required to interpret and to use such scales and scores with your students. In addition, you will be expected to explain the meaning of reports of these scores to your students and their parents.

TYPES OF NORM GROUPS

Before you can understand and use norm-referenced scores you need to understand the meaning of norms and norm groups. As we've already stated, a norm group is the large representative sample of students for which test manuals report performance. The performance of a norm group on a particular assessment represents the present, average status of that group of students on that particular assessment. A group's current average does not represent a standard, however, nor does it establish what your school or your students should attain. Your state's content and performance standards and your curriculum's learning targets tell you what students should achieve. Comparing your students and school to norm groups can help you, however, decide the general range of performance to expect from your students, provided your students are similar to those in the norm group. As you will see, test publishers may provide information on several different groups when reporting norm-referenced scores.

Multiple Norm-Group Comparisons

Ordinarily, a student is a member of more than one group. For example, a 14-year-old, eighth-grade boy with a hearing impairment took a standardized mathematics concepts test and obtained a raw score of 32. This may represent a percentile rank of:

- 99 in a national group of deaf eighth graders.
- 94 in the test publishers' national eighth-grade standardization sample.
- 89 in the group of eighth graders in his local community.
- 80 in the group of eighth graders currently enrolled with him in an advanced mathematics course.

Depending on the decisions you must make, referencing a student's score to more than one norm group may be in order. Vocational counseling decisions, for example, may require that you compare a student's profile of abilities and achievements to each of several occupational or vocational groups about which the student is seeking career information. Comparing the person only to "students in general" may offer less information for career exploration.

Local Norms

For many of your norm-referenced interpretations, the most appropriate group with which you should compare a student is the **local norm group**: the group of students in the same grade in the same school district. It is this group with which you and the students will interact the most. Local percentile ranks or standard scores are easy to compile for a school's testing program, and your director of testing should provide them to you every time a standardized test is administered. Publishers also offer this service for their customers—frequently at extra cost, however.

National Norms

Most norm-referenced, standardized achievement and aptitude batteries have what are called **national norms**. In principle, the national norm groups are supposed to be representative of the students in the country, and some publishers expend a great deal of effort to ensure representativeness. But each publisher uses a somewhat different definition of what constitutes a truly representative national sample and conducts the sampling processes differently. The result is that the norms from different publishers are not comparable. You should note, however, that no publisher's norming sample exactly mirrors the nation's schools. A school's participation in a publisher's norming sample is voluntary. Sometimes this creates a self-selection bias in a given publisher's norms that may distort the norms in favor of schools that have used that publisher's tests in the past (Baglin, 1981). A more detailed description of how publishers obtain norming samples is given in Chapter 18.

National norms need not be composed simply of students in general at a grade level. A publisher may provide

separate male/female norms or may provide separate norms for students with certain disabilities. Sometimes modal-age norms are provided. **Modal-age norms** include, from among all students at a particular grade level, only those near the most typical chronological age for that grade.

Special Norm Groups

For some tests **special norm groups** are formed. Examples include students with deafness or blindness, students with mental retardation, students enrolled in a certain course of study or curriculum, and students attending regional schools. A student may belong to more than one special group, of course.

School Averages Norms

School averages norms consist of a tabulation of the average (mean) score from each school building in a national sample of schools and provide information on the relative ordering of these averages (means). This distribution of averages is much less variable than the distribution of individual student scores. Figure 17.1 illustrates this difference in variability for one publisher's reading test.

If your school principal wants to know how the school's third-grade average score compares with that of other school buildings, then the principal needs to use school averages norms. For individual students' norms, a distribution of individual scores is made and used as the basis for norm-referencing. But individual student scores vary widely, so much so that comparing a school's average to that group may lead to misinterpretations.

Study the following example to get some idea of what your school district may gain from using school averages norms.

Example

Example of how using the wrong norms may lead to underestimating how well a school is doing

In Lincoln School the average spring fifth-grade developmental standard score on the *Iowa Tests of Basic Skills* (Reading Comprehension subtest) is 250 (see Figure 17.1). The principal looked up this number in the individual student norms table and erroneously concluded that the school ranks higher than 85% (PR = 85 for individuals) of the schools. (In Figure 17.1, look at the row labeled "*NPR of Avg. SS: Student Norms*.") Actually, the school is much better, ranking at the top 1% (PR = 99 for school averages, "*NPR of Avg. SS: School Norms*").

In general, if someone uses individual score norms erroneously and the school is above average, the results will underestimate that school's standing among other schools; those whose schools are below average will overestimate

FIGURE 17.1 Comparison of the distributions of students' scores and school averages for the Reading Comprehension subtest of the *Iowa Tests of Basic Skills*, Grade 5, spring norms.

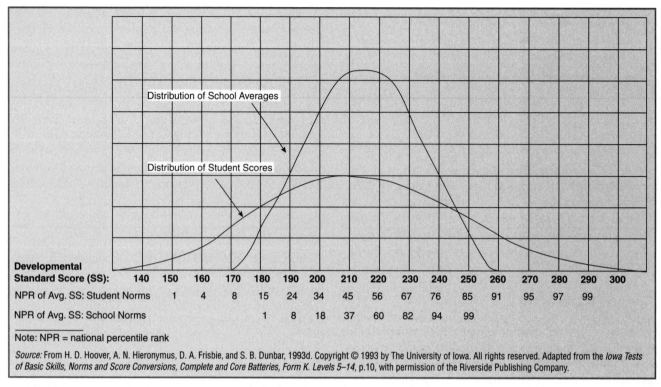

Developmental Standard Score (SS):	140	150	160	170	180	190	200	210	220	230	240	250	260	270	280	290	300
NPR of Avg. SS: Student Norms		1	4	8	15	24	34	45	56	67	76	85	91	95	97	99	
NPR of Avg. SS: School Norms					1	8	18	37	60	82	94	99					

Note: NPR = national percentile rank

Source: From H. D. Hoover, A. N. Hieronymus, D. A. Frisbie, and S. B. Dunbar, 1993d. Copyright © 1993 by The University of Iowa. All rights reserved. Adapted from the *Iowa Tests of Basic Skills, Norms and Score Conversions, Complete and Core Batteries, Form K. Levels 5–14*, p.10, with permission of the Riverside Publishing Company.

their standing among other schools. You can verify this principle by checking several developmental standard score values and percentile ranks in Figure 17.1.

Not all publishers provide school averages norms. Some publishers say that school averages norms mix together very small and very large schools. They say that mixing schools that are very different makes the data in a school averages norms table difficult to interpret correctly.

Using Publishers' Norms

Know When the Assessment Was Normed You obtain the most accurate estimate of a student's standing in a norm group when the student is tested on a date nearest the time of year the publisher established the norms. Publishers commonly interpolate and extrapolate to develop norm tables: They may provide spring norm tables, for example, even though no tests were actually administered to the norm group in the spring. Each publisher's empirical norming dates are different, but the publisher should state the dates in the test manual or technical report. To be accurate, your school should administer a standardized test within 2 or 3 weeks before or after the midpoint date of the publisher's empirical norming period.

Criteria for Evaluating Norms It is generally accepted (APA et al., 1974) that published norms data should satisfy three Rs: relevance, representativeness, and recency. **Relevance** means that the norm group(s) a publisher provides should

be the group(s) to which you will want to compare your students. **Representativeness** means that the norm sample must be based on a carefully planned sample. The test publisher should provide you with information about the subclassifications (gender, age, socioeconomic level, etc.) used to ensure representativeness. Remember that the sample size is not as crucial as its representativeness. (Of course, if the population of students is very large, a representative sample should necessarily be large.)

Recency means that the norms are based on current data. As the curriculum, schooling, and social and economic factors change, so will students' performance on tests. Further, if your school uses the same form of a test year after year, scores will generally increase because the students become familiar with the format, and teachers tend to prepare students specifically for that test (Linn, Graue, & Sanders, 1990; Shepard, 1990; Wiser & Lenke, 1987). If the norms are not recent, they will mislead, conveying the impression that your students are learning better than they really are.

Using Norms Tables

Test manuals contain tables—called *norms tables*—for converting raw scores to different kinds of norm-referenced scores. No computation is required: You need "only" look up the score. Only is in quotes because, as trivial a task as it may seem, looking up scores in a table and copying them into a student's record is something teachers seem to have a hard time doing correctly. Studies of the kinds of errors found in federal program evaluations indicate that using the wrong norms table and misreading a table are common problems (Crane & Bellis, 1978; Finley, 1977; Johnson & Thomas, 1979; Moyer, 1979). Specimen tables are shown later in this chapter, along with a discussion of the particular scores, so that you can practice using the tables.

OVERVIEW OF NORM-REFERENCED SCORES

Norm-referenced scores are derived from the raw scores of an assessment. You should be aware that many types of norm-referenced scores exist. Space permits discussion of only the ones you will most often encounter, which are represented in the concept map shown in Figure 17.2. If you are interested in pursuing the study of norm-referenced scores in greater detail, consult the very readable book, *Test Scores and What They Mean* (Lyman, 1998).

PERCENTILE RANKS

We begin at the leftmost branch of norm-referencing schemes in Figure 17.2. The **percentile rank** tells the percentage of the students in a norm group that have scored *lower* than the raw score in question. The percentile rank is perhaps the most useful and easily understood norm-referenced score. Figure 17.3 is an example of a

publisher's norms table that gives percentile ranks for each raw score.

The raw score obtained from the assessment is located in the correct column in the body of the table, and the corresponding percentile rank is read out. For example, suppose a seventh grader named Veronica takes the *Differential Aptitude Tests (DAT)* on October 23, and she scores 48 in Mechanical Reasoning. Her percentile rank from the norms table in the last example is 98. She is above average in the norm group of seventh-grade females in mathematics; her raw score exceeds 98% of the females in the standardization group.

Notice there are three sets of percentile ranks in the example table—one for the seventh-grade boys, one for the seventh-grade girls, and one for the combined group. This is common practice for norm-referenced assessments in which there are large differences between males and females.

A raw score of 48 has a percentile rank of 90 for boys. This lower percentile rank for boys for the same raw score reflects that seventh-grade boys do much better as a group on this Mechanical Reasoning test. As a result, 48 does not rank as high for boys as it does for girls. When the boys and girls are combined, the resulting distribution is shown in the "Combined" column of the table in the last example.

Which gender norms should teachers and counselors use? The answer depends on how they will use the test scores. The *DAT*, for example, provides a profile of each student's strengths and weaknesses in eight cognitive areas.

FIGURE 17.2 Organization of major score-referencing schemes.

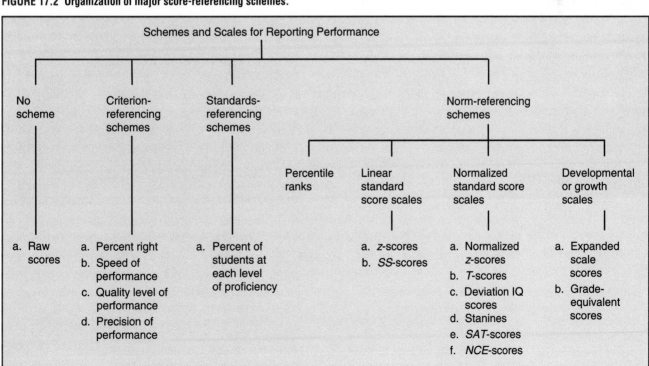

FIGURE 17.3 Example of a percentile norms table: *Differential Aptitude Tests, Level 1, Form C.*

MECHANICAL REASONING											
MALE				FEMALE				COMBINED			
Raw Score	%-ile Rank	Sta-nine	Scaled Score	Raw Score	%-ile Rank	Sta-nine	Scaled Score	Raw Score	%-ile Rank	Sta-nine	Scaled Score
60	99	9	343	60	99	9	343	60	99	9	343
59	99	9	330	59	99	9	330	59	99	9	330
58	99	9	316	58	99	9	316	58	99	9	316
57	99	9	307	57	99	9	307	57	99	9	307
56	99	9	301	56	99	9	301	56	99	9	301
55	99	9	296	55	99	9	296	55	99	9	296
54	99	9	292	54	99	9	292	54	99	9	292
53	98	9	288	53	99	9	288	53	99	9	288
52	97	9	285	52	99	9	285	52	99	9	285
51	95	8	282	51	99	9	282	51	98	9	282
50	94	8	279	50	99	9	279	50	97	9	279
49	92	8	277	49	99	9	277	49	97	9	277
48	90	8	274	48	98	9	274	48	95	8	
47	88	7	272		98	9	272	47			
46	85	7				9	270	46			
45	82	7				9	268				
44	79					9	266				234
				23	15				14	3	232
				22	14				13	3	231
				21	13	2		21	10	2	229
			227	20	12	2		20	8	2	227
19	6	2	226	19	10	2	226	19	7	2	226
18	5	2	224	18	9	2	224	18	5	2	224
17	4	2	222	17	7	2	222	17	4	2	222
16	3	1	220	16	6	2	220	16	3	1	220
15	2	1	218	15	4	1	218	15	3	1	218
14	2	1	216	14	3	1	216	14	2	1	216
13	1	1	214	13	2	1	214	13	2	1	214
12	1	1	212	12	2	1	212	12	1	1	212
11	1	1	209	11	1	1	209	11	1	1	209
10	1	1	207	10	1	1	207	10	1	1	207
9	1	1	204	9	1	1	204	9	1	1	204
8	1	1	201	8	1	1	201	8	1	1	201
7	1	1	198	7	1	1	198	7	1	1	198
6	1	1	194	6	1	1	194	6	1	1	194
5	1	1	190	5	1	1	190	5	1	1	190
4	1	1	185	4	1	1	185	4	1	1	185
3	1	1	178	3	1	1	178	3	1	1	178
2	1	1	169	2	1	1	169	2	1	1	169
1	1	1	155	1	1	1	155	1	1	1	155

Teachers and counselors use this profile to help a student plan for further schooling and careers. The *DAT* publishers encourage using separate-gender norms:

> Although at first glance it may appear that reporting norms for females and males separately represents an undesirable form of sex discrimination; in fact, exactly the opposite may be true.
>
> The two sexes typically score differently on some tests of the DAT. In particular, males tend to score higher than females on the Mechanical Reasoning test and to a lesser extent on the Space Relations test, while females earn higher scores on the Perceptual Speed and Accuracy test and to a lesser extent on the Spelling test. Some of these differences may be of considerable consequence in educational and vocational planning. . . .
>
> The use of separate-sex norms not only provides the opportunity for both males and females to be compared with the performance of students of the same sex, but also with students of the opposite sex. . . .

In spite of the recent changes in the job world, there are still many career fields dominated by one sex or the other. Thus, in counseling a female who wishes to enter a mechanical field, her scores on the Mechanical Reasoning test should be compared with those of males at the same grade level. On the other hand, in counseling a male who wishes to enter a clerical or an editorial field, his score on the Perceptual Speed and Accuracy test, as well as Spelling, should be compared with those of females at the same grade level. . . .

Because females and males tend to perform about the same on many of the tests of the DAT, it is entirely possible that, with the increasing changes in the job market, the sex differences . . . will diminish over time. (Psychological Corporation, 1991, pp. 31–33)

Be sure to use the norms table that corresponds to the time of year during which the student takes the assessment. In our example, a raw score of 48 in the fall of the year corresponds to a percentile rank of 99. If you looked up a raw score of 48 in the spring norms table, it would have a slightly lower percentile rank. This lower percentile rank reflects that students learn or improve during the year.

As with all scores, you should not interpret percentile ranks too precisely. For example, a student with a percentile rank of 44 and a student with a percentile rank of 46 differ little. Therefore, for many educational decisions you should interpret these scores as essentially equivalent. Some publishers, to reflect that all scores contain measurement error, report percentile bands or uncertainty intervals instead of a single percentile rank. These percentile bands are based on the assessment's standard error of measurement (see Chapter 4).

The advantages and limitations of percentile ranks are summarized as follows:

Advantages

1. Easily understood by pupils, parents, teachers, and others.
2. Clearly reflect the norm-referenced character of the interpretation.
3. Permit a person's performance to be compared to a variety of norm groups.
4. Can be used to compare a student's relative standing in each of several achievement or ability areas.

Limitations

5. Can be confused with percentage correct scores.
6. Can be confused with some other types of two-digit derived scores.
7. Differences between *PR*s in the middle of the scale tend to be overinterpreted. Differences of the same magnitude near the tails of a distribution tend to be underinterpreted.

Because percentile ranks are easy to understand, your school district will most likely report them. Percentile ranks are also easy to calculate. Figure I.8 in Appendix I shows the procedure. The same procedure can be used for results from your classroom or for your entire district.

Remember that percentile ranks are specific to the group being referenced. After your students take a standardized test, the publisher will probably report both the **local percentile ranks** and the **national percentile ranks**. Your student Robert, for example, may have a national percentile rank of 40 and a local percentile rank of 30. Local percentile ranks are lower than national percentile ranks only when the population of students in a local school system scores higher, on the average, than the national standardization sample. You must keep in mind the reference group when you interpret percentile ranks.

LINEAR STANDARD SCORES

A **linear standard score** tells how far a raw score is from the mean of the norm group, the distance being expressed using standard deviation units.[1] The second branch of the norm-referencing schemes diagram in Figure 17.2 shows two types of linear standard scores. Both are discussed in this section.

In general, linear standard scores have the same-shaped distribution as the raw scores from which they are derived (this is not true of percentile ranks and nonlinear standard scores) and can be used to make two distributions more comparable by placing them on the same numerical scale. Linear standard scores are called linear because if you plot each raw score against its corresponding linear standard score in a graph and then connect these points, you will always have a straight line.

z-Scores

The fundamental linear standard score is the **z-score**, which tells the number of standard deviation units a raw score is above (or below) the mean of a given distribution. Other linear standard scores are computed from z-scores. Equation 17.1 explains.

$$z = \frac{X - M}{SD} \qquad \text{[Eq. 17.1]}$$

where

X represents the raw score

M represents the mean (average) raw score of the group

SD represents the standard deviation of the raw scores for that group

[1]The standard deviation is an index that measures the spread of scores in a distribution. The standard deviation is denoted *SD* in this book and is explained in Appendix I.

Here is an example of how to apply this equation:

Example

Example of calculating a linear z-score using Equation 17.1

Suppose Ashley's raw score was 38 on Test A. Suppose further that the test mean is 44 and the standard deviation is 4. The corresponding z-score is calculated as follows:

$$z = \frac{38 - 44}{4} = \frac{-6}{4} = -1.5$$

The z-score tells the number of standard deviations a raw score is above or below the mean. For example, if a student's raw score falls below the mean a distance equal to one and one half times the standard deviation of the group, the student's z-score equals -1.50. A z-score is negative when the raw score is below the mean, positive when the raw score is above the mean, and equal to zero when the raw score is exactly equal to the mean.

An advantage of using z-scores is that they communicate students' norm-referenced achievement expressed as a distance away from the mean. In many groups, the majority of students' scores cluster near the mean, usually within one standard deviation on either side of the mean. A distance of one standard deviation above the mean is $z = +1.0$; a distance of one standard deviation below the mean is $z = -1.0$. Thus, you would interpret a student whose z-score is between $+1.0$ and -1.0 as having typical or average attainment. (Remember, this is a norm-referenced framework, not a criterion-referenced framework. That is, the interpretation is relative to others and not absolute.) Similarly, you would interpret a student with $z = -1.5$ or less as having atypically low attainment because few students have z-scores of -1.5 or less. You interpret a student with $z = +1.5$ or greater as having atypically high attainment because relatively few students attain z-scores of $+1.50$ or greater.

Another advantage of using z-scores is to put raw scores with different metrics on the same norm-referenced scale. Consider the following example, in which the same students are measured in both pounds and kilograms. Notice what happens when each student's measurements are transformed to z-scores.

Example

Example showing how a student's z-scores remain the same even though the measurement scale changes

	Weight in kilograms		Weight in pounds	
Student	X	z	X	z
A	48	−1.52	105.2	−1.52
B	52	−0.17	114.4	−0.17
C	54	−0.51	118.8	−0.51
D	6	1.18	123.2	1.18

Even though the pounds mean and standard deviation are different from the kilograms mean and standard deviation, the students' relative positions in the distributions are the same. This is expressed by the z-scores (which are identical for pounds and kilograms), not by the pounds and kilograms raw scores.

The z-score has several practical disadvantages. It is difficult to explain to students and parents, because understanding it requires an understanding of the mean and standard deviation. Another practical disadvantage is that plus and minus signs are used. Transcription errors, resulting in omitted or interchanged algebraic signs, are frequent. Further, you will find it difficult to explain to students (or parents) why assessment performances are reported as negative and/or fractional numbers. For example, a student may say, "I got 15 of the 45 questions right. How could my score be -1.34?" Likewise, the decimal point is subject to frequent transcription error.

These practical problems are easily overcome, however, by transforming the z-score to other types of scores. These additional transformations maintain the conceptual norm-referenced advantage of z-scores while overcoming their practical limitations.

SS-Scores

The second type of score under the linear standard score branch of Figure 17.2 is the SS-score. An **SS-score** tells the location of a raw score in a distribution having a mean of 50 and a standard deviation of 10. To remedy some of the disadvantages of z-scores, some publishers apply a modification (transformation) to eliminate both the negative scores and the fractional portion of the z-scores. Equation 17.2 for an SS-score shows how these two things are accomplished:

$$SS = 10z + 50$$
$$= (10 \text{ times the } z\text{-score}) + 50 \qquad \text{[Eq. 17.2]}$$

First, z-scores are computed; then, each z-score is transformed to an SS-score: Each z is multiplied by 10, the product rounded to the nearest whole number, and finally 50 is added. Multiplying by 10 and rounding eliminates the z-score's decimal. Adding 50 eliminates the z-score's negative value. Here is an example of how to use the equation.

Example

Example showing how a student's z-score is transformed into an SS-score.

Suppose Ashley's z-score was computed to be -1.5. (See the earlier example.) To convert this to an SS-score, multiply it by 10 and add 50 to the result. Thus,

$$SS = 10(-1.5) + 50$$
$$= -15 + 50 = 35$$

The result of applying this conversion to the z-scores is that the distribution of SS-scores will have a mean of 50 and a standard deviation of 10. Once you know this fact, you can interpret anyone's *SS*-score, essentially by doing a mental conversion back to a *z*-score.

> ### Example
>
> *Example showing how to interpret a student's SS-score by converting it back to a z-score*
>
> Ashley's *SS*-score is 35; a score of 35 is 15 points or 1.5 standard deviations below 50, the mean. Thus, Ashley's *z*-score is −1.5.

SS-scores have the advantage of not changing the shape of the original raw score distribution. The distribution of *SS*-scores always has a mean of 50 and a standard deviation of 10. The *SS*-score is interpretable in terms of standard deviation units while avoiding negative numbers and decimal fractions. A disadvantage is that a person needs to understand the concepts of standard deviation and linear transformation to interpret them.

Comparison of Linear Standard Scores

It may help you understand these scores if we display the numerical relationship between them. Because all linear standard score systems reflect essentially the same information, interpreting their meaning is easy once you know the multiplier and the added constant. The next example shows how each type of score is related to the other and to the raw scores.[2]

> ### Example
>
> *Example comparing z-scores and SS-scores for the same raw score*
>
> | Raw score in a group with $M = 41$ and $SD = 3$ | Linear standard scores corresponding to each raw score | |
> | --- | --- | --- |
> | | z-score | SS-score |
> | 32 | −3.0 | 20 |
> | 35 | −2.0 | 30 |
> | 38 | −1.0 | 40 |
> | 41 | 0.0 | 50 |
> | 44 | +1.0 | 60 |
> | 47 | +2.0 | 70 |
> | 50 | +3.0 | 80 |

NORMAL DISTRIBUTIONS

Shortly we will discuss the normalized standard score branch of Figure 17.2. However, first we need to discuss normal distributions of scores.

[2]The values of *M* and *SD* have been set arbitrarily.

Definition

Assessment developers have found it advantageous to transform the scores to a common distributional form: a normal distribution. A **normal distribution**, sometimes called a *normal curve*, is a mathematical model invented in 1733 by Abraham deMoivre (Pearson, 1924). It is defined by a particular equation that depends on two specific numbers: the mean and the standard deviation, signifying that many normal distributions exist and each has a different mean and/or standard deviation. Figure 17.4 shows several different normal curves. Each of these was obtained by using the normal curve equation and plotting points on a graph. In Figure 17.4 (A), each normal distribution has the same mean but a different standard deviation. Although each is centered on the same point on the *X*-scale, some appear flatter and more spread out because their standard deviation is larger. Figure 17.4 (B) shows three normal curves, each with the same standard deviation but each with a different mean. The degree of spread is the same for each, but each is centered on a different point on the score scale.

Every normal curve is smooth and continuous; each has a symmetrical, bell-shaped form. In theory, a normal curve never touches the baseline (horizontal axis) but is asymptotic to it, extending out to infinity in either direction from the mean. Graphs of actual raw-score distributions are nonsymmetrical and jagged. For actual raw-score distributions, the lowest possible score is 0 and the highest possible score equals the total number of items on the assessment. An idea of how an actual distribution compares to the mathematically defined normal curve may be obtained from Figure 17.5. Both distributions have the

FIGURE 17.4 Illustrations of different normal distributions.

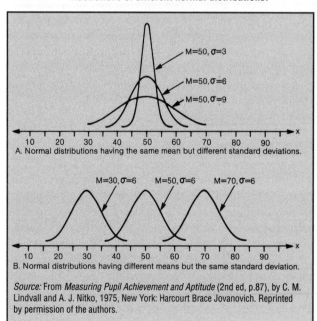

A. Normal distributions having the same mean but different standard deviations.

B. Normal distributions having different means but the same standard deviation.

Source: From *Measuring Pupil Achievement and Aptitude* (2nd ed, p.87), by C. M. Lindvall and A. J. Nitko, 1975, New York: Harcourt Brace Jovanovich. Reprinted by permission of the authors.

FIGURE 17.5 Example of a mathematically defined normal curve (smooth curve) superimposed on an actual distribution (histogram) of average eighth-grade mathematics standard scores for 575 schools. Both distributions have the same mean and standard deviation.

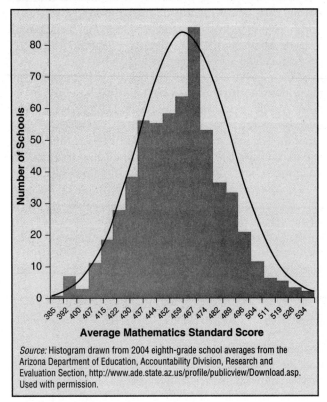

Average Mathematics Standard Score

Source: Histogram drawn from 2004 eighth-grade school averages from the Arizona Department of Education, Accountability Division, Research and Evaluation Section, http://www.ade.state.az.us/profile/publicview/Download.asp. Used with permission.

same mean and the same standard deviation. This normal curve approximates the actual distribution but does not match it exactly.

Natural Law Versus Normal Distributions

Early users of normal curves believed that somehow natural laws dictated that nearly all human characteristics were distributed in a random or chance fashion around a mean or average value. This view of the normal curve's applicability was, perhaps, begun by deMoivre (1756), but it was adamantly held to be true for intellectual and moral qualities by Quetelet (1748) (Dudycha & Dudycha, 1972; Landau & Lazarsfeld, 1968).

This thought—that somehow the distributions of human characteristics are by nature normal distributions—has carried over to mental measurement. It is frequently held, too, that because assessment scores have a bell-shaped distribution, this indicates that not just the scores but also the human abilities *underlying* the scores are normally distributed. This converse statement is, of course, not true. The assessment's score distribution depends not only on the underlying abilities of the persons tested but also on the properties of the assessment procedure itself. An assessment developer can, by judicious selection of tasks, make the score distribution have any shape: rectangular,

skewed bimodal, symmetrical, and so on (Lord, 1953). (See Appendix I for shapes of distributions.) These nonnormal score distribution shapes could appear in the data, for example, even though the underlying ability of the group is normal in form. Similarly, score distributions could appear to be normal in shape even though the underlying ability of the group is non-normal in form.

From your own experience, you know that you can control the shape of a test score distribution. For example, if all items on a test are easy, there will be a lot of high scores and few low scores. A very difficult test will have many low scores and few high scores. The point is, the normal distribution is a convenient model, but you should not believe it is a natural representation of educational achievement outcomes.

Percentile Ranks and *z*-Scores in a Normal Distribution

To understand the relationship between percentile ranks and normal curve *z*-scores you need to study carefully the graph at the top of Figure 17.6. If we cut up a normal distribution into sections one standard deviation wide, each section will have a fixed percentage of cases (see Figure 17.6) or **area under the normal curve**. For example, a section that is one standard deviation wide and located just above the mean contains approximately 34% of the area. The comparable section just below the mean contains, by symmetry, 34% as well. Together those two sections contain 68% of the area. Thus, 68% of the area in a normal distribution will be within one standard deviation of the mean; 95% will be within two standard deviations; and 99.7% of the area will fall within three standard deviations. Therefore, if a distribution is normal, nearly all of the scores will span a range equivalent to six standard deviations.

You can use these facts about the percentage of cases in various segments to determine the correspondence between percentile ranks and *z*-scores in a normal distribution. To emphasize that we are speaking only of a normal distribution, Figure 17.6 denotes the *z*-scores as z_n. This percentile rank correspondence, the same for all normal distributions, permits an easy interpretation of standard scores in normal distributions. For example, look at the graph in Figure 17.6 and the two scales below the graph. The percentage of cases below $z_n = -2.00$ is 2.27% (= 0.13 + 2.14). (Figure 17.6 also shows *T*-scores, which we will explain later in this chapter.) Thus, in a normal distribution the percentile rank corresponding to $z_n = -2.00$ is (rounded) 2. Other z_n-scores' percentile ranks can be computed similarly from Figure 17.6, as shown in the examples below. The chart under the drawing in Figure 17.6 provides more complete information on percentile rank correspondences between z_n-scores and normal curves.

FIGURE 17.6 Relationships among percentile ranks, *z*-scores, and *T*-scores in a normal distribution.

%ile rank	z_n	T	%ile rank	z_n	T	%ile rank	z_n	T	%ile rank	z_n	T
0.05	-2.6	24									
1	-2.3	27	26	-0.6	44	51	0.0	50	76	0.7	57
2	-2.1	29	27	-0.6	44	52	0.1	51	77	0.7	57
3	-1.9	31	28	-0.6	44	53	0.1	51	78	0.8	58
4	-1.8	32	29	-0.6	44	54	0.1	51	79	0.8	58
5	-1.7	33	30	-0.5	45	55	0.1	51	80	0.8	58
6	-1.6	34	31	-0.5	45	56	0.2	52	81	0.9	59
7	-1.5	35	32	-0.5	45	57	0.2	52	82	0.9	59
8	-1.4	36	33	-0.4	46	58	0.2	52	83	1.0	60
9	-1.3	37	34	-0.4	46	59	0.2	52	84	1.0	60
10	-1.3	37	35	-0.4	46	60	0.3	53	85	1.0	60
11	-1.2	38	36	-0.4	46	61	0.3	53	86	1.1	61
12	-1.2	38	37	-0.3	47	62	0.3	53	87	1.1	61
13	-1.1	39	38	-0.3	47	63	0.3	53	88	1.2	62
14	-1.1	39	39	-0.3	47	64	0.4	54	89	1.2	62
15	-1.0	40	40	-0.3	47	65	0.4	54	90	1.3	63
16	-1.0	40	41	-0.2	48	66	0.4	54	91	1.3	63
17	-0.9	41	42	-0.2	48	67	0.4	54	92	1.4	64
18	-0.9	41	43	-0.2	48	68	0.5	55	93	1.5	65
19	-0.9	41	44	-0.2	48	69	0.5	55	94	1.6	66
20	-0.8	42	45	-0.1	49	70	0.5	55	95	1.7	67
21	-0.8	42	46	-0.1	49	71	0.6	56	96	1.8	68
22	-0.8	42	47	-0.1	49	72	0.6	56	97	1.9	69
23	-0.7	43	48	-0.1	49	73	0.6	56	98	2.1	71
24	-0.7	43	49	-0.0	50	74	0.6	56	99	2.3	73
25	-0.7	43	50	-0.0	50	75	0.7	57	99.9	3.1	81

*Values are rounded. To "normalize" scores, enter table with actual percentile rank and read out z_n or T.

Example

How to determine the percentile rank corresponding to selected z_n-scores in a normal distribution

z_n	PR (rounded)	How calculated
3.0	0.1	= 0.13
2.0	2	= 0.13 + 2.14
1.0	16	= 0.13 + 2.14 + 13.59
0.0	50	= 0.13 + 2.14 + 13.59 + 34.13
1.0	84	= 50 + 34.13
2.0	98	= 50 + 34.13 + 13.59
3.0	99.9	= 50 + 34.13 + 13.59 + 2.14

NORMALIZED STANDARD SCORES

Now that you have a little background on the meaning of a normal curve, let's return to the third branch of Figure 17.2: normalized standard scores. The figure shows five types of normalized standard scores. We will discuss all of them in this section.

Test publishers may transform raw scores to a new set of scores that is distributed normally (or nearly so). Such transformation changes the shape of the original distribution, squeezing and stretching the scale to make it conform to a normal distribution. Once this is accomplished, various types of standard scores can be derived, and each can have an appropriate normal curve interpretation. The general name for these derived scores is **normalized standard scores**. These are also termed *area transformations*, as opposed to linear transformations, which we presented earlier in this chapter. This section reviews five of the common varieties reported in test manuals and shown in Figure 17.2.

Normalized *z*-Scores

When the *z*-scores have percentile ranks corresponding to what we would expect in a normal distribution, they are called **normalized *z*-scores** (z_n) and the following symbol is used:

z_n = the *z*-score corresponding to a given percentile rank in a normal distribution

If a distribution of raw scores is not normal in form, the percentile ranks of its *z*-scores will not correspond to what would be expected in a norm distribution. You may be surprised to learn, however, that one can create a set of "normalized" *z*-scores for any nonnormal distribution. After making this transformation, the new set of scores is more nearly like a normal distribution. **"Normalizing" a set of scores** is done in the following way: (a) determine the percentile rank of each raw score in the norm group, (b) look up each percentile rank in a normal curve table (e.g., the chart in Figure 17.4), and (c) read out the z_n-value that corresponds to each. The resulting z_n-values are "normalized." That is, they are the *z*-scores that *would have been attained if the distribution had been normal in form*.

To show you how the process works, and to illustrate the difference between *z* and z_n, consider the scores in the next example. The scores and the percentile ranks came from our example of the class of 25 students that showed how percentile ranks were calculated (Figure I.8 in Appendix I).

Example

Illustration of normalized z-scores and (actual) linear z-scores corresponding to the distribution of 25 test scores shown in the previous example in Table I.8

Raw score	%ile rank	Normalized[a] standard scores (z_n)	Linear[b] standard scores (z)
36	98	2.05	2.43
33	96	1.75	1.64
32	94	1.55	1.38
31	90	1.28	1.12
30	88	1.18	0.86
29	84	0.99	0.59
28	72	0.58	0.33
27	54	0.10	0.07
26	32	+0.47	+0.20
25	16	+0.99	+0.46
24	10	+1.28	+0.72
22	8	+1.41	+1.25
21	6	+1.55	+1.51
15	4	+1.75	+3.09
14	2	+2.05	+3.36

Notes: [a] z_n-values are obtained by looking up the percentile ranks in Figure 17.6 and reading out the corresponding z_n-values.
[b] z-values are obtained by using the actual distribution of scores in Table I.8 (Appendix I) and by applying the equation:

$$z = \frac{X - M}{SD}$$

where $M = 26.75$ and $SD = 3.80$.

Next, you look up each percentile rank in Figure 17.6, and read out the corresponding z_n. The results appear in the example. For the sake of comparison, the actual, linear *z*-scores are computed via Equation 17.1, using $M = 26.75$ and $SD = 3.8$. The difference between the normalized and linear *z*-scores represents the "stretching and squeezing" necessary to make the original distribution correspond more nearly to a normal distribution.

Normalized *T*-Scores (McCall's *T*)

The second type of score in the normalized standard score branch of Figure 17.2 is a *T*-score. A **normalized *T*-score** tells the location of a raw score in a normal distribution having a mean of 50 and a standard deviation of 10. The normalized *T*-score is the counterpart to the linear *SS*-score. Thus,

$$T = 10z_n + 50 \qquad \text{[Eq. 17.3]}$$

The difference between Equation 17.3 and Equation 17.2 ($SS = 10z + 50$) is that z_n is a normalized standard score instead of a linear standard score.

Normalized *T*-scores have the same advantages over normalized *z*-scores as *SS*-scores have over linear *z*-scores, with the additional advantage that *T*-scores have the percentile rank interpretations of a normal curve. Here is an example.

> ### Example
>
> *Examples of how to interpret T-scores using a normal curve like the one shown in Figure 17.6*
>
> 1. Joey's *T*-score is 40. This means he is one standard deviation below the mean of the norm group, and his percentile rank is approximately 16.
> 2. Betty's percentile rank is 84. This means her *T*-score is 60, and she is a distance of one standard deviation above the norm-group mean.

Figure 17.6 shows the correspondence between percentile ranks, *T*-scores, and z_n scores in a normal distribution. That figure can help you convert percentile ranks directly to *T*-scores without using Equation 17.3.

Deviation IQ Scores

The third type of normalized standard score shown in Figure 17.2 is the deviation IQ score used with certain assessments of mental ability. A **deviation IQ score (DIQ = score)** tells the location of a raw score in a normal distribution having a mean of 100 and a standard deviation of 15 or 16. The norm group is usually made up of all those students with the same chronological age, regardless of grade placement. For example, if the test developer sets the standard deviation at 16, *DIQ*s are given by

$$DIQ = 16z_n + 100 \qquad \text{[Eq. 17.4]}$$

These *DIQ*s as shown in Equation 17.4 are interpreted in a way similar to *T*-scores, but with reference to the normal distribution having a mean of 100 and a standard deviation of 16. Here is an example.

> ### Example
>
> *The meaning of DIQ-scores.*
>
> 1. Meghan has *DIQ* = 116. This means she has scored one standard deviation above the mean of her age group and the percentile rank of her score is 84.
> 2. Sherry has *DIQ* = 100. This means she has scored at the mean of her age group and the percentile rank of her score is 50.

Usually, assessment manuals provide tables that permit you to convert raw scores directly to *DIQ*s.

FIGURE 17.7 Illustration of a normal distribution showing stanines, percentile ranks, and percentage of cases having each stanine.

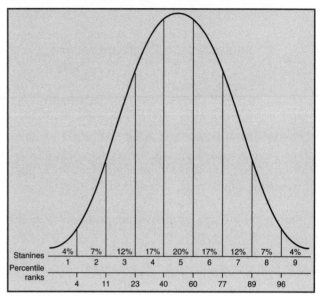

Stanines

The fourth normalized standard score shown in Figure 17.2 is the stanine. A **stanine score** tells the location of a raw score in a specific segment of a normal distribution. Publishers frequently recommend using **national stanines** for norm-referenced interpretation of achievement and aptitude assessments. You will see an example of a publisher's test table that uses stanines along with percentile ranks if you look at the *DAT Mechanical Reasoning Test* norms table in Figure 17.3.

Figure 17.7 illustrates the meaning of a stanine score. A normal distribution is divided into nine segments, numbered from a low of 1 through a high of 9. Scores falling within the boundaries of these segments are assigned one of these nine numbers (hence, the term *stanine* from "standard nine"). Each segment is one half a standard deviation wide, except for stanines 1 and 9. The percentage of the cases in a normal curve falling within each segment is shown in Figure 17.7, along with the range of percentile ranks associated with each.

All persons with scores falling within an interval are assigned the stanine of that interval. For example, all persons with scores having percentile ranks from 11 through 22 are assigned a stanine of 3; all from 23 through 29 a stanine of 4; and so on. Twelve percent of the persons in the norm group would be assigned a stanine of 3 and 17% a stanine of 4. When raw scores from normal distributions are converted to stanines, the stanines have a mean of 5 and a standard deviation equal to 2. Here is an example of how stanines are interpreted. As you read these examples, refer to Figure 17.6.

Example

How to interpret stanine scores

1. Sophia received a stanine of 5 on the mathematics subtest of a standardized test. This means her raw score on the test was in the middle 20% of the norm group.

2. Jesse received a stanine of 9 in the reading subtest of a standardized test. This means his raw score on the test was in the top 4% of the norm group.

3. Blake's stanine on the spelling subtest of the standardized test was 3. This means that his raw score was in the lower 20% of the norm group. Specifically, his percentile rank was between 11 and 22.

Among the advantages claimed for stanines: They are single-digit numbers only, have approximately equal units all along the score scale, and do not imply an exactness greater than that warranted by the assessment.

Not all assessment experts agree with using stanines for norm-referenced interpretations. Some hold that stanines present more difficult interpretative problems than percentile ranks, especially for reliable assessments, because stanines reflect coarse groupings of scores (Hoover et al., 1993b).

As with percentile ranks, stanines are specific to the reference group on which they are calculated. Some test publishers report both local and national stanines. For a specific student, these two stanines may be different, depending on how the student ranks in each reference group.

The example in Appendix I (Figure I.4) shows how you can transform any set of scores into stanines. The example uses the distribution of 25 scores we used earlier in Figure I.8.

SAT-Scores

The fifth score in the normalized standard score branch of Figure 17.2 is the *SAT*-score. The *SAT Reasoning Test* (SAT) results are reported using this type of score. The *SAT*-score is a normalized standard score from a distribution that has a mean of 500 and a standard deviation of 100. The *SAT*-score scale is based on a reference group of 1,052,000 students who graduated from high school in 1990 and who took the *SAT* in either their junior or senior year (Dorans, 1994). The scores of this reference group were normalized, the mean set to 500, and the standard deviation set to 100. This is shown in Equation 17.5.

$$SAT\text{-score} = 100z_n + 500 \qquad [\text{Eq. 17.5}]$$

Tests given after 1990 are statistically equated to the performance of the 1990 reference group. This ensures that the scores have the same meaning from year to year. Thus, an *SAT*-score tells the location of a current student's score in the 1990 normal distribution that has a mean of 500 and a standard deviation of 100. Percentile ranks corresponding to each current year's scores are provided to test users to facilitate interpretation for the current year.

Normal Curve Equivalents

The sixth type of normalized standard score in Figure 17.2 is the normal curve equivalent. The **normal curve equivalent** (*NCE*) is a normalized standard score with a mean of 50 and a standard deviation of 21.06. It was developed primarily for use with federal program evaluation efforts (Tallmadge & Wood, 1976). Its primary value is evaluating gains from various educational programs that use different publishers' tests. Although some publishers present norm tables for *NCE*s in their assessment manuals, using these scores for reporting individual student results is not recommended because they are too easily confused with percentile ranks. *NCE*-values are found by the formula shown in Equation 17.6. Their highest possible value is 99 and their lowest possible value is 1.

$$NCE = 21.06z_n + 50 \qquad [\text{Eq. 17.6}]$$

As stated previously, *NCE*-scores have a mean of 50 and a standard deviation of 21.06. By comparison, *T*-scores have a mean of 50 and a standard deviation of 10. Why choose a standard deviation of 21.06? This choice of standard deviation was made so the *NCE*-scores would span the range 1 to 99.

The following example shows the relationship between selected percentile ranks, *NCE*-scores, and stanines.

Example

Correspondences between selected percentile ranks, NCE-scores, and stanines

Percentile rank	NCE	Stanine
1	1	1
5	15	2
10	23	2
20	32	3
25	36	4
30	39	4
35	42	4
40	45	5
45	47	5
50	50	5
55	53	5
60	55	6
65	58	6
70	61	6
75	64	6
80	68	7
85	72	7
90	77	8
95	85	8
99	99	9

As you can see in the table, percentile ranks of 1, 50, and 99 are identical in value to *NCE*-scores. At other points, however, percentile ranks and *NCE*-scores differ: *NCE*-scores are less spread out than percentile ranks in the middle of the distribution and more spread out than

percentile ranks at the lower and upper extremes. Notice the *NCE*-scores look very similar to percentile ranks. For this reason they are often confused with percentile ranks. Although some publishers present *NCE* norms tables in their standardized test manuals, we do not recommend *NCE*-scores for reporting individual student results because of this percentile rank confusion.

You may notice the relationship of the *NCE*-score to stanines. If you move the *NCE* decimal point to the left one digit and round to the nearest whole number, you will roughly have the stanine. For example, an *NCE* = 72 has a stanine equivalent of 7; *NCE* = 58 a stanine equivalent of 6; and so on. This rough correspondence stems from the fact that both *NCE*-scores and stanines are based on a normal distribution, and *NCE*-scores and percentile ranks have the same range.

DEVELOPMENTAL AND EDUCATIONAL GROWTH SCALES

We turn now to the fourth branch of the norm-referencing schemes in Figure 17.2. The normalized standard score scales discussed so far are specific to a particular grade level or age group. If a score scale is specific to a particular grade, you cannot use it to measure growth as a student moves from one grade to the next. The next example illustrates why you cannot use percentile ranks and *T*-scores to evaluate a student's educational growth.

Example

Why percentile ranks and T*-scores cannot be used to measure growth*

1. Suppose Billy tested at the 84th percentile in Grades 5, 6, and 7. Although Billy would be growing in skills and knowledge, his percentile rank (84) has stayed the same. The number, 84, by reflecting only location in each grade's norm group, does not communicate Billy's growth.

2. Similarly, suppose Ashley's *T*-score determined separately for each grade's norm group remained nearly the same from year to year, say about 60. Ashley in fact exhibited educational growth each year as she moved through the grades. The *T*-score, because it remains constant, does not communicate growth.

You would find it useful, however, if your students' educational growth were reported on one scale of numbers that spanned the school years. Survey achievement batteries, for example, usually span several grades—say 2nd through 8th, or 9th through 12th. If the score scale of such batteries failed to link the assessments from several grade levels to a single developmental score scale, you could not measure your students' growth over those years. We now turn to a discussion of the two scales shown in the developmental or growth

scales branch of Figure 17.2: the extended normalized standard score scale and the grade-equivalent score scale.

EXTENDED NORMALIZED STANDARD SCORE SCALES

Basic Idea of the Extended Normalized Score Scales

An **extended normalized standard score** tells the location of a raw score on a scale of numbers that is anchored to a lower grade reference group. Educators find that a "ruler" or achievement continuum on which a student's progress can be measured over a wide range of grades is very useful. On this continuum, low scores represent the lowest levels of educational development and high scores the highest level of educational development. Publishers refer to this type of scale with a variety of names, for example: *obtained scale score, scale score, extended standard score, developmental standard score,* or *growth-scale values.*

Development of Extended Score Scales

Although each publisher prepares expanded scales somewhat differently, and the numbers obtained are not comparable from publisher to publisher, extended scaled scores share the same goals and the same general method of development: (a) a base or anchor group is chosen and normalized *z*-scores are developed that extend beyond the range of scores for this anchor group; (b) a series of assessments is administered with common items given to adjoining groups (e.g., second and third graders take a common set of items, then third and fourth graders, and so on); (c) distributions of scores are tabulated and normalized for each grade; and (d) through these overlapping items, all of the groups are placed on the extended *z*-score scale of the anchor group. This extended *z*-scale becomes the ruler or growth scale spanning the several grades.

The extended *z*-scale is then transformed again to a scale that removes the unpleasant properties (such as negative numbers and decimals) of the *z*-scores. The new scale may range from 00 to 99, from 000 to 999, or any other set of positive integers, depending on the publisher; there are no standards for what this range should be. Figure 17.8 illustrates how a publisher establishes such scales in a hypothetical case. The scaled scores reported in the example in Figure 17.1 are an actual example of how a test manual reports expanded standard scores.

Item Response Theory Method[3]

Recent technical advances have resulted in some publishers offering schools two choices of how extended standard scores can be calculated. One method uses the traditional

[3]A full explanation of the IRT method is beyond the scope of this book.

FIGURE 17.8 Hypothetical example of how scores on a series of achievement tests are converted to a common extended score scale. The successive groups are located on the scale by linking together the overlapping tests in a special administration.

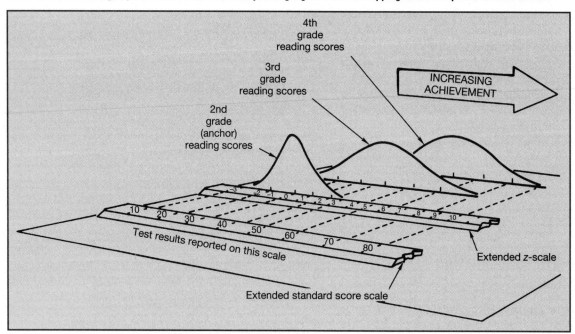

raw score for students (i.e., number right score) as a beginning step for calculating. This is the method we described above. A second method uses **item response theory (IRT)** in which a mathematical equation is fit to the publisher's sample of students' item responses. The results are then used to derive a score scale. According to this method, a student's score depends on the pattern of her right or wrong answers. **IRT pattern scoring** considers whether a student answered an easy or difficult item correctly, and how sharply that item distinguishes students of different achievement levels. This means, for example, that two students who answer correctly the same number of items may get different scaled scores if the pattern of correctly answered items is very different for the two students.

The advantage is that the resultant extended standard scores can have lower measurement error and greater reliability than traditional number-right scores. The disadvantages are (a) the direct link between the number correct and the extended scale score is broken (when certain equations are used), and (b) the method does not work well for every type of test and every population of students.

To learn more about item response theory you may consult http://edres.org/irt for links to different tutorials. On that site you will also find an introductory book, *The Basics of Item Response Theory* (Baker, 2001), that you may read online.

Recommendations

Although program evaluators and school researchers generally prefer to use extended standard scores, their meaning is not immediately apparent to teachers, parents, and students. To understand what they mean you have to compare a

student's score with the average score of students in that grade. Some educators consider this an advantage because it lessens the chance of overinterpreting scores. On the other hand, if no one knows what they mean, they will not be used, and therefore the scores will be underutilized.

Extended standard scores tend to show that on the average students have less achievement growth in the upper elementary grades than in the lower grades. Note that extended standard scores show different standard deviations for school subjects and progressively increasing standard deviations as grade levels increase. Thus, you cannot compare a student's extended assessment score from one subject area to another. In this respect, they share a common property with grade-equivalent scores, discussed next.

GRADE-EQUIVALENT SCORES

Basic Idea of Grade-Equivalent Scores

A **grade-equivalent score** *(GE)* tells the grade placement at which a raw score is average. *GE*s are educational development scores most often used with achievement tests at the elementary school level. A grade-equivalent score is reported as a decimal fraction, such as 3.4 or 7.9. The whole number part of the score refers to a grade level, and the decimal part refers to a month of the school year within that grade level. For example, you read a grade-equivalent score of 3.4 as "third grade, fourth month"; similarly, you read 7.9 as "seventh grade, ninth month." Suppose 6.3 is the grade-equivalent score corresponding to the raw score 31. This means that the average in the norm group during the third month of sixth grade was 31. The example below shows how the grade-equivalent scale is laid out.

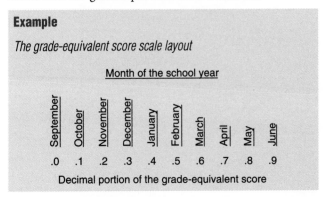

Example

The grade-equivalent score scale layout

Month of the school year

September	October	November	December	January	February	March	April	May	June
.0	.1	.2	.3	.4	.5	.6	.7	.8	.9

Decimal portion of the grade-equivalent score

When using these scores, you assume that the time between June and September (i.e., the summer months) represents an increment of one tenth (or 1 month) on the grade-equivalent scale (see above). By defining the grade-equivalent scale this way, the average of the scores shows 10 months' growth every year. (However, you should not expect every student to show 1 month's growth each summer.)

Overall Usefulness of Grade-Equivalent Scores

Grade-equivalent scores are useful for reporting a pupil's educational development. If a standardized test is administered periodically throughout a student's school years, the resulting grade-equivalent scores can help monitor the student's educational progress using a grade-based educational development scale. To a lesser extent, grade equivalents can be used to evaluate a student's grade placement. *The problem with grade placement interpretations of GE scores is that they depend on the how well the test content matches what was taught to the students up to the point at which the test was administered—the poorer this match, the less valid are grade placement interpretations.*

Grade-equivalent scores (and extended standard score) cannot be used to compare a student's strengths and weaknesses across different subject matters. Nor can they be used to determine a student's rank among his or her peers. An explanation of these limitations follows in the remainder of this section.

Development of Grade-Equivalent Scores

Understanding how the test publisher obtains grade equivalents will help you avoid misinterpretation. There is no need, of course, for you to compute them because test manuals provide the needed conversion tables.

The development process is illustrated with a reading test, but the same process applies to all subject areas. Suppose a publisher wishes to assess reading from Grades 1 through 8 and develop grade equivalents. The publisher creates a series of overlapping tests that spans the desired

grades: one test for first and second grades, one for second and third, and so on. Each test is appropriate for specific grade levels. The publisher administers the appropriate tests to a large national sample at each grade level. Usually, the publisher does this once or twice during the year (fall and/or spring) because it is impossible to administer them continuously throughout the year. The dates on which tests are administered are called **empirical norming dates**. These overlapping tests are then linked using an expanded score scale. This allows the raw scores from the different tests to be placed on a grade-based reading ability scale. The process is called *vertical linking* or *vertical equating* because the links go up the grades.

On this common scale, large differences in reading ability exist in the norm group at each grade level. Therefore, at each grade level there is a spread of reading scores. These distributions of reading scores are shown in Figure 17.9. In this illustration, the publisher administered the assessments only once during the year—in February (Month = 0.5)—so the figure graphs the distributions directly above 1.5, 2.5, 3.5, and so forth.

Setting the Grade-Equivalent Scale The publisher's first step is to locate and plot on a graph the median score (the mean score is used sometimes instead) in each grade's norm group. For instance, in the figure first graders in the norm group taking the test in February have an average (median) score of 10. February is the fifth month. Thus, the median raw score of 10 has a grade-equivalent score of 1.5 because the grade placement of this median is 1.5. Norm-group second graders in February have an average score of 15, and their corresponding grade equivalent is 2.5. Grade equivalents for Grades 4 and 5 are found similarly from the medians plotted in Figure 17.9.

Interpolation and Extrapolation Actual grade equivalents can be obtained only for those points in time when the publisher administered the tests. Grade equivalents for other points are obtained by interpolation or extrapolation. In Figure 17.9, notice that a solid line connects the medians of the actual distributions. This solid line is used to **interpolate** or estimate the values of the in-between grade equivalents. For example, the raw score 13 is not an actual median of a norm-group distribution. However, we draw a horizontal line from 13 across the graph until it intersects with the solid line and then drop a perpendicular line down to the grade placement scale. The grade placement corresponding to this vertical line (2.1) becomes the interpolated grade equivalent that corresponds to a raw score of 13.

Consider a raw score of 8. A grade equivalent for this score can be obtained only by **extrapolating** or extending the line beyond the norm groups actually tested according to the trend of the medians. The dashed lines in Figure 17.9 represent this extension. Thus, the extrapolated grade equivalent of the raw score 8 is 1.1. If the extrapolation is incorrect, so will be the grade equivalent.

FIGURE 17.9 **Hypothetical example of data used to obtain grade-equivalent scores.**

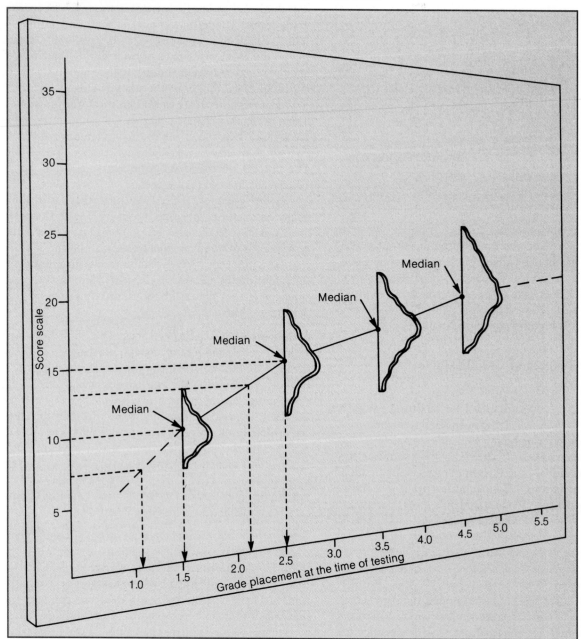

The next example summarizes what has been said so far about extrapolation and interpolation in relation to Figure 17.9. Before reading further, be sure you understand how these numbers were obtained from the figure.

Example

Raw score to grade-equivalent conversion table for the hypothetical data in Figure 17.9

Raw score	Grade equivalent	How obtained
9	1.4	extrapolation
10	1.5	actual data
11	1.7	interpolation
12	1.9	interpolation
13	2.1	interpolation
14	2.3	interpolation
15	2.5	actual data
16	2.8	interpolation
17	3.2	interpolation
18	3.5	actual data
19	4.0	interpolation
20	4.5	actual data
21	4.6	extrapolation

An example of an actual conversion table from a published test is shown in Figure 17.10. You will use this type of conversion table when you consult a publisher's norms

FIGURE 17.10 Part of grade-equivalent table for the *Metropolitan Achievement Tests* (7th Edition), *Forms S/T, Fall Norms*. Notice that you enter the table with the (expanded) scaled scores and read the grade-equivalent scores in the margins. The expanded scaled scores are obtained first from another table (not shown), which you enter with raw scores.

Grade Equiv.	Word Recognition	Reading Vocabulary	Reading Comprehension	Prereading/ Total Reading	Concepts & Problem Solving	Procedures	Grade Equiv.
7.9	665	661	656	659	644	650	7.9
7.8	663–664	660	654–655	657–658	642–643	648–649	7.8
7.7	661–662	659	—	655–656	641	647	7.7
7.6	660	658	653	654	640	—	7.6
7.5	—	657	—	—	639	646	7.5
7.4	—	656	—	—	638	645	7.4
7.3	659	655	652	653	637	—	7.3
7.2	—	654	—	—	636	644	7.2
7.1	658	653	651	652	635	643	7.1
7.0	657	651–652	650	651	634	642	7.0
6.9	656	650	649	650	633	641	6.9
6.8	653–655	648–649	647–648	647–649	632	639–640	6.8
6.7	651–652	646–647	645–646	645–646	630–631	638	6.7
6.6	649–650	644–645	643–644	643–644	628–629	636–637	6.6
6.5	647–648	642–643	642	641–642	626–627	634–635	6.5
6.4	646	640–641	640–641	640	624–625	632–633	6.4
6.3	644–645	638–639	639	638–639	622–623	629–631	6.3
6.2	642–643	636–637	637–638	636–637	620–621	626–628	6.2
6.1	641	634–635	635–636	635	618–619	623–625	6.1
6.0	639–640	632–633	633–634	633–634	616–617	621–622	6.0
5.9	637–638	630–631	631–632	631–632	614–615	618–620	5.9
5.8	634–636	628–629	630	628–630	613	616–617	5.8
5.7	632–633	626–627	628–629	626–627	611–612	614–615	5.7
5.6	630–631	624–625	626–627	625	610	611–613	5.6
5.5	628–629	622–623	624–625	623–624	609	608–610	5.5
5.4	626–627	620–621	623	621–622	608	606–607	5.4
5.3	624–625	618–619	622	619–620	607	604–605	5.3
5.2	622–623	616–617	621	618	606	602–603	5.2
5.1	620–621	614–615	620	617	605	600–601	5.1
5.0	618–619	612–613	618–619	616	603–604	597–599	5.0
4.9	616–617	610–611	617	615	601–602	595–596	4.9
4.8	613–615	607–609	615–616	613–614	599–600	592–594	4.8
4.7	611–612	604–606	613–614	610–612	597–598	590–591	4.7
4.6	608–610	601–603	610–612	607–609	595–596	587–589	4.6
4.5	605–607	598–600	607–609	603–606	592–594	584–586	4.5
4.4	602–604	595–597	604–606	600–602	590–591	581–583	4.4
4.3	599–601	592–594	601–603	598–599	587–589	577–580	4.3
4.2	596–598	589–591	598–600	596–597	585–586	573–576	4.2
4.1	593–595	586–588	596–597	594–595	582–584	569–572	4.1
4.0	589–592	583–585	594–595	591–593	580–581	566–568	4.0

Source: From the *Multilevel Norms Book: Metropolitan Achievement Test: Seventh Edition.* Copyright © 1993 by Harcourt Assessments, Inc. Reproduced by permission. All rights reserved.

booklet to convert your students' raw scores to grade equivalents. Practice looking up student's score with Figure 17.10.

What to Keep in Mind When Interpreting Grade Equivalents

Spring-to-Fall Drops: Summer Losses One special concern in the process of interpreting grade equivalents is the phenomenon of summer achievement losses. In some subject

areas—arithmetic, for example—students' performance loses some of its edge over the summer months (Beggs & Hieronymus, 1968; DeVito & Long, 1977; Tallmadge, 1973; Tallmadge & Horst, 1974; Tallmadge & Wood, 1976). A performance drop over the summer months has several meanings: (a) the assumption of an over-the-summer growth of one month is not true in every subject area, (b) educational growth is not regular and uniform for many children, and (c) using fall-to-spring gains in grade-equivalent scores to evaluate an instructional program may lead to wrong conclusions. The third point is less problematic when the test publisher has separate fall and spring norms and when a school system tests on dates very close to the dates on which the publisher's norms were established.

Grade Equivalents and Curriculum Correspondence It would be a misconception to say that students ought to have the same placement as their grade-equivalent scores. To understand why, recall Figure 17.9 and how grade equivalents are based on the median. By definition, half the students in the norm groups at a particular grade placement will have scores above the median. Thus, half the students in the norm group have grade-equivalent scores higher than their actual grade placement. Second, recall that a publisher uses a series of tests, rather than a single test, to establish grade equivalents. You can't interpret a third grader's grade-equivalent score of, say, 5.7 on a mathematics test covering third-grade content to mean that this student ought to be placed in fifth-grade mathematics. The test shows that the student did very well on third-grade content, but the student was not assessed on fifth-grade mathematics. Many factors, of course, besides a single assessment result determine whether the student should receive an accelerated placement. Some test publishers, however, may develop their test batteries so that third-grade students are administered fifth-grade content for purposes of developing a grade-equivalent scale. In such cases, it may be appropriate to say cautiously that the third graders with a grade equivalent of 5.7 do know some fifth-grade content (Hoover et al., 1993b).

The meaning of grade-equivalent scores as describing a student's learning status in a subject depends very much on the subject matter. In reading, for example, students' educational growth may be less tied to the curriculum sequence than it is mathematics. In such cases, third-grade students with grade equivalents of 5.7 may well be reading much like a fifth grader; and a fifth grader with a grade equivalent of 3.7 may well be reading like a third grader.

Grade Equivalents and Mastery Sometimes teachers, parents, and school administrators misinterpret grade equivalents as meaning mastery of a particular fraction of a curricular area. For example, a parent may erroneously think that a student's grade equivalent of 3.5 in mathematics means the student has mastered 5/10ths of the local school's third-grade mathematics curriculum. The most that can be said about this student, however, is that his test score equals the average score of the norm group when it was in the 5th month of third grade. This is unlikely to mean mastery of third-grade mathematics because the test does not systematically sample the entire domain of third-grade mathematics in the student's local curriculum.

Grade Equivalents and What Was Covered in the Class The more closely the test items match the material you emphasized in the classroom before the test was administered, the more likely your students are to score well above grade level

on these nationally standardized tests. You may teach the content of some test items after the testing date. As a result, your students may perform poorly when tested but will learn the material before the end of the school year. Answering three or four items wrong will significantly lower a student's grade-equivalent score. If your teaching sequence and the testing sequence are not aligned, inferring mastery is problematic. This points out the norm-referenced character of grade-equivalent scores and illustrates that criterion-referenced interpretations are difficult to make from them.

Grade Equivalents From Different Tests Cannot Be Interchanged Grade-equivalent (and other norm-referenced) scores depend on the particular items placed on the test and the particular norm group used. You would be misinterpreting grade equivalents, for example, if you said, "A grade equivalent of 3.7 on the *ABC Reading Assessment* means the same thing as a grade equivalent of 3.7 on the *DEF Reading Assessment*." The results from two different publishers' assessments are simply not comparable except under special conditions (Bianchini & Loret, 1974a, 1974b; Jaeger, 1973; Peterson et al., 1989).

Grade Equivalents for Different Subjects Cannot Be Compared Another misinterpretation is to compare a student's mathematics grade equivalent with the student's reading grade equivalent. This is invalid. Consider the following hypothetical assessment results for three third-grade students.

Example			
			Survey subtest
		Reading	**Mathematics**
John	GE	4.9	4.9
	PR	78	90
Howard	GE	4.9	4.3
	PR	78	78
Susan	GE	4.9	4.6
	PR	78	84

Notice that John has two identical grade equivalents, but their corresponding percentile ranks are *different*. Howard has two different grade equivalents but has *identical* percentile ranks. Finally, Susan has one grade equivalent higher than another, yet her higher grade equivalent has a lower percentile rank than her *lower* grade equivalent.

The reason for the phenomena is that scores for one subject area are more diverse than those of another, resulting in different patterns of interpolation when grade equivalents are prepared. Expanded standard scores cannot be used to compare a student's performance in different areas, either.

What should you use to describe a student's relative strengths and weaknesses in different subject areas? *Use percentile ranks to compare a student's scores from different subjects* if all students in the norm group took the same tests in all subjects. Thus, in the preceding illustration, John is somewhat better in mathematics and in reading, Howard is about the same in both subjects, and Susan is slightly better in mathematics than in reading. Because these are norm-referenced interpretations, "better" implies "compared with other persons."

"Normal" Growth Sometimes teachers and school administrators use grade equivalents to answer questions of what educational growth they should expect of a student. This is not a good practice and the results of doing it are unsatisfactory. One view of **normal growth** is this: "A student ought to exhibit a growth of 1.0 grade-equivalent units from one grade to the next." Under this view, a student taking the test in second grade and scoring 1.3, for example, would need to score 2.3 in third grade, 4.3 in fifth, and so on to show "normal" or expected growth.

This *grade-equivalent view of normal growth* cannot be supported at all percentile ranks. Figure 17.11 shows examples of what will happen to three hypothetical students on the mathematics subtest of two published tests if this view is adopted.

The students have these characteristics: Student A is one year behind in terms of grade equivalents, Student B is at grade level, and Student C is one year ahead. Each year, the students' grade equivalents show a one-year "growth" over the preceding year. But look at the percentile ranks corresponding to their scores: Student A, who starts out one year behind, has to *exceed more persons* in the norm group to maintain a one-year-behind grade equivalent. Being one year behind in second grade means being at the 16th or 17th percentile. However, one year behind in Grade 8 means being around the *41st or 42nd percentile.* One has to move from the bottom of the group toward the middle. An opposite phenomenon occurs for Student C, who begins one grade ahead at around the *86th or 92nd*

percentile. In this case, the student can fall behind more and more students and still be "one year ahead." Students who are at grade level (Student B) have raw scores equal to the average. By definition, the average at a grade is assigned one year's growth from the preceding year. Thus, only students who are exactly at the average each year will maintain their percentile rank from year to year.

An alternate norm-referenced definition is the *percentile view of normal growth*: A student shows normal growth if that student maintains the same position (i.e., percentile rank) in the norm from year to year. Figure 17.12 shows examples of what happens to a student's grade-equivalent score if that student's *percentile rank stays the same each year.*

Lower scoring students (such as Students A and D)—even though they do not change their position in the norm group—have grade equivalents indicating they are further and further behind. (An opposite trend occurs for initially high-scoring students.) The exact magnitude of this falling-behind phenomenon will vary from one publisher's test to another's and depends on the student's percentile rank. The grade-equivalent scales of some tests are created to minimize the falling-behind effect. Students close to the 50th percentile will exhibit less of the falling-behind effect than will those further from the center of the distribution. The reasons for this effect are two: (a) the line connecting the medians of the distributions at each grade level (see Figure 17.9) tends to flatten out at higher grades rather than being a diagonal line, and (b) scores at upper grades become more spread out, spanning a larger range than scores at lower grades.

Unequal Units You should be aware that the grade-equivalent score scale does not have a one-to-one correspondence with the number of questions a student answers correctly on a test. This means, for example, that students in the

FIGURE 17.11 Examples of changes in the percentile ranks for three hypothetical students as each "gains" one year in grade-equivalent units from second through eighth grade.

| Grade placement at the time of testing | Metropolitan Achievement Tests, Total Mathematics | | | | | | Iowa Tests of Basic Skills, Total Mathematics | | | | | |
| | Student A: "Below grade level" | | Student B: "On grade level" | | Student C: "Above grade level" | | Student A: "Below grade level" | | Student B: "On grade level" | | Student C: "Above grade level" | |
	GE	PR	GE	PR	GE	PR	GE	PR	GE	PR	GE	PR
2.3	1.3	16	2.3	63	3.3	86	1.3	18	2.3	54	3.3	92
3.3	2.3	29	3.3	64	4.3	85	2.3	18	3.3	55	4.3	85
4.3	3.3	34	4.3	63	5.3	80	3.3	28	4.3	56	5.3	77
5.3	4.3	37	5.3	61	6.3	77	4.3	34	5.3	54	6.3	71
6.3	5.3	36	6.3	57	7.3	73	5.3	34	6.3	52	7.3	66
7.3	6.3	39	7.3	60	8.3	70	6.3	38	7.3	52	8.3	65
8.3	7.3	42	8.3	55	9.3	60	7.3	41	8.3	53	9.3	64

FIGURE 17.12 Examples of changes in the grade-equivalent score for four hypothetical students as each student's percentile rank remains the same from second through eighth grade.

| Grade placement at the time of testing | Metropolitan Achievement Tests, Total Mathematics | | | | Iowa Tests of Basic Skills, Total Mathematics | | | |
| | Student A: "Below grade level" (PR = 16 each year) | | Student B: "Above grade level" (PR = 84 each year) | | Student C: "Below grade level" (PR = 16 each year) | | Student D: "Above grade level" PR = 84 each year | |
	GE	"Grades behind"	GE	"Grades ahead"	GE	"Grades behind"	GE	"Grades ahead"
3.3	2.1	1.2	4.8	1.5	2.1	1.2	4.7	1.4
4.3	2.6	1.7	6.3	2.0	2.8	1.5	5.9	1.6
5.3	3.1	2.2	7.7	2.4	3.3	2.0	7.3	2.0
6.3	3.9	2.4	9.0	2.7	4.0	2.3	8.8	2.5
7.3	4.5	2.8	10.1	2.8	4.7	2.6	10.3	3.0
8.3	5.1	3.2	10.6	2.3	5.1	3.2	11.9	3.6

Source: Data reproduced from *The Metropolitan Achievement Test: Seventh Edition, Fall Norms Table.* Copyright © 1993 by Harcourt Assessment, Inc. Reproduced by permission. All rights reserved. Other data are adapted from Hoover, Hieronymus, Frisbie, & Dunbar (1993c). *Iowa Tests of Basic Skills: Norms and Score Conversion, Complete and Core Batteries, Form K.* Copyright © 1993 by The University of Iowa. All rights reserved. Reproduced with permission of the Riverside Publishing Company.

middle of the distribution who get one more item correct are likely to raise their grade-equivalent scores by only one tenth (i.e., one "month"). For students in the upper part of the distribution, however, one additional correct item may result in an increment of several tenths (several "months" of growth). As a result of these unequal units, calculating averages using grade equivalents becomes problematic.

Grade Mean Equivalents Because it is problematic to average grade-equivalent scores, some publishers (e.g., CTB/McGraw-Hill) have tried other ways to give schools information on how well their students performed on the average. One technique is to report the **grade mean equivalent** that tells the grade placement of a group's average extended scale score. Instead of averaging grade-equivalent scores directly, you first average the extended scale scores. Second, you look up the grade-equivalent that corresponds to this average extended scale score. For example, if a fourth-grade class's average (mean) reading expanded scale score on the *TerraNova* assessment was 641, this would convert to a grade equivalent of 4.9. This means that 641 is the national average for all norm-group students who have completed the 9th month of Grade 4 (CTB/McGraw-Hill, 1997). This averaging of extended scores is also problematic, however. There is evidence to suggest that extended score scales do not have equal units of measurement either, even though some test developers claim they do (Hoover, 1984a, 1984b). If this is the case, then their averages and the grade mean equivalents on which they are based would be just as problematic as averaging grade equivalents.

Recommendations

In light of the problems with grade equivalents, you may wonder why they are used at all. Indeed, many assessment specialists believe they should be eliminated. Yet such

scores are popular with teachers and administrators who are generally unaware of the complex criticisms. Teachers and school administrators have a real need for at least some crude measure of educational development or growth that they can relate to years of schooling. Despite the technical difficulties in doing so, grade equivalents seem intuitively to be a "natural metric." Some assessment specialists recommend extended standard scores as measures of growth, but they possess many of the same interpretive problems as grade equivalents, and because they cannot be easily referenced to grade levels, their interpretation can be confusing.

You should use grade-equivalent scores as coarse indicators of educational development or growth but do so only when you report them with their corresponding percentile ranks. Grade equivalents are norm-referenced growth indicators. If you want information about the content of a student's learning, you need to look carefully at the kinds of performances the student can do. To do that, you need to review for each student the kinds of test items the student answered correctly. When you do this, of course, you are making criterion-referenced interpretations.

Summary of Grade Equivalents

As a summary of grade-equivalent scores, consider the situation in which a school administered a published, norm-referenced achievement test to third graders in May. Further, assume that the school's teachers have judged the assessment to match the curriculum validly and to be an appropriate way to assess the students. Finally, assume that the publisher's norms are appropriate. Then, even with all these nice assumptions, each of the following statements[4]—except

[4]Statements 1 through 6 are adapted from Lindvall and Nitko (1975, p. 98). Statements 7 and 8 have been paraphrased and adapted from Hills (1976, pp. 87–88).

the first—are *false*:

1. Pat's Reading subtest grade-equivalent score is 3.8. This suggests that she is an average third-grade reader.

2. Ramon's Arithmetic subtest grade equivalent is 4.6. This means that he knows arithmetic as well as the typical fourth grader who is at the end of the 6th month of school.

3. Melba's Arithmetic subtest grade equivalent is 6.7. This suggests that next year she ought to take arithmetic with the sixth graders.

4. Debbie's Reading subtest grade equivalent is 2.3. This means she has mastered three tenths of the second-grade reading skills.

5. John's grade-equivalent profile is Vocabulary = 6.2, Reading = 7.1, Language = 7.1, Work-Study Skills = 7.2, Arithmetic = 6.7. This means that his weak areas are vocabulary and arithmetic.

6. Two of Sally's grade equivalents are Language = 4.5 and Arithmetic = 4.5. Because her language and arithmetic grade equivalents are the same, we conclude that her language and arithmetic ability are about equal.

7. Half of this school's third graders have grade equivalents below grade level. This means that instructional quality is generally poor.

8. This year Mrs. Murray was assigned all of the students whose assessment scores were in the bottom quarter. The average of her class's grade equivalents this May was further below grade level than the class's average last year. This means that Mrs. Murray's instruction has been ineffective for the class as a whole.

COMPARISON OF VARIOUS NORM-REFERENCED SCORES

Figure 17.13 summarizes the various norm-referenced scores discussed in this chapter. Although each type of score describes the student's location in a norm group, each does so differently. The easiest type of score to explain to parents and students is a percentile rank. Various types of linear standard scores require an understanding of the mean and standard deviation for their meaning to become clear. Usually you will need to interpret normalized standard scores in conjunction with percentile ranks. From test to test, normalized

FIGURE 17.13 How to interpret different types of norm-referenced scores.

Type of score	Interpretation	Score	Examples of interpretations
Percentile rank Linear standard score (*z*-score)	Percentage of scores in a distribution below this point. Number of standard deviation units a score is above (or below) the mean of a given distribution.	$PR = 60$ $z = +1.5$ $z = -1.2$	"60% of the raw scores are lower than this score." "This raw score is located 1.5 standard deviations *above* the mean." "This raw score is located 1.2 standard deviations *below* the mean."
Linear standard score (*SS*-score or 50 ± 10 system)	Location of score in a distribution having a mean of 50 and a standard deviation of 10. (Note: For other systems, substitute in these statements that system's mean and standard deviation.)	$SS = 65$ $SS = 38$	"This raw score is located 1.5 standard deviations *above* the mean in a distribution whose mean is 50 and whose standard deviation is 10." "This raw score is located 1.2 standard deviations *below* the mean in a distribution whose mean is 50 and whose standard deviation is 10."
Stanine	Location of a score in a specific segment of a normal distribution of scores.	Stanine = 5 Stanine = 9	"This raw score is located in the middle 20% of a normal distribution of scores." "This raw score is located in the top 4% of a normal distribution of scores."
Normalized standard score (*T*-score or normalized 50 ± 10 system)	Location of score in a normal distribution having a mean of 50 and a standard deviation of 10. (Note: For other systems, substitute in these statements that system's mean and standard deviation [e.g., *DIQs* have a mean of 100 and a standard deviation of 16: this is a 100 ± 16 system].)	$T = 65$ $T = 38$	"This raw score is located 1.5 standard deviations above the mean in a normal distribution whose mean is 50 and whose standard deviation is 10. This score has a percentile rank of 84." "This raw score is located 1.2 standard deviations below the mean in a normal distribution whose mean is 50 and whose standard deviation is 10. This score has a percentile rank of 12."
Extended standard score	Location of a score on an arbitrary scale of numbers that is anchored to some reference group.		(No interpretation is offered here because the systems are so arbitrary and unalike.)
Grade-equivalent score	The grade placement at which the raw score is average.	$GE = 4.5$	"This raw score is the obtained or estimated average for all pupils whose grade placement is at the 5th month of the fourth grade."

Source: Adapted from *Measuring Student Achievement and Aptitude* (2nd ed., p. 99), by C. M. Lindvall and A. J. Nitko, 1975, New York: Harcourt Brace Jovanovich. Reproduced by permission of the authors.

standard scores will have the same percentage of cases associated with them. Consequently, their meaning remains fairly constant as long as a normal distribution can be assumed. Grade equivalents and extended standard scores provide scores along an educational growth continuum, but because of their inherent technical complexities, teachers and school administrators may misinterpret them. Limit using grade equivalents to gross estimates of yearly student growth. Use them only when you accompany them with percentile ranks. Use percentile ranks to compare an individual student's performance in different curriculum areas.

GENERAL GUIDELINES FOR SCORE INTERPRETATION

Teachers and school administrators should consider the following points when interpreting student scores on norm-referenced standardized tests (Prescott, Balow, Hogan, & Farr, 1978):

1. *Look for unexpected patterns of scores.* An assessment should confirm what a teacher knows from daily interactions with a student; unusually high or low scores for a student should be a signal for exploring instructional implications.

2. *Seek an explanation for patterns.* Ask why a student is higher in one subject than another. Check for motivation, special interests, special difficulties, and so on.

3. *Don't expect surprises for every student.* Most students' assessment results should be as you expect from their performance in class. A valid assessment should confirm your observations.

4. *Small differences in subtest scores should be viewed as chance fluctuations.* Use the standard error of measurement (Chapter 4) to help decide whether differences are large enough to have instructional significance.

5. *Use information from various assessments and observation to explain performance on other assessments.* Students low

FIGURE 17.14 Parent's copy of a score report along with computerized interpretations.

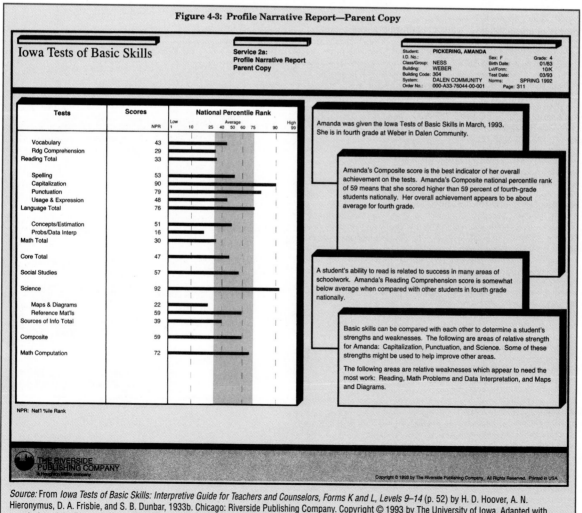

Source: From *Iowa Tests of Basic Skills: Interpretive Guide for Teachers and Counselors, Forms K and L, Levels 9–14* (p. 52) by H. D. Hoover, A. N. Hieronymus, D. A. Frisbie, and S. B. Dunbar, 1933b. Chicago: Riverside Publishing Company. Copyright © 1993 by The University of Iowa. Adapted with permission of the Riverside Publishing Company.

in reading comprehension may perform poorly on the social studies subtest, for example.

You may wish to try your hand at implementing these general guidelines by reviewing the case presented in Figure 17.14. Your interpretation of Amanda Pickering's report may be different from that of the computer.

INTERPRETING SCORES TO PARENTS

A teacher has the most direct contact with parents regarding norm-referenced score reports. Parents call the teacher first if they have questions about students' standardized test results. You must be prepared, therefore, to explain students' test results to their parents. Studying the concepts and principles in this chapter is a prerequisite for effectively communicating to parents.

Types of Questions Parents Ask and Suggested Ways of Answering Them

Figure 17.15 contains examples of many of the questions parents ask when they receive standardized test results from a school. The questions are organized into five categories: standing, growth, improvement needed, strengths, and intelligence. You should be prepared to answer questions in these categories. The table contains suggestions for answering each category of questions. Note that we indicate which type of norm-referenced score to use. Although other scores might be used, we believe the ones suggested will be most helpful to your explanation.

Notice, too, that we suggest always using a student's classroom performance to complement and explain the student's standardized test results. Because in the majority of cases students' standardized test performance will be very consistent with their classroom performance, using students' classroom performance to illustrate their standardized test performance will help you reinforce to the parents your assessment of the students.

Parent Misunderstandings

Parents also have misunderstandings about what norm-referenced test scores mean. We have already discussed many of the misconceptions and limitations in this chapter. The following list *summarizes common parent misunderstandings* that you need to be clear about before you can help parents correct them:

1. The grade-equivalent score tells which grade the student should be in. . . .
2. The percentile rank and percent-correct scores mean the same thing. . . .
3. The percentile rank norm group consists of only the students in a particular classroom. . . .
4. "Average" is the standard to beat. . . .
5. Small changes in percentile ranks over time are meaningful. . . .
6. Percent-correct scores below 70 are failing. . . .
7. If you get a perfect score, your percentile rank must be 99. . . . (Hoover et al., 1993b, pp. 103–105)

FIGURE 17.15 How to answer parents' questions about standardized test results.

Category	Examples of questions	Suggestions for answering
Standing	• How is my child doing compared to others? • Is my child's progress normal for his or her grade?	Use percentile ranks to describe standing. Explain that a standardized test gives partial information only. Use information from classroom performance to explain progress.
Growth	• Has my child's growth been as much as it should be?	Use grade-equivalent scores to show progress from previous years. Use composite scores (i.e., all subjects combined) to show general growth; use scores from each subject to explain growth in particular curricular areas. Obtain past performance information from the child's cumulative folder. Use information from classroom performance to explain growth.
Improvement needed	• Does my child have any learning weaknesses? • How can I help improve my child's learning?	Use percentile ranks to identify relative weaknesses. Use information about a student's performance to clusters of similar questions to pinpoint weaknesses. Use information from class performance to explain specific weaknesses. Don't overemphasize weaknesses. Explain a student's relative strengths, too; give specific suggestions as to how parents can help.
Strengths	• What does my child do well?	Use percentile ranks to pick out areas of relative strengths. Use class information to illustrate the point. Make suggestions for how parents can help improve these areas even more.
Intelligence	• How smart is my child? Is my child gifted?	Explain that an achievement test is not an intelligence test. Explain that an achievement test is very sensitive to what was taught in class and that high scores may only reflect specific opportunities to learn. Use class information to illustrate your points.

Source: This figure is based on suggestions in Hoover et al., 1993b.

Summary

Three Referencing Frameworks

- By themselves, raw scores on educational and psychological tests are difficult to interpret: You need to reference them to a well-defined norm group and to a well-defined domain of performances.
- Norm-referencing frameworks compare a student's performance with well-defined groups of other students who took the same test. Norm-referencing answers the question, "How did this student do compared to other students?"
- Criterion-referencing frameworks compare a student's performance against the domain of performances on the assessment samples. Criterion-referencing answers the question, "How much of the targeted learning did this student achieve?" For many of your daily teaching decisions, criterion-referencing frameworks are most useful.
- Standards-referencing frameworks combine elements of criterion-referencing and norm-referencing, answering the question, "Has the student reached the state-defined proficiency level?" Standards-referencing is used for state accountability reporting.

Using Norms

- There are many groups to which a student may be compared. These are called norm groups, and they include local, national, and special norm groups.
- The average score in a school building should be compared only to school averages norms.
- Three criteria you may use for judging the quality of norm data are relevance to your school, representativeness of the publisher's sampling plan, and recency of the norm-group test administration.

Meaning of Norm-Referenced Scores

- The most common criterion-referenced scores are percentage correct, speed of performance, quality ratings, and precision of performance.
- The most common norm-referenced scores are percentile ranks, linear standard scores, normalized standard scores, and grade-equivalent scores. These are found in test publishers' norms tables.
- Linear standard scores include z-scores, SS-scores, and SAT-scores. Normalized standard scores include z_n-scores, T-scores, stanine scores, NCE-scores, DIQ-scores, and extended scale scores.

Normal Distributions

- A normal curve helps you interpret the relationship between normalized standard scores and percentile ranks. You should not believe, however, that students' aptitudes, intelligences, or achievements are naturally normally distributed. A normal curve is not a law of nature for educational assessments. It is a tool to help you interpret test results.

Grade-Equivalent Scores

- Grade-equivalent scores help you interpret a student's standardized test performance by providing a grade-based scale of educational development. Grade equivalents are not criteria or standards, however.
- Among the misconceptions that teachers and school administrators sometimes have about grade equivalents are (a) growth over the summer is the same in each subject, (b) students are expected to have the same placement as their grade-equivalent scores, (c) students should have grade-equivalent scores equal to or higher than their grade placement, (d) grade equivalents tell what fraction of the curriculum a student has mastered, (e) a student's grade equivalents for one curriculum subject can be compared to those of other subjects, (f) grade-equivalent scores from different publishers' tests mean the same thing, and (g) a student should gain one year in grade-equivalent scores for each year in school. Remember that these are misconceptions: If you believe any one of these seven statements, you are wrong.
- When interpreting or explaining a student's grade-equivalent scores to others, you should include the student's percentile rank in the explanation.

Comparison of Various Norm-Referenced Scores

- Figure 17.13 summarizes and compares the various norm-referenced scores.

General Guidelines for Score Interpretation

- You should review a student's profile of scores on a standardized test (a) to identify unusually high or low scores, (b) with a questioning attitude as to why the student obtained a particular score, (c) expecting to confirm what you already know about the student rather than encounter "surprises," (d) without overemphasizing small differences in scores, and (e) in light of the other knowledge you have about the student's performance on other assessments and in your classroom.
- You should be prepared to use norm-referenced scores and classroom performance to answer parents' questions about their children's standing, growth, needed improvement, strengths, and intelligence. Suggestions for doing so are given in Figure 17.15.

Important Terms and Concepts

area under the normal curve
derived scores
empirical norming dates
extended normalized standard score
grade-equivalent scores (*GE*)
grade mean equivalent
interpolation versus extrapolation
IRT pattern scoring
item response theory (IRT)
linear standard scores (*z*, *SS*)
modal-age norms
normal curve equivalent (*NCE*)
normal distribution
normal growth (grade-equivalent view, percentile rank view)
normalized standard scores (z_n, *T, DIQ, NCE, SAT*)
normalizing a set of scores
norm groups (local, national, special)
norm-referencing versus criterion-referencing
percentile ranks (local and national)
raw scores
relevance, representativeness, and recency of norm data
SAT-score
school averages norms
standards-referencing framework
stanine scores (national stanine)

Exercises and Applications

1. A student takes a test during the middle of the school year. By mistake, the student's teacher uses the norms tables published for the end of the school year to look up the student's percentile rank. What effect does this error have on the percentile ranks the teacher reports? What would be the effect in this case if the teacher used the norms tables from the beginning of the year?

2. Read each of these statements and decide to which norm-referenced score(s) each mainly refers. Justify your choice(s) to your classmates.
   a. In this skewed distribution, John's score places him one standard deviation below the mean.
   b. Bob's test score is the same as the average score of students tested in the 4th month of fifth grade.
   c. Because Bill's score increased this year, I know that his general educational development has increased, even though his position in the norm group remained the same.
   d. Nancy's score is 5 because it is located in the middle 20% of a normal distribution.

3. Judge each of the following statements true or false. Explain the basis for your judgment in each case.
   a. A person's percentile rank is 45. This means that the person's raw score was the same as 45% of the group assessed.
   b. Sally's arithmetic assessment score is 40. The class's mean score is 45, and its standard deviation is 10. Therefore, Sally is located 1 standard deviation below the mean.
   c. The norms tables show that the distribution of deviation IQ scores on a school ability test is approximately normal in form. This means that for the people in the norm groups, the intellectual ability that naturally underlies the scores is normally distributed.

4. Figure 17.16 shows several types of normalized scores. Use the relationships between the scores to complete the table and thereby show how various scores are related to one another. The first two are completed for you. You may use Figure 17.6 for assistance.

5. Figure 17.17 shows part of a norms table that might appear in a manual of a standardized achievement test. The table shows selected raw scores, grade-equivalent scores, and percentile

FIGURE 17.16 Use with Exercise 4.

Percentile rank	Stanine	z_n	DIQ ($SD = 15$)	T-score
99.9	9	+3.00		
98				
84				
50				
16				
2				
0.1				

ranks for the publisher's standardization sample (i.e., norm group). Assume that (a) the local school system has judged the test's content to be a good match to its curriculum, (b) the norm data were collected during the 7th month of the fourth grade, (c) the norms are appropriate for use with the local school system, (d) the publisher has computed grade equivalents and percentile ranks in the usual way and with no errors, and (e) the school tested the students in April.

Use the table and your knowledge of norm-referenced frameworks to judge each of the following statements as true or false. Explain and justify your judgment in each case.
   a. James is a fourth-grade student with a grade-equivalent profile of $V = 6.2$, $R = 5.6$, $L = 5.6$, $W = 5.6$, $A = 6.2$. Decide whether each of the following conclusions is true or false, and explain the basis for your judgment.
      i. James should be in fifth grade.
      ii. James is strongest in vocabulary and arithmetic.
      iii. James's scores are above average for his grade.
   b. Fourth grader Sue's raw score on reading is 50, and on language it is 30. Decide whether each of the following conclusions is true or false, and explain your decision.
      i. Sue is more able in reading because her raw score in reading is higher.
      ii. Because Sue's grade-equivalent scores are equal, she is equally able in reading and vocabulary (relative to the norm group).
      iii. Sue is more able in language than reading (relative to the norm group) because her percentile rank in language is higher.

FIGURE 17.17 Use with Exercise 5.

Raw score	Vocabulary (V) GE	PR	Reading (R) GE	PR	Language (L) GE	PR	Work-study (W) GE	PR	Arithmetic (A) GE	PR
5	1.8	1	1.6	1	1.9	1	2.3	1	2.5	1
20	4.1	34	3.3	17	4.4	41	5.6	74	5.5	65
30	5.1	61	4.2	36	5.6	75	7.0	96	6.2	74
40	6.2	74	4.8	52	6.4	86	7.6	99	6.9	97
50	7.0	96	5.6	74	7.9	99	8.0	99	7.7	99
70			8.1	99						

18 Finding and Evaluating Published Assessments

LEARNING TARGETS

After studying this chapter, you should have learned the following:

Locating a Published Test and Its Published Review

1. Name the major print and nonprint sources of information about published assessments. [1, 3, 6]

2. Describe the kinds of sources you would use in locating an assessment instrument to use for a specific purpose, professional reviews of assessment instruments, names and addresses of assessment publishers, technical information about an assessment, and assessment specialists who could answer your questions about a particular assessment instrument. [1, 3, 6]

Locating an Unpublished Test and Computerized Testing Information

3. Describe the sources you would use in locating an unpublished assessment instrument for a specific purpose. [1, 3, 6]

4. Describe the sources you would use to locate computerized tests and testing services. [1, 3, 6]

Restrictions on Purchasing and Using Tests

5. Explain your responsibilities and the assessment developers' responsibilities for using a test properly. [1, 3, 4, 7]

6. Describe the contents and uses of the *Standards for Educational and Psychological Testing* and the *Code of Fair Testing Practices in Education (Revised)* [1, 3, 4, 7]

Evaluating and Selecting a Test

7. Identify the steps necessary to locate and evaluate specific published assessment instruments. [1, 3]

8. Explain the local school district factors to consider before adopting a published assessment. [1, 3, 4]

9. Name several nontest factors that must be reported along with assessment results when evaluating a school's or district's effectiveness. [4, 7, 6]

10. State what materials you need to obtain from the publisher to review an assessment procedure properly. [1, 3]

11. Identify and explain the major categories of information you should include in your evaluation report before recommending that a published assessment instrument be purchased. [1, 3]

How a Standardized Test Is Developed

12. Describe the major research and development steps for developing a standardized test. [1, 3]

Important Terms and Concepts

13. Explain how the terms and concepts listed at the end of this chapter apply to educational assessment. [6]

420

ABOUT THIS CHAPTER

This chapter is organized as follows. First, we discuss how to locate a published test and find out basic information about it. We discuss several print, Internet, and personal contact resources. Next, we discuss how to locate evaluative reviews of a test. We examine print resources, Internet resources, and personal contacts for obtaining test reviews. Third, we examine how to locate tests that are not published. These tests may have been used in various research projects. Fourth, we discuss how to find information about computerized tests and testing services. Fifth, we look at purchasing tests. There are restrictions for purchasing tests that you should know about before you try to buy a test. Sixth, we discuss how to evaluate the quality of a test that you or your school district are considering for adoption. We present an outline of a systematic approach to evaluating the test and writing an evaluation report. Finally, we describe the steps a reputable

test publisher takes when developing a test. Part of your test evaluation is your judgment as to whether the publisher of the test you have in mind has followed these steps appropriately.

LOCATING A PUBLISHED TEST

Suppose you want to locate a test that you can use to diagnose students' reading problems, assess students' self-concept, or assess some other category of students' characteristics. How do you locate possible tests for such purposes if you do not even know the name(s) of the particular test(s)? You can begin your search in one of three ways: (a) search printed materials, (b) search online resources, or (c) make personal contacts with persons who may know what you are looking for. Figure 18.1 is an overview of the available sources for locating a test. We describe each of these resources in this section.

FIGURE 18.1 Where to look to locate a tool.

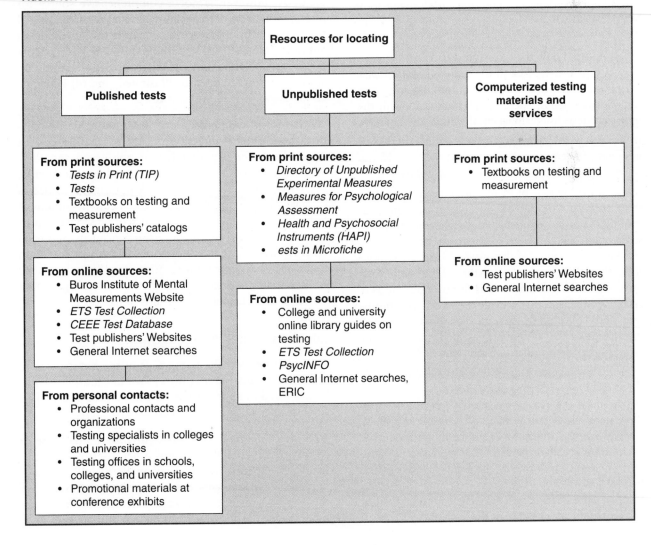

Locating Published Tests From Print Sources

Four print resources are available. Three of these resources are likely to be in your library: *Tests in Print*, *Tests*, and textbooks on testing and measurement. The fourth, test publishers' catalogs, are not likely to be in a library.

Tests in Print (TIP) VII The ***Tests in Print*** seventh edition (Murphy, Plake, Impara, & Spies, 2006) is a test bibliography that contains information on more than 4,000 commercially available instruments. You can use this source to identify appropriate tests, locate reviews of tests in the *Mental Measurements Yearbooks* (discussed later), and find publishers' addresses. To appear as an entry in *Tests in Print*, a test must be currently in print and must be published in English. Each entry includes the following information: a description of the test and its purpose, information on population and scoring, test editions available and their price, name of the publisher, and location of the test's review in the *Mental Measurements Yearbook*. (See the top portion of Figure 18.4 for an example of a *TIP* entry.) The *TIP VII* also provides listing notations on out-of-print tests.

You locate a test by using one of the book's five indexes.

1. If you know or have some idea of the test's name, look in the *Index of Titles*. The index lists all of the tests in *TIP VII* plus all those that are out of print.

2. If you do not know the test name, but know the category or type of test, look in the *Classified Subject Index*. All tests in the book are grouped into 18 categories (e.g., Social Studies, Speech & Hearing, etc.), with the individual tests listed alphabetically under the category.

3. If you know the name of the test author or person who has reviewed the test in one of the *Mental Measurements Yearbooks*, look in the *Index of Names*.

4. If you know the type of score a test may yield, look in the *Score Index*. For example, you may recall from your reading that a test contained an "aggression/hostility" score or an "enjoyment of mathematics" score, but do not know the names of the respective tests. The *Score Index* lists all such scores alphabetically for the tests included in *TIP VI*. The entries in this index are very specific to the tests that provide the scores. This means that your definition of the score may differ from a test publisher's or that different publishers may score the same student trait under different names. Thus, check all alternative or related score names before concluding that a test is not included in *TIP VII*.

5. If you know the acronym for a test but not its complete name, look in the *Index of Acronyms*. You may want to use this index, for example, if you recall that there is a test called the *DAT* that was used in counseling and want to locate it. The *Index of Acronyms* lists two *DAT*s: *Dental Admissions Test* and *Differential Aptitude Tests*. Because you want the counseling test, it is likely the latter rather than the former.

***Tests: A Comprehensive Reference for Assessments in Psychology, Education, and Business* (Fifth Edition)** This reference (Maddox, 2003) lists and describes approximately 2,000 tests, but gives no evaluations of them. (The test evaluations are given in *Test Critiques*, a companion volume, described later.) *Tests* is divided into three primary groups—psychology, education, and business—and 90 subcategories. Each listing describes the test and its purpose, for whom it is intended, scoring procedures, costs, and publisher.

The organization of the indexes makes locating tests easy. *Tests* has several indexes: title, publisher, computer-scoring, hearing impaired, visually impaired, physically impaired, out of print, tests found in the fourth but not in the fifth edition, and foreign language availability. Publishers' Websites are also listed.

Textbooks on Testing and Measurement A number of textbooks list, describe, and (sometimes) review selected tests. If you are looking for a test in a specific area, looking in the index of a textbook in the area may be a useful way to see which tests are frequently used. (Appendix K in this book lists a selection of published tests in several areas.) A textbook, however, is not a comprehensive source for information about tests because (a) tests are often selected for inclusion primarily for their merits in illustrating an author's point, (b) space permits only a few tests being mentioned, (c) often only the most popular or easily available tests are mentioned or illustrated, and (d) no single author is aware of all available tests.

Test Publishers' Catalogs An important way to get information about a test is directly from the test publisher. (See Appendix L for a partial list of publishers and their Websites.) Most test publishers have catalogs that describe the tests they publish in detail. A publisher's catalog is especially helpful for finding out about current editions of tests along with information about scoring services, costs, and how to obtain specimen sets, test manuals, and technical reports. Current information of this sort is seldom found in other print sources. Your school's testing office and the testing and measurement office of a college or university usually maintain collections of recent catalogs.

Locating Published Tests Online

Buros Test Locator The home page of the Buros Institute of Mental Measurements (http://www.unl.edu/buros) may be navigated to locate its database of published tests. This site lists over 4,000 commercially available tests.

ETS Test Collection ETS Test Collection is a database of approximately 20,000 tests and other assessment instruments. It contains information on both published and unpublished instruments. Some of the instruments listed in the database are out of print, some are available from publishers, some are available from the test authors, and some are available for purchase and downloading from ETS. Some of the tests are from outside the United States. You may search for a test type, author, or title. Click the "Search Help" button from the Test Collection home page for further assistance in searching. You can access the *ETS Test Collection* database directly at http://www.ets.org/testcoll.

CEEE Test Database This contains tests that are used with limited English proficiency students. The database is maintained by the Region III Comprehensive Center of the Center for Equity and Excellence in Education (George Washington University). Some tests are assessments of English proficiency. Others are subject-matters achievement tests in other languages (e.g., Spanish, Arabic, etc.). The tests are organized into groups: Diagnosis, District Evaluation, Identification, Language Dominance, Placement, Proficiency, Program Exit, Progress, and Program Evaluation. You may search by title or key word, as well as scroll through the list of tests under each grouping. The database may be accessed at http://r3cc.ceee.gwu.edu/standards_assessments/EAC/HOME.HTM.

Test Publishers' Websites As we discussed earlier, an important way to get information about a test is directly from the test publisher. (See Appendix L for a partial list of publishers and their Websites.) Most test publishers have Websites that describe the tests they publish in detail. A publisher's Website is especially helpful for finding out about current editions of tests along with information about scoring services, costs, and how to obtain specimen sets, test manuals, and technical reports. Current information of this sort is seldom found in other print sources. Remember, however, that publishers' Websites are marketing tools, not objective sources of test information.

General Internet Searches If you are unable to locate a test through one of these **online sources**, you could try searching the Internet with the test title, author's name, or subject area. Include the word "test" or "assessment" with the subject-area key word to help narrow the search. Usually, searching through http://www.eric.ed.gov will yield more relevant hits for educational tests than a general search, say on Google. You may try searching on *PsycINFO*, too, in your library.

Locating Published Tests Through Personal Contacts

Professional Contacts and Organizations Figure 18.2 lists organizations that may help you locate published tests. Larger testing companies and agencies usually have an information and/or advisory office to answer questions over their toll-free telephone numbers. Professional organizations, such as the National Council on Measurement in Education, can sometimes help by referring you to a member in your local area who can be of assistance. Some professional associations whose focus is not on assessment per se may have special

FIGURE 18.2 Examples of organizations that provide information on educational assessment.

Professional associations prepare periodicals and other publications related to educational assessment, work toward improved assessment usage, and may be contacted to identify members who are experts in certain areas of educational assessment.
1. American Educational Research Association (Washington, DC) [http://www.aera.net]
2. Association for Assessment in Counseling and Education (Arlington, VA) [http://aac.ncat.edu]
3. International Reading Association (IRA) (Newark, DE) [http://www.reading.org]
4. National Association of Test Directors (NATD) [http://www.natd.org]
5. National Council on Measurement in Education (NCME) (Washington, DC) [http://www.ncme.org]

Educational Research Information Center (ERIC). Online services are provided.
1. Search ERIC [http://searcheric.org]

Research centers and regional laboratories invest in research on technical or policy issues in educational assessment. They have catalogs of these publications and sometimes answer inquiries about specific assessment issues.
1. Buros Institute of Mental Measurements (University of Nebraska) [http://www.unl.edu/buros]
2. Center for the Study of Testing, Evaluation, and Educational Policy (Boston College) [http://www.csteep.bc.edu]
3. Center for Research on Evaluations, Standards, and Student Testing (CRESST) (UCLA) [http://www.cse.ucla.edu]
4. Northwest Regional Educational Laboratory (NREL) (Portland, OR) [http://www.nwrel.org]
5. Comprehensive Regional Assistance Centers [www.ccnetwork.org/where.html]
6. Mid-continent Regional Educational Laboratory (Mcrel)(Aurora, CO) [http://www.mcrel.org]

Nonprofit testing corporations offer a wide range of assessment services, conduct assessment research, and disseminate assessment information.
1. American College Testing Program (ACT) (Iowa City, IA) [http://www.act.org]
2. Educational Testing Service (ETS) (Princeton, NJ) [http://www.ets.org]

Nonprofit advocacy and public interest groups research matters of legality, individual rights, and public policy related to assessment.
1. National Center for Fair and Open Testing (Fair Test) (Cambridge, MA) [http://www.fairtest.org]

interest groups that are interested in specific issues such as performance, critical thinking, or classroom assessment. In some areas, federally funded research and development centers and regional laboratories have technical assistance offices that can help with testing problems. In some states, county-based school agencies, state-related school agencies, or technical assistance centers are specially organized to offer assistance in reviewing and using tests.

Testing Specialists in Colleges and Universities Testing and measurement professors at colleges and universities usually work in departments of educational research, educational psychology, measurement and statistics, counseling and guidance, or psychology. Ask the department chairperson for recommendations of persons to call.

Testing Offices in Schools, Colleges, and Universities The director of your school testing office or the school psychologist is frequently a useful resource. Many larger colleges and universities have testing offices designed to help their faculties and students with testing problems, and such offices are usually available to answer questions from the public as well.

Promotional Exhibits at Conferences If you attend a professional conference you may go to the exhibit area. The exhibits will have books and instructional materials, and may also have exhibits by test publishers. The exhibitor may have a test you are seeking or may put you in contact with a sales representative in your area with the information you seek.

LOCATING EVALUATIONS OF PUBLISHED TESTS

In the preceding section we discussed how to find a test. But finding a test is only one part of the information you need to evaluate a published test. You will also need to locate published reviews of the test, preferably by reviewers who are competent assessment specialists and who are not associated with the test publisher. In this section we discuss three places to look for reviews of the test you have located: (a) printed materials, (b) online resources, or (c) personal contacts with persons who may know about the test. Figure 18.3 gives an overview of the resources that are available for locating test reviews. We describe each of these resources in this section.

Locating Evaluations of Published Tests From Print Sources

Three print resources are likely to be in your academic library: *Mental Measurements Yearbook*s, *Test Critiques*, and professional journals.

Mental Measurements Yearbooks (MMYs) Among the most useful resources for locating information on tests are the publications of the Buros Institute of Mental Measurements (located at the University of Nebraska). The late Oscar K. Buros founded the institute and began a series of test bibliographies and ***Mental Measurements Yearbooks (MMYs)***. The *Mental Measurements Yearbooks* (Buros, 1938 through present) are a series of volumes that critically evaluate many of the currently available published tests in English. Each volume supplements rather than replaces the earlier editions, so it is occasionally necessary to consult earlier volumes to obtain complete coverage of a test. One or more experts review each test especially for the *MMYs*, and each volume gives excerpted journal reviews as well. Each *Mental Measurements Yearbook* contains original reviews of hundreds of tests.

Each test entry is organized into five sections. The *description section* contains a test title, age or grade levels, publication dates, special comments, number and type of part scores, authors, publishers, references, and bibliographic information. Each entry is cross-referenced to previous reviews in earlier *MMYs*. The *development section* evaluates how well the publisher developed the test using professionally accepted standards, including the use of empirical data in the development process (recall our discussion of empirically developed test in Chapter 16). The *technical section* evaluates the tests standardization procedure, reliability, and validity. The *commentary section* contains the reviewer's overall evaluation of the test. The *summary section* is a concise wrap-up of the reviewer's opinion of the test. Names and addresses of hundreds of test publishers are listed in each *MMY*. A disadvantage of the printed *MMYs* is that because of the publication lag, editions of tests reviewed may not correspond to publishers' new editions.

To locate a test evaluation, you need to know the *MMY* volume in which the test appears. If your test title appears in *Tests in Print VII*, that publication will tell you the

FIGURE 18.3 Where to locate published reviews of tests.

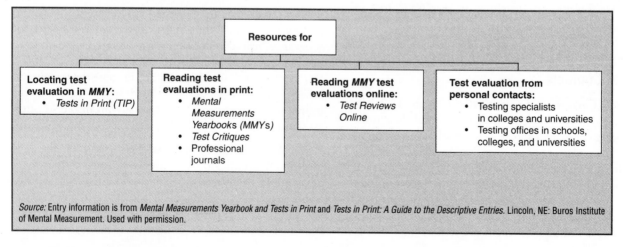

Source: Entry information is from *Mental Measurements Yearbook and Tests in Print and Tests in Print: A Guide to the Descriptive Entries*. Lincoln, NE: Buros Institute of Mental Measurement. Used with permission.

review's *MMY* volume and entry number. You may also use the *Test Reviews Online* described in the last section by accessing it on the Internet through the Buros Institute home page. Figure 18.4 shows how a page in the *MMY* is laid out. This will give you a better sense of what to expect from this resource. For an online lesson in how to use an *MMY* test review see Nitko (2005b) at http://www.unl.edu/buros/bimm/html/lesson01.html.

Test Critiques (Volumes I–XI) Test Critiques (Keyser & Sweetland, 1994) is a series of volumes that reviews the most frequently used tests in business, education, and psychology. A testing specialist reviews each test. Entries cover an introduction to the test, practical uses and applications, technical aspects, and an overall evaluation of the test. You may use *Tests: A Comprehensive Reference for Assessments in Psychology, Education, and Business*, described earlier,

FIGURE 18.4 Layout of a *Mental Measurements Yearbook* review entry for a hypothetical test.

Entry Number: The number cited in all indexes when referring to this test.

Title: Test titles are printed in boldface type; secondary or series titles are set off from main titles by colon.

Population: A description of the groups for which the test is intended.

Administration: Individual or group administration is indicated.

Distribution: This is noted only for tests that are put on a special market by the publisher.

Special Editions: Various types of special editions are listed here.

Author: All test authors' names are reported, exactly as printed on the test materials.

Cross References: For tests that have been previously listed in a Buros publication, cross references to the reviews, excerpts, and references will be noted here. "9:1410," for example, refers to test 1410 in the *Ninth Mental Measurements Yearbook*; "T4:3010" refers to test 3010 in *Tests in Print IV*.

[420]
The Hypothetical Test: Reading.
Purpose: Designed to "measure achievement in reading."
Population: Grades 9–12.
Publication Dates: 1989–1994.
Acronym: HYPE.
Scores, 3: Vocabulary, Comprehension, and Total.
Administration: Individual or group.
Forms, 3: Survey, Abbreviated, Complete Battery.
Restricted Distribution: Distribution of Survey Form restricted to school principals.
Price Data, 1995: $70 per complete kit including 100 tests, scoring key, and manual ('94, 120 pages); $9 per scoring key; $32 per manual.
Special Editions: Braille edition available.
Time: 50 (60) minutes.
Comments: May be self-scored.
Author: Jane J. Doe.
Publisher: Hypothetical Tests, Inc.
Cross References: See T4:3010 (2 references); for reviews by John Roe and Robert Smith of an earlier edition, see 9:1410 (6 references).

Review of the Hypothetical Test: Reading by John J. Smith, Associate Professor of Instruction and Learning, State University, Jonestown, Any State

The actual text of the test review would be here. Space does not permit including a review.

Purpose: A brief, clear statement describing the purpose of the test; often these are quotations from the test manual.

Publication Date: The inclusive range of publication dates.

Acronym: Acronym by which the test may be commonly known.

Scores: The number of explicit scores is presented along with the descriptions of what they are intended to measure.

Forms: All available forms, parts, and levels are listed.

Price Data: Price information is reported for test packages, answer sheets, accessories, and specimen sets.

Time: This is the amount of time to take, and administer, the test. The first number is the actual working time examinees are allowed, and the second (parenthesized) number is the total time needed to administer the test.

Comments: Special notations and comments.

Publisher: The publisher's full address can be found in the Publishers Directory and Index.

Source: Entry information is from "*Mental Measurements Yearbook* and Tests in Print: A Guide to the Description Entries." Lincoln, NE: Buros Institute of Mental Measurement. Used with Permission.

Source: Entry information is from *Mental Measurements Yearbook and Tests in Print* and *Tests in Print: A Guide to the Descriptive Entries*. Lincoln, NE: Buros Institute of Mental Measurement. Used with permission.

to locate the *Test Critiques* volume in which the test is found.

Professional Journals Professional journals in a field often review tests that have potential application in a particular area, such as reading, mathematics, child development, or learning disabilities. Specialized testing and measurement journals review tests that have a wide appeal to school practitioners and psychologists. Among the journals often reporting test reviews (Buros, 1978) are *Developmental Medicine and Child Neurology; Journal of Educational Measurement; Journal of Learning Disabilities; Journal of Personality Assessment; Journal of Reading; Journal of School Psychology; Journal of Special Education; Measurement and Evaluation in Guidance; Modern Language Journal; Psychological Reports; Psychology in the Schools;* and *Reading Teacher.*

Bibliographic information about these and other journals (including those that review testing books) appears at the back of some *Mental Measurements Yearbooks.* Journal references are indexed in such sources as the *Education Index, Dissertation Abstracts, Research Studies in Education, Psychological Abstracts,* and *Research in Education* (ERIC).

Locating Evaluations of Published Tests Online

One source for obtaining test reviews online is *Test Reviews Online* from the Buros Institute (http://www.unl.edu/buros). Test reviews from *MMY*s 9 through 16 are available. Approximately 2,000 test reviews are available, but can be seen and downloaded only for a fee. This is an excellent resource for someone who does not have ready access to the print sources but who does have Internet access and a credit card.

Locating Evaluations of Published Tests Through Personal Contacts

Testing Specialists in Colleges and Universities Just as your professional contacts may help you locate a test, these same people may help you evaluate a test. Testing and measurement professors at colleges and universities usually work in departments of educational research, educational psychology, measurement and statistics, counseling and guidance, or psychology. Call the department chairperson for recommendations of persons to call. A testing specialist may have personal experience with a particular test and be willing to share that experience with you.

Testing Offices in Schools, Colleges, and Universities The director of your school testing office or the school psychologist may be a useful resource. Many larger colleges and universities have testing offices designed to help their faculties and students with testing problems. Such offices are usually available to answer questions from the public, as well.

LOCATING COMPUTERIZED TESTING MATERIALS

General Internet Searches

You may have some luck searching for computerized testing products using Google or another search engine. Be sure to use "computer testing + education" as the search term; otherwise, you will get lots of false links. Most sites you find will be selling computerized testing products, so you cannot find objective expert evaluations of products at these sites.

Test Publishers' Websites

Test publishers may have several computerized testing products, which will be listed on their Websites. Again, these sites are marketing tools, so you will not find objective evaluations of the products at the sites. A list of Websites for companies offering computer-assisted testing is provided in the Companion Website to this textbook (http://www.prenhall.com/nitko). A list of test publishers and their URLs is given in Appendix L of this book.

LOCATING UNPUBLISHED TEST MATERIALS

Not all test materials are published. Many tests have been used in research and evaluation projects. Some of these are available, if you can find them. We describe some sources for locating these types of tests in this section.

Locating Unpublished Tests from Print Sources

ETS Test Collection Earlier we discussed the online *ETS Test Collection* as an online database of tests. Many of the tests in this database are unpublished.

Tests in Microfiche Tests in Microfiche contains more than 800 unpublished tests used in education, business, and psychology. It is available in many college and university libraries in their microforms collections.

Directory of Unpublished Experimental Measures This directory edited by Goldman and Mitchell (1997) lists unpublished tests and surveys in a variety of educational and psychological areas. The listings are arranged in 24 categories and include tests' availability, purpose, content, format, and related research. Each volume has a cumulative index that lists all the approximately 5,000 tests across the earlier volumes.

Measures for Psychological Assessment: A Guide to 3,000 Original Sources and Their Applications This volume, edited by Chun, Cobb, and French (1975), is a bit dated but provides annotated descriptions of tests and instruments used in published research.

Health and Psychosocial Instruments (HAPI) This resource is available on CD-ROM (contact Evelyn Perloff, Behavior Measurement Database Service, P.O. Box 110287, Pittsburgh, PA 15232-0787, 412-687-6850) and online through Ovid Technologies (a vendor of databases) at http://www.ovid.com/. It includes instruments from journal articles in health sciences, nursing, psychology, and social sciences.

Locating Unpublished Tests Online

College and University Library Subject Guides Some academic libraries in colleges and universities provide online subject guides in testing and measurement. These may include links to bibliographies of unpublished tests and survey instruments. Two examples are: *Tests and Testing Information* (Corby, 2002) at Michigan State University (http://www.lib.msu.edu/corby/psychology/) and *Test and Measures in the Social Sciences: Tests Available in Compilation Volumes* (Hough, 2005) at the University of Texas Arlington (http://libraries.uta.edu/helen/lests&meas/testmaniframe.htm/). You should check your local library for *subject guides on testing and measurement.*

ETS Test Collection We discussed earlier this database of approximately 20,000 tests and other assessment instruments. It contains information on both published and unpublished instruments. You can access the *ETS Test Collection* database directly at http://www.ets.org/testcoll.

General Internet Searches If you are unable to locate a test through one of the preceding sources, you could try searching the Internet with the test title, author's name, or subject area. Include the word "test" or "assessment" with the subject-area key word to help narrow the search. Usually, searching through ERIC will yield more relevant hits for educational tests than a general search, say on Google. You may try searching on *PsycINFO*, too, in your library.

RESTRICTIONS ON PURCHASING AND USING TESTS

Purchasing Restrictions

Although you may find the name of a test you want to use, its availability may be restricted. To guard against assessment abuse, some publishers restrict the sale of test materials. The publisher's catalog will list any restrictions on test purchasing: The sale of certain tests, especially individually administered intelligence and personality tests, is restricted to qualified psychologists. Typically, publishers label the tests according to the severity of the restrictions in purchasing:

Level A–may be ordered on official letterhead by an agency or organization in which qualified persons will administer and interpret the results. The agency or institution would employ persons who meet the recommendations of the *Standards for Educational and Psychological Testing* (1999). An individual who is ordering would have to verify completion of sufficient training and a course in test interpretation and use from a recognized program.

Level B–individuals will need to verify that they have had sufficient graduate-level training (typically a master's degree) and supervised experience to administer and interpret the test being ordered. Membership in an appropriate professional association may be required. The recommendations of the *Standards* would be followed.

Level C–individuals need to verify that they have a Ph.D. or related degree in psychology or education as well as appropriate coursework and supervised training in administration and interpretation of the test being ordered.

Sales restrictions vary with the publisher, each implementing a somewhat different policy on establishing a purchaser's qualifications and selling tests. The test user must be sure to acquire the requisite training and experience before purchasing a test. A form needs to be completed, signed, and submitted to the publisher for approval before a test can be purchased.

If you are a practicing teacher and want to review the achievement tests your school district uses, then you should contact the district's testing director. If you are taking a course in which you are expected to write an evaluation of a test, you should ask your instructor how to proceed. Your university may have a testing office that contains specimen sets of tests for this purpose. If you must order a test, your instructor will likely need to prepare a letter for you to include with the order explaining the assignment and how the test will be used. Start your search for a test early. Last-minute searches will likely result in problems completing your assignment.

The previously mentioned *Standards for Educational and Psychological Testing* gives the test publisher the responsibility for telling the user the qualifications needed to interpret test results properly. However, *Standards* (American Educational Research Association [AERA], American Psychological Association, & National Council on Measurement in Education, 1985) states, "A test user should know his own qualifications and how well they match the qualifications required for use of specific tests" (p. 58). *Standards* is discussed in the following paragraphs.

Guidelines for Proper Test Development and Use

Test Standards A useful publication for evaluating educational and psychological tests is the *Standards for Educational and Psychological Testing* (AERA et al., 1999). This was the publication cited in the preceding paragraphs on test-ordering restrictions. This is a set of standards for publishers and users of tests prepared jointly by the American Educational Research Association, the American

Psychological Association, and the National Council on Measurement in Education. The *Standards* describe various kinds of information that a publisher should provide in a test manual and accompanying materials. It includes suggestions for how a test should be developed as well as guidelines for how a test should be used. Further information can be obtained by calling the National Council on Measurement in Education.

The Code The ideas and concepts in the *Standards* are directed to the professional tester rather than to measurement students and the public. However, the Joint Committee on Testing Practices (2004) prepared a set of major obligations for professionals (like yourself) who use tests in formal educational testing programs. These obligations, described in the *Code of Fair Testing Practices in Education (Revised)*, are included in Appendix B. The *Code* will be especially useful to you as you evaluate a test or your school's testing program. The *Code* lists separate obligations for test users and for test developers. *The Code of Professional Responsibilities in Educational Measurement* (NCME, 1995) also describes professional obligations and is reproduced in Appendix C. (See also Chapter 5.)

EVALUATING AND SELECTING A TEST

Because tests play important roles in the educational system, school officials should select them carefully. Before your district adopts a test, a committee of parents, teachers, and administrators should carefully examine and evaluate it. This section describes a systematic procedure for conducting such a review and evaluation. Part of your professional responsibility as a teacher is to participate and offer informed judgments when serving on such test selection committees. School administrators who select tests without the informed judgment of teachers run the risk of egregious errors. Because no test can perfectly match a school district's needs, comparing the merits of one test with another is an important step in choosing the better product.

Clarify Your Purpose

The first step in reviewing a test is to pinpoint the specific purpose(s) for obtaining student information and to find out who will be using the information to make decisions. The more specific you are about the purposes and conditions under which assessment information will be used, the better you will be able to select the appropriate procedure. At this point, reread Chapter 3, which discusses test score validity.

Things you need to keep clearly in mind as you begin your selection include:

1. *The school setting in which the assessment will be used*—type of community, ages or grades of students, persons who will be helped by an appropriate assessment, and

persons who will be in charge of using the assessment results.

2. *The specific decisions, purposes, and/or uses intended for the assessment results*—identifying specific reading skills needing remediation, appraising a student's emotional needs or areas of anxiety as a prelude to counseling, appraising a student's aptitude for mechanical activities that a counselor will discuss during guidance sessions, or surveying general levels of reading and mathematics achievement to report curriculum evaluation information to the school board.

3. *The way you believe that using test scores or other assessment information will help improve the decision, serve the purpose, or solve the problem*—the better you can articulate, from the outset, what you expect an assessment procedure to accomplish, the better you will be able to evaluate the many options open to you and to choose the most satisfactory one.

4. *The need to strike a balance between the strengths and limitations of performance tasks relative to multiple-choice tests*—such factors as time, cost, in-depth assessment of narrow curricular areas, and less in-depth assessment of broad areas of the curriculum. The assessment procedure you select will be the result of compromises on several dimensions, so it is helpful to think about these early in the process.

Put the New Assessment Plans into Local Context

Before you set out to select a new assessment procedure, you should take stock of the assessments already being used in the district. For example, what type of assessments do teachers already do, of what quality are these assessments, and do they serve the perceived need?

External Assessments Versus Teacher-Crafted Assessments You will need a perspective on what an external assessment contributes beyond the school-based assessments currently used by teachers. Externally imposed assessments do not match a local curriculum framework exactly. You may decide, for example, that it will be wiser and instructionally more effective to spend the district's money improving teacher-crafted assessment procedures rather than purchasing an **external assessment procedure** such as a standardized test. *In general, a school district should rely on teacher-crafted assessments for 90% to 95% of its assessment needs.* Principals, because they are responsible for the quality of the instruction in their schools, bear a special responsibility to evaluate teacher-crafted assessments to ensure they are of high quality. Sadly, principals are often ignorant of how high-quality, teacher-crafted assessments impact students' learning.

State-Mandated Assessments Versus Standardized Tests States have mandated standardized assessment programs. These programs may be basic skills assessments, accountability programs, or more complex assessments. To reduce redundancy, the assessment a school district purchases should supplement the mandated assessment and serve other, nonduplicating purposes. There has been an increase in mandated state assessments following the federal NCLB legislation. Content and performance standards have been defined, and states are required to attend to these to participate in federal funding. Chapter 16 gave a set of guidelines for selecting a standardized achievement test that is compatible with state-mandated assessment requirements.

Instructional Value of Standardized Tests As discussed in Chapter 16, standardized assessments with norms and educational development scales are most helpful to (a) assess students' relative strengths and weaknesses across curricular areas, (b) assess students' growth within a specific curricular area, and (c) provide an "independent, external" assessment of students' accomplishments relative to a standardization sample. *You should weigh these purposes against teacher-based assessments; use instructional benefit to students as a criterion.*

Evaluating a School District Sometimes a school district wishes to use an external assessment, such as a standardized test, to evaluate itself. School officials should be aware that not only do single tests provide an especially poor foundation on which to evaluate teachers and curricula, but also that program evaluation itself is a technical area requiring well-prepared professional evaluators. Very

often, qualified program evaluation personnel are not on a district's payroll. Being unaware of the need for a professional program evaluator, school officials often assign the task to persons professionally trained in other areas, such as school psychologists or guidance counselors. Superintendents wanting to use assessments for program evaluation may wish to consult curriculum evaluation experts before designing these evaluation strategies. One suggestion is to contact the American Educational Research Association (http://www.aera.net) and ask about contacting a member of Division H who lives near your school district. Figure 18.5 summarizes some factors affecting the difficulty of the school's educational task. Information about these factors should be used along with test results to help interpret a school's effectiveness.

Qualifications of the Staff Another consideration is the qualifications of a school district's staff in relation to the assessment procedure proposed. For example, specially trained professionals are needed to administer and interpret individual intelligence and personality tests, as well as group-administered scholastic ability tests. If such professionals are in short supply in a district, you will want to use other assessment procedures. Similarly, using performance assessments and portfolios requires educating teachers about scoring and interpreting these procedures. This will cost time and money that a district may not have. Sometimes partial implementation may be helpful, such as assessing students at some grades and not others.

FIGURE 18.5 Facts to be reported in addition to standardized test results when evaluating school effectiveness.

Attendance   Includes absences of staff and students from school and parents from participation in parent-teacher organizations.

Holding power   Includes graduation and dropout rates.

Parent involvement   Includes parent-teacher organizations, volunteers, and parent-staffed programs.

Diversity   Includes staff and student gender, ethnicity, and home language and staff responsibilities.

Economic conditions   Includes parent income levels and students receiving free or reduced-cost lunches.

Stability   Includes percent of staff and students new to a school district.

Experience   Includes years of teaching experience and years of education beyond the initial qualifications.

Staff development   Includes in-service programs, peer mentoring, collaboration with businesses or colleges, and courses taken.

Programs for students   Includes study skills, counseling, dropout and at-risk prevention, reentry, cross-age tutoring, extracurricular, and summer school.

Achievement   Includes performance of students at the next higher educational level; longitudinal patterns of achievement test results, student awards and honors, per-student library loans, National Merit scholars, college entrance test results, and out-of-class student accomplishments.

School environment   Includes incidents of vandalism and violence, gang-related activities, types of disciplinary actions, special services, extracurricular activities, and library facilities.

Instructional variables   Includes length of day, year, and class periods; amount of time per subject per week; number of students using extended day academic program; homework actually assigned; and percent of school days devoted exclusively to academic learning.

Fiscal   Includes average teacher, staff, and administrator salaries; expenditures per student.

Source: Adapted from "Putting Test Scores in Perspective: Communicating a Complete Report Card for Your Schools," by K. K. Matter, in *Understanding Achievement Tests: A Guide for School Administrators* (pp. 121–129) by L. M. Rudner, J. C. Conoley, and B. S. Plake (Eds.), 1989. Washington, DC: ERIC Clearinghouse on Tests, Measurement, and Evaluation.

Review the Actual Assessment Materials

Locate Tests and Reviews of Them   If you have done your homework as just described, you will be in a good position to locate assessments and to begin reviewing them. The information sources described earlier in this chapter will help you identify assessments that approximate your needs. Of particular help in identifying tests and obtaining descriptions of them are the following:

> *Tests in Print VII*
> *Mental Measurements Yearbooks*
> *Tests*
> *ETS Test Collection*
> Test publishers' catalogs

The following sources are helpful for locating reviews of tests:

> *Mental Measurements Yearbooks*
> *Test Critiques*
> Professional journals

Obtain Copies of the Test to Review   After narrowing your choices to a few assessment procedures that appear to suit your needs, you should obtain copies of the assessment materials and tasks; detailed descriptions of the assessment content and rationale behind its selection; materials related to scoring, reporting, and interpreting assessment results; information about the cost of the assessment materials and scoring service; and technical information about the assessment. (See our earlier discussion about restrictions in ordering tests.)

Much of this material is bundled together in a **specimen set,** which is designed as a marketing tool as well as for critical review of materials. As a result, not all materials you will need to review a test intelligently are included. For example, some publishers' specimen sets do not include complete copies of the assessment booklets or scoring guidelines. You will need to order these separately.

Technical Information About a Test's Quality   Technical information about a test's quality is not found in a publisher's catalog. A test's **technical manual** gives information about how the test was developed, reliability coefficients, standard errors of measurement, correlational and validity studies, equating methods, item analysis procedures, and norming-sample data. Technical manuals are not typically included in specimen sets and must be ordered separately from the tests. Often the publisher prepares several technical reports for a standardized test. Although school testing directors should have copies of the technical manuals for the tests the school uses, too often they do not. Some colleges and universities that maintain test collections for their faculty and students may have technical manuals. Usually, you will need to order the technical manual directly from the test's publisher.

Committee Should Review All Materials   Once you obtain the materials, the committee can review them. Be sure to compare similar assessments against the purposes you had in mind for using the assessments. It might be helpful for the committee to obtain input from noncommittee members for certain parts of the assessment: for example, mathematics teachers for the mathematics section, reading teachers for the reading assessment, and so forth. You could also call upon a college or university faculty member to help: For example, a testing and measurement faculty member may be better qualified to review and/or explain technical material. Contact the National Council on Measurement in Education (http://www.ncme.org) for the names of specialists who live near your school district.

Achievement Tests Must Match the Curriculum   It is important to match each test item with your state's standards and state or local curriculum. You do this by obtaining the complete list of standards or learning targets, organized by grade level. Two persons independently read each test item and record which standard or learning target it matches. When all items have been matched, the persons compare their results and reconcile the differences. The findings are summarized in a table that lists each standard and the I.D. number of the test items matching each. The number of nonmatching items is also recorded. This should be done separately for each grade, because a test's items may appear at a grade level that is different than the grade at which the corresponding learning target is taught. If there are a lot of these grade-sequence mismatches, the test will not be suitable for your school district. Be sure to note especially the match between the kinds of thinking and performance activities implied by the standards and the test items. Often the content matches, but the thinking processes and performances required do not. An example of how to do this is found in Nitko et al., (1998). As we discussed in Chapter 3, one should examine whether a test and the standards are aligned with respect to content span, depth of understanding required, topical emphasis, expected student performance, and applicability of the test for all students (La Marca et al., 2000). You should review Chapter 3 on these points.

Finally, find out the month during which the district plans to administer the test. Then, determine what proportion of the test's items assess content that will have been taught before testing begins. When a test assesses content students have not yet been taught, scores are lowered. (See Chapter 17 for further discussion of this point in connection with grade-equivalent scores.)

Pilot the Test   If possible, you should administer the assessment to a few students to get a feel for how students might respond. This would be especially important with writing tasks or performance tasks. You may find that for some otherwise appealing performance tasks, student time limits or instructions are not sufficient and confusion results.

This is less likely if the assessment was professionally developed and standardized on a national sample.

A Sample Outline for Your Test Review

It will help your review if you systematically organize relevant information in one or two pages. Using a form is a concise way of sharing information among committee members or with others who may help make decisions about the choice. Figure 18.6 suggests what information to

FIGURE 18.6 Suggested outline for recording relevant information for reviewing and evaluating an assessment procedure.

Identifying information
1. Title, publisher, copyright date
2. Purpose of the test as described by the publisher
3. Grade level(s), subject(s), administrative time
4. Cost per student, service costs
5. Types of scores and norms provided

Content and curricular evaluation
1. Publisher's description and rationale for specific types of tasks
2. Quality and clarity of the tasks themselves
3. Currency of the content and match to recent curricular trends
4. Match of the tasks to each of the school district's curricula
5. Inclusion of ethnic and gender diversity in the task content

Instructional use evaluation
1. Publisher's description and rationale for how the assessment results may be used by teachers to improve instruction
2. Local teachers' evaluations of how the assessment results could be used for improving their instruction
3. Overlap of assessment with the existing teacher-based assessment procedures

Technical evaluation
1. Representativeness, recency, and local relevance of the national norms
2. Types of reliability coefficients and their values (use average values if necessary)
3. Summary of the evidence regarding the validity of the assessment for the purpose(s) you have in mind for using it
4. Quality of the criterion-referenced information the assessment provides
5. Likelihood that the assessment will have adverse effects on students with disabilities, minority students, and female students

Practical evaluation
1. Quality of the manual and teacher-oriented materials
2. Ease of administration and scoring
3. Cost and usefulness of the scoring services
4. Estimated annual costs (time and money) if the assessment procedure is adopted for the district
5. Likely public reaction to using the assessment procedure

Overall evaluation
1. Comments of reviewers (e.g., *MMY* or *Test Critiques*)
2. Conclusions about the positive aspects of the assessment
3. Conclusions about the negative aspects of the assessment
4. Summary and recommendation about adoption

List of references and sources used

record for your review in such a form. You will find an online lesson in how to use this form along with reviews from the *MMY* to systematically review a test in Nitko (2005a) at http://www.unl.edu/buros/bimm/html/lesson02.html.

HOW A STANDARDIZED TEST IS DEVELOPED

As an informed consumer of assessments, you must be aware of the steps a publisher should follow when developing a test, as well as the activities involved in each of these steps. Your judgment of how well the publisher carried out each step should be part of your evaluation of the quality of an assessment procedure.

A standardized test should be the product of a carefully conducted program of research and development. The activities involved in each step are briefly described in this section. Such a well-run development program involves the work of many persons and includes the following steps (Robertson, 1990, pp. 62–63).

1. Preliminary ideas.
2. Evaluate proposal (approve/reject).
3. Make formal arrangement (sign contract if publication is approved).
4. Prepare test specifications.
5. Write items.
6. Conduct item tryout.
   a. Prepare tryout sample specifications.
   b. Prepare participants.
   c. Prepare tryout materials.
   d. Administer tryout items.
   e. Analyze tryout data.
7. Assemble final test form(s).
8. Conduct national standardization.
   a. Prepare standardization sample specifications.
   b. Obtain participants.
   c. Prepare standardization materials.
   d. Administer tests.
   e. Analyze data.
   f. Develop norms tables.
9. Prepare final materials.
   a. Establish publication schedule.
   b. Write manual.
   c. Prepare test books and answer forms.
   d. Manufacture/produce/print materials.
10. Prepare marketing plan.
    a. Initiate direct mail promotion.
    b. Initiate space advertising.
    c. Train sales staff.
    d. Attend professional meetings and conventions.
11. Publish.

More details about these steps and what test developers are expected to do at each stage of development are found in the *Standards for Educational and Psychological Testing* (AERA et al., 1999).

Note, however, that many assessments available in the marketplace do not follow all steps, because to do so is quite costly and time consuming. Unfortunately, if a publisher omits steps during the developmental process, the publisher will probably omit those concerned with collecting and analyzing data used to improve the quality of the test and/or to support the validity of the claims made for the test. Shortcutting assessment development steps usually means lowering validity, so beware of poorly developed assessments.

Summary

Locating a Published Test and Its Published Review

- There are numerous sources you may use to locate information about tests. These include
  - Buros Institute of Mental Measurements
  - Comprehensive Center of the Center for Equity and Excellence
  - Educational Testing Service
  - Professional associations
  - Test publishers
- Other test information sources include
  - Testing and measurement textbooks
  - Professional contacts and organizations
  - Test standards
  - Online services through Internet

Locating an Unpublished Test and Computerized Testing Information

- There are several sources to locate information about unpublished tests. These include
  - *Directory of Unpublished Experimental Measures*
  - *Health and Psychosocial Instruments (HAPI)*
  - *ETS Test Collection*
  - *Tests in Microfiche*
  - *PsycINFO*
- There are several sources to locate information about computerized tests and testing services tests. These include
  - Textbooks on testing and measurement
  - The Companion Website for this book (http://www.prenhall.com/nitko)
  - Publishers' catalogs and Websites
  - Internet searches

Restrictions on Purchasing and Using Tests

- Qualifications for assessment purchase were discussed. Although a publisher is obliged to tell you and other prospective users what qualifications are necessary to use and interpret an assessment, you bear the ultimate responsibility of knowing your own qualifications and whether they match those required for using the assessment properly.

Evaluating and Selecting a Test

- Before evaluating and selecting a published assessment instrument, you should:
  - Clearly identify the purposes for which you want to use the results.
  - Think about new assessments in your local educational context, including the type of nontest information you need to report (see Figure 18.5).
  - Identify the sources likely to have the information you need.

- Obtain specimen sets, administration manuals, and technical manuals for all assessments you are evaluating.
- Prepare a summary report of your review of each assessment procedure using an outline similar to that in Figure 18.6.

How a Standardized Test Is Developed

- One aspect of evaluating a published assessment is judging how carefully it was built.
- A professionally developed assessment should have gone through several research and development steps before being made available to consumers.
- Professional standards for test development are described in the *Standards for Educational and Psychological Testing*.
- You should include in your test evaluation your judgment of how well the publisher has followed each of these steps.

Important Terms and Concepts

ETS Test Collection
external assessment procedure
Mental Measurements Yearbooks (**MMYs**)
online sources
specimen set
Standards for Educational and Psychological Testing
technical manual
Test Critiques
Tests in Microfiche
Tests in Print

Exercises and Applications

1. Describe the types of assessment information you would find in each of the following sources:
   a. *Mental Measurements Yearbook*
   b. *Tests in Print*
   c. *Tests*
   d. *Test Critiques*
   e. *ETS Test Collection*
   f. *Standards for Educational and Psychological Testing*
   g. a test publisher's catalog
   h. http://www.ncme.org
2. Describe how each of the following professional organizations may help you obtain test information:
   a. Association for Assessment in Counseling and Education
   b. International Reading Association
   c. National Association of Test Directors
   d. National Council on Measurement in Education
3. Read each of these statements and identify the one source that would most likely contain the information the speaker is requesting.
   a. "I want to know what kinds of instruments are available to assess attitudes of female students toward work, home, marriage, and family life."
   b. "I want to know what professionals in the field think of this criterion-referenced test."
   c. "What services does a publisher provide for interpreting assessment results, and what are the charges?"
   d. "I want to know the newest instruments developed for assessing perceptual-motor development of primary school students."

4. Suppose you have already located a particular test and you want the specific information about it implied by the following statements. What source would you consult first for each statement?
   a. "What are the reliability coefficients for their test?"
   b. "What kind of norms does the publisher provide?"
   c. "How do test specialists view the quality of the procedures the publisher followed when developing the test?"
   d. "What research studies and reports have used this assessment instrument?"

5. Using the procedures described in this chapter, locate a specific standardized assessment instrument you believe can serve a purpose you have identified.
   a. Then, following the procedures described in this chapter, review and evaluate this assessment instrument in relation to your stated purpose. Write your review and evaluation using the outline given in Figure 18.6, using headings and subheadings appropriately.
   b. Share your evaluation with others in this course.

19 Scholastic Aptitude, Career Interests, Attitudes, and Personality Tests

LEARNING TARGETS

After studying this chapter, you should have learned the following:

Assessing Scholastic and Other Aptitude Tests

1. Explain why it is important to assess and use information about students' general intellectual skills and aptitudes in teaching. [4, 1]

2. Explain why aptitude tests do not describe a student's future capacity to learn or to succeed. [4, 1]

3. Distinguish between aptitude and achievement tests. [4, 7, 9]

4. Explain how the fixed conditions under which most students must learn increase the ability of aptitude tests to predict their success. [4, 3]

5. Explain the factors that keep students' aptitude test scores stable or consistent over time. [4, 3]

6. Explain the factors that tend to cause scholastic aptitude test scores to change over time. [4, 3]

7. Explain the advantages and disadvantages of using omnibus, two-score, and multiple-factor aptitude tests for educational decisions. [4, 3]

8. Describe some of the popular group-administered tests of scholastic aptitude, including some of the types of scores teachers are likely to receive with reports about students. [6, 3]

9. Explain the advantages of using group tests of specific aptitudes in education. [6, 7, 3]

10. Explain the advantages of using individually administered tests of general scholastic aptitude in assessing students. [4, 3, 6, 7]

11. Describe the popular individually administered tests of general scholastic aptitude in terms of their content, the ages of students for whom they are used, and the types of scores they report. [4, 6, 7]

12. Explain why it is necessary to assess systematically a low-functioning student's adaptive behavior. [4, 6]

Assessing Vocational and Career Interests

13. Explain the benefits of using information from vocational interest inventories in addition to achievement and aptitude information when counseling a student on further schooling and career choices. [4, 6, 7]

Assessing Attitudes and Personality

14. Distinguish among the concepts of achievement, aptitude, attitude, interests, and values. [4, 1]

15. Explain the two major approaches to building career interest inventories. [4, 6]

16. Describe the content, organization, and types of scoring of a career interest inventory. [4, 6]

17. Distinguish among expressed, manifested, tested, and inventoried tests. [4, 6]

18. Explain the factors you should keep in mind when using the results of attitude assessments with your students. [4, 6, 7]

19. Explain the two major approaches to assessing personality characteristics. [4]

20. Discuss the usefulness of students' personality assessment results for a classroom teacher. [4]

Important Terms and Concepts

21. Explain how the terms and concepts listed at the end of this chapter apply to educational assessment. [6]

ABOUT THIS CHAPTER

This chapter begins by exploring tests used to assess general scholastic aptitude.[1] You may be required to administer and interpret some of these tests for students in your classroom. Other types of general scholastic aptitude tests are administered and interpreted only by qualified persons such as school psychologists. You need to be familiar with these tests, nevertheless, because you may be required to read and interpret the psychologist's report or participate in an individual educational planning team.

Second, we discuss instruments that assess career and job interests. These instruments, in combination with information from scholastic aptitude tests, help students see how closely their current pattern of interests match those of men and women who have been successful in different types of jobs. Teachers and guidance counselors can assist in reviewing and interpreting these test results and in guiding students' career explorations.

Next, we discuss assessment of students' attitudes. Students' attitudes reflect their disposition toward school, family, and other institutions. Most school districts profess that positive attitudes toward school, family, community, work, and further learning are important learning targets.

Fourth, we explain assessment of personality characteristics. These assessment procedures should be administered and interpreted only by a qualified psychologist. Nevertheless, you may be required to read and interpret a psychologist's report for some of your students.

APTITUDES FOR LEARNING

General Versus Specific Intellectual Skills

Assessments of the kind discussed in this chapter describe a learner's **general intellectual skills**, rather than describing the **specific intellectual skills** a learner needs in, say, next week's geometry lessons. When the knowledge or skills a student needs for an upcoming lesson are specific and narrow, the student's present level of knowledge and skills are the best predictor of his learning success. For most of these specific, day-to-day instructional decisions, you will have to develop your own assessment procedures.

General Intellectual Skills and Aptitudes Measurement

A student's past performance in a specific course is not very helpful in establishing expectations for learning new material whenever (a) the student must learn to perform in ways that are quite different from those learned in the past,

(b) the student's past performance has been very erratic, (c) previous test scores or school grades are known to be very unreliable or invalid, or (d) the student's record of past performance is not available.

Consider a ninth grader, for example, who wants to study Spanish for the first time, having had no previous foreign language training or experience. A test of Spanish language knowledge provides no information about this student's chances of succeeding in an upcoming Spanish course. In such cases, an assessment of more general intellectual skills and abilities *related to language learning* will predict success better. Usually such tests assess English language skills and concepts, acquired auditory learning skills, and applied memory skills. Similarly, a student transferring from another school system or moving from one educational level to the next may have complete records, but the meaning of these records may be unclear. To clarify them, a school may test the student with an instrument assessing broad intellectual skills or scholastic aptitude.

School officials can use a number of ways to predict a student's likely success in an educational program. Three examples are the student's (a) level of past achievement for the same specific type of performance as the new performance the student needs to learn, (b) level of general scholastic ability, and (c) ability in several specific aptitudes related to the new performance to be learned. The validity of these predictors is related to the specificity of the performance the school wants to predict. If a school wants to predict a very specific performance (for example, solving quadratic equations), then (a) a student's prior achievement of a very similar kind is the best predictor, (b) a student's general scholastic aptitude is the next best predictor, and (c) assessment of specific aptitudes is least preferred. If the school wants to predict a very general performance (such as overall school performance as measured by first-year-student grade point average), then the preferred order of predictors is (a) general scholastic aptitude assessment, (b) assessments of prior specific achievement, and (c) assessments of specific abilities (Snow, 1980).

Aptitude Tests Measure Learned Behavior

Capacity Is Not Fixed Tests assessing aptitude or intellectual skills reflect only past learning. They do not directly assess innate ability or "capacity." Further, because we cannot obtain a sample of performance from the future, they cannot directly assess future ability. We have to be content to use past and present learning to predict future learning. It is important to recognize that a student's "aptitude for learning" implies learning through a specific type of instructional approach. If you change the instructional approach drastically, the student's aptitude for learning changes as well. A student's aptitude is influenced also by a number of facts of development (including biological makeup), experience in the environment (including interactions with other persons), and a complex interaction of the two.

[1]We discussed multiple intelligences theory and its assessment implications in Chapter 11. Because the creator of that theory is opposed to creating tests that separately measure students' intelligences (Gardner in Checkley, 1997), we have chosen not to discuss such tests in this chapter.

The very idea of "capacity" places some upper limit on a student's ability to learn. This limitation is likely to be untrue in general. For example, a student's capacity to do algebra may depend on the way a teacher currently teaches it, on the mathematics concepts the student learned previously, and on the motivational level a teacher stimulates in the student, as well as on some kind of native endowment. It seems reasonable to conclude that both developmental (life history) and instructional conditions affect one's particular potentials. As Cronbach (1977) observed: "So long as a way is open to invent better conditions of development, no one knows the limit of human potentialities" (p. 274).

Aptitude-Achievement Distinctions It sometimes troubles teachers to see assessment instruments bearing titles such as *readiness, intelligence, general mental ability*, and "*aptitude for* X," but containing items closely resembling those found on achievement tests. The troublesome aspect appears to be related in part to a teacher's failure to distinguish between the abstract concepts of **aptitude** and **achievement** and the observations we make to infer the state of a person's aptitude and achievement. We can define an aptitude for X as the present state of a person that indicates the person's expected future performance in X if the conditions of the past and present continue into the future (see Carroll, 1974). A student's present aptitude (or state) could be indicated in many ways.

> Thus: [An] "aptitude test" is only one indicant of aptitude. Other indicants of aptitude could include scores on achievement tests, data on prior performance in activities similar to those for which we wish to predict success, and information derived from procedures for assessing personality, interest, attitude, physical prowess, physiological state, etc. (Carroll, 1974, p. 287)

Scholastic aptitude tests deliberately set out to assess a student's reasoning rather than the student's recall of factual knowledge or ability to use well-learned rules on problems practiced in school. These tests differ from traditional standardized achievement tests in at least three ways:

> First, tests of reasoning ability, especially mathematical reasoning, require a relatively small declarative knowledge base. The . . . amount of mathematical knowledge required by the typical SAT [for example] is rarely beyond that taught in a first year high school algebra course and an introductory semester of geometry. . . . [The SAT places heavy demands, however, on] procedural knowledge or, more precisely, the procedural use of declarative knowledge. . . .
>   A second way in which reasoning tests differ from subject matter tests is in the quite deliberate way in which they were constructed to not depend upon specific subject matter content. The verbal reasoning skills measured by the SAT-V, for example, have no specific secondary school course sequence on which they can be referred.
>   A final way in which verbal and mathematical reason tests

differ from at least some achievement tests is in degree of problem-solving and reasoning, as distinct from simple memory. Tests in subject matters such as geography, foreign languages, and history make primary demands on memory but minimal demands on problem-solving skills and reasoning. (Bond, 1989, pp. 429–430)

Teaching Conditions for Aptitude Development

Nonadaptive Teaching An important part of the definition of aptitude given earlier was the continuance of past learning conditions into the future. One thing that makes aptitude tests useful predictors of future school success is that schools are generally not very adaptive to individual learners. Thus, the conditions under which students learn this year are usually quite similar to last year's learning conditions.

Underemphasizing Adaptive Teaching When a student must learn under the same conditions from year to year, there is a danger that teachers will believe that the results of the student's scholastic aptitude testing determine what the student is able to accomplish. That is, once they see a student's present aptitude level, they will do little to modify learning conditions to improve the student's aptitude. Past psychological conceptions of the learner have led some educators to overemphasize the (a) consistency of the general scholastic ability of learners, (b) passivity of learners as receivers of information, and (c) categorical placement of learners into educational tracks with narrow ranges of instructional options. They have *underemphasized* the (a) adaptivity and plasticity of learners, (b) learners' ability to actively construct information during problem solving, and (c) responsibility of educational systems to adapt to learners' initial performance levels (Glaser, 1977).

Invalidity for Instructional Placement Unfortunately, the aptitude tests described in this chapter have not been validated for use in assigning students to different kinds of instructional methods. Rather, they have been built to predict how well students will perform when they must adapt to the fixed type of instruction. You should view the tests' helpfulness for decision making in that light.

Scholastic Aptitude Test Score Stability

Importance of Score Stability An important school concern is whether a student's scholastic aptitude remains constant or stable over time. If a student's scholastic aptitude test score changed erratically every year, you would have no confidence that it assessed a useful characteristic. Although on a student-by-student basis scores may systematically rise or decline, a definite tendency exists for a student to maintain similar, but not identical, ranking in the student's age group throughout his school years. In general, changes in students' rankings on general scholastic aptitude tests tend to be greater (a) as the time interval between the two testings grows and (b) the younger the students were at the time of the initial testing. Although groups of students tend to maintain their relative position in the distribution of aptitude scores, important changes in individual students do occur. Therefore, if a school wants to use a student's scholastic aptitude score for guidance or placement decisions, it should bear in mind that there are sufficient differences in individual students' patterns of score change to justify reassessment each time a decision is made (Sattler, 1988).

Factors for Score Stability Among the factors that work to keep students' rankings on aptitude tests about the same over time are (Anastasi, 1988; Ausubel, Novak, & Hanesian, 1978; Sattler, 1988):

1. The genetic makeup of students remains stable.

2. If a student's socioeconomic level, family configuration, and sociocultural influences remain stable over a long period, these contribute to aptitude stability.

3. Development and prerequisite learning is rarely reversible, so earlier development and learning continues to exert similar impact on new development and learning.

4. If the content assessment by different scholastic aptitude tests is similar, students' scores will be similar from one testing to the next.

Reasons for Score Changes Among factors that work to change students' rankings on aptitude tests from one testing to another are the following:

1. *Errors of measurement*—Even if the person's "true score" were to stay the same, the obtained score is likely to be different due to a test's unreliability (see Chapter 4).

2. *Test differences*—The content of tests produced by different publishers will vary. Also, the content of the same publisher's test may vary with the age level of the student taking the test. Tests designed for young children are more concrete and perceptual; those designed for older children are more abstract and verbal.

3. *Norm-group differences*—The norms of different publishers' tests are not comparable. Because mental ability scores are norm-referenced, differences in scores may be due to differences in norms.

4. *Special interventions and enriched environments*—If a person's environment dramatically and persistently becomes more intellectually nurturing, that person's scores on a scholastic aptitude test are likely to increase. Conversely, if the person becomes physically or emotionally ill or deprived in a way that interferes with intellectual development, then aptitude scores may decrease.

GROUP TESTS OF SCHOLASTIC APTITUDES

Types of Group Aptitude Tests

Advantage The principal advantage of group testing over individual testing is the efficiency and cost savings gained by testing many persons at the same time. The ease with which group tests can be administered and scored has contributed greatly to schools adopting them.

Number of Aptitudes Reported There are different types of group aptitude tests. The **omnibus test** contains items assessing different abilities that comprise general scholastic aptitude, but it provides only a single score. A two-score test also assesses several different kinds of specific abilities, but reports only two scores, usually verbal/quantitative or verbal/nonverbal. The items on the verbal section of the test, for example, may assess several kinds of specific verbal abilities, but only one verbal ability score is reported.

Some school ability tests report three scores, such as verbal, quantitative, and nonverbal. **Nonverbal tests** assess how well students process symbols and content that have no specific verbal labels, such as discerning spatial patterns and relations or classifying patterns and figures. **Multiple-aptitude tests** assess several different abilities separately and provide an ability score for each. Multiple-aptitude tests, for example, may provide separate scores for verbal reasoning, verbal comprehension, numerical reasoning, and figural reasoning.

Type of Test to Use The type of group scholastic aptitude test a school should use depends on how the staff will use the scores. Multiple-aptitude tests are most useful for providing information about a student's profile of strengths and weaknesses to make better decisions about further schooling or planning a career. Omnibus tests are most useful when a school wants an estimate of a student's general level of school ability for purposes of predicting his future success under standard classroom conditions. Examples of a two-score and multiple-score aptitude tests are given in the following sections. Others are listed in Appendix K.

Two-Score Test: *Otis-Lennon School Ability Test*

Test Content The *Otis-Lennon School Ability Test* (*OLSAT*) provides verbal and nonverbal part scores as well as a total score. The identification of a test item as verbal versus nonverbal depends on whether the student must understand English to answer the item. For example, Numeric Inference is classified as quantitative reasoning because English language is not necessary to succeed on the items. Once the directions for the subtest are understood, an examinee could answer the questions without knowing English. Arithmetic Reasoning, on the other hand, is classified as verbal reasoning because it "is made up of verbal problems, does not depend on computation, and depends on understanding English" (Harcourt Educational Measurement, 2003). Figure 19.1 describes the clusters and types of items the *OLSAT* contains.

Test Organization The *OLSAT* is organized into seven levels: Level A (kindergarten), Level B (Grade 1), Level C (Grade 2), Level D (Grade 3), Level E (Grades 4 and 5), Level F (Grades 6, 7, and 8), and Level G (Grades 9, 10, 11, and 12). Not all of the different types of items are given at every grade. Items at the lower grade levels are pictorial, do not require reading, and are teacher-paced. Items at the upper levels are self-administered: Students read the directions and answer the items without teacher-pacing. In Grades K through 3, the test items are organized into three sections, each section containing distinct item types. However, in Grades 4 through 12, similar types of items are not grouped together into subtests, but are arranged into a **spiral format**, similar to that shown in Figure 19.2. One item of each type is presented; then the sequence is repeated, but with more difficult items.

Norm-Referencing Scheme The publisher of the *OLSAT* uses several norm-referencing schemes to report the verbal, nonverbal, and total test results. These are illustrated on the individual student report shown in Figure 19.3. These types of scores are described in the following list. The letters in this description correspond to the letters in Figure 19.3. (You should review norm-referencing schemes in Figure 17.13 if you are uncertain of the terminology.)

1. **Age-based scores** compare this student with norm-group students who are the same age, regardless of grade placement. In addition to raw scores, *OLSAT* reports (1) *School Ability Index (SAI)*, a normalized standard score with mean 100 and standard deviation of 16; (2) *national percentile rank (PR)*; (3) *national stanine (S)*; and (4) *normal curve equivalent (NCE)*.

2. **Grade-based scores** compare this student with norm-group students who have the same grade placement, regardless of their age. The scores reported in this section are (1) *scaled score*, an expanded scaled score that allows you to track growth in scholastic aptitude over several years because the scale spans all grades; (2) *national percentile rank (PR)*; (3) *national stanine (S)*; (4) *local percentile rank (PR)*; (5) *local stanine (S)*; and (5) *local normal curve equivalent (NCE)*.

3. *Percentile bands* show the uncertainty interval for the student's scores that are reported in Sections A and B of Figure 19.3. Uncertainty bands are formed by

FIGURE 19.1 Description of the kinds of items on the *OLSAT*.

	Cluster description	Types of items
Verbal clusters	*Verbal comprehension* is dependent on the ability to perceive the relational aspects of words and word combinations, to derive meaning from types of words, to understand subtle differences among similar words and phrases, and to manipulate words to produce meaning.	Following Directions Antonyms Sentence Completion Sentence Arrangement
	Verbal reasoning is dependent on the ability to infer relationships among words, to apply inferences to new situations, to evaluate conditions in order to determine necessary versus optional, and to perceive similarities and differences.	Aural Reasoning Arithmetic Reasoning Logical Selection Word/Letter Matrix Verbal Analogies Verbal Classification Inference
Nonverbal clusters	*Pictorial reasoning* assesses the ability in young children to reason using pictorial representations. These items assess the ability to infer relationships among objects, to evaluate objects for similarities and differences, and to determine progressions and predict the next step in those progressions.	Picture Classification Picture Analogies Picture Series
	Figural reasoning items assess the ability to use geometric figures to infer relationships, to perceive progressions and predict the next step in those progressions, to generalize from one set of figures to another and from dissimilar sets of figures, and to manipulate spatially.	Figural Classification Figural Analogies Pattern Matrix Figural Series
	Quantitative reasoning items assess the ability to use numbers to infer relationships, derive computational rules, and predict outcomes according to computational rules.	Number Series Numerical Inference Number Matrix

Source: Adapted from *Otis-Lennon School Ability Test: Eighth Edition, Directions for Administering, Levels E/F/G*. Copyright © 2003, 2002 by Harcourt Assessment, Inc. Reproduced by permission. All rights reserved.

FIGURE 19.2 Examples of the type of items on the *Otis-Lennon School Ability Test* (8th ed.).

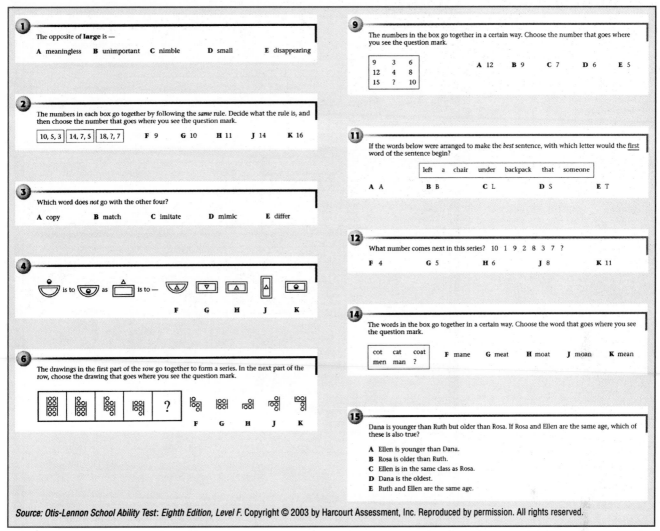

adding and subtracting one *SEM* to the student's score. (See the discussion of *SEM* in Chapter 4.)

4. *Cluster scores* are the raw scores for each of the five clusters at a particular grade level (see Figure 19.1). Below average, average, and above average describe cluster performance in terms of stanines: below average includes stanines 1, 2, 3; average scores fall into stanines 4, 5, 6; and above-average stanines are 7, 8, 9. Stanines are different for the spring and fall standardization groups.

5. *Computer-generated narrative* explains the results in simplified language.

Interpretation of Results Although the *OLSAT* is a two-score test, its authors encourage you to use the total test results as the main interpretive piece of information. They believe that because verbal and nonverbal abilities are needed to succeed in school, the total score is the best overall indicator. They recognize, however, that much of what you teach students relates to verbal learning. Thus, if

a student is very much higher in nonverbal than in verbal ability, you might be alerted that the student may have good scholastic ability but may have difficulty in highly verbal subjects. Students with higher verbal than nonverbal ability may experience more difficulty with quantitative subjects. The authors recommend that you consider score differences larger than two stanines as meaningful. You should interpret smaller differences much more cautiously because they may represent only measurement error.

Other possible causes for a verbal-nonverbal difference include bilingualism, reading problems, learning disability, hearing impairment, visual impairment, anxiety, illness, or irregularities in test administration. You should request a readministration of the *OLSAT* if a student has a large verbal-nonverbal difference. If retesting verifies a difference and you want further diagnostic information, then you should request assessment with an individual test such as the *Wechsler Intelligence Scale for Children*, fourth edition (described later in this chapter).

FIGURE 19.3 An individual student's report showing the type of scores reported for the *Otis-Lennon School Ability Test*.

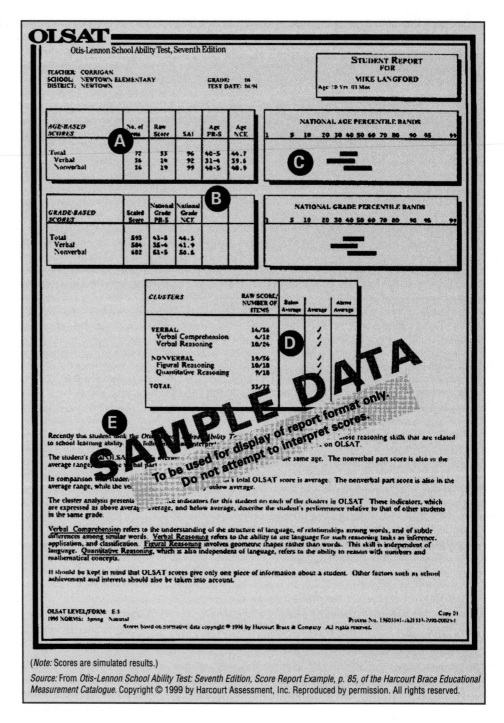

(*Note:* Scores are simulated results.)

Achievement/Ability Comparisons If you administer the *OLSAT* along with either the *Stanford Achievement Test* or the *Metropolitan Achievement Tests,* a score called the Achievement/Ability Comparison (AAC) is part of a student's test report. The AAC describes, for each achievement survey battery subtest, how this student's achievement compares to norm-group students who have the same *OLSAT* total score.

To do this, students in the grade-base *OLSAT* norm group are first sorted into stanines. Second, the students

within each *OLSAT* stanine are then sorted into stanines for the achievement test subtest (e.g., reading comprehension stanines for all students whose *OLSAT* stanine is 5). Third, within each achievement subtest group from Step two, students are clustered into high (stanines 7, 8, 9), middle (stanines 4, 5, 6), and low (stanines 1, 2, 3) groups. The student's *OLSAT* stanine is reported along with his achievement subtest stanines.

For example, Don's *OLSAT* stanine is 5. Don also took the *Stanford Achievement Test* and scored stanines of 4, 5, and 6 in Total Reading, Total Mathematics, and Spelling, respectively. Compared to the entire norm group for the achievement test, these stanines fall in the middle of the distribution. However, if we look only at those students who attained an *OLSAT* stanine of 5, Don will be in the low AAC range in Total Reading, in the middle AAC range in Total Mathematics, and in the high AAC range in Spelling. These AAC results tell us that compared to other students with the same scholastic aptitude as Don, he is below average in Total Reading, average in Total Mathematics, and above average in Spelling.

Multiple-Aptitude Test: *Differential Aptitude Tests*

Purpose The battery of *Differential Aptitude Tests (DAT)* was originally developed in 1947 to satisfy the needs of guidance counselors and consulting psychologists working in schools, social agencies, and industry (Bennett, Seashore, & Wesman, 1974). The tests were revised in 1962, 1972, 1982, and 1990.

The primary purpose of the tests is to provide information about a student's profiles with respect to different cognitive abilities. This information is used for guiding and counseling students in junior and senior high schools (Grades 7 through 12) as they prepare for career decisions. There are two levels: Level 1 (Grades 7–9) and Level 2 (Grades 10–12). The *DAT* are also used with adults for vocational and educational counseling and as part of a battery of tests for job selection.

Test Content The *Differential Aptitude Tests* report scores for each of the eight subtests shown in Figure 19.4. An additional ninth score, Scholastic Aptitude, which is a combination of the Verbal Reasoning and Numerical Reasoning scores, is reported: This score is used to assess general scholastic aptitude. Figure 19.4 also shows examples of items from each subtest.

Gender-Specific Norms The *DAT* have separate male and female norms, as well as combined norms. Separate norms allow comparisons of a student with his or her own gender, as well as with members of the opposite gender. Cross-gender comparisons may help a student consider an occupation or educational program that he or she would have overlooked. This may surprise you and may seem like a form of gender discrimination. However, because the tests are used for guidance and counseling, this purpose is better served by these separate norms, given the realities of the current job market. This issue was discussed in Chapter 17 in connection with separate gender norms of the *DAT*.

Advantage of the **DAT** An advantage of using a multiple-aptitude battery such as the *DAT* instead of an omnibus or two-score aptitude test is the opportunity it provides for finding some aptitude for which a student has a relative strength. For example, a student may have low general scholastic ability (Verbal Reasoning and Numerical Reasoning) but have high Perceptual Speed and Accuracy or high Mechanical Reasoning. This provides the counselor with some information on aptitude that can be used to encourage a student.

Combining Aptitude With Interest Assessment The *DAT* comes with an optional *Career Interest Inventory*. Using the results of this instrument along with aptitude scores, achievement scores, and school grades can help a student make realistic career or further education decisions. The interest inventory presents sentences describing activities in various types of work and school situations. Students indicate their degree of agreement with the sentences. (Interest inventories are described in greater detail in this chapter.)

GROUP TESTS OF SPECIFIC APTITUDES

The kinds of general scholastic aptitude tests illustrated earlier are widely used in schools, but other types used for special decisions should be mentioned, too. Among these are readiness tests, high school and college admissions tests, and tests of aptitude for specific subjects.

Readiness Testing

Schools often use **readiness tests** as supplemental information to make instructional decisions for first-grade pupils. Often such tests are used to supplement a kindergarten teacher's judgment about a youngster's general developmental and readiness level for first-grade work, especially reading, where grouping by readiness level is a common practice. Because readiness tests measure a child's acquired learning skills, they are frequently classified as achievement tests rather than aptitude tests. (The discussion at the beginning of this chapter described the distinction between aptitude and achievement used in this book.)

Teachers frequently use readiness tests to help form instructional groups (for example, for reading instruction). When used in this way, they should be considered placement tests. Because teachers use readiness tests to predict implicitly a pupil's likely success in instruction, we have classified them as aptitude tests in this book, although they also may be classified as achievement tests.

You should keep in mind the test author's point of view when selecting a readiness test. The author's viewpoint of what constitutes "readiness to learn" will determine the test content (as does an author's viewpoint for every test, of course). If you want to use the scores on a readiness test to make a statement about whether a student has mastered specific prerequisites, you must carefully examine the actual test items to see if they measure the kinds of skills and abilities you expect each student to have acquired before entering the new instruction.

FIGURE 19.4 Brief descriptions, time limits, number of items, and a sample item from each subtest of the *Differential Aptitude Tests* (5th ed.).

Verbal Reasoning (25 min., 40 items)

Measures the ability to see relationships among words; may be useful in predicting success in business, law, education, journalism, and the sciences.

SAMPLE ITEM

Which answer contains the missing words to complete this sentence?

. . . . . is to fin as bird is to . . . . .

  A water — — feather
  B shark — — nest
*C fish — — wing
  D flipper — — fly
  E fish — — sky

Numerical Reasoning (30 min., 40 items)

Measures the ability to perform mathematical reasoning tasks; important in jobs such as bookkeeping, lab work, carpentry, and toolmaking.

SAMPLE ITEM

What number should replace R in this correct addition example?

$$\begin{array}{r} 7R \\ + \ R \\ \hline 88 \end{array}$$

  A 9
  B 6
  C 4
  D 3
*E None of these

Abstract Reasoning (20 min., 40 items)

A nonverbal measure of the ability to reason using geometric shapes or designs; important in fields such as computer programming, drafting, and vehicle repair.

SAMPLE ITEM

Choose the Answer Figure that should be the next figure (or fifth one) in the series.

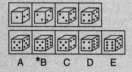

A   *B   C   D   E

Perceptual Speed and Accuracy (6 min., 200 items)

Measures the ability to compare and mark written lists quickly and accurately; helps predict success in performing routine clerical tasks.

SAMPLE ITEM

Look at the underlined combination of letters or numbers and find the same one on the answer sheet. Then fill in the circle under it.

```
1  XY Xy XX YX Yy      Xy Yy YX XX XY     nn mn nv nm mm
2  6g 6G G6 Gg g6      ○  ○  ●  ○  ○      ○  ○  ○  ●  ○
3  nm mn mm nn nv      g6 Gg 6g G6 6G     BD BB Bd Db Bb
4  Db BD Bd Bb BB      ○  ○  ○  ○  ●      ●  ○  ○  ○  ○
```

Mechanical Reasoning (25 min., 60 items)

Understanding basic mechanical principles of machinery, tools, and motion is important for occupations such as carpentry, mechanics, engineering, and machine operation.

SAMPLE ITEM

Which load will be easier to pull through soft sand?

A   B   C

Space Relations (25 min., 50 items)

Measures the ability to visualize a three-dimensional object from a two-dimensional pattern, and to visualize how this object would look if rotated in space; important in drafting, architecture, design, carpentry, and dentistry.

SAMPLE ITEM

Choose the one figure that can be made from the pattern.

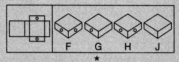

F   G   H   J

Spelling (10 min., 40 items)

Measures one's ability to spell common English words; a useful skill in many academic and vocational pursuits.

SAMPLE ITEM

Decide which word is not spelled correctly in the group below.

*A paragraf
  B dramatic
  C circular
  D audience

Language Usage (15 min., 40 items)

Measures the ability to detect errors in grammar, punctuation, and capitalization; needed in most jobs requiring a college degree.

SAMPLE ITEM

Decide which of the four parts of the sentence below contains an error. If there is no error, mark the space on your answer sheet for the letter next to No Error.

Jane and Tom/ is going/ to the office/ this morning.
    A   *B   C   D

E No Error

Admissions Testing

Multiple-Assessment for Admission Test scores, previous grades, letters of recommendation, interviews, and biographical information on out-of-school accomplishments are among kinds of information colleges and selective high schools use to make admissions decisions. Some private and parochial high schools, for example, use a battery of achievement and aptitude tests to screen applicants.

Testing sessions are usually held at the local high school, and its staff generally administers the tests.

College Admissions Tests Two widely used college admissions testing programs are the College Entrance Examination Board's *SAT Reasoning Test*[2] and the *ACT Assessment Program* published by American College Testing. Both programs administer secure tests. Both administer the tests through local testing centers (usually high schools and colleges) on preestablished dates several times during the year. Although the tests are secure prior to their administration, students can obtain copies of their test booklets and answers after they have taken them. For both programs, test booklets and answer sheets are returned to their respective publishers for scoring, recording, and processing results to the colleges the students designate.

SAT Reasoning Test The College Entrance Examination Board (CEEB), currently located in New York City, was formed around 1899 to help selective colleges in the northeastern United States coordinate their admissions testing requirements. The tests developed out of that effort around 1926 and were created by Carl Brigham, associate secretary for the CEEB (Donlon & Angoff, 1971). Educational Testing Service in Princeton, New Jersey, currently develops the test for the CEEB. More than 2 million college candidates take the test each year.

The program includes the *SAT Reasoning Test* and *SAT Subject Tests*. Students generally take one or both types during their junior or senior year of high school. Only the *SAT Reasoning Test* is discussed in this chapter. There is a new version of the *SAT Reasoning Test* beginning in 2006. It has three parts: a Critical Reading section, a Mathematics section, and a Writing section. The Critical Reading section emphasizes reading and word knowledge. Two types of multiple-choice items are used, with questions based on short and long reading passages. (Analogy questions, a feature of past *SAT*s, have been eliminated.) The Mathematics section emphasizes quantitative thinking using arithmetic, algebra (both Algebra I and II content), and geometry knowledge. It includes items on topics such as estimation, exponential growth, absolute value, functional notation, linear functions, manipulations with exponents, and tangent lines. Two types of items are used: standard multiple-choice and student-produced response. For student-produced response items, examinees "bubbled in" their numerical answers on a special answer sheet (there are no choices). The Writing section contains both multiple-choice grammar (identifying error in sentences, and improving sentences and paragraphs) items and a 20-minute written essay. In the essay, candidates are asked to develop a point of view on an issue, and are evaluated on their ability to reason and use evidence to support their

ideas. The test booklets and answer sheets are sent to the Educational Testing Service (ETS) for scoring, recording, and processing scores to the colleges the student designates. A student's essay responses are posted on a Website that college admission officers can access and read.

ACT Information Program The *ACT Assessment Program* was formed in 1959, with the ideas and help of E. F. Lindquist, among others. This admissions testing program was originally conceived to be of a different character than the *SAT* program. Whereas initially CEEB was concerned primarily with the private selective colleges of the northeast, the ACT program initially sought to serve midwestern public colleges and universities. What these colleges needed was help in (a) eliminating the few incapable students who were applying, (b) providing guidance services for those admitted, and (c) measuring broad educational development rather than narrower verbal and quantitative aptitudes (Lindquist in Feister & Whitney, 1968). Today American College Testing in Iowa City is as active a research and test development enterprise as is Educational Testing Service. More than 1.2 million college candidates take the test each year.

The *ACT Assessment Program* has four components: *Tests of Educational Development*, Course/Grade Information, Student Profile, and *ACT Interest Inventory*. The *Tests of Educational Development* consists of four multiple-choice subtests: English, Mathematics, Reading, and Science Reasoning. In addition, there is an optional writing test. The English Test emphasizes standard written English conventions and rhetorical skills. The Mathematics Test emphasizes quantitative reasoning and problem solving using pre-algebra, algebra, geometry, and trigonometry knowledge. The Reading Test contains passages representative of topics in social studies, natural sciences, fiction, and humanities. The items focus on using inference and reasoning for reading comprehension. The Science Reasoning Test contains several sets of related data tables, diagrams, and verbal descriptions drawn from biology, chemistry, physics, and earth/space science. The items focus on interpreting data, interpreting experimental results, and reasoning with respect to alternative viewpoints. The developers view the test items as "work samples"–simulations of the kinds of learning activities typically required of the first-year college student.

The Course/Grade Information section asks candidates to self-report their grades in 30 courses from what is usually included in a college preparatory curriculum in English, mathematics, natural sciences, social studies, language, and the arts. The Student Profile section asks candidates to report 200 pieces of information including educational plans, interests, and needs; special educational needs, interests, and goals; college extracurricular plans; financial aid; high school extracurricular activities; out-of-class accomplishments; and so on. Among other purposes, this questionnaire permits the student to indicate any

[2]Before 1994 this was called the *Scholastic Aptitude Test (SAT)*.

special talents and accomplishments not reflected in course grades (such as winning a state debate). The *ACT Interest Inventory* consists of a list of activities, and students indicate whether they would like, dislike, or are indifferent about doing each activity on the list. The interest inventory helps students get a better idea of how their career interests fit into the mainstream of various major areas of college.

INDIVIDUALLY ADMINISTERED TESTS OF GENERAL SCHOLASTIC APTITUDES

Stanford-Binet Intelligence Scale

History The *Stanford-Binet Intelligence Scale* is a widely used, individually administered test of general scholastic aptitude. First prepared in 1916 by Lewis M. Terman as a translation and revision of the *Binet-Simon Scale*, the test was revised in 1937 (with Maud A. Merrill), revised again in 1960, renormed in 1972, revised and renormed in 1986, and revised and renormed for the 2003 (fifth edition by Gale Roid). See Becker's (2003) *History of the* Stanford-Binet Intelligence Scales.

Content The *Stanford-Binet V* is used with a wide range of ages, from 2 years old through adults age 85+. You can gain an idea of the nature and content of this assessment instrument by studying the diagram that follows. The diagram shows that the subtests are clustered into five nonverbal areas (factors) and five verbal areas (factors). The scores from the five nonverbal factors are combined to obtain the Nonverbal IQ; the scores from the five verbal factors are combined to obtain the Verbal IQ.

Structure of the Stanford-Binet V

- **Full Scale IQ**
  - **Nonverbal IQ**
    - **Nonverbal Fluid Reasoning**
      Object Series
      (routing test)
    - **Nonverbal Knowledge**
      Procedural Knowledge,
      Picture Absurdities
    - **Nonverbal Quantitative Processing**
      Quantitative Reasoning
    - **Nonverbal Visual-Spatial Processing**
      Form Board,
      Form Patterns
    - **Nonverbal Working Memory**
      Delayed Response,
      Block Span
  - **Verbal IQ**
    - **Verbal Fluid Reasoning**
      Early Reasoning,
      Verbal Absurdities,
      Verbal Analogies
    - **Verbal Knowledge**
      Vocabulary
      (routing test)
    - **Verbal Quantitative Reasoning**
      Quantitative Reasoning
    - **Verbal Visual-Spatial Processing**
      Position and Direction
    - **Verbal Working Memory**
      Memory for Sentences,
      Last Word

Not all items in each subtest are administered because within each subtest items are arranged in order of increasing difficulty. The object series and vocabulary subtest is given first and is used as a routing test. The student's performance on this test, along with the student's age or estimated ability, tells the psychologist the difficulty level on the other tests at which he or she should begin testing the student. If a quick (and less reliable) estimate of the Full Scale IQ is desired, the psychologist can stop after administering the verbal and nonverbal routing tests. The standard scores on these two tests are combined to obtain an Abbreviated Full Scale IQ score.

Scores A student's raw score on each subtest is converted to a normalized standard score called a **standard age score (SAS)** for the subtest. The *SAS*s for each of the 10 subtests have a mean of 10 and standard deviation of 3 in the norm group having the same age as the student being tested. The 10 *SAS*-scores from the subtests are combined in different ways to make 9 different composite scores. There are four kinds of composite scores: Factor Index Scores, Domain Scores, Abbreviated Score, and Full-Scale Score. All the composite scores are deviation IQs (*DIQs*) with a mean of 100 and a standard deviation of 15, as explained in Chapter 17, Equation 17.4. Within each composite score type, there are from one to five different *DIQ*-scores. The diagram below shows how these four composite scores are formed.

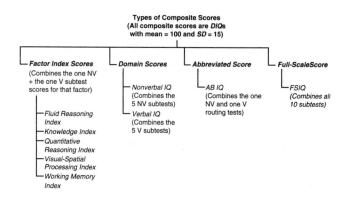

Types of Composite Scores
(All composite scores are *DIQs* with mean = 100 and *SD* = 15)

- **Factor Index Scores**
  (Combines the one NV
  + the one V subtest
  scores for that factor)
  - Fluid Reasoning Index
  - Knowledge Index
  - Quantitative Reasoning Index
  - Visual-Spatial Processing Index
  - Working Memory Index
- **Domain Scores**
  - Nonverbal IQ
    (Combines the 5 NV subtests)
  - Verbal IQ
    (Combines the 5 V subtests)
- **Abbreviated Score**
  - AB IQ
    (Combines the one NV and one V routing tests)
- **Full-ScaleScore**
  - FSIQ
    (Combines all 10 subtests)

The subtest scores and the different composite scores are used by school psychologists or counseling psychologists along with other information (e.g., school records, other test results, interviews, and reports from teachers and parents) for (a) describing a profile of a student's intellectual skills and abilities, (b) classifying a student into a diagnostic category (e.g., attention deficit disorder/hyperactivity disorder), or (c) placing a student into a special educational program (e.g., a gifted program).

The concepts of **mental age** and intelligence quotient (IQ) are no longer used with tests such as the *Stanford-Binet V* (or any other modern intelligence test). Thus, the ratio IQ (=100 times mental age divided by chronological age) has been replaced by the *DIQ*.

Norm-Referenced Character Tests of scholastic aptitude describe a student's ability as the student's location in a norm group having the same age as the student. If the student's intellectual development does not keep pace with others in the norm group, the student will receive a lower *DIQ*. Norms become outdated and from time to time a test will have to be renormed.

Wechsler Intelligence Scales

Another widely used set of individual tests is the *Wechsler Intelligence Scales*. This set consists of three different intelligence tests, each designed for use with a different age level: (a) *Wechsler Preschool and Primary Scale of Intelligence–III* (*WPPSI–III*), 2 years, 6 months to 7 years, 3 months; (b) *Wechsler Intelligence Scale for Children–IV* (*WISC–IV*), 6 to 16 years, 11 months; and (c) *Wechsler Adult Intelligence Scale–III* (*WAIS–III*), 16 to 89 years.

General Design All the Wechsler tests have a similar general design, although the items are not identical. The items are organized into subtests. The items within a subtest are similar in content but differ in difficulty. (The subtests on the different scales–*WPPSI*, *WISC*, and *WAIS*–contain different types of items, however.) Subtests are clustered into groups to represent different factors or aspects of general ability. These form a hierarchical pattern of abilities as shown below, but with some slight differences for the different age-level tests:

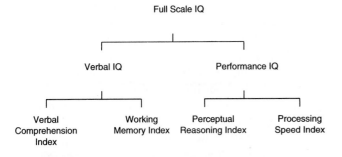

The four factors at the lowest level of the hierarchy are described as follows (Psychological Corporation, 2003):

Verbal Comprehension: One's ability to listen to, understand, and give spoken responses to verbal questions. It includes skills in understanding information presented verbally, using words to think and reason, and using words to express thoughts.

Working Memory: One's ability to learn new information and retain it in memory as one completes a task. It includes skills in paying attention, in concentrating, and in mental reasoning.

Perceptual Reasoning: One's ability to examine and think about pictures and designs, and solve problems without using words. It involves skills working quickly with visual information to solve nonverbal problems.

Processing Speed: One's ability to scan symbols and make judgments about them quickly. It involves skills in paying attention, hand-eye coordination, and mental problem solving.

Scores All the Wechsler scales report subtest results as normalized, standard scores (mean = 10, standard deviation = 3). All of the scales report Performance IQ, Verbal IQ, and the total or Full Scale IQ. These three are *DIQ*-scores (mean = 100, standard deviation = 15). The four factor indexes are also *DIQ*-scores with mean 100 and standard deviation of 15. The norm group to which a student is referenced is the group of students with the same age.

WAIS–III The *Wechsler Adult Intelligence Scale–III* is used with ages 16 to 89 years. It overlaps with the *WISC–III* for age 16. It contains 14 subtests, but only 11 are used to calculate the four indexes as follows (supplemental subtests are in parentheses):

Verbal Comprehension Index:	Vocabulary, Similarities, Information, (Comprehension)
Working Memory Index:	Digit Span, Arithmetic, (Letter-Number Sequencing)
Perceptual Organization Index:	Block Design, Matrix Reasoning, Picture Completion, (Picture Arrangement)
Processing Speed Index:	Digit-Symbol Coding (Symbol Search)

The *WAIS–III* is generally considered to be a reasonably valid and reliable tool for assessing general cognitive ability. Following are some of its limitations (Sattler, 1992b): (a) It does not provide low enough scores for persons with severe mental retardation, (b) it does not provide high enough scores for persons with extremely gifted mental ability, and (c) the range of subtest scaled scores is restricted for some age groups.

WISC–IV The *Wechsler Intelligence Scale for Children–IV* is used with children ages 6 years through 16 years, 11 months. It contains 10 core and 5 supplemental subtests. In the Verbal Comprehension category are Similarities, Vocabulary, and Comprehension (Information and Word Reasoning are supplemental subtests). In the Perceptual Reasoning category are Block Design, Picture Concepts, and Matrix Reasoning (Picture Completion is a supplemental subtest). In the Working Memory category are Digit Span and Letter-Number Sequencing (Arithmetic is a supplemental subtest). In the Processing Speed category is Coding and Symbol Search (Cancellation is a supplemental subtest).

The *WISC–IV* was standardized with the *Wechsler Individual Achievement Test – II* (*WIAT–II*), an individually administered basic skills achievement test. This makes it possible to compare mental ability results from the *WISC–IV* with the *WIAT–II*, a comparison often made for students experiencing learning difficulties in school. This assists in the process of establishing individual education plans (IEPs).

The *WISC–IV* is generally considered to be a good test of overall mental ability. Among its strengths (Sattler, 1992b) are its (a) high-quality norms; (b) good reliability and validity; (c) usefulness in diagnosing cognitive abilities of most students; (d) good features of the materials, administration, and scoring; and (e) extensive research literature. Among its limitations (Sattler, 1992b) are its (a) lack of usefulness for extremely low- and high-ability children, (b) restriction of the range of scores for certain subtests and age levels, (c) lack of appropriate norms when a subtest is substituted, (d) susceptibility to large practice effects on the Performance Scale, and (e) potential for penalizing students who do not place a premium on speed of responding. Like the *Stanford-Binet V*, the *WISC–IV* is used by psychologists, along with other information, for developing students' profiles of intellectual skills and abilities, classification in diagnostic categories, or placement in special educational programs. The *SB–V* and *WISC–IV* are different tests; you should not expect them to come to the exact same conclusion about a student.

WPPSI–III The *Wechsler Preschool and Primary Scale of Intelligence–III* is used with children ages 2 years, 6 months years through 7 years, 3 months. It overlaps with the *WISC–IV* for ages 6 years through 7 years, 3 months. For this overlapping age range, the *WISC–IV* is recommended (Sattler, 1992b). The *WPPSI–III* contains 15 subtests, 8 of which are supplemental subtests. In the Verbal category are Information, Vocabulary, and Word Reasoning (Comprehension and Similarities are supplemental subtests). In the Performance category are Block Design, Matrix Reasoning, and Picture Concepts (Picture Completion and Object Assembly are supplemental subtests). The Processing Speed or visual-motor category contains Coding and Symbol Search. The Full Scale IQ uses scores from the three Verbal, the three Performance, and one of the Processing Speed subtests.

Kaufman Assessment Battery for Children

General Description The *Kaufman Assessment Battery for Children–II* (*KABC–II*) is an individually administered test of general intelligence (Kaufman & Kaufman, 2004). It is used with children ages 3 through 18. The *KABC–II* differs in several ways from other approaches to measuring scholastic aptitude described thus far: (a) The subtests were derived from a differential psychological model (Cattell-Horn-Carroll [CHC] model; see Alfonso, Flanagan, & Radwan, 2005) and neuropsychological theory (Luria model; see Das, 2002); (b) a psychologist must decide before testing which one of the two interpretive models to

use with a particular child and base the overall score only on the chosen model; and (c) there is a deliberate attempt to organize the testing to make it "fairer" to students not in the mainstream culture and for certain students with language-affected disabilities. In the norming sample, non-mainstream ethnic groups had average scores that were slightly higher when the Luria model was used than when the CHC model was used. The use of different models for defining cognitive ability is helpful, too, when professionals are developing IEPs for students.

Content The *KABC–II* is organized into five scales. The scales and their subtests are organized as follows. The names in brackets are the scale names when the CHC model is used.

- *Sequential Processing Scale [Short-Term Memory]* (G_{sm})[3] One's ability to remember an ordered series of images or ideas and use this memory to do a task. Requires repeating a sequence of numbers or identifying a sequence of pictures that the examiner says. Includes two subtests (and one supplemental subtest): Number Recall and Word Order (Hand Movements).

- *Simultaneous Processing Scale [Visual Processing]* (G_v) One's ability to consider an array of information and process the parts of the array simultaneously to do the task. This form of thinking requires the student to visualize and integrate the elements in the array presented, so it is called visual processing ability. Consists of six subtests (and one supplemental subtest): Face Recognition, Triangles, Conceptual Thinking, Pattern Recognition, Rover, and Block Counting (Gestalt Closure).

- *Planning Ability Scale [Fluid Reasoning]* (G_f) One's ability to understand a nonverbal problem, generate a hypothesis about how to solve it, test that solution, and revise it if necessary. Students must use verbal reasoning to solve the nonverbal problems. Includes two subtests: Pattern Reasoning and Story Completion.

- *Learning Ability Scale [Long-Term Storage and Retrieval]* (G_{lr}) One's ability to successfully complete different types of tasks that require learning something new. Some tasks require immediate recall of the newly learned information and others require using that information after a period of delay. Includes two subtests: Atlantis and Rebus.

- *Knowledge Scale [Crystallized Ability]* (G_c) One's ability to express one's knowledge and understanding of objects and events in the mainstream culture. Students are asked to express their knowledge of words and facts, when questions are asked verbally and

[3]The notation used is *G* with a subscript. The *G* represents "general ability factor," first postulated by Spearman (1927). This factor can be decomposed into subfactors like the ones defined here for the CHC model. The subscript on the *G* denotes the subfactor.

through pictorial stimuli. They respond either verbally or by pointing. Consists of three subtests: Riddles, Expressive Vocabulary, and Verbal Knowledge.

Illustrations of items similar to those on each subtest and the age levels for which each subtest is appropriate are found on the publisher's Website in the *Sampler* pages at http://www.agsnet.com/PDF/kabcsampler.pdf. A readable explanation of the Luria model and the CHC model, a full description of the *KABC–II*, and the history of the *KABC–II* are found in Kaufman, Lichtenberger, Fletcher-Janzen, and Kaufman (2005).

Scores The *KABC–II* provides *DIQ*-scores (mean = 100, standard deviation = 15) for each of the five scales: Sequential Processing, Simultaneous Processing, Planning Ability, Learning Ability, and Knowledge. Each of the subtests within these scales is reported as a normalized standard score (mean = 10, standard deviation = 3). In addition, there are three *DIQ* composite scores: the *Mental Processing Index* (*MPI*), the *Fluid-Crystallized Index* (*FCI*), and the *Non-Verbal Index* (*NVI*). Any one student can be assigned only *MPI* and *NVI* or *FCI* and *NVI*.

You will recall that the examiner must choose to use either the Luria model or the CHC model before testing a student. If the examiner chooses the Luria model, then the student can receive the *MPI* composite but not the *FCI* composite; if the examiner chooses the CHC model, the student receives the *FCI* composite, not the *MPI*. The difference is that the *MPI* does not include the Knowledge/Crystallized Ability (*G$_c$*) subtest because it is not administered under the Luria model. Here is the structure:

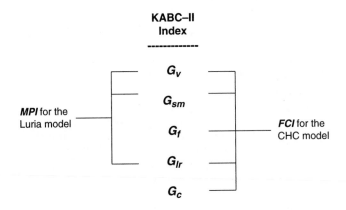

Usefulness of the KABC–II Approach The authors suggest the following uses for the *FCI* and *MPI* (Kaufman et al., 2005):

- The *FCI* (i.e., all five areas) should be used for the majority of students; when there is a suspicion of a reading, written expression, or mathematics disability; for a child with mental retardation; for a child with Attention-Deficit/Hyperactivity Disorder (ADHD); for a child with an emotional or behavioral disorder; and with a child who is gifted.

- The *MPI* (i.e., exclude administration of the Knowledge component) should be used with children from bilingual backgrounds; with nonmainstream cultural backgrounds whose verbal development is problematic; with language disorders; with autism; and with deafness or hearing loss.

Until the research on the *KABC–II* has been completed we cannot properly evaluate these proposed uses.

ASSESSING ADAPTIVE BEHAVIOR

Meaning of Adaptive Behavior

Tests such as the *Stanford-Binet*, the *WISC*, and the *KABC* measure general scholastic ability. A school setting, of course, is not the only environment in which persons are expected to cope. Some students may appear to teachers and other school personnel to suffer from mental retardation, but their families, neighbors, and peers accept the students and consider the students normal in all other facets of life (Mercer, 1973). It is recommended, therefore, that before labeling a student as having mental retardation, the student's ability to cope with the demands of his or her environment outside classroom learning be assessed (Grossman, 1983). According to the American Association on Mental Retardation (2002), "*mental retardation* is a disability characterized by significant limitations both in intellectual functioning and in *adaptive behavior* as expressed in conceptual, social, and practical adaptive skills. This disability originates before age 18" [emphasis added].

Adaptive behavior assessment focuses on how independently students can care for themselves and how well they can cope with the demands placed on them by the immediate culture in which they are living. Thus, these types of assessments focus on a student's success as a family member, consumer, wage earner, member of a nonacademic peer group, person interacting with adults, and person caring for his or her health and physical needs—that is, skills in the three domains of conceptual, social, and practical adaptive skills. A psychological report for a student often includes assessment of the student's adaptive behavior as well as his or her general scholastic aptitude. This section presents one example.

Vineland Adaptive Behavior Scales (VABS)

The *Vineland Adaptive Behavior Scales–II* (*VABS–II*), revised and renormed by Sparrow, Cicchetti, and Balla in 2005, is a developmental checklist that assesses adaptive behavior in five areas: Communication (expressive, receptive, and written); Daily Living Skills (domestic tasks, personal habits, behavior outside the home); Socialization (interpersonal relations, play and leisure skills, coping); Motor Skills (gross and fine motor); and Maladaptive

Behavior (inappropriate and undesirable behavior). The first three areas are assessed for children from birth through 90 years (and low-functioning adults). Motor Skills assessment is limited to children younger than 9 years and the Maladaptive Behavior area to children 5 years and older. A trained interviewer completes the assessment by interviewing a child's parent or caregiver.

The *VABS–II* has four editions: (1) Interview Edition, Survey Form, which provides standard scores for each of the five areas as well as a total adaptive behavior score (ages birth to 90); (2) Interview Edition, Expanded Form, which in addition to the standard scores provides specific, detailed information for preparing educational and habilitation programs (ages birth to 90); (3) Classroom Edition, for ages 3 to 22, which a teacher completes as a questionnaire and which provides standard scores for four adaptive behavior areas as well as a total adaptive behavior score; and (4) Parent/Caregiver Rating forms. A qualified professional is needed to interpret the scores. *The VABS–II* provides national norms for all editions. For the two interview editions, special supplemental norms are available for adults with mental retardation (residential and nonresidential), children with hearing impairments, children with visual impairments, and children with emotional disturbances (the latter three groups in residential settings).

According to the authors, the *VABS–II* may be used for diagnosing adaptive behavior deficits, determining eligibility for special services, planning intervention programs, and tracking progress in development. The authors have planned for its use with populations of individuals with mental retardation, autism spectrum disorders (ASDs), ADHD, posttraumatic brain injury, hearing impairment, and dementia/Alzheimer's disease.

ASSESSING VOCATIONAL AND CAREER INTERESTS

What Are Interests?

Attitudes, Interests, and Values Three characteristics of students are closely related: attitudes, interests, and values. Questionnaires very often assess these characteristics. The questionnaires appear similar because, when responding to the questionnaire, a student reads several statements and expresses his or her degree of agreement with the statements. You must remember, however, that in spite of their similarity, the three concepts are not identical.

To interpret assessment results properly, you must distinguish among these three concepts. An **attitude** is a positive or negative feeling about a physical object, a type of people, a particular person, a government or other social institution's policy, ideas, or the like. For example, when a student expresses agreement with the statement, "My mathematics class helps me become a better person," the student is expressing his attitude toward the mathematics class.

Interests, on the other hand, are preferences for specific types of activities when a person is not under external pressure. For example, when a student expresses agreement with the statement, "I enjoy working on the mathematics problems my teacher assigns," the student is expressing her interest in a mathematics activity.

Values, unlike attitudes and interests, are long-lasting beliefs of the importance of certain life goals, a lifestyle, a way of acting, or a way of life. For example, when a student expresses agreement with the statement, "I consider it more important to be one of the best students in mathematics than to be one of the best players in a football game," the student is expressing his valuing of mathematics success over football (athletic) success.

When studying ways of assessing attitudes, interests, and values, keep in mind that the methods you use for assessing them are "highly susceptible to faking, require frank responses from the subject, and are therefore able to assess only the characteristics that the individual is able to, or wishes to, reveal" (Mehrens & Lehmann, 1991, p. 405).

Focus on Career Interests This cluster of interests is important as students begin to prepare themselves for further schooling and for the world of work. No single piece of information is sufficient for a student to use in making vocational decisions, of course. However, the student's interest in various activities associated with specific types of work or work environments is an important consideration. Besides knowing the duty requirements of the job market, and his own abilities and aptitudes, a student should also understand his own interests regarding work-related activities. Thus, the types of career interest inventories described next can provide one source of information to help a student make educational and vocational choices.

Expressed, Manifested, Tested, and Inventoried Interests

Interest inventories of the type described in this section are limited to only vocational interests or career interests. Even career interests are narrowed even further. You may find it useful to distinguish among expressed, manifested, tested, and inventoried interests (Super, 1947, 1949).

Expressed Interests **Expressed interests** are obtained when you ask students directly about their interests. The interests a student verbally professes when you ask the student directly may not express her true preferences: A youngster may express an interest in being a doctor, for example, because she perceives it as something parents expect. Or a teenager may say she wants to be a mortician just to see the reaction of her parents.

Manifested Interests **Manifested interests** are deduced from what a student actually does, or the activities in which the student actually participates. When you attempt to deduce students' interests from their activities, you may be in error, also. For example, you may conclude a boy is interested in athletics because he participates in the junior high track team, but you later find out he only wants to be with his friends after school.

Tested Interests   **Tested interests** are those you infer from the results of assessing a student's information and knowledge of a particular subject matter. For example, you may hypothesize that a student who has a lot of scientific knowledge and information has more interest in science than a student who knows little about science. Such knowledge assessments are not used very often in current vocational counseling practice.

Inventoried Interests   **Inventoried interests** are identified through various paper-and-pencil tests or interest inventories. A limitation here is that the interests you discover through a particular interest inventory do not represent all interests or even all career interests. Further, as with other forms of educational and psychological assessment, you should not assume that the interest patterns identified with one publisher's interest inventory are the same ones that could be identified with others. When counseling students, keep in mind that you should use all three interests—expressed, manifested, and inventoried—to assess a student's interest pattern (Davis, 1980).

Vocational Interest Inventories

Vocational interest inventories are formal paper-and-pencil questionnaires that help students express their likes and dislikes about a very wide range of work and other activities. A student's pattern of interests is then determined from these responses. This profile or pattern of interests becomes one source of information a student can use for career exploration, counseling, and decision making.

Building Interest Inventories   The traditional rationale for describing a person's inventoried interests is a variation on the "birds of a feather flock together" theme (Darley & Hagenah, 1955). This philosophy has been called the **people-similarity rationale** (Cole & Hanson, 1975, p. 6):

> Rationale 1. If a person likes the same things that people in a particular job like, the person will be satisfied with the job.

Certain parts of the *Kuder Occupational Interest Survey* (*KOIS*) and the *Strong Interest Inventory* (*SII*) follow this rationale. Both the *KOIS* and the Occupational Scales of the *SII*, for example, are **empirically keyed scales**, made up of items especially selected because research has shown that responses to these items clearly differentiate between the persons who are currently and happily employed in a particular occupation and people in general.

A second rationale has been called the **activity-similarity rationale** (Cole & Hanson, 1975, p. 6):

> Rationale 2. If people like activities similar to the activities required by a job, they will like those job activities and consequently be satisfied with their job.

Inventories built using this rationale present the students with lists of activities that are similar to those required of persons working in certain jobs or studying certain subjects. The developers assume that if a person has an identifiable pattern of likes and dislikes common to a particular job, that person will be satisfied with that job. Among the inventories developed using this rationale are the *ACT Interest Inventory* and the *Ohio Vocational Interest Survey, Second Edition* (*OVIS–II*).

Formats of Interest Items   Figure 19.5 shows sample items from two vocational interest inventories. Notice that the items from one inventory, the *ACT*, ask students to rate each activity or statement on a like/dislike continuum. Items from the other inventory, the *KOIS*, present activities in sets of three (triads). These latter items ask the student to mark the one activity in the triad that the student most ("M") likes and the one activity the student least ("L") likes. This is equivalent to asking a student to rank the three activities from most liked to least liked. This approach, called a **forced-choice item format**, was designed to overcome the tendency for some students to have very high personal standards for "like," whereas others have very low standards. When this difference in standards occurs, two students who may in fact have the *same order* of likes or dislikes for an activity may mark their answer sheets differently. Measurement experts have criticized the forced-choice format, however, because using it results in a statistical artifact that causes a negative correlation among the scales of the inventory.

Item Content   The pioneers of the interest inventory technique used a variety of content to survey interests, including asking examinees likes and dislikes of job titles, school subject matter, hobbies, leisure activities, work activities, types of persons, and type of reading material, and assessing examinees' personal characteristics (Davis, 1980). Over time, however, the concept of interests narrowed to the world of work and careers. Today the content of most inventories is limited exclusively to lists of activities, and most are concerned with work activities. An exception is the *SII*, which uses a large variety of content. The 291 items on the *SII* measure a person's interest in relation to persons working in a wide range of careers.

Interest Inventory Use   Among the uses made of scores on vocational interest inventories are these: (a) to reassure people about tentative choices, (b) to give people a structure for understanding the world of work, (c) to help people resolve conflicting alternatives, (d) to help people plan their personal development, (e) to call attention to desirable alternatives that the average person usually does not know about or overlooks, (f) to help people understand

FIGURE 19.5 **Examples of items on two interest process inventories.**

The *ACT Interest Inventory*

I would *dislike* doing this activity . . . . D

I am *indifferent* (don't care one way or the other) I

I would *like* doing this activity L

1. Explore a science museum
2. Play jazz in a combo
3. Help settle an argument between friends

Kuder Occupational Interest Survey, Form DD

* 1.	Visit an art gallery . . . . M		L
	Browse in a library . . . . M		L
	Visit a museum . . . . M		L
2.	Collect autographs . . . . M		L
	Collect coins . . . . M		L
	Collect stones . . . . M		L

Notes:

*M=most liked, L=least liked

Sources: The test items from the *ACT Interest Inventory*, p. 10 in Registering for the ACT Assessment. Copyright by ACT, Inc. Reproduced by permission of the publisher.

The items from the *Kuder Occupational Interest Survey, Form DD* are reproduced by permission. Published by National Career Assessment Services Inc.™, P.O. Box 277, Adel, Iowa 50003. 800-314-8972/ www.kuder.com. Copyright © by National Career Assessment Services, Inc™. All rights reserved.

---

their job dissatisfaction, (g) to help employers select people who will be better workers, (h) to help people plan their career advancement, and (i) to aid in the scientific study of the world of work and to link this research to other research in the social sciences (Holland, 1975, p. 22).

Strong Interest Inventory

A number of vocational interest inventories are listed in Appendix K. One of the inventories, the *Strong Interest Inventory (SII)*, is briefly described here.

Organization The 2004 revision, which is used with persons 14 years old and older, is composed of 291 items. A person is presented with occupations, subject areas, activities, leisure activities, and people and rates each item on a 5-point scale: strongly like, like, indifferent, dislike, or strongly dislike. The responses are then scored via a computer (tests cannot be scored locally) and reported as standard scores on various scales. The *SII* results are reported to the examinee in four ways: (a) 6 General Occupational Themes, which describe a person's overall pattern of occupational interests; (b) 30 Basic Interest Scales, which describe the somewhat narrower categories of interest areas a person likes within the 6 General Occupational Themes; (c) 211 Occupational Scales, which describe the extent to which a person's likes and dislikes are similar to persons working in specific occupations; and (d) 5 Personal Style Scales.

General Occupational Themes The person receives a score on each of six areas, which were adapted from Holland (1973). These are Realistic, Conventional, Investigative, Enterprising, Artistic, and Social. A counselor can use the student's profile regarding these areas to help a student understand his or her overall or general pattern of interests, work activities, personal values, and how he or she appears to be oriented to the world of work. A normalized standard score (*T*-score) is reported for each of the six themes.

Basic Interest Scales The 30 scales are grouped in clusters under each of the six themes. For example, six of the Basic Interest Scales—Teaching and Education, Social Sciences, Human Resources and Training, Healthcare Services, Religion and Spirituality, and Counseling and Helping— are clustered under the general occupational theme of Social. The Basic Interest Scales are intermediate between the General Occupational Themes and the more specific Occupational Scales (described next). The Basic Interest Scales describe the clusters of interests a student has. These activity areas may be common to several specific occupations (for example, there are many types of teachers).

Occupational Scales Paralegal, respiratory specialist, florist, artist, and social science teacher are some of the occupational scales. The occupational scales are organized under each of the six general occupation themes. A person receives a standard score for each occupation based on the combined male and female norms. This score describes how similar the student's pattern of likes and dislikes is to persons who are experienced and satisfied in each occupation. In the report to the student within each General Occupational Theme, occupations are ordered according to the student's similarity to persons of their own gender. Occupations first on the list are those for which the student's *SII* responses are most similar to persons of their own gender who are working in that occupation.

Special Scales There are five Personal Style Scales describing how the student approaches learning, people, and the workplace. These are: Work Style, Learning Environment, Leadership Style, Risk Taking, and Team Orientation. In addition to these scales, there is a special administrative index, the Typicality Index. This index is used to assess the consistency of a student's responses to items that are very highly correlated in the norm group in an attempt to detect random and atypical response patterns. A counselor uses this index to help decide whether a student responded well enough to make the results meaningful. If not, the counselor will need to explore with the student individually why the student did not respond consistently to very similar items.

Male-Female Differences Although the *SII* has a single booklet for both males and females, there are 122 Occupational Scales for men and 122 Occupational Scales for women for a total of 244 Occupational Scales. The authors have kept scale reporting separate for each gender because (a) there are large differences in the strength of interests in the two genders in many areas and (b) combined-sex (unisex) scales appear less valid for many occupations. Students may understand their interests better if they can compare them to both like-gender and opposite-gender norms. This may be especially helpful to students who are thinking of entering occupations dominated by the gender opposite of their own.

ASSESSING ATTITUDES

Attitudes and Their Characteristics

Attitudes are characteristics of persons that describe their positive and negative feelings toward particular objects, situations, institutions, persons, or ideas. When discussing attitudes and using the results of attitude inventories, you should keep in mind the following points (Mehrens & Lehmann, 1991):

- A student learns attitudes, and once learned they direct or guide the students' actions.
- You cannot observe a student's attitudes directly; you must infer them from the student's actions or from responses to an attitude questionnaire.
- Different ways of constructing attitude scales include Thurstone, Guttman, Likert, Semantic Differential,

and Item Response Theory. These methods are not interchangeable.
- Because it is difficult to construct an attitude scale, you may need to look seriously into the validity and reliability of the results before you use one.
- Because students can fake their responses to attitude questionnaires, you should interpret the results very cautiously.

When interpreting students' attitudes, keep in mind that they differ in both **direction** and **intensity**. Two students may hold the same positive attitude (direction), but the students may differ greatly regarding the strength of feeling (intensity) they attach to that attitude.

Students' attitudes will also differ in **affective saliency** or emotionality. Two students may have the same positive attitude, but one may become much more emotional than the other regarding it.

The attitudes of older students and adults are changeable, but it is much easier to change the attitudes of younger students.

ASSESSING PERSONALITY DIMENSIONS

A variety of techniques have been developed to measure various aspects of personality. Personality tests and vocational tests are the two most numerous varieties of tests. A person using a personality test must be trained in psychological interpretation of the results. This usually requires extensive graduate work in counseling or school psychology and a lengthy supervised internship. Thus, for the most part, teacher-training programs leave teachers unqualified to administer and interpret personality tests. Teachers will encounter the results of such tests, however, if they are part of a child study team or if they read psychological reports of students. Thus, some familiarity with a few basic concepts of personality measurement is in order.

Assessment Approaches

The kind of personality tests a counselor or psychologist uses depends primarily on the psychological orientation of the particular professional. Currently, there is no standard model or conception of personality, nor do counselors and psychologists agree on which particular aspects of personality are most important to assess. The implication of this diversity is that the kinds of personality tests used in psychological reports a teacher may encounter depend on the background and training of the psychologist assigned to a given student's case.

Projective Techniques

Projective Hypothesis Two broad methods for assessing personality dimensions are projective techniques and structured techniques. **Projective techniques** present the examinee with ambiguous stimuli and ask the examinee to respond to them. The proponents of this technique assume that an examinee's interpretations of these vague stimuli will reveal the examinee's innermost needs, feelings, and conflicts, even though the examinee is unaware of what he or she is revealing. This assumption is known as the **projective hypothesis** (Frank, 1939). A trained examiner is needed to interpret an examinee's responses. Examples of projective personality tests are the *Rorschach Test*, the *Thematic Apperception Test* (*TAT*), word association tests, various sentence-completion tests, certain picture arrangement tests, and various figure drawing tests.

Rorschach   The *Rorschach Test*, for example, presents to the examinee one at a time several cards on which inkblots are printed. The examinee is asked to tell what each inkblot means or to describe the things seen in the inkblot. Because the examinee's responses are based on associations, the *Rorschach* is classified as an **association test**. The psychologist analyzes the content of the responses as well as the process and manner in which the subject responds. As a result of this analysis, the psychologist generates hypotheses about the subject's personality dynamics that the psychologist can explore with the client and can confirm or reject during subsequent interview sessions.

Thematic Apperception Test (TAT)   The *TAT* pictures are more structured than the *Rorschach* inkblots. They show surrealistic pictures of scenes involving one or more persons. The examinee is asked to tell a story about the picture: What happened before the event pictured? What is happening at the moment? Who are the characters? What are their feelings? How will the story end? Because examinees must construct stories, the *TAT* is sometimes classified as a **construction test**. The psychologist analyzes the content of the story in terms of H. A. Murray's (1938) personality theory of "needs" and "press," generating hypotheses about the examinee's personality for further exploration during interviews.

Sentence-Completion Assessments   Sentence **completion tests of personality** ask the examinee to complete sentences related to various aspects of self and interpersonal relations (e.g., "Compared with most families, mine . . . "). The results of content analyses are used similarly to generate hypotheses about a subject's personality.

Structured Techniques

Definition   **Structured personality assessment techniques** follow very specific rules for administering, scoring, and interpreting the tests. Usually they follow a response-choice format: yes-no, true-false, or multiple-choice. Examples of structured personality tests are the *Guilford-Zimmerman Temperament Survey*, the *Minnesota Multiphasic Personality Inventory–Second Edition*, the *California Psychological Inventory*, the *Sixteen Personality*

Factors Questionnaire–Fifth Edition, and the *Personality Inventory for Children–Second Edition*.

Self-Report Characteristic   Each test is sometimes referred to as a **self-report personality inventory** because it requires the examinee to respond to the items in a way that describes his or her personal feelings. For instance, examinees may be asked whether the statement, "I usually express my personal opinions to others," is true of themselves.

Dimensions of Personality   Another characteristic of structured personality inventories is that the items are related to various scales or personality dimensions. The *Guilford-Zimmerman Temperament Survey*, for example, reports an examinee's profile with respect to 10 scales: general activity, restraint, ascendance (leadership), sociability, emotional stability, objectivity, friendliness, thoughtfulness, personal relations, and masculinity.[4]

Usefulness of Tests for the Teacher

Self-report personality inventories require persons to (Thorndike et al., 1991) (a) read and comprehend each item, (b) be able to understand their own actions enough to know whether a given statement is true of them, and (c) be willing to respond honestly and frankly. Reading in the context of personality testing requires that students understand the items well enough to be able to decide the degree to which the statements apply to their own lives. To decide whether a statement applies, a student must view that behavior objectively, which may not be within the repertoire of a poorly adjusted student. Finally, if a student is neither able nor willing to respond frankly to the items, a distorted personality description may result. This lack of frankness may occur more often when testing children who feel vulnerable or threatened if they reveal their feelings to the teacher or, more generally, to the school.

Considering the shortcomings of self-report personality and adjustment inventories, some measurement experts answer the questions of whether to use them in the following way: "these instruments have a limited role in education and should be used in educational settings only when the results are to benefit the examinee and will be interpreted by a person with adequate clinical training and experience" (Thorndike et al., 1991, p. 416).

Summary

Assessing Scholastic and Other Aptitude Tests

- Tests of general scholastic ability or intelligence describe a learner's general intellectual skill rather than the specific abilities needed to learn a particular lesson or task.
- Information about general intellectual skills becomes important when trying to forecast a pupil's future academic performance in general and when the conditions for future

---

[4]*Masculinity* is the term these authors use.

learning are expected to remain similar to the past learning conditions.

- General scholastic ability test scores are less valid when predicting very specific kinds of academic learning, but more valid when predicting more global kinds of academic accomplishments.

- A person's capacity to learn is a function of biological makeup, experience in the environment, and a complex interaction of the two. The capacity of a person to learn something new will depend on previous learning, the way the new material is taught, the pupil's motivation, and a host of other factors, as well as the pupil's native endowment.

- Both achievement tests and aptitude tests can reflect a person's present aptitude level. Test items that best predict future attainment, however, tend to be found on aptitude tests.

- All predictions made from aptitude test scores assume that the same learning conditions that existed in the past will extend into the future.

- This chapter discusses three general types of group-administered scholastic aptitude tests: an omnibus test, a two-score test, and a multiple-aptitude test. Suggestions for using these test scores appear.

- School readiness tests are also described.

- High school and college admissions tests are designed to predict success at the next higher level of schooling. The chapter describes two college admissions tests.

- As a group, pupils' scholastic aptitude test scores tend to be stable over time.

- In general, test-retest correlations for scholastic ability tests (a) tend to become lower (less stable) as the time interval between the testings grows, and (b) for a fixed interval between testings, they tend to be lower for younger children than for older children.

- Some factors that contribute to the relative stability of aptitude scores are (a) the cumulative nature of intellectual skills, (b) the stability of a person's environment, and (c) the generative nature of earlier acquired prerequisite skills.

- Some factors that contribute to changes in a person's aptitude scores are (a) errors of measurement, (b) test and norm differences, and (c) special interventions and enriched environments.

- Growth in intellectual skills in the early years seems to be associated with an environment that is emotionally supportive and accepting and in which there are many opportunities for experiencing and reinforcing a person's cognitive successes.

- The *Stanford-Binet Intelligence Scale*, the *Wechsler Intelligence Scales*, and the *Kaufman Assessment Battery for Children* are examples of individually administered tests of general scholastic aptitude. The text describes each and the similarities and differences among them.

- Behavior checklists help psychologists assess whether a student has acquired normal, age-appropriate adaptive behaviors. These behaviors indicate a child can cope with the social and physical environment, especially outside the school context. A comprehensive assessment requires ascertaining the level of the pupil's adaptive behavior (as well as the level of general academic skills).

Assessing Vocational and Career Interests

- Vocational interest inventories are paper-and-pencil questionnaires that help individuals express their likes and dislikes about certain work-related activities. Individuals' patterns of likes and dislikes are used to help them explore and make decisions about careers.

- Interest inventories contain one of two item formats: (a) a rating format in which persons rate the degree to which they like the activities presented to them, or (b) a forced-choice ranking format in which the persons must rank the activities presented from best liked to least liked.

- Nearly all vocational interest inventories limit the activities in the items to work-related activities. The *Strong Vocational Interest Bank* of the *Strong Interest Inventory* is an exception because of the diversity of item content it includes (e.g., occupational titles, school subjects, amusements, work- and nonwork-related activities, types of people, and personal characteristics).

Assessing Attitudes and Personality

- Attitudes describe a person's feelings toward particular objects, situations, institutions, persons, or ideas.

- Several factors to consider before you use the results of an attitude questionnaire are presented.

- The choice of the particular kind of personality test often depends on the training and orientation of the psychologist examining the person.

- Projective tests of personality present ambiguous stimuli and assume that the examinee's responses reflect the person's underlying psychological needs and personality dispositions.

- Structured personality tests usually use a response-choice format. Examinees either rank or rate statements in terms of how well the statements describe themselves. Structured personality test scores describe a person's normative standing on each of several dimensions or aspects of personality.

- Teachers probably should not administer and interpret personality tests because (a) the tests are subject to distortion by pupils, (b) such tests have limited predictive validity when used alone, (c) paper-and-pencil inventories depend on the examinee's reading ability and insight into his or her own behavior, (d) teachers generally do not have the requisite coursework and supervised training necessary to interpret them, and (e) teachers seldom have the time needed to explore the meaning of a test score with an individual pupil.

Important Terms and Concepts

abstract/visual reasoning subtests
adaptive behavior
affective saliency
age-based scores versus grade-based scores
aptitude (versus achievement)
association test of personality
attitudes
completion test of personality
construction test of personality
direction and intensity of attitude
empirically keyed scales
expressed interests, inventoried interests, manifested interests, tested interests

figural reasoning
forced-choice item format
general versus specific intellectual skills
interests
mental age
multiple-aptitude tests
nonverbal tests
omnibus test
people-similarity rationale versus activity-similarity rationale
pictorial reasoning
projective hypothesis
projective personality test techniques
quantitative reasoning
readiness test
short-term memory subtests
spiral format
standard age score (*SAS*)
structured (self-report) personality assessment techniques
values
verbal comprehension tests
verbal reasoning tests
vocational interest inventories

Exercises and Applications

1. Describe several school situations in which it is less helpful to know a student's level of specific skill development than to know a student's general intellectual skill development in setting expectations for learning new material.

2. Read each of the following statements of educational needs. For each statement choose the type of test that possibly could meet the stated need. Next to each type of test you selected for a need, put a plus sign (+) if you believe the need can actually be met by the type of test you selected, and a minus sign (–) if you believe the need cannot actually be met by the test. Defend your choices. Choose from among the tests in this set to respond to this exercise:

OLSAT, DAT, readiness tests, *SAT, ACT*, aptitude tests for a specific subject, *SB–V, WISC–IV, KABC–II*.

   a. "In addition to finding out a student's verbal and quantitative aptitudes, I would like to know how well the student processes symbols and other nonverbal material."
   b. "I'd like to give all ninth graders a test that would provide information helpful to them in making career decisions."
   c. "I would like to know which of my fifth-grade students could learn computer programming quickly and well."
   d. "I need a general ability test for a student who recently arrived from Cuba."
   e. "I need a college admissions test that gives me information that I can use in guidance and counseling activities as well as in admissions."

3. Both the *DAT* and *SVIB–SII* report results on separate general norms. Explain why they do so, and discuss whether this practice is helpful to the career and further schooling planning of females.

4. What are the nine uses of interest inventories scores cited by Holland (1975)?
   a. Visit your school's guidance department and determine whether its counselors use interest inventories scores in any of these ways.
   b. Share your findings with your classmates.

5. Read the following statements. Each statement expresses a student's status with respect to achievement, aptitude, attitude, interest, or values. Classify each statement into one of the five categories.
   a. "I am in control of my learning in this class at all times."
   b. "I like science fiction stories better than biographies."
   c. "I think my math class is boring."
   d. "It is more important for me to be in personal control of my working hours than to earn a high salary."
   e. "I am constantly striving to be the best student in this school."

Standards for Teacher Competence in Educational Assessment of Students

Developed by the American Federation of Teachers, National Council on Measurement in Education, and National Education Association

The standards are intended for use as:

- a guide for teacher educators as they design and approve programs for teacher preparation
- a self-assessment guide for teachers in identifying their needs for professional development in student assessment
- a guide for workshop instructors as they design professional development experiences for in-service teachers
- an impetus for educational measurement specialists and teacher trainers to conceptualize student assessment and teacher training in student assessment more broadly than has been the case in the past

1. Teachers Should Be Skilled in Choosing Assessment Methods Appropriate for Instructional Decisions.

Skills in choosing appropriate, useful, administratively convenient, technically adequate, and fair assessment methods are pre-requisite to good use of information to support instructional decisions. Teachers need to be well-acquainted with the kinds of information provided by a broad range of assessment alternatives and their strengths and weaknesses. In particular, they should be familiar with criteria for evaluating and selecting assessment methods in light of instructional plans.

Teachers who meet this standard will have the conceptual and application skills that follow. They will be able to use the concepts of assessment error and validity when developing or selecting their approaches to classroom assessment of students. They will understand how valid assessment data can support instructional activities such as providing appropriate feedback to students, diagnosing group and individual learning needs, planning for individualized educational programs, motivating students, and evaluating instructional procedures. They will understand how invalid information can affect instructional decisions about students. They will also be able to use and evaluate assessment options available to them, considering among other things the cultural, social, economic, and language backgrounds of students. They will be aware that different assessment approaches can be incompatible with certain instructional goals and may impact quite differently on their teaching.

Teachers will know, for each assessment approach they use, its appropriateness for making decisions about their pupils.

Source: From *Standards for Teacher Competence in Educational Assessment of Students* (pp. 1–4) by American Federation of Teachers, National Council on Measurement in Education, and National Education Association, 1990, Washington, DC: National Council on Measurement in Education. Copyright 1990 by the National Council on Measurement in Education. Reprinted by permission of the publisher.

Moreover, teachers will know where to find information about and/or reviews of various assessment methods. Assessment options are diverse and include text- and curriculum-embedded questions and tests, standardized criterion-referenced and norm-referenced tests, oral questioning, spontaneous and structured performance assessments, portfolios, exhibitions, demonstrations, rating scales, writing samples, paper-and-pencil tests, seatwork and homework, peer- and self-assessments, student records, observations, questionnaires, interviews, projects, products, and others' opinions.

2. Teachers Should Be Skilled in Developing Assessment Methods Appropriate for Instructional Decisions.

While teachers often use published or other external assessment tools, the bulk of the assessment information they use for decision-making comes from approaches they create and implement. Indeed, the assessment demands of the classroom go well beyond readily available instruments.

Teachers who meet this standard will have the conceptual and application skills that follow. Teachers will be skilled in planning the collection of information that facilitates the decisions they will make. They will know and follow appropriate principles for developing and using assessment methods in their teaching, avoiding common pitfalls in student assessment. Such techniques may include several of the options listed at the end of the first standard. The teacher will select the techniques which are appropriate to the intent of the teacher's instruction.

Teachers meeting this standard will also be skilled in using student data to analyze the quality of each assessment technique they use. Since most teachers do not have access to assessment specialists, they must be prepared to do these analyses themselves.

3. Teachers Should Be Skilled in Administering, Scoring and Interpreting the Results of Both Externally-produced and Teacher-produced Assessment Methods.

It is not enough that teachers are able to select and develop good assessment methods; they must also be able to apply them properly. Teachers should be skilled in administering, scoring, and interpreting results from diverse assessment methods.

Teachers who meet this standard will have the conceptual and application skills that follow. They will be skilled in interpreting informal and formal teacher-produced assessment results, including pupils' performances in class and on homework assignments. Teachers will be able to use guides for scoring essay questions and projects, stencils for scoring response-choice questions, and scales for rating performance assessments. They will be able to use these in ways that produce consistent results.

Teachers will be able to administer standardized achievement tests and be able to interpret the commonly reported scores: percentile ranks, percentile band scores, standard scores, and grade equivalents. They will have a conceptual understanding of the summary indexes commonly reported with assessment results: measures of central tendency, dispersion, relationships, reliability, and errors of measurement.

Teachers will be able to apply these concepts of score and summary indices in ways that enhance their use of the assessments that they develop. They will be able to analyze assessment results to identify pupils' strengths and errors. If they get inconsistent results, they will seek other explanations for the discrepancy or other data to attempt to resolve the uncertainty before arriving at a decision. They will be able to use assessment methods in ways that encourage students' educational development and that do not inappropriately increase students' anxiety levels.

4. Teachers Should Be Skilled in Using Assessment Results When Making Decisions About Individual Students, Planning Teaching, Developing Curriculum, and School Improvement.

Assessment results are used to make educational decisions at several levels: in the classroom about students, in the community about a school and a school district, and in society, generally, about the purposes and outcomes of the educational enterprise. Teachers play a vital role when participating in decision-making at each of these levels and must be able to use assessment results effectively.

Teachers who meet this standard will have the conceptual and application skills that follow. They will be able to use accumulated assessment information to organize a sound instructional plan for facilitating students' educational development. When using assessment results to plan and/or evaluate instruction and curriculum, teachers will interpret the results correctly and avoid common misinterpretations, such as basing decisions on scores that lack curriculum validity. They will be informed about the results of local, regional, state, and national assessments and about their appropriate use for pupil, classroom, school, district, state, and national educational improvement.

5. Teachers Should Be Skilled in Developing Valid Pupil Grading Procedures Which Use Pupil Assessments.

Grading students is an important part of professional practice for teachers. Grading is defined as indicating both a student's level of performance and a teacher's valuing of that performance. The principles for using assessments to obtain valid grades are known and teachers should employ them.

Teachers who meet this standard will have the conceptual and application skills that follow. They will be able to devise,

implement, and explain a procedure for developing grades composed of marks from various assignments, projects, in-class activities, quizzes, tests, and/or other assessments that they may use. Teachers will understand and be able to articulate why the grades they assign are rational, justified, and fair, acknowledging that such grades reflect their preferences and judgments. Teachers will be able to recognize and to avoid faulty grading procedures such as using grades as punishment. They will be able to evaluate and to modify their grading procedures in order to improve the validity of the interpretations made from them about students' attainments.

6. Teachers Should Be Skilled in Communicating Assessment Results to Students, Parents, Other Lay Audiences, and Other Educators.

Teachers must routinely report assessment results to students and to parents or guardians. In addition, they are frequently asked to report or to discuss assessment results with other educators and with diverse lay audiences. If the results are not communicated effectively, they may be misused or not used. To communicate effectively with others on matters of student assessment, teachers must be able to use assessment terminology appropriately and must be able to articulate the meaning, limitations, and implications of assessment results. Furthermore, teachers will sometimes be in a position that will require them to defend their own assessment procedures and their interpretations of them. At other times, teachers may need to help the public to interpret assessment results appropriately.

Teachers who meet this standard will have the conceptual and application skills that follow. Teachers will understand and be able to give appropriate explanations of how the interpretation of student assessments must be moderated by the student's socioeconomic, cultural, language, and other background factors. Teachers will be able to explain that assessment results do not imply that such background factors limit a student's ultimate educational development. They will be able to communicate to students and to their parents or guardians how they may assess the student's educational progress. Teachers will understand and be able to explain the importance of taking measurement errors into account when using assessments to make decisions about individual students. Teachers will be able to explain the limitations of different informal and formal assessment methods. They will be able to explain printed reports of the results of pupil assessments at the classroom, school district, state, and national levels.

7. Teachers Should Be Skilled in Recognizing Unethical, Illegal, and Otherwise Inappropriate Assessment Methods and Uses of Assessment Information.

Fairness, the rights of all concerned, and professional ethical behavior must undergird all student assessment activities, from the initial planning for and gathering of information to the interpretation, use, and communication of the results. Teachers must be well-versed in their own ethical and legal responsibilities in assessment. In addition, they should also attempt to have the inappropriate assessment practices of others discontinued whenever they are encountered. Teachers should also participate with the wider educational community in defining the limits of appropriate professional behavior in assessment.

Teachers who meet this standard will have the conceptual and application skills that follow. They will know those laws and case decisions which affect their classroom, school district, and state assessment practices. Teachers will be aware that various assessment procedures can be misused or overused resulting in harmful consequences such as embarrassing students, violating a student's right to confidentiality, and inappropriately using students' standardized achievement test scores to measure teaching effectiveness.

Code of Fair Testing Practices in Education (Revised)

Prepared by the Joint Committee on Testing Practices

The *Code of Fair Testing Practices in Education (Code)* is a guide for professionals in fulfilling their obligation to provide and use tests that are fair to all test takers regardless of age, gender, disability, race, ethnicity, national origin, religion, sexual orientation, linguistic background, or other personal characteristics. Fairness is a primary consideration in all aspects of testing. Careful standardization of tests and administration conditions helps to ensure that all test takers are given a comparable opportunity to demonstrate what they know and how they can perform in the area being tested. Fairness implies that every test taker has the opportunity to prepare for the test and is informed about the general nature and content of the test, as appropriate to the purpose of the test. Fairness also extends to the accurate reporting of individual and group test results. Fairness is not an isolated concept, but must be considered in all aspects of the testing process.

The *Code* applies broadly to testing in education (admissions, educational assessment, educational diagnosis, and student placement) regardless of the mode of presentation, so it is relevant to conventional paper-and-pencil tests, computer-based tests, and performance tests. It is not designed to cover employment testing, licensure or certification testing, or other types of testing outside the field of education. The *Code* is directed primarily at professionally developed tests used in formally administered testing programs. Although the *Code* is not intended to cover tests made by teachers for use in their own classrooms, teachers are encouraged to use the guidelines to help improve their testing practices.

The *Code* addresses the roles of test developers and test users separately. Test developers are people and organizations that construct tests, as well as those that set policies for testing programs. Test users are people and agencies that select tests, administer tests, commission test development services, or make decisions on the basis of test scores. Test developer and test user roles may overlap, for example, when a state or local education agency commissions test development services, sets policies that control

the test development process, and makes decisions on the basis of the test scores.

Many of the statements in the *Code* refer to the selection and use of existing tests. When a new test is developed, when an existing test is modified, or when the administration of a test is modified, the *Code* is intended to provide guidance for this process.

The *Code* is not intended to be mandatory, exhaustive, or definitive, and may not be applicable to every situation. Instead, the *Code* is intended to be aspirational, and is not intended to take precedence over the judgment of those who have competence in the subjects addressed.

The *Code* provides guidance separately for test developers and test users in four critical areas:

A. Developing and Selecting Appropriate Tests
B. Administering and Scoring Tests
C. Reporting and Interpreting Test Results
D. Informing Test Takers

The *Code* is intended to be consistent with the relevant parts of the Standards for Educational and Psychological Testing (American Educational Research Association [AERA], American Psychological Association [APA], and National Council on Measurement in Education [NCME], 1999). The *Code* is not meant to add new principles over and above those in the Standards or to change their meaning. Rather, the *Code* is intended to represent the spirit of selected portions of the Standards in a way that is relevant and meaningful to developers and users of tests, as well as to test takers and/or their parents or guardians. States, districts, schools, organizations and individual professionals are encouraged to commit themselves to fairness in testing and safeguarding the rights of test takers. The *Code* is intended to assist in carrying out such commitments.

The *Code* has been prepared by the Joint Committee on Testing Practices, a cooperative effort among several professional organizations. The aim of the Joint Committee is to act, in the public interest, to advance the quality of testing practices. Members of the Joint Committee include the American Counseling Association (ACA), the American Educational Research Association (AERA), the American Psychological Association (APA), the American Speech-Language-Hearing Association (ASHA), the National Association of School Psychologists (NASP), the National Association of Test Directors (NATD), and the National Council on Measurement in Education (NCME).

A. Developing and Selecting Appropriate Tests*

Test Developers

Test developers should provide the information and supporting evidence that test users need to select appropriate tests.

1. Provide evidence of what the test measures, the recommended uses, the intended test takers, and the strengths and limitations of the test, including the level of precision of the test scores.
2. Describe how the content and skills to be tested were selected and how the tests were developed.
3. Communicate information about a test's characteristics at a level of detail appropriate to the intended test users.
4. Provide guidance on the levels of skills, knowledge, and training necessary for appropriate review, selection, and administration of tests.
5. Provide evidence that the technical quality, including reliability and validity, of the test meets its intended purposes.
6. Provide to qualified test users representative samples of test questions or practice tests, directions, answer sheets, manuals, and score reports.
7. Avoid potentially offensive content or language when developing test questions and related materials.
8. Make appropriately modified forms of tests or administration procedures available for test takers with disabilities who need special accommodations.
9. Obtain and provide evidence on the performance of test takers of diverse subgroups, making significant efforts to obtain sample sizes that are adequate for subgroup analyses. Evaluate the evidence to ensure that differences in performance are related to the skills being assessed.

Test Users

Test users should select tests that meet the intended purpose and that are appropriate for the intended test takers.

1. Define the purpose for testing, the content and skills to be tested, and the intended test takers. Select and use the most appropriate test based on a thorough review of available information.
2. Review and select tests based on the appropriateness of test content, skills tested, and content coverage for the intended purpose of testing.
3. Review materials provided by test developers and select tests for which clear, accurate, and complete information is provided.
4. Select tests through a process that includes persons with appropriate knowledge, skills, and training.
5. Evaluate evidence of the technical quality of the test provided by the test developer and any independent reviewers.
6. Evaluate representative samples of test questions or practice tests, directions, answer sheets, manuals, and score reports before selecting a test.
7. Evaluate procedures and materials used by test developers, as well as the resulting test, to ensure that potentially offensive content or language is avoided.
8. Select tests with appropriately modified forms or administration procedures for test takers with disabilities who need special accommodations.
9. Evaluate the available evidence on the performance of test takers of diverse subgroups. Determine to the extent feasible

*Many of the statements in the *Code* refer to the selection of existing tests. However, in customized testing programs test developers are engaged to construct new tests. In those situations, the test development process should be designed to help ensure that the completed tests will be in compliance with the *Code*.

which performance differences may have been caused by factors unrelated to the skills being assessed.

B. Administering and Scoring Tests

Test Developers

Test developers should explain how to administer and score tests correctly and fairly.

1. Provide clear descriptions of detailed procedures for administering tests in a standardized manner.
2. Provide guidelines on reasonable procedures for assessing persons with disabilities who need special accommodations or those with diverse linguistic backgrounds.
3. Provide information to test takers or test users on test question formats and procedures for answering test questions, including information on the use of any needed materials and equipment.
4. Establish and implement procedures to ensure the security of testing materials during all phases of test development, administration, scoring, and reporting.
5. Provide procedures, materials and guidelines for scoring the tests, and for monitoring the accuracy of the scoring process. If scoring the test is the responsibility of the test developer, provide adequate training for scorers.
6. Correct errors that affect the interpretation of the scores and communicate the corrected results promptly.
7. Develop and implement procedures for ensuring the confidentiality of scores.

Test Users

Test users should administer and score tests correctly and fairly.

1. Follow established procedures for administering tests in a standardized manner.
2. Provide and document appropriate procedures for test takers with disabilities who need special accommodations or those with diverse linguistic backgrounds. Some accommodations may be required by law or regulation.
3. Provide test takers with an opportunity to become familiar with test question formats and any materials or equipment that may be used during testing.
4. Protect the security of test materials, including respecting copyrights and eliminating opportunities for test takers to obtain scores by fraudulent means.
5. If test scoring is the responsibility of the test user, provide adequate training to scorers and ensure and monitor the accuracy of the scoring process.
6. Correct errors that affect the interpretation of the scores and communicate the corrected results promptly.
7. Develop and implement procedures for ensuring the confidentiality of scores.

C. Reporting and Interpreting Test Results

Test Developers

Test developers should report test results accurately and provide information to help test users interpret test results correctly.

1. Provide information to support recommended interpretations of the results, including the nature of the content, norms or comparison groups, and other technical evidence. Advise test users of the benefits and limitations of test results and their interpretation. Warn against assigning greater precision than is warranted.
2. Provide guidance regarding the interpretations of results for tests administered with modifications. Inform test users of

potential problems in interpreting test results when tests or test administration procedures are modified.

3. Specify appropriate uses of test results and warn test users of potential misuses.
4. When test developers set standards, provide the rationale, procedures, and evidence for setting performance standards or passing scores. Avoid using stigmatizing labels.
5. Encourage test users to base decisions about test takers on multiple sources of appropriate information, not on a single test score.
6. Provide information to enable test users to accurately interpret and report test results for groups of test takers, including information about who were and who were not included in the different groups being compared, and information about factors that might influence the interpretation of results.
7. Provide test results in a timely fashion and in a manner that is understood by the test taker.
8. Provide guidance to test users about how to monitor the extent to which the test is fulfilling its intended purposes.

Test Users

Test users should report and interpret test results accurately and clearly.

1. Interpret the meaning of the test results, taking into account the nature of the content, norms or comparison groups, other technical evidence, and benefits and limitations of test results.
2. Interpret test results from modified test or test administration procedures in view of the impact those modifications may have had on test results.
3. Avoid using tests for purposes other than those recommended by the test developer unless there is evidence to support the intended use or interpretation.
4. Review the procedures for setting performance standards or passing scores. Avoid using stigmatizing labels.
5. Avoid using a single test score as the sole determinant of decisions about test takers. Interpret test scores in conjunction with other information about individuals.
6. State the intended interpretation and use of test results for groups of test takers. Avoid grouping test results for purposes not specifically recommended by the test developer unless evidence is obtained to support the intended use. Report procedures that were followed in determining who were and who were not included in the groups being compared and describe factors that might influence the interpretation of results.
7. Communicate test results in a timely fashion and in a manner that is understood by the test taker.
8. Develop and implement procedures for monitoring test use, including consistency with the intended purposes of the test.

D. Informing Test Takers

Test Developers or Test Users

Under some circumstances, test developers have direct communication with the test takers and/or control of the tests, testing process, and test results. In other circumstances the test users have these responsibilities.

Test developers or test users should inform test takers about the nature of the test, test taker rights and responsibilities, the appropriate use of scores, and procedures for resolving challenges to scores.

1. Inform test takers in advance of the test administration about the coverage of the test, the types of question formats, the directions, and appropriate test-taking strategies. Make such information available to all test takers.
2. When a test is optional, provide test takers or their parents/guardians with information to help them judge whether a test should be taken—including indications of any consequences that may result from not taking the test (e.g., not being eligible to compete for a particular scholarship)—and whether there is an available alternative to the test.
3. Provide test takers or their parents/guardians with information about rights test takers may have to obtain copies of tests and completed answer sheets, to retake tests, to have tests rescored, or to have scores declared invalid.
4. Provide test takers or their parents/guardians with information about responsibilities test takers have, such as being aware of the intended purpose and uses of the test, performing at capacity, following directions, and not disclosing test items or interfering with other test takers.
5. Inform test takers or their parents/guardians how long scores will be kept on file and indicate to whom, under what circumstances, and in what manner test scores and related information will or will not be released. Protect test scores from unauthorized release and access.
6. Describe procedures for investigating and resolving circumstances that might result in canceling or withholding scores, such as failure to adhere to specified testing procedures.
7. Describe procedures that test takers, parents/guardians, and other interested parties may use to obtain more information about the test, register complaints, and have problems resolved.

Note: The membership of the working group that developed the *Code of Fair Testing Practices in Education* and of the Joint Committee on Testing Practices that guided the working group is as follows:
  Peter Behuniak, PhD; Lloyd Bond, PhD; Gwyneth M. Boodoo, Phd; Wayne Camara, PhD; Ray Fenton, PhD; John J. Fremer, PhD (Cochair); Sharon M. Goldsmith, PhD; Bert F. Green, PhD; William G. Harris, PhD; Janet E. Helms, PhD; Stephanie H. McConaughy, PhD; Julie P. Noble, PhD; Wayne M. Patience, PhD; Carole L. Perlman, PhD; Douglas K. Smith, PhD; Janet E. Wall, EdD (Cochair); Pat Nellor Wickwire, PhD; Mary Yakimowski, PhD. Lara Frumkin, PhD, of the APA served as staff liaison.

The Joint Committee intends that the *Code* be consistent with and supportive of existing codes of conduct and standards of other professional groups who use tests in educational contexts. Of particular note are the Responsibilities of Users of Standardized Tests (Association for Assessment in Counseling, 1989), APA Test User Qualifications (2000), ASHA Code of Ethics (2001), Ethical Principles of Psychologists and Code of Conduct (1992), NASP Professional Conduct Manual (2000), NCME Code of Professional Responsibility (1995), and Rights and Responsibilities of Test Takers: Guidelines and Expectations (Joint Committee on Testing Practices, 2000).

Code of Professional Responsibilities in Educational Measurement

Prepared by the NCME Ad Hoc Committee on the Development of a Code of Ethics: Cynthia B. Schmeiser, ACT–Chair; Kurt F. Geisinger, State University of New York; Sharon Johnson-Lewis, Detroit Public Schools; Edward D. Roeber, Council of Chief State School Officers; William D. Schafer, University of Maryland

Preamble and General Responsibilities

As an organization dedicated to the improvement of measurement and evaluation practice in education, the National Council on Measurement in Education (NCME) has adopted this Code to promote professionally responsible practice in educational measurement. Professionally responsible practice is conduct that arises from either the professional standards of the field, general ethical principles, or both.

The purpose of the Code of Professional Responsibilities in Educational Measurement, hereinafter referred to as the Code, is to guide the conduct of NCME members who are involved in any type of assessment activity in education. NCME is also providing this Code as a public service for all individuals who are engaged in educational assessment activities in the hope that these activities will be conducted in a professionally responsible manner. Persons who engage in these activities include local educators such as classroom teachers, principals, and superintendents; professionals such as school psychologists and counselors; state and national technical, legislative, and policy staff in education; staff of research, evaluation, and testing organizations; providers of test preparation services; college and university faculty and administrators; and professionals in business and industry who design and implement educational and training programs.

This Code applies to any type of assessment that occurs as part of the educational process, including formal and informal, traditional and alternative techniques for gathering information used in making educational decisions at all levels. These techniques include, but are not limited to, large-scale assessments at the school, district, state, national, and international levels; standardized tests; observational measures; teacher-conducted assessments; assessment support materials; and other achievement, aptitude, interest, and personality measures used in and for education.

Although NCME is promulgating this Code for its members, it strongly encourages other organizations and individuals who engage in educational assessment activities to endorse and abide by the responsibilities relevant to their professions. Because the Code pertains only to uses of assessment in education, it is recognized that uses of assessments outside of educational contexts,

such as for employment, certification, or licensure, may involve additional professional responsibilities beyond those detailed in this Code.

The Code is intended to serve an educational function: to inform and remind those involved in educational assessment of their obligations to uphold the integrity of the manner in which assessments are developed, used, evaluated, and marketed. Moreover, it is expected that the Code will stimulate thoughtful discussion of what constitutes professionally responsible assessment practice at all levels in education.

Section 1: Responsibilities of Those Who Develop Assessment Products and Services

Those who develop assessment products and services, such as classroom teachers and other assessment specialists, have a professional responsibility to strive to produce assessments that are of the highest quality. Persons who develop assessments have a professional responsibility to:

1.1 ensure that assessment products and services are developed to meet applicable professional, technical, and legal standards.

1.2 develop assessment products and services that are as free as possible from bias due to characteristics irrelevant to the construct being measured, such as gender, ethnicity, race, socioeconomic status, disability, religion, age, or national origin.

1.3 plan accommodations for groups of test takers with disabilities and other special needs when developing assessments.

1.4 disclose to appropriate parties any actual or potential conflicts of interest that might influence the developers' judgment or performance.

1.5 use copyrighted materials in assessment products and services in accordance with state and federal law.

1.6 make information available to appropriate persons about the steps taken to develop and score the assessment, including up-to-date information used to support the reliability, validity, scoring and reporting processes, and other relevant characteristics of the assessment.

1.7 protect the rights to privacy of those who are assessed as part of the assessment development process.

1.8 caution users, in clear and prominent language, against the most likely misinterpretations and misuses of data that arise out of the assessment development process.

1.9 avoid false or unsubstantiated claims in test preparation and program support materials and services about an assessment or its use and interpretation.

1.10 correct any substantive inaccuracies in assessments or their support materials as soon as feasible.

1.11 develop score reports and support materials that promote the understanding of assessment results.

Section 2: Responsibilities of Those Who Market and Sell Assessment Products and Services

The marketing of assessment products and services, such as tests and other instruments, scoring services, test preparation services, consulting, and test interpretive services, should be based on information that is accurate, complete, and relevant to those considering their use. Persons who market and sell assessment products and services have a professional responsibility to:

2.1 provide accurate information to potential purchasers about assessment products and services and their recommended uses and limitations.

2.2 not knowingly withhold relevant information about assessment products and services that might affect an appropriate selection decision.

2.3 base all claims about assessment products and services on valid interpretations of publicly available information.

2.4 allow qualified users equal opportunity to purchase assessment products and services.

2.5 establish reasonable fees for assessment products and services.

2.6 communicate to potential users, in advance of any purchase or use, all applicable fees associated with assessment products and services.

2.7 strive to ensure that no individuals are denied access to opportunities because of their inability to pay the fees for assessment products and services.

2.8 establish criteria for the sale of assessment products and services, such as limiting the sale of assessment products and services to those individuals who are qualified for recommended uses and from whom proper uses and interpretations are anticipated.

2.9 inform potential users of known inappropriate uses of assessment products and services and provide recommendations about how to avoid such misuses.

2.10 maintain a current understanding about assessment products and services and their appropriate uses in education.

2.11 release information implying endorsement by users of assessment products and services only with the users' permission.

2.12 avoid making claims that assessment products and services have been endorsed by another organization unless an official endorsement has been obtained.

2.13 avoid marketing test preparation products and services that may cause individuals to receive scores that misrepresent their actual levels of attainment.

Section 3: Responsibilities of Those Who Select Assessment Products and Services

Those who select assessment products and services for use in educational settings, or help others do so, have important professional responsibilities to make sure that the assessments

are appropriate for their intended use. Persons who select assessment products and services have a professional responsibility to:

3.1 conduct a thorough review and evaluation of available assessment strategies and instruments that might be valid for the intended uses.

3.2 recommend and/or select assessments based on publicly available documented evidence of their technical quality and utility rather than on unsubstantiated claims or statements.

3.3 disclose any associations or affiliations that they have with the authors, test publishers, or others involved with the assessments under consideration for purchase and refrain from participation if such associations might affect the objectivity of the selection process.

3.4 inform decision makers and prospective users of the appropriateness of the assessment for the intended uses, likely consequences of use, protection of examinee rights, relative costs, materials and services needed to conduct or use the assessment, and known limitations of the assessment, including potential misuses and misinterpretations of assessment information.

3.5 recommend against the use of any prospective assessment that is likely to be administered, scored, and used in an invalid manner for members of various groups in our society for reasons of race, ethnicity, gender, age, disability, language background, socioeconomic status, religion, or national origin.

3.6 comply with all security precautions that may accompany assessments being reviewed.

3.7 immediately disclose any attempts by others to exert undue influence on the assessment selection process.

3.8 avoid recommending, purchasing, or using test preparation products and services that may cause individuals to receive scores that misrepresent their actual levels of attainment.

Section 4: Responsibilities of Those Who Administer Assessments

Those who prepare individuals to take assessments and those who are directly or indirectly involved in the administration of assessments as part of the educational process, including teachers, administrators, and assessment personnel, have an important role in making sure that the assessments are administered in a fair and accurate manner. Persons who prepare others for, and those who administer, assessments have a professional responsibility to:

4.1 inform the examinees about the assessment prior to its administration, including its purposes, uses, and consequences; how the assessment information will be judged or scored; how the results will be kept on file; who will have access to the results; how the results will be distributed; and examinees' rights before, during, and after the assessment.

4.2 administer only those assessments for which they are qualified by education, training, licensure, or certification.

4.3 take appropriate security precautions before, during, and after the administration of the assessment.

4.4 understand the procedures needed to administer the assessment prior to administration.

4.5 administer standardized assessments according to prescribed procedures and conditions and notify appropriate persons if any nonstandard or delimiting conditions occur.

4.6 not exclude any eligible student from the assessment.

4.7 avoid any conditions in the conduct of the assessment that might invalidate the results.

4.8 provide for and document all reasonable and allowable accommodations for the administration of the assessment to persons with disabilities or special needs.

4.9 provide reasonable opportunities for individuals to ask questions about the assessment procedures or directions prior to and at prescribed times during the administration of the assessment.

4.10 protect the rights to privacy and due process of those who are assessed.

4.11 avoid actions or conditions that would permit or encourage individuals or groups to receive scores that misrepresent their actual levels of attainment.

Section 5: Responsibilities of Those Who Score Assessments

The scoring of educational assessments should be conducted properly and efficiently so that the results are reported accurately and in a timely manner. Persons who score and prepare reports of assessments have a professional responsibility to:

5.1 provide complete and accurate information to users about how the assessment is scored, such as the reporting schedule, scoring process to be used, rationale for the scoring approach, technical characteristics, quality control procedures, reporting formats, and the fees, if any, for these services.

5.2 ensure the accuracy of the assessment results by conducting reasonable quality control procedures before, during, and after scoring.

5.3 minimize the effect on scoring of factors irrelevant to the purposes of the assessment.

5.4 inform users promptly of any deviation in the planned scoring and reporting service or schedule and negotiate a solution with users.

5.5 provide corrected score results to the examinee or the client as quickly as practicable should errors be found that may affect the inferences made on the basis of the scores.

5.6 protect the confidentiality of information that identifies individuals as prescribed by state and federal law.

5.7 release summary results of the assessment only to those persons entitled to such information by state or federal law or those who are designated by the party contracting for the scoring services.

5.8 establish, where feasible, a fair and reasonable process for appeal and rescoring the assessment.

Section 6: Responsibilities of Those Who Interpret, Use, and Communicate Assessment Results

The interpretation, use, and communication of assessment results should promote valid inferences and minimize invalid ones. Persons who interpret, use, and communicate assessment results have a professional responsibility to:

6.1 conduct these activities in an informed, objective, and fair manner within the context of the assessment's limitations and with an understanding of the potential consequences of use.

6.2 provide to those who receive assessment results information about the assessment, its purposes, its limitations, and its uses necessary for the proper interpretation of the results.

6.3 provide to those who receive score reports an understandable written description of all reported scores, including proper interpretations and likely misinterpretations.

6.4 communicate to appropriate audiences the results of the assessment in an understandable and timely manner, including proper interpretations and likely misinterpretations.

6.5 evaluate and communicate the adequacy and appropriateness of any norms or standards used in the interpretation of assessment results.

6.6 inform parties involved in the assessment process how assessment results may affect them.

6.7 use multiple sources and types of relevant information about persons or programs whenever possible in making educational decisions.

6.8 avoid making, and actively discourage others from making, inaccurate reports, unsubstantiated claims, inappropriate interpretations, or otherwise false and misleading statements about assessment results.

6.9 disclose to examinees and others whether and how long the results of the assessment will be kept on file, procedures for appeal and rescoring, rights examinees and others have to the assessment information, and how those rights may be exercised.

6.10 report any apparent misuses of assessment information to those responsible for the assessment process.

6.11 protect the rights to privacy of individuals and institutions involved in the assessment process.

Section 7: Responsibilities of Those Who Educate Others About Assessment

The process of educating others about educational assessment, whether as part of higher education, professional development, public policy discussions, or job training, should prepare individuals to understand and engage in sound measurement practice and to become discerning users of tests and test results. Persons who educate or inform others about assessment have a professional responsibility to:

7.1 remain competent and current in the areas in which they teach and reflect that in their instruction.

7.2 provide fair and balanced perspectives when teaching about assessment.

7.3 differentiate clearly between expressions of opinion and substantiated knowledge when educating others about any specific assessment method, product, or service.

7.4 disclose any financial interests that might be perceived to influence the evaluation of a particular assessment product or service that is the subject of instruction.

7.5 avoid administering any assessment that is not part of the evaluation of student performance in a course if the administration of that assessment is likely to harm any student.

7.6 avoid using or reporting the results of any assessment that is not part of the evaluation of student performance in a course if the use or reporting of results is likely to harm any student.

7.7 protect all secure assessments and materials used in the instructional process.

7.8 model responsible assessment practice and help those receiving instruction to learn about their professional responsibilities in educational measurement.

7.9   provide fair and balanced perspectives on assessment issues being discussed by policymakers, parents, and other citizens.

Section 8: Responsibilities of Those Who Evaluate Educational Programs and Conduct Research on Assessments

Conducting research on or about assessments or educational programs is a key activity in helping to improve the understanding and use of assessments and educational programs. Persons who engage in the evaluation of educational programs or conduct research on assessments have a professional responsibility to:

8.1   conduct evaluation and research activities in an informed, objective, and fair manner.

8.2   disclose any associations that they have with authors, test publishers, or others involved with the assessment and refrain from participation if such associations might affect the objectivity of the research or evaluation.

8.3   preserve the security of all assessments throughout the research process as appropriate.

8.4   take appropriate steps to minimize potential sources of invalidity in the research and disclose known factors that may bias the results of the study.

8.5   present the results of research, both intended and unintended, in a fair, complete, and objective manner.

8.6   attribute completely and appropriately the work and ideas of others.

8.7   qualify the conclusions of the research within the limitations of the study.

8.8   use multiple sources of relevant information in conducting evaluation and research activities whenever possible.

8.9   comply with applicable standards for protecting the rights of participants in an evaluation or research study, including the rights to privacy and informed consent.

Afterword

As stated at the outset, the purpose of the *Code of Professional Responsibilities in Educational Measurement* is to serve as a guide to the conduct of NCME members who are engaged in any type of assessment activity in education. Given the broad scope of the field of educational assessment as well as the variety of activities in which professionals may engage, it is unlikely that any code will cover the professional responsibilities involved in every situation or activity in which assessment is used in education. Ultimately, it is hoped that this Code will serve as the basis for ongoing discussions about what constitutes professionally responsible practice. Moreover, these discussions will undoubtedly identify areas of practice that need further analysis and clarification in subsequent editions of the Code. To the extent that these discussions occur, the Code will have served its purpose.

To assist in the ongoing refinement of the Code, comments on this document are most welcome. Please send your comments and inquiries to:

Executive Officer
National Council on
Measurement in Education
1230 Seventeenth Street, NW
Washington, DC 20036-3078

Summaries of Taxonomies of Educational Objectives: Cognitive, Affective, and Psychomotor Domains

FIGURE D.1 **Categories and subcategories of the Bloom et al. taxonomy of cognitive objectives.**

1.00 Knowledge
    1.10 Knowledge of Specifics
    1.11 Knowledge of Terminology Knowledge of the referents for specific symbols (verbal and nonverbal)....
    1.12 Knowledge of Specific Facts Knowledge of dates, events, persons, places, etc.
    1.20 Knowledge of Ways and Means of Dealing with Specifics
    1.21 Knowledge of Conventions Knowledge of characteristic ways of treating and presenting ideas and phenomena.
    1.22 Knowledge of Trends and Sequences Knowledge of the processes, directions, and movements of phenomena with respect to time.
    1.23 Knowledge of Classifications and Categories Knowledge of the classes, sets, divisions, and arrangements that are regarded as fundamental for a given subject field, purpose, argument, or problem.
    1.24 Knowledge of Criteria Knowledge of the criteria by which facts, principles, and conduct are tested or judged.
    1.25 Knowledge of Methodology Knowledge of the methods of inquiry, techniques, and procedures employed in a particular subject field as well as those employed in investigating particular problems and phenomena.
2.00 Comprehension
    2.10 Translation Comprehension as evidenced by the care and accuracy with which the communication is paraphrased or rendered from one language or form of communication to another.
    2.20 Interpretation The explanation or summarization of a communication.
    2.30 Extrapolation The extension of trends or tendencies beyond the given data to determine implications, consequences, corollaries, effects, etc., that are in accordance with the conditions described in the original communication.
3.00 Application The use of abstractions in particular and concrete situations. The abstractions may be in the form of general ideas, rules of procedures, or generalized methods.
4.00 Analysis
    4.10 Analysis of Elements Identification of the elements included in a communication.
    4.20 Analysis of Relationships The connections and interactions between elements and parts of a communication.
    4.30 Analysis of Organized Principles The organization, systematic arrangement, and structure that hold the communication together.
5.00 Synthesis
    5.10 Production of a Unique Communication The development of a communication in which the writer or speaker attempts to convey ideas, feelings, and/or experiences to others.
    5.20 Production of a Plan or Proposed Set of Operations The development of a plan of work or the proposal of a plan of operations.
    5.30 Derivation of a Set of Abstract Relations The development of a set of abstract relations either to classify or to explain particular data or phenomena, or the deduction of propositions and relations from a set of basic propositions or symbolic representations.
6.00 Evaluation
    6.10 Judgments in Terms of Internal Evidence Evaluation of the accuracy of a communication from such evidence as logical accuracy, consistency, and other internal criteria.
    6.20 Judgments in Terms of External Criteria Evaluation of material with reference to selected or remembered criteria.

Source: Adapted from *Taxonomy of Educational Objectives Book 1. Cognitive Domain* (pp. 201–207) Edited by Benjamin S. Bloom et al. Published by Allyn and Bacon, Boston, MA. Copyright © 1984 by Pearson Education. Reprinted with permission of the publisher.

FIGURE D.2 **Gagné's levels of complexity in human skills, characteristics of responses to tasks assessing these capacities, and examples of specific objectives written for each capacity.**

Type of ability or capacity	Characteristics of responses to assessment tasks	Example of a specific learning target
1. **Discrimination:** ability to respond appropriately to stimuli that differ. The stimuli can differ in one or more physical attributes such as size, shape, or tone. (capacity verb: *discriminates*)	The leader's response must indicate that the learner has distinguished between the different stimuli. The leader may do this by indicating "same" or "different."	Given two cardboard cutouts, one a triangle shape and the other a square shape, the leader can point to the one that is a "square."
2. **Concrete concept:** ability to identify a stimulus as belonging to a particular class or category. The members of the class have one or more physical properties in common. (capacity verb: *identifies*)	The learner's response must indicate that two or more members of the class have been identified.	Given several differently shaped figures of various colors and shapes, half of which have triangular shapes, the learner can point to all the "triangles."
3. **Defined concept:** ability to demonstrate what is meant by a defined class of objects, events, or relations—that is, demonstrate an understanding of a concept. (capacity verb: *classifies*)	The learner's response must go beyond memorization to identify specific instances of the defined concept and to show how these instances are related to each other (and are thereby members of the same concept or category).	Given descriptions and brief biographies of each of several different persons not born in this country, the learner is able to identify all the persons who are immigrants and state their relationship to each other.
4. **Rule:** ability to make responses that indicate a rule is being applied in a variety of different situations. (capacity verb: *demonstrates*)	The learner's response must indicate that a particular rule is being applied in one or more concrete instances, but the learner need not be able to state the rule.	Given a "story" problem of the type presented in class involving two single-digit addends, the pupil is able to add the digits correctly.
5. **Higher-order rule:** (problem solving): ability to form a new (for the learner) rule to solve a problem, by combining two or more previously learned rules. (capacity verb: *generates*)	The learner's response must indicate that a new complex rule has been "invented" and applied to solve a problem that is new or novel for the learner. Once the rule is invented, the learner should be able to apply it to other situations (transfer of learning).	Given an announcement about a specific job opening for which the learner is qualified, the learner is able to generate and write an appropriate letter of application for that job.
6. **Cognitive strategies:** ability to use internal processes to choose and change ways to focus attention, learn, remember, and/or think. (capacity verb: *adopts*)	The learner's responses provide only a way of inferring that internal cognitive strategies were used. Among the cognitive strategies a learner may use are rehearsing (practicing), elaborating, organizing information, and metacognition. It is sometimes necessary to ask a learner to "think aloud" while performing a task in order to discover the cognitive processes the learner is using.	Given the task of learning a list of new Spanish vocabulary words, the learner is able to associate an English word with an "acoustical link" to help memorize the Spanish words' definitions.

Source: Table and excerpts adapted from *Principles of Instructional Design* (3rd ed., pp. 12, 57–68), by Robert M. Gagne, Leslie J. Briggs, & Walter W. Wager. Copyright © 1988. Reprinted by permission of Wadsworth, a division of Thomson Learning: www.thomsonrights.com. Fax 800-730-2215.

FIGURE D.3 **Summary of the Quellmalz taxonomy.**

Classification	Definition	Illustration	Relation to Bloom taxonomy
Recall	Most tasks require that students recognize or remember key facts, definitions, concepts, rules, and principles. Recall questions require students to repeat verbatim or to paraphrase given information. To recall information, students need most often to rehearse or practice it, and then to associate it with other, related concepts. The Bloom taxonomy levels of knowledge and comprehension are subsumed here, since verbatim repetition and translation into the student's own words represent acceptable evidence of learning and understanding.	Who was the main character in the story?	Recall Comprehension
Analysis	In this operation, students divide a whole into component elements. Generally, the different part/whole relationships and the parts of cause/effect relationships that characterize knowledge within subject domains are essential components of more complex tasks. The components can be the distinctive characteristics of objects or ideas, or the basic actors of procedures or events. This definition of analysis is the same as that in the Bloom taxonomy.	What are the different story parts?	Analysis
Comparison	These tasks require students to recognize or explain similarities and differences. Simple comparisons require attention to one or a few very obvious attributes or component processes, while complex comparisons require identification of the differentiation among many attributes or component actions. This category relates to some of the skills in the Bloom level of analysis. The separate comparison category emphasizes the distinct information processing required when students go beyond breaking the whole into parts in order to compare similarities and differences. This is akin to the Bloom level of synthesis.	How was this story like the last one?	Analysis
Inference	Both deductive and inductive reasoning fall into this category. In deductive tasks, students are given a generalization and are required to recognize or explain the evidence that relates to it. Applications of rules and "if then" relationships require inference. In inductive tasks, students are given the evidence or details and are required to come up with the generalization. Hypothesizing, predicting, concluding, and synthesizing all require students to relate and integrate information. Inductive and deductive reasoning relate to the Bloom levels of application and synthesis. Application of a rule is one kind of deductive reasoning; synthesis, putting parts together to form a generalization, occurs in both inductive and deductive reasoning.	What might be a good title for this story?	Application Synthesis
Evaluation	These tasks require students to judge quality, credibility, worth, or practicality. Generally, we expect students to use established criteria and explain how these criteria are or are not met. The criteria might be established rules of evidence, logic, or shared values. Bloom's levels of synthesis and evaluation are involved in this category. To evaluate, students must *assemble* and *explain* the interrelationship of evidence and reasons in support of their conclusion (synthesis). Explanation of criteria for reaching a conclusion is unique to evaluative reasoning.	Is this a good story? Why or why not?	Synthesis Evaluation

Source: Adapted from *Measuring Thinking Skills in the Classroom* (Table 1, pp. 8 and 19), revised edition, by R. J. Stiggins, E. Rubel and E. Quellmalz. Copyright 1988. Washington, DC: National Educatonal Association. Adapted by permission of the NEA Professional Library.

FIGURE D.4 Categories and subcategories of the Krathwohl et al. taxonomy of affective objectives with illustrative statements of objectives.

Category	Definition	Learning targets
1.0 Receiving (attending)		
1.1 Awareness	Be conscious of something ... take into account a situation, phenomenon, object, or state of affairs....	Develops awareness of aesthetic factors in dress, furnishings, architecture, city design, good art, and the like.
1.2 Willingness to Receive	Being willing to tolerate a given stimulus, not to avoid it.... Willing to take notice of the phenomenon and give it ... attention....	Appreciation (tolerance) of cultural patterns exhibited by individuals from other groups—religious, social, economic, national, etc.
1.3 Controlled or Selected Attention	The control of attention, so that when certain stimuli are presented they will be attended to.... The favored stimulus is selected and attended to despite competing and detracting stimuli....	Alertness toward human values and judgments on life as they are recorded in literature.
2.0 Responding		
2.1 Acquiescence in Responding	"Obedience" or "compliance." ... There is a passiveness so far as the initiation of behavior is concerned....	Follows school rules on the playground.
2.2 Willingness to Respond	The learner is sufficiently committed to exhibiting the behavior that he does so not just because of fear ... but "on his own" or voluntarily....	Volunteers to help classmates who are having difficulty with the science project.
2.3 Satisfaction in Response	The behavior is accompanied by a feeling of satisfaction, an emotional response, generally of pleasure, zest, or enjoyment.	Finds pleasure in reading for recreation.
3.0 Valuing		
3.1 Acceptance of a Value	The emotional acceptance of a proposition or doctrine upon what one considers adequate ground....	Continuing desire to develop the ability to speak and write effectively.
3.2 Preference for a Value	The individual is sufficiently committed to a value to pursue it, to seek it out, to want it....	Assumes responsibility for drawing reticent members of a group into conversation.
3.3 Commitment	"Conviction" and "certainty beyond a doubt." ... Acts to further the thing valued ..., to extend the possibility of ... developing it, to deepen ... involvement with it....	Devotion to those ideas and ideals that are the foundation of democracy.
4.0 Organization		
4.1 Conceptualization of a Value	The quality of abstraction or conceptualization is added (to the value or belief which permits seeing) ... how the value relates to those he already holds or to new ones....	Forms judgments as to the responsibility of society for conserving human and material resources.
4.2 Organization of a Value System	To bring together a complex of values ... into an ordered relationship with one another....	Weighs alternative social policies and practices against the standards of the public welfare rather than the advantage of ... narrow interest groups.
5.0 Characterization by a Value or Value Complex		
5.1 Generalized Set	Gives an internal consistency to the system of attitudes and values.... Enables the individual to reduce and order the complex world ... and to act consistently and effectively in it.	Judges problems and issues in terms of situations, issues, purposes, and consequences involved rather than in terms of fixed, dogmatic precepts or emotional wishful thinking.
5.2 Characterization	One's view of the universe, one's philosophy of life, one's *Weltanschauug*....	Develops for regulation of one's personal and civic life a code of behavior based on ethical principles consistent with democratic ideals.

Source: Adapted from *Taxonomy of Educational Objectives: Book 2: Affective Domain* (pp. 176–185), by David R. Krathwohl, Benjamin S.Bloom, and Bertram B. Masia (Eds.). Published by Allyn and Bacon, Boston, MA. Copyright © 1964 by Pearson Education. Reprinted by permission of the publisher.

FIGURE D.5 **Categories and subcategories of the Harrow taxonomy of psychomotor and perceptual objectives.**

Classification Levels and Subcategories	Definitions	Learning Targets

1.00 Reflex Movements
    1.10 Segmental Reflexes
    1.20 Intersegmental Reflexes
    1.30 Suprasegmental Reflexes
	Actions elicited without conscious volition in response to some stimuli.	Flexion, extension, stretch, postural adjustments.

2.00 Basic-Fundamental Movements
    2.10 Locomotor Movements
    2.20 Non-Locomotor Movements
    2.30 Manipulative Movements
	Inherent movement patterns which are formed from a combining of reflex movements and are the basis for complex skilled movement.	Walking, running, jumping, sliding, hopping, rolling, climbing, pushing, pulling, swaying, swinging, stooping, stretching, bending, twisting, handling, manipulating, gripping, grasping finger movements.

3.00 Perceptual Abilities
    3.10 Kinesthetic Discrimination
    3.20 Visual Discrimination
    3.30 Auditory Discrimination
    3.40 Tactile Discrimination
    3.50 Coordinated Abilities
	Interpretation of stimuli from various modalities providing data for the learner to make adjustments to his environment.	The *outcomes* of perceptual abilities are observable in *all purposeful* movement.
		Examples:
		Auditory—following verbal instructions.
		Coordinated—jumping rope, punting, catching.

4.00 Physical Abilities
    4.10 Endurance
    4.20 Strength
    4.30 Flexibility
    4.40 Agility
	Functional characteristics of organic vigor which are essential to the development of highly skilled movement.	Distance running, distance swimming, weight lifting, wrestling, touching toes, back bend, ballet exercises, shuttle run, typing, dodgeball.

5.00 Skilled Movements
    5.10 Simple Adaptive Skill
    5.20 Compound Adaptive Skill
    5.30 Complex Adaptive Skill
	A degree of efficiency when performing complex movement tasks which are based upon inherent movement patterns.	All skilled activities which build upon the inherent locomotor and manipulative movement patterns of classification level two.

6.00 Non-Discursive Communication
    6.10 Expressive Movement
    6.20 Interpretive Movement
	Communication through bodily movements ranging from facial expressions through sophisticated choreographies.	Body postures, gestures, facial expressions, all efficiently executed skilled dance movements and choreographies.

Source: Adapted from *A Taxonomy of the Psychomotor Domain: A Guide for Developing Behavioral Objectives* (pp. 104–106), by A. J. Harrow, 1972, White Plains, NY: Longman. Reprinted by permission of the author.

FIGURE D.6a The knowledge dimension of a revision of Bloom's Taxonomy of Educational Objectives.

Major types and subtypes	Examples
A. Factual Knowledge—The basic elements students must know to be acquainted with a discipline or solve problems in it	
AA. Knowledge of terminology	Technical vocabulary; musical symbols
AB. Knowledge of specific details and elements	Major national resources, reliable sources of information
B. Conceptual Knowledge—The interrelationships among the basic elements within a larger structure that enable them to function together	
BA. Knowledge of classifications and categories	Periods of geological time; forms of business ownership
BB. Knowledge of principles and generalizations	Pythagorean theorem; law of supply and demand
BC. Knowledge of theories, models, and structures	Theory of evolution; structure of Congress
C. Procedural Knowledge—How to do something; methods of inquiry; and criteria for using skills, algorithms, techniques, and methods	
CA. Knowledge of subject-specific skills and algorithms	Skills used in painting with watercolors; whole-number division algorithm
CB. Knowledge of subject-specific techniques and methods	Interviewing techniques; scientific method
CC. Knowledge of criteria for determining when to use appropriate procedures	Criteria used to determine when to apply a procedure involving Newton's second law; criteria used to judge the feasibility of using a particular method to estimate business costs
D. Metacognitive Knowledge—Knowledge of cognition in general as well as awareness and knowledge of one's own cognition	
DA. Strategic knowledge	Knowledge of outlining as a means of capturing the structure of a unit of subject matter in a textbook; knowledge of the use of heuristics
DB. Knowledge about cognitive tasks, including appropriate contextual and conditional knowledge	Knowledge of the types of tests particular teachers administer; knowledge of the cognitive demands of different tasks
DC. Self-knowledge	Knowledge that critiquing essays is a personal strength, whereas writing essays is a personal weakness; awareness of one's own knowledge level business costs

Source: Adapted from *A Taxonomy for Learning, Teaching, and Assessing* (pp. 46, 67–68), by Lorin W. Anderson and David R. Krathwohl (Eds.). Published by Allyn and Bacon, Boston, MA. Copyright © 2001 by Pearson Education. Reprinted by permission of the publisher.

FIGURE D.6b The cognitive process dimension of a revision of Bloom's Taxonomy of Educational Objectives.

Categories & cognitive processes	Alternative names	Definitions and examples
1. Remember—Retrieve relevant knowledge from long-term memory		
1.1 Recognizing	Identifying	Locating knowledge in long-term memory that is consistent with presented material (e.g., Recognize the dates of important events in U.S. history)
1.2 Recalling	Retrieving	Retrieving relevant knowledge from long-term memory (e.g., Recall the dates of important events in U.S. history)
2. Understand—Construct meaning from instructional messages, including oral, written, and graphic communication		
2.1 Interpreting	Clarifying, paraphrasing, representing, translating	Changing from one form of representation (e.g., numerical) to another (e.g., verbal) (e.g., Paraphrase important speeches and documents)
2.2 Exemplifying	Illustrating, instantiating	Finding a specific example or illustration of a concept or principle (e.g., Give examples of various artistic painting styles)
2.3 Classifying	Categorizing, subsuming	Determining that something belongs to a category (e.g., concept or principle) (e.g., Classify observed or described cases of mental disorders)
2.4 Summarizing	Abstracting, generalizing	Abstracting a general theme or major point(s) (e.g., Write a short summary of the events portrayed on a videotape)
2.5 Inferring	Concluding, extrapolating, interpolating, predicting	Drawing a logical conclusion from presented information (e.g., In learning a foreign language, infer grammatical principles from examples)
2.6 Comparing	Contrasting, mapping, matching	Detecting correspondences between two ideas, objects, and the like (e.g., Compare historical events to contemporary situations)
2.7 Explaining	Constructing models	Constructing a cause-and-effect model of a system (e.g., Explain the causes of important 18th-century events in France)

FIGURE D.6b (*continued*)

Categories & cognitive processes	Alternative names	Definitions and examples
3. Apply—Carry out or use a procedure in a given situation		
3.1 Executing	Carrying out	Applying a procedure to a familiar task (e.g., Divide one whole number by another whole number, both with multiple digits)
3.2 Implementing	Using	Applying a procedure to an unfamiliar task (e.g., Use Newton's Second Law in situations in which it is appropriate)
4. Analyze—Break material into its constituent parts and determine how the parts relate to one another and to an overall structure or purpose		
4.1 Differentiating	Discriminating, distinguishing, focusing, selecting	Distinguishing relevant from irrelevant parts or important from unimportant parts of presented material (e.g., Distinguish between relevant and irrelevant numbers in a mathematical word problem)
4.2 Organizing	Finding coherence, integrating, outlining, parsing, structuring	Determining how elements fit or function within a structure (e.g., Structure evidence in a historical description into evidence for and against a particular historical explanation)
4.3 Attributing	Deconstructing	Determine a point of view, bias, values, or intent underlying presented material (e.g., Determine the point of view of the author of an essay in terms of his or her political perspective)
5. Evaluate—Make judgments based on criteria and standards		
5.1 Checking	Coordinating, detecting, monitoring, testing	Detecting inconsistencies or fallacies within a process or product; determining whether a process or product has internal consistency; detecting the effectiveness of a procedure as it is being implemented (e.g., Determine if a scientist's conclusions follow from observed data)
5.2 Critiquing	Judging	Detecting inconsistencies between a product and external criteria, determining whether a product has external consistency; detecting the appropriateness of a procedure for a given problem (e.g., Judge which of two methods is the best way to solve a given problem)
6. Create—Put elements together to form a coherent or functional whole; reorganize elements into a new pattern or structure		
6.1 Generating	Hypothesizing	Coming up with alternative hypotheses based on criteria (e.g., Generate hypotheses to account for an observed phenomenon)
6.2 Planning	Designing	Devising a procedure for accomplishing some task (e.g., Plan a research paper on a given historical topic)
6.3 Producing	Constructing	Inventing a product (e.g., Build habitats for a specific purpose)

Source: Adapted from *A Taxonomy for Learning, Teaching, and Assessing* (pp. 46, 67–68), by Lorin W. Anderson and David R. Krathwohl (Eds.). Published by Allyn and Bacon, Boston, MA. Copyright © 2001 by Pearson Education. Reprinted by permission of the publisher.

Categories of Learning Targets Derived from the Dimensions of Learning Model

Declarative Knowledge

Procedural Knowledge

Complex Thinking

A. Effectively translates issues and situations into meaningful tasks that have a clear purpose.
B. Effectively uses a variety of complex reasoning strategies.

REASONING STRATEGY 1: COMPARISON Comparison involves describing the similarities and differences between two or more items. The process includes three components that can be assessed:

a. Selects appropriate items to compare.
b. Selects appropriate characteristics on which to base the comparison.
c. Accurately identifies the similarities and differences among the items, using the identified characteristics.

REASONING STRATEGY 2: CLASSIFICATION Classification involves organizing items into categories based on specific characteristics. The process includes four components that can be assessed:

a. Selects significant items to classify.
b. Specifies useful categories for the items.
c. Specifies accurate and comprehensive rules for category membership.
d. Accurately sorts the identified items into the categories.

REASONING STRATEGY 3: INDUCTION Induction involves creating a generalization from implicit or explicit information and then describing the reasoning behind the generalization. The process includes three components that can be assessed:

a. Identifies elements (specific pieces of information or observations) from which to make inductions.
b. Interprets the information from which inductions are made.
c. Makes and articulates accurate conclusions (inductions) from the selected information or observations.

REASONING STRATEGY 4: DEDUCTION Deduction involves identifying implicit or explicit generalizations or principles (premises) and then describing their logical consequences. The process includes three components that can be assessed:

a. Identifies and articulates a deduction based on important and useful generalizations or principles implicit or explicit in the information.
b. Accurately interprets the generalizations or principles.
c. Identifies and articulates logical consequences implied by the identified generalizations or principles.

REASONING STRATEGY 5: ERROR ANALYSIS Error analysis involves identifying and describing specific types of errors in information or processes. It includes three components that can be assessed:

a. Identifies and articulates significant errors in information or in process.
b. Accurately describes the effects of the errors on the information or process.
c. Accurately describes how to correct the errors.

REASONING STRATEGY 6: CONSTRUCTING SUPPORT Constructing support involves developing a well-articulated argument for or against a claim. The process includes three components that can be assessed:

a. Accurately identifies a claim that requires support rather than a fact that does not require support.
b. Provides sufficient or appropriate evidence for the claim.
c. Adequately qualifies or restricts the claim.

REASONING STRATEGY 7: ABSTRACTING Abstracting involves identifying and explaining how the abstract pattern in one situation or set of information is similar to or different from the abstract pattern in another situation or set of information. The process includes three components that can be assessed:

a. Identifies a significant situation or meaningful information that is a useful subject for the abstracting process.
b. Identifies a representative general or abstract pattern for the situation or information.
c. Accurately articulates the relationship between the general or abstract pattern and another situation or set of information.

REASONING STRATEGY 8: ANALYZING PERSPECTIVES Analyzing perspectives involves considering one perspective on an issue and the reasoning behind it as well as an opposing perspective and the reasoning behind it. The process includes three components that can be assessed:

a. Identifies an issue on which there is disagreement.
b. Identifies one position on the issue and the reasoning behind it.

Source: Adapted from *Assessing Student Outcomes: Performance Assessment Using the Dimensions of Learning Model* (pp. 65–93), by R. J. Marzano, D. Pickering, and J. McTighe, 1993. Alexandria, VA: Association for Supervision and Curriculum Development. (Copyright by McREL Institute, 2550 South Parker Road, Aurora, CO 80014.) Adapted by permission.

c. Identifies an opposing position and the reasoning behind it.

REASONING STRATEGY 9: DECISION MAKING Decision making involves selecting among apparently equal alternatives. It includes four components that can be assessed:

a. Identifies important and appropriate alternatives to be considered.
b. Identifies important and appropriate criteria for assessing the alternatives.
c. Accurately identifies the extent to which each alternative possesses each criteria.
d. Makes a selection that adequately meets the decision criteria and answers the initial decision question.

REASONING STRATEGY 10: INVESTIGATION Investigation is a process involving close examination and systematic inquiry. There are basic types of investigation:

• *Definitional Investigation*: Constructing a definition or detailed description concept for which such a definition or description is not readily available or accepted.
• *Historical Investigation*: Constructing an explanation for some past event for an explanation is not readily available or accepted.
• *Projective Investigation*: Constructing a scenario for some future event or hypothetical past event for which a scenario is not readily available or accepted.

Each type of investigation includes three components that can be assessed:

a. Accurately identifies what is already known or agreed upon about the concept (definitional investigation), the past event (historical investigation), or the future event (projective investigation).
b. Identifies and explains the confusions, uncertainties, or contradictions about the concept (definitional investigation), the past event (historical investigation), or the future event (projective investigation).
c. Develops and defends a logical and plausible resolution to the confusions, uncertainties, or contradictions about the concept (definitional investigation), the past event (historical investigation), or the future event (projective investigation).

REASONING STRATEGY 11: PROBLEM SOLVING Problem solving involves developing and testing a method or product for overcoming obstacles or constraints to reach a desired outcome. It includes four components that can be assessed:

a. Accurately identifies constraints or obstacles.
b. Identifies viable and important alternatives for overcoming the constraints or obstacles.
c. Selects and adequately tries out alternatives.
d. If other alternatives were tried, accurately articulates and supports the reasoning behind the order of their selection, and the extent to which each overcame the obstacles or constraints.

REASONING STRATEGY 12: EXPERIMENTAL INQUIRY Experimental inquiry involves testing hypotheses that have been generated to explain phenomenon. It includes four components that can be assessed:

a. Accurately explains the phenomenon initially observed using appropriate and accepted facts, concepts, or principles.
b. Makes a logical prediction based on the facts, concepts, or principles underlying the explanation.

c. Sets up and carries out an activity or experiment that effectively tests the prediction.
d. Effectively evaluates the outcome of the activity or experiment in terms of the original explanation.

REASONING STRATEGY 13: INVENTION Invention involves developing something unique or making unique improvements to a process to satisfy an unmet need. It includes four components that can be assessed:

a. Identifies a process or product to develop or improve to satisfy an unmet need.
b. Identifies rigorous and important standards or criteria the invention will meet.
c. Makes detailed and important revisions in the initial process or product.
d. Continually revises and polishes the process or product until it reaches a level of completeness consistent with the criteria or standards identified earlier.

Information Processing

A. Effectively interprets and synthesizes information.
B. Effectively uses a variety of information-gathering techniques and resources.
C. Accurately assesses the value of information.
D. Recognizes where and how projects would benefit from additional information.

Effective Communication

A. Expresses ideas clearly.
B. Effectively communicates with diverse audiences.
C. Effectively communicates in a variety of ways.
D. Effectively communicates for a variety of purposes.
E. Creates quality products.

Collaboration/Cooperation

A. Works toward the achievement of group goals.
B. Demonstrates effective interpersonal skills.
C. Contributes to group maintenance.
D. Effectively performs a variety of roles within a group.

Habits of Mind

A. Is aware of own thinking.
B. Makes effective plans.
C. Is aware of and uses necessary resources.
D. Evaluates the effectiveness of own actions.
E. Is sensitive to feedback.
F. Is accurate and seeks accuracy.
G. Is clear and seeks clarity.
H. Is open-minded.
I. Restrains impulsivity.
J. Takes a position when the situation warrants it.
K. Is sensitive to the feelings and level of knowledge of others.
L. Engages intensively in tasks even when answers or solutions are not immediately apparent.
M. Pushes the limits of own knowledge and ability.
N. Generates, trusts, and maintains own standards of evaluation.
O. Generates new ways of viewing a situation outside the boundaries of standard convention.

Assessment of Metacognition

Definition of Metacognition

There are many facets to teaching students to use thinking skills. In Chapter 2 we discussed several frameworks for identifying thinking skills that should be incorporated into your teaching and assessment practices. One broad area of thinking that has received considerable attention in recent years from researchers and curriculum specialists is students' abilities to monitor and control their own thinking in relation to the cognitive tasks they are performing. Monitoring and controlling one's own thinking processes are complex skills themselves. The cluster of such related skills is known as metacognitive skills.

Metacognition is defined as "one's knowledge concerning one's own cognitive processes and products or anything related to them. . . . For example, I am engaging in metacognition . . . if I notice that I am having more trouble learning A than B; if it strikes me that I should double check C before accepting it as a fact. . . . Metacognition refers, among other things, to the active monitoring and consequent regulation and orchestration of these processes . . . usually in the service of some concrete goal or objective" (Flavell, 1976, p. 232).

As can be surmised, students engage in metacognitive thinking when they are aware of their thoughts as they perform specific learning activities and then use this awareness to control what they are doing (Marzano et al., 1988).

Types of Metacognitive Skills

The metacognitive cluster of skills can be organized in several ways. The Marzano et al. (1988) organization gives a brief overview of this domain of learning targets.

I. **Self-regulation skills** are used by students when they are aware that they can control their commitment, attitudes, and attention toward academic tasks.
  A. *Commitment to an academic task* is a student's conscious decision to choose to do the task, whether or not it is fun for the student.
  B. *Positive attitude toward an academic task* is a student's belief that she can perform the task and that the main determiner of success on it is her own efforts, not luck, natural talent, or help from others.
  C. *Controlling attention to the requirements of an academic task* occurs when a student recognizes that he must control

the level and focus of his attention to match the requirements of the task to be performed.
II. **Types of knowledge** used by students must be appropriate for performing the academic task at hand.
  A. *Declarative knowledge* is exhibited when a student knows what needs to be done, knows factual information, or knows that something is to be done.
  B. *Procedural knowledge* is exhibited when a student is able to perform a task or to apply strategies to complete tasks.
  C. *Conditional knowledge* is exhibited when a student is aware of why certain procedures or strategies are used or in what circumstances one procedure or strategy is preferred over another.
III. **Executive control skills** are used by students when they evaluate, plan, and check their own progress in completing an academic task.
  A. *Evaluation skills* are used when a student assesses her current state of knowledge before, during, and at the completion of an academic task; identifies available and still-needed resources for completing the academic task; and identifies the goals and subgoals of the academic task.
  B. *Planning skills* are used by a student before and during the completion of an academic task when the student deliberately chooses procedures and strategies to do the task.
  C. *Regulating processes skills* are used by a student while completing an academic task when the student monitors his progress toward completing the task successfully.

These categories of skills are not hierarchical and, in practice, students usually use them in combination to complete academic tasks.

Assessing Metacognition with Paper-and-Pencil Instruments

Suggestions for how to model and teach these skills are found in other sources (Good & Brophy, 2002; Marzano et al., 1988). Here we give some examples of simple ways to assess students' perceptions of whether they use these skills.

Teachers have found this type of assessment information useful for planning instruction (Tittle, 1989; Tittle, Hecht, & Moore, 1993). To create an instrument, you need to identify a specific instructional activity on which to focus the items. For example, you may wish to focus on students' metacognitions during class, while working with others, while doing homework or other assignments and projects, or when they complete tests or other assessment activities used for summative evaluation (Tittle et al., 1993). Then, using the subcategories of metacognitive skills, write statements describing a student's thoughts, beliefs, or awareness about the specific type of activity. Write both positive and negative statements (i.e., "good" and "poor" metacognitions) for each category. Give each student a copy of the list and ask him or her to indicate how often he or she does the things in each statement.

Figure F.1 shows some examples of statements related to various metacognitions that may occur when students work on a social studies research paper. Students are asked to identify how often they engage in the thoughts, actions, or beliefs listed.

The statements are arranged to follow the outline of metacognitive skills discussed earlier. The statements are in pairs: The odd-numbered member of the pair is a positive statement, and the even-numbered one is a negative statement. The codes in the brackets identify the skill in the outline and whether the statement is positively or negatively worded. Remember that Figure F.1 is just a list of examples, not a sample instrument per se. In an actual instrument you would scramble the order of positive and negative statements so as not to have a pattern, omit the codes, and have more than two statements per category. Also, you might not assess some categories because of the nature of the particular activity on which you are focusing. Note that such an instrument may be inappropriate for primary children, whose reading skills may not be sufficient to understand it.

FIGURE F.1 Examples of positively and negatively phrased items that assess how students report using metacognitions when preparing a social studies research paper.

Directions to students: These questions ask about how often you do some things when you write a research paper in social studies. Circle the number that tells how often you do each thing.				

Never or almost never 1	Sometimes 2	Often 3	Always or almost always 4				Don't Know DK
1. When the paper is not a lot of fun, I work very hard to do a good job on it. [I.A,+]				1	2	3	4	DK
2. When the paper is not a lot of fun, I do not work very hard on it. [I.A,−]				1	2	3	4	DK
3. I do a good job on the paper even though I am less talented than other students. [I.B,+]				1	2	3	4	DK
4. I have to get really lucky to do a good job on the paper. [I.B,−]				1	2	3	4	DK
5. When I read articles related to my paper, I read only those parts related to my topic. [I.C,+]				1	2	3	4	DK
6. When reading articles about the topic of my paper, I give equal attention to everything in the article. [I.C,−]				1	2	3	4	DK
7. My research papers have an introductory section that tells why the topic is important. [II.A,+]				1	2	3	4	DK
8. My research papers list the facts about the topic but do not give my interpretation of the meaning of the facts. [II.A,−]				1	2	3	4	DK
9. I make tables in my research papers to compare information on the topic. [II.B,+]				1	2	3	4	DK
10. I do not use note cards when preparing my research paper. [II.B,−]				1	2	3	4	DK
11. Before I decide to use a graph or a chart I ask myself which idea in the paper it supports. [II.C,+]				1	2	3	4	DK
12. I use lots of graphs or charts in my research reports. [II.C,−]				1	2	3	4	DK
13. One of the first things I do when I start my paper assignment is to make a list of what I already know about the topic. [III.A,+]				1	2	3	4	DK
14. Before I do anything else on the paper I go to the library to find all the books and articles about my topic. [III.B,−]				1	2	3	4	DK
15. After I complete my research paper I ask myself what I learned about the topic. [III.A,+]				1	2	3	4	DK
16. After I complete my research paper, I do not think about the topic anymore. [III.A,−]				1	2	3	4	DK
17. When I am ready to begin collecting information, I ask myself what sources would be best to use first. [III.B,+]				1	2	3	4	DK
18. No matter what the topic of my paper, I go first to the encyclopedia to look up the topic. [III.B,−]				1	2	3	4	DK
19. While I am writing the paper I think about whether it meets the criteria for a good research report. [III.C,+]				1	2	3	4	DK
20. As soon as I have a little information on the topic, I begin writing the paper. [III.C,−]				1	2	3	4	DK

Notes: Codes in brackets refer to outline in the text.

Examples of Alternative Blueprints for a Summative Unit Assessment

FIGURE G.1 **A checklist for judging the quality of a teacher's plan for a summative unit assessment.**

1.	Does your plan clarify the purpose(s) of the assessment and what you expect it to tell you about each student?	Yes	No
2.	Does your plan indicate the main subject-matter topics and performances you want to assess?	Yes	No
3.	Will your plan help you to judge whether the assessment tasks match the major content topics and learning targets you have specified?	Yes	No
4.	Have you clearly identified the elements of knowledge and performance that *all* students need to know?	Yes	No
5.	Does your plan give the most important learning targets the heaviest weights in the total score? Are the least important learning targets given the least weight? (You may wish to give certain tasks more weight than others.)	Yes	No
6.	Do you know what kind(s) of assessment tasks should be used to assess each content-thinking skill combination? Are these tasks the best ways to assess the combination?	Yes	No
7.	Have you estimated the amount of time students need to complete this assessment? Is this estimated time realistic?	Yes	No
8.	Have you estimated the amount of time you will need to evaluate the students' responses? (Consider how this time might be shortened, without reducing the validity of the results, by changing some of the tasks, rearranging tasks on a page, or using the capabilities of a microcomputer or other scoring device.)	Yes	No

Note: Revise your assessment plan if you answered no to one or more of the questions in the checklist.

Source: Adapted from *Teacher's Guide to Better Classroom Testing: A Judgmental Approach* (p. 26), by A. J. Nitko and T-C. Hsu, 1987, Pittsburgh, PA: Institute for Practice and Research in Education, School of Education, University of Pittsburgh. Adapted by permission of the authors.

FIGURE G.2 **Complete specifications with modified taxonomy headings.**

Content outline	Recalling information taught or read	Applying knowledge in situations very similar to those taught	Applying knowledge in a new or novel context

I. *Basic Parts of Cell*
  A. *Nucleus*
  B. *Cytoplasm*
  C. *Cell membrane*
	1. *Names and tells functions of each part of cell*	8. *Labels parts of cell shown on a line drawing*	11. *Given photographs of actual plant and animal cells, labels the parts*

40% of Total = 8 pts	37% of Row = 3 pts	37% of Row = 3 pts	26% of Row = 2 pts

II. *Plant vs. Animal cells*
  A. *Similarities*
  B. *Differences*
    1. *cell wall vs. membrane*
    2. *food manufacture*
	2. *Explains differences between plant and animal cells*
	3. *Describes the cell wall and cell membrane*		

10% of Total = 2 pts	100% of Row = 2 pts	__% of Row = __pts	__%of Row = __pts

III. *Cell Membrane*
  A. *Living nature of*
  B. *Diffusion*
  C. *Substances diffused by cells*
	4. *Lists substances diffused and not diffused by cell membranes*
	5. *Gives definition of diffusion*
		9. *Distinguishes between diffusion and oxidation*	

20% of Total = 4 pts	75% of Row = 3 pts	25% of Row = 1 pts	__% of Row = __pts

IV. *Division of Cells*
  A. *Phases in division*
  B. *Chromosomes and DNA*
  C. *Plant vs. Animal cell division*
	6. *Gives definitions of division, chromosomes, and DNA*
	7. *States differences between plant and animal cell division*
		10. *Given the numbers of chromosomes in a cell before division, states the number in each cell after division*	

30% of Total = 6 pts	67% of Row = 4 pts	33% of Row = 2 pts	__% of Row = __pts

Source: Adapted from *Teacher's Guide to Better Classroom Testing: A Judgmental Approach* (p. 4) by A. J. Nitko and T-C Hsu, 1987, Pittsburgh, PA: Institute for Practice and Research in Education, School of Education, University of Pittsburgh. Adapted by permission of the authors.

FIGURE G.3 **Blueprint without objectives stated.**

Content outline	Recalling information taught or read	Applying knowledge in situations very similar to those taught	Applying knowledge in a new or novel context

I. *Basic Parts of Cell*
  A. *Nucleus*
  B. *Cytoplasm*
  C. *Cell membrane*
	1 item, scored 0–3 (short-answer)	1 item, scored 0–3 (label parts of cell drawing)	2 items, each scored 0–1 (label parts of cell photographs)

40% of Total = 8 pts	37% of Row = 3 pts	37% of Row = 3 pts	26% of Row = 2 pts

II. *Plant vs. Animal cells*
  A. *Similarities*
  B. *Differences*
    1. *cell wall vs. membrane*
    2. *food manufacture*
	2 items, each scored 0–1 (short-answer)		

10% of Total = 2 pts	100% of Row = 2 pts	__% of Row = __pts	__% of Row = __pts

III. *Cell Membrane*
  A. *Living nature of*
  B. *Diffusion*
  C. *Substances diffused by cells*
	2 items, one scored 0–2, the other scored 0–1 (short-answer)	2 items, each scored 0–1 (multiple-choice)	

20% of Total = 4 pts	75% of Row = 3 pts	25% of Row = 1 pts	__% of Row = __pts

IV. *Division of Cells*
  A. *Phases in division*
  B. *Chromosomes and DNA*
  C. *Plant vs. Animal cell division*
	4 items, each scored 0–1 (definitions, short-answer)	1 item, scored 0–1 (short-answer)	

30% of Total = 6 pts	67% of Row = 4 pts	33% of Row = 2 pts	__% of Row = __pts

Source: Adapted from *Teacher's Guide to Better Classroom Testing: A Judgmental Approach* (p. 4) by A. J. Nitko and T-C Hsu, 1987, Pittsburgh, PA: Institute for Practice and Research in Education, School of Education, University of Pittsburgh. Adapted by permission of the authors.

FIGURE G.4 **Blueprint using only a list of learning targets.**

Objectives of the unit	Number of items	Number of points
1. Names and tells functions of each cell part.	1	3
2. Explains differences between plant and animal cells.	1	1
3. Describes the cell wall and cell membrane.	1	1
4. Lists substances diffused and not diffused through cell membrane.	1	2
5. Gives definition of diffusion.	1	1
6. Gives definition of division, chromosomes, and DNA.	3	3
7. States differences between plant and animal cell division.	1	1
8. Labels parts of a cell when shown a line drawing.	3	3
9. Distinguishes between diffusion, oxidation, and fission.	2	2
10. Given the number of chromosomes in a cell before division, states the number in each cell after division.	1	1
11. Given photographs of plant and animal cells, identifies parts of cells without using prompts.	2	2
	Total points = 17	Total points = 20

Source: From *Teacher's Guide to Better Classroom Testing: A Judgmental Approach* (p. 39), by A. J. Nitko and T-C. Hsu, 1993. Pittsburgh, PA: Institute for Practice and Research in Education, School of Education, University of Pittsburgh. Reprinted by permission.

FIGURE G.5 **Blueprint using only a content listing.**

Major topics of unit	Number of items	Number of points per item	Total number of points
I. Basic Parts of a Cell			
A. Nucleus	2	2	4
B. Cytoplasm	3	1	3
C. Cell membrane	1	1	1
	subtotal = 6		subtotal = 8
II. Plant vs. Animal Cells			
A. Similarities	1	1	1
B. Differences			
1. cell wall vs. cell membrane	1	1	1
2. food manufacture	0		0
	subtotal = 2		subtotal = 2
III. Cell Membrane			
A. Living nature of	0		0
B. Diffusion	2	1	2
C. Examples of different substances	1	2	2
	subtotal = 3		subtotal = 4
IV. Division of Cells			
A. Phases in division	2	1	2
B. Role of chromosomes and DNA	2	1	2
C. Plant vs. animal cell division	2	1	2
	subtotal = 6		subtotal = 6
	Total test items = 17		Total test points = 20

Source: From *Teacher's Guide to Better Classroom Testing, A Judgmental Approach* (p. 38), by A. J. Nitko and T-C. Hsu, 1993. Pittsburgh, PA: Institute for Practice and Research in Education, School of Education, University of Pittsburgh. Reprinted by permission of the authors.

Scoring Guide for Oregon's Writing Assessment

Writing Scoring Guide: Middle School Student Version

Ideas and Content Communicating knowledge of the topic, including relevant examples, facts, anecdotes and details		
6 **The writing is exceptionally clear, focused and interesting. It holds the reader's attention. Main ideas stand out and are developed by strong support and rich details that fit the audience and purpose. The writing has** • a clear focus and control. • main idea(s) that stand out. • details that are on topic and carefully selected; when needed, use of resources provides strong, accurate, believable support. • an appropriate amount of detail (not too much or too little) to support an in-depth explanation or exploration of the topic; the writing makes connections and shares insights. • main ideas and selected details that fit the purpose and hold the reader's attention from beginning to end.	**5** **The writing is clear, focused and interesting. It holds the reader's attention. Main ideas stand out and are developed by supporting details that fit the audience and purpose. The writing has** • a clear focus and control. • main idea(s) that stand out. • details that are on topic and carefully selected; when needed, use of resources provides strong, accurate, believable support. • an appropriate amount of detail (not too much or too little) to support a thorough explanation or exploration of the topic; the writing makes connections and shares insights. • main ideas and selected details that fit the purpose and hold the reader's attention from beginning to end.	**4** **The writing is clear and focused. The reader can easily understand the main ideas. Support is present, but may be limited or somewhat general. The writing has** • a clear purpose. • clear main ideas. • details that are on topic, but may be too general or limited; when needed, resources are used to provide accurate support. • details that may sometimes be too many or too few for a thorough explanation or exploration of the topic; some connections and insights may be present. • main ideas and selected details that fit the purpose and hold the reader's attention most of the time from beginning to end.
3 **The writing has main idea(s), but they may be too broad or simplistic. Supporting detail is often too limited, overly general, or sometimes off the topic. The writing has** • a purpose that is easy to find. • main idea(s) that are easy to find but overly obvious or predictable; main points or conclusions repeat ideas often heard. • support of main ideas, but there aren't enough supporting details, or they are too general, predictable, or somewhat off topic. • details that may not be based on reliable resources; may be based on clichés, stereotypes, or sources of information that are biased, uninformed, or unreliable.	**2** **The writing has main idea(s), but they are undeveloped, and the purpose is somewhat unclear. The writing has** • an unclear purpose that requires the reader to guess the main ideas. • minimal development, lacking details. • details, when included, are not well connected to the main ideas and clutter the paper. • details that are frequently repeated.	**1** **The writing lacks main idea(s) or purpose. The writing has** • ideas that are very limited or simply unclear. • few or no attempts to develop ideas; the paper is too short to demonstrate the development of an idea.

Source: From *Writing Scoring Guide: Middle School Student Version* (pp. 1–7), by Oregon Department of Education, 1996. Salem, OR: Office of Assessment and Evaluation, author. Reprinted by permission.

Organization
Structuring information in logical sequence, making connections and transitions among ideas, sentences, and paragraphs

6

The organization makes the central idea(s) and supporting details clear. The order and structure are strong and move the reader easily through the writing. The writing has
- effective (and sometimes creative) ideas, details, and examples in an order that is easy to follow.
- a strong and inviting introduction that draws the reader in and a strong conclusion that leaves the reader satisfied
- smooth, effective transitions that tie together ideas, sentences and paragraphs; the reader can move easily from one part to the next.
- details placed where they work well and make the most sense.

5

The organization helps clarify the central idea(s) and supporting details. The order and structure are strong and move the reader through the writing. The writing has
- ideas, details, and examples in an order that makes sense and is easy to follow.
- an inviting introduction that draws the reader in and a conclusion that leaves the reader satisfied.
- smooth transitions that tie together ideas, sentences, and paragraphs; the reader can move easily from one part to the next.
- details placed where they work well and make the most sense.

4

The organization is clear and functional. Order and structure are present, but may seem like a formula. The writing has
- clear sequencing.
- an organization that may be predictable.
- an introduction that is recognizable but may not be especially inviting; a developed conclusion that is functional but may seem repetitive and ordinary.
- transitions that work but they may be awkward or common.
- a body that is easy to follow with details that fit where placed.
- an organization which helps the reader, despite some weaknesses.

3

An attempt to organize the writing has been made, but it doesn't work well in places or is too obvious. The writing has
- attempts to put ideas in order, but the order is sometimes unclear.
- a beginning and an ending, but they are either too short or too obvious (e.g., "My topic is . . ."; "These are all the reasons that . . .")
- a limited number of transitional words that are used too many times (e.g., "and," "then," "but," "so," "or," "for," "yet," numbering)
- a structure that is too obvious, almost like a formula.
- details that seem out of order and confuse the reader.
- an organization that helps the reader in some places but breaks down in others.

2

The writing lacks a clear organizational structure. An occasional attempt at organizing is made, but the writing is difficult to follow and the reader has to reread large sections. The writing may seem incomplete. The writing has
- some attempts to organize ideas, but the order does not make the meaning clear.
- a missing or extremely undeveloped introduction, body, or conclusion.
- few or no transitions; when present they are ineffective or overused.
- details are randomly placed; the reader is frequently confused.

1

The writing doesn't hold together; the writing seems haphazard and disjointed. Even after rereading, the reader is still confused. The writing has
- ideas that are not in a clear or logical order.
- no recognizable beginning or ending.
- few or no transitions.
- arrangement and pace of ideas that either drag or feel rushed.

Voice **Expressing ideas in an engaging and credible way for audience and purpose**		
6 **The writer has chosen an appropriate voice for the topic, purpose and audience and shows a deep sense of involvement with the topic. The writing is interesting and sincere. The writing has** • an effective level of closeness to the audience or distance from it (e.g., a narrative should have a strong personal voice, while a research paper may require a more objective voice; both should be lively or interesting). • an exceptionally strong sense of purpose and audience. • a sense that the topic has come to life; when appropriate, shows use of originality, liveliness, honesty, conviction, excitement, humor, suspense and/or use of outside resources.	**5** **The writer has chosen an appropriate voice for the topic, purpose and audience and shows involvement with the topic. The writing is interesting and seems sincere. The writing has** • an appropriate level of closeness to the audience or distance from (e.g., a narrative should have a strong personal voice, while a researched report may require a more objective voice; both could be lively or interesting.) • a strong sense of purpose and audience. • a sense that the topic has come to life; when appropriate, the writing shows originality, liveliness, honesty, conviction, excitement, humor, suspense and/or use of outside resources.	**4** **A voice is present, and there is a sense of involvement with the topic. In places, the writing is interesting and seems sincere. The writing has** • a questionable or inconsistent level of closeness or distance from the audience. • a sense of purpose and audience but may not use a consistently appropriate voice. • originality, liveliness, humor and/or use of outside resources, when appropriate; however, at times voice may be too casual or formal.
3 **The writer doesn't seem particularly involved with the topic or may seem either too personal or too impersonal. The writing has** • a voice that doesn't seem to match the topic, purpose, and audience. • a limited sense that the paper was written for a particular audience. • a sense in places of the writer behind the words; however, this may shift or disappear a line or two later. • limited ability to shift from a casual, informal voice to one that is more objective when that is necessary.	**2** **The writing provides little sense of involvement or evidence of a suitable voice. The writing has** • little or no sense that the writer cares about the topic; the writing is largely flat, lifeless, stiff, or mechanical. • little or no awareness of matching the topic, purpose and audience. • little or no sense of the writer behind the words; there are only a few places where the reader and writer can feel a connection. • a voice that is likely to be overly formal or overly personal.	**1** **The writing lacks a sense of involvement and a suitable voice. The writing has** • no sense that the writer cares about the topic; the writing is flat, lifeless, stiff, or mechanical. • no sense that the piece was written for an audience. • no hint of the writer behind the words; there are few if any places where the reader feels connected to the writer. The writing doesn't get the reader involved.

Word Choice
Selecting functional, precise and descriptive words
appropriate for audience and purpose

6	5	4
Words communicate the intended message in an exceptionally interesting, accurate and natural way. The writer uses a rich, broad range of words that have been carefully chosen and thoughtfully placed. The writing has • accurate, powerful and specific words; word choices make the writing interesting and lively. • fresh, original expression; if slang is used, it is for a reason and works very well. • vocabulary that has variety and gets noticed but is also natural and doesn't seem to be trying to impress the reader. • ordinary words used in an unusual way. • words that create strong pictures in the reader's mind; metaphors and similes may be used.	**Words communicate the intended message in an interesting, accurate, and natural way. The writer uses a broad range of words that have been carefully chosen and thoughtfully placed. The writing has** • accurate, specific words; word choices make the writing more interesting and lively. • fresh, clear expression; if slang is used, it is for a reason and works well. • vocabulary that may have variety and get noticed but is also natural and doesn't seem to be trying to impress the reader. • ordinary words used in an unusual way. • words that create clear pictures in the reader's mind; metaphors and similes may be used.	**Words communicate the intended message. The writer uses a variety of words that work and are appropriate for the topic, audience and purpose. The writing has** • words that work but do not necessarily make the writing more interesting and lively. • expression that works; however, slang, if used, does not always seem to match the purpose or seem effective. • some attempts at colorful language; however, they may occasionally seem overdone. • rare experiments with language; however, the writing may have some especially good moments, and it generally avoids clichés.
3	2	1
Language is ordinary. The writer does not use a variety of words, producing a sort of "generic" paper with commonly used words and phrases. Words may be too technical or loaded with jargon. The writing has • words that work, but that are rarely interesting. • expression that seems ordinary and general; any slang is used for a reason and is effective. • words that are accurate for the most part, although misused words may sometimes appear. • attempts at colorful language that do not fit or seem natural; they seem forced or trying to impress. • too many clichés and overused expressions. • overuse or ineffective use of technical jargon.	**The language is monotonous and/or misused, taking away from the meaning and impact. The writing has** • words that are flat or not specific enough. • words or expressions that are either so common or used so often that they detract from the message. • images that don't work because they are not clear or are absent altogether.	**The writing shows a limited vocabulary, or is so filled with words not used correctly that the meaning is unclear. Only the most general idea comes through because the language is not specific enough. The writing has** • general, vague words that do not make the point. • a small set of words used over and over. • words that simply do not work; they seem too general or just plain wrong.

Sentence Fluency
Developing flow and
rhythm of sentences

6
The writing has an effective flow that is smooth and natural. The sentences are put together so they are consistently varied and interesting. The sentences make the piece easy and interesting to read. The writing has
- a natural, fluent sound; it glides along with one sentence flowing effortlessly into the next.
- extensive variation in sentence lengths, patterns, and beginnings that make the writing interesting.
- a sentence structure that helps the reader understand the text by highlighting key ideas and relationships.
- strong control over sentence structure; if fragments are used at all, they work well.
- natural-sounding dialogue, if dialogue is used at all.

5
The writing has a smooth, natural flow. Sentences are put together so they are varied and interesting. The sentences make the piece easy and interesting to read aloud. The writing has
- a natural, fluent sound; it glides along with one sentence flowing into the next.
- a variety of sentence lengths, patterns, and beginnings that make the writing interesting.
- sentence structure that helps the reader understand the meaning.
- control over sentence structure; if fragments are used at all, they work well.
- natural-sounding dialogue, if dialogue is used at all.

4
The writing flows; however, connections between phrases or sentences may be less than fluid. Sentences are somewhat varied, making oral reading easy. The writing has
- a natural sound; the reader can move easily through the piece, although it may lack a sense of rhythm.
- some repeated sentence lengths, patterns and beginnings that detract somewhat from overall impact.
- strong control over simple sentences; less control over more complex sentences. If fragments are used at all, they are usually effective.
- dialogue, if used at all, that usually sounds natural but can sound artificial.

3
The writing tends to be choppy rather than smooth. Sometimes awkward constructions force the reader to slow down or reread. The writing has
- some passages that are easy to read aloud and some that are choppy.
- some variety in sentence lengths, patterns, and beginnings, although a few are used repeatedly.
- simple sentence used correctly, but more complex sentences may have problems; if fragments are used, they may not be effective.
- sentences that are correct, but are not very interesting or appealing.
- dialogue that may not sound unnatural or not true-to-life, if it is used.

2
The writing tends to be choppy or rambling. Awkward construction often forces the reader to slow down and reread. The writing has
- large portions of the text that are difficult to follow or read aloud.
- sentence patterns that are monotonous (e.g., subject-verb or subject-verb-object).
- a large number of awkward, choppy, or rambling sentence structures.

1
The writing is difficult to follow or to read aloud. Sentences tend to be choppy, incomplete, rambling, or just very awkward. The writing has
- sentences that may be hard to read aloud easily.
- confusing word order that often makes the meaning hard to follow.
- sentence patterns that frequently make meaning unclear.
- sentences that are fragmented, confusing, choppy, or rambling on and on.

Conventions
Demonstrating knowledge of spelling, grammar, punctuation, capitalization, usage, paragraphing

6

The writing demonstrates mastery of a variety of standard conventions, even in complex and less common situations. Errors, if any, are not obvious or significant. The writing has

- correct use of punctuation, including commas, semicolons, apostrophes and colons, in a variety of situations to add meaning.
- correct spelling, even of difficult words.
- paragraphing that strengthens the impact and organization.
- correct capitalization.
- correct grammar and usage that contribute to clarity and style.
- skill in using a wide range of conventions in a sufficiently long and complex piece.
- little or no need for editing.

5

The writing demonstrates strong control of standard conventions which effectively contribute to the message. Errors are so few and so minor that they do not distract the reader. The writing has

- correct grammar and usage.
- sound paragraphing.
- effective use of punctuation.
- correct spelling, even of difficult words.
- few capitalization errors.
- skill in using a wide range of conventions in a sufficiently long and complex piece.
- little need for editing.

4

The writing demonstrates competent handling of standard conventions. Minor errors are distracting but not confusing. The writing has

- correct end-of-sentence punctuation; minor and very few or no instances of confusion with commas, semi-colons, apostrophes or colons.
- common or key words spelled correctly.
- paragraph breaks that are logically placed.
- correct capitalization; errors, if any, are in uncommon cases.
- occasionally incorrect grammar and usage; problems do not confuse or change the meaning.
- a need for some minor editing.

3

The writing shows a limited control of standard conventions. Errors begin to interfere with readability. The writing has

- errors in grammar, usage, and capitalization that do not block meaning but do distract the reader.
- paragraphs that sometimes run together or begin at ineffective points.
- end-of-sentence punctuation that is usually correct, but internal punctuation contains frequent errors.
- spelling errors that distract the reader; misspelling of common words sometimes occurs.
- some control over basic conventions, but the text is too simple or too short to show mastery.
- a significant need for editing.

2

The writing shows little understanding of standard conventions. Errors often distract and confuse the reader, requiring the reader to reread passages. The writing has

- many places where punctuation is left out or incorrect.
- frequent spelling errors, even of common words.
- random paragraph indentations or none at all.
- many capitalization errors, including sentence beginnings and names.
- errors in grammar and usage that confuse the reader or change the meaning or are inappropriate for audience and purpose.
- a need for major revisions and corrections.

1

Numerous errors in conventions repeatedly distract the reader and make the writing difficult to read. The writing has

- very limited skill in using conventions.
- punctuation (including ends of sentences) that tends to be omitted, haphazard, or incorrect.
- frequent spelling errors that significantly interfere with readability.
- paragraphing that may be irregular or absent.
- capitalization that appears to be random.
- a need for extensive editing.

Citing Sources
Use only on classroom assignments requiring research
**Indicating the sources of information presented, including all ideas, statements,
quotes and statistics that are taken from sources and that are not common knowledge**

6

The writing demonstrates exceptionally strong commitment to the quality and significance of research and the accuracy of the written document. Documentation is used to avoid plagiarism and to enable the reader to judge how believable or important a piece of information is by checking the source. The writer has

- acknowledged borrowed material by introducing the quotation or paraphrase with the name of the authority.
- punctuated all quoted materials; errors, if any, are minor.
- paraphrased material by rewriting it using writer's style and language.
- provided specific in-text documentation for each borrowed item.
- provided a bibliography page listing every source cited in the paper; omitted sources that were consulted but not used.

5

The writing demonstrates a strong commitment to the quality and significance of research and the accuracy of the written document. Documentation is used to avoid plagiarism and to enable the reader to judge how believable or important a piece of information is by checking the source. Errors are so few and so minor that the reader can easily skim right over them unless specifically searching for them. The writer has

- acknowledged borrowed material by introducing the quotation or paraphrase with the name of the authority; key phrases are directly quoted so as to give full credit where credit is due.
- punctuated all quoted materials; errors are minor.
- paraphrased material by rewriting using writer's style and language.
- provided specific in-text documentation for borrowed material.
- provided a bibliography page listing every source cited in the paper; omitted sources that were consulted but not used.

4

The writing demonstrates a commitment to the quality and significance of research and the accuracy of the written document. Documentation is used to avoid plagiarism and to enable the reader to judge how believable or important a piece of information is by checking the source. Minor errors, while perhaps noticeable, do not blatantly violate the rules of documentation. The writer has

- acknowledged borrowed material by sometimes introducing the quotation or paraphrase with the name of the authority.
- punctuated all quoted materials; errors, while noticeable, do not impede understanding.
- paraphrased material by rewriting using writer's style and language.
- provided in-text documentation for most borrowed material.
- provided a bibliography page listing every source cited in the paper; included sources that were consulted but not used.

3

The writing demonstrates a limited commitment to the quality and significance of research and the accuracy of the written document. Documentation is sometimes used to avoid plagiarism and to enable the reader to judge how believable or important a piece of information is by checking the source. Errors begin to violate the rules of documentation. The writer has

- enclosed quoted materials within quotation marks; however, incorrectly used commas, colons, semicolons, question marks or exclamation marks that are part of the quoted material.
- included paraphrased material that is not properly documented.
- paraphrased material by simply rearranging sentence patterns.

2

The writing demonstrates little commitment to the quality and significance of research and the accuracy of the written document. Frequent errors in documentation result in instances of plagiarism and often do not enable the reader to check the source. The writer has

- enclosed quoted materials within quotation marks; however, incorrectly used commas, colons, semicolons, question marks or exclamation marks that are part of the quoted material.
- attempted paraphrasing but included words that should be enclosed by quotation marks or rephrased into the writer's language and style.
- altered the essential ideas of the source.
- included citations that incorrectly identify reference sources.

1

The writing demonstrates disregard for the conventions of research writing. Lack of proper documentation result in plagiarism and do not enable the reader to check the source. The writer has

- borrowed abundantly from an original source, even to the point of retaining the essential wording.
- no citations that credit source material.
- included words or ideas from a source without providing quotation marks.
- included no bibliography page listing sources that were used.

Basic Statistical Concepts

It is necessary for you to have an understanding of a few basic statistical concepts to better understand the results of your classroom assessments, to better summarize assessment results when you grade students, to interpret your students' norm-referenced test scores, to understand the basic data in published test manuals, and to understand assessment summary reports provided by your school district or state. This appendix focuses on concepts rather than on computations. However, the computations of certain statistical indices are illustrated so you will understand the origin of their numerical values.

Although you may believe that mathematics or computations are your weak suit, you should not shy away from learning the few techniques shown in this appendix. With the availability of inexpensive calculators, computations become simple and accurate with only a little practice. Some computerized gradebook programs will make a few calculations, also. You should buy an inexpensive scientific calculator that has a "correlation" or "r" function. Such a calculator will allow you to enter the scores from your assessments and painlessly carry out calculations for all of the statistical indices in this appendix.

Statistical methods are techniques to summarize scores so that you may better understand how a group of students has performed and how well an individual student has performed relative to others in the group. A *statistical index* (or *statistic*) is a summary number that concisely captures a specific feature of a group of scores. For example, measures of central tendency focus on an average or typical score for a group. Measures of variability focus on quantifying the extent to which students' scores differ from one another. This appendix presents four categories of statistical methods that you will find most useful in understanding test scores and other assessment results: (1) distribution of scores, (2) typical or average score, (3) variability of scores, and (4) degree to which two sets of scores are correlated.

Describing Distributions of Test Scores

Suppose the scores shown in Figure I.1 are scores of our students on two tests you gave. The arrangement of the scores in the table is similar to how they might be arranged in your grade-book: Students' names are arranged alphabetically with their mark next to their names. This arrangement does not make it easy to answer such questions as:

1. How many students in the class have similar scores?
2. What scores do most students obtain?

FIGURE I.1 **List of students in a class and their scores on two tests.**

Name	Test 1	Test 2
1. Anthony	89	94
2. Ashley	75	68
3. Blake	74	72
4. Chad	84	77
5. Donald	56	66
6. Edward	80	68
7. Festina	66	68
8. George	86	73
9. Harriet	68	73
10. Irene	98	86
11. Jesse	65	78
12. Katherine	44	60
13. Lorraine	45	53
14. Marya	61	75
15. Nancy	75	76
16. Oprah	68	54
17. Peter	55	53
18. Quincy	70	68
19. Robert	69	65
20. Sally	60	47
21. Tina	73	74
22. Ula	75	88
23. Veronica	71	73
24. Wallace	43	61
25. William	83	87
26. Xavier	95	83
27. Yvonne	96	85
28. Zena	75	70

3. Are the scores widely scattered along the score scale, or do they bunch together?
4. Does the pattern of scores in the class appear unusual in some way? Or are they as expected?
5. Does any student score unusually higher or lower than his or her classmates?

Ranking Scores

One simple way to begin answering questions such as these is to rank the scores. Most people know how to do this already. To rank the scores, *order them from largest to smallest.* The largest score is assigned a rank of 1; the next largest, a rank of 2; and so on, down to the smallest score. In this way all of the raw scores (marks) are transformed into ranks.

Figure I.2 demonstrates the procedure for score from Test 1. Notice what is done when students have the same score. In this case they are tied for the ranks. The tie is resolved by awarding each of the persons whose scores are tied the average of the ranks for which they are tied. For example, four students have a score of 75 and thus are tied for ranks 9, 10, 11, and 12. Rather than arbitrarily awarding one person a rank of 9, and another a rank of 10, and so on, each person is awarded the average of the tied ranks, that is:

$$\frac{9 + 10 + 11 + 12}{4} = 10.5$$

A simple ranked list of scores helps you answer some basic questions about how well your class performed on a test. The list shows quickly the highest and lowest scores. It shows how the scores are spread out and which scores occur most often. This ranked list may be all you need to understand how your students performed on a test. However, ranked lists are not easily understood if the number of students is very large: for example, the score of all fourth graders in the school district or in the state. A better way to organize the scores in such cases is discussed later.

Interpretations of simple ranks of this sort depend on the number of students in the group. For example, suppose I told you that of all the classes in testing and measurement I have taught, your class ranked second. You might be proud as a group until I also told you that I have taught only one other class. Adding another 13 classes might result in your class's rank

FIGURE I.2 Rank order of students from Figure I.1 according to their scores on Test 1.

Name	Test 1	Rank	
Irene	98	1	
Yvonne	96	2	
Xavier	95	3	
Anthony	89	4	
George	86	5	
Chad	84	6	
William	83	7	
Edward	80	8	
Zena	75	10.5	
Ula	75	10.5	Four scores
Nancy	75	10.5	tied for ranks
Ashley	75	10.5	9, 10, 11, and 12
Blake	74	13	
Tina	73	14	
Veronica	71	15	
Quincy	70	16	
Robert	69	17	
Oprah	68	18.5	Two scores tied
Harriet	68	18.5	for ranks 18 and 19
Festina	66	20	
Jesse	65	21	
Marya	61	22	
Sally	60	23	
Donald	56	24	
Peter	55	25	
Lorraine	45	26	
Katherine	44	27	
Wallace	43	28	

dropping, say, from second to 15th: Although the class's rank has changed from second to 15th, its relative position–dead last–has not changed. The point is that a student's rank cannot be fully interpreted without knowing the number of other students being ranked. This problem is largely overcome by using *percentile ranks* (see Chapter 17). We show you how to calculate percentile ranks in Figure I.8.

Stem-and-Leaf Displays

A simple way to organize a large group of scores is to prepare a stem-and-leaf display. Figure I.3 illustrates the procedure for the scores of the 28 students in Figure I.1 for each of the two tests. The "stem" is the tens' digit and the "leaves" are the ones' digits of the score. For example, consider the scores 80, 83, 84, 86, and 89 from Test 1. The tens' digit is 8 and is written in the stem column. The ones' digits 0, 3, 4, 6, and 9 are the leaves and are written in the row to the right of the 8.

The stem-and-leaf display has the advantage of showing how the entire group of scores is distributed along the score scale when they are grouped together by intervals of 10. That is, it organizes the scores into the groupings of 40s, 50s, 60s, 70s, 80s, and 90s. With the ones' digits displayed, you can easily "reconstitute" individual values of the scores. This is useful if you need to make future calculations. In the "Frequency" column, the number of scores is written in each row.

Notice that tens' digits in the stem column (0, 1, 2, etc.) are ordered from lowest to highest. When you turn the page on its side, the display is a type of graph: The length of the "leaves" row is proportional to the frequency of the scores.

The scores in Figure I.3 are grouped into interval widths of 10. You could also group the scores into narrower intervals, say five digits wide, as shown in Figure I.4. The stem 4 represents the scores 40, 41, 42, 43, and 44; the stem 4* represents the scores 45, 46, 47, 48, and 49. Figures I.3 and I.4 contain the same information, but are organized slightly differently. Notice, too, that you can easily construct a ranked list from a stem-and-leaf display, because the individual score values are easily recovered from the display.

Frequency Distributions

When the number of scores to be organized is very large, ranked lists and stem-and-leaf displays are cumbersome. In such cases, the collection of scores is organized into a figure called a *frequency distribution*. This figure shows the number of persons obtaining various scores. Figure I.5 shows frequency distributions for the two tests.

Notice that the figure shows scores grouped into intervals of five points on the score scale: 95–99, 90–94, 85–89, and so on. Grouping scores into intervals is a common practice when the students' scores span a wide range of values. The advantage is that the table shows the distribution of scores in a more compact space. The number of intervals is set at some convenient value, say 10 or 12. A common practice is to make the width of the interval an odd number, because then the midpoint of the interval is a whole number. Whole-number midpoints are desirable when the information in the table is to be used to construct a graph or for later calculations. The midpoints of each interval are shown in Figure I.5. Often the midpoints are not presented when the table can be interpreted without that information. Similarly, the "Tally" column is seldom shown in a finished table. Its only purpose is to make it easier and more accurate to count the scores in each interval. At the bottom of the frequency column you

FIGURE I.3 Stem-and-leaf display of the distribution of the students' scores from Figure I.1.

	Test 1				Test 2	
Stem	Leaves	Frequency		Stem	Leaves	Frequency
0				0		
1				1		
2				2		
3				3		
4	3 4 5	3		4	7	1
5	5 6	2		5	3 3 4	3
6	0 1 5 6 8 8 9	7		6	0 1 5 6 8 8 8 8	8
7	0 1 3 4 5 5 5 5	8		7	0 2 3 3 3 4 5 5 6 7 8	10
8	0 3 4 6 9	5		8	3 5 6 7 8	5
9	5 6 8	3		9	4	1
		N=28				N=28

FIGURE I.4 Stem-and-leaf display of the scores from Figure I.1 when the internal width equals 5.

	Test 1				Test 2	
Stem	Leaves	Frequency		Stem	Leaves	Frequency
0				0		
0*				0*		
1				1		
1*				1*		
2				2		
2*				2*		
3				3		
3*				3*		
4	3 4	2		4		
4*	5	1		4*	7	1
5		0		5	3 3 4	3
5*	5 6	2		5*		0
6	0 1	2		6	0 1	2
6*	5 6 8 8 9	5		6*	5 6 8 8 8 8	6
7	0 1 3 4	4		7	0 2 3 3 3 4	6
7*	5 5 5 5	4		7*	5 6 7 8	4
8	0 3 4	3		8	3	1
8*	6 9	2		8*	5 6 7 8	4
9		0		9	4	1
9*	5 6 8	3		9*		0
		N = 28				N = 28

FIGURE I.5 Frequency distributions of the scores in Figure I.1. (Interval widths equal 5.)

	Test 1				Test 2		
Interval	Tally	Midpoint	Frequency	Interval	Tally	Midpoint	Frequency
95–99	|||	97	3	95–99		97	0
90–94		92	0	90–94	|	92	1
85–89	||	87	2	85–89	||||	87	4
80–84	|||	82	3	80–84	|	82	1
75–79	||||	77	4	75–79	||||	77	4
70–74	||||	72	4	70–74	⧸⧹⧹⧹|	72	6
65–69	⧸⧹⧹⧹	67	5	65–69	⧸⧹⧹⧹|	67	6
60–64	||	62	2	60–64	||	62	2
55–59	||	57	2	55–59		57	0
50–54		52	0	50–54	|||	52	3
45–49	|	47	1	45–49	|	47	1
40–44	||	42	2	40–44		42	0
			28				28

should record the sum of the frequencies. This is N, the total number of scores in the collection.

You can calculate the width of the interval to use as follows. Subtract the lowest score in the group from the highest score. Divide this difference by 12. The interval width to use is the nearest odd number to this quotient. For example, for Test 1, the highest score is 98 and the lowest is 43. Thus, $(98 - 43) \div 12$ is 4.56, and the nearest odd number is 5. For Test 2, this calculation is 3.91 and the nearest odd number is 3. However, if you want to compare the distributions of Tests 1 and 2, it is best to use the same interval width. Thus, we have used a width of 5 for each test distribution. This illustrates that there are no hard and fast rules for fixing interval widths.

To make the table, it is best to make the lower limit of the interval a multiple of the interval width. This makes it easier to construct the table. Thus, the lower limit of the highest interval in Figure I.5 is 95, the next is 90, next is 85, and so on. Be sure that the highest interval contains the highest score. You need not continue the intervals below the interval containing the lowest score. Thus, the lowest interval in Figure I.5 is 40–44.

The *grouped frequency distribution*, as Figure I.5 is called, provides the same convenient summary of the distribution of scores as the stem-and-leaf display. However, unlike the stem-and-leaf display, information about the specific numerical values of the scores in each interval is lost: Only the frequency of the scores falling into the interval is recorded. Unlike the stem-and-leaf display, however, the frequency distribution table can summarize large collections of scores in a compact, easy-to-interpret format.

Frequency Polygons and Histograms

Frequency distributions are often graphed because graphs permit an increased understanding of the distribution of scores. Two common types of graphs of frequency distribution are the histogram and frequency polygon. For both, a scale of score values is marked off on a horizontal axis. The *histogram* (sometimes called a *bar graph*) represents the frequency of each score by a rectangle. The height of each rectangle is made equal to (or proportional to)

the frequency of the corresponding score. Figure I.6A shows a histogram for the Test 1 scores of Figure I.5. A *frequency polygon* for these same scores is shown in Figure I.6B. A dot is made directly above the score-value to indicate the frequency. (If no one has obtained a particular score-value, the dot is made at 0.) The dots are then connected with straight lines to make the polygon.

A graph communicates in an easy manner the shape or form of a frequency distribution. Using the names of these shapes is a compact way of describing how the scores are distributed.

Figure I.7 shows a variety of distributional forms, their corresponding names, and examples of measurement situations that might give rise to them.

Frequency Distributions and Graphs

The illustrations of Figure I.7 are idealized and do not represent actual distributions. Nevertheless, it is helpful to have a mental picture of these distributional forms because, in practice, actual test score distributions resemble the ideal forms at least roughly. Test manuals and school and state reports often describe score distributions using the terms.

Score distribution shape depends on both the test taker and the test

The shape of a score distribution reflects the characteristics of the test as well as the ability of the group being tested. There is no single "natural" or "normal" shape toward which the test scores of a given group of students tends. A test composed of items that are not too difficult and not too easy for a particular group is likely to result in distributions of scores similar to those illustrated by A, B, or C of Figure I.7. This same group, with the same ability, could take a test in the same subject made up of items that few persons could answer correctly or a test made up of "easy" items. In these latter cases, skewed distributions (F or G) might result. It is not accurate, therefore, to come to a conclusion about the *underlying ability* distribution of a group of students by examining only the shape of the distribution of observed test scores. The characteristics of the test the group took also need to be made a part of the decision.

FIGURE I.6 Histogram and frequency polygon for the scores of Test 1 from Figure I.5.

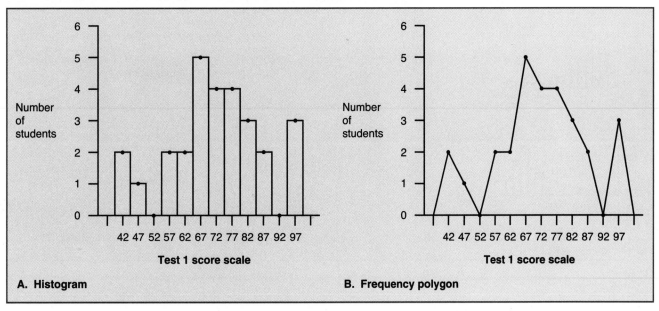

A. Histogram

B. Frequency polygon

FIGURE I.7 Histograms showing various forms of frequency distributions

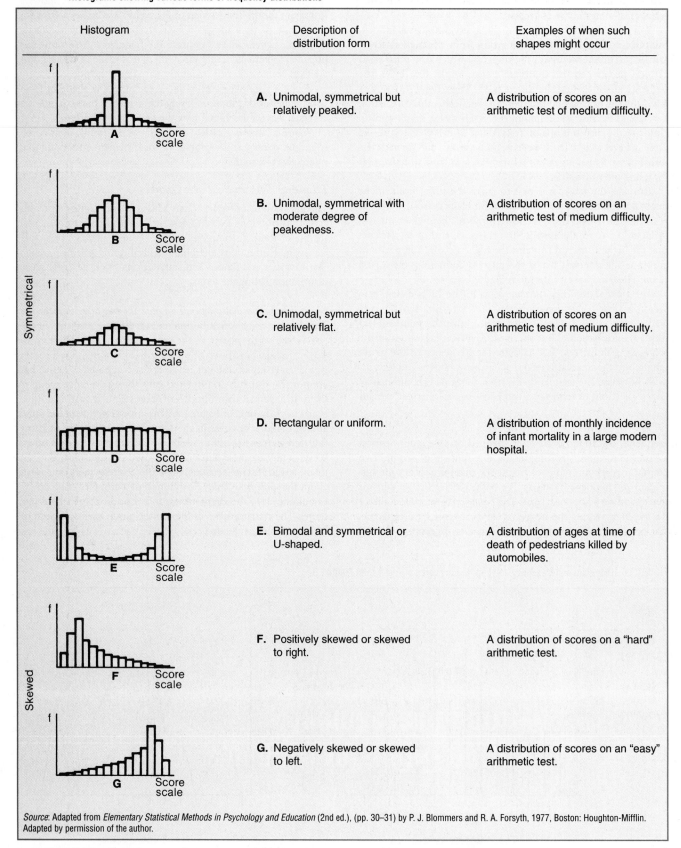

Histogram	Description of distribution form	Examples of when such shapes might occur
A	**A.** Unimodal, symmetrical but relatively peaked.	A distribution of scores on an arithmetic test of medium difficulty.
B	**B.** Unimodal, symmetrical with moderate degree of peakedness.	A distribution of scores on an arithmetic test of medium difficulty.
C	**C.** Unimodal, symmetrical but relatively flat.	A distribution of scores on an arithmetic test of medium difficulty.
D	**D.** Rectangular or uniform.	A distribution of monthly incidence of infant mortality in a large modern hospital.
E	**E.** Bimodal and symmetrical or U-shaped.	A distribution of ages at time of death of pedestrians killed by automobiles.
F	**F.** Positively skewed or skewed to right.	A distribution of scores on a "hard" arithmetic test.
G	**G.** Negatively skewed or skewed to left.	A distribution of scores on an "easy" arithmetic test.

(Left vertical labels: Symmetrical for A–E, Skewed for F–G)

Source: Adapted from *Elementary Statistical Methods in Psychology and Education* (2nd ed.), (pp. 30–31) by P. J. Blommers and R. A. Forsyth, 1977, Boston: Houghton-Mifflin. Adapted by permission of the author.

Choice between Histogram or Polygon   For many classroom purposes, you could use either a polygon or a histogram; the choice between them is rather arbitrary. The polygon emphasizes the continuous nature of the attribute that underlies the scores you see on the test; the histogram emphasizes the discrete nature. Although observed test *scores* usually are discrete whole numbers (0, 1, 2, . . .), the underlying characteristic a test is designed to measure is often thought of as continuous rather than discrete.

Comparing Two Distributions   It is sometimes useful to compare two or more frequency distributions by graphing on the same axes using polygons, rather than histograms. A graph could compare, for example, a class of students before and after instruction, or it could compare two different classes of students. Such a graph would display the forms of the distributions, the variability or disbursement of scores, and the place(s) along the score scale where the scores tend to cluster.

Calculating Percentile Ranks   Percentile ranks tell the percentage of the scores in a distribution that are below a particular point on the score scale. We explained the concept of percentile ranks in Chapter 17. We show how to calculate percentile ranks in Figure I.8.

Measures of Central Tendency

It is quite common when interpreting assessment results to speak of the "average score," as we speak of the "average student," "being above average in spelling," or "of average intelligence."

There are many ways to define averages, but we describe only three: *mode, mean,* and *median.* The *mode* is the score that occurs most frequently in relation to other scores in the collection. Thus, the modal score is average in the sense of being most popular or most probable in the group. The *mean,* or more precisely the *arithmetic mean,* is found by summing the scores and dividing by their number. Thus, the mean is the average that takes into account all of the scores and is the "center of gravity" of the collection. The *median* is the score point that divides the score scale so 50% of the scores in the collection are above it and 50% are below it. This makes the median a typical score in the sense of coming nearest in the aggregate to all the scores.

Mode

You find the mode by listing the scores and identifying the most frequently occurring. In Figure I.9, the mode of the Test 1 distribution is 75, and the mode of the Test 2 distribution is 68. You could identify the mode from either a stem-and-leaf display or a frequency distribution.

If in one distribution two scores occur with approximately equal frequency, there are two modes. Such a distribution is said to be *bimodal.* A distribution with one mode is *unimodal.*

The mode is the point on the score scale where a large number of scores in a distribution are located. If there is more than one mode, there are concentrations of scores at more than one score level. You should note that a distribution may not have a mode. For example, the uniform distribution in Figure I.7D does not have a mode.

Mean

To calculate the mean, add the scores and divide by their number. The formula is

$$M = \frac{Sum\ of\ all\ the\ scores}{Total\ number\ of\ scores}$$

$$= \frac{\Sigma X}{N}$$

where M represents the mean, N represents the total number of scores involved, and Σ represents "sum of." The means of the Test 1 and Test 2 scores in Figure I.9 are 71.4 and 71.3, respectively.

An important property of the mean is that its value is affected by every one of the scores in the collection, because the sum on which it is based includes every score. When you want an average that focuses on the total rather than the typical or most frequent, choose the mean. The mean reflects the highest and lowest scores, whereas the mode reflects only the most frequent. This influence of extremely high or low scores may be undesirable because such scores are not typical scores for the distribution. The median is preferred when you want an average to focus on typical performance and to be uninfluenced by extremely high or extremely low scores.

Median

A simple way to calculate the median is to arrange the scores by rank, and then count to the point on the score scale that has the same number of scores above it as below it. If there is an even number of scores in the collection, the median is halfway between the two middle scores. If there is an odd number of scores, the median is the middle score.

In Figure I.9, the median for Test 1 is 72; the median for Test 2 is 72.5. Notice that the median does not have to be a score that any person has attained. This is so because the median is a point on the score scale that divides the distribution into halves. The mean also need not be a score anyone attained; however, the mode must be a score that many persons attained.

Because the median separates the distribution into two halves, it is also the *50th percentile.* Further, it does not sum up all of the scores. As a result, its value is not affected by extremely high or low scores (as the mean is). The median is the average to use when you do not want an average that is sensitive to such extreme scores.

Measures of Variability

Although averages summarize the central tendency of a group of scores, they do not summarize how the scores spread out over the score scale. For example, the mean reading test scores of two seventh-grade classes may be 75. However, in one class the scores may range widely from 55 to 95, while in the other the scores may range only from 70 to 80. Obviously, the students in the latter class are more nearly alike in their reading achievement than the students in the former class. You will need to cater to more widely different reading levels when teaching the former class than when teaching the latter.

This section describes three measures of the spread or variability of a set of scores: the *range,* the *interquartile range,* and the *standard deviation.*

Range (R)

The range is a simple index of spread. It is the difference between the highest and lowest scores in the set. For the two tests in Figure I.9, the range is 55 for Test 1 (98 − 43 = 55) and 47 for Test 2 (94 − 47 = 47). Although for either test the range is relatively

FIGURE I.8 **Example of how to calculate percentile ranks for a class of 25 students.**

Raw	Tally	Frequency	Cumulative frequency	$PR = \dfrac{\frac{1}{2}\left[\begin{array}{c}\text{number of persons}\\\text{having the score}\end{array}\right] + \left[\begin{array}{c}\text{number of persons}\\\text{below the score}\end{array}\right]}{\text{total number of persons}} \times 100$
36	/	1	25	$98 = \dfrac{.5 + 24}{25} \times 100$
35		0	24	96
34		0	24	96
33		0	24	$96 = \dfrac{0 + 24}{25} \times 100$
32	/	1	24	$94 = \dfrac{.5 + 23}{25} \times 100$
31	/	1	23	$90 = \dfrac{.5 + 22}{25} \times 100$
30		0	22	$88 = \dfrac{0 + 22}{25} \times 100$
29	//	2	22	$84 = \dfrac{1 + 20}{25} \times 100$
28	////	4	20	$72 = \dfrac{2 + 16}{25} \times 100$
27	ⅢⱢ	5	16	$54 = \dfrac{2.5 + 11}{25} \times 100$
26	ⅢⱢ /	6	11	$32 = \dfrac{3 + 5}{25} \times 100$
25	//	2	5	$16 = \dfrac{1 + 3}{25} \times 100$
24	/	1	3	$10 = \dfrac{.5 + 2}{25} \times 100$
23		0	2	8
22		0	2	$8 = \dfrac{0 + 2}{25} \times 100$
21	/	1	2	$6 = \dfrac{.5 + 1}{25} \times 100$
20		0	1	4
19		0	1	4
18		0	1	4
17		0	1	4
16		0	1	4
15		0	1	$4 = \dfrac{0 + 1}{25} \times 100$
14	/	1	1	$2 = \dfrac{.5 + 0}{25} \times 100$
		$N = 25$		

Step-By-Step

1. List the possible scores in descending order (Column 1). (You may group the scores into intervals if you wish.)
2. Tally the number of students attaining each score (Column 2).
3. Sum the number of students attaining each score (Column 3).
4. Add the frequencies consecutively, starting at the bottom of the column with the lowest score. Place each consecutive sum in the cumulative frequency column (Column 4). E.g., 0 + 1 = 1, . . . , 2 + 1 = 3, 3 + 2 = 5, etc.
5. Calculate the percentile rank of each score (Column 5). Below is an example for the score 27.
   (a) Calculate one-half of the frequency of the score (1/2 × 5 = 2.5).
   (b) Add the result in (a) to the cumulative frequency just below the score (2.5 + 11 = 13.5).
   (c) Divide the result in (b) by the total number of scores (13.5 ÷ 25 = .54).
   (d) Multiply the result in (c) by 100 (.54 × 100 = 54).

large, it is smaller for Test 2, showing the scores are spread over a smaller part of the score scale. The procedure may be summarized as follows:

$$R = highest\ score - lowest\ score$$

A weakness of the range as an index of variability is that it is based on only two scores. It ignores the scores between the highest and lowest scores. Another problem with the range is that a change in either the highest or lowest score in the set can radically alter its value.

Interquartile Range (IR)

The interquartile range describes the spread of the middle 50% of the scores. It is the difference between the third and the first quartiles. *Quartiles* are points that divide the group of scores into quarters. The first quartile (Q_1) is the point *below which* the lowest 25% of the students score. The third quartile (Q_3) is the point *above which* the highest 25% of the students score. The second quartile (Q_2) is the median.

To obtain the interquartile range, you first order the scores and proceed similarly to calculating the median. That is, count down from the highest score 25% of the scores to locate Q_3 and up from the lowest score 25% to calculate Q_1. The interquartile range is the difference between these two values:[1]

$$IR = Q_3 - Q_1$$

In Figure I.9, $Q_3 = 83$ and $Q_1 = 61$ for Test 1. That is, for Test 1 the 75th percentile is 83 and the 25th percentile is 61. The $IR = [83 - 61] = 22$ for this test. Thus, the middle 50% of the scores on Test 1 have a 22-point spread. For Test 2, $Q_3 = 73$, $Q_1 = 65$, and $IR = [73 - 65] = 8$. The middle 50% of the students have only an 8-point spread on Test 2.

Standard Deviation (SD)

The most frequently used index of variability is the standard deviation. Large numerical values of this index indicate that the scores are spread out away from the mean. Small values indicate that the scores tend to cluster near the mean. The standard deviation is the average amount by which the scores differ from the mean score.[2] In some test reports the squared standard deviation (SD^2), or *variance*, is used.

The definitional formula for the standard deviation is:

$$SD = \sqrt{\frac{\Sigma(X-M)^2}{N}}$$

$$= \sqrt{\frac{sum\ of\ the\ squared\ deviations\ from\ the\ mean}{total\ number\ of\ scores}}$$

[1]Some books divide the interquartile range by 2 to obtain the *semi-interquartile range (SIR)*. This value indicates the approximate distance you would need to move on the score scale above and below the median to encompass the middle 50% of the scores.
[2]This is not strictly correct, but as a practical matter little interpretive harm regarding assessment results is done by thinking of the standard deviation in this way.

FIGURE I.9 **Scores on Test 1 and Test 2 ranked separately and showing measures of central tendency.**

Test 1	Test 2
98	94
96	88
95	87
89	86
86	85
84	83
83	78
80	77
75	76
75	75
75 Mode = 75	74
75	73
74	73
73	73
71 ← Median = 72	73 ← Median = 72.5
70	72
69	70
68	68
68	68 Mode = 68
68	68
66	68
65	66
61	65
60	61
56	60
55	54
45	53
44	53
43	47
$\Sigma X = 1,999$	$\Sigma X = 1,995$
$M = (1,999) \div 28 = 71.4$	$M = (1,995) \div 28 = 71.3$

Many inexpensive scientific calculators and microcomputer programs have procedures for calculating the standard deviation. You should use one of these to calculate *SD*. If you want to calculate the standard deviation using a calculator that does not have this procedure built in, follow these steps:

1. First arrange the scores into a frequency distribution, as in Figure I.5 and reproduced in Figure I.10.
2. Apply a computational formula such as the one shown here. (You can find other computational formulas in an applied statistics text.)

$$SD = \sqrt{\frac{\Sigma f(X^2)}{N} - M^2}$$

$$= \sqrt{\frac{sum\ of\ the\ product\ of\ the\ square\ of\ each\ score\ and\ its\ frequency}{total\ number} - [square\ of\ the\ mean]}$$

This is not as hard to compute as it looks:

Steps	Symbols
1. Square each interval midpoint.	1. X^2
2. Multiply each square by its frequency.	2. $f(X^2)$
3. Add together all of these products.	3. $\Sigma f(X^2)$
4. Divide by the total number.	4. $\dfrac{\Sigma f(X^2)}{N}$

FIGURE I.10 **Computing the standard deviation of Test 1 scores after they are organized into a frequency distribution.**

Score Interval	Midpoint	Frequency (f)	Step 1 (X^2)	Step 2 $f(X^2)$
95–99	97	3	9,409	28,227
90–94	92	0	8,464	0
85–89	87	2	7,569	15,138
80–84	82	3	6,724	20,172
75–79	77	4	5,929	23,716
70–74	72	4	5,184	20,736
65–69	67	5	4,489	22,445
60–64	62	2	3,844	7,688
55–59	57	2	3,249	6,498
50–54	52	0	2,704	0
45–49	47	1	2,209	2,209
40–44	42	2	1,764	3,528
		$n = 28$		150,357

The formula is:

$$SD = \sqrt{\frac{\Sigma f(X^2) - M^2}{N}}$$ (*Note that using the grouped data above, M = 71.8*)

Putting the numbers into the formula:

$$SD = \sqrt{\frac{150,357}{28} - (71.8)^2}$$

After Steps 4 and 5:

$$SD = \sqrt{5,369.89 - 5,155.24}$$

Then Step 6:

$$SD = \sqrt{214.65}$$

Step 7 gives the final result: $SD = 14.65$

5. Square the mean. (If the mean has not been computed already, you need to compute it.)

6. Subtract the square of the mean from the result found in Step 4. (Stop here if you want only the variance.)

7. Take the square root of the difference. This is the standard deviation.

5. M^2

6. $\dfrac{\Sigma f(X^2)}{N} - M^2$

7. $\sqrt{\dfrac{\Sigma f(X^2)}{N} - M^2}$

Figure I.10 illustrates these calculations for Test 1. (Note that in this example, the result obtained from Figure I.10 is not the same result you would obtain if you did not group the scores into intervals. Grouping scores results in some error. However, the result is still useful.)

Calculating Stanines Stanines are normalized standard scores that tell the location of a raw score in one of nine specific segments of a normal distribution. Stanines were explained in Chapter 17. We show how to calculate stanines in Figure I.11.

The Correlation Coefficient

Calculating the correlation coefficient requires using a calculator or a computer. Some scientific calculators have this capability already built in as a statistical function, so all you need to do is enter the paired scores of students. However, this section illustrates the calculation for those with calculators that do not have the correlation coefficient function built in.

For practical work, you can use the following computational formula:

$$r = \frac{N(\Sigma XY) - (\Sigma X)(\Sigma Y)}{\sqrt{[N(\Sigma X^2) - (\Sigma X)^2][N(\Sigma Y^2) - (\Sigma Y)^2]}}$$

This formula is illustrated in Figure I.12 with the scores from the two tests in Figure I.1. In this example, Test 1 is symbolized X and Test 2 is symbolized Y. Figure I.13 shows the calculation.

If you have already computed the standard deviations and means of each variable, then the following formula (which is equivalent to the previous equation) will save you some computational labor.

$$r_{xy} = \frac{\dfrac{\Sigma XY}{N} - M_x M_y}{(SD_x)(SD_y)}$$

To illustrate with the data in Figure I.13, for which

$$M_x = 71.39, M_y = 71.25$$
$$SD_x = 14.81, SD_y = 11.57$$

FIGURE I.11 **How to transform raw scores into stanines.**

You may transform any set of scores to stanines by applying the normal curve percentage relationship implied by Figure 17.7. These theoretical percentages are:

Stanine	Percent of scores	Stanine	Percent of scores
9	top 4%	4	next 17%
8	next 7%	3	next 12%
7	next 12%	2	next 7%
6	next 17%	1	bottom 4%
5	middle 20%		

The preferred procedure is to begin assigning stanines at the middle of the score distribution (i.e., assigning stanine = 5 first) and then work toward each end. This procedure helps to make the resulting distribution of stanines more symmetric than if you started at the top or bottom. I illustrate the procedure below using the 25 students' scores shown in percentile rank calibration example given earlier (Figure I.8).

Step-by-step	Results from percentile ranks example	Comments
1. Make a frequency distribution or list the scores in order from high to low .	See PR example, first and third columns.	
2. Locate the median or middle score.	25 scores × ½ = 12.5 scores. Therefore, the middle score is 27.	Round the median to a whole number.
3. Use the theoretical percentages to determine how many scores should be assigned a stanine of 5.	20% of 25 = 5 scores.	
4. Assign stanines of 5 to the number of scores calculated in Step 3. (You should include scores just above and below the median if necessary to come as close as possible to the desired number .)	It so happens that in the PR example exactly 5 persons had a score of 27, so that we do not need to look to adjacent values. (See below.)	Remember that *all* equal scores must have the same stanine assigned to them.

Scores	Stanines	Actual number	Theoretical number
36	9	1	1
32–35	8	1	2
29–31	7	3	3
28	6	4	4
27	5	5	5
26	4	6	4
24–25	3	3	3
15–23	2	1	2
14	1	1	1

5. Working up from the scores assigned stanine 5, use the theoretical percentages to assign scores to stanine categories of 6, 7, 8, and 9. Come as near to the theoretical percentages as possible.

6. Repeat the procedure for the scores that are below those assigned stanine 5.

7. It is important that you assign all equal scores the same stanine.

FIGURE I.12 **Example calculating a correlation coefficient.**

Steps	Symbols	Examples
1. List everyone's pair of scores.	1. X, Y	1. *Blake:* $X = 74$, $Y = 72$
2. Square each score.	2. X^2, Y^2	2. *Blake:* $X^2 = (74)^2 = 5,476$ $Y^2 = (72)^2 = 5,184$
3. Multiply the scores in each pair.	3. XY	3. *Blake:* $XY = 74 \times 72$ $= 5,328$
4. Sum the X, Y, X^2, Y^2, and XY columns.	4. $\Sigma X, \Sigma Y$ $\Sigma X^2 \, \Sigma Y^2$ ΣXY	4. $\Sigma X = 1,999$, $\Sigma X^2 = 148,635$ $\Sigma Y = 1,995$, $\Sigma Y^2 = 145,761$ $\Sigma XY = 145,902$

5. Put the sums into equation.

$$r = \frac{28\,(145,902) - (1,999)\,(1,995)}{\sqrt{[28(148,635) - (1,999)^2]\,[(145,761) - (1995)^2]}}$$

$$= \frac{4,085,256 - 3,988,005}{\sqrt{(4,161,780 - 3,996,001)\,(4,081,308 - 3,980,025)}}$$

$$= \frac{97,251}{\sqrt{(165,779)\,(101,283)}} = \frac{97,251}{129,578.53} = .75$$

FIGURE I.13 **Computing a correlation coefficient between the scores in Figure I.1**

Names	Test 1		Test 2		Cross Products
	X	X²	Y	Y²	XY
Anthony	89	7,921	94	8,836	8,366
Ashley	75	7,625	68	4,624	5,100
Blake	74	5,476	72	5,184	5,328
Chad	84	7,056	77	5,929	6,468
Donald	56	3,136	66	4,356	3,696
Edward	80	6,400	68	4,624	5,440
Festina	66	4,356	68	4,624	4,488
George	86	7,396	73	5,329	6,278
Harriet	68	4,624	73	5,329	4,964
Irene	98	9,604	86	7,396	8,428
Jesse	65	4,225	78	6,084	5,070
Katherine	44	1,936	60	3,600	2,640
Lorraine	45	2,025	53	2,809	2,385
Marya	61	3,721	75	5,625	4,575
Nancy	75	5,625	76	5,776	5,700
Oprah	68	4,624	54	2,916	3,672
Peter	55	3,025	53	2,809	2,915
Quincy	70	4,900	68	4,624	4,760
Robert	69	4,761	65	4,225	4,485
Sally	60	3,600	47	2,209	2,820
Tina	73	5,329	74	5,476	5,402
Ula	75	5,625	88	7,744	6,600
Veronica	71	5,041	73	5,329	5,183
Wallace	43	1,849	61	3,721	2,623
William	83	6,889	87	7,569	7,221
Xavier	95	9,025	83	6,889	7,885
Yvonne	96	9,216	85	7,225	8,160
Zena	75	7,625	70	4,900	5,250
	1,999	148,635	1,995	145,761	145,902

we have:

$$r = \frac{\frac{145,902}{28} - (71.39)(71.25)}{(14.81)(11.57)} = .75$$

(The slight difference you obtain from these two equations is due to rounding error.)

Calculating Basic Statistics with the Excel Spread Sheet

Many of the statistics in this appendix can be calculated very easily using the Microsoft Excel spreadsheet program. The first figure in this appendix (Figure I.1) shows the scores on two tests for a class of 28 students. We use the scores in this table to illustrate how to use the Excel program. You need to type students' names and scores into the spreadsheet as shown in the example on the next page. Notice that the rows are labeled with numbers and the columns are labeled with letters. These column letters and row numbers appear automatically and cannot be changed.

To calculate the mean (M) of the scores for Test 1, click on cell B31. Then type = AVERAGE(B2:B29) and press the return key. (Be sure to include the equal sign and no space before the word AVERAGE.) This tells the program to calculate the average of the scores that are in cells B2 through B31. The value of the mean (= 71.39) will appear in the B31 cell. To calculate the standard deviation (SD) of scores for Test 1, click on cell B32. Then type = STDEVP(B2:B29) and press the return key. The SD (= 14.65) of the scores in cells B2 through B29 will appear in cell B32. Similarly, if you type = AVERAGE(C2:C29) into cell C31 and press return, the mean of Test 2 (= 71.25) will appear in cell C31. If you type =STDEVP(C2:C29) into cell C32, the SD (= 11.37) will appear in cell C32.

To calculate the correlation coefficient, you need to tell the program the two columns of scores that are involved. Click on cell B33, then type =CORREL(B2:B29,C2:C29). This tells the program to correlate the Test 1 scores in cells B2 through B29 with the Test 2 scores in cells C2 through C29. Press the return key and the correlation, r = .75, appears in cell B33.

	A	B	C
1	Names	Test 1	Test 2
2	Anthony	89	94
3	Ashley	75	68
4	Blake	74	72
5	Chad	84	77
6	Donald	56	66
7	Edward	80	68
8	Festina	66	68
9	George	86	73
10	Harriet	68	73
11	Irene	98	86
12	Jesse	65	78
13	Katherine	44	60
14	Lorraine	45	53
15	Marya	61	75
16	Nancy	75	76
17	Oprah	68	54
18	Peter	55	53
19	Quincy	70	68
20	Robert	69	65
21	Sally	60	47
22	Tina	73	74
23	Ula	75	88
24	Veronica	71	73
25	Wallace	43	61
26	William	83	87
27	Xavier	95	83
28	Yvonne	96	85
29	Zena	75	70
30			
31	Mean	71.39	71.25
32	Std Dev	14.65	11.37
33	Correlation	.75	

Enter students' names and scores into these rows and columns

Type =STDEVP (B2:B29) into this cell

Type =AVERAGE(B2:B29) into this cell

Type =CORRELL(B2:B29,C2:C29) into this cell

APPENDIX J

Computational Procedures for Various Reliability Coefficients

FIGURE J.1 Example of how to compute the Spearman-Brown double length and the Rulon split-halves reliability estimates.

A. Pupil's item scores and total test scores[a]

Pupils	Items on test 1	2	3	4	Total score (X)
Alan	1	0	0	0	1
Isaac	1	1	0	0	2
Leslie	0	0	1	1	2
Miriam	0	0	0	0	0
Rebecca	1	1	0	1	3
Robert	1	1	1	1	4

$$M = \frac{\Sigma X}{N} = \frac{12}{6} = 2; \ (SD_x)^2 = \frac{\Sigma(X - M)^2}{N} = \frac{10}{6} = 1.67$$

[a]An item is scored 1 if it is answered correctly; 0 otherwise.

B. Computation for Spearman-Brown formula

Pupils	Half-test scores odd items (1 + 3)	even items (2 + 4)	Computing correlation between halves[b] z-scores for: odd	even	Product $(z_o \cdot z_e)$
Alan	1	0	0	−1.22	0
Isaac	1	1	0	0	0
Leslie	1	1	0	0	0
Miriam	0	0	−1.72	−1.22	2.10
Rebecca	1	2	0	+1.22	0
Robert	2	2	+1.72	+1.22	2.10
Means	1.0	1.00			
SDs	0.58	0.82	$r_{nn} = \frac{\Sigma z_o z_e}{N} = \frac{4.6}{6} = 0.70$		

Spearman-Brown
   double length

$$\text{reliability estimates} = \frac{2r_{nn}}{1 + r_{nn}} = \frac{(2)(.70)}{1 + .70} = 0.82$$

[b]Other procedures may be used for computing the correlation coefficient (see Figure I.12).

C. Computation for Rulon formula

Pupils	Half-test scores[c] odd items (1 + 3)	even items (2 + 4)	Difference between half-test scores
Alan	1	0	1
Isaac	1	1	0
Leslie	1	1	0
Miriam	0	0	0
Rebecca	1	2	−1
Robert	2	2	0

Variance of differences $= (SD_{diff})^2 = 0.33$
Variance of total scores $= (SD_x)^2 = 1.67$
Rulon split-halves
   reliability estimate

$$= 1 - \frac{(SD_{diff})^2}{(SD_x)^2}$$

$$= 1 - \frac{0.33}{1.67} = 0.80$$

[c]Neither the Spearman-Brown nor the Rulon formula is restricted to an odd-even split. Other splits may be used (see text).

FIGURE J.2 Example of how to compute the Kuder-Richardson formula 20 (KR20) and the Kuder-Richardson formula 21 (KR21) reliability estimates.

A. Computing KR20

Pupils	Items on test[a]				Total score[b] (X)
	1	**2**	**3**	**4**	
Alan	1	0	0	0	1
Isaac	1	1	0	0	2
Leslie	0	0	1	1	2
Miriam	0	0	0	0	0
Rebecca	1	1	0	1	3
Robert	1	1	1	1	4
Fraction passing each item (p-values)	.67	.50	.33	.50	$M = 2.0$ $(SD_x)^2 = 1.667$
$(1-p)$	.33	.50	.67	.50	
$p(1-p)$	.222	.250	.222	.250	$\Sigma p(1-p) = 0.944$

$$KR20 = \left[\frac{k}{k-1}\right]\left[1 - \frac{\Sigma p(1-p)}{(SD_x)^2}\right] = \left[\frac{4}{(4-1)}\right]\left[1 - \frac{0.944}{1.667}\right]$$

$$= (1.333)(1 - .566) = (1.333)(.434) = .58$$

[a]An item is scored 1 if it is answered correctly; 0 otherwise.
[b]The mean and variance are computed in Appendix I.

B. Computing KR21

Pupils	Total score[a] (X)
Alan	1
Isaac	2
Leslie	2
Miriam	0
Rebecca	3
Robert	4

$M = 2.0$; $(SD_x)^2 = 1.667$

$$KR21 = \left[\frac{k}{k-1}\right]\left[1 - \frac{M(k-M)}{k(SD_x)^2}\right]$$

$$= \left[\frac{4}{4-1}\right]\left[1 - \frac{2(4-2)}{4(1.667)}\right]$$

$$= (1.333)\left[1 - \frac{4}{6.668}\right]$$

$$= (1.333)(1 - .600)$$

$$= .53$$

[a]The mean and variance are computed in Appendix I.

C. Comparing the values of various reliability estimates for the same test[a]

Estimating procedure	Numerical value
Spearman-Brown	.82[b]
Rulon	.80[b]
KR20	.58
KR21	.53

[a]See Appendix I also.
[b]Based on an odd-even split.

FIGURE J.3 **Example of how to compute a coefficient alpha reliability estimate for a set of essay questions or judges' ratings.**

Persons	Questions or judges				Total score (X)
	I	**II**	**III**	**IV**	
Aaron	4	3	4	4	15
Dorcas	2	5	5	5	17
Katherine	3	5	5	3	16
Kenneth	1	3	1	1	6
Lee	5	5	5	4	19
Peter	4	3	4	4	15
$(SD_i)^2$ values	1.81	1.00	2.00	1.58	$(SD_x)^2 = 16.89$

$\Sigma(SD_i)^2 = 1.81 + 1.00 + 2.00 + 1.58 = 6.39$

$$\alpha = \left[\frac{k}{k-1}\right]\left[1 - \frac{\Sigma(SD_i)^2}{(SD_x)^2}\right] = \left[\frac{4}{4-1}\right]\left[1 - \frac{6.39}{16.89}\right] = (1.33)(1-.38) = (1.33)(.62) = .82$$

FIGURE J.4 **Example of computing the general Spearman-Brown reliability estimate.**

A. Formula

$$r_{nn} = \frac{nr_{11}}{1 + (n-1)r_{11}}$$

B. Example

Q. A teacher has a 10-item test with reliability coefficient equal to 0.40. What would be the reliability if the teacher added 15 new items similar to those currently on the test?

A. Here $r_{11} = 0.40$ and $n = \frac{25}{10} = 2.5$. (The new test would be 25 items long, hence, 2.5 times as long as the original test.) Thus, the new test reliability is:

$$r_{nn} = \frac{(2.5)(0.40)}{1 + (2.5 - 1)(0.40)}$$

$$= \frac{1.00}{1 + 0.6} = \frac{1.0}{1.6} = .625$$

C. Results of applying the formula to various values of r_{11} and n

Original reliability	Number of times original test is lengthened (n)				
	2	**3**	**4**	**5**	**6**
.10	.18	.25	.31	.36	.40
.20	.33	.43	.50	.56	.60
.30	.46	.56	.63	.68	.72
.40	.57	.67	.73	.77	.80
.50	.67	.75	.80	.83	.86
.60	.75	.82	.86	.88	.90
.70	.82	.88	.90	.92	.93
.80	.89	.92	.94	.95	.96
.90	.95	.96	.97	.98	.98

FIGURE J.5 **Example of how to compute percentage agreement and the kappa coefficient. The kappa coefficient adjusts the percent agreement for chance agreement that is not related to the assessment procedure.**

A. General layout of the data

| | | Results from Test 1 | | |
		Mastery	Nonmastery	Marginal totals
Results from Test 2	Mastery	a	b	$a + b$
	Nonmastery	c	d	$c + d$
	Marginal totals	$a + c$	$b + d$	$N = a + b + c + d$

B. Formulas

P_A = total percentage agreement in figure

$$= \frac{a}{N} + \frac{d}{N} = \frac{a + d}{N}$$

P_c = percent agreement expected because of the composition of the group

$$= \left(\frac{a + b}{N} \times \frac{a + c}{N} \right) + \left(\frac{c + d}{N} \times \frac{b + d}{N} \right)$$

$$\kappa = \frac{P_A - P_c}{1 - P_c}$$

C. Numerical example

| | | Results from Test 1 | | |
		Mastery	Nonmastery	Marginal totals
Results from Test 2	Mastery	11	4	15
	Nonmastery	1	9	10
	Marginal totals	12	13	25

$$P_A = \frac{11}{25} + \frac{9}{25} = \frac{11 + 9}{25} = \frac{20}{25} = 0.80$$

$$P_C = \left(\frac{15}{25} \times \frac{12}{25} \right) + \left(\frac{10}{25} \times \frac{13}{25} \right) = \frac{180}{625} + \frac{130}{625} = \frac{310}{625} = 0.50$$

$$\kappa = \frac{0.8 - 0.50}{1 - 0.50} = \frac{0.30}{0.50} = 0.60$$

A Limited List of Published Tests

FIGURE K.1 **Selected published tests.**

Title	Age/Grade level	Publisher[1]	Review[2]
Multilevel survey achievement batteries (group)			
• Iowa Tests of Basic Skills, Forms K, L, M	K–9	RP	**11**:184, **14**:159
• Iowa Tests of Educational Development, Forms K, L, M, A, B	Gr. 9–12	RP	**10**:156, **14**:160, **16**
• Metropolitan Achievement Tests, 8th Ed.	Gr. 1–12	HEM	**12**:232, **16**
• Stanford Early School Achievement Test	K–1.5	HEM	**11**:378
• Stanford Achievement Test, 10th Ed.	Gr. 2–12	HEM	**12**:371, **13**:292, **16**
• TerraNova, 2nd Ed.	K–12	CTBMH	**13**:40, **16**
• TerraNova, Comprehensive Tests of Basic Skills, 5th Ed.	K–12	CTBMH	**11**:81, **14**:383
• Tests of Achievement and Proficiency, Forms K, L, M	Gr. 9–12	RP	**11**:455, **14**:396
Multilevel survey achievement batteries (individual)			
• Peabody Individual Achievement Test—R	K–12	AGS	**11**:280, **14**:279
• Kaufman Test of Educational Achievement—R	1–12	AGS	**10**:161, **14**:191
• Wide Range Achievement Test—3	K–12	JA	**10**:389, **12**:414, **16**
Multilevel criterion-referenced achievement tests			
• Degrees of Reading Power—Revised	1–12	TASA	**12**:101, **14**:111
• Key Math—Revised	K–9	AGS	**11**:191, **14**:194
Reading survey tests			
• Gates–MacGinite Reading Tests, 4th Ed.	K–12	RP	**11**:146, **16**
Reading diagnostic tests			
• Stanford Diagnostic Reading Test, 4th Ed.	Gr. 1–12	HEM	**9**:1178, **13**:294
• Woodcock Diagnostic Reading Battery	K–Adult	RP	**10**:391, **14**:422
Adaptive behavior inventories			
• Vineland Adaptive Behavior Scales–II	0–90 yrs.	AGS	**10**:381
Individual general ability/scholastic aptitude tests			
• Bayley Scales of Infant Development, 2nd Ed.	1–42 mo.	HEM	**10**:26, **13**:29
• Columbia Mental Maturity Scale	3–10 yrs.	HEM	**8**:210
• Draw A Person: A Quantitative Scoring System	5–17 yrs.	PC	**11**:114
• Kaufman Assessment Battery for Children, 2nd Ed.	2–12 yrs.	AGS	**9**:562, **16**
• McCarthy Scales of Children's Abilities	2–8 yrs.	HEM	**9**:671
• Peabody Picture Vocabulary Test—III	2–Adult	AGS	**9**:926, **14**:280
• Porteus Mazes	3–Adult	PC	**9**:965
• Raven Progressive Matrices	5–Adult	PC	**9**:1007
• Stanford-Binet Intelligence Scale, 5th Ed.	2–Adult	RP	**10**:342, **16**
• System of Multicultural Pluralistic Assessment	5–11 yrs.	PC	**9**:1222
• Wechsler Adult Intelligence Scale—3rd Ed.	16–89 yrs.	PC	**9**:1350, **14**:415
• Wechsler Intelligence Scale for Children, 4th Ed.	6–16 yrs.	HEM	**12**:412, **16**
• Wechsler Preschool and Primary Scale of Intelligence, 3rd Ed.	3–7 yrs.	PC	**11**:466, **16**

[1] See Appendix L for names and addresses of publishers.
[2] The boldface number is the number of the *MMY* volume; the number after the colon is the entry number. If the entry number is missing, it was not available at the time of publication

FIGURE K.1 *(Continued)*

Group-administered tests of scholastic aptitude			
• ACT Assessment	Gr. 10–12	ACT	**12**:139
• Closed High School Placement Test	Gr. 8	STS	**8**:26, **14**:80
• Cognitive Abilities Test—Form 6	K–12	RP	**10**:66, **13**:71, **16**
• Kuhlman Anderson Tests	Gr. K–12	STS	**9**:579
• Otis-Lennon School Ability Test, 7th Ed.	Gr. K–12	PC	**11**:274
• College Board SAT Reasoning Test	Gr. 121	ETS	**9**:244
Multiple aptitude batteries			
• Differential Aptitude Test, 5th Ed.	Gr. 7–12	PC	**12**:118
• Flanagan Aptitude Classification Test	Gr. 9–12	SRA	**7**:675
• USES Nonreading Aptitude Test	Gr. 9–Adult	USGPO	**9**:1305
Vocational interest inventories			
• Hall Occupational Orientation Inventory, 2nd Ed.	Gr. 3–Adult	STS	**12**:175, **16**
• Harrington-O'Shea Career Decision-Making System, 4th Ed.	Gr. 7–Adult	AGS	**12**:179, **16**
• Jackson Vocational Interest Survey—Revised	Gr. 9–Adult	SAS	**14**:187, **15**:129
• Kuder Occupational Interest Survey—R, Form DD	Gr. 10–12	CTBMH	**10**:167
• Kuder General Interest Survey, Form E	Gr. 6–12	CTBMH	**12**:209
• Self-Directed Search, Forms R, E, & CP, 4th Ed.	Gr. 7–Adult	PAR	**14**:345
• Strong Interest Inventory, 4th Ed.	16 yrs.–Adult	CPP	**12**:374, **15**:248.

List of Test Publishers and Their Websites

See the current *Mental Measurements Yearbook*, or *MMY*, the Buros Institute of Mental Measurements (http://www.unl.edu/buros), or the Association of Test Publishers (http://testpublishers.org) for additional names and addresses.

American College Testing Program (ACT)
2201 N. Dodge Street
PO Box 168
Iowa City, IA 52243
http://www.act.org

American Council on Education (ACE)
Suite 800
1 Dupont Circle
Washington, DC 20036
http://www.acenet.edu

American Guidance Service (AGS)
4201 Woodland Road
PO Box 99
Circle Pines, MN 55014-1796
http://www.agsnet.com

CTB/McGraw-Hill (CTBMH) Publishers Test Service
20 Ryan Ranch Road
Monterey, CA 93940-5703
http://www.ctb.com

Center for Applied Linguistics (CAL)
4646 40th Street NW
Washington, DC 20016
http://www.cal.org

The College Board (CEEB)
45 Columbus Avenue
New York, NY 10023-6992
http://www.collegeboard.org

CPP (formerly Consulting Psychologist Press)
1055 Joaquin Road, Suite 200
Mountain View, CA 94043
http://www.cpp-db.com

Educational and Industrial Testing Service (EDITS Online)
http://www.edits.net

Educational Records Bureau, Inc. (ERB)
220 East 42nd Street
New York, NY 10017
http://www.erbtest.org

Educational Testing Service (ETS)
Rosedale Road
PO Box 6736
Princeton, NJ 08541-6736
http://www.ets.org

Harcourt Educational Measurement (HEM)
19500 Bulverde Boulevard
San Antonio, TX 78259-3701
http://www.harcourtassessment.com

Institute for Personality and Ability Testing (IPAT)
PO Box 1188
Champaign, IL 61824-1188
http://www.ipat.com

PRO-ED (PE)
8700 Shoal Creek Boulevard
Austin, TX 78757-6897
http://www.proedinc.com

The Psychological Corporation (PC)
19500 Bulverde Boulevard
San Antonio, TX 78259-3701
http://www.PsychCorp.com

Riverside Publishing Co. (RP)
425 Spring Lake Drive
Itasca, IL 60143-2079
http://www.riverpub.com

Scholastic Testing Service, Inc. (STS)
480 Meyer Road
Bensenville, IL 60106
http://www.ststesting.com

Scott, Foresman (SF)
1900 East Lake Avenue
Glenview, IL 60025-2055
http://www.scottforesman.com

Sigma Assessment Systems (SAS)
PO Box 610984
Port Huron, MI 48061-0984
http://www.sigmaassessmentsystems.com

Slosson Educational Publishers, Inc.
538 Buffalo Road
PO Box 280
East Aurora, NY 14052-0280
http://www.slosson.com

Touchstone Applied Science Associates, Inc.
4 Hardscrabble Heights

PO Box 382
Brewster, NY 10509-0382
http://www.tasa.com

United States Government Printing Office (USGPO)
732 North Capital Street NW
Washington, DC 20401
http://www.gpo.gov

Western Psychological Services (WPS)
12031 Wilshire Boulevard
Los Angeles, CA 90025-1251
http://www.wpspublish.com

absolute achievement: The achievement of specific learning targets and content without regard to what other students have achieved. See also **criterion-referencing** and **relative achievement**.

absolute standards grading: Evaluating student progress by comparing the student's achievement against content standards, performance standards, or learning targets rather than against the achievement of other students. See also **criterion-referencing**.

abstract/visual reasoning subtests: A subtest of a scholastic aptitude battery that contains items in which the examinee is expected to reason using geometric shapes, sequences, and patterns.

access to assessment results: Students and parents can see all of their assessment results. Others can do so only on a need-to-know basis or by special permission of the parents or students.

accountability testing: Assessment that is used to hold individual students or school officials responsible for ensuring that students meet state standards.

achievement dimensions: The continua of knowledge, skills, and abilities that you want students to learn as a result of your teaching. See also **content achievement dimensions** and **lifelong achievement dimensions**.

action verb: An active verb that describes an observable performance in a learning target.

activity-similarity rationale for assessing interests: Interest inventories built using this rationale present the students with lists of activities that are similar to those required of persons working in certain jobs or studying certain subjects.

adaptive assessment task: A computer-assisted assessment in which a student's response to one task will determine what the next presentation will be.

adaptive behavior: Behaviors indicating a child can cope with the normal social and physical environment that is appropriate for his or her age, especially outside the school context.

adaptive testing strategy: An assessment method that makes the next stage in the assessment dependent on whether a student's response to the previous stage was correct or incorrect.

affective domain: A collection of educational outcomes and learning targets that focus on feelings, interests, attitudes, dispositions, and emotional states.

affective saliency: The degree of emotionality with which students hold particular attitudes.

age-based scores versus grade-based scores: *Age-based scores* use as a norm group only those students with the chronological age that is typical for a particular grade placement. *Grade-based scores* include all students at a particular grade placement, regardless of their chronological age.

algorithmic knowledge assessment: A diagnostic assessment that identifies whether a student knows the proper algorithm or procedure to follow to complete a given problem or task correctly. See also **component competencies of problem solving**.

alignment studies: Empirical studies involving the collection of ratings from trained judges and summaries of students' responses to testing. Their aim is to describe, as objectively as possible, the degree to which the actual test items on a state's assessment instrument(s) are matched to the educational content and performance standards set by that state.

"all of the above": A possible alternative or option for a multiple-choice item; all of the preceding alternatives are correct answers to this multiple-choice question.

alternate-forms reliability coefficient [delayed]: A procedure for estimating reliability that is used when one wants to study how scores are influenced by differences in both content and testing occasion. The procedure is to administer to the same group of students one form of an assessment on one occasion and an alternate form on another occasion.

alternate-forms reliability coefficient [same occasion]: A procedure for estimating reliability that is used when one wants to study the consistency of scores from two different, but comparable, samples of test items that were administered on the same occasion. The procedure is to administer two forms of an assessment to the same group of students on the same (or nearly the same) occasion and to correlate the scores. Also known as the *equivalent-forms reliability coefficient* or the *parallel-forms coefficient*.

alternate solution strategies: Different, but equally correct, procedures or methods for obtaining a correct solution to a problem or for producing the correct product.

alternative assessment: Usually refers to performance assessment. The "alternative" in alternative assessment usually means in opposition to standardized achievement tests and to multiple-choice (true-false, matching, completion) item formats. See also **performance assessment**.

alternatives: The list of choices from which an examinee answering a multiple-choice item must select the correct or best answer. Also known as *choices, options*, and *response choices*.

ambiguous alternatives: A type of multiple-choice and matching exercise item-writing flaw that results in *upper group students* being unable to distinguish between the correct answer and one or more of the distractors in a multiple-choice item (Sax, 1989).

analysis: A category in the Bloom et al. (1956) *Taxonomy of Educational Objectives*. Learning targets in this category ask students to identify the parts of a piece of information, explain the interconnections and relationships among the parts, or explain the organization or structure of the piece of information. See also **application, comprehension, evaluation, knowledge,** and **synthesis**.

analytic rubric, analytic scoring rubric: A rule that you use to rate or score the separate parts or traits (dimensions) of a student's product or process first, then sum these part scores to obtain a total score. See also **holistic rubric** and **rubrics**.

analyze arguments: The ability to identify the details of the arguments presented in verbal statements, discussions, scientific or political reports, cartoons, and so on.

annotated holistic rubrics: Rules you use to conduct holistic rating of a student's product or process, then rate or describe a few characteristics that are strengths and weaknesses to support your holistic rating. See also **rubrics**.

annotated holistic scoring rubric: See **annotated holistic rubrics**.

knowledge assessment, schematic knowledge assessment, and **strategic knowledge assessment.**

comprehension: A category in the Bloom et al. (1956) *Taxonomy of Educational Objectives.* Learning targets in this category ask students to paraphrase or explain concepts in their own words. See also **application, analysis, evaluation, knowledge,** and **synthesis.**

computer-prepared narrative reports: An automated report of a school's, a grade's, or an individual's performance on a standardized test.

concept: A name that represents a category of things such as persons, objects, events, or relationships.

concept mapping: A graphical way to represent how a student understands relationships among the major concepts in a subject.

concrete concept: A class, whose members have in common one or more physical, tangible qualities that can be heard, seen, tasted, felt, or smelled.

concurrent validity evidence: The extent to which individuals' current status on a criterion can be estimated from their current performance on an assessment instrument. See also **predictive validity evidence.**

confidentiality: The right of students to have their test results kept private, known only to authorized persons, and not released to those outside the school except by student-approved release.

constructed-response format: A test question in which the examinee is expected to respond to an item using his or her own ideas and words rather than choosing an answer from among two or more options.

construction test of personality: A type of personality test in which the examinee tells a story about a picture.

content achievement dimensions: Continua that include the specific declarative and procedural learning targets you want students to achieve.

content analysis of the responses: An analysis of students' responses to written open-ended items. Responses are organized into meaningful categories to identify in the class common errors and misconceptions.

content centered: A criterion for a well-stated learning target: A learning target should describe the specific subject-matter content to which a student should apply the performance learned. See also **performance centered** and **student centered.**

content relevance: Validity evidence that focuses on whether the assessment tasks belong in the user's definition of what the assessment should include.

content representativeness: Validity evidence that focuses on whether the assessment tasks are representative of a larger domain of performance.

content standards: Statements about the subject-matter facts, concepts, principles, and so on that students are expected to learn.

content-based method for grading: See **quality-level method for grading.**

context-dependent items: See **interpretive exercises.**

context-dependent tasks: See **interpretive exercises.**

continuous assessment: The daily process by which you gather information about students' progress in achieving the curriculum's learning targets (Nitko, 1995).

continuum of learning: See **achievement dimensions.**

correct-answer variety: A multiple-choice item format in which one of the alternatives is unarguably the correct answer to the question or problem posed by the stem.

correcting records: The professional responsibility to correct mistakes in school records, especially about student assessments. See also **purging records.**

correction for guessing formulas: An algebraic formula used with response-choice items for adjusting each student's raw score by estimating how many items on which the examinee guessed. See also **response-choice items.**

correction variety of true-false items: An item format that requires students to judge a proposition, as does the true-false variety, but students are also required to correct any false statement to make it true.

correlation coefficient: A statistical index that quantifies, on a scale of −1 to +1, the degree of relationship between the scores from one assessment and the scores from another.

credentialing: Decision processes in which persons who meet specified requirements (usually involving passing a test or other assessment) are awarded a certain status and given a credential.

criteria for judging a planned assessment: These include (a) matching tasks to learning targets, (b) covering important skills, (c) selecting appropriate assessment task formats, (d) making assessments understandable, (e) satisfying validity criteria, (f) using the appropriate length of the assessment, (g) ensuring equivalence, and (h) identifying appropriate complexity and difficulty of tasks.

criterion-referenced grading framework: The assignment of grades by comparing a student's performance to a defined set of standards to be achieved, targets to be learned, or knowledge to be acquired.

criterion-referencing: A score-interpreting framework that compares a student's test performance against the domain of performances that the assessment samples to answer the question, "How much of the targeted learning did this student achieve?"

critical thinking: This is "reasonable, reflective thinking that is focused on deciding what to believe or do" (Ennis, 1985, p. 54). Critical-thinking educational goals focus on developing students who are fair-minded, are objective, reach sound conclusions, and are disposed toward seeking clarity and accuracy (Marzano et al., 1988).

curricular relevance: Validity evidence that focuses on the degree of overlap between a specific curriculum and the specific tasks on a particular assessment.

deadwood alternative: An alternative of a multiple-choice or matching item that no examinee chooses and, hence, is nonfunctional.

debate: A special type of oral performance that pits one student against another to logically argue issues. Assessment focuses on the logical and persuasive quality of the argument and the rebuttals.

deciding on an action: One of the abilities in critical thinking and problem solving.

decision consistency index: A statistical index used to describe the consistency of decisions made from scores rather than the consistency of the scores themselves.

declarative knowledge: The facts, ideas, generalizations, and theories you want a student to learn.

decontextualized knowledge: The use of knowledge without its real-world context or application.

defined concept: The name of a class, the members of which can be defined in the same way by attributes that are not tangible and which frequently involve relationships among other concepts.

Sometimes called *abstract* or *relational concepts* (Gagné, 1970). See also **concept** and **concrete concept**.

deficits in learning: Student learning needs identified by diagnostic assessment. Depending on the diagnostic approach used, deficits in learning can be low standing, relative to peers, on certain content or low performance on measures of prerequisite skills needed for particular learning targets.

degree of authenticity: The extent to which a test task represents an important real-world activity. See also **authentic assessment**.

demonstration: An on-demand complex performance assessment in which a student shows he or she can use knowledge and skills to complete a well-defined, "right or best way to do it" task.

derived score: A score obtained by statistically transforming a raw score in a way that increases its norm-referenced meaning. See also **percentile rank, raw score**, and **standard score**.

descriptive graphic rating scale: An improved version of the graphic rating scale in which the ambiguous single words (e.g., *frequently*) are replaced with short behavioral descriptions of the various points along the scale. See also **rating scale** and **graphic rating scale**.

developmental learning targets: Skills and abilities that are continuously developed throughout life. Learning targets such as these are more aptly stated at a somewhat higher level of abstraction than mastery learning targets. See also **mastery learning targets**.

diagnostic assessment: Assessment of a student's learning difficulties that serves two related purposes: (a) to identify which learning targets a student has not mastered and (b) to suggest possible causes or reasons why the student has not mastered the learning targets.

dichotomous item scoring: Scoring an item in such a way that there are only two possible scores.

differential item functioning (DIF): An approach to studying item fairness at the level of individual test items rather than looking simply at average differences in an item's performance. The approach studies whether persons of the same ability, but from two different groups, performed differently on the item.

dimensions: See **achievement dimensions**.

DIQ-**score:** A type of normalized standard score, called a deviation IQ score. The distribution of such scores has a mean of 100 and a standard deviation of 15 (or 16 in some tests).

direct assessment: An assessment procedure that allows a student's learning target achievement to be expressed directly as it is intended by the learning target.

direction and intensity of attitude: Two of the ways students' attitudes may differ. Direction means that the attitude may be positive or negative. Intensity refers to the strength of feeling of a student's attitude. See also **attitudes**.

directions for matching: The instructions for a matching exercise that explain the basis the student is expected to use in matching the premises with the correct responses.

disaggregate the test results: To separate the test results for the total population of students in order to report separately for subgroups of students such as students who are poor or minorities, students with limited English proficiency, and students with disabilities, in addition to reporting on the total population.

dispositions toward critical thinking: The tendencies or habitual uses of critical thinking abilities.

distractor rationale taxonomy: A way to categorize the developmental level represented by an incorrect response choice in order to obtain diagnostic information from students' wrong answers to multiple-choice items (King, Gardner, Zucker, & Jorgensen, 2004).

distractors: Alternatives in a multiple-choice item that are not the correct or best answer to the question or problem posed by the stem, but that appear to be correct or plausible answers to less knowledgeable examinees.

domain of achievement: A description of all possible tasks that might be appropriate for assessing achievement for a particular set of learning targets.

double negatives: The use of two negating forms of words in close sequence in a test item.

dramatization: A performance assessment method that combines verbalizations, oral and elocution skills, and movement performances.

due process: Whether a person was treated fairly before a judgment was made against the person. *Substantive due process* concerns the appropriateness of the requirement (e.g., passing the test) and the purpose (e.g., maintaining high-quality teaching). *Procedural due process* focuses on the fairness with which the examinee was treated in the proceeding that led to a judgment.

educational defensibility principle of test preparation: "No test preparation practice should increase students' test scores without simultaneously increasing student mastery of the content domain tested" (Popham, 1991, p. 13).

educational goals: Statements of "those human activities which contribute to the functioning of a society (including the functioning of an individual *in* society), and which can be acquired through learning" (Gagné, Briggs, & Wagner, 1988, p. 39).

effective communication: A category of learning targets that asks students to demonstrate their communication skills such as communicating to the right audience, using the most appropriate communication method for the purpose at hand, and developing appropriate communication products.

electronic portfolio: A portfolio that is crafted as an electronic folder on a computer, a removable disk, or on a Web page. Entries are digitized files and may include text documents, photos, video clips, and other digitized material.

elements of a complete test plan: These include (a) content topics to assess, (b) types of thinking skills to assess, (c) specific learning targets to assess, and (d) emphasis (number of tasks or points) for each learning target to be assessed. See also **table of specifications**.

emotionality: The bodily and autonomic arousal that accompanies test anxiety. See also **four factors of test anxiety**.

empirical norming dates: Refers to the dates during the school year when tests were actually administered to students during the process of developing the grade-equivalent scores.

empirically documented tests: Refers to standardized tests that have data to support the development of the test, the selection of items, claims to reliability, and claims to validity.

empirically keyed scales: Interest inventory scales made up of items especially selected because research has shown that persons' responses to these items clearly differentiate between those who are currently and happily employed in a particular occupation and people in general.

enhanced multiple-choice items: Multiple-choice items that assess combinations of skills and knowledge in ways that require students to apply what they know.

equivalence: In the context of classroom assessment, the degree to which past and present students are required to know and perform tasks of similar (but not identical) complexity and difficulty to get the same grade on the same content of the units. See also **table of specifications**.

error score: The score an examinee would obtain if you could quantify the amount of error in the examinee's obtained score. See also **obtained score** and **true score**.

ethical principles: Rules or guidelines that suggest what is right or wrong with students' behaviors—especially with regard to how students are treated as far as testing and evaluation are concerned.

ethical test preparation practices: The range of practice activities that you can provide your students to improve their performance on an assessment and still claim that the students' test results are a valid assessment of their achievement in the broader curriculum domain for your school district or state.

ethnic and gender stereotyping: Depiction of races or genders in assessment material that is subtly or blatantly offensive to any subgroup of students or depicts races or genders in over-simplified inappropriate ways. See also **role stereotype**.

ETS Test Collection: Educational Testing Service database of approximately 20,000 tests and other assessment instruments. It contains information on both published and unpublished instruments.

evaluation: The process of making value judgments about the worth of a student's product or performance. Also, a category in the Bloom et al. (1956) *Taxonomy of Educational Objectives*. See also **application, analysis, comprehension, knowledge,** and **synthesis**.

evaluation variables: See **assessment variables**.

everyday understandings of terms and phenomena: Students' understandings of meanings that do not have a sound scientific or technical explanation. These explanations may be partly correct or entirely incorrect. See also **schema (schemata)**.

exemplar: The individual members of the concept category (also called *instances* or *examples*). Also, examples of student work that illustrate or exemplify different levels on a scoring rubric.

expectancy table: A grid or two-way table that shows how criterion scores are related to test scores. It describes how likely it is for a person with a specific score to attain each criterion score level.

experiment: An on-demand performance used to assess a student's ability to plan, conduct, and interpret the results of an empirical research study that focuses on answering specific research questions or on investigating specific research hypotheses.

experiment-interpretation items: A type of context-dependent exercise in which an experiment and its results are presented to the examinee and the examinee must explain the results or choose the correct explanation from among several explanations presented.

expository writing: A type of writing that has as its purpose to give an explanation to and information for the reader.

expressed interests: What students will tell you their career or occupational interests are when you ask them directly. See also **interests, inventoried interests, manifested interests,** and **tested interests**.

extended normalized standard score: A type of normalized standard score that tells the location of a raw score on an achievement scale that spans multiple grades anchored to a lower grade reference group.

extended response essay item: A type of essay question that requires students to write essays in which they are free to express their own ideas, to show interrelationships among their

ideas, and to organize their own answers. Usually no single answer is considered correct.

external assessment procedure: An assessment procedure that comes from outside the local school district and was not crafted by teachers in the district. A state's assessment and a standardized test are two examples.

external structure: Validity evidence that focuses on the pattern of relationships between assessment scores, and external variables or criteria. See also **internal structure**.

external uses of test results: Uses of standardized test results for purposes outside the classroom. Among external uses of test results are (Hieronymus, 1976) the following: (a) to help school officials make decisions about curriculum or instructional changes; (b) to help educational evaluators describe the relative effectiveness of alternate methods of instruction and some of the factors moderating their effectiveness; (c) to help educational researchers describe the relative effectiveness of innovations or experiments in education; and (d) to help school superintendents describe to school boards the relative effectiveness of the local educational enterprise.

extrapolation: The process of estimating an unknown number that lies outside the range of available data. Used extensively with standardized achievement tests to estimate the grade-equivalent scores of examinees whose raw scores lie well below or above the available data.

facial bias: According to this approach, an assessment is biased if it contains offensive stereotypes in its use of language or in pictures in the assessment tasks and materials (Cole & Nitko, 1981).

failing grade: The letter grade that indicates that a student has achieved far below the expectations for that grade level in a subject. The letter grade associated with a failing grade is usually F.

failing work versus failing to try: Two categories of student failure (Brookhart, 1999): (a) doing work that is of very poor quality (i.e., *failing work*) and (b) not doing the work at all (i.e., *failing to try*).

fair assessment or test: An assessment or test that provides scores that (a) are interpreted and used appropriately for specific purposes, (b) do not have negative or adverse consequences as a result of the way they are interpreted or used, and (c) promote appropriate values.

feedback to students: Information about how a student can improve his or her work, usually given by a teacher to a student on the basis of observation and diagnosis of performance on *formative assessments* or *classroom activities*. See also **formative uses of assessments**.

figural reasoning: The ability to reason using geometric figures: to infer relationships among the figures, to identify the similarities and differences among figures, and to identify progressions and predict the next figure in the progression.

filler alternative: A type of multiple-choice item-writing flaw in which a nonplausible alternative is added to an item primarily for the purpose of increasing the number of alternatives rather than as a useful functioning distractor.

fixed-percentage method for grading: Assigning grades by using percentages as bases for marking and grading papers. The relationship between percentage correct and letter grade is arbitrary.

focusing the item: Asking a direct question or writing the item in a way that the specific question the student is to answer is clear.

foils: See **distractors**.

forced-choice item format: A technique used by interest inventories that presents activities in items in sets of three (triads). These items ask the student to mark the one activity in the triad that the student most ("M") likes and the one activity the student least ("L") likes. This is equivalent to asking a student to rank the three activities from most liked to least liked.

formative evaluation of schools, programs, or materials: Judgment about the worth of curricula, materials, and programs made while they are under development leading to suggestions for ways to redesign, refine, or improve them. See also **summative evaluation of schools, programs, or materials**.

formative evaluation of students' achievement: Judgment about the quality of students' achievement made while the students are still in the process of learning. Such judgments help you guide a student's next learning steps. See also **summative evaluation of students' achievement**.

formative uses of assessments: Using assessment results to improve your teaching and to help you guide students' learning. See also **summative uses of assessment**.

four factors of test anxiety: Students' anxiety reactions to assessment on four related factors: tension, worry, test-irrelevant thinking, and bodily reactions (Sarason, 1984).

four principles for validation: Rules about interpretations, uses, values, and consequences that help you judge whether your assessment results have sufficient validity for their intended purposes.

frequency: The number of persons that have a particular score.

frequency distribution: A table that shows the number of persons in a group having each possible score.

frequency polygon: A line graph of a frequency distribution.

functional alternatives: Response choices in a multiple-choice item that work effectively as distractors or correct answers. If no examinee in the lower scoring group chooses a particular alternative, it is considered nonfunctional. See also **distractors**.

gender representation: The number and ways that males and females are discussed or pictured in test items. See also **role stereotype**.

gender stereotype: See **role stereotype**.

general learning targets: Statements of expected learning outcomes derived from educational goals that are more specific than the goals but not specific enough to be useful as classroom learning targets. See also **educational goals** and **specific learning targets**.

general scoring rubric: Guideline for scoring that applies across many different tasks, not just to one specific task. It may be used in its generic format or serve as a general framework for developing more specific rubrics. Also called *generic scoring rubric*.

general versus specific intellectual skills: *General intellectual skills* are a student's overall abilities to engage successfully in academic learning in general or on the average. *Specific intellectual skills* are the student's abilities to engage successfully in learning one subject or one academic area.

generalizability of assessment results: Validity evidence that focuses on the extent to which students' scores on a test can be generalized to their performance on the broader curriculum of the school district or state.

grade mean equivalent: A norm-referenced score that tells the grade placement of a group's average expanded scale score.

gradebook program: A computer program combining a spreadsheet and database that allows you to enter students' names and grades and then automatically calculates averages and letter grades.

grade-equivalent score *(GE)*: A norm-referenced growth scale score that tells the grade placement at which a raw score is average. A grade-equivalent score is reported as a decimal fraction, such as 3.4. The whole number part of the score refers to a grade level, and the decimal part refers to a month of the school year within that grade level.

grading: The process of summing up students' achievement in a subject through the use of letters such as A, B, C, D, and F.

grading for summative purposes: Assigning grades for the purposes of providing you, other teachers, school officials, students, parents, postsecondary educational institutions, and potential employers with a report about how well a student has achieved the curriculum learning targets.

grading framework: A logically consistent way of conceptualizing the meaning of grades that is well reasoned and consistent with your teaching approach.

grading on a curve: A method for assigning grades that ranks students' marks from highest to lowest, and assigns grades (A, B, C, etc.) on the basis of this ranking. See also **ranking scores**.

grading variables: The subset of variables, selected from among all the reporting variables, on which you may base your grades (Frisbie & Waltman, 1992). You use the grading variables to describe a student's accomplishments in the subject. See also **reporting variables**.

grammatical clue: A type of multiple-choice and matching item flaw in which the correct grammatical relationship between words in the stem and words in the correct alternate clue the examinee as to which alternative is correct. Similarly, incorrect grammatical relationships between words in the stem and distractors clue the examinee that those distractors can be eliminated from consideration.

graph and table reading abilities: The abilities needed to understand and use information presented in a table or a graph.

graphic rating scale: A rating scale that contains an unbroken line to represent the particular achievement dimension and on which you rate a student's performance or product. See also **rating scale** and **descriptive graphic rating scale**.

greater-less-same items: A multiple-choice-item format that presents an examinee with a pair of concepts, phrases, quantities, and so on that have a greater-than, same-as, or less-than relationship and requires the examinee to identify what that relationship is.

grouped frequency distribution: A table showing the number of persons having specified intervals of scores. Unlike a frequency distribution, a grouped frequency distribution organizes the score scale into intervals, and then displays the number of persons with scores in each interval. See also **frequency distribution**.

group project: A long-term performance activity that requires two or more students to work together. The major purpose of a group project *as an assessment technique* is to evaluate whether students can work together in cooperative and appropriate ways to create a high-quality product. See also **individual project** and **project**.

group-referenced grading: See **norm-referenced grading**.

growth and learning-progress portfolio: A portfolio containing a selection of a sequence of a student's work that demonstrates progress or development toward achieving the learning target(s). See also **portfolio** and **best-work portfolio**.

growth-standards grading framework: See **self-referenced grading framework**.

habits of mind: The types of learning targets that ask students to demonstrate their ability for self-regulation, critical thinking, and/or creative thinking.

halo effect: A type of error that occurs when a teacher's general impression of the student affects how the teacher rates the student on specific dimensions.

heterogeneous alternatives: A type of item-writing flaw in which one or more alternatives of a multiple-choice item or matching exercise do not belong to the same set of things. See also **homogeneous alternatives**.

heuristic: Any one of several general strategies that may help solve a given problem.

high-quality information: Assessment information that has high validity for the decisions for which you want to use it.

high-stakes assessments (tests): Assessments (or tests) of which the results are used for decisions that result in serious consequences for school administrators, teachers, or students.

histogram: A bar graph of a frequency distribution in which each frequency is represented by a rectangle. See also **frequency distribution**.

holistic rubric, holistic scoring rubric: Rubric that requires a teacher to rate or score a student's product or process as a whole without first scoring parts or components separately. See also **analytic rubric** and **rubrics**.

homogeneous alternatives; homogeneous premises and responses: A desirable item-writing practice in which each alternative of a multiple-choice or matching exercise is a member of the same set of "things," *and* each alternative is appropriate to the question asked or problem posed by the stem or premises.

homogeneous tasks: All of those tasks in one assessment that measure the same trait or ability.

homogeneous versus heterogeneous test: All items on a *homogeneous* test will measure one ability, whereas the items on a *heterogeneous* test will assess a combination of abilities.

IDEAL problem solver: A way of organizing general problem-solving skills into a five-stage process (Bransford & Stein, 1984):

I	Identify the problem
D	Define and represent the problem
E	Explore possible strategies
A	Act on the strategies
L	Look back and evaluate the effects of your activities

identifying assumptions: The ability to identify the unstated bases that are part of someone's reasoning about what to believe or do. A part of what is meant by critical thinking.

identifying errors in performance: A diagnostic assessment approach that identifies a student's errors, rather than reporting only a number-right total score reflecting overall performance on a particular learning target.

ill-structured problem: A type of problem in which the problem-solver must (a) organize the information to understand it; (b) clarify the problem itself; (c) obtain all the information needed, which may not be immediately available; and (d) recognize that there may be several equally correct answers.

imaginative writing: A type of writing in which the writer describes something that did not, often could not, happen.

incomplete stem: A type of multiple-choice item-writing flaw in which the stem does not contain enough information for the examinee to know what question or problem the item poses.

independent scoring of essays: When two or more raters score the same student's essay responses without consulting or collaborating with each other.

indirect assessment: A type of assessment that assesses part of the entire learning target or assesses the learning target in a context that is not intended by the learning target. See also **direct assessment**.

individual education plan (IEP): An educational plan designed by a child study team (including a teacher) and agreed to by the student's parents or guardians describing what learning targets the student should attain, the time frame for attaining them, the proposed methods for attaining them, and the methods of evaluating the student's progress in achieving the learning targets.

individual project: A long-term performance activity during which students work independently and that results in a product that is one student's work: a model, a functional object, a substantial report, or a collection. See also **group project** and **project**.

informal assessment techniques: Impromptu methods you use to gather information that guides and fine-tunes your thinking while you are teaching, to plan your next teaching activities, and to diagnose the causes of students' learning difficulties.

information processing: A category of learning targets requiring students to demonstrate different ways of gathering, synthesizing, and/or evaluating information needed for a particular purpose.

informed consent: Giving approval to release information or participate in an activity after understanding (1) the extent to which personal information will remain anonymous, (2) the extent participation is voluntary, (3) who (or what agency) is requesting the information and for what purpose, and (4) what will happen to the information after it is collected.

in-level versus out-of-level testing: *Out-of-level testing* is using a standardized test designed for a certain grade level with students above or below that level; *in-level testing* is using a standardized test designed for students at that grade level.

instructional features of an assessment procedure: Features that permit an assessment's use for classroom teaching.

instructional objective: See **specific learning targets**.

intensity of attitude: See **direction and intensity of attitude**.

interacting with others: A critical thinking strategy requiring the use of rhetorical devices to persuade, explain, or argue.

interests: A person's preferences for specific types of activities when he or she is not under external pressure. See also **attitudes** and **values**.

internal structure: Validity evidence that focuses on the interrelationships among the individual tasks (items) on an assessment, and the relationship between the individual tasks and the total scores. See also **external structure**.

interpolation: The process of finding an unknown number that is between two known numbers. Used extensively in estimating the grade-equivalent scores of students who are not tested on the empirical norming dates of a standardized achievement test.

interpretive exercises: A set of items or assessment tasks that require the student to use reading material, graphs, tables, pictures, or other material to answer the items. See also **interpretive materials**.

interpretive materials: The reading material, graphs, pictures, tables, or other material that accompany a set of items and that the examinee must use to answer the questions or problems posed by the item.

interquartile range: The difference between the third and fourth quartiles. It is the range spanned by the middle 50% of the scores. See also **quartiles.**

inter-rater reliability: A procedure for estimating reliability used when you want to study the extent to which a student would obtain the same score if a different teacher had scored the paper or rated the performance.

inventoried interests: Career and vocational interests that are identified through various paper-and-pencil tests or interest inventories. See also **interests, expressed interests, manifested interests,** and **tested interests.**

IRT pattern score: A norm-referenced expanded-scale score derived from a mathematical equation that is fit to the publisher's sample of students' item responses. *IRT* stands for *item response theory.*

item: See **task (item).**

item analysis: The process of collecting, summarizing, and using information from students' item responses to make decisions about how each item is functioning.

item analysis report (on a standardized test): A report that shows for each grade the proportion of students who answered each item on a standardized test correctly.

item bank: A file of previously used items, usually along with the statistics about each item, that can be drawn upon to create new tests.

item difficulty index (p and p^*): The fraction of the total group answering a dichotomously scored item correctly. The item difficulty for a constructed-response and performance item, denoted p^*, is simply the average score for the group for that item.

item difficulty level: See **item difficulty index (p and p^*).**

item discrimination index (D and D^*): For dichotomously scored items, D is the difference between the fraction of the upper group answering the item correctly and the fraction of the lower group answering it correctly. The discrimination index describes the extent to which a particular test item is able to differentiate the higher scoring students from the lower scoring students. See also **upper, middle, and lower scoring groups.**

item file: See **item bank.**

item response theory (IRT) score: See **IRT pattern score.**

judging credibility: The ability to evaluate the quality of the evidence someone uses in supporting a position.

judging deductions: The ability to apply logical thinking when analyzing statements and conclusions.

judging inductions: The ability to draw valid conclusions by generalizing from given information. Students who have the ability to judge inductions identify the conclusions that best explain the given evidence (Norris & Ennis, 1989).

judging value definitions: The ability to identify when inferences have been made on the basis of values, what these values are, and when to use your own values to make inferences.

key: The correct answer to any type of item or assessment task.

keyed alternative: The alternative in a multiple-choice or true-false item that is correct.

keyed answer: See **keyed alternative.**

keylist items: See **masterlist items.**

knowledge: A category in the Bloom et al. (1956) *Taxonomy of Educational Objectives.* Learning targets in this category ask students to recall information about facts, generalizations, processes and methods of doing things, theories, and so on. See also **application, analysis, comprehension, evaluation,** and **synthesis.**

knowledge structure assessment: A diagnostic assessment approach that identifies how a student (a) perceives the structure or organization of several concepts and facts of the subject, and (b) processes concepts and facts to solve problems in the subject.

Kuder-Richardson formula 20 reliability ($KR20$): A procedure for studying reliability when the focus is on consistency of scores on the same occasion and similar content, but when repeated testing or alternate forms testing are not possible. See also **coefficient alpha reliability.**

Kuder-Richardson formula 21 reliability ($KR21$): A procedure for studying reliability for the same purposes as Kuder-Richardson formula 20, except that this formula is used when the dichotomously scored test items are equally difficult, thus allowing for a simplified calculation procedure. See also **Kuder-Richardson formula 20 reliability ($KR20$).**

learning hierarchy assessment: A diagnostic assessment approach that uses the prerequisite treelike ordering of learning targets to identify which learning targets a student has mastered and which have yet to be mastered.

learning objective: See **specific learning targets.**

learning target: See **specific learning targets.**

leniency error: A type of rating error that occurs when a teacher tends to rate almost all students toward the high end of the scale and avoids using the low end. It is the opposite of a severity error. See also **severity error.**

letter grades method of reporting student progress: A summative evaluation of student achievement that uses letters (e.g., A, B, C, D, F) to describe a student's achievement in each subject area.

letter to parents method of reporting student progress: A summative evaluation letter written by a teacher to describe a student's achievement in each subject area.

lifelong achievement dimensions: A category of achievement learning targets that cut across curricula or may be useful outside school, such as complex thinking, information processing, effective communication, cooperation and collaboration, and habits of mind (Marzano et al., 1993).

linear standard scores (z, SS): Norm-referenced scores that tell the location of the raw scores in relation to the mean and standard deviation of the distribution of all scores.

linguistic knowledge assessment: A diagnostic assessment approach that identifies the key terms and key phrases a student must understand to translate the problem statement into an internal model that can be solved. See also **component competencies of problem solving.**

linked items: An item-writing flaw in which the answer to one or more items depends on obtaining the correct answer to a previous item.

linking: See **linked items.**

local norm group: See **norm group (local, national, special).**

local percentile rank: The percentile rank of a student in the distribution of scores for the school district the student attends.

logic rule method for grading: The use of a set of decision rules, based on student performance during a marking period, to assign grades. See also **quality-level method for grading** and **rubrics.**

logical error: A type of rating error that occurs when a teacher gives similar ratings on two or more dimensions of performance that the teacher believes are logically related but that are in fact unrelated.

long performance task: Performance activities that cannot be completed in a short class period but require students to work at the task over several days or months.

mandated tests: Tests that students must take because the law says they are required to do so. State assessment programs are usually mandated.

manifested interests: Students' vocational and career interests that are deduced from what a student actually does, or the activities in which the student actually participates. See also **interests, expressed interests, inventoried interests,** and **tested interests**.

map-reading abilities: The abilities needed to obtain and use information from maps.

marking period: The period over which a teacher's summative evaluation of each student's achievement in each subject area is reported to the student, parents, and school officials.

masterlist items: A matching exercise that has three parts: (a) directions to students, (b) the masterlist of options, and (c) a list or set of stems.

mastery learning targets: Statements of what students can do at the end of instruction. Sometimes these are called "can do" statements (Forsyth, 1976), specific learning outcomes, or behavioral objectives. See also **developmental learning targets**.

mastery of specific objectives: A diagnostic assessment approach that identifies the specific learning targets a student has and has not mastered. See also **learning hierarchy assessment**.

matching exercise (basic): This format presents a student with three things: (a) directions for matching, (b) a list of premises, and (c) a list of responses. The student's task is to match each premise with one of the responses, using the criteria described in the directions as a basis for matching.

maximum performance assessment: Assessment of students when you set the conditions so that students are able to earn the best score they can. See also **typical performance assessment**.

MAZE item type: Reading comprehension assessment that is a multiple-choice adaptation of the cloze reading exercise. See also **cloze reading exercise**.

mean: An average score found by summing all of the scores and dividing by their number. Also known as the *arithmetic mean*.

meaningfully arranged alternatives: Arranging the alternatives of a multiple-choice or matching exercise in logical, numerical, or alphabetical order so they will be less confusing to examinees.

measurement: A procedure for assigning numbers (usually called *scores*) to a specified attribute or characteristic of a person in such a way that the numbers describe the degree to which the person possesses the attribute. See also **assessment, evaluation,** and **test**.

measurement error: See **error score**.

median: The point on the score scale at which 50% of the scores are below and 50% are above.

median score method: A procedure for combining several component grades into a composite report card grade. All scores are converted to the same scale, usually a rubric or grade (A, B, C, D, F) scale, and the median mark is used as the composite grade.

mental age: The age at which the student's score on a scholastic aptitude test is average. This concept is no longer used in modern scholastic aptitude testing.

***Mental Measurements Yearbook* (MMYs):** A set of volumes published by the Buros Institute of Mental Measurement that contains reviews of tests published in the English language.

mental model: The way a person mentally represents or characterizes a problem before attempting to solve it.

metacognition: Knowledge of one's cognitive processes, including monitoring and regulating one's own learning.

minimum assessment-taking skills: Those skills for how to act during a test that a student needs to do his or her best.

minimum attainment method: A procedure for combining several component grades into a composite report card grade by the following process: determine which components of students' final grades are more important to demonstrating the students' achievement of the learning targets; specify, for each of these "more important" components, the minimum level of performance you will accept for each of the final grade levels; and establish rules for what levels of performance you will accept, at each final grade level, on each of the "less important" components. These rules form a set of decision rules for how to assign grades.

miskeyed items: Items for which the answer designated as correct in the answer key is wrong. An item may be miskeyed if a larger number of upper group students selects a particular wrong response.

modal-age norms: Norms that include, from among all students at a particular grade level, only those near the most typical chronological age for that grade.

mode: The most frequently occurring score in a distribution.

multilevel survey battery: A survey battery of standardized tests that spans a wide range of grades in each school subject. See also **single-level test**.

multiple marking system: A system of reporting summative evaluation of educational progress to students and parents using several kinds of symbols and marks. Multiple marking systems usually take the form of a report card and report on academic achievement, attendance, deportment, and nonacademic achievement.

multiple true-false variety of true-false items: This format looks similar to a multiple-choice item. However, instead of selecting one option as correct, the student treats every option as a separate true-false statement.

multiple-aptitude tests: Tests that assess several different abilities separately and provide an ability score for each. See also **omnibus test** and **two-score test**.

multiple-assessment strategy: Combining the results from several different types of assessments (such as homework, class performance, quizzes, projects, and tests) to improve the validity of your decisions about a student's attainments.

multiple-choice item: This item format consists of a stem that poses a question or sets a problem and a set of two or more response choices for answering the question or solving the problem. Only one of the response choices is the correct or best answer.

multiple intelligences assessment menu: A list of alternative ways to assess students that is organized so that each way corresponds to each type of intelligence in Gardner's theory.

multiple intelligences theory: Howard Gardner's (1983, 1991, 1993) theory that all persons have not one, but eight intelligences, although some persons are stronger in some of these areas than others.

narrative report method of reporting student progress: A detailed, written report describing what each student has learned in relation to the school's curriculum framework and the student's effort in class.

narrative writing: A type of writing in which the author describes something that really happened, usually a personal experience of the writer.

national norms: See **norm group (local, national, special)**.

national percentile rank: A student's percentile rank in the national sample of students who took the test.

national stanines: Stanines are scores derived from a test publisher's national norm sample. See also **stanine**.

naturally occurring performance: Performance not done at the request of a teacher or school authority but which occurs in the normal course of daily activities.

NCE-score: See **normal curve equivalent (NCE)**.

negative correlation: A type of relationship between two sets of scores that occurs when high scores on one assessment are associated with low scores on the other; low scores on one are associated with high scores on the other. See also **correlation coefficient** and **positive correlation**.

negatively discriminating item: An item that high-scoring students tend to answer incorrectly and low-scoring students tend to answer correctly.

negatively skewed distribution: A frequency distribution of scores in which the scores are piled up at the upper end of the score scale and spread thinly toward the lower end of the score scale. See also **positively skewed distribution**.

negatively worded stem: A multiple-choice stem that contains "not" or some other negative word. For example, "Which of the follow persons did NOT invent the cotton gin?"

nondiscriminating item: An item for which the number of correct discriminations equals the number of incorrect discriminations (so that an equal number of upper and lower group students answers the item correctly).

"none of the above": A multiple-choice alternative that means that none of the preceding alternatives is the correct answer to the question or problem posed by the stem.

non-paper-and-pencil task: An assessment task in which performance is not primarily evaluated by the student's written response.

nonverbal tests: Tests that elicit and assess nonverbal responses such as assembling objects, completing experiments, performing a psychomotor activity, and so on. See also **verbal tests** and **performance assessment**.

norm group (local, national, special): A well-defined group of students who have been given the same assessment under the same conditions (same time limits, directions, equipment and materials, etc.). See also **special norms**.

normal curve equivalent (NCE): A normalized standard score with a mean of 50 and a standard deviation of 21.06. This choice of standard deviation was made so the NCE-scores would span the range 1 to 99. It was developed primarily for use with federal program evaluation efforts (Tallmadge & Wood, 1976).

normal distributions: A set of theoretical distributions that takes on a bell-shaped and unimodal form through the use of a special mathematical formula.

normal growth (grade-equivalent view, percentile rank view): The *grade-equivalent view* of normal growth is that a student ought to exhibit a growth of 1.0 grade-equivalent unit from one grade to the next. Under this view, a student taking the test in second grade and scoring 1.3, for example, would need to score 2.3 in third grade, 4.3 in fifth, and so on to show "normal" or expected growth. The *percentile rank view* of normal growth is that a student shows normal growth if that student maintains the same position (i.e., percentile rank) in the norm from year to year.

normalized standard scores (z_n, T, DIQ, NCE, SAT): A category of scores in which the raw scores have been changed or transformed into other scores that are distributed more like a normal distribution.

normalizing a set of scores: The process used to transform the original raw scores in a distribution into a new set of scores that are distributed more like a normal distribution.

norm-referenced grading framework: A framework for assigning grades on the basis of how a student's performance (achievement) compares with other students in the class: Students performing better than most classmates receive the higher grades.

norm-referencing: A framework for interpreting a student's score by comparing his or her test performance with the performance of other students in a well-defined group who took the same test.

novel material: A new situation, problem, or context for applying previously learned knowledge or skills.

numbers method of reporting student progress: A summative evaluation of a student's achievement in each subject that is reported using either numbers (e.g., 5, 4, 3, 2, 1) or percentages.

numerical rating scale: A scale for which you must mentally translate judgments of quality or degree of achievement into numerical ratings.

objectivity: The degree to which two or more qualified evaluators of a student's performance will agree on what quality rating or score to assign to it.

obtained score: The scores students actually receive when you assess them. These scores include ratings from open-ended tasks such as essays, number-right scores from multiple-choice or short-answer tests, and standard scores or grade-equivalent scores from norm-referenced standardized tests. See also **error score** and **true score**.

odd-even split halves reliability coefficient: A procedure for estimating reliability when the focus is on consistency of scores on different samples of content on the same occasion, but when alternate forms have not been built. The items from one test are divided into two groups—the odd-numbered items in one group and the even-numbered in another. The full-test reliability is estimated from these two groups. See also **Spearman-Brown double length reliability formula** and **split-halves reliability coefficient**

omnibus test: A type of test containing items assessing several different abilities that comprise general scholastic aptitude, but that reports only a single score. See also **multiple-aptitude tests** and **two-score test**.

on-demand task: An assessment in which the teacher or other authority decides what and when materials should be used, specifies the instructions for performance, describes the kinds of outcomes toward which students should work, tells the students they are being assessed, and gives students opportunities to prepare themselves for the assessment.

online services: Internet services for locating tests, test reviews, and other assessment information.

open-response task: An assessment task allowing multiple correct answers. See also **closed-response task**.

optional essay questions: Presenting students with several different essays and allowing them to select which one(s) to answer.

options: See **alternatives**.

oral presentation: A performance assessment task that permits students to verbalize their knowledge and use their oral skills in the form of interviews, speeches, or other spoken activities.

overgeneralizing a concept: To identify things by a concept name when they are similar to the members of the concept class but do not actually belong to it.

overinterpreting score differences: Placing too much emphasis on small differences of students' obtained scores on a test or small differences in the obtained scores of one student on two different tests.

overlapping alternatives: A type of multiple-choice item-writing flaw in which the meaning of one alternative overlaps with or includes the meaning of another alternative.

paper-and-pencil assessments: Assessment techniques for which students write their responses to the questions. Written homework, seatwork, and tests are typical paper-and-pencil assessment techniques.

paper-and-pencil task: Assessment that requires students not only to record their answers but also to write explanations, articulate their reasoning, and express their own approaches toward solving a problem. Sometimes referred to as a *paper-and-pen* task.

parallel forms: Two forms (versions) of an assessment that are made up of tasks carefully matched to the same blueprint so the tests are as nearly alike as possible, even though they do not have any items in common.

parallel forms reliability coefficient: See also **alternate forms reliability coefficient [same occasion]**.

parent-teacher conferences method of reporting student progress: A personal meeting between the parent(s) and the teacher that involves a summative report of a student's achievement in each subject.

partial credit: Giving the student some portion of an item's maximum possible points because the student's response is partially correct.

partial knowledge: The incomplete knowledge a student possesses and uses to respond to an item.

partial ordering of students: Placing students into two or more categories; the categories themselves are ordered, but there is *no ordering of individuals within a category*.

participation: Students with disabilities have the right, and sometimes the obligation, to be assessed, including taking part in accountability assessment programs.

passage dependency: The degree to which correct answers to questions on a reading comprehension test depend on the students actually reading and comprehending the passage.

passing score: The score that identifies students who have attained the minimum level of knowledge needed to benefit from further instruction on the topic. This may vary from one learning target to the next.

Pearson product-moment correlation coefficient: A type of correlation coefficient that is the average product of the linear z-scores corresponding to the paired scores in the set being correlated. It is denoted by ρ or r. See also **correlation coefficient**.

people-similarity rationale for assessing interests: The traditional view of describing a person's inventoried interests based on the rationale that "if a person likes the same things that people in a particular job like, the person will be satisfied with the job" (Cole & Hanson, 1975, p. 6).

percentage of agreement: An index of the consistency of decisions made by two independent judges. It is the percentage of students for whom the two judges reached the same decision.

percentages method of reporting student progress: A summative evaluation of a student's achievement in each subject that uses the average percentage of schoolwork marked correct.

percentile rank: A norm-referenced score that tells the percentage of persons in a norm group scoring lower than a particular raw score. See also **local percentile rank** and **national percentile rank**.

perfect matching: When a matching exercise has an equal number of premise statements and response statements.

performance assessment: Any assessment technique that requires students physically to carry out a complex, extended *process* (e.g., present an argument orally, play a musical piece, or climb a knotted rope) or produce an important *product* (e.g., write a poem, report on an experiment, or create a painting). The complexity of the task distinguishes performance assessments from the short answers, decontextualized math problems, or brief (one class period) essay tasks found on typical paper-and-pencil assessments.

performance centered: A criterion for a well-stated learning target: A learning target should describe what a student is able to do (or to perform) after completing instruction. See also **content centered** and **student centered**.

performance standards: Statements about the things students can perform or do once the content standards are learned. See also **content standards** and **standards**.

performance task: One activity or item in a performance assessment. See also **performance assessment**.

permanent record card: The official summative record by grade level of a student's achievement in each subject and his or her attendance in a particular school.

personal bias: A type of rating error that occurs when a teacher has a general tendency to use inappropriate or irrelevant stereotypes favoring boys over girls, whites over blacks, working families over welfare recipients, or particular families and individual students a teacher likes over others the teacher may dislike.

persuasive writing: A type of writing in which the writer attempts to convince the reader of the writer's point of view. The writer may want the reader to accept his or her idea or to take some actions that the writer supports.

pictorial reasoning: The ability to reason using pictures. For example, to infer relationships among the pictured objects, to identify the similarities and differences among pictures, and to identify progressions and predict the next picture in the progression.

placement decision: A decision in which persons are assigned to different levels of the same general type of instruction, education, or work; no one is rejected, but all remain within the institution to be assigned to some level (Cronbach, 1990; Cronbach & Gleser, 1965). See also **classification decision** and **selection decision**.

plausible distractor: An incorrect alternative of a multiple-choice or matching exercise that seems correct to less knowledgeable students.

poorly functioning distractor: A distractor in a multiple-choice item that virtually no one in the lower scoring group chooses.

portfolio: A limited collection of a student's work used for assessment purposes either to present the student's best work(s) or demonstrate the student's educational growth over a given time span.

portfolio culture model: An instructional approach advocating that students' portfolios become the center of a teacher's instructional planning and teaching activities so the teacher and the students will interact intensively with the portfolio contents (Duschl & Gitomer, 1991; Niyogi, 1995).

portfolio entry sheet (caption): A sheet for each entry in a portfolio that contains the following information: name of the student, date of entry, title or description of the entry, some indication of the learning target or purpose for including the entry, and why this particular entry is important or valuable.

positive correlation: A type of relationship between two sets of scores that occurs when high scores on one assessment are associated with high scores on the other; low scores on one are associated with low scores on the other. See also **correlation coefficient** and **negative correlation**.

positive or negative consequences of decisions: What happens to students as a result of taking an assessment. Positive consequences mean some desirable things happen (e.g., getting extra help in reading); negative consequences mean some undesirable things happen (e.g., being labeled as stupid because one needs extra help in reading).

positively discriminating item: An item for which the proportion of upper scoring students getting high scores is larger than the proportion of lower scoring students getting high scores on it.

positively skewed distribution: A frequency distribution of scores in which the scores are piled up at the lower end of the score scale and spread thinly toward the upper end of the score scale. See also **negatively skewed distribution**.

predictive validity evidence: A type of external structure validity evidence showing the extent to which individuals' future performance on a criterion can be predicted from their prior performance on an assessment instrument. See also **concurrent validity evidence** and **external structure**.

preinstruction unit assessment framework: A plan to help assess cognitive and affective learning targets of an upcoming unit.

premises, premise list: The leftmost list of statements or elements in a matching exercise.

prerequisite knowledge and skill deficits assessment: A diagnostic assessment approach that identifies what a student needs to know before he or she can profit from new instruction. The approach uses task analysis to identify entry requirements and might also identify a learning hierarchy of prerequisites. See also **learning hierarchy assessment**.

prewriting activities: Before writing, a writer clarifies the purpose for writing, begins to organize thoughts, brainstorms, and tries out new ideas. The writer discusses the ideas with others, decides what the format and approach to writing will take, and determines the primary audience. A plan for the piece develops.

principle: A rule that describes what to do or the relationships between two concepts.

principle-governed thinking: Thinking that is manifested when a person consistently uses appropriate rules to identify how two or more concepts are related.

privacy: Keeping a student's assessment results closed to those who are unauthorized to have access to them. See also **confidentiality**.

problem: The presence of obstacles to attaining a desired outcome so that immediate attainment of a goal is not possible without further mental processing.

problem-sorting task: An assessment task that presents several types of word problems in science or mathematics to the student. The student's task is to read the problems, group them into like problems, and then explain why the problems in each group are alike.

procedural knowledge: The skills, methods, rules, and procedures you want a student to learn in order to carry out a process.

procedure checklist: A checklist of the steps necessary to complete a process correctly. See also **checklist**.

process assessment: Assessment that focuses on the procedure a student uses to complete a task rather than the final product produced. See also **product versus process**.

product assessment: Assessment that focuses on the final product a student produces rather than on the process the student uses to create that product. See also **product versus process**.

product checklist: A checklist of the necessary and important characteristics of the product a student is required to produce that is used to evaluate the quality of the work.

product versus process: The tangible thing a student produces is called a *product*. The procedure a student follows to complete a task or to produce the product is called a *process*.

professional ethics principle of test preparation: "No test-preparation practice should violate the ethical standards of the education profession" (Popham, 1991, p. 13).

professional responsibility: Acting toward students in a way that is ethical and consistent with one's role as a professional person.

profile of strengths and weaknesses assessment: A diagnostic assessment approach that identifies a student's norm-referenced pattern of achievement in several topical areas. See also **unreliable profile**.

profile report (on a standardized test): An individual student home report showing a student's results from a standardized test. This report is usually computer-prepared and is given to parents or guardians.

project: A long-term activity that results in a student product: a model, a functional object, a substantial report, or a collection.

projective hypothesis: The assumption that an examinee's interpretations of vague stimuli (such as inkblots) will reveal the examinee's innermost needs, feelings, and conflicts, even though the examinee is unaware of what he or she is revealing (Frank, 1939).

projective personality test techniques: Assessment techniques that present the examinee with ambiguous stimuli (such as inkblots) and ask the examinee to respond to them.

proposition: Any sentence that can be said to be true or false. See also **true-false variety**.

psychometric issues: Issues about assessment, especially bias in assessment, that concern the technical or statistical properties of the assessment in question.

psychomotor domain: A collection of educational outcomes and learning targets that focus on motor skills and perceptual processes.

pupil-teacher conferences method of reporting student progress: A method of reporting a student's summative achievement evaluation by means of a direct meeting between the teacher and student.

purging records: Destroying recorded information no longer needed for making decisions about a student so persons who are unauthorized to have access to that information cannot use it.

quality-level method for grading: A method for assigning letter grades in which the type of student performance required for each letter grade is specified beforehand. See also **logic rule method for grading** and **rubrics**.

quantitative reasoning: Reasoning with numerical quantities. For example, to infer relationships among the numbers, to identify the similarities and differences among numbers and patterns, and to identify progressions and predict the next number in the progression.

quartiles: Points on the score scale that divide the group of scores into quarters.

question variety: A type of short answer item in which the item itself is a direct question, and the answer is a word or phrase following it.

race representation: The number of times and the way in which each race is depicted in assessment items and materials. See also **role stereotype**.

race role-stereotype: See **role stereotype**.

random guessing: Responding to an item using chance rather than using your knowledge.

range: The difference between the highest and lowest scores in a set. It is used as a simple index of the spread of the scores in the set.

rank ordering, ranking: Ordering the scores from largest to smallest.

rater: The person, often a teacher, who judges the quality or level of achievement of a student's work, performance, or product using criteria and a rating scale. See also **rating scale**.

rater drift: A type of rating error that occurs when the raters, whose ratings originally agreed, begin to redefine the rubrics for themselves. As a result, the raters no longer produce ratings that agree.

rating scale: A scoring rubric that helps a teacher assess the degree to which students have attained the achievement dimensions in the performance task. See also **checklist**.

rating scale method of reporting student progress: A summative evaluation of a student's achievement that uses a rating scale to describe the degree of mastery. See also **rating scale**.

raw score: The number of points (marks) you assign to a student's performance on an assessment. Points may be assigned based on each task, or points awarded on separate parts of the assessment.

readiness test: An assessment of a student's general developmental skills needed for first-grade work, especially reading, where grouping by readiness level is a common practice.

recency of norm data: How current the norm data are. As the curriculum, schooling, and social and economic factors change, so will the currency of the data.

relational concepts: See **defined concept**.

relative achievement: The level of a student's achievement expressed in terms of comparisons to peers rather than by describing the specific learning targets the student has achieved. See also **absolute achievement** and **criterion-referencing**.

relative standards grading: See **norm-referenced grading framework**.

relevance of norm data: The extent to which the norm group a publisher provides is the appropriate group to which you want to compare your students' performance on the test.

reliability: The amount of consistency of assessment results (scores). Reliability is a limiting factor for validity.

reliability coefficient: Any of several statistical indices that quantifies the amount of consistency in assessment scores. See also **reliability**.

reliability decay: A rating error that results in the scores from multiple raters becoming less consistent over time.

reliability of ratings: The consistency of students' ratings over time, different samples of content, and different raters. See also **reliability**.

report card: The document that reports the summative achievement grades to students and parents.

reporting variables: A subset, from among all the assessment variables, that a school district will expect a teacher to report to parents and for official purposes (Frisbie & Waltman, 1992).

representativeness (of norm data): The extent to which the norm sample is based on a carefully planned sample that represents the target population. The test publisher should provide you with information about the subclassifications (gender, age, socioeconomic level, etc.) used to ensure representativeness.

response-choice items: Test items that provide students with alternatives from which to choose to answer the question or solve the problem posed.

response list: The list of plausible response alternatives in a matching exercise. This list is placed to the right of the premise list when crafting exercises. See also **premises**.

restricted-response essay items: Essay prompts or instructions that restrict or limit both the substantive content and the form of the written response.

right-wrong variety of true-false items: This item format presents a computation, equation, or language sentence that the student judges as correct or incorrect (right or wrong).

role stereotype: Depiction in assessment materials of races or genders in oversimplified activities or work roles that convey the impression that such persons' capacities are limited in some way.

rubric method for grading: See **logic rule method for grading** and **quality-level method for grading**.

rubrics: A coherent set of rules you use to evaluate the quality of a student's performance: They guide your judgments and ensure that you apply the rules consistently from one student to the next. See also **checklist** and **rating scale**.

SAT-score: A normalized standard score from a distribution that has a mean of 500 and a standard deviation of 100.

scaffolding: The degree of support, guidance, and direction you provide students when they set out to complete the task.

scatter diagram (scattergram): A graph on which paired scores are plotted to show their relationship.

scenario: An assessment technique that presents a realistic situation and assesses how the student performs in this situation.

schema (schemata): The way knowledge is represented in a person's mind through networks of connected concepts, information, rules, problem-solving strategies, and conditions for actions (Marshall, 1990).

schema-driven problem solving: When a person recognizes a particular problem as part of or very similar to an existing schema and applies the solution strategy stored in that schema to solve the new problem (Gick, 1986). See also **schema (schemata)**.

schematic knowledge assessment: A diagnostic assessment approach that identifies whether a student has formed an internal representation or model of the problem. See also **component competencies of problem solving**.

school averages norms: A tabulation of the average (mean) score from each school building in a national sample of schools that provides information on the relative ordering of these averages (means).

score band: See **uncertainty interval**.

scorer reliability: See **inter-rater reliability** and **decision consistency index**.

scoring key: A rubric or list of rules that shows the correct answer and the kinds of partially correct answers that are to receive various amounts of credit.

scoring rubric: See **rubrics**.

selection decision: A decision in which an institution or organization decides that some persons are acceptable whereas others are not; those unacceptable are rejected and are no longer the concern of the institution or organization. See also **classification decision** and **placement decision**.

self-evaluation checklist: A checklist that students use to evaluate their own performance.

self-referenced grading framework: The assignment of grades by comparing a student's performance with your perceptions of his or her capability.

severity error: A rating error that occurs when a teacher tends to assign almost all ratings toward the low end of the scale. It is the opposite of a leniency error. See also **leniency error**.

short performance task: A performance task that can be completed within one class period or less. See also **long performance task**.

short-answer variety: This item format requires a student to respond with a word, short phrase, number, or symbol.

short-term memory subtests: Assessments of a person's ability to remember patterns, objects, words, and numbers immediately after they are heard, seen, or read.

simulation: On-demand event that happens under controlled conditions and that attempts to mimic naturally occurring events.

single-level test: A standardized survey battery that is used only at one grade level or one narrow range of grade levels. See also **multilevel survey battery**.

Six + 1 Traits® of Writing: A framework and scoring rubrics for assessing general writing ability that focuses on evaluating a student on seven writing traits for each essay: ideas, organization, voice, word choice, sentence fluency, conventions, and presentation.

sizing-up uses: Using assessment information to form a general impression of a student's strengths, weaknesses, learning characteristics, and personality at the beginning of a course or of the year.

skewed distribution: A description of a frequency distribution in which the scores are piled up on one end of the score scale and thinly spread out toward the other. See also **negatively skewed distribution** and **positively skewed distribution**.

SOAP: An acronym for the following elements that should appear in the prompt to stimulate good writing on the part of the student (Albertson, 1998):

S   *Subject*—inform the student who or what the piece is supposed to be about.

O   *Occasion*—inform the student what is the occasion or situation that requires that the piece be written.

A   *Audience*—inform the student who the intended audience is.

P   *Purpose*—inform the student what the purpose is supposed to be: Is it to inform or narrate? To be imaginative? To be persuasive?

Spearman-Brown double length reliability formula: A procedure for estimating reliability when the focus of the study is on consistency of students' scores from one sample of items to another equivalent sample of items from the same content domain, but when only one form of the test exists. See also **odd-even split halves reliability procedure** and **split-halves reliability coefficient**.

special norms: Percentile rank or standard-score norms developed for specific subpopulations of students such as deaf students, Catholic schools, and so on.

specific determiner: A word or phrase (e.g., *always*, *never*, *often*, *usually*, and so on) in a true-false or multiple-choice item that "overqualifies" a given statement and gives the student an unintended clue to the correct answer (Sarnacki, 1979).

specific learning targets: A clear statement about what students are to achieve by the end of a unit of instruction. See also also **educational goals** and **general learning targets**.

specific scoring rubric: A scoring rubric that results from adapting the general scoring framework to a particular task. See also **general scoring rubric**.

specimen set: A packet of materials from a test publisher containing a sample of the test, sample computer reports, promotional materials, and (occasionally) a technical report of the test's quality.

speeded assessment: Any assessment that focuses on how quickly a student can perform.

spiral format: An arrangement of items in a test whereby similar types of items are not grouped together into subtests, but are arranged in a pattern so that one item of each type is presented; then the sequence is repeated, but with more difficult items.

split-halves reliability coefficient: Any method for estimating reliability on a single occasion by studying the relationship between students' scores on each half of the full-length test. See also **domain of achievement**, **Spearman-Brown double length formula**, and **odd-even split-halves reliability procedure**.

SS-score: A type of linear standard score that tells the location of a raw score in a distribution having a mean of 50 and a standard deviation of 10. See also **linear standard score** and **raw score**.

SS-score method for making composites: A method for preparing students' composite marks for purposes of norm-referenced grading that preserves the influence (weights) you want the components of the composite to have.

stability coefficient: Any of several methods for estimating reliability that study the consistency of students' scores from one occasion to the next. See also **alternate forms reliability coefficient [delayed]**, **alternate forms reliability coefficient [same occasion]**, and **test-retest reliability coefficient**.

stages in crafting performance tasks: Three stages of developing a performance task are: (a) being very clear about the performance you want to assess, (b) crafting the task, and (c) crafting a way to score and record the results (Stiggins, 1994).

stakeholders: Persons or groups with an interest in the results of an assessment, usually because they will be affected by decisions made about them using the test results.

standard age score *(SAS)*: Normalized standard score with a mean of 50 and standard deviation of 8 in the norm group having the same age as the student being tested.

standard deviation: An index of the spread of the scores in a distribution calculated by taking the square root of the mean squared deviation of the scores from the arithmetic mean of the scores.

standard deviation method of grading: A norm-referenced grading method that uses the standard deviation of the class' scores as a unit of measure on the grading scale: A teacher computes the standard deviation of the scores and uses this number to mark off segments on the number line that define the boundaries for grade assignment. See also **standard deviation**.

standard error of measurement (SEM): An estimate of the standard deviation or the spread of a hypothetical obtained-score distribution resulting from repeated testing of the same person with the same assessment. See also **obtained score** and **standard deviation**.

standard or quality dimension: See **achievement dimensions**.

standard score: A category of transformed scores that changes the mean, standard deviation, and sometimes the shape of the distribution of the original scores so they are more easily interpreted. See also **linear standard scores (z,SS)** and **normalized standard scores (z_n, T, DIQ, NCE, SAT)**.

standardized patient format: Originally used to assess the clinical skills of medical candidates and practicing doctors, an actor is trained to display the symptoms of a particular disorder. Each medical candidate meets and interviews this standardized patient to diagnose the illness and to prescribe treatment.

standardized test: A test for which the procedures, administration, materials, and scoring rules are fixed so that as far as possible the assessment is the same at different times and places.

standards: Statements about what students are expected to learn. Some states call these statements *essential skills, learning expectations, learning outcomes, achievement expectations,* or other names. Often there are two sets of standards: content and performance. See also **content standards** and **performance standards**.

Standards for Educational and Psychological Testing: Guidelines and recommendations prepared by the American Educational Research Association, the American Psychological Association, and the National Council on Measurement in Education for the development and use of educational and psychological assessments.

standards-referencing: A score-interpreting framework that compares a student's test performance to clearly defined levels of achievement of proficiency. These levels are established using both criterion-referencing and norm-referencing techniques. See also **criterion-referencing** and **norm referencing**.

stanine scores: A type of normalized standard score that tells the location of a raw score in one of nine specific segments of a normal distribution. Thus, stanine is derived from standard nine.

state-mandated assessments: Tests and other assessments that the law requires to be administered to all students at designated grade levels.

statement-and-comment items: Items used to assess students' ability to evaluate a given set of interpretations of quoted comments using learned criteria.

statistic (statistical index): A summary number that concisely captures a specific feature of a group of scores.

stem: The part of a multiple-choice item that asks a question or poses a problem to be solved.

strategic knowledge assessment: An assessment approach that pinpoints a student's ability to identify the proper sequence of steps or the proper processes needed to reach the answer. See also **component competencies of problem solving**.

strip key: A strip of paper on which the correct answers to completion items are written in a column in such a manner that when the strip is put on a student's test paper, the correct answers line up with the locations of the student's responses.

structure a task: To provide written or oral guidance to a student for how to complete a task, what resources to use, how long the response must be, and so on. The more guidance you give, the more structured the task is said to be. See also **scaffolding**.

structured (self-report) personality assessment techniques: These assessment procedures have a specific set of response-choice items; follow very specific rules for administering, scoring, and interpreting the tests; and require examinees to respond to the items in a way that describes their personal feelings (e.g., examinees may be asked whether the statement, "I usually express my personal opinions to others," is true of themselves).

structured task (exercise): See **structure a task** and **scaffolding**.

student centered: A criterion for a well-stated learning target: A learning target should describe what a student is to learn. See also **performance centered** and **content centered**.

student progress reporting methods: Any one of several ways in which schools and teachers report each student's achievement to parents and for the official school records. These include letter grades, number grades, percentage grades, checklists, rating scales, narrative reports, pupil-teacher conferences, parent-teacher conferences, and letters to parents.

student self-assessment: Involving students in judging the quality of their own work against learning targets and in deciding what actions they need to take to improve. See also **formative uses of assessments**.

subtest: A short test that is scored separately but is part of a longer battery of tests. The longer battery is comprised of two or more subtests.

summative evaluation of schools, programs, or materials: Judgments about the worth of programs, curricula, or materials after they are completed with the idea of suggesting whether they should be adopted or used. See also **formative evaluation of schools, programs, or materials**.

summative evaluation of students' achievement: Judgments about the quality or worth of students' achievement after the instructional process is completed. See also **formative evaluation of students' achievement**.

summative uses of assessment: See **summative evaluation of students**.

surface feature: A diagnostic assessment approach that uses the immediate external feature of the content of a test or test item describe a student's achievement. This is contrasted with the deeper features of how a student perceives the structure or organization of that content, and processes information and knowledge to solve problems using that content knowledge. See also **knowledge structure assessment**.

symmetrical distribution: A frequency distribution of scores in which it is possible for the graph of the distribution to be folded along a vertical line so that the two halves of the figure coincide

synthesis: A category in the Bloom et al. (1956) *Taxonomy of Educational Objectives.* Learning targets in this category ask students to combine parts into a whole that was not there before.

table of specifications: This chart describes the major content categories and skills that a test assesses. It describes the percentage of tasks (items) for each content-skills combination included on the test.

tabular (matrix) items: A type of matching exercise in which the student matches to elements from several lists of *responses* (e.g., presidents, political parties, famous firsts, and important events) with elements from a common list of *premises*.

tandem arrangement of alternatives: A type of multiple-choice item-writing flaw in which the alternatives are arranged in a paragraphlike continuous stream of text instead of the more desirable list arrangement of one alternative placed beneath the other.

task (item): The questions, exercises, and activities appearing on an assessment procedure. Typically, the term *item* is used to refer to paper-and-pencil test exercises.

task format: The way a task or item appears on an assessment. Typical formats include multiple-choice, true-false, matching, short-answer, and essays, among others.

task-directed thoughts: Thoughts and test-taking actions that focus on completing the assessment tasks and thereby reduce any tensions that are associated with them (Mandler & Sarason, 1952). See also **task-irrelevant thoughts**.

task-irrelevant thoughts: Thoughts and test-taking actions that are self-preoccupied, centering on what could happen if a student fails a test or on a student's own helplessness, and sometimes on a desire to escape from the test situation as quickly as possible (Mandler & Sarason, 1952). One of the four test anxiety factors. See also **task-directed thoughts** and **four factors of test anxiety**.

task-referenced grading: See **criterion-referenced grading framework**.

task-specific rubrics: Scoring rubrics in which the description of quality levels refers to the specific task and expected responses. See also **general scoring rubric** and **rubrics**.

taxonomies of instructional learning targets: Highly organized schemes for classifying learning targets (instructional objectives) into various levels of complexity. See also **cognitive domain, affective domain,** and **psychomotor domain**.

teaching actions after assessing: The things you do to use the assessment results you obtain to improve your teaching and your students' learning.

technical manual: A publication prepared by a test developer that explains the technical details of how the test was developed, how the norms were created, the procedures for selecting test items, the procedures for equating different forms of the test, and reliability and validity studies that have been completed for the test.

tension: One of the four test anxiety factors in which students feel very uneasy, jittery, distressed, anxious, and so on before taking a test. See also **four factors of test anxiety**.

test: An instrument or systematic procedure for observing and describing one or more characteristics of a student using either a numerical scale or a classification scheme. See also **assessment, evaluation,** and **measurement**.

test anxiety: Increased emotional tension among students who want to do well on a test that results in bodily and autonomic arousal and thoughts about the negative consequences of failure and how a student's performance will compare to others. See also **worry, emotionality,** and **four factors of test anxiety**.

Test Critiques: A series of volumes that reviews the most frequently used tests in business, education, and psychology. Published by the Test Corporation of America.

test level: The grade level or narrow range of grade levels for which a standardized test is targeted.

tested interests: Students' vocational and career interests inferred from the results of an assessment of a student's information and knowledge of a particular subject matter. See also **interests, expressed interests, inventoried interests,** and **manifested interests**.

test-retest reliability coefficient: A procedure for estimating reliability when the focus of the study is the consistency of the students' scores from one occasion to the next on the same test items.

Tests in Microfiche: A collection of more than 800 unpublished tests used in education, business, and psychology. Published by the Educational Testing Service.

Tests in Print: A test bibliography that contains information on more than 2,900 commercially available instruments. Published by the Buros Institute of Mental Measurements.

test-takers' rights: The rights of those who take tests to information from and fair treatment by those who administer tests and use the results.

testwiseness: A student's ability to use the characteristics of both the assessment materials and the assessment situation to attain a higher score than the student's knowledge would otherwise warrant.

textbookish phrasing: A type of item-writing flaw in which the item is worded very similarly to how textbooks phrase the information.

three fundamental principles for crafting assessments: The basic principles that underlie virtually all of the more specific suggestions for crafting assessment tasks (items). They are: (a) focus only on educationally important learning targets, (b) elicit only the performances that are relevant to the learning target being assessed, and (c) neither prevent nor inhibit a student's ability to demonstrate that he or she has obtained the learning target.

top-down approach to rubric crafting: Adopting a conceptual framework that defines the achievement dimensions that need to be assessed before starting to craft the rubric. See also **bottom-up approach to rubric crafting**.

total points method for grading: A criterion-referenced method of assigning grades in which each component included in the final composite grade is given maximum point value (e.g., quizzes may count 10 points, exams may count a maximum of 50 points each, and projects may count a maximum of 40 points each); letter grades are assigned on the basis of the number of total points a student accumulated over the marking period.

tricky item: An item for which an option's correctness depends on a trivial fact, an idiosyncratic standard, or an easily overlooked word or phrase.

true score: The hypothetical score you would obtain if you subtracted the examinee's error score from the examinee's obtained score. See also **error score** and **obtained score**.

true-false variety: An item format consisting of a statement or proposition that the student must judge as true or false. See also **proposition**.

T-score: A type of normalized standard score that tells the location of a raw score in a normal distribution having a mean of 50 and a standard deviation of 10. The normalized *T*-score is the counterpart to the linear *SS*-score.

two-category method of reporting student progress: A method for reporting summative evaluations of student achievement that uses only two levels of achievement such as pass-fail.

two-score test: A type of test that assesses several kinds of specific abilities, but reports only two scores, usually verbal/quantitative or verbal/nonverbal. See also **omnibus test** and **multiple-aptitude tests**.

types of test-anxious students: There are three types of test-anxious students: those who do not have good study skills and fail to understand how the main ideas of the subject you are teaching are related and organized; those who do have a good grasp of the material and good study skills but have built up fears of failure associated with assessment and evaluation; and those who believe they have good study habits but who do not.

typical performance assessment: Gathering information about what a student would do under ordinary or everyday conditions. See also **maximum performance assessment**.

uncertainty interval: The score interval within which an examinee's true score is likely to be. The endpoints of this interval are calculated by (a) subtracting the standard error of measurement from an examinee's obtained score (lower endpoint) and (b) adding the standard error of measurement to the examinee's obtained score (upper endpoint). Also referred to as the score band. See also **obtained score, standard error of measurement (SEM),** and **true score**.

undergeneralizing a concept: Not being able to include in a concept all of the things that fit that concept name.

underinterpreting score differences: A type of score-interpretation error that occurs when differences in scores between two students or differences in scores of one student on two tests are ignored even though the differences are not due simply to error of measurement. Some action should be taken. See also **overinterpreting score differences**.

unimodal distribution: A frequency distribution of scores in which there is one pileup of scores (i.e., one mode). See also **bimodal distribution**.

unit of instruction: A teaching sequence covering from 1 to 7 weeks of lessons, depending on the students and topics you are teaching.

unreliable profile: The set of a student's scores on each subtest in a battery is called a *profile*. Unreliable subtest scores result in patterns for which a student's strengths and weaknesses may be exaggerated or masked by chance errors of measurement. Hence, the profile is unreliable. See also **profile of strengths and weaknesses assessment**.

upper, middle, and lower scoring groups: The three groups into which you divide the class before conducting an item analysis. The groups are formed after ranking students on the basis of their total score on the test that includes the items you will be analyzing.

validity: The soundness of your interpretations and uses of students' assessment results.

validity coefficient: A predictive or concurrent correlation that is used as one piece of external structure evidence to support the validity of an assessment. See also **correlation coefficient, concurrent validity evidence, external structure,** and **predictive validity evidence**.

values: A person's long-lasting beliefs of the importance of certain life goals, a lifestyle, a way of acting, or a way of life. See also **attitudes** and **interests**.

verbal clues: See **grammatical clue** and **specific determiner**.

verbal comprehension tests: Tests that assess the students' ability to understand verbal material and to use language to express themselves.

verbal reasoning tests: Tests that assess students' ability to see relationships among words, read critically, and reason with words.

verbal tests: Tests that have as their main purpose to elicit and assess the verbal responses of students such as how they define words, explain their answers, or define similarities or differences between concepts. See also **nonverbal tests** and **performance assessment**.

vocational interest inventories: Formal paper-and-pencil questionnaires that help students express their likes and dislikes about a wide range of work and other activities. A pattern of vocational and career interests is then determined from the students' responses.

well-structured problems: Problems are presented as assessment tasks that are clearly laid out: All the information students need is given, the situations are very much the same as students were taught in class, and there is usually one correct answer that students can attain by applying a procedure that was taught (Frederiksen, 1984).

window dressing: The use of words that tend to "dress up" an item stem to make it sound as though it is testing something of practical importance, when it does not (Ebel, 1965).

within-classroom uses of test results: Uses of the results of a standardized test within a teacher's classroom, such as describing the educational developmental levels of each student or describing specific qualitative strengths and weaknesses in students.

worry: One of the cognitive aspects of test anxiety: a person's thoughts about the negative consequences of failure and how his or her performance will compare to others'. See also **four factors of test anxiety**.

writing process: Most writing results from an orderly process that includes drafting, feedback, revisions, and polishing.

writing traits (writing dimensions): The several characteristics or qualities that can be used to evaluate writing quality. Each characteristic is expressed as a continuum of quality. See also **Six + 1 Traits® of Writing**.

yes-no variety of true-false items: An item format that asks a direct question, to which a student's answers are limited to yes or no.

yes-no with explanation variety of true-false items: An item format that asks a direct question and requires the student to respond yes or no and explain why his or her choice is correct.

z-score: A type of linear standard score that tells the number of standard deviation units a raw score is above or below the mean of a given distribution. The mean and standard deviation of the distribution of z-scores are always zero and one, respectively. See also **linear standard score** and **raw score**.

z_n-score A type of normalized standard score: z_n-scores have percentile ranks corresponding to what would be expected in a normal distribution. See also **normalized standard scores**.

Achieve. (2004). *Measuring up 2004: A report on language arts literacy and mathematics standards and assessments for New Jersey*. Washington, DC: Author.

Airasian, P. W. (1979). A perspective on the uses and misuses of standardized achievement tests. *NCME, Measurement in Education, 10*(3), 1–12.

Airasian, P. W. (1991a). *Classroom assessment*. New York: McGraw-Hill.

Airasian, P. W. (1991b). Perspective on measurement instruction. *Educational Measurement: Issues and Practice, 10*(1), 13–16.

Albertson, B. (1998). *Creating effective writing prompts*. Newark: Delaware Reading and Writing Project, Delaware Center for Teacher Education, University of Delaware.

Alexander, P. A. (1992). Domain knowledge: Evaluating themes and emerging concerns. *Educational Psychologist, 27*, 33–51.

Aleyideino, S. C. (1968). The effects of response methods and item types upon working time scores and grade-equivalent scores of pupils differing in levels of achievement. *Dissertation Abstracts International, 29*, 1774A–1775A. (University Microfilms No. 68–16, 773)

Alfonso, V. C., Flanagan, D. P., & Radwan, S. (2005). The impact of the Cattell-Horn-Carroll theory on test development and interpretation of cognitive and academic abilities. In D. P. Flanagan & P. L. Harrison (Eds.), *Contemporary intellectual assessment: Theories, tests, and issues* (2nd ed., pp. 185–202). New York: Guilford.

Algozzine, R. (1993). Including students with disabilities in systemic efforts to measure outcomes: Why ask why? In J. E. Ysseldyke & M. L. Thurlow (Eds.), *Views on inclusion and testing accommodations for students with disabilities* (pp. 5–18). Minneapolis: National Center on Educational Outcomes, University of Minnesota.

Allen, R., Bettis, N., Kurfman, D., MacDonald, W., Mullis, I. V. S., & Salter, C. (1990). *The geography learning of high school seniors*. Princeton, NJ: National Assessment of Educational Progress, Educational Testing Service.

American Association on Mental Retardation. (2002). *Definition of mental retardations*. Retrieved July 29, 2005, from http://www.aamr.org/Policies/faq_mental_retardation.shtml

American College Testing Program. (1994). *ACT Interest Inventory*. Princeton, NJ: Author.

American Council on the Teaching of Foreign Languages. (1989). *Oral proficiency interview: Tester training manual*. Yonkers, NY: Author.

American Counseling Association. (1995). *The ACA code of ethics*. Retrieved from http://www.counseling.org/resources/ethics.htm

American Educational Research Association. (2000). *Ethical standards of the American Educational Research Association*. Retrieved from http://www.aera.net

American Educational Research Association, American Psychological Association, & National Council on Measurement in Education. (1985). *Standards for educational and psychological testing*. Washington, DC: American Psychological Association.

American Educational Research Association, American Psychological Association, & National Council on Measurement in Education. (1999). *Standards for educational and psychological testing*. Washington, DC: American Educational Research Association.

American Federation of Teachers, National Council on Measurement in Education, & National Education Association. (1990). *Standards for teacher competence in educational assessment of students*. Retrieved from http://www.unl.edu/buros/bimm/html/subarts.html

American Psychological Association. (2002). *Ethical principles of psychologists and code of conduct*. Retrieved from http://www.apa.org/ethics/homepage.html

American Psychological Association. (1974). *Standards for educational and psychological tests*. Washington, DC: American Psychological Association.

American School Counselor Association. (2004). *Ethical standards for school counselors*. Retrieved from http://www.schoolcounselor.org

Anastasi, A. (1976). *Psychological testing* (4th ed.). Upper Saddle River, NJ: Merrill/Prentice Hall.

Anastasi, A. (1988). *Psychological testing* (6th ed.). Upper Saddle River, NJ: Merrill/Prentice Hall.

Anderson, J. R. (1987). Skill acquisition: Compilation of weak-method problem solutions. *Psychological Review, 94*, 199–210.

Anderson, L. W., Krathwohl, D. R., Airasian, P. W., Cruikshank, K. A., Mayer, R. E., Pintrich, P. R., et al. (Eds.). (2001). *A taxonomy for learning, teaching, and assessing: A revision of Bloom's Taxonomy of Educational Objectives* (Complete ed.). New York: Longman.

Anderson, R. C. (1972). How to construct achievement tests to assess comprehension. *Review of Educational Research, 42*, 145–170.

Anderson, R. C. (1977). The notion of schemata and educational enterprise: General discussion of the conference. In R. C. Anderson, R. J. Spiro, & W. E. Montague (Eds.), *Schooling and acquisition of knowledge*. Hillsdale, NJ: Erlbaum.

Anderson, R. C. (1984). Some reflections on the acquisition of knowledge. *Educational Researcher, 13*, 5–10.

Armstrong, T. (1994). *Multiple intelligences in the classroom*. Alexandria, VA: Association for Supervision and Curriculum Development.

Arter, J. A. (1998, April). *Teaching about performance assessment*. Paper presented at the annual meeting of the National Council on Measurement in Education, San Diego, CA.

Arter, J., & McTighe, J. (2001). *Scoring rubrics in the classroom*. Thousand Oaks, CA: Corwin Press.

Arter, J. A., & Spandel, V. (1992). NCME instructional module: Using portfolios of student work in instruction and assessment. *Educational Measurement: Issues and Practice, 11*(1), 36–44.

Arter, J. A., & Stiggins, R. J. (1992, April). *Performance assessment in education*. Paper presented at the annual meeting of the American Educational Research Association, San Francisco, CA.

Association for Assessment in Counseling and Education. (2003). *Responsibilities of Users of Standardized Tests (RUST)* (3rd ed.). Retrieved from http://aac.ncat.edu/Resources/documents/RUST2003%20VII%20Final.pdf

Ausubel, D. P., Novak, J. D., & Hanesian, H. (1978). *Educational psychology: A cognitive view* (2nd ed.). New York: Holt, Rinehart & Winston.

Azwell, T., & Schmar, E. (Eds.). (1995). *Report on report cards: Alternatives to consider*. Portsmouth, NH: Heinemann.

Baglin, R. F. (1981). Does "nationally" normed really mean nationally? *Journal of Educational Measurement, 18*, 92–107.

Baker, E. L. (1992). Issues in policy, assessment, and equity. In *Proceedings of the National Research Symposium on Limited English Proficiency Student Issues: Vol. 1 and 2: Focus on Evaluation and Measurement*. Washington, DC.

Baker, E. L., & O'Neil, H. F., Jr. (1994). Performance assessment and equity: A view from the USA. *Assessment in Education, 1*, 11–26.

Baker, F. (2001). *The basics of item response theory*. ERIC Clearinghouse on Assessment and Evaluation, University of Maryland. College Park, MD. Available from http://edres.org/irt

Ballstaedt, S. P., & Mandl, H. (1985). *Diagnosis of knowledge structure in text learning*. (Technical Report 37). Turbingen: University of Turbingen, Deutsches Institute für Fernstudien.

Barker, K., & Ebel, R. L. (1981). A comparison of difficulty and discrimination values of selected true-false item types. *Contemporary Educational Psychology, 7*, 35–40.

Barone, J. B. (1991). Strategies for the development of effective performance exercises. *Applied Measurement in Education, 4*, 305–318.

Barrett, H. C. (2000). Create your own electronic portfolio: Using off-the-shelf software to showcase your own and students' work. *Learning and Leading with Technology*.

Retrieved from http://electronicportfolios. com/portfolios/iste2k.html

Beck, M. D. (1974). Achievement test reliability as a function of pupil-response procedures. *Journal of Educational Measurement, 11*, 109–114.

Becker, K. A. (2003). *History of the Stanford-Binet Intelligence Scales: Content and psychometrics.* Retrieved July 28, 2005, from http://www.assess.nelson.com/pdf/ sb5-asb1.pdf

Beggs, D. L., & Hieronymus, A. N. (1968). Uniformity of growth in the basic skills throughout the school year and during the summer. *Journal of Educational Measurement, 5*, 91–97.

Bejar, I. I. (1984). Educational diagnostic assessment. *Journal of Educational Measurement, 21*, 175–189.

Bellanca, J. A., & Kirschenbaum, H. (1976). An overview of grading alternatives. In S. B. Simon & J. A. Bellanca (Eds.), *Degrading the grading myths: A primer of alternatives to grades and marks.* Washington, DC: Association for Supervision and Curriculum Development.

Bennett, G. K., Seashore, H. G., & Wesman, A. G. (1974). *Fifth edition manual for the Differential Aptitude Tests (Forms S and T).* New York: Psychological Corporation.

Benson, J. (1989). Structural components of statistical test anxiety in adults: An exploratory model. *Journal of Experimental Psychology, 57*, 247–261.

Benson, J., & El-Zahhar, N. E. (1994). Further refinement and validation of the Revised Test Anxiety Scale. *Structural Equation Modeling, 1*, 203–221.

Bianchini, J. C., & Loret, P. G. (1974a). *Anchor test study supplement. Final report* (Vol. 1). (ERIC Document Reproduction Service No. ED092601)

Bianchini, J. C., & Loret, P. G. (1974b). *Anchor test study supplement. Final report* (Vol. 31). (ERIC Document Reproduction Service No. ED092632)

Black, P., & Wiliam, D. (1998). Assessment and classroom learning. *Assessment in Education, 5*, 7–74.

Blank, R. K. (2002). Using surveys of enacted curriculum to evaluate quality of instruction and alignment with standards. *Peabody Journal of Education, 77*(4), 86–121.

Blommers, P. J., & Forsyth, R. A. (1977). *Elementary statistical methods in psychology and education* (2nd ed.). Boston: Houghton Mifflin.

Bloom, B. S. (1968). Learning for mastery. *Evaluation Comment, 1*, 1–12.

Bloom, B. S., Englehart, M. D., Furst, E. J., Hill, W. H., & Krathwohl, D. R. (1956). *Taxonomy of educational objectives: The classification of educational goals, Handbook I: Cognitive domain.* White Plains, NY: Longman.

Bloom, B. S., Hastings, J. T., & Madaus, G. F. (1971). *Handbook on formative and summative evaluation of student learning.* New York: McGraw-Hill.

Bond, L. (1989). The effects of special preparation on measures of scholastic ability. In R. L. Linn (Ed.), *Educational measurement* (3rd ed., pp. 429–444). Upper Saddle River, NJ: Merrill/Prentice Hall.

Boothroyd, R. A., McMorris, R. F., & Pruzek, R. (1992, April). *What do teachers know about testing and how did they find out?* Paper presented at the annual meeting of the National Council on Measurement in Education, San Francisco, CA.

Boruch, F. R. (1971). Maintaining confidentiality of data in educational research: A systemic analysis. *American Psychologist, 26*, 413–430.

Bransford, J. D., & Stein, B. S. (1984). *The IDEAL problem solver.* New York: W. H. Freeman.

Brelend, H. M., Camp, R., Jones, R. J., Morris, M. M., & Rock, D. A. (1987). *Assessing writing skill.* (Research Monograph No. 11.). New York: College Entrance Examination Board.

Brennan, R. L. (2001). An essay on the history and future of reliability from the perspective of replications. *Journal of Educational Measurement, 38*, 295–317.

Brennan, R. L., & Plake, B. S. (1991). Survey of programs and employment in educational measurement. *Educational Measurement: Issues and Practice, 10*(2), 32.

Brookhart, S. M. (1991). Letter: Grading practices and validity. *Educational Measurement: Issues and Practice, 10*(1), 35–36.

Brookhart, S. M. (1993). Teachers' grading practices: Meaning and values. *Journal of Educational Measurement, 30*, 123–142.

Brookhart, S. M. (1999). Teaching about communicating assessment results and grading. *Educational Measurement: Issues and Practice, 18*(1), 5–13.

Brookhart, S. M. (2004). *Grading.* Upper Saddle River, NJ: Prentice Hall/Merrill Education.

Brown, W. (1910). Some experimental results in the correlation of mental abilities. *British Journal of Psychology, 3*, 296–322.

Buren, A., & Lewis, S. (1994). *Regional writing portfolio audit meetings: Final report.* Frankfort: Kentucky Department of Education.

Buros, O. K. (Ed.). (1938). *The nineteen thirty-eight mental measurements yearbook.* New Brunswick, NJ: Rutgers University Press.

Buros, O. K. (Ed.). (1978). *The eighth mental measurements yearbook.* Highland Park, NJ: Gryphon Press.

Burton, R. R. (1982). Diagnosing bugs in a simple procedural skill. In D. Sleeman & J. S. Brown (Eds.), *Intelligent tutoring systems* (pp. 157–183). New York: Academic Press.

Campbell, L. (1997). Variations on a theme: How teachers interpret MI theory. *Educational Leadership, 55*(1), 14–18.

Campbell, R. N. (1928). *An account of the principles of measurement and calculations.* London: Longmans, Green.

Carlson, S. B. (1985). *Creative classroom testing: Ten designs for assessment and instruction.* Princeton, NJ: Educational Testing Service.

Carroll, J. B. (1961). The nature of the data or how to choose a correlation coefficient. *Psychometrika, 26*, 347–372.

Carroll, J. B. (1963). A model of school learning. *Teachers College Record, 64*, 723–733.

Carroll, J. B. (1974). The aptitude-achievement distinction: The case of foreign language aptitude and proficiency. In D. R. Green (Ed.), *The aptitude-achievement distinction: Proceedings of the Second CTB/McGraw-Hill Conference on Issues in Educational Measurement.* Monterey, CA: CTB/McGraw-Hill, Inc.

Cashen, V. M., & Ramseyer, G. C. (1969). The use of separate answer sheets by primary age children. *Journal of Educational Measurement, 6*, 155–158.

Center for the Study of Testing, Evaluation, and Educational Policy. (1992, October). *The influence of testing on teaching math and science in grades 4–12.* Boston: Boston College.

Champagne, A. B., Hoz, R., & Klopfer, L. E. (1984). *Construct validation of the cognitive structure of physics concepts.* Paper presented at the annual meeting of the American Educational Research Association, New Orleans, LA.

Champagne, A. B., & Klopfer, L. E. (1980). *Using the ConSAT: A memo to teachers.* (LRDC Reports to Educators RTE/4). Pittsburgh, PA: University of Pittsburgh, Learning Research and Development Center.

Champagne, A. B., Klopfer, L. E., & Gunstone, R. F. (1982). Cognitive research and the design of science instruction. *Educational Psychologist, 17*, 31–53.

Checkley, K. (1997). The first seven . . . and the eighth: A conversation with Howard Gardner. *Educational Leadership, 55*(1), 8–13.

Chun, K. T., Cobb, S., & French J. R. P., Jr. (Eds.). (1975). *Measures for psychological assessment: A guide to 3,000 original sources and their applications.* Ann Arbor, MI: Institute for Social Research.

Clark, J. L. (1992). The Toronto Board of Education's Benchmarks in Mathematics. *The Arithmetic Teacher: Mathematics Education Through the Middle Grades, 39*(6), 51–55.

Clarke, J. H. (1990). *Patterns of thinking: Integrating learning skills in content thinking.* Boston: Allyn & Bacon.

Clarridge, P. B., & Whitaker, E. M. (1997). *Rolling the elephant over: How to effect large-scale change in the reporting process.* Portsmouth, NH: Heinemann.

Cleary, T. A. (1968). Test bias: Prediction of grades of negro and white students in integrated colleges. *Journal of Educational Measurement, 5*, 115–124.

Coffman, W. E. (1971). Essay examinations. In R. L. Thorndike (Ed.), *Educational measurement* (2nd ed.). Washington, DC: American Council on Education.

Cohen, J. (1960). A coefficient of agreement for nominal scales. *Educational and Psychological Measurement, 20*, 37–46.

Cohen, S. A., & Hyman, J. S. (1991). Can fantasies become facts? *Educational Measurement: Issues and Practice, 10*(1), 20–23.

Cole, N. S. (1973). Bias in selection. *Journal of Educational Measurement, 10*, 237–255.

Cole, N. S. (1978, March). *Approaches to examining bias in achievement test items.* Paper presented at the annual meeting of the American Personnel and Guidance Association, Washington, DC.

Cole, N. S., & Hanson, G. R. (1975). Impact of interest inventories on career choice. In E. E. Diamond (Ed.), *Issues of sex bias and sex fairness in career interest measurement.* Washington, DC: Career Education Program, National Institute of Education, Department of Health, Education, and Welfare.

Cole, N. S., & Moss, P. A. (1989). Bias in test use. In R. L. Linn (Ed.), *Educational measurement* (3rd ed., pp. 201–219). Upper Saddle River, NJ: Merrill/Prentice Hall.

Cole, N. S., & Nitko, A. J. (1981). Instrumentation and bias: Issues in selecting measures for educational evaluations. In R. A. Berk (Ed.), *Educational evaluation methodology: The state of the art.* Baltimore: Johns Hopkins University Press.

Cole, N. S., & Zieky, M. J. (2001). The new faces of fairness. *Journal of Educational Measurement, 38*, 369–382.

Collis, K. F. (1991). *Assessment of the learned structure in elementary mathematics and science.* Paper presented at the Assessment in the Mathematical Sciences Conference, Victoria, Australia.

Committee on Education and the Workforce. (2005). *Full history of the ESEA effort: Press releases, summaries, and information related to H.R. 1, the Reauthorization of the Elementary and Secondary Education Act.* Retrieved from http://edworkforce.house.gov/democrats/eseainfo.html

Connolly, A. J., Nachtman, W., & Pritchett, E. M. (1976). *Manual: KeyMath diagnostic arithmetic test.* Circle Pines, MN: American Guidance Service.

Consulting Psychologists Press, Inc. (1994). *Strong interest inventory.* Palo Alto, CA: Author.

Corby, K. (2002). *Tests and testing information.* East Lansing: Michigan State University, University Library.

Council of Chief State School Officers. (2005). *Alignment analysis.* Washington, DC: Author. Available from http://www.ccsso.org/Projects/alignment_analysis

Cowan, J. (1972, February). Is freedom of choice in examinations such an advantage? *The Technical Journal.*

Crane, L., & Bellis, D. (1978). *Preliminary results of Illinois pilot district edits.* Unpublished memorandum to Technical Assistance Center Directors.

Cronbach, L. J. (1951). Coefficient alpha and the internal structure of tests. *Psychometrika, 16*, 297–334.

Cronbach, L. J. (1963). Course improvement through evaluation. *Teachers College Record, 64*, 672–683.

Cronbach, L. J. (1971). Test validation. In R. L. Thorndike (Ed.), *Educational measurement* (2nd ed.). Washington, DC: American Council on Education.

Cronbach, L. J. (1977). *Educational psychology* (3rd ed.). New York: Harcourt Brace Jovanovich.

Cronbach, L. J. (1988). Five perspectives on validity argument. In H. Wainer (Ed.), *Test validity* (pp. 3–17). Hillsdale, NJ: Erlbaum.

Cronbach, L. J. (1989). Construct validation after thirty years. In R. L. Linn (Ed.), *Intelligence: Measurement, theory, and public policy* (pp. 147–171). Urbana: University of Illinois Press.

Cronbach, L. J. (1990). *Essentials of psychological testing* (5th ed.). New York: Harper & Row.

Cronbach, L. J., & Gleser, G. C. (1965). *Psychological tests and personnel decisions* (2nd ed.). Urbana: University of Illinois Press.

Cronbach, L. J., & Snow, R. E. (1977). *Aptitudes and instructional methods: A handbook for research on interactions.* New York: Irvington.

CTB Macmillan/McGraw-Hill. (1992). *Listening and speaking checklist, Grades 9–12: California Achievement Tests* (5th ed.). Monterey, CA: Author.

CTB/McGraw-Hill. (1985). *Kuder Occupational Interest Survey, Form DD.* Monterey, CA: Author.

CTB/McGraw-Hill. (1993). *California Achievement Tests, Class management guide* (5th ed.). Monterey, CA: Author.

CTB/McGraw-Hill. (1997). *Winter norms book: TerraNova.* Monterey, CA: Author.

Culler, R. E., & Holahan, C. J. (1980). Test anxiety and academic performance: The effects of study-related behaviors. *Journal of Educational Psychology, 72*, 16–20.

Cyert, R. M. (1980). Problem solving and educational policy. In D. T. Tuma & F. Reif (Eds.), *Problem solving and education: Issues in teaching and research.* Hillsdale, NJ: Erlbaum.

Darden, A. D. (2000). Thoughtful conversations: Student-teacher writing conferences. *Trade Secrets: Teaching Tips for Elementary, Middle, and High School Teachers, 20*(1), 3–5.

Darley, J. G., & Hagenah, T. (1955). *Vocational interest measurement.* Minneapolis: University of Minnesota Press.

Darlington, R. B. (1971). Another look at "cultural fairness." *Journal of Educational Measurement, 8*, 71–82.

Darlington, R. B. (1976). A defense of "rational" personnel selection, and two new methods. *Journal of Educational Measurement, 13*, 43–52.

Das, J. P. (2002). A better look at intelligence. *Current Directions in Psychological Science, 11*(1), 28–33.

Davey, B., & Rindone, D. A. (1990, April). *Anatomy of a performance task.* Paper presented at the annual meeting of the American Educational Research Association, Boston, MA.

Davis, B. G., & Trimble, C. S. (1978). *Consumable booklets vs. single answer sheets with non-consumable booklets.* Frankfort: Kentucky State Department of Education. (ERIC Document Reproduction Service No. ED160656)

Davis, R. V. (1980). Measuring interests. In D. A. Payne (Ed.), *New directions for testing and measurement: Recent developments in affective measurement* (No. 7). San Francisco: Jossey-Bass.

DeLandsheere, V. (1988). Taxonomies of educational objectives. In J. P. Keeves (Ed.), *Educational research, methodology, and measurement: An international handbook* (pp. 345–354). Oxford: Pergamon Press.

DeVito, P. J., & Long, J. V. (1977, April). *The effects of spring-spring vs. fall-spring testing upon the evaluation of compensatory educational programs.* Paper presented at the annual convention of the American Educational Research Association, New York City.

Diamond, J. J., & Evans, W. J. (1972). An investigation of the cognitive correlates of testwiseness. *Journal of Educational Measurement, 9*, 145–150.

Donlon, T. F., & Angoff, W. H. (1971). The Scholastic Aptitude Test. In W. H. Angoff (Ed.), *The College Board Admissions Testing Program: A technical report on research and development activities relating to the Scholastic Aptitude Test and achievement tests.* New York: College Entrance Examination Board.

Dorans, N. J. (1994, May). *Choosing and evaluating a scale transformation: Centering and realigning SAT score distributions.* Princeton, NJ: Educational Testing Service.

Douglas, H. R., & Tallmadge, M. (1934). How university students prepare for new types of examinations. *School and Society, 39*, 318–320.

Downing, S. M., Baranowski, R. A., Grosso, L. J., & Norcini, J. J. (1995). Stem type and cognitive ability measured: The validity evidence for multiple true-false items in medical specialty certification. *Applied Measurement in Education, 8*, 187–197.

Dudycha, A. L., & Dudycha, L. W. (1972). Behavioral statistics: An historical perspective. In R. E. Kirk (Ed.), *Statistical issues: A reader for the behavioral sciences.* Monterey, CA: Brooks/Cole.

Dunbar, D. A., Float, B., & Lyman, F. J. (1980, November). *Report card revision steering committee final report.* Mount Lebanon, PA: Mount Lebanon School District.

Dunbar, S. B., Koretz, D., & Hoover, H. D. (1991). Quality control in the development and use of performance assessments. *Applied Measurement in Education, 4*(4), 289–303.

Duran, R. P. (1989). Testing of linguistic minorities. In R. L. Linn (Ed.), *Educational measurement* (3rd ed., pp. 573–587). Upper Saddle River, NJ: Merrill/Prentice Hall.

Duschl, R. A., & Gitomer, D. H. (1991). Epistemological perspectives on conceptual change: Implications for educational practice. *Journal of Research in Science Teaching, 28*, 839–858.

Ebel, R. L. (1951). Writing the test item. In E. F. Lindquist (Ed.), *Educational measurement.* Washington, DC: American Council on Education.

Ebel, R. L. (1965). *Measuring educational achievement.* Upper Saddle River, NJ: Prentice Hall.

Ebel, R. L. (1972). *Essentials of educational measurement* (2nd ed.). Upper Saddle River, NJ: Prentice Hall.

Ebel, R. L. (1974). Shall we get rid of grades? *Measurement in Education, 5*(4), 1–2.

Ebel, R. L. (1979). *Essentials of educational measurement* (3rd ed.). Upper Saddle River, NJ: Prentice Hall.

Ebel, R. L., & Frisbie, D. A. (1991). *Essentials of educational measurement* (5th ed.). Upper Saddle River, NJ: Prentice Hall.

Ebel, R. L., & Stuit, D. B. (1954). *Technical Bulletin No. 8.* Iowa City: University Examinations Service, State University of Iowa.

Egawa, K., & Azwell, T. (1995). Telling the story: Narrative reports. In T. Azwell & E. Schmar (Eds.), *Report on report cards: Alternatives to consider.* Portsmouth, NH: Heinemann.

Einhorn, H. J., & Bass, A. R. (1971). Methodological considerations relevant to discrimination in employment testing. *Psychological Bulletin, 75,* 261–269.

Ennis, R. H. (1985). Goals for a critical thinking curriculum. In A. Costa (Ed.), *Developing minds: A resource book for teaching thinking.* Alexandria, VA: Association for Supervision and Curriculum Development.

Equal Employment Opportunity Commission, Civil Service Commission, Department of Justice, Department of Labor, & Department of the Treasury. (1979). Adoption of questions and answers to clarify and provide a common interpretation of the uniform guidelines on employee section procedures. *Federal Register, 44* (Publication Number: 11996–12006).

Equal Employment Opportunity Commission, Civil Service Commission, Department of Labor, & Department of Justice (1978, August 25). Uniform guidelines on employee selection procedures. *Federal Register, 43* (Publication Number: 38290–38315).

Ergene, T. (2003). Effective interventions on test anxiety reduction: A meta-analysis. *School Psychology International, 24,* 313–328.

Ericsson, K. A., & Simon, H. A. (1999). *Protocol analysis: Verbal reports as data.* Cambridge: Massachusetts Institute of Technology.

Evaluation Center. (1995). *An independent evaluation of the Kentucky Instructional Results Information System (KIRIS).* Frankfort: Kentucky Institute for Education Research.

Feister, W. J., & Whitney, D. R. (1968). An interview with D. E. F. Linquist. *Epsilon Bulletin, 42,* 17–28.

Feldt, L. S. (1967). A note on the use of confidence bands to evaluate the reliability of a difference between two scores. *American Educational Research Journal, 4,* 139–145.

Feldt, L. S. (1976, December). *New uses of Iowa Tests of Educational Development as an instrument for evaluation.* Paper presented at the Sixty-First Annual Education Conference, Evaluation in the Schools, Iowa City, IA.

Feldt, L. S. (2002). Estimating the internal consistency reliability of tests composed of testlets varying in length. *Applied Measurement in Education, 15,* 33–48.

Feldt, L. S., & Brennan, R. L. (1989). Reliability. In R. L. Linn (Ed.), *Educational measurement* (3rd ed.). New York: Macmillan.

Ferguson, R. L. (1970). A model for computer-assisted criterion-referenced measurement. *Education, 81,* 25–31.

Fillenbaum, S., & Rapoport, A. (1971). *Structures in the subjective lexicon.* New York: Academic Press.

Finley, C. J. (1977, October 24). *Errors in reporting data in Iowa.* Unpublished memoranda to Technical Assistance Center Directors.

Fischer, R. J. (1994). The Americans with Disabilities Act: Implications for measurement. *Educational Measurement: Issues and Practice, 13*(4), 17–26, 37.

Fisher, T. H. (1980). The courts and your minimum competency testing program—A guide to survival. *NCME Measurement in Education, 11*(1), 1–12.

Flanagan, J. C. (1967). Functional education for the seventies. *Phi Delta Kappan, 49,* 27–32.

Flanagan, J. C. (1969). Program for learning in accordance with needs. *Psychology in the Schools, 6,* 133–136.

Flaugher, R. L. (1978). The many definitions of test bias. *American Psychologist, 33,* 671–679.

Flavell, J. H. (1976). Metacognitive aspects of problem solving. In L. B. Resnick (Ed.), *The nature of intelligence* (pp. 231–235). Hillsdale, NJ: Erlbaum.

Forsyth, R. A. (1976, March). *Describing what Johnny can do* (Iowa Testing Program, Occasional Paper, No. 17). Iowa City: University of Iowa.

Frank, L. K. (1939). Projective methods for the study of personality. *Journal of Psychology, 8,* 389–413.

Frederiksen, N. (1984). Implications of cognitive theory for instruction in problem-solving. *Review of Educational Research, 54,* 363–407.

Freeman, D. J., Kuhs, T. M., Knappen, L. B., & Porter, A. C. (1982). A closer look at standardized tests. *Arithmetic Teacher, 29*(7), 50–54.

Frisbie, D. A. (1992). The multiple true-false format: A status review. *Educational Measurement: Issues and Practice, 11*(4), 21–26.

Frisbie, D. A., & Becker, D. F. (1990). An analysis of textbook advice about true-false tests. *Applied Measurement in Education, 4,* 67–83.

Frisbie, D. A., & Waltman, K. K. (1992). Developing a personal grading plan. *Educational Measurement: Issues and Practice, 11*(3), 35–42.

Gaffney, R. F., & Maguire, T. O. (1971). Use of optically scored test answer sheets with young children. *Journal of Educational Measurement, 8,* 103–106.

Gagné, R. M. (1962). The acquisition of knowledge. *Psychological Review, 69,* 355–365.

Gagné, R. M. (1968). Learning hierarchies. *Educational Psychologist, 6,* 1–9.

Gagné, R. M. (1970). Instructional variables and learning outcomes. In M. C. Wittrock & F. Wiley (Eds.), *Evaluation of instruction.* New York: Holt, Rinehart & Winston.

Gagné, R. M., & Briggs, L. J. (1979). *Principles of instructional design* (2nd ed.). New York: Holt, Rinehart & Winston.

Gagné, R. M., Briggs, L. J., & Wager, W. W. (1988). *Principles of instructional design* (3rd ed.). New York: Holt, Rinehart & Winston.

Gagné, R. M., Major, J. R., Garstens, H. L., & Paradise, N. E. (1962). Factors in acquiring knowledge of a mathematical task. *Psychological Monographs, 76*(7, whole No. 526).

Gagné, R. M., & Paradise, N. E. (1961). Abilities and learning sets in knowledge acquisition. *Psychological Monographs, 75*(14, whole No. 518).

Gardner, H. (1983). *Frames of mind: The theory of multiple intelligences.* New York: Basic Books.

Gardner, H. (1991). *The unschooled mind: How children think and how schools should teach.* New York: Basic Books.

Gardner, H. (1993). Educating for understanding. *American School Board Journal, 180,* 20–24.

GI Forum, et al. vs. Texas Education Agency, et al. (January 7, 2000). U.S. District Court (Civil Action SA – 97-CA-1278-EP).

Gick, M. L. (1986). Problem-solving strategies. *Educational Psychologist, 21,* 99–120.

Glaser, R. (1963). Instructional technology and the measurement of learning outcomes. *American Psychologist, 18,* 519–521.

Glaser, R. (1968). Adapting the elementary school curriculum to individual performances. *Proceedings of the 1967 Invitational Conference on Testing Problems,* pp. 3–36. Princeton, NJ: Educational Testing Service.

Glaser, R. (1977). *Adaptive education: Individual diversity and learning.* New York: Holt, Rinehart & Winston.

Glaser, R. (1982). Instructional psychology: Past, present, and future. *American Psychologist, 37,* 292–305.

Glaser, R. (1984). Education and thinking: The role of knowledge. *American Psychologist, 39,* 93–104.

Glaser, R., Lesgold, A., & Lajoie, S. (1985). Toward a cognitive theory for the measurement of achievement. In R. R. Ronning, J. Gloveer, J. C. Conoley, & J. C. Witt (Eds.), *The influence of cognitive psychology on testing and measurement* (pp. 41–85). Hillsdale, NJ: Erlbaum.

Glaser, R., & Nitko, A. J. (1971). Measurement in learning and instruction. In R. L. Thorndike (Ed.), *Educational measurement* (2nd ed., pp. 625–670). Washington, DC: American Council on Education.

Goldman, B. A., & Mitchell, D. F. (Eds.). (1997). *Directory of unpublished experimental measures.* Dubuque, IA: William C. Brown.

Gong, B., Venezky, R., & Mioduser, D. (1992). Instructional assessments: Level for systemic change in science education classrooms. *Journal of Science Education and Technology, 1,* 157–175.

Good, T. L., & Brophy, J. E. (2002). *Looking in classrooms* (9th ed.). Boston: Allyn & Bacon.

Goodwin, D. L. (1966). *Training teachers in reinforcement techniques to increase student* task-oriented behavior: An experimental evaluation. In L. J. Cronbach, G. C. Gleser, H. Nanda, & N. Rajaratmam, *The dependability of behavioral measurements: Theory of generaliz-ability of scores and profiles.* New York: Wiley.

Gow, D. T. (Ed.). (1976). *Design and development of curricular materials: Instructional design articles* (Vol. 2). Pittsburgh: University Center for International Studies, University of Pittsburgh.

Green, K. (1984). Effects of item characteristics on multiple-choice item difficulty. *Educational and Psychological Measurement, 44,* 551–561.

Greene, H. A., Jorgensen, A. N., & Gerberich, J. R. (1942). *Measurement and evaluation in the elementary school.* New York: Longmans, Green.

Greene, H. A., Jorgensen, A. N., & Gerberich, J. R. (1943). *Measurement and evaluation in the secondary school.* New York: Longmans, Green.

Greeno, J. G. (1976). Cognitive objectives of instruction: Theory of knowledge for solving problems and answering questions. In D. Klahr (Ed.), *Cognition and instruction.* Hillsdale, NJ: Erlbaum.

Greeno, J. G. (1978). Nature of problem-solving abilities. In W. K. Estes (Ed.), *Handbook of learning and cognitive processes* (Vol. 5). Hillsdale, NJ: Erlbaum.

Gronlund, N. E. (1973). *Preparing criterion-referenced tests for classroom instruction.* New York: Macmillan.

Gronlund, N. E. (1976). *Measurement and evaluation in teaching* (3rd ed.). Upper Saddle River, NJ: Merrill/Prentice Hall.

Gross, A. L., & Su, W. (1975). Defining a "fair" or "unbiased" selection model: A question of utilities. *Journal of Applied Psychology, 60,* 345–351.

Grossman, H. J. (1983). *Classification in mental retardation.* Washington, DC: American Association on Mental Deficiency.

Gulliksen, H. (1950). *Theory of mental tests.* New York: Wiley.

Gulliksen, H. (1986). Perspective on educational measurement. *Applied Psychological Measurement, 10,* 109–132.

Haertel, E., & Calfee, R. (1983). School achievement: Thinking about what to test. *Journal of Educational Measurement, 20,* 119–131.

Hakstain, A. R. (1969, February). *The effects of type of examination anticipated on student test preparation and performance.* Paper presented at the annual meeting of the American Educational Research Association, Washington, DC.

Haladyna, T. M., & Downing, S. M. (1989a). A taxonomy of multiple-choice item-writing rules. *Applied Measurement in Education, 2,* 37–50.

Haladyna, T. M., & Downing, S. M. (1989b). Validity of a taxonomy of multiple-choice item-writing rules. *Applied Measurement in Education, 2,* 51–78.

Haladyna, T. M, Downing, S. M., & Rodriguez, M. C. (2002). A review of multiple-choice item writing guidelines for classroom assessment. *Applied Measurement in Education, 15,* 309–334.

Hambleton, R. K., & Murphy, E. (1992). A psychometric perspective on authentic measurement. *Applied Measurement in Education, 5,* 1–16.

Hambleton, R. K., & Sheehan, D. S. (1977). On the evaluation of higher-order science instructional objectives. *Science Education, 61,* 307–315.

Harcourt Educational Measurement. (1992). *Integrated Assessment System: Science Performance Assessment.* San Antonio, TX: Author.

Harcourt Educational Measurement. (2003). *Otis-Lennon School Ability Test (8th ed.) Levels E/F/G. Directions for administering.* San Antonio, TX: Author.

Harmin, M. (1994). *Inspiring active learning: A handbook for teachers.* Alexandria, VA: Association for Supervision and Curriculum Development.

Harris, W. S. (1973). Agreement among NCME members on selected issues in educational measurement. *Journal of Educational Measurement, 10,* 63–70.

Harrow, A. J. (1972). *A taxonomy of the psychomo-tor domain: A guide for developing behavioral objectives.* White Plains, NY: Longman.

Hawkes, H. E., Lindquist, E. F., & Mann, C. R. (Eds.) (1936). *The construction and use of achievement examinations: A manual for secondary school teachers.* Boston: Houghton Mifflin.

Hembree, R. (1988). Correlates, causes, effects and treatment of test anxiety. *Review of Educational Research, 58,* 47–77.

Henrysson, S. (1971). Gathering, analyzing, and using data on test items. In R. L. Thorndike (Ed.), *Educational measurement* (2nd ed.). Washington, DC: American Council on Education.

Herman, J. L., Aschbacher, P. R., & Winters, L. (1992). *A practical guide to alternative assessment.* Alexandria, VA: Association for Supervision and Curriculum Development.

Herman, W. E. (1990). Fear of failure as a distinctive personality trait measure of test anxiety. *Journal of Research and Development in Education, 23,* 180–185.

Herndon, E. B. (1980). *Your child and testing.* Washington, DC: National Institute of Education, U.S. Department of Education.

Hewson, M. G. A. B., & Hamlyn, D. (1984). The influence of intellectual environment on conceptions of heat. *European Journal of Science Education, 6,* 245–262.

Hieronymus, A. N. (1976, December). *Uses of Iowa Tests of Basic Skills in evaluation.* Paper presented at the Sixty-First Annual Education Conferences, Iowa City, IA.

Hieronymus, A. N., & Lindquist, E. F. (1971). *Iowa Tests of Basic Skills: Teacher's guide to administration, interpretation, and use* (Levels Ed., Form 6). Iowa City, IA: Riverside.

Hieronymus, A. N., & Lindquist, E. F. (1974a). *Iowa Tests of Basic Skills: Manual for administrators, supervisors, and counselors* (Levels ed., Forms 5 & 6). Iowa City, IA: Riverside.

Hieronymus, A. N., & Lindquist, E. F. (1974b). *Iowa Tests of Basic Skills: Teacher's guide for*

administration, interpretation, and use (Forms 5 & 6). Iowa City, IA: Riverside.

Highland, R. W. (1955). *A guide for use in performance testing in Air Force technical schools* (ASPRL-TM-55-1). Lowry Air Force Base, CO: Armament Systems Performance Personnel Research Laboratory.

Hills, J. R. (1976). *Exercises in classroom measurement.* Upper Saddle River, NJ: Merrill/Prentice Hall.

Hills, J. R. (1990). Response to two letters: Grading practices and improving standardized test scores. *Educational Measurement: Issues and Practice, 9*(3), 33.

Hirsch, E. D., Jr. (1977). *The philosophy of composition.* Chicago: University of Chicago Press.

Holland, J. L. (1973). *Making vocational choices: A theory of careers.* Upper Saddle River, NJ: Prentice Hall.

Holland, J. L. (1975). The use and evaluation of interest inventories. In E. E. Diamond (Ed.), *Issues of sex bias and sex fairness in career interest measurement.* Washington, DC: Career Education Program, National Institute of Education, Department of Health, Education, and Welfare.

Hoover, H. D. (1984a). The most appropriate scores for measuring educational development in the elementary schools: GE. *Educational Measurement: Issues and Practice, 3*(4), 8–14.

Hoover, H. D. (1984b). Rejoinder to Burket. *Educational Measurement: Issues and Practice, 3*(4), 16–18.

Hoover, H. D., Hieronymus, A. N., Frisbie, D. A., & Dunbar, S. B. (1993a). *Directions for administration: Iowa Tests of Basic Skills, Levels 9–14, Forms K and L.* Chicago: Riverside.

Hoover, H. D., Hieronymus, A. N., Frisbie, D. A., & Dunbar, S. (1993b). *Interpretive guide for teachers and counselors: Iowa Tests of Basic Skills, Levels 9–14, Forms K and L.* Chicago: Riverside.

Hoover, H. D., Hieronymus, A. N., Frisbie, D. A., & Dunbar, S. B. (1993c). *Iowa Tests of Basic Skills: Norms and score conversions, complete and core batteries, Form K.* Chicago: Riverside.

Hoover, H. D., Hieronymus, A. N., Frisbie, D. A., & Dunbar, S. B. (1993d). *Iowa Tests of Basic Skills: Score conversions, complete and core batteries, Form K.* Chicago: Riverside.

Hopkins, K. D., Stanley, J. C., & Hopkins, B. R. (1990). *Educational and psychological measurement and evaluation* (7th ed.). Upper Saddle River, NJ: Prentice Hall.

Horvath, F. G. (1991). *Assessment in Alberta: Dimensions of authenticity.* Paper presented at the annual meeting of the National Association of Test Directors and the National Council on Measurement in Education, Chicago, IL.

Hough, H. (2005). *Tests and measures in social science: Tests available in compilation volumes.* University of Texas at Arlington, Central Library, Health Sciences. Retrieved from http://libraries.uta.edu/helen/test&meas/testmainframe.htm

Huynh, H. (1976). On the reliability of decisions in domain-referenced testing. *Journal of Educational Measurement, 13,* 253–264.

Ismail, M. (1994). *Development and validation of a multicomponent diagnostic test of arithmetic word problem solving ability for sixth-grade students in Malaysia.* Unpublished doctoral dissertation, University of Pittsburgh, Pittsburgh, PA.

Iwanicki, E. F. (1980). A new generation of standardized achievement test batteries: A profile of their major features. *Journal of Educational Measurement, 17,* 155–162.

Jaeger, R. M. (1973). The national test-equating study in reading: Pre-Anchor Test Study. *NCME Measurement in Education, 4,* 1–8.

Jaeger, R. M. (1989). Certification of student competence. In R. L. Linn (Ed.), *Educational measurement* (3rd ed., pp. 485–514). New York: Macmillan.

Jaeger, R. M. (1990). Setting standards on teacher certification tests. In J. Millman & L. Darling-Hammond (Eds.), *The new handbook of teacher evaluation: Assessing elementary and secondary school teachers* (pp. 295–321). Newbury Park, CA: Sage.

Jakwerth, P. R., Stancavage, F. B., & Reed, E. D. (1999). *An investigation of why students do not respond to questions* (NAEP validity studies). Palo Alto, CA: American Institutes for Research.

Jenkins, J. R., & Deno, S. J. (1971). Assessing knowledge of concepts and principles. *Journal of Educational Measurement, 8*(1), 95–101.

Johnson, H. M. (1928). Some fallacies underlying the use of psychological tests. *Psychological Review, 35,* 328–337. In T. Engen & N. Levy (Eds.), *Selected readings in the history of mental measurement* (1955). Providence, RI: Brown University.

Johnson, H. M. (1936). Pseudo-mathematics in the mental and social sciences. *American Journal of Psychology, 48,* 342–351. In T. Engen & N. Levy (Eds.), *Selected readings in the history of mental measurement* (1955). Providence, RI: Brown University.

Johnson, P. E. (1967). Some psychological aspects of subject-matter structure. *Journal of Educational Psychology, 58,* 75–85.

Johnson, R. T., & Thomas, W. P. (1979, April). *User experiences in implementing the RMC Title I evaluation modes.* Paper presented at the annual meeting of the American Educational Research Association, San Francisco, CA.

Joint Advisory Committee. (1993). *Principles for fair student assessment practices for education in Canada.* Edmonton, Alberta: Author, Centre for Research in Applied Measurement and Evaluation, University of Alberta.

Joint Committee on Standards for Educational Evaluation. (1988). *The personnel evaluation standards: How to assess systems for evaluating educators.* Thousand Oaks, CA: Corwin Press. Available from http://www.wmich.edu/evalctr/jc

Joint Committee on Standards for Educational Evaluation. (1994). *The program evaluation standards: How to assess evaluations of educational programs.* Thousand Oaks, CA: Sage. Available from http://www.wmich.edu/evalctr/jc

Joint Committee on Standards for Educational Evaluation. (2003). *The student evaluation standards: How to improve evaluations of students.* Thousand Oaks, CA: Corwin Press.

Joint Committee on Testing Practices. (1999). *Rights and responsibilities of test takers: Guidelines and expectations.* Retrieved January 23, 2006, from http://www.apa.org/science/ttrr.html

Joint Committee on Testing Practices. (2004). *Code of fair testing practices in education (revised).* Washington, DC: Science Directorate, American Psychological Association. Available from http://www.apa.org/science/fairtestcode.html

Jones, L. V. (1971). The nature of measurement. In R. L. Thorndike (Ed.), *Educational measurement* (2nd ed.). Washington, DC: American Council on Education.

Jones, R. W. (1994). *Performance and alternative assessment techniques: Meeting the challenges of alternative evaluation strategies.* Paper presented at the Second International Conference on Educational Evaluation and Assessment, Pretoria, Republic of South Africa.

Ju, T-P. (1989). *The development of a microcomputer-assisted measurement tool to display a person's knowledge structure.* Unpublished doctoral dissertation, University of Pittsburgh, Pittsburgh, PA.

Kane, M. T. (1992). An argument-based approach to validity. *Psychological Bulletin, 112,* 527–535.

Kane, M. T. (2001). Current concerns in validity theory. *Journal of Educational Measurement, 38,* 319–342.

Kane, M. T. (2002). Validating high-stakes testing programs. *Educational Measurement: Issues and Practice, 21*(1), 31–41.

Karweit, N. L., & Wasik, B. A. (1992). *A review of the effects of extra-year kindergarten programs and transitional first grades* (CDS Report 41). Baltimore: Center for Research on Effective Schooling for Disadvantaged Students, Johns Hopkins University.

Kaufman, A. S., & Kaufman, N. L. (2004). *Kaufman Assessment Battery for Children, Second Edition.* Circle Pines, MN: American Guidance Service.

Kaufman, A. S., Lichtenberger, E. O., Fletcher-Janzen, E., & Kaufman, N. L. (2005). *Essentials of KABC-II Assessment.* San Francisco: Jossey-Bass.

Keller, F. S. (1968). Goodbye teacher. *Journal of Applied Behavior Analysis, 1,* 79–89.

Keller, F. S., & Sherman, J. G. (1974). *PSI: The Keller Plan handbook.* Menlo Park, CA: Benjamin-Cummings.

Kelly, T. L. (1939). The selection of upper and lower groups for the validation of test items. *Journal of Educational Psychology, 30,* 17–24.

Kentucky Department of Education. (1993a). *KIRIS Assessment Portfolio: Mathematics, Grade 4, 1993–1994.* Frankfort, KY: Office of Assessment and Accountability.

Kentucky Department of Education. (1993b). *Portfolios and you.* Frankfort, KY: Office of Assessment and Accountability.

Kentucky Department of Education. (1993c). *Teacher's guide: Kentucky Mathematics Portfolio.* Frankfort, KY: Office of Assessment and Accountability.

Kentucky Department of Education. (1994). *KIRIS Mathematics Portfolio Assessment, Grade 8: Scoring training manual, 1992–93, Addenda 1994.* Frankfort, KY: Office of Assessment and Accountability.

Keyser, D. J., & Sweetland, R. C. (Eds.) (1994). *Test critiques: Volume 10.* Austin, TX: PRO-ED.

Khattri, N., Reeve, A. L., & Adamson, R. J. (1997). *Studies of education reform: Assessment of student performance.* Washington, DC: Office of Educational Research and Improvement.

King, K. V., Gardner, D. A., Zucker, S., & Jorgensen, M. A. (2004, July). *The distractor rationale taxonomy: Enhancing multiple-choice items in reading and mathematics* (Harcourt Assessment Report). San Antonio, TX: Harcourt Assessment.

King, W. L., & Janow, J. E. (1990). *Testing accommodations for students with disabilities.* Washington, DC: Association on Handicapped Student Services in Postsecondary Education.

Kintsch, W. (1974). *The representations of meaning in memory.* Hillsdale, NJ: Erlbaum.

Klaus, C. H., Lloyd-Jones, R., Brown, R., Littlefair, W., Mullis, I., Miller, D., et al. (1979). *Composing childhood experience: An approach to writing and learning in the elementary grade*s (Experimental version). St. Louis: CEMREL.

Klausmeier, H. J. (1975). An alternative form of schooling. In K. Talmage (Ed.), *Systems of individual education.* Berkeley, CA: McCutchan.

Klopfer, L. E. (1969). *An operational definition of "understand."* Unpublished manuscript, Learning Research and Development Center, University of Pittsburgh, Pittsburgh, PA.

Klopfer, L. E. (1971). Evaluation of learning in science. In B. S. Bloom, J. T. Hastings, & G. F. Madaus (Eds.), *Handbook on formative and summative evaluation of student learning.* New York: McGraw-Hill.

Koretz, D., Stecher, B., Klein, S., & McCaffrey, D. (1994). The Vermont Portfolio Assessment Program: Findings and implications. *Educational Measurement: Issues and Practice, 13*(3), 5–16.

Kracke, E. A. (1953). *Civil service in early Sung China: 960–1067.* Cambridge, MA: Harvard University Press.

Krathwohl, D. R. (2002). A revision of Bloom's Taxonomy: An overview. *Theory Into Practice, 41*(4), 212–218.

Krathwohl, D. R., Bloom, B. S., & Masia, B. B. (1964). *Taxonomy of educational objectives: Book 2. Affective domain.* White Plains, NY: Longman.

Kryspin, W. J., & Feldhusen, J. F. (1974). *Developing classroom tests.* Minneapolis: Burgess.

en
E
Nurs
as
C
Ode
ne
O'D
Jo
22
Oost
ed
Sa
Oost
C
th
Jo
Oswa
et
Su
Otis,
m
An
Parke
M
mi
Re
Parke
sch
in
an
Pauls
(1
Ed
Pears
of
40
Pelle
R.
W
Perfo
Wi
Re
Perki
co
Re
Perl,
pa
Ch
Peter
(1
R.
(3r
Pfanz
Yo
Philli
of
Ed
56
Philli
ac
rig
93
Philli
Re
Ne
ww

Kuder, G. F., & Richardson, M. W. (1937). The theory of the estimation of test reliability. *Psychometrika, 2*, 151–160.

Kuhn, D. (1999). A developmental model of critical thinking. *Educational Researcher, 28*(2), 16–25, 46.

Kunder, L. H., & Porwoll, P. J. (1977). *Reporting student progress: Policies, procedures, and systems.* Arlington, VA: Educational Research Service.

La Marca, P. M., Redfield, D., Winter, P. C., Bailey, A., & Despriet, L. H. (2000). *State standards and state assessment systems: A guide to alignment.* Washington, DC: Council of State School Officers.

Landau, D., & Lazarsfeld, P. F. (1968). Quetelet, Adolphe. *International encyclopedia of the social sciences, 13*, 247–257.

Lane, S. (1992). The conceptual framework for the development of a mathematics performance assessment instrument. *Educational Measurement: Issues and Practice, 12*(2), 16–23.

Lane, S., Parke, C., & Moskal, B. (1992). *Principles for developing performance assessments.* Paper presented at the annual meeting of the American Educational Research Association, San Francisco, CA.

Lane, S., & Stone, C. A. (2002). Strategies for examining the consequences of assessment and accountability programs. *Educational Measurement: Issues and Practice, 21*(1), 23–30.

Langenfeld, T. E., & Crocker, L. M. (1994). The evaluation of validity theory: Public school testing, the courts, and incompatible interpretations. *Educational Assessment, 2*, 149–165.

Lawshe, C. H., & Balma, M. J. (1966). *Principles of personnel testing* (2nd ed.). New York: McGraw-Hill.

Liebert, R. M., & Morris, L. W. (1967). Cognitive and emotional components of test anxiety: A distinction and some initial data. *Psychological Reports, 20*, 975–978.

Lindquist, E. F. (1936). The theory of test construction. In H. E. Hawkes, E. F. Lindquist, & C. R. Mann (Eds.), *The construction and use of achievement examinations: A manual for secondary school teachers.* Boston: Houghton Mifflin.

Lindquist, E. F. (1951). Preliminary considerations in objective test construction. In E. F. Lindquist (Ed.), *Educational measurement.* Washington, DC: American Council on Education.

Lindquist, E. F., & Mann, C. R. (1936). The construction of tests. In H. E. Hawkes, E. F. Lindquist, & C. R. Mann (Eds.), *The construction and use of achievement examinations: A manual for secondary school teachers.* Boston: Houghton Mifflin.

Lindvall, C. M. (1964). Introduction. In C. M. Lindvall (Ed.), *Defining educational objectives: A report of the Regional Commission on Educational Coordination and the Learning Research and Development Center.* Pittsburgh, PA: University of Pittsburgh Press.

Lindvall, C. M. (1967). *Measuring pupil achievement and aptitude.* New York: Harcourt, Brace and World.

Lindvall, C. M. (1976). Criteria for stating IPI objectives. In D. T. Gow (Ed.), *Design and development of curricular materials: Instructional design articles* (Vol. 2). Pittsburgh, PA: University Center for International Studies, University of Pittsburgh.

Lindvall, C. M., & Bolvin, J. O. (1967). Programmed instruction in the schools: An application of programming principles in "Individually Prescribed Instruction." In P. Lange (Ed.), *Programmed instruction: 66th Yearbook, Part II* (pp. 217–254). Chicago: National Society for the Study of Education.

Lindvall, C. M., & Cox, R. C. (1970). Evaluation as a tool in curriculum development: The IPI evaluation program. *AERA Monograph Series on Curriculum Evaluation* (Publication No. 5). Chicago: Rand McNally.

Lindvall, C. M., & Nitko, A. J. (1975). *Measuring pupil achievement and aptitude* (2nd ed.). New York: Harcourt Brace Jovanovich.

Linn, R. L. (1973). Fair test use in selection. *Review of Educational Research, 43*, 139–161.

Linn, R. L. (1993). Educational assessment: Expanded expectations and challenges. *Educational Evaluation and Policy Analysis, 15*, 1–16.

Linn, R. L. (1994). Performance assessment: Policy, promises, and technical measurement standards. *Educational Researcher, 23*(4), 4–14.

Linn, R. L., & Baker, E. (1997, Summer). CRESST conceptual model for assessment. *Evaluation Comment, 7*(1), 1–22.

Linn, R. L., Baker, E. L., & Dunbar, S. B. (1991). Complex, performance-based assessment: Expectations and validation criteria. *Educational Researcher, 20*(8), 5–21.

Linn, R. L., Graue, M. E., & Sanders, N. M. (1990). Comparing state and district test results to national norms: The validity of claims that "everyone is above average." *Educational Measurement: Issues and Practice, 9*(3), 5–14.

Linn, R. L., & Gronlund, N. E. (1995). *Measurement and assessment in teaching* (7th ed.). Upper Saddle River, NJ: Prentice Hall.

Lord, F. M. (1953). The relation of test scores to the trait underlying the test. *Educational and Psychological Measurement, 13*, 517–549.

Lord, F. M. (1977). A study of item bias using item characteristic curve theory. In Y. H. Poortinga (Ed.), *Basic problems in cross-cultural psychology.* Amsterdam: Swets and Vitlinger.

Lord, F. M., & Novick, M. R. (1968). *Statistical theories of mental test scores.* Reading, MA: Addison-Wesley.

Lyman, H. B. (1998). *Test scores and what they mean* (6th ed.). Boston: Allyn & Bacon.

Maddox, T. (Ed.). (2003). *Tests: A comprehensive reference for assessments in psychology, education, and business* (5th ed.). Austin, TX: PRO-ED.

Mandler, G., & Sarason, S. B. (1952). A study of anxiety and learning. *Journal of Abnormal and Social Psychology, 47*, 166–173.

Marshall, J. C. (1967). Composition errors and essay examinations grades reexamined. *American Educational Research Journal, 4*, 375–385.

Marshall, J. C., & Powers, J. M. (1969). Writing neatness, composition errors, and essay grades. *Journal of Educational Measurement, 6*, 97–101.

Marshall, S. P. (1990). Generating good items for diagnostic tests. In N. Frederiksen, R. Glaser, A. Lesgold, & M. G. Shafto (Eds.), *Diagnostic monitoring of skill and knowledge acquisition* (pp. 433–452). Hillsdale, NJ: Erlbaum.

Marshall, S. P., Pribe, C. A., & Smith, J. D. (1987). *Schema knowledge structure for representing and understanding arithmetic story problems* (Report No. SE 047 910). San Diego, CA: San Diego State University, Center for Research in Mathematics and Science Education. (ERIC Document Reproduction Service No. ED281716)

Marzano, R. J., Brandt, R. S., Hughes, C. S., Jones, B. F., Presseisan, B. Z., Rankin, S. C., et al. (1988). *Dimensions of thinking: A framework for curriculum and instruction.* Alexandria, VA: Association for Supervision and Curriculum Development.

Marzano, R. J., Pickering, D. J., Arredondo, D. E., Blackburn, G. J., Brandt, R. S., & Moffett, C. A. (1992). *Dimensions of Learning teacher's manual.* Alexandria, VA: Association for Supervision and Curriculum Development.

Marzano, R. J., Pickering, D., & McTighe, J. (1993). *Assessing student outcomes: Performance assessment using the Dimensions of Learning Model.* Alexandria, VA: Association for Supervision and Curriculum Development.

Matter, K. K. (1989). Putting test scores in perspective: Communicating a complete report card for your schools. In L. M. Rudner, J. C. Conoley, & B. S. Plake (Eds.), *Understanding achievement tests: A guide for school administrators* (pp. 121–129). Washington, DC: ERIC Clearinghouse on Tests, Measurement, and Evaluation.

Mayer, R. E., Larkin, J. H., & Kadane, J. B. (1984). A cognitive analysis of mathematical problem-solving ability. In R. J. Sternberg (Ed.), *Advances in the psychology of human intelligence.* Hillsdale, NJ: Erlbaum.

McCormick, R. A. (1974). Proxy consent in the experimental situation. *Perspectives in Biology and Medicine, 18*, 2–20.

McDonnell, L. (1997). *The politics of state testing: Implementing new student assessments. CSE Technical Report 424.* Los Angeles: National Center for Research on Evaluation, Standards, and Student Testing, UCLA.

McGregor, D. M. (1935). Scientific measurement and psychology. *Psychological Review, 24*, 246–266.

McKeachie, W. J., Pollie, D., & Spiesman, J. (1985). Relieving anxiety in classroom examinations. *Journal of Abnormal and Social Psychology, 50*, 93–98.

Mealey, D. L., & Host, T. R. (1992). Coping with test anxiety. *College Teaching, 40*, 147–150.

Roberts, M. (1994, October). Testing accommodations for students with disabilities. *Teaching Times*, 7–8.

Robertson, G. J. (1990). A practical model for test development. In C. R. Reynolds & R. W. Kamphaus (Eds.), *Handbook of psychological and educational assessment of children: Intelligence and achievement* (pp. 62–85). New York: Guilford Press.

Rodriguez, M. C. (2005). Three options are optimal for multiple-choice items: A meta-analysis of 80 years of research. *Educational Measurement: Issues and Practice, 24*(2), 3–13.

Royer, J. M., Cisero, C. A., & Carlo, M. S. (1993). Techniques and procedures for assessing cognitive skills. *Review of Educational Research, 63*, 201–243.

Rozeboom, W. W. (1966). Scaling theory and the nature of measurement. *Synthese, 16*, 170–233.

Rudner, L. M., & Boston, C. (1994). Performance assessment. *The ERIC Review, 3*(1), 2–12.

Rulon, P. J. (1939). A simplified procedure for determining the reliability of a test by split halves. *Harvard Educational Review, 9*, 99–103.

Salvia, J., & Ysseldyke, J. E. (2004). *Assessment in special and inclusive education* (9th ed.). Boston: Houghton Mifflin.

Sanders, N. M. (1966). *Classroom questions: What kinds?* New York: Harper & Row.

Sarason, I. G. (Ed.). (1980). *Test anxiety: Theory, research, and application*. Hillsdale, NJ: Erlbaum.

Sarason, I. G. (1984). Stress, anxiety, and cognitive interference: Reactions to tests. *Journal of Personality and Social Psychology, 46*, 929–938.

Sarnacki, R. E. (1979). An examination of test-wiseness in the cognitive test domain. *Review of Educational Research, 49*, 252–279.

Sattler, J. M. (1988). *Assessment of children* (3rd ed.). San Diego, CA: Author.

Sattler, J. M. (1992). *Assessment of children: WSC-III and WPPSI-R supplement*. San Diego, CA: Author.

Sax, G. (1974). *Principles of educational measurement and evaluation*. Belmont, CA: Wadsworth.

Sax, G. (1980). *Study guide for Principles of Educational Measurement and Evaluation* (2nd ed.). Belmont, CA: Wadsworth.

Sax, G. (1989). *Principles of educational and psychological measurement and evaluation*. Belmont, CA: Wadsworth.

Scannell, D. P., & Marshall, J. C. (1966). The effects of selected composition errors on the grades assigned to essay examinations. *American Educational Research Journal, 3*, 125–130.

Schmeiser, C. B. (1992). Ethical codes in the professions. *Educational Measurement: Issues and Practice, 11*(4), 5–11.

Schmidt, W. H. (1983). Content bias in achievement tests. *Journal of Educational Measurement, 20*, 165–178.

Scriven, M. (1967). *The methodology of evaluation*. AERA monograph series on curriculum evaluation (Publication No. 1). Chicago: Rand McNally.

Shalaway, L. (1998). *Learning to teach . . . Not just for beginners*. New York: Scholastic Professional Books.

Shank, R. C., & Ableson, R. (1977). *Scripts, plans, goals and understanding*. Hillsdale, NJ: Erlbaum.

Shannon, G. A. (1973). *The construction of matching tests: An empirical statement*. Unpublished master's thesis, University of Pittsburgh, Pittsburgh, PA.

Shavelson, R. J. (1985). *Schemata and teaching routines: A historical perspective*. Paper presented at the annual meeting of the American Educational Research Association, Chicago, IL.

Shavelson, R. J., & Baxter, G. P. (1991). Performance assessment in science. *Applied Measurement in Education, 4*, 347–362.

Shavelson, R. J., & Stanton, G. C. (1975). Construct validation: Methodology and application to three measures of cognitive structure. *Journal of Education Measurement, 12*, 67–85.

Shavelson, R. J., & Stern, P. (1981). Research on teachers' pedagogical thoughts, judgments, decisions, and behavior. *Review of Educational Research, 51*, 455–498.

Shepard, L. A. (1990). Inflated test score gains: Is the problem old norms or teaching the test? *Educational Measurement: Issues and Practice, 9*(3), 15–22.

Shepard, L. A. (1991). Interview on assessment issues with Lorrie Shepard. *Educational Researcher, 20*(3), 21–23.

Shepard, L. A. (1993). Evaluating test validity. *Review of Research in Education, 19*, 405–450.

Shuell, T. J. (1990). Phrases of meaning learning. *Review of Educational Psychology, 60*, 531–548.

Silver, E. A., Smith, M. S., & Nelson, B. S. (1995). The QUASAR Project: Equity concerns meet mathematics education reform in middle school. In W. Secada, E. Fennema, & L. Byrd (Eds.), *New directions for equity in mathematics education*. New York: Cambridge University Press.

Silver, H., Strong, R., & Perini, M. (1997). Integrating learning styles and multiple intelligences. *Educational Leadership, 55*(1), 22–27.

Simon, H. A. (1973). The structure of ill-structured problems. *Artificial Intelligence, 4*, 181–201.

Sireci, S. G. (2005). Unlabeling the disabled: A perspective on flagging scores from accommodated test administrations. *Educational Researcher, 34*(1), 3–12.

Slakter, M. J., Koehler, R. A., & Hampton, S. H. (1970). Grade level, sex, and selected aspects of test-wiseness. *Journal of Educational Measurement, 7*, 119–122.

Slavin, R. E. (1988). Cooperative learning and student achievement. *Educational Leadership, 46*(2), 31–33.

Smith, J., & Walker, J. (2002). Using electronic gradebooks. *Principal, 82*(2), 64–65.

Smith, M. L. (1997). *Reforming schools by reforming assessment: Consequences of the Arizona Student Assessment Program (ASAP): Equity and teacher capacity building* (CSE Technical Report 425). Los Angeles: National Center for Research on Evaluation, Standards, and Student Testing, UCLA.

Snow, R. E. (1980). Aptitudes and achievement. In W. B. Schrader (Ed.), *Measuring achievement: Progress over a decade. Proceedings of the 1979 ETS Invitational Conference. New Directions for Testing and Measurement* (No. 5). San Francisco: Jossey-Bass.

Spandel, V., & Stiggins, R. J. (1990). *Creating writers: Linking assessment and writing instruction*. New York: Longman.

Sparrow, S. S., Cicchetti, D. V., & ., Balla, D., (2005). *Vineland Adaptive Behavior Scales: Second Edition*. Circle Pines, MN: American Guidance Service.

Spearman, C. (1910). Correlation calculated from faulty data. *British Journal of Psychology, 3*, 271–295.

Spearman, C. E. (1927). *The abilities of man, their nature and measurement*. New York: Macmillan.

Stalnaker, J. M. (1936). A study of optional questions in examinations. *School and Society, 44*, 829–832.

Stalnaker, J. M. (1951). The essay type of examination. In E. F. Lindquist (Ed.), *Educational measurement*. Washington, DC: American Council on Education.

Stanley, J. C. (1971). Reliability. In R. L. Thorndike (Ed.), *Educational measurement* (2nd ed.). Washington, DC: American Council on Education.

Stanley, J. C., & Hopkins, K. D. (1990). *Educational and psychological measurement* (7th ed.). Upper Saddle River, NJ: Prentice Hall.

Sternberg, R. J. (1984). Preface. In R. J. Sternberg (Ed.), *Mechanisms of cognitive development*. San Francisco: W. H. Freeman.

Stevens, S. S. (1951). Mathematics, measurement, and psychophysics. In S. S. Stevens (Ed.), *Handbook of experimental psychology*. New York: Wiley.

Stiggins, R. J. (1987). Design and development of performance assessments: An NCME instructional module. *Educational Measurement: Issues and Practice, 6*(3), 33–42.

Stiggins, R. J. (1994). *Student-centered classroom assessment*. Upper Saddle River, NJ: Merrill/Prentice Hall.

Stiggins, R. J., Conklin, N. F., & Associates. (1992). *In teachers' hands: Investigating the practice of classroom assessment*. Albany, NY: SUNY Press.

Stiggins, R. J., Frisbie, D. A., & Griswold, P. A. (1989). Inside high school grading practices: Building a research agenda. *Educational Measurement: Issues and Practice, 8*(2), 5–14.

Stiggins, R. J., Rubel, E., & Quellmalz, E. (1986). *Measuring thinking skills in the classroom*.

Washington, DC: National Educational Association.

Stodola, Q. (1961). *Making the classroom test: A guide for teachers* (No. 4. Evaluation and Advisory Services). Princeton, NJ: Educational Testing Service.

Strang, H. R. (1977). The effects of technical and unfamiliar options upon guessing on multiple-choice test items. *Journal of Educational Measurement, 14,* 253–260.

Subkoviak, M. J. (1976). Estimating reliability from a single administration of a criterion-referenced test. *Journal of Educational Measurement, 13,* 265–276.

Subkoviak, M. J. (1980). Decision consistency approaches. In R. A. Berk (Ed.), *Criterion-referenced measurement: The state of the art.* Baltimore: Johns Hopkins University Press.

Super, D. E. (1947). Vocational interest and vocational choice. *Educational and Psychological Measurement, 7,* 375–384.

Super, D. E. (1949). *Appraising vocational fitness.* New York: Harper & Row.

Suppes, P. (1974). A survey of cognition in handicapped children. *Review of Educational Research, 44,* 145–176.

Suppes, P., & Zinnes, J. L. (1963). Basic measurement theory. In R. D. Luce, R. R. Bush, & E. Galanter (Eds.), *Handbook of mathematical psychology* (Vol. 1). New York: Wiley.

Surber, J. R. (1984). Mapping as a testing and diagnostic device. In C. D. Holley & D. F. Dansereau, *Spatial learning strategies: Techniques, applications, and related issues* (pp. 213–233). Orlando, FL: Academic Press.

Surber, J. R., & Smith, P. L. (1981). Testing for misunderstanding. *Educational Psychologist, 16,* 165–174.

Swaminathan, H., Hambleton, R. K., & Algina, J. (1974). Reliability of criterion-referenced tests: A decision-theoretic formulation. *Journal of Educational Measurement, 11,* 263–267.

Swiderek, B. (1997). Parent conferences. *Journal of Adolescent and Adult Literacy, 40,* 580–581.

Tallmadge, G. K. (1973, March). *An analysis of the relationship between reading and mathematics achievement gains and per pupil expenditures in California Title I projects: Fiscal year 1972* (AIR-35100-3/73-FR). Palo Alto, CA: American Institutes for Research.

Tallmadge, G. K., & Horst, D. (1974). *A procedural guide for validating achievement gains in educational projects* (revised, RMC Report UR-240). Los Altos, CA: RMC Research Corporation.

Tallmadge, G. K., & Wood, C. T. (1976). *User's guide* (ESEA Title I Evaluation and Reporting System). Mountain View, CA: RMC Research Corporation.

Taylor, C. S. (1998). An investigation of scoring methods for mathematics performance-based assessments. *Educational Assessment, 5,* 195–224.

Taylor, E. D., & Nuttall, D. L. (1974). Question choice in examinations: An experiment in geography and science. *Educational Research, 16,* 143–150.

Terry, P. W. (1933). How students review for objective and essay tests. *Elementary School Journal, 33,* 592–603.

Terwilliger, J. S. (1971). *Assigning grades to students.* Glenview, IL: Scott, Foresman.

Terwilliger, J. S. (1989). Classroom standard-setting and grading practices. *Educational Measurement: Issues and Practice, 8,* 15–19.

Thorndike, E. L. (1910). Handwriting. *Teachers College Record, 11,* 1–93.

Thorndike, R. L. (1949). *Personal selection: Test and measurement technique.* New York: Wiley.

Thorndike, R. L. (1951). Reliability. In E. F. Lindquist (Ed.), *Educational measurement.* Washington, DC: American Council on Education.

Thorndike, R. L. (1971). Concepts of culture fairness. *Journal of Educational Measurement, 8,* 63–70.

Thorndike, R. L., & Hagen, E. P. (1977). *Measurement and evaluation in psychology and education* (4th ed.). New York: Wiley.

Thorndike, R. M., Cunningham, G. K., Thorndike, R. L., & Hagen, E. P. (1991). *Measurement and evaluation in psychology and education* (5th ed.). New York: Macmillan.

Tippets, E., & Benson, J. (1989). The effect of item arrangement on test anxiety. *Applied Measurement in Education, 2,* 289–296.

Tittle, C. K. (1989). Validity: Whose construct is it in the teaching and learning context? *Educational Measurement: Issues and Practice, 8*(1), 5–13, 34.

Tittle, C. K., Hecht, D., & Moore, P. (1993). Assessment theory and research for classrooms: From taxonomies to constructing meaning in context. *Educational Measurement: Issues and Practice, 12*(4), 13–19.

Touchstone Applied Science Associates. (1995a). *Degrees of reading power and degrees of word meaning: An overview.* Brewster, NY: Author.

Touchstone Applied Science Associates. (1995b). *DRP catalog.* Brewster, NY: Author.

Tryon, G. S. (1980). The measurement and treatment of test anxiety. *Review of Educational Research, 50,* 343–372.

Tuckman, B. W. (1988). *Testing for teachers* (2nd ed.). San Diego, CA: Harcourt Brace Jovanovich.

Tuinman, J. J., Farr, R., & Blanton, B. E. (1972). Increases in test scores as a function of material rewards. *Journal of Educational Measurement, 9,* 215–223.

Tyler, F. T., & Chalmers, T. M. (1943). The effect on scores of warning junior high school pupils of coming tests. *Journal of Educational Research, 37,* 290–296.

Tyler, R. W. (1934). *Constructing achievement tests.* Columbus: Ohio State University.

Tyler, R. W. (1966). The objectives and plans for a National Assessment of Educational Progress. *Journal of Educational Measurement, 3,* 1–4.

United States Supreme Court. (1971). *Griggs et al., Petitioners vs. Duke Power Company* (Publication No. 125, 401 U.S. 424, decided March 8, 1971).

Urevbu, A. O. (1984). School science curriculum and innovation: An African perspective.

European Journal of Science Education, 6, 217–225.

U.S. Department of Education. (2005, May 10). *New flexibility for states raising achievement for students with disabilities.* No Child Left Behind. Retrieved from http://www.ed.gov/policy/elsec/guid/raising/disab-factsheet.pdf

U.S. Department of Education. (n.d.). *Accountability.* Retrieved from http://www.ed.gov/nclb/accountability/index.html

Valencia, S. W., & Place, N. A. (1994). Literacy portfolios for teaching, learning, and accountability: The Bellevue Literacy Assessment Project. In S. W. Valencia, E. H. Hiebert, & P. P. Afferbach (Eds.), *Authentic reading assessment: Practices and possibilities.* Newark, DE: International Reading Association.

Vallance, T. R. (1947). Comparison of essay and objective examinations as learning experiences. *Journal of Educational Research, 41,* 279–288.

Vernon, P. E. (1962). The determinants of reading comprehension. *Educational and Psychological Measurement, 22,* 269–286.

Viadero, D. (1995). New assessments have little effect on contract, study finds. *Education Week, 14*(40), 6.

Wagner, R. K., & Sternberg, R. J. (1984). Alternate conceptions of intelligence and their implications for education. *Review of Educational Research, 54,* 179–223.

Waltman, K. K., & Frisbie, D. A. (1994). Parents understanding of their children's report cards. *Applied Measurement in Education, 2,* 223–240.

Wang, M. C. (1980). Adaptive instruction: Building on diversity. *Theory Into Practice, 19,* 122–128 (Reprinted as *Reports to Educators 5.*) Pittsburgh, PA: University of Pittsburgh, Learning Research and Development Center.

Wang, X., Wainer, H., & Thissen, D. (1995). On the viability of some untestable assumptions in equating exams that allow examinee choice. *Applied Measurement in Education, 8,* 211–225.

Waples, D., & Tyler, R. W. (1930). *Research methods and teacher problems.* New York: Macmillan.

Webb, N. L. (1999). *Summary report: Alignment analyses of standards and assessments for four states in science and mathematics* (Council of Chief State School Officers and National Institute for Science Education). Madison: Wisconsin Center for Education Research, University of Wisconsin–Madison.

Wechsler, D. (1939). *The measurement of adult intelligence.* Baltimore: Williams & Wilkins.

Weidemann, C. C. (1926). How to construct the true-false examination. *Teachers College, Columbia University. Contributions to Education* (No. 225). New York: Bureau of Publications, Teachers College, Columbia University.

Wesley, E. B., & Wronski, S. P. (1958). *Teaching social studies in high schools* (4th ed.). Boston: D.C. Heath.

Wesman, A. G. (1971). Writing the test item. In R. L. Thorndike (Ed.), *Educational measurement*

(2nd ed.). Washington, DC: American Council on Education.

Whitney, D. R., & Sabers, D. L. (1970, May). *Improving essay examinations III: Use of item analysis* (Technical Bulletin No. 11). Iowa City: University Evaluation and Examination Service, University of Iowa.

Wick, J. W. and others. (1989). *School attitude measure* (2nd ed.). Iowa City, IA: American Techtronics.

Wiggins, G. (1990). *The case for authentic assessment* (EDD-TM-9010). Washington, DC: ERIC Clearinghouse on Tests, Measurement, and Evaluation, American Institutes for Research.

Williams, R. L. (1975). THE BITCH-100: A culture-specific test. *Journal of Afro-American Issues, 3,* 103–116.

Wilson, J. A. (1976). Question choice in A-level physics. *Curriculum Studies, 8,* 71–78.

Wine, J. (1971). Test anxiety and direction of attention. *Psychological Bulletin, 76,* 92–104.

Wiser, B., & Lenke, J. M. (1987, April). *The stability of achievement test norms over time.* Paper presented at the annual meeting of the National Council on Measurement in Education, Washington, DC.

Wolf, D. P. (1989). Portfolio assessment: Sampling student work. *Educational Leadership, 46*(2), 4–10.

Wood, R. (1977). Multiple choice: A state of the art report. *Evaluation in Education: International Progress, 1,* 191–280.

Woolfolk, A. E. (1995). *Educational Psychology* (6th ed.). Boston: Allyn & Bacon.

Woolfolk, A. (2005). *Educational Psychology* (9th ed.). Boston: Allyn & Bacon.

Young, M. J. (1993). *Quantitative measures for the assessment of declarative knowledge structure characteristics.* Unpublished doctoral dissertation, University of Pittsburgh, Pittsburgh, PA.

Young, M. J., & Zucker, S. (2004). *The standards-referenced interpretive framework: Using assessments for multiple purposes* (Harcourt Assessment Report). San Antonio, TX: Harcourt Assessment.

Zeidner, M. (1998). *Test anxiety: The state of the art.* New York: Plenum Press.

Zoref, L., & Williams, P. (1980). A look at content bias in IQ tests. *Journal of Educational Measurement, 17,* 313–322.

Zucker, S., Sassman, C., & Case, B. J. (2004). *Cognitive labs (Harcourt Technical Report).* San Antonio, TX: Harcourt Assessment. Available from http://harcourtassessment.com/hai/Images/resource/library/pdf/CognitiveLabs_Final.pdf